A Guide to the Companies Act 2006

The Companies Act 2006 is a historic piece of legislation. It is by far the largest Act in the history of UK Parliament covering three volumes of legislation, consolidating many parts of the Companies Acts 1985–1989.

A Guide to the Companies Act 2006 is a section-by-section analysis with detailed commentary on the legal and practical implications of the Act. This book traces the development of company law reform before the Companies Act 2006, with a consideration of the various committees established to address company law reform, and the 'six phases' culminating in the Companies Act 2006. It is comprehensive and wide-ranging in its analysis, tackling all of the major individual areas of reform.

The book is also supported by a Companion Website, which contains useful appendices including a table of destinations and origins, with the latest Ministerial Statements on duties of company directors; practice direction and rules on derivative actions; and registration of floating charges in Scotland.

This book is an invaluable resource for practitioners, students, industrialists, directors and secretaries.

The Companion Website is available at:
http://www.routledgecavendish.com/textbooks/9780415421072

Dr Saleem Sheikh, LLB (Hons), LLM (Lond), PhD (Lond) is a solicitor.

A Guide to the Companies Act 2006

Dr Saleem Sheikh

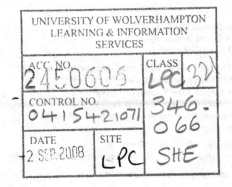

Routledge·Cavendish
Taylor & Francis Group
LONDON AND NEW YORK

First published 2008
by Routledge-Cavendish
2 Park Square, Milton Park, Abingdon, Oxon OX14 4RN

Simultaneously published in the USA and Canada
by Routledge-Cavendish
270 Madison Ave, New York, NY 10016

*Routledge-Cavendish is an imprint of the Taylor & Francis Group,
an informa business*

© 2008 Saleem Sheikh

Typeset in Times by
RefineCatch Limited, Bungay, Suffolk
Printed and bound in Great Britain by
TJ International, Padstow, Cornwall

British Library Cataloguing in Publication Data
A catalogue record for this book is available from the British Library

Library of Congress Cataloging-in-Publication Data
Sheikh, Saleem.
   A guide to the Companies Act 2006 / Saleem Sheikh.
      p. cm.
   1. Corporation law–Great Britain. 2. Great Britain. Companies Act
2006. I. Title.
   KD2074.54.S54 2008
   346.41′066—dc22

                                                            2007039132

ISBN10: 0–415–42107–1 (pbk)
ISBN13: 978–0–415–42107–2 (pbk)

Table of Contents

Acknowledgements

In writing this book, I wish to acknowledge the support and encouragement of my wife, Shabena and my children, Iram, Kamil and Sohail. Their patience and support is to be admired and respected during the long hours of working on this book.

My parents, Tahir and Fahmida, have been a constant source of inspiration to me.

This book is also dedicated to the memory of the late, Professor John Parkinson, who made an indelible impact to the contribution of company law, including his invaluable contributions as part of the team on the Company Law Review Group. His works and contributions will continue to make an effective impact on company lawyers, academics, students and industrialists.

I am also grateful to my publishers Routledge-Cavendish and particularly Sonny Leong, for having the trust and confidence in me to write this book, even though the delivery of the manuscripts were delayed owing to the voluminous nature of the CA 2006.

My appreciation is due to the kind support and assistance of the staff at the Institute of Advanced Legal Studies, and the London School of Economics and Political Science.

I also wish to take this opportunity to acknowledge the perceptive clarity of the Explanatory Notes to the CA 2006, provided by the Department of Trade and Industry. I have included some of the Explanatory Notes in this book with my own commentary on the legal and practical implications of the CA 2006.

Preface

A fair, modern and effective framework of company law is crucial to the UK's economic performance. The UK was one of the first countries to establish a legal framework to regulate the organisation and management of companies within the corporate governance system. The strength of company law continues to make the UK a prime location for investors.

Before 2006, companies legislation in the UK was perceived as largely Victorian and antiquated. The CA 1985 proceeded on the basis of 'think large companies first', with little attention paid to the needs of private companies and small businesses. The CA 1985 was also a product of administrative burden and regulation for private companies, with layer upon layer of provisions added to the legislation as exemptions to the public company provisions – and only then as an afterthought for private companies – particularly in the areas of share capital, financial assistance and company meetings.

In 1998, the Labour Government embarked on wide ranging consultation with interested parties, resulting in a series of consultation documents on a broad range of company law issues. This culminated in the publication of two White Papers in 2002 and 2005 leading to the enactment of the CA 2006.

The CA 2006 is a remarkable piece of legislation spanning over three volumes, setting out in comprehensive detail a wide spectrum of company law areas ranging from company formation; company constitution and corporate capacity; re-registration in altering company status; company and business names; members and exercise of their rights; directors – their appointment and removal; general and specific duties and liabilities of directors; company secretary; the registrar of companies; share capital; meetings and resolutions; debentures; accounts; auditors; derivative claims; takeovers; mergers; and control of political funds by companies. The philosophy of the CA 2006 is based on the following premise: (i) 'think small first'; (ii) reduction of administrative and regulatory burdens; (iii) ensuring clarity and conciseness in the legislation; and (iv) reducing costs to companies.

The CA 2006 also embraces a sense of corporate social responsibilities by creating a new 'social law'. It creates an awakening of social consciousness in directors. Directors are now the conscience or gatekeepers for various stakeholders of the corporation. They are required to have regard to these potential claimants as well as the shareholders. They are now required to discharge their corporate social responsibilities by way of statutory regulation as part of their duties.

The CA 2006 is perceived as radical legislation, which will have a significant impact on the functioning of companies, including the role of directors and main officers within the corporate governance system.

Table of Cases

Table of Statutes and Statutory Instruments

Table of European Legislation

Glossary

Combined Code   The Stock Exchange's Principles of Good Governance and Code of Best Practice

Cohen Committee   The Committee on Company Law Amendment, chaired by Mr Justice Cohen

DTI's Consultation Papers   A series of consultation papers issued by the DTI from the period 1998–2002 on company law reform

Company Law Review   The DTI's review of company law launched in March 1998

Company Law Review Group   A group set up by the DTI comprising academic accountants, industrialists and other specialists in the area of company law as part of the company law reform in the UK

ESRC Centre for Business Research   Economic and Social Research Council, Centre for Business Research at the University of Cambridge

General law   In England the common law and equity and in Scotland the common law

Greene Committee   The Company Law Committee established by Lord Greene on Company Law Reform

Jenkins Committee   The Company Law Committee, chaired by Lord Jenkins

Listings Rules   The Listings Rules for the official list of the Stock Exchange

Model Code   A code of dealing for transactions in securities by directors, certain employees and connected persons, which appears in an appendix to Chapter 16 of the Listing Rules

Myners, P.   Report on Institutional Investment in the UK, 20 December 2004

Prentice Report   A report presented by Dr Dan Prentice (as he was then) to the Department of Trade and Industry in 1986 on reform of the *ultra vires* doctrine

Sandler Report   Medium and Long-term Retail Savings Review (9 July 2002)

Stock Exchange   London Stock Exchange Limited

Table A   CA 1985, Table A (SI 1985/805, Schedule)

Abbreviations

1985 Act	Companies Act 1985
AC	Appeals Cases
ACCA	Association of Chartered Certified Accountants
ADR	Alternative Dispute Resolution
AGM	Annual General Meeting
AIM	Alternative Investment Markets
ALL ER	All England Law Reports
APB	Auditing Practices Board
ASB	Accounting Standards Board
BCC	Butterworths Company Cases
BCLC	Butterworths Company Law Cases
CA	Court of Appeal
CA 1948	Companies Act 1948
CA 1967	Companies Act 1967
CA 1985	Companies Act 1985
CA 1989	Companies Act 1989
CA 2006	Companies Act 2006
C(AICE) Act 2004	Companies (Audit, Investigations and Community Enterprise) Act 2004
CBI	Confederation of British Industry
CEO	Chief Executive Officer
ChD	Chancery Division
CFD	Contract for Difference
c.i.c.	Community Interest Company
CLR	Company Law Review
CPS	Crown Prosecution Service
CSR	Corporate Social Responsibilities
D & O Insurance	Directors' and Officers' Liability Insurance
DTI	Department of Trade and Industry (now known as the Department for Business, Enterprise and Regulatory Reform)
EC	European Community

ECU	European Currency Unit
EEA	European Economic Area
EEC	European Economic Community
ESCB	European System of Central Banks
EU	European Union
FRC	Financial Reporting Council
FRRP	Financial Reporting Review Panel
FRS	Financial Reporting Standard
FSA	Financial Services Authority
FSMA	Financial Services and Markets Act 2000
GB	Great Britain
HL	House of Lords
IA 1986	Insolvency Act 1986
IAS	International Accounting Standards
ICAEW	Institute of Chartered Accountants in England and Wales
ICAS	Institute of Chartered Accountants in Scotland
ICSA	Institute of Chartered Secretaries and Administrators
IoD	Institute of Directors
ISC	Institutional Shareholders' Committee
LPA 1907	Limited Partnerships Act 1907
NED	Non-Executive Directors
OECD	Organization of Economic Co-operation and Development
OFR	Operating and Financial Review
NI	Northern Ireland
NGO	Non-Governmental Organisation
PA 1890	Partnership Act 1890
PC	Privy Council
PPERA	Political Parties, Elections and Referendums Act 2000
PIRC	Pensions Investment Research Consultants Ltd
plc	Public limited company
PRO NED	Promotion of Non-Executive Directors
PSM	Professional Securities Market
QC	Queen's Counsel
RTE	Right to Enfranchise
RTM	Right to Manage
SE	Societas Europaea (European Public Limited-Liability Company)
SFO	Serious Fraud Office
SI	Statutory Instrument
TLR	Times Law Reports
UK	United Kingdom
UKHL	UK House of Lords

| UKLA | United Kingdom Listing Authority |
| WLR | Weekly Law Reports |

Introduction

The CA 2006 has been described as 'an historic piece of legislation',[1] 'long overdue' and a 'huge piece of legislation . . . undertaking a root-and-branch reform of the law'; an 'archaeological approach to company law'; 'gargantuan'; 'this monster'; 'incredibly long';[2] 'rather like peeling back the layers of an onion';[3] 'lengthy and complex';[4] an Act that is 'pro-small business';[5] 'a model of how legislation should be introduced'.[6] It is by far the largest Act in the history of Parliament covering three volumes of legislation. According to Lord Hodgson, 'company law reform may not set many parliamentary pulses racing – but it has a huge influence for good or ill on British industry and commerce'.[7]

During the debates in the House of Lords on the Company Law Reform Bill (as it was then),[8] Lord Sainsbury of Turville remarked that over 150 years

---

[1] During the Lords sitting on 2 November 2006, Lord Hodgson remarked that the extraordinary fact of the Company Law Reform Bill (as it was then) was the number of amendments that had to be considered, which was quite remarkable for this Bill, and he echoed his statement that 'a journey of a thousand miles begins with a single statement'. The Companies Act was now in three volumes instead of two with some 1,264 clauses instead of 885. This was owing to the Government accepting the Lords' advice to consolidate previous Companies Acts into the new Act. 'The name change may have confused some people; nevertheless, history will show that the effort was worthwhile.'

[2] See Lord Hodgson, HL Debates, 11 Jan 2006.

[3] Lord Sharman, HL Debates, 11 Jan 2006. However, Lord Sharman was not in support of the previous Company Law Reform Bill, and together with Lord Hodgson, he expressed concern and disappointment that the Company Law Reform Bill (as it was then) was not a consolidating Bill. It would mean that the CA 1985 would end up partly repealed with parts of companies legislation contained both in the CA 1985 and the new Companies Act.

[4] Baroness Bottomley of Nettlestone, HL Debates, 11 Jan 2006.

[5] Lord Borrie, HL Debates, 11 Jan 2006.

[6] Lord Gordon of Strathblane, HL Debates, 11 Jan 2006.

[7] HL, Hansard Debates, 11 Jan 2006.

[8] The Bill was previously referred to as the Company Law Reform Bill until a later consolidation introduced a new Companies Bill. According to the House of Lords debates, Lord Clinton-Davis advocated a need for consolidation. However, Lord Sainsbury contended that following

ago, his predecessor Robert Lowe, described as the 'father of modern company law' (later First Viscount Sherbrooke), brought forward the Bill that created the joint stock limited liability company. It was the first nationwide codification of company law in the world. Over the past decades, company law in the UK has continued to maintain an impressive record with a large number of incorporations, including foreign firms incorporating in the UK. The primary attraction was due to the speed and cost-effectiveness for companies to set up in the UK rather than any other EU Member State.

According to Lord Sainsbury, improvements could still be made to the companies legislation in the UK, particularly as companies operated internationally, and the UK would need to take account of international developments. Further, if owners and investors were to continue to invest in UK companies, there was a perceived need to retain their confidence in the UK corporate governance system. Although a number of Companies Acts had been enacted in the past, the CA 1985 had been the centrepiece of company law until the Company Law Reform Bill (and later the Companies Bill) was introduced. There has been a need constantly to update UK company law in response to changes in the way that companies conducted business, taking account of a previous review by independent experts.

The CA 2006 has ensured simplification of the needs of small businesses and on deregulation, which represented a break from the past. The CA 2006 was expected to produce savings for businesses of around £250 million a year, of which £100 million a year would benefit small businesses, including significant savings relating to moves from paper to electronic communications, as well as simplifications in the procedures for private companies to take their decisions. The CA 2006 provided clearer structure and language than its predecessor.

The CA 2006 has four main objectives. First, enhancing shareholder engagement and a long-term investment culture; second, ensuring better regulation and a 'think small first' approach;[9] third, making it easier to set up and run a company; and fourth, providing flexibility for the future. Better regulation was at the heart of the CA 2006. Lord Sainsbury noted that company law in the UK was originally designed for large companies with numerous public investors, but that over 90 per cent of companies had five or fewer shareholders. The CA 2006 had lifted the burden of unnecessary provisions

---

consultation, the need for consolidation was not a major objective. He stated that it would not be possible to have a consolidated Bill that would hold for a lengthy period of time: it was neither desirable nor what people wanted. See HL debates: 11 Jan 2006.

[9] However, according to Lord Wedderburn of Charlton, the Bill (as it was then) did not 'think small first' in its deregulation of formalities or AGM's but the Bill 'thinks private company first' and the two are not the same. 'Think private company' is a very different proposition from 'think small'. HL Debates, 11 Jan 2006.

on private companies, with emphasis on deregulation and ensuring that private companies are able to operate their business smoothly and effectively, without unnecessary regulatory burdens. The CA 2006 followed the important principle of enabling shareholders to be the primary regulators of corporate behaviour rather than the State. Companies existed for the benefit of their members collectively, and needed the freedom and flexibility to create wealth. Corporate law and governance had to be designed to encourage and enable companies to create the internal structures and controls that would promote trust and transparency, and lead to better performance.

The CA 2006 upholds the primacy of the main objective of companies previously reinforced in case law – namely, profit maximisation for the benefit of the company's shareholders. Under Part 10, s 172 of the CA 2006, directors have a duty to promote the success of the company for the benefit of the members as a whole.

However, profit maximisation is not the only objective of companies. A company has a soul. It has a corporate conscience. It exercises corporate social responsibilities in society. It discharges philanthropic functions. It cares about the environment, its customers, its suppliers, and the wider community. A corporation is now benevolent. Its directors are trustees – the gatekeepers, custodians or guardians for the potential claimants on the corporation. The CA 2006 creates a wakening of social consciousness in company directors. Section 172(1) of the CA 2006 requires directors to exercise their corporate social responsibilities towards groups wider than shareholders – it creates a 'social law'. It requires directors to have regard to the interests of other potential claimants on the corporation including the employees; the company's business relationships with suppliers, customers and others; the impact of the company's operations on the community and the environment; the desirability of the company maintaining a reputation of a high standard of business conduct; and the need to act fairly as between members of the company. Directors now have a legal and social obligation to discharge their duties by a consideration of these claims on the corporation.

This book comprises 33 chapters.

Chapter 1 provides an overview of company law reform in the United Kingdom. It traces the historical development of the company law reform debate as long ago as 1844, beginning with the Companies Act 1844, which allowed companies to incorporate by registration. This chapter proceeds to consider some of the significant influential government committees that were established to consider company law reform in the UK until 1998. They included the UK Loreburn Committee; the Wrenbury Committee; the Greene Committee; the Cohen Committee; and the Jenkins Committee. Reform of the *ultra vires* doctrine was later addressed by the Prentice Report. The position after 1998 is then addressed with a consideration of the 'six phases' that led to the enactment of the CA 2006. In these phases, wide consultation was undertaken by the DTI through the Steering Committee, resulting in the publication of various consultation documents.

Chapter 2 provides highlights of the significant areas of reform under the CA 2006 that will have a major legal and practical impact on the operation and functioning of companies. It considers the timeline of the passage of the Companies Bill culminating in the CA 2006, with significant debates in both Houses of Parliament. It analyses the structure and style of the CA 2006; the Parts and the Schedules; the remaining provisions under the CA 1985 and the CA 1989; the preamble to the CA 2006; territorial extent and devolution; regulations and orders; the provisions in force; a summary of the main highlights of the CA 2006; and consideration of two guidance documents issued by the Department of Trade and Industry, in respect of the CA 2006 provisions that have a significant impact on private companies. A more detailed analysis of the areas highlighted is considered in the subsequent chapters to this book.

Chapter 3 sets out the procedure for company formation. It provides a definition of a 'company' and the 'Companies Acts' as applied to various parts of the CA 2006. It considers the general introductory provisions and sets out the types of companies that may be established, with particular reference to limited and unlimited companies; private and public companies; companies limited by guarantee and having share capital; and community interest companies.

This chapter also considers the process of forming a company. In particular, it addresses the function of the Memorandum of Association. It will be noted that the Memorandum of Association no longer forms part of a company's constitution: it serves a very limited purpose. There are new provisions on requirements for registration including registration of documents; statement of capital and initial shareholdings; statement of guarantee; statement of proposed officers; and statement of compliance. This chapter also considers the registration procedure, including the issue of certificate of incorporation and effect of registration.

Consideration is also given to a company's registered office and provisions dealing with directors' residential addresses.

Chapter 4 addresses the company's constitution with a definition as to what constitutes a company's constitution (with a wider meaning provided under s 257 of the CA 2006 in respect of Part 10 of the CA 2006 concerning directors). It proceeds to consider a company's Articles of Association, which now have an elevated status under the CA 2006. It considers the power of the Secretary of State to prescribe model articles; and default application of model articles. There are provisions dealing with amendment to the articles; entrenchment provisions of the articles; notice to registrar of existence of restriction on amendment of articles; the effect of alteration of articles on a company's members; the requirement to send registrar a copy of the amended articles; and registrar's notice to comply in case of failure with respect to amended articles.

This chapter also considers resolutions and agreements affecting a company's constitution; and the requirement for copies of resolutions or agreements to be forwarded to the registrar. This chapter sets out new provisions in respect of a statement of a company's objects, thereby allowing companies the freedom to engage in commercial dealings without any restrictions. There are other provisions addressed in this chapter with respect to a company's constitution, including the constitutional documents to be provided to members and the effect of a company's constitution.

Owing to the close association with the company's constitution, this chapter also considers a company's capacity, and sets out important changes in respect of provisions dealing with a company's capacity; power of directors to bind the company; constitutional limitations in transactions involving directors or their associates; and constitutional limitations in respect of companies that are charities.

It also considers the formalities of doing business under the law of England and Wales or Northern Ireland with particular reference to company contracts; execution of documents; common seal; execution of deeds; execution of deeds or other documents by attorney; execution of documents by companies; official seal for use abroad; official seal for share certificates; pre-incorporation contracts, deeds and obligations'; and bills of exchange and promissory notes.

Chapter 5 deals with re-registration as a means of altering corporate status. It deals with various types of re-registrations, including a private company becoming public; a public company becoming private; a private limited company becoming unlimited; an unlimited private company becoming limited; and a public company becoming private and limited.

Chapter 6 sets out significant changes to provisions on a company's name. It considers prohibited names; names suggesting connection with government or public authority; other sensitive words or expressions; the duty to seek comments from government departments or other specified body; and permitted characters. It also deals with indications of company types or legal forms, with particular reference to public and private companies and available exemptions.

This chapter also addresses provisions dealing with similarity to other names with respect to the name on the registrar's index, or in respect of which a person has goodwill. It introduces 'company name adjudicators', and sets out the procedural rules on the governance of company names adjudicators, including their decisions being made public.

The chapter sets out other powers of the Secretary of State with reference to the provision of misleading information, as well as misleading indication of activities. There are also provisions dealing with change of name, the procedures involved and the effect of registration. This chapter also addresses trading disclosures dealing with the requirement to disclose company name, including the civil and criminal consequences of failure to make required disclosures.

Chapter 6 also deals with business names and sets out the provisions replacing the Business Names Act 1985. It addresses restricted or prohibited names; sensitive words or expressions; and misleading names. It considers disclosure required in case of sole traders or partnerships including consequence of failure to make the required disclosure.

Chapter 7 considers shareholders and exercise of their rights. It sets out who are members of a company and analyses the provisions dealing with the register of members, including rights to inspect and require copies of company records, and penalties for failure to comply.

This chapter also sets out provision for special cases with reference to share warrants, single member companies and companies holding their own shares as treasury shares. It also addresses the power of the court to rectify the register, and time limits for claims arising from entries in the register. It also addresses overseas branch registers and the procedures involved.

There are also provisions concerned with prohibition of a subsidiary being a member of its holding company.

Chapter 7 also addresses the exercise of members' rights. It considers the effect of provisions in a company's Articles of Association as to the enjoyment or exercise of members' rights. It also sets out information rights, and exercise of rights where shares are held on behalf of others.

The final aspect of this chapter is concerned with the protection of members against unfair prejudice. It sets out the grounds for application, and the orders the court may make in the event that the applicant is successful.

Chapter 8 sets out the appointment and removal of directors. It deals with the requirement to have directors, including the procedure for appointing a director, with the minimum age for appointment; provisions affecting existing under-age directors; and the validity of acts of directors. This chapter also makes provision for the register of directors, with the particulars of directors to be registered and a duty to notify the registrar of changes.

This chapter also considers the procedure for removal of a director and a director's right to protest against removal.

Chapter 9 sets out some of the most important changes introduced by the CA 2006 on directors' duties. It sets out a codification of directors' general duties, with particular reference to the duties to act within powers; to promote the success of the company; to exercise independent judgment; to exercise reasonable care, skill and diligence; to avoid conflicts of interests; not to accept benefits from third parties; and to declare any interest in a proposed transaction or arrangement. It considers the civil consequences of breach of general duties; and the particular circumstances of consent, approval or authorisation by members.

Chapter 10 considers the specific duties and liabilities of directors, with particular reference to the declaration of interests in existing transaction or arrangement and creates an offence of failure to declare an interest; and it also deals with cases of declared interest regarding companies with a sole director, and cases of declared interest in an existing transaction by a shadow director.

This chapter also sets out transactions with directors requiring approval of members. The main transactions highlighted are service contracts; substantial property transactions; loans, quasiloans and credit transactions and payments for loss of office. It then addresses directors' service contracts with new provisions on length of service contract that require approval from shareholders. There are also provisions dealing with contracts with sole members who are directors.

Particular consideration is also given to directors' liabilities, with provisions protecting directors from liability and ratifying the acts of directors.

Finally, this chapter sets out the supplementary provisions that include provision for employees on cessation or transfer of business; records of directors' meetings; and definitions of director, shadow director and related offices.

Chapter 11 is concerned with company directors with respect to foreign disqualification. It sets out the power to disqualify; the power to make persons liable for company debts; and the power to require statements to be sent to the registrar of companies.

Chapter 12 addresses the role of a company secretary with particular reference to private secretaries and secretaries of public companies. It also considers provisions that apply to both private companies with a secretary, and to public companies.

There are additional requirements for public companies in respect of requirements for AGMs, and additional requirements for quoted companies with respect to website publication of poll results and independent reports on polls. These are all considered in this chapter.

Chapter 13 concerns the registrar of companies. It sets out the provisions on the registrar with functions, the registrar's official seal and fees payable to the registrar. It also addresses certificates of incorporation; registered numbers; delivery of documents to the registrar; requirements for property delivery; public notice of receipt of certain documents; the register; inspection of the register; correction or removal of material on the register; the registrar's index of company names; language requirements with respect to translation and transliteration.

Chapter 14 concerns resolutions and meetings with procedural aspects set out. There are general provisions about resolutions, with reference to ordinary and special resolutions and voting aspects. This chapter then addresses the aspect of written resolutions, with a consideration of general provisions about written resolutions; circulation of written resolutions; and agreeing to written resolutions.

It also addresses resolutions at meetings with general provisions about resolutions at meetings; calling meetings; notice of meetings; members' statements; procedure at meetings; proxies; adjourned meetings; electronic communications; and applications for class meetings.

Chapter 15 sets out provisions governing a company's share capital. It addresses the aspect of shares and share capital of a company; allotment of shares; allotment of equity securities with reference to existing shareholders' right of pre-emption; payment for shares; share premiums; and, in respect of public companies, the independent valuation of non-cash considerations.

This chapter also addresses the issue of alteration of share capital by discussing how share capital may be altered; the subdivision or consolidation of shares; and redenomination of share capital.

Chapter 16 addresses the certification and transfer of securities. It considers share certificates and their issue on allotment of shares. There are provisions dealing with the transfer of securities and provisions on share warrants.

It also deals with the evidencing and transfer of title to securities without written instrument.

Chapter 17 concerns information about interests in a company's shares. It considers notice requiring information about interests in shares; orders imposing restriction on shares; the powers of members to require a company to act; register of interests disclosed; and the definition of interest in shares.

This chapter also sets out provisions on classes of share and class rights, including reduction of capital with procedure for private companies and public companies.

Chapter 18 concerns distributions and defines the term 'distribution'. It sets out the general rules on distributions and the justification of distribution by reference to accounts, with supplementary provisions on accounting matters; distributions in kind; and the consequences of unlawful distribution.

Chapter 19 addresses acquisition by a limited company of its own shares. It sets out the general provisions, followed by provisions dealing with shares held by a company's nominee; and shares held by or for a public company. It also addresses the issue of financial assistance and exemptions; redemption with particular reference to redeemable shares with terms and manner of redemption as well as financing of redemption; the purchase of own shares with general provisions and reference to authority for purchase of own shares, authority for off-market purchase and authority for market purchase.

This chapter also considers redemption or purchase by a private company out of capital as well as treasury shares.

Chapter 20 addresses provisions on debentures. It sets out the definition of a debenture and provisions governing the register of debenture holders.

Chapter 21 concerns company charges in England and Wales or Northern Ireland, with the requirement to register company charges; charges in other jurisdictions; the register of charges; avoidance of certain charges;

and company's records and registers. Similar provisions are set out for Scotland.

Chapter 22 deals with accounts and reports. It sets out provisions for companies subject to the small companies regime, and the regime governing quoted and unquoted companies. It also considers accounting records, including offences for breach of the duty to keep accounting records. It addresses a company's financial year and procedure for alteration of the financial year.

It also considers a company's annual accounts with provisions concerning individual accounts; group accounts (small companies); group accounts (other companies); and general provisions on group accounts; including certain information to be given in the 'Notes to the Accounts.'

This chapter also sets out provisions on directors' reports and on setting out the contents of such reports. There are also provisions for quoted companies in respect of directors' remuneration reports. It also deals with the publication of accounts and reports. There are provisions dealing with public companies: laying of accounts and reports before the general meeting; in quoted companies, members' approval of directors' remuneration reports; the filing of accounts and reports; revision of defective accounts and reports; and liability for false or misleading statements in reports.

Chapter 23 concerns audit and auditors. It addresses the requirement for audited accounts; the appointment of auditors; the functions of an auditor; the removal or resignation of auditors; and auditors' liability.

Chapter 24 deals with statutory auditors. It defines a statutory auditor. It then addresses statutory auditors by reference to individuals or firms, including eligibility for appointment; independence requirement; the effect of appointment of a partnership; supervisory bodies; professional qualifications; information; and enforcement.

This chapter also addresses the Auditors General with reference to eligibility for appointment; the conduct of audits; The Independent Supervisor; the supervision of Auditors General; reporting requirements; information; enforcement; proceedings; and grants.

It considers the register of auditors and registered third-country auditors.

Chapter 25 sets out new provisions on derivative claims and proceedings by members in England and Wales or Northern Ireland and in Scotland. It considers the nature of derivative proceedings including procedural aspects.

Chapter 26 addresses arrangements and reconstructions. It sets out provisions for meetings of creditors or members; court sanctions for compromise or arrangement; and reconstructions and amalgamations.

Chapter 27 deals with mergers and divisions of public companies. This chapter sets out detailed provisions on merger and requirements applicable to merger with exceptions. It also sets out provisions on division, with the requirements to be complied with in case of division with exceptions.

Chapter 28 is concerned with takeovers. There are new provisions governing the Takeover Panel and its rules; and its rulings and directions. The powers of the Panel are set out with reference to its powers to require documents and information; the Panel's duty of co-operation; hearings and appeals; contravention of rules; and funding. It also considers impediments to takeovers with reference to opting in and opting out.

This chapter analyses provisions dealing with the concepts of 'squeeze out' and 'sell out'.

Chapter 29 deals with dissolution and restoration to the register. It considers striking off and the registrar's power to strike off a defunct company, and voluntary striking off.

This chapter also deals with the property of a dissolved company and property vesting as bona vacantia. It considers the issue of restoration to the register, including administrative restoration to the register and restoration to the register by the court.

Chapter 30 concerns offences under the Companies Acts. It addresses the liability of officers in default; the liability of the company as officer in default; and its application to bodies other than companies.

Chapter 31 addresses transparency obligations and related matters, with particular reference to the transparency directive.

Chapter 32 addresses the control of political donations and expenditure by companies. It considers the nature of donations or expenditure; the remedies in case of unauthorised donations or expenditure; and exemptions applicable in certain circumstances.

Chapter 33 deals with miscellaneous aspects of certain areas considered under the CA 2006. They include fraudulent trading; company investigations which makes amendments to the CA 1985, with respect to power of Secretary of State to give directions to inspectors; resignation, removal and replacement of inspectors; power to obtain information from former inspectors; power to require production of documents; and disqualification orders.

This chapter also contains supplementary provisions for companies setting out provisions for company records; service addresses; sending or supplying documents or information; requirements as to independent valuation; and notice of appointment of certain officers.

Further, this chapter contains miscellaneous provisions dealing with the regulation of actuaries; information as to exercise of voting rights by institutional investors; disclosure of information under the Enterprise Act 2002; expenses of winding up; and commonly held associations.

Dr Saleem Sheikh
London
December 2007

Chapter 1

Company Law Reform

Introduction

1.1 The UK companies legislation was long in need of reform – but reform of what kind? The debate had largely centred on whether legislation or self-regulation was the best way forward towards reforming company law. The system of company law in the UK was largely fragmented comprising self-regulation, best practice, case law and legislation. There was no coherent framework governing company law nor any attempt to modernise the whole spectrum of company law. Before 2006, company law in the UK proceeded on the basis of 'think large first' approach – priority being accorded to public companies with scant attention being paid to private companies and small business, as they were usually an afterthought – as exceptions to the public company provisions.

Prior to introduction of incorporation of companies and limited liability concepts, partnerships and unincorporated associations were the common forms of business organisations in the UK. Partnerships, in particular, were regulated by principles of common law and equity, partnership agreements, including statutory regulation under the Partnership Act 1890 and the Limited Partnerships Act 1907. Liability for these forms of business organisations was based on the concept of agency under actual or apparent authority.

The incorporation of joint stock companies under the Companies Act 1844 required them to register their constitution in the form of a deed of settlement at Companies House.[10] The deed of settlement was an extended

---

[10] The Joint Stock Companies Act 1844 allowed companies to incorporate by registration. The 1844 Act only allowed for provisional registration with partial incorporation for a joint stock company, which later permitted full incorporation and complete registration. However, the 1844 Act did not confer limited liability status for companies and the effect was that members could still be liable without limit for the company's losses. The limited liability status was introduced by the Limited Liability Act 1855. Before the 1844 Act, incorporation was only permissible by Royal Charter or a Private Act of Parliament limited to particular industries at

form of partnership deed, and the 1844 Act required such companies to provide a statement of the nature and purpose of their business. Joint stock companies had no independent corporate personality. Section 25 of that Act stated that the main powers and privileges of a deed of settlement company included a power to 'perform all other Acts necessary for carrying into effect the purposes of such Company, and in all respects as other Partnerships are entitled to do'. Although the Companies Act 1844 referred to the term 'company', the deed of settlement company was only still an extended form of partnership that had been granted certain quasi-corporate attributes.

Since the Companies Act 1844 was enacted, there has been much discussion on how company law should best be regulated, including a wider debate: 'in whose interests should the company operate'? The Jenkins Committee reporting in 1962[11] advocated some changes to companies legislation with the need for greater disclosure of information, but its reforms merely tinkered at the edges of companies legislation without consideration of the specific needs of small businesses and private companies, or the need for flexibility in the company law regime. Jenkins's response to company law reform was yet more disclosure of information, and adding further layers of regulation and bureaucracy. This has been the pattern throughout the history of company law reform in the UK. Layer after layer of further domestic legislation, and EC legislation, have been added on to companies' legislation, which favoured large public companies. UK companies legislation did not take account of the perceived needs of the small businesses or private companies of which a majority were registered at Companies House. Instead, the companies legislation proceeded on the basis of providing a series of exemptions for small

---

the time. Many businesses comprised unincorporated associations with unlimited liability status conferred on them. The 1844 Act created a registrar of joint stock companies that allowed registration of joint stock companies by a two-stage procedure. First provisional registration upon payment of a fee that did not confer corporate status; and then another fee, which completed the corporate status formalities. The 1844 Act also did not allow for a separate regime for insolvency and liquidation of companies. Thus, the 1844 Act conferred unlimited liability status with the effect that the shareholders were still liable to the creditors for the company's debts. Some shareholders purported to limit their liability by entering into individual shareholder contracts with creditors. In some cases, complex drafting of deeds of settlement for establishing joint stock companies produced the effect of a company limited by liability thereby requiring creditors to sue shareholders individually rather than jointly and severally. Before enactment of the Limited Liability Act 1855, some attempt to give credence to a 'limited liability' clause was considered in *Hallett v Dowdall* (1852) 21 LJQB 98. The court held that a standard 'limited liability' clause that was included in a joint stock company's contracts with creditors was effective. However, inserting such a clause into a joint stock company's deed of settlement would not bind creditors even if they had express notice of it. See subsequently the Joint Stock Companies Act 1856 and the Companies Act 1862 that further allowed incorporation with limited liability which was possible by allowing seven members out of the 25 members to become shareholders of the company.

[11] Board of Trade, *Report of the Company Law Committee*, Cmnd. 1749 (1962).

private companies from the public company provisions. However, this did not fit well within the overall framework of company law in the UK, owing to a lack of coherent framework of the companies statutes, which were far from user-friendly. The CA 1985 witnessed complicated and largely irrelevant provisions that impacted on small private companies such as financial assistance, reduction of capital and the capital maintenance provisions, including unsatisfactory provisions for a single-member company.

It was only in the late 1990s that bold initiatives were taken to modernise UK company law radically, owing to various global corporate scandals such as Enron, WorldCom and BCCI. These scandals showed the need to strengthen the corporate governance system in UK companies, and triggered a provoking debate on how best to strengthen and modernise UK company law, but also to ensure that the law would be modern, flexible, easily accessible, user-friendly, and one that took account of the needs of small private limited liability companies.

In the late 1990s, the Labour Government, through the Department of Trade and Industry (DTI), established a Steering Committee charged with the task of looking at all aspects of UK company law and providing recommendations for company law reform. The Steering Committee comprised members from various sectors including directors, chairmen, academics, judiciary, industrialists and specialist consultants. It established various company law review groups to consider a wide spectrum of company law, and to provide suggestions and recommendations for company law reform.

Chapter 1 provides a chronological analysis of the various phases and developments in the history of UK company law reform before 1998, with a consideration of the work of three influential Government committees charged with the responsibility of reforming company law at various stages of UK company law modernisation, namely, the Greene, Cohen and Jenkins Committees.

It then proceeds to consider the position after 1998 culminating in a series of consultation documents issued by the DTI through the Steering Committee during the late 1990s until 2000, commenting on a whole spectrum of company law including the Steering Committee's recommendations on modernising the company law regime in the UK. It summarises the main aspects and recommendations set out in the consultation documents that had a significant impact on company law reform. It also examines the rationale for modernising company law, including two White Papers published by the Government in 2002 and 2005. The Law Commissions of England and Wales and of Scotland were also instrumental in their in-depth study of some key aspects of UK company law that had an impact on reforming companies legislation. They worked in parallel on some of the areas of company law reform addressed by the Steering Committee. The Law Commissions in particular jointly published controversial and radical discussion papers on directors' duties and shareholders' remedies that were largely accepted by the

Labour Government. This period from 1998 could be characterised as one that allowed proposals for the development of a modern structure for company law and implementation. The Government put forward the rationale for a change to the current UK company law regime, consulted as widely as possible and developed policies that led to the implementation of the CA 2006.

The Position Before 1998

1.2 Company law had its origins in the enactment of various Companies Acts, case law, principles of contract law, trusts, common law, confidentiality and fiduciary duties. Company law in the UK had largely borrowed legal principles from common law and equity for its development, supplemented the regulation of company law regime by legislation.

Company law reform in the UK proceeded on the basis of Government committees being established almost every 20 years by successive Governments. The committees would usually be chaired by a senior judge with recommendations that would lead to changes to existing companies legislation, or the enactment of new companies legislation with major consolidation such as the Companies Act 1908, Companies Act 1929 and the Companies Act 1948. Two of the earliest committees to report and make recommendations on company law reform were the Loreburn Committee reporting in 1905 and the Wrenbury Committee in 1918. However, their terms of reference were limited, and their recommendations did not radically amend the companies legislation at that time.

A more comprehensive report was provided by the Greene Committee reporting in 1926 on *Company Law Amendment*.[12] The Greene Committee's terms of reference extended to a whole spectrum of company law in connection with the Companies Acts 1908 to 1917. According to the Greene Committee, the system of company law and practice in force in England and Scotland had been gradually evolved to meet the needs of the community at large and the commercial community in particular. It considered that in general, the companies legislation fulfilled this objective in a 'highly satisfactory manner'. It was a system well understood by those who had to deal with it; it had stood the test of years and should not be altered in any manner of principle, except where alteration was imperatively demanded. Its philosophy was not to avoid radically amending the companies legislation if the provisions were working in practice, and only to make such amendments as were absolutely necessary in the circumstances. This approach has been followed by successive committees established in considering company law reform in the UK.

The Greene Committee was satisfied that the great majority of limited companies both public and private were honestly and conscientiously

---

[12] Company Law Amendment (Greene Committee) (1925–1926).

managed. Cases in which fraud or lesser forms of dishonesty or improper dealing were comparatively few, and the public interest which such cases naturally aroused, tended to divert attention from the vast number of honestly conducted concerns to create an exaggerated idea of the evils connected with limited companies and their activities. The Committee realised that the system of limited liability left opportunities for abuse. However, this was part of the price the community was required to pay for the adoption of a system that would be beneficial to its trade and industry. The Committee did not recommend major changes in the deregulation of private companies.[13]

The Committee considered a wide spectrum of company law reform ranging from the objects clause[14] and change of name to capital maintenance, meetings and liquidation of a company. One important area for consideration by the Committee was directors' liability in the management of a company's affairs. A common practice had been established in the Articles of Association exempting directors from liability for loss except when it was due to their 'willful neglect or default'.[15] Another common form of article exempted directors in every case except actual dishonesty.[16] The Committee considered that this type of article gave an unjustifiable protection to directors. Under the article, a director could with impunity be guilty of the grossest negligence, provided that he did not consciously do anything that he recognised to be improper. According to the evidence before the Committee, in a great majority of companies in the UK, directors conscientiously endeavoured to perform their duties. The exemption of directors' liability for everything except actual dishonesty would need to be amended by legislation.

---

[13] According to the Greene Committee: 'A number of suggestions were made to us, the object of which was to remove certain of the restriction imposed by the present law upon limited companies and those concerned in their formation and management. Here again, we have not felt justified in making any recommendation except such as appeared to us to be called for by a strong body of business opinion as to which we have satisfied ourselves that no undesirable consequences are likely to follow. In dealing with an instrument so nicely balanced as the existing law relating to limited companies there is always the danger that some alteration, apparently desirable in itself, may have unexpected repercussions throughout the whole mechanism.'

[14] Previously, the Wrenbury Committee in paras 53–55 of its report had criticised the modern form of memorandum and recommended that the objects of the company should alone be inserted in the memorandum and its powers relegated to the articles. The Greene Committee did not agree with the Wrenbury Committee's recommendations here by reasoning that the weight of commercial opinion was against the suggested change. The Greene Committee also opposed a shortened form of the memorandum, stating that although this may be convenient, commercial opinion was against it, and the desirability of having one document only to which reference could be made when the question of *ultra vires* arose appeared to outweigh all other considerations. The Greene Committee 'purposely' made no recommendations to changes to Table A.

[15] See for example, *Re City Equitable Fire* [1925] Ch 407.

[16] See *Brazilian Rubber Estates* [1911] 1 Ch 425.

The Committee thought that 'to attempt by statute to define the duties of directors would be a hopeless task' and the proper course would be to prohibit articles and contracts directed at relieving directors and other officers of a company from their liability under the general law of negligence, and breach of duty or breach of trust. This type of enactment would not cause any hardship to a conscientious director or make his position more onerous, and it would not discourage otherwise desirable persons from accepting office. A director who accepted office did not consciously do so upon the footing that he may be as negligent as he pleased without incurring liability. It was only when the director had been negligent and the company had suffered a loss, that he was content to take shelter behind this article. The Committee recommended that any conduct or provision (whether in the company's articles or otherwise) whereby a director, manager or other officer of the company was excused from or indemnified against his liability under the general law for negligence or breach of duty or breach of trust, should be declared void.

The Committee noted that private companies had been subjected to a certain amount of criticism on the evidence before the Committee. Although this criticism may have been justified in some cases, the Committee was satisfied that the great majority of private companies on the register were honestly conducted. Much of the criticism was directed to cases of fraudulent trading by undischarged bankrupts and others through the medium of a private company and cases of directors holding debentures which they enforced at a time convenient for themselves. The Committee did not, therefore, feel that any alteration to the law was required to meet the 'special' cases of private companies. This was a disappointing report, as the Committee had missed the opportunity to consider radical reforms for small businesses and private companies, even though the majority of the companies registered at Companies House were private companies. The 'think public companies first' approach prevailed. The unfounded fear was that small businesses would incorporate under the cloak of a company with all the privileges of limited liability and incorporation, and conduct fraudulent trading, become bankrupt and then liquidate the company with no remedy for creditors. This was perceived by the Committee as an abuse of privilege of incorporation. There were no statistics put forward to the Committee as evidence to demonstrate that such abuse of incorporation was taking place with respect to small businesses and private companies. Many of the Greene Committee's recommendations were included in the Companies Act 1929, which consolidated previous companies legislation.

The Cohen Committee reported in 1945 in its Report on *Company Law Amendment*.[17] The areas considered for company law reform were quite

---

[17] Board of Trade, Report of the Committee on Company Law Amendment (June 1945), Cmnd 6659.

extensive ranging from memoranda of association, the names of companies, capital maintenance, prospectuses, private companies, charges, nominee shareholders and financial aspects.[18] The Cohen Committee shared the Greene Committee's view that a great majority of limited companies both public and private were honestly and conscientiously managed. The system of limited liability companies had been, and was, beneficial to the trade and industry of the country, and essential to the prosperity of the nation as a whole. The Companies Acts had been amended from time to time to bring them into accord with changing conditions, but if there were to be any flexibility, opportunities for abuse would inevitably exist. However, it recommended that the fullest practicable disclosure of information concerning the activities of companies would lessen such opportunities and accord with a wakening social consciousness. The Committee took account of the view that business should not be fettered unnecessarily, and that the best way to govern companies was to make available as much information as was reasonably required to the shareholders and creditors of the companies concerned and the general public.[19]

The Cohen Committee also examined the relationship between shareholders and directors. It stated that the illusory nature of the control theoretically exercised by shareholders over directors had been accentuated by the dispersion of capital among an increasing number of shareholders, who paid little attention to their investments so long as satisfactory dividends were forthcoming, who lacked sufficient time, money and experience to make full use of their rights as occasion arises and who were, in many cases, too numerous and too widely dispersed to be able to organise themselves. The shareholders were perceived as voiceless – absentee shareholders.[20] A large part of the Cohen Committee's recommendations were included in the CA 1948 by consolidating previous companies legislation.

The Jenkins Committee reporting in 1962 also considered reforms to the

---

[18] The Committee's terms of reference were 'to consider and report what major amendments are desirable in the Companies Act 1929, and, in particular, to review the requirements prescribed in regard to the formation and affairs of companies and the safeguards afforded for investors and for the public interest'.

[19] On the issue of objects and powers in a Memorandum of Association, the Cohen Committee was of the view that a practice had grown up of drafting memoranda of association very widely and at great length to enable the company to engage in any form of activity and to confer on it all ancillary powers which it might conceivably require in connection with such activities. The Committee believed that the doctrine of *ultra vires* was an illusory protection for the shareholders and yet may be a pitfall for third parties dealing with the company. Accordingly, the doctrine served no useful purpose and was a cause of unnecessary prolixity and vexation. It recommended that every company should, notwithstanding anything omitted from its Memorandum of Association, have as regards third parties the same powers as an individual.

[20] This concept is similar to the one proposed by Berle and Means in 1933. See *The Modern Corporation and Private Property* (1933).

company law system in the UK and principally to the CA 1948, which was the principal companies legislation at the time, including a review of directors' duties and the rights of shareholders.[21]

The Jenkins Committee acknowledged that since enactment of the Companies Act 1862, later enactments had greatly increased the volume and complexity of the law relating to companies. Even the CA 1948 comprised a total of 462 sections with 18 schedules. It advocated the need for a reduction in this 'unwieldy mass of legislation', but the Committee did not make recommendations contributing towards a reduction in the legislative provisions. In effect, its main conclusions and recommendations sought to further increase the level of disclosure of information for companies and added a number of provisions to the CA 1948. The Committee did not propose major reforms in the area of company law. It suggested that the elaboration of law under the Companies Acts was justified as having been found necessary, in order to keep effective control over the growing and changing uses of the company system as an instrument of business and finance, and the possibilities of abuse inherent in the system. The Committee believed that it would be wrong in principle to disturb in any important respect long-standing provisions designed to serve these ends, unless they had clearly outlived their usefulness or were demonstrably objectionable on other grounds.

According to the Jenkins Committee, it was necessary for the protection of shareholders, creditors and intending investors that the activities of companies and those responsible for their management should be subject to a considerable degree of statutory regulation and control. However, controls and regulations carried to excess could defeat their own object. It was undesirable to impose restrictions that would seriously hamper the activities of honest business people in order to defeat an occasional wrongdoer, and the importance of not placing unreasonable fetters upon business which was conducted in an efficient and honest manner.

The Committee noted the increase of private companies registered at Companies House[22] and observed the Board of Trade's evidence of the 'irresponsible multiplication of companies, particularly of "one-man" companies'; to the dangers of abuse through the incorporation with limited liability of very small under-capitalised businesses; and to the fact that at the time incorporation was frequently used as a cheap means of protecting a name. The Committee was satisfied that the proliferation of very small companies could lead to abuse and gave rise to ever-increasing administrative difficulties.

---

[21] The Jenkins Committee's terms of reference were to review and report upon the provisions and the working of the CA 1948, the Prevention of Fraud (Investments) Act 1958, except insofar as it relates to industrial and provident societies and building societies, and the Registration of Business Names Act 1916; to consider in the light of modern conditions and practices, including the practice of take-over bids, what should be the duties of directors and the rights of shareholders; and generally to recommend what changes in the law are desirable.

[22] By the end of 1961, there were 403,000 private companies and 16,000 public companies.

However, the Committee was not persuaded that a single-member company should be established and instead opted for two shareholders to be needed upon incorporation of a company. This was designed to discourage irresponsible incorporations; and a change would enable one person, by merely signing a piece of paper and complying with certain statutory requirements, to convert himself into a company, and to repeat this performance as often as he wished.

The Committee retained the *ultra vires* principle in respect of objects and powers of a company. It decided that the best course would be to attempt no general repeal of the existing *ultra vires* doctrine to companies registered under the Companies Acts, but instead to provide protection to third parties contracting with companies.[23]

On the issue of directors' duties, the Jenkins Committee noted that the Companies Act 1945 expressly imposed certain duties on directors, but they were not exhaustive. The larger part of the duties and responsibilities were determined by extensive and complex case law, which could not be found in the Companies Act. The Committee also noted that certain advocates of company law reform had proposed a codification of directors' duties by legislation. Others had suggested that there should be a Directors' Code which would not have the force of law. The Committee shied away from recommending any codification of directors' duties. Instead, it adopted the statement of the General Council of the Bar that any attempt to define the duties of directors more clearly would involve the risk that since it would be impossible to define such duties exhaustively, there would be inevitable

---

[23] This would be achieved by abrogating the rule in *Royal British Bank v Turquand* (1855) 5 E. & B. 248 that third parties are fixed with constructive notice of the contents of a company's memorandum and Articles of Association. The Committee recommended that a contract entered into between a company and another party (including a shareholder contracting otherwise than in his capacity as a shareholder) contracting with the company in good faith, should not be held invalid as against the other party on the ground that it was beyond the powers of the company; he should not, however, be allowed to enforce the contract without submitting to perform his part of it as far as it is unperformed. Further, by entering into such contract, the other party should be entitled to assume without investigation that the company is in fact possessed of the necessary power; and should not by reason of his omission so to investigate, be deemed not to have acted in good faith, or be deprived of his right to enforce the contract on the ground that at the time of entering into it, he had constructive notice of any limitations on the powers of the company, or on the powers of any director or other person to act on the company's behalf, imposed by its memorandum or Articles of Association. The other party should not be deprived of his right to enforce the contract on the ground that he had actual knowledge of the contents of the memorandum and articles at the time of entering into the contract if he honestly and reasonably failed to appreciate that they had the effect of precluding the company (or any director or other person on its behalf) from entering into the contract in question. The Jenkins Committee also recommended that every company should have certain specified powers, except to the extent that they are excluded, expressly or by implication, by its memorandum; such powers being those which any company would normally need in order to pursue its objects.

lacunae which might make it more difficult to determine in any particular set of circumstances what these duties were. However, the Committee was in favour of a statement expressing the fiduciary relationship of directors towards their companies, provided that any such reference did not override or replace any existing duties under the law. A general statement of the basic principles underlying this relationship could be useful for directors and others concerned with company management.[24]

It is interesting to note that even in 1965, the Jenkins Committee advocated some regulation of directors' fiduciary duties, even as a general principle. It recommended that the Companies Act should provide that a director should observe the utmost good faith towards a company in any transaction with it or on its behalf, and should act honestly in the exercise of his powers and the discharge of the duties of his office. Further, a director should not make use of any money or other property of the company or of any information acquired by virtue of his position as a director or officer of the company, to gain directly or indirectly an improper advantage for himself at the expense of the company. A director who committed a breach of these provisions would be liable to the company for any profit made by him, and for any damage suffered by the company as a result of the breach.

The Jenkins Committee favoured active shareholder involvement in companies and was against the 'passive' investor concept. It commented: 'But, unless the affairs of the company have gone badly wrong there is seldom any controversy. The directors of reputable companies would much prefer that meetings should be better attended and that more interest should be taken by members in the company's affairs. Members on the other hand are persistently reluctant to concern themselves with the management of their companies, and, so long as satisfactory dividends are paid, are content to leave everything to the directors. This works well in the great majority of cases but untoward events, which might have been averted by greater interest on the part of shareholders, do occur.'[25]

---

[24] As an example, the Committee referred to one of the fiduciary duties established in *Percival v Wright* [1902] 2 Ch 421. This case was authority for the proposition that no fiduciary duty was owed by a director to individual members of the company, but only to the company itself.

[25] With regards to the relationship between shareholders and directors, the Jenkins Committee stated that the Companies Act at the time provided shareholders with powerful weapons provided they chose to use them. This must, however, be balanced against the directors' ability to manage their company efficiently and they must, within broad limits, have a free hand to do what they consider best in the interests of the company. The Jenkins Committee was generally satisfied that as a general rule, directors exercised their powers in what they conceived to be in the best interests of their companies and pay due regard to the desirability of referring to their shareholders for approval, whenever it was practicable to do so, any proposals of fundamental importance which they have in view, or failing that, of keeping their shareholders adequately informed of such developments. Jenkins recommended more disclosure of information to shareholders and transparency in respect of the company's activities such as the directors' report and that all directors should be made responsible for the accuracy of this report.

The Committee recommended more disclosure of information to shareholders to protect shareholders' interests. It also stated however that if directors were to manage their companies efficiently they must, within broad limits, also have a free hand to do what they considered in the best interests of the company. The Committee was generally satisfied that directors did exercise their delegated powers in what they considered to be in the best interests of their companies and pay due regard to the desirability of referring to their shareholders for approval, whenever it was practicable to do so, any proposals of fundamental importance.

The Jenkins Committee's approach to company law reform was yet more disclosure of information and transparency – more bureaucracy and administration. The Committee hardly made any attempt to address the practical and real needs of small businesses and private companies. As with previous company law reform committees, it was convinced that to allow flexibility for private limited companies would create room for abuse of the privilege of incorporation, and the Committee left no room for further reform in this area. As a result, the Jenkins Committee's recommendations were added to subsequent companies legislation some of which provisions were largely irrelevant to small companies. The Jenkins Committee's recommendations did not lead to any consolidation of the Companies Act at the time and reforms proceeded by way of amendments to the CA 1948. There was no significant consolidation until the CA 1985. The CA 1985 consolidated many of the provisions of the CA 1948. With the accession of the UK to the European Economic Community in 1972, the CA 1985 also included a harmonisation and unification of European company laws.[26] The CA 1989 was not a consolidating legislation, but was enacted to implement the Seventh EU Directive on consolidated accounts and the Eighth Directive on the regulation of auditors. The CA 1989 also considered further reforms to the *ultra vires* doctrine and reference to the doctrine of constructive notice, reforms to company charges, increasing the investigatory powers of the Department of Trade and Industry into company investigations, reform of competition laws regarding mergers, the deregulation of private companies and amendments to the financial services legislation, previously the Financial Services Act 1986 (now the Financial Services and Markets Act 2000).

Separate Acts were enacted that had an impact on the CA 1985 such as the Business Names Act 1985, insolvency legislation by way of the Insolvency Act 1986, and the previous Financial Services Act 1986.

---

[26] For example, under s 9 of the European Communities Act 1972, the UK implemented the First Directive on company law harmonisation with particular reference to the *ultra vires* doctrine and directors' authority. Further, the Companies Act 1980 implemented the Second Directive of the European Union on share capital and classification of companies. The Companies Act 1981 implemented the Fourth Directive on company accounts. There were also Directives issued by the European Union on the listing to the stock exchanges of other member states.

Reform of The *Ultra Vires* Rule – The Prentice Report

1.3 In 1986, the Department of Trade and Industry commissioned Dr D.D. Prentice to review the *ultra vires* doctrine with a view to making recommendations in this area. A consultative document was produced in order to seek comments from various interested parties. According to the Department of Trade and Industry, '. . . in practice, it (i.e. the *ultra vires* doctrine) represents an obstacle to enterprise and works so capriciously that it is doubtful whether it offers any real protection to anyone'.[27]

The Prentice Report recommended the complete abolition of the *ultra vires* doctrine since it no longer served any useful purpose. His recommendations, inter alia, were that a company should not be affected by the contents of any document merely because it was registered by the registrar of companies or with the company (this could be made the subject of appropriate exceptions); a company should be bound by the acts of its board or individual director; a third party should be under no obligation to determine the scope of the authority of a company's board or an individual director, or the contents of a company's articles or memorandum (this should extend to documents which have to be registered under s 380 CA 1985);[28] a third party who has actual knowledge that a board or an individual director does not posses authority to enter into a transaction on behalf of the company should not be allowed to enforce against the company but the company should be free to ratify it. The same result should obtain where a third party has actual knowledge that the transaction falls outside the company's objects, but in this case ratification should be by special resolution; knowledge in this context will require understanding and it will only be the knowledge of the individual entering into the particular transaction that will be relevant. As regards actual knowledge, Prentice recommended that the rules should be modified where a third party is an officer or director of the company, and in this situation constructive knowledge should be sufficient to render the transaction unenforceable, and for this purpose, constructive knowledge that may reasonably be expected of a person carrying out the functions of that director or officer of that company.

Although the CA 1989 had virtually repealed the *ultra vires* doctrine, the Act had not adopted the recommendations proposed by Prentice. It instead inserted a new s.3A CA 1985 ('Statement of Company's Objects').[29] This

---

[27] Department of Trade and Industry, *Reform of the Ultra Vires Rule: A Consultative Document*, at para 2 p.1. On the criticisms of the *ultra vires* doctrine, see especially para 12 pp.13–14 of the report.

[28] CA 1985, s 380 required a company to forward a copy of all elective, special, extraordinary and certain ordinary resolutions to Companies House within 15 days of these being passed. The registrar would then record these resolutions.

[29] CA 1989, s 110.

provided that where the memorandum states that the company's object is to carry on business as a 'general commercial company', the company can carry out any trade or business whatsoever. It also had power to do all such things as are incidental or conducive to the carrying of any trade or business by it, including philanthropic acts. Section 3A was intended to encourage the companies to use the 'short form' objects clause rather than the 'long form' objects clause, which was widely drafted to avoid the *ultra vires* doctrine.

Further steps towards the virtual abolition of the *ultra vires* doctrine were achieved by substituting for the original s 35 above new ss 35, 35A and 35B Companies Act as amended.[30] The new s 35, *inter alia*, provided that the validity of an act committed by a company cannot be questioned on the ground of lack of capacity by reason of anything in the company's memorandum. This meant that neither the company nor the third party could rely on the strict *ultra vires* doctrine. The new ss 35A and 35B (CA 1985) were concerned with directors' lack of authority and constructive notice respectively. Section 35A, *inter alia*, provided that, where a third party was dealing with the company in good faith, the board of directors would be deemed to have authority to exercise all the company's power (unless the Companies Act required the powers to be exercised by another body) and to be able to delegate such authority, notwithstanding, in either event, any limitations in the company's constitution on the board's authority. Section 35B was to be read with s 711A of the CA 1985, with the result that a third party dealing with the company was no longer deemed to have notice of the contents of any corporate documents even though they may be registered at Companies House. This effectively abolished the doctrine of constructive notice.

The period up to 1998 could be characterised as one of consolidation of company laws in the United Kingdom. The establishment of various company law committees did not make significant reforms to the Companies Acts to modernise the company law framework. Almost all committees avoided a major overhaul of company law. The interests of small businesses and private companies were largely ignored by the committees, which preferred instead to add to the layer of existing provisions a series of exemptions for private companies as an afterthought, giving further credence to public companies over private companies, despite the fact that a majority of companies registered were private companies.

This period can also be characterised as one in which the 'think public company first' approach prevailed. Very little consideration was given to the needs of small businesses and private companies. Layer after layer of provisions were added onto subsequent companies legislations exempting private companies from complying with public company provisions. Rather than a period of deregulation, this period can be categorised as yet more

---

[30] As inserted by CA 1989, s 108.

disclosure of information by the company, and unnecessary bureaucracy, with some of the public company provisions largely irrelevant to private companies.

The Position in 1998

1.4 A step towards a radical reform of the company law regime in the UK, was witnessed in the Labour Government's commitment to a series of consultation documents issued by the Department of Trade and Industry (as it was then), that began in 1998 and continued until the latter part of 2000. The Government signalled its firm intention to establish a Steering Group that would be charged with reviewing the whole spectrum of UK company law, and to make recommendations with a view to enacting new legislation.[31]

The period from 1998 until 2005 was one of wide consultation by the Government, providing a rationale for change, addressing the defects inherent in the existing company law regime and providing recommendations including publication of various parts of the Companies Bill at various stages of consultation, with detailed scrutiny of the Companies Bill in both Houses of Parliament.[32]

There was a wide perception that the existing company law framework comprised a 'patchwork' of legislation – much of which dated back to Victorian times and was costly for companies to comply with. It was particularly onerous for small companies and businesses which were required to comply with provisions that were largely applicable to public companies, many being irrelevant and inapplicable to private companies. For larger companies, there was the added issue of complying with the corporate governance combined code of best practice. However, company law did not set out any coherent definition as to the role, responsibilities and duties of directors, shareholders or auditors.[33]

This section sets out a summary of the main issues considered in each of the key consultation documents issued by the Department of Trade culminating in the CA 2006.

---

[31] According to one member of the Steering Committee: 'Company law provides Government's framework for the orderly conduct of British business. It is a truism that such a framework needs to be coherent so that it can encourage sound entrepreneurial activity and enhance the confidence in the UK as a good place for business activity . . . But the present framework of company law is . . . anything but coherent. It is a patchwork of piecemeal legislation – and latterly corporate governance codes as well – built up over a century or more.' Foreword by Rosemary Radcliffe, *A Practitioner's Guide to The Company Law Review* (2001).

[32] The Bill began its life as the Company Law Reform Bill, which was not a consolidation of companies legislation and only amended parts of the CA 1985. However, at a later stage in Parliament, the Bill was changed to the Companies Bill as a consolidating measure.

[33] See Foreword by Rosemary Radcliffe, n.31 above, at p.xx1.

The Six Phases

1.5 From 1998, company law reform in the UK can be characterised into six phases:

(a) Phase one – the Launch;
(b) Phase two – the Strategic Framework;
(c) Phase three – Developing the Framework;
(d) Phase four – Completing the Structure;
(e) Phase five – Final Report; and
(f) Phase six – the White Papers.

Phase One – The Launch

1.6 Phase one can be considered as the launch phase for the debate on company law reform in the UK. It was a period in which the essential foundations were established for a review of the whole spectrum of company law; the rationale for change; the establishment of a steering committee charged with responsibility for the review; and wide consultation. The philosophy for change was also addressed, including the benefits of reform.

Establishing the foundations – Modern Company Law: For A Competitive Economy

1.6.1 The initial consultation stages in developing a new, coherent framework for the UK company law regime began in 1998 when the Labour Government's Board of Trade prepared the setting for a radical reform of UK company law in its consultation document *Modern Company Law: For A Competitive Economy*.[34] This document can be described as the launch document towards company law reform.[35] The Board's then President,

---

[34] Board of Trade, *Modern Company Law For A Competitive Economy* (1998).

[35] *A Practitioner's Guide to The Company Law Review*, n 31 above, at p 1 (Jonathan Rickford, Project Director of the Review). According to Rickford, what was required was 'a modern law for a modern world', based on a comprehensive re-examination of the law as a coherent interrelated system. At a later stage, the Steering Group stated there was a need for 'a framework of company law which promotes the competitiveness of British companies, strikes a proper balance between the interests of those concerned with companies, in the context of straightforward, cost-effective and fair regulation, and promotes consistency, predictability and transparency in the law.' The launch document received over 200 responses with no dissent on the need for reform. According to Rickford, the structure of the review was to be participative, open, multi-disciplinary and layered. The Steering Group was chaired by a senior DTI civil servant, but included senior board members of both public and private companies, professions, academic lawyers, a High Court Judge, economists, accountants and experts in the regulation and business strategy. During the course of the review, the Steering Committee issued 10 major, and some minor consultation documents and letters which were all published

Margaret Beckett, stated that company law lay at the heart of UK economy. Although technical, and often left to be handled by specialists, it provided the legal basis for all companies, and was fundamental to the UK's competitiveness. The Government introduced a 'fundamental review of the framework of core company law'. It argued that 40 years had passed since the last major review of company law and much of the structure of corporate law was a legacy of nineteenth-century legislators.[36] Although the review was under the aegis of the Board of Trade, much of the work was undertaken by a multi-disciplinary Steering Committee with detailed specialised company law aspects delegated to a series of working groups and sub-committees comprising academics, industrialists, other professionals and unions. The Steering Committee was required to report within three years.[37]

by the DTI. The consultation process was structured in four phases with each being completed by a new consultation document consolidating progress and opening up new issues. Phase 1 was *The Strategic Framework* (February 1999); Phase 2 was *Developing the Framework* (March 2000); Phase 3 was *Completing the Structure* (November 2000); and Phase 4 was *The Final Report* (May 2001). The Steering Group had maintained overall control of the review through its project director. It also set the strategy and decided all major issues of principle and settled all major publications. Much of the work of analysing the issues and proposing policy solutions was delegated to Working Groups, Sub-Groups and more informal ad hoc working parties – comprising almost 20, each led by a Steering Group member. Experts from various perspectives were invited to participate in these issues on a basis of personal independence, but with the authority to test ideas through their own networks. This approach enabled them to develop and test ideas in an atmosphere of expert, multi-disciplinary 'give-and-take', without any defending of vested interests. Further, this discipline also operated in the Steering Committee. Each major consultation document was considered by the Review Consultative Committee. This Committee was designed as a representative committee. It included delegates of all major representative bodies in industry, commerce and professions with an interest in company law and leading individual experts; and of non-government institutions, and of main government departments. In total, this Committee comprised 60 members. It met every quarter, and was briefed about every meeting, and provided a forum for interested bodies to influence, discuss, share and co-ordinate their views as work proceeded.

[36] In a debate in the House of Commons, Margaret Beckett stated: 'The review is an important part of the Government's strategy to modernise the nation. While much of the relevant statute has stood the test of time, the review will ensure that company law statute can continue to underpin the growth, competitiveness and accountability of British companies into the twenty-first century. It will, for example, consider, whether, taking account of partnership law and the proposed Limited Liability Partnership, business has the right choice of legislative vehicles for growth. It will address the complexity of the current legislation, and ensure a structure that is clear to users; and it will seek a flexible framework of regulation which is cost effective for companies, and fair to all interests.' HC Deb, 4 March 1998 cc 636–7W.

[37] The Steering Committee and all parties in the House of Commons had emphasised the importance of the independence of the Committee from any government influence. The work of the Committee received favourable cross-Party support. The Steering Committee presented its 'Final Report' to the Government in May 2001. Shortly thereafter, the Labour Government announced its intention to legislate on company law.

The President epitomised the fragmented and antiquated nature of UK companies legislation: 'Our current framework of company law is essentially constructed on foundations which were put in place by Victorians in the middle of the last century. There have been numerous additions, amendments and consolidations since then, but they have created a patchwork of regulation that is immensely complex and seriously out of date. The resulting costs and problems may not be obvious to all, but they are real and substantial nonetheless.'[38]

There was a need to ensure that UK established a framework of company law that was up to date, competitive and designed for the next century. These three concepts were categorised as the 'three key pillars' in UK's approach towards competitiveness. The consultation document set out a wide review of the companies legislation, without necessarily affecting the underlying company law principles that had stood the test of time. The review would actively consider the current balance of obligations and responsibilities, and seek to ensure that they were clearly expressed for the non-specialist.

The Labour Government considered that the time was right to embark on a fundamental review of the framework of core company law. Many of the key features of companies legislation were put in place in the middle of last century. Although there have been numerous changes and additions through the years, it had been almost 40 years since the last broad review of company law. The current framework of company law had as a result become seriously out-dated in key respects, notwithstanding the increasing globalisation of the economy. Rapid progress in information technology had meant that in a number of areas of company law, present arrangements had held back rather than facilitated competitiveness, growth and investment.

The object of company law review has been to bring forward proposals for a modern law for the modern world. The UK companies legislation was required to have an updated framework, promoting competitiveness of UK companies, which contributed to national competitiveness and increased prosperity. The consultation document envisaged the establishment of a Steering Committee and Working Groups with broad representation, a Consultative Committee, and the publication for comment of key documents from time to time.[39] The review would be wide ranging, but businesses would not have to fear large-scale upheaval of familiar requirements.

---

[38] Margaret Beckett, President of the Board of Trade (1998), Foreword to *Modern Company Law: For A Competitive Economy*.

[39] The Steering Group would oversee the management of the project and ensure that its outcome was clear in concept, internally coherent, well-articulated and expressed and workable. The Steering Group would be small, comprising senior lawyers, representatives of business (large and small), a Scottish representative, Chairs of Working Groups and the Project Director. The Steering Group would be chaired by the Director, Company Law and Investigations and the DTI. The review would be handled with maximum openness and independence on the basis of

The consultation document highlighted one end of the spectrum, the range of small start-up type companies and the other end of the spectrum, large companies registered at Companies House.[40] All these companies were subject to the same broad framework of company law, namely the then CA 1985, which brought together or 'consolidated' previous legislation. Some of the provisions of the CA 1985 varied according to the type and size of company, but the same basic principles applied to all companies, small and large, even though some of the principles may not have been applicable to smaller start-up type companies. The philosophy behind the CA 1985 was that one size fitted all companies.

Many of the key principles such as limited liability, registration on a public register and disclosure of information about the company's financial state, were put in place in the middle of the nineteenth century. There had been two reforms that had a significant impact on company law in the UK. First, the Joint Stock Companies Act 1844 required all new businesses with more than 25 participants to be 'incorporated', namely, to set up as companies with a legal status and personality of their own, rather than as conventional partnerships. The 1844 Act also stated that such companies should be set up by the simple process of registration (rather than by Act of Parliament or royal charter), and created the post of Registrar of Companies, which continues to this day. The Act also provided for 'publicity' or disclosure in particular through companies' constitutions and annual accounts being filed with the Registrar of Companies.

The second main Act was the Limited Liability Act 1855. This introduced the concept of limited liability for shareholders in respect of their liability for the company's debts, if it became bankrupt, and liability was limited to the amount of share capital they had invested. It was felt important that the company's creditors should be aware of the limited liability status of the company, and the requirement for companies to have 'limited' or 'Ltd' in their name.

Following the above legislation, businesses mostly fell into two categories: incorporated companies and conventional partnerships. The numbers of incorporated companies increased steadily mainly towards the end of the nineteenth century. In numerical terms, by 1914 about 65,000 companies were

wide consultation. Simplification and rationalisation would be key themes at the heart of the review from the beginning. The Government was also determined to ensure that the new arrangements would support business activity and promote growth and competitiveness within a balanced framework rather than to act as a brake or unnecessary constraint.

[40] In 1998, the DTI estimated that there were about 1.14 million UK companies registered at Companies House ranging from the smallest start-up businesses to large long-established companies operating internationally. There were relatively few companies operating at the larger end of the scale – only 2,450 had their shares publicly traded on the London Stock Exchange.

registered; and by 1945, about 200,000. The principal rules for partnership were brought together in the Partnership Act 1890.

Developments in UK company law in the nineteenth century arose largely from reactions to scandals and mischief arising from the wide scope allowed by the Victorian legislation, which in general had only a light regulatory touch. The Board of Trade in fact appointed a Committee at intervals of around 20 years to review company law.[41] The resulting recommendations were introduced in an amending Companies Act. The old and the new laws were then 'consolidated' into a new comprehensive Companies Act. These major consolidations took place in 1908, 1929 and 1948. One significant review of company law took place under the Jenkins Committee, which was appointed in 1960 and reported in 1962. A number of its recommendations were enacted piecemeal in the companies legislation of 1967, 1980 and 1981. These reviews largely concentrated on current scandals and perceived deficiencies in protecting investors or preventing fraud. The ultimate result was the constant addition of new rules and regulations to companies legislation without any re-examination of its fundamental principles. Company law, therefore, grew in bulk and complexity, but no attempt was made to slim down the basic structure and remove sections designed to deal with practices and situations which had often died out.

To add to further complications to the existing legislation, additional legislation was tacked on, owing to the UK's entry into the EC in 1972, reflecting the need to reflect EC Directives in UK companies legislation adopted under the EC harmonisation programme. According to the late Professor Gower, this left the legislation 'in a worse state than at any time this century'.

The legislation up to 1985 was consolidated in the form of the CA 1985. This was swiftly followed by the then Insolvency Acts 1985 and 1986 (later only the Insolvency Act 1986) and the Financial Services Act 1986 (later the Financial Services and Markets Act 2000). These latter Acts represented a major structural change in the legislation by removing insolvency law and securities regulation from companies legislation and establishing them as distinct areas of law.

This period also witnessed the enactment of the CA 1989. It largely implemented the Seventh EC Company Law Directive on Consolidated Accounts, and the Eighth EC Company Law Directive on Audits, but also included some 'domestic' reforms following the Prentice Report. The 1989 Act was the most recent Act in company law, though a number of provisions of this Act and the CA 1985 had been modified by the use of Order-making powers, that is, the power to make minor changes without a new Act of Parliament.

---

[41] See, for example, the Wrenbury Committee; the Loreburn Committee; the Greene Committee; the Cohen Committee and the Jenkins Committee.

The history of company law has; therefore, witnessed the great reforms of the nineteenth century. There have been a series of additions to the existing legal framework resulting from the need to tackle perceived deficiencies and shortcomings. However, over the years there has also been increasing concern in all company-related circles that the company law framework had become obsolescent, and it was also clear that gradual piecemeal reform could not significantly reduce the amount and complexity of current arrangements.

The consultation document highlighted some of the main issues that needed to be addressed in order to radically reform UK company law. It advocated that the structure of UK company law was not just outdated, but that it also contributed to problems and costs for business. The Government was keen to emphasise that this overhaul of UK company law was not just an academic exercise to 'tidy up' the complex area of law, but that new arrangements were required to establish a more effective, and cost-effective, framework of law for companies to improve their competitiveness, and contribute further to national growth and prosperity. The new arrangements would be based on principles of 'consistency', 'predictability' and 'transparency'. They would also compare favourably with the company law framework of other developed economies.

One of the major problems with the UK company law framework was its sheer complexity. Arrangements could not be fully effective if companies and their directors could not clearly identify and understand their legal responsibilities. The problem was particularly acute for small companies without ready access to legal advice. Many issues were highlighted by the Board of Trade: one was over-formal language – Table A to the Companies Acts set out a model form memorandum and Articles of Association and provided the basic constitutional framework for most companies. Providing such models was widely regarded as helpful for smaller companies. However, Table A was written in technical, legalistic language and would have been of more practical use if it were re-written in plain English. Another issue was excessive detail – there were many small points that made the legislation more complicated than it needed to be, such as the distinction between special and extraordinary resolutions at general meetings. There was a real problem in understanding the legislation due to such detail. Another issue highlighted was over-regulation – difficulties arose from the overall approach of the legislation. For example, a major part of the CA 1985 was concerned with rules to ensure that companies maintained their capital, namely, the finance raised from the issue of shares. Although this was an important area of the CA 1985, which was designed to reduce the risk of insolvency, it was too detailed, and was widely believed to increase the cost, and reduce the flexibility, of companies' management of their capital. Comparison with other countries, such as Canada, suggested that a framework that was easier to operate and gave greater general freedoms would be possible. Some aspects such as the requirement for shares to have a nominal or 'par' value could be abandoned. Among other advantages, this would enable a simpler statement of share capital in companies' accounts. There was also a case for reform of the complicated and costly court procedures that companies were required to go through if they were to reduce their share capital.

Another major aspect concerned the complex structure of the CA 1985. The difficulty was understanding all the specific rules in the Companies Act directed at particular classes of company, such as small private companies. Some parts of that Act, such as the disclosure of who owned shares, applied only to public companies. Other parts of the Act, such as those on capital maintenance and the enforcement of fair dealing by directors, contained rules that were different in their application for public and private companies. These rules were often mixed together in a way that made it difficult to distinguish between those that applied to public and those to private companies. The objective of company law review was, therefore, to consider how best to set out companies legislation so that it showed clearly the legal responsibilities of small companies and their directors.

One consequence of the complexity was that companies often incurred substantial costs in terms of management time and professional fees. This was evident in the rule that prevented companies from giving financial assistance to another person to buy their shares. These rules were difficult to comprehend for small companies.

The companies legislation was, therefore, poorly laid out and complicated owing to many changes being made to meet 'short-term' needs and problems, rather than to lay sound foundations for likely future developments. Sometimes too, company law just failed to achieve its purpose.

Some of the companies legislation was obsolescent or ineffective. For example, companies were required to keep on their register of members not only the name and address of each member, but also the date on which he or she became or ceased to be a member. This provision dated back to 1856! This would have been useful at a time before limited liability became widely used, when shareholders could still be personally liable for all the company's debts, and it might have been important to establish when a person became a shareholder for that reason. However, in modern times, in relation to listed companies, and the modern capital markets, recording these dates appears to serve little purpose. Another example concerned s 3A CA 1985 on the statement of the 'objects' or purpose of the company. Such a statement was required in the company's Memorandum of Association. Those setting up companies were often anxious to make sure that no constraints were placed on the future direction that their company might take, and hence describe its 'objects' at great length in order to allow for every conceivable circumstance. In order to avoid the need for such 'boilerplate' statements, s 3A was inserted in that Act to allow companies to describe themselves as a 'general commercial company', but it had been little used because it was still not regarded as covering every eventuality. The practice, therefore, grew of adding a s 3A clause at the end of a long form objects clause to cover every eventuality!

The companies legislation created obstacles to progress. Essentially the Companies Acts were backward looking, seeking to deal with problems that had arisen in the past rather than to facilitate modern practices. They risked impending efficiency. They limited the use of information technology in company administration. Reform was needed so that Companies House could pursue its modernisation plans aimed at allowing filing electronically rather than in paper form. Specific rules would then be adapted for AGMs to allow votes to be registered electronically by those not attending in person.

A further major issue has been the relationship between company law and corporate governance. The Cadbury Committee reporting in 1992 defined corporate governance as 'the system by which companies are directed and controlled' and concerned issues such as the composition and structure of boards of directors (such as the role of non-executive directors and the audit committee) and the accountability of boards to shareholders. It could have a major impact on the overall direction of the company and its commercial prospects. During the 1990s, three Committees had carried out major studies on corporate governance: the Cadbury Committee; the Greenbury Committee; and the Hampel Committee. The report of each committee had set out recommendations as to what was considered best practice in various aspects of corporate governance. These principles now form part of the London Stock Exchange regulations.

The consultation document emphasised that best practice principles could work side-by-side with legislation and may not be incompatible. Some of the areas highlighted for legal underpinning were: (i) duties of directors and the need to legislate as proposed by the Law Commissions of England and Wales and Scotland;[42] (ii) the conduct of annual general meetings which should be designed to make it easier for shareholders to table resolutions, and to attend and vote at AGMs if they did not hold shares in their name; (ii) shareholders' control over directors' pay with more transparency.

The Government, therefore, decided that the time was right for a thorough review of core company law. This meant the stripping out of obsolescent and

---

[42] This subject was widely discussed during the 1990's including *Tomorrow's Company* inquiry by the Royal Society of Arts; and the report, *Promoting Prosperity* by the Commission on Public Policy and British Business. The Commission concluded: 'Certainly it is important not to constrain directors to do anything against the long-interests of shareholders; rather, they should be free from an excessively narrow interpretation of their fiduciary responsibilities which could actually work against the company's interests.' The Commission went on to recommend that the Government should clarify directors' duties to enable directors to take a broader view of their responsibilities.

over-complex provisions and the repair of defective ones. There was a need for clear and simple arrangements which would better capture the balance of obligations, protections and responsibilities that were required to underpin the modern marketplace and technological environment rather than act as a brake; and be sufficiently flexible to cater for future developments. An up-to-date company law framework based on principles of consistency, predictability and transparency was particularly important in the context of a globalised economy, in terms both of competing for inward investment, and producing internationally competitive companies.[43]

The Board of Trade's objectives in undertaking company law review[44] were to promote a framework for the formation and constitution of British businesses which, through an effective combination of law and non-statutory regulation:

- supported the creation, growth and competitiveness of British companies and partnerships;
- promoted an internationally competitive framework for business, so that the UK continued to be an attractive place to do business;
- provided straightforward, cost-effective and fair regulation that balances the interests of business with those of shareholders, creditors and others; and

---

[43] In respect of the international dimension, the consultation document noted that the company law framework introduced by the Victorians had immense influence worldwide. Other countries, both within the British Empire and beyond, often followed the UK in introducing similar arrangements. For the most part of 150 years, broadly similar frameworks were put in place in many countries around the world. However, in more recent years, the UK's framework for company law has been perceived to be out of date. Major reviews have occurred in Canada, South Africa, Australia, New Zealand and Hong Kong. Commonwealth countries were increasingly developing their own model of company law, tailored to local circumstances and no longer looking to the UK for inspiration. The consultation documentation stated that in an increasingly globalised economy, the national framework of company law could not be considered in isolation. It represented part of the nation's infrastructure. This could best be seen in relation to business mobility. The Government was determined to ensure that the nation's framework of company law did not through increasing obsolescence become a disincentive to establishing business in the UK.

[44] The review concerned modernisation of company law. It was not reviewing the Insolvency Acts or the regulation of Financial Services. The task of the review was to develop a legal framework, based on the principles reflected in the Companies Acts, that covered the requirements for the birth, existence and death of companies. It would identify the fundamental rules governing the procedures for incorporation, the basic constitutional structure and the cessation of existence. It would examine the rights and responsibilities of the entity and its participants and identify the areas that should contain mandatory rules to protect the interests of shareholders, creditors, employees and other participants. It would also consider the issue of sanctions and enforcement including shareholder remedies. The review of company law would not extend to charity law or co-operatives.

- promoted consistency, predictability and transparency and underpins high standards of company behaviour and corporate governance.[45]

Modern Company Law: For A Competitive Economy, therefore, paved the way for the essential terms of reference and principles, that would guide a future Steering Committee in its review of UK company law reform and to make recommendations.

Phase one can be categorised as the launch phase for the reform of company law in the UK, and the establishment of terms of reference for the Steering Committee charged with the task of undertaking the review.

Phase Two – Modern Company Law For A Competitive Economy – The Strategic Framework

1.7 Phase Two of company law reform was concerned with the strategic framework. This was the first consultation document issued by the Steering Group that took forward the proposals set out by the DTI in the Launch Phase.

In February 1999, the Company Law Review Steering Group (the Group) published a consultation document entitled *Modern Company Law For A Competitive Economy – The Strategic Framework*.[46] This document was the first of a series of consultation documents to be issued by the Group set up to take forward a fundamental review of UK company law. The consultation document described in detail the work of the Group so far as the proposed arrangements for taking it forward. It also analysed a number of key substantive issues for the purpose of consultation and indicated a preferred way forward in some cases; and examined issues relating to legislative form of implementation and the institutional structures for

---

[45] The proposed terms of reference were: to consider how core company law can be modernised in order to provide a simple, efficient and cost-effective framework for carrying out business activity which (a) permits the maximum amount of freedom and flexibility to those organising and directing the enterprise; (b) at the same time protects, through regulation where necessary, the interests of those involved with the enterprise, including shareholders, creditors and employees; and (c) is drafted in clear, concise and unambiguous language that can be readily understood by those involved in business enterprise. The terms of reference also included considering whether company law, partnership law, and other legislation that establishes the legal form of business activity together provide an adequate choice of vehicle for business at all levels; to consider the proper relationship between company law and non-statutory standards of corporate behaviour; to review the extent to which foreign companies operating in Great Britain should be regulated under British company law.

[46] Department of Trade and Industry, *Modern Company Law For A Competitive Economy – The Strategic Framework* (A Consultative Document from The Company Law Review Steering Group) (February 1999).

on-going reform.[47] The Strategic Framework was the initial strategic and analytical phase in the development of company law reform. It set out the work already carried out by the review and details for taking company law reform forward. The consultation document also considered some key areas for consideration including presumptions in favour of minimising complexity and maximising the accessibility of rules.[48]

The Group emphasised that the objective of their review was to modernise company law, to ensure it was well fitted to meet the current and foreseeable future needs of company law users. This could involve some deregulation, but the objective was to suit the law to the needs of all participants, and of other relevant interests, rather than to reduce regulatory safeguards. The Group's focus was, therefore, on provisions that, in form or substance, no longer served their proper purpose, or that could be adjusted better to do so, and on needs for which there was currently no provision.

According to the Group, company law reform should also be aimed at facilitating productive and creative activity in the economy in the most competitive and efficient[49] way forward to benefit everyone, with freedom for managers and other controlling companies, ensuring that in order to maximise wealth and welfare, they were enabled to exercise their proper function in managing resources. The law should not be involved in substituting for the business judgments involved, but to provide optimal conditions for their exercise. Companies should not be required to operate at the legal boundary but must adopt a wide range of non-legal standards including best practice.[50]

The Group advocated that there should be freedom for companies but also protection from abuse. This did not mean that the law should merely facilitate and secure freedom for management and controllers of companies.[51] The Group advocated that the need for high standards of conduct should be maintained. Such standards were important components in promoting competitiveness and efficiency. Management must respond to the needs of

---

[47] The objectives of company law review were also the competitiveness of British companies; an attractive regime for overseas companies; a proper balance of the interests of those concerned with companies in the context of straightforward; cost effective and fair regulation; and the promotion of consistency, predictability and transparency in company law.

[48] See *The Company Law Reform Bill [HL]* Bill 190 2005–2006, Research Paper 06/30, 2 June 2006, Timothy Edmonds.

[49] The term 'efficient' referred to maximum output and contribution to prosperity at minimum cost, rather than simple efficiency in the popular sense.

[50] The Group emphasised that a competitive economy would rely as little as possible on costly and inflexible legal mechanisms. The most efficient law would often derive from well tried best practice or provide the best conditions for its development.

[51] There had to be a trade-off between freedom and abuse, and between freedom and efficiency. Abuse would damage the efficiency and the credibility of business and of the productive system.

shareholders and others and to ensure that corporate activity responded also to wider economic, environmental and social needs.[52]

The Group also highlighted the need to ensure comprehensive reform to produce a coherent framework. This was in contrast to the patchwork of largely core and prescriptive additions, accumulated as a result of episodic and reactive reform. Comprehensive reform was essential to produce a competitive and efficient outcome.

Although the companies legislation had many strengths and benefits, it did not measure up well against the modern company law objectives. However, UK company law failed in terms of responsiveness to the shape of modern businesses, and the accessibility of the language in which it was expressed. Some of the relevant provisions were hard to find and understand, and expensive to administer. Anti-abuse provisions took the form of unduly wide prohibitions, sometimes introduced for broad or now-superseded reasons, overlaid with complex exemptions, to which were attached a further layer of conditions and safeguards. Although the purpose might have been reasonably clear in theory, it bore little relationship to modern commercial reality, particularly in the context of the wide range of purposes to which the law was put. Further, elaborate prescriptive structures, such as the capital maintenance doctrine, had been built up on the back of theories that now had very little relevance. Legal obscurity would also lend support to outdated views such as the proper scope of managerial discretion.

External changes had exacerbated the problems for company law in the UK. The globalisation of economies and international trading had witnessed deficiencies in UK companies legislation. The increasing international mobility of business and capital, the globalisation of brands and the ability of firms to operate internationally, without local incorporation, also raised the need to review systems for regulating overseas businesses in Great Britain. Further, the UK's membership of the European Union had led to the increasing openness of the UK market and that of its EU partners as part of the globalisation process. Also, UK became party to the Community legal

---

[52] This included the concept of 'corporate social responsibility' – the so-called 'externalities' identified by the Group and the need for wider considerations to be taken into account. The Group recognised the concern that introduction of extraneous considerations into rules governing continuing relationships within companies may prevent management from focusing on the key business of managing to generate wealth. However, the Group also recognised that the corporate sector remained the most important component of the productive economy; the laws governing its constitution, management and accountability already recognised wider interests. Best practice often went further. Companies could be viewed largely as contractual entities, created and controlled under agreements entered into by members and directors. The Group did not accept that there could be no place for law in securing that companies took account of the wider interests. It was a question of public policy whether company law was an appropriate vehicle to achieve this, and what constraints and conditions should be attached to corporate status and limited liability.

harmonisation process as part of the single market enterprise. As Continental European traditions were typically more prescriptive and regulatory than the UK's, this led to some difficulties in adjusting domestic British law, and the harmonisation programme created some problems in considering reforms.

The UK had also witnessed changing patterns of regulation. Companies were now subject to a range of regulatory control beyond traditional company law. This included the Stock Exchange, the Financial Services Authority, the Takeover Panel and other accountancy bodies, issuing rules and exercise enforcement powers. All these bodies were specialised and brought particular skills thereby making the resulting picture inevitably more complex.

Information technology has also made a significant impact on the development of a competitive economy in the UK. Company law in the UK had not kept pace with such developments in technology.

The UK company law regime had not addressed the changing patterns of ownership with many small owner-managed businesses registered with limited liability – yet the legislation failed to address their needs. In large companies, ownership and control had become increasingly concentrated with institutional investors holding about 80 per cent of shares in UK companies. The growth in the influence of institutional investors had led to the development of a more effective market in corporate control which was a further non-legal constraint on the power of managers.[53]

The Group highlighted the importance of small and closely-held companies and the role they played in the UK economy and competitiveness. UK company law had paid little attention to the peculiar needs of small firms, either in accessibility and simplicity or in substantive provision. The start-up and development of such businesses was an important process for which the law should provide an optimal climate.

---

[53] The Group also referred to the 'modern asset mix' as part of the overall reform of the company law regime. This referred to the pattern of productive activity, which in many sectors of the economy was shifting to becoming increasingly human resource and knowledge based. Asset structures were also changing and becoming increasingly 'soft' in the sense that a significant portion of the value or capacity of a business was to be found in intangibles rather than in tangible assets such as buildings and machinery. The skills of the workforce were also a particularly important resource. The concept of modern asset mix was an important concept developed by the Group beyond its terms of reference. Thus, traditional concepts in company law such as fixed and current assets in the balance sheet, including the profit and loss account, although important, needed to be considered alongside other real sources of wealth and the resources over which directors should exercise effective stewardship and provide accountability in a wide range of areas, including skills, the know-how and motivation of employees and the company's relationships with creditors, suppliers and customers; the company's reputation and the interests of the public. This required better management processes and the development and operation of effective systems to monitor and manage these areas. These aspects were hardly reflected in directors' stewardship nor reflected in company accountability and reporting.

The Group developed some 'Guiding Principles' for company law review. Although the terms of reference for company law reform were provided to the Group by the DTI, the Group also developed its approach with the need for modern company law, to meet modern needs and an overall philosophy embraced by certain Guiding Principles that pervaded throughout company law reform analysis. They were:

- *Facilitation of transactions – A Presumption Against Prescription*. This was concerned with the facilitation of effective wealth generation in the widest sense possible and the benefits to the wider community. According to the Group, businesses were likely to achieve this if they had the freedom to make economic choices and if provided with all relevant information. This guiding principle promoted freedom with transparency. There was a need for companies to be responsive to change, to leave space for developing best practice and to enable competitive efficiency. There should be freedom of activity for participants. A key role for company law was as a means of facilitating the operation of market forces, through contractual and other mutual relationships. These operated in markets and other areas where accountability ('transparency') enabled the effective assertion of claims by external interests, and an appropriate response by managements and shareholders. The key markets included capital markets and the markets for managerial skills and corporate control. Companies were involved in a range of interrelated contracts and other relationships enabling claims and demands to be efficiently met. Therefore, freedom of contract and exchange supported by transparency requirements should be the approach wherever possible. The law should acknowledge the diversity of economic activity and provide participants with the means to devise the best legal solution for themselves exercising their own commercial and other judgment and freedom of choice within the network of non-legal constraints and pressures.[54] According to the Group, wider and public interests might require that any informed market choices should be overridden or replaced by interventionist regulation. This would be necessary in cases of market failure, a director's conflict of interest or an overriding public interest including the need to secure fundamental standards of professional integrity, honesty and fair dealing.[55]

---

[54] Company law reform had to take account of the costs and benefits and the effectiveness of the protections concerned. In this context, the flexibility of civil enforcement, with costs borne by the wrong-doer, had great advantages over criminal sanctions, which required public resources that were already overstretched. Civil enforcement could be expensive and inefficient. This suggested that where detailed prescription was nevertheless justified, the sensitive application of 'self-regulatory' rules would often be a preferable approach where available in effective form.

[55] See Rickford, n 35 above, at p 5.

- *Accessibility – Ease of Use and Identification of the Law.* Competitiveness required the minimum complexity and maximum accessibility, both in terms of substance of the law and the way in which it was communicated. It should be easier to find out which requirements applied and what they meant. This had implications both for substance and the language used and for the way in which it was assembled and arranged. Sometimes the law had to provide for complex situations. The current structure of UK company law was essentially based on the needs of the large company with a wide shareholding. Special exemptions and derogations were allowed for smaller companies and more informally managed entities. In general, the same law applied to all companies whether large or small, public or private. This required radical restructuring of the legislation.
- *Regulatory boundaries – Proper Jurisdiction.* Rule making and enforcement should be assigned to the most suitable body among the various regulatory jurisdictions that operated in this field. Further, overlaps, duplications and conflicts should be avoided. This could be achieved by separating the rules for major companies subject to such jurisdictions.[56]

The Group considered eight key issues in its review of company law reform. They were: the scope of company law; problems of the small or closely-held company; various regulatory and self regulatory bodies; international aspects of the law; company formation; company powers; capital maintenance; and electronic communications and information.[57]

As part of its remit, the Group considered what should be the proper scope for company law, that is, in whose interests should it be designed to serve and

---

[56] The task of the Group was not to make recommendations of a 'distributive' kind. Although it was the proper purpose of company law to facilitate the creation of wealth, it was not to establish some basis of fairness for allocating the benefit of such wealth.

[57] The Group also took account of the regulatory framework of the European dimension with particular reference to Directives and Regulations, European Union Law and the European Convention on Human Rights which constrained and shaped the opens open to UK company law reform regime. The Group also took account of the comparative dimension taking account of the work of Professor Cally Jordan for the Hong Kong review of company law reform and the Centre for Law and Business at the University of Manchester on Continental Europe. The Group considered briefly the Commonwealth developments in Canada (where reform of company law led to a radical reappraisal and simplification of company law based on the USA model); New Zealand where the Companies Act were fundamentally simplified; Australia enacted the Corporation Law which came into force in 1991; South Africa and Hong Kong; and the USA with the Model Business Corporations Act and the American Law Institute's Principles of Corporate Governance.

the legal means by which it should do so.[58] The present structure of the law reflected three purposes.[59] Companies were formed and managed for the benefit of shareholders, but subject to the safeguards for the benefit of actual and potential creditors. Accounting and disclosure requirements operated for the benefit of actual, and potential shareholders and creditors, and through public disclosure of information, for the benefit of the community as a whole. The issue of whose interests should be protected was an important aspect for the Group. Although participants in the company were interested parties in the company's prosperity, a wider range of people were also dependent on the company's performance. These included the wider public where, for example, environmental damage may affect the local community, or the closure of a local plant thereby making employees redundant. The issue for debate was whether directors ought to consider the wider interests of groups that were also dependent on the company. This could be considered as a wider debate on the corporate social responsibilities of companies, and directors' steward-ship of the wider group of claimants on the corporation. Curiously, company law in the UK has never witnessed such a debate as that in America in the 1930s between Berle and Dodd.[60] The Steering Group considered that enforceability of action against directors by wider constituency groups may be unworkable and impracticable and could result in unnecessary litigation against directors and costs. A more practical solution would be to provide directors with wider discretion to consider the interests of various constituents but with less accountability towards them.

The law on the formation and management of companies served the interests of shareholders by conferring on them ultimate control of the

[58] The Group cited 'shareholder value' as an example. This was a concept which disciplined and focused the powers of directors towards accountability to shareholders. As the law stood, it was essentially for the members of the company to define the objects which they wished it to achieve. For example, a company could be set up for a social or charitable objective, and in those circumstances, it would be for the directors to operate the undertaking to achieve that objective, which could be said to represent value for shareholders in the context. The Group was of the view that the objectives of 'shareholder value' ', 'shareholder wealth' and broader 'welfare' were therefore flexible and developing concepts. The law must be defined in a way that left room for all these variations and for an effective combination of legal engineering with wider market and societal dynamics.

[59] The review of company law reform was essentially concerned with *law* reform and not with the wider ethical or managerial issues about the behaviour and standards of participants in companies. The focus was on the components of such reform – namely, directors' and share-holders' powers and duties, their extent and limitations, and related rights, remedies and liabilities.

[60] See A. Berle and G. Means, *The Modern Corporation and Private Property* (1933); J. Weiner, *The Berle-Dodd Dialogue on the Concept of the Corporation* (1964) 64 Columbia Law Review 1,458; A. Berle in the preface to *The Corporation in Modern Society* (1960), E. Mason (ed) p.i; E.M. Dodd, *For Whom Are Corporate Managers Trustees?* (1932) 45 Harv Law Rev 1145; and A. Berle, *For Whom Corporate Managers Are Trustees: A Note* (1932) 45 Harv Law Rev 1,365.

undertaking. Shareholders purchased their shares in the company and in return, the law conferred control over management to ensure that the proceeds of that investment were managed in the shareholders' interests to ensure the value of shares increased over time. Shareholders were entitled to obtain the benefit of that value by distributions or sale of their shares or realising their value on a company's winding up. The directors were required to manage the business on their behalf, being obliged by fiduciary duties which required them to act honestly, in their judgment, for the company's benefit. In other words, for the benefit of shareholders as a whole. Directors were also required to exercise the powers conferred on them for their proper purposes and subject to the duty of care and skill.[61] Failure by directors to comply with their duties could lead them open to civil claims or dismissal. The law had recognised that it was essential for directors to have discretion in the way they managed, and that the courts would not interfere in business judgments. The system of ultimate control was subject to the overriding obligation to ensure creditors were not wrongly exposed to insolvency, through general duties imposed by company and insolvency law[62] and special safeguards which applied to protect creditors in particular transactions, such as distributions of profits or capital. This system was also subject to wider duties of accountability that applied to the enterprise as a whole, members and management.

The Group considered the main arguments for reform. The principal objective of reform should be to achieve competitiveness and efficient creation of the wealth and other benefits for all participants in the enterprise. The aim should also be to minimise the negative impacts of corporate activity on participants and to maximise their welfare.

The Group argued that the present scheme of law failed to recognise adequately that business normally best generated wealth where participants operated harmoniously as teams, and that managers should recognise the wider interests of the community in their activities. There had been much debate about how a wide range of interests of various participants on the corporation could best be balanced. Various commentators had argued that management had escaped effective shareholder control and that in consequence many companies were inefficient. Others have argued that pressures from shareholders, or managerial perceptions of such pressures, had inhibited long-term investment in value-creating internal and external relationships, as well as in physical assets and other intangibles. Not all such relationships needed to be co-operative or long-term; but often relationships of this kind were important ingredients of success. These included relationships between the company's employees and suppliers. The Group stated that

[61] Directors were also subject to the duty to act fairly as between members. See too the City Code on Takeovers and Mergers.
[62] See for example, *West Mercia Safety Wear v Dodd* [1988] BCLC 250.

in modern business, it was arguably no longer necessary the case that shareholders were the sole repositories of residual risk which could not be diversified anyway.

The issue of in whose interests should the company be operated was a major aspect of the Steering Group's analysis in the Consultation document. The Group went beyond the scope of its terms of reference by highlighting two perspectives on this issue: *enlightened shareholder value* and *pluralist approaches*.

The 'enlightened shareholder value' perspective advocated that the ultimate objective of companies was to generate maximum value for shareholders, which was the best means of securing overall prosperity and welfare. Others, however, have argued that in practice, neither maximum value for shareholders nor overall prosperity and welfare may be achieved. This was owing to the fact that management may fail to recognise that the way to success was in many cases through building long-term relationships that depend on trust. An exclusive focus on short-term gains was erroneous, and incompatible with the cultivation of co-operative relationships, which were likely to involve short-term costs but would bring greater benefits in the long term. Thus, the 'enlightened shareholder value' approach advocated that directors owed their duties exclusively to shareholders, but it also recognised the need for wider interests to be properly understood, assessed and managed and for an inclusive long-term and balanced strategic view to be taken of these wider interest groups.[63]

According to the 'pluralist approach', the ultimate objective of maximising shareholder value would not achieve maximum prosperity and welfare. Instead, company law should be modified to include other objectives so that a company was required to serve a wider range of interests, not subordinate to, or as a means of achieving, shareholder value but as valid in their own right.[64] This approach involved a need to balance potentially conflicting interests with some sacrifice on the part of shareholders in favour of some other interest. Therefore, if directors' duties were still to be envisaged as owed to 'the company', the company could no longer be regarded as just the association of shareholders that created it, and their successors in title. It needed to be regarded as embracing others who made commitments to it, usually employees, suppliers and customers. This pluralist approach favoured

---

[63] According to the Steering Committee: 'It is in our view clear, as a matter of policy, that in many circumstances directors should adopt and broader and longer-term ("inclusive") view of their role. This is indeed now widely acknowledged. But we do not accept that there is anything in the present law of directors' duties which requires them to take an unduly narrow or short-term view of their functions. Indeed they are obliged honestly to take account of all the considerations which contribute to the success of the enterprise.' at. para 5.1.19, above.

[64] As an example, see M. Blair, *Ownership and Control: Rethinking Corporate Governance for the Twenty-First Century* (1955); and J. Kay and A. Silberston, 'Corporate Governance' in *National Institute Economic Review*, August 1995.

directors' duties being owed to wider groups of interests and not just the shareholders.[65]

The enlightened shareholder value was linked to directors' duties and s 309 of the CA 1985.[66] The objective of the enlightened shareholder value was to maximise shareholder welfare and, therefore, directors' duties did not need to be reformed. In company law, directors were required to act honestly and in good faith for the company's benefit. Directors must act in the best interests of shareholders both present and future. They must also exercise their powers for a proper purpose. The Group stated that in many circumstances, the directors should adopt the broader and longer-term view of their role. They could also take a narrow or short-term view of their functions and obliged honestly to take account of all the considerations which contribute to the company's success. Therefore, company law provisions did not require any

---

[65] According to the Steering Group: 'At the minimum, implementation of the pluralist view would require a reform of the law of directors' duties to permit *them* to further the interests of non-shareholder participants – that is employees, customers and suppliers – even if this were to the detriment of shareholders. A possible variant would be a duty *requiring* them to promote the success of the company as a business enterprise in this way – i.e. with the interests of none of the participants, including the shareholders', being regarded as overriding. Such directors' duties would need to be expressed subjectively to confer a wide range of discretion, but we would not favour the contentious issues involved being litigable. At the same time we also see difficulties in merely enabling directors to diverge from the enlightened shareholder value objective, since there would be no formal remedy for abuse of the powers conferred (though the provisions against the directors furthering their own interests would remain in place). Arguably this could create a dangerously broad and unaccountable discretion, unless sufficient add-itional safeguards can be devised. More extensive reform in a pluralistic direction might require changes in the *shareholders' control* over the company through their ability to deter-mine the composition of the board. This seems inevitably to raise the the question of constitu-encies other than members having power to nominate board members, or of there being some self-selecting or internally appointed component on the board tasked with securing broader objectives . . . but we note here that arguments are not being strongly expressed currently for employee, or wider, representation on company board as mandatory requirement and that even in the most well developed version of employee participation in Germany, ultimate control of the company does not in fact rest in the hands of members, through the casting vote of the chairman (appointed by the members) of the supervisory board. There is however an argument that such arrangements for modifying board composition could be structured in a way which reduced to some degree the pressure of members on management and created a system of broader accountability. Proposals to alter board composition to require wider representation as a mandatory requirement would represent a very radical change to British corporate culture and would be unlikely tocommand wide support. There must in any case be doubt whether their objective cannot be more satisfactorily achieved through a regime of enlightened share-holder value combined with improved information flow and greater disclosure.' See below at paras 5.1.30–5.1.32.

[66] CA 1985, s 309 provided that the matters to which the directors of the company are to have regard in the performance of their functions include the interests of the company's employees in general, as well as the interests of its members. The duty imposed by s 309 on the directors was owed by them to the company (and the company alone) and was enforceable in the same way as any other fiduciary duty owed to a company by its directors.

change, and the Steering Group rejected the pluralist approach in favour of the enlightened shareholder value perspective.

The Group stated that there was also evidence that the law was not well recognised and understood. For example, s 309 of the CA 1985 was a statutory declaration of an enlightened shareholder value duty, requiring that directors consider the interests of employees in reaching a view as to what was in the company's best interests. However, the duty was to the company and the company alone. Employees had no remedy under this section. Still, this section would serve as an immunity for directors, who would be able to resist legal actions by the shareholders based on the grounds that the directors had neglected their normal fiduciary duty to them in favour of employees.[67]

According to the Group, there was a need to clarify the law in this area. The object would be to ensure that directors recognised their obligation to have regard to the need, where appropriate, to build long-term trusting relationships with employees, suppliers, customers and others, in order to secure the company's success over time.[68] This could be achieved by primary legislation that would need to be expressed in subjective terms, to ensure that the difficult decisions involved in evaluating the relevant benefits were reserved to the directors' business judgment. However, legislation may not be flexible and responsive to changing needs. Alternatively, it may be possible to produce a public statement of directors' position but not in a binding legal form such as a 'highway code', to ensure the law was properly understood and applied.

According to the pluralist approach, the present law, in making shareholders' interests ultimately overriding, may create, or reinforce, an environment in which relationships of trust were difficult to sustain. This increased the level of inefficient risk between those managing companies and employees, suppliers and others, on whom the company depended for the factors of production and who depended in turn on the company for secure environment within which to make the commitments necessary to provide them. As the duties of directors was ultimately to further the interests of shareholders, those who wanted to make a commitment to the company, such as employees and suppliers, would be reluctant to do so, owing to the level of risk to which they were exposed. The pluralist view, therefore, asserted that the present law failed to cater for these considerations. Its directors should be accountable for the stewardship of the company's assets and the maximisation of their value for the benefit of all contributors and not just its shareholders. Only against the background of a regime that permitted or required directors to treat non-member participants in that way could they be expected to undertake the necessary commitments. In modern companies, it was no

[67] See *Fulham Football Club v Cabra Estates* [1994] 1 BCLC 363.
[68] See now CA 2006, s 172.

longer necessarily the case that shareholders were the sole repositories of residual risk that could not be diversified away. The economic case for giving shareholders ultimate control of the company was no longer valid. Other participants may be in this position. The relationships with such participants should be regarded as important assets which directors should be bound to manage effectively.[69]

The Group also considered the argument that companies should respond to a range of demands beyond the interests of their members and that company law should reflect this. There were claims that corporations should behave ethically and should respond to a wide range of public interests. Although companies generated wealth, they also caused some external 'harm' that society disapproved of – such as damage to health and safety, abusive employment or contracting practices, and environmental damage. Although there was specific legislation dealing with these issues, it did not interfere with the profit maximisation motive but operated subject to the constraints imposed by the need for profit maximisation. The Group believed that although such legislation was of prime importance, it was slow to be introduced and adjusted, relied on minimum rather than aspirational standards and could not be adjusted to specific circumstances.

There were two views on the issue of considering wider potential claimants on the corporation: first, that companies that were properly managed and controlled by directors and members, would employ long-term vision and insight in their own enlightened self-interest and ensure that they took proper account of these wider objectives. Corporations depended to a large extent on their reputation for commercial success; they were under increasing scrutiny from governments, regulators, the press, pressure groups and non-governmental organisations (NGOs) and the communities in which they operated.

Another view, which was a pluralistic one, was that to work properly such

---

[69] However, there are counter arguments to the pluralist view. First, it may be argued that in practice a broad enlightened shareholder value approach would provide an adequate environment for the development of such relationships. It is not clear that the trade-offs of shareholders' interests against those of other participants that the pluralist approach envisages would be necessary in practice. Second, it is not self-evident that the normal process of bargaining between suppliers and consumers of factors of production is incapable of generating appropriate safeguards or incentives for all sides. If there are problems because parties lack the information necessary for efficient bargaining it should be possible for institutional arrangements to overcome these within the framework of company law. Third, it may be argued that if there are deficiencies in this area they are best made good by changes in other areas of the law and public policy, or in best practice, rather than by making changes in company law, which might have unpredictable and damaging effects. Fourth, that to change the present focus of directors on increasing the value of business over time, subject to clear single-channel accountability to members, in favour of some broader objective involving the trade-off of interests of members and others, would dangerously distract management into a political balancing style at the expense of economic growth and international competitiveness.

market mechanisms required a fuller system of disclosure than company law currently provided, and that there should also be readiness on the part of companies to sacrifice their own self-interest in appropriate cases. It could be possible to increase accountability through greater transparency. Alternatively, directors' duties could be adjusted. However, the adoption by directors of high ethical standards was unlikely to be held by the court to be beyond the permissible judgments about the optimal positioning of the company. It would be improbable that shareholders would seek to exercise their powers to castigate such practices. However, as a matter of principle, it may be argued that the law should be changed to allow directors discretion to sacrifice commercial advantage for ethical or public objectives.

The Group also considered the issue of corporate philanthropy and other forms of corporate community support. Much of the activity found in this area had a commercial foundation, because, for example, it could help build the company's positive reputation with customers and others. It was also possible that director might engage in corporate generosity towards deserving causes that had little if any genuine relationship with the commercial interests of their companies. If this was considered desirable it should be properly authorised in law, subject to proper transparency or other safeguards.

According to the Group, consideration also needed to be given to transparency and public accountability. This was partly catered for by disclosure of a company's accounts and reports and publication at Companies House. This enabled the public to evaluate a company's performance and bring pressure to bear on the company as a whole. Enhanced reporting would also reduce short-term pressures by shareholders on directors. Effective reporting regimes could improve the climate of opinion on issues of acceptable and desirable corporate behaviour. Reporting requirements would still provide some discipline against abuse. The Group noted that company law paid little attention for 'soft' assets and resources. These would include the level of stability of the workforce, established and trading relationships with suppliers, and the value of the company's reputation and brands, which were an important indicator of ongoing relationships of confidence with customers. In many of these areas, there were no adequate standards and benchmarks for reporting capable of carrying the weight that was needed to establish effective pressures to ensure that there was an adequate response to this range of interests. The Group attached great importance to the potential of company law to achieve a proper measure of corporate responsiveness to wider interests through transparency and accountability.

Company law reform also needed to cater for the needs of small and closely-held companies. A company could be regarded as 'small' either because of its economic significance or because of the small number of its shareholders. In the latter case, shareholders were usually also involved in the company's management and such companies are usually described as 'closely-held' or 'close companies'. Small companies were the greatest proportion registered at Companies House. However, the Companies Acts were structured around the needs of larger, publicly-owned companies with a division between the shareholders/investors and the directors who were in charge of, and accountable to shareholders for, day-to-day management. Many provisions of the Acts imposed duties on directors and provided protection for shareholders against abuses of directors' powers.

However, as the Group noted, over the years, many detailed additions and adaptations had been made to the Acts to cater for the needs of private companies,[70] 'single member companies', companies of smaller economic size, and companies wishing to operate through written procedures between members, rather than meetings, or by dispensing with some key formalities. The written resolution and elective regime applied to private companies and was helpful for small private companies wishing to opt out of normal governance requirements. However, these procedures and regimes were little used in practice because of the requirement of member unanimity.

Further, many of the CA 1985 provisions did not apply to small private companies either in law or practice and many that did, were not well designed to cater for their real needs. Owing to its structure, building on the large business model and then making detailed adaptations, the Act was opaque and inaccessible for small business users. To determine which parts of the CA 1985 actually applied to small companies required a thorough knowledge of the whole Act, what exemptions or adaptations were available, and under what conditions. The Group stated that the law should be accessible to those managing and advising small companies and relevant to their requirements. There was concern that the 'regulatory' requirements set out in the Act mainly for the protection of the company's creditors was largely overly burdensome and failed to serve the purposes for which they were designed.

According to the Group, there was a clear case for providing the most competitive legal form possible for the typical small commercial business seeking limited liability and transferable shares. The Group considered two types of approaches in developing models for small companies, namely the *free standing* approach and the *integrated* approach. The 'free standing' approach involved creating a separate, free-standing, limited liability vehicle for small companies, probably involving separate legislation. Eligibility criteria would be based on the economically small closely-held, company where the shape of the regulation could be tailored and would be relatively light when compared with the full Companies Act provisions. Such companies

---

[70] These were defined for the first time by the Companies Act 1907, s 37. The 1907 Act exempted private companies from various provisions including those on prospectuses and the filing of accounts and directors' reports.

would need to revert to the Companies Act regime should they develop beyond these limits. Some of the jurisdictions adopting this approach have been the South African Close Corporation, the US Limited Liability Company and the Limited Liability Partnership. The 'integrated approach' would be within the single Companies Act regime, with such regime adopted in New Zealand.

According to the Group, the main advantage of a stand-alone small companies vehicle was that it would be tailored more closely to the needs of those companies, unlike the existing CA 1985. The legislation might be relatively concise and designed specifically for a limited class of users. However, the consequence of being tailored in this way would be that the legislation would not provide an integrated regime within which a company that ceased to satisfy the criteria could continue to operate. But the levels at which these criteria would be set were arbitrary. The criteria would also present major problems of transition. The Group, however, favoured the integrated approach, which would involve both changes in form and substance to the existing legislation. The components of the legislation would be the following:

- Companies legislation should be reframed so that the basic model was the private company, and private company provisions should be presented as a single integrated whole. Provisions relating to public and listed companies should be drafted so that they were separated and dealt with as an additional set, in a separate Act or within part of the Act. In this case, the users of the legislation who were concerned only with private companies should have no need to consider them.
- Small companies should benefit from changes that would be made to the law applying to private companies generally. The legislation would be simplified and brought into line with current business needs.
- A new set of articles to suit the needs of close companies would need to be devised such as a special version of Table A, designed for companies in which all the shareholders are involved in management.
- Consideration should also be given to whether it should be possible for private companies in general, or a more restricted class of closely-held companies, to adopt a form that is exempt from a wide range of Companies Act requirements, allowing them greater freedom to customise their constitutions to their individual needs. A similar possibility would be a reformed written resolution procedure that required unanimity but could be changed to require only a majority vote.

The Group also considered proposals for simplifying the law relating to company formation and maintenance of share capital. These included:

- clarification and reform of the rules relating to capacity of companies and their agents and validity of transactions with third parties.[71] The Group stated there was a case, in the interests of simplification, for ending the distinction between memorandum and articles, and providing instead a single constitution document. Further, it would be made explicit that in all relations with third parties, a company was deemed to have the capacity to do anything a legal person was capable of doing. This would be so regardless of anything in the company's constitution. The requirement on companies to include an objects clause in their constitution on their formation would disappear. Companies would continue to be free, if they chose, to limit the authority of their directors to bind the company, as an in-built constraint on their freedom vis-à-vis the shareholders. This could be done either by the constitution (articles) or by a shareholder resolution made under it; but no such limitation would affect the rights of an independent third party dealing with the board of a company or an agent authorised by the board in good faith, even if they were aware of it. Existing companies could choose whether or not to retain their existing objects clauses. However, these should cease to have the effect of limiting the authority of any agent of the company as against third parties, without prejudice to their limiting effect as against shareholders. Existing companies would continue to be free, like newly-formed ones, to limit the authority of directors to bind the company by or under the constitution, with the same effects. Further, the special minority protection in relation to resolutions to alter a company's objects would be abolished. The shareholders could bring proceedings to restrain the commission of any action of the directors, or of any person authorised by them, that was beyond their powers as set out in the constitution or in a resolution, but this would not affect the validity of a commitment already entered into. The Group intended to abolish the 'deemed notice' concept in full:[72]

[71] A requirement had grown up to include long-form objects clauses in memoranda of association. An objects clause had a dual significance: it restricted the capacity of the company so that transactions outside the objects of the company were void and thus *ultra vires*; and it also limited the authority of directors (or anyone else) as agents of the company to bind the company as their principal. The powers of directors to bind the company or authorise others to do so might also be limited by or under the company's Articles. Over a period of time, the position of corporate capacity became unsatisfactory for both companies and third parties. This devalued the objects clause as a means of informing the world of the company's business, without entirely removing the risk faced by third parties if the founders of the company had failed to think of everything. The result was that prudent third parties needed to study the objects clause carefully to ensure that they were not caught out by some trivial defect in the long and tortuous wording.

[72] The companies legislation would be silent on the authority of officers or agents of the company, below board level and persons authorised by the board, which would be governed by the normal rules of agency law, subject to the provision for existing companies which removes any limitation on the authority of agents by virtue of the objects clause so far as third parties are concerned.

- removing the need for court approval of capital reduction;
- introducing a simplified financial assistance regime, dependent on member approval and solvency certification; and
- introducing no par value shares.

The Group also considered issues regarding capital maintenance. The principle of capital maintenance was as old as limited liability. The law gave the shareholder the privilege of limiting his liability, so that once he had paid, or promised to pay on call, an amount equal to the nominal value of the shares he took up, he had no further responsibility for the company's debts. In order to protect members and creditors, a body of rules was established; such rules were designed to prevent the capital so provided from being extracted or otherwise eroded, except as a result of trading or other business events. The most important rules were those concerning reduction of capital, purchase by company of own shares, financial assistance by a company for a third party's acquisition of its shares and distribution of profits.

However, creditors and potential creditors did not any longer regard the amount of a company's issued share capital as a significant matter when deciding whether or not to extend credit to it. Whilst the existence of a substantial share capital may sometimes be regarded as a comfort, sophisticated creditors paid more regard to the size of the company's total resources, including non-distributable reserves, and to its cash generation.

On the issue of reduction of capital, the Group considered some of the provisions for effecting reduction of capital to be outdated, in particular, the need for a special resolution and reference to the court for approval of the reduction, even where there was no conceivable threat to creditors. The reduction process was effectively the same as in the Companies Act 1867. Although the legislative provisions have become more flexible, however, a company wishing to reduce capital could find that the court required it to provide an expensive bank guarantee to cover present and future claims of its existing creditors however financially sound the company may be, making creditors better protected than they would be, at the company's expense. The Group did not regard this rule as efficient. The reduction of capital process was used to return capital to shareholders, and to write off losses.

The Group stated that the distinction between share capital (including share premium) and other funds should be retained. However, reduction of capital should become a simpler and more efficient process. It would be preferable for companies to be permitted to reduce capital with the sanction of a special resolution (ensuring the appropriate endorsement by shareholders of the change in status of funds, which they envisaged as a contribution towards the trading capacity of the company); and following the declaration of solvency by the directors (to ensure reasonable, but not excessive, protection of creditors from the risk of insolvency).

The declaration of solvency would be required to address the position of the company immediately following the reduction. However, the declaration need not take the form of a statutory declaration. The directors should be required to make a proper enquiry and then to reach a judgment on solvency. Directors who made a declaration without having reasonable ground for the opinion expressed should be liable to a fine and could be made personally liable for any losses to creditors resulting from a reduction made in circumstances that they should have known were likely to lead to insolvency.

On the issue of financial assistance, the Group noted that there were provisions under the CA 1985 which, subject to exceptions, prohibited companies and their subsidiaries from giving financial assistance for the purpose of acquisition of shares of the company. The Group was firmly of the view that changes to the existing law should be made in this area. It did not regard the financial assistance provisions as strictly necessary for the maintenance of capital. Private companies should be permitted to give all kinds of financial assistance if approved, in general meeting, by the company's members other than any who had a special interest in the outcome, and preceded by a declaration of solvency regarding the situation following the giving of the assistance. Shareholder approval would be necessary in all cases, but an ordinary resolution of disinterested members was sufficient and it was appropriate for assistance to be permissible out of capital, so long as it was approved and creditors were protected.

The Group also addressed the issue of regulation and the boundaries of the law. Many of the areas such as directors' duties, company disclosure, company management, and the role of directors and of the general meeting, were not regulated by the Act. However, there was substantial secondary legislation made under the Act such as the Takeovers and Mergers Code, the Stock Exchange Rules and the Code on corporate governance.

The nature of the obligation and the consequences of breach were different in each case. In some areas, two or three layers of regulation were superimposed. There were merits and drawbacks to different forms of regulation. Regulation by and enforcement under statute had the merit of democratic legitimacy in the making of rules. Enforcement through the courts was open and independent of rule-making. Ministers were accountable publicly for the effective operation of the rules. However, such statutory regulation also had drawbacks. In a field where commercial practice and technology were constantly evolving, it was often difficult to respond with appropriate changes in the law, unless the need to do so had been anticipated and secondary legislation powers provided. Also, the perceived need to foresee and provide for every eventuality had led to a level of complexity in the statute beyond the capacity of those without legal training to assimilate. Non-statutory regulation enabled flexibility and dynamism in the development of rules and other guidance, while it tends to permit in some contexts a higher level of generality or vagueness in expression, combined with more sensitive discretionary enforcement to meet the merits of varying cases. The drawbacks could include lack of precision; lack of transparency in both rule making and enforcement activities; and suspicion, that the authorities administering the rules may tend to favour their own member or clients, or wider commercial considerations.

The Group considered that there may be scope in rationalising the present regulatory structure. The present structure did, however, offer the benefit of familiarity even if it sometimes appeared to lack logic. A distinction needed to be drawn between the form of legislation, in terms of precision, flexibility and sanctions, and the nature of the competent body and the function that it performs, whether prescribing the rules or enforcing them or both. The general trend should be away from prescriptive rules set out in the statute and enforced by criminal sanctions. These might in appropriate cases be replaced by more flexible rules in the form of codes of practice, expressed in sufficiently general terms to permit the exercise of judgment and common sense in their application to individual cases. The administration of such rules would be a public law function and appropriate safeguards would be required. Responsibility for this could rest with either a public or a private body: and the availability of effective sanctions would be a key factor in the decision.

The Group considered technology was of vital importance in the modernisation of company law in the UK. The new technologies represented a major resource for the competitive operation of companies with potential for greater efficiency. Technology was, therefore, a high priority for company law reform. Companies could make more use of the internet to communicate with their shareholders as well as dealings with Companies House. The objectives were:

- Ensuring competitiveness by enabling the widest possible use of the new media by companies, reducing costs and ensuring ease of compliance;
- Promoting greater efficiency and quality of service at the Registrar of Companies;
- Promoting transparency and availability of information;
- Promoting participation and higher standards of governance.

The approach to technology should be based on the following principles:

- In general participants should be enabled to exploit the new technologies on the basis of a facilitative and technology-neutral approach;
- Security was an important consideration, but a proportionate approach should be adopted, recognising that current systems were far from absolutely secure and that a balance should be maintained, recognising that in some respects the new technologies were more secure than old;
- Legal changes should be in a flexible form, able to be readily adapted to changing applications and patterns of abuse;

- As far as companies were concerned, the permissive rather than prescriptive approach may also need to change over time such as more extensive or different reporting requirements may be desirable for large companies;
- The law should continue to ensure reasonable access to company information for individuals recognising that domestic access to modern forms of communication such as internet was limited.

Over the years, the Companies Acts have attempted to address the technology issue. Company records were in the form of a 'register, index, minute book or accounting records' and these records were to be kept in 'bound books' or by recording in any other manner including in non-legible, form and for inspection to be available by a provision of a legible copy of the recording. The Companies Registry allowed the Registrar to receive material in non-legible form and to lay down how this was to be presented and authenticated, and to maintain it and to send out in such form as approved by the Registrar.

There had not been much use of electronic forms of communication and this should be an essential means of communication. The Group considered that reform should take place in the following areas:

- meetings of directors and members – it should be provided that a meeting would be valid if all the participants had a reasonable opportunity to participate, whether or not they were all in one place, which could include 'virtual' meetings;
- communications between companies and members – with the consent of members, it should be possible for a company to communicate any information electronically, including by informing members of its availability on the internet. This should include notices calling meetings and related information, and proxy forms. Similarly, where members wish to do so, they should be able to communicate with their companies electronically in matters such as registering forms of proxy on digital forms in advance of general meetings;
- information held at company's offices – various information was required to be held and available for inspection at company offices. However, much of the information was also required to be registered at Companies House. Company law reform should take account of the widening use of the internet in this area;
- information on business communications – the CA 1985 required disclosure of various information on company documents and correspondence. Electronic commerce now provided effective substitutes, and modifications to the law in order to ensure equivalent protection appeared desirable.

Phase Two was, therefore, concerned with the Strategic Framework. It set out a comprehensive basis and foundation for a radical reform of the UK company law regime across the whole spectrum of UK company law. Although at times acting outside its terms of reference, the Steering Group had established the essential principles and policy arguments for reform, on which specific working groups would provide detailed analysis and engage in wide consultation on key areas of company law.

Law Commission Report: Shareholder Remedies

1.8 From time to time during the company law review process, the Law Commissions of England and Wales and Scotland had joined forces to work alongside the Group's work on various aspects of company law reform. The work of the Law Commissions was distinct from the Group's terms of reference, but enabled the Group to consider some of the invaluable recommendations provided by the Law Commissions.

Two timely reports published by the Law Commission that had an impact on the Group's work were *Shareholder Remedies* and *Directors' Duties*.

The Law Commission published its report on *Shareholder Remedies* in 1997.[73] It recommended law reform designed to make shareholder remedies more affordable and more appropriate in modern conditions.[74] The focus of the Law Commission's work in this area was exclusively on remedies available to a minority shareholder,[75] who was dissatisfied with the manner in which the company of which he is a member was run. This may be owing to a breach of duty by the directors; or because of the way in which the majority shareholders had used their voting power to cause the company to act in a manner that unfairly prejudiced the interests of the minority shareholder; or it may be that the requirements of the company's constitution had not been properly complied with.

The Law Commission identified two main problems on shareholders' remedies: the first one was the obscurity and complexity of the law relating to the ability of the shareholder to bring proceedings on behalf of the company. He may wish to do so to enforce liability for a breach by one of the directors of his duties to the company. Generally, it was for the company itself with the will of a majority of its members, to bring any such proceedings, as this is the rule in *Foss v Harbottle*. However, where the wrongdoing directors control

---

[73] Law Commission Report, *Shareholder Remedies*, Report No: 246 (1997).

[74] The terms of reference given by the Lord Chancellor and the President of the Board of Trade in February 1995 were 'to carry out a review of shareholder remedies with particular reference to: – the rule in *Foss v Harbottle* (1843) 2 Hare 461 and its exceptions; sections 459 to 461 of the CA 1985; and the enforcement of the rights of shareholders under the Articles of Association; and to make recommendations.'

[75] This applied to one or more members not holding the majority of voting rights capable of being cast at general meetings. See Knox J in *Re Baltic Real Estate Ltd (No 1)* [1993] BCLC 498; and *Re Baltic Real Estate (No 2)* [1993] BCLC 503.

the majority of the votes, they may prevent legal proceedings being brought. Although there were exceptions to the rule in *Foss v Harbottle*, the Law Commissions were of the view that the exceptions were rigid, old fashioned and unclear.[76] The law was inaccessible and procedures lengthy and costly.[77]

The second main problem related to the efficiency and cost of the remedy that was widely used by minority shareholders to obtain some personal remedy in the event of the unsatisfactory conduct of a company's business. The remedy was provided in ss 459–461 of the CA 1985. The remedy was often used where there was a breakdown in relations between the owner–managers of small private companies, and one of them was prevented from taking part in management. The dissatisfied shareholder could obtain various reliefs but the most popular one was a court order requiring the majority shareholders to purchase his shares. The Law Commissions considered that proceedings under s 459 of the CA 1985 were costly and cumbersome. Many cases that went to trial often lasted weeks and the costs of litigation were substantial.[78]

The Law Commissions identified three main shareholder remedies. First, the 'unfair prejudice' remedy, in which a member sought redress for action by the company that injures his interest as a member. Second, the derivative action, in which a member sought to enforce a claim belonging to his company. Third, action to enforce the company's constitution, which included the extent to which a shareholder could insist on the affairs of the company being conducted in accordance with the Articles of Association.

The Law Commissions had in an earlier consultation document identified six 'guiding principles' for their proposals in relation to reform of the law and procedure relating to shareholder remedies. They were: (i) *proper plaintiff* – usually the company should be the only party to enforce a cause of action belonging to it. Accordingly, a member should be able to maintain proceedings about wrongs done to the company only in exceptional circumstances; (ii) *internal management* – an individual member should not be able to pursue proceedings on behalf of a company about matters of internal management, that is, matters that the majority were entitled to regulate by ordinary resolution; (iii) *commercial decisions* – the court should continue to have regard to decisions of directors on commercial matters if the decision was made in good faith, on proper information and in the light of the relevant considerations, and appears to be a reasonable decision for directors to have taken.[79] In those circumstances, the court should not substitute its own judgment for

---

[76] See too Law Commission Consultation Paper No 142, paras 1.6 and 14.1–14.4.

[77] See *Smith v Croft (No 2)* [1988] Ch 114.

[78] See for example, *Re Elgindata Ltd* [1991] BCLC 959, where the hearing lasted 43 days. See too on costs in civil litigation, Lord Woolf's *Access to Justice, The Final Report to the Lord Chancellor on the Civil Justice System in England and Wales (July 1996)*.

[79] See for example, *Howard Smith v Ampol Petroleum* [1974] AC 821; *Re Burton & Deakin Ltd* [1977] 1 WLR 390; and *Re D'Jan of London Ltd* [1994] 1 BCLC 561.

that of the directors; (iv) *sanctity of contract* – a member is taken to have agreed to the terms of the memorandum and Articles of Association when he became a member, whether or not he appreciated what they meant at the time. The law should continue to treat him so bound unless he could show that the parties had come to some other agreement or understanding that was not reflected in the articles or memorandum; (v) *freedom from unnecessary shareholder interference* – shareholders should not be able to involve the company in litigation without good cause, or where they intended to cause the company or the other shareholders embarrassment or harm rather than genuinely pursue the relief claimed. Otherwise the company could be 'killed by kindness',[80] or waste money or management time in dealing with unwarranted proceedings; and (vi) efficiency and cost effectiveness – all shareholder remedies should be made as efficient and cost effective as could be achieved in the circumstances.

The unfair prejudice remedy and the derivative action were specialist remedies, and the former was far more common in practice than the latter. The unfair prejudice remedy was most commonly used by private companies of which, as at 3 August 1997, there were some 1,080,671 in Great Britain. The Law Commissions recommended statutory and other changes to simplify the remedy, and help reduce its high cost to litigant and taxpayer alike. The derivative action was not common but it was an important mechanism of shareholder control of corporate wrongs. The current law was archaic. The Law Commission's principal recommendation was for a new rule of court that would set out, in a modern and accessible form, the circumstances in which the courts would permit the derivative action to be brought. The underlying policy, which was restrictive of the circumstances in which a derivative action may be brought, would not be not affected.

The Law Commission's view was that prevention was better than cure. Litigation was time-consuming and costly. In order to minimise reliance on shareholder remedies, it was recommended that a new article should be added to Table A, which was the statutory model form of a company's Articles of Association. This contained a basic dispute resolution mechanism, and would encourage shareholders in future to have pre-agreed routes to resolve disputes without litigation.

Below follows a summary only of the main recommendations of the Steering Group following its consideration of the Law Commissions' report on *Shareholder Remedies*, in order to avoid duplication of the recommendations.

- The problems of the excessive length and cost of many proceedings brought under s 459 of the CA 1985 should be dealt with primarily by active case management by the courts.

---

[80] *Prudential Assurance Co Ltd v Newman Industries Ltd (No 2)* [1982] Ch 204.

- Greater use should be made of the power to direct that preliminary issues be heard, or that some issues be tried before others.
- The court should have the power to dismiss any claim or part of a claim or defence thereto which, in the opinion of the court, has no realistic prospect of success at full trial.
- The Lord Chancellor should consider changes to the 1986 Rules (governing unfair prejudice proceedings) so as to include an express reference to the power to adjourn at any stage to enable the parties to make use of mechanisms for ADR for disposing of the case or any issue in it, together with provisions for reporting back to the court as to the outcome along the lines of the 1996 Commercial Court Practice Statement.
- The court should use its power pro-actively to determine how facts are to be proved.
- In shareholder proceedings, the court should have the power to exclude an issue from determination if it can do substantive justice between the parties on the other issues and determining it would therefore serve no worthwhile purpose.
- In proceedings under s 459 of the CA 1985, the court should have greater flexibility than at present to make costs orders to reflect the manner in which the successful party has conducted the proceedings and the outcome of individual issues.
- There should be legislative provision for presumptions in proceedings under ss 459–461 of the CA 1985 that, in certain circumstances, (a) where a shareholder has been excluded from participation in the management of the company, the conduct will be presumed to be unfairly prejudicial by reason of the exclusion; and (b), if the presumption is not rebutted and the court is satisfied that it ought to order a buy-out of the petitioner's shares, it should do so on a pro rata basis.
- The following conditions should be present for the presumptions to apply:

  (1) the company was a private company limited by shares;
  (2) the petitioner has been removed as a director or has been prevented from carrying out all or substantially all of his functions as a director;
  (3) immediately before the exclusion from participation in the management, (a) the petitioner held shares in his sole name giving him not less than 10 per cent of the rights to vote at general meetings of the company on all or substantially all matters, and (b) all, or substantially all of the members of the company the were directors. (For the purposes of (b), only one joint holder should be counted as a member).

- The first presumption should provide that, where these conditions are present, the affairs of the company would be presumed to have been conducted in a manner that is unfairly prejudicial to the petitioner, unless the contrary was shown.

- The second presumption should provide that where the first presumption had not been rebutted and the court was satisfied that it ought to make an order, that one or more of the respondents should purchase the petitioner's shares, and the shares should be valued on a pro rata basis unless the court otherwise orders.
- The Group recommended that, if its recommendations for the presumptions are implemented, the Vice Chancellor should be invited to consider whether there should be a practice direction requiring the petitioner to serve a notice on the other members of the company, and the company requiring them to purchase his shares valued on a pro rata basis before he starts his proceedings if he then intends to rely on the second presumption.

Imposition of limitation period

- The Group recommended that there should be a time limit for bringing claims under s 459 of the CA 1985, but that the length of the limitation period and the other relevant details (such as the date from which the limitation period should run) should be considered in the context of the Law Commission's current project on limitation.

Adding winding up to the remedies available under section 461 of the Companies Act 1985

- The Group recommended that winding up should be added to the remedies available to a petitioner in proceedings under s 459 of the CA 1985.
- The Group recommended that a petitioner should require the court's leave to apply for winding up in proceedings under ss 459–461 of the CA 1985.
- The Group recommended that a petitioner should also require the leave of the court to apply for a winding up order under s 122(1)(g) of the Insolvency Act 1986 in conjunction with an application under s 459 of the CA 1985.
- The Group recommended that where a petition under s 459 of the CA 1985 is amended to include a claim for winding up (whether under s 122(1)(g) of the IA 1986 or under the new provision) the winding up should be deemed to commence from the date of the amendment.
- The Group recommended that the Vice-Chancellor should be invited to consider whether there should be an amended practice direction setting out a standard form validation order where winding up is sought under the new provision.

Power to determine relief as between respondents

- The Group recommended that the Lord Chancellor consider changes to the 1986 Rules (governing unfair prejudice proceedings) so as to give the court the procedural powers to allow contribution and indemnity claims in proceedings under s 459 of the CA 1985 if this matter is not dealt with in the general rules introduced under the Civil Procedure Act 1997.

Advertisement of section 459 petitions

- The Group recommended that the Lord Chancellor consider changes to the 1986 Rules (governing unfair prejudice proceedings) so as to include an express provision stating that no advertisement of s 459 of the CA 2006 petitions should take place except in accordance with an order of the court, and so as to confirm the meaning given by the courts to 'advertisement' in this context by providing an appropriate definition.

Articles of Association

- The Group recommended that appropriate provisions should be included in Table A to encourage parties to sort out areas of potential dispute at the outset. In particular, the Group drafted a shareholders' exit article, and recommended its inclusion in Table A.

A new derivative action

- The Group recommended that there should be a new derivative procedure with more modern, flexible and accessible criteria for determining whether a shareholder can pursue the action.

The Group made the following recommendations on the details of the procedure.

Availability of the new derivative action

- The new procedure should only be available if the cause of action arises as a result of an actual or threatened act or omission involving (a) negligence, default, breach of duty or breach of trust by a director of the company, or (b) a director putting himself in a position where his personal interests conflict with his duties to the company. The cause of action may be against the director or another person (or both).
- For these purposes, director should include a shadow director.
- The derivative action should be available only to members of the company.

Extent to which the common law rule should be abrogated

- The new derivative procedure should replace the common law derivative action entirely.

Notice requirements

- Unless the court otherwise ordered, a claimant should be required to give notice to the company of its intention to bring a derivative action at least 28 days before the commencement of proceedings.
- The notice should specify the grounds of the proposed derivative action.

Company fails diligently to pursue proceedings

- A shareholder should be able to apply to continue, as a derivative action, proceedings commenced by the company where:
- the claim was capable of being pursued as a derivative action;
- the company had failed to prosecute the claim diligently; and
- the manner in which the company had commenced and continued the action amounted to an abuse of the process of the court.

Consideration by the court

- Where a derivative action was brought, the court must fix a case management conference.
- Unless the court otherwise directed, the claimant must seek leave to continue the derivative action at the case management conference.

Issues relevant to the grant of leave

- There should be no threshold test on the merits.
- In considering the issue of leave, the court should take account of all the relevant circumstances without limit.

These should include the following:

- the good faith of the applicant (which should not be defined);
- the interests of the company (having regard to the views of directors on commercial matters);
- the fact that the wrong has been, or may be, approved by the company in general meeting (but effective ratification should continue to be a complete bar);
- the fact that the company in general meeting had resolved not to pursue the cause of action;

- the views of an independent organ that for commercial reasons the action should or should not be pursued;
- the availability of alternative remedies.
- The court should not grant leave to continue the proceedings if it is satisfied that the action is not in the interests of the company.

Other relevant provision

- The action should be brought on behalf of all the company's members other than any who are defendants, and a decision of the court should be binding on all the members on whose behalf the action is brought. However, any decision of the court should not be enforced against a person who was not a party to the proceedings without the court's permission.
- The court may adjourn a hearing to enable a meeting of shareholders to be convened for the purpose of considering a resolution affecting the claim.
- No proceedings brought by a shareholder under the provisions relating to derivative actions may be discontinued or compromised without the leave of the court.

Reform of section 14 of the Companies Act 1985

- The Group did not recommend any reform of s 14 of the CA 1985.

Pre-action discovery

- The Group did not recommend any extension to the right to disclosure of documents specifically for shareholder proceedings.

The Law Commissions: *Company Directors: Regulating Conflicts of Interests and Formulating a Statement of Duties*

1.9 In September 1999, the Law Commissions of England and Wales and Scotland jointly published a consultation paper on company directors with particular emphasis on regulating conflicts of interest and formulating a statement of duties.[81] The Law Commissions were contributing to the wider

---

[81] The Law Commission and The Scottish Law Commission, *Company Directors: Regulating Conflicts of Interests and Formulating a Statement of Duties* (September 1999), Law Com No 261, Scot Law Com No 173.

Company Law Review debate.[82] The Commissions looked at directors' fiduciary duties and their duty of skill and care.

The Commissions considered full codification and partial codification of directors' duties. Full codification would be a statutory statement of all a director's fiduciary duties and his duty of skill and care. It would be an exhaustive statement and would entirely replace the general law. A partial codification would be a statement of the main, settled duties, including the director's duty of care. It would not be exhaustive. The general law would continue to apply in those areas not covered by statute. It would, however, be superseded in relation to the duties set out in the statement.

The Commissions considered that full codification might make the law more consistent, certain, accessible and comprehensible. However, some duties were not well settled and it might be difficult to state them in statutory form, which could restrict the ability of the law to develop. The case against full codification was the difficulty of defining the standard of care that a director must show in carrying out his functions, and to set out the standard in statute would freeze it at the time of enactment.

Many of the Commission's recommendations were accepted by the Group in subsequent company law reviews.

Below follows the recommendations of the Steering Group on directors' duties, taking account of the Commission's views. References to the sections are to the CA 1985. The Group recommended that:

- There should be a statutory statement of a director's main fiduciary duties and his duty of care and skill.
- The statement should so far as possible be drafted in broad and general language.
- It should not be exhaustive, i.e. it should state that a director is subject to other duties that have not been codified.
- Forms 10(2) and 288a should contain the statutory statement of duties, and when a director signs the forms he should acknowledge that he has read his statement.
- The DTI should consider the most effective way of producing and distributing a pamphlet explaining a director's duties.
- A director's duty of care, skill and diligence to his company should be set out in statute; the standard should be judged by a twofold objective/

[82] The Law Commissions' terms of reference were (i) to review Part X of the Act with a view to considering how the provisions could be simplified and modernised; (ii) to consider a case for a statutory statement of the duties owed by directors to their company under the general law, including their fiduciary duties and their duty of care; (iii) to review additional provisions of the Companies Acts which the Commissions consider should be reviewed at the same time as part of the above work; and (iv) to make recommendations.

subjective test; and regard should be had to the functions of the particular director and the circumstances of the company.

- There should not be a statutory business judgment rule.
- There should not be a statutory provision setting out the circumstances in which a director may delegate his powers to others and rely on information provided by others without incurring liability.
- Sections 312–6, 319, 320–22 and 330–44 of the CA 1985 should not be replaced.
- Sections 312–6 of the CA 1985 should not apply to covenanted payments. Since the point has not been conclusively established by English case law, the Group also recommended that the section be amended to make the position clear.
- The compensation of loss of office which by virtue of para 8(2) of Sched 6 of the CA 1985 must be shown in the notes to the annual accounts should be shown for each director separately. The components of the compensation package set out in para above should be shown in the notes to those accounts.
- No amendments should be made to ss 312–316 of the CA 1985 to make express reference to former directors.
- Sections 312–316 of the CA 1985 should not be extended so that they apply to payments to connected persons.
- Where a director receives a payment for a loss of some office with the company in the context of the loss of office as a director, ss 312–316 of the CA 1985 should apply to that payment. However, in line with its earlier recommendations, ss 312–315 of the CA 1985 should not apply to any such payment which is a covenanted payment.
- Section 314 of the CA 1985 should not be amended to cover takeovers by scheme of arrangement and the Commissions therefore recommend against it.
- Section 314 of the CA of the 1985 should be amended so as expressly to cover unconditional offers.
- Directors to whom ss 312–316 of the CA 1985 apply should include those of holding companies.
- There should be no change to the majorities required for approvals under ss 312–315 of the CA 1985.
- Sections 312–316 of the CA 1985 should not be amended to require disclosure of details of other payments being made to the director.
- There should not be any introduction of a mechanism for deemed shareholder approval into ss 312–315 of the CA 1985.
- There should be statutory remedies as suggested above, where payment is received in breach of ss 312–316 of the CA 1985, and s 315 of the CA 1985 does not apply. A provision similar to s 313 (2) of the CA 1985 should for consistency be inserted into s 312 (CA 1985). In addition, there should be separate section or group of sections setting out in one

place the statutory civil remedies for breach of the provisions of article X of the CA 1985.

- If the offeree shareholders seek to enforce their claims under s 315 of the CA 1985, their claim should prevail over any claim to which the company may be entitled, arising from the same facts, unless the court otherwise orders.
- Section 311 of the CA 1985 may safely be repealed: it had not changed as a result of the consultation, and accordingly the Group recommended its repeal.
- Immaterial interests should be excluded from the disclosure obligation in s 317 of the CA 1985 by providing that the section should not apply where the director satisfies the court that the interest did not give rise to the real risk of an actual conflict of interest and his position as the holder of that interest and his position as a director of the company; or the director satisfies the court that the rest of the board were aware of the nature and extent of his interest before the directors approved the transaction.
- Section 317 of the CA 1985 should continue to require disclosure of interests, whether or not the transaction comes before, or requires the approval of, the board or a committee of the board.
- Section 317 of the CA 1985 should be subject to exceptions for the interests of directors in their own service agreements.
- The Group did not recommend exemption from disclosure of interests in arrangements for the benefit of all employees.
- The Group did not recommend that there should be exempted from disclosure under s 317 of the CA 1985 interests that a director has, by reason only that he is a director of another company in the same group or has a non-beneficial shareholding in it.
- An exemption from disclosure under s 317 of the CA 1985 should provide that a director should disclose the interests of connected persons if he would have to disclose them on his own behalf.
- The introduction of a requirement to keep a register of directors' interests not that the proposed register should be open to inspection by shareholders. There should be no further requirement for disclosure in the annual accounts.
- A sole director should be exempt form the requirements of s 317 of the CA 1985, but the director's interests should be recorded in the register of directors' interests as the Group recommended above, or, if that recommendation were not accepted, in a written memorandum or minutes of the directors' meeting following the general meeting. The Group did not recommend that a sole director should disclose his interests to the company in a general meeting.
- The Group did not recommend disqualifying directors of public companies (or companies generally) from voting on matters in which they are interested.

- Section 317 of the CA 1985 should be amended so as to require a director to disclose the nature and extent of his interests.
- The criminal penalty for breach of s 317 of the CA 1985 should be replaced by a civil remedy, by which the contract or transaction would be voidable at the instance of the company unless the court otherwise directs; the contract or transaction would cease to be voidable in circumstances analogous to those set out in s 322(2) of the CA 1985, save that the protection of third parties (under s 322(2) (CA 1985)) would extend to the parties to the contract or transaction including connected persons.
- Whether the transaction was voidable or not, the liability of a director and/or a connected person would be: to account for any profits from the transaction; and to indemnify the company for any loss resulting from the transaction in either case to the extent that the court thinks just and equitable; and the connected person would incur no liability under either head unless he knew of the failure to disclose.
- The Secretary of State should not be able to disapply s 318 of the CA 1985 where the company is already bound, in his opinion, by sufficient disclosure under the Listing Rules; disclosure under s 318 of the CA 1985 should be extended to contracts for services and non-executive directors' letters of appointment; s 318(5) and (11) of the CA 1985 should be repealed as they are no longer appropriate; s 318 of the CA 1985 should not be amended to inquire into the disclosure of particulars of terms collateral to service contracts; the statutory limit on the duration of directors' service contracts without shareholder approval should be reduced from five years to three years although the Group suggest that further consideration should be given to the position of small companies in the course of the Company Law Review. The Group also recommend that the three-year limit should be applied to rolling contracts; and no mechanism for deemed shareholder approval should be introduced into s 319 of the CA 1985.
- The Group made no recommendation on whether to allow public inspection of directors' service contracts.
- Section 320 of the CA 1985 should be amended so as to allow a company to enter into a contract that is conditional on the company first obtaining shareholder approval.
- Section 320 of the CA 1985 should be amended in order to clarify that it does not apply to covenanted payments under service agreements or to other payments to which s 316(3) of the CA 1985 applies.
- Section 321 of the CA 1985 should be amended to introduce new exemptions for transactions with administrators. The Group also recommended that where there is reason to believe that the company's assets were insufficient to make a payment to shareholders, or for some other good reason, administrative receivers should have the option of

applying to the court for approval of a transaction as an alternative to shareholder approval.

- Section 320 of the CA 1985 should not be amended so as to give the Secretary of State power to exempt listed companies.
- Section 320 of the CA 1985 should not be amended so as to displace the requirement of shareholder approval where independent non-executive directors approve the transaction; where shareholders do not object within a specified period; or where an expert reports that in his opinion the transaction was fair and reasonable.
- Subject to its recommendation that consideration be given to the introduction of a single code of remedies, s 322 of the CA 1985 should not be amended to the effect that the company would have no remedy where the defendant/defender shows that it was not prejudiced by the transaction.
- Subject to the Group's recommendation that consideration be given to the introduction of single code remedies, ss 322A and 322B of the CA 1985 should be retained as they stood.
- Sections 323 and 327 of the CA 1985 should be replaced.
- Section 324 of the CA 1985 should not be amended to exempt non-beneficial shareholdings but it should be amended so as to give the Secretary of State the power by regulation to vary the rules in Part 1 of Schedule 13, for determining whether a person had an interest in shares or debentures for the purposes of ss 324–326 of the CA 1985 and s 346 of the CA 1985.
- Section 329 of the CA 1985 should be amended so that a company was bound to transmit to the relevant exchange such information as the company is bound to enter into the register of directors' interests without notification by the director pursuant to s 325(3) and (4) of the CA 1985.
- If s 323 of the CA 1985 were repealed, s 324 (2)(b) of the CA 1985 should be extended to cover the taking of options.
- Retaining the prohibition in s 330(3), (4), (6) and (7) of the CA 1985 on companies making loans to (or entering into analogous transactions with) their directors or the companies and not just relevant companies. This, however, was subject to the outcome of the Company Law Review, which may favour the introduction of special provisions for small companies. The Group recommended the retention of existing exemptions to the prohibitions in s 330 of the CA 1985, and that those in ss 339–40 of the CA 1985 should be retained in their current form. The Group did not recommend the introduction of an additional exemption for loans made the consent of shareholders.
- The obligation under Schedule 6 of the CA 1985 to disclose interests in transactions should apply to interests that are material to the director in question or the company. The Group also recommended the repeal of paragraphs of that Schedule.

- Schedule 6, Part II of the CA 1985 should be retained and not replaced by FRS 8.
- The director should be placed under a duty to give notice to the company of such matters relating to himself and (so far as known to him) his connected persons as may be necessary for the purposes of Schedule 6, Part II of the CA 1985.
- The exception for transactions in the ordinary course of business in para 20 of the CA Schedule 6 of the CA 1985 should be retained and it should be extended to apply to transactions which are not intra-group.
- The level of detail of disclosure of the incidents of quasi loans and credit transactions and related guarantees and security should in principle be the same as that required under sub-paras (d) and (e) of para 22 of Schedule 6 of the CA 1985 (loans).
- The exemption in para 23 of Schedule 6 of the CA 1985 should be extended to credit transactions.
- There should be minimum exception for loans and quasi loans on similar lines to those set out in para 24 of Schedule 6 of the CA 1985.
- Where the deeming provision in s 340(7) of the CA 1985 is applied for the purpose of Schedule 6, a director should, wherever possible, be required to give an estimate of the value of the transaction.
- The Group did not consider that a company should be exempted from an obligation to disclose transactions in which a director has a material interest, merely because that interest is as a director of the other company. Accordingly, the Group recommended that para 18(a) of Schedule 6 of the CA 1985 should not apply to transactions disclosable under paras 15(c) and 16(c).
- The Group made no recommendation as to whether ss 343 and 344 of the CA 1985 were necessary or desirable.
- The current definition for 'connected persons' be extended so as to include cohabitants; the current definition should be extended to include infant children of the cohabitant if they lived with the director and the cohabitant, and the cohabitant is a connected person; the current definition should be extended to same-sex cohabitants, adult children, parents and siblings; and the Company Law Review would consider simplifying the circumstances in which a director was associated with a company through his control of another company.
- The Group's recommendation was not to amend s 346 of the CA 1985 so as to give the Secretary of State the power to vary by regulations the list of connected persons.
- Part X of the CA 1985 should continue to apply to acts committed outside the jurisdiction. The Group also recommended that s 347 be amended so as to include references to ss 322A and 322B of the CA 1985.
- The Group also published a draft *Statement of Directors' Duties*, which it

proposed to include in a future Companies Act. Set out below is a text of the draft:

DRAFT STATEMENT OF DIRECTORS' DUTIES

General

1)   The law imposes duties on directors. If a person does not comply with his duties as a director he may be liable to civil or criminal proceedings and he may be disqualified form acting as a director.

2)   Set out below there is a summary of the main duties of a director to his company. It is not a complete statement of a director's duties, and the law may change anyway. If a person is not clear about his duties as a director in any situation he should seek advice.

Loyalty

3)   A director must act in good faith in what he considers to be the interests of the company.

Obedience

4)   A director must act in accordance with the company's constitution (such as the Articles of Association) and must exercise his powers only for the purposes allowed by law.

No secret profits

5)   A director must not use the company's property, information or opportunities for his own or anyone else's benefit unless he is allowed to by the company's constitution or the use has been disclosed to the company in general meeting and the company has consented to it.

Independence

6)   A director must not agree to restrict his power to exercise an independent judgment. But if he considers in good faith that it is in the interests of the company for a transaction to be entered into and carried into effect, he may restrict his power to exercise an independent judgment by agreeing to act in a particular way to achieve this.

Conflict of interest

7)   If there is a conflict between an interest or duty of a director and a interest of the company in any transaction, he must account to the company for any benefit he receives from the transaction. This applies whether or not the company sets aside the transaction. But he does not have to account for the benefit if he is allowed to have the interest or duty by the company's constitution or the interest or duty has been disclosed to and approved by the company in general meeting.

Care, skill and diligence

8)   A director owes the company a duty to exercise the care, skill and diligence

which would be exercised in the same circumstances by a reasonable person having both:

a) the knowledge and experience that may reasonably be expected of a person in the same position as the director, and

b) the knowledge and experience which the director has.

Interests of employees, etc.

9) A director must have regard to the interests of the company's employees in general and its members.

Fairness

10) A director must act fairly as between different members.

Effect of this statement

The law stating the duties of directors is not affected by this statement or by the fact that, by signing this document, a director acknowledges that he has read the statement.

Modern Company Law For A Competitive Economy: Company General Meetings and Shareholder Communication

1.10 In October 1999, the Group published a trilogy of consultation documents on specific areas of company law that required wide consultation and on which the Group had previously made progress.

One of the first consultative documents was entitled: *Modern Company Law For A Competitive Economy: Company General Meetings and Shareholder Communication*.[83] The Group considered that meetings and shareholder communication were of wide public interest that required consultation. AGMs were considered the key mechanism whereby shareholders held managers of companies to account. They were the focus for conveying much information to shareholders, and they provided the forum for the direct questioning of the company's management. In addition, AGMs normally provided the mechanism for taking certain formal decisions such as the election of directors.

AGMs have been perceived as the key mechanism for promoting transparency and accountability in the management of the company's affairs. However, there had been wide consensus that AGMs did not achieve these objectives very satisfactorily.[84] The Group's task was to examine what improvements in law and practice could be made to AGMs without imposing undue burdens on company boards. The consultation document also

---

[83] The Company Law Review Steering Group, *Modern Company Law For A Competitive Economy: General Meetings and Shareholder Communication* (October 1999).

[84] For example, there were no statutory requirements as to the agenda of an AGM.

considered communication technology and its applications for company law reform, including communication with shareholders and conducting company general meetings. Many companies were taking advantage of new technology, and it was important that the law did not inhibit such development but facilitated and encouraged them.

Although provisions in the CA 1985 dealt with convening and conducting meetings, in practice they were inadequate. The Group noted that a general meeting of shareholders could be an effective mechanism for quasi-democratic control of directors if most of the votes were held by members other than the directors or those under their influence; and if most of the members were able and willing to participate in the meeting. However, in practice, the position was rather different. At one extreme, there was a large number of small, mainly owner-managed companies whose shares were held wholly or mainly by the directors and those actively engaged in the company, or their families. Such companies were run for the most part informally and without reference to company law unless something went wrong. A formal meeting of members served little purpose where the directors and members were largely the same people, and the extent of compliance by such companies with a requirement to hold an AGM was conjectural. The elective regime that allowed private companies to elect to dispense with the AGM was recognition of that situation.

For public companies, at least those whose shares were listed on a stock exchange, the general meeting failed for quite different reasons to provide the reality of democratic accountability and control. There were many thousands – sometimes hundreds of thousands or even millions – of individual shareholders of such companies; they lived in all parts of UK, and many lived abroad. It was quite impracticable for more than a small minority of them to attend a general meeting on a working weekday at a single location in the UK.

Moreover, 70 to 80 per cent of the shares in listed companies were registered in the names not of individuals but of financial institutions. It was unusual for representatives of these institutions to attend any company general meetings. They exercised their membership rights in different way. Typically, a large listed company would publish preliminary results within a few weeks of the end of the financial year, followed up to three months later by the publication of the full statutory accounts, which were then laid before the AGM shortly thereafter. It was the preliminary results rather than the full statutory accounts that were the main influence on the share price. In the interval between the publication of preliminary results and full accounts, the company would typically hold a considerable number of meetings, either one-to-one with individual institutions or with analysts representing institutions. These discussions would be conducted in scrupulous observance of the constraints of the insider-dealing legislation; but often searching questions were asked of the directors and a substantial amount of information was conveyed about the company's past performance and future plans and prospects – far more than the individual shareholder would glean from the annual report and accounts. Well before the AGM, the institutions were able to take an informed view of the matters to be decided; they would then lodge their proxy forms with the company, so that in the vast majority of cases the outcome of the meeting was determined in advance. The AGM was not the debating, information-exchanging and decision-taking body that it purported to be. Individual shareholders had neither the participation rights nor the quality of information that the theory arguably implied.

Recently, proceedings at the AGMs of some leading companies were dominated by representatives of pressure groups exercising their rights as shareholders to draw attention to wider social or environmental concerns. It was believed that some shareholders acquired a few shares for this specific purpose. According to the Group, it was entirely reasonable that the directors should face challenges on the wider implications of the company's activities and policies; but in some cases, the objectives of the groups concerned had seemed to be disruption rather than enlightenment, and self-advertisement rather than genuine monitoring of the company's operations; and their activities have reduced the value of the AGM for the 'genuine' private shareholder.

For a large company, the direct cost of arranging an AGM, including in some cases the cost of security arrangements to ensure that the business was transacted without disruption, was considerable. Even more significant was the opportunity cost of the very substantial amount of directors' and senior managers' time that was needed to prepare for an unpredictable debate on any aspect on the company's business. This would be justified if the AGM provided a genuine forum of accountability. But in most cases it did not.

The Group highlighted two ways of responding to the ineffectiveness of the AGM in fulfilling its role in the governance of public companies. The first was to extend to plcs a right to dispense with the AGM; the second was to improve the legislative provisions relating to the AGM to enable it better to fulfil its role. The two were not mutually exclusive.

The rationale for enabling plcs to dispense with the holding of the AGM would be that the AGM was in many cases ineffective in fulfilling the functions assigned to it in theory, and the companies should have the option of replacing it with something less cumbersome in order to achieve the indispensable governance functions of the institutions. Those functions would however remain important, and it would be very necessary for the law to ensure that they are fulfilled no less – and preferably more – effectively in those plcs that decided to dispense with the AGM. It would be necessary for this purpose for the law to ensure:

(a) that all shareholders had timely access to whatever information on performance and prospects it was decided to require the company to disclose;

(b)   that the shareholders were able both to decide on matters put to them for decision by the directors, and themselves to put forward matters for decision; and

(c)   that the shareholders had the opportunity to debate this information amongst themselves, and to question the directors and hold them to account.

According to the Group, item (c) was more dubious, given that the reality of the position was that such debates did not make any difference in practice in the vast majority of cases. The Group thought it could be replaced by a requirement that any private meetings with substantial shareholders to explain the interim announcement or the final results should be recorded, and the record made available to the shareholders.

The Group believed that to fulfil these functions without an AGM, it would be necessary for the law to make separate provision for the accountability of directors to shareholders, and to decisions taken by shareholders. Thus debate between the members and questions to the directors could take place at a series of meetings in different locations (if appropriate); and voting could take place by post or electronically, without a meeting. But if it was thought essential to preserve shareholder participation at a level of effectiveness no lower that that provided by the AGM, and if the availability of the information that the company was required to publish each year was necessary if shareholders were to participate in an informed way, detailed rules would be needed. The law would have to provide a carefully modulated sequence of events – dispatch of report and accounts – period for 'live' meetings and circulation of records of meetings (if any) – opportunity for formulation of shareholder resolutions – circulation of resolutions – opening of voting – closing of voting. The spread of electronic communication had reduced the time all this would take. But there would need to be minimum periods between each stage to enable shareholder input to be considered and effective, and there would also need to be an overall time limit if decisions are not to be taken based on information that was even more out-of-date than before. The resulting legislation would be quite complex, and the process cumbersome and probably more expensive.

It would also be necessary for the law to set out procedures by which a plc would dispense with the AGM. It would be impracticable to require unanimity among the members of a widely held public company for a decision to dispense with the AGM. But to require a special resolution (needing a 75 per cent majority) would often enable the board of a listed plc to secure enough support from the institution to dispense with the AGM regardless of the views of individual shareholders. The Group thought that a possible compromise might be to require the support of holders of 90 per cent of the votes (i.e. not just of those actually voting) at an annual or extraordinary general meeting of the company, by analogy with the holders of 10 per cent of the votes required to requisition an EGM. A subsequent resolution to reinstate the AGM might then be deemed to succeed if supported by holders of more than 10 per cent of the votes.

The CA 1985 did not define what may count as a 'meeting', but the great majority of AGMs of listed UK companies took place at a specified time, in a single location in the UK, with voting during the course of the meeting. Companies had on occasions accommodated some shareholders in an over-flow room with two-way audio–visual communication with the 'main' meeting room, and it was understood that the law accepted this as a single meeting for the purposes of s 366 of the CA 1985. Provided that there was two-way real-time communication between all locations, there seemed no reason why a 'meeting' held at a number of locations, including all overseas locations, should not be recognised by the law as a company general meeting. Rapid advances in communication technology were providing a wide range of modes of 'real-time' communication between geographically separated locations, and the extent to which the law would, without further assistance, recognise these things as 'meetings' was unclear.

According to the Group, it would be possible to go one stage further and envisage an interactive 'virtual' meeting held in no location; the directors' presentations would be posted on an electronic company bulletin board accessible to shareholders, and the shareholders' interventions and the directors' responses would also be posted on the bulletin board. Such a 'meeting' would probably have to remain open for several days. Such a procedure could potentially offer even wider shareholder access, but at the cost of the discipline on the directors of face-to-face real-time contact with shareholders. It was suggested that this option should be open to plcs with unanimous shareholder agreement, as an alternative to dispensing with the AGM altogether, but there could be a case for allowing this approach with a lesser majority requirement.

Section 366(2) of the CA 1985 required companies to hold an AGM in every calendar year except that the first could be held at any time within 18 months of incorporation; and s 366(3) of the CA 1985 required that each AGM must be held not more than 15 months after the previous one. According to the Group, if it was accepted that a main purpose of an AGM was to require an account of stewardship by directors to shareholders, it would be more logical to relate the timing of the AGM to the availability of the annual accounts and directors' report. It was, therefore, suggested that companies should be required to hold their AGM (including the first AGM after incorporation) with time allowed for the laying and delivering of accounts and reports.[85] (This period was seven months for a public company and ten months for a private company.) In the case of a newly formed company, the

---

[85] CA 1985, s 244.

effect of the change proposed would be to put back the latest permitted date of the first AGM from 18 to 21 or 22 months after incorporation.

There were currently no statutory requirement as to the business to be transacted at the AGM as such. However, s 241 of the CA 1985 required the directors to lay before the company in general meeting copies of the annual accounts, the directors' report and the auditors' report on the accounts. In addition, s 385 of the CA 1985 required the company, at the general meeting at which the accounts were laid, to appoint auditors for the period until the next annual accounts are laid; and s 390A of the CA 1985 required the company in general meeting to fix the remuneration of the auditors or determine the manner in which the remuneration will be fixed.

It was common practice for each of these requirements to be met at the AGM. In addition, the Articles commonly provided for the AGM to re-elect retiring directors and to elect new directors, including the confirmation of directors appointed to casual vacancies since the previous AGM.[86] A three-year rotation is also covered in the codes on corporate governance.[87]

It was suggested that the law should be clarified, in line with almost universal practice, by obliging companies to transact the following business at the AGM with respect to shareholders:

- lay before them the annual accounts;
- lay before them the directors' report;
- lay before them the auditor's report;
- appoint auditors for the coming year;
- re-elect directors retiring and seeking re-election in accordance with any annual requirement in the Articles;
- elect new directors to fill vacancies; and
- confirm by election the appointment of any director appointed (other than by general meeting) since the previous AGM to fill any casual vacancy.

The requirement that the remuneration must be fixed in general meeting, or in such manner as the company may in general meeting determine, was usually met in the latter manner, by delegation. The Group thought that there was a case for removing the requirement from the statute altogether, and leaving the manner of fixing the auditors' remuneration to the company's constitution.

In addition to these recurring items, there were a number of points on which companies were required by statute to take decisions in general meeting (not necessarily the AGM) but which may not arise every year. These included:

---

[86] See Table A 1985, articles 73ff.   [87] Combined Code, para A6.

- directors' authority to issue shares;[88]
- directors' authority to issue shares without pre-emption;[89]
- alteration of share capital;[90]
- reduction of capital;[91]
- authority to purchase own shares;[92] and
- approval of certain long-term directors' contracts.[93]

In the first, second, fourth and fifth cases, the requirement for decision in the general meeting derived from the Second Directive. The first two cases were in practice recurrent because although the authorities in question had a maximum duration of five years, they were normally renewed annually. The sixth should be assumed to remain as a requirement, pending consideration of directors' remuneration. It was suggested that these requirements for decisions in general meeting should remain, but without specifying the AGM.

If these suggestions were accepted, the agenda for AGM would thus compromise:

- recurring items required by the statute or the Articles to be decided by the AGM;
- non-recurring items (if any) required by the statute or the Articles to be decided in the general meeting;
- any other resolution proposed by the directors; and
- resolutions proposed by the shareholders and accepted for consideration by the directors.

It had been suggested, as a means of combating disruption from pressure groups, that the legislation might confirm a company's right to restrict the right of some members of the company, or some of a class of member, to attend a general meeting, by reference to the number, value and percentage of their shares in the company. Possible thresholds for the right to attend might be 1 per cent of the shares or a holding of £500m market value. The Group saw serious difficulties in this idea: it would be seen as 'anti-democratic' and aimed at stifling legitimate criticism of companies, and it would be difficult to pick a threshold high enough to discourage pressure groups that did not also deprive significant numbers of 'genuine' members of one of the main membership rights.

The requirements under the CA 1985 were for notice in writing of 21 (calendar) days for AGMs and for meetings at which a special resolution was to be considered. The notice required for other meetings was 14 days, except for unlimited companies where it was seven days. The report of the

[88] CA 1985, s 80.   [89] CA 1985, s 95.   [90] CA 1985, s 121.
[91] CA 1985, s 135.   [92] CA 1985, s 165.   [93] CA 1985, s 319.

Committee on Corporate Governance (the Hampel Committee) recommended as a matter of good practice that listed companies should give at least 20 working days' notice for their AGM, to enable institutional shareholders to consult their clients.[94] It had also been drawn to the Group's attention that a longer notice period may help institutional shareholders who held shares through custodians to communicate voting instructions to the custodian and ensure that these were acted on. This could help to increase the proportion of shares voted from the present disappointing levels. However, against that, the introduction of electronic communication should make it easier to conduct the necessary communications within the present notice period.

Section 366 of the CA 1985 required that the notice of an AGM shall specify the meeting as the AGM. That apart, there were no statutory requirements for the content of a meeting notice. Table A in the CA 1985, Article 38, provided that a meeting shall specify the time and place of the meeting and the general nature of the business to be transacted. At common law, sufficient notice was required of the nature of the business to enable a member to decide whether to attend. It seemed desirable that the notice should be required to include also:

- the text of resolutions proposed by directors and shareholders. (This was already the case with extraordinary and special resolutions. But they were often detailed and expressed in technical language difficult for the layman to understand); and
- an explanation that appeared sufficient to the proposers to explain the motivation of any proposed resolution. (This would include relevant biographical details in the case or resolutions to elect or re-elect directors.)[95]

Matters such as the quorum for a meeting, the arrangements for a substitute chairman where one was needed, and the right to propose the adjournment, were currently left to the Articles.

In this recent report of its Committee of Inquiry into Vote Execution, the National Association of Pension Funds (NAPF) found that levels of voting at AGMs of major plcs remained at around 40 per cent;[96] acceptance by

---

[94] Hampel Report, para 5.24.

[95] This point was covered in the Combined Code, para A.6.2.

[96] National Association of Pension Funds, Committee of Inquiry into Voting Execution, 5 July 1999. The Committee looked at two key issues: first, whether the low voting rate achieved by pension funds reflected the intentions of trustee boards; and second, the nature of the problems within the current system of voting. The Inquiry concluded that the low voting figure partly reflected conscious decisions by some institutions and fund managers not to vote on routine items of corporate business, but it also reflected on a complex and antiquated system. The Inquiry's key recommendations were that (i) regular, considered voting should be regarded as a fiduciary responsibility of trustee boards; (ii) trustee boards should record their policy

institutions of voting as a fiduciary responsibility, together with closer co-ordination between institutions and custodians and the introduction of electronic voting levels; but the legal framework relating to voting at general meetings was also an inhibiting factor.

In most respects, the procedure for voting at general meetings is provided for in the company's Articles. Table A 1985, Articles 46 and 54 provide that voting shall be by show of hands (one vote for each shareholder actually present or represented in the case of a corporate shareholder; but not proxies unless the Articles so provide) unless a poll is demanded (one share, one vote) before or after the declaration of the result. Many companies follow this. But it is open to a company to provide that all votes shall be by poll. Section 373 of the CA 1985 set out the right of members to demand a poll. The only questions on which the Articles could rule out the demand for a poll were the election of the chairman and the adjournment of the meeting.[97] A demand for a poll could not be made ineffective if it was made by at least five members with the right to vote or by members representing at least 10 per cent of the total voting rights.[98] It was provided in Articles that a poll (other than on the election of the chairman or on the adjournment) may be fixed by the chairman to take place up to 30 days after the poll was demanded, and the meeting was not closed until the poll was taken.[99]

According to the Group, voting a by show of hands had the merit of enabling uncontroversial resolutions to be disposed of quickly, and the right of the chairman on the one hand and a relatively small number of members on the other to demand a poll was a safeguard against a decision being taken against the wish of holders of a majority of the shares. But given the unrepresentative nature of the attendance at AGMs of large companies, voting by show of hands seemed anomalous – particularly so if Table A applied, and proxies had no votes.[100] The case for retaining voting by a show of hands was weakest for listed companies.

The Group believed that a possible way both of rationalising the voting procedure and adding substance to the meeting itself might be to defer voting until after the meeting – beginning at the end of the meeting and ending some time later. (An interval of two weeks might be appropriate.) Shareholders attending the meeting could reflect before voting; and those unable to attend would not lodge proxies before the meeting but would vote themselves afterwards. Boards with close and harmonious relations with major shareholders

wide consultation. Simplification and rationalisation would be key themes at the heart of the review from the beginning. The Government was also determined to ensure that the new arrangements would support business activity and promote growth and competitiveness within a balanced framework rather than to act as a brake or unnecessary constraint.

[97] CA 1985, s 373(1)(a).   [98] CA 1985, s 373(1)(b).   [99] Table A 1985, article 49.
[100] Table A 1985, articles 54 and 58.

would, as now, be confident of support in the vote; but in some cases boards would go into the meeting knowing that they already had the votes to achieve their desired outcome. This could give the meeting a more real 'democratic' significance, leaving open the possibility, at least, that the course of the debate might influence the outcome. In particular, institutions could assess the directors' performance at the meeting, and any media at public reaction, before casting their vote. Votes might be cast either at the place(s) of the meeting at the conclusions of the business, or by post or, if authorised by the constitution, and agreed by the members, by telephone or electronically. It would, however, be necessary to provide for voting at the meeting on procedural matters. Voting by proxy would still be permitted, but would in practice be replaced by postal or electronic voting after the meeting.

One particular problem with deferred voting was that of amendments. It was an unsatisfactory feature of current procedure that meetings could be delayed for long periods while a poll was taken on an amendment. On the other hand, to invite shareholders to vote, after a meeting, on a resolution to amend the original motion and then on a conditional basis on both the amended and the unamended resolution, would be to invite confusion. The solution could be to provide that no amendment shall be considered unless notice of the intention to propose it had been given the company a reasonable period before the meeting with the support of, say, 10 per cent of the share capital. The proposed amendment could then be discussed at the meeting, and the law could provide for the voting to take place in relation to two alternative resolutions – amended and unamended. It might also be necessary to correct errors and to conform the resolution to changed circumstance.

At present, there was no way of distinguishing between a failure to vote on a resolution and a considered abstention. It had been suggested that the inclusion on the ballot paper for company resolutions of abstention as a third option would provide shareholders, and particularly institutions, with a means of demonstrating their disquiet with a proposal, without having to face up to the implication for the value of their investment if it were defeated.

Section 376 of the CA 1985 provided that the company must circulate a resolution proposed by shareholders representing at least 5 per cent of the voting rights or by at least 100 shareholders with shares on which at least £100 on average has been paid up. Circulation was at the shareholders' expense. Following the DTI consultation on the subject, Ministers approved the following proposed modifications. Shareholders' resolutions would have to be circulated by the directors free of charge, if they were:

(a)   received by a date specified by the directors as reasonably necessary to enable them to be included in the report mailing;

(b)   signed by members representing at least 5 per cent of voting rights (as now) or by at least 100 members with an average holding of a market value of at least £500.

Companies could refuse to circulate resolutions repetitious of others to be considered at the same meeting, or which had been defeated within the previous five years.

Section 372 of the CA 1985 provided that a proxy may vote on a poll and may speak at a meeting of a private company; but he could not speak at a meeting of a public company, nor vote on a show of hands at either a public or a private company meeting, unless permitted to do so by the Articles. It also provided, unless otherwise provided in the Articles, that each member of a private company may appoint only one proxy to attend and vote on his behalf. Following the DTI consultation on the subject, Ministers have approved the following proposed modifications. Section 372 of the CA 1985 would be amended:

(a)   to require proxies to be permitted to speak at meetings of public as well as of private companies, and to vote on a show of hands at either; and

(b)   to inquire all companies to permit a member to appoint a proxy for each beneficial holding at a given meeting, thus ensuring that where a nominee or trustee member has beneficial holders who wish to vote in different ways, their wishes could be accommodated.

An extraordinary resolution was a resolution which must be passed by a 75 per cent majority at a meeting, of which notice is given specifying the resolution as a special resolution (s 378 of the CA 1985). Extraordinary resolutions were required in the following cases:

•   for a variation of class rights in certain cases (s 125(2) of the CA 1985);
•   under the Insolvency Act, in connection with various aspects of winding up (e.g. voluntary winding up by reason of inability to meet liabilities – s 84(1)(c) of the CA 1985); and
•   where the Articles so require and the act does not require a special or elective resolution.

The Group believed that it was desirable to preserve a category of resolutions requiring an enhanced majority for certain very important decisions, and this was in any case necessary to comply with requirements of the Second Directive (on withdrawal of pre-emption rights and reduction of capital). In the case of capital reduction (Article 30 of the Directive) there was also a requirement that the meeting notice should state the purpose of the resolution. The Group doubted however whether it was necessary to preserve the extraordinary resolution as a separate category, given that the only difference was that it may be passed at an EGM with 14 days' notice, and that the notice required by a special resolution may be reduced with the agreement of holders of 95 per cent of the voting rights. The Jenkins Committee recommended the abolition of such resolutions in 1962.[101]

An extraordinary general meeting (EGM) was defined as any general meeting which is not called as an AGM.[102] A meeting may be called either:

(a)   by the directors on their own initiative;[103] or
(b)   by the directors on a requisition by members holding at least 10 per cent of voting rights.[104]

It was suggested that the above proposals for AGMs should also apply to EGMs with the following variations.

An EGM was typically called to conduct specific business that could not wait for the next AGM. There were therefore no rules about when an EGM may be held. It was suggested that this should remain the position.

Under the CA 1985, the statutory minimum notice period for an EGM was seven (calendar) days for an unlimited company and 14 days for a company of any other type. However, if it was proposed to pass a special resolution, the minimum notice period was 21 days. Table A also included a 21-day notice period for a resolution to appoint a director.

If it was decided to move to a minimum notice period of 20 working days for AGMs, it would be logical to do the same for EGMs at which it was proposed to pass a special resolution. In that event, a minimum notice period for the EGMs might be ten working days (five for an unlimited company).

It was up for consideration whether, if voting after the meeting was introduced for AGMs, this should also extend to EGMs. The argument of improved accountability applies with equal force to EGMs; but the urgency of the business at many EGMs might require decisions on the spot.

It was suggested that the right of the shareholders to have their resolutions circulated should not extend to EGMs, apart of course from the case of an EGM requisitioned by shareholders, where it should extend only to the objects stated in the requisition.

Under s 368 of the CA 1985, if members holding at least 10 per cent of the voting rights requisitioned the directors to call an EGM with stated objects, the directors must do so. If the directors failed to do so within 21 days, the requisitionists could do so themselves and recover reasonable expenses from the company. There were safeguards to prevent the directors from calling the meeting for a distant date in the future. It was suggested that the substance of these provisions should be retained.

[101] Jenkins Committee, op cit., Cmnd 1749, para 461.
[102] Table A 1985, Art 36.
[103] Table A 1985.
[104] CA 1985, s 368.

The DTI at the time had already issued for consultation proposals that a Bill to promote electronic commerce should include provisions that would enable companies, where the shareholder agreed: (a) to transmit to him by electronic means information required by the CA 1985; or (b) to place such information on the website or electronic forum, notifying him that access was available. Such provisions would cover:

- annual accounts;
- directors' report;
- notices of meetings; and
- proxy forms.

The consultation letter also proposed a provision enabling a shareholder, if he wished, to return to the company an appointment of a proxy instrument by electronic means, as an alternative to a hard copy instrument, where the company decided to permit this. However, if voting took place after the AGM, or if public companies were permitted to dispense with the AGM altogether, it would seem appropriate that provisions for electronic transmission should extend to the voting itself. Even without these changes, some companies may wish to offer electronic voting as an option.

The Group considered that institutional holders of shares listed plcs benefited from fuller information about the company's performance and prospects than individual shareholders. The Hampel Committee was concerned about this. In para 5.24 of their report, the Committee stated:

> The Group also consider that, as far as is practicable, private individuals should have to the same information from companies as institutional shareholders. In time, as it becomes possible to communicate with shareholders through electronic media, companies will be able to make their presentations to institutional investors available to a wider audience more readily. For the time being, companies who value links with private shareholders cultivate them by, for example, arranging briefings for client brokers and regional shareholders seminars. The Group commend such initiatives.

The Group considered that the time was now ripe to develop these ideas into more concrete proposals. For example, listed plcs with widely dispersed shareholdings might hold a series of meetings in different locations, open to all shareholders, in the period between the publication of the annual report and accounts and the commencement of voting on the AGM resolutions. Only the last meeting, at the conclusion of which the voting began, would be the statutory AGM; but the agenda for the meeting could be the same throughout, and the separation of the voting procedure from the AGM would in practice give almost equal rights to those attending any of the meetings.

Electronic communication had developed rapidly even over the last year or two, and many companies were taking advantage of this to communicate with their shareholders through company websites. It was now feasible for companies to supplement the shareholder communications required by the statute by placing on such websites much of the information now available only to institutions and analysts, thus reducing the present disparity of information, at least for those individual shareholders able to receive electronic communications.

The Group thought that answers to some of the above questions could be different for different categories of company, e.g. private and public companies; listed and unlisted companies; companies in particular sectors. One option would be to give the Secretary of State a general power to delegate the making of rules relating to company general meetings to a regulatory body. This might enable rules to be tailored more closely to the requirements of particular classes of company or particular sectors, and for the rules to be changed more quickly and conveniently in response to changing circumstances. The bodies to whom such a power might be delegated might include, for example, the Financial Services Authority (FSA), the Financial Reporting Council (FRC) or the London Stock Exchange.

Modern Company Law For A Competitive Economy: Company Formation and Capital Maintenance

1.11 In October 1999, the Group produced a second consultation document entitled: *Modern Company Law For A Competitive Economy: Company Formation and Capital Maintenance*.[105]

The Group considered radical proposals concerning the formation of new companies under future legislation. The Group advocated that the main principle should be the 'think small first' approach and the need to assist small private companies in the company law reform process.

Another radical proposal concerned the company's constitution under the Memorandum of Association and Articles of Association. The Group proposed that new companies should in the future have their constitution in one document, broadly corresponding to the Articles. This would be presented for registration along with a new registration form containing information that must be on the public register and containing much of what is now included in the Memorandum. The information would not however include an account of the company's authorised share capital: it was proposed to abolish the concept of authorised share capital as distinct from issued share capital.

---

[105] Department of Trade and Industry, *Modern Company Law For A Competitive Economy: Company Formation and Capital Maintenance* (October 1999).

The provisions of the constitution, like those of the Articles, could be amended by special resolution. The more onerous requirements for changes to the Memorandum including court approval would be removed. However, it would be possible for companies on formation, or later, to entrench provisions in the constitution, so that they could be changed only unanimously.

The Group's view was that it should remain possible to form a new company of any of the existing types – a company limited by shares, either public or private; a company limited by guarantee; or an unlimited company. The law should continue to offer model constitutions for companies of each type. It should also be possible to form a company of any type with a single member only.

Under the CA 1985, the founder members of a new company were the subscribers to the Memorandum. It was proposed to define the founder members as the persons who signed the new registration form as members. Their names would be entered in the company's register of members, and from then on the company's members would be those whose names were from time to time registered on the register.

The Group proposed to clarify the relationship between the company and its members by providing that the company's constitution was binding as between the company and its members and between the members themselves.

The Group proposed to retain the present system of registration for new companies with some modifications. The founder members would submit to the registrar of companies the new registration form and a copy of the company's constitution. These would be accompanied by a formal statement of compliance, which would no longer have to be in the statutory declaration. If the registrar was satisfied with these documents, and that the proposed name complied with regulations in force at the time, he would issue a certificate of incorporation, which would be conclusive.

The Group also considered the company's objects, its capacity and the powers of directors to bind the company. It proposed to abolish, at least for private companies, the requirement that a company must have objects. It also proposed that, in its relations with third parties, a company should have unlimited capacity and thus completely abolishing the *ultra vires* concept. However, it would remain possible for members to bring proceedings to restrain the directors from acting contrary to the company's constitution, including its objects if the company had any. It would also become possible for the shareholders to ratify such an act by the directors.

The concept of 'good faith' would still remain in favour of genuine third parties, but 'insiders' connected with the directors would not be protected in this way. It would also remain possible for members to take proceedings to restrain directors from exceeding their powers. The Group also proposed to abolish the concept of 'deemed notice', so that a person would no longer be presumed to have notice of something merely because it was disclosed at Companies House or in the company's own records available for inspection.

The Group also considered the rules that restricted the freedom of companies to return to their shareholders funds that were originally subscribed for shares. It also covered the rules ensuring that full value was received for shares on issue including, for public companies, the requirement that a minimum amount of share capital should be subscribed in the first place.

The original purpose of many of the capital maintenance rules was to protect creditors by preventing companies from dissipating funds subscribed for shares. However, major creditors attached very little importance to the amount of a company's share capital.

At present, there were two rules for both public and private companies, designed to ensure that full value was received when shares were issued. The shares must be paid up in money or money's worth; and they may not be issued at a discount to their nominal or par value. It was proposed to keep the former rule but to abolish for private companies the requirement for shares to have a par value. Instead, a share would represent simply a proportion of the value of the company.

For private companies, the abolition of par values meant that the concept of share premium is also superseded. It should be replaced by a simple rule that when new shares are issued, the undistributable reserves are increased by the net proceeds of the shares. For public companies, the present rules on share premium would remain but there should be some tightening of the rules on its application.

The Group proposed a major relaxation of the rules governing the reduction of share capital. Instead of the present provisions, which required public or private companies to seek court approval in every case, the Group proposed that a company should be able to decide by special resolution to reduce its share capital, provided that the decision was supported by a solvency statement.

The Group also considered financial assistance by a company for the acquisition of its own shares. The Group favoured abolishing all restrictions on financial assistance and significant relaxations of the 'whitewash' procedure for private companies.

The Group proposed to retain the present rules on redeemable shares and purchase by a company of its own shares. The Group considered that it might not be necessary to retain the special procedure by which a private company may redeem its shares out of capital.

The Group proposed that the rules governing dividends and other distributions by companies to their shareholders should be limited expressly to distributions to shareholders in their capacity as such. The statutory distribution rules should in the future displace existing common law rules.

Modern Company Law For A Competitive Economy: Reforming the Law Concerning Overseas Companies

1.12 Also in October 1999, the Group published its third consultation document on reforming the law concerning overseas companies.[106]

The Group noted that under the CA 1985, there were two registration regimes for companies, one for 'branches' and one for places of business which are not branches.

The regime for branches implemented the requirements of the EC Eleventh Company Law Directive.[107] The Directive did not, however, define 'branch'. But decisions of the European Court of Justice in the related area of judgments indicated that a branch implied a place of business which had the appearance of permanency, and which had a management and was otherwise physically equipped to negotiate business with third parties directly, and whose head office was abroad.

The place of business regime predated the Directive requirements, and continued to apply to places of business which are not branches. A 'place of business' encompassed both a presence less substantial than a branch and one where the central management and control of the company was in the UK.

Overseas companies that set up either a branch or any other place of business were required to register certain particulars at the Companies registry. The registration requirements were similar, but not identical, under the two regimes. Slightly more information was required in relation to branches than to other places of business. In particular, while both regimes required information about the overseas company itself (e.g. details of the company's directors and secretary, and a copy of the company's constitution), the branch regime required more information to be provided about the business established in Great Britain (e.g. details of the people empowered to represent the branch).

The requirements to file accounts also differed:

- under the branch regime, companies originating within the EC must file full accounts, prepared and audited in accordance with the requirements of their 'home' Member State. Companies formed outside the EC must file home state audited accounts, if any, but must otherwise file 'section 700' accounts; and
- under the place of business regime, companies must file s 700 (CA 1985) accounts.

---

[106] Department of Trade and Industry, *Company Law For A Competitive Economy: Reforming the Law Concerning Overseas Companies* (October 1999).

[107] Eleventh Council Directive 89/666/EEC of 21 December 1989 concerning disclosure requirements in respect of branches opened in a Member State by certain types of company governed by the law of another State.

The accounts required under s 700 of the CA 1985 were considerably less detailed than those required for companies incorporated here. In addition, the Group believed that the present s 700 (CA 1985) requirements were unsatisfactory.

The existence of the two regimes raised to a number of problems:

- it created some confusion and uncertainty for overseas companies wanting to establish a presence here: it was not always clear whether they should register under the branch or the place of business regime;
- the arrangement was further complicated by transitional provisions that applied when a company needed to transfer from the branch to a place of business regime, or vice versa, and by the fact that companies may need to register separately in England and Wales and in Scotland; and
- there was no obvious reason why less information should be available in respect of some overseas companies than others: where information was needed in order to protect third parties, the need would seem to be just as relevant to business carried out under the place of business regime as under the branch regime.

Responses to the Group's last consultation document revealed broad support for simplifying Part XXIII of the CA 1985, and in particular for adopting a single regime that would apply to all businesses registering at present under either the place of business or branch regimes.

The Group's proposal was, therefore, for a single regime based on the requirements of the Eleventh Directive. Under the proposals any overseas company establishing a place of business in the UK would be required to file certain information at the companies registry. (Under the new regime, 'place of business' would include all those businesses which at present have to register as branches.)

Overseas companies registered under the existing place of business regime needed to file less information than those registered under the branch regime. One effect of the Group's proposals would, therefore, be to increase slightly the filing requirement for certain overseas companies, by standardising the regime that requires greater disclosure.

The Group believed that all third parties in the UK who did business with overseas companies should have the same level of protection, without the somewhat artificial distinction between different types of overseas company that exist at present. The Group also believed that the slight increase in disclosure requirements for some overseas companies would be more than compensated for by the benefits of a single set of rules for all such companies – especially in terms of the greater clarity and certainty that the new regime would offer the overseas companies themselves.

The Group proposed that the requirements governing the accounts that overseas companies had to file should be simplified and improved:

- an overseas company should be required to file the accounts and reports that its home state requires it to prepare;
- where a company was not required to file accounts in its home state, the Group propose either: to restate the s 700 (CA 1985) requirements in a clear way with some modifications; or to simplify and update the requirements based on the most important requirements of the current UK reporting regime.

The consultation document also set out a number of other proposals for simplifying and standardising the rules applying to overseas companies. In particular:

- the number of multiple registrations of places of business would be kept to a minimum: for example, where an overseas company operates here from a number of locations within a common management structure, only one registration should be required;
- companies incorporated in the Channel Islands and Isle of Man should be covered by the same provisions as other overseas companies (at present Channel Island and Isle of Man companies that register under the place of business regime have to file an annual return, which is not required of other overseas companies);
- there would be no requirement for companies registered in Northern Ireland or Gibraltar (which are treated as part of the United Kingdom by the Eleventh Directive and the present branch regime) to register places of business that they establish here;
- all overseas companies subject to winding up or insolvency procedures should have to file certain information at the companies registry (at present this requirement applies in respect of branches but not other places of business);
- the requirements in the Eleventh Directive for overseas companies to disclose information on their business stationery (such as the company name, head office address and company number) should be extended to all overseas companies;
- criminal penalties should be imposed where an overseas company does not comply with the various filing requirements, but failure to comply should not prevent the company from enforcing transactions which it had entered into; and
- the registrar of companies should be able to de-register an overseas company where it was clear that the company has ceased to exist or that it no longer had a place of business here.

Phase Three

1.13 This Phase was concerned with the Group building upon the progress it had made in the series of consultation documents it had issued in 1999 and the responses it had received to those documents. The Group also took account of the Law Commission's publications on *Shareholder Remedies* and *Directors' Duties*. Phase three was, therefore, considered as developing the framework established in previous phases.

Modern Company Law For A Competitive Economy: Developing The Framework

1.14 In March 2000, the Group issued a consultation document *Modern Company Law For A Competitive Economy: Developing The Framework*.[108] This document analysed and made proposals on the key areas of 'governance' of companies (i.e. the main rules governing their operation and control, including transparency rules) and on small and private companies. This was the second strategic consultation document from the Group. It included proposals on the scope of UK company law; directors' duties; and the accounting aspects for small and large companies.

The Group addressed the 'scope' issue – namely, 'in whose interests should companies be run?'[109] It rejected the pluralist perspective and advocated an endorsement for the concept and development of enlightened shareholder value. The Group argued that the overall objective of wealth generation and competitiveness for the benefit of all could best be achieved through the twin components of:

- an 'inclusive' approach to directors' duties, which required directors to have regard to all the relationships on which the company depended and to the long-term, as well as the short-term, implications of their actions, with a view to achieving company success for the benefit of shareholders as a whole;[110] and
- wider public accountability: this was to be achieved principally through

---

[108] Department of Trade and Industry, *Company Law For A Competitive Economy: Developing the Framework* (March 2000). This document was similar to the Group's February 1999 document. It was wide-ranging and addressed a number of corporate issues in detail.

[109] The Group emphasised that the role of company law was to facilitate the exercise of effective business choices so as to maximise wealth and welfare. This included providing flexibility in the modern company law regime to allow the various legal vehicles for conducting business to develop in changing economic, social and technical conditions.

[110] The company law regime before the new Act was that the law required directors to operate their companies for the benefit of shareholders. This obligation was reflected in the powers of shareholders to hold directors to account, which included powers of appointment, dismissal and control of the company constitution.

improved company reporting, which for public and very large private companies would require the publication of a broad operating and financial review, which would explain the companies performance, strategy and relationships (e.g. with employees, customer and suppliers as well as the wider community).

The Group considered the role of directors. It:

- put forward a legislative restatement of directors' duties on high level principles; it included an 'inclusive' duty of compliance and loyalty and an objective duty of care, skill and diligence;[111]
- proposed amendments to Part X of the CA 1985, on conflicted transactions by directors;
- examined the detailed rules on directors and their relationships with the company, including liability to third parties and training, qualifications and terms and conditions.
- examined – primarily in the context of listed companies – the role of non-executive directors; and raised various issues on the function and content of the Combined Code on Corporate Governance;
- assessed economic evidence on the functioning of the governance system and corporate control and of capital markets.

The Group examined the role of shareholders in company governance. It made proposals for:

- strengthening the relationship between companies and the beneficial holders of shares who were not registered as members;
- improvements in rules on notice, timing agendas, voting and resolutions for general meetings; the Group concluded that to permit public companies to dispense with annual general meetings would be premature, but suggested there should be provisions to relieve them of this requirement in cases where developing technology offered alternative mechanisms with comparable safeguards;

---

[111] According to the Group, a statutory statement of directors' duties with a list of considerations was the preferred way forward. It set out the 'inclusive' nature of this duty. The list of considerations was relevant to a well-managed company, that is, the company's dependency on employees and participants in the supply chain (including suppliers of finance and customers, direct and indirect), community and environmental policies and its reputation. These are matters to be considered in order to reach the properly considered, or 'calculated', view required in the core part on the duty of good faith principle. These considerations were subordinate to the objective of success on behalf of shareholders and were to be regarded as of value to the extent that they contribute to that objective. The list was not exhaustive; the core duty would require directors to consider other factors if they were to be regarded as relevant. Nor would all the interests which were listed be equally, or even at all, relevant in every case: see paras 3.55–3.56.

- reform of the remedies available to minority shareholders, including reform of the personal rights of shareholders under the company constitution, of s 459 of the CA 1985 (the 'unfair prejudice' remedy), and the law on actions brought by shareholders on behalf of the company ('derivative actions').

The Group proposed that for the listed companies the preliminary statement of results should become a statutory document distributed to all shareholders and published on a company website. The full report would then be filed within 90 days of the year end and published on the web. It would be available to shareholders on request.

The Group proposed that all rules on the form and content of accounts and reports, including the statutory preliminary statement, should be delegated to an appropriate rule-making body, reserving for legislation only the overall framework, essentially prescribing the documents to be provided, their purpose and the time limits for filing and laying before the General Meeting.

Under the Group's proposals, public and very large private companies would include in their full annual report a new statutory operating and financial review, which would enable the user to assess the performance and prospects of the business, including its wider relationships (e.g. with employees and suppliers), its reputation and its impact on the community and the environment. The content of the review would be partly prescribed by statute, with the detailed requirements being laid down in standards. The director's report would be replaced for large companies partly by the operating and financial review and partly by a supplementary statement, and for small ones by a cover sheet to the accounts. The statement or cover sheet would contain any public interests disclosures prescribed by the Secretary of State.

The Group proposed that both the scope of audit and the range of auditors' liability should be widened. This would be balanced by a removal of the bar on auditors agreeing a limit on their liability with the company and clarification of the law on contributory fault by companies.

The Group's approach here has been based on principles set out in the *Strategic Framework Consultation Document*: that legislation should provide a coherent, self-contained statement of the law for a small and private company to which more detailed provisions could be added for larger and public companies (think small first); and that this should form part of the overall framework of the Act, thereby avoiding the legislative constraints and unexpected traps that might otherwise arise when a company ceased to be eligible for small company treatment (the integrated approach). The emphasis was on simplifying the law for all private companies where possible. Within this overall simplified framework the Group then proposed a set of provisions specially suited to the needs of small companies. The latter regime was to be the norm, i.e. it would apply to all private companies, unless they positively opted out. While designed for smaller companies, it would not be formally restricted to them: by avoiding rigid eligibility thresholds the Group aims also to avoid the consequent traps and inhibitions to growth.

The Group also examined proposals for simplifying the law for private companies generally, by shortening minimum notice periods for meetings, allowing companies to relax the requirements for resolutions in writing, further simplifying the capital maintenance rules, relaxing the restrictions on the power of directors to issue shares, removing the requirement to have a company secretary, making provision for arbitration of shareholder disputes and simplifying the model constitution.

To this would be added a regime designed for small companies, which would apply automatically on formation unless excluded. This would include the existing 'elective' regime, which enabled private companies to opt out of certain requirements relating to meetings, but requires a specific decision to do so. There would also be more flexible provisions on notice of meetings, the appointment of auditors and written resolutions.

The Group then considered whether the law could be further simplified for 'owner-managed' companies (i.e. companies where the owners and directors are the same people) for whom a distinction between the board and the general meeting is arguably superfluous. Three options were considered: conferring the power of the general meeting on the board; conferring the power of the board on the general meeting; and relaxing the rules on general meeting for owner-managed companies so as to enable general meetings to take place as if they were board meetings. All three models had both benefits and drawbacks.

The Group proposed a simpler form of report and accounts, to be prepared and filed by small companies (i.e. those satisfying two of the following criteria: turnover of less than £4.8 million; gross assets of less than £2.4 million; fewer than 50 employees). The Group suggested that the distinction between accounts prepared for shareholders and those filed at Companies House should be abolished: the abbreviated accounts presently filed by some companies saved no costs and provided inadequate information for users. The accounts should be filed within seven months of the year end (rather than ten months as at present). The separate category of medium-sized companies would be abolished. The Group proposed exemption from audit for companies that satisfy two of the following criteria: turnover of less than £1 million; gross assets of less than £500,000; fewer than 25 employees. A new form of independent assurance, substantially short of audit, is proposed (an independent professional review) for small companies above this threshold.

The Group did not propose any change in the law on companies limited by guarantee. It suggested that charitable companies should have a separate form of incorporation overseen by the Charity Commission. The Group suggested that this regime should not extend to other not-for-profit companies, whether formed for a public purpose or not. The Group opposed the introduction of new barriers to the formation of limited companies, believing that the risks are better regulated in other ways, including transparency requirements and insolvency law.

The Group examined the requirements for companies to disclose information, whether by maintaining and granting access to their own registers and recorders and records or by filing information at Companies House. It suggested some reform of the register of members, its maintenance and structure, access to that register by members and others and the use that may be made of the information it contained. It proposed some other small changes to the maintenance of certain company records, and disclosure of company ownership and officers at Companies House. It examined the requirement for the registrar to publish certain information in the national gazette and propose a limited power for the registrar to rectify the public register.

The Group put forward proposals to simplify procedures for restoring dissolved companies to the register (including an administrative process which would remove the need to go to court in some cases) and to reduce the risks of inadvertent striking off.

Modern Company Law For A Competitive Economy: Capital Maintenance – Other Issues

1.15 This consultation document was issued in July 2000 and focused on a small number of residual technical issues to the main consultation document on capital maintenance previously issued by the Group. This included issues on no par value shares; distribution of profits and assets with reference to *Aveling Barford*;[112] 'realised' profits and losses; and specific rules relating to distributable profits.

---

[112] *Aveling Barford v Perion Ltd* [1989] BCLC 626. This case involved a sale by one company to another, associated (but not grouped) by reason of a common controlling shareholder company, of land at an undervalue, which was known to both sides. Aveling Barford owned land that was surplus to requirements, but suitable for development. It sold the land to Perion for £350,000. At the time the land was believed to be worth 800,000 pounds sterling and the bank to which the land was charged as security valued the land at £1.15 million sterling. A few months later, the land was sold to a third party for £1.5 million. At the time of the sale the transferor company's accounts showed net assets below the level of its share capital (i.e. it had negative reserves). The effect of the transaction was thus substantially to extract a valuable asset, for the benefit of the owner, from a company that was not free to make distributions, thus avoiding the distribution rule and constraints on the reduction of capital. However, the transaction was not expressed as a reduction of capital in that the company's share capital and undistributable reserves remained intact on the liabilities side of the balance sheet. It has held that the transaction was void because (i) it was an unlawful reduction of capital at common law, being a disguised distribution or return of capital to shareholders in circumstances where there were no assets available for distribution, and, therefore, *ultra vires* and incapable of ratification by the shareholders; and (ii) a breach of duty by the directors that was known to the purchaser. The transferee company was merely a constructive trustee and had to account to the transferor company for the profit on the resale of the property.

Modern Company Law For A Competitive Economy: Registration of Company Charges

1.16 In 2000, the Group published another consultation document *Modern Company Law For A Competitive Economy: Registration of Company Charges.* The Group reviewed the law and practice of company charges including the Crowther[113] and Diamond[114] Reports; the development of the charges system in UK; and the options available for the way forward. The main options included:

- retain the legislation contained in Part XII of the CA 1985;
- retain the main core procedural provisions of the present legislation, including the Registrar's conclusive certificate, but incorporate certain improvements introduced in the unimplemented Part IV of the CA 1989, including updating the list of registerable charges and the new provisions for overseas companies;
- a more radical option, involving the replacement of the present 'transaction' filing system (registration only after a charge had been created) with a 'notice' filing system (with registration before or after creation of a charge).

Following wide consultation, the Group would include its recommendations in subsequent publications.

Phase three can be characterised as one in which the Group set out policies, introduced concepts, provided recommendations and proposed further consultation with interested parties based on the work established in the previous phases.

Phase Four

1.17 Phase four involved completing the structure, and followed the same pattern as *Developing the Framework*, with a mixture of policy decisions, new proposals and further ideas for consultation.

Modern Company Law for a Competitive Economy: Completing the Structure

1.18 In November 2000, the Group issued its consultation document: *Modern Law for a Competitive Economy: Completing the Structure.*[115] This

---

[113] *The Report of the Committee on Consumer Credit*, HMSO, Cmnd. 4596 (1971). See too: *Reform of the Law on Consumer Credit*, HMSO, Cmnd. 5427, (1973); *Insolvency Law and Practice, Report of the Review Committee*, HMSO, Cmnd. 8558, (1982).

[114] *A Review of Security Interests in Property*, by Professor A L Diamond, HSMO, ISBN 011 514664 4, 1989.

[115] Department of Trade and Industry, *Modern Company Law For A Competitive Economy: Completing the Structure* (November 2000).

consultation document took forward the proposals on which the Group consulted in *Developing the Framework*, revising them in the light of responses and inviting further comments on a limited number of issues that emerged from the consultation. It also set out proposals in areas not previously addressed in consultation, where views were sought across a broader range of issues.

The consultation document addressed the needs of small and private companies. It covered three areas:

• the need to make the law accessible to all who used it, particularly those involved with small companies. The Group wanted to ensure that any new Act met the needs of small private companies. This included focusing on substance, simplifying the law, removing unnecessary restrictions or obligations, and producing a coherent overall framework; and to reflect the needs of small companies in the form that the law took. The law should, therefore, be expressed clearly, and drafted in a way that people would find it easy to use.[116] The law must also be expressed in a way that was clear and accessible. The legislation should be structured in such a way that the provisions that applied to small companies were easily identifiable. While some parts of the legislation would inevitably be complex, owing to the complexity of the underlying policy or business practices, the Group advocated that it should be possible to simplify those parts of the law likely to be most frequently relied on by small companies. This could require simpler policies, or simple, clear, exemptions in complex areas rather than merely simpler drafting. This included proposals that the minimum period of notice for all meetings of private companies be set at 14 days. Further, small companies should be allowed to pass written resolutions without achieving unanimity, and the requirement to notify the auditors of a written resolution served no useful purpose. The Group proposed to abolish the application of ss 151–158 of the CA 1985 to private companies; that the directors' declaration of solvency, required in the proposed new procedure for reduction of capital, need not be supported by an auditor's report; and to abolish the requirement for alterations or reductions of share capital or purchase of own shares to be authorised in the articles. The requirement in s 80 of the CA 1985 for shareholder authorisation to allot shares should not apply to private companies. The Group also recommended abolishing the requirement

---

[116] The Group stated that a poorly drafted law could impose significant costs, especially on business. However, accuracy and certainty should not be sacrificed unduly in an attempt to make the law merely superficially more accessible. For example, over-simplification or imprecise language may make the law apparently more readable, particularly for the non-specialist; but it was likely to give rise to greater uncertainty.

for a company secretary.[117] However, private companies should be able, if they wished, appoint a secretary to carry out secretarial functions if they so choose. The Group recommended a system of alternative dispute resolution (ADR) (including arbitration) schemes to resolving disputes. Table A (Articles of Association) should be modified radically to reflect the needs of private companies;

- the specific proposals to simplify the company law and accounting requirements for private companies put forward in *Developing the Framework*; there was a large measure of support for these proposals and the Group intended to proceed with them; and
- the distinction between private and public companies.

The Group largely confirmed the position on 'scope' as set out in *Developing the Framework*, in particular the proposals for an inclusive statement of directors' duties (i.e. one requiring directors to promote the success of the company in the interests of its members but taking account of all relevant considerations, including the implications for the company of their decisions over time and of wider relationships, such as those with employees, suppliers, customers and the wider community);[118] and for improved transparency, principally through the proposed operating and financial review (OFR) to be prepared by public companies and large private companies.

Concerning the proposals in *Developing the Framework* in relation to directors and the rules in Part X of the CA 1985 on enforcement of fair dealing by the directors, the Group largely supported the responses received. There was little support for change on the Combined Code, and no change was proposed in this area at this stage except on payments on loss of office and some greater transparency in relation to non-executive directors (NEDs) and employment contracts.

As set out in *Developing the Framework*, the Group examined in more detail the issue of companies' and directors' liability to third parties. It made

---

[117] There had been advocates for retaining the company secretary arguing that the abolition would assist only sole director companies, since those with two or more may easily designate one of the directors as secretary; and the secretary was an important element in the corporate governance of private companies; and the existence of a secretary helped to ensure that a company complied with its statutory obligations and helped to prevent abuse. The Group was not convinced of any of these arguments.

[118] The Group emphasised that the directors' statement should be expressed at a sufficiently high level of generality that it could be capable of judicial development within its terms. The Group did not see any merit in defining 'fiduciary' so long as the intention of achieving substantial continuity with the present law was achieved. The Group believed that the relevant provisions could be drafted so that general principles of statutory interpretation would ensure that to the extent that they enacted the common law, the existing authorities would be capable of being invoked to explain the nature of the duties that they codified. The Group agreed that the duties must be subject to the overriding duties of directors towards creditors in an insolvency or threatened insolvency situation. See too Insolvency Act 1986, s 214 (wrongful trading).

proposals on a company's vicarious liability and contributory fault for frauds committed by directors in the course of their authority. The Group suggested that the Department of Trade and Industry (DTI) should discuss with the Lord Chancellor's Department and the Scottish Executive the scope for general provisions ensuring that the law applies effectively to all employers and principals in such cases (whether corporate bodies or not).

The Group also addressed the role of shareholders. It confirmed the proposals of *Developing the Framework* and developed further the proposals on the rights of minority shareholders and the limits on the majority. It proposed that: all members should have a personal right to enforce any obligation under the constitution; the unfair prejudice remedy should remain subject to the principles laid down in *O'Neil v Philips*;[119] derivative actions should be put on a statutory basis, extending only to breach of duty by a director, and capable of being blocked by ratification; and subject to those provisions the majority should be constrained only: (i) by the requirement that decisions should be taken *bona fide* in the best interest of the members as a whole, in cases of alteration of the constitution or of class rights; and (ii) in all cases, by the disqualification of those seeking to ratify or otherwise prevent the pursuit of their own wrong done by a person to whose influence they were subject.

In the light of responses to *Developing the Framework*, the Group put forward significantly revised proposals in relation to the financial reporting documents to be prepared by companies and the timetable for their publication. In particular the Group proposed that quoted companies should publish their full annual report on their Group website as soon as it is available and, at the latest, within 90 days of the year end; at least 15 days must elapse before the notice of the Annual General Meeting (AGM) is circulated to shareholders, to facilitate the tabling of shareholders' resolutions; the accounts should be laid before the AGM and filed within 150 days; and quoted companies should continue to be able to offer summary financial statements (SFS) as an alternative to the full annual report. The proposal for the preliminary announcement to be circulated to all shareholders has been dropped, but the requirement for it to be published on the company's website should be retained. The proposals for other public companies are also revised in view of the changes for quoted companies.

In respect of the proposals in *Developing the Framework* for greater delegation of detailed accounting requirements to a standards-setting body, the Group broadly confirmed its previous recommendations in this area. A number of further important points were raised on the proposals relating to audit and auditors' liability; in particular it was proposed that, if the range of the duty of care of auditors were to be extended to potential investors and

---

[119] [1999] BCLC 425.

creditors, the duty of the company and its directors should be similarly extended, but that claimants should be required to prove that they have taken all reasonable steps to protect themselves from loss.

The capital maintenance proposals had already been the subject of extensive consultation. The Group set out briefly the way forward on the issues proposed in the consultation document *Capital Maintenance: Other Issues*, published in June 2000. The main point was that the Group did not now propose to proceed with no par value shares for private companies, given that EU directive constraints preclude this step for public companies.

The Group addressed responses on companies' other disclosure obligations. It proposed that the DTI and Companies House should explore the scope for enabling directors to put a 'service address' on the public record, with their residential address being available only to certain regulatory and enforcement agencies, or on the order of the court. The Group confirmed proposals to restrict the use that could be made of companies' register of members. It proposed that companies should be allowed to set a 'record date' for the purposes of determining who was entitled to receive a notice of meetings or to attend and vote. It confirmed proposals to control company names that were misleading or registered for an improper purpose, and to simplify procedures for restoring dissolved companies to the register.

The Group confirmed support for a separate form of incorporation designed for charities, to be taken forward by the Charity Commission. A similar proposal was being considered for Scottish charities by an independent Scottish Charity Law Review Commission.

On groups of companies, the Group invited views on a proposal for an optional regime that would provide for less onerous reporting and auditing requirements for subsidiary companies where the parent company guarantees their liabilities. The Group also invited views on whether the prohibition on a subsidiary holding shares in its parent should be extended to apply to entities other than bodies corporate. (e.g. certain kinds of partnership) over which the parent had control.

The Group examined the scope for streamlining the ways in which companies could restructure, provided for in s 425 of the CA 1985 and ss 428–430 of the CA 1985, and s 110 of the Insolvency Act 1986. The Group made proposals for: a simpler statutory merger procedure within wholly-owned group of companies; and for 'jurisdictional migration', to enable companies to change their place of incorporation (i.e. to migrate into or out of Great Britain or to move between England and Wales and Scotland) without winding up and re-incorporation.

The Group proposed a new institutional structure to underpin a new Act; examined the areas to be devolved to a rule-making body; and considered how the law could best be kept up to date, and the best mechanism for ensuring proper consideration of legislative and rule-making.

A Companies Commission was proposed, with continuing oversight of developments in company law, and with a duty to prepare an annual report on the state of company law and to advise on proposals for new legislation (including secondary legislation) and on other topics referred to it by Ministers. Subsidiary bodies would be responsible for: setting detailed rules on both accounting and reporting and other areas delegated to it (such as rules on the conduct of AGMs or corporate governance codes): enforcing reporting and accounting requirements; and ensuring that due account is taken of the needs and concerns of private companies. There were also proposals for a specialist tribunal to hear cases brought by the enforcement body.

The consultation document also set out criteria for a coherent framework of criminal and civil sanctions; considered other ways to encourage compliance, such as warning letters and reminders, and extra-legal remedies such as 'naming and shaming'; suggested improvements to a number of specific sanctions; and invited views on detailed proposals for codifying civil remedies for breach of directors' duties, based on the personal remedies available under s 322 of the CA 1985. Finally it considered ways of strengthening the protection against 'phoenix companies', where directors of a failed company mislead the market into believing that it is continuing to trade, or alternatively where they mislead the market into believing that a successor company is unrelated to a previous company whose debts have been abandoned

In the fourth phase, *Developing the Framework* therefore proceeded to focus on two main initiatives: first, simplifying the legal requirements for small companies; and second, supporting a new framework of institutions to develop and apply company law in the future.

Phase Five

1.19 This phase was concerned with the last report published by the Group on company law reform that was presented to the Secretary of State for Trade and Industry. It set out the final recommendation of the Group on company law reform.

Modern Company Law For a Competitive Economy: Final Report

1.20 In July 2001, the Group published its *Modern Company Law For A Competitive Economy: Final Report*. The report stated that it was 'the most fundamental review for at least 40 years – and arguably in the law's 150 year history'. This was a significant report in two volumes, which also contained draft sections for a new Companies Bill.

The *Final Report* contained two volumes. Volume 1 set out the Group's final recommendations on company law reform. Volume 2 contained a selection of draft clauses for a new Companies Bill in order to demonstrate how a new Companies Bill could be drafted more clearly than its predecessors, so as to achieve the objectives set out in the *Final Report* that any new legislation should be written in clear, plain English and be user-friendly.

The *Final Report* reported on a wide spectrum of company law reform that the Group had previously addressed in various consultation documents. The *Final Report* considered three main aspects: (i) simplifying and modernising the law for small companies; (ii) providing a legal framework for companies that reflects the needs of the modern economy; and (iii) ensuring a flexible and responsive institutional structure.

Simplifying and Modernising the Law for Private Companies

1.21 The Report highlighted the following main recommendations:

* Small companies would be able to adopt a simple statutory model constitution instead of the memorandum and Articles of Association.
* For private companies, there would not be any need for shareholder authorisation for the allotment of shares.
* Private companies should be able to incorporate through a modern and simple process removing the present requirement for a statutory declaration on incorporation, combining the memorandum and Articles of Association into a single document, and revoking the present requirement for an 'objects' clause to define what transactions the company has capacity to enter into, thereby giving companies unlimited objects.
* Companies should be able to implement electronic voting by shareholders.
* Companies should be able to migrate to and from Great Britain more easily.
* Companies should be able to re-register as other kinds of company more simply.
* Companies should no longer have to maintain a mortgage or charges register.
* The 'unanimous consent rule' that already exists in the common law would be codified and extended. The effect is that any decision that a company has the power to make would be valid even if it had not observed all the required legal formalities, provided that all members of the company gave their consent.
* Written resolutions in private companies would no longer require unanimous endorsement. Instead, the normal thresholds for special and ordinary resolutions would apply to written resolutions. This would allow small companies to take certain decisions more easily, without the obligation of holding a general meeting.
* The 'elective' regime, under which private companies can resolve to dispense with some of the Act's formalities (holding an AGM, and laying of

accounts and the annual appointment of auditors at the AGM) will become the default for such companies. If a company wishes to be bound by these requirements (e.g. it wants to hold an AGM), then it would have to make an election to do so. The default regime will be that no AGM need be held unless the company makes a positive decision to be covered by that obligation.

- Private companies would no longer need to appoint a company secretary, though they may still choose to do so.
- Alternative dispute resolution would be promoted for settling disputes between shareholders in private companies as an alternative to the courts, and in particular a special arbitration scheme for shareholders would be created.
- Financial reporting and audit for small companies would be simplified. More small companies would be able to prepare simpler 'small company accounts' as a result of raising the thresholds in the UK to the maxima permitted in EC law. The turnover threshold below which a statutory audit need not be prepared would be £4.8 million also (the EC limit again). And, while statutory accounts for small companies will be simplified, the additional facility of small companies to file 'abbreviated accounts' for public disclosure would be removed.
- Private companies would have to file their accounts within seven months of their year-end, rather than the ten currently allowed.
- Private companies will not have to comply with the complex rules prohibiting a company from giving any form of financial assistance to assist in the sale and purchase of its shares so that the 'whitewash' procedure will no longer apply.
- Public companies should have exemptions from the rules restricting them from giving any form of financial assistance to assist in the sale and purchase of their shares clarified and revised.
- In common with large private companies, public companies should have to publish an operating and financial review as part of their annual report.
- Public companies should hold their AGM and file their accounts within six months of their year end, but shareholders, by unanimous consent, should be able to dispense with the requirements to hold AGMs.
- Public quoted companies should circulate members' resolutions free of charge with the AGM papers.
- Public quoted companies should publish their report and accounts on the internet at least 15 days before settling the AGM papers for circulation.

Providing a legal framework for companies that reflects the needs of the modern economy

1.22 The *Final Report* highlighted a broad spectrum of corporate governance reforms. Some of the main recommendations included:

- Directors should have a clear authoritative statement of their duties. The duties of company directors, which arose outside of statute law, would be codified into a statutory statement. The statement would both define the principles that directors must observe and the standards to which those duties are fulfilled. In addition to duties of obedience to the company's constitution, of loyalty (which would oblige a director to act to serve the purposes of the company), of exercising independent judgment and of exercising care, skill and diligence, there would be duties to have regard to the interests of creditors (where there is a risk of insolvency) and to control conflicts of interest.
- As part of the principle of acting in good faith to promote the success of the company, the proposed statement required a director to take account in good faith of all practicable material factors. Notes in the draft statement included among material factors, the need for the company to foster its business relationships with employees, suppliers and customers; the need to have regard to the impact of its operations on communities and the environment and the need to maintain a reputation for high standards of business conduct.
- Directors should face a limit on the contractual notice period in service contracts of three years on first appointment and one year thereafter, unless the shareholders have authorised otherwise.
- Directors should be able to provide a service address instead of their personal address on the public record at Companies House, but personal addresses should still be available to certain public authorities and to others such as shareholders and creditors on application to the court.
- Directors should also face tougher criminal sanctions for offences involving dishonesty and fraudulent trading.
- There should be strict rules on insolvency including revised restrictions on transactions between directors and their companies, restrictions on directors and companies re-using the names of insolvent companies, and interim disqualification pending final disqualification proceedings.
- Directors should have any criminal convictions for breaches of the Companies Act disclosed in the annual report.
- Directors should not have to stand for annual reappointment (unless the company's constitution provided otherwise) if aged over 70 and a director of a public company.
- The Combined Code would remain as the key governance code for quoted companies. As now, it should require companies to comply with

its requirements or explain why ('comply or explain'), rather than create binding obligations.

- It would be easier for shareholders who hold their shares in 'nominee' accounts (where the identity of the beneficial shareholder is not clear from the register) to exercise their rights. While the *Final Report* recommended voluntary measures, it also called for the Secretary of State to have reserve powers to enforce mandatory ones.
- Listed companies would have to circulate members' resolutions free of charge as AGM papers. This removes a potential cost barrier to shareholder participation.
- Institutional investors, who typically own more than half the shares in major companies would have to disclose how they have exercised their rights as members (e.g. on company votes) if they manage funds on behalf of others. Companies would have to disclose their main relationships with financial annual reports. Voting on important company resolutions would be audited.
- Large companies would have to disclose broad strategic information about their OFR.
- To improve the disclosure of quoted companies, the annual report and accounts would have to be filed within six months of the end of the financial year (currently seven months is allowed; at an earlier stage, the Review was proposing five). The documents would be available earlier on the company's website, where they would have to appear within four months. Fifteen days would have to elapse between the website publication and the circulation of notice of the AGM, to allow shareholders time to table resolutions.
- Directors and employees would be under stricter obligations to provide information to auditors. Directors would have to recognise that such information is needed for the audit. A criminal penalty will apply to a director's failure to supply information that he knows is material.
- The duty of care owed by auditors would not be extended beyond its current common law requirement (set in *Caparo*). A liability in contract (by agreement with the company) and in tort (through notice in the auditor's report, which would bind those who rely on the report). Any limitation would have to be reasonable, within the terms of the Unfair Contract Terms Act 1977.

Ensuring a Flexible and Responsive Institutional Structure

1.23

- The Group's Consultation document, *Completing the Structure*, had set out a proposed set of institutions to oversee the development and detailed operation of company law. While the main elements of that framework were carried forward into the *Final Report*, some alterations were made to the names of the bodies and their respective responsibilities.

- The Company Law and Reporting Commission (CLRC – which was originally to be called the Companies Commission) would keep company law and governance under review, reporting annually to the Secretary of State. The government would be obliged to consult the CLRC on the proposed secondary legislation, and the CLRC would also issue authoritative guidance within its field of reference.

- The Standards Board (which was originally called the Standards Committee) would make detailed substantive rules on accounting and reporting disclosures, including the standards for a new qualitative report, the Operating and Financial Review. It would also keep the Combined Code under review and have powers to make rules about the disclosure of governance matters under the Code and other forms of corporate disclosure. The Board would not however have the power to make the Code's substantive obligations.

- A Private Companies Committee would have an advisory role on areas of company law and reporting, which are of relevance to private companies.

- A Reporting Companies Review Panel (originally the Monitoring and Enforcement Committee) will take on the Financial Reporting Review Panel's task of monitoring compliance with reporting requirements.

Other Recommendations

1.24

- A new form of corporate entity reserved for charities would be developed (this became the Community Interest Companies set up under the Companies (Audit, Investigations and Community Enterprise Act) 2004.
- Companies would have to disclose any criminal sanctions against the company in their annual reports.
- The incidence of criminal sanctions on officers and employees for defaults in company law would be clarified and more precisely targeted.

Phase Five can, therefore, be characterised as one in which the Group presented its *Final Report* to the Department of Trade and Industry. The *Final Report* covered a wide spectrum of company law reform addressed in previous consultation documents with a volume containing selected provisions of a Companies Bill. It should be noted that not all the *Final Report* recommendations were accepted by the Government, and in that some cases, amendments were made to some of the Report's recommendations.

Phase Six

1.25 This phase can be characterised as one in which the Government reflected upon the recommendations of the Group and the Law Commissions, and published two White Papers on the scope of company law reform, including drafts of parts of the Companies Bill, for consideration by interested parties. At least another two years passed from the last consultation document before the Labour Government issued its first White Paper on company law reform.

Modernising Company Law: White Paper (July 2002)

1.26 In July 2002, the Labour Government published its first White Paper on company law reform, *Modernising Company Law*.[120] The then Secretary of State for Trade and Industry, Patricia Hewitt, highlighted the state of British company law, and stated that when British company law was created in the nineteenth century, it was a source of competitive advantage. However, it had now become a competitive disadvantage. The law had become encrusted with amendments and case law over generations. It had failed to adapt to meet the changing role of small enterprises, IT and international markets. The law needed to change: it needed to modernise and reform and it needed to be fit for the twenty-first century and beyond.

The White Paper emphasised that company law was central to UK prosperity. It was important, therefore, that it was up to date and able to meet the needs of a modern dynamic economy. The White Paper set out the Government's core proposals for simplifying and modernising the law. It aimed to provide a legal framework for all companies that reflected the needs of the modern economy; and to ensure that the framework could be kept up to date in the future. The White Paper addressed the issue of why reform was largely overdue and needed. This was because company law had a direct impact on enterprise. It could actively promote and encourage enterprise – or hold it back. The Government was strongly committed to promoting enterprise and believed that company law reform had an important part to play in making it as easy as possible to start and run companies while maintaining adequate safeguards against abuse. Further, inefficiencies and failings in company law could have a significant impact on the economy as a whole, with unnecessary burdens for small companies. The law needed to be clearer, more certain and more accessible. The present framework of UK company law had developed through a series of partial reviews and piecemeal alterations. This had made it increasingly bulky and complex. The way it was written made it particularly difficult to identify those provisions that applied to smaller companies. For example, the main rules on accounts were set out in one place, with no

---

[120] Department of Trade and Industry, *Modernising Company Law* (July 2002) (Cm 5553–1).

indication that there was any simpler provision elsewhere for smaller companies. It took another 20 pages to find these – and it would be easy to overlook them.

British company law was largely created in the nineteenth century. It recognised that the right to limited liability brought with it certain responsibilities, and that its advantages should be matched by arrangements for accountability. Whilst these basic principles remained true prior to 2006, the details were in need of significant modernisation and reform. A thorough overhaul was needed to make the law clearer and accessible. This would produce savings for companies, freeing them up from unnecessary red tape and improving competitiveness.

The Government, therefore, established the independent Company Law Review to develop proposals for reform. Its *Final Report* was widely welcomed, and the White Paper was the first part of the Government's response. In conjunction, the Government was also at that time taking a number of other initiatives to promote improved corporate governance, such as the independent review of the role and effectiveness of non-executive directors led by Derek Higgs,[121] and the work undertaken in the wake of the collapse of Enron, which would feed into the Companies Bill and Act as appropriate.

According to the White Paper, the current company law was designed around the needs of big public companies with additional provisions for other companies. This reflected the origins of company law in the mid-nineteenth century, when the joint-stock company was seen as an ideal model for raising money for large capital projects, such as railway building. The Government believed that the starting point for company law should be small companies – to 'think small first' – with additional or different provisions for larger companies being brought in where necessary. The law needed to balance various interests, for example, those of shareholders, directors, employees, creditors and customers, but it must also avoid unjustified burdens. The Government advocated that the law should be flexible, so that it could adapt easily to development and changing technology. Further, the most appropriate way forward was to tailor the core of company law to fit the smallest companies, which were mostly private companies, and that a clear distinction was made between public and private companies.

The Government proposed to modernise and simplify the ways in which companies took decisions, including by:

- removing the requirement for private companies to hold Annual General Meetings (AGMs) unless members wanted them;[122]

---

[121] D. Higgs, *The Role and Effectiveness of Non-Executive Directors* (20 January 2003).

[122] This would require an ordinary resolution to 'opt in' and to lay accounts and appoint auditors at such meetings. For public companies, the requirement to hold an AGM would be retained though it would be possible unanimously to dispense with AGMs.

- simplifying the rules on written resolutions to make it easier for private companies to take decisions.[123]

The Government wanted also to increase transparency. In future:

- company constitutions would be a single document that would obviate the need for objects clauses. There would be simpler, clearer models for both private and public companies;[124]
- AGMs would be held within six months of the financial year-end for public companies and where required within ten months for private companies;
- shareholders would be able to require a scrutiny of a poll;[125] and
- proxies were to have extended rights.

The Government was also keen to see institutional investors playing a more effective role in corporate governance.

The Government agreed with the Review that the primary role of directors should be to promote the success of the company for the benefit of its shareholders as a whole, and that directors' general duties to the company should be codified, broadly as proposed by the Review. The Government also proposed to prepare clear guidance for new directors on what these duties meant.[126]

The Government also proposed to prohibit corporate directors.

---

[123] The Government's aim was to maintain the simplicity of the current written procedure while also ensuring that all members receive adequate information about written resolutions. In particular, the Government believed that companies should send proposed resolutions to all members at the same time, as far as it was practicable.

[124] Shareholders of a company would be able to amend the single constitution by special resolution. They would also be able – if they all agreed – to make it more difficult to make changes, by requiring a higher majority or even unanimity. Anyone doing business with the company in good faith would not need to be concerned about the details of the company's constitution.

[125] The scrutiny would cover the activity both of the company and its registrar, and examine the procedure for establishing the admissibility of votes and proxies, the voting procedure and the procedure for counting votes. The scrutiny would be conducted by a registered auditor, not necessarily the company's own auditor, and the object would be to give an opinion on whether the procedure for the recording and counting of proxies and votes was adequate to ensure that the statement of votes cast was accurately stated. The scrutiny would have to be completed within a month of the meeting and the scrutineer's report sent to the members.

[126] Directors were also required to recognise, as the circumstances required, the company's need to foster relations with its employees, customers and suppliers, its need to maintain its business reputation, and its need to consider the company's impact on the community and the working environment. All directors of the company should be subject to the same set of general duties regardless of any particular duties they might have under service agreements as employees. All new directors would receive a leaflet setting out the requirements and responsibilities expected of directors, such as filing accounts, making returns and providing other information to Companies House.

The Government believed that company reporting should provide accurate, accessible information at reasonable cost.

The Government proposed to replace the current directors' report. For small companies, it believed all that was needed was a short, simple, supplementary statement. It also proposed to simplify the accounts for around 15,000 companies by increasing the definition of a small company for accounting purposes to the EU maximum (£4.8 million turnover, £2.4 million balance sheet total, 50 employees). As it was important that company accounts should be generally available, the Government proposed to abolish the option for small and medium-sized companies to file abbreviated accounts at Companies House. It also proposed to reduce the time allowed to file accounts to seven months for private companies.

The White Paper provided that the largest companies would have to provide an Operating and Financial Review (OFR), i.e. a narrative report on a company's business, its performance and future plans. Quoted companies would also be required to prepare a directors' remuneration report.

For the first time quoted companies would also be required to publish their accounts on their website within four months of their year-end.

The Government did not propose to adopt the idea of an independent professional review as an alternative to an audit for some small company accounts. It would however assess the impact of the July 2000 increase in the audit threshold for small firms to £1 million before deciding whether to propose a further increase.

The aspects of auditing were under consideration as part of the work to improve corporate governance following the collapse of Enron.

The White Paper stated that the Government believed it was important to keep the law up to date and ensure it continued to meet all users' needs. It proposed therefore largely to follow the Review's recommendations to put those elements that were likely to need regular amendment into secondary legislation, and to enable some detailed rule-making to be devolved to one or more specified bodies.

The Government proposed the establishment of a single body, based on the current Accounting Standards Board (ASB), but with a suitably adapted membership and constitution, making detailed rules on matters such as the form and content of financial statements (except where international accounting standards apply), disclosure requirements for the OFR, and the form and content of the summary statement. A successor body to the Financial Reporting Review Panel (FRRP), with a broader remit, would enforce these 'form and content' rules on public and large private companies in the same way that the FRRP enforced current accounting law and standards. Companies House would continue to enforce these rules for smaller private companies.

The rule-making body would also take over from the UK Listing Authority the responsibility for making rules to require listed companies to disclose their compliance with the Combined Code on Corporate Governance. The body should also decide when any further review of the Code is necessary, though the Code will remain a non-statutory document.

The Government did not intend to pursue the Review's recommendations to create a statutory Company Law and Reporting Commission and a Private Companies Committee. While it shared the Review's objectives, these could be achieved without legislation.

The Government proposed to simplify and update the law on company formation and capital maintenance, particularly for private companies. It would also abolish the requirement for private companies to appoint company secretaries (although they will of course be free to do so voluntarily).

The Government also proposed to simplify the law regulating companies incorporated overseas and operating in Great Britain.

The work to develop a new Companies Bill also took account of a number of other initiatives. Part of UK company law has been the implementation of series of European directives, the oldest of which was now 35 years old. The Government had welcomed the European Commission's initiatives to review and reform European company law, with the appointment of a high level group to review a wide range of company law issues at a European level. In addition, there were number of more specific initiatives under way at that time:

- the increasingly international nature of business meant that it was important that the very largest companies adopt common accounting standards. From 1 January 2005 all companies admitted to trading on the London Stock Exchange (and any other European regulated market) will need to compile their consolidated accounts in accordance with the EU Regulation on the Application of International Accounting Standards (IAS), which was adopted on 7 June 2002;
- the European Commission had also proposed changes to the other European rules on the annual reports and accounts of companies. These were mainly designed to remove any conflict between the current Fourth and Seventh Company Law Directives and IAS;
- the EC had adopted a regulation to allow the formation of a new public company vehicle, the Societas Europea, for businesses with interest in more than one Member State, with effect from October 2004;
- negotiations were under way in Brussels on a new prospectus directive on the information that has to be published when a company makes a public offer of securities are admitted to trading on a regulated market;
- the European Commission had also consulted on a new directive on the continuing obligations of listed companies to make information available to the market. Its proposals covered both annual and quarterly financial reporting and ongoing disclosures, including, for example, major shareholdings and of some corporate governance information;

- the UK Listing Authority has also announced that it would conduct its own review of the UK Listings Rules;
- the European Commission had also proposed changes to the First Company Law Directive (which dates from 1968) to take account of technological developments;
- the Government had requested Derek Higgs to carry out an independent review of the role and effectiveness of non-executive directors. Though the Government had an open mind, it had indicated that its preferred starting point in this area was if possible, an approach based on best practice, not regulation or legislation;
- the Government had also established a co-ordination group, comprising Government and the principal regulators, to ensure the arrangements for financial reporting and auditing were effective in the light of the collapse of Enron in the United States. The Treasury Select Committee was also undertaking an enquiry into the financial regulation of public companies;
- the Law Commissions were carrying out a review of the law on company charges, at the request of the Government;
- the Cabinet Office Performance and Innovation Unit had recommended that the Government should prepare a regulatory impact assessment of the options for greater disclosure of beneficial interests in the shares of unquoted companies; and
- the Performance and Innovation Unit's separate work on the voluntary and charitable sector was taking forward the Review's recommendation that there should be a separate form of incorporation for charities.

The Government would take account of all these developments as appropriate in carrying forward work on a new Companies Bill.

Company Law Reform: White Paper (March 2005)

1.27 In March 2005, the UK Government published a White Paper, *Company Law Reform*, setting out the Government's proposals for comprehensive reform of the UK company law framework and to align this with modern business needs.[127] According to the Secretary of State for Trade and Industry, 'a fair, modern, and effective framework of company law is crucial to our performance as an economy, and as a society'.[128] However, over a period of time, UK company law (a model adopted in many nations) has become outdated, and risks presenting obstacles to the ways companies want and need to do business in today's world. The White Paper built on the work undertaken

---

[127] Department of Trade and Industry, *Company Law Reform*, March 2005, Cmnd 6456.
[128] Foreword by The Rt Hon Patricia Hewitt, White Paper, p 3.

in the Company Law Review[129] (CLR) and the Government's White Paper[130] 2003 and a partial draft to Company Law Reform Bill (the Bill) published at that time. According to the Secretary of State, the CLR had been universally recognised as providing a thorough and authoritative assessment of the changes that needed to be made, and provided the essential blueprint for the reforms now proposed by the Government. For these reasons, the Government had been committed to ensuring the legal and regulatory frameworks within which business operated and promoted enterprise, growth and the right conditions of employment, would be provided.

The White Paper stated that the UK system of company law and corporate governance was vital to the legal and regulatory framework. It set out the legal basis on which companies are formed, operated and managed. It also set out the rules for company boards and shareholders, and for the exercise of decisions on business growth and investment, and to ensure those in control of the company are held accountable for their actions for the proper exercise of corporate power. The Government, therefore, believed that a genuinely modern and effective framework for company law could promote enterprise, enhance competitiveness and stimulate investment.[131] The system of UK company law and corporate governance should be one that (i) facilitates enterprise by making it easy to set up and grow a business; (ii) encourages the efficient allocation of capital by giving confidence to investors; (iii) promotes long-term company performance through shareholder engagement and effective dialogue between business and investors; and (iv) maintains the UK's position as a central place to set up and operate a business and to reflect the global marketplace in which companies must operate if they are to be successful. There were also steps internationally and at the European level towards global convergence, such as facilitating cross-boarder incorporations, mergers and acquisitions, accounting standards, strengthening shareholders' rights and third-party protection and rebuilding investors' confidence.[132]

---

[129] Department of Trade and Industry, Company Law Review, 2003.

[130] Department of Trade and Industry, White Paper, 2003.

[131] According to the Government, an effective framework of company law and corporate governance is a key building block of a modern economy. An ineffective or outmoded framework of company law can inhibit productivity and growth and undermine investment confidence. This is witnessed by high profile corporate collapses in recent years – such as Enron, WorldCom and Parmalat.

[132] This is the 'global challenge' that must be addressed in the company law reform framework. For example, there is now a move towards global convergence of accounting standards so that companies should be able to prepare their accounts on the same basis, whenever they are listed. At the European level, there is already a large body of European law impacting on companies and where the Commission's Company Law and Corporate Governance Action Plan is focused on fostering global efficiency and competitiveness of EU businesses, strengthening shareholders' rights and third-party protection and rebuilding investor confidence.

The White Paper stated that Britain had kept pace with the international and European company law developments. In 1998, it commissioned the CLR[133] to take a long-term and fundamental consideration of the UK's underpinning system of company law, and to see how it could be brought up to date. The CLR, however, had been perceived as part of a wider programme of action to facilitate enterprise, encourage investment and promote long-term company performance. Various initiatives had been introduced by the Government to achieve these objectives. They have included:

(a)   Companies (Audit, Investigations and Community Enterprise) Act 2004. This Act was introduced to ensure better oversight and stronger regulation of the accounting and audit profession, to increase investor confidence in company reporting and enforcement, and to strengthen powers to investigate companies. The Act also encouraged the development of the social enterprise sector to enable the formation of a new type of company known, as the 'community interest company', whose profits and assets must be used for the benefit of the community.

(b)   The Government had laid draft regulations that would require all quoted companies to produce an Operating and Financial Review (OFR). The OFR was a new form of narrative report, in which companies would need to describe future strategies, resources, risks and uncertainties, including policies in relation to employees and the environment where these areas were relevant to future strategy and performance. The OFR ensured transparency and improvement in company reporting, and in developing relationships with employees, customers, suppliers and others that support long-term value creation.

(c)   The Government also introduced the Directors' Remuneration Report Regulations 2002. They required quoted companies to disclose and seek shareholder approval for their executive remuneration policies, and to disclose how remuneration relates to performance.[134]

Legislation had not been the only mechanism in achieving the Government's objectives towards company law reform and modernisation. Other mechanisms have included the Financial Reporting Council's powers of oversight and enforcement. A new Combined Code on Corporate Governance was also published in July 2003, incorporating many of the changes recommended by Higgs, aimed at strengthening the independence and effectiveness of non-executive directors. In order to promote more effective shareholder engagement, the Government welcomed the Institutional Shareholder Committee's

---

[133] The CLR comprised an independent group of experts, practitioners and from industry.

[134] The government has also raised the audit thresholds for turnover and balance sheet totals to £5.6m and £2.8m respectively.

principles in October 2002, with a commitment to reflect these principles in fund management contracts and insurance fund practice. The Government has also considered the investment chain of relationships of institutional investors to investigate how well the chain works, through the Myners, Sandler and Higgs reviews, and has undertaken a comprehensive reform programme. A separate report by Paul Myners to the Shareholder Voting Working Group focused on the practical steps that market participants must take to improve the effectiveness of the voting process, and the DTI has agreed to implement the report's legislative recommendations.

The new Combined Code also strengthened the role of the audit committee following a report from Robert Smith. The DTI had also worked with business to take forward other recommendations of Higgs and Tyson that aimed at extending the diversity and effectiveness of company boards.[135]

According to the White Paper, the company law reform programme was focused on four key objectives:

1   *Enhancing shareholders engagement and a long-term investment culture*
     This required an effective dialogue between those who own the company and those who control it, in order to ensure a good understanding and effective engagement between the two groups. This required defining clearly the different roles and responsibilities, and there must be an efficient and transparent mechanism for ensuring that views were heard and decisions taken. There were provisions in the Bill that would provide better guidance for directors on their responsibilities and duties, ensuring more effective and efficient communication with shareholders, and making it easier for shareholders, including indirect investors, to exercise their rights of ownership. The proposed changes in this area aimed to ensure that directors and shareholders work together as a team to promote the company's long-term performance and value creation.

2   *Ensuring better regulation and a 'think small first' approach*
     When companies laws were first enacted in UK, they were mainly designed for large companies with many public investors. Currently, the companies legislation operated by allowing smaller private companies certain exemptions to the provisions applicable to public companies. Recently, many of the companies established were smaller and private, with different needs to those of public companies. The companies legislation was, therefore, burdensome and created unnecessary regulation and obstacles for smaller private companies as well as costs and expenses that could not be justified for such companies. Therefore, the new law should recognise smaller private companies not as an exception, but as a rule. The Government intended to remove unnecessary burdens on smaller

---

[135] See DTI, *Better Boards* (December 2004).

companies, and to enable such companies and their advisors to access guidance readily on what they needed to know about the law.

3   *Making it easier to set up and run a company*

Although, compared to other countries, it was easier to set up a company in the UK, there were still some procedural requirements that could complicate both the setting up of a company and its initial operation. These included the need for smaller companies to appoint a company secretary or to hold an Annual General Meeting. Where appropriate, the Bill would seek to remove such obstacles.

4   *Providing flexibility, for the future*

According to the Government, there should be flexibility built into the company law framework to ensure it could be kept up to date in the future.[136]

Enhancing Shareholder Engagement and a Long-Term Investment Culture

1.28 According to the Government, companies worked best when the respective roles and responsibilities of directors and members or shareholders were clearly understood, where there was effective communication and engagement between directors and shareholders, and there were efficient mechanisms for taking decisions essential to the company's operation. The Government wished to ensure greater transparency and accountability, and there was more opportunity for all shareholders to play an informal part in company business.

A new Companies Bill would, therefore, provide more clarity on the duties of directors, and to ensure these duties are clearly understood. The Bill would provide that while directors must promote the success of the company for the benefit of shareholders, this could only be achieved by taking due account of longer-term performance and wider interests, including the interest of employees and the impact of the company's operations on the community and environment.

The White Paper was committed towards improving shareholder dialogue. According to the White Paper, shareholders had a key role to play in driving long-term company performance and economic prosperity. However, communication channels between shareholders and the company could become complex, with the result that communication up and down the investment chain and the exercise of ownership rights and responsibilities had become more difficult. Steps had been taken by the Government to increase shareholder engagement such as action requiring all quoted companies to seek shareholder approval for the directors' remuneration report.

---

[136] This would be subject to appropriate processes of public consultation and parliamentary scrutiny.

The White Paper highlighted the importance of access to timely, transparent company information. Shareholders should, therefore, have access to clear and meaningful information to enable them to have constructive dialogue and increase their engagement with the company in which they held shares. Some of the proposed measures that the Bill intended to include were:

(a)   Holding an AGM that would be linked to the reporting cycle, to ensure shareholders have a timely opportunity to hold directors to account.

(b)   Quoted companies would be required to put on their website the preliminary announcements of their annual results and their full accounts and reports. This information must be made available to the public and not just shareholders.

(c)   Under the proposed Bill, shareholders of quoted companies would have a right, within a 15-day holding period after the accounts become available, to propose a resolution to be moved at the general meeting where the accounts were to be laid (such as the AGM). Such resolutions would be circulated at the company's expense.

(d)   Quoted companies would also be required to disclose on their websites the results of polls at general meetings. This would ensure increased transparency for shareholders, whether as registered shareholders of the company or as indirect investors, of decisions taken at general meetings.

(e)   Shareholders of quoted companies would also have a new rights where a certain minority so request, to require an independent scrutiny of any polled vote.

With the advent of modern technology and improved communication, there was more opportunity to reduce the costs and expenses in improving transparency of dialogue between companies and shareholders. When company law was first enacted in the UK, it did not envisage such technology with many of its provisions being reduced to paperwork and documentation, thereby preventing companies and shareholders from enjoying all the cost savings and other benefits that modern technology could bring.

Accordingly, the Government intended to allow all companies, subject to shareholder approval, to be able to use electronic communications with shareholders as the default position, permitting (but not mandating) companies to use websites and e-mail to communicate with their registered members. However, it would be possible for individuals to request paper communication as not everyone would have access to modern technology.

According to the Government, when investors – whether major institutional investors or retail investors – bought shares in listed companies, they were increasingly likely to hold their shares through an intermediary or a chain of intermediaries. This made it difficult for indirect investors to have any direct relationship with the company. The Bill, therefore, proposed to enhance the ability of indirect investors (those not holding legal title to the company's shares in which they invest), to play a fuller role in corporate proceedings. With regard to indirect investors, the Bill further proposed:

(a) Indirect investors exercising rights through proxy, by nominating one or more proxies who could, on their behalf, attend and speak at meetings, demand a poll and vote on a show of hands or poll. These mechanisms would enable indirect investors to have participation rights in the company.

(b) The exercise of governance rights by indirect shareholders so that where a company made provisions in its articles to enfranchise indirect investors, then to the extent provided in the company's Articles, reference to registered members and their rights in primary legislation should be extended to include those designated by the registered member.

(c) The Bill also proposed to include a reserve power for the Secretary of State to compel some or all public companies to provide information electronically to persons having an interest in shares of the registered member requests. At that time, only the intermediary (as the registered member) received a pack of information, which was not then usually passed on to the indirect investors.

At present, the law on directors' duties was fragmented. Some of the directors' duties could be identified from case law rather than in the Companies Act. However, one of the difficulties was that those who became company directors might not understand their obligations under the law. Further, such obligations may not be understood by some of the members of companies in whose interests directors should be acting.

According to the Government, directors' duties were essential to company law and such duties must be widely known and understood. The Bill would introduce a new statutory statement of directors' general duties. It was intended that the statutory statement would replace existing common law and equitable rules. Therefore, the duties would be owed to the company alone and only the company would be able to enforce them.

The statutory statement would be drafted in a way that reflected modern business needs and the wider expectations of responsible business behaviour. The Government would apply the principle of 'enlightened shareholder value' – namely, that the principal objective of directors should be the company's success for the benefit of its members as a whole. However, in order to achieve this objective, directors would need to take a properly balanced view of the implications of decisions over time and foster effective relations with employees, customers and suppliers, and more widely in the community. The enlightened shareholder value approach would drive long-term company performance and maximise overall competitiveness and wealth and welfare for all.

The statutory statement would also address circumstances where there was a conflict between a director's duties to the company and his/her personal interests or duties to others. The Bill was not intended to impose impractical and onerous requirements that would stifle entrepreneurial activity. The Bill would also provide that the company's rights may be waived by the board, acting independently of any conflicted director.

The statutory statement would not change the current remedies available for breaches of duties, including payment of damages by way of compensation where the director's action is considered negligent and the restoration of company property where assets have been misappropriated.

Further, the statutory duties would apply to all persons acting as director. They would apply equally to shadow directors with some variations where required.

It was intended that the statutory statement would be flexible to allow the law to respond to changing business needs and circumstances. There would be scope for the courts to interpret and develop its provisions in a way that reflected the nature and effect of its principles.

The statutory statement would also be widely accessible and understood. It was intended that the government would publish plain language guidance explaining statutory duties to all interested parties.

Under Part 10 of the CA 1985 (as amended), there were a number of provisions dealing with situations where a director has a conflict of interest. However, Part 10 was considered to be very complex and fragmented and the Government intended to reform Part 10 with the following objectives:

(a)   the Bill would simplify the overall structure so that the provisions are more accessible to directors and other users – particularly those transactions requiring shareholder approval;

(b)   the Bill would deregulate where the existing provisions are unnecessary or excessive – for example, companies would be able to make loans to directors with shareholder approval;

(c)   the Bill would remove existing loopholes, for example, by requiring directors to disclose the interests of connected persons if they would have to be disclosed if these interests would have to be disclosed on the director's own behalf, and by broadening the definition of a director's service contract in relation to the requirement that it might be open to inspection by shareholders;

(d)   the Bill would reflect modern business behaviour, for example, by requiring disclosure of interests to other directors as soon as is reasonably practicable;

(e)   the Bill would clarify the law where the existing provisions are unclear or incomplete, for example, by making it clear that the rules as to *ex gratia* payments for loss of office do not extend to other payments that a company is bound to make to a director on his retirement, or other loss of office, because of a legal obligation.

The Government believed that the law on directors' liability must be carefully balanced; the law must be firm and robust to deal fairly with cases where something has gone wrong, either owing to negligence or dishonesty. However, the law should also encourage individuals to become directors and for such directors to take informed and rational risks. As from 6 April 2005, companies may indemnify directors against most liabilities to third parties; and pay directors' legal costs upfront, provided that the director repays if he/she is convicted in any criminal proceedings or judgment given against him/her in any civil proceedings brought by the company.

British company law was flexible in allowing all legal persons, such as companies, to be company directors in the same way as if they were individuals. The Government believed that this flexibility could be abused by those who wish to conceal who was controlling a company. Accordingly, the Government proposed that the Bill should include a requirement that at least one director be a natural person. This was intended to ensure that every company will have at least one individual who could be held accountable for the company's actions.

However, the Bill would allow each company to set its own rules for who appoints its directors. The company should be responsible for ensuring that it appoints persons who not only understand their duties, but also take full responsibility for their actions and omissions. The Bill would also provide that 16 would be the minimum age for a person to be a director. Any child under 16 appointed after publication of the White Paper, would not be entitled to financial compensation in respect of early termination from office resulting from the introduction of the prohibition.

In most cases, minority shareholders commonly use the derivative action procedure to enforce company rights where directors have breached their duties – and such actions hold directors to account for the proper exercise of their duties in pursuit of their company's short-term and long-term interests. Derivative actions are only available at common law and not under statute. The Government, therefore, intended to enact a provision in the Bill to put derivative actions on a statutory footing.

The Government wished to encourage confidence in the statutory audit to ensure a strong, competitive and high quality audit market. Following a company's failure, those who have suffered loss may look to the auditors as having the 'deepest pockets' of all those they can pursue for compensation. The Government intended to reform this area – such reform will have three main elements: (i) legislating to allow shareholders to agree limitations on auditors' liability; (ii) some specific improvements to the quality of the audit process; and (iii) the establishment of an on-going process by which further enhancements to quality and competition can be identified and then implemented. The Government believed it would be inappropriate to change the law regarding who can sue auditors in civil courts. However, owing to the importance of audited financial statements, the Government proposed to make it a criminal offence knowingly or recklessly to given an incorrect audit opinion.

The Government proposed that shareholders should be able to agree a limit to an auditor's liability for damage incurred by a company, to such an amount determined by the Courts to be just and equitable having regard to the relative extent of responsibility of the auditor for the damage incurred.

In particular, the Government proposed:

(a)   such a limitation would apply in situations where damage to the company has been caused through the (mis)conduct of an audit, to the extent the Court considers just and equitable in the circumstances of the case;
(b)   the company would be left to recover, as part of a separate action, the loss suffered for which some other defendant (e.g. another professional advisor) was responsible;
(c)   the auditor would continue to be fully liable for any fraud to which he/she was a party;
(d)   the company could not agree in advance a monetary limit to the auditor's liability;

only those causes of action arising after commencement of the legislation would be subject to the proposed provisions.

The effect of the Government's proposals would mean that with the authority of the shareholders, the company's directors would negotiate the scope, terms and cost of the audit contract. Directors would need to decide how much weight should be given to factors that might influence the terms of the audit, such as cost and availability of insurance, attitudes to risk taken by the directors, shareholders and auditors, and the directors' perception of the level of competition between audit firms. Where shareholders have given explicit agreement, the contract with auditors could include a limitation of the auditors' liability. Accordingly, the Government proposed that shareholder agreement to such limitation should be required each year and in advance of each year's audit.

The Government also proposed that the existence of any limitation of liability would be shown in the company's annual financial statements. The auditor should also provide a list of all companies with which it has agreed a limitation of liability in its own annual financial statements.

Auditors had made some proposals to the Government for improvements in audit transparency and to support shareholder involvement in the audit process. They included: (i) the publication of audit engagement letters, which would increase transparency and enable third parties to understand better the scope of the audit and the terms on which it has been undertaken; (ii) shareholders should be able to question auditors about the audit, which might involve enabling shareholders to question the auditor in advance of an AGM, or by writing to the auditor, via the company, with reasonable questions. All queries must relate to the auditors' report or to the conduct of audit; (iii) publication of auditor resignation statements, to enable investors to understand the reasons for the resignation; and (iv) the audit lead partner should sign and print his/her name on the audit reports. This would serve to improve audit standards by encouraging further personal responsibility for the actions taken by the audit team.

Ensuring Better Regulation and 'Think Small First' Approach

1.29 As stated earlier, a large part of UK company law has traditionally been written for public companies rather than small private companies. Legislation has merely added provisions for private companies as a tailpiece to the provisions applying to public companies.[137] The Government, therefore, wanted to reset the balance and make the law easier to understand and follow. There is emphasis on much greater simplicity and clarity of language. The Government intended that the new law should be presented in an accessible and user-friendly manner. In complex areas of company law, the Government proposed that such areas should be supplemented by clear and comprehensive guidance, such as directors' duties and on the principles of 'Think Small First'.

There would also be improved website communication with Companies House so that web incorporation would be possible by 2007 and hence easier access to relevant material on the website.

On resolutions and meetings, the Government proposed to include measures in the Bill to streamline company decision-making processes to make them easier for small, private companies to understand and follow.

A deregulation procedure will apply to private companies as regards AGMs. It was proposed that private companies would not be required to lay their accounts or to appoint an auditor at the AGM. However, no statutory provision would be needed for those companies that wished to continue to hold an AGM, to lay their accounts and appoint an auditor, if they had one, at the AGM. They would be able to incorporate the necessary provisions into their constitution voluntarily if they wished.

With regard to written resolutions, the Bill proposed to make it easier for private companies to take decisions by written resolution. It would provide that in future, a simple or 75 per cent majority of those eligible to vote would

---

[137] For example, CA 1985, Part 7 on accounts and audit, which are difficult to follow. Also provisions on meetings and resolutions applying largely to public companies.

be required for a written ordinary resolution or a written special resolution to be passed, rather than unanimity. However, shareholders would still have the right to call a general meeting if they wished. The Bill proposed to retain the existing provision whereby members holding 10 per cent of the vote would be able to requisition a general meeting.

There would also be a simplification of notice periods and short notice requirements. At that time, 21 days' notice must be given for an AGM and 14 for an EGM. The Bill would equalise the minimum notice period for all company meetings to 14 days. However, companies could set a longer notice period if they wished. Consent to short notice is fixed at 95 per cent but private companies can elect to reduce this to 90 per cent. The Bill proposed to make this figure the default for private companies, so that members holding 90 per cent of voting rights should be able to agree to a meeting being held at short notice.

However, the Bill would not codify the principle of 'unanimous consent'. At common law, any decision taken (however informally) by all of a company's shareholders together constitutes a decision of the company. Therefore, the principle of unanimous consent would continue to apply at common law.

There will be no legislative provisions clarifying the concept of dispersed meetings, because common law already allows a valid general meeting to be held using overflow rooms with audio–visual links to enable participants to see and hear what is going on in the other rooms and to be seen and heard by those in other rooms.

The White Paper proposed legislative changes to the company's constitution – namely the Articles of Association, which regulate the internal affairs of the company and provide freedom for shareholders to make their own rules, subject to some legal constraints. Table A (Articles) provides model Articles for companies limited by shares. It also operates as a 'default' set of Articles for such companies, namely, that the Articles of a company limited by shares will be set out in Table A if the company does not register Articles at Companies House, or to the extent that any Articles which it does register do not exclude or modify Table A provisions.

According to the Government, Table A was no longer an appropriate form of model Articles. Although it has been revised on many occasions, it still remained a product of the mid-nineteenth century in language and substance, and was largely drafted from the viewpoint of a public company rather than that of a private company: 'successive revisions to Table A have tended to include increasingly elaborate provisions, designed to cover every conceivable event or set of circumstances that a company may find itself in, however unlikely it is that the majority of companies who are using Table A would ever find themselves in those circumstances'.[138]

---

[138] White Paper, p 33.

A large part of the Table A provisions are, therefore, irrelevant to many companies using Table A. Although new provisions had been added to Table A, some of the redundant provisions remained, and the 'one-size-fits-all' approach was not practical. Further: (i) Table A was now considered to be user-unfriendly, poorly laid out and often unintelligible to non-specialists; (ii) a large part of Table A was taken up with matters that are remote from the concerns of smaller companies; and (iii) Table A did not take account of relatively recent changes in the law such as the introduction of single member companies.

These were some of the reasons for the Government to consider reforms to Table A. There should be a radically simplified set of model articles for private companies limited by shares, reflecting the way that small companies operate. Further, there should be a separate set of model articles for public companies limited by shares similar in scope to the current Table A but with clearer layout and drafting. There should also be a full set of model articles for private companies limited by guarantee. Also, there should be comprehensive, clear and concise guidance for small companies who are using, or thinking of using, model articles.

Companies set up under the new legislation would have the new set of model articles, which would operate as default provisions for the types of company for which they are prescribed, in the same way as Table A did before revision. Existing companies would be able to replace their current articles (whether or not these are set out in Table A) with new model Articles, if their shareholders passed a special resolution to do so.

It was proposed that the Bill would contain a power for the Secretary of State to prescribe, by secondary legislation, stand-alone model articles for public companies, private companies limited by shares and private companies limited by guarantee. It is intended that the private company articles would wholly replace Table A for those private companies limited by shares, which would in the future be formed under the new ACT and would play an important role in simplifying the law for small companies. The private company articles would apply by default where a company did not register its own articles at Companies House (to the extent that the company in question had not specifically excluded or modified the model articles). However, Table A would continue to provide the model articles for companies formed before the new model articles came into force.

The aim of drafting the new model articles was to avoid archaic and legalistic language and to reduce the number of provisions in the articles to ensure more accessibility to the directors and shareholders of small companies than previously. The model articles would be aimed largely at small, owner-managed companies. The articles for private companies contain the minimum number of rules that it is envisaged a typical private company limited by shares will need and that the shareholders will want.

It will be open to any private company limited by shares when using the private company articles to add to, amend or delete rules from the model articles as they see fit, or adopt completely different articles of their own.

A majority of private companies are likely to take advantage of the written resolution procedure as part of decision making by members, thereby obviating the need for a meeting to be called. In the event members of private companies require a meeting, the procedure for the conduct of such meetings will be set out in a new Act.

The White Paper envisaged draft guidance notes on private company articles, which would be available from Companies House by the time new private company articles come into force. The draft guidance would seek to explain, in plain English, what Articles of Association are, and how private companies' articles work.

The Government intended to provide separate model articles for public companies. Their content would be similar to Table A and would include more detailed rules for more complex circumstances.

The Government also proposed that it should no longer be a requirement for private companies to appoint a company secretary. However, shareholders can continue to require that a company secretary be appointed if they require or otherwise leave it for the directors to decide.

The White Paper also addressed the nature of offences to be included in the Bill and for these to be applied consistently across the legislation. This would include refinements to the 'officer in default' framework, to make it clear which individuals in which circumstances should be made liable for breach. The White Paper in this regard was shifting away from imposing any criminal liability from the company itself in certain circumstances. Accordingly, directors would be liable where they authorise, participate in, permit or fail to take action to prevent a default, including monitoring failures where appropriate. De facto directors would also be included in this provision.

The White Paper provided that secretaries should be liable, if directors had properly charged them with the relevant function (or if the function has been conferred on them by the articles), where they authorise, participate in, permit or fail to take active steps to prevent the default.

Corporate managers were also subject to personal liability. These comprise relatively senior employees, with a policy and decision-making role that can affect the enterprise substantially, and have responsibility for the function which is the subject of the breach. The draft clauses of the Bill used the term 'senior executive' instead of 'manager', to describe the category of person envisaged. This would cover senior employees within the company but not external third parties.

Delegates would be another category of persons who could be personally liable on a case-by-case basis under the Bill. The term 'delegate' covers individuals to whom a particular function has properly been delegated, by or under the authority of the directors or secretary.

The clauses in the Bill provided that for delegation to be 'proper', it must be reasonable in all the circumstances. The White Paper makes it clear that delegation would not be the same as assignment. Even a 'proper' act of delegation would not remove potential liability from those delegating, albeit they would be able to adduce the delegation as evidence of their having taken reasonable steps to secure compliance. Decisions on whether delegates should be targeted in a particular offence can only be decided on a case-by-case basis.[139]

The White Paper aimed to ensure that targeting sanctions on a company's officers would make it essential for every company to comply with the requirements to have officers. Accordingly, the Government proposes to give the Registrar of Companies power to issue a notice requiring a company to comply with the requirement within a specific period. There would be a criminal sanction following on a company's failure to comply with the notice.[140]

According to the Government, the company's register of members was an integral part of the constitutional apparatus. The register was necessary to ensure that members can be contacted, and such a register should be made available for public inspection. The Bill, however, makes some deregulatory changes to make it easier for companies to maintain their registers. The Bill would keep the public right both to inspect and to obtain a copy of a company's register of members, both supported by the ability to apply for a court order if the company refuses.

The Government also proposed to amend the capital maintenance and share provisions which were very complex and difficult to understand. The Bill, therefore, proposed to introduce a number of deregulatory measures for private companies on capital maintenance. The Bill abolished financial assistance provisions for private companies, so that they would no longer be prevented from providing financial assistance for the purchase of their own shares.

Making it Easier to Set Up and Run a Company

1.30 The White Paper highlighted that the law on the formation of companies was one of the most frequently used parts of the Companies Act. Although the process of establishing a company was not cumbersome compared with international standards, the White Paper believed there should be some changes made in substance to make the process smoother and more efficient.

---

[139] As an example, if a statutory function is one that many companies often and reasonably outsource to informed third parties, those third parties may be brought within the frame of liability for breach.

[140] Other sanctions include amending CA 1985, s 458 so that the penalty for fraudulent trading would be increased from seven to ten years.

Accordingly, the following aspects were addressed in the Bill, with a focus on the practicalities:

- one person should be able to form any type of company;
- the key rules on the internal workings of the company should be in one document (the 'articles');
- there should be separate model articles for private companies limited by shares and public companies;
- unless a company positively chooses to restrict its objects, neither the company's capacity, nor the authority of the directors to bind the company, should be limited by them;
- members should be able to choose to entrench elements of the company's articles (making certain provisions harder to amend subsequently than would otherwise be the case); and
- companies should be able to migrate between different parts of the UK.

Flexibility in the Future

1.31 In its consultation document *Flexibility and Accessibility*,[141] the Government proposed that changes to company law in future could be made by a special form of secondary legislation (rather than by primary legislation), both to reform and to restate the law. This would help company law remain flexible in the future, and accessible to all those who use it – particularly smaller firms.

The Government did not propose to introduce a new body to oversee the review of company law, which had included the Company Law and Reporting Commission and the Private Companies Committee. The Government wanted to ensure that Companies Act inspectors would undertake effective management of large investigations. The Government was considering administrative measures to help avoid prolonged and unduly expensive inspections. It proposed to introduce a new power to enable the Secretary of State to direct Companies Act inspectors, both at the outset of and during the life of an inspection, as to the scope, conduct, timing and certain other matters in relation to their investigation, and to discontinue an investigation.

There would also be an amendment to s 8 of the Company Directors Disqualification Act 1986, so that the Secretary of State could make a decision to apply to the Courts for the disqualification of a company director in the light of any information obtained by Companies Act inspectors, without the need for the information to be included in a report by such inspectors.

---

[141] Published by the Government in May 2005, and seeking views on specific proposals to introduce new legislative powers as part of the Bill.

Phase six was, therefore, concerned with proposals put forward by the Government on issues raised by the *Final Report*. The Government did not accept all the *Final Report*'s proposals.[142]

[142] In 2005, the DTI published a document entitled *Company Law Reform: Small Business Summary*. It stated that an effective framework of company law and corporate governance promoted enterprise and stimulated investment. The Government was determined to ensure that the UK system made it easy to set up and grow a business. A thorough overhaul of the law was needed to make it more suited to the needs of small business. This summary sets out the main DTI proposals of the Company Law Reform Bill (as it was then) affecting small business. Currently company law was written with the large company in mind. The provisions that applied to private companies are often expressed as an exception to the provisions applying to public companies, making them hard to understand. The Government was committed to restructure those parts of the law most relevant to small companies (such as the model Articles of Association and the requirements on accounts and audit) so that the provisions that apply to them are easier to find. It would also use simpler, clearer language. The Government stated that it could not eliminate the complexity in company law, (as this would reduce flexibility for companies), so to make it easier to understand for both companies and their advisors, it must be supplemented by clear and comprehensive guidance. Small companies would easily be able to identify the basic day-to-day requirements that applied to them. The Government would increase the coverage of Companies House plain English guidance and ensure it followed the principles of 'think small first'. Increasingly, small companies were using the Companies House website. Companies House would continue to improve their website for their customers, including a wider range of web-based guidance, better links to related websites and on-line access to up-to-date companies legislation. During 2007, Companies House would be offering web incorporation and this would be supported by easier access to relevant material, for example the new shortened and simplified private company Articles of Association. The main changes to company law affecting small companies would be as follows: There would be separate model Articles of Association for private companies that would contain the minimum key rules on the internal workings of the company. These would be shorter and clearer. The Government would abolish the requirement for private companies to have a company secretary. The general duties that a director owed to the company were currently established in case law rather than statute making it hard for them to be widely understood. The Bill would include a statutory statement of directors' general duties both to make the law in this area more accessible and to change the law where it no longer applied to modern business practice. The Government would provide clear guidance for new directors on what these duties mean. Directors would automatically have the option of filing a service address on the public record (rather than their private home address). Private companies would not need to hold an annual general meeting unless they positively opted to do so. It would be easier for companies to take decisions by written resolution rather than holding a meeting, as such resolutions may in future be carried with simple or 75 per cent majority of eligible votes rather than requiring unanimity as at present. Companies would be able to make greater use of electronic communications for communications with shareholders. The provisions on accounts and audit would be restated to make them much easier to understand for small companies and their advisors. The Government would be retaining the option for small- and medium-sized companies to file abbreviated accounts with Companies House. The deadline for private companies to file their annual reporting documents would be reduced from a ten-month year-end to seven, reflecting both improvements in technology and the increased rate at which information would become out of date. In order to keep the law up to date and ensure it met users' needs, the Government would provide a power to allow the reform or restatement of company law to be made in future by a special form of secondary legislation, subject to strong requirements for public consultation and Parliamentary scrutiny.

Conclusion

1.32 This chapter has addressed the substantive proposals that have been made by various committees and the DTI over a period of time since the first Companies Act in the UK was enacted. The period before 1998 was largely reflective of the recommendations made by the Loreburn Committee, the Wrenbury Committee, the Greene Committee, the Cohen Committee, and the Jenkins Committee (together, the Committees). Many of these Committees' recommendations were incorporated in subsequent Companies Acts. The recommendation of these Committees were largely in the nature of additional disclosure of information, as they believed this would lead to more transparency and accountability, without recognising the additional burdens to companies that this would entail. Rather than deregulation, the additional provisions further regulated companies and allowed little flexibility. Although the Committees recognised the importance of small companies and that there were more private companies than public companies registered at Companies House, the Committees shied away from making specific recommendations applicable to the small private company or business. Many of the recommendations of the Committees were simply added on to the existing companies' legislation and considered as exceptions for small companies, without properly addressing the needs of such companies.

Company law in the UK was antiquated and archaic: it did not meet the demands of a modern UK competitive economy, nor the increasing use of IT from which company law could benefit. The result had been fragmented legislation with no coherence or logic, that was incomprehensible to many small businesses, bureaucratic and unsympathetic to the needs of small companies and clearly not user-friendly.

The position after 1998 could be characterised as one of from policy to implementation. In 1998, the Labour Government seized on the initiative for the need to radically reform the UK company law regime. It recognised the perceived inadequacies of the companies legislation, which was hopelessly out of date and needed to be modernised in all respects. It set about appointing a Steering Committee whose task would be to review all aspects of UK company law thoroughly and to make recommendations. Between 1998 and 2000, the Steering Committee issued various consultation documents culminating in two White Papers in 2002 and 2005 respectively, leading to the CA 2006.

COMPANY LAW REFORM – CHECKLIST

Date	Document	Coverage
1905	Loreburn Committee Report	Examined limited aspects of company law
1918	Wrenbury Committee Report	Examined limited aspects of company law
1925–6	Greene Committee Report	Report on the whole spectrum of company law in connection with the Companies Acts 1908 to 1917
1945	Cohen Committee Report	Consideration of various aspects of company law including objects clause; directors' duties; accounting aspects; financial assistance; relationship between directors and shareholders
1962	Jenkins Committee Report	Examined the CA 1948; considered whole spectrum of company law
1986	Department of Trade and Industry: The Prentice Report	Reform of the *Ultra vires* rule
1997	Law Commission Report: Shareholder Remedies	Law Commissions of England, Wales and Scotland on radical reform of shareholder remedies
1997	Law Commission Report: Regulating Conflicts of Interest and Formulating a Statement of Directors' Duties	Law Commissions of England and Wales and Scotland on radical reform of directors' duties to be placed on a statutory footing
1998	Modern Company Law for a Competitive Economy	Established the foundations for a new company law regime
1999	Company Law Steering Group – The Strategic Framework	Detailed analysis of whole spectrum of company law requiring radical change
1999	Company Law Steering Group: Modern Company Law for a Competitive Economy: Company General Meetings and Shareholder Communication	Considered proposed reforms to general meetings and effective communication between shareholders
1999	Company Law Steering Group: Modern Company Law for a Competitive Economy: Company Formation and Capital Maintenance	Detailed proposals on reform of law relating to company set-up (types of companies) and capital maintenance including financial assistance

Continued

Date	Document	Coverage
1999	Company Law Steering Group: Modern Company Law For a Competitive Economy: Reforming the Law Concerning Overseas Companies	Proposals on reforming the laws concerning overseas companies
2000	Company Law Steering Group: Modern Company Law for a Competitive Economy: Developing the Framework	Made key proposals on governance of companies and small and private companies
2000	Company Law Steering Group: Modern Company Law For A Competitive Economy: Capital Maintenance – Other Issues	Focused on a small number of residual technical issues on capital maintenance
2000	Company Law Steering Group: Modern Company Law for a Competitive Economy: Registration of Company Charges	Reviewed previous reports on company charges and proposed options
2000	Company Law Steering Group: Modern Company Law for a Competitive Economy: Completing the Structure	Took forward proposals of previous consultation documents towards final phase
2001	Final Report presented by the Steering Group	Set out the Group's final recommendations on a wide spectrum of company law reform areas addressed in previous consultation documents
2002	White Paper: Modernising Company Law	Examined the Company Law Steering Group's proposals and formulation of Government policies with publication of draft Companies Bill
2005	White Paper: Company Law Reform	Final White Paper issued with publication of draft Companies Bill

Chapter 2

Overview of the Act

Introduction

2.1 This chapter provides an overview of the CA 2006. It sets out the main highlights of the CA 2006 that are likely to have a significant impact on companies, including legal and practical implications. The areas highlighted are considered in more detail in subsequent chapters.

This chapter considers the timeline leading to the enactment of the CA 2006. It analyses the structure and style of the CA 2006; the Parts and the Schedules to the CA 2006; the remaining provisions under the CA 1985 and the CA 1989; the preamble to the CA 2006; territorial extent and devolution; regulations and orders; the provisions in force; a summary of the main highlights of the CA 2006; and consideration of two guidance documents, issued by the Department of Trade and Industry (now known as the Department for Business, Enterprise and Regulatory Reform), in respect of the CA 2006 provisions applicable to private companies.

Timeline of the CA 2006

2.2 Following wide consultation and the publication of two White Papers by the Government in 2002 and 2005 respectively, the Company Law Reform Bill (as it was then known) (the 'Bill') was introduced to Parliament in late 2005. The Bill amended and restated many of the provisions of the CA 1985, and parts of the CA 1989. Approximately two-thirds of the CA 1985 was proposed to be repealed by the Bill. The Bill also purported to codify certain provisions of case law, namely in the area of directors' duties. In some areas, the Bill made textual amendments to the CA 1985 or other legislation. New provisions were also included in the Bill, (for example, statements of objects; entrenchment of articles; a financial assistance regime for private companies; and the appointment of company names adjudicators).

The Bill was not a consolidating measure, a fact that was considered with dissatisfaction by some[143] who advocated the need for consolidation. However, owing to the need to modernise UK company law and lobbying from various sectors of the industries and professions, the Bill became a consolidating measure during Summer 2006, and the Bill became known as the Companies Bill. This required a large number of clauses to be scrutinised by both the House of Lords and the House of Commons towards the latter part of 2006, with perceptive debates in both Houses on some of the clauses to the Companies Bill.

Structure and Style

2.3 The CA 2006 comprises 47 Parts with a total of 1,300 sections and 16 Schedules. This can be compared to the previous CA 1985, which had a total of 747 sections and 25 Schedules. The increase in the number of provisions to the CA 2006 was owing to the need to modernise company law in the UK, and to take account of the developing changes both nationally and in the European Community, in the form of regulations and directives (see for example, the Transparency Directive;[145] and the Takeovers Directive).[146]

Part 1 of the CA 2006 restates almost all of the provisions of the CA 1985, as well as the provisions of the CA 1989, and the Companies (Audit, Investigations and Community Enterprise) Act 2004 (C(AICE) Act 2004. The CA 2006 also codifies certain provisions of case law, particularly in respect of fiduciary and common law duties of directors.[147]

The CA 2006 is more orderly, and more logically structured than the CA 1985. It has been written in clear and concise language – varying the structure of the sentences with a division into paragraphs and sub-paragraphs, to ensure that the section is fully understood in its meaning and context. The parliamentary draftsman has also sought to use plain, simple language taking account of the wide spectrum of audience to whom the CA 2006 applies, and to ensure that the sections of the CA 2006 are not overwhelming in their effect and application. Some of the sections and paragraphs are shorter to ensure clarity and conciseness.

---

[143] See for example, Lord Clinton-Davis who advocated some degree of consolidation when the Company Law Reform Bill was presented to the House of Lords. (HL Debates 11 Jan 2006). However, Lord Sainbury contended that it was simply not possible to have a consolidated Bill that would hold for a lengthy period of time – it was neither desirable, necessary, nor what people wanted. But see Lord Sharman, who expressed his concern and disappointment that the Bill was not a consolidating one. The resultant effect would leave the CA 1985 partly repealed and company law contained in both the CA 1985 and the Bill: HL Debates 11 Jan 2006.

[144] (Facing page) See CA 2006 Commencement Timetable issued by the Department of Trade and Industry. Appendix 1.

[145] See Chapter 32.

[146] See Chapter 29.

[147] See CA 2006, Part 10; see further Chapter 9.

Companies Act 2006 Timeline

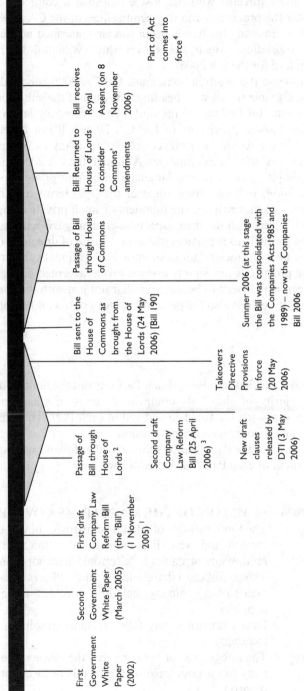

First Government White Paper (2002)

Second Government White Paper (March 2005)

First draft Company Law Reform Bill (the 'Bill') (1 November 2005) [1]

Passage of Bill through House of Lords [2]

Second draft Company Law Reform Bill (25 April 2006) [3]

New draft clauses released by DTI (3 May 2006)

Takeovers Directive Provisions in force (20 May 2006)

Bill sent to the House of Commons as brought from the House of Lords (24 May 2006) [Bill 190]

Summer 2006 (at this stage the Bill was consolidated with the Companies Acts 1985 and 1989) – now the Companies Bill 2006

Passage of Bill through House of Commons

Bill Returned to House of Lords to consider Commons' amendments

Bill receives Royal Assent (on 8 November 2006)

Part of Act comes into force [4]

1 The Bill was introduced in the House of Lords on 1 November 2005 and entitled the 'Company Law Reform Bill'. It was introduced by Lord Sainsbury.
2 The Bill passed through the Report stage and Third reading stages in the House of Lords on 19 October 2006.
3 The Bill was amended in the Grand Committee of the House of Lords and reprinted on 25 April 2006.
4 The Act comes into force in stages set out by the DTI. [144]

However, a novice director who has just established a company and is learning to master the provisions and the technicalities of the CA 2006, may well be justified in throwing his hands up in the air – alarmed at the sheer volume of the legislation, which spans over three volumes! Is this an appropriate standard for the CA 2006?

In order to appease the position somewhat, the CA 2006 subdivides the sections into manageable topics with headings for each of the sub-topics for ease of reference, and for finding the relevant area of company law without difficulty. However, some provisions of the CA 2006 will not be easy to understand for some directors and officers of the company as opposed to 'professional directors' of public companies. Although the CA 2006 attempts to balance the simplicity of style and language with appropriate choice of words and expression, in some cases, some of the legal terms may not be easily understood – particularly for the founders of small private companies who are not well-versed with the finer aspects of company law with its technical phrases and terms. This is particularly so in the case of directors' duties, which uses terms such a 'fiduciary' and 'common law' without explanation or elaboration. The provisions just simply assume this as accepted background knowledge. Directors will need to become familiar not just with the common law and fiduciary duties, but also the general statutory duties and developing case law.

The Parts

2.4 The CA 2006 is divided into Parts. Each Part sets out the main company law topic. A majority of the Parts comprise a series of Chapters. The Chapters further subdivide the topic considered in each Part. The Chapters contain sections on the topic under consideration.

A general overview of the Parts can be summarised as follows with specific details of the content of each Part considered below:

PART OF CA 2006	SUMMARY OF THE MAIN AREAS COVERED
Parts 1–7	The fundamentals of what a company is, how it can be formed and what it can be called – the provisions remove any obstacles to 'electronic incorporation'
Parts 8–12	The members (shareholders) and officers (management) of a company including directors' duties and liabilities
Parts 13 and 14	How companies may take decisions (resolutions and meetings)
Parts 15 and 16	The safeguards for ensuring that the officers of a company are accountable to the members (accounts and reports)

Parts 17–25	Raising share capital, capital maintenance, annual returns and company charges
Parts 26–28	Company reconstructions, mergers and takeovers
Parts 29–39	The regulatory framework, application to companies not formed under the Companies Acts, and other company law provisions
Parts 40–42	Overseas disqualification of directors, business names and statutory auditors
Part 43	Transparency obligations
Parts 44–47	Miscellaneous and general

The Schedules

2.5 The Schedules set out the main company law topics addressed in some of the Parts and sections of the CA 2006. Some of the Schedules are divided into Parts, which are a further sub-division of the Schedule. The function of the Schedules is to supplement the context of the Parts and sections to which they refer, and to elucidate on the areas highlighted in the section(s) concerned.

The Schedules are:

SCHEDULES TO THE CA 2006	SUMMARY OF THE MAIN AREAS COVERED
Schedule 1	Connected persons: references to an interest in shares or debentures
Schedule 2	Specified persons, descriptions of disclosures, etc. for the purpose of CA 2006, s 948
Schedule 3	Amendments of remaining provisions of the CA 1985 relating to offences
Schedule 4	Documents and information sent or supplied to a company
Schedule 5	Communications by a company
Schedule 6	Meaning of 'subsidiary', etc.: supplementary provisions
Schedule 7	Parent and subsidiary undertakings: supplementary provisions
Schedule 8	Index of defined expressions
Schedule 9	Removal of special provisions about accounts and audit of charitable companies
Schedule 10	Recognised supervisory bodies
Schedule 11	Recognised professional qualifications
Schedule 12	Arrangements in which registered third country auditors are required to participate

Schedule 13	Supplementary provisions with respect to delegation order
Schedule 14	Statutory auditors: consequential amendments
Schedule 15	Transparency obligations and related matters: minor and consequential amendments
Schedule 16	Repeals

What remains of previous legislation after the CA 2006?

2.6 The following provisions remain after the CA 2006:

- Part 14 of the CA 1985 on company investigations that go wider than companies (although this area has been amended by Part 32 of the CA 2006 – see ss 1035–1039 (CA 2006));
- Part 2 of the Companies (Audit, Investigations and Community Enterprise) Act 2004 dealing with the provisions on community interest companies.

The non-company law provisions that remain are:

- Part 18 of the CA 1985 (floating charges and receivers (Scotland));
- Part 3 of the CA 1989 (powers to require information and documents to assist overseas regulatory authorities);
- Sections 112–116 of the CA 1989 (provisions about Scottish incorporated charities);
- Part 7 of the CA 1989 (provisions about financial markets and insolvency);
- Schedule 18 of the CA 1989 (amendments and savings consequential upon changes in law made by the CA 1989);
- Sections 14 and 15 of the C(AICE) Act 2004 (supervision of accounts and reports);
- Sections 16 and 17 of the C(AICE) Act 2004 (bodies concerned with accounting standards).

In non-company law areas, the CA 2006 makes amendments to other legislation. This includes the Financial Services and Markets Act 2000, and also makes new provision of various kinds. The main areas where provision of this kind is made are:

- Overseas disqualification of company directors (Part 40 of the CA 2006 – company directors: foreign disqualification);
- Business names (Part 41 of the CA 2006) – this replaces the Business Names Act 1985;
- Statutory auditors (Part 42 of the CA 2006) – replacing Part 2 of the CA 1989; and

- Transparency obligations (Part 43 of the CA 2006) – amending Part 6 of the Financial Services and Markets Act 2000.

The Preamble

2.7 The Preamble to the CA 2006 states that the objective of the Act is to reform company law and restate the greater part of the enactments[148] relating to companies; to make other provisions relating to companies and to other forms of business organisation;[149] to make provision about directors' disqualification,[150] business names,[151] auditors and actuaries;[152] to amend Part 9 of the Enterprise Act 2002;[153] and for connected purposes.

The Preamble, therefore, sets out the primary objectives of the CA 2006 with emphasis on wide-ranging areas across the whole spectrum of UK company law regime. The CA 2006 also restates many provisions of the CAs of 1985 and 1989, and the Companies (Audit, Investigations and Community Enterprise) Act 2004 (C(AICE) Act 2004).

Some of the provisions also codify particular aspects of case law such a directors' duties.[154]

Territorial Extent And Devolution

2.8 The CA 2006 also extends company law to the whole of the United Kingdom. Section 1299 of the CA 2006 states that, except as otherwise provided (or the context otherwise requires), the provisions of the CA 2006 extend to the whole of the UK. The territorial scope of the CA 2006 applies as follows:

Northern Ireland

2.8.1 In respect of Northern Ireland, company law is a devolved matter. The provisions of Great Britain company law have generally been replicated in

---

[148] The term 'enactment' is defined to include (a) an enactment contained in subordinate legislation within the meaning of the Interpretation Act 1978 (c.30); (b) an enactment contained in, or in an instrument made under, an Act of the Scottish Parliament; and (c) an enactment contained in, or in an instrument made under, Northern Ireland legislation within the meaning of the Interpretation Act 1978: CA 2006, s 1293.

[149] See Chapter 3.

[150] See Chapter 11.

[151] See Chapter 6.

[152] See Chapter 33. On actuaries, see CA 2006, Part 44, ss 1274–1276 which amends the Companies (Audit, Investigations and Community Enterprise) Act 2004.

[153] Part 9 of the Enterprise Act 2002 is concerned with restrictions on disclosure of information. It adds s 241A to the Enterprise Act 2002 dealing with civil proceedings. See CA 2006, s 1281 (disclosure of information under the Enterprise Act 2002). See further Chapter 33.

[154] See further Chapter 9 on codification of some of directors' fiduciary and common law duties.

separate Northern Ireland legislation. The CA 2006 provides for a single company law regime applying to the whole of the United Kingdom, so that companies will be United Kingdom companies rather than Great Britain companies or Northern Ireland companies as at present. This does not affect the legislative competence of Northern Ireland; company law remains a transferred matter, and the CA 2006 could be separately amended or repealed in Northern Ireland if that were so desired.

It should be noted that where a provision describes a particular section as restating or replacing a provision in the CA 1985, the CA 1989, or the C(AICE) Act 2004, this should be read as applying equally to the corresponding provision of the Companies (Northern Ireland) Order 1986, the Companies (Northern Ireland) Order 1990, or the Companies (Audit, Investigations and Community Enterprise) Order 2005.

Part 45 of the CA 2006 addresses the territorial scope of the Act to Northern Ireland. It provides that the Companies Acts (as defined by s 2 of the CA 2006) extend to Northern Ireland.[155] Further, the enactments in force in Great Britain relating to SEs (Societas Europaea) extend to Northern Ireland.[156]

The CA 2006 also provides for extension of Great Britain enactments relating to certain other forms of business organisation. The following, therefore, extend to Northern Ireland: limited liability partnerships; limited partnerships; open-ended investment companies; European Economic Interest Groupings.[157]

In respect of business names, the provisions of Part 41 of the CA 2006 (business names) extend to Northern Ireland.[158]

---

[155] CA 2006, s 1282(1). The following cease to have effect: the Companies (Northern Ireland) Order 1986 (SI 1986/1032 (NI 6)); the Companies Consolidation (Consequential Provisions) (Northern Ireland) Order 1986 (SI 1986/1035 (NI 9); and Part 3 of the Companies (Audit, Investigations and Community Enterprise) Order 2005 (SI 2005/1967 (NI 17)). See CA 2006, s 1284(2).

[156] CA 2006, s 1285 (1). The following enactments cease to have effect: the European Public Limited-Liability Company Regulations (Northern Ireland) 2004 (SR 2004/417); and the European Public Limited-Liability Company (Fees) Regulations (Northern Ireland) 2004 (SR 2004/418): CA 2006, s 1285(2). The term 'SE' refers to a European Public Limited-Liability Company (or Societas Europea) within the meaning of Council Regulation 2157/2001/EC of 8 Oct 2001 on the Statute for a European Company.

[157] CA 2006, s 1286(1). The following cease to have effect: the Limited Liability Partnerships Act (Northern Ireland) 2002 (c 12 (NI)); the Limited Partnerships Act 1907 (c 24) as it formerly had effect in Northern Ireland; the Open-Ended Investment Companies Act (Northern Ireland) 2002 (c 13 (NI)); and the European Economic Interest Groupings Regulations (Northern Ireland) 1989 (SR 1989/216): see CA 2006, s 1286(2).

[158] CA 2006, s 1287(1). Accordingly, the Business Names (Northern Ireland) Order 1986 (SI 1986/1033) (NI 7) ceases to have effect: CA 2006, s 1287(2).

Scotland

2.8.2 Company law is a reserved matter and the Companies Acts extend to the whole of Great Britain. However, there are several areas where, in legislating about companies, the Act deals with matters which are devolved. These are:

- Changes in Part 41 of the CA 2006 to the regulation of business names (a devolved matter) – these correspond to changes in Part 5 of the CA 2006 to the regulation of company names (a reserved matter);
- statutory guidance to prosecutors and other enforcement authorities in relation to a new offence knowingly or recklessly causing an audit report to be misleading, false or deceptive – even though the offence itself is a reserved matter, guidance is to be issued by the Lord Advocate in Scotland;[159]
- certain changes relating to exemptions from audit requirements for companies that are charities;[160]
- conferral of a power on the Auditor General to specify public bodies for his audit.[161]

These were the subject of a legislative consent motion agreed to by the Scottish Parliament on 16 March 2006.

---

[159] CA 2006, s 509. This provides that the Lord Advocate may issue guidance for the purpose of helping relevant regulatory authorities to determine how they should carry out their functions in cases where behaviour occurs that appears to involve the commission of an offence under CA 2006, s 507 (offences in connection with auditor's report); and has been, or is being or may be investigated pursuant to arrangements under CA 2006, Sched 10, para 15 (investigation of complaints against auditors and supervisory bodies), or of a kind mentioned in CA 2006, Schedule 10, para 24 (independent investigation for disciplinary purposes of public interest cases).

[160] CA 2006, s 1175.

[161] CA 2006, s 483. This is concerned with Scottish public sector companies with reference to audit by the Auditor General for Scotland. The Scottish Ministers may by order provide for the accounts of a company having its registered office in Scotland to be audited by the Auditor General for Scotland: s 483(1). An order under CA 2006, s 483(1) may be made in relation to a company only if it appears to the Scottish Ministers that the company exercises in or as regards Scotland functions of a public nature none of which relate to reserved matters (within the meaning of the Scotland Act 1998); or is entirely or substantially funded from a body having accounts falling within para (a) or (b) of s 483(3) CA 2006: s 483(2). The accounts are (a) accounts in relation to which the Public Finance and Accountability (Scotland) Act 2000, s 21 (asp1) (audit of accounts: Auditor General for Scotland) applies; (b) accounts which are subject to audit by the Auditor General for Scotland by virtue of an order under this section: s 483(3). An order under s 483(1) may make such supplementary or consequential provision (including provision amending an enactment) as the Scottish Ministers think expedient: s 483(4). An order under s 483(1) will not be made unless a draft of the statutory instrument containing it has been laid before, and approved by resolution of, the Scottish Parliament.

Wales

2.8.3 Company law is not transferred to the Welsh Assembly. There are no provisions under the CA 2006 that impact on devolved competencies.

Crown Dependencies

2.9 Part 28 of the CA 2006 (takeovers) contains provisions enabling it to be extended by Order in Council to the Isle of Man, or any of the Channel Islands. This reflects the existing jurisdiction of the Takeover Panel (as the takeover regulator), and has been agreed by the relevant Island authorities. If the power were to be exercised, there would be further prior consultation with these authorities.[162]

Regulations and Orders

2.10 The CA 2006 is the primary legislation that will apply to companies directly once all the provisions come into force. However, a number of provisions will need to be set out in secondary legislation – mainly in regulations or orders made by statutory instrument. The CA 2006 makes references throughout the various Parts to various regulations and orders. Section 1288 of the CA 2006 states that unless otherwise provided, regulations and orders under the CA 2006 must be made by statutory instrument.

Some regulations and orders are subject to a *negative resolution procedure*. This means that the statutory instrument containing the regulation or order will be subject to annulment in pursuance of a resolution of either House of Parliament.[163]

Other regulations and orders are subject to an *affirmative resolution procedure*. This means that the regulations or order must not be made unless a draft of the statutory instrument containing them has been laid before Parliament, and approved by a resolution of each House of Parliament.[164]

In some provisions under the CA 2006, regulations or orders that are subject to *approval after being made* must be laid before Parliament after being made;[165] and cease to have effect at the end of 28 days, beginning with the day on which they were made, unless during that period they are approved by resolution of each House.[166] In determining the period of 28 days, no account will be taken of any time during which Parliament is dissolved, or during which both Houses are adjourned for more than four days.[167]

---

[162] See CA 2006, s 965. This provides that Her Majesty may by Order in Council direct that any of the provisions of CA 2006, Part 28, Chapter 1 extend, with such modifications as may be specified in the Order, to the Isle of Man or any of the Channel Islands.

[163] CA 2006, s 1289.   [164] CA 2006 s 1290.   [165] CA 2006, s 1291(1)(a).

[166] CA 2006, s 1291(1)(b).

[167] CA 2006 s 1291(2). See further supplementary provisions on regulations under CA 2006, s 1292.

The Department for Business Enterprise and Regulatory Reform has recently issued draft regulations as part of the implementation of the CA 2006.[168]

Provisions in Force

2.11 Some of the provisions of the CA are already in force. Other provisions will gradually be implemented over a period of time up to the end of 2008.[169]

---

[168] The draft regulations are: the Small Companies and Group (Accounts and Directors' Report) Regulations 2008; the Large and Medium-sized Companies and Group (Accounts and Reports) Regulations 2008; the Companies (Summary Financial Statement) Regulations 2008; the Companies (Revision of Defective Accounts and Reports) Regulations 2008; the Insurance Accounts Directive (Miscellaneous Insurance Undertakings) Regulations 2008; the Bank Accounts Directive (Miscellaneous Banks) Regulations 2008; the Partnership (Accounts) Regulations 2008: the Companies Act 2006 (Accounts and Reports) (Amendment) Regulations 2008; the Companies (Prescribed Particulars of Company Charges) Regulations 2007; the Companies (Trading Disclosures) Regulations 2008; the Companies (Company Records and Fees) Regulations 2007; the Companies (Particulars of Usual Residential Address) Regulations 2008; the Companies (Disclosure of Audit Remuneration and Liability Limitation Agreements) Regulations 2007; the Companies (Registrar of Companies) Regulations 2008; the Companies (Unregistered Companies) Regulations 2008; the Non-Companies Acts (Companies Authorised to Register) Regulations 2008; the Companies (Company and Business Names) (Miscellaneous Provisions) Regulations 2007; the Company Names Adjudicator Rules 2007; the Companies (Registration) Regulations 2007; the Companies (Model Articles) Regulations 2007; and the Independent Supervisor Appointment Order 2007.

[169] On 2 November 2006, in the House of Lords, Lord Sainsbury made a statement to the Lords explaining when the provisions of the Act would come into force. The Government intended to publish further consultation papers as to the implementation of the Act for existing companies for 2008 including transitional provisions. The Government would implement the provisions on company communications to shareholders and others in January 2007. This would include provisions facilitating electronic communication. These provisions were being implemented before other implementation provisions as they would bring considerable savings to businesses with significant and tangible benefits. The Government would consult in February 2008 on its detailed implementation plans. Its intention was to commence all parts of the Act by October 2008. The Government would continue to work with stakeholders in implementing the Act. It would also work with the business community to ensure widespread and effective communication of the Act's provisions, so that all parties fully understood the new provisions and were in a position to take advantage of the benefits. According to Lord Sainsbury, all the company law provisions in the Companies Acts 1985, 1989 and 2005 had been brought into the Act, other than the self-standing provisions on community enterprise companies and the provisions on investigations, which go wider than companies. The non-company parts of those Acts that would remain related to some Scots law provisions, which were now devolved to and have been replaced by the Scottish Parliament; provisions about the Financial Reporting Council and the operation of that body and its subsidiaries, but not about how companies generally conduct themselves; and provisions about assisting overseas regulatory authorities in relation to financial markets, the Financial Reporting Review Panel and insolvency, all of which related more to financial services rather than company law. The CA 2006 is the primary legislation that will apply to companies directly once all the provisions come into force. However, a number of provisions will need to be set out in secondary legislation –

Implementation Dates for the Companies Act 2006

2.12 This is the timetable for implementation of the CA 2006.

2006	
Date	
8 November	Companies Bill received Royal Assent and became the Companies Act 2006. The following provisions came into force on 8 November 2006:[170] • Part 43 of the CA 2006 (transparency obligations and related matters), except the amendment in para 11(2) of Schedule 15 of the definition of 'regulated market' in Part 6 of the Financial Services and Markets Act 2000 (c 8);[171] • Part 44 of the CA 2006 (miscellaneous provisions), namely, s 1274 CA 2006 (grants to bodies concerned with actuarial standards, etc.); and s 1276 CA 2006 (application of provisions to Scotland and Northern Ireland); • Part 46 of the CA 2006 (general supplementary provisions),[172] except s 1295 and Schedule 16 of the CA 2006 (repeals); and • Part 47 of the CA 2006 (final provisions).[173]
7 December	Companies Act published in electronic form (available at www.opsi.gov.uk).
21 December	Companies Act 2006 (Commencement No 1, Transitional Provisions and Savings) Order 2006 ((2006)/3428) laid before Parliament.
21 December	Companies (Registrar, Languages and Trading Disclosures) Regulations 2006 (2006/3429) laid before Parliament.
22 December	Implementation Briefing on First Commencement Order made available.
29 December	Companies admitted to the Official List, AIM and PLUS Markets required to announce total number of voting rights.

mainly in regulations or orders made by statutory instrument. There are a number of powers in the Act to make secondary legislation, not all of which the Government intends to exercise on commencement of the Act. Where powers in the CA 1985 have been restated in the CA 2006, work is ongoing to look at whether existing statutory instruments made under the 1985 Act should remain. See also written Ministerial Statement on implementation of various parts of the CA 2006 by Margaret Hodge, Minister for Industry and the Regions, HC Hansard, 28 Feb 2007.

[170] CA 2006, s 1300 (commencement). The other provisions of the CA 2006 will come into force on such day as may be appointed by order of the Secretary of State or the Treasury.

[171] Part 47 deals with Short Title; Extent; and Commencement: see CA 2006, ss 1298–1300.

[172] See CA 2006, ss 1265–1273.

[173] CA 2006, Part 46 deals with regulations and orders with particular reference to statutory instrument; negative resolution procedure; approval after being made; and supplementary issues. It also deals with definition of the term 'enactment' and consequential and transitional provisions. See CA 2006, ss 1288–1297.

2007	
Date	
1 January	Companies Act 2006 (Commencement No.1, Transitional Provisions and Savings) Order 2006 (2006/3428) came into force. This sets the 1 January, 20 January and 6 April implementation and repeal dates which are referred to below.[174]
	The Companies (Registrar, Languages and Trading Disclosures) Regulations 2006 (2006/3429) came into force. These Regulations implement provisions of the First Company Law Amendment Directive (EEC 2003/58/EC) relating to electronic communications with the Registrar of Companies and related matters. These Regulations also introduced additional disclosure requirements for websites and company order forms by amending ss 349 and 351 of the CA 1985.[175]
1 January	The following provisions of the Companies Act 2006 came into force on 1 January 2007:
	(a) s 1068(5) (registrar's duty to accept delivery by electronic means of documents subject to Directive disclosure requirements);
	(b) s 1077 (public notice of receipt of certain documents);
	(c) s 1078 (documents subject to Directive disclosure requirements);
	(d) s 1079 (effect of failure to give public notice);

[174] This was the first Commencement Order made under the CA 2006. Part 47 and certain provisions in Parts 43, 44 and 46 CA 2006 came into force on the passing of the CA 2006.

[175] These Regulations implement provisions of Directive 2003/58/EC of the European Parliament and Council of 15 July 2003 amending 65/151/EEC, as regards requirements in respect of certain types of companies (O.J. L221, 4.9.2003, p.13). They do so amending the Companies Act 1985 and the Companies (Northern Ireland) Order 1986 so far as not yet repealed by the Companies Act 2006, and by supplementing provisions of the Companies Act 2006 brought into force on the same date as these Regulations. Regulation 2 applies when the registrar of companies provide a copy in electronic form of material on the registrar to a person requesting that the copy be certified as a true copy. The registrar's certificate must be certified by an electronic signature which is uniquely linked to the registrar by means under his sole control and which is linked to the certificate and the copy in such a way that the subsequent changes are detectable. Regulation 3 amends the 1985 Act and the 1986 Order (except of limited liability partnerships) by no longer requiring the copies certain documents delivered to the registrar to be office copies (i.e, hard copies). The effect of regulation 4 is that when a contract for the allotment of shares paid up other than in cash is delivered to the registrar, it need not be in English but must be accompanied by a certified translation into English. Regulation 5 enables companies to deliver to the registrar any of the documents to which Council Directive 68/151/EEC (O.J. L65, 14.3.1968, p.8) applies (listed in section 1078 CA 2006) in any of the official languages of the European Union if accompanied by a certifies translation into English. Regulations 6 and 7 and Schedules 1 and 2 amend the 1985 Act, the 1986 Order, the Insolvency Act 1986 and the Insolvency (Northern Ireland) Order 1989 so as to include websites and documents in electronic form in provisions requiring the company's name, registered number, registered office and other particulars, and the fact that the company is being wound up (where that is so), to appear on correspondence, publications and other documents.

(e)   s 1080 (the register);

(f)   ss 1085–1092 (inspection etc of the register);

(g)   ss 1102–1107 (language requirements: translation); and

(h)   s 1111 (registrar's requirements as to certification or verification).

The following provisions of the Companies Act 2006 came into force on 1 January 2007 so far as necessary for the purposes of the provisions mentioned above:

(a)   s 2 (the Companies Acts);

(b)   s 1068(1)–(4), (6) and (7) (registrar's requirements as to form, authentication and manner of delivery);

(c)   s 1114 (application of provisions about documents and delivery);

(d)   section 1117 (registrar's rules);

(e)   s 1120 (application of provisions to overseas companies);

(f)   s 1168 (hard copy and electronic form and related expressions);

(g)   in s 1173 (minor definitions: general), the definitions of 'Gazette' and 'working day'; and

(h)   s 1284 (extension of Companies Acts to Northern Ireland).

20 January

The following provisions of the Companies Act 2006 came into force on 20 January 2007:

(a)   ss 308 (manner in which notice to be given) and 309 (publication of notice of meeting on website);

(b)   s 333 (sending documents relating to meetings, etc. in electronic form);

(c)   s 463 (liability for false or misleading statements in reports);

(d)   ss 791–810, 811(1)–(3), 813 and 815–828 (information about interests in a company's shares); and

(e)   ss 1143–1148 and Schedules 4 and 5 (the company communications provisions).

The following provisions of the Companies Act 2006 came into force on 20 January 2007 so far as necessary for the purposes of the provisions mentioned above:

(a)   section 2 (the Companies Acts):

(b)   ss 1121, 1122, 1125–1131 and 1133 (provisions relating to offences);

(c)   s 1168 (hard copy and electronic form and related expressions);

(d)   in s 1173 (minor definitions: general), the definition of 'working day'; and

(e)   s 1284 (extension of Companies Acts to Northern Ireland).

The provisions of the Companies Act 2006, so far as not brought into force by s 1300 (1) of that Act or article 2 or the preceding provisions of this article, came into force on 20 January 2007 for the purpose of enabling the exercise of powers to make orders or regulations by statutory instrument.

6 April	The following provisions of the Companies Act 2006 came into force on 6 April 2007:

(a)   s 1063 (fees payable to registrar), so far as not in force by virtue of article 3(3);

(b)   s 1176 (power of Secretary of State to bring civil proceedings on company's behalf);

(c)   s 1177 (repeal of certain provisions about company directors);

(d)   s 1178 (repeal of requirement that certain companies publish periodical statement);

(e)   s 1179 (repeal of requirement that Secretary of State prepare annual report); and

(f)   s 1281 (disclosure of information under the Enterprise Act 2002).

Section 1,295 of, and Schedule 16 to, the Companies Act 2006 (repeals) came into force on 6 April 2007 so far as relating to the repeal of:

(a)   the provisions of the 1986 Order corresponding to the provisions of the 1985 Act repealed by the provisions mentioned in para (1)(b)–(e);

(b)   s 41 of the 1985 Act and Article 51 of the 1986 Order (authentication of documents on behalf of company); and

(c)   ss 293 and 294 of the 1985 Act and Articles 301 and 302 of the 1986 Order (age limits for directors).

The following provisions of the Companies Act 2006 came into force on 6 April 2007 so far as necessary for the purposes of the provisions mentioned above:

(a)   s 1060 (the registrar of companies);

(b)   s 1061 (the registrar's functions); and

(c)   s 1284 (extension of Companies Acts to Northern Ireland).

The coming into force of s 1063 by virtue of para (1)(a) does not extend to Northern Ireland.

The following provisions of the Companies Act 2006 came into force on 6 April 2007:

(a)   s 2 (the Companies Acts);

(b)   ss 942–992 and Schedule 2 (takeovers, etc.);

(c)   section 1043 (unregistered companies);

(d)   section 1170 (meaning of 'EEA State' and related expressions); and

(e)   section 1284(1) (extension of Companies Acts to Northern Ireland) so far as it relates to:
    (i)   the provisions mentioned in sub-paras (a), (b) and (c) above, and
    (ii)   Part 2 of the 2004 Act (community interest companies).

The following provisions of the Companies Act 2006 came into force on 6 April 2007 so far as necessary for the purposes of the provisions mentioned above:

(a)   s 546 (issued and allotted share capital);

(b)   s 558 (when shares are allotted);

	(c) ss 1121–1123 and 1125–1133 (provisions relating to offences);
	(d) ss 1134, 1135 and 1138 (company records);
	(e) s 1139 (service of documents on a company);
	(f) s 1140 (service of documents on directors, secretaries and others);
	(g) s 1168 (hard copy and electronic form and related expressions); and
	(h) in s 1173 (minor definitions: general), the definitions of 'body corporate', 'the Gazette' and 'regulated market'.
July	A draft of the Companies Act 2006 (Commencement No 3, Consequential Amendments, Transitional Provisions and Savings) Order 2007, was laid before Parliament under ss 1290 and 1294(6) of the CA 2006 for approval by resolution of each House of Parliament. This Order is now in force (S.I. 207 No 2194).
1 October	The following provisions of the Companies Act 2006 came into force on 1 October 2007:
	(a) ss 29 and 30 (resolutions and agreements affecting a company's constitution);
	(b) ss 116–119 (inspection of register of members);
	(c) ss 145–153 (exercise of members' rights);
	(d) in Part 10 (a company's directors): s 154 (companies required to have directors); s 160 (appointment of directors of public company to be voted on individually); s 161 (validity of acts of directors); ss 168 and 169 (removal of directors); ss 170–181 (general duties of directors), except ss 175–177 (duty to avoid conflicts of interest, duty not to accept benefits from third parties and duty to declare interest in proposed transaction or arrangement); ss 188–226 (transactions with directors requiring approval of members); ss 227–230 (directors' service contracts); s 231 (contract with sole member who is also a director); ss 232–239 (directors' liabilities); ss 247–259 (supplementary provisions);
	(e) ss 260–269 (derivative claims and proceedings by members);
	(f) in Part 13 (resolutions and meetings): ss 281–287 (general provisions about resolutions); ss 288–300 (written resolutions); ss 301–307, 310–326, 327(1), (2)(a) and (b) and (3), 328, 329, 330(1)–(5), (6)(a) and (b) and (7), 331, 332, 334 and 335 (resolutions at meetings); ss 336–340 (public companies: additional requirements for AGMs); ss 341–354 (additional requirements for quoted companies); ss 355–359 (records of resolutions and meetings); ss 360 and 361 (supplementary provisions);
	(g) s 417 (contents of directors' report: business review);
	(h) ss 485–488 (appointment of auditors of private companies);
	(i) s 993 (fraudulent trading);

(j)   ss 994–999 (protection of members against unfair prejudice);

(k)   ss 1035–1039 and 1124 and Schedule 3 (company investigations: amendments);

(l)   ss 1121–1123 and 1125–1133 (general supplementary provisions relating to offences), as they apply to offences under Part 14 or 15 of the 1985 Act.

Sections 362–379 of the Companies Act 2006 (control of political donations and expenditure), with the exception of the provisions specified in article 5 of this Order (which relate to independent election candidates), came into force in Great Britain on 1 October 2007.

The following provisions of the Companies Act 2006 came into force on 1 October 2007 so far as necessary for the purposes of the provisions mentioned above:

(a)   s 17 (a company's constitution);

(b)   s 385 (quoted and unquoted companies);

(c)   s 540(1) and (4) (shares);

(d)   s 545 (companies having a share capital);

(e)   s 546 (issued and allotted share capital);

(f)   s 548 (equity share capital);

(g)   s 629 (classes of shares);

(h)   ss 1121, 1122, 1125 and 1127–1133 (provisions relating to offences); (i) s 1158 (meaning of 'UK-registered company'); (k) in section 'corporation'), 'firm' and 'working day'. (j) ss 1168 (hard copy and electronic form and related expressions); and 1173 (minor definitions: general), the definitions of body corporate;

Section 1284 of the Companies Act 2006 (Extension of Companies Acts to Northern Ireland) came into force on 1 October 2007 so far as necessary for the purposes of the provisions mentioned in para (1)(a)–(j).

1 November	Ss 362–379 of the Companies Act 2006 (control of political donations and expenditure), with the exception of the provisions specified in article 5 of this Order (which relate to independent election candidates), came into force in Northern Ireland on 1 November 2007. The following provisions of the Companies Act 2006 came into force on 1 November 2007 so far as necessary for the purposes of the provisions mentioned in para (I) (a) s 546 (issued and allotted share capital); (b) s 1158 (meaning of 'UK-registered company'); (c) in s 1173 (minor definitions: general), the definition of 'body corporate'; and (d) s 1284 (extension of Companies Acts to Northern Ireland).
15 December	Section 1068 of the Companies Act 2006 (registrar's requirements as to form, authentication and manner of delivery), other than subsection (5), (which is already wholly in force (a)), comes into force on 15 December 2007 so far as necessary for the purposes of any regulations made before that date in implementation of

> Directive 2005/56/EC of the European Parliament and of the
> Council of 26 October 2005 on cross-border mergers of limited
> liability companies.
>
> The following provisions of the Companies Act 2006 come into
> force on 15 December 2007 so far as necessary for the purposes of
> the provisions mentioned above:
>
> (a) s 1168 (hard copy and electronic form and related
>   expressions); and
> (b) s 1284 (extension of Companies Acts to Northern Ireland).

2008	
1 October	The following provisions of the Companies Act 2006 (which have the effect of applying the provisions about control of political donations and expenditure to independent election candidates) come into force on 1 October 2008:
	(a) in s 362(a), the words 'and to independent election candidates';
	(b) in s 363(2)(a), the words 'or an independent election candidate to whom';
	(c) s 363(3);
	(d) in s 363(4), the words 'or independent election candidate' and 'independent candidate';
	(e) s 364(3);
	(f) in s 365(1)(a) and (b)(i), the words 'or an independent election candidate';
	(g) in s 366(1)(a), the words 'or to an independent election candidate';
	(h) in s 367(3)(a), the words 'or independent election candidates';
	(i) in s 387(2), the words 'or to an independent election candidate'.
	Section 1284 of the Companies Act 2006 (extension of Companies Acts to Northern Ireland) comes into force on 1 October 2008 so far as necessary for the purposes of the provisions mentioned above.

Note:
Certain provisions have been put back until 1 October 2009 (see Written Statement by the
Government dated 13 December 2007). They include: (i) general introductory provisions (ss 1–6);
(ii) company formation (ss 7–16); (iii) company's constitution (ss 17–38); (iv) company's name (ss
53–85); (v) company's registered office (ss 86–88); (vi) re-registration as a means of altering a
company's status (ss 89–111); (viii) company's members (ss 112–144); (ix) company's share capital
(ss 540–657); (x) acquisition by limited company's of its own shares (ss 658–737); (xi) company's
annual return (ss 854–859); (xii) company charges (ss 860–894); (xiii) dissolution and restoration
to register (ss 1000–1034); (xiv) UK companies not formed under the Companies Acts (ss
1040–1043); (xv) overseas companies (ss 1044–1059); (xvi) registrar of companies (ss 1060–1120);
(xvii) company directors: foreign disqualification (ss 1182–1191); (xiii) business names (ss
1192–1208). The revised timetable is set out in the Companion Guide at www.berr.gov.uk/files/
file42238.doc.

Tables of Destinations and Origins

2.13 Annex A on the Companion Website sets out the Commencement Timetable issued by Margaret Hodge, on 28 February 2006. Annex B sets out the Table of Destinations, and Annex C sets out the Table of Origins. The Companion Website can be found at http://www.routledge-cavendish.com/textbooks/9780415421072.

Highlights of the Companies Act 2006

2.14 The highlights to the CA 2006 are considered by reference to a summary of Parts 1–47, including two guidance notes issued by the DTI on the application of the CA 2006 to private companies.

Part 1

This is concerned with general introduction provisions, and sets out the types of companies that may be established with particular reference to limited and unlimited companies; private and public companies; companies limited by guarantee and having share capital; and community interest companies. The purpose of this Part is also to set out the definitions of a 'company' and the 'Companies Acts'.[176]

Part 2

Part 2 concerns company formation. It sets out the procedure of forming a company. In particular, it addresses the function of the Memorandum of Association. It will be noted that the Memorandum of Association no longer forms part of a company's constitution: it serves a very limited purpose.

This Part sets out new provisions on requirements for registration, including registration of documents; statement of capital and initial shareholdings; statement of guarantee; statement of proposed officers; and statement of compliance. Part 2 also considers the registration procedure, including the issue of certificate of incorporation and the effect of registration.

Part 3

This Part deals with a company's constitution with a definition as to what constitutes a company's constitution (with a wider meaning provided under s 257 of the CA 2006 in respect of Part 10 of the CA the CA 2006 concerning directors). Part 2 proceeds to consider a company's Articles of Association, which now have an elevated status under the CA 2006. It considers the power

---

[176] See further Chapter 3.

of the Secretary of State to prescribe model articles; and default application of model articles. There are provisions dealing with amendment to the articles; entrenchment provisions of the articles; notice to registrar of existence of restriction on amendment of articles; the effect of alteration of articles on the company's members; the requirement to send the registrar a copy of amended articles; and registrar's notice to comply in case of failure with respect to amended articles.

Part 3 also considers resolutions and agreements affecting a company's constitution; and the requirement for copies of resolutions or agreements to be forwarded to the registrar. This Part introduces new provisions on a statement of company's objects, thereby allowing companies the freedom to engage in commercial dealings without any restrictions. There are other provisions with respect to a company's constitution, including the constitutional documents to be provided to members and the effect of a company's constitution.[177]

Part 4

Part 4 is concerned with a company's capacity, and makes important changes in respect of provisions dealing with a company's capacity; the power of directors to bind the company; constitutional limitations in transactions involving directors or their associates; and constitutional limitations in respect of companies that are charities.

This Part also considers the formalities of doing business under the law of England and Wales or Northern Ireland, with particular reference to company contracts; execution of documents; common seal; execution of deeds; execution of deeds or other documents by attorney; execution of documents by companies; official seal for use abroad; official seal for share certificates; pre-incorporation contracts, deeds and obligations; and Bills of exchange and promissory notes.[178]

Part 5

This Part introduces significant changes to provisions on a company's name. It considers prohibited names; names suggesting connection with government or public authority; other sensitive words or expressions; duty to seek comments of government department or other specified body; and permitted characters.

Part 5 deals with indications of company type or legal form with particular reference to public and private companies and exemptions available.

This Part addresses provisions dealing with similarity to other names with

---

[177] See further Chapter 4.   [178] See further Chapter 4.

respect to name on the registrar's index, or in respect of which a person has goodwill. This Part introduces 'company name adjudicators' and sets out the procedural rules on the governance of the company names adjudicators, including their decisions being made public.

Part 5 sets out other powers of the Secretary of State with reference to the provision of misleading information, as well as misleading indication of activities. There are also provisions dealing with change of name, the procedures involved, and the effect of registration. Part 5 also addresses trading disclosures dealing with the requirement to disclose a company name, including the civil and criminal consequences of failure to make required disclosures.[179]

Part 6

This is a short Part setting out requirements for a company's registered office, change of address and has particular reference to Welsh companies.[180]

Part 7

Part 7 addresses the procedure of re-registration as a means of altering a company's status. It deals with various types of re-registrations, including a private company becoming public; a public company becoming private; a private limited company becoming unlimited; an unlimited private company becoming limited; and a public company becoming private and limited.[181]

Part 8

This Part is concerned with a company's members. It sets out who are members of a company and sets out provisions dealing with register of members, including rights to inspect and require copies and offences for failure to comply.

Part 8 also makes provision for special cases with reference to share warrants, single member companies, and a company holding its own shares as treasury shares. It also addresses the power of the court to rectify the register and time limits for claims arising from entry in register.

Part 8 addresses overseas branch registers and the procedures involved.

There are also provisions concerned with a prohibition on a subsidiary being a member of its holding company.[182]

---

[179] See further Chapter 6.   [180] See further Chapter 3.   [181] See further Chapter 5.
[182] See further Chapter 7.

Part 9

Part 9 concerns exercise of members' rights. It addresses the effect of provisions in a company's Articles of Association as to enjoyment or exercise of members' rights. It also sets out information rights; and the exercise of rights where shares are held on behalf of others.[183]

Part 10

Part 10 contains some of the most important provisions in the CA 2006. It concerns a company's directors. It deals with the requirement to have directors, including the procedure for appointment of a director with minimum age for appointment; existing under-age directors; and the validity of acts of directors. This Part makes provision for the register of directors, with the particulars of directors to be registered and the duty to notify the registrar of changes.

This Part considers the procedure for removal of a director and a director's right to protest against removal.

Part 10 codifies directors' general duties with particular reference to the duty to act within powers; the duty to promote the success of the company; the duty to exercise independent judgment; duty to exercise reasonable care, skill and diligence; the duty to avoid conflicts of interest; the duty not to accept benefits from third parties; and the duty to declare interest in proposed transactions or arrangements. It considers the civil consequences of breach of general duties; and particular circumstances of consent, approval or authorisation by members.

This Part considers declaration of interests in existing transactions or arrangements and creates an offence of the failure to declare an interest; it deals with cases of declaration of interest for a company with a sole director, and declarations of interest in existing transactions by a shadow director.

Part 10 also addresses transactions with directors requiring the approval of members. The main transactions highlighted are service contracts; substantial property transactions; loans, quasi loans and credit transactions; and payments for loss of office.

This Part addresses directors' service contracts with new provisions on length-of-service contracts that require approval from shareholders. There are also provisions dealing with contracts with sole members who are directors.

Part 10 addresses directors' liabilities, with provisions protecting directors from liability and ratification of acts of directors.

There are also new provisions concerning directors' residential addresses, and protection from disclosure, replacing the confidentiality orders under the CA 1985.

---

[183] See further Chapter 7.

Part 10 also makes supplementary provisions that include provision for employees on cessation or transfer of business; records of meetings of directors; and definitions of director, shadow director and related offices.[184]

Part 11

Part 11 concerns new provisions on derivative claims and proceedings by members in England and Wales or Northern Ireland and in Scotland. It considers the nature of derivative proceedings including procedural aspects.[185]

Part 12

This Part concerns company secretaries with particular reference to private secretaries and secretaries of public companies. There are also provisions that apply to both private companies with a secretary and to public companies.[186]

Part 13

Part 13 concerns resolutions and meetings with procedural aspects set out. There are general provisions about resolutions with reference to ordinary and special resolutions and voting aspects. This Part then addresses the aspect of written resolutions with a consideration of general provisions about written resolutions; circulation of written resolutions; and agreeing to written resolutions.

Part 13 also addresses resolutions at meetings with general provisions about resolutions at meetings; calling meetings; notice of meetings; members' statements; procedure at meetings; proxies; adjourned meetings; electronic communications; and applications to class meetings.

There are additional requirements for public companies in respect of requirements for AGMs; and additional requirements for quoted companies with respect to the website publication of poll results and independent report on poll.[187]

Part 13 also sets out provisions dealing with resolutions and meetings.

Part 14

Part 14 addresses the control of political donations and expenditure by companies. It considers the nature of donations or expenditure; the remedies in

---

[184] See further Chapters 8, 9 and 10.   [185] See further Chapter 25.
[186] See further Chapter 12.   [187] See Chapter 14.

case of unauthorised donations or expenditure; and exemptions applicable in certain circumstances.[188]

Part 15

This Part deals with accounts and reports. It sets out provisions for companies subject to the small companies regime and the regime governing quoted and unquoted companies.

Part 15 also considers accounting records, including offences for breach of the duty to keep accounting records.

This Part addresses a company's financial year and procedure for alteration of the financial year.

Part 15 also considers a company's annual accounts with provisions concerning individual accounts; group accounts (small companies); group accounts (other companies); and general provisions on group accounts; including certain information to be given in notes to the accounts.

Part 15 sets out provisions on directors' reports and setting out the contents of such reports. There are also provisions for quoted companies in respect of directors' remuneration reports. It also deals with publication of accounts and reports. There are provisions dealing with public companies: laying accounts and reports before general meeting; quoted companies: members' approval of directors' remuneration reports; the filing of accounts and reports; the revision of defective accounts and reports; and liability for false or misleading statements in reports.[189]

Part 16

Part 16 deals with audit. It addresses the requirement for audited accounts; the appointment of auditors; functions of auditor; removal or resignation of auditors; and auditors' liability.[190]

Part 17

This Part sets out provisions governing a company's share capital. It addresses the aspect of shares and share capital of a company; allotment of shares; allotment of equity securities with reference to existing shareholders' right of pre-emption; payment for shares; share premiums; and in respect of public companies – the independent valuation of non-cash consideration.

Part 17 also addresses the issue of alteration of share capital with how share capital may be altered; the subdivision or consolidation of shares; and redenomination of share capital.

---

[188] See Chapter 33.   [189] See further Chapter 22.   [190] See further Chapter 23.

This Part sets out provisions on classes of shares and class rights, including the reduction of capital, with procedures for private and public companies.[191]

Part 18

This Part addresses acquisition by a limited company of its own shares. It sets out the general provisions, followed by provisions dealing with shares held by a company's nominee; and shares held by or for a public company.

Part 18 also considers financial assistance for purchase of a limited company's own shares, setting out the meaning of financial assistance; circumstances in which financial assistance is prohibited; and exceptions from the prohibition.

Part 18 addresses the issue of redeemable shares, with terms and manner of redemption as well as financing of redemption; the purchase of own shares with general provisions and reference to authority for purchase of own shares, authority for off-market purchase and authority for market purchase.

This Part also considers redemption or purchase by private company out of capital as well as treasury shares.[192]

Part 19

This is a short Part addressing provisions on debentures. It sets out the definition of a debenture, and provisions governing the register of debenture holders.[193]

Part 20

Part 20 sets out the differences between private and public companies. It addresses the prohibition of public offers by private companies; and the minimum share capital requirement for public companies.[194]

Part 21

Part 21 deals with the certification and transfer of securities. It considers share certificates and their issue on allotment of shares. There are provisions dealing with transfer of securities and provisions on share warrants.

This Part also deals with evidencing and transfer of title to securities without written instrument.[195]

---

[191] See further Chapter 15.   [192] See further Chapters 19 and 21.
[193] See further Chapter 20.   [194] See further Chapter 15.   [195] See further Chapter 16.

Part 22

This Part concerns information about interests in a company's shares. It considers notice requiring information about interests in shares; orders imposing restrictions on shares; powers of members to require a company to act; register of interests disclosed; and a definition of interest in shares.[196]

Part 23

This Part concerns distributions and defines the term 'distribution'. It sets out the general rules on distributions and the justification of distribution by reference to accounts, with supplementary provisions on accounting matters; distributions in kind; and the consequences of unlawful distribution.[197]

Part 24

This Part deals with a company's annual accounts. It is very short but sets out the duty to deliver annual returns, the contents of an annual return, and failure to deliver an annual return.[198]

Part 25

Part 25 considers a company charges in England and Wales or Northern Ireland, with the requirement to register company charges; charges in other jurisdictions; the register of charges; avoidance of certain charges; and the company's records and registers. Similar provisions are set out for Scotland.[199]

Part 26

This Part considers arrangements and reconstructions. It sets out provisions for meetings of creditors or members; the courts' sanctions for compromises or arrangements; and reconstructions and amalgamations.[200]

Part 27

Part 27 deals with mergers and divisions of public companies. It sets out detailed provisions on merger and requirements applicable to merger with exceptions.

This Part also sets out provisions on division with requirements to be complied with in case of division with exceptions.[201]

---

[196] See further Chapter 17.   [197] See further Chapter 18.   [198] See further Chapter 22.
[199] See further Chapter 21.   [200] See further Chapter 26.   [201] See further Chapter 27.

Part 28

This Part is concerned with takeovers. There are new provisions governing the Takeover Panel and its rules; its rulings and directions. The powers of the Panel are set out with reference to the power to require documents and information; the Panel's duty of co-operation; hearings and appeals; contravention of rules; and funding.

Part 28 also considers impediments to takeovers with reference to opting in and opting out. This Part makes provisions for the concepts of 'squeeze out' and 'sell out'.[202]

Part 29

This Part covers the offence of fraudulent trading.[203]

Part 30

Part 30 applies to protection of members against unfair prejudice. It sets out who may petition, and powers of the court to make orders if unfair prejudice is shown.[204]

Part 31

Part 31 deals with dissolution and restoration to the register. It deals with striking off and the registrar's power to strike off defunct companies, and voluntary striking off. This Part also deals with the property of dissolved company and property vesting as *bona vacantia*.

Part 31 also considers the issue of restoration to the register, with administrative restoration to the register and restoration to the register by the court.[205]

Part 32

This Part addresses company investigations and makes amendments to the CA 1985 with respect to power of Secretary of State to give directions to inspectors; the resignation, removal and replacement of inspectors; powers to obtain information from former inspectors; powers to require production of documents; and disqualification orders.[206]

---

[202] See further Chapter 28.   [203] See further Chapter 33.   [204] See further Chapter 7.
[205] See further Chapter 29.   [206] See further Chapter 33.

Part 33

This Part deals with provisions concerning UK companies not formed under the companies legislation and provisions for unregistered companies.[207]

Part 34

This Part applies to overseas companies and sets out details for registration of particulars and other requirements concerning annual reports, trading disclosures and company charges, including offences.[208]

Part 35

This Part concerns the registrar of companies. It sets out the provisions applicable to the registrar with functions, the registrar's official seal and fees payable to registrar.

This Part also addresses certificates of incorporation; registered numbers; delivery of documents to the registrar; requirements for property delivery; public notice of receipt of certain documents; the register; inspection of the register; correction or removal of material on the register; the registrar's index of company names; language requirements with respect to translation and transliteration.[209]

Part 36

This Part deals with offences under the Companies Acts. It addresses the liability of an officer in default; liability of the company as officer in default; and application to bodies other than companies.[210]

Part 37

This Part contains supplementary guidelines for companies setting out provisions for company records; service addresses; sending or supplying documents or information; requirements as to independent valuation; and notice of the appointment of certain officers.[211]

Part 38

This Part contains interpretation of definitions used in the CA 2006.

---

[207] See further Chapter 3.　　[208] See further Chapter 3.　　[209] See further Chapter 13.
[210] See further Chapter 30.　　[211] See further Chapter 33.

Part 39

This Part concerns minor amendments.

Part 40

Part 40 applies to company directors with respect to foreign disqualification. It sets out the power to disqualify; the power to make persons liable for company debts; and the power to require statements to be sent to the registrar of companies.[212]

Part 41

This Part deals with business names and replaces the Business Names Act 1985. It addresses restricted or prohibited names; sensitive words or expressions; and misleading names.

Part 41 also concerns the disclosure required in case of individuals or partnerships, including the consequences of failure to make the required disclosure.[213]

Part 42

This Part deals with statutory auditors. It defines a statutory auditor. This Part addresses statutory auditors by reference to individuals or firms, including eligibility for appointment; the independence requirement; the effect of appointing a partnership; supervisory bodies; professional qualifications; information; and enforcement.

Part 42 also addresses the Auditors General with reference to eligibility for appointment; the conduct of audits; the Independent Supervisor; supervision of Auditors General; reporting requirements; information; enforcement; proceedings; and grants.

This Part considers the register of auditors and registered third-country auditors.[214]

Part 43

This Part addresses transparency obligations and related matters, with particular reference to the transparency directive.[215]

---

[212] See further Chapter 11.   [213] See further Chapter 6.   [214] See Chapter 24.
[215] See Chapter 31.

Part 44

This Part contains miscellaneous provisions dealing with the regulation of actuaries; information as to the exercise of voting rights by institutional investors; disclosure of information under the Enterprise Act 2002; expenses of winding up; and commonhold associations.[216]

Part 45

This Part contains provisions applying to Northern Ireland.

Part 46

This Part contains general supplementary provisions including regulations and orders; the meaning of 'enactment'; consequential and transitional provisions.

Part 47

Part 47 contains the final provisions on the CA 2006 including short title, extent and commencement.

The Law Applicable to Private Companies under the CA 2006

2.15 In February 2007, the Department of Trade and Industry published two documents to assist private companies to better understand the new regime under the CA 2006 governing private companies. Company law in the UK had been updated to ensure it reflected modern conditions and reality. The first document was entitled *The Companies Act 2006 – a summary of what it means for private companies*; and the second document was entitled *Private Company Information*.

The Companies Act 2006 – a summary of what it means for private companies

2.16 This document sets out the new choices for private companies and the deregulation procedure that will make it easier for private companies to run smoothly and efficiently.

---

[216] See Chapter 33.

New choices: How decisions are taken by shareholders –
from October 2007

2.16.1 Written resolutions signed by shareholders are an alternative to call-ing meetings of shareholders, and it will be much more easier to use them. Written resolutions will no longer need to be signed by all the shareholders. Instead, the required majority will be similar to that for shareholder meetings – a simple majority of the eligible shares for ordinary resolutions, or 75 per cent for special resolutions.

Proposed written resolutions will no longer have to be notified to the aud-itors (and following other recent reforms, most small companies are no longer required to have auditors).

Decisions can be made more quickly – from January 2007

2.16.2 Companies can choose to make more use of electronic methods. Reso-lutions can be circulated by e-mail or by other electronic methods such as websites, with shareholder agreement. This will speed up the decision-making process, and means most small businesses will be able to make most shareholders' decisions more quickly, without the need for a general meeting.

Shareholder meetings can be streamlined – from October 2007

2.16.3 Private companies will no longer hold an annual general meeting. Shareholders can demand a meeting if at least 10 per cent (5 per cent in certain circumstances) wish to. Shareholders still have the right to receive accounts.

Shareholder meetings for private companies can now all be on a 14-day notice period, unless different arrangements are specified in a company's articles.

There will be choice over whether to have a company secretary –
from April 2008

2.16.4 Private companies will not have to appoint a company secretary unless they choose to do so. But if a company does decide to have one, the secretary will have the same authority and responsibilities as now, and will continue to be registered at Companies House.

A new option on filing directors' addresses – from October 2008

2.16.5 Directors will be required to file a service address on the public record at Companies House, which may, for example, be their company's address, rather than their private home address. A director's private address will be held as protected information at Companies House.

It will be simpler to reduce share capital – from October 2008

2.16.6 As an alternative to the current process requiring court approval, private companies can in future choose to reduce their capital by special resolution, supported by a solvency statement by each of the directors. As every small company will know, these simpler procedures are similar to those that apply currently when a company redeems or purchases its own shares out of capital.

Giving financial assistance for purchase of a private company's own shares is no longer prohibited – from October 2008

2.16.7 The previous statutory rule that companies cannot give financial assistance for the purchase of their own shares is to be abolished for private companies. Previously, private companies who wished to give such financial assistance had to comply with a 'whitewash' procedure. The new arrangements should make transactions easier.

Directors' conflicts of interest – from October 2008

2.16.8 Directors have always had a duty to avoid a situation in which they have an interest that conflicts or may conflict with the company's interests, unless the matter has been duly authorised. At the moment, only the shareholders can authorise such a conflict of interest. In future, in the case of existing companies, it will be possible for those directors who do not have an interest in the matter, to authorise it if this is specifically permitted by the company's articles. (In the case of new private companies incorporated on or after 1 October 2008, it will be possible for those directors who do not have an interest in the matter to authorise it, unless this is specifically prohibited by the company's articles.)

Forming a company – from October 2008

2.16.9 The Memorandum of Association will now become a historic document which, with various accompanying documents, will simply record the facts at the time of incorporation.

From October 2008, the articles rather than the memorandum will set out the principles covering the way the company conducts its business.

From October 2008, new companies registering under the CA 2006 will be able, if they wish, to take advantage of new default model Articles of Association for private companies. These will be set out in clearer language and reflect the way many small companies operate. Existing companies can also choose to adopt these new articles.

There will be no requirement in future, either in the Memorandum or the articles, for companies to state their objects. So companies need not be restricted in what they do: but they can choose to be restricted if they wish.

New or revised requirements
Electronic documents – from January 2007

2.16.10 Electronic communications, including e-mails and websites, will in future need to include the company's name, number, registered office and other particulars (as business letters are already required to do).

New accounting arrangements – from April 2008

2.16.11 The deadline for private companies to file annual accounts and reports will reduce from ten months to nine, reflecting increased use of new technology.

The exemption from preparing consolidated accounts by medium-sized groups has now been changed so as to apply only to small groups.

At least one person as a director – from October 2008

2.16.12 All companies must now have at least one actual person as a director and cannot just have companies acting as directors.

Child directors – from October 2008

2.16.13 A new minimum age of 16 is set for directors. Existing under-age directors will cease to be directors from October 2008.

Confirmation of existing responsibilities – directors' duties

2.16.14 The general duties of directors have until now been developed in case law. In order to make the rules more accessible, the CA 2006 confirms the existing case law by stating that the duty of directors is to act in a way that they consider most likely to promote the success of the company for the benefit of its shareholders as a whole and that, in doing so, they will need to have regard where appropriate to long-term factors, the interests of other stakeholders and the community, and the company's reputation.

Private Company Information

2.17 The DTI published another document in respect of private company information under the CA 2006. The document is intended to point out those changes to the previous law which are likely to be of most significance to the generality of private companies.

Memorandum of Association

2.17.1 Under the CA 2006, the role of the Memorandum of Association is greatly reduced for both existing companies and new companies. In future it will contain only very limited information: the names of the subscribers; the fact that they wish to form a company; and that they agree to become members of the company and, if the company has share capital, take at least one share in the company each. It will be primarily an historical record rather than one affecting the ongoing operation of the company. Information that was previously provided in the memorandum on formation will in future be provided to the registrar in the form of a series of statements made in the application for registration or in the articles. The formation provisions have been drafted with a view to supporting electronic incorporation, and it is envisaged that the required information could be provided to the registrar in the form of a series of data entries or alternatively in hard copy.

For existing companies (i.e. those existing before the Act comes into force), this means that any provisions contained in their memorandum which go beyond that limited information will, from October 2008, be regarded as provisions of their Articles of Association.

Objects

2.17.2 The memorandum used to contain the company's objects. For new companies, this will not be necessary, as the default position under the CA 2006 is that a company's objects are unrestricted (s 31(1) of the CA 2006). Existing companies may wish to take advantage of this change by resolving to remove a statement of objects from their articles that were previously in the memorandum. Companies should note that they would be required to give notice of such a change to the registrar.

Shares

2.17.3 The previous style of memorandum also set out the company's authorised share capital or, if it was a guaranteed company, the terms of the guarantee. From October 2008, new companies will not be required to specify their authorised share capital. Instead, they will need to deposit an initial statement of capital or, as appropriate, a statement of guarantee when incorporating. This will then need to be updated by the company when appropriate, for example, when new shares are issued.

Shares will still be required to have a nominal value.

Although authorised share capital has been abolished for new companies, for existing companies it will continue to operate as a restriction in the articles. It will act as a ceiling on the number of shares that can be allotted. Existing companies will need to amend their articles to abolish reference to authorised share capital if they want to allow the company to allot shares beyond that ceiling.

Most private companies have only one class of share. In these companies, directors will be able to allot further shares of that class, subject to any rights of pre-emption in either the articles or the CA 2006 (and subject to any ceiling set out as in the previous paragraph), without prior authorisation from the members, as is currently required. This new power is subject to provision in the articles: a company may need to amend its articles if it wants the power to apply. Alternatively it may wish to consider whether the articles should prohibit the directors' ability to allot shares without first getting the members' approval, or whether it wants to place some other restriction on the directors' allotment powers.

The pre-emption rights conferred by the CA 2006 may be disapplied either in the articles or by special resolution, namely s 569(1), so some companies may wish to consider amending their articles to permit this.

In private companies with more than one class of share, or where private companies wish to allot shares of a new class, the directors will require authorisation for allotting shares by an ordinary resolution of the members. Such authorisation can be general or in relation to a specific allotment, and can only be for a maximum of five years. This is a change from the present rule, as private companies can currently give authorisation for an indefinite period.

The previous statutory rule that companies cannot give financial assistance for the purchase of their own shares has been abolished for private companies. Previously, private companies who wished to give such financial assistance had to comply with a 'white-wash' procedure.

Private companies may in future reduce their capital by passing a special resolution, coupled with a statement by each of the directors that the company is solvent. Previously a reduction of capital required the approval of the court. The new procedure is subject to any provision in the articles restricting or prohibiting reduction of capital. These procedures are similar to those that apply to other ways of achieving reductions of capital, such as the redemption or purchase by the company of its own shares out of capital.

Model articles

2.17.4 Model articles (which were set out in Table A under the old arrangements) will continue to be prescribed. The Secretary of State will now prescribe different sets of model articles for the most common types of company: private companies limited by shares; private companies limited by guarantee; and public companies.

Model articles are 'default' in the sense that they apply where the company either has not provided for its own articles, or where its articles do not cover a particular subject. As before, companies can exclude some or all of the model articles. The new model articles for private companies will eliminate much of the complex regulation that used to be contained in Table A but is not relevant to small companies.

Existing companies will still be subject to the model articles that were in force at the time the company was registered, unless a company has subsequently chosen to make different arrangements. However, existing companies can adopt the new model articles instead if they wish, by members passing an appropriate special resolution. New companies registering from 1 October 2008 will have the new model articles as a default, unless they choose to register different articles.

Entrenchment of articles

2.17.5 Provisions of the articles can now be entrenched. Articles can say that certain of their provisions can only be amended or altered if specific conditions are met or procedures followed. Existing companies may wish to take advantage of this new provision by amending their articles.

Directors: minimum requirements

2.17.6 Under the CA 2006, all companies must have at least one natural person as a director, so a company cannot be the sole director of another company. If a company's only director is a company, it will need to appoint a natural person.

A new minimum age of 16 is set for directors. In future if the company appoints a younger person as a director his appointment will be void. Existing under-age directors will cease to be directors from 1 October 2008.

Directors: other changes

2.17.7 Companies are no longer required to maintain a register of dealings in their shares by directors and their spouses, civil partners or children. Directors in future will not be required to provide details of their other directorships.

Directors' general duties

2.17.8 Directors' general duties to their companies are, for the first time, comprehensively set out in the CA 2006. The general duties of directors have been developed until now in case law. In order to make the rules more accessible, the CA 2006 confirms existing case law by stating that the primary duty of directors is to act in a way that they consider most likely to promote the success of the company for the benefit of its shareholders as a whole and that, in doing so, they will need to have regard where appropriate to long-term factors, the interests of other stakeholders and the community, and the company's reputation. While the Act generally codifies the case-law position, there are two major changes.

Firstly, the CA 2006 says that a director proposing to enter into a transaction with the company need only disclose his interest to the board, rather than seek the approval of shareholders. Companies are able to make provision on these lines in their articles, and this is what the majority of companies have done. Secondly, in future non-conflicted directors of private companies can authorise what would otherwise be a director's conflict of interest (other than transactions with the company itself), rather than refer it to shareholders for approval as previously, so long as nothing in the articles invalidates this. However, if a conflict is already permitted by articles then this will continue to be the case: see s 180(4)(b).

Loans, quasi loans and credit transactions to or in favour of directors (ss 197–214 of the CA 2006) are no longer prohibited, but are now subject to member approval if there is adequate disclosure and the criminal offence has been repealed.

Ratification of breaches (s 239 of the CA 2006): negligence, default, breach of duty and breach of trust by directors continue to be ratifiable by the members. In future, for an effective ratification a company will need to disregard the votes of the director in default and any person connected with him. This does not affect the unanimous consent rule, so if all the members are defaulting directors and/or connected persons and they all vote to ratify the default, then that vote is effective. However, directors and shareholders still cannot ratify certain breaches, for example those that impact on creditors.

Directors' addresses

2.17.9 Every company continues to be required to keep a register of directors. However, in order to protect directors as appropriate, the CA 2006 now provides that the register should contain service addresses for the directors rather than requiring details of their residential address. The service address can, for example, be a residential address or stated simply as 'the company's registered office'.

The company must also keep a separate register of the directors' residential addresses. Both the service and the residential address (or the fact that the service address is the residential address) will need to be supplied to the Registrar of Companies. However, the residential address (or the fact that the service address is the residential address) will generally remain confidential to the company, the Registrar and certain specified public bodies and credit reference agencies. It will therefore be withheld from the public register. However, there may be certain circumstances where the residential address has to be disclosed, such as if communications from the registrar remain unanswered or communications are not coming to the director's attention.

Company secretary

2.17.10 Private companies will, from 6 April 2008, no longer be obliged to have a company secretary, although they may continue to have one if they wish. If they no longer wish to have a secretary they need do nothing, apart from the secretary resigning or his or her appointment being terminated. The CA 2006 says that a director or person authorised by the directors can do anything required to be done by or to the secretary (see s 274(b) of the CA 2006). If a private company does continue to have, or appoints, a secretary then s/he will have the same status as previously.

Executing documents

2.17.11 Affixing a common seal is relatively rare now. Apart from that, documents such as contracts can, as previously, be executed by companies, either by the signatures of two directors, or by the signatures of one director and the secretary if there is one. Documents can also be signed by just one director, so long as s/he signs in the presence of a witness.

Company names: change

2.17.12 A company can now set its own procedure in its articles for changing its name (s 791). Existing companies may wish to amend their articles to allow this.

Company names: objection

2.17.13 Anyone may now object to a company's name if it either interferes with a name in which they have goodwill, or is so similar to such a name that it would suggest a link between them and the company which is misleading. If the objection is upheld the company may be directed to change its name (see generally s 69 of the CA 2006). However, a company can only be required to change its name if it cannot show any of the specified legitimate reasons for it to have the name, or if it can be shown to have chosen the name because of its value to someone else, with the intention of blocking its use by that person, or in effect, selling it.

Trading disclosures

2.17.14 The current requirement is for the company name to appear legibly on a sign outside all its business premises, including the registered office, and in all business communications. This includes (a) all business letters, (b) all notices and other official publications, (c) all websites, (d) all bills of exchange, promissory notes, endorsements, cheques, orders for money or goods purporting to be signed by or on behalf of the company, and (e) all bills of parcels, invoices, receipts, letters of credit. In addition, the company's business letters, order forms and websites have to include the company's place of registration, its registered number, and the address of its registered office. A company's name, number, registered office and other particulars, currently required to be displayed on business letters and other documents, must now also be provided on electronic documents, as well as on any company website or order form (see The Companies Act 2006: Registrar, Languages and Trading Disclosures Regulations 2006).

There is also a new provision permitting the Secretary of State to require companies to supply, on request, specified information to those they deal with in the course of their business (s 82(1)(c) of the CA 2006).

Register of members

2.17.15 The register of members continues to be open to the inspection of members without charge and any other person on payment of the requisite fee. However, requests for inspection must in future outline details about the person seeking the information, whether the information obtained will be disclosed to others, and what the purpose for the request is. If the company does not think it is a proper purpose, it may apply to the court for, and the court may grant, an order that the company need not comply with the request.

Communications

2.17.16 The CA 2006 makes it much easier for companies to communicate electronically, either by e-mail or another electronic form or through a website. The general principle is that companies should be able to communicate in hard copy or electronically. These provisions came into force in January 2007.

Hard copy documents or information sent to a company or by a company can continue to be in hard copy form, by sending the document by post or by hand to the relevant address.

Electronic documents or information can only be sent to or by a company electronically, if the company or recipient respectively has agreed generally that all documents/information will be sent electronically, or has agreed specifically in relation to a particular document/information. It should be noted that various provisions of the CA 2006 deem a company to have agreed to receiving documents/information electronically: for example, if a company gives an electronic address in any document containing or accompanying a written resolution, then it is regarded as having agreed that documents or information relating to it can be sent to the company electronically at that address unless it says otherwise.

The CA 2006 also allows companies to agree that information or documents are validly sent to it or by it in any way that the company agrees with the sender or recipient respectively, unless those provisions of the CA 2006 apply, which allow information to be supplied by companies only in particular ways.

Companies should therefore consider whether they wish to have agreements, especially general agreements with members, that communications can be received in certain ways, especially electronically.

The CA 2006 now allows a company to provide information to members on a website. This can only be done where the recipient has agreed to it being done that way. However, if the members generally agree that websites might be used for communication, or if there is such provision in the articles, then individual members will generally be regarded as having agreed, if they are asked for agreement and do not respond within 28 days. Companies may wish to consider proposing an appropriate resolution or change to the articles.

Every time new information is made available on the website, the company will need to inform the relevant members of this, either in hard copy or electronically. Companies wishing to the make best use of the provisions will probably wish to secure members' agreement to e-mail communication.

Shareholders will always be entitled to request hard copies of documents or information.

Resolutions and meetings

2.17.17 The CA 2006 abolishes the current obligation for private companies to hold annual general meetings. Companies will still be able to hold shareholder meetings if they wish to; and meetings can be instituted by the directors at any time, or by members representing 10 per cent of voting shares (5 per cent if it is more than 12 months since the members met). Companies may still need to hold a meeting in certain circumstances, since they will not be able to dismiss a director or an auditor before his term of office by written resolution (see s 288(2)(a) of the CA 2006).

The vast majority of decision-making in private companies is obviously carried out by the directors. However, the members or shareholders of the company also have a role in taking various decisions – such as the appointment of the directors, amending the articles, etc. In small companies, of course, the shareholders and directors will often be the same people. The CA 2006 therefore makes it easier to use written resolutions for decisions by shareholders, and is drafted on the basis that most decision-making by members in private companies will be by written resolution, rather than by calling meetings of shareholders.

In future, written resolutions can be proposed either by the directors or by members representing either 5 per cent of members eligible to vote or whatever lower percentage the company's articles provide. Articles can be amended to substitute a lower percentage.

Previously, written resolutions required unanimity. Now, the CA 2006 refers to two types of resolution: ordinary, which to be passed requires a simple majority of those eligible to vote; and special, which requires 75 per cent of those eligible to vote to be in favour. Written resolutions will no longer have to be notified to the auditors since, following other recent reforms, most small companies are no longer required to have auditors.

The CA 2006 does not override provisions in the articles that require a higher majority than the Act specifies for a particular action. So, if the CA 2006 requires only an ordinary resolution as it does in the majority of cases, but the articles require a special resolution or unanimity, then the provision in the articles will need to be complied with.

As from 1 October 2007, any provision in a company's articles that provides that a member voting by proxy will have fewer votes than if he votes in person, will be invalid. Where the company does decide to have meetings, the arrangements have not changed significantly. Since the AGM requirement has been abolished, private company meetings are now all on 14 days' notice unless the articles say otherwise. Now 90 per cent, rather than 95 per cent, of members can agree to hold a meeting on short notice (although the articles can specify a higher percentage up to but not exceeding 95 per cent).

Proxies

2.17.18 Shareholders can now appoint more than one proxy at a meeting, up to a maximum of one proxy per share. This right will override any conflicting provision in a company's articles.

Accounts, reports and audit

2.17.19 The time for private companies to file their accounts with the Registrar of Companies has been reduced from ten months to nine months from the year end. The medium-sized group exemption from preparing consolidated accounts has now been removed: in future only small groups will be so exempt.

In recognition of the abolition of the requirement for private companies to hold an AGM, they will now no longer be required to send out their annual accounts prior to a general meeting.

Instead, the annual accounts, or summary financial statements if appropriate, must be sent to members by the time they are due to be filed with the Registrar of Companies. Accounting provisions will be separately set out for small private companies under regulations to be made in 2008 (save for a few provisions common to all companies that will remain in the CA 2006).

Many small private companies are exempt from audit. Small private companies who do not take advantage of the audit exemption and so have audits will be affected by certain changes in the CA 2006. As there will no longer be a requirement for annual general meetings, an auditor will be deemed to be reappointed for the following year unless the company takes steps to end his appointment, or to appoint a different auditor. It will also now be possible for the company, by ordinary resolution, to choose to agree a limitation of the auditor's liability for a financial year.

Annual return

2.17.20 There is no change to current arrangements on the face of the CA 2006, but the regulations will provide for exemptions from the requirements for details of shareholders and their shareholding so that, in the case of private companies, shareholders' addresses are no longer required.

Chapter 3

Company Formation

Introduction

3.1 The objective of Part 1 of the CA 2006 is to set out general introductory provisions and to define the terms 'company' and the 'Companies Acts', which are used throughout the various provisions of the CA 2006.

Part 1 proceeds to define the companies that are covered under the Companies Acts and distinguishes between various types of companies, namely limited and unlimited companies; private and public companies; companies limited by guarantee and having share capital; and community interest companies. A distinction is also made between public and private companies. Part 1 comprises six sections.

Part 1 also defines the term 'Companies Acts', but it will be noted that although the term substantially consolidates a large part of previous companies legislation, there still remain some provisions in the CA 1985 and CA 1989 that have not been consolidated under the CA 2006.

Part 2 of the CA 2006 addresses company formation. It sets out the mechanism and process leading to a company's registration, including the new documents and statements that are required to be lodged at Companies House as part of the incorporation and registration process.

The provisions dealing with a company's registered office are considered in this chapter.

This chapter sets out provisions contained in Part 10 of the CA 2006 in connection with directors' residential addresses, and the procedure for directors to obtain a non-disclosure certificate under the circumstances set out in Part 10, either on formation of the company, or any time after formation.

This chapter also addresses the position of United Kingdom companies that are not formed under the companies legislation, but authorised to register under the CA 2006, including unregistered companies and overseas companies as they are referred to in Part 2 of the CA 2006.

These sections replace equivalent provisions in the CA 1985. The CA 2006 creates a single company law regime for the whole of the UK,[217] and, where a note on this or a subsequent Part of the CA 2006 describes a particular provision as restating a provision in the CA 1985, this should be read as applying equally to the corresponding provisions in the Companies (Northern Ireland) Order 1986.

Definition of 'Company'

3.2 Section 1 of the CA 2006 sets out the definition of 'company'[218] for the purposes of the Companies Acts.[219] Section 1(1) defines a 'company' as one that is formed and registered under the CA 2006, that is, either:

(a)   formed and registered after commencement of Part 1 of the CA 2006[220] – these will be the 'new' companies that are established under the CA 2006 regime; or

(b)   a company that immediately before the commencement of Part 1 of the CA 2006, was formed and registered under:

- the CA 1985 (c 6);or
- the Companies (Northern Ireland) Order 1986 (SI 1986/1032) (NI 6); or
- was an existing company[221] for the purposes of the CA 1985 or the Companies (Northern Ireland) Order.

These refer to 'existing' companies or companies that were established before Part 1 of the CA 2006 came into force.

A company formed under the CA 1985 or the Companies (Northern Ireland) Order 1986, or an 'existing' company for the purposes of the CA 1985 or the 1986 Order, is to be treated on commencement, as if it was formed and registered under the CA 2006. Therefore, the CA 2006 regime will apply to both the new companies formed under Part 1 of the CA 2006, and

---

[217] CA 2006, s 1299 ('Extent') provides that except as otherwise provided (or the context otherwise requires), the provisions of CA 2006 extend to the whole of the United Kingdom.

[218] Previously, under CA 1985, s 735(1)(a), the term 'company' was defined as a company formed and registered under the CA 1985, or an existing company.

[219] See CA 2006, s 2 on the definition of 'Companies Acts'.

[220] CA 2006, s 1(1)(a).

[221] Under CA 1985, s 735(1)(b), an 'existing company' was defined as a company formed and registered under the former Companies Acts, but it did not include a company registered under the Joint Stock Companies Acts, the Companies Act 1862 or the Companies (Consolidation) Act 1908 in what was then Ireland. Reference to the 'former Companies Acts' meant the Joint Stock Companies Acts, the Companies Act 1862, the Companies (Consolidation) Act 1908, the Companies Act 1929, and the Companies Acts 1948 to 1983: CA 1985, s 735(1)(c).

companies established prior to the commencement of Part 1 of the CA 2006.[222]

Under s 1(2) of the CA 2006, certain provisions of the Companies Acts also apply to other types of companies. They are:

(a) companies registered, but not formed under the CA 2006 (these are dealt with under Chapter 1 of Part 33 of the CA 2006 – these provisions refer to companies not formed under the companies legislation but authorised to register);[223] and

(b) bodies incorporated in the United Kingdom, but not registered under the CA 2006 (these are dealt with under Chapter 2 of Part 33 of the CA 2006 – these provisions refer to unregistered companies).[224]

Part 34 of the CA 2006 applies to companies incorporated outside the United Kingdom and known as 'overseas companies'.[225]

The effect of s 1 of the CA 2006 is to restate s 735(1) (a) and (b) of the CA 1985. It provides a definition of 'company', (which refers to companies formed and registered under the Companies Acts). It also provides other references to provisions in the CA 2006 that relate to companies that are registered, but not formed, under this Act, namely unregistered companies and overseas companies.

Section 1(2) of the CA 2006 refers to the recognition of other regimes for companies established under Chapter 1 of Part 33 of the CA 2006 (companies authorised to register under the companies legislation – ss 1040–1042 of the CA 2006), or Chapter 2 of Part 34 of the CA 2006 (unregistered companies – s 1043 of the CA 2006). Sections 1040–1042 of Part 33 of the CA 2006 deal with UK companies that are not formed under the companies legislation, but that are authorised to register under the CA 2006.

Definition of 'Companies Acts'

3.3 Section 2(1) of the CA 2006 defines the term 'Companies Acts' as comprising:

(a) the company law provisions of CA 2006.[226] The provisions of CA 2006 that apply are Parts 1–39 and Parts 45–46;[227]

(b) Part 2 of the Companies (Audit, Investigations and Community Enterprise) Act 2004 (c 27) (community interest companies);[228] and

---

[222] CA 2006, s 1(1)(b).   [223] CA 2006, s 1(2)(a).   [224] CA 2006, s 1(2)(b).
[225] CA 2006, s 1(3).   [226] CA 2006, s 2(1)(a).   [227] CA 2006, s 2(2)(a) and (b).
[228] CA 2006, s 2(1)(b).

(c)   the provisions of the CA 1985 (c 6) and the Companies Consolidation (Consequential Provisions) Act 1985 (c 9) that remain in force.[229]

Although it is a consolidation legislation, the CA 2006 does not replace all existing companies legislation – only parts of it. Section 2 of the CA 2006 highlights that any reference to 'Companies Acts' in the CA 2006 includes those provisions of the Acts listed in s 2(1)(c) of the CA 2006 that remain in force (as well as the company law provisions of the CA 2006, and Part 2 of the Companies (Audit, Investigations and Company Enterprise) (C(AICE) Act 2004).

Section 2 of the CA 2006 makes it clear that the CA 2006 is a substantial reform and restatement of the companies legislation. Prior to June 2006, the Government had intended that the Company Law Reform Bill (as it was then) should be read together with the CA 1985 and the CA 1989 and that there would not be any consolidation. However, in June 2006, the Government abandoned this approach, particularly as it was continuously emphasised by the Government and reinforced by the Company Law Review Group, that one of the objectives of company law review was to reform and modernise UK company law. Accordingly, during the latter part of 2006, the Company Law Reform Bill became the Companies Bill, which consolidated much of the previous companies legislation.

Types of company

3.4 The Company Law Review Group in its *Final Report* recommended that the law should provide for the relative ease of formation of new companies of each of the types that are currently available. This recommendation was accepted by the Government and included in the CA 2006, which retained all of the current forms of companies.

Limited and unlimited companies

3.4.1 Section 3 of the CA 2006 sets out the distinction between limited and unlimited companies. A company is a *limited company* if the liability of its members is limited by its constitution. A company may be limited by shares or limited by guarantee.[230]

A company *limited by shares* is a company whose shareholders have limited their liability to the amount, if any, unpaid on shares held by them.[231]

A company *limited by guarantee* is a company whose shareholders have limited their liability to such amount as they undertake to contribute to the company's assets in the event the company is wound up.[232]

[229] CA 2006, s 2(1)(c).   [230] CA 2006, s 3(1).   [231] CA 2006, s 3(2).
[232] CA 2006, s 3(3).

An *unlimited company* is a company that has no limit on the liability of its members.[233]

Section 3 of the CA 2006 replaces s 1(2)(a), (b) and (c) of the CA 1985. It is concerned with types of companies. It updates the Companies Acts definitions of 'limited company' and 'unlimited company' to reflect changes to what is to be included in a company's Memorandum of Association.[234] As under the CA 1985, a company may be limited by shares or by guarantee. Where there is no limit on the liability of the company's members, a company is an 'unlimited company'.

Private and public companies

3.4.2 Section 4 of the CA 2006 states that a *private company* is any company that is not a public company.[235]

A *public company* is a company limited by shares or by guarantee. Its certificate of incorporation must state that it is a public company.[236] To obtain this certificate, the company will need to comply with the provisions of the CA 2006 (or former Companies Acts) as regards registration or re-registration as a public company on or after the relevant date.[237] It must also have a share capital. There is a minimum share capital requirement (the 'authorised minimum'), which is currently set at £50,000 having remained unchanged under CA 2006.

Section 4 of the CA 2006 replaces s 1(3)[238] and s 735(2) of the CA 1985.[239] It sets out definitions of 'private company' and 'public company'.

Section 4(4) of the CA 2006 refers to Part 20 of the CA 2006 for the two major differences between private and public companies. Under Part 20, s 755 of the CA 2006 states that a private company may not offer securities to the public, or allot or agree to allot any securities of the company with a view to their being offered to the public, including consequences of contravention. Part 20 also sets out the minimum share capital requirements for public companies. Section 756 of the CA 2006 states that a company that is a public company (otherwise than by virtue of re-registration as a public company) must not do business or exercise any borrowing powers, unless the registrar has issued it with a trading certificate. The trading certificate will only be

[233] CA 2006, s 3(4).   [234] See CA 2006, s 8.   [235] CA 2006, s 4(1).

[236] CA 2006, s 4(2).

[237] The 'relevant date' is: (i) in relation to registration or re-registration in Great Britain, 22 December 1980; (ii) in relation to registration or re-registration in Northern Ireland, 1 July 1983: CA 2006, s 4 (3).

[238] CA 1985, s 1(3)(a), however, required the public company to state in its Memorandum of Association that it was a public company. The Memorandum of Association under the CA 2006 now has a different function.

[239] CA 1985, s 735(2) provided that the terms 'public company' and 'private company' have the meanings given by CA 1985, s 1(3).

issued if the registrar is satisfied that the nominal value of the company's allotted share capital is not less than the authorised minimum. Section 763 of the CA 2006 states that the authorised minimum amount is £50,000. There are penalties for conducting business without a trading certificate.[240]

Companies limited by guarantee and having a share capital

3.4.3 Section 5 of the CA 2006 states that a company can no longer be formed (or registered) as a company limited by guarantee and with share capital.[241] This provision has been in force in Great Britain since 22 December 1980, and in Northern Ireland since 1 July 1983.[242]

Any provision in the constitution of a company limited by guarantee, that purports to divide the company's undertaking into shares or interests, is a provision for share capital. This applies whether or not the nominal value or number of the shares or interests is specified by the provision.[243]

Section 5 of the CA 2006 replaces s 1(4) of the CA 1985.[244] This provision was originally introduced by s 1(2) of the CA 1980. Before the CA 1980, companies limited by guarantee could also have a share capital for other purposes, which could include providing votes to its shareholders. However, since 22 December 1980, a company limited by guarantee cannot be formed with a share capital.

Community interest companies

3.4.4 Section 6 of the CA 2006 provides that in accordance with Part 2 of the Companies (Audit, Investigations and Community Enterprise) Act 2004 (c 27), the following can become a community interest company: a company limited by shares or a company limited by guarantee and not having a share capital; or a company limited by guarantee and having a share capital.

The other provisions of the Companies Acts apply to a community interest company subject to Part 1 of the CA 2006.[245] The objective here is to highlight the fact that in some respects, the requirements imposed on community interest companies are different from the requirements imposed on other registered companies.

Section 6 of the CA 2006 on community interest companies is a new provision. The Companies (Audit, Investigations and Community Enterprise) Act 2004 (C(AICE)) came fully into force on 1 July 2005. Section 26 to Part 2 of that Act created a new company vehicle, known as the 'community interest

---

[240] See CA 2006, s 767.   [241] CA 2006, s 5 (1).   [242] CA 2006, s 5(2)(a) and (b).

[243] CA 2006, s 5 (3)

[244] CA 1985, s 1(4) provided that with effect from 22 December 1980, a company cannot be formed as, or become, a company limited by guarantee with a share capital.

[245] CA 2006, s 6(2).

company' or c.i.c. (if not a public company) or 'cwmni buddiant cymunedol', or c.b.c. (if to be registered in Wales); or 'community interest public limited company', or 'community interest plc' (if public company) or 'cwmni buddiant cymunedol cyhoeddus cyfyngedig', or 'cwmni buddiant cymunedol c.b.c.' (if registered in Wales). The community interest company is designed for use by social enterprises.[246]

[246] Part 2 of the Companies (Audit, Investigations and Community Enterprise) Act 2004 establishes a new type of company, the community interest company, for use by social enterprises wishing to operate as companies. This Part also establishes the Regulator of Community Interest Companies (the Regulator), whose role will be to maintain public confidence in the c.i.c. model. The c.i.c. is intended to be used primarily by non-profit-distributing enterprises providing benefit to a community. Such businesses are presently active in areas such as childcare, social housing, leisure and community transport. Many of them already incorporate as companies, either as a company limited by guarantee (CLG) or a company limited by shares (CLS). The special characteristics of the c.i.c. are intended to make it a particularly suitable vehicle for some types of social enterprise – essentially, those that wish to work for community benefit within the relative freedom of the non-charitable company form, but with an assurance of non-profit-distribution status. Companies that are formed as, or become, c.i.c.s will continue to be subject to the general framework of company law. In particular, c.i.c.s and directors of c.i.c.s will have to comply with their obligations and duties under the Companies Acts and the common law, as modified by this Act. The c.i.c. will be a new variant of existing forms of company. It can take the form of a CLG or CLS, and existing companies limited by guarantee with a share capital will also be able to become a c.i.c. C.i.c.s will be registered as companies with the registrar of companies in the usual way, and will be subject to the usual regulatory constraints and powers associated with company status, including the oversight of the Department of Trade and Industry's Companies Investigation Branch. The distinguishing features of the c.i.c. will be: (a) in order to become a c.i.c., a company will have to satisfy a community interest test, confirming that it will pursue purposes beneficial to the community and will not serve an unduly restricted group of beneficiaries. The test is whether a reasonable person might consider the c.i.c.'s activities to benefit the community – it is therefore wider and simpler than the charitable test of public benefit; (b) companies of a particular description may be excluded from c.i.c. status by regulations; it is anticipated that political parties, companies controlled by political parties, and political campaigning organisations will be excluded in this way; (c) c.i.c.s will not be able to have charitable status, even if their objects are entirely charitable. However, charities (and all other organisations except political parties) will be able to establish c.i.c.s as subsidiaries; (d) each c.i.c. will be required to produce an annual community interest company report containing key information relevant to c.i.c. status. The report will be placed on the public register of companies; (e) c.i.c.s will have an asset lock – that is, they will ordinarily be prohibited from distributing any profits they make to their members; (f) however, it is intended that regulations will allow c.i.c.s that are limited by shares to issue dividend-paying 'investor shares'. The dividend payable on such shares will be subject to a cap; (g) when a c.i.c. is wound up, its residual assets will not be distributed to its members. Instead, they will pass to another suitable organisation that has restrictions on the distribution of its profits, for example another c.i.c. or a charity; (h) the Regulator will approve applications for c.i.c. status, receive copies of the community interest company reports and police the requirements of c.i.c. status, including compliance with the asset lock. He will have close links with the registrar of companies. The key role of the Regulator will be to maintain public confidence in the c.i.c. model. He will aim to impose the minimum necessary regulatory burden on c.i.c.s, but will have powers to investigate abuses of c.i.c. status and to take action where necessary,

Section 6 of the CA 2006 provides a reference to the provisions in the C(AICE) Act, which enable a company to be formed as or become a c.i.c. Community Interest Companies are registered under the same legislation as other registered companies, but have to complete certain additional formalities and are subject to certain additional elements of regulation. (C(AICE)) establishes a 'Regulator of Community Interest Companies' to ensure smooth functioning of c.i.c.s, including providing guidance and assistance about any matters relating to c.i.c.s. There are also detailed rules as to the establishment of a c.i.c. with regards to the constitution, financial reports, decisions, audit, investigations, civil proceedings, the appointment of directors or managers, assets, transfer of shares and distribution of assets on winding up.

Establishing a Company

3.5 Part 2 of the CA 2006 is concerned with formation of companies, with particular reference to the method of forming a company, and requirements for registration, including the documents involved. Part 2 replaces equivalent provisions in the CA 1985.

As from 1 January 2007, the registrar of companies (registrar) offers a web incorporation facility for those who wish to incorporate a company online. This implements a recent amendment to the First Company Law Directive (68/151/EEC). The sections in Part 2 have been prepared with the objective, in particular, of removing any obstacles to the formation of companies online, and to ensure a smooth process towards facilitating such incorporation.

Part 2 comprises ten sections.

Method of forming a company

3.6 Sections 7 and 8 of the CA 2006 contain general provisions on company formation. Section 7(1) of the CA 2006 is concerned with the method of company formation. It states that a company can be formed by one or more persons if two requirements are complied with: first, by subscribing their names to a Memorandum of Association (see s 8 of the CA 2006);[247] and

---

for instance to remove directors, freeze assets or apply to the courts for a c.i.c. to be wound up. He will also set the cap on c.i.c. dividends. Sections 26–29 of the Act introduce the concept of the c.i.c. and establish the Regulator, Appeal Officer and Official Property Holder. Sections 30–35 set out special requirements which c.i.c.s must satisfy. The processes for becoming a c.i.c. are set out in ss 36–40. Sections 41–51 set out the supervisory powers of the Regulator. The conditions under which it is possible to cease being a c.i.c. are set out in ss 52–56. Supplementary ss 57–63 provide for various aspects of c.i.c. operation and regulation, including fees and information gateways for the Regulator.

[247] CA 2006, s 7(1)(a).

second, complying with the registration requirements (see ss 9–13 of the CA 2006).[248] A company may not, however, be so formed for an unlawful purpose.[249]

Section 7 of the CA 2006 replaces s 1(1) and (3A) of the CA 1985. It set out the new provisions on forming a company. In line with the recommendations of the Company Law Review Group, it is provided that a single person can form any type of company (and not just a private company).[250]

A company can only be formed if two requirements are complied with. First, the subscribers must subscribe to the company's Memorandum of Association. In this respect, s 7 of the CA 2006 makes references to compliance with s 8 of the CA 2006, as to the nature and content of the Memorandum of Association. Second, there must be compliance with the requirements as to registration and reference is made to ss 9–13 of the CA 2006. These sections deal with the registration documents required (s 9 of the CA 2006); the statement of capital and initial shareholding (s 10); a statement of guarantee (s 11); a statement of proposed officers (s 12); and a statement of compliance (s 13). Some of these statements are new introductions by CA 2006, owing to the now limited function of the Memorandum of Association.

It is also made clear and reproduced from the existing CA 1985 requirement that a company cannot be formed for an 'unlawful purpose'.[251] A company can only be established for a lawful purpose. The term 'unlawful purpose' is not defined. However, in *R v Registrar of Joint Stock Companies, ex pte More*,[252] a group of Irish people sought to incorporate a company whose objects would be to market Irish Sweepstake tickets. This activity was lawful in Ireland but not in the UK. The registrar refused to register this company, and a mandamus was sought by the applicants to overturn the registrar's decision. The Court of Appeal upheld the registrar's decision to refuse to register the company, on the basis that the proposed company's activities were not lawful. However, in *R v Registrar of Companies ex pte Bowen*,[253] a mandamus was made against the registrar, on the basis that the activity was lawful, and all the statutory conditions had been complied with by the proposed company and its founders. The registrar was, therefore, bound to register the company.

It is submitted that the term 'unlawful purpose' must relate to the activities or objects in which the company is engaged. The activities may be considered illegal, or contrary to public interest or morals, either upon incorporation or after the company is established.

[248] CA 2006, s 7(1)(b).   [249] CA 2006, s 7(2).   [250] *Final Report*, para 9.2.
[251] CA 2006, s 7(2). See too CA 1985, s 1(1), which required that the shareholders were to be associated 'for a lawful purpose'. See too CA 1985, s 1(3A), which allowed one person (a single member) to form a company 'for a lawful purpose'.
[252] [1931] 2 KB 197.   [253] [1914] 2 KB 1161.

Memorandum of Association

3.7 Section 8(1) of the CA 2006 provides that a Memorandum of Association is a memorandum stating that the subscribers wish to engage in two aspects. First they agree to form a company under the CA 2006.[254] This evidences their intention to establish a company. Second, the subscribers also agree to become members of the company and, in the case of a company that is to have a share capital, to take at least one share each.[255] This confirms that by taking their respective allocation of shares, they will be shareholders in the company.

The memorandum must be in the prescribed form and must be authenticated by each subscriber.[256]

Section 8 of the CA 2006 replaces s 2 of the CA 1985, which had set out the legal requirements for the content of the Memorandum of Association.[257] It remains the requirement under the CA 2006 that individuals who wish to form a company must still subscribe to the Memorandum of Association.

The Memorandum of Association under CA 2006, however, now serves a more limited and restricted purpose: it only evidences the intention of the subscribers to the memorandum, at a particular point in time, to form a company and become members of that company on formation. Where a company is limited by shares, the memorandum will also provide evidence of members' agreement to take at least one share each in the company. Apart from this, the memorandum serves no other purpose.

The 'new look' Memorandum of Association of a company formed under the CA 2006 will look radically different from that of a company registered under the CA 1985. In future, it will not be possible to amend or update the memorandum of a company formed under the CA 2006. There are no provisions in the CA 2006 allowing for an amendment to the Memorandum of Association.[258] The memorandum of such a company will essentially be a 'snapshot' of part of the company's constitution at the time of registration.

---

[254] CA 2006, s 8(1)(a).   [255] CA 2006, s 8(1)(b).   [256] CA 2006, s 8(2)

[257] CA 1985, s 2 required the memorandum, *inter alia*, to contain the company's objects; the subscribers; name of the company; the company's share capital; that the member's liability was limited; and the registered address of the company. The memorandum under the CA 1985 was, therefore, detailed and an important part of a company's constitution.

[258] Previously, under CA 1985, s 4, a company could alter its objects by special resolution. The alteration did not have effect until it was confirmed by the court. CA 1985, s 5 set out a detailed procedure that allowed an applicant to object to the alteration to the company's objects clause (see s 5(2)(a) and (b) as to who could object). Further, the courts order could (if the court thought fit) provide for the purchase by the company of the shares of any members of the company, and for the reduction of its share capital. The court could also make such alterations to the companies memorandum and articles as would be required in consequence of that provision: see CA 1985, s 5(5). If the court order required the company not to make any, or any specified, alteration in its memorandum or articles, the company did not then have power without leave of court to make any such alteration in breach of that requirement: CA 1985, s 5(6).

The memorandum will be a much shorter document in comparison to the format previously, under the CA 1985.

Provisions in the memoranda of exiting companies, which are of a type that will be in the memoranda of companies formed under the CA 2006, will be treated as provisions in the articles.[259] Existing companies will, therefore, be able to alter or update provisions in their constitution, which are now set out in their memoranda, by amending their articles (such as share capital; registered address; objects, etc).

These changes to the memorandum are based on the Company Law Review Group's recommendation that there should be a single company constitution.[260] In line with the principles behind this recommendation, in future, key information regarding the internal allocation of powers between the directors and members of a company, will be set out in one document: the Articles of Association. The Articles of Association, therefore, become one of the most important documents of a company's constitution.

For companies formed under the CA 2006, constitutional information of this type will be set out in the Articles of Association and not the Memorandum of Association. Existing companies will not be required to amend their articles to reflect this change, but they may they do so if they wish. They may want to amend their articles in any event to reflect changes to the law that are made in the CA 2006, for example, in future, companies formed under the CA 2006, and existing companies, will have unrestricted objects unless they specifically restrict them.

Existing companies are currently able to 'entrench' elements of their constitution in the Memorandum of Association (that is, provide that a particular provision may not be altered, or may only be altered if certain conditions are met). In future, it will be possible for companies to entrench elements of their constitution in their articles,[261] and where the memorandum of an existing company contains a 'provision of entrenchment', this will be treated as a provision in the company's articles with effect from the date that the CA 2006 came into force.[262]

Other than the purpose of the Memorandum of Association under CA 2006 as evidencing a subscriber's intention to form a company and to agree to become a member of the company, it is difficult to see what other purpose is served by the new style Memorandum of Association. Of course, the Memorandum of Association must be delivered to the registrar at Companies House together with other documents. However, it is disappointing that recommendations as long ago as 1986, by Dr Dan Prentice (as he was then), for abolishing the Memorandum of Association have not found their way into CA 2006. Prentice recommended there should only be one single document comprising the company's constitution. This would have required the

---

[259] See further CA 2006, s 28.   [260] See *Final Report*, para 9.4.   [261] CA 2006, s 23.
[262] CA 2006, s 29.

abolition of both the Memorandum of Association and the Articles of Association, which would have been renamed under one single document as the 'company's constitution'. The memorandum would in effect have been integrated into the Articles of Association.

A new-look Memorandum of Association under the CA 2006 will be a much shorter document than it was under the CA 1985. The subscribers must set out the memorandum in a prescribed form. Further, it must be authenticated by each subscriber, which will give validity to the Memorandum of Association, by adding their signatures next to their names.

The Companies (Registration) Regulations 2007 provide that the Memorandum of Association of a company having a share capital must be in the form set out in Schedule 1 to the Regulations (see para 2(a)); and for a company not having a share capital in the form set out in Schedule 2 to the Regulations (see para 2(b)).

Requirements for registration

3.8 Sections 9–13 of the CA 2006 set out the practical requirements for incorporation. This is achieved by setting out the prescribed form documentation that is required to register the company. Many of these details were previously set out in the old-style Memorandum of Association under the CA 1985, and could easily have been included in the new-style company's constitution. The details are now to be included in separate forms to be lodged at Companies House. It could be argued that far from simplifying the process of registration, the CA 2006 has added yet further bureaucratic layers by requiring completion of additional documentation that could have been included in a single company's constitution. Various 'statements' are required to be completed before the registrar will proceed to incorporate the company. These are: (i) statement of capital and initial shareholdings; (ii) statement of guarantee (if applicable); (iii) statement of proposed officers; and (iv) statement of compliance. This is in addition to the application for registration form that must be completed.

Registration documents

3.9 Section 9(1) of the CA 2006 states that the Memorandum of Association must be delivered to the registrar together with the following documents: (i) an application for registration of the company; (ii) the documents required by s 9 of the CA 2006; and (iii) a statement of compliance.

Application for registration

3.10 The application for registration must contain the following details:[263]

---

[263] CA 2006, s 9(2).

- the company's proposed name;[264]
- whether the company's registered office is to be situated in England and Wales (or Wales), in Scotland or in Northern Ireland;[265]
- whether the liability of the company's members is to be limited and if so whether it is to be limited by shares or by guarantee;[266]
- whether the company is to be a private or a public company;[267]
- where a company is to have a share capital, a statement of the company's capital and initial shareholdings, the details of which are set out in s 10 of the CA 2006;[268]
- in the case of a company that is to be limited by guarantee, the application must also contain a statement of guarantee, the details of which are set out in s 11 of the CA 2006;[269]
- a statement of the company's proposed officers, the details of which are set out in s 12 of the CA 2006;[270]
- a statement of the intended address of the company's registered office (that is, the postal address of the company's registered office), as opposed to a statement confirming the jurisdiction in which the company's registered office it to be situated, which is also required;[271]
- a copy of any proposed Articles of Association (to the extent that the company does not intend to use the model articles under s 20 of the CA 2006);[272]
- if the application is delivered by a person who acts as agent for the subscribers to the Memorandum of Association, it must state that agent's name and address;[273]
- the company's Memorandum of Association in a new-look 'short form' style; and
- a statement of compliance.

The application must be delivered to the registrar of companies depending upon where the company is situated – either of England and Wales (or Wales), Scotland, or Northern Ireland.[274]

---

[264] CA 2006, s 9(2). On the company's name, see CA 2006, Part 5.

[265] CA 2006, s 9(2)(b). On the company's registered office, see CA 2006, Part 6, ss 86–88.

[266] CA 2006, s 9(2)(c). As to who are the 'members' of the company, see CA 2006, s 112. CA 2006, s 11(1) states that the subscribers of a company's memorandum are deemed to have agreed to become members of the company, and on its registration become members and must be entered as such in its register of members. CA 2006, s 112(2) states that every other person who agrees to become a member of a company, and whose name is entered in its register of members, is a member of the company. See further CA 2006, Chapter 2, Part 8 as to the register of members.

[267] CA 2006, s 9(2)(d).   [268] CA 2006, s 9(4)(a).   [269] CA 2006, s 9(4)(b).

[270] CA 2006, s 9(4)(c).   [271] CA 2006, s 9(5)(a).   [272] CA 2006, s 9(5)(b).

[273] CA 2006, s 9(3).   [274] CA 2006, s 9(6).

Section 9 of the CA 2006 replaces ss 2 and 10 of the CA 1985.[275] It sets out the types of information or 'documents' that must be delivered to the registrar when an application for registration is made, and the manner in which that information must be delivered to the registrar. Previously, a large part of this information would have been contained in the company's Memorandum of Association such as the name, registered office and company's capital, including liability of the members.

However, changes to the manner in which certain information is delivered to the registrar are required as a result of the changes that have been made to the Memorandum of Association under the CA 2006. In future, information that is currently set out in the memorandum, will be provided to the registrar in accordance with the provisions of s 9 of the CA 2006, which prescribes, amongst other aspects, the contents of the application for registration.

It should be noted that the application may be delivered in person by the subscribers to the Memorandum of Association, or by a person acting as their agent, but that the agent must state its name and address on the application. This would apply, for example, to company formation agencies, accountants, lawyers, and others establishing a company for the subscribers.

Under the CA 2006, it will also be possible to form a company online, and the various types of information referred to in s 9 of the CA 2006 are, therefore, capable of being delivered as a series of data entries as well as on paper, or such other form as the registrar may permit or prescribe. These provisions have been designed to ensure that online registration can be effected. The registrar has power to prescribe the form and manner in which documents are to be delivered to her.

Statement of capital and initial shareholdings

3.11 Where a company is to have a share capital, s 10(1) of the CA 2006 provides that the statement of capital and initial shareholdings that is required to be delivered to the registrar, must comply with this section. The statement must set out the following details:

- the total number of shares of the company to be taken on formation by the subscribers to the Memorandum of Association;[276]
- the aggregate nominal value of those shares;[277]

---

[275] CA 1985, s 10 concerned documents to be sent to the registrar which included the company's Memorandum and Articles of Association accompanied by particulars of the first director(s) and secretary of the company; a statement of the usual residential address of the director or secretary; a statement of the intended situation of the company's registered office on incorporation; and where a memorandum was delivered by a person as agent for the subscribers, a statement of that person's name and address.

[276] CA 2006, s 10(2)(a).   [277] CA 2006, s 10(2)(b).

- for each class of shares: (i) prescribed particulars of the rights attached to the shares; (ii) the total number of shares of that class; and (iii) the aggregate nominal value of shares of that class;[278] and (iv) the amount to be paid up and the amount (if any) to be unpaid on each share (whether on account of the nominal value of the share or by way of premium);[279]
- such information as may be prescribed for the purpose of identifying the subscribers to the Memorandum of Association.[280]

With respect to each subscriber to the memorandum, the statement must also contain the following details:

- the number, nominal value (of each share) and class of shares to be taken by him on formation.[281] Further, where a subscriber to the memorandum is to take shares of more than one class, the information that is required (as to the number, nominal value and class of shares), for each class of shares;[282] and
- the amount to be paid up and the amount (if any) to be unpaid on each share (whether on account of the nominal value of the share or by way of premium).[283]

Section 10 of the CA 2006 replaces ss 2(5)(a) and (c), (6) and (6A) of the CA 1985 (which refer to the memorandum). It sets out the contents to be included in the statement of capital and initial shareholdings.

Previously under the CA 1985, in the case of a limited company with a share capital, the memorandum was required to state the amount of the share capital with which the company proposed to be registered and the nominal value of each of its shares. This was known as the 'authorised share capital', and acted as a ceiling on the amount of capital that could be issued (although it could be increased pursuant to an ordinary resolution). The Company Law Review Group recommended that the requirement for a company to have authorised share capital should be abolished.[284]

The CA 2006, therefore, gives effect to this recommendation and now, the memorandum will only contain very limited information regarding a company's founder members, that is, the subscribers to the memorandum. Information about the shares subscribed to by those signing the memorandum, which was previously set out in the memorandum itself, will now be provided to the registrar in the form of two statements made in the application for registration: a statement of initial shareholdings and a statement of share capital.

---

[278] CA 2006, s 10(2)(c).   [279] CA 2006, s 10(2)(d).

[280] CA 2006, s 10(3). The statement of capital and initial shareholdings must contain the name and address of each subscriber to the Memorandum of Association – see para 3 to the Companies (Registration) Regulations 2007.

[281] CA 2006, s 10(4)(a).   [282] CA 2006, s 10(5).   [283] CA 2006, s 10(4)(b).

[284] *Final Report*, para 10.6.

Like the statement of share capital and the statement of guarantee, the statement of initial shareholdings must contain the names and addresses of the subscribers to the memorandum. The requirement in all cases is for a contact address – there is no requirement for the person making the statement to give his/her home address.

A statement of capital is essentially a 'snapshot' of a company's share capital at a particular point in time. In this context, it requires information to be provided with respect to the share capital to be taken by the subscribers on formation.

The requirement for a statement of capital under the CA 2006 is new, and not in any previous Companies Acts. For public companies, this requirement is linked to the abolition of authorised share capital. It implements (as far as public companies are concerned) Article 2 of the Second Company Law Directive (77/91/EC) (the Second Directive) which states: 'the statutes or instruments of incorporation of the company shall always give at least the following information . . . when the company has no authorised capital, the amount of the subscribed capital.'

Section 10(2)(c)(i) of the CA 2006 refers to 'prescribed particulars of the rights attached to the shares' (and elsewhere where a statement of capital is called for). This is a reference to such particulars as may be prescribed by the Secretary of State by statutory instrument.

Whilst the Second Company Law Directive only applies to public companies, it is important that the information on the public register is up to date. A statement of capital will, therefore, be required where it is proposed that a company formed under CA 2006 will have a share capital on formation and, with limited exceptions (in particular, where there has been a variation of class rights which does not affect the company's aggregate subscribed capital) wherever a company having a share capital makes an alteration to its share capital (whether under CA 2006, or the remaining provisions of the CA 1985, which deal with alterations to a company's share capital).

Statement of guarantee

3.12 Section 11(1) of the CA 2006 deals with the statement of guarantee required to be delivered for a company that is limited by guarantee. The statement must contain the names and addresses of the subscribers to the memorandum – the objective being to identify the subscribers to the memorandum.[285] It must also state that each member undertakes that, if the company is wound up while he/she is a member, or within one year after he/she

---

[285] CA 2006, s 11(2). The statement of guarantee must contain the name and address of each subscriber to the Memorandum of Association – see para 4 to the Companies (Registration) Regulations 2007.

ceases to be a member, he/she will contribute to the assets of the company such amount as may be required for the following:

- payment of the debts and liabilities of the company contracted before he/she ceases to be a member;[286]
- payment of the costs, charges and expenses of winding up;[287] and
- adjustment of the rights of the contributories among themselves[288]

not exceeding a specified amount.

Section 11 of the CA 2006 replaces s 2(4) of the CA 1985. It sets out the contents of the statement of guarantee that must accompany the application for registration, where it is proposed that a company will be limited by guarantee on formation.

The statement of guarantee is essentially an undertaking, given by the founder members of the company, to contribute to the assets of the company up to a specified amount in the event of it being wound up. New members must also agree to make the same contribution. It demonstrates a firm and certain intention, as well as good faith on the part of the founders, in establishing the company.

A member of a company limited by a guarantee is only liable to contribute to the assets of a company if it is wound up during the time that he is a member, or within one year of him/her ceasing to be a member.

The undertaking is quite onerous and must not be taken lightly by the founders. It includes payments for all debts and liabilities that the company has incurred, not just with third parties, but also internally with its directors (such as payment for breach of service contract with one of its directors). The undertaking by the founder also includes payment of the costs, charges and expenses of winding up, which will include the liquidator's fees, and any other amounts owing to third parties under the winding-up priority order; and adjustment of the rights of contributors among themselves not exceeding a certain amount.

Statement of proposed officers

3.13 Section 12(1) of the CA 2006 provides that the statement of the company's proposed officers required to be delivered to the registrar must contain the required particulars of:

- the person who is, or persons who are, to be the first director or directors of the company;[289]

---

[286] CA 2006, s 11(3)(a).   [287] CA 2006, s 11(3)(b).   [288] CA 2006, s 11(3)(c).
[289] CA 2006, s 12(1)(a).

- where a company is to be a private company, any person who is (or the persons who are) to be the first secretary (or joint secretaries) of the company;[290]
- where a company is to be a public company, the person who is (or the persons who are) to be the first secretary (or joint secretaries of the company).[291]

Section 12(2) of the CA 2006 provides that the reference to *required particulars* are to the required particulars that must be stated in the company's register of directors and register of directors' residential addresses[292] or, as the case may be, its register of secretaries.[293]

The statement of proposed officers must also contain consent by each of the persons named as a director, as secretary or as one of joint secretaries, to act in the relevant capacity. If all the partners in a firm are to be joint secretaries, consent may be given by one partner on behalf of them all.[294]

Section 12 of the CA 2006 replaces s 10 of the CA 1985. Under s 10 of the CA 1985, details of the first director(s) and the secretary or joint secretaries, were required to be given to the registrar at the time of application for registration, together with other documents for registration. This requirement is carried forward under the CA 2006, but there are two deregulatory changes under the CA 2006 that should be noted: first, as recommended by the Company Law Review Group in its *Final Report*,[295] the CA 2006 now provides that all directors will have the option of their home address being kept on a separate record to which access will be restricted.[296] In order to benefit from this option, a director will have to provide a service address for the public record; second, as recommended by the Company Law Review Group in its *Final Report*,[297] it reflects the abolition of the requirement for private companies to have a secretary.[298]

Statement of compliance

3.14 Section 13(1) of the CA 2006 provides that the statement of compliance required to be delivered to the registrar, is a statement that the requirements of CA 2006 as to registration are complied with. The registrar may accept the statement of compliance as sufficient evidence of compliance.[299]

---

[290] CA 2006, s 12(1)(b).   [291] CA 2006, s 12(1)(c).

[292] See also CA 2006, ss 162–166 (register and particulars of directors). On directors' residential addresses, see CA 2006, Part 10, Chapter 8.

[293] See also CA 2006, ss 277–279 (register and particulars of secretaries).

[294] CA 2006, s 12(3).   [295] *Final Report*, para 11.46.

[296] See further CA 2006, Part 10, Chapter 8.   [297] *Final Report*, para 4.7.

[298] CA 2006, s 270 (Private company not required to have a secretary).

[299] CA 2006, s 13(2).

Section 13 of the CA 2006 replaces s 12(3) and (3A) of the CA 1985. Previously, where an application for registration of a company was made in paper form, the application had to be accompanied by a statutory declaration (made before a solicitor or commissioner of oaths) confirming that the requirements of the CA 1985 in respect of registration, and of matters precedent and incidental to it, had been complied with.[300] This statutory declaration had to be made by one of the persons whom it was proposed would be a founder or secretary of the company (that is, on registration), or a solicitor engaged in the formation of the company.

Where the application for registration was made in electronic form, in place of the statutory declaration required under s 12(3) of the CA 1985, the same person could, alternatively, deliver an 'electronic statement' to the registrar. This statement had to confirm that the requirements referred to in section 12(1) of the CA 1985 had been met, and the registrar had discretion whether to accept such a statement as sufficient evidence of compliance.[301]

Based on the recommendations of the Company Law Review Group in its *Final Report*,[302] the previous requirement under the CA 1985 for a statutory declaration or electronic statement, here and elsewhere in CA 2006, has been replaced by a requirement only to make a statement of compliance. This statement does not need to be witnessed or sworn before a solicitor engaged in the company formation, and may be made in paper or electronic form. It will be for the registrar rules under s 1068 of the CA 2006 (registrar's requirements) to specify who may make this statement (and the form of it).[303] As with all documents delivered to, or statement made to, the registrar, it is an offence to make a false statement of compliance.[304]

Registration and its effect

3.15 Sections 14–16 of the CA 2006 are concerned with the process of registration with legal and practical implications of effects of registration.

---

[300] See CA 1985, s 12.   [301] See CA 1985, s 12(3A).   [302] See *Final Report*, para 9.5.

[303] Under CA 2006 s 1068(1), the registrar may impose requirements as to form, authentication and manner of delivery of documents required or authorised to be delivered to the registrar under any enactment.

[304] See CA 2006, s 1112 (general false statement offence). This section provides that it is an offence for a person knowingly or recklessly to deliver or cause to be delivered to the registrar, for any purpose of the Companies Acts, a document, or to make to the registrar, for any such purpose, a statement that is misleading, false or deceptive in a material particular. This is a criminal offence. A person guilty of an offence is liable on conviction on indictment, to imprisonment for a term not exceeding two years or a fine (or both). On summary conviction in England and Wales to imprisonment for a term not exceeding 12 months or to a fine not exceeding the statutory maximum (or both); and in Scotland or Northern Ireland, to imprisonment for a term not exceeding six months or to a fine not exceeding the statutory maximum or both: CA 2006, s 1112(2).

Registration

3.16 Under s 14 of the CA 2006, if the registrar is satisfied that the requirements of the CA 2006 as to registration are complied with, he/she must register the documents delivered to him/her.

This section replaces s 12(1) of the CA 1985. As in the CA 1985, where the registrar is satisfied that all the requirements of the CA 2006 as to registration have been met, she will register the documents delivered to her and issue a certificate of incorporation under s 15 of the CA 2006.[305]

The registrar has the sole discretion to decide whether requirements of the CA 2006 as to registration have been met. There is no guidance provided under the CA 2006 as to when the registrar is 'satisfied' that all requirements under the CA 2006 have been complied with. However, in practice, the registrar must consider all the documents and information delivered to her, and upon examination of the provisions of the CA 2006, determine that all aspects have been complied with. There is no question of any 'substantial' compliance by the company. Either there is compliance under the CA 2006 or there is not. If there is no compliance, the registrar cannot register the documents delivered. Further information and/or documents may be obtained from the founders of the company to satisfy the requirement of compliance.

The registrar must also consider that the company has been established for a lawful purpose in order to demonstrate compliance under the CA 2006.[306]

Provided all documents and information are in order, and not in contravention of the requirements under CA 2006, and the company is not set up for an unlawful purpose, the registrar will have no discretion to refuse registration.

Issue of certificate of incorporation

3.17 Section 15(1) of the CA 2006 provides that on registration of a company, the registrar of companies must provide a certificate that the company is incorporated. The certificate must state the following:[307]

- name and registered number of the company;[308]
- date of its incorporation;[309]
- whether it is a limited or unlimited company, and if it is limited, whether it is limited by shares or limited by guarantee;[310]

---

[305] CA 1985, s 12(1) provided that the registrar of companies would not register a company's memorandum unless satisfied that all the requirements of the CA 1985 in respect of registration and of matters precedent or incidental to it had been complied with.
[306] See CA 2006, s 7(2).   [307] CA 2006, s 15(2).   [308] CA 2006, s 15(2)(a).
[309] CA 2006, s 15(2)(b).   [310] CA 2006, s 15(2)(c).

- whether it is a private or a public company;[311] and
- whether the company's registered office is situated in England and Wales (or Wales), in Scotland or in Northern Ireland.[312]

The certificate must be signed by the registrar or authenticated by the registrar's official seal.[313] The certificate will be 'conclusive evidence' that the requirements of CA 2006 as to registration have been complied with, and that the company is duly registered under the CA 2006.[314]

Section 15 of the CA 2006 replaces s 13(1), (2), (6) and (7) of the CA 1985.[315] It sets out the specific contents of the certificate of incorporation that must be issued by the registrar on registration of a company. The certificate of incorporation is conclusive evidence: that the requirements of the CA 2006 as to registration have been met; that the company has been registered; and (where relevant) that the company has been registered as a limited company or a public company.

Each company will have its own unique registration number, which will be used for filing and identification purposes. The date of incorporation ensures that the company has been legally formed and a private company can trade as from that date and also important for accounting purposes.

There is one change as to what the certificate of incorporation is required to state which was not in the CA 1985: in future, the certificate of incorporation will include details of whether the company's registered office is situated in England and Wales (or in Wales), in Scotland or in Northern Ireland. It has been the registrar's practice to include this information in the certificate of incorporation, but there was no requirement for this under the CA 1985. The certificate will also state, in caseswhere the company is limited, whether it is limited by shares or by guarantee.

As to the conclusivity of the certificate of incorporation, s 15(4) of the CA 2006 provides that the certificate will be 'conclusive evidence that the requirements of the CA 2006 as to registration have been complied with, and that the company is duly registered under the CA 2006. This provision

---

[311] CA 2006, s 15(2)(d).   [312] CA 2006, s 15(2)(e).   [313] CA 2006, s 15(3).

[314] CA 2006, s 15(4).

[315] CA 1985, s 13(1) provided that on registration of a company's memorandum, the registrar of companies was required to give a certificate of incorporation and in the case of a limited company, that it was a limited company. Under CA 1985, s 13(2), the certificate may be signed by the registrar or authenticated by his official seal. CA 1985, s 13(6) stated that where the company was a public company, the certificate of incorporation was required to state that the company was a public company. CA 1985, s 13(7) provided that a certificate of incorporation was conclusive evidence that the requirements of the CA 1985 in respect of registration and of matters precedent and incidental to it had been complied with, and that the association was a company authorised to be registered and was duly registered under the CA 1985. Further, if the certificate contained a statement that the company was a public company, that the company was such a company.

remains unchanged from the CA 1985 although the CA 1985 provided for wider conclusivity that included 'matters precedent and incidental' to registration requirements under the CA 1985, which expression is not included in the CA 2006.

On the issue of conclusivity, in *Jubilee Cotton Mills Ltd v Lewis*,[316] the House of Lords stated that the certificate issued by the registrar was conclusive evidence as to the date of the company's incorporation, even though the date was erroneously set out in the certificate.[317] Section 15(4) of the CA 2006 provides that the certificate will be conclusive evidence that the formalities for establishing a company under the CA 2006 have been complied with, but it is not conclusive evidence that the company's objects are in fact legal. If the company's objects are illegal, the certificate cannot be issued by the registrar.[318] In *Bowman v Secular Society Ltd*,[319] the House of Lords allowed the Attorney General to apply for certiorari to have the company's registration cancelled, owing to the illegality of the company's objects.

Effect of registration

3.18 Section 16 of the CA 2006 is concerned with the effect of registering a company. It provides that registration of a company has the following effects as from the date of incorporation:

- the subscribers to the memorandum, together with such other persons as may from time to time become members of the company, are a body corporate by the name stated in the certificate of incorporation;[320]
- that body corporate is capable of exercising all the functions of an incorporated body;[321]
- the status and registered office of the company are as stated in, or in connection with, the application for registration;[322]
- in the case of a company having a share capital, the subscribers to the memorandum become holders of the shares specified in the statement of capital and initial shareholdings;[323] and
- the persons named in the statement of proposed officers are deemed to have been appointed to that office, namely: as director; or as secretary or joint secretary of the company.[324]

---

[316] [1924] AC 958.   [317] See too *Cotman v Brougham* [1918] AC 514.

[318] See too CA 2006, s 7(2), which states that a company may not be so formed for an unlawful purpose.

[319] [1917] AC 406. Also *R v Registrar of Companies, ex pte A-G* [1991] BCLC 476; and *Princess of Reuss v Bos* (1871) LR 5 HL 176.

[320] CA 2006, s 16(2).   [321] CA 2006, s 16(3).   [322] CA 2006, s 16(4).

[323] CA 2006, s 16(5).   [324] CA 2006, s 16(6).

Section 16 of the CA 2006 replaces ss 13(3)–(5) of the CA 1985.[325] It does not make any substantive changes to the current provisions and provides, amongst other things, that the subscribers to the memorandum, together with such other persons as may from time to time become members of the company, are a body corporate by the name stated in the certificate of incorporation. This means that on registration, a company becomes a legal person in its own right from the people who own it (the members) and the people who manage it (the directors).[326] However, in respect of a public company, an additional certificate as to the amount of allotted share capital in the company must be obtained before it can commence business or borrow.

The list of effects of registration set out in s 16 of the CA 2006 should not be considered as exhaustive. It should be considered in conjunction with traditional effects and other corporate attributes.[327] They include:

- A company's perpetual succession. A company may continue to function subject to compliance with all applicable legislation until final dissolution of the company.
- A company being a separate legal independent entity can sue in its name or be sued.
- A company can own property in its own name.
- A company can create a fixed and/or floating charge.
- A company has the ability to obtain loans/facilities.
- The corporation can be charged for manslaughter, including breaches of legislation that would impose criminal sanctions against the corporation, such as health and safety legislation.[328]
- Although the body corporate is capable of exercising all the functions of an incorporated company, it still must comply with the law as well as the Companies Acts and other legislation to which it may be subject.

[325] CA 1985, s 13(3) stated that from the date mentioned in the certificate, the subscribers of the memorandum together with such other persons as may from time to time become members of the company, shall be a body corporate by the name contained in the memorandum. The body corporate is then capable of exercising all the functions of an incorporated company, but with such liability on the part of its members to contribute to its assets in the event of its being wound up: CA 1985, s 13(4). Further, CA 1985, s 13(5) provided that the persons named as directors, secretary or joint secretary were, on the company's incorporation, deemed to have been respectively appointed as its first directors, secretary or joint secretaries.

[326] See *Salomon v A Salomon & Co Ltd* [1897] AC 22 and cases concerning 'piercing the corporate veil' including *Lee v Lee's Air Farming Ltd* [1961] AC 12; *Smith, Stone & Knight Ltd v Birmingham Corp* [1939] 4 All ER 116; *Gilford Motor Co Ltd v Horne* [1933] Ch 935; *DHN Food Distributors Ltd v London Borough of Tower Hamlets* [1976] 23 All ER 462; *Woolfson v Strathclyde Regional Council* (1978) 38 P & CR 521.

[327] See *The Case of Sutton's Hospital* (1612) 10 Co Rep 1a.

[328] See Corporate Manslaughter and Corporate Homicide Act 2007, which addresses issues of management failure and the position at common law of gross negligence manslaughter.

A Company's Registered Office

General

3.19 The provisions dealing with a company's registered office are set out in Part 6 of the CA 2006. This contains three sections on requirements for the registered office.

Registered office

3.20 Section 86 of the CA 2006 requires every company to have at all times a registered office and for that office to be the company's address, to which communications and notices may be sent. Section 1139 of the CA 2006 states that the service of a document on a company is effective if it is sent to its registered office. Section 86 of the CA 2006 replaces s 287(1) of the CA 1985.

Change of address of registered office

3.21 Section 87 of the CA 2006 is concerned with changing the address of a company's registered office. It states that a company may change the address of its registered office by giving notice to the registrar.[329] The change takes effect only upon the notice being registered by the registrar, but until the end of the period of 14 days beginning with the date on which it is registered, a person may validly serve any document on the company at the address previously registered.[330]

Once a company has given notice to the registrar of change of registered office, the company may act on the change from such date, and it has 14 days from the date within which to comply with any changes it may wish to make. The duties on a company may include keeping available for inspection at its registered office any register, index or other document;[331] or to mention the address of its registered office in any document.[332]

There is a defence for the company if it cannot perform its duties within the time period owing to change of registered office. Section 87(4) of the CA 2006 provides that where a company unavoidably ceases to perform at its registered address any such duty as set out in s 87(3)(a) of the CA 2006 in circumstances in which it was not practicable to give prior notice to the registrar of a change in the address of its registered office, but later resumes performance of that duty at other premises as soon as practicable;[333] and gives notice accordingly to the registrar of a change in the situation of its registered office with 14 days of doing so,[334] the company will not be treated as having failed to comply with that duty.

---

[329] CA 2006, s 87(1).   [330] CA 2006, s 87(2).   [331] CA 2006, s 87(3)(a).
[332] CA 2006, s 87(3)(b).   [333] CA 2006, s 87(4)(a).   [334] CA 2006, s 87(4)(b).

Section 87 of the CA 2006 replaces s 287(3), (4), (5) and (6) of the CA 1985. It retains the procedure in the CA 1985 for a company wishing to change the address of its registered office where both the new and old address are in the same part of the UK, i.e. Northern Ireland, Scotland, or England and Wales. In the case of a Welsh company (see s 88 of the CA 2006) both the new and old address must be in Wales. The company must give notice to the registrar of the intended address.

The change of registered office does not take effect until the new address is on the public record: this is to ensure there cannot be any period during which a company does not have an address that is effective for the service of documents on the company.

Section 87 of the CA 2006 provides for a fortnight's overlap between the new and old addresses: during this period, both addresses are effective for the service of documents on the company. The company has a fortnight, starting from the date of the notice under s 87(2) of the CA 2006, in which to make changes arising from changing the address of its registered office (for example, to its documents for correspondence, etc).

Section 87 of the CA 2006 also covers the possibility of an unplanned change in registered office, for example, in the event of a fire or another unforseeable event. It provides the company with a fortnight in which to regularise its arrangements as regards the duty in s 87(3)(a) of the CA 2006 (the duty of a company to make available for inspection at its registered office any register, index or other document). It provides the company with a 14-day breathing space, where it is not be treated as having failed to comply with the duty to make certain records available for inspection at its registered office.

Sections 87(3) and (4) of the CA 2006 are necessary, as there are criminal sanctions if the company fails to make certain records available for inspection at its registered office, or to comply with requirements to include its address in certain documents (such requirements may be imposed by regulations under s 82 of the CA 2006 (requirement to disclose company name, etc).

Welsh companies

3.22 Section 88 of the CA 2006 deals with the position of registered office for Welsh companies. In the Companies Acts, the definition of a 'Welsh company' means a company as to which it is stated in the register that its registered office is to be situated in Wales.[335]

A company whose registered office is in Wales,[336] and as to which it is stated in the register that its registered office is to be situated in England and Wales,[337] may by special resolution, require the register to be amended so that

---

[335] CA 2006, s 87(1).　　[336] CA 2006, s 88(2)(a).　　[337] CA 2006, s 88(2)(b).

it states that the company's registered office is to be situated Wales.[338] Similar provision applies where its registered office is in Wales and it may by special resolution change to England and Wales.[339]

Once the company has passed a special resolution, it must give notice to the registrar. The registrar is required to amend the register accordingly;[340] and issue a new certificate of incorporation, altered to meet the circumstances of the case.[341]

The purpose of s 88 of the CA 2006 is to provide a definition of a Welsh company. This is a company whose registered office address must be in Wales. A company can be set up as a Welsh company by delivering to the registrar a statement on formation that its registered office is to be situated in Wales.[342]

Section 88 of the CA 2006 retains the existing provision whereby a company may become a Welsh company by passing a special resolution (so that the register states that its registered office is to be situated 'in Wales'). As recommended by the Company Law Review Group, s 88(3) of the CA 2006 provides a mechanism whereby a company can cease to be a Welsh company (that is, so that the register states that its registered office is to be situated in 'England and Wales'). This is a new provision. Under the CA 1985, while a company could choose to restrict the address of its registered office to Wales on formation or subsequently by special resolution, it was not possible under the CA 1985 for a Welsh company to drop the restriction so that its registered office address could be changed to anywhere in England and Wales.

Welsh companies may deliver documents to the registrar in Welsh.[343] Welsh companies may also end their company name with Welsh versions of the statutory indicators of legal status. For example, 'cyfyngedig' in place of 'limited' or 'c.c.c.' in place of 'plc'.[344] When a company ceases to be a Welsh company using the procedure under this clause, it may no longer take advantage of these provisions.

Where a company passes a special resolution under s 88(2) or (3) of the CA 2006 (and so becomes or ceases to be Welsh company), s 88(4) of the CA 2006 provides that the registrar will amend the register and issue the company with a new certificate of incorporation.

Companies Not Formed Under Companies Legislation

3.23 The definition of 'company' and 'Companies Acts' under the CA 2006 is wide in scope. Under s 1(2) of the CA 2006, certain provisions of the Companies Acts apply to companies registered, but not formed, under the

---

[338] CA 2006, s 88(2).   [339] CA 2006, s 88(3).   [340] CA 2006, s 88(4)(a).
[341] CA 2006, s 88(4)(b).   [342] See CA 2006, s 9(2)(b).   [343] See CA 2006, s 1104.
[344] See CA 2006, ss 58 and 59.

CA 2006 – the regime of which is governed by Chapter 1 of Part 33 of the CA 2006. This section addresses the provisions of Chapter 1 of Part 33 of the CA 2006.

Companies not formed under companies legislation but authorised to register

3.24 Chapter 1 of Part 33 of the CA 2006 is concerned with companies that are not formed under companies legislation, but are nevertheless authorised to register under the CA 2006. Section 1040 of the CA 2006, applies to the following entities:

- any company that was in existence on 2 November 1862 (including any company registered under the Joint Stock Companies Acts);[345] and
- any company formed after that date (whether before or after commencement of the CA 2006):

  (i)   in pursuance of an Act of Parliament (other than the CA 2006 or any of the former Companies Acts);[346] or
  (ii) in pursuance of letters patent;[347] or
  (iii) that is otherwise duly constituted according to law.[348]

Any of the above companies may on making an application register under the CA 2006.[349] Such a company may register as an unlimited company, or as a company limited by shares, or as a company limited by guarantee.[350] Section 1040(4) of the CA 2006 elucidates on those companies established by an Act of Parliament or in pursuance of letters patent. It states that a company that has the liability of its members limited by an Act of Parliament or letters patent, may not register under s 1040 of the CA 2006, unless it is a joint stock company; and may not register under s 1040 of the CA 2006 as an unlimited company, or a company limited by guarantee.

A company that is not a joint stock company may not register under s 1040 of the CA 2006 as a company limited by shares.[351] Further, the registration of a company under s 1040 of the CA 2006 is not invalid by reason that it has taken place with a view to the company being wound up.[352]

Section 1040 of the CA 2006 replaces s 680 of the CA 1985. Companies incorporated within the United Kingdom, but not formed under the Companies Acts (or certain earlier companies legislation), may apply to register under the CA 2006. The types of company that can take advantage of this provision are listed in s 1040(1) of the CA 2006. They include companies

---

[345] CA 2006, s 1040(1)(a).   [346] CA 2006, s 1040(b)(i).   [347] CA 2006, s 1040(b)(ii).
[348] CA 2006, s 1040(b)(iii).   [349] CA 2006, s 1040(2)   [350] CA 2006, s 1040(3).
[351] CA 2006, s 1040(5).   [352] CA 2006, s 1040(6).

formed before 2 November 1862; companies formed by private Act of Parliament and companies incorporated by royal charter.

The company may apply to register as a company limited by shares, a company limited by guarantee or as an unlimited company. Section 1,040(4) and (5) of the CA 2006 imposes restrictions on this choice. So, a company with limited liability may not register as an unlimited company, and only a company with share capital may register as a company limited by shares.

A company may wish to apply to register under the CA 2006 in order to take advantage of legislation applying to companies registered under the Companies Acts. Section 1040(6) of the CA 2006 makes clear that a company may register even if it is in order to take advantage of certain provisions of the Insolvency Act 1986 not available to unregistered companies. For example, under s 221(4) Insolvency Act 1986, unregistered companies may not be wound up under that Act voluntarily (except in accordance with the EC regulation on insolvency proceedings).

The definition of a 'joint stock company' is set out in s 1041 of the CA 2006. For the purposes of s 1040, a 'joint stock company' is a company:

(a)   having a permanent paid up or nominal share capital of a fixed amount divided into shares, also of fixed amount, or held or transferable as stock, or divided and partly held in one way and partly in the other;[353] and

(b)   formed on the principle of having for its members the holders of those shares or that stock, and no other persons.[354]

A joint stock company that satisfies the above definition when registered with limited liability under the CA 2006, is deemed a company limited by shares.[355] The definition is the same as that under s 683 of the CA 1985 Act. Section 1040(2) of the CA 2006 allows some joint stock companies to register under the Companies Acts as a company limited by shares.

Under s 1042 of the CA 2006, the Secretary of State has power to make provision by regulations in respect of the following:

• for and in connection with registration under s 1040 of the CA 2006;[356] and

• as to the application of the provisions of the Companies Acts to companies so registered.[357]

Regulations made under s 1042 of the CA 2006 may make provision

---

[353] CA 2006, s 1040(1)(a).   [354] CA 2006, s 1041(1)(b).   [355] CA 2006, s 1041(2).

[356] CA 2006, s 1042(1)(a). See the Non-Companies Acts Companies Authorised to Register Regulations 2008, which make provision in connection with the registration of a company following an application under s 1040 CA 2006.

[357] CA 2006, s 1042(1)(b).

corresponding to any provision formerly made by Chapter 2 of Part 22 to the CA 1985.[358]

Section 1042(2) of the CA 2006 confers a new power on the Secretary of State to make regulations in connection with the registration of company following an application under s 1040(1) of the CA 2006 (application by UK company not formed under the Companies Acts to register under the Companies Acts). Regulations made under this section will replace the provisions made by ss 681, 682–690 and Schedule 21 of the CA 1985. The regulations will cover the procedural requirements for registration, the conditions to be satisfied before registration, and the documents to be supplied on an application for registration. The regulations will also set out the consequences of registration, including the status of the company following registration and the application of the Companies Acts to such companies following registration.

Any regulations made under s 1042 of the CA 2006 are subject to the negative resolution procedure.[359]

Unregistered companies

3.25 Section 1(2) of the CA 2006 also states that certain provisions of the Companies Acts apply to bodies incorporated in the United Kingdom but not registered under the CA 2006. This regime applies to unregistered companies and governed by Chapter 2 of Part 33 of the CA 2006.

Section 1043 of the CA 2006 applies to bodies corporate incorporated in and having a principal place in the United Kingdom, other than:

- bodies incorporated by, or registered under, a public general Act of Parliament;[360] or
- bodies not formed for the purpose of carrying on a business that has for its object the acquisition of gain by the body or its individual members;[361] or
- bodies for the time being exempted by s 1043 of the CA 2006 by direction of the Secretary of State;[362] or

---

[358] CA 2006, s 1042(2). Chapter 2 of Part 22 to the CA 1985 concerned companies not formed under companies legislation but authorised to register. CA 1985, s 680 addressed the issue of companies capable of being registered under Chapter II; s 681 (procedural requirements for registration); s 682 (change of name on registration); s 683 (definition of 'joint stock company'); s 684 (requirements for registration by joint stock companies)' s 685 (registration of joint stock company as public company); s 686 (other requirements for registration); s 687 (name of company registering); s 688 (certificate of registration under this Chapter); s 689 (effect of registration); and s 690 (power to substitute memorandum and articles for deed of settlement).

[359] CA 2006, s 1042(3).   [360] CA 2006, s 1043(1)(a).   [361] CA 2006, s 1043(1)(b).

[362] CA 2006, s 1043(1)(c).

- open-ended investment companies.[363]

The Secretary of State may make provision by regulations applying specified provisions of the Companies Acts to all, or any specified description of, the bodies to which s 1043 of the CA 2006 applies.[364] The regulations may provide that the specified provisions of the Companies Acts apply subject to any specified limitations and to such adaptations and modifications (if any) as may be specified.[365] The term 'specified' means specified in the regulations.[366]

However, s 1043 of the CA 2006 does not repeal or revoke in whole or in part any enactment, royal charter or other instrument constituting or regulating any body in relation to which provisions of the Companies Acts are applied by regulations made under this section;[367] or restrict the power of Her Majesty to grant a charter or in lieu or supplementary to any such charter.[368]

However, in relation to any such body, the operation of any such enactment, charter or instrument is suspended insofar as it is inconsistent with any of those provisions as they apply for the time being to that body.

Section 1043 of the CA 2006 replaces s 718 of the CA 1985. It confers a power on the Secretary of State to apply provisions of the Companies Acts to certain unregistered companies. These are companies incorporated and having their principal place of business in UK, but not formed or registered under the Companies Acts, or any other public general Act of Parliament. Some examples include companies formed by letters patent, or by private Act of Parliament. Section 1043(1) of the CA 2006 exempts certain other companies, including those exempted by direction of the Secretary of State.

Regulations under s 1143 of the CA 2006 replace the provisions made by Schedule 22 of the CA 1985.[369] The regulations may apply specified provisions of the Companies Acts to specified descriptions of unregistered company and may make limitations, adaptations and modifications to the application of the Companies Acts to unregistered companies. The regulations are subject to the negative resolution procedure.[370]

Overseas companies

3.26 Section 1(3) of the CA 2006 refers to an overseas company that may be established. Part 34 of the CA 2006 governs the regime for overseas companies. An 'overseas company' is defined as a company incorporated outside the United Kingdom.[371] It enables various registration, reporting and

---

[363] CA 2006, s 1043(1)(d).
[364] CA 2006, s 1043(2). See the Companies (Unregistered Companies) Regulations 2008.
[365] CA 2006, s 1043(3).   [366] CA 2006, s 1043(5)   [367] CA 2006, s 1043(4)(a).
[368] CA 2006, s 1043(4)(b).
[369] CA 1985, Schedule 22 was concerned with provisions of that Act applying to unregistered companies.
[370] CA 2006, s 1043(6).   [371] CA 2006, s 1044.

disclosure requirements to be imposed on overseas companies. Sections 1044–1059 of the CA 2006 deal with the regime governing overseas companies, including registration of particulars of overseas companies, accounts and reports, and offences.

Part 34 of the CA 2006, together with the regulations to be made under it, replace the provisions made by Part 23 and Schedules 21A–D of the CA 1985. Regulations made under this Part will continue to implement the requirements of the Eleventh Company Law Directive (89/666/EEC), which imposes disclosure requirements on overseas companies that set up branches in the United Kingdom.

As originally enacted, Part 23 of the CA 1985 Act applied to companies incorporated outside Great Britain that established a place of business in Great Britain. Subsequently, the Eleventh Company Law Directive imposed a different set of disclosure requirements on those overseas companies with branches in the United Kingdom. The branch disclosure requirements also differed depending on whether or not the overseas company was incorporated within another EEA State. The result was that there were effectively two parallel regimes that applied to overseas companies.

The Company Law Review Group set out their initial analysis of the rules for regulating companies formed abroad in Chapter 5.6 of the *Strategic Framework*, and then put forward their provisional detailed conclusions in their consultation document of October 1999 entitled *Reforming the Law Concerning Overseas Companies*. The Company Law Review Group presented their conclusions in paras 11.21–11.33 of the *Final Report*.

Section 1044 of the CA 2006 defines an 'overseas company' for the purposes of the Companies Acts as a company incorporated outside the United Kingdom. This is wider than the definition of an overseas company in s 744 of the CA 1985, which it replaces. Section 744 of the CA 1985 referred to companies incorporated outside Great Britain that established a place of business in Great Britain.[372] However, the definition under s 1044 of the CA 2006 is wider, to include connection with the United Kingdom that gives rise to the various disclosure obligations imposed under Part 34 of the CA 2006.

The Secretary of State is empowered to make regulations applying ss 43–52 of the CA 2006 (formalities of doing business and other matters) to overseas companies. This is, however, subject to such exceptions, adaptations or modifications as may be specified in the regulations.[373]

---

[372] CA 1985, s 744 (expressions used in the CA 1985) defined an 'overseas company' as (a) a company incorporated elsewhere than in Great Britain which, after the commencement of this Act, establishes a place of business in Great Britain; and (b) a company so incorporated which has, before that commencement, established a place of business and continues to have an established place of business in Great Britain at that commencement. The expression 'place of business' included a share transfer or share registration office.

[373] CA 2006, s 1045(1).

Regulations made under s 1045 of the CA 2006 are subject to a negative resolution procedure.[374]

Part 34 of the CA 2006 addresses the issue of registration of particulars for an overseas company. Section 1046 of the CA 2006 gives the Secretary of State a new power to make regulations to require overseas companies to register with the registrar of companies. The regulations will require an overseas company to deliver with the registrar of companies a return containing specified particulars for registration, and to deliver to the registrar specified documents with the return. The regulations may require particular information to be included in the registration: for example, an address for the company and details of its directors. The regulations may also require particular documents to be sent to the registrar, such as a copy of the company's constitution.

In the case of a company other than a Gibraltar company, the regulations must require the company to register particulars if the company opens a branch in the United Kingdom.[375] However, the regulations may, in the case of a Gibraltar company, require the company to register particulars if the company opens a branch in the United Kingdom.[376] Further, the regulations may, in any case, require the registration of particulars in such other circumstances as may be specified.[377] Section 1046(2) of the CA 2006, ensures that the regulations implement the requirements of the Eleventh Company Law Directive (89/666/EEC), under which an overseas company must register of the company opens a branch in the UK.

The regulations may require the overseas company to inform the registrar of companies of any changes in the details or documents it has registered. In particular, where a company has registered particulars under s 1046 of the CA 2006 and any alteration is made in the specified particulars,[378] or in any document delivered with the return,[379] the regulations may provide that the company must deliver to the registrar for registration, a return containing specified particulars of the alteration. The term 'specified' means as specified in the regulations.[380]

The regulations may also make provision requiring the return to be delivered for registration to the registrar for a specified part of the United Kingdom,[381] and requiring it to be delivered before the end of a specified period.[382] The regulations may set deadlines for sending the information to the registrar of companies. They may also determine whether the overseas company should register with the registrar for England and Wales, the

[374] CA 2006, s 1045(2).   [375] CA 2006, s 1046(2)(a).

[376] CA 2006, s 1046(2)(b). The term 'branch' means a branch within the meaning of the Eleventh Company Law Directive (89/666/EEC). 'Gibraltar Company' means a company incorporated in Gibraltar (CA 2006, s 1046(3)).

[377] CA 2006, s 1046(2).   [378] CA 2006, s 1046(4)(a).   [379] CA 2006, s 1046(4)(b).

[380] CA 2006, s 1046(7).   [381] CA 2006, s 1046(5)(a).   [382] CA 2006, s 1046(5)(b).

registrar for Scotland or the registrar for Northern Ireland. Section 1046(6) of the CA 2006 states that the regulations may make different provision according to the place where the company is incorporated,[383] and the activities carried on (or proposed to be carried on) by the company.[384] For example, an overseas company that opens a branch in Scotland may be required to register with the registrar of companies for Scotland. This is, however, without prejudice to the general power to make different provision for different cases.

The Eleventh Company Law Directive imposes different disclosure requirements depending on where the overseas company setting up the branch is incorporated. Different reporting requirements are imposed on credit and financial institutions. Therefore, regulations under s 1046 of the CA 2006 may take different provision according to the place where the company is incorporated and the activities carried on by it. All regulations made under s 1046 of the CA 2006 will be subject to the affirmative resolution procedure.[385]

Registered name of overseas company

3.27 Section 1047 of the CA 2006 applies to overseas companies that are required to register with the registrar of companies by regulations made under s 1046 of the CA 2006 (duty to register particulars). Overseas companies registered under that section will be required to provide a name for registration. The name will be entered on the index of company names (governed by s 1099 of the CA 2006).[386]

The company may register its corporate name (by which is meant its registered or legal name in its place of incorporation),[387] or another name referred to as an alternative name in accordance with s 1048 of the CA 2006.[388] All companies are free to choose whether to register their corporate name or an alternative name, subject to the restrictions imposed by s 1047(4) and (5) of the CA 2005. A name other than the corporate name can be registered only if it complies with the requirements imposed on the names of companies formed and registered under the of the CA 2006. Likewise, unless the overseas company is incorporated in an EEA State, its corporate name can only be registered if it complies with these requirements. The only requirements of Chapters 1 to 4 of Part 5 of the CA 2006 (company's name) that do not apply, are the requirements for the names of certain types of company to end with certain words (ss 58 and 59 of the CA 2006). These rules are not appropriate for overseas companies as they are specific to the types of company formed under the Companies Acts.

---

[383] CA 2006, s 1046(6)(a).   [384] CA 2006, s 1046(6)(b).   [385] CA 2006, s 1046(8).
[386] CA 2006, s 1047(1).   [387] CA 2006, s 1047(2)(a).   [388] CA 2006, s 1047(2)(b).

Under s 1047(3) of the CA 2006, where the overseas company is incorporated in an EEA State (defined in s 1170 of the CA 2006), it may always register its corporate name, even if it does not comply with the requirements imposed on the names of companies formed under the CA 2006, other than the requirement relating to permitted characters (contained in s 57 of the CA 2006). Section 1047(3), together with s 1048 of the CA 2006 (registration under an alternative name) replaces s 694 of the CA 1985.

Section 1047(4) of the CA 2006 states that in any other case, the following provisions of Part 5 of the CA 2006 (a company's name) will apply in relation to registration of the name of an overseas company:

(a)   s 53 of the CA 2006 (prohibited names);[389]
(b)   ss 54–56 of the CA 2006 (sensitive words and expressions);[390]
(c)   s 65 of the CA 2006 (inappropriate use of indications of company type or legal form);[391]
(d)   ss 66–74 of the CA 2006 (similarity to other names);[392]
(e)   s 75 of the CA 2006 (provision of misleading information, etc);[393]
(f)   s 76 of the CA 2006 (misleading indication of activities).[394]

Further, s 57 of the CA 2006 (permitted characters) will apply in every case to an overseas company.[395] Any reference in s 1047(4) and (5) to a change of name will be read as a reference to registration of a different name under s 1048 of the CA 2006.[396]

Registration under an alternative name

3.28 Section 1048 of the CA 2006 addresses registration under an alternative name. It enables an overseas company to be registered under an alternative name rather than its corporate name. It also enables an overseas company to change the name by which it is registered. To do so, it must deliver a statement to the registrar of companies with its proposed new name for registration.[397] As long as the proposed name complies with the requirements for registration (see s 1047 of the CA 2006), the registrar of companies will enter it on the index of company names in place of the name previously registered.

Section 1048(3) of the CA 2006 also provides that whatever name an overseas company is registered under, whether its corporate name or an

---

[389] CA 2006, s 1047(4)(a).   [390] CA 2006, s 1047(4)(b).   [391] CA 2006, s 1047(4)(c).
[392] CA 2006, s 1047(4)(d).   [393] CA 2006, s 1047(4)(e).   [394] CA 2006, s 1047(4)(f).
[395] CA 2006, s 1047(5).   [396] CA 2006, s 1047(6).
[397] CA 2006, ss 1048(1) and (2). Section 1048(1) applies where an overseas company is required to register particulars under CA 2006, s 1046; and s 1048(2) applies where an overseas company has registered an alternative name with the registrar of companies.

alternative, it is treated as being its corporate name for the purposes of the law in the United Kingdom. The change of name will not affect the references in s 1048 of the CA 2006 or s 1047 of the CA 2006 to the company's corporate name;[398] nor will it affect any rights or obligations of the company;[399] or render defective any legal proceedings that are continued or commenced by or against the company.[400]

Accounts and reports: general

3.29 Part 34 of the CA 2006 also sets out other requirements that apply to the establishment of an overseas company. The Secretary of State has power to make regulations requiring overseas companies that are required to register particulars under s 1046 of the CA 2006, to prepare appropriate accounts and a directors' report;[401] and cause to be prepared such an auditor's report.[402] The requirement must be like those imposed on companies formed and registered under the CA 2006.[403] The accounts, directors' report and auditor's report requirements applying to companies formed and registered under the CA 2006 appear in Part 15 (accounts and reports) and Part 16 (audit) of the CA 2006.

Regulations under s 1049 of the CA 2006 may modify those requirements set out in Part 15 and Part 16 of the CA 2006 in their application to overseas companies as appropriate.[404] Regulations under s 1049 of the CA 2006 may require the overseas company to deliver to the registrar of companies copies of the accounts and reports prepared in accordance with the regulations;[405] alternatively the overseas company may be required to deliver to the registrar a copy of the accounts and reports that it has prepared, and have them audited in accordance with the law of the country in which it is incorporated.[406]

Regulations under s 1049 of the CA 2006 replace ss 699AA–703 and Schedule 21D of the CA 1985. The regulations will be subject to the negative resolution procedure.[407]

Accounts and reports: credit or financial institutions

3.30 Section 1050 of the CA 2006 applies only to credit or financial institutions incorporated or formed outside the United Kingdom and Gibraltar,[408] with their head office outside the United Kingdom and Gibraltar,[409] but

---

[398] CA 2006, s 1048(4)(a).   [399] CA 2006, s 1048(4)(b).   [400] CA 2006, s 1048(4)(c).
[401] CA 2006, s 1049(1)(a).   [402] CA 2006, s 1049(1)(b).   [403] CA 2006, s 1049(1).
[404] CA 2006, s 1049(2).   [405] CA 2006, s 1049(3)(a).   [406] CA 2006, s 1049(3)(b).
[407] CA 2006, s 1049(4).   [408] CA 2006, s 1050(1)(a).   [409] CA 2006, s 1050(1)(b).

having a branch in the UK.[410] The term 'branch' refers to a place of business that forms a legally dependent part of the institution and conducts directly all or some of the operations inherent in its business.[411]

This section confers on the Secretary of State a power to make regulations specifically in respect of like accounts and directors' report;[412] and cause to be prepared such an auditor's report[413] by these credit or financial institutions, as would be required if the institution were a company formed and registered under the CA 2006. The regulations apply with or without modifications all or any of the provisions of Part 15 (accounts and reports) and Part 16 (audit) of the CA 2006.[414] Further, the Secretary of State may under the regulations require an institution to deliver to the registrar copies of the accounts prepared in accordance with the regulations,[415] or accounts and reports that it is required to prepare and have audited under the law of the country in which the institution has its head office.[416]

Reference to 'credit institution' and 'financial institution' are both defined in s 1173 of the CA 2006.

The regulations under this section will implement requirements of the Bank Branches Directive 89/117/EEC of the Council, of 13 February 1989. The definition of 'branch' for the purposes of this section (s 1050(2) of the CA 2006 is based on article 1(3) of Directive 2000/12/EC of the European Parliament and of the Council of 20 March 2000 relating to the taking up and pursuance of the business of credit institutions. The power to make regulations under this section is similar to that under s 1049 of the CA 2006 (accounts and reports: general).

The regulations replace s 699A and Schedule 21C of the CA 1985. The regulations are subject to the negative resolution procedure.[417]

Trading disclosures

3.31 Section 1051 of the CA 2006 addresses the issue of trading disclosures for overseas companies. It confers on the Secretary of State a power to make regulations as to the specified information that overseas companies carrying on business in the United Kingdom must provide:

(a) companies must display specified information in specified locations. For example, a sign with their name outside every branch;[418]
(b) they must give specified information in specified descriptions of document or communication. For example, their name and country of incorporation on every invoice;[419] or

---

[410] CA 2006, s 1050(1)(c).   [411] CA 2006, s 1050(2).   [412] CA 2006, s 1050(3)(a).
[413] CA 2006, s 1050(3)(b).   [414] CA 2006, s 1050(4).   [415] CA 2006, s 1050(5)(a).
[416] CA 2006, s 1050(5)(b).   [417] CA 2006, s 1050(6).   [418] CA 2006, s 1051(1)(a).
[419] CA 2006, s 1051(1)(b).

(c)   they must provide specified information on request to those they deal
with in the course of business.[420]

The regulations must in every case require a company that has registered
particulars under s 1046 of the CA 2006, to disclose the name registered by it
under s 1047 of the CA 2006.[421] Further, the regulations may make provision
as to the manner in which any specified information is to be displayed, stated
or provided.[422]

The regulations may also make provision, corresponding to that made in
ss 83 (civil consequences of failure to make required disclosure) and 84 (criminal consequences of failure to make required disclosure) of the CA 2006, in
respect of a failure by a company formed and registered under the Companies Acts to comply with the trading disclosure requirements imposed on
them by regulations under s 82 of the CA 2006.[423]

Regulations under s 1051 of the CA 2006, like those under s 82 of the CA
2006, are subject to the affirmative resolution procedure.[424] Regulations made
under s 1051 of the CA 2006 replace s 693 of the CA 1985. Section 1051 of
the CA 2006 complements the similar power under s 82 of the CA 2006 to
make regulations imposing trading disclosure obligations in companies
formed and registered under the Companies Acts.

Company charges

3.32 There are specific provisions dealing with company charges applicable
to overseas companies. Section 1052 of the CA 2006 provides that the
Secretary of State may by regulations make provision about the registration
of specified charges over property in the United Kingdom of a registered
overseas company.[425] The regulations would enable the Secretary of State to
make provision about the following:

(a)   a registered overseas company that has particulars registered in more
than one part of the United Kingdom;[426] or has property in more than
one part of the United Kingdom;[427]

(b)   the circumstances in which the property is to be regarded as being or not
being, in the United Kingdom, or in a particular part of the United
Kingdom;[428]

---

[420] CA 2006, s 1051(1)(c).   [421] CA 2006, s 1051(2)(a).   [422] CA 2006, s 1051(2)(b).
[423] CA 2006, s 1051(3).   [424] CA 2006 s 1051(5).
[425] CA 2006, s 1052(1). The term 'registered overseas company' means an overseas company that
has registered particulars under CA 2006, s 1046(1): CA 2006, s 1053(6).
[426] CA 2006, s 1052(2)(a)(i).   [427] CA 2006, s 1052(2)(a)(ii).   [428] CA 2006, s 1052(2)(b).

(c)   the keeping by a registered overseas company of records and registers about specified charges and their inspection;[429]

(d)   the consequences of a failure to register a charge in accordance with the regulations;[430]

(e)   the circumstances in which a registered overseas company ceases to be subject to the regulations.[431]

The regulations may apply, with or without modifications any of the provisions of Part 25 of the CA 2006 (company charges).[432] Further, the regulations may modify any reference in an enactment to Part 25, or to a particular provision of that Part, so as to include a reference to the regulations or to a specified provision of the regulations.[433] The regulations are subject to negative resolution procedure.[434]

This section applies to overseas companies that are required to register particulars under s 1046 of the CA 2006. It gives the Secretary of State power to make regulations about the registration by those companies of charges they grant over property in the United Kingdom. Section 1052(2) of the CA 2006 sets out some of the matters that may be dealt with in such regulations. Sections 1052(3) and (4) provide the regime for overseas companies to mirror specified provisions in Part 25 of the CA 2006, with modifications. Section 1052 of the CA 2006 replaces s 409 (charges on property in England and Wales created by an overseas company) and s 424 (extension of Chapter 2) of the CA 1985.

Other returns

3.33 Overseas companies that are required to register particulars under s 1046 of the CA 2006 are subject to the requirement to file other returns in certain circumstances.[435] Section 1053(2) of the CA 2006 confers on the Secretary of State a power to make regulations requiring those companies to deliver returns to the registrar if they are being wound up;[436] or become or cease to be the subject of insolvency proceedings, or composition or any analogous proceedings.[437] The regulations may also require the liquidator of such companies to deliver returns to the registrar.[438]

The regulations may specify the circumstances in which a return is to be made to the registrar:[439] for example, on termination of the winding-up of a company. The regulations may specify the particulars to be given in the

---

[429] CA 2006, s 1052(2)(c).   [430] CA 2006, s 1052(2)(d).   [431] CA 2006, s 1052(2)(e).

[432] CA 2006, s 1052(3).

[433] CA 2006, s 1052(4). The term 'specified' means as specified in the regulations: CA 2006, s 1053(6).

[434] CA 2006, s 1052(5).   [435] CA 2006, s 1053(1).   [436] CA 2006, s 1053(2)(a)(i).

[437] CA 2006, s 1053(2)(a)(ii).   [438] CA 2006, s 1053(2)(b).   [439] CA 2006, s 1053(3)(a).

return;[440] as well as the period within which it is to be made.[441] They may require notice to be given to the registrar of the appointment of a judicial factor in Scotland[442] and may, to that end, include any provision corresponding to the equivalent obligation placed on companies incorporated in the United Kingdom by s 1154 of the CA 2006 (duty to notify registrar of certain appointments).[443]

The regulations replace ss 703P and 703Q of the CA 1985. The regulations are subject to the affirmative resolution procedure.[444]

Offences

3.34 The offences for breach of Part 34 of the CA 2006 are set out in s 1054 of the CA 2006. Section 1054(1) of the CA 2006 ensures that the regulations will be able to specify the person or persons who would be responsible for complying with any specified requirement of the regulations. It allows regulations to provide for offences, including the person or persons who would be liable in the event of any specified contravention of the regulations;[445] and circumstances that are, or are not, to be a defence on a charge of such an offence.[446]

The regulations must not provide for imprisonment.[447] The maximum level of penalty permissible under the regulations on indictment is an unlimited fine and on summary conviction a fine not exceeding level 5 on the standard scale, or for continued contravention, or a daily contravention, a daily default fine not exceeding one-tenth of that.[448]

The objective of s 1054 of the CA 2006 is to ensure that the regulations will be able to specify the person or persons who would be responsible for complying with any specified requirement of the regulations. It allows regulations to provide for offences, including who would be liable in the event of any contravention and what might be considered a defence if a charge were to be brought.

Disclosure of individual's residential address: protection from disclosure

3.35 Under s 1055 of the CA 2006, if the regulations under s 1046 of the CA 2006 require an overseas company to register an individual's usual residential address, then the regulations must also provide for its protection on the same basis as is provided for the director's residential addresses in Chapter 8 of Part 10 of the CA 2006.

[440] CA 2006, s 1053(3)(b).   [441] CA 2006, s 1053(3)(c).   [442] CA 2006, s 1053(4.
[443] CA 2006, s 1053(5).   [444] CA 2006, s 1053(6).   [445] CA 2006, s 1054(2)(a).
[446] CA 2006, s 1054(2)(b). The term 'specified' means as specified in the regulations: CA 2006, s 1054(4).
[447] CA 2006, s 1054(3)(a).   [448] CA 2006, s 1054(3)(b).

Requirement to identify persons authorised to accept service of documents

3.36 Under s 1056 of the CA 2006, every overseas company required by regulations under s 1046 of the CA 2006 to register with the registrar of companies, must register particulars identifying every person resident in the United Kingdom, who is authorised to accept service of documents on the company's behalf;[449] or make a statement that there is no such person.[450]

The process as to how a document may be served on a registered overseas company is set out in s 1139(2) of the CA 2006, and the company communication provisions under ss 1144–1148 of the CA 2006 and Schedules 4 and 5 of the CA 2006.

Section 1056 of the CA 2006 replaces the provision made by s 691(1)(b)(ii) and para 3 (e) of Schedule 21A to the CA 1985.

Registrar to whom returns, notices, etc. to be delivered

3.37 Section 1057 of the CA 2006 makes a provision for regulations in respect of overseas companies that are required to register, or have registered, particulars under s 1046 of the CA 2006 on more one part of the United Kingdom.[451] Such regulations may set out what should happen, for example, if the overseas company has registered branches in Scotland and in Northern Ireland. The Secretary of State may provide by regulations that, in the case of such a company, anything authorised or required to be delivered to the registrar under Part 34 of the CA 2006 must be delivered to the registrar for each part of the United Kingdom in which the company is required to register or has registered particulars;[452] or to the registrar for such part or parts of the United Kingdom as may be specified or determined in accordance with the regulations.[453]

The regulations may require the returns or notices to be delivered to each registrar with which the company is registered, or to the registrar for such part or parts of the United Kingdom as the regulations may specify.

Regulations made under s 1057 of the CA 2006 are subject to the negative resolution procedure.[454]

Duty to give notice of ceasing to have registerable presence

3.38 Where an overseas company has registered particulars with the registrar following the opening of a branch in the United Kingdom, s 1058 of the CA

---

[449] CA 2006, s 1056(a).   [450] CA 2006, s 1056(b).   [451] CA 2006, s 1057(1).
[452] CA 2006, s 1057(2)(a).   [453] CA 2006, s 1057(2)(b).   [454] CA 2006, s 1057(3).

2006 will enable regulations to require the overseas company to give notice to the registrar if it subsequently closes that branch.[455]

In addition, an overseas company that has registered particulars in other circumstances specified by regulations under s 1046 of the CA 2006, may be required by regulations to give notice to the registrar if those circumstances cease to obtain.[456] The regulations will require the notice to be delivered to the registrar for the part of the United Kingdom in which the original return of particulars was delivered,[457] and may set deadlines for sending the information to the registrar.[458]

Regulations made under s 1058 of the CA 2006 will be subject to negative resolution procedure.[459]

Application of provisions in case of relocation of branch

3.39 Section 1059 of the CA 2006 deals with relocation of a branch. It provides that the relocation of a branch from one part of the United Kingdom to another is to be treated as a closing of the branch in one part and an opening in another. For example, if an overseas company moves a branch from Scotland to Wales, it must inform the registrar for Scotland that it is closing the branch. It must also inform the registrar for England and Wales that it is opening a branch in Wales. Section 1059 of the CA 2006 replaces the provision made by s 695A(4) of the CA 1985.

Directors' Residential Addresses: Non-Disclosure Certificate

The position before the CA 2006

3.40 Under the CA 1985 (and previous Companies Acts), the usual residential address of every director was required to be entered on the public record held by the registrar, and each company of which he is director in its register of directors.

Access to the public record as held by the registrar was made in a variety of ways, including daily bulk downloading by some subscribers. There was also a public right to inspect companies' registers of directors. There was an exception for directors at serious risk of violence or intimidation, for example, from political activists and terrorists. Under ss 723B–723E of the CA 1985, introduced by the Criminal Justice and Police Act 2001, directors could apply for a 'confidentiality order'. A director with a confidentiality order provided a single service address in addition to his usual residential

---

[455] CA 2006, s 1058(1)(a).   [456] CA 2006, s 1058(1)(b).   [457] CA 2006, s 1058(2).
[458] CA 2006, s 1058(3).   [459] CA 2006, s 1058(4).

address. The services address was entered on the public record; the usual residential address was kept on a secure register to which access was restricted to specified enforcement authorities. The historic record was not affected by the confidentiality order.

Section 723B of the CA 1985 allowed a present or prospective director or company secretary or permanent representative to apply to the Secretary of State for Trade and Industry for a confidentiality order, which had the effect of disapplying the requirement that his usual residential address be available for inspection on the public record. The application was required to be accompanied by a service address, which would appear on the public record in place of the residential address. The objective was to offer protection for those who may be at serious risk of violence or intimidation if their home address became public knowledge. The Secretary of State would determine whether the grounds for such an application had been met. This section enabled further provision to be made about confidentiality orders, including provision for the payment of fees on the making of an application to fund the cost of setting up and maintaining the system of confidentiality orders, the manner in which applications for such orders were to be made, including the information to be given by applicants and the procedure for determining how the decision on the application was to be reached, and provision for the period for which the confidentiality orders were to remain in force and the grounds for revoking such orders.

Section 723C of the CA 1985 set out the effect of a confidentiality order. This was to remove the right of public access to the usual residential address of the directors concerned, which was to be held as a confidential record by Companies House, and to require the company's annual return to show the service address, rather than the usual home address of the director. The section provided for Regulations to make provision for similar protection for usual residential addresses filed on the company's own register of directors. It also provided for Regulations to make provision for the inspection of the confidential records and for applications for access. The section also enabled provision to be made as to the conditions governing the choice of service address. It was anticipated that certain public bodies such as law enforcement agencies would have automatic access rights to the private address under the Regulations; the Regulations would cover the means by which those not afforded automatic rights would be able to apply to be given access by the court.

Section 723D of the CA 1985 provided for the construction of the terms used in ss 723B and 723C of the CA 1985. The terms defined included 'relevant company', 'permanent representative of a company', 'confidential records' and 'confidentiality order'. It also enabled the court, which could, if the Regulations provided, approve applications for access to the confidential record – to be identified in the regulations. The section enabled regulations to provide that documents delivered after the coming into force of a confidentiality order could be treated as having been delivered at the time that they were required by law to be delivered. This sought to ensure that companies would not delay presenting information that they were required to do by law in order to take advantage of the possible granting of a confidentiality order. This section also made clear that it was not necessary to make an application for a confidentiality order for the company in which the applicant sought to become a director to have been incorporated or established a branch at the time of the application.

Section 723E(1) of the CA 1985 enabled regulations to be made providing for it to be an offence for a person to give false information knowingly or recklessly when applying for a confidentiality order, or for providing confidential information in breach of the regulations made under s 723C of the CA 1985.

The Company Law Review Group considered it essential that directors' residential addresses be filed with the central register, so that enforcement and regulatory bodies as well as regulators, and in some circumstances creditors and shareholders, could discover the individual's residential address. However, they were concerned that unrestricted public access to directors' residential addresses was being abused. They considered that there should not be any discretion as to whether particular address should or should not be placed on the public record. Therefore, welcoming the introduction of the confidentiality order regime, they recommended all directors be given the option of either, as now, providing their residential address for the public record; or, providing both a service address and their residential address, with the service address being on the public record and the residential address being on a separate secure register to which would be restricted. Access to the restricted register would be available to certain public authorities. Other parties, such as members and creditors, should have a right to apply to the court for access to a director's residential address.[460]

The position under the CA 2006

3.41 Chapter 8 to Part 10 of the CA 2006 implements the recommendation by the Company Law Review Group. These provisions replace the confidentiality order regime under the CA 1985.

Protected information

3.42 Section 240 of the CA 2006 and Chapter 8 to Part 10 of the CA 2006 make provision for protecting, in the case of a company director who is an individual, the information as to his usual residential address;[461] and the

---

[460] Company Law Review Group, *Final Report*, para 11.46.
[461] CA 2006, s 240(1)(a).

information that his service address is his usual residential address.[462] Chapter 8 of the CA 2006 refers to this information as 'protected information'.[463] Information does not cease to be protected information on the individual ceasing to be a director of the company. Further, the references in Chapter 8 of the CA 2006 to a director include, to that extent, a former director.[464]

Section 240 of the CA 2006 sets out the information about directors' usual residential addresses, recorded under Chapter 1 to Part 10 of the CA 2006, that will be protected under the new provisions.

Protected information: restriction on use or disclosure by company

3.43 Section 241 of the CA 2006 states that a company must not use or disclose protected information about any of its directors, except for communicating with the director concerned;[465] or in order to comply with any requirement of the Companies Acts as to particulars to be sent to the registrar;[466] or in accordance with s 244 of the CA 2006 (disclosure under court order).[467]

Section 241(1) of the CA 2006 does not prohibit any use or disclosure of protected information with the consent of the director concerned.[468]

Section 241 of the CA 2006 provides for the protection that a company must give to the information covered by s 240 of the CA 2006. It prohibits the company from using the individual's home address without his consent, except for communicating with him, or to comply with an obligation to send information to the registrar or when required by a court.

Protected information: restriction on use or disclosure by the registrar

3.44 Section 242 of the CA 2006 requires that the registrar must omit protected information from the material on the register that is available for inspection where it is contained in a document, delivered to him, in which such information is required to be stated;[469] and in the case of a document having more than one part, it is contained in a part of the document in which such information is required to be stated.[470]

The registrar is not obliged to check other documents or (as the case may be) other parts of the document to ensure the absence of protected information;[471] or to omit from the material that is available for public inspection anything registered before this Chapter comes into force.[472]

The registrar must not use or disclose protected information except as permitted by s 243 of the CA 2006 (permitted use or disclosure by

---

[462] CA 2006, s 240(1)(b).   [463] CA 2006, s 240(2).   [464] CA 2006, s 240(3).
[465] CA 2006, s 241(1)(a).   [466] CA 2006, s 241(1)(b).   [467] CA 2006, s 241(1)(c).
[468] CA 2006, s 241(2).   [469] CA 2006, s 242(1)(a).   [470] CA 2006, s 242(1)(b).
[471] CA 2006 s 242(2)(a).   [472] CA 2006, s 242(2)(b).

registrar);[473] or in accordance with s 244 of the CA 2006 (disclosure under court order).[474]

Section 242 of the CA 2006 provides for protection by the registrar of information that is covered by s 240 of the CA 2006. The registrar need only protect information where it is submitted on a form where directors' usual residential addresses are required and entered in the appropriate place. The registrar is not obliged to check all documents submitted to him to ensure that an address has not been inadvertently disclosed. The protection is not retrospective: it does not apply to information on the public record when these provisions come into force. The CA 2006 makes separate provision in s 1088 of the CA 2006, for removal of addresses from the register in circumstances specified by regulations.

Permitted use or disclosure by the registrar

3.45 Section 243 of the CA 2006 states that the registrar may use protected information for communicating with the director in question.[475]

The registrar may disclose protected information to a public authority[476] specified for the purposes of s 243 of the CA 2006 by regulations made by the Secretary of State[477] or to a credit reference agency.[478]

The Secretary of State may make provision by regulations specifying the conditions for the disclosure of protected information in accordance with s 243 of the CA 2006;[479] and providing for the charging of fees.[480]

The Secretary of State may make provision by regulations requiring the registrar, on application, to refrain from disclosing protected information relating to a director to a credit reference agency.[481]

The regulations under s 243(4) of the CA 2006 may make provision as to who may make an application;[482] the grounds on which an application may be made;[483] the information to be included in and documents to accompany an application;[484] and how an application is to be determined.[485]

The provision under s 243(5)(d) of the CA 2006 may in particular confer a discretion on the registrar;[486] and provide for a question to be referred to a

---

[473] CA 2006, s 242(3)(a).   [474] CA 2006, s 242(3)(b).   [475] CA 2006, s 243(1).

[476] The term 'public authority' includes any person or body having functions of a public nature.

[477] CA 2006, s 243(2)(a).

[478] CA 2006, s 243(2)(b). The term 'credit reference agency' means a person carrying on a business comprising the furnishing of information relevant to the financial standing of individuals, being information collected by the agency for that purpose: CA 2006, s 243(7).

[479] CA 2006, s 243(3)(a).   [480] CA 2006, s 243(3)(b).

[481] CA 2006, s 243(4). See the Companies (Particulars of Usual Residential Address) Regulations 2008 which make provisions relating to applications under ss 243 and 1088 CA 2006.

[482] CA 2006, s 243(5)(a).   [483] CA 2006, s 243(5)(b)   [484] CA 2006, s 243(5)(c).

[485] CA 2006, s 243(5)(d).   [486] CA 2006, s 243(6)(a).

person other than the registrar for the purposes of determining the application.[487]

Regulations made under s 243 of the CA 2006 are subject to negative resolution procedure.[488]

This section provides for certain kinds of permitted use or disclosure of a director's home address, that is, directors' home addresses and whether a service address is a home address.

Section 243(1) of the CA 2006 provides that the registrar may use the protected information for communicating with the director in question. Section 243(2) of the CA 2006 provides that the registrar may disclose protected information to a public authority or credit reference agency (as defined under the Consumer Credit Act 1974, but which should be read with s 243(3) and (4) of the CA 2006). Section 243(3) of the CA 2006 confers power on the Secretary of State to make regulations specifying conditions that must be met before the registrar may disclose protected information. The regulations may also provide for fees to be paid by the authority or agency seeking the address. Section 243(4) of the CA 2006 provides power to make regulations specifying the circumstances in which an application can be made for a director's address not to be revealed to a credit reference agency.

Disclosure under court order

3.46 Section 244 of the CA 2006 states that the court may make an order for the disclosure of protected information by the company or by the registrar in the following circumstances: if there is evidence that service of documents at a service address other than the director's usual residential address is not effective in bringing them to the notice of the director;[489] or it is necessary or expedient for the information to be provided in connection with the enforcement of an order or decree of the court.[490] Further, the court must otherwise be satisfied that it is appropriate to make the order.

An order for disclosure by the registrar is to be made only if the company does not have the director's usual residential address;[491] or has been dissolved.[492] The order may be made on the application of a liquidator, creditor or member of the company, or any other person appearing to the court to have a sufficient interest.[493]

The order must specify the persons to whom, and purposes for which, disclosure is authorised.[494]

Section 244 of the CA 2006 provides for two circumstances in which the court may require the company to disclose protected information. The first circumstance is that the service address is not effective; the second is that the

[487] CA 2006, s 243(6)(b).   [488] CA 2006, s 243(8).   [489] CA 2006, s 244(1)(a).
[490] CA 2006, s 244(1)(b).   [491] CA 2006, s 244(2)(a).   [492] CA 2006, s 244(2)(b).
[493] CA 2006, s 244(3).   [494] CA 2006, s 244(4).

home address is needed for the enforcement of an order or decree of the court. If the company cannot provide the address, the court may require the registrar to reveal it.

Section 244(3) of the CA 2006 provides that the application for the order may be made not only by a liquidator, creditor or member of the company, but also by anyone with sufficient interest.

Circumstances in which registrar may put address on the public record

3.47 Section 245 of the CA 2006 states that the registrar may put a director's usual residential address on the public record if communications sent by the registrar to the director and requiring a response within a specified time period remain unanswered;[495] or there is evidence that service of documents at a service address provided in place of the director's usual residential address is not effective in bringing them to the notice of the director.[496]

The registrar must give notice of the proposal to the director;[497] and to every company of which the registrar has been notified that the individual is a director.[498] The notice must state the grounds on which it is proposed to put the director's usual residential address on the public record;[499] and specify a period within which representations may be made before that is done.[500]

It must be sent to the director at his usual residential address, unless it appears to the registrar that service at that address may be ineffective to bring it to the individual's notice, in which case it may be sent to any service address provided in place of that address.[501]

The registrar must take account of any representations received within the specified period.[502] What is meant by putting the address on the public record is set out in s 246 of the CA 2006.[503]

The objective of s 245 of the CA 2006 is that if a service address is not effective, then the home address can be put on the public record. It provides for the registrar to send a warning notice, with a specified period for representations before the intended action, both to the director and to every company of which he is a director. The registrar must take account of any representations made within the specified period in deciding whether to proceed as provided by s 245 of the CA 2006.

Putting the address on the public record

3.48 Section 246 of the CA 2006 states that the registrar, on deciding in accordance with s 245 of the CA 2006 that a director's usual residential address is to be put on the public record, must proceed as if notice of a

---

[495] CA 2006, s 245(1)(a).   [496] CA 2006, s 245(1)(b).   [497] CA 2006, s 245(2)(a).
[498] CA 2006, s 245(2)(b).   [499] CA 2006, s 245(3)(a).   [500] CA 2006, s 245(3)(b).
[501] CA 2006, s 245(4).   [502] CA 2006, s 245(5).   [503] CA 2006, s 245(6).

change of registered particulars had been given stating that address as the director's service address;[504] and stating that the director's usual residential address is the same as his service address.[505]

The registrar must give notice of having done so to the director;[506] and to the company.[507] On receipt of the notice, the company must enter the director's usual residential address in its register of directors as his service address;[508] and state in its register of directors' residential addresses that his usual residential address is the same as his service address.[509]

If the company has been notified by the director in question of a more recent address as his usual residential address, it must enter that address in the register of directors as the director's service address;[510] and give notice to the registrar as on a change of registered particulars.[511]

If a company fails to comply with s 246(3) or (4) of the CA 2006, an offence is committed by the company;[512] and every officer of the company who is in default.[513] A person guilty of an offence under s 246(5) of the CA 2006 is liable under summary conviction to a fine not exceeding level 5 on the standard scale and, for continued contravention, a daily default fine not exceeding one-tenth of level 5 on the standard scale.[514]

A director whose usual residential address has been put on the public record by the registrar under s 246 of the CA 2006, may not register a service address other than his usual residential address for a period of five years from the date of the registrar's decision.

The effect of s 246 of the CA 2006 is to provide that, if the registrar is putting a director's home address on the public record under s 245 of the CA 2006, then the registrar updates the public record as if she had been notified that the service address is the director's home address. She must also notify both the director and every company of which he/she is a director. The companies must each put the director's home address on its register of directors as his/her service address. And for the next five years, the director may not register a service address other than his usual residential address.

---

[504] CA 2006, s 246(1)(a).   [505] CA 2006, s 246(1)(b).   [506] CA 2006, s 246(2)(a).
[507] CA 2006, s 246(2)(b).   [508] CA 2006, s 246(3)(a).   [509] CA 2006, s 246(3)(b).
[510] CA 2006, s 246(4)(a).   [511] CA 2006, s 229(4)(b).   [512] CA 2006, s 246(5)(a),
[513] CA 2006, s 246(5)(b).   [514] CA 2006, s 246(6).

Company's Constitution and Corporate Capacity

Introduction

4.1 The provisions dealing with a company's constitution are set out in Part 3 of the CA 2006. Part 3 comprises four chapters. It replaces similar provisions in the CA 1985. It starts by defining (non-exhaustively) 'a company's constitution' (because the definition is used in a wider context in Part 10 of the CA 2006), and then makes provision about the main constituent parts of a company's constitution (the Articles of Association and certain classes of members' resolutions and agreements), including their legal effects, how they are to be notified to the registrar and made available to members, and how changes to them are to be dealt with. Chapter 1 of Part 3 is concerned with introductory provisions to the company's constitution. Chapter 2 deals with the Articles of Association. Chapter 3 concerns resolutions and agreements affecting a company's constitution; and Chapter 4 considers miscellaneous and supplementary provisions.

Owing to the related constitutional issues, this chapter also considers a company's capacity and related matters. These are governed by Part 4 of the CA 2006, which contains provisions that include a company's capacity; the power of directors to bind the company; execution of documents and deeds; company seal; and pre-incorporation contracts.

A company's constitution

4.2 Chapter 1 of Part 3 of the CA 2006 sets out the introductory aspects to and the scope of a 'company's constitution'. Section 17 of the CA 2006 provides that unless the context otherwise requires, references in the Companies Acts to a 'company's constitution' include the company's articles;[515] and any resolutions and agreements to which Chapter 3 of Part 3 of the CA 2006 applies (see s 29 of the CA 2006).[516]

---

[515] CA 2006, s 17(a).   [516] CA 2006, s 17(b).

Section 17 of the CA 2006 is a new provision. It sets out a non-exhaustive definition of 'a company's constitution', which will apply throughout the CA 2006, and the 'Companies Acts',[517] unless the context requires a wider or more restricted meaning, such as, for example, s 257 of the CA 2006, which expands the definition of a company's constitution with a wider significance for the purpose of Part 10 of the CA 2006 (company directors).[518] The concepts of a company's constitution and the rights and obligations arising under it are used both in Part 3 and elsewhere in CA 2006.

The definition of 'a company's constitution' is expressed to be non-exhaustive because it 'includes' a company's articles and any resolutions and agreements to which Chapter 3 of Part 3 of the CA 2006 applies. In addition to the provisions of companies' articles, and the resolutions and agreements to which Chapter 3 of Part 3 of the CA 2006 applies,[519] the contents of certain other documents will be of constitutional relevance for certain purposes. For example, a company's certificate of incorporation summarises key information applicable to the company by setting out whether it is a public or private company.[520] The Memorandum of Association is clearly no longer part of a company's constitution. Previously, the Memorandum of Association was the dominant constitutional document and in the event of any inconsistency between the two, the memorandum prevailed over the Articles of Association.[521] This is no longer the position under the CA 2006. The memorandum will simply represent a 'snapshot' of a company at the time of incorporation.

---

[517] See too CA 2006, s 2 on the definition of 'Companies Acts'. See too CA 2006, s 29, which refers to resolutions and agreements affecting a company's constitution. The resolutions include any special resolution; any resolution or agreement agreed to by all the members of a company that, if not so agreed to, would not have been effective for its purpose unless passed by a special resolution; any resolution or agreement agreed to by all the members of a class of shareholders that, if not agreed to, would not have been effective for its purpose unless passed by some particular majority or otherwise in some particular manner; any resolution or agreement that effectively binds all members of a class of shareholders of shareholders though not agreed to by all those members; any other resolution or agreement to which Chapter 3 of CA 2006, Part 3 applies by virtue of any enactment: CA 2006, s 29(1).

[518] CA 2006, s 257 also refers to 'the company's constitution', which term includes any resolution or other decision come to in accordance with the constitution; and any decision by the members of the company, or a class of members, that is treated by virtue of any enactment or rule of law as equivalent to a decision by the company.

[519] As described in CA 2006, s 29 (resolutions and agreements affecting a company's constitution).

[520] See CA 2006, s 15 on the issue of certificate of incorporation including conclusivity.

[521] See for example, *Ashbury Railway Carriage and Iron Co Ltd v Riche* (1875) LR 7 HL 653 at 671, where Lord Cairns LC stated that 'the memorandum is, as it were, the area beyond which the actions of the company cannot go; inside that area the shareholders may make such regulations for their own government as they think fit'. See too, *Guinness v Land Corpn of Ireland* (1882) 22 Ch D 349 per Bowen LJ at 379.

Articles of Association

General

4.3 Under the CA 2006, a company's constitution includes its Articles of Association. A company's articles are internal rules, chosen by the company's members, which govern a company's internal affairs. They form a statutory contract between the company and its members, and between each of the members, and are an integral part of a company's constitution. Previously, companies could divide their constitutional rules between their memoranda and their articles, with the terms of their memoranda being capable of being altered after formation in some respects, but not in others. The memoranda prevailed over the articles in the event of a conflict between the two constitutions. However, under the CA 2006, the memorandum is now a very simple document of purely historic significance, evidencing an intention to form a company, and all the company's key internal rules on matters such as the allocation of powers between the members of a company and its directors must now be set out in the articles. The articles are now the superior or dominant form of a company's constitution. It will no longer be necessary to read both the company's articles and memorandum together to determine the scope of a company's constitution,[522] or to resolve any ambiguities, because under the CA 2006, the Articles of Association will contain all provisions that are necessary for the proper functioning of the company.

The articles are intended to give flexibility to both directors and shareholders in the effective governance of the company, and to provide some degree of transparency in the relationship between directors and shareholders.

Articles of Association

4.4 Section 18(1) of the CA 2006 provides that a company must have Articles of Association prescribing regulations for the company. Unless it is a company to which model articles apply by virtue of s 20 of the CA 2006 (default application of model articles in case of limited company), it must register the Articles of Association.[523]

Section 18(3) of the CA 2006 prescribes the format of the Articles of Association. The Articles of Association registered by a company must be contained in a single document;[524] and be divided into paragraphs numbered consecutively.[525] Any references in the Companies Acts to a company's 'articles' are to its Articles of Association.[526]

[522] See for example, *Angostura Bitters (Dr J.G.B. Siegert & Sons) Ltd v Kerr* [1933] AC 550.
[523] CA 2006, s 18(2).   [524] CA 2006, s 18(3)(a).   [525] CA 2006, s 18(3)(b).
[526] CA 2006, s 18(4).

Section 18 of the CA 2006 replaces s 7 of the CA 1985.[527] It carries forward the requirement that all registered companies must have Articles of Association. The provisions of this section have been updated to reflect the changes made by s 19 of the CA 2006, which give the Secretary of State the power to prescribe model articles for different descriptions of companies. As result of this change, some types of company that are currently required to register articles with the relevant registrar of companies (for example, companies limited by guarantee), will have the option of not registering articles, but instead relying on the 'relevant model articles' for that description of company. The relevant model articles will be those prescribed by the Secretary of State as the default articles, if none have been registered.

It will not be possible for the articles to be contained in separate or different documents, as s 18 of the CA 2006 provides that the articles must be contained in a single document, and must be divided into consecutively numbered paragraphs. This position has not altered from that under the CA 1985. It is submitted that where the articles are lodged at Companies House as more than one document, the registrar should strictly reject this under CA 2006, based on the 'single document' rule.

It should be noted that companies formed under the CA 1985 had freedom to make such rules about their internal affairs as they saw fit. However, if a company's articles contained anything that was contrary to the provisions of the CA 1985, or contrary to general law, then that provision would have no effect and would not be upheld. This principle also applies to articles of companies that are formed under the CA 2006.

Power of Secretary of State to prescribe model articles

4.5 Section 19(1) of the CA 2006 provides that the Secretary of State may by regulations prescribe model Articles of Association for companies. However, different model articles may be prescribed for different descriptions of company.[528] A company may adopt all or any of the provisions of model articles.[529]

Any amendment of model articles by regulations under s 19 of the CA

---

[527] CA 1985, s 7 was concerned with articles prescribing regulation for companies. It stated that there may in the case of a company limited by shares, and there shall in the case of a company limited by guarantee or unlimited, be registered with the Memorandum, Articles of Association signed by the subscribers to the memorandum and prescribing regulations for the company: CA 1985, s 7(1). Further, CA 1985, s 7(3) provided that the articles must be printed, be divided into paragraphs numbered consecutively; and be signed by each subscriber of the memorandum in the presence of at lease one witness who must attest the signature.

[528] CA 2006, s 19(2). See the Companies (Model Articles) Regulations 2007 which prescribe model form of articles of association for private companies limited by shares (regulation 2 and Schedule 1); private companies limited by guarantee (regulation 3 and Schedule 2); and public companies (regulation 4 and Schedule 3).

[529] CA 2006, s 19(3).

2006 does not affect a company registered before the amendment takes effect. The term 'amendment' includes addition, alteration or repeal.[530]

Default application of model articles

4.6 Section 20(1) of the CA 2006 provides that on the formation of a limited company, if the articles are not registered;[531] or, if articles are registered, insofar as they do not exclude or modify the relevant model articles,[532] then the relevant model articles (so far as practicable) will form part of the company's articles, in the same manner and to the same extent as if articles in the form of those articles had been duly registered.

The term 'relevant model articles' means the model articles prescribed for a company of that description as in force at the date on which the company is registered.[533]

Previously, s 8 of the CA 1985 enabled the Secretary of State to prescribe model forms of articles for companies registered under that Act.[534] The forms of model articles were prescribed in the Companies (Tables A–F) Regulations 1985 (SI 1985/805). Articles for certain special types of companies, for example, common hold associations, right to manage (RTM) companies, and right to enfranchise (RTE) companies were prescribed by regulations made under the Acts that created these types of company.

Although ss 8 and 8A of the CA 1985 allowed the Secretary of State to prescribe forms of articles (and memoranda) for a number of different types of company under s 8 of the CA 1985, which gave him a power to prescribe model articles for partnership companies), he was only able to prescribe 'default' model articles for companies limited by shares. 'Default' model articles are model articles that apply to companies of a particular description, where they have not registered any articles of their own, or have not made provision for a particular matter for which there is a corresponding model article. Default model articles apply to a company of the description for which they are prescribed, only to the extent that it has not modified the default provision in question in their own registered articles nor excluded it, or the model articles in their entirety, from the registered articles.

---

[530] CA 2006, s 19(4). Regulations made under CA 2006, s 19 are subject to negative resolution procedure: CA 2006, s 19(5).

[531] CA 2006, s 20(1)(a).   [532] CA 2006, s 20(1)(b).   [533] CA 2006, s 20(2).

[534] Under the CA 1985, s 8(1) provided that the Articles of Association may adopt all or any of the regulations contained in Table A. Section 8(2) provided that in the case of the company limited by shares, if articles are not registered, in so far as the articles do not exclude or modify Table A, the regulations of Table A as in force at the date of the company's registration shall constitute the company's articles. Section 8(4) provided that the articles of companies limited by guarantee with and without share capital, shall be respectively in the forms set out in Tables D, C and E, as prescribed in regulations made by the Secretary of State or as near that form as circumstances admit. These model articles were not required to be followed but simply as guidance with allowance for flexibility.

The rationale behind this is that the model articles should operate as a 'safety net', which enables the members and directors of such companies to take decisions in circumstances where a company has failed to provide the appropriate authority in its registered articles (or failed to register articles at all).

Sections 19 and 20 of the CA 2006 replace s 8 of the CA 1985.[535] In line with the Company Law Review Group's recommendation in *Company Formation and Capital Maintenance*,[536] the Secretary of State will have the power under CA 2006 to prescribe model articles, including 'default' model articles, for different descriptions of companies formed under the CA 2006.

Existing companies will be free to adopt, wholly or in part, the model articles prescribed for companies of a particular description formed under CA 2006.[537] For example, an existing private company limited by shares, may prefer to adopt the model articles for private companies limited by shares, or indeed the model articles for public companies formed under CA 2006 (with or without modifications) in place of the Table A articles, or previous articles of its own devising.

As with Table A, the adoption of model articles by companies formed under CA 2006 will be entirely a matter for individual companies. They will be able to incorporate (with or without amendment) provisions from the model articles, and/or add to those provisions, and/or exclude such provisions as they think fit.

They will also be able to adopt the provisions of model articles by reference. This is a common practice, which enables a company that wishes to incorporate specific provisions of the model articles into its own registered articles to do so, without the necessity of having to copy out the provision in question. For example, a company's registered articles may have the following variations in its Articles of Association:

- 'The model articles apply except for model articles x, y, and z'; or
- 'The company's articles are A, B and C, plus model articles g, p, and q'; or
- 'Model article n applies but is amended as follows . . .'

Companies have found such techniques useful in the past and they will continue to be permitted under CA 2006.

Alteration of Articles

4.7 There are seven provisions dealing with alterations of articles contained in Chapter 2 of Part 3 of the CA 2006.

---

[535] CA 2006, s 20 deals with default application of model articles.
[536] See para 2.22.
[537] See for example, CA 2006, s 19(3), which provides that a company may adopt all or any of the provisions of model articles.

Amendment of articles

4.8 Section 21(1) of the CA 2006 states that a company may alter its articles by special resolution.

Where a company is a charity, this is subject to in England and Wales, s 64 Charities Act 1993 (c 10);[538] and in Northern Ireland, Article 9 Charities (Northern Ireland) Order 1987 (SI 1987/2048) (NI 19).[539]

Where a company is registered in the Scottish Charity Register, this is subject to s 112 of the CA 1989 (c 40);[540] and section 116 Charities and Trustee Investment (Scotland) Act 2005 (asp 10).[541]

Section 21 of the CA 2006 provides for a mechanism to change a company's Articles of Association. It replaces an equivalent provision in s 9 of the CA 1985.

Under s 21(2) and (3) of the CA 2006, this general principle is subject to certain rules in charities legislation about the liability of companies that are charities to change their constitution and the effects that such changes have. There are separate but broadly similar rules for English and Welsh, Scottish and Northern Irish charities.

Previously under s 9 of the CA 1985, a company could alter its articles, but this was subject to the provisions of the CA 1985, and to the conditions contained in a company's articles. The proviso is not contained in s 21 of the CA 2006. Over the years, there has developed a principle in English company law, that the power to alter articles must be exercised '*bona fide* for the benefit of the company as a whole' and this expression appears to have been inextricably linked to s 9 of the CA 1985, as well as its predecessor. This concept derives from partnership law, and adopted by English company law to ensure that the majority did not abuse its powers of expulsion to the detriment of the minority.[542]

---

[538] CA 2006, s 21(2)(a).   [539] CA 2006, s 21(2)(b).   [540] CA 2006, s 21(3)(a).
[541] CA 2006, s 21(3)(b).
[542] See for example, *Blisset v Daniel* (1853) 10 Hare 493. In *Allen v Gold Reefs of West Africa Ltd* [1900] 1 Ch 656, Lindley MR stated that the power must 'be exercised subject to those general principles of law and equity which are applicable to all powers conferred on majorities and enabling them to bind minorities. It must be exercised, not only in the manner required by law, but also bona fide for the benefit of the company as a whole, and it must not be exceeded. These conditions are always implied, but are seldom, if ever, expressed.' In *Greenhalgh v Arderne Cinemas Ltd* [1951] Ch 286 at 291, Evershed MR stated that 'I think it is plain that "bona fide for the benefit of the company as a whole" means not two things but one thing. It means that the shareholder must proceed upon what, in his honest opinion, is for the benefit of the company as a whole . . . the phrase, "the company as a whole", does not (at any rate in such a case as the present) mean the company as a commercial entity, distinct from the corporators; it means the corporators as a general body. That is to say, the case may be taken of a hypothetical member and it may be asked whether what is proposed is, in his honest opinion of those who voted in its favour, for the person's benefit.' The test of bona fide for the company's benefit cannot be used in every conceivable situation for the aid of the minority:

The cases have shown that the courts will not thrust upon shareholders the determination as to what is for the benefit of the company, as this is a matter for the directors.[543] In *Shuttleworth v Cox Bros & Co (Maidenhead) Ltd* [1927] 2 KB 9, the Court of Appeal per Bankes LJ stated that the courts will interfere with the alteration of articles if the alteration is 'so oppressive as to cast suspicion on the honesty of the persons responsible for it, or so extravagant that no reasonable man could really consider it for the benefit of the company'.

In *Greenhalgh v Arderne Cinemas Ltd*, Evershed MR stated that '. . . a special resolution of this kind would be liable to be impeached if the effect of it were to discriminate between majority shareholders and the minority shareholders, so as to give the former an advantage of which the latter were deprived'.

The cases have also shown that provided the alteration is bona fide and within the powers, it will be upheld by the courts.

However, shareholders do not need to take the company's interests into account. They are not obliged to act in the best interests of the company. They do not owe duties to the company or the directors. They are not partners with the company. They are not trustees for the company. They are not the company's keepers or keepers of the company's conscience. They can vote against the interests of the company. Their intentions may be *male fide* but they owe no duties to directors or the company.

The provision dealing with altering a company's Articles of Association does not require that the alteration should be *'bona fide* for the benefit of the company'. Neither s 9 of the CA 1985 (previously) nor s 21 of the CA 2006 requires that the test for alteration should be the *bona fide* test. It is submitted that the only words used in the provision are that the alteration must be by special resolution.

Many of the cases on alteration of the company's articles have applied the concept of *bona fide* into the alteration process. In *Brown v British Abrasive Wheel Co*,[544] there were two groups of shareholders in the company with the majority shareholders wishing to put more capital into the company with a view to ousting the minority shareholders. The minority shareholders

---

Pender v Lushington (1877) 6 Ch D 70; *Mills v Mills* (1938) 60 CLR 150. Shareholders owe no duties or obligations to the company: they may vote as they please: *Phillips v Manufacturers' Securities Ltd* (1917) 116 LT 290. Cases have also shown that the power to alter articles must not oppress the minority or be exercised fraudulently: *Cook v Deeks* [1916] 1 AC 554; *Menier v Hooper's Telegraph Works* (1874) 9 Ch App 350. The courts will not presume fraud or oppression or abuse of power and the burden of proving that the power has not been properly exercised is on the complainant – usually the minority shareholder: *Peter's American Delicacy Co Ltd v Heath* (1939) 61 CLR 457.

[543] See for example, *Carruth v ICI Ltd* [1937] AC 707.
[544] [1919] 1 Ch 290.

challenged the alteration. The court was of the opinion that the alteration was not *bona fide* for the company's benefit. In *Dafen Tinplate Co Ltd v Llanelly Steel Co* (1907) Ltd,[545] an alteration to the articles that contained a power to buy out minority shareholders at fair value was held by the court as not *bona fide* for the benefit of the company. However, in *Sidebottom v Kershaw, Leese & Co Ltd*,[546] the Court of Appeal upheld an alteration to the articles which provided for minority shareholders to be bought out if they competed with the company. In this case, one of the shareholders actually competed with the company. In *Shuttleworth v Cox Bros & Co (Maidenhead) Ltd*, the Court upheld the power to alter the articles on grounds that the director in question was disrupting the company's business and the power to terminate his office by way of alteration to the company's articles was *bona fide* for the company's benefit. However, the *bona fide* for the benefit of the company test was rejected by the Australian court in *Gambotto v WCP Ltd*.[547]

It is submitted that any alteration to the Articles of Association should proceed on the following basis. First, consideration must be given to s 21 of the CA 2006, which requires any alteration of articles to be effected by a special resolution. Second, the company must examine the powers and the procedures conferred on the directors and shareholders for amending the company's articles as set out in the company's Articles of Association. Voting will be by special resolution unless the articles provide otherwise. Third, directors will also be under a statutory obligation to consider their duties and powers as set out in Chapter 2 of Part 10 of the CA 2006. Directors must also have regard to the interests of minority shareholders when proposing amendments to the company's articles. It is submitted that the test should no longer be whether the alteration is '*bona fide* for the benefit of the company'. This is reading words that have never existed in statutory form, and have been adapted from partnership law to suit company law purposes. The test was originally employed in partnership law in consideration of the partnership agreement expulsion clauses where a partner was unlawfully expelled from a partnership. The *bona fide* test is a figment of company law, as there never has been any statutory wording of this type to justify its use. The 'test of *bona fide* for the benefit of the company' should not be the 'rescue clause' for the minority shareholders.

Entrenched provisions of the articles

4.9 Section 22(1) of the CA states that a company's articles may provide that specified provisions of the articles may not be altered or repealed, or may be altered or repealed only if conditions are met, or procedures are complied

---

[545] [1920] 1 Ch 124.   [546] [1920] 1 Ch 154.   [547] (1955) 182 CLR 432.

with, that are more restrictive than those applicable in the case of a special resolution. This is known as 'provision for entrenchment'.

Provision for entrenchment may only be made in the company's articles on formation,[548] or by an amendment of the company's articles agreed to by all the members of the company.[549] Further, provision for entrenchment does not prevent amendment of the company's articles by agreement of all the members of the company;[550] or by order of a court or other authority having power to alter the company's articles.[551] Section 22 of the CA 2006 does not affect any power of a court or other authority to alter a company's articles.[552]

Section 22 of the CA 2006 is a new provision. It replaces the practice under s 17(2)(b) of the CA 1985,[553] whereby companies were able to entrench elements of their constitution by putting them in their memoranda, and providing that they could not be altered. This will not now be possible under the CA 2006 as the memorandum serves a different purpose altogether.

Section 22 of the CA 2006 allows companies to provide in their articles that specified provisions may be amended or repealed only if conditions are met that are more restrictive than would apply in the case of a special resolution. Such a provision is referred to as a 'provision for entrenchment'. Companies formed under the CA 2006 will not be allowed to provide in their articles that an entrenchment provision can never be repealed or amended.

Notice to registrar of existence of restriction on amendment of articles

4.10 Section 23(1) of the CA 2006 states that if a company's articles on formation contain provision for entrenchment;[554] or a company's articles are amended so as to include such provision;[555] or are altered by order of a court or other authority so as to restrict or exclude the power of the company to amend its articles,[556] the company must give notice of that fact to the registrar.

Similarly, where a company's articles are amended so as to remove provision for entrenchment;[557] or are altered by order of the court or other authority so as to remove such provision;[558] or so as to remove any other restriction on, or any exclusion of, the power of the company to amend its articles,[559] the company must give notice of that fact to the registrar.

Section 23 of the CA 2006 is a new provision. It requires a company to give

---

[548] CA 2006, s 22(2)(a).   [549] CA 2006, s 22(2)(b).   [550] CA 2006, s 22(3)(a).
[551] CA 2006, s 22(3)(b).   [552] CA 2006, s 22(4).
[553] CA 1985, s 17(2)(b) provided that CA 1985, s 17 (conditions in memorandum that could have been in articles) did not apply where the memorandum itself provided for or prohibited the alteration of all or any of the conditions referred to in CA 1985, s 17 and did not authorise any variation or abrogation of the special rights.
[554] CA 2006, s 23(1)(a).   [555] CA 2006, s 23(1)(b).   [556] CA 2006, s 23(1)(c).
[557] CA 2006, s 23(2)(a).   [558] CA 2006, s 23(2)(b)(i).   [559] CA 2006, s 23(2)(b)(ii).

notice to the registrar when an entrenching provision is included in its articles (whether on formation or subsequently), or when the company's articles are altered by order of a court or other authority, so as to restrict or exclude the power of the company to amend its articles.

There is a corresponding requirement as to notice where the company amends its articles so as to remove a provision for entrenchment, or where the articles are altered by order of a court or other authority so as to remove a provision for entrenchment or any other restriction on, or any exclusion of, the power of the company to amend its articles.

Statement of compliance where amendment of articles restricted

4.11 Section 24 of the CA 2006 applies where a company's articles are subject to provision for entrenchment;[560] or to an order of a court or other authority restricting or excluding the company's power to amend the articles.[561]

If a company amends its articles;[562] and is required to send to the registrar a document making or evidencing the amendment,[563] the company must deliver with that document a statement of compliance.

The statement of compliance required is a statement certifying that the amendment has been made in accordance with the company's articles and, where relevant, any applicable order of a court or other authority.[564] The registrar may rely on the statement of compliance as sufficient evidence of the matters stated in it.[565]

Section 24 of the CA 2006 is a new provision. Where a company's articles contain provision for entrenchment, or where the articles are subject to an order of a court or other authority restricting or excluding the company's power to amend its articles and the company subsequently amends its articles, it is required to send to the registrar the document making or evidencing the amendment. The document must be accompanied by a 'statement of compliance'.

The statement of compliance must certify that the amendment to the company's articles has been made in accordance with the company's articles (including any provision for entrenchment) or, where relevant, in accordance with any order of the court or other authority that is in force at the time of the amendment.

The objective of ss 23 and 24 of the CA 2006 is to ensure that the registrar, and any person searching the public register, is put on notice that the articles contain entrenching provisions and that special rules therefore apply to the company's articles.

---

[560] CA 2006, s 24(1)(a).   [561] CA 2006, s 24(1)(b).   [562] CA 2006, s 24(2)(a).
[563] CA 2006, s 24(2)(b).   [564] CA 2006, s 24(3).   [565] CA 2006, s 24(4).

Effect of alteration of articles on company's members

4.12 The effect of alteration of articles on a company's members is governed by s 25(1) of the CA 2006. This states that a member of a company is not bound by an alteration to its articles after the date on which he became a member, if and so far as the alteration requires him to take or subscribe for more shares in the company than the number held by him at the date on which the alteration is made;[566] or if the alteration has the effect in any way of increasing his liability to the company as at that date, to contribute to the company's share capital or otherwise to pay money to the company.[567]

Section 25(1) of the CA 2006 does not, however, apply where a member agrees in writing, either before or after the alteration is made, to be bound by the alteration.[568]

Section 25 of the CA 2006 restates s 16 of the CA 1985. The only difference is that s 16 also applied to alterations of a company's memorandum. A company formed under CA 2006 will not be able to or need to alter its memorandum.

This section retains the principle that a member of a company is not bound by any alteration made to the articles subsequent to his becoming a member if the alteration has the effect of increasing his liability to the company, or requiring him to take more shares in the company. A member may however give his written consent to such an alteration and, where he does, he will be bound by it.

Registrar to be sent copy of amended articles

4.13 Section 26(1) of the CA 2006 states that where a company amends its articles, it must send to the registrar a copy of the articles as amended, not later than 15 days after the amendment takes effect.

Section 26 of the CA 2006 does not require a company to set out in its articles any provisions of model articles that are applied by the articles;[569] or that are applied by virtue of s 20 of the CA 2006 (default application of model articles).[570]

If a company fails to comply, an offence is committed by the company;[571] and by every officer of the company who is in default.[572] A person guilty of an offence is liable on summary conviction to a fine not exceeding level 3 on the standard scale and, for continued contravention, a daily default fine not exceeding one-tenth of level 3 on the standard scale.[573]

Section 26 of the CA 2006 replaces an equivalent provision in s 18(2) and (3) of the CA 1985. The time period for lodging the amended articles is 15

---

[566] CA 2006, s 25(1)(a).   [567] CA 2006, s 25(1)(b).   [568] CA 2006, s 25(2).
[569] CA 2006, s 26(2)(a).   [570] CA 2006, s 26(2)(b).   [571] CA 2006, s 26(3)(a).
[572] CA 2006, s 26(3)(b).   [573] CA 2006, s 26(4).

days after the amendment takes effect. The time period is strict, but there are detailed provisions contained in s 27 of the CA 2006 that apply where the company fails to comply with respect to the amended articles.

The First Company Law Directive (68/151/EEC) requires Member States to take such measures as are required to ensure that companies disclose certain constitutional information, which will then be made available to the public in a central register. In particular, companies are to be required to disclose (i) their 'instrument of constitution, and the statutes if they are contained in a separate instrument; (ii) any amendments to these instruments; and (iii) 'after every [such] amendment . . . the complete text of the instrument or statutes as amended to date'. For United Kingdom companies, the 'instrument of constitution' equates to the memorandum, and the 'statutes' equate to the articles. The central registers are those kept by the registrars of companies for England and Wales, Scotland and Northern Ireland.

Registrar's notice to comply in case of failure with the respect to amended articles

4.14 Section 27(1) of the CA 2006 states that if it appears to the registrar that a company has failed to comply with any enactment requiring it to send to the registrar a document making or evidencing an alteration in the company's articles;[574] or to send to the registrar a copy of the company's articles as amended,[575] the registrar may give notice to the company requiring it to comply.

The notice must state the date on which it is issued;[576] and require the company to comply within 28 days from the notice date.[577] If the company complies with the notice within the specified time, no criminal proceedings may be brought in respect of the failure to comply with s 27(1) of the CA 2006.[578]

If the company does not comply with the notice within the specified time, it is liable to a civil penalty of £200. This civil penalty is in addition to any liability to criminal proceedings in respect of the failure set out in s 27(1) of the CA 2006.[579] The penalty may be recovered by the registrar and is to be paid into the Consolidated Fund.[580]

This section is a new provision. It gives the registrar a means of ensuring that companies comply with the obligation set out in s 26 of the CA 2006 without having to resort to criminal proceedings. However, the offence of failing to file amended articles is retained under s 26(3) of the CA 2006.

Where the registrar becomes aware of any default in complying with s 26 of

---

[574] CA 2006, s 27(1)(a).   [575] CA 2006, s 27(1)(b).   [576] CA 2006, s 27(2)(a).
[577] CA 2006, s 27(2)(b).   [578] CA 2006, s 27(3).   [579] CA 2006, s 27(4).
[580] CA 2006, s 27(5).

the CA 2006 (or any similar provision of another enactment that was in force at the time of the default, for example, s 18(2) of the CA 1985), he may give notice to the company requiring it to rectify the breach within 28 days. Where the company complies with the registrar's notice, the company will avoid prosecution for its initial failure to comply. If the company does not comply within the specified time, it will be liable to a civil penalty of £200, recoverable by the registrar as a debt. This is in addition to any liability to criminal proceedings that may be imposed.[581]

Existing companies: provisions of memorandum treated as provisions of articles

4.15 Section 28(1) of the CA 2006 states that provisions that immediately before commencement of Part 3 of the CA 2006 were contained in a company's memorandum, but are not provisions of the kind mentioned in s 8 of the CA 2006 (provisions of new-style memorandum) are to be treated after the commencement of Part 3 of the CA 2006 as provisions of the company's articles.

This applies not only to substantive provisions but also to provision for entrenchment (as defined in s 22 of the CA 2006).[582]

The provisions of Part 3 of the CA 2006 regarding provision for entrenchment apply to such provisions as they apply to provisions made on the company's formation, except that the duty under 23(1)(a) of the CA 2006 to give notice to the registrar does not apply.[583]

This section contains supplementary provisions. For companies formed under the CA 2006, the memorandum will contain limited information evidencing the intention to form a company. The memoranda of existing companies, on the other hand, will contain key constitutional information of a type which will in future be set out in the articles or provided to the registrar in another format.[584] Section 28(1) of the CA 2006 provides that such material is to be treated for the future as part of the company's articles.

Section 28(2) of the CA 2006 makes it clear that where the memorandum of an existing company contains a provision for entrenchment at the date that Part 3 of of the CA 2006 comes into force, this will be deemed, with effect from that date, to be a provision for entrenchment in the company's articles.

Resolutions and agreements affecting a company's constitution

4.16 This is governed by Chapter 3 of Part 3 of the CA 2006. Chapter 3 replaces equivalent provisions in the CA 1985 on the registration of

---

[581] See, for example, CA 2006, s 26(4).   [582] CA 2006, s 28(2).   [583] CA 2006, s 28(3).
[584] See CA 2006, Part 2.

resolutions and agreements, and on making these available to members. Chapter 3 contains two sections.

Resolutions and agreements affecting a company's constitution

4.17 Section 29(1) of the CA 2006 applies to the following resolutions and agreements affecting a company's constitution:

- any special resolution;[585]
- any resolution or agreement agreed to by all the members of a company that, if not so agreed to, would not have been effective for its purpose unless passed as a special resolution;[586]
- any resolution or agreement agreed to by all the members of a class of shareholders that, if not so agreed to, would not have been effective for its purpose unless passed by some particular majority or otherwise in some particular manner;[587]
- any resolution or agreement that effectively binds all members of a class of shareholders though not agreed to by all those members;[588]
- any other resolution or agreement to which Chapter 3 applies by virtue of any enactment.[589]

The references to a 'member of a company', or of a class of members of a company, do not include the company itself where it is such a member by virtue only of its holding shares as treasury shares.[590]

Section 29 of the CA 2006 replaces s 380(4) of the CA 1985. It lists the resolutions and agreements that must be sent to the registrar for registration (as set out in s 30 of the CA 2006), and made available to members on request: see s 32 of the CA 2006.

Copies of resolutions or agreements to be forwarded to and recorded by registrar

4.18 Section 30 of the CA 2006 states that a copy of every resolution or agreement to which Chapter 3 of Part 3 of the CA 2006 applies, or (in the case of a resolution or agreement that is not in writing), a written memorandum setting out its terms, must be forwarded to the registrar within 15 days after it is passed or made.[591]

If a company fails to comply, an offence is committed by the company;[592] and by every officer who is in default.[593] A liquidator of the company is

---

[585] CA 2006, s 29(1)(a).   [586] CA 2006, s 29(1)(b).   [587] CA 2006, s 29(1)(c).
[588] CA 2006, s 29(1)(d).   [589] CA 2006, s 29(1)(e).   [590] CA 2006, s 29(2).
[591] CA 2006, s 30(1).   [592] CA 2006, s 30(2)(a).   [593] CA 2006, s 30(2)(b).

treated as an officer of the company.[594] Section 30(3) of the CA 2006 provides that a person guilty of an offence under this section is liable on summary conviction to a fine not exceeding level 3 on the standard scale and, for continued contravention, a daily default fine not exceeding one-tenth of level 3 on the standard scale.[595]

Section 30 of the CA 2006 restates s 380(1), (5) and (7) of the CA 1985 and Schedule 24 of the CA 1985. Where a company passes a resolution or agreement of the type listed in s 29 of the CA 2006, it must forward a copy of the resolution (or in the case of a resolution or agreement that is not in writing – a written memorandum) to the registrar for registration within 15 days of the date on which the resolution was passed or made and recorded by him/her. If a company fails to do this, the company and every officer of it who is in default commit an offence.

Where a resolution or agreement which affects a company's constitution is not in writing, the company is required to provide the registrar with a written memorandum setting out the terms of the resolution or agreement in question.

Miscellaneous And Supplementary Provisions

4.19 Chapter 4 of Part 3 of the CA 2006 addresses the miscellaneous and supplementary provisions in connection with a company's constitution. It is concerned with the company's objects and other aspects in dealing with a company's constitution. Chapter 4 contains 8 sections.

Statement of company's objects

4.20 Section 31 of the CA 2006 provides that unless a company's articles specifically restrict the objects of a company, its objects are unrestricted.[596]

Where a company amends its articles so as to add, remove or alter a statement of the company's objects, it must give notice to the registrar.[597] On receipt, the registrar must register that notice;[598] and the amendment is not effective until entry of that notice on the register.

Any such amendment does not affect any rights or obligations of the company or render defective any legal proceedings by or against it.[599]

Section 31 of the CA 2006 applies to companies which are charities that are subject to s 64 of the Charities Act 1993 in England and Wales;[600] and in Northern Ireland subject to the Charities (Northern Ireland) Order 1987 (SI 1987/2048 (NI)).[601] In the case of a company that is entered in the Scottish

---

[594] CA 2006, s 30(4).   [595] CA 2006, s 30(3).   [596] CA 2006, s 31(1).
[597] CA 2006, s 31(2)(a).   [598] CA 2006, s 31(2)(b).   [599] CA 2006, s 31(3).
[600] CA 2006, s 31(4)(a).   [601] CA 2006, s 31(4)(b).

Charity Register, s 31 of the CA 2006 also applies, subject to the provisions of the Charities and Trustee Investment (Scotland) Act 2005 (asp 10).[602]

The position before the CA 2006

4.20.1 Before the CA 2006, commercial companies had the option of adopting a short form objects clause under s 3A of the CA 1985 (Statement of company's objects: general commercial company) that stated:[603]

> Where the company's memorandum states that the object of the company is to carry on business as a general commercial company:
>
> (a) the object of the company is to carry on any trade or business whatsoever; and
> (b) the company has power to do all such things as are incidental or conducive to the carrying on of any trade or business by it.

There were, however, several unresolved issues concerning s 3A of the CA 1985. First, it was not clear what interpretation was to be given to the words 'general commercial company'; clearly not all companies were general commercial companies. Second, most companies still preferred to draft the 'long form' objects clause which was the common form of practice before the CA 1989. It was arguable that the long form objects clause would still be the common form objects clause even after the 1989 Act.

A new s 35 of the CA 1985, as inserted by s 108 of the CA 1985. This provided, *inter alia*, that: 'the validity of an act done by a company shall not be called be into question on the ground of lack of capacity by reason of anything in the company's memorandum'.[604]

Therefore there was not be any legal argument whether a company or a third party may question the validity of the company's act on grounds of alleged *ultra vires*. Neither the company nor the third party could rely on the strict *ultra vires* doctrine to set aside an act or a transaction.

However, s 35 of the CA 1985 provided a mechanism that would effectively limit the scope of corporate activities, as s 35(2) stated that a shareholder could bring proceedings 'to restrain the doing of an act which but for sub-s (1) would be beyond the company's capacity'.[605] A shareholder could bring proceedings by way of an injunction against the company where the company has already entered into a legal obligation.

Directors still had obligations to the company under s 35(3) of the CA

---

[602] CA 2006, s 31(5).   [603] As inserted by CA 1989, s 110(1).
[604] Section 35 was not restricted to the company's objects clause but extended to anything in the company's memorandum.
[605] This section overcame the procedural obstacles of the rule in *Foss v Harbottle*.

1985, which stated, *inter alia*, that 'it remains the duty of the directors to observe any limitations on their powers flowing from the company's memorandum'.

Curiously, s 35 of the CA 1985 provided for a two-stage procedure for absolving a director who had entered into an *ultra vires* transaction. Shareholders could pass two special resolutions at a general meeting. Each of the special resolutions served a specific purpose. The first special resolution applied to an *ultra vires* act or transaction. Such a transaction could be ratified by the company in a general meeting. The second special resolution indemnified a director or any other person who entered into the act or transaction.

Therefore, the 'internal' effects of the *ultra vires* doctrine survived under s 35 of the CA 1985 as between directors and shareholders.

Section 35A was concerned with limitations on the powers of directors. It amended the old s 35 and provided that: 'in favor of a person dealing with as company in good faith, the power of the board of directors to bind the company or authorise others to do so, is deemed to be free of any limitation under the company's constitution'.[606]

Section 35A provided that a person 'deals with' the company 'if he is a party to any transaction or other act to which the company is a party'.[607] The act or transaction that was entered into had to be approved by the board of directors acting collectively or by any person authorised by them. Section 35A also provided that a third party would not be acting in bad faith by reason of his knowing that the act was beyond the powers of directors under the company's constitution. A third party would be presumed to have acted in good faith unless the contrary was proved.[608]

Any limitations imposed upon the powers of directors were ineffective as against the third party. These were limitations in the company's memorandum or Articles of Association including those imposed by the resolutions of the general meeting. Section 35A had similar provisions to s 35,

---

[606] The word 'constitution' has been substituted for 'memorandum or articles' which appeared in the previous s 35 in recognition of the fact that some companies may not have memorandum or articles within the meaning of CA 1985, ss 680 and 718. Gower suggest that s 35A should be interpreted to read as follows: 'In favour of a person dealing with the company in good faith the board of directors shall be deemed to have authority to exercise all the powers of the company excepts such as the Act requires to be exercised by some other organ, and authorise others to do so, notwithstanding, in either event, any limitations in the company's constitution on the boards authority.' (Gower, *Principles of Modern Company Law*, p 178). Section 35A still presented problems since it did not give any protection to the third party who has dealt with 'another organ' of the company, such as the general meeting of shareholders.

[607] It did not now matter whether a person is dealing with the company as an insider or an outsider as was the case under *Royal Bank v Turquand* (1856) 6 E & B 327.

[608] The court could apply the test of 'good faith' as established by Nourse J in *Barclays Bank Ltd v TOSG Trust Fund, op cit*, n 20.

which allows the member the right to apply for an injunction but only in respect of future corporate acts. However, there was no reference under s 35A to ratification by a double special resolution procedure, as there was in s 35 of the CA 1985. Therefore, if an act or transaction was beyond the powers of directors or any other person, it could be ratified by an ordinary resolution.[609] The third party was further protected by the abolition of the doctrine of constructive notice under s 35B. The third party was not required to inquire whether the act or transaction with the company was valid under the company's constitution.[610]

The position under the CA 2006

The position under the CA 2006 is that s 31 of the CA 2006 provides for a new approach to the question of a company's objects. Based on a recommendation of the Company Law Review Group in its *Final Report*,[611] a different approach is taken under the CA 2006. Instead of companies being required to specify their objects, they will now have unlimited objects, unless the objects are specifically restricted by the articles. This will mean that unless a company makes a deliberate choice to restrict its objects, the objects will have no bearing on what it can do. The objective has been to ensure freedom for companies to engage in commercial dealings without any impediment or limitations in the objects clause. The *ultra vires* doctrine is no longer applicable. Some companies will continue to restrict their objects. Companies that are charities will need to restrict their objects (under charities legislation) and some community interest companies may also choose to do so. It should be noted that the company can only be set up for a lawful purpose.[612]

Assume, for example, that a company decides to restrict its objects clause in the Articles of Association, so that it will not provide any donations to charities, nor engage in any 'philanthropic' activities, except by a resolution of the shareholders at a general meeting. In breach of the restriction in its articles, the company provides financial donations to charities, and seconds some of its employees to local organisations, to discharge its corporate social responsibilities, and to demonstrate that it is a good, responsible and caring corporate citizen in society. Is the corporation to be held in breach of s 31 of

---

[609] *Grant v UK Switchback Rys* (1880) 40 Ch D 135.

[610] Section 35B was required to be read in light of CA 1985, s 711A, which stated: '(1) A person shall not be taken to have notice of any matter merely because of its being disclosed in any document by the registrar of companies (and thus available for inspection) or made available by the company of inspection. (2) This does not affect the question whether person is affected by notice of any matter by reason of a failure to make such inquiries as ought to be made.' Section 711A would therefore protect a third party who was not dealing with the directors but with another officer of the company.

[611] *Final Report*, para 9.10.

[612] CA 2006, s 79(2) states that a company may not be so formed for an unlawful purpose.

the CA 2006, even though it is behaving as a good corporate citizen? The effect of s 31 of the CA 2006 is that this provision would have been breached owing to a restriction in its Articles of Association, and directors would be held accountable for their actions in respect of their general duties set out in Part 10 of the CA 2006, unless they could demonstrate they acted in good faith to promote the success of the company.

The effect of s 31(2) of the CA 2006 is that where a company changes its articles to add, remove or alter a statement of the company's objects, it must give notice to the registrar. The registrar must register the notice, and the alteration will not take effect until it has been so registered.

Section 31(3) of the CA 2006 ensures that such an amendment to the company's articles will not affect any rights or obligations of the company, or render defective any legal proceedings by or against it.

Companies that are charities will apply s 31 of the CA 2006 in respect of their objects, but the charities will be subject to the charities legislation depending upon the jurisdiction where the charities were established.

It should be noted that the directors of a company are under a duty to observe the company's constitution. This is made particularly clear in s 171 of the CA 2006, which refers to a director's duty to act within her powers, although restrictions in objects will, as now, have little effect outside of the internal workings of the company because of the effect of s 39 of the CA 2006 (a company's capacity) and s 40 of the CA 2006 (power of directors to bind the company) except in the case of charities where modified rules again apply.[613]

Other provisions with respect to a company's constitution

Constitutional documents to be provided to members

4.21 Section 32 of the CA 2006 states that a company must on request by any member, send to him a copy of the following documents:

- an up-to-date copy of the company's articles;[614]
- a copy of any resolution or agreement relating to the company to which Chapter 3 of Part 3 of the CA 2006 applies (resolutions and agreements affecting a company's constitution) and that is for the time being in force;[615]
- a copy of any document required to be sent to the registrar under s 34(2) of the CA 2006 (notice where the company's constitution altered by enactment);[616] or s 35(2)(a) of the CA 2006 (notice where order of court or other authority alters the company's constitution);[617]

[613] See CA 2006, s 42.   [614] CA 2006, s 32(1)(a).   [615] CA 2006, s 32(1)(b).
[616] CA 2006, s 32(1)(c)(i).   [617] CA 2006, s 32(1)(c)(ii).

- a copy of any court order under s 899 of the CA 2006 (order sanctioning compromise or arrangement), or s 900 of the CA 2006 (order facilitating reconstruction or amalgamation);[618]
- a copy of any court order under s 996 of the CA 2006 (protection of members against unfair prejudice: powers of the court) that alters the company's constitution;[619]
- a copy of the company's current certificate of incorporation, and of any past certificates of incorporation;[620]
- in the case of a company with a share capital, a current statement of capital.[621] The statement of capital is a statement of the total number of shares of the company;[622] the aggregate nominal value of those shares;[623] for each class of shares (i) prescribed particulars of the rights attached to the shares;[624] (ii) the total number of shares of that class;[625] (iii) the aggregate nominal value of shares of that class;[626] and the amount paid up and the amount (if any) unpaid on each share (whether on account of the nominal value of the share or by way of premium): s 33(2) of the CA 2006;[627]
- in the case of a company limited by guarantee, the statement of guarantee.[628]

If a company makes default in complying, an offence is committed by every officer of the company who is in default.[629] A person guilty of an offence is liable on summary conviction to a fine not exceeding level 3 on the standard scale.[630]

Section 32 of the CA 2006 replaces s 19 of the CA 1985 and Schedule 24 of the CA 1985. It gives members the right to obtain from the company copies of the company's articles and certain other documents of constitutional importance.

The provision in the of the CA 1985 which enabled a company to charge its members 5p for a copy of its articles and/or memorandum has been removed. This information must in future be provided to the members (on request) free of charge.

The effect of a company's constitution

4.22 Section 33(1) of the CA 2006 provides that the provisions of a company's constitution bind the company and its members, to the same extent as if there were covenants on the part of the company and of each member to observe those provisions.

Money payable by a member to the company under its constitution is a

---

[618] CA 2006, s 32(1)(d). [619] CA 2006, s 32(1)(e). [620] CA 2006, s 32(1)(f).
[621] CA 2006, s 32(1)(g). [622] CA 2006, s 32(2)(a). [623] CA 2006, s 32(2)(b).
[624] CA 2006, s 32(2)(c)(i). [625] CA 2006, s 32(2)(c)(ii). [626] CA 2006, s 32((2)(c)(iii).
[627] CA 2006, s 32(2)(d). [628] CA 2006, s 32(1)(h). [629] CA 2006, s 32(3).
[630] CA 2006, s 32(4).

debt due from him to the company. In England and Wales and Northern Ireland it is of the nature of an ordinary contract debt.[631]

The position before the CA 2006 was governed by s 14 of the CA 1985.[632] Cases under s 14 of the CA 1985 had demonstrated that the Articles of Association are a statutory contract.[633] Further, the articles bind members in their capacity as such.[634] Section 14 of the CA 1985 had the effect of binding the company and its members to the articles on which either can sue or be sued.[635] The articles are also a contract between the shareholders.[636] On some occasions, the courts have stated that the articles did not create an enforceable contract between a company and a person who was not a shareholder of the company (also known as an 'outsider').[637]

The position is now governed by section 33(1) of the CA 2006 which replaces s 14(1) of the CA 1985. Its effect is that the provisions of a company's constitute a special kind of contract, whose terms bind the company and its members from time to time. Like s 14(1) of the CA 1985, s 33 of the CA 2006 will continue to be excepted from the general principle set out in s 1 Contracts (Rights of Third Parties) Act 1999, so that provisions of a company's constitution will not confer any rights on persons other than the company and its members. Unlike s 14(1) of the CA 1985, s 33 of the CA 2006 refers to 'company's constitution', rather than its 'memorandum and articles'. This reflects the new division of formation and constitutional information between the memorandum, articles and other constitutional documents. Unlike s 14(1) of the CA 1985, s 33(1) of the CA 2006 does not refer to the section being 'subject to the provisions of this Act', as was the position under s 14(1) of the CA 2006.

Section 33(1) of the CA 2006 has been updated and there is no change in the law – namely, that the constitution binds both the company and its members.

Section 33(2) of the CA 2006 replaces s 14(2) of the CA 1985.

---

[631] CA 2006, s 33(2).

[632] CA 1985, s 14 provided that subject to the provisions of this Act, the memorandum and articles, when registered, bind the company and its members to the same extent as if they respectively had been signed and sealed by each member, and contained covenants on the part of each member to observe all the provisions of the memorandum and of the articles.

[633] *Bratton Seymour Service Co Ltd Ltd v Oxborough* [1992] BCLC 693.

[634] *Hickman v Kent or Romney Marsh Sheepbreeders' Association* [1915] Ch 881; *Beattie v E & F Beattie Ltd* [1938] Ch 708.

[635] *Pender v Lushington* (1877) 6 Ch D 70.

[636] *Welton v Saffrey* [1897] AC 299; *London Stock and Bag Co v Dixon and Lugton Ltd* [1943] 2 All ER 763; *Re Greene, Greene v Greene* [1949] Ch 333; *Wood v Odessa Waterworks Co* (1889) 42 CH D 636.

[637] *Eley v Positive Government Security Life Assurance Co Ltd* (1876) 1Ex D 88, see too *Browne v La Trinbidad* (1887) 37 Ch D 1; *Cumbrian Newspaper Group Ltd v Cumberland and Westmorland Herald Newspaper and Printing Co Ltd* [1886] 3 WLR 26; *Swabey v Port Darwin Gold Mining Co* (1892) 66 LT 253; *Re New British Iron Co ex pte Beckwith* [1898] 1 Ch 324.

Notice to registrar where company's constitution altered by enactment

4.23 Section 34 of the CA 2006 applies where a company's constitution is altered by an enactment, other than an enactment amending the general law.[638] The company must give notice of the alteration to the registrar, specifying the enactment, not later than 15 days after the enactment comes into force. In the case of a special enactment, the notice must be accompanied by a copy of the enactment.[639]

If the enactment amends the company's articles;[640] or resolution or agreement to which Chapter 3 of Part 3 of the CA 2006 applies (resolutions and agreements affecting a company's constitution),[641] the notice must be accompanied by a copy of the company's articles, or the resolution or agreement in question, as amended.

The term 'special enactment' means an enactment that is not a public general enactment and includes any Act for confirming a provisional order;[642] any provision of a public general Act in relation to the passing of which any of the standing orders of the House of Lords or the House of Commons relating to Private Business applied;[643] or any enactment to the extent that it is incorporated or applied for the purpose of a special enactment.[644]

If a company fails to comply, an offence is committed by the company;[645] and every officer of the company who is in default.[646] A person guilty of an offence is liable on summary conviction to a fine not exceeding level 3 on the standard scale and, for continued contravention, a daily default fine not exceeding one-tenth of level 3 on the standard scale.[647]

Section 34 of the CA 2006 replaces s 18 of the CA 1985 and Schedule 24 of the CA 1985.

The provisions of a company's constitution may be altered by legislation, rather than by a resolution or agreement of the company's members. Such legislation will either be of general relevance to all companies: (for example, a new Companies Act clause saying that provisions of a certain type in any company's articles are void), or to all companies of a particular type (for example, new common hold legislation changing the provisions prescribed for inclusion in the articles of all commonhold associations) or it will be relevant only to a particular company (for example, a private Act amending the articles of a specific company established by an earlier Act).

In keeping with the principles underlying s 26 of the CA 2006 (that the registrar be sent a copy of amended articles), it is important that those searching the register of companies should be able to be made aware of the

---

[638] CA 2006, s 34(1).   [639] CA 2006, s 34(2).   [640] CA 2006, s 34(3)(a).
[641] CA 2006, s 34(3)(b).   [642] CA 2006, s 34(4)(a).   [643] CA 2006, s 34(4)(b).
[644] CA 2006, s 34(4)(c).   [645] CA 2006, s 34(5)(a).   [646] CA 2006, s 34(5)(b).
[647] CA 2006, s 34(6).

changes to companies articles that legislation may effect. However, there is a balance to be struck between maintaining transparency on the one hand and inundating the registrar and searchers with mountains of paper that will be of little practical use to persons searching the public register (and whose contents are generally available in any event) on the other. Section 34 of the CA 2006 therefore does not require companies to send copies of most public general Acts that alter their articles (such as Companies Acts or new commonhold legislation) to the registrar. It does, however, require 'special enactments' (as defined in s 34(3) of the CA 2006) to be sent to the registrar by companies whose articles are altered by the enactment in question.

Where an enactment to which s 34 of the CA 2006 applies alters a company's articles, or where such an enactment alters a resolution or agreement affecting the company's constitution, the company is obliged to send a copy of the articles, or the resolution or agreement in question, as altered, to the registrar.

The procedural rules for sending such legislation to the registrar, and the penalties for non-compliance with them, are as for s 26 of the CA 2006.

Notice to registrar where company's constitution altered by order

4.24 Section 35 of the CA 2006 provides that where a company's constitution is altered by an order of a court or other authority, the company must give notice to the registrar of the alteration not later than 15 days after the alteration takes effect.[648] The notice must be accompanied by a copy of the order;[649] and, if the order amends the company's articles;[650] or a resolution or agreement to which Chapter 3 applies (resolutions and agreements affecting the company's constitution),[651] a copy of the company's articles, or the resolution or agreement in question, as amended must be sent to the registrar.

If a company fails to comply, an offence is committed by the company;[652] and every officer of the company who is in default.[653] A person guilty of an offence is liable on summary conviction to a fine not exceeding level 3 on the standard scale and, for continued contravention, a daily default fine not exceeding one-tenth of level 3 on the standard scale.[654]

Section 35 of the CA 2006, however, does not apply where provision is made for another enactment for the delivery to the registrar of a copy of the order in question.[655]

Section 35 of the CA 2006 is a new provision, which provides for a mechanism for registering alterations that are made to the company's constitution by an order of the court or some other authority such as, for example, the

---

[648] CA 2006, s 35(1).   [649] CA 2006, s 35(2)(a).   [650] CA 2006, s 35(2)(b)(i).
[651] CA 2006, s 35(2)(b)(ii).   [652] CA 2006, s 35(3)(a).   [653] CA 2006, s 35(3)(b).
[654] CA 2006, s 35(4).   [655] CA 2006, s 35(5).

Charity Commission. It obliges companies to give notice of such alterations to the registrar, and to supply a copy of the articles, or the resolution or agreement in question, as altered, to the registrar.

Documents to be incorporated in or accompany copies of articles issued by company

4.25 Section 36 of the CA 2006 requires that every copy of a company's articles issued by the company must be accompanied by the following:

- a copy of any resolution or agreement relating to the company to which Chapter 3 of Part 3 of the CA 2006 applies (resolutions and agreements affecting a company's constitution);[656]
- where the company has been required to give notice to the registrar under s 34(2) of the CA 2006 (notice where company's constitution is altered by enactment), a statement that the enactment in question alters the effect of the company's constitution;[657]
- where the company's constitution is altered by a special enactment (see s 34(4) of the CA 2006), a copy of the enactment;[658] and
- a copy of any order required to be sent to the registrar under s 35(2)(a) of the CA 2006 (order of court or other authority altering company's constitution).[659]

Section 36 of the CA 2006 replaces s 380(2), (6) and (7) of the CA 1985 and Schedule 24 of the CA 1985. The effect of s 34 of the CA 2006 is that every copy of a company's articles that it issues must be accompanied by various documents: in particular various resolutions, agreements, enactments or orders that affect or evidence alterations to the company's constitution, unless the effect of the resolution, agreement, enactment or order has been incorporated into the company's articles or is no longer in force.

The objective of s 36 of the CA 2006 is that information provided on a request for a copy of the company's articles should be up to date, but the company should not be obliged to provide the same information twice, that is, in different forms.

Supplementary Provisions

Right to participate in profits otherwise than as member is void

4.26 Section 37 of the CA 2006 states that in the case of a company limited by guarantee and not having a share capital, any provision in the company's

---

[656] CA 2006, s 36(1)(a).   [657] CA 2006, s 36(1)(b).   [658] CA 2006, s 36(1)(c).
[659] CA 2006, s 36(1)(d).

articles, or in any resolution of the company, purporting to give a person a right to participate in the divisible profits of the company otherwise than as a member is void.

Section 37 of the CA 2006 restates s 15 of the CA 1985. The effect of this provision is to provide that a company limited by guarantee without a share capital cannot, by means of a provision in its articles or a resolution of its members, confer on any person a right to participate in its divisible profits otherwise than as a member. As under the CA 1985, there is no statutory restriction on the members of such companies participating in their profits, unless they have sought exemption from the use of the word 'limited' in their names.

Application to single member companies of enactment and rules of law

4.27 Section 38 of the CA 2006 provides that any enactment or rule of law applicable to companies formed by two or more persons or having two or more members applies with any necessary modification in relation to a company formed by one person or having only one person as a member.

Under s 7 of the CA 2006 (method of forming a company) it will be possible for a single person to form any type of company. Section 38 of the CA 2006 provides that in future any enactment or rule of law that is applicable to companies formed by two or more persons (or having two or more members) applies (with any necessary modifications) to companies formed with one member (or having only one person as a member). This is already the case in respect of private limited companies.[660]

A Company's Capacity and Related Matters

4.28 Part 4 of the CA 2006 is concerned with a company's capacity and related matters. It replaces various provisions in Chapter 3 of Part 1 of the CA 1985. Sections 39 and 40 of the CA 2006 replace ss 35, 35A and 35B of the CA 1985, which contained provisions derived from the First Company Law Directive (68/151/EEC), with regard to power of directors to bind the company and the effect of the *ultra vires* doctrine.

Part 4 also addresses other related matters that include the formalities of doing business under the law of England and Wales or Northern Ireland, with a consideration of company contracts, execution of documents, common seal and execution of deeds. Other related matters are also considered, including the official seal for use abroad, the official seal for the share

---

[660] See the Companies (Single Member Private Limited Companies) Regulations 1992 (SI 1992/1699).

certificate, pre-incorporation contracts, and bills of exchange and promissory notes.

Capacity of Company and Power of Directors to bind it

4.29 Sections 39–42 of the CA 2006 consider the scope of a company's capacity and the powers of directors to bind the company including their application to charities.

A company's capacity

4.30 Section 39(1) of the CA 2006 applies to a company's capacity to enter into obligations or undertake an act. It states that the validity of a company's acts will not be called into question on the ground of lack of capacity by reason of anything in a company's constitution.

This section is modified in its application to charities.[661]

Section 39 of the CA 2006 replaces s 35(1) of the CA 1985, which made similar provision for restrictions on capacity contained in the memorandum.

The position before the Companies Act 1989

4.30.1 The aim of the *ultra vires* doctrine as it applied to companies was to protect investors and creditors against unauthorised corporate activities and the depletion of their funds. In the strict sense of the term, any transaction that was beyond the company's capacity as defined in its objects clause in the Memorandum of Association, would be void and could not be ratified by the members. The common form of business organisations before the establishment of joint stock companies in 1844 was a partnership, but the *ultra vires* doctrine had no application to partnerships. Their liability was based on the concept of agency under actual or apparent authority, and any change in the nature of partnership business required unanimous consent.[662]

The incorporation of joint stock companies under the Companies Act 1844 required them to register their constitution, in the form of a deed of settlement, at Companies House. The deed of settlement was an extended form of partnership deed and the 1844 Act required such companies to provide a statement of the nature and purpose of their business. These companies had no corporate personality and, therefore, the *ultra vires* doctrine did not apply to them. Section 25 of that Act stated that the main powers and privileges of a deed of settlement company included a power to perform all other Acts necessary for carrying into effect the purposes of such a Company,

---

[661] CA 2006 s 39(2).   [662] See now in particular the Partnership Act 1890, ss 5, 6, 9 and 24.

and in all respects as other Partnerships are entitled to do. Although the 1844 Act referred to the word 'company', the deed of settlement company was still only an extended form of partnership, which had been granted certain corporate attributes. The doctrine also did not apply to chartered corporations even though they had a legal personality distinct from their members.[663] Subsequent legislation, particularly the Joint Stock Companies Act 1856, defined the limits and boundaries of corporate capacity when entering into transactions. This was achieved by compelling registered incorporated companies to state their object(s) or purpose(s), which could not be altered later by the members in a general meeting.

The *ultra vires* doctrine was first applied in its strict sense to registered and statutory companies in the mid-nineteenth century, with particular application to the railway and public utility companies. In the landmark decision of *Ashbury Railway Carriage and Iron Co v Riche*,[664] the House of Lords was concerned with the effect of the railway company entering into a transaction that was not permitted by its objects clause. It held that a company incorporated under the Companies Acts had the capacity to commit only those actions that were expressly or impliedly authorised by its Memorandum of Association. The House of Lords clearly distinguished actions that were *ultra vires* the directors because they were beyond the powers delegated to them under their company's articles, and, therefore capable of ratification by the members, from those actions that were *ultra vires* the company because they were beyond the objects as expressed in the memorandum. These latter acts were correctly termed *ultra vires* and not ratifiable by the members in general meeting.[665]

The strict rule in the *Ashbury* case was relaxed in subsequent cases, which gradually diminished the scope of the doctrine. Various devices were used to mitigate the extreme effects of the doctrine. In *A-G v Great Eastern Railway Co*,[666] the House of Lords concluded that, in addition to the express powers given to the company under its memorandum, a company had implied powers to do whatever was reasonably incidental to the carrying out of the express objects. Lord Selborne LC stated that 'the doctrine ought reasonably, and not unreasonably to be understood and applied . . .'.[667] The doctrine could also be circumvented by the corporate practice of providing an

---

[663] This was confirmed in the case of *Sutton's Hospital* (1612) 10 Co Rep 1a, 23a. See too *British South Africa Co v De Beers* [1910] 1 Ch 354.

[664] (1875) LR 7 HL 653. For a discussion of the rationale of the application of the *ultra vires* doctrine to registered companies, see Hornsey (1949) 61 Jur Rev 263.

[665] The term *ultra vires* was used in a wider sense by Vinelot J in *Rolled Steel Products (Holdings) Ltd v British Steel Corp* (1982) 3 All ER 1057 at 1076–1077 to refer to a transaction that was within the company's express or implied powers but entered into a furtherance of an unauthorised purpose. This was rejected by the Court of Appeal on the grounds of creating uncertainty in commercial transactions: [1986] Ch 246.

[666] (1880) 5 App Cas 473 HL.   [667] *Ibid*, at p 478.

extensive list of objects and powers in the memorandum and allowing companies the freedom to engage in a wide range of activities without being restricted by the doctrine. Although the House of Lords in *Cotman v Brougham*[668] viewed this activity as a 'pernicious practice: confusing power with purpose', Lord Wrenbury felt he had to 'yield to it' but nevertheless expressed his dissatisfaction:

> It has arrived now at a point at which the fact is that the function of the memorandum is taken to be not to specify, not to disclose, but to bury beneath a mass of words the real object or objects of the company, with the intent that every conceivable form of activity shall be found included somewhere within its terms.[669]

This issue was resolved by the judicial practice of analysing and construing various objects and powers in the memorandum and defining the main as opposed to the ancillary objects of the company's activities. The courts applied the *ejusdem generis* rule of construction, by deciding that the powers could only be used in relation to the company's objects. This became known as the 'main objects rule of construction'. In *Re Haven Gold Mining Co*,[670] the court held that, where the company's objects were expressed in a series of paragraphs; it would look for those paragraphs that contained the company's main objects. All other sub-paragraphs would be considered ancillary to its main objects.

Some companies nevertheless evaded the distinction between powers and objects and thereby avoided the application of the *ultra vires* rule. This was achieved by the practice of including a provision at the end of the objects clause, which stated that the objects could not be construed restrictively and that each of the paragraphs should be interpreted as a separate and an independent object. This was known as the *Cotman v Brougham* clause.[671] The courts subsequently took a restrictive view of this form of clause. In *Re Introductions Ltd v National Provincial Bank Ltd*, Harman J considered that not all powers could be objects: 'You cannot have an object to do every mortal thing you want, because that is to have no object at all'.[672]

The legal rationale of allowing the main objects rule of construction to defeat the *ultra vires* doctrine was extended to subjective objects clauses. These were drafted to empower a company 'to carry on any other trade or business whatever, which can in the opinion of the board of directors, be advantageously carried on by, in connection with, or ancillary to, any of the

---

[668] (1918) AC 514.   [669] *Ibid*, at p 523.

[670] (1882) 20 Ch D 151. See too *Re German Date Coffee Co* (1882) 20 Ch D 169.

[671] (1918) Ac 514. Cf: the earlier disapproval of this form of clause by Swinfen Eady J in *Stephens v Mysore Reefs (Kangundy) Mining Co Ltd* [1902] 1 Ch 745.

[672] (1970) Ch 199 at p 209 noted by Leigh (1970) 33 MLR 81.

above businesses or general business of the company'. The validity of this clause was upheld by the Court of Appeal in *Bell Houses Ltd v City Wall Properties Ltd*,[673] where the court applied a 'natural and ordinary meaning' to the clause and concluded that, so long as the directors honestly and genuinely formed the view that a particular business could be carried on advantageously, any activity undertaken in reliance of such a clause would be within the company's capacity.

The doctrine sometimes imparted unfairly on innocent third parties to the transaction. Because of the doctrine of constructive notice, which deems a party to have notice of the company's objects and capacity, in some circumstances, the doctrine could have a very unfair impact on third parties.[674]

Upon joining the European Community in January 1973, the UK was required to implement the First Directive of the European Community on Company Law. Article 9 of the Directive required all Member States to provide protection for third parties dealing with companies.[675] It stated that 'acts done by the organs of the company shall be binding upon it even if those acts are not within the objects of the company, unless such acts exceed the powers that the law confers or allows to be conferred on those organs'.

Article 9 also provided that if Member States could not comply with this provision, they could implement an alternative provision which stated that:

> the company shall not be bound where such acts are outside the objects of the company, if it proves that the third party knew that the act was outside those objects or could not in view of the circumstances have been unaware of it; disclosure of the statutes shall not of itself be sufficient proof thereof.

The United Kingdom implemented the latter alternative in the form of s 9 of

---

[673] (1966) 1 QB 207 and noted by Wedderburn (1966) 29 MLR 673; Baker (1966) 82 LQR 463; and Polack (1966) CLJ 174. A subjective object clause had been upheld in *HA Stephen Son & Son Ltd v Gillanders Arbuthnot & Co* (1931) 45 CLR 476. See too *Peruvian Railways Co v Thames and Mersey Marine Insurance, Re Peruvian Railways Co.* (1867) 2 Ch App 617 per Cairns LJ at p 624. However, in *Re Crown Bank* (1890) 44 Ch D 634, the court doubted whether the clause complied with the Companies Act but the New Zealand Registrar of Companies had accepted the validity of such a clause in *Christchurch City Corp v Flamingo Coffee Lounge Ltd* (1959) NZLR 986. See too Board of Trade, *Report of the Committee Law on Company Amendment* (1945) Cmmd 6659 at para 12; and Board of Trade, *Report of the Company Law Committee* (1962) Cmmd 1749 at para 40, p 12.

[674] *Re Jon Beauforte (London) Ltd* [1953] 2 WLR 465. Also on the issue of constructive notice, see *Royal British Bank v Turquand* (1856) 6 E & B 327.

[675] 68/151/EEC. First Council Directive of 9 March 1968 on coordination of the safeguards which, for the protection of the interests of he members and others, are required by members states of companies within the meaning of the second paragraph of Article 58 of the Treaty of Rome with a view to making such safeguards equivalent throughout the Community: OJ No 1968 L 65/8. See too D.D. Prentice, *EEC Directive on Company Law and Financial Markets* (1991).

the European Communities Act 1972, which was later consolidated and became s 35 of the CA 1985.[676] It stated:

> (1) In favour of a person dealing with a company in good faith, any transaction decided on by the directors is deemed to be one within the capacity of the company to enter into, and the power of the directors to bind the company is deemed to be free of any limitation under the memorandum or articles.
>
> (2) A party to a transaction so decided on is not bound to inquire as to the capacity of the company to enter into it or as to such limitation on the powers of the directors, and is presumed to have acted in good faith unless the contrary is proved.

The effect of s 35 was that a company would be bound by the decision of its directors regardless of whether or not the transaction with the third party was outside the company's objects clause, unless it could be shown that the third party was not acting in good faith. It was presumed that the third party was acting in good faith unless the contrary could be proved. The third party was not, however, required to examine the company's articles or memorandum to enquire into any limitations imposed on directors or the company's capacity to act by virtue of the contents of the constitution.

Section 35 did not completely abolish the *ultra vires* rule. It could not be relied upon by the company and only protected the third party dealing with the company in good faith. The section did not provide any definition of the words 'good faith'. It was also unclear whether 'directors' could also include a sole director. In construing s 35, some courts considered the First Directive as an aid to the section's interpretation.[677]

The requirement of 'good faith' was considered in *International Sales and Agencies v Marcus*, where Lawson J decided that:

> ... the test of good faith in someone entering into obligations with a company will be found either in proof of his actual knowledge that the transaction was *ultra vires* the company or where it can be shown that such a person could not in view of all the circumstances have been unaware that he was a party to a transaction *ultra vires*.[678]

In *Barclays Bank Ltd v TOSG Trust Fund Ltd*, Nourse J was emphatic that

---

[676] For a critical discussion of s 9 European Communities Act 1972 see especially Prentice (1973) 89 LQR 518; Wyatt (1978) 94 LQR 182; Sealy and Collier (1973) Camb LJ 112; Green (1983) JBL 303; Collier (1986) CLJ 207; Ventris (1973) 36 MLR 687; Pennington (1987) 8 Co Law 104–106.

[677] *International Sales and Agencies v Marcus* [1982] 3 All ER 551 per Lawson J, noted (1983) 46 MLR 204; (1982) CLJ 244. See too *TCB v Gray* (1986) Ch 621, noted by J Birds (1986) 7 Co Law 104; Collier (1986) CLJ 207.

[678] *Ibid*, at p 559.

the test of good faith was not objective but subjective, requiring a person to act 'genuinely and honestly in the circumstances of the case'.[679]

In 1985, the Court of Appeal reconsidered the *ultra vires* rule in *Rolled Steel Products v British Steel Corp.*[680] Browne-Wilkinson LJ clarified the confusion that had existed in previous cases:

> The critical distinction is, therefore, between acts done in excess of the capacity of the company on the one hand and acts done in excess or abuse of the powers of the company on the other. If the transaction is beyond the capacity of the company it is in any event a nullity and wholly void: whether or not the third party had notice of the invalidity, property transferred or money paid under such a transaction will be recoverable from a third party. If, on the other hand, the transaction (although in excess or abuse of powers) is within the capacity of the company, the position of the third party depends upon whether or not he had notice that the transaction is beyond the capacity of the company or merely in excess or abuse of its power: in either event the shareholders will be able to restrain the carrying out of the transaction or hold liable those who have carried it out. Only if the question of ratification by all the shareholders arises will it be material to consider whether the transaction is beyond the capacity of the company since it is established that, although all the shareholders can ratify a transaction within the company's capacity, they cannot ratify a transaction falling outside its objects.[681]

However, this statement by Browne-Wilkinson LJ identified the proper definition to be attributed to the *ultra vires* doctrine. There clearly exists a distinction between 'acts done in excess of the capacity of the company' and 'acts done in excess or abuse of the powers of the company'. Unfortunately, this distinction was not maintained by the courts in some cases decided before *Rolled Steel Products*. Where a company acts in excess of its capacity, then its acts are *ultra vires*, but where it abuses its powers, it is liable to legal sanctions; the question of its acts being *ultra vires* does not arise. An abuse of power by the company can be disregarded if it is ratified by the company's shareholders. It is in light of this distinction that one should consider whether acts of corporate philanthropy in the form of donations or other forms of monetary or non-monetary consideration should be regarded as *ultra vires* or an abuse of power by the company. It is, however, to be emphasised that

---

[679] (1984) BCLC 1 at p 18.

[680] (1985) 3 All ER 52. See Clark (1985) 6 Co Law 185; (1986) 102 LQR 109; Green (1983) JBL 303.

[681] *Ibid*, at p 92. See too Department of Trade and Industry, *Reform of the Ultra Vires Rule: A Consultative Document* at para 2, p 1. on the criticisms of the *ultra vires* doctrine see especially para 12 pp 13–14 of the report.

corporate philanthropy may be justified provided it is not regarded as an act in abuse of the power of the company.

The position under the Companies Act 1989

4.30.2 Although the CA 1989 has virtually repealed the *ultra vires* doctrine, the Act has not adopted the recommendations proposed by Prentice.

It instead inserted a new s 3A of the CA 1985 ('Statement of Company's Objects').[682] This provided that where the memorandum states that the company's object is to carry on a business, the company can carry on any trade or business whatsoever. It also has power to do all such things as are incidental or conducive to the carrying on of any trade or business by it, including philanthropic acts. Section 3A was intended to encourage to use 'short form' objects clause rather than the 'long form' objects clause.

Further steps towards the virtual abolition of the *ultra vires* doctrine were achieved by substituting for the original s 35 of the CA 1985 above new ss 35, 35A and 35B of the CA 1985 as amended.[683] Section 35 of the CA 1985 *inter alia*, provided that the validity of an act done by a company cannot be questioned on the *ground* of lack of capacity by reason of anything in the company's memorandum. This meant that neither the company nor the third party can rely on the strict *ultra vires* doctrine. Sections 35A and 35B were concerned with directors' lack of authority and constructive notice respectively. Section 35A, *inter alia*, provided that, where a third party was dealing with the company in good faith, the board of directors would be deemed to have authority to exercise all the company's powers, except where the Companies Act requires the powers to be exercised by another body and by others so authorised to, notwithstanding, in either event, any limitations in the company's constitution on the board's authority. Section 35B was read together with s 711A of the CA 1985, with the result that a third party dealing with the company is no longer deemed to have notice of the contents of any corporate documents even though they may be registered at Companies House. This abolished the doctrine of constructive notice.

The position under the CA 2006

4.30.3 Section 39 of the CA 2006 provides that any acts that are undertaken by the company (namely its corporate capacity) will not be questioned regardless of anything in its constitution.

Section 39 of the CA 2006 does not contain provisions corresponding to s 35(2) and (3) of the CA 1985. It is considered that the combination of the fact that under the CA 2006, a company may have unrestricted objects (and

---

[682] CA 1989, s 110.   [683] As inserted by CA 1989, s 108.

where it has restricted objects, the directors' powers are correspondingly restricted), and the fact that a specific duty on directors to abide the company's constitution is provided for in s 171 of the CA 2006 (duty to act within powers), makes these provisions unnecessary.

It should be noted that s 39 of the CA 2006 is independent of s 31 of the CA 2006 (statement of company's objects). Section 31 states that the company's objects are unrestricted unless the restrictions are set out in the Articles of Association. The combined effect of ss 39 and 31 of the CA 2006 means that there are no limits to the company's capacity or the objects in which it can engage. A company has complete freedom in its commercial dealings with third parties. The effect is that the 'act' in which the company is engaged cannot be questioned, thereby abolishing the remnants of any external effects of the *ultra vires* doctrine.

However, some companies may choose to restrict the scope of their objects under s 31 of the CA 2006. Although under s 39 of the CA 2006, the company's act will not be called into question even though the objects specifically limited the scope of a company's capacity as set out in the articles or the company's constitution (the latter having a wider meaning), the internal effects of the *ultra vires* doctrine still remain. Directors will be held accountable to their shareholders for engaging in prohibited objects or acts. This also has implications for the powers of directors to undertake prohibited acts. In practice, it means that the powers of directors will also be constrained or restricted from entering into prohibited acts or objects, as directors would have exceeded the company's capacity. If directors engaged in such prohibited acts, they would be held accountable before the shareholders for their actions and this would constitute a breach of statutory duty of the powers vested in directors.

Power of directors to bind the company

4.30.4 Section 40(1) of the CA 2006 provides that in favour of a person dealing with a company in good faith, the power of the directors to bind the company, or authorise others to do so, is deemed not to be constrained by the company's constitution. This means that a third party dealing with a company in good faith need not be concerned about whether a company is acting within its constitution.

Section 40(2) of the CA 2006 further elucidates on the expressions used in s 40(1) of the CA 2006. Thus, a person 'deals with' a company if he is a party to any transaction or other act to which the company is a party.[684] Further, a person dealing with a company is not bound to enquire as to any limitation on the powers of the directors to bind the company or authorise others to do

---

[684] CA 2006, s 40(2)(a).

so.[685] He is presumed to have acted in good faith unless the contrary is proved;[686] and he is not to be regarded as acting in bad faith by reason only of his knowing that an act is beyond the powers of the directors under the company's constitution.[687]

The references to limitations on the directors' powers under the company's constitution include limitations deriving from a resolution of the company or of any class of shareholders;[688] or from any agreement between the members of the company or any class of shareholders.[689]

The *intra vires* aspect of relations between directors and shareholders is still preserved. Section 40(4) of the CA 2006 provides that it does not affect any right of a member of the company to bring proceedings to restrain the doing of an action that is beyond the powers of the directors. This allows shareholders to bring an action (usually seeking an injunction) to prevent directors from entering into future obligations that are beyond their power. However, no such proceedings lie in respect of an act to be done in fulfillment of a legal obligation arising from a previous act of the company. Neither does this affect any liability incurred by the directors, or any other person, by reason of directors exceeding their powers.[690] This is subject to s 41 of the CA 2006 (transactions with directors or their associates); and s 42 of the CA 2006 (companies that are charities).[691]

The position before the CA 2006 was governed by ss 35A and 35B of the CA 1985. Section 40 of the CA 2006 now provides safeguards for a person dealing with a company in good faith. It restates s 35A of the CA 1985.

Section 40(2)(b)(i) of the CA 2006 replaces part of s 35B of the CA 1985: an external party is not bound to enquire whether there are any limitations on the power of directors. The first part of s 35B of the CA 1985, which referred to the memorandum, has not been carried forward under the CA 2006. This was concerned with restrictions in a company's constitution that limited a company's ability to act and consequently the powers of directors to bind the company under the *ultra vires* doctrine. Under the CA 2006, the objects no longer affect the company's capacity to act and so this part of s 35 of the CA 1985 was not required.

Constitutional limitations: Transactions involving directors or their associates

4.31 Section 41 of the CA 2005 applies to a transaction if, or to the extent that, its validity depends on s 40 of the CA 2006 (powers of directors deemed to be free of limitations under company's constitution in favour of person

---

[685] CA 2006, s 40(2)(b)(i).   [686] CA 2006, s 40(2)(b)(ii).   [687] CA 2006, s 40(2)(b)(iii).
[688] CA 2006, s 40(3)(a).   [689] CA 2006, s 40(3)(b).   [690] CA 2006, s 40(5).
[691] CA 2006, s 40(6).

dealing with company in good faith). It provides that nothing in s 41 of the CA 2006 is to be read as excluding the operation of any other enactment or rule of law by virtue of which the transaction may be called in question or any liability to the company may arise.[692]

Where a company enters into a transaction of the type contemplated in s 41(1) of the CA 2006,[693] and the parties to the transaction include a director of the company or of its holding company;[694] or a person connected with any such director,[695] the transaction is voidable at the instance of the company. This section refers to a transaction with an 'insider', such as a director or a person connected with a director.

Irrespective whether the transaction is voided, the 'insider' and any director of the company who authorised the transaction, is liable to account to the company for any gain he has made directly or indirectly by the transaction as a result of the transaction;[696] and to indemnify the company for any loss or damage that the company has incurred resulting from the transaction.[697]

As now, under s 41(4) of the CA 2006, a transaction will cease to be voidable in certain circumstances. They are:

- if restitution of any money or assets that have been lost as a result of the transaction is no longer possible;[698] or
- the company is indemnified for any loss or damage resulting from the transaction;[699] or
- rights acquired *bona fide* for value and without actual notice of the directors' exceeding their powers by a person who is not a party to the transaction would be affected by the voiding the transaction;[700] or
- the transaction is affirmed by the company.[701]

However, where the 'insider' is not a director of the company, it may be possible for him to avoid liability under s 41(3) of the CA 2006, if he can show that at the time he entered into the transaction with the company, he did not know that the directors were exceeding their powers.[702]

Nothing in the preceding provisions of s 41 of the CA 2006 affects the rights of any party to the transaction not within s 41(2)(b)(i) or (ii) of the CA 2006. However, the court may, on application of the company or any such party, make an order affirming, severing or setting aside the transaction on such terms as appear to the court to be just.[703] The words 'transaction'

---

[692] CA 2006, s 41(1).   [693] CA 2006, s 41(2)(a).   [694] CA 2006, s 41(2)(b)(i).
[695] CA 2006, s 41(2)(b)(ii).   [696] CA 2006, s 41(3)(a).   [697] CA 2006, s 41(3)(b).
[698] CA 2006, s 41(4)(a).   [699] CA 2006, s 41(4)(b).   [700] CA 2006, s 41(4)(c).
[701] CA 2006, s 41(4)(d).   [702] CA 2006, s 41(5).   [703] CA 2006, s 41(6).

includes any act;[704] and the reference to a person connected with a director has the same meaning as Part 10 of the CA 2006 (company directors).[705]

This section restates s 322A of the CA 1985.

Constitutional limitations: companies that are charities

4.32 Section 42 of the CA 2006 provides that the protection afforded to an eternal party by ss 39 and 40 of the CA 2006 will not apply to the acts of a company which is a charity, except in favour of a person who does not know at the time the act is done that the company is a charity;[706] or gives full consideration in money or money's worth in relation to the act in question and does not know (as the case may be) that the act is not permitted by the company's constitution;[707] or that the act is beyond the powers of the directors.[708]

Where a company that is a charity purports to transfer or grant an interest in its property, the fact that (as the case may be) the act was not permitted by the company's constitution;[709] or the directors in connection with the act exceeded any limitation on their powers under the company's constitution,[710] does not affect the title of a person who subsequently acquires that property or an interest in it for full consideration without actual notice of any such circumstances affecting the validity of the company's act.

In any proceedings arising out of ss 42(1) or (2) of the CA 2006, the burden of proving that a person knew that the company was a charity;[711] or that a person knew that an act was not permitted by the company's constitution or was beyond the powers of the directors,[712] lies on the person asserting that fact.

Where a company is registered as a charity in England and Wales and Northern Ireland, and it seeks to affirm an act that was beyond the powers of the directors (see s 41 of the CA 2006 – transactions with directors or their associates), such affirmation may only be given if the company has received the prior written consent of the Charity Commissioners in England and Wales,[713] or the Department for Social Development in Northern Ireland.[714]

Corresponding provisions for charities that are registered in Scotland can be found in s 112 of the CA 1989.[715]

Section 42 of the CA 2006 restates the substance of s 65 Charities Act 1993. It is a qualification of the rules in s 39 of the CA 1989 (a company's capacity) and s 40 of the CA 2006 (power of the directors to bind the company).

---

[704] CA 2006, s 41(7)(a).   [705] CA 2006, s 41(7)(b).   [706] CA 2006, s 42(1)(a).
[707] CA 2006, s 42(1)(b)(i).   [708] CA 2006, s 42(1)(b)(ii).   [709] CA 2006, s 42(2)(a).
[710] CA 2006, s 42(2)(b).   [711] CA 2006, s 42(3)(a).   [712] CA 2006, s 42(3)(b).
[713] CA 2006, s 42(4)(a).   [714] CA 2006, s 42(4)(b).   [715] CA 2006, s 42(5).

Formalities of doing business under the law of England and Wales or Northern Ireland

Company contracts

4.33 Section 43 of the CA 2006 provides that a contract may be entered into by a company under the law of England and Wales and Northern Ireland, by the company itself, by writing under its common seal;[716] or on behalf of the company by a person acting under its authority, express or implied.[717]

Any formalities required by law in the case of a contract made by an individual also apply, unless a contrary intention appears, to a contract made by or on behalf of a company.[718]

This section restates the provisions of s 36 of the CA 1985.

Execution of documents

4.34 Section 44(1) of the CA 2006 provides that under the law of England and Wales or Northern Ireland, a document is executed by a company by the affixing of its common seal;[719] or by signature in accordance with s 44 of the CA 2006.[720]

A document is validly executed by a company if it is signed on behalf of the company by two authorised signatories;[721] or by a director of the company in the presence of a witness who attests the signature.[722]

The following are 'authorised signatories' for the purposes of s 44(2) of the CA 2006. They are: every director of the company;[723] and in the case of a private company with a secretary or a public company, the secretary (or any joint secretary) of the company.[724]

A document that is signed in accordance with s 44(2) of the CA 2006 and expressed in whatever words, to be executed by the company, has the same effect as if executed under the common seal of the company.[725]

In favour of a purchaser, a document is deemed to have been duly executed by a company if it purports to be signed in accordance with s 44(2) of the CA 2006. The word 'purchaser' means a purchaser in good faith for valuable consideration and includes a lessee, mortgagee or other person who for valuable consideration acquires an interest in property.[726]

Where a document is to be signed by a person on behalf of more than one company, it is not duly signed by that person unless he signs it separately in each capacity.[727]

---

[716] CA 2006, s 43(1)(a).   [717] CA 2006, s 43(1)(b).   [718] CA 2006, s 43(2).
[719] CA 2006, s 44(1)(a).   [720] CA 2006, s 44(1)(b).   [721] CA 2006, s 44(2)(a).
[722] CA 2006, s 44(2)(b).
[723] CA 2006, s 44(3)(a). This includes a single director of a company.
[724] CA 2006, s 44(3)(b).   [725] CA 2006, s 44(4).   [726] CA 2006, s 44(5).
[727] CA 2006, s 44(6).

The references under s 44 of the CA 2006 to a document being (or purporting to be) signed by a director or secretary are to be read, in a case where the office is held by a firm, as references to its being (or purporting to be) signed by an individual authorised by the firm to sign on its behalf.[728] Section 44 of the CA 2006 also applies to a document that is (or purports to be) executed by a company in the name of or on behalf of another person whether or not that person is also a company.[729]

Section 44 of the CA 2006 largely restates s 36A of the CA 1985.

Common seal

4.35 Section 45 of the CA 2006 provides that a company may have a common seal, but need not have one.[730] A company that has a common seal must have its name engraved in legible characters on the seal.[731] If a company fails to comply, an offence is committed by the company[732] and every officer of the company who is in default.[733]

An officer of a company, or a person acting on behalf of a company, commits an offence if he uses, or authorises the use of, a seal purporting to be the seal of the company on which its name is not engraved as required by s 45(2) of the CA 2006.[734] A person guilty of an offence is liable on summary conviction to a fine not exceeding level 3 on the standard scale.[735] Section 45 of the CA 2006 does not form part of the law of Scotland.[736]

Section 45 replaces s 36A(3) and s 350 of the CA 1985.

Execution of deeds

4.36 Section 46(1) of the CA 2006 states that a document is validly executed by a company as a deed for the purposes of s 1(2)(b) Law of Property (Miscellaneous Provisions) Act 1989, and for the purposes of the law of Northern Ireland if, and only if, it is duly executed by the company;[737] and it is delivered as a deed.[738] For the purposes of s 46(1)(b) of the CA 2006, a document is presumed to be delivered upon its being executed, unless a contrary intention is proved.[739]

This section re-enacts s 36A, inserted into the of the CA 1985 by the Regulatory Reform (Execution Of Deeds and Documents) Order 2005 (SI 2005/1906). The only change is to extend the application for the purposes of the law of Northern Ireland.

[728] CA 2006, s 44(7).   [729] CA 2006, s 44(8).   [730] CA 2006, s 45(1).
[731] CA 2006, s 45(2).   [732] CA 2006, s 45(3)(a).   [733] CA 2006, s 45(3)(b).
[734] CA 2006, s 45(4).   [735] CA 2006, s 45(5).   [736] CA 2006, s 45(6).
[737] CA 2006, s 46(1)(a).   [738] CA 2006, s 46(1)(b).   [739] CA 2006, s 46(2).

Execution of deeds or other documents by attorney

4.37 Section 47 of the CA 2006 provides that under the law of England and Wales or Northern Ireland a company may, by instrument executed as a deed, empower a person, either generally or in respect of specified matters, as its attorney to execute deeds or other documents on its behalf.[740] A deed or document so executed, whether in the United Kingdom or elsewhere, has effect as if executed by the company.[741]

This section replaces s 38 of the CA 1985. The CA 1985 did not require the appointment of the attorney to be by deed, nor did it state anything about deeds executed on behalf of the company in the United Kingdom.

Section 47 of the CA 2006 makes clear that the method for a company appointing an attorney is by instrument executed as a deed, which is the same method by which an individual appoints an attorney.

Formalities of doing business under the law of Scotland

Execution of documents by companies

4.38 Section 48(1) of the CA 2006 provides that the section forms part of the law of Scotland only.[742] Notwithstanding the provision of any enactment, a company need not have a company seal.[743] For the purposes of any enactment, providing for a document to be executed by a company by affixing its common seal;[744] or referring (in whatever terms) to a document so executed,[745] a document signed or subscribed by or on behalf of the company in accordance with the provisions of the Requirements of Writing (Scotland) Act 1955 has effect as if so executed.[746]

This section restates s 36B of the CA 2006. It makes clear that no seal is required regardless of any other statutory provision. The only change is the addition of s 49(1) of the CA 2006 which makes clear that this section forms part of the law of Scotland only.

Other matters

Official seal for use abroad

4.39 Section 50(1) of the CA 2006 provides that a company that has a common seal may have an official seal for use outside the UK. The official seal must be a facsimile of the company's seal, with the addition on its face of the place or places where it is to be used.[747] The official seal when duly affixed to a

---

[740] CA 2006, s 47(1).   [741] CA 2006, s 47(2).   [742] CA 2006, s 48(1)
[743] CA 2006, s 48(2).   [744] CA 2006, s 48(3)(a).   [745] CA 2006, s 48(3)(b).
[746] CA 2006, s 48(3).   [747] CA 2006, s 49(2).

document has the same effect as the company's seal. The latter does not however extend to Scotland.[748] A company having its official seal for use outside the United Kingdom may by writing under its common seal;[749] or as respects Scotland, by writing subscribed in accordance with the Requirements of Writing (Scotland) Act 1995,[750] authorise any person appointed for the purpose to fix an official seal to any deed or other document to which the company is a party.

As between the company and a person dealing with such an agent, the agent's authority continues during the period mentioned in the instrument conferring the authority;[751] or if no period is mentioned, until notice of the revocation or termination of the agent's authority has been given to the person dealing with him.[752]

The person affixing the official seal must certify in writing on the deed or other document to which the seal is affixed the date on which, and place at which, it is affixed.[753]

This section re-enacts s 39 of the CA 1985. It sets out the circumstances and manner in which a company may use its common seal outside the United Kingdom.

Official seal for share certificates, etc

4.40 Section 50(1) of the CA 2006 provides that a company that has a common seal may have an official seal for use for sealing securities issued by the company;[754] or for sealing documents creating or evidencing securities so issued.[755] The official seal must be a facsimile of the company's seal, with the addition on its face of the word 'Securities';[756] and when duly affixed to the document has the same effect as the company's common seal.[757]

This section restates s 40 of the CA 1985. It enables a company that has a common seal to have an official seal for sealing securities issued by the company and for sealing documents creating or evidencing securities so issued.

Pre-incorporation contracts, deeds and obligations

4.41 Section 51(1) of the CA 2006 provides that a contract that purports to be made by or on behalf of a company at a time when the company has not been formed has effect, subject to any agreement to the contrary, as one made with the person purporting to act for the company or as agent for it, and he is personally liable on the contract accordingly.

Section 51(1) of the CA 2006 applies to the making of a deed under the law

---

[748] CA 2006, s 49(3).   [749] CA 2006, s 49(4)(a).   [750] CA 2006, s 49(4)(b).
[751] CA 2006, s 49(5)(a).   [752] CA 2006, s 49(5)(b).   [753] CA 2006, s 49(6).
[754] CA 2006, s 50(1)(a).   [755] CA 2006, s 50(1)(b).   [756] CA 2006, s 50(2)(a).
[757] CA 2006, s 50(2)(b).

of England and Wales or Northern Ireland;[758] and to the undertaking of an obligation under the law of Scotland,[759] as it applies to the making of a contract.

Section 51 of the CA 2006 restates s 36C of the CA 1985. A company is not bound by a contract purportedly made on its behalf before it came into existence unless the obligations are novated, that is, a new contract must come into existence after incorporation on the same terms as the old one. Novation may be expressed or implied.[760]

Bills of exchange and promissory notes

4.42 Section 52 of the CA 2006 provides that a bill of exchange or promissory note is deemed to have been made, accepted or endorsed on behalf of a company if made, accepted or endorsed in the name of, or by or on account of, the company by a person acting under its authority.

This section restates s 37 of the CA 1985. A bill of exchange is an unconditional order in writing, addressed by one person to another, signed by the person giving it, requiring the person to whom it is addressed to pay on demand or at a fixed or determinable future time a sum certain in money to or to the order of a specified person, or to its bearer. A promissory note is an unconditional promise in writing made by one person to another, signed by the maker, engaging to pay, on demand or at a fixed or determinable future time, a sum certain in money to, or to the order of, a specified person or to its bearer. Where someone acting under a company's authority makes, accepts, or endorses such an instrument in the name of the company, or on its behalf, this clause treats this as if these actions had been done by the company.

---

[758] CA 2006, s 51(2)(a).   [759] CA 2006, s 51(2)(b).

[760] See *Phonogram Ltd v Lane* [1982] QB 938; *Cotronic (UK) Ltd v Dezonie* [1991] BCLC 721; *Badgerhill Properties Ltd v Cottrell* [1991] BCLC 805; *Rover International Ltd v Cannon Film Sales Ltd (No 2)* (1987) 3 BCC 369. For the common law position see *Kelner v Baxter* (1866) LR 2 CP 174; *Newborne v Sensolid (GB) Ltd* [1954] 1 QB 45; *Re Northumberland Avenue Hotel Co Ltd* (1886) 33 Ch D 16; *Howard v Patent Ivory Manufacturing Co* (1888) 38 Ch D 156; and European Communities Act 1972, s 9(2), later enacted with some amendments under CA 1985, s 36C.

Chapter 5

Company Re-registration

Introduction

5.1 Part 7 of the CA 2006 is concerned with the re-registration of companies as a means of altering a company's status. It replaces equivalent provisions in Part 2 of the CA 1985. There are some substantive changes, as well as amendments reflecting the new provisions of the CA 2006 about registration. Part 7 comprises 23 sections.

Alteration of status by re-registration

5.2 Section 89 of the CA 2006 sets out the types of companies that may alter their status by re-registering. It provides that a company may by re-registration alter its status from a private company to a public company;[761] or from a public company to a private company;[762] or from a private limited company to an unlimited company;[763] or from an unlimited private company to a limited company;[764] or from a public company to an unlimited private company.[765]

This section provides for various mechanisms under CA 2006 by which a company may alter its status. As recommended by the Company Law Review Group,[766] it retains the current possibilities for re-registration, but there is one significant change to the CA 1985 regime: in line with the recommendation of the Company Law Review Group Final Report,[767] in future a public company will be able to re-register as an unlimited private company without first having to re-register as private limited.[768]

---

[761] CA 2006, ss 90–96.   [762] CA 2006, ss 97–101.   [763] CA 2006, ss 102–104.
[764] CA 2006, ss 105–107.   [765] CA 2006, ss 109–110.   [766] *Final Report*, para 11.16.
[767] *Final Report*, para 11.11.   [768] See CA 2006, s 109.

Private company becoming public

Re-registration of private company as public

5.3 Section 90(1) of the CA 2006 provides that a private company (whether limited or unlimited) may be re-registered as a public company limited by shares, if a special resolution that it should be so re-registered is passed;[769] and the conditions in s 90(2) of the CA 2006 are met;[770] and an application for re-registration is delivered to the registrar under s 94 of the CA 2006, together with other documents required by s 94;[771] and a statement of compliance.[772]

The conditions to be met are:

- that the company has a share capital;[773]
- that the requirements of s 91 of the CA 2006 are met as regards its share capital;[774]
- that the requirements of s 92 of the CA 2006 are met as regards its net assets;[775]
- if s 93 of the CA 2006 applies (recent allotment of shares for non-cash consideration), the requirements of that section are met;[776] and
- that the company has not previously been re-registered as unlimited.[777]

The company must make such changes in its name;[778] and in its articles[779] as are necessary in connection with its becoming a public company.[780] If the company is unlimited, it must also make such changes in its articles as are necessary to its becoming a company limited by shares.

Section 90 of the CA 2006 replaces s 43(1)(a) and (2) of the CA 1985, and s 48 of the CA 1985. It enables a private company (whether limited or unlimited) to re-register as a public company provided certain conditions are met. These conditions are set out in s 90(2)–(4) of the CA 2006. They include a requirement for the company to make such alterations to its name and Articles of Association ('articles'), as are necessary to reflect the fact that the company will be a public company. This will be particularly important for private companies formed under the CA 2006 who are using the model articles: in particular, the new model articles for private companies limited by shares formed under the CA 2006 will be written with such companies in mind, and are unlikely to be suitable for use by a newly re-registered public company.

Under s 48 of the CA 1985, an unlimited private company with a share

---

[769] CA 2006, s 90(a).   [770] CA 2006, s 90(1)(b).   [771] CA 2006, s 90(1)(c)(i).
[772] CA 2006, s 90(1)(c)(ii).   [773] CA 2006, s 90(2)(a).   [774] CA 2006, s 90(2)(b).
[775] CA 2006, s 90(2)(c).   [776] CA 2006, s 90(2)(d).   [777] CA 2006, s 90(2)(e).
[778] CA 2006, s 90(3)(a).   [779] CA 2006, s 90(3)(b).   [780] CA 2006, s 90(4).

capital will be able to re-register as a public company and this is reflected in s 90(4) of the CA 2006.

Section 90(2)(e) of the CA 2006 retains the requirement that a private company may not re-register as a public company, if it has previously re-registered as an unlimited company. The intention behind this provision is that a company should not be able to enjoy the benefits of limited liability, or avoid the obligations that are attached to this, for example, the increased reporting requirements, by continually swapping from limited to unlimited status.

Requirement as to share capital

5.4 With regards to the requirement as to share capital, s 91(1) of the CA 2006 provides that the following requirements must be met at the time the special resolution is passed that the company should be re-registered as a public company:

(a) the nominal value of the company's allotted share capital must not be less than the authorised minimum;[781]

(b) each of the company's allotted shares must be paid up at least as to one-quarter of the nominal value of that share and the whole of any premium on it;[782]

(c) if any shares in the company or any premium on them have been fully or partly paid up by an undertaking given by any person that he or another do work or perform services (whether for the company or any other person), the undertaking must have been performed or otherwise discharged;[783]

(d) if shares have been allotted as fully or partly paid up as to their nominal value or any premium on them otherwise than in cash, and the consideration for the allotment consists of or includes an undertaking to the company (other than one to which paragraph (c) applies), then either the undertaking must have been performed or otherwise discharged;[784] or there must have been a contract between the company and some person pursuant to which the undertaking is to be performed within five years from the time the special resolution is passed.[785]

For the purpose of determining whether the requirements in s 91(1)(b), (c) and (d) of the CA 2006 are met, the following may be disregarded:

---

[781] CA 2006, s 91(1)(a).   [782] CA 2006, s 91(1)(b).   [783] CA 2006, s 91(1)(c).
[784] CA 2006, s 91(1)(d)(i).   [785] CA 2006, s 91(1)(d)(ii).

(a)   shares allotted:

   (i)   before 22 June 1982 in the case of a company then registered in Great Britain;[786] or

   (ii)   before 31 December 1984 in the case of a company then registered in Northern Ireland;[787]

(b)   shares allotted in pursuance of an employees' share scheme by reason of which the company would, but for this subsection, be precluded under s 91(1)(b) of the CA 2006 (but not otherwise) from being re-registered as public company.[788]

No more than one-tenth of the nominal value of the company's allotted share capital is to be disregarded under s 91(2)(a) of the CA 2006. For this purpose the allotted share capital is treated as not including shares disregarded under s 91(2)(b) of the CA 2006.[789]

Shares disregarded under s 91(2) of the CA 2006 are treated as not forming part of the allotted share capital for the purposes of s 91(1)(a) of the CA 2006.[790]

A company must not be re-registered as a public company if it appears to the registrar that the company has resolved to reduce its share capital;[791] that the reduction is made under s 626 of the CA 2006 (reduction in connection with redenomination of share capital);[792] that it is supported by a solvency statement in accordance with s 643 of the CA 2006;[793] that has been confirmed by an order of the court under s 648 of the CA 2006;[794] or it must also be shown that the effect of the reduction is, or will be, that the nominal value of the company's allotted share capital is below the authorised minimum.[795]

Section 91 of the CA 2006 re-states ss 45 and 47(3) of the CA 1985. It sets out the requirement as to share capital of a company that it is proposing to re-register as a public company. These requirements carry forward the provisions of the CA 1985, for example, the company's share capital must not be less than the authorised minimum (defined in s 533 of the CA 2006), and each of the company's allotted shares must be paid up at least as to a quarter of the nominal value of that share and the whole of any premium on it.

Section 91(5) of the CA 2006 replaces s 47(3) of the CA 1985. It provides that the registrar must not issue a new certificate of incorporation on re-registration, if the court has made an order confirming a reduction of capital, which has the effect of bringing the company's allotted share capital below the authorised minimum (which remains at £50,000 but may be satisfied in

---

[786] CA 2006, s 91(2)(a)(i).   [787] CA 2006, s 91(2)(a)(ii).   [788] CA 2006, s 91(2)(b).
[789] CA 2006, s 91(3).   [790] CA 2006, s 91(4).   [791] CA 2006, s 91(5)(a).
[792] CA 2006, s 91(5)(b)(i).   [793] CA 2006, s 91(5)(b)(ii).   [794] CA 2006, s 91(5)(b)(iii).
[795] CA 2006, s 91(5)(c).

sterling or euros – see s 763 of the CA 2006), or if the company has reduced its capital via the solvency statement procedure for capital reductions[796] or in connection with a redenomination of share capital (see s 626 of the CA 2006).[797]

Requirement as to net assets

5.5 Section 92 of the CA 2006 provides that a company applying to re-register as a public company must obtain the following balance sheet prepared as at a date not more than seven months before the date on which the application is delivered to the registrar;[798] an unqualified report by the company's auditor on that balance sheet;[799] and a written statement by the company's auditor that in his opinion at the balance sheet date, the amount of the company's net assets was not less than the aggregate of its called-up share capital and undistributable reserves.[800]

Between the balance sheet date and the date on which the application for re-registration is delivered to the registrar, there must be no change in the company's financial position that results in the amount of its net assets becoming less that the aggregate of its called-up share capital and undistributable reserves.[801]

The term 'unqualified report' in s 92(1)(b) of the CA 2006 means:

(a)   if the balance sheet was prepared for a financial year of the company, a report stating without material qualification of the auditor's opinion that the balance sheet has been properly prepared in accordance with the requirements of this Act;[802]

(b)   if the balance sheet was not prepared for a financial year of the company, a report stating without material qualification of the auditor's opinion that the balance sheet has been properly prepared in accordance with the provisions of this Act which would have applied if it had been prepared for a financial year of the company.[803]

For the purposes of an auditor's report on a balance sheet that was not prepared for a financial year of the company, the provisions of the CA 2006 will apply with such modifications as are necessary by reason of that fact.[804]

For the purposes of s 92(3) of the CA 2006, a qualification is material unless the auditor states in his report that the matter giving rise to the qualification is not material for the purpose of determining (by reference to the company's balance sheet) whether at the balance sheet date, the amount of

[796] See CA 2006, s 642.   [797] See CA 2006, s 626.   [798] CA 2006, s 92(1)(a).
[799] CA 2006, s 92(1)(b).   [800] CA 2006, s 92(1)(c).   [801] CA 2006, s 92(2).
[802] CA 2006, s 92(3)(a).   [803] CA 2006, s 92(3)(b).   [804] CA 2006, s 92(4).

the company's net assets was not less than the aggregate of its called-up share capital and undistributable reserves.[805]

Section 92 of the CA 2006 restates s 43 (3)(b)–(c) and (4) and s 46 of the CA 1985. It makes no substantive changes to these provisions, and the requirements as to net assets for a public company remain unchanged (as under the CA 1985, these are determined by reference to the company's most recent balance sheet).

Recent allotment of shares for non-cash consideration

5.6 Section 93 of the CA 2006 applies where shares are allotted by the company in the period between the date as at which the balance sheet required by s 92 of the CA 2006 is prepared and the passing of the resolution that the company should re-register as a public company;[806] and the shares are allotted as fully or partly paid up as to their nominal value or any premium on them otherwise than in cash.[807]

Section 93(2) of the CA 2006 provides that the registrar will not entertain an application by the company for re-registration as a public company unless the requirements of s 593(1)(a) and (b) of the CA 2006 have been complied with (independent valuation of non-cash considerations; valuer's report to the company not more than six months before allotment);[808] or the allotment is in connection with a share exchange;[809] or a proposed merger with another company.[810]

An allotment is in connection with a share exchange, if the shares are allotted in connection with an arrangement under which the whole or part of the consideration for the shares allotted is provided by the transfer to the company allotting the shares of shares (or shares of a particular class) in another company;[811] or the cancellation of shares (or shares of a particular class) in another company;[812] and the allotment is open to all the holders of the shares of the other company in question (or, where the arrangement applies only to shares of a particular class, to all the holders of the company's shares of that class) to take part in the arrangement in connection with which the shares are allotted.[813]

In determining whether a person is a holder of shares for the purposes of s 93(3) of the CA 2006, the following will be disregarded: shares held by, or by a nominee, of the company allotting the shares;[814] shares held by, or by a

---

[805] CA 2006, s 92(5). The terms 'net assets' and 'undistributable reserves' have the same meaning as in CA 2006, s 831 (net asset restriction on distributions by public companies).

[806] CA 2006, s 93(1)(a).   [807] CA 2006, s 93(1)(b).   [808] CA 2006, s 93(2)(a).

[809] CA 2006, s 93(2)(b)(i). See too CA 2006, s 93(3)–(5).

[810] CA 2006, s 93(2)(b)(ii). See too CA 2006, s 93(6).

[811] CA 2006, s 93(3)(a)(i).   [812] CA 2006, s 93(3)(a)(ii).   [813] CA 2006, s 93(3)(b).

[814] CA 2006, s 93(4)(a).

nominee, of the holding company of the company allotting the shares,[815] a subsidiary of the company allotting the shares,[816] or a subsidiary of the holding company of the company allotting the shares.[817]

It is immaterial, for the purposes of deciding whether an allotment is in connection with a share exchange, whether or not the arrangement in connection with which the shares are allotted involves the issue to the company allotting the shares of shares (or shares of a particular class) in the other company.[818]

Section 93(6) of the CA 2006 relates back to the definition of a proposed merger set out in s 93(2)(b)(ii) of the CA 2006. It states that there is a proposed merger with another company if one of the companies concerned proposes to acquire all the assets and liabilities of the other in exchange for the issue of its shares or other securities to shareholders of the other (whether or not accompanies by a cash payment). 'Another company' includes any body corporate.[819]

For the purposes of s 93 of the CA 2006, the consideration for an allotment does not include any amount standing to the credit of any of the company's reserve accounts, or of its profit and loss account, that has been applied in paying up (to any extent) any of the shares allotted or any premium on those shares;[820] and 'arrangement' means any agreement, scheme or arrangement, including an arrangement sanctioned in accordance with Part 26 of the CA 2006 (arrangements and reconstructions);[821] s 110 Insolvency Act 1986 (c.45) or Article 96 of the Insolvency (Northern Ireland) Order 1989 (SI 1989/2405 (NI 19)) (liquidation in winding up accepting shares as consideration for sale of company's property).[822]

Section 93 of the CA 2006 restates s 44 of the CA 1985. Where there has been an allotment of shares for non-cash consideration between the date of the balance sheet required under s 92 of the CA 2006 (requirements as to net assets) and the date the company passed the resolution to re-register as a public company, the registrar will not entertain an application for re-registration unless the consideration for the allotment has been valued in accordance with s 108 of the CA 1985 (valuation and report).

Application and accompanying documents

5.7 Section 94 of the CA 2006 deals with the application and accompanying documents for re-registration as a public company. An application for re-registration as a public company must contain a statement of the company's

---

[815] CA 2006, s 93(4)(b)(i).   [816] CA 2006, s 93(4)(b)(ii).   [817] CA 2006, s 93(4)(b)(iii).
[818] CA 2006, s 93(5).   [819] CA 2006, s 93(6).   [820] CA 2006, s 93(7)(a).
[821] CA 2006, s 93(7)(b)(i).   [822] CA 2006, s 93(7)(b)(ii).

proposed name on re-registration;[823] and a statement of the company's proposed secretary.[824]

The application must be accompanied by a copy of the resolution that the company should re-register as a public company (unless a copy has already been forwarded to the registrar under Chapter 3 of Part 3);[825] a copy of the company's articles as proposed to be amended;[826] a copy of the balance sheet and other documents referred to in s 92(1) of the CA 2006;[827] and if s 93 of the CA 2006 applies (recent allotment of shares for non-cash consideration), a copy of the valuation report (if any) under s 93(2)(a) of the CA 2006.[828]

The statement of compliance required to be delivered together with the application is a statement that the requirements of this Part as to re-registration as a public company have been complied with.[829]

The register may accept the statement of compliance as sufficient evidence that the company is entitled to be re-registered as a public company.[830]

Section 94 of the CA 2006 restates s 43(1)(b), (2)(a), (3)(a) and (e) and s 47(2) of the CA 1985. It prescribes the contents of the application for re-registration. There is one important change, which is required as a result of the abolition of the requirement under the CA 1985 for private companies to have a company secretary – see s 270 of the CA 2006. In future, where a private company, which is proposing to re-register as a public company, does not have a company secretary, the application for re-registration must include a statement of the company's proposed secretary where the company does not already have a secretary. The contents of this statement are prescribed in s 95 of the CA 2006.

The application for re-registration must be accompanied by a statement of compliance – see s 90(1)(c)(ii) – which replaces the present requirement for a statutory declaration (or its electronic equivalent), contained in s 43(3)(e) and 3(A) of the CA 1985, with a requirement to make this statement.

Statement of proposed secretary

5.8 Section 95(1) of the CA 2006 provides that the statement of the company's proposed secretary must contain the required particulars of the person who is or the persons who are to be (or continue to be) the secretary or joint secretaries of the company. The required particulars are the particulars that will be required to be stated in the company's register of secretaries.[831]

The statement must also contain a consent by a person named as secretary, or each of the persons named as joint secretaries, to act in the relevant

---

[823] CA 2006, s 94(1)(a).   [824] CA 2006, s 94(1)(b).   [825] CA 2006, s 94(2)(a).

[826] CA 2006, s 94(2)(b).   [827] CA 2006, s 94(2)(c).   [828] CA 2006, s 94(2)(d).

[829] CA 2006, s 94(3).   [830] CA 2006, s 94(4).

[831] Section 95(2). See too CA 2006, ss 277–279.

capacity. If all the partners in a firm are to be joint secretaries, consent may be given by one partner on behalf of all of them.[832]

Section 95 of the CA 2006 is a new provision, which is required as a result of the abolition of the requirement for private companies to have a company secretary (see s 270 of the CA 2006). Where a private company is proposing to re-register as a public company and the company does not already have a company secretary, the application for re-registration must include details of the persons who will act as company secretary or joint secretaries on re-registration. The statement of proposed secretary must also contain a consent given by each of the persons named in the statement, to act as company secretary or joint secretaries. If all partners in a firm are to be joint secretaries, one partner in the firm must give consent to act on behalf of all the partners.

Issue of certificate of incorporation on re-registration

5.9 Section 96 of the CA 2006 states that where, on application for re-registration as a public company, the registrar is satisfied that the company is entitled to be so re-registered, the company must be re-registered accordingly.[833] The registrar must issue a certificate of incorporation altered to meet the circumstances of the case.[834] The certificate must state that it is issued on re-registration and the date on which it is issued.[835]

On issue of the certificate, the company by virtue of the issue of the certificate becomes a public company;[836] the changes in the company's name and articles take effect,[837] and the person or persons named in the statement under s 95 of the CA 2006 (statement of proposed secretary) as secretary or joint secretary of the company are deemed to have been appointed to that office.[838]

The certificate is conclusive evidence that the requirements of the CA 2006 as to re-registration have been complied with.[839]

This section replaces s 47 of the CA 1985. As previously under the CA 1985, where the registrar is satisfied that a company is entitled to be re-registered as a public company, he will issue a new certificate of incorporation (which must state that it is being issued on the re-registration of the company). On the issue of a new certificate of incorporation under this section; the company becomes a public company; the change to its name and any amendments that were made to the company's articles take effect; and the person (or persons) named as secretary (or joint secretaries) in the statement of proposed secretary (see s 95 of the CA 2006) is deemed to have been appointed as such.

As now, the certificate of incorporation on re-registration is conclusive

---

[832] CA 2006, s 95(3).   [833] CA 2006, s 96(1).   [834] CA 2006, s 96(2).
[835] CA 2006, s 96(3).   [836] CA 2006, s 96(4)(a).   [837] CA 2006, s 96(4)(b).
[838] CA 2006, s 96(4)(c).   [839] CA 2006, s 96(5).

evidence that the company is now a public company, and that the requirements of the CA 2006 as regards re-registration to have been met.

Public company becoming private

Re-registration of public company as private limited company

5.10 Section 97 of the CA 2006 makes provision for a public company to re-register as a private company. A public company may be re-registered as a private limited company if the following conditions are satisfied:

(a)   a special resolution that it should be so re-registered is passed;[840]
(b)   the conditions specified below are met;[841] and
(c)   an application for re-registration is delivered to the registrar in accordance with s 100 of the CA 2006 together with:

    (i)   the other documents required by that section;[842] and
    (ii) a statement of compliance.[843]

The conditions are that:

(a)   where no application under s 98 of the CA 2006 for cancellation of the resolution has been made:

    (i)   having regard to the number of members who consented to or voted in favour of the resolution, no such application may be made;[844] or
    (ii) the period in which such an application could be made has expired.[845] Or

(b)   where such an application has been made:

    (i)   the application has been withdrawn;[846] or
    (ii) an order has been made confirming the resolution and a copy of that order has been delivered to the registrar.[847]

The company must make such changes to its name,[848] and Articles of Association,[849] as are necessary in connection with its becoming a private company limited by shares or, as the case may be, by guarantee.

    Section 97 of the CA 2006 replaces s 53 of the CA 1985. It enables a public

---

[840] CA 2006, s 97(1)(a).   [841] CA 2006, s 97(1)(b).   [842] CA 2006, s 97(1)(c)(i).
[843] CA 2006, s 97(1)(c)(ii).   [844] CA 2006, s 97(2)(a)(i).   [845] CA 2006, s 97(2)(a)(ii).
[846] CA 2006, s 97(2)(b)(i).   [847] CA 2006, s 97(2)(b)(ii).   [848] CA 2006, s 97(3)(a).
[849] CA 2006, s 97(3)(b).

company to re-register as a private limited company if the conditions specified in s 97(2) of the CA 2006 are met.

The conditions are the same is those previously under s 53 of the CA 1985 but with two important changes. First, consistent with the approach taken elsewhere in the CA 2006, for example, the sections on the re-registration of a private company as public, s 97(1)(c)(ii) of the CA 2006 introduces a new requirement for a statement of compliance. Second, s 97(2) of the CA 2006 introduces new provisions enabling an application for the re-registration of a company from public to private limited to be processed within a 28-day period, during which dissenting members may apply to the court, under s 98 of the CA 2006, for an order cancelling the resolution for re-registration, provided that the registrar is satisfied that such an application cannot be made. The change reflects the registrar's current practice.

As before, the company must make such changes to its name and Articles of Association as are necessary in connection with it becoming a private company limited by shares or, as the case may be, a private limited guarantee.

Application to court to cancel resolution

5.11 Section 98 of the CA 2006 states that where a special resolution by a public company to be re-registered as a private limited company has been passed, an application to the court for the cancellation of the resolution may be made by any of the following:

(a) by the holders of not less in the aggregate than 5 per cent in nominal value of the company's issued share capital or any class of the company's issued share capital (disregarding any shares held by the company as treasury shares);[850]
(b) if the company is not limited by shares, by no less than 5 per cent of its members;[851] or by not less than 50 of the CA the company's members;[852] but not by a person who has consented to or voted in favour of the resolution.

The application must be made within 28 days after the passing of the resolution and may be made on behalf of the persons entitled to make it by such one or more of their number as they may appoint for the purpose.[853]

On the hearing of the application the court must make an order either cancelling or confirming the resolution.[854] The court may:

---

[850] CA 2006, s 98(1)(a).   [851] CA 2006, s 98(1)(b).   [852] CA 2006, s 98(1)(c).
[853] CA 2006, s 98(2).   [854] CA 2006, s 98(3).

272 A Guide to the Companies Act 2006

(a)   make that order in such terms and conditions as it thinks fit,[855]
(b)   if it thinks fit, adjourn the proceedings in order that an arrangement
       may be made to the satisfaction of the court for the purchase of the
       interests of dissentient members,[856] and
(c)   give such directions and make such orders, as it thinks expedient for
       facilitating or carrying into effect any such arrangement.[857]

The court's order may, if the court thinks fit, provide for the purchase by the
company of the shares of any of its members and for the reduction accordingly of the company's capital;[858] and make such alteration in the company's
articles as may be required in consequence of that provision.[859]

      The court's order may, if the court thinks fit, require the company not to
make any, or any specified, alterations in its articles without the leave of the
court.[860]

      Section 98 of the CA 2006 restates s 54(1)–(3), (5)–(6), and (8) of the CA
1985. As previously under CA 1985, where a public company has passed a
special resolution to re-register as a private limited company, the requisite
majority of the company's members (see s 98(1) of the CA 2006) may apply
to the court for the cancellation of this resolution. Such an application to the
court must be made within 28 days of the resolution to re-register being
passed, and on hearing the application the court may confirm or cancel the
resolution or make such other order as it thinks fit.

Notice to registrar of court application or order

5.12 Section 99 of the CA 2006 states that on making an application under
s 98 of the CA 2006 (application to court to cancel a resolution) the applicants, or the person making the application on their behalf, must immediately
give notice to the registrar.[861]

      On being served with notice of any such application, the company must
immediately give notice to the registrar.[862]

      Within 15 days of the making of the court's order on the application, or
such longer period as the court may at any time direct, the company must
deliver to the registrar a copy of the order.[863]

      If a company fails to comply with s 99(2) or (3) of the CA 2006 an offence
is committed by the company;[864] and every officer of the company who is
in default.[865] A person guilty of an offence is liable on summary conviction
to a fine not exceeding level 3 on the standard scale and, for continued

---

[855] CA 2006, s 98(4)(a).   [856] CA 2006, s 98(4)(b).   [857] CA 2006, s 98(4)(c).
[858] CA 2006, s 98(5)(a).   [859] CA 2006, s 98(5)(b).   [860] CA 2006, s 98(6).
[861] CA 2006, s 99(1).   [862] CA 2006, s 99(2).   [863] CA 2006, s 99(3).
[864] CA 2006, s 99(4)(a).   [865] CA 2006, s 99(4)(b).

contravention, a daily default fine not exceeding one-tenth of level 3 on the standard scale.[866]

This section replaces s 54(4) (7) and (10) of the CA 1985. As previously under the CA 1985, where an application is made to the court under s 98 of the CA 2006 (that is, to cancel a resolution for re-registration as a private limited company), the company must immediately give notice to the registrar. Similarly, where the court has made an order in connection with such an application, the company must deliver a copy of that to the registrar within 15 days of the order being made (or such longer time as the court may direct).

Section 99(1) of the CA 2006 is a new provision that requires the dissenting members, on making an application to court seeking to cancel the resolution for re-registration from public to private, to give notice direct to the registrar. This ensures that the registrar is aware of any applications that have been made under s 98 of the CA 2006, and will enable the registrar to process the application for re-registration without further delay where the registrar is satisfied that no application to court may be made.

Section 99(4) of the CA 2006 carries forward the offence in s 54(10) of the CA 1985. Where the company fails to give notice to the registrar or fails to deliver a copy of the order made by the court under s 98 of the CA 2006 to the registrar within the prescribed time limits (see s 99(2) and (3) of the CA 2006, the company and every officer of the company who is in default commits an offence. The penalty for this offence is set out in s 99(5) of the CA 2006.

Application and accompanying documents

5.13 Section 100(1) of the CA 2006 states that an application for re-registration as a private limited company must contain a statement of the company's proposed name on re-registration. The application must be accompanied by a copy of the resolution that the company should re-register as a private limited company (unless a copy has already been forwarded to the registrar under Chapter 3 of Part 3 of the CA 2006);[867] and a copy of the company's articles as proposed to be amended.[868]

The statement of compliance required to be delivered with the application will be a statement that the requirements of Part 7 of the CA 2006 as to re-registration as a private limited company have been complied with.[869]

The registrar may accept the statement of compliance as sufficient evidence that the company is entitled to be re-registered as a private limited company.[870]

Section 100 of the CA 2006 replaces s 53(1)(b) of the CA 1985. It

[866] CA 2006, s 99(5).   [867] CA 2006, s 100(2)(a).   [868] CA 2006, s 100(2)(b).
[869] CA 2006, s 100(3).   [870] CA 2006, s 100(4).

prescribes the documents/information that must accompany the application for re-registration where a company is proposing to re-register from public to private limited. Consistent with the approach taken in the CA 2006 with other forms of registration, in future the application for re-registration as a private limited company must be accompanied by a statement of compliance. Previously, there was no requirement for a statutory declaration (or electronic equivalent) where a public company re-registers as a private limited company.

Issue of certificate of incorporation on re-registration

5.14 Section 101(1) of the CA 2006 provides that if on an application for re-registration as a private limited company, the registrar is satisfied that the company is entitled to be so re-registered, the company must be re-registered accordingly.

The registrar must issue a certificate of incorporation altered to meet the circumstances of the case.[871] The certificate must state that it is issued on re-registration and the date on which it is issued.[872]

On the issue of the certificate the company by virtue of the issue of the certificate becomes a private limited company,[873] and the changes in the company's name and articles taken effect.[874] The certificate becomes conclusive evidence that the requirements of the CA 2006 as to re-registration have been complied with.[875]

Section 101 of the CA 2006 re-states s 55 of the CA 1985. As previously under the CA 1985, where the registrar is satisfied that a company is entitled as a private limited company, he will issue a new certificate of incorporation (which must state that it is being issued on re-registration of the company). On the issue of a new certificate of incorporation under this section, the company becomes a private limited company and the change to its name and any amendments that were required to be made to the articles take effect.

The certificate of incorporation on re-registration issued under this section is conclusive that the company is now a private limited company and that the requirements of the CA 2006 as regards re-registration have been met.

Private limited company becoming unlimited

Re-registration of private limited company as unlimited

5.15 Section 102(1) of the CA 2006 provides that a private limited company may be re-registered as an unlimited company if:

---

[871] CA 2006, s 101(2).   [872] CA 2006, s 101(3).   [873] CA 2006, s 101(4)(a).
[874] CA 2006, s 101(4)(b).   [875] CA 2006, s 101(5).

(a)   all the members of the company have assented to its being so re-registered,[876]
(b)   the condition specified below is met,[877] and
(c)   an application for re-registration is delivered to the registrar in accordance with s 103 of the CA 2006, together with the other documents required by that section, and a statement of compliance.[878]

The condition that must be satisfied is that the company has not previously been re-registered as limited.[879]

The company must make such changes in its name and its articles as are necessary in connection with its becoming an unlimited company,[880] and if it is to have a share capital, as are necessary in connection with its becoming an unlimited company having a share capital.[881]

For the purpose of s 102 of the CA 2006, a trustee in bankruptcy of a member of the company is entitled, to the exclusion of the member, to assent to the company's becoming unlimited;[882] and the personal representative of a deceased member of the company may assent on behalf of the deceased.[883]

The term 'a trustee in bankruptcy of a member of the company' in s 102(4)(a) of the CA 2006 includes a permanent trustee or an interim trustee (within the meaning of the Bankruptcy (Scotland) Act 1985 (c 66)) on the sequestrated estate of a member of the company;[884] a trustee under a protected trustee deed (within the meaning of the Bankruptcy (Scotland) Act 1985) granted by a member of the company.[885]

Section 102 of the CA 2006 replaces s 49(1)–(2) and (9), of the CA 1985. As under the CA 1985, s 102 of the CA 2006 permits a private company that is limited by share or, as the case may be, by guarantee, to re-register as an unlimited private company, providing that certain conditions are met (see s 102(2) of the CA 2006) and all of the members have given their assent to the company being so re-registered. In the case of a deceased member, assent may be given by the personal representative of the deceased member's estate. Where a member is bankrupt, assent may be given by his trustee in bankruptcy (to the exclusion of the member in question).

An 'unlimited company' is a company not having any limit on the liability of its members. As now, a company may not re-register as an unlimited company, if it has previously been re-registered as limited (having previously been unlimited).

The application for re-registration as an unlimited company must be accompanied by a statement of compliance.

---

[876] CA 2006, s 102(1)(a).   [877] CA 2006, s 102(1)(b).   [878] CA 2006, s 102(1)(c).
[879] CA 2006, s 102(2).   [880] CA 2006, s 102(3)(a).   [881] CA 2006, s 102(3)(b).
[882] CA 2006, s 102(4)(a).   [883] CA 2006, s 102(4)(b).   [884] CA 2006, s 102(5)(a).
[885] CA 2006, s 102(5)(b).

Application and accompanying documents

5.16 Section 103(1) of the CA 2006 states that an application for re-registration as an unlimited company must contain a statement of the company's propose name on re-registration.

Section 103(2) of the CA 2006 states that the application must be accompanied by the prescribed form of assent to the company's being registered as an unlimited company, authenticated by or on behalf of all the members of the company;[886] and a copy of the company's articles as proposed to be amended.[887]

The statement of compliance required to be delivered together with the application is a statement that the requirements of this Part is to re-registration as an unlimited company have been complied with.[888]

The statement must contain a statement by the directors of the company that the persons by whom or on whose behalf the form of assent is authenticated constitute the whole membership of the company,[889] and if any of the members have not authenticated that form themselves, that each person who authenticated it on behalf of a member was lawfully empowered to do so.[890]

The registrar may accept the statement of compliance as sufficient evidence that the company is entitled to be re-registered as an unlimited company.[891]

Section 103 of the CA 2006 replaces s 49(4)–(8A) of the CA 1985. It prescribes the contents of the application for re-registration where a company is proposing to re-register from private limited to unlimited, and the documents/information that must accompany this application. The previous requirement under the CA 1985 for a statutory declaration made by the directors on application for re-registration as an unlimited company has been replaced by a requirement for a statement of compliance. Unlike other statements of compliance made under the CA 2006 (see, for example s 14 of the CA 2006) the statement of compliance made on application for re-registration as an unlimited company must contain a statement made by the directors confirming that the persons by whom or on whose behalf the form of assent is subscribed constitute the whole membership of the company; and if any of the members have not subscribed that form themselves, that the directors have taken all reasonable steps to satisfy themselves that each person who subscribed it on behalf of a member was lawfully empowered to do so.

The contents of the director's statement carry forward the provisions of s 49(8) of the CA 1985 (prescribed form of assent to company being registered as unlimited).

---

[886] CA 2006, s 103(2)(a). As to the form of assent for re-registration of private limited company as unlimited see regulation 5 and Schedule 3 of the Companies (Registration) Regulations 2007.
[887] CA 2006, s 103(2)(b).   [888] CA 2006, s 103(3).   [889] CA 2006, s 103(4)(a).
[890] CA 2006, s 103(4)(b).   [891] CA 2006, s 103(5).

Issue of certificate of incorporation on re-registration

5.17 Section 104(1) of the CA 2006 states that if on an application for re-registration of a private limited company as an unlimited company, the registrar is satisfied that the company is entitled to be so re-registered, the company shall be re-registered accordingly.

The registrar must issue a certificate of incorporation altered to meet the circumstances of the case.[892] The certificate must state that it is issued on re-registration and the date on which it is issued.[893] On the issue of the certificate the company by virtue of the issue of the certificate becomes an unlimited company,[894] and the changes in the company's name and articles take effect.[895] The certificate is conclusive evidence that the requirements of the CA 2006 as to re-registration have been complied with.[896]

Section 104 of the CA 2006 restates s 50 of the CA 1985. Where the registrar is satisfied that a company is entitled to be re-registered as an unlimited company, he will issue a new certificate of incorporation (which must state that it is being issued on re-registration of the company). On the issue of a new certificate of incorporation under this section, the company becomes an unlimited company and the change to its name and any amendments that were required to be made to the articles take effect.

The certificate of incorporation on re-registration is conclusive evidence that the company is now an unlimited company, and that the requirements of the CA 2006 as regards re-registration have been met.

Unlimited private company becoming limited

Re-registration of unlimited company as limited

5.18 Under s 105(1) of the CA 2006, an unlimited company may be re-registered as a private limited company if a special resolution that it should be so re-registered is passed,[897] the condition specified below is met,[898] and an application for re-registration is delivered to the registrar in accordance with s 106 of the CA 2006, together with the other documents required by that section,[899] and a statement of compliance.[900]

The condition is that the company has not previously been re-registered as unlimited.[901] The special resolution must state whether the company is to be limited by shares or by guarantee.[902]

The company must make such changes in its name;[903] and in its articles;[904]

---

[892] CA 2006, s 104(2).   [893] CA 2006, s 104(3).   [894] CA 2006, s 104(4)(a).
[895] CA 2006, s 104(4)(b).   [896] CA 2006, s 104(5).   [897] CA 2006, s 105(1)(a).
[898] CA 2006, s 105(1)(b).   [899] CA 2006, s 105(1)(c)(i).   [900] CA 2006, s 105(1)(c)(ii).
[901] CA 2006, s 105(2).   [902] CA 2006, s 105(3).   [903] CA 2006, s 105(4)(a).
[904] CA 2006, s 105(4)(b).

as are necessary in connection with its becoming a company limited by shares or, as the case may be, by guarantee.

Section 105 of the CA 2006 replaces s 51 (1)–(3) and (6) of the CA 1985. It permits an unlimited company to re-register as a private limited company if certain conditions are met (see s 105(2) of the CA 2006). As before, a re-registration from unlimited to limited requires a special resolution of the company's members, (which must specify whether the company is to be limited by shares or limited by guarantee). The company must also make such changes to its name and articles as are required to reflect the change in the company's status. As was the case under s 51(6) of the CA 1985, this section does not permit the re-registration of an unlimited company as a private company (this section provides for the re-registration of an unlimited company as a private limited company. There is a new requirement for a statement of compliance).

Application and accompanying documents

5.19 Section 106(1) of the CA 2006 provides that an application for re-registration as a limited company must contain a statement of the company's proposed name on re-registration. The application must be accompanied by a copy of the resolution that the company should re-register as a private limited company (unless a copy has already been forwarded to the registrar under Chapter 3 of Part 3) of the CA 2006;[905] if the company is to be limited by guarantee, a statement of guarantee;[906] and a copy of the company's articles as proposed to be amended[907] must accompany the application.

Section 106(3) of the CA 2006 provides that the statement of guarantee required to be delivered in the case of a company that is to be limited by guarantee must state that each member undertakes that, if the company is wound up while he is a member, or within one year after he ceases to be a member, he will contribute to the assets of the company such amount as may be required for payments of the debts and liabilities of the company contracted before he ceases to be a member,[908] payment of the costs, charges and expenses of winding up,[909] and adjustment of the rights of the contributories among themselves, not exceeding a specified amount.[910]

The statement of compliance required to be delivered together with the application is a statement that the requirements of this Part as to re-registration as a limited company have been complied with.[911] The registrar may accept the statement of compliance as sufficient evidence that the company is entitled to be re-registered as a limited company.[912]

---

[905] CA 2006, s 106(2)(a).   [906] CA 2006, s 106(2)(b).   [907] CA 2006, s 106(2)(c).
[908] CA 2006, s 106(3)(a).   [909] CA 2006, s 106(3)(b).   [910] CA 2006, s 106(3)(c).
[911] CA 2006, s 106(4).   [912] CA 2006, s 106(5).

Section 106 of the CA 2006 replaces s 51 (3), (4) and (5) of the CA 1985 and contains new provisions. It prescribes the contents of application for re-registration, where an unlimited private company is proposing to re-register as private limited and the documents/information that must accompany this application. Where the company is to be limited by guarantee, s 106(2)(b) of the CA 2006 requires the application for re-registration to be accompanied by a 'statement of guarantee'. There is no requirement for a statement of capital and initial shareholdings where the company is to be limited by shares. this is unnecessary because the company will be required to make a return of allotments to the registrar, under s 555 of the CA 2006 as soon as it allots shares subsequent to its registration and the return must be accompanied by a statement of capital.

Issue of certificate of incorporation on re-registration

5.20 Section 107(1) of the CA 2006 provides that if on an application for re-registration of a private unlimited company as a limited company, the registrar is satisfied that the company is entitled to be so re-registered, the company must be re-registered accordingly.

The registrar must issue a certificate of incorporation altered to meet the circumstances of the case.[913] The certificate must state that it is issued on re-registration and the date on which it is so issued.[914]

On the issue of the certificate the company by virtue of the issue of the certificate becomes an limited company,[915] and the changes in the company's name and articles take effect.[916] The certificate is conclusive evidence that the requirements of the CA 2006 as to re-registration have been complied with.[917]

This section restates s 52 of the CA 1985. It provides that, where the registrar is satisfied that a company is entitled to be re-registered as a private company, he will issue a new certificate of incorporation (which must state that it is being issued on the re-registration of the company). On the issue of a new certificate of incorporation under this section, the company becomes a private limited company, and the change to its name and any amendments that were required to be made to the articles take effect.

The certificate of incorporation on the re-registration issued under s 107 of the CA 2006 is conclusive evidence that the company is now private limited company, and that the requirements of the CA 2006 as regards re-registration have been met.

---

[913] CA 2006, s 107(2).   [914] CA 2006, s 107(3).   [915] CA 2006, s 107(4)(a).
[916] CA 2006, s 107(4)(b).   [917] CA 2006, s 107(5).

Statement capital required where company already has share capital

5.21 Section 108 of the CA 2006 states that a company which on re-registration under s 107 of the CA 2006 already has allotted share capital, must within 15 days after the re-registration deliver a statement of capital to the registrar.[918]

This does not apply if the information that would be included in the statement has already been sent to the registrar in a statement of capital and initial shareholdings (see s 10 of the CA 2006),[919] or a statement of capital is contained in an annual return (see s 856(2) of the CA 2006).[920]

The statement of capital must state with respect to the company's share capital on re-registration:

(a)   the total number of shares of the company,[921]
(b)   the aggregate nominal value of those shares,[922]
(c)   for each class of shares:

    (i)   prescribed particulars of the rights attached to the shares,[923]
    (ii)   the total number of shares of that class,[924] and
    (iii)   the aggregate nominal value of shares of that class,[925] and

(d)   the amount paid up and the amount (if any) unpaid on each share (whether on account of the nominal value of the share or by way of premium).[926]

If default is made in complying with this section, an offence is committed by the company,[927] and every officer of the company who is in default.[928] A person guilty of an offence under this section is liable on summary conviction to a fine not exceeding level 3 on the standard scale and, for continued contravention, a daily default fine not exceeding one-tenth of level 3 on the standard scale.[929]

Section 108 of the CA 2006 is a new provision which requires a company that has re-registered from unlimited having a share capital to private limited by shares, to file a statement of capital with the registrar in certain circumstances. The statement must be delivered to the registrar within 15 days of the company's re-registration and, where the company fails to observe this requirement, the company and every officer of the company who is in default, commits an offence (see s 108(4) of the CA 2006).

---

[918] CA 2006, s 108(1).   [919] CA 2006, s 108(2)(a).   [920] CA 2006, s 108(2)(b).
[921] CA 2006, s 108(3)(a).   [922] CA 2006, s 108(3)(b).   [923] CA 2006, s 108(3)(c)(i).
[924] CA 2006, s 108(3)(c)(ii).   [925] CA 2006, s 108(3)(c)(ii).
[926] CA 2006, s 108(3)(d).   [927] CA 2006, s 108(4)(a).
[928] CA 2006, s 108(4)(b).   [929] CA 2006, s 108(5).

The provision is necessary because unlimited companies are required to provide a statement of capital to the registrar in a limited number of circumstances only: in particular, where the company has a share capital on formation (see s 10 of the CA 2006) or where an unlimited company having a share capital makes an annual return to the registrar under s 854 of the CA 2006. Consequently, where an unlimited company having a share capital re-registers as private limited by shares under s 107 of the CA 2006, in contrast to other companies that are limited by shares, the information on the public register pertaining to the company's subscribed capital may be out of date (in particular if the company has allotted further shares subsequent to its formation or, as the case may be, its last annual return).

The requirement for a statement of capital in this section puts companies that have re-registered as private limited by shares under s 107 of the CA 2006 on the same footing as other companies limited by shares on the register, and ensures that the information on the public register is up to date. The company will, however, be exempted from the requirement to provide a statement of capital on re-registration where there has been no change to the company's total subscribed capital since it was first formed and registered or, as the case may be, since the company filed its most recent annual return (see s 108(2) of the CA 2006).

Public company becoming private and unlimited

Re-registration of public company as private and unlimited

5.22 Section 109(1) of the CA 2006 states that a public company limited by shares may be re-registered as an unlimited private company with a share capital, if all the members of the company have assented to its being so re-registered,[930] the condition specified below is met,[931] and an application for re-registration is delivered to the registrar in accordance with s 109 of the CA 2006, together with the other documents required by that section,[932] and a statement of compliance.[933]

The condition is that the company has not previously been re-registered as limited;[934] or as unlimited.[935]

The company must take such changes in its name;[936] and in its articles, as are necessary in connection with its becoming an unlimited private company.[937]

---

[930] CA 2006, s 109(1)(a).   [931] CA 2006, s 109(1)(b).   [932] CA 2006, s 109(1)(c)(i).
[933] CA 2006, s 109(1)(c)(ii).   [934] CA 2006, s 109(2)(a).   [935] CA 2006, s 109(2)(b).
[936] CA 2006, s 109(3)(a).   [937] CA 2006, s 109(3)(b).

A trustee in bankruptcy of a member of the company is entitled, to the exclusion of the member, to assent to the company's becoming re-registered;[938] and the personal representative of a deceased member of the company may assent on behalf of the deceased.[939]

The term 'a trustee in bankruptcy of a member of the company' in s 109(4)(a) of the CA 2006 includes a permanent trustee or an interim trustee (within the meaning of the Bankruptcy (Scotland) Act 1985) of the sequestrated estate of a member of the company;[940] and a trustee under a protected trustee deed (within the meaning of the Bankruptcy (Scotland) Act 1985) granted by a member of the company.[941]

Section 109 of the CA 2006 is a new provision, which, as recommended by the Company Law Review Group in its *Final Report*,[942] enables a public company to re-register as a private unlimited company with share capital without first having to re-register as a private limited company. The conditions specified in s 109(2) of the CA 2006 must be met and all of the members must give their assent to the company being so re-registered. In the case of a deceased member, assent may be given by the personal representative of the deceased member's estate. Where a member is bankrupt, assent may be given by his trustee in bankruptcy (to the exclusion of the member in question).

A public company may not re-register as an unlimited private company under this section if it has previously been re-registered as limited or as unlimited (s 109(2) of the CA 2006). The intention behind this subsection (which is based on s 90(2)(e) of the CA 2006) is that a company should not be able to enjoy the benefits of limited liability or avoid the obligations that are attached to this, for example, the increased reporting requirements, by continually swapping from limited to unlimited status.

Application and accompanying documents

5.23 Section 110(1) of the CA 2006 states that an application for re-registration as a public company as an unlimited private company must contain a statement of the company's proposed name on re-registration.

The application must be accompanied by the prescribed form of assent to the company's being registered as an unlimited company, authenticated by or on behalf of all the members of the company,[943] and a copy of the company's articles as proposed to be amended.[944]

The statement of compliance required to be delivered together with the application is a statement that the requirements of this Part as to re-registration as a unlimited private company have been complied with.[945]

---

[938] CA 2006, s 109(4)(a).   [939] CA 2006, s 109(4)(b).   [940] CA 2006, s 109(5)(a).
[941] CA 2006, s 109(5)(b).   [942] *Final Report*, para 11.11.
[943] CA 2006, s 110(2)(a). As to the prescribed form of assent, see regulation 6 and Schedule 4 of the Companies (Registration) Regulations 2007.
[944] CA 2006, s 110(2)(b).   [945] CA 2006, s 110(3).

Section 109(4) of the CA 2006 states that the statement must contain a statement by the directors of the company that the persons by whom or on whose behalf the form of assent is authenticated constitute the whole membership of the company,[946] and if any of the members have not authenticated that form themselves, that each director have taken all reasonable steps to satisfy themselves that each person who authenticated it on behalf of a member was lawfully empowered to do so.[947]

The registrar may accept the statement of compliance as sufficient evidence that the company is entitled to be re-registered as an unlimited private company.[948]

This section is a new provision. It prescribes the contents of the application for re-registration from public to unlimited private, and the documents/information that must accompany this application. There is a requirement for a statement compliance and in contrast the statement of compliance that is required here, must contain a statement made by the directors confirming that the persons by whom or on whose behalf the form of assent is subscribed constitute the whole membership of the company; and if any of the members have not subscribed that form themselves, that the directors have taken all reasonable steps to satisfy themselves that each person who subscribed it on behalf of a member was lawfully empowered to do so.

This mirrors the requirements of the statement of compliance in s 103 of the CA 2006.

Issue of certificate of incorporation on re-registration

5.24 Section 111(1) of the CA 2006 states that if on an application for re-registration of a public company as an unlimited private company, the registrar is satisfied that the company is entitled to be so re-registered, the company shall be re-registered accordingly.

The registrar must issue a certificate of incorporation altered to meet the circumstances of the case.[949] The certificate states that it is issued on re-registration and the date on which it is so issued.[950]

On the issue of the certificate, the company by virtue of the issue of the certificate becomes an unlimited private company,[951] and the changes in the company's name and articles take effect.[952]

The certificate will be conclusive evidence that the requirements of the CA 2006 as to re-registration have been complied with.[953]

Section 111 of the CA 2006 is a new provision, which requires the registrar to issues a new certificate of incorporation if satisfied that a public company

---

[946] CA 2006, s 110(4)(a).   [947] CA 2006, s 110(4)(b).   [948] CA 2006, s 110(5).
[949] CA 2006, s 111(2).   [950] CA 2006, s 111(3).   [951] CA 2006, s 111(4)(a).
[952] CA 2006, s 111(4)(b).   [953] CA 2006, s 111(5).

is entitled to register as private and unlimited. On the issue a new certificate of incorporation (which must state that it is being issued on the re-registration of the company), the company becomes a private unlimited company and the change to its name and any amendments that were made the articles take effect.

The certificate of incorporation is conclusive evidence that the company is now a private unlimited company and that the requirements of the CA 2006 as regards re-registration have been met.

Chapter 6

Company and Business Names

Introduction

6.1 Part 6 of the CA 2006 applies to the name under which a company is registered, sometimes called the 'corporate name'. This Part regulates the choice of name. The rules are primarily intended to ensure that third parties dealing with a company are not misled. There are no property rights in companies' registered names as such. While there is no requirement for a company to use its registered name in the course of business, Part 6 also requires a company to disclose its name in specified circumstances.

The CA 2006 includes new sections, ss 70–74, which provide for the appointment of company names adjudicators in cases where there is dispute over registering a company name. Section 71 of the CA 2006 safeguards the independence of the adjudicators, and s 74 of the CA 2006 provides a right of appeal to the court.

Part 5 comprises 6 Chapters. Chapter 1 addresses the general requirements with reference to prohibited names, and sensitive words and expressions; Chapter 2 concerns indications of company type or legal form; Chapter 3 deals with similarity to other names; Chapter 4 contains other powers of the Secretary of State in respect of corporate names; Chapter 5 sets out the procedure for change of name; and Chapter 6 deals with trading disclosures.

This chapter also considers the provisions on business names set out in Part 41 of the CA 2006. This Part comprises three Chapters. Chapter 1 sets out the restricted or prohibited names; Chapter 2 deals with disclosure required in case of individual or partnership; and Chapter 3 deals with supplementary provisions. Part 41 repeals the Business Names Act 1985.

Part 6 of the CA 2006 must now be read with the Companies (Company and Business Names) (Miscellaneous Provisions) Regulations 2007.

A Company's Name

6.2 Chapter 1 of Part 5 of the CA 2006 sets out the general requirements in respect of a company's name. It contains five sections dealing with prohibited names; sensitive words and expressions; and permitted characters.

Prohibited names

6.3 Section 53 of the CA 2006 provides that a company must not be registered under the of the CA 2006 by a name if, in the opinion of the Secretary of State, its use by a company could constitute an offence;[954] or it is offensive.[955]

Section 53 of the CA 2006 replaces s 26(1)(d) and (e) of the CA 1985.[956] It retains the existing prohibition of companies registering names that cannot be used without commission of an offence; and of those that are offensive.

Sensitive words and expressions

Names suggesting connection with government or public authority

6.4 Section 54(1) of the CA 2006 states that the approval of the Secretary of State is required for a company to be registered under the CA 2006 by a name that would be likely to give the impression that the company is connected with Her Majesty's Government, any part of the Scottish administration, or Her Majesty's Government in Northern Ireland;[957] or local authority;[958] or any public authority specified in any regulations made by the Secretary of State.[959]

This section replaces s 26(2)(a) of the CA 1985.[960] It prevents a name being registered without the Secretary of State's approval, if it suggests a connection with Her Majesty's Government, a local authority or – which represents

---

[954] CA 2006, s 53(1)(a).

[955] CA 2006, s 53(1)(b).

[956] CA 1985, s 26(1)(d) stated that a company could not be registered under the CA 1985 by a name the use of which by the company would in the opinion of the Secretary of State constitute a criminal offence; or under CA 1985, s 26(1)(e) which in the opinion of the Secretary of State is offensive.

[957] CA 2006, s 54(1)(a).

[958] CA 2006, s 54(1)(b). A 'local authority' means a local authority within the meaning of the Local Government Act 1972, the Common Council of the City of London or the Council of the Isles of Scilly (CA 2006, s 54(2)(a)); or a council constituted under s 2 of the Local Government etc. (Scotland) Act 1994 (CA 2006, s 54(2)(b)); or a district council in Northern Ireland: CA 2006, s 54(2)(c).

[959] CA 2006, s 54(1)(c). The term 'public authority' includes any person or body having functions of a public nature: CA 2006, s 54(2).

[960] This provided that except with the approval of the Secretary of State a company could not be registered under the CA 1985 by a name which in the opinion of the Secretary of State would be likely to give the impression that the company was connected in any way with Her Majesty's Government or with any local authority.

a change from the CA 1985 – any part of the Scottish administration, or Her Majesty's Government in Northern Ireland. A new power allows similar protection to be extended to other public authorities.

Regulations made under s 54 of the CA 2006 are subject to the affirmative resolution procedure.[961]

Other sensitive words or expressions

6.5 Section 55(1) of the CA 2006 requires the prior approval of the Secretary of State for the adoption of a name that includes words or expressions specified in regulations made by the Secretary of State, before a company can be registered under the CA 2006.

Section 55 of the CA 2006 replaces s 26(2)(b) and 29(1)(a) of the CA 1985.[962]

Section 55(2) of the CA 2006 provides for the procedure to be used for making the regulations. Regulations under this section are subject to approval after being made. Some of the words and expressions protected by the current Regulations (The Company and Business Names Regulations 1981) include British, English, Scottish and Welsh; chamber of commerce, charity, her Majesty, midwife, police, university.

Duty to seek comment of government department or other specified body

6.6 Under s 56(1) of the CA 2006, the Secretary of State may by regulations under s 54 of the CA 2006 (name suggesting connection with government or public authority);[963] or s 55 of the CA 2006 (other sensitive words or expressions)[964] require that, in connection with an application for the approval of the Secretary of State under that section, the applicant must seek the view of a specified Government department or other body. The term 'specified' means specified in the regulations.[965]

The applicant seeking approval must request the specified department or other body in writing to indicate whether (and if so why) it has any objections to the proposed name.[966] The applicant must, when registering the company, send the registrar a statement that a request has been made under s 56 of the CA 2006;[967] and the statement must be accompanied by a copy of any response received.[968] Similarly, where a request for a change of a company's

---

[961] CA 2006, s. 54(3).

[962] CA 1985, s 26(2)(b) stated that a company could not be registered without prior approval of the Secretary of State where a name included any word or expression specified in regulations under CA 1985, s 29. CA 1985, s 29(1)(a) enabled the Secretary of State to make regulations specifying words or expressions for the registration of which or as part of a company's corporate name for which his approval was required under CA 1985, s 26(2)(b).

[963] CA 2006, s 56(1)(a).   [964] CA 2006, s 56(1)(b).   [965] CA 2006, s 56(5).

[966] CA 2006, s 56(2).   [967] CA 2006, s 56(3)(a).   [968] CA 2006, s 56(3)(b).

name is made, the notice of change sent to the registrar must be accompanied by a statement by a director or secretary of the company that a request has been made under s 56 of the CA 2006;[969] and a copy of the response received.[970]

Section 56 of the CA 2006 replaces s 29(1)(b), (2), (3) and (4) of the CA 1985. It provides powers for the Secretary of State to specify whose view must be sought when seeking approval for a name. For example, under the present Regulations, the approval of the General Dental Council is required for the use of either 'dental' or 'dentistry'. The new regulations would be able to replicate this. They could also require the approval of, say, the House Authorities for names suggesting a connection with Parliament.

Permitted characters, etc.

6.7 Section 57(1) of the CA 2006 states that the Secretary of State may make provision by regulations as to the letters or other characters, signs or symbols (including accents and other diacritical marks), and punctuation that may be used in the name of a company registered under the CA 2006.[971] He may also specify a standard style or format for the name of a company for the purposes of registration.[972]

The regulations may prohibit the use of specified characters, signs or symbols when appearing in a specified position (in particular, at the beginning of a name).[973] A company may not be registered under the CA 2006 by a name that consists of or includes anything that is not permitted in accordance with the regulations.[974] Regulations under this section are subject to negative resolution procedure.[975] The term 'specified' means specified in the regulations.[976]

Section 57 of the CA 2006 is a new provision. It provides power for regulations to specify what letters, symbols, etc. may be used in a company's registered name; the regulations may also specify a permitted format for a name (for example, to prevent the use of superscript or subscript).

Indications of Company Type or Legal Form

6.8 Chapter 2 of Part 5 of the CA 2006, deals with indications of company type or legal form, and considers the required indications for limited companies, including inappropriate use of company type or legal form. It contains eight sections.

---

[969] CA 2006, s 56(4)(a).   [970] CA 2006, s 56(4)(b).

[971] CA 2006, s 57(1)(a). See the Companies (Company and Business Names) (Miscellaneous Provisions) Regulations 2007 – in particular regulations 2 and 3 and Schedules 1 and 2.

[972] CA 2006, s 57(1)(b).   [973] CA 2006, s 57(2).   [974] CA 2006, s 57(3).

[975] CA 2006, s 57(4).   [976] CA 2006, s 57(5).

Public limited companies

6.9 Section 58 of the CA 2006 states that the name for a limited company that is a public company must end with 'public limited company' or 'plc'.[977] In the case of a Welsh company, its name may instead end with 'cwmni cyfyngedig cyhoeddus' or 'ccc'.[978] The section does not apply to community interest companies, but see ss 33(3) and (4) Companies (Audit, Investigations and Community Enterprise) Act 2004.[979]

Section 58 of the CA 2006 replaces s 25(1) of the CA 1985 (and also s 27(4)(b) and (d) of the CA 1985 in its application to s 25(2) of the CA 2006). It brings together in a single provision all the alternative statutory indicators of legal status, that must be used by a public company as part of its registered name, i.e. 'public limited company' or the Welsh equivalent, or the specified abbreviations rather than randomly set out, as was the position under the CA 1985.

Private limited companies

6.10 Under s 59 of the CA 2006, the name of a limited company that is a private company must end with 'limited or 'Ltd'.[980] In the case of a Welsh company its name may instead end with 'cyfyngedig' or 'cyf'.[981] Certain companies are exempt from this requirement.[982] However, s 59 of the CA 2006 does not apply to community interest companies, but see ss 33(1) and (4) Companies (Audit, Investigations and Community Enterprise) Act 2004.[983]

Section 59 of the CA 2006 replaces s 25(2) of the CA 1985 (and also s 27(4)(a) and (c) of the CA 1985 in their application to s 25(2) of the CA 1985).

Exemption from requirement as to use of 'limited'

6.11 Section 60(1) of the CA 2006 states that a private company is exempt from s 59 of the CA 2006 (requirement to have name ending with 'limited' or

[977] CA 2006, s 58(1).   [978] CA 2006, s 58(2).

[979] C(AICE)A 2004, s 33(3) states that the name of a community interest company which is a public company must end with (a) 'community interest public limited company', or (b) 'community interest plc'. Section 33(4) states that the name of such a company may (instead) end with (a) 'cwmni buddiant cymunedol cyhoeddus cyfyngedig', or (b) 'cwmni buddiant cymunedol c.c.c.', if the memorandum of the company states that the company's registered office is to be situated in Wales.

[980] CA 2006, s 59(1). See regulation 4 of the Companies (Company and Business Names) (Miscellaneous Provisions) Regulations 2007 regarding exemption from requirement to use 'limited'.

[981] CA 2006, s 59(2).

[982] CA 2006, s 59(3). See CA 2006, s 60 (exemption from requirement as to use of 'limited').

[983] C(AICE)A 2004, s 33(1) states that the name of a community interest company which is not a public company must end with (a) 'community interest company', or (b) 'c.i.c'. Section 33(4) states 'But the name of such a company may (instead) end with (a) "cwmni buddiant cymunedol cyhoeddus cyfyngedig", or (b) "cwmni buddiant cymunedol c.c.c.", if the memorandum of the company states that the company's registered office is to be situated in Wales.'

permitted alternative) in three circumstances: (i) if it is a charity;[984] or (ii) is exempted from the requirement under s 59 of the CA 2006 by regulations made by the Secretary of State;[985] or (iii) it meets the conditions set out in s 61 of the CA 2006 (continuation of existing exemption: companies limited by shares); or s 62 of the CA 2006 (continuation of existing exemption: companies limited by guarantee).[986]

The registrar may refuse to register a private limited company by a name that does not include the word 'limited' (or a permitted alternative), unless a statement has been delivered to him that the company meets the conditions for exemption.[987] The registrar may accept the statement as sufficient evidence of the matters stated in it.[988]

Regulations under this section are subject to the negative resolution procedure.[989]

Section 60 of the CA 2006 restricts the exemption to companies already exempt and, unlike the CA 1985, to charities and to other companies exempted by regulations. So long as they continue to meet the conditions, those companies already exempt will continue to be exempt, unless and until they change their registered name.

Continuation of existing exemption: companies limited by shares

6.12 Section 61(1) of the CA 2006 applies to a private company limited by shares (a) that on 25 February 1982 was registered in Great Britain;[990] and had a name by virtue of a license under s 19 of the CA 1948 (or corresponding earlier legislation), did not include the word 'limited' or any of the permitted alternatives;[991] or (b) that on 30 June 1983, was registered in Northern Ireland;[992] and had a name that by virtue of a license under s 19 of the Companies Act (Northern Ireland) 1960 (or corresponding earlier legislation), did not include the word 'limited' or any of the permitted alternatives.[993]

Section 61 of the CA 2006 replaces s 30(2) of the CA 1985. It specifies the two conditions[994] that must be met for a company currently exempt in order to continue to qualify for exemption from s 59 of the CA 2006 provided the company does not change its name.[995]

The first condition is that the objects of the company are the promotion of commerce, art, science, education, religion, charity, or any profession and anything incidental or conducive to any of those objects.[996] The second condition is that the company's articles require its income to be applied in

[984] CA 2006, s 60(1)(a).   [985] CA 2006, s 60(1)(b).   [986] CA 2006, s 60(1)(c).
[987] CA 2006, s 60(2).   [988] CA 2006, s 60(3).   [989] CA 2006, s 60(4).
[990] CA 2006, s 61(1)(i).   [991] CA 2006, s 61(1)(ii).   [992] CA 2006, s 61(b)(i).
[993] CA 2006, s 61(b)(ii).   [994] CA 2006, s 61(2)(a).   [995] CA 2006, s 61((2)(b).
[996] CA 2006, s 61(3).

promoting its objects;[997] prohibit the payment of dividends or any return of capital, to its members;[998] and require all the assets that would otherwise be available to its members generally to be transferred on its winding up either to another body with objects similar to its own, or to another body to the objects of which are the promotion of charity and anything incidental or conducive thereto (whether or not the body is a member of the company).[999]

Sections 60 and 61 of the CA 2006 replace s 30 of the CA 1985. Section 30 of the CA 1985 exempted certain companies from the requirement for their names ending with 'limited'. Exempt companies were also exempt from some of the requirements regarding publication of their name, but they still had to disclose their limited status in correspondence. Those currently exempt are those with a licence granted under s 19 of the CA 1948 Act, and those who have delivered a statutory declaration to the registrar that the company complies with the requirements for the exemption. These requirements are, in effect, that the company is non-profit-making, and its objects are the promotion of commerce, art, science, education, religion, charity or any profession.

Sections 60 and 61 of the CA 2006 which replace s 30(2) and (3) of the CA 1985 specify the conditions that must be met for a company currently exempt to continue to qualify for the exemption: its objects must continue to satisfy the criteria for their exemption and its articles must both preclude distribution of dividends to its members and also, in the event of it being wound up, require its assets to be passed to a body with similar objects. For companies limited by shares benefiting from an exemption under the of the CA 1948 (or its Northern Irish equivalent), there is a new requirement that the articles prevent a distribution of capital. This is linked to the change in s 63(4) of the CA 2006 in respect of private company exemption.

Continuation of existing exemption: companies limited by guarantee

6.13 Section 62 of the CA 2006 provides that a private company limited by guarantee that immediately before the commencement of Part 5 of the CA 2006 was exempt by virtue of s 30 of the CA 1985 or Article 40 of the CA the Companies (Northern Ireland) Order 1986/1032 (NI6) from the requirement to have a name including the word 'limited' or a permitted alternative;[1000] and had a name that did not include the word 'limited' or any of the permitted alternatives may qualify for exemption from s 59.[1001] Such a company is exempt from s 59 of the CA 2006 (requirement to have a name ending with 'limited' or any of the permitted alternatives), so long as it continues to meet the following two conditions and does not change its name.

The first condition is that the objects of the company are the promotion of

---

[997] CA 2006, s 61(4)(a).   [998] CA 2006, s 61(4)(b).   [999] CA 2006, s 61(4)(c).
[1000] CA 2006, s 62(1)(a).   [1001] CA 2006, s 62(1)(b).

commerce, art, science, education, religion, charity or any profession and anything incidental or conducive to any of the objects.[1002]

The second condition is that the company's articles requires its income to be applied in promoting its objects;[1003] prohibit the payment of dividends to its members;[1004] and require all the assets that would otherwise be available to its members generally to be transferred on its winding up either (i) to another body with objects similar to its own;[1005] or (ii) to another body of the objects of which are the promotion of charity and anything incidental or conducive thereto,[1006] (whether or not the body is a member of the company).

Exempt company: restriction on alteration of articles

6.14 Section 63(1) of the CA 2006 states that a private company that is exempt under ss 61 or 62 of the CA 2006 from the requirement to use 'limited' (or a permitted alternative) as part of its name;[1007] and whose name does not include 'limited' or any of the permitted alternatives,[1008] must not amend its articles so that it ceases to comply with the conditions for exemption under that section.

Breach of s 63(1) of the CA 2006 leads to an offence being committed by the company,[1009] and every officer of the company who is in default. A shadow director is also treated as an officer of the company.[1010]

A person guilty of an offence under this section is liable on summary conviction to a fine not exceeding level 5 on the standard scale and, for continued contravention, to a daily default time not exceeding one-tenth of level 5 on the standard scale.[1011]

This section replaces ss 31(1) and (5) of the CA 1985. It prohibits a company benefiting from an exemption under the CA 1985 or the CA 1948 (or their Northern Irish equivalents) from changing its articles in such a way that

---

[1002] CA 2006, s 62(2).   [1003] CA 2006, s 62(3)(a).   [1004] CA 2006, s 62(3)(b).
[1005] CA 2006, s 62(3)(c)(i).   [1006] CA 2006, s 62(3)(c)(ii).   [1007] CA 2006, s 63(1)(a).
[1008] CA 2006, s 63(1)(b).   [1009] CA 2006, s 63(2)(a).   [1010] CA 2006, s 63(2)(b)
[1011] CA 2006, s 63(3). CA 2006, s 64(4) deals with exemptions for certain companies. It states that where before the commencement of CA 2006, s 63(4): (a) a company was exempt by virtue of s 30 of the CA 1985 or Article 40 of the Companies (Northern Ireland) Order 1986 (SI 1986/ 1032 (NI 6) from the requirement to have a name including the word 'limited' (or a permitted alternative); and (b) the company's memorandum or articles contained provision preventing an alteration of them without the approval of (i) the Board of Trade or a Northern Ireland department (or any other department or Minister), or (ii) the Charity Commission, that provision and any condition of any such licence as is mentioned in s 61(1)(a) or (b)(ii) requiring such provision, shall cease to have effect. This does not apply if, or to the extent that, the provision is required by or under any other enactment. CA 2006, s 64(5) states that it is hereby declared that any such provision as is mentioned in subs (4)(b) formerly contained in a company's memorandum was at all material times capable, with the appropriate approval, of being altered or removed under CA 1985, s 17 or Article 28 of the Companies (Northern Ireland) Order 1986 (SI 1986/1032) (NI 6) (or corresponding earlier enactments).

it no longer meets the requirements for the exemption. It is an offence to change the company's articles in such a way. Many companies with an exemption under the CA 1948 (or its Northern Irish equivalent), were made to include a provision in their memorandum preventing an amendment to their memorandum or articles without the consent of the then Board of Trade, (there were a number of variations in this theme). Sections 63(4) and (5) of the CA 2006 make provision to remove this administrative burden.

Power to direct change of name in case of company ceasing to be entitled to exemption

6.15 Section 64(1) of the CA 2006 states that if it appears to the Secretary of State that a company whose name does not include 'limited' or any of the permitted alternatives, has ceased to be entitled to exemption under s 60(1)(a) or (b) of the CA 2006;[1012] or in the case of a company within ss 61 or 62 (which impose conditions on the objects and articles of the company), has carried on any business other than the promotion of any of the objects mentioned in s 61(3) or s 62(2) of the CA 2006;[1013] or has acted inconsistently with the provision required by s 61(4)(a) or (b), or s 62(3)(a) or (b) of the CA 2006,[1014] then the Secretary of State may direct the company to change its name so that it ends with 'limited' or one of the permitted alternatives.

The direction by the Secretary of State must be in writing and must specify the period within which the company is to change its name.[1015]

A change of name in order to comply with a direction under s 64 of the CA 2006 may be made by resolution of the directors. This is without prejudice to any other method of changing the company's name.[1016]

Where a resolution of the directors is passed in accordance with s 64(3) of the CA 2006, the company must give notice to the registrar of the change. Sections 80 and 81 of the CA 2006 apply as regards the registration and effect of the change.[1017] If a company fails to comply with a direction, an offence is committed by the company and every officer of the company who is in default.[1018] A person liable on summary conviction to a fine not exceeding level 5 on the standard scale and, for continued contravention, to a daily default fine not exceeding one–tenth of level 5 on the standard scale.[1019] A company that has been directed to change its name may not, without approval of the Secretary of State, subsequently change its name so that it does not include 'limited' or one of the permitted alternatives. This does not apply to a change of name on re-registration or on conversion to a community interest company.[1020]

Section 64 of the CA 2006 replaces s 31(2)–(4) to (6) of the CA 1985. It

[1012] CA 2006, s 64(1)(a).   [1013] CA 2006, s 64(1)(b)(i).   [1014] CA 2006, s 64(1)(b)(ii).
[1015] CA 2006, s 64 (2).   [1016] CA 2006, s 64 (3).   [1017] CA 2006, s 64 (4).
[1018] CA 2006, s 64 (5).   [1019] CA 2006, s 64 (6).   [1020] CA 2006, s 64 (7).

gives the Secretary of State power to withdraw a private company's exemption from the requirement for its name to conclude with 'limited' if the company no longer meets the criteria that applied when it was granted the exemption.

Inappropriate use of indications of company type or legal form

6.16 Section 65(1) of the CA 2006 provides that the Secretary of State may make provision by regulations prohibiting the use in a company name of specified words, expressions or other indications that are associated with a particular type of company or form of organisation;[1021] or that are similar to words, expressions or other indications associated with a particular type of company or form of organisation.[1022] The regulations may prohibit the use of words, expressions or other indications in a specified part, or otherwise than in a specified part, of a company's name;[1023] in conjunction with, or otherwise than in conjunction with, such other words, expressions or indications as may be specified.[1024]

A company must not be registered under the CA 2006 by a name that consists of or includes anything prohibited by regulation.[1025]

Regulations under s 65 of the CA 2006 are subject to negative resolution procedure.[1026]

Section 65 of the CA 2006 replaces s 26(1)(a), (b), (bb) and (bbb) of the CA 1985 (prohibition on registration of certain names). These paragraphs restricted the use of various words, expressions and abbreviations that were indicators of legal status for various types of commercial entity, e.g. plc., community interest company, open-ended investment company, etc. Some of the restrictions applied to the use of the particular indicator at the end of a company's name; some anywhere other than at the end of the name; and some anywhere in a company's name.

Section 65 of the CA 2006 provides power to make regulations prohibiting the inclusion in a company's name of specified words, expressions and abbreviations. The only words that can be specified in the regulations are those associated with a particular type of company or form or organisation, or those confusingly similar to such words and expressions. Section 65 of the CA 2006 also provides power to require or prohibit the statutory indicators of being used in conjunction with specified other words.

[1021] CA 2006, s 65(1)(a).   [1022] CA 2006, s 65(1)(b).   [1023] CA 2006, s 65(2)(a).
[1024] CA 2006, s 65(2)(b). The word 'specified' means specified in the regulations: CA 2006, s 65(4).
[1025] CA 2006, s 65(3).   [1026] CA 2006, s 65 (5).

Similarity to other name or registrar's index

6.17 Section 66(1) of the CA 2006 states that a company must not be registered under the CA 2006 by a name that is the same as another name appearing in the registrar's index of company names. This section retains the prohibition contained in s 26(1)(c) of the CA 1985, on a company adopting a name that is already on the registrar's index of company names – which includes not only the names of Companies Act companies, but various other business entities.[1027]

The Secretary of State may make provision by regulations supplementing s 66 of the CA 2006.[1028] The regulations may make provision as to matters that are to be disregarded;[1029] and as to words, expressions, signs or symbols that are, or are not, to be regarded as the same,[1030] for the purposes of s 66 of the CA 2006. The Secretary of State is, therefore, empowered to make regulations to replace the detailed rules contained in s 26(3) of the CA 1985 as to what is to be disregarded; and what words, expressions, signs, letters and symbols are to be taken as the same when comparing a proposed and an existing name.

At present only 'and' and '&' are taken as the same. Section 66 of the CA 2006 would provide power also to treat the following as the same:

- currency symbols (e.g. £, $) and their respective English word equivalents;
- '%' and 'per cent';
- '1', '2', '3', etc. and 'one', 'two', 'three', etc.

The prohibition of names that, under these rules, are the same as an existing name will not be discretionary. But in future, it will be possible for there to be exceptions.

Section 66(4) of the CA 2006 states that the regulations may provide that registration by a name that would otherwise be prohibited under s 66 of the CA 2006 is permitted in specified circumstances;[1031] or with specified consent;[1032] and that if those circumstances obtain, or that consent is given at the time a company is registered by a name, a subsequent change of circumstances or withdrawal of consent does not affect the registration.[1033] Regulations under this section are subject to negative resolution procedure.[1034]

Power to direct change of name in case of similarity to existing name

6.18 Section 67 of the CA 2006 replaces s 28(2) of the CA 1985, which

---

[1027] See CA 2006, s 1099.
[1028] CA 2006, s 66(2). See regulation 7 and Schedule 2 of the Companies (Company and Business Names) (Miscellaneous Provisions) Regulations 2007.
[1029] CA 2006, s 66(3)(a).   [1030] CA 2006, s 66(3)(b).   [1031] CA 2006, s 66(4)(a)(i).
[1032] CA 2006, s 66(4)(b)(ii).   [1033] CA 2006, s 66(4)(b).   [1034] CA 2006, s 66(5).

provides the Secretary of State with power to direct a company to change its newly adopted name, if in the opinion of the Secretary of State it has been registered in a name that is the same as an existing name, or too like a name appearing at the time of registration in the registrar's index of company names,[1035] or a name that should have appeared in that index at the time.[1036] The objective is to prevent the public being confused by the simultaneous appearance on the register of two very similar names, when the similarity is such that the later name was not caught by the non-discretionary prohibition of adopting a name effectively the 'same as' an existing name.[1037]

Section 67(1) of the CA 2006 covers two circumstances. First, any delay in the entry on the index of company names of the new names of entities that are not UK companies. Companies House enters all names immediately, but there may be delays outside their control. If the name had already been taken by the other entity before the company adopted it, then the registrar will direct the company to change its name. Second, the visual difference between the new name and an existing name being so small, that third parties are likely to be confused by the simultaneous appearance of both names on the index of company names.

Section 67(2) of the CA 2006 empowers the Secretary of State to make regulations supplementing s 67 of the CA 2006, to replace the detailed rules contained in s 26(3) of the CA 1985 as to the matters that are to be disregarded;[1038] and what words, expressions, signs or symbols that are or are not to be regarded as the same when comparing a proposed and existing name.[1039]

The regulations may provide that no direction is to be given in respect of a name in specified circumstances,[1040] or if specified consent is given;[1041] and that a subsequent change of circumstances or withdrawal of consent does not give rise to grounds for a direction under s 67 of the CA 2006.[1042] Section 67(4) of the CA 2006 provides for a power to make regulations permitting names that would otherwise be regarded as 'too alike' in certain circumstances or where consent is given.

Regulations under this section are subject to negative resolution procedure.[1043]

Direction to change name: supplementary provisions

6.19 The direction to change name and supplementary provisions are set out in s 68 of the CA 2006. This section replaces s 28(4) and (5) of the CA 1985 as they apply to s 28(2) of the CA 1985. Section 68 of the CA 2006 applies in

---

[1035] CA 2006, s 67(1)(a).   [1036] CA 2006, s 67(1)(b).   [1037] See CA 2006, s 66.
[1038] CA 2006, s 67(3)(a).   [1039] CA 2006, s 67(4)(b).   [1040] CA 2006, s 67(4)(i).
[1041] CA 2006, s 67(4)(ii).
[1042] CA 2006, s 67(4)(b). The term 'specified' means specified in the regulations: CA 2006, s 67(6).
[1043] CA 2006, s 67(5).

respect of a direction under s 67 of the CA 2006 (power to direct change of name in case of similarity to existing name).[1044] It provides for deadlines for the Secretary of State's giving the direction to change the name and for the company's compliance. Any such direction must be given within 12 months of the company's registration by the name in question;[1045] and must specify the period within which the company is to change its name.[1046] The Secretary of State may by further direction extend that period. However, any such direction must be given before the end of the period for the time being specified.[1047]

A direction under s 67 or s 68 of the CA 2006 must be in writing.[1048]

If a company fails to comply with the direction, an offence is committed by the company, and every officer of the company who is in default. A shadow director will also be treated as an officer of the company.[1049] A guilty of an offence is liable on summary conviction to a fine not exceeding level 3 on the standard scale and, for continued contravention, a daily default fine not exceeding one-tenth of level 3 on the standard scale.[1050]

Similarity to other name in which person has goodwill

6.20 The following sections, ss 69–74 of the CA 2006 are new provisions. They are a result of the Company Law Review Group's recommendation[1051] that there should be provision for a person to apply for a company to be directed to change its name, if the applicant can show that the name was chosen with the principal intention of seeking money from him, or preventing him registering the name, where it is one in which he has previously acquired reputation or goodwill. The provisions also introduce company names adjudications.

Objection of company's registered name

6.21 Section 69 of the CA 2006 is a new provision. It provides for any person, known as an 'applicant' and not just a company, to object to a company's registered name in the following two circumstances: first, that it is the same as a name associated with the applicant in which he has goodwill;[1052] or second, that it is sufficiently similar to such a name that its use in the United Kingdom would be likely to mislead by suggesting a connection between the company and the applicant.[1053]

The objection must be made by application to a 'company names adjudicator', as set out in s 70 of the CA 2006.[1054] The company concerned must be the

[1044] CA 2006, s 68 (1).   [1045] CA 2006, s 68(2)(a).   [1046] CA 2006, s 68(2)(b).
[1047] CA 2006, s 68(3).   [1048] CA 2006, s 68(4).   [1049] CA 2006, s 68(5).
[1050] CA 2006, s 68(6).   [1051] *Final Report*, para 11.50.   [1052] CA 2006, s 69(1)(a).
[1053] CA 2006, s 69(1)(b).
[1054] CA 2006, s 69(2). See regulations 3–13 of the Company Names Adjudicator Rules 2007.

primary respondent to the application. Any of its members or directors may be joined as respondents.[1055]

Section 69(4) of the CA 2006 lists a set of circumstances raising a presumption that a name was adopted legitimately. If the ground specified in s 69(1)(a) or (b) of the CA 2006 is established, then the respondents must show that one of the following applies:

(a)   that the name was registered before the commencement of the activities on which the applicant relies to show goodwill.[1056] The expression 'goodwill' means reputation of any description;[1057] or

(b)   that the company is operating under the name;[1058] or is proposing to do so and has incurred substantial start-up costs in preparation;[1059] or was formerly operating under the name and is now dormant;[1060] or

(c)   that the name was registered in the ordinary course of a company formation business and the company is available for sale to the applicant on the standard terms of that business;[1061] or

(d)   the name was adopted in good faith;[1062] or

(e)   that the interests of the applicant are not adversely affected to any significant extent, (for example, where the applicant has hardly used the name at all).[1063]

The objection will be upheld if the respondents cannot demonstrate any of the above.

If the facts mentioned in s 70(4)(a), (b) or (c) of the CA 2006 are established, the objection will also be upheld, if the applicant shows that the main purpose of the respondents (or any of them) in registering the name, was to obtain money (or other consideration) from the applicant or to prevent him from registering the name.[1064] If the objection is not upheld under s 69(4) or (5) of the CA 2006, it must be dismissed.[1065]

Company names adjudicators

6.22 Section 70 of the CA 2006 applies to 'company names adjudicators'. This section is a new provision. It empowers the Secretary of State to appoint persons to be company names adjudicators.[1066] The persons appointed must have such legal or other experience as, in the Secretary of State's opinion, makes them suitable for appointment.[1067]

The adjudicator holds office in accordance with the terms of his

---

[1055] CA 2006, s 69(3).   [1056] CA 2006, s 69(4)(a).   [1057] CA 2006, s 69(7).
[1058] CA 2006, s 69(4)(b)(i).   [1059] CA 2006, s 69(4)(b)(ii).   [1060] CA 2006, s 69(4)(b)(iii).
[1061] CA 2006, s 69(4)(c).   [1062] CA 2006, s 69(4)(d).   [1063] CA 2006, s 69(4)(e).
[1064] CA 2006, s 69(5).   [1065] CA 2006, s 69(6).   [1066] CA 2006, s 70(1).
[1067] CA 2006, s 70(2).

appointment.[1068] He is eligible for re-appointment when his term of office ends.[1069] He may resign at any time by notice in writing given to the Secretary of State.[1070] He may be dismissed by the Secretary of State on the ground of incapacity or misconduct.[1071]

One of the adjudicators must be appointed Chief Adjudicator. He must perform such functions as the Secretary of State may assign to him.[1072] The other adjudicators will undertake such duties as the Chief Adjudicator may determine.[1073]

The Secretary of State may appoint staff for the adjudicators;[1074] pay remuneration and expenses to the adjudicators and their staff;[1075] defray other costs arising in relation to the performance by the adjudicators of their functions;[1076] and compensate persons for ceasing to be adjudicators.[1077]

Procedural rules

6.23 Section 71 of the CA 2006 provides that the Secretary of State may make rules about proceedings before a company names adjudicator.[1078] The rules may, in particular, make provision on the following:

- as to how an application is to be made and the form and content of an application or other documents;[1079]
- the fees to be charged;[1080]
- the service of documents and the consequences of failure to serve them;[1081]
- as to the form and manner in which evidence is to be given;[1082]
- circumstances in which the hearings are required and those in which they are not;[1083]
- the cases to be heard by more than one adjudicator;[1084]
- setting time limits for anything required to be done in connection with the proceedings (and allowing such time limits to be extended, even if they have expired);[1085]
- enabling the adjudicator to strike out an application, or any defence, in whole or in part on the ground that it is vexatious, has no reasonable prospect of success or is otherwise misconceived;[1086] or failure to comply with the requirements of the rules;[1087]

[1068] CA 2006, s 70(3)(a).   [1069] CA 2006, s 70(3)(b).   [1070] CA 2006, s 70(3)(c).
[1071] CA 2006, s 70(3)(d).   [1072] CA 2006, s 70(4).   [1073] CA 2006, s 70(5).
[1074] CA 2006, s 70(6)(a).   [1075] CA 2006, s 70(6)(b).   [1076] CA 2006, s 70(6)(c).
[1077] CA 2006, s 70(6).
[1078] CA 2006, s 71(1). See the Company Names Adjudicator Rules 2007.
[1079] CA 2006, s 71(2)(a).   [1080] CA 2006, s 71(2)(b).   [1081] CA 2006, s 71(2)(c).
[1082] CA 2006, s 71(2)(d).   [1083] CA 2006, s 71(2)(e).   [1084] CA 2006, s 71(2)(f).
[1085] CA 2006, s 71(2)(g).   [1086] CA 2006, s 71(2)(h)(i).   [1087] CA 2006, s 71(2)(h)(ii).

- conferring power to order security for costs (in Scotland, caution for expenses);[1088]
- how far proceedings are to be held in public;[1089] or
- requiring one party to bear the costs (in Scotland, expenses) of another and as to the taxation (or settling) the amount of such costs (or expenses).[1090]

The rules may confer on the Chief Adjudicator power to determine any matter that could be the subject of provision in the rules.[1091] Rules under s 71 of the CA 2006 must be made by statutory instrument, which must be subject to annulment in pursuance of a resolution of either House of Parliament.[1092]

Section 71 of the CA 2006 is a new provision. It provides power to make regulations for the proceedings before a company names adjudicator. The list of matters that the rules may cover is not exhaustive. It also enables the rule to confer on the Chief Adjudicator power to determine any matter that could be the subject of the rules made under this power.

Decision of adjudicator to be made available to public

6.24 Under s 72 of the CA 2006, a company names adjudicator must, within 90 days of determining an application under s 69 of the CA 2006, make his decision and his reasons for it available to the public.[1093] The adjudicator may do so by means of a website, or by such other means as appear to him to be appropriate.[1094]

Order requiring name to be changed

6.25 Section 73 of the CA 2006 is a new provision. If an objection made under s 69 of the CA 2006 is upheld, then the adjudicator must make an order to direct the company with the offending name to change its name to one that does not similarly offend.[1095] The adjudicator can also require all respondents to take such steps as are within their power to make, or facilitate the making, of that change;[1096] and not to cause or permit any steps to be taken calculated to result in another company being registered with a name that is an offending name.[1097]

The term 'offending name' means a name that, by reason of its similarity to the name associated with the applicant in which he claims goodwill, would be likely to be the subject of a direction under s 67 of the CA 2006 (power of

[1088] CA 2006, s 71(2)(i).   [1089] CA 2006, s 71(2)(j).   [1090] CA 2006, s 71(2)(k).
[1091] CA 2006, s 71(3).   [1092] CA 2006, s 71(4).   [1093] CA 2006, s 72(1).
[1094] CA 2006, s 72(2).   [1095] CA 2006, s 73(1)(a).   [1096] CA 2006, s 73(1)(b)(i).
[1097] CA 2006, s 73(1)(b)(ii).

Secretary of State to direct change of name);[1098] or to give rise to a further application under s 69 of the CA 2006.[1099] A deadline must be set for the change. The order must specify a date by which the respondent company's name is to be changed, and may be enforced in England and Wales or Northern Ireland in the same way as an order of the High Court;[1100] or in Scotland in the same way as a decree of the Court of Session.[1101]

If the offending name is not changed by the respondent company in accordance with the order by the specified date, then the adjudicator will determine a new name for the company.[1102] If the adjudicator determines a new name for the respondent company, he must give notice of his determination to the applicant,[1103] to the respondents,[1104] and to the registrar.[1105] A company's name is changed when the change takes effect under s 81(1) of the CA 2006 (on the issue of the new certificate of incorporation).[1106]

Appeal from adjudicator's decision

6.26 The appeal from adjudicator's decision is governed by s 74 of the CA 2006. A company that has received a direction from the company names adjudicator can appeal to a court against the decision. An appeal from any decision of a company names adjudicator lies to the court to uphold or dismiss an application under s 70 of the CA 2006.[1107] This section is a new provision.

Notice of appeal against a decision upholding an application, must be given before the date specified in the adjudicator's order by which the respondent company's name is to be changed.[1108] If notice of appeal is given against a decision upholding an application, the effect of the adjudicator's order is suspended.[1109]

On appeal, the court will either affirm the adjudicator's decision to uphold the application;[1110] or reverse the adjudicator's decision to dismiss the application.[1111] The court may (as the case may require), specify the date by which the adjudicator's order is to be complied with, remit the matter to the adjudicator or to make any order that the adjudicator might have made.[1112]

If the court determines a new name for the company, it must give notice of the determination to the parties to the appeal;[1113] and to the registrar.[1114]

[1098] CA 2006, s 73(2)(a).   [1099] CA 2006, s 73(2)(b).   [1100] CA 2006, s 73(3)(a).
[1101] CA 2006, s 73(3)(b).   [1102] CA 2006. s 73(4).   [1103] CA 2006, s 73(5)(a).
[1104] CA 2006, s 73(5)(b).   [1105] CA 2006, s 73(5)(c).   [1106] CA 2006, s 73(6).
[1107] CA 2006, s 74(1).   [1108] CA 2006, s 74(2).   [1109] CA 2006, s 74(3).
[1110] CA 2006, s 74(4)(a).   [1111] CA 2006, s 74(4)(b).   [1112] CA 2006, s 74(4).
[1113] CA 2006, s 74(5)(a).   [1114] CA 2006, s 74(5)(b).

Other powers of the Secretary of State

6.27 Chapter 4 of Part 5 of the CA 2006 contains other powers of the Secretary of State with regard to the company name. It comprises two sections dealing with misleading information.

Provision of misleading information

6.28 Section 75 of the CA 2006 deals with the provision of misleading information. It replaces s 28(3) of the CA 1985 and it supports that section and s 28(4)–(6) of the CA 1985. It empowers the Secretary of State to direct a company to change its name within a specified period in two circumstances. First, if misleading information has been given for the purposes of a company's registration by a particular name to enable the adoption of the name.[1115] Second, if an undertaking or assurance has been given for that purpose to enable the adoption of the name and has not been fulfilled.[1116]

The direction can only be made up to five years after the adoption of the name.[1117] It must also specify the period within which the company is to change its name.[1118] The Secretary of State may by a further direction extend the period within which the company is to change its name. Any such direction must be given before the end of the period for the time being specified.[1119] The direction must be in writing.[1120]

It is an offence to fail to comply with the direction. An offence is committed by the company,[1121] and every officer of the company who is in default.[1122] A shadow director is treated as an officer of the company.[1123] A person guilty of an offence is liable on summary conviction to a fine not exceeding level 3 on the standard scale and, for continued contravention, a daily default fine not exceeding one-tenth of level 3 on the standard scale.[1124]

Misleading indication of activities

6.29 Section 76 of the CA 2006 is concerned with misleading indication of activities. It replaces s 32 of the CA 1985. The Secretary of State is empowered to direct a company to change its name, regardless of how long the company has had the name, in the specified circumstances. The circumstances are that, in his opinion, not only does the name by which the company is registered give a misleading indication of the nature of the company's activities, but also that it is likely to cause harm to the public as a result.[1125]

The direction must be in writing.[1126]

[1115] CA 2006, s 75(1)(a).   [1116] CA 2006, s 75(1)(b).   [1117] CA 2006, s 75(2)(a).
[1118] CA 2006, s 75(2)(b).   [1119] CA 2006, s 75(3).   [1120] CA 2006, s 75(3).
[1121] CA 2006, s 75(5)(a).   [1122] CA 2006, s 75(5)(b).   [1123] CA 2006, s 75(5).
[1124] CA 2006, s 75(6).   [1125] CA 2006, s 76(1).   [1126] CA 2006, s 76(2).

There are time limits for compliance with the direction. The direction must be complied with within six weeks from the date of the direction, or such longer period as the Secretary of State may think fit to allow. This does not apply if an application is made to the court under this section.[1127] The company may apply to the court to set the direction aside. The application must be made with the period of three weeks from the date of the direction.[1128] The court may set the direction aside or confirm it. If the court confirms the direction, it specifies the deadline for compliance.[1129]

It will be an offence for failure to comply with the direction. The offence would be committed by the company,[1130] and every officer of the company who is in default.[1131] A shadow director is treated as an officer of the company.[1132] A person guilty of an offence is liable on summary conviction to a fine not exceeding level 3 on the standard scale and, for continued contravention, daily default fine not exceeding one-tenth of level 3 on the standard scale.[1133]

Change of Name

6.30 Chapter 5 of Part 5 of the CA 2006 sets out the provisions dealing with change of company name. It comprises five sections.

Section 77 of the CA 2006 is concerned with change of name and the various mechanisms for effecting a change of name. It replaces s 28(1) of the CA 1985.[1134] Companies can change their name by special resolution;[1135] or by other means provided for by the company's articles.[1136] This means that the company will be able to determine the procedures for changing its own name.

A company's name may also be changed under the following mechanisms:

- by resolution of the directors acting under s 64 of the CA 2006 (change of name to comply with direction of Secretary of State under that section);[1137] or
- on the determination of a new name by order of the company names adjudicator if an objection under s 73 of the CA 2006 is upheld (powers of adjudicator on upholding objection to company name);[1138] or

---

[1127] CA 2006, s 76(3).   [1128] CA 2006, s 76(4).   [1129] CA 2006, s 76(5).
[1130] CA 2006, s 76(6)(a).   [1131] CA 2006, s 76(6)(b).   [1132] CA 2006, s 76(6).
[1133] CA 2006, s 76(7).
[1134] CA 1985, s 28(1) provided that a company could by special resolution change its name (but subject to CA 1985, s 31 in the case of a company which had received a direction under subs (2) of that section from the Secretary of State). CA 1985, s 31 applied to companies that were exempt under CA 1985, s 30.
[1135] CA 2006, s 77(1)(a).   [1136] CA 2006, s 77(1)(b). See CA 2006, s 79.
[1137] CA 2006, s 77(2)(a).   [1138] CA 2006, s 77(2)(b).

- on the determination of a new name by the court under s 74 of the CA 2006 (appeal against decision of company names adjudicator);[1139] or
- under s 1033 of the CA 2006 (company's name on restoration to the register).[1140]

Change of name by special resolution

6.31 Section 78 of the CA 2006 deals with the procedural issues involved in a change of name by special resolution. It is a new provision. It provides that where a change of name has been agreed to by a company by special resolution, the company must notify the registrar of the special resolution for a change of name. This requirement is in addition to the obligation to forward a copy of the special resolution to the registrar.[1141]

Sections 78(2) and (3) of the CA 2006 address the particular situation where a company has passed a special resolution to change its name, but the change is not to take place until some other event has occurred (for example, a merger). It introduces a special procedure for such a special resolution. This section does not provide a means by which a company can reserve a name. Rather, it provides for the situation where a special resolution to change a name has been passed, and therefore must be notified – but where its conditions have not been met. The statutory restrictions on the choice of name, including the prohibition of a new name being the same as a name already on the register, will be applied only after this section's requirements have been satisfied. Section 78(2) of the CA 2006 provides that where a change of name by special resolution is conditional on the occurrence of an event, the notice to the registrar to the change must specify that the change is conditional;[1142] and state whether the event has occurred.[1143]

If the notice states that the event has not occurred, the registrar is not required to act under s 80 of the CA 2006 (registration and issue of new certificate of incorporation) until further notice.[1144] When the event occurs, the company must give notice to the registrar stating that it has occurred.[1145] The registrar may rely on the statement as sufficient evidence of the matters stated in it.[1146]

The objective of s 78(3) of the CA 2006 is that the registrar will not act on the notice to change the name, until she has been notified that the specified event has occurred, and that he can do so as soon as he receives such notice.

[1139] CA 2006, s 77(2)(c).   [1140] CA 2006, s 77(2)(d).   [1141] CA 2006, s 78(1).
[1142] CA 2006, s 78(2)(a).   [1143] CA 2006, s 78(2)(b).   [1144] CA 2006, s 78(3)(a).
[1145] CA 2006, s 78(3)(b).   [1146] CA 2006, s 78(3).

Change of name by means provided for in company's articles

6.32 Another mechanism for changing a company's name is by means provided for in a company's articles. This is addressed in s 79 of the CA 2006. This section is a new provision supplementing the new provision (s 77(1)(b) of the CA 2006). Where a change of a company's name has been made by other means provided for by its articles, the company is required to provide the registrar with both a notice of the name change[1147] and a statement that the change has been made in accordance with the company's articles.[1148]

The registrar may rely on the statement as sufficient evidence of the matters stated in it.[1149] This ensures the registrar can act on the notice to change the name as soon as he receives it.

Change of name: registration and issue of new certificate of incorporation

6.33 Section 80 of the CA 2006 deals with change of name in respect of registration and issue of new certificate of incorporation. This section, which replaces in part s 28(6) of the CA 1985[1150] and in total s 32(5) of the CA 1985, provides for the procedures that the registrar must perform before a company's proposed new name is effective. It applies where the registrar receives notice of a change of a company's name.[1151]

If the registrar is satisfied that the new name complies with the requirements and formalities for change of name;[1152] and that the requirements of the Companies Acts, and any relevant requirements of the company's articles, with respect to a change of name, are complied with,[1153] the registrar must enter the new name on the register in place of the former name. The effect is to provide for the checks both that the name meets all the requirements for a company's name, and that the necessary documents have been provided to the registrar. On the registration of the new name, the company must be issued a certificate of incorporation by the registrar with the new name, which may be altered to meet the circumstances of the case.[1154]

Effect of change of name

6.34 Section 81 of the CA 2006 addresses the effect of change of name. It replaces s 28(6) of the CA 2006 in part and in total s 28(7) of the CA 1985. It

---

[1147] CA 2006, s 79(1)(a).   [1148] CA 2006, s 79(1)(b).   [1149] CA 2006, s 79(2).

[1150] CA 1985, s 28(6) provided that where a company changed its name, the registrar was required (subject to CA 1985, s 26) to enter the new name on the register in place of the former name. He was also required to issue a certificate of incorporation altered to meet the circumstances of the case; and the change of name had effect from the date on which the altered certificate was issued.

[1151] CA 2006, s 80(1).   [1152] CA 2006, s 80(12)(a).   [1153] CA 2006, s 80(2)(b).

[1154] CA 2006, s 80(3).

provides that the new name is effective from the date on which the altered certificate of incorporation is issued.[1155] The change of name does not affect the company's rights or obligations, or render defective any legal proceedings by or against it in its previous name.[1156] Any legal proceedings that might have continued or commenced against it by its former name may be continued or commenced against it by its new name.[1157]

Trading Disclosures

6.35 Chapter 6 addresses the issue of trading disclosures. This Chapter contains four sections.

Requirement to disclose company name

6.36 Section 82 of the CA 2006 is concerned with the requirement to disclose its company name. This section replaces ss 348(1), 349(1) and 351(1) and (2) of the CA 1985 and, insofar as it applies to companies, s 4(1) of the Business Names Act 1985. It empowers the Secretary of State to make regulations requiring every company:

(a)   to display a sign with its name and specified other information at specified locations;[1158]
(b)   to include its name and specified information in specified documents and communications;[1159]
(c)   to provide its name and specified information to those they deal with in the course of their business.[1160] This is a new provision insofar as it applies to companies doing business under their registered names.

The term 'specified' means specified in the regulations.[1161]

The regulations must in every case require disclosure of the name of the company.[1162] They must also make provision as to the manner in which any specified information is to be displayed, stated or provided.[1163] The regulations may provide that, for the purposes of any requirement to disclose a company's name, any variation between a word or words required to be part of the name and a permitted abbreviation of that word or those words (or vice versa) will be disregarded.[1164]

Regulations under s 82 of the CA 2006 are subject to affirmative resolution procedure.[1165]

[1155] CA 2006, s 81(1).   [1156] CA 2006, s 81(2).   [1157] CA 2006, s 81(3).
[1158] CA 2006, s 82(1)(a). See the Companies (Trading Disclosures) Regulations 2008 – particularly regulations 2–9.
[1159] CA 2006, s 82(1)(b).   [1160] CA 2006, s 82(1)(c).   [1161] CA 2006, s 82(4).
[1162] CA 2006, s 82(2)(a).   [1163] CA 2006, s 82(2)(b).   [1164] CA 2006, s 82(3).
[1165] CA 2006, s 82(5).

Civil consequences of failure to make required disclosure

6.37 Section 83(1) of the CA applies to any legal proceedings brought by a company to which s 82 of the CA 2006 (requirement to disclose company name) applies, to enforce a right arising out of a contract made in the course of a business in respect of which the company was, at the time the contract was made, in breach of the regulations made under the section.

The proceedings will be dismissed if the defendant (in Scotland, the defender) to the proceedings shows either:

- that he has a claim against the claimant (pursuer) arising out of the contract that he has been unable to pursue by reason of the latter's breach of the regulations;[1166] or
- that he has suffered some financial loss in connection with the contract by reason of the claimant's (pursuer's) breach of the regulations.[1167]

The exception is that the court before which the proceedings are brought, must be satisfied that it is just and equitable to permit the proceedings to continue.

Section 83 of the CA 2006 does not affect the right of any person to enforce such rights as he may have against another person in any proceedings brought by that person.[1168]

Section 83 of the CA 2006 replaces s 5 of the Business Names Act 1985 in its application to companies. As recommended by the Company Law Review Group,[1169] it follows the precedent of the Business Names Act 1985 as regards the civil remedy for failure to comply with the information requirements made in regulations under s 82 of the CA 2006. Section 83 of the CA 2006 does not include provision for personal civil liability of officers in default in s 349(4) of the CA 1985.[1170]

Criminal consequences of failure to make required disclosures

6.38 Section 84 of the CA 2006 deals with the criminal consequences for failure to make the required disclosures. It states that regulations under s 82 of the CA 2006 may provide that where a company fails, without reasonable excuse, to comply with any specified requirement of regulations under that

---

[1166] CA 2006, s 83(2)(a).   [1167] CA 2006, s 83(2)(b).   [1168] CA 2006, s 83(3).
[1169] *Final Report*, para 11.57.
[1170] CA 1985, s 349(4) provided that if an officer of a company or a person on its behalf signed or authorised to be signed on behalf of the company any bill of exchange, promissory note, endorsement, cheque or order for money or goods in which the company's name is not mentioned as required by CA 1985, s 349(1) he was liable to a fine; and he was further personally liable to the holder of the bill of exchange, promissory note, cheque or order for money or goods for the amount of it (unless it was duly paid by the company).

section, then an offence is committed by the company;[1171] and every officer who is in default.[1172]

The regulations may also provide that a person guilty of an offence is liable on summary conviction to a fine not exceeding level 3 on the standard scale and, in the case of continued contravention, to a daily default fine not exceeding one-tenth of level 3 on the standard scale.[1173]

The regulations may provide that for the purposes of any provision made under s 84(1) of the CA 2006, a shadow director of the company will be treated as an officer of the company.[1174]

The term 'specified' means specified in the regulations.[1175]

Section 84 of the CA 2006 replaces ss 348(2), 349(2) and (3) and 351(5) of the CA 1985 and, in its application to companies, part of s 7 of the Business Names Act 1985. It makes it an offence not to comply with the requirements, to be specified in the regulations, for every company to disclose its name and specified other information.

Minor variations in form of name to be left out of account

6.39 Section 85 of the CA 2006 states that in considering a company's name, no account is to be taken of whether upper or lower characters (or a combination of the two) are used;[1176] whether diacritical marks or punctuation are present or absent;[1177] or whether the name is in the same format or style as is specified under s 57(1)(b) of the CA 2006 for the purposes of registration.[1178] The proviso is that there must be no real likelihood of names differing only in those respects being taken to be different names.[1179] This does not affect the operation of regulations under s 57(1)(a) of the CA 2006 permitting only specified characters, diacritical marks or punctuation.[1180]

This section is a new provision. It means that the company's name as used to comply with the disclosure requirement need not be exactly the same as the registered name. The permitted differences are the case of the letters, the use of punctuation, accents, etc. and formatting. However the differences must not result in there being risk of confusion.

Business Names

Introduction

6.40 Part 41 of the CA 2006 sets out provisions on business names. The provisions replace the Business Names Act 1985. It comprises three Chapters.

[1171] CA 2006, s 84(1)(a)(i).   [1172] CA 2006, s 84(1)(a)(ii).   [1173] CA 2006, s 84(1)(b).
[1174] CA 2006, s 84(2).   [1175] CA 2006, s 84(3).   [1176] CA 2006, s 85(1)(a).
[1177] CA 2006, s 85(1)(b).   [1178] CA 2006, s 85(1)(c).   [1179] CA 2006, s 85(1).
[1180] CA 2006, s 85(2).

Chapter 1 addresses restricted or prohibited names. Chapter 2 is concerned with disclosure required in case of an individual or partnership. Chapter 3 comprises supplementary provisions.

Restricted or prohibited names

6.41 Chapter 1 comprises eight sections on restricted or prohibited names.

Application of this Chapter

6.42 Chapter 1 applies to any person carrying on business[1181] in the United Kingdom.[1182] The provisions of this Chapter do not prevent an individual carrying on business under a name consisting of his surname[1183] without any addition other than a permitted addition;[1184] or individuals carrying on business in partnership[1185] under a name consisting of the surnames of all the partners without any addition other than a permitted addition.[1186]

The following are the permitted additions in the case of an individual, his forename or initial;[1187] in the case of a partnership (i) the forenames of individual partners or the initials of those forenames;[1188] or where two or more individual partners have the same surname, the addition of 's' at the end of that surname;[1189] in either case (under s 1192(2)(a) or (b)) of the CA 2006, an addition merely indicating that the business is carried on in succession to a former owner of the business.[1190]

Section 1192 of the CA 2006 partly replaces s 1 of the Business Names Act 1985. It ensures that the restrictions on the use of names in the course of business apply to all persons carrying on business in the United Kingdom, other than certain individuals or partnerships. In particular the restrictions apply to all companies (and not, as previously in the Business Names Act,

---

[1181] The term 'business' includes a profession: CA 2006, s 1208.

[1182] CA 2006, s 1192.

[1183] The term 'surname' in relation to a peer or person usually known by a British title different from his surname, means the title by which he is known: CA 2006, s 1208.

[1184] CA 2006, s 1192(2)(a).

[1185] The term 'partnership' means a partnership within the Partnership Act 1890; or a limited partnership registered under the Limited Partnerships Act 1907; or a firm or entity of a similar character formed under the law of a country or territory outside the United Kingdom: CA 2006, s 1208.

[1186] CA 2006, s 1192(2)(b). As to business names, see regulation 6 of the Companies (Company and Business Names) (Miscellaneous Provisions) Regulations 2007.

[1187] CA 2006, s 1192(3)(a). The term 'initial' includes any recognised abbreviation of a name. It means that the restrictions on names in Chapter 1 to CA 2006, Part 41 not only would apply to, for example, James Alexander Scotland as if he were to trade as 'James Alexander Scotland' or 'J.A. Scotland', but also if he were to trade as 'Jimmy Scotland', or 'Jim A. Scotland'. However, the restrictions would apply if he were to trade as 'Scotland Bakers', or 'John Scotland': see CA 2006, s 1208.

[1188] CA 2006, s 1192(3)(b)(i).   [1189] CA 2006, s 1192(3)(b)(ii).   [1190] CA 2006, s 1192(c).

just to any company capable of being wound up under the Insolvency Act 1986 that trades under a name other than that under which it is registered). The restrictions also apply to any partnership whose members include a company (and not, as in the Business Names Act, only if the name under which such a partnership does business includes names for the corporate partners other than those under which they are registered).

As previously under the Business Names Act, the restrictions do not apply to individuals if they trade either alone or in partnership under their surnames augmented only by their forenames and/or initials. Sole traders and individuals carrying on business in partnership are also excluded from the scope of the Chapter, if the only addition to their name show's the business previous ownership.

The main effect of the wider coverage is that controls apply to all overseas companies carrying on business in the United Kingdom. It also removes any uncertainty as to whether the controls apply to business entities other than companies incorporated under the Companies Acts.

Sensitive words or expressions

6.43 Section 1193 of the CA 2006 applies to sensitive words or expressions used in business names with particular reference to a name suggesting connection with government or public authority.

A person must not, without the approval of the Secretary of State, carry on business in the United Kingdom under a name that would be likely to give the impression that the business is connected with Her Majesty's Government, any part of the Scottish administration or Her Majesty's Government in Northern Ireland;[1191] or any local authority;[1192] or any public authority specified for the purposes of this section by regulations made by the Secretary of State.[1193]

The term 'local authority' means a local authority within the meaning of the Local Government Act 1972 (c 70), the Common Council of the City of London or the Council of the Isles of Scilly;[1194] or a council constituted under s 2 of the Local Government, etc. (Scotland) Act 1994 (c 39);[1195] or a district council in Northern Ireland.[1196]

The term 'public authority' includes any person or body having functions of a public nature.

Regulations under this section are subject to affirmative resolution procedure.[1197]

A person who contravenes this section commits an offence.[1198] Where an

[1191] CA 2006, s 1193(1)(a).   [1192] CA 2006, s 1193(1)(b).   [1193] CA 2006, s 1193(1)(c).
[1194] CA 2006, s 1193(2)(a).   [1195] CA 2006, s 1193(2)(b).   [1196] CA 2006, s 1193(2)(c).
[1197] CA 2006, s 1193(3).   [1198] CA 2006, s 1193(4).

offence is committed by a body corporate, an offence is also committed by every officer of the body who is in default.[1199] A person guilty of an offence under s 1193 of the CA 2006 is liable on summary conviction to a fine not exceeding level 3 on the standard scale and, for continued contravention, a daily default fine not exceeding one-tenth of level 3 on the standard scale.[1200]

Other sensitive words or expressions

6.44 Section 1194 of the CA 2006 considers other sensitive words or expressions. A person must not, without the approval of the Secretary of State, carry on business in the United Kingdom under a name that includes a word or expression for the time being specified in regulations made by the Secretary of State under this section.[1201]

Regulations under this section are subject to approval after being made.[1202]

A person who contravenes s 1194 of the CA 2006 commits an offence.[1203] Where an offence under this section is committed by a body corporate, an offence is also committed by every officer of the body who is in default.[1204] A person guilty of an offence under this section is liable on summary conviction to a fine not exceeding level 3 on the standard scale and, for continued contravention, a daily default fine not exceeding one-tenth of level 3 on the standard scale.[1205]

Requirement to seek comments of government department or other relevant body

6.45 In specific situations, s 1195 of the CA 2006 imposes a requirement to seek comments of government department or other relevant body. The Secretary of State may by regulations under s 1193 of the CA 2006 (name suggesting connection with government or public authority),[1206] or s 1194 of the CA 2006 (other sensitive words or expressions),[1207] require that, in connection with an application for the approval of the Secretary of State under that section, the applicant must seek the view of a specified Government department or other body.

Where such a requirement applies, the applicant must request the specified department or other body (in writing) to indicate whether (and if so why) it has any objections to the proposed name.[1208] He must submit to the Secretary of State a statement that such a request has been made and a copy of any response received from the specified body.[1209] If these requirements are not

[1199] CA 2006, s 1193(5). [1200] CA 2006, s 1193(6). [1201] CA 2006, s 1194(1).
[1202] CA 2006, s 1194(2). [1203] CA 2006, s 1194(3). [1204] CA 2006, s 1194(4).
[1205] CA 2006, s 1194(5). [1206] CA 2006, s 1196(1)(a). [1207] CA 2006, s 1194(1)(b).
[1208] CA 2006, s 1194(2). [1209] CA 2006, s 1194(3).

complied with, the Secretary of State may refuse to consider the application for approval.[1210]

The term 'specified' means specified in the regulations.[1211]

Withdrawal of Secretary of State's approval

6.46 Section 1196 of the CA 2006 applies to approval given for the purposes of s 1193 of the CA 2006 (name suggesting connection with government or public authority), or s 1194 of the CA 2006 (other sensitive words or expressions).[1212]

If it appears to the Secretary of State that there are overriding considerations of public policy that require such approval to be withdrawn, the approval may be withdrawn by notice in writing given to the person concerned.[1213]

The notice must state the date as from which approval is withdrawn.[1214]

Sections 1193 to 1196 of the CA 2006 replace ss 2, 3, 6 and 7 of the Business Names Act 1985. Section 1199 of the CA 2006 contains savings equivalent to those in s 2(2) of the Business Names Act. These sections require prior approval for the use of any name for carrying on business for which a company would require approval before it could be registered under it. (Sections 54 to 56 of the CA 2006, replacing ss 26(2) and 29 of the CA 1985, apply corresponding restrictions to company names). The differences between the requirements under these sections and the requirements under the Business Names Act 1985 are:

- Section 1193(1)(a) of the CA 2006 requires prior approval for names likely to give the impression that the business is connected with Her Majesty's Government in Northern Ireland;
- Section 1193(1)(c) of the CA 2006 provides a power for the Secretary of State to specify in regulations the public authorities, such that prior approval will be required for names likely to give the impression that the business is connected with them;
- The definition of local authority in s 1193(2) of the CA 2006 is brought up to date for Scotland and includes district council in Northern Ireland;
- Section 1195(4) of the CA 2006 provides that the Secretary may refuse to consider an application for approval that is not compliant with the statutory requirements.

Section 1196 of the CA 2006 provides that approval for the use of a name may be withdrawn in appropriate circumstances.

[1210] CA 2006, s 1194(4).   [1211] CA 2006, s 1194(5).   [1212] CA 2006, s 1196(1).
[1213] CA 2006, s 1196(2).   [1214] CA 2006, s 1196(3).

Misleading names

6.47 Sections 1197 and 1198 of the CA 2008 apply to misleading names.

Name containing inappropriate indication of company type or legal form

6.48 Section 1197 of the CA 2006 addresses the situation where a name contains an inappropriate indication of a company type or legal form. The Secretary of State may make provision by regulations prohibiting a person from carrying on business in the United Kingdom under a name consisting of or containing specified words, expressions or other indications that are associated with a particular type of company or form of organisation;[1215] or that are similar to words, expressions or other indications associated with a particular type of company or form of organisation.[1216]

The regulations may prohibit the use of words, expressions or other indications in a specified part, or otherwise than in a specified part, of a name;[1217] or in conjunction with, or otherwise than in conjunction with, such other words, expressions or indications as may be specified.[1218]

The term 'specified' means specified in the regulations.[1219]

Regulations under this section are subject to negative resolution procedure.[1220]

A person who uses a name in contravention of regulations commits an offence.[1221] Where an offence under this section is committed by a body corporate, an offence is also committed by every officer of the body who is in default.[1222] A person guilty of an offence under s 1197 of the CA 2006 is liable on summary conviction to a fine not exceeding level 3 on the standard scale and, for continued contravention, a daily default fine not exceeding one-tenth of level 3 on the standard scale.[1223]

Section 1197 of the CA 2006 replaces ss 33, 34 and 34A of the CA 1985. Rather than making it an offence on the face of the Act to use prohibited words, this section provides that the Secretary of State may by regulations make it an offence to carry on business under names using indicators of particular legal status, or similar words, unless entitled to do so. It complements ss 58 and 59 of the CA 2006, which control the use of statutory indicators (eg. 'Ltd' and plc') in companies' registered names.

[1215] CA 2006, s 1197(1)(a). [1216] CA 2006, s 1197(1)(b). [1217] CA 2006, s 1197(2)(a).
[1218] CA 2006, s 1197(2)(b). [1219] CA 2006, s 1197(3). [1220] CA 2006, s 1197(4).
[1221] CA 2006, s 1197(5). [1222] CA 2006, s 1197(6). [1223] CA 2006, s 1197(7).

Name giving misleading indication of activities

6.49 Section 1198 of the CA 2006 states that a person must not carry on business in the United Kingdom under a name that gives so misleading an indication of the nature of the activities of the business as to be likely to cause harm to the public.[1224]

A person who uses a name in contravention of this section commits an offence.[1225] Where an offence is committed by a body corporate, an offence is also committed by every officer of the body who is in default.[1226] A person guilty of an offence under this section is liable on summary conviction to a fine not exceeding level 3 on the standard scale and, for continued contravention, a daily default fine not exceeding one-tenth of level 3 on the standard scale.[1227]

This section makes it an offence to use a business name that gives so misleading an indication of the nature of the activities of the business as to be likely to cause harm to the public. This section complements s 76 of the CA 2006 which gives the Secretary of State power to direct a company to change its registered name in these circumstances.

Supplementary

Savings for existing lawful business names

6.50 Section 1199 of the CA 2006 applies in relation to ss 1192 to 1196 of the CA 2006 (sensitive words or expressions), and s 1197 of the CA 2006 (inappropriate indication of company type or legal form).[1228]

Those sections do not apply to the carrying on of a business by a person who carried on the business immediately before the date on which this Chapter came into force;[1229] and continues to carry it on under the name that immediately before that date was its lawful business name.[1230]

Where a business is transferred to a person on or after the date on which this Chapter came into force,[1231] and that person carries on the business under the name that was its lawful business name immediately before the transfer,[1232] those sections do not apply in relation to the carrying on of the business under that name during the period of 12 months beginning with the date of the transfer.

The term 'lawful business name', in relation to a business, means a name under which the business was carried on without contravening s 2(1) of the Business Names Act 1985 (c 7) or Article 4(1) of the Business Names

---

[1224] CA 2006, s 1198(1).   [1225] CA 2006, s 1198(2).   [1226] CA 2006, s 1198(3).
[1227] CA 2006, s 1198(4).   [1228] CA 2006, s 1199(1).   [1229] CA 2006, s 1199(2)(a).
[1230] CA 2006, s 1199(2)(b).   [1231] CA 2006, s 1199(3)(a).   [1232] CA 2006, s 1199(3)(b).

(Northern Ireland) Order 1986 (SI 1986/1033 NI7));[1233] or, since this Chapter has come into force, the provisions of this Chapter.[1234]

Section 1199 of the CA 2006 provides exemptions for those continuing to use a name that was lawful before the CA 2006 came into force. The exemption is from both the requirement for prior approval, and from using names that include a protected indicator of company status. It also retains the existing provision for when a business is transferred: providing the name was previously lawful, the business may continue under that name for 12 months even if otherwise it would not be lawful for whoever is now carrying on the business (see s 1199(3) of the CA 2006).

Disclosure Required In Case of Individual or Partnership

6.51 Chapter 2 of Part 41 of the CA 2006 addresses the nature of disclosure required in the case of an individual or partnership. It comprises seven sections.

This Chapter re-enacts for individual and partnerships the Business Names Act 1985 provisions relating the information that must be displayed at places of business and in correspondence. These sections ensure that a business's suppliers and customers can discover the legal identity of the person with whom they are doing business and can serve documents upon it. Section 1203 of the CA 2006 makes special provision for large partnerships so that not all the partners' names are required in all business documents, provided certain conditions are met.

Application of this Chapter

6.52 Section 1200 of the CA 2006 applies to an individual or partnership carrying on business in the United Kingdom under a business name.[1235] Any references in this Chapter to 'a person to whom this Chapter applies' are to such an individual or partnership.

The term a 'business name' means a name other than in the case of an individual, his surname without any addition other than a permitted addition;[1236] or in the case of a partnership the surnames of all partners who are individuals;[1237] and the corporate names of all partners who are bodies corporate,[1238] without any addition other than a permitted addition.

The following are the permitted additions in the case of an individual, his forename or initial;[1239] in the case of a partnership the forenames of individual partners or the initials of those forenames;[1240] or where two or more

---

[1233] CA 2006, s 1199(4)(a).   [1234] CA 2006, s 1199(4)(b).   [1235] CA 2006, s 1200(1).
[1236] CA 2006, s 1200(2)(a).   [1237] CA 2006, s 1200(2)(b)(i).
[1238] CA 2006, s 1200(2)(b)(ii).   [1239] CA 2006, s 1200(3)(a).   [1240] CA 2006, s 1200(3)(b)(i).

individual partners have the same surname, the addition of 's' at the end of that surname;[1241] in either case, an addition merely indicating that the business is carried on in succession to a former owner of the business.[1242]

Section 1200 of the CA 2006 partly replaces s 1 of the Business Names Act 1985. It provides that Chapter 2 applies to sole traders if they trade under any name other than their true surnames augmented only by their forenames and/ or initials. (Section 1208 of the CA 2006 defines 'initial' to include any recognised abbreviation of a name.) It also applies to partnerships unless their name comprises the surnames of all its human partners (augmented only by their forenames and/or initials) and the registered names of its other partners.

It also excludes sole traders and partnerships if the only addition to their name shows the business's previous ownership.

This section ensures that the coverage of this Chapter is the same as the Business Names Act 1985 except that, unlike that Act, it does not apply to any companies. The comparable requirements for companies are in Part 5, Chapter 6 of the CA 2006.

Information required to be disclosed

6.53 Section 1201 of the CA 2006 states that the 'information required by this Chapter' is, in the case of an individual, his name;[1243] in the case of a partnership, the name of each member of the partnership;[1244] and in relation to each person so named, an address in the United Kingdom at which service of any document relating in any way to the business will be effective.

This section replaces s 4(1)(a)(i)(ii) and (iv) of the Business Names Act 1985. It specifies the information that is to be the subject of disclosure under this Chapter (i.e. names and addresses for service).

Disclosure requirements

Disclosure required: business documents, etc.

6.54 Section 1202 of the CA 2006 sets out the disclosure required in business documents and similar documents. A person to whom this Chapter applies must state the information required by this Chapter, in legible characters, on all business letters,[1245] written orders for goods or services to be supplied to the business,[1246] invoices and receipts issued in the course of the business,[1247] and written demands for payment of debts arising in the course of the business.[1248] This subsection applies subject to s 1203 of the CA 2006 (exemption for large partnerships if certain conditions met).

[1241] CA 2006, s 1200(3)(b)(ii).   [1242] CA 2006, s 1200(3)(c).   [1243] CA 2006, s 1201(a).
[1244] CA 2006, s 1201(b).   [1245] CA 2006, s 1202(1)(a).   [1246] CA 2006, s 1202(1)(b).
[1247] CA 2006, s 1202(1)(c).   [1248] CA 2006, s 1202(1)(d).

A person to whom this Chapter applies must ensure that the information required by this Chapter is immediately given, by written notice, to any person with whom anything is done or discussed in the course of the business and who asks for that information.[1249] The Secretary of State may by regulations require that such notices be given in a specified form.[1250]

Regulations under this section are subject to negative resolution procedure.[1251]

Exemption for large partnerships if certain conditions met

6.55 Section 1203 of the CA 2006 is concerned with exemption for large partnerships if certain conditions are met. It states that s 1202(1) of the CA 2006 (disclosure required in business documents) does not apply in relation to a document issued by a partnership of more than 20 persons if the following conditions are met.[1252]

The conditions are that the partnership maintains at its principal place of business a list of the names of all the partners;[1253] no partner's name appears in the document, except in the text or as a signatory;[1254] and the document states in legible characters the address of the partnership's principal place of business and that the list of the partners' names is open to inspection there.[1255]

Where a partnership maintains a list of the partners' names for the purposes of this section, any person may inspect the list during office hours.[1256]

Where an inspection required by a person in accordance with this section is refused, an offence is committed by any member of the partnership concerned who without reasonable excuse refused the inspection or permitted it to be refused.[1257] A person guilty of an offence under s 1203(4) of the CA 2006 is liable on summary conviction to a fine not exceeding level 3 on the standard scale and, for continued contravention, a daily default fine not exceeding one-tenth of level 3 on the standard scale.[1258]

Sections 1202 and 1203 of the CA 2006 replace s 4(1)(a) and (2)–(7) of the Business Names Act 1985. They are designed to ensure that customers and suppliers of sole traders know the true identity of the person with whom they are dealing, and have an address for him/her which is effective for the service of documents relating to the business. Further, that customers and suppliers of partnerships with 20 or fewer partners know the identity of every partner, and the address that is effective for the service of documents relating to the business. Additionally, that customers and suppliers of larger partnerships know the address that is effective for the service of documents relating to the

[1249] CA 2006, s 1202(2).   [1250] CA 2006, s 1202(3).   [1251] CA 2006, s 1202(4).
[1252] CA 2006, s 1203(1).   [1253] CA 2006, s 1203(2)(a).   [1254] CA 2006, s 1203(2)(b).
[1255] CA 2006, s 1203(2)(c).   [1256] CA 2006, s 1203(3).   [1257] CA 2006, s 1203(4).
[1258] CA 2006, s 1203(5).

business, and either the identity of every partner, or the address at which they can discover the identity of every partner.

Large partnerships are not permitted to choose which partner's names are included in the documents: they must either include the names of all partners or none (except in the text or as a signatory) (see s 1202(2)(b) of the CA 2006).

Section 1202 of the CA 2006 also provides power for regulations relating to the form of a notice giving the trader's or partners' name(s) and address in response to any person who asks for the information in the course of business. For companies' registered names, equivalent provision may be made in regulations in s 82 of the CA 2006.

Disclosure required: business premises

6.56 Section 1204 of the CA 2006 provides that a person to whom this Chapter applies must, in any premises where the business is carried on,[1259] and to which customers of the business or suppliers of goods or services to the business have access,[1260] display in a prominent position, so that it may easily be read by such customers or suppliers, a notice containing the information required by this Chapter.

The Secretary of State may by regulations require that such notices be displayed in a specified form.[1261]

Regulations under this section are subject to negative resolution procedure.[1262]

Section 1204 of the CA 2006 replaces s 4(1)(b) of the Business Names Act 1985 so far as it applies to sole traders and partnerships. It makes provision to enable customers and suppliers to discover the name(s) and the address for service of documents when visiting any business premises of the trader or partners.

Consequences of failure to make required disclosure

Criminal consequences of failure to make required disclosure

6.57 Section 1205 of the CA 2006 sets out the criminal consequences for failure to make the required disclosure. A person who without reasonable excuse fails to comply with the requirements of s 1202 of the CA 2006 (disclosure required: business documents etc), or s 1204 of the CA 2006 (disclosure required: business premises),commits an offence.[1263]

Where an offence is committed by a body corporate, an offence is also

---

[1259] CA 2006, s 1204(1)(a).   [1260] CA 2006, s 1204(1)(b).   [1261] CA 2006, s 1204(2).
[1262] CA 2006, s 1204(3).   [1263] CA 2006, s 1205(1).

committed by every officer of the body who is in default.[1264] A person guilty of an offence under s 1205 of the CA 2006 is liable on summary conviction to a fine not exceeding level 3 on the standard scale and, for continued contravention, a daily default fine not exceeding one-tenth of level 3 on the standard scale.[1265]

References in s 1205 of the CA 2006 to the requirements of s 1202 or 1204 of the CA 2006 include the requirements of regulations under that section.[1266]

Section 1205 of the CA 2006 provides that certain provisions in Part 36 of the CA 2006 (offences under the Companies Acts) also apply to offences under this Part. It replaces and expands upon s 7 of the Business Names Act 1985 so far as it applies to sole traders and partnerships. It retains the existing offences for failure to comply with the requirements relating to disclosure of name and address in documents and notices.

Civil consequences of failure to make required disclosure

6.58 Section 1206 of the CA 2006 applies to any legal proceedings brought by a person to whom this Chapter applies to enforce a right arising out of a contract made in the course of a business in respect of which he was, at the time the contract was made, in breach of s 1202(1) or (2) of the CA 2006 (disclosure in business documents etc) or s 1204(1) of the CA 2006 (disclosure at business premises).[1267]

The proceedings will be dismissed if the defendant (in Scotland, the defender) to the proceedings shows that he has a claim against the claimant (pursuer) arising out of the contract that he has been unable to pursue by reason of the latter's breach of the requirements of this Chapter,[1268] or that he has suffered some financial loss in connection with the contract by reason of the claimant's (pursuer's) breach of those requirements,[1269] unless the court before which the proceedings are brought is satisfied that it is just and equitable to permit the proceedings to continue.

The references in s 1206 of the CA 2006 to the requirements of this Chapter include the requirements of regulations under this Chapter.[1270]

Section 1206 of the CA 2006 does not affect the right of any person to enforce such rights as he may have against another person in any proceedings brought by that person.[1271]

Section 1206 of the CA 2006 replaces s 5 of the Business Names Act 1985 so far as it applies to sole traders and partnerships. It provides legal rights to anyone who has sustained losses as a result of failure to comply with this Chapter's requirements by a sole trader or partnership.

[1264] CA 2006, s 1205(2).   [1265] CA 2006, s 1205(3).   [1266] CA 2006, s 1205(4).
[1267] CA 2006, s 1206(1).   [1268] CA 2006, s 1206(2)(a).   [1269] CA 2006, s 1206(2)(b).
[1270] CA 2006, s 1206(3).   [1271] CA 2006, s 1206(4).

Supplementary

6.59 Chapter 3 of Part 41 of the CA 2006 deals with supplementary aspects to business names.

Application of general provisions about offences

6.60 Section 1207 of the CA 2006 states that the provisions of ss 1121–1123 of the CA 2006 (liability of officer in default) and 1125–1131 of the CA 2006 (general provisions about offences) apply in relation to offences under this Part as in relation to offences under the Companies Acts. This section replaces s 7(6) of the Business Names Act 1985.

Chapter 7

Shareholders and the Exercise of their Rights

Introduction

7.1 Part 8 of the CA 2006 is concerned with company members and comprises four Chapters. It sets out a definition of who constitutes a 'member' of a company in order to exercise certain statutory rights within the company, as part of the corporate governance process. It also deals with the register of members; overseas branch registers; and prohibition on a subsidiary being a member of its holding company.

This chapter also addresses the provisions dealing with the exercise of members' rights. This is governed by Part 9 of the CA 2006.

Consideration is also given in this chapter to the protection of members against unfair prejudice contained in Part 30 of the CA 2006.[1272]

The members of a company

7.2 Chapter 1 of Part 8 of the CA 2006 deals with members of a company. It comprises only one section, and sets out when a person is considered to be a member of the company. Section 112(1) of the CA 2006 states that the subscribers of a company's memorandum are deemed to have agreed to become members of the company, and on its registration, become members and must be entered as such in its register of members.

Every other person who agrees to become a member of a company, and whose name is registered in its register of members, is a member of the company.[1273]

Section 112 of the CA 2006 restates s 22 of the CA 1985.[1274] There are additional words to make it clear that the subscribers to the memorandum

---

[1272] See CA 2006, ss 994–999.   [1273] CA 2006, s 112(2).

[1274] CA 1985, s 22 stated that the subscribers of a company's memorandum are deemed to have agreed to become members of the company, and on its registration shall be entered as such in its register of members.

become members on registration of the company, even if the company fails to enter their names in the register of members.

Register of Members

7.3 Chapter 2 of Part 8 to the CA 2006 is concerned with the register of members. It comprises 16 sections.

There is an obligation under s 113(1) of the CA 2006 for a company to keep a register of its members. The following details must be entered in the register of members:

- names and addresses of the members;[1275]
- the date on which each person was registered as a member;[1276] and
- the date on which any person ceased to be a member.[1277]

Where a company has share capital, there must be entered in the register, with the names and addresses of the members, a statement of the shares held by each member distinguishing each share by its number (as long as the share has a number);[1278] and where the company has more than one class of issued shares, by its class.[1279] There must also be entered in the register, a statement of the amount paid or agreed to be considered as paid on the shares of each member.[1280]

If the company has converted any of its shares into stock, and given notice of the conversion to the registrar, the register of members must show the amount of stock held by each member, instead of the amount of shares, and the particulars relating to the shares.[1281]

In the case of joint holders of shares or stock in a company, the company's register of members must state the names of each joint holder. In other respects, joint holders will be regarded for the purposes of Chapter 2 of Part 8 of the CA 2006 as a single member and accordingly, the register must show a single address.[1282]

Where a company does not have share capital, but has more than one class of member, there must be entered in the register, with the names and addresses of the members, a statement of the class to which each member belongs.[1283]

If a company makes a default in complying with s 113 of the CA 2006, an offence will be committed by the company;[1284] and every officer of the company who is in default.[1285] A person guilty of an offence is liable on summary

---

[1275] CA 2006, s 113(2)(a).   [1276] CA 2006, s 113(2)(b).   [1277] CA 2006, s 113(2)(c).
[1278] CA 2006, s 113(3)(a)(i).   [1279] CA 2006, s 113(3)(a)(ii).   [1280] CA 2006, s 113(3)(b).
[1281] CA 2006, s 113(4).   [1282] CA 2006, s 113(5).   [1283] CA 2006, s 113(6).
[1284] CA 2006, s 113(7)(a).   [1285] CA 2006, s 113(7)(b).

conviction to a fine not exceeding level 3 on the standard scale and, for continued contravention, a daily default fine not exceeding one-tenth of level 3 on the standard scale.[1286]

Section 113 of the CA 2006 replaces s 352(1)–(5) of the CA 1985 Act. The only new provision is s 113(5) of the CA 2006 states that for the purposes of Chapter 2 of Part 8 to the CA 2006, joint holders of shares are to be treated as a single member and the register only needs to show one address, although all their names must be stated in the register.

Register to be kept available for inspection

7.4 Section 114 of the CA 2006 states that a company's register of members must be kept available for inspection either at its registered office;[1287] or at a place specified in regulations under s 1136 of the CA 2006.[1288] Section 1136 of the CA 2006 states that the Secretary of State may make provision by regulations specifying places, other than the company's registered office, at which a company's records that are required to be kept available for inspection under a relevant provision, may be so kept in compliance with that provision.[1289] The regulations may specify a place by reference to the company's principal place of business, the part of the United Kingdom in which the company is registered, the place at which the company keeps any other records available for inspection, or in any other way.[1290] The regulations may also provide that a company does not comply with a relevant provision by keeping company records available for inspection at a place specified in the regulations, unless conditions specified in the regulations are met.[1291]

A company must give notice to the registrar of the place where its register of members is kept available for inspection, and of any change in that place.[1292] However, a notice will not be required if the register has, at all times since it came into existence (or in the case of a register in existence on the relevant date, at all times since then), been kept available for inspection at the company's registered office.[1293] The 'relevant date' is 1 July 1948, where a company is registered in Great Britain;[1294] and 1 April 1961, where a company is registered in Northern Ireland.[1295]

If a company makes a default for 14 days in complying with s 114(2) of the CA 2006, an offence will be committed by the company;[1296] and every officer of the company who is in default.[1297] A person guilty of an offence will be liable on summary conviction to a fine not exceeding level 3 on the standard

---

[1286] CA 2006, s 113(8).   [1287] CA 2006, s 114(1)(a).
[1288] CA 2006, s 114(1)(b). See CA 2006, s 1136(2), which refers to the register of members.
[1289] CA 2006, s 136(1).   [1290] CA 2006, s 136(3).   [1291] CA 2006, s 136(4).
[1292] CA 2006, s 114(2).   [1293] CA 2006, s 114(3).   [1294] CA 2006, s 114(4)(a).
[1295] CA 2006, s 114(4)(b).   [1296] CA 2006, s 114(5)(a).   [1297] CA 2006, s 114(5)(b).

scale and, for continued contravention, a daily default fine not exceeding one-tenth of level 3 on the standard scale.

Section 114 of the CA 2006 replaces s 353 of the CA 1985.[1298] Under the CA 1985, the register of members was required to be kept at the registered office of the company, except that if the company had appointed a third party to maintain or update the register, it could be kept at the office where that work was done, subject to that office being in the jurisdiction where the company was registered.

However, under the CA 2006 the requirement (here and in relation to other registers) is to keep the register available for inspection at a specified location. It is immaterial where the work of compiling or updating the register is carried out.

Index of members

7.5 Section 115 of the CA 2006 states that every company which has more than 50 members, must keep an index of the names of the company members, unless the register of members is in such a form as to constitute in itself an index.[1299]

The company is required to make any necessary alteration in the index, within 14 days after the date on which any alteration is made in the register of members.[1300] The index must contain, in respect of each member, a sufficient indication to enable the account of that member in the register to be readily found.[1301] There is an obligation to ensure that the index is, at all times, kept available for inspection at the same place as the register of members.[1302]

In the event of any default is made in complying with s 115 of the CA 2006, an offence will be committed by the company;[1303] and every member of the company who is in default.[1304] A person guilty of an offence is liable on summary conviction to a fine not exceeding level 3 on the standard scale and, for continued contravention, a daily default fine not exceeding one-tenth of level 3 on the standard scale.

Section 115 of the CA 2006 replaces s 354 of the CA 1985. There is no change in the obligation of a company with more than 50 members to

---

[1298] CA 1985, s 353 stated that a company's register of members was required to be kept at its registered office, except that if the work of making it up was done at another office of the company, it could be kept there; and if the company arranged with some other person for the making up of the register to be undertaken on its behalf by that other, it could be kept at the office of the other at which the work was done. However, it must not be kept, in the case of a company registered in England and Wales, at any place elsewhere than in England and Wales or, in the case of a company registered in Scotland, at any place elsewhere than in Scotland.

[1299] CA 2006, s 115(1).   [1300] CA 2006, s 115(2).   [1301] CA 2006, s 115(3).
[1302] CA 2006, s 115(4).   [1303] CA 2006, s 115(5)(a).   [1304] CA 2006, s 115(5)(b).

maintain an index of the names of the members, (which the company is obliged to do, unless the register itself is kept in such a form as to constitute an index).

Rights to inspect and request copies

7.6 Section 116(1) of the CA 2006 provides that the register and the index of members' names must be open to the inspection of any member of the company without charge;[1305] and any other person on payment of such fee as may be prescribed.[1306]

Any person may require a copy of a company's register of members, or of any part of it, on payment of such fee as may be prescribed.[1307]

A person seeking to exercise either of the rights provided under s 116 of the CA 2006, must make a request to the company to that effect.[1308] The request must contain the following information:

- In the case of an individual, his name and address;[1309]
- In the case of an organisation, the name and address of an individual responsible for receiving information on its behalf;[1310]
- The purpose for which the information is to be used;[1311] and
- Whether the information will be disclosed to any other person and, if so, the name and address of the individual or organisation, and the purpose for which the information is sought.[1312]

Section 116 of the CA 2006 replaces s 356 of the CA 1985.[1313] Section 356 of the CA 1985 stated that the obligation to make the register available for

---

[1305] CA 2006, s 116(1)(a).   [1306] CA 2006, s 116(1)(b).   [1307] CA 2006, s 116(2).
[1308] CA 2006, s 116(3).   [1309] CA 2006, s 116(4)(a).   [1310] CA 2006, s 116(4)(b).
[1311] CA 2006, s 116(4)(c).   [1312] CA 2006, s 114(4)(d).

[1313] CA 2006, s 356 was concerned with inspection of register and index. It provided that except when the register of members was closed under the CA 1985, the register and index of members' names must be open to the inspection of any member of the company without charge, and of any other person on payment of such fee as may be prescribed. Any member of the company or other person could require a copy of the register, or of any part of it, on payment of such fee as may be prescribed; and the company was required to send a copy of the register to be sent to the person so requesting within ten days beginning with the day next following that on which the requirement was received by the company. Where inspection was refused, or a copy that was required by a person was not sent within the prescribed period, the company and every officer of it who was in default was liable in respect of each offence to a fine. In the case of such refusal or default, the court could make an order compelling an immediate inspection of the register and index, or direct that the copies required should be sent to the persons requiring them. CA 1985, s 358 was concerned with power to close the register. It stated that the company could, on giving notice by advertisement in a newspaper circulating in the district in which the company's registered office was situated, close the register of members for any time or times not exceeding on the whole 30 days in each year. CA 2006, s 116 does not now include the power to close.

inspection was subject to an exception when the register was closed under s 358 of the CA 1985. The power to close the register is not included in s 116 of the CA 2006, and the obligation under s 116(1) of the CA 2006 is absolute. The Company Law Review Group recommended in its *Final Report* that information in a company's register of members should be made available only for certain specified purposes.[1314] Section 116 of the CA 2006 adopts this recommendation.

The section modifies the rights of inspection and the right to be provided with copies of the register of members and its index. It should be noted that s 1137 of the CA 2006 provides power for the Secretary of the State to make regulations about the inspection of records and provision of copies, and to set fees.

Sections 114(3) and (4) of the CA 2006 are new provisions. They require those seeking to inspect or to be provided with a copy of the register of members to provide their names and addresses, the purpose for which the information will be used and, if the access is sought on behalf of others, similar information for them.

Register of members: responses to requests for inspection or copy

7.7 Section 117 of the CA 2006 considers the legal and practical implications of a response to a request for inspection or copy of the resister of members pursuant to s 116 of the CA 2006. Where a company receives a request under s 116 of the CA 2006, it must, within five working days, either comply with the request,[1315] or apply to the court.[1316]

If the company applies to the court, it must notify the person making the request.[1317] If on application, the court is satisfied that the inspection or copy is not sought for a proper purpose, the court will direct the company not to comply with the request,[1318] and the court may further order the company's costs (in Scotland, expenses) on the application, be paid in whole or in part by the person who made the request, even if he is not a party to the application.[1319] If the court makes such a direction, and it appears to the court that the company is or may be subject to other requests made for similar purpose (whether made by the same person or other persons), it may direct that the company is not to comply with such a request. The order must contain such provision as appears to the court appropriate to identify the requests to which it applies.[1320] If on application, the court does not direct the company not to comply with the request, the company must comply with the request

---

[1314] *Final Report*, para 11.44.   [1315] CA 2006, s 117(1)(a).   [1316] CA 2006, s 117(1)(b).
[1317] CA 2006, s 117(2).   [1318] CA 2006, s 117(3)(a).   [1319] CA 2006, s 117(3)(b).
[1320] CA 2006, s 117(4).

immediately upon the court giving its decision or, as the case may be, the proceedings being discontinued.[1321]

Section 117 of the CA 2006 is a new provision. It provides a procedure by which the company can refer the matter to the court, if it thinks that the request may not be for a proper purpose. This section replaces the 10-day deadline for compliance with a request that was set out in s 356(3) of the CA 1985, with a 5-day period within which the company must either comply with the request or apply to the court for relief from the obligation. If the company applies for relief from the obligation, it will be subject to ss 117(3) and (4) of the CA 2006. Section 117(3) of the CA 2006 provides that if the court is satisfied that access to the register of members is not sought for a proper purpose, it will direct the company not to comply with the request, and further may require the person who made the request to pay the company's costs. Section 117(4) of the CA 2006 provides that the court may also require the company not to comply with other requests made for similar purposes. If the court does not make an order under s 117(3) of the CA 2006, or if proceedings are discontinued, the company must immediately comply with the request.

Register of members: refusal of inspection or default in providing copy

7.8 Section 118 of the CA 2006 is concerned with the effect of refusal to comply with request for inspection or default in providing a copy of the register. If an inspection required under s 116 of the CA 2006 is refused, or default is made in providing a copy required under that section, otherwise than in accordance with an order of the court, an offence is committed by the company,[1322] and every officer of the company who is in default.[1323] A person guilty of an offence is liable on summary conviction to a fine not exceeding level 3 on the standard scale and, for continued contravention, a daily default fine not exceeding one-tenth of level 3 on the standard scale.[1324] In the case of any such refusal or default, the court may by order compel an immediate inspection or, as the case may be, direct that the copy required be sent to the person requesting it.[1325]

Section 118 of the CA 2006 replaces s 356(5) and (6) of and Schedule 24 to the CA 1985.[1326] This section retains the existing sanctions for failure to

---

[1321] CA 2006, s 117(5).   [1322] CA 2006, s 118(1)(a).   [1323] CA 2006, s 118(1)(b).
[1324] CA 2006, s 118(2).   [1325] CA 2006, s 118(3).
[1326] CA 1985, s 24 was concerned with punishment for offences under the CA 1985. CA 1985, s 356(5) provided that if an inspection required under this section was refused, or if a copy so required was not sent within the proper period, the company and every officer of it who was in default was liable in respect of each offence to a fine. CA 1985, s 356(6) provided that in the case of such refusal or default, the court could by order compel an immediate inspection of the register and index, or direct that the copies required be sent to the persons requiring them.

comply with a request. They do not apply if the court has directed that the company need not comply with the request.

Register of members: offences in connection with request for or disclosure of information

7.9 Section 119 of the CA 2006 addresses the offences in connection with requests for or disclosure of information. It is an offence for a person knowingly or recklessly to make in a request under s 116 of the CA 2006 (register of members: right to inspect or require copy), a statement that is misleading, false or deceptive in a material particular.[1327]

It is also an offence for a person in possession of information obtained by exercise of either of the rights conferred by s 116 of the CA 2006 to do anything that results in the information being disclosed to another person;[1328] or fail to do anything with the result that the information is disclosed to another person,[1329] and in both cases, knowing or having reason to suspect that person may use the information for a purpose that is not a proper purpose.

A person guilty of an offence is liable on conviction on indictment, to imprisonment for a term not exceeding two years or a fine (or both);[1330] if on a summary conviction in England and Wales, to imprisonment for a term not exceeding 12 months or to a fine not exceeding the statutory maximum (or both);[1331] if in Scotland or Northern Ireland, to imprisonment for a term not exceeding six months, or to a fine not exceeding the statutory maximum (or both).[1332]

Section 119 of the CA 2006 is a new provision. It creates two offences in connection with a request for or disclosure of information relating to the register of members. First, in relation to the new requirement in s 116 of the CA 2006 to provide information in a request for access, it is an offence knowingly or recklessly to make a statement that is misleading, false or deceptive in a material particular. Second, it is an offence to disclose information from a company's register of members obtained under s 116 of the CA 2006 knowing or having reason to suspect that the other person may use the information for a purpose that is not a proper purpose.

Information as to state of register and index

7.10 With regards to the information as to the state of register and index that the company is required to provide, the position is governed by s 120 of the CA 2006. When a person inspects the register, or the company

---

[1327] CA 2006, s 119(1).   [1328] CA 2006, s 119(2)(a).   [1329] CA 2006, s 119(2)(b).
[1330] CA 2006, s 119(3)(a).   [1331] CA 2006, s 119(3)(b)(i).   [1332] CA 2006, s 119(2)(b)(ii).

provides him with a copy of the register or any part of it, the company must inform him of the most recent date (if any) on which alterations were made to the register and confirm that there were no further alterations to be made.[1333]

When a person inspects the index of members' names, the company must inform him whether there is any alteration to the register that is not reflected in the index.[1334] If the company fails to provide the information required under s 120(1) or (2) of the CA 2006, an offence will be committed by the company;[1335] and every officer of the company in default.[1336] A person guilty of an offence is liable on summary conviction to a fine not exceeding level 3 on the standard scale.[1337]

Section 120 of the CA 2006 is a new provision. It implements the Company Law Review Group's recommendation that companies be required to advise anyone exercising their right of inspection or right to demand a copy of the register of index, whether the information is up to date and, if not, the date to which it has been made up.[1338] Failure to provide this information renders the company and any officer in default liable to a fine.

Removal of entries relating to former members

7.11 Section 121 of the CA 2006 states that an entry relating to a former member of the company may be removed from the register after the expiration of ten years from the date on which he ceased to be a member.

This section replaces s 352(6) of the CA 1985.[1339] Based on a recommendation by the Company Law Review Group in its *Final Report*,[1340] it reduces the period for which the entry of a past member must be kept from 20 years to ten years.

Share warrants

7.12 Section 121 of the CA 2006 is concerned with share warrants. Under s 122(1) of the CA 2006, on the issue of a share warrant the company must enter in the register of members the following details:

• the fact of the issue of a warrant;[1341]

[1333] CA 2006, s 120(1).   [1334] CA 2006, s 120(2).
[1335] CA 2006, s 120(3)(a).   [1336] CA 2006, s 120(3)(b).
[1337] CA 2006, s 120(4).   [1338] See *Final Report*, para 11.43.
[1339] CA 1985, s 352(6) provided that an entry relating to a former member of the company could be removed from the register after the expiration of 20 years from the date on which he ceased to be a member.
[1340] *Final Report*, para 11.40.   [1341] CA 2006, s 122(1)(a)(i).

- a statement of the shares included in the warrant, distinguishing each share by its number so long as the share has a number;[1342] and
- the date of the issue of the warrant.[1343]

The company must also amend the register, if necessary, so that no person is named on the register as the holder of the shares specified in the warrant.[1344]

Until the warrant is surrendered, the particulars specified in s 122(1)(a) of the CA 2006 are deemed to be those required by the CA 2006 to be entered in the register of members.[1345]

The bearer of a share warrant may, if the articles of the company so provide, be deemed a member of the company within the meaning of the CA 2006, either to the full extent or for any purposes defined in the articles.[1346]

Subject to the company's articles, the bearer of a share warrant is entitled, on surrendering it for cancellation, to have his name entered as a member in the register of members.[1347]

The company is responsible for any loss incurred by any person, by reason of the company entering in the register the name of a bearer of a share warrant, in respect of the shares specified in it, without the warrant being surrendered and cancelled.[1348]

On the surrender of a share warrant, the date of the surrender must be entered in the register.[1349]

Section 122 of the CA 2006 replaces s 355 of the CA 1985, and implements the Company Law Review Group's recommendation in making clear that shares need not first be issued in registered form, but can be issued directly in warrant to bearer form.[1350]

Single member companies

7.13 The CA 2006 addresses the position in respect of the register with regards to single member companies. The position is governed by s 123 of the CA 2006. If a limited company is formed under the CA 2006 with only one member, there must be entered in the company's register of members, with the name and address of the sole member, a statement that the company has only one member.[1351]

If the number of members of a limited company falls to one, or if an unlimited company with only one member becomes a limited company on re-registration, there is a requirement that upon the occurrence of that event, there must be entered in the company's register of members, with the name and address of the sole member the following details: a statement that the

---

[1342] CA 2006, s 122(1)(a)(ii).   [1343] CA 2006, s 122(1)(a)(iii).   [1344] CA 2006, s 122(1)(b).
[1345] CA 2006, s 122(2).   [1346] CA 2006, s 122(3).   [1347] CA 2006, s 122(4).
[1348] CA 2006, s 122(5).   [1349] CA 2006, s 122(6).
[1350] *Completing the Structure*, para 5.41.   [1351] CA 2006, s 123(1).

company has only one member;[1352] and the date on which the company became a company having only one member.[1353]

If the membership of a limited company increases from one to two or more members, there must upon the occurrence of that event be entered in the company's register of members, with the name and address of the person who was formerly the sole member, the following details: a statement that the company has ceased to have only one member;[1354] and the date on which that event occurred.[1355]

If a company defaults in complying, an offence will be committed by the company;[1356] and every officer of the company who is in default.[1357] A person guilty of an offence is liable on summary conviction to a fine not exceeding level 3 on the standard scale and, for continued contravention, a daily default fine not exceeding one-tenth of level 3 on the standard scale.[1358]

Section 123 of the CA 2006 replaces s 352A of the CA 1985 (a statement that a company only has one member), which implements the Twelfth Company Law Directive (89/667/EEC) on single member private limited liability companies. This section requires a statement to be entered in a company's register of members that it has only one member, if that is the case on incorporation, or at a later date – if the latter, the date on which it so became must also be entered. It also requires a statement that the company has ceased to have only one member, together with the date of the increase. It should be noted that s 352A of the CA 1985 applied to private companies alone, whereas s 123 of the CA 2006 applies to both private and public companies.

Company holding its own shares as treasury shares

7.14 Section 124 of the CA 2006 is concerned with a company holding its own shares as treasury shares. Where a company purchases its own shares in circumstances in which s 724 of the CA 2006 (treasury shares) applies, the requirements of s 113 of the CA 2006 (register of members) need not be complied with, if the company cancels all of the shares forthwith after the purchase;[1359] and if the company does not cancel all of the shares forthwith after the purchase, any share that is so cancelled will be disregarded for the purposes of that section.[1360]

Where a company holds shares as treasury shares, the company must be entered in the register as the member holding those shares.[1361]

Section 124 of the CA 2006 replaces s 352(3A) of the CA 1985 as regards the entries to be made in the register of members where a company holds treasury shares. The effect of that provision is unchanged.

[1352] CA 2006, s 123(2)(a).   [1353] CA 2006, s 123(2)(b).   [1354] CA 2006, s 123(3)(a).
[1355] CA 2006, s 123(3)(b).   [1356] CA 2006, s 123(4)(a).   [1357] CA 2006, s 123(4)(b).
[1358] CA 2006, s 123(5).   [1359] CA 2006, s 124(1)(a).   [1360] CA 2006, s 124(1)(b).
[1361] CA 2006, s 124(2).

Power of court to rectify register

7.15 The CA 2006 contains provisions dealing with the power of the court to rectify the register, which carries forward familiar provisions contained in the of the CA 1985. Section 125 of the CA 2006 provides that if the name of any person is, without sufficient cause, entered in or omitted from the company's register of members;[1362] or a default is made or unnecessary delay takes place in entering on the register the fact of any person having ceased to be a member;[1363] the 'person aggrieved', or any member of the company, or the company, may apply to the court for rectification of the register.

The court can either refuse the application, or it may order rectification of the register and payment by the company of any damages sustained by any party aggrieved.[1364] On such an application, the court may decide any question relating to the title of a person who is a party to the application to have his name entered in or omitted from the register, whether the question arises between members or alleged members, or between members or alleged members on the one hand and the company on the other hand, and generally may decide any question necessary or expedient to be decided for rectification of the register.[1365] In the case of a company required by the CA 2006 to send a list of its members to the registrar of companies, the court, when making an order for rectification of the register, must by its order, direct notice of the rectification to be given to the registrar.[1366]

Section 125 of the CA 2006 restates s 359 of the CA 1985. There is no change of substance.

Trusts not to be entered on register

7.16 Section 126 of the CA 2006 states that no notice of any trust, expressed, implied or constructive, is be entered on the register in England and Wales or Northern Ireland, or be receivable by the registrar.

This section restates s 360 of the CA 1985. The only change is in consequence of its extension to Northern Ireland.

Register to be evidence

7.17 Section 127 of the CA 2006 states that the register of members is *prima facie* evidence of any matters which are directed or authorised by the CA 2006 to be inserted in it.

This section restates s 361 of the CA 1985. Its effect is unchanged.

[1362] CA 2006, s 125(1)(a).   [1363] CA 2006, s 125(1)(b).
[1364] CA 2006, s 125(2).   [1365] CA 2006, s 125(3).
[1366] CA 2006, s 125(4).

Time limit for claims arising from entry in register

7.18 There are time limits for claims arising from entry in the register. Section 128 of the CA 2006 states that liability incurred by a company from the making or deletion of an entry in the register of members;[1367] or from a failure to make or delete such entry,[1368] will not be enforceable more than ten years after the date on which the entry was made or deleted or, as the case may be, the failure first occurred.

This is without prejudice to any lesser period of limitation (and in Scotland, to any rule that the obligation giving rise to the liability prescribes before the expiry of that period).[1369]

This section replaces s 352(7) of the CA 1985. Based on a recommendation by the Company Law Review Group in its *Final Report*, it reduces the time limit for claims relating to entries in the register from 20 years to ten years.[1370]

Overseas branch registers

7.19 Chapter 3 of Part 8 to the CA 2006 is concerned with overseas branch registers. It has seven sections. It restates the provisions of the CA 1985, namely, s 362 and Parts I and II of Schedule 14 of the CA 1985, regarding overseas branch registers. It enables companies in specified circumstances to keep, in a specified country or territory, a register of those members resident in that country or territory. An overseas branch register is deemed to be part of the company's register of members. The CA 2006 provision on overseas branch registers differ from the CA 1985 provisions in two respects. First, rather than providing for an Order in Council, s 129(3) of the CA 2006 provides the Secretary of State with power to make regulations as to the circumstances in which a company is to be regarded as keeping an overseas branch register. Second, s 131 of the CA 2006 provides power to modify the provisions of Chapter 2 relating to the company's register of members, in their application to overseas branch registers.

Under s 129(1) of the CA 2006, a company having a share capital may, if it transacts business in a country or territory to which Chapter 3 of the CA 2006 applies, cause to be kept there a branch register of members resident there. This is known as an 'overseas branch register'.

Chapter 3 applies to the following territories:

- Any part of Her Majesty's dominions outside the United Kingdom, the Channel Islands and the Isle of Man;[1371]
- Bangladesh; Cyprus; Dominica; The Gambia; Malaysia; Malta; Nigeria; Pakistan; Guyana; The Hong Kong Special Administrative Region of

---

[1367] CA 2006, s 128(1)(a).   [1368] CA 2006, s 128(1)(b).   [1369] CA 2006, s 128(2).
[1370] *Final Report*, para 11.40.   [1371] CA 2006, s 129(2)(a).

the People's Republic of China; India; Ireland; Kenya; Kiribati; Lesotho; Malawi; Seychelles; Sierra Leone; Singapore; South Africa; Sri Lanka; Swaziland; Trinidad and Tobago; Uganda; Zimbabwe.[1372]

The Secretary of State may make provision by regulations as to the circumstances in which a company is to be regarded as keeping a register in a particular country or territory.[1373] The regulations relating to these registers is subject to negative resolution procedure.[1374]

Notice of opening of overseas branch

7.20 Section 130 of the CA 2006 is concerned with notice of opening of overseas branch registers. A company that begins to keep an overseas branch register must give notice to the registrar within 14 days of doing so, stating the country or territory in which the register is kept.[1375] If default is made in complying, an offence will be committed by the company;[1376] and every officer of the company who is in default.[1377] A person guilty of an offence is liable on summary conviction to a fine not exceeding level 3 on the standard scale and, for continued contravention, a daily default fine not exceeding one-tenth of level 3 on the standard scale.[1378]

Keeping of overseas branch register

7.21 The position of keeping of overseas branch register is governed by s 131 of the CA 2006. An overseas branch register is regarded as part of the company's register of members. It is referred to as 'the main register'.[1379] The Secretary is empowered to make regulations modifying any provision of Chapter 2 (register of members) as it applies in relation to an overseas branch register.[1380] Any regulations under s 131 of the CA 2006 are subject to negative resolution procedure.[1381] Subject to the provisions of the CA 2006, a company may by its articles make such provision as it thinks fit as to the keeping of overseas branch registers.[1382]

[1372] CA 2006, s 129(2)(b).   [1373] CA 2006, s 129(2).
[1374] CA 2006, s 129(4). Under CA 2006, s 129(5) references (a) in any Act or instrument (including, in particular, a company's articles) to a dominion register, or (b) in articles registered before 1 November 1929 to a colonial register, are to be read (unless the context otherwise requires) as a reference to an overseas branch register kept under CA 2006, s 129.
[1375] CA 2006, s 130(1).   [1376] CA 2006, s 130(2)(a).   [1377] CA 2006, s 130(2)(b).
[1378] CA 2006, s 130(3).   [1379] CA 2006, s 131(1).   [1380] CA 2006, s 131(2).
[1381] CA 2006, s 131(3).   [1382] CA 2006, s 131(4).

Register or duplicate to be kept available for inspection in UK

7.22 Section 132 of the CA 2006 states that a company that keeps an over-seas branch register must keep available for inspection the register;[1383] or a duplicate of the register duly entered up from time to time,[1384] at the place in the United Kingdom where the company's main register is kept available for inspection.

Any such duplicate is treated for all purposes of the CA 2006 as part of the main register.[1385]

If default is made in complying, an offence is committed by the com-pany;[1386] and every officer of the company who is in default.[1387] A person guilty of an offence under s 131(3) of the CA 2006 is liable on summary conviction to a fine not exceeding level 3 on the standard scale and, for continued contravention, a daily default fine not exceeding one-tenth of level 3 on the standard scale.[1388]

Transactions in shares registered in overseas branch register

7.23 Under s 133 of the CA 2006, shares registered in an overseas branch register must be distinguished from those registered in the main register.[1389] No transaction with respect to shares registered in an overseas branch regis-ter may be registered in any other register.[1390] An instrument of transfer of a share registered in an overseas branch register is regarded as a transfer of property situated outside the United Kingdom;[1391] and unless executed in a part of the United Kingdom, is exempt from stamp duty.[1392]

Jurisdiction of local courts

7.24 Section 134 of the CA 2006 states that a competent court in a country or territory where an overseas branch register is kept, may exercise the same jurisdiction as is exercisable by a court in the United Kingdom to rectify the register (see s 125 of the CA 2006);[1393] or in relation to a request for inspection or a copy of the register (see s 117 of the CA 2006).[1394]

The offences of refusing inspection or failing to provide a copy of the register (see s 118 of the CA 2006);[1395] and of making a false, misleading or deceptive statement in a request for inspection or a copy (see s 119 of the CA 2006),[1396] may be prosecuted summarily before any tribunal having summary criminal jurisdiction in the country or territory where the register is kept.

[1383] CA 2006, s 132(1)(a).   [1384] CA 2006, s 132(1)(b).   [1385] CA 2006, s 132(2).
[1386] CA 2006, s 132(3)(a).   [1387] CA 2006, s 132(3)(b).   [1388] CA 2006, s 132(4).
[1389] CA 2006, s 133(1).   [1390] CA 2006, s 133(2).   [1391] CA 2006, s 133(3)(a).
[1392] CA 2006, s 133(3)(b).   [1393] CA 2006, s 134(1)(a).   [1394] CA 2006, s 134(1)(b).
[1395] CA 2006, s 134(2)(a).   [1396] CA 2006, s 134(2)(b).

Section 134 of the CA 2006 extends only to those countries and territories to which para 3 of Schedule 14 to the CA 1985 (which made similar provision) extended immediately before the coming into force of this Chapter.[1397]

Discontinuance of overseas branch register

7.25 Section 135 of the CA 2006 addresses the position of discontinuance of an overseas branch register. A company may discontinue an overseas branch register.[1398] If it does so, all the entries in that register must be transferred to some other overseas branch register kept in the same country or territory;[1399] or to the main register.[1400]

The company must give notice to the registrar within 14 days of the discontinuance.[1401]

If default is made in complying, an offence is committed by the company;[1402] and every officer of the company who is in default.[1403] A person guilty of an offence under s 135(4) of the CA 2006 is liable on summary conviction to a fine not exceeding level 3 on the standard scale and, for continued contravention, a daily default fine not exceeding one-tenth of level 3 on the standard scale.[1404]

Prohibition on subsidiary being member of its holding company

7.26 Chapter 4 of Part 8 of the CA 2006 is concerned with prohibition on a subsidiary being a member of its holding company. This Chapter is a restatement of the provisions of s 23 of the CA 1985 and Schedule 2 of the CA 1985 as it applies for the purposes of that section. Unless in circumstances covered by an exception, a company cannot be a member of its own holding company. There is no change in substance to the provision in the CA 1985.

Prohibition on subsidiary being member of its holding company

7.27 Section 136 of the CA 2006 provides that except as provided by Part 8, Chapter 4 of the CA 2006, a body corporate cannot be a member of a company that is its holding company;[1405] and any allotment or transfer of shares in a company to its subsidiary will be void.[1406] However, the exceptions are provided for in s 138 of the CA 2006 (subsidiary acting as personal representative or trustee), and s 141 of the CA 2006 (subsidiary acting as authorised dealer in securities).[1407]

[1397] CA 2006, s 134(3).   [1398] CA 2006, s 135(1).   [1399] CA 2006, s 135(2)(a).
[1400] CA 2006, s 135(2)(b).   [1401] CA 2006, s 135(3).   [1402] CA 2006, s 135(4)(a).
[1403] CA 2006, s 135(4)(b).   [1404] CA 2006, s 135(5).   [1405] CA 2006, s 136(1)(a).
[1406] CA 2006, s 136(1)(b).   [1407] CA 2006, s 136(2).

Section 136 of the CA 2006 prohibits a company from holding the shares of its own holding company. The prohibition applies to all bodies corporate. Section 137 of the CA 2006 is a saving for certain shares acquired before the date on which the prohibition originally came into force.

Shares acquired before prohibition became applicable

7.28 Section 137 of the CA 2006 is concerned with shares that are acquired before the prohibition in s 136 of the CA 2006 becomes applicable. Where a body corporate became a holder of shares in a company before the relevant date;[1408] or on or after that date and before the commencement of this Chapter in circumstances in which the prohibition in s 23(1) of the CA 1985 or Article 33(1) of the Companies (Northern Ireland) Order 1986 (SI 1986/1032 (NI 6)) (or any corresponding earlier enactment), as it then had effect, did not apply;[1409] or on or after the commencement of this Chapter in circumstances in which the prohibition in s 136 of the CA 2006 did not apply,[1410] it may continue to be a member of the company.

The 'relevant date' for the purposes of s 137(1)(a) of the CA 2006 is 1 July 1948 in the case of a company registered in Great Britain;[1411] and 1 April 1961 in the case of a company registered in Northern Ireland.[1412]

So long as it is permitted to continue as a member of a company by virtue of s 137 of the CA 2006, an allotment to it of fully paid shares in the company may be validly made by way of capitalisation of reserves of the company.[1413]

But, so long as the prohibition in s 136 of the CA 2006 would (apart from s 137 of the CA 2006) apply, it has no right to vote in respect of the shares mentioned in s 137(1) of the CA 2006 above, or of any shares allotted as mentioned in s 137(2) of the CA 2006 above, on a written resolution or at meetings of a company or at any class of its members.[1414]

Subsidiary acting as a personal representative or trustee

7.29 Section 138 of the CA 2006 applies to a subsidiary acting as a personal representative or trustee The prohibition in s 136 of the CA 2006 (prohibition on subsidiary being a member of its holding company) does not apply where the subsidiary is concerned only as personal representative;[1415] or as trustee,[1416] unless, in the latter case, the holding company or a subsidiary of it is beneficially interested under the trust.

For the purpose of ascertaining whether the holding company or a subsidiary is so 'interested', the following are to be disregarded:

[1408] CA 2006, s 137(1)(a).   [1409] CA 2006, s 137(1)(b).   [1410] CA 2006, s 137(1)(c).
[1411] CA 2006, s 137(2)(a).   [1412] CA 2006, s 137(2)(b).   [1413] CA 2006, s 137(3).
[1414] CA 2006, s 137(4).   [1415] CA 2006, s 138(1)(a).   [1416] CA 2006, s 138(1)(b).

(a)   any interest held only by way of security for the purposes of a transaction entered into by the holding company or subsidiary in the ordinary course of a business that includes the lending of money;[1417]

(b)   any interest within s 139 of the CA 2006 (interests to be disregarded: residual interest under a pension scheme or an employees' share scheme); or s 140 of the CA 2006 (interests to be disregarded: employers rights of recovery under a pension scheme or an employees' shares scheme);[1418]

(c)   any rights that the company or subsidiary has in its capacity as trustee, including in particular any right to recover its expenses or be remunerated out of the trust property, and any right to be indemnified out of the trust property for any liability incurred by reason of any act or omission in the performance of its duties as trustee.[1419]

Interests to be disregarded: residual interest under pension scheme or employees' share scheme

7.30 Section 139 of the CA 2006 is concerned with interests to be disregarded – namely, the residual interest under a pension scheme or an employees' share scheme.

Where shares in a company are held on trust for the purposes of a pension scheme or employees' share scheme, there shall be disregarded for the purposes of s 138 of the CA 2006 any residual interest that has not vested in possession.[1420]

The term 'residual interest' is defined as a right of a company or subsidiary (the residual beneficiary) to receive any of the trust property on the event of:

(a)   all the liabilities arising under the scheme having been satisfied or provided for;[1421] or

(b)   the residual beneficiary ceasing to participate in the scheme;[1422] or

(c)   the trust property at any time exceeding what is necessary to satisfy the liabilities arising or expected to arise under the scheme.[1423]

In respect of s 139(2) of the CA 2006 the reference to a right includes a right dependent on the exercise of discretion vested by the scheme in the trustee of another person;[1424] and the reference to liabilities arising under a scheme includes liabilities that have resulted from the exercise of any such discretion.[1425]

For the purposes of s 139 of the CA 2006, a residual interest vests in possession in the following circumstances:

[1417] CA 2006, s 138(2)(a).   [1418] CA 2006, s 138(2)(b).   [1419] CA 2006, s 138(2)(c).
[1420] CA 2006, s 138(1).   [1421] CA 2006, s 139(2).   [1422] CA 2006, s 139(2)(b).
[1423] CA 2006, s 139(2)(c).   [1424] CA 2006, s 139(3)(a).   [1425] CA 2006, s 139(3)(b).

(a)   in a case within s 139(2)(a) of the CA 2006, on the occurrence of the event mentioned there (whether or not the amount of the property receivable pursuant to the right is ascertained);[1426]

(b)   in a case within s 139(2)(b) or (c) of the CA 2006, when the residual beneficiary becomes entitled to require the trustee to transfer to him any of the property receivable pursuant to the right.[1427]

The term 'pension scheme' means a scheme for the provision of benefits consisting of or including relevant benefits for or in respect of employees or former employees.[1428] The term 'relevant benefits' here means any pension, lump sum, gratuity or other like benefit to be given on retirement or on death or in anticipation of retirement or, in connection with past service, after retirement or death.[1429] The term 'employee' is to be read as if a director of a company were employed by it.[1430]

Interests to be disregarded: employer's rights of recovery under pension scheme or employees' share scheme

7.31 Section 140 of the CA 2006 considers interests to be disregarded in respect of employer's rights of recovery under a pension scheme or an employees' share scheme.

Where shares in a company are held on trust for the purposes of a pension scheme or employees' share scheme, there shall be disregarded for the purposes of s 138 of the CA 2006 any charge or lien on, or set-off against, any benefit or other right or interest under the scheme for the purpose of enabling the employer or former employer of a member of a scheme to obtain the discharge of a monetary obligation due to him from the member.[1431]

In the case of a trust for the purposes of a pension scheme there shall also be disregarded any right to receive from the trustee of the scheme, or as trustee of the scheme to retain, an amount that can be recovered or retained, under s 61 of the Pension Schemes Act 1993 (c 48) or s 57 of the Pension Schemes (Northern Ireland) Act 1993 (c 49) (deduction of contributions equivalent premium from refund of scheme contributions) or otherwise, as reimbursement or partial reimbursement for any contributions equivalent premium paid in connection with the scheme under Part 3 of that Act.[1432]

The term 'pension scheme' means a scheme for the provision of benefits consisting of including relevant benefits for or in respect of employees or former employees. 'Relevant benefits' here means any pension, lump sum, gratuity or other like benefit given or to be given on retirement or on death or

---

[1426] CA 2006, s 139(4)(a).   [1427] CA 2006, s 139(4)(b).   [1428] CA 2006, s 139(5).
[1429] CA 2006, s 139(6)(a).   [1430] CA 2006, s 139(6)(b).   [1431] CA 2006, s 140(1).
[1432] CA 2006, s 140(2).

in anticipation of retirement or, in connection with past service, after retirement or death.[1433]

The terms 'employer' and 'employee' are to be read as if a director of a company were employed by it.[1434]

Subsidiary acting as authorised dealer in securities

7.32 Section 141 of the CA 2006 deals with the subsidiary acting as an authorised dealer in securities. The prohibition in s 136 of the CA 2006 (prohibition on a subsidiary being a member of its holding company) does not apply where the shares are held by the subsidiary in the ordinary course of its business as an intermediary.[1435]

A person is an intermediary if he:

(a) carries on a bona fide business of dealing in securities;[1436]
(b) is a member of an EEA exchange (and satisfies any requirements for recognition as a dealer in securities laid down by that exchange) or is otherwise approved or supervised as a dealer in securities under the laws of EEA State;[1437] and
(c) does not carry on an excluded business.[1438]

However, the following are excluded businesses:

(a) a business that consists wholly or mainly in the making or managing of investments;[1439]
(b) a business that consists mainly or wholly in, or is carried on wholly or mainly for the purposes of, providing services to persons who are connected with the person carrying on the business;[1440]
(c) a business that consists in insurance business;[1441]
(d) a business that consists in managing or acting as trustee in relation to a pension scheme, or that is carried on by the manager or trustee of such a scheme in connection with or for the purposes of the scheme;[1442]
(e) a business that consists in operating or acting as trustee in relation to a collective investment scheme, or that is carried on by the operator or trustee of such a scheme in connection with and for the purposes of the scheme.[1443]

For the purposes of s 141 of the CA 2006:

(a) the question whether the person is connected with another shall be

---

[1433] CA 2006, s 140(3).   [1434] CA 2006, s 140(4).   [1435] CA 2006, s 141(1).
[1436] CA 2006, s 141(2)(a).   [1437] CA 2006, s 141(2)(b).   [1438] CA 2006, s 141(2)(c).
[1439] CA 2006, s 141(3)(a).   [1440] CA 2006, s 141(3)(b).   [1441] CA 2006, s 141(3)(c).
[1442] CA 2006, s 141(3)(d).   [1443] CA 2006, s 141(3)(e).

determined in accordance with s 839 of the Income and Corporation taxes Act 1988 (c 1);[1444]

(b) 'collective investments scheme' has the meaning given in s 236 of the Financial Services and Markets Act 2000 (c 8);[1445]

(c) 'EEA exchange' means a market that appears on the list drawn up by an EEA State pursuant of Article 16 of Council Directive 93/22/EEC on investment service in the securities field;[1446]

(d) 'insurance business' means business that consists in the effecting or carrying out of contracts of insurance;[1447]

(e) 'securities includes:

   (i)   options,
   (ii) futures, and
   (iii) contracts for differences, and rights or interests in those investments.[1448]

(f) 'trustee' and 'the operator' in relation to a collective investment scheme shall be construed in accordance with s 237(2) of the Financial Services and Markets Act 2000.

The expressions used in s 141 of the CA 2006 that are also used in the provisions regulating activities under the Financial Services and Markets Act 2000 (c 8) have the same meaning here as they do in those provisions.[1449]

Protection of third parties in other cases where subsidiary acting as a dealer in securities

7.33 Section 142 of the CA 2006 deals with protection of third parties in other cases where a subsidiary acts as a dealer in securities. It applies where a subsidiary that is a dealer in securities has purportedly acquired shares in its holding company in contravention of the prohibition in s 136 of the CA 2006;[1450] and a person acting in good faith has agreed, for value and without notice of the contravention, to acquire shares in the holding company from the subsidiary or from someone who has purportedly acquired the shares after their disposal by the subsidiary.[1451]

A transfer to that person of the shares mentioned in s 142(1)(a) of the CA 2006 has the same effect as it would have had if their original acquisition by the subsidiary had not been in the contravention of the prohibition.[1452]

[1444] CA 2006, s 141(4)(a).   [1445] CA 2006, s 141(4)(b).   [1446] CA 2006, s 141(4)(c).

[1447] CA 2006, s 141(4)(d).   [1448] CA 2006, s 141(4)(e).

[1449] CA 2006, s 141(5). See also FSMA 2000, s 22, orders made under that section, and Schedule 2 to that Act.

[1450] CA 2006, s 142(1)(a).   [1451] CA 2006, s 142(1(b).   [1452] CA 2006, s 142(2).

Application of provisions to companies not limited by shares

7.34 Section 143 of the CA 2006 states that in relation to a company other than a company limited by shares, the references in this Chapter to shares are to be read as references to the interest of its members as such, whatever the form of the interest.

Application of provisions to nominees

7.35 Under s 144 of the CA 2006, the provisions of Chapter 4 of Part 8 of the CA 2006 apply to a nominee acting on behalf of a subsidiary as to the subsidiary itself.

Sections 138 and 141 of the CA 2006 provide for exceptions from the prohibition where the subsidiary is acting as personal representative or trustee, or as a dealer in securities.

Exercise of Members' Rights

7.36 Part 9 of the CA 2006 is concerned with the exercise of members' rights. The Company Law Review Group considered the rights of persons other than registered shareholders in Chapter 4, *Developing the Framework* and Chapter 5, *Completing the Structure*, presenting their recommendations in Chapter 7 of the *Final Report*. The new provisions in Part 9 have been developed with these recommendations in mind and are designed to make it easier for investors to exercise their governance rights fully and responsibly. Previously, when investors, whether major institutional investors or retail investors, bought shares in a listed company, they were increasingly likely to hold their shares through an intermediary or a chain of intermediaries. This meant that it was an intermediary's name that appeared on the register of members. As a result, investors typically had to rely on contractual arrangements with the intermediaries, both to obtain information from the company and also to give any instructions they wish about how shares should be voted.

Part 9 introduces new provisions dealing with the ability of indirect investors to exercise governance rights. The first section in Part 9 removes any doubts as to the ability of companies to make provision in their articles for others to enjoy and exercise membership rights, and enables indirect investors to enjoy information rights through the registered member.

The next group of sections provides that indirect investors in traded companies can be nominated by the registered member to receive company documents and information. It is up to the registered member, typically a broker, to decide whether to nominate or not.

The last two sections in Part 9 make it easier for registered members to exercise rights in different ways to reflect the underlying holdings and allow indirect investors to participate in, for example, requests for resolutions at the AGM. The provisions of this Part 9 should be considered together with ss 324–331 on proxies in Part 13 of the CA 2006, which enable the registered member to appoint indirect investors as proxies to exercise voting rights.

It should be noted that the information rights and exercise of other rights where shares are held on behalf of others, can be initiated and enforced with the company only by the registered member. Part 9 does not compel the registered member to confer such rights on third parties. It will be for indirect investors, such as shareholders through a nominee, to choose a nominee operator who offers such rights as part of their service.

Effect of provisions in a company's articles

Effect of provisions of articles as to enjoyment or exercise of members' rights

7.37 Section 145 of the CA 2006 applies where provision is made by a company's articles enabling a member to nominate another person or persons as entitled to enjoy or exercise all or any specified rights of the member in relation to the company.[1453]

So far as is necessary to give effect to that provision, anything required or authorised by any provision of the Companies Acts to be done by or in relation to the member shall instead be done, or (as the case may be) may instead be done, by or in relation to the nominated person (or each of them) as if he were a member of the company.[1454]

This applies, in particular, to the rights conferred by the following sections:

(a) ss 291 and 293 of the CA 2006 (the right to be sent proposed written resolution);[1455]

(b) s 292 of the CA 2006 (the right to require circulation of written resolutions);[1456]

(c) s 303 of the CA 2006 (the right to require directors to call a general meeting);[1457]

(d) s 310 of the CA 2006 (the right to notice of general meetings);[1458]

(e) s 314 of the CA 2006 (the right to require circulation of a statement);[1459]

(f) s 324 of the CA 2006 (the right to appoint a proxy to act at a meeting);[1460]

(g) s 338 of the CA 2006 (the right to require circulation of resolutions for AGM of a public company);[1461] and

(h) s 423 of the CA 2006 (the right to be sent a copy of annual accounts and reports).[1462]

[1453] CA 2006, s 145(1).   [1454] CA 2006, s 145(2).   [1455] CA 2006, s 145(3)(a).
[1456] CA 2006, s 145(3)(b).   [1457] CA 2006, s 145(3)(c).   [1458] CA 2006, s 145(3)(d).
[1459] CA 2006, s 145(3)(e).   [1460] CA 2006, s 145(3)(f).   [1461] CA 2006, s 145(3)(g).
[1462] CA 2006, s 145(3)(h).

Section 145 of the CA 2006 and any such provision as is mentioned in s 145(1) of the CA 2006 do not confer rights enforceable against the company by anyone other than the member;[1463] and do not affect the requirements for an effective transfer or other disposition of the whole or part of a member's interest in the company.[1464]

Section 145 of the CA 2006 allows a company's articles to enable a member to identify another person or persons as entitled to enjoy or exercise all or any specified rights of a member. The articles may specify that this entitlement can apply only to certain rights or to all rights, except the right to transfer the shares. Section 145(4) of the CA 2006 states that the right to transfer shares must remain as under the CA 1985, with the member whose name is on the register.

Section 145(2) of the CA 2006 states that where a company makes relevant provision in its articles, all the relevant references in the Companies Acts to 'member' should be read as if the reference to member were a reference to the person or persons nominated by the member. Section 145(3) of the CA 2006 provides a non-exhaustive list of the provisions.

The effect of s 145(4)(a) of the CA 2006 is that non-members do not have direct enforceable rights against the company. They should enforce their rights through the member whose name is on the register, and who has the right to enforce the articles.

Information rights

7.38 Information rights are considered in ss 146 to 150 of the CA 2006. These sections introduce new provisions enabling indirect investors to be appointed by the registered member to receive information that is sent to members by the company. These provisions only apply to companies traded on a regulated market. The Secretary of State may extend or limit the classes of companies to which these provisions apply through power provided under s 151 of the CA 2006.

Traded companies: nomination of persons to enjoy information rights

7.38.1 Section 146 of the CA 2006 applies to a company whose shares are admitted to trading on a regulated market.[1465] A member of such a company who holds shares on behalf of another person may nominate that person to enjoy information rights.[1466]

The term 'information rights' means the right to receive a copy of all communications that the company sends to its members generally, or to any

---

[1463] CA 2006, s 145(4)(a).   [1464] CA 2006, s 145(4)(b).   [1465] CA 2006, s 146(1).
[1466] CA 2006, s 146(2).

class of its members that includes the person making the nomination;[1467] and the rights conferred by s 431 or s 432 of the CA 2006 (the right to require copies of accounts and reports);[1468] and s 1145 of the CA 2006 (the right to require a hard copy version of documents or information provided in another format).[1469]

The reference in s 146(3)(a) of the CA 2006 to communications that a company sends to its members generally includes the company's annual accounts and reports. For the application of s 426 of the CA 2006 (the option to provide a summary financial statement) in relation to a person nominated to enjoy information rights, see s 426(5) of the CA 2006.[1470]

A company need not act on a nomination purporting to relate to certain information rights only.[1471]

Section 146(1) and (2) of the CA 2006 provide new rights for members of companies whose shares are traded on regular markets, to nominate those on whose behalf they hold shares, to receive information that is sent to members direct from the company and to exercise certain rights.

Section 146(3) of the CA 2006 sets out what is meant by 'information rights', namely the right to receive all communications that the company sends to members, the right to require copies of accounts and reports (as in ss 431 or 432 of the CA 2006), and the right to require hard copy versions of documents (see s 1145 of the CA 2006).

Section 146(4) of the CA 2006 refers to s 426 of the CA 2006, which allows under certain circumstances for summary financial statements rather than full accounts to be sent out as part of the general information. These must also be sent to nominated persons.

Section 146(5) of the CA 2006 provides that the company does not need to respond to a nomination that specifies only certain information rights.

Information rights: form in which copies to be provided

7.38.2 Section 147 of the CA 2006 applies as regards the form in which copies are to be provided to a person nominated under s 146 of the CA 2006 (nomination of person to enjoy information rights).[1472]

If the person to be nominated wishes to receive hard copy communications, he must request the person making the nomination to notify the company of that fact;[1473] and provide an address to which such copies may be sent.[1474] This must be done before the nomination is made.

If having received such a request the person making the nomination notifies the company that the nominated person wishes to receive hard copy

---

[1467] CA 2006, s 146(3)(a).   [1468] CA 2006, s 146(3)(b)(i).   [1469] CA 2006, s 146(3)(b)(ii).
[1470] CA 2006, s 146(4).   [1471] CA 2006, s 146(5).   [1472] CA 2006, s 147(1).
[1473] CA 2006, s 147(2)(a).   [1474] CA 2006, s 147(2)(b).

communications;[1475] and provides the company with that address,[1476] the right of the nominated person is to receive hard copy communications accordingly.

This is subject to the provisions of Parts 3 and 4 of Schedule 5 of the CA 2006 (communications by company), under which the company may take steps to enable it to communicate in electronic form, or by means of a website.[1477]

If no such notification is given (or no address is provided), the nominated person is taken to have agreed that documents or information may be sent or supplied to him by the company by means of a website.[1478]

That agreement may be revoked by the nominated person;[1479] and does not affect his right under s 1145 of the CA 2006 to require a hard copy version of a document or information provided in any other form.[1480]

The effect of s 147 of the CA 2006 deals with the way in which information is to be provided to a nominated person. Section 147(2) of the CA 2006 explains that if a nominated person wants communications to be in hard copy, they must ask the member, providing a postal address, before the nomination is made. If the member then passes this on to the company, under s 147(3) of the CA 2006, the nominated person will have the right to receive hard copy communications.

Termination or suspension of nomination

7.39 Section 148 of the CA 2006 applies to termination or suspension of nomination. The following provisions apply in relation to a nomination under s 146 of the CA 2006 (nomination of a person to enjoy information rights).[1481]

The nomination may be terminated at the request of the member or of the nominated person.[1482]

The nomination ceases to have effect on the occurrence in relation to the member or the nominated person of any of the following: in the case of an individual, death or bankruptcy;[1483] or in the case of a body corporate, dissolution or the making of an order for the winding up of the body otherwise than for the purposes of reconstruction.[1484]

In s 148(3) of the CA 2006, the reference to bankruptcy includes the sequestration of a person's estate;[1485] and a person's estate being the subject of a protected trust deed (within the meaning of the Bankruptcy (Scotland) (c 66) of the CA 1985);[1486] and the reference to the making of an order for winding up is to the making of such an order under the Insolvency Act 1986 (c 45) or the Insolvency (Northern Ireland) Order 1989 (SI 1989/2405 (NI

[1475] CA 2006, s 147(3)(a).   [1476] CA 2006, s 147(3)(b).   [1477] CA 2006, s 147(4).
[1478] CA 2006, s 147(5).   [1479] CA 2006, s 147(6)(a).   [1480] CA 2006, s 147(6)(b).
[1481] CA 2006, s 148(1).   [1482] CA 2006, s 148(2).   [1483] CA 2006, s 148(3)(a).
[1484] CA 2006, s 148(3)(b).   [1485] CA 2006, s 148(4)(a)(i).   [1486] CA 2006, s 148(4)(a)(ii).

19));[1487] or any corresponding proceeding under the law of a country or territory outside the United Kingdom.[1488]

The effect of any nominations made by a member is suspended at any time when there are more nominated persons than the member has shares in the company.[1489]

Where the member holds different classes of shares with different information rights;[1490] and there are more nominated persons than he has shares conferring a particular right,[1491] the effect of any nominations made by him is suspended to the extent that they confer that right.

Where the company enquires of a nominated person whether he wishes to retain information rights;[1492] and does not receive a response within the period of 28 days beginning with the date on which the company's enquiry was sent,[1493] the nomination ceases to have effect at the end of that period. Such an enquiry is not to be made of a person more than once in any 12-month period.

The termination or suspension of a nomination means that the company is not required to act on it. It does not prevent the company from continuing to do so, to such extent or for such period as it thinks fit.[1494]

Section 148 of the CA 2006 provides that a nomination will stop having effect on the request of the nominated person or the member (s 148(2) of the CA 2006), or on the death, bankruptcy or winding-up of the nominated person or the member (s 148(3) of the CA 2006).

Section 148(5) of the CA 2006 explains that all nominations made by member will be suspended if there are more nominations than the total number of shares. Section 148(6) of the CA 2006 makes similar provision where there are different classes of shares.

Information as to possible rights in relation to voting

7.40 Section 149 of the CA 2006 applies where a company sends a copy of a notice of a meeting to a person nominated under s 146 of the CA 2006 (nomination of person to enjoy information rights).[1495]

The copy of the notice must be accompanied by a statement that he may have a right under an agreement between him and the member by whom he was nominated to be appointed, or to have someone else appointed, as a proxy for the meeting;[1496] and if he has no such right or does not wish to exercise it, he may have a right under such an agreement to give instructions to the member as to the exercise of voting rights.[1497]

[1487] CA 2006, s 148(4)(b)(i).   [1488] CA 2006, s 148(4)(b)(ii).   [1489] CA 2006, s 148(5).
[1490] CA 2006, s 148(6)(a).   [1491] CA 2006, s 148(6)(b).   [1492] CA 2006, s 148(7)(a).
[1493] CA 2006, s 148(7)(b).   [1494] CA 2006, s 148(8).   [1495] CA 2006, s 149(1).
[1496] CA 2006, s 149(2)(a).   [1497] CA 2006, s 149(2)(b).

Section 149(3) of the CA 2006 states that s 325 of the CA 2006 (notice of meeting to contain statement of a member's rights in relation to appointment of proxy) does not apply to the copy, and the company must either omit the notice required by that section;[1498] or include it but state that it does not apply to the nominated person.[1499]

Section 149 of the CA 2006 requires the company, when sending a meeting notice to nominated persons, to include a statement that the nominated person may have voting rights that he can exercise through the person who nominated him.

Information rights: status of rights

7.41 Section 150 of the CA 2006 applies as regards the rights conferred by a nomination under s 146 of the CA 2006 (nomination of a person to enjoy information rights).[1500]

Enjoyment by the nominated person of the rights conferred by the nomination is enforceable against the company by the member, as if they were rights conferred by the company's articles.[1501]

Any enactment, and any provision of the company's articles, having effect in relation to communications with members, has a corresponding effect (subject to any necessary adaptations) in relation to communications with the nominated person.[1502]

In particular where under any enactment, or any provision of the company's articles, the members of a company entitled to receive a document or information are determined as at a date or time before it is sent or supplied, the company need not send or supply it to a nominated person whose nomination was received by the company after that date or time;[1503] or if that date or time falls in a period of suspension of his nomination;[1504] and where under any enactment, or any provision of the company's articles, the right of a member to receive a document or information depends on the company having a current address for him, the same applies to any person nominated by him.[1505]

The rights conferred by the nomination are in addition to the rights of the member himself;[1506] and do not affect any rights exercisable by virtue of any such provision as is mentioned in s 145 of the CA 2006 (provisions of a company's articles as to enjoyment or exercise of members' rights).[1507]

A failure to give effect to the rights conferred by the nomination does not affect the validity of anything done by or on behalf of the company.[1508]

[1498] CA 2006, s 149(3)(a).   [1499] CA 2006, s 149(3)(b).   [1500] CA 2006, s 150(1).
[1501] CA 2006, s 150(2).   [1502] CA 2006, s 150(3).   [1503] CA 2006, s 150(4)(a)(i).
[1504] CA 2006, s 150(4)(a)(ii).   [1505] CA 2006, s 150(4)(b).   [1506] CA 2006, s 150(5)(a).
[1507] CA 2006, s 150(5)(b).   [1508] CA 2006, s 150(6).

The references in s 150 of the CA 2006 to the rights conferred by the nomination are to the rights referred to in s 146(3) of the CA 2006 (information rights);[1509] and where applicable, the rights conferred by s 147(3) (the right to hard copy communications) and s 149 of the CA 2006 (information as to possible voting rights).[1510]

The objective of s 150 of the CA 2006 is to deal with rights arising from a nomination under s 146 of the CA 2006, and provides that it is the member, rather than the nominated person, who can enforce the rights against the company.

Information rights: power to amend

7.42 Section 151 of the CA 2006 provides that the Secretary of State may by regulations amend the provisions of ss 146–150 of the CA 2006 (information rights) so as to extend or restrict the classes of companies to which s 146 applies;[1511] make other provision as to the circumstances in which a nomination may be made under that section;[1512] or extend or restrict the rights conferred by such a nomination.[1513]

The regulations may make such consequential modifications of any other provisions of this Part, or of any other enactment, as appear to the Secretary of State to be necessary.[1514]

The regulations under s 151 of the CA 2006 are subject to affirmative resolution procedure.[1515]

The effect of s 151 of the CA 2006 is to give power for the Secretary of State to amend the provisions of ss 146–150 of the CA 2006. The power allows for changes in the companies covered, the circumstances in which nominations can be made and the rights covered by nomination.

Exercise of rights where shares held on behalf of others

7.43 Sections 152–153 of the CA 2006 enable indirect investors through the registered member to exercise voting and requisition rights by making it easier for registered members to exercise rights in different ways that will reflect underlying holdings and by allowing those on whose behalf they hold shares to participate in requisitions. These two sections apply to all types of companies.

[1509] CA 2006, s 150(7)(a).   [1510] CA 2006, s 150(7)(b).   [1511] CA 2006, s 151(1)(a).
[1512] CA 2006, s 151(1)(b).   [1513] CA 2006, s 151(1)(c).   [1514] CA 2006 s 151(2).
[1515] CA 2006, s 151(3).

Exercise of rights where shares held on behalf of others: exercise in different ways

7.44 Under s 152 of the CA 2006 where a member holds shares in a company on behalf of more than one person, rights attached to the shares;[1516] and rights under any enactment exercisable by virtue of holding the shares, need not all be exercised, and if exercised, need not all be exercised in the same way.[1517]

A member who exercises such rights but does not exercise all his rights, must inform the company to what extent he is exercising the rights.[1518]

A member who exercises such rights in different ways must inform the company of the ways in which he is exercising them and to what extent they are exercised in each way.[1519]

If a member exercises such rights without informing the company that he is not exercising all his rights;[1520] or that he is exercising his rights in different ways,[1521] the company is entitled to assume that he is exercising all his rights and is exercising them in the same way.

The objective of s 152 of the CA 2006 is to provide that a member can choose to split his holding and exercise rights attached to shares in different ways. This is to accommodate members who hold shares on behalf of more than one person, each of whom may want to exercise rights attaching to their shares in different ways. For example, it enables votes to be cast in different ways. Section 152(4) of the CA 2006 provides that if the member does not make it clear to the company in what way he is exercising his rights, the company can assume that all rights are being dealt with in the same way.

Exercise of rights where shares held on behalf of others: members' requests

7.45 Section 153 of the CA 2006 applies for the purposes of the following sections:

(a)   s 314 of the CA 2006 (power to require circulation of statements);[1522]

(b)   s 338 of the CA 2006 (public companies: power to require circulation of resolutions for AGM);[1523]

(c)   s 342 of the CA 2006 (power to require independent reports on polls);[1524] and

(d)   s 527 of the CA 2006 (power to require website publication of audit concerns).[1525]

[1516] CA 2006, s 152(1)(a).   [1517] CA 2006, s 152(1)(b).   [1518] CA 2006, s 152(2).
[1519] CA 2006, s 152(3).   [1520] CA 2006, s 152(4)(a).   [1521] CA 2006, s 152(4)(b).
[1522] CA 2006, s 153(1)(a).   [1523] CA 2006, s 153(1)(b).   [1524] CA 2006, s 153(1)(c).
[1525] CA 2006, s 153(1)(d).

A company is required to act under any of those sections if it receives a request in relation to which the following conditions are met: it is made by at least 100 persons;[1526] and it is authenticated by all the persons making it;[1527] and in the case of any of those persons is not a member of the company, it is accompanied by a statement of the full name and address of a person (the member) who is a member of the company and holds shares on behalf of that person;[1528] that the member is holding those shares on behalf of that person in the course of business;[1529] of the number of shares in the company that the member holds on behalf of that person;[1530] of the total amount paid up on those shares;[1531] that those shares are not held on behalf of anyone else or, if they are, that the other person or persons are not among the other persons making the request;[1532] that some or all of those shares confer voting rights that are relevant for the purposes of making a request under the section in question;[1533] and that the person has the right to instruct the member how to exercise those rights.[1534]

In the case of any of those persons who is a member of the company, it is accompanied by a statement that he holds shares otherwise than on behalf of another person;[1535] or that he holds shares on behalf of one or more other persons but those persons are not among the other persons making the request;[1536] it is accompanied by such evidence as the company may reasonably require of the matters mentioned in paras (c) and (d);[1537] the total amount of the sums paid up on shares held as mentioned in para (c);[1538] and shares held as mentioned in para (d),[1539]divided by the number of persons making the request, is not less than £100; the request complies with any other requirements of the section in question as to contents, timing and otherwise.[1540]

Section 153 of the CA 2006 deals with four situations where the shareholder threshold required to trigger a right is 100 shareholders holding £100 each on average of paid-up capital. Indirect investors are able to count towards the total, subject to certain conditions being met, intended to ensure that only genuine indirect investors are allowed to count towards the total, that the same shares cannot be used twice and that the indirect investors' contractual arrangements with the member allow the former to give voting instructions.

[1526] CA 2006, s 153(2)(a).   [1527] CA 2006, s 153((2)(b).   [1528] CA 2006, s 153(2)(c)(i).
[1529] CA 2006, s 153(2)(c)(ii).   [1530] CA 2006, s 153(2)(c)(iii).
[1531] CA 2006, s 153(2)(c)(iv).   [1532] CA 2006, s 153(2)(c)(v).
[1533] CA 2006, s 152(2)(c)(vi).   [1534] CA 2006, s 153(2)(c)(viii).
[1535] CA 2006, s 153(2)(d)(i).   [1536] CA 2006, s 153(2)(d)(ii).   [1537] CA 2006, s 153(2)(e).
[1538] CA 2006, s 153(2)(f)(i).   [1539] CA 2006, s 153(2)(f)(ii).   [1540] CA 2006, s 153(2)(g).

Unfair Prejudice

Protection of members against unfair prejudice

7.46 Part 30 of the CA 2006 sets out the provisions for the protection of members against unfair prejudice. It comprises six sections. Sections 994–998 of the CA 2006 restate ss 459, 460 and 461 of the CA 1985, which provide a remedy where a company's affairs are being conducted in a manner which is unfairly prejudicial to the interests of its members.

Over the years, the courts in the UK have been concerned to protect the interests of minority shareholders and ensure that the majority shareholders do not usurp the powers of the company for their own purpose and benefit. One effective remedy for minority shareholders has been the use of ss 459–461 of the CA 1985. Section 459 of the CA 1985 provided a remedy for a shareholder where a company's affairs were being conducted in a manner that was unfairly prejudicial to the interests of its members generally, or some part of its members including the shareholder.

Some of common allegations that have been made under s 459 of the CA 1985 have included:

(a)   misappropriation or diversion of corporate assets;
(b)   failure to provide or disclose information;
(c)   improper increases of share capital; and/or excessive remuneration, and non-payment (or payment) of inadequate dividends.

A shareholder was required to demonstrate there had been unfairly prejudicial conduct. Once this has been established, the court had a wide discretion to consider the remedies available under s 461 of the CA 1985. This provided that the court could make such order as it thought fit for giving relief in respect of the matters of which the petitioner complained.

Before the enactment of s 210 of the CA 1948 (the pre-cursor to s 459 of the CA 1985), a minority shareholder was usually unable to obtain redress from the courts to prevent majority shareholders from acting in an 'oppressive' manner. The courts could, however, apply the remedy of winding up the company on just and equitable grounds, but this remedy was considered too draconian, and was only used in very limited circumstances.

The development of s 210 of the CA 1948 owed its origins to the Cohen Committee report in 1945. The Cohen Committee drew attention to the need to strengthen the position of those entitled to a minority shareholding, where directors refused to register a transfer of shares and where directors received an undue proportion of profit by way of directors' remuneration, thereby depriving shareholders of dividends. The Committee considered the position of the minority shareholders in resisting oppression by majority shareholders, usually in private companies. It concluded that winding up a company would not necessarily benefit minority shareholders, as the break-up value of the assets may be small, or the only available purchaser may be the majority whose oppression has driven the minority to seek redress. It recommended that the court should have the power to impose upon the parties to a dispute whatever settlement the court considered just and equitable. The court must have unfettered discretion.

As a result of the Committee's recommendation, s 9 of the Companies Act 1947 was enacted (which later became s 210 of the CA 1948). There were not may reported cases on s 210, and the matter fell to be considered by the Jenkins Committee in 1962, which drew attention to a number of defects in s 210 and proposed several changes in the law. Its recommendations formed the basis of what was eventually enacted as s 75 of the Companies Act 1980 which later became s 459 of the CA 1985.

Petition by company member

7.47 Section 994 of the CA 2006 sets out the petition by a company member, thereby ensuring the locus standi for a member to bring an action. A member of a company may apply to the court by petition for an order under Part 30 of the CA 2006 on the ground:

(a)   that the company's affairs are being or have been conducted in a manner that is unfairly prejudicial to the interests of members generally, or of some part of its members (including at least himself);[1541] or

(b)   that an actual or proposed act or omission of the company (including an act or omission on its behalf) is or would be so prejudicial.[1542]

These provisions restate s 459(1) of the CA 1985.

The provisions of Part 30 of the CA 2006 also apply to a person who is not a member of a company, but to whom shares in the company have been transferred or transmitted by operation of law, as they apply to a member of a company.[1543]

This provision restates s 459(2) of the CA 1985.

In s 994 of the CA 2006, and so far as applicable for the purposes of this section in the other provisions of Part 30 of the CA 2006, the term 'company' means a company within the meaning of of the CA 2006;[1544] or a company that is not such a company but is a statutory water company within the meaning of the Statutory Water Companies Act 1991 (c 58).[1545]

This provision restates s 459(3) of the CA 1985.

[1541] CA 2006, s 994(1)(a).   [1542] CA 2006, s 994(1)(b).   [1543] CA 2006, s 994(2).
[1544] CA 2006, s 994(3)(a).   [1545] CA 2006, s 994(3)(b).

Petition by Secretary of State

7.48 Section 995 of the CA 2006 sets out the petition by the Secretary of State. It applies to a company in respect of which:

(a) the Secretary of State has received a report under s 437 of the CA 1985 (c 6) (inspector's report);[1546]

(b) the Secretary of State has exercised his powers under s 447 or s 448 of the CA 1985 (powers to require documents and information or to enter and search premises);[1547]

(c) the Secretary of State or the Financial Services Authority has exercised his or its powers under Part 11 of the Financial Services and Markets Act 2000 (c 8) (information gathering and investigations);[1548] or

(d) the Secretary of State has received a report from an investigator appointed by him or the Financial Services Authority under that Part.[1549]

If it appears to the Secretary of State that in the case of such a company, that the company's affairs are being or have been conducted in a manner that is unfairly prejudicial to the interests of members generally or of some part of its members;[1550] or an actual or proposed act or omission of the company (including an act or omission on its behalf) is or would be so prejudicial,[1551] he may apply to the court by petition for an order under this Part.

This provision restates s 460(1) and (1A) of the CA 1985.

The Secretary of State may do this in addition to, or instead of, presenting a petition for the winding up of the company.[1552]

In this s 995 of the CA 2006, and so far as applicable for the purposes of this section in the other provisions of Part 30 of the CA 2006, the term 'company' means any body corporate that is liable to be wound up under the Insolvency Act 1986 (c 45) or the Insolvency (Northern Ireland) Order 1989 (SI 1989/2405 (NI 19)).[1553] This means the provision restates s 460(2) of the CA 1985 but also extends now to Northern Ireland.

Powers of the court under this Part

7.49 Section 996 of the CA 2006 sets out the powers of the court to make an order(s). If the court is satisfied that a petition under Part 30 of the CA 2006 is well-founded, it may make such order as it thinks fit for giving relief in respect of the matters complained of.[1554]

[1546] CA 2006, s 995(1)(a).   [1547] CA 2006, s 995(1)(b).   [1548] CA 2006, s 995(1)(c).
[1549] CA 2006, s 995(1)(d).   [1550] CA 2006, s 995(2)(a).   [1551] CA 2006, s 995(2)(b).
[1552] CA 2006, s 995(3).   [1553] CA 2006, s 995(4).   [1554] CA 2006, s 996(1).

Without prejudice to the generality of s 996(1) of the CA 2006, the court's order may provide any of the following:

(a)   regulate the conduct of the company's affairs in the future;[1555]
(b)   require the company:

    (i)   to refrain from doing or continuing an act complained of;[1556] or
    (ii)   to perform an act that the petitioner has complained it has omitted to perform;[1557]

(c)   authorise civil proceedings to be brought in the name and on behalf of the company by such person or persons and on such terms as the court may direct;[1558]
(d)   require the company not to make any, or any specified, alterations in its articles without the leave of the court;[1559]
(e)   provide for the purchase of the shares of any members of the company by other members or by the company itself and, in the case of a purchase by the company itself, the reduction of the company's capital accordingly.[1560]

Supplementary provisions

7.50 Section 996 of the CA 2006 restates much of s 461 of the CA 1985, re-organised for the purpose of clarity. Under s 996(d) of the CA 2006, there is now no reference to the Memorandum of Association as the latter cannot now be amended.

Application of general rule-making powers

7.51 Section 997 of the CA 2006 deals with the application of general rule-making powers. The power to make rules under s 411 of the Insolvency Act 1986 (c 45) or Article 359 of the Insolvency (Northern Ireland) Order 1989 (SI 1989/2405 (NI 19)), so far as relating to a winding-up petition, applies for the purposes of a petition under Part 30 of the CA 2006.

This section restates s 461(6) of the CA 1985, but now also extends to Northern Ireland.

Copy of order affecting company's constitution to be delivered to registrar

7.52 Section 998 of the CA 2008 is concerned with the copy of the order affecting the company's constitution to be delivered to the registrar. Where

---

[1555] CA 2006, s 996(2)(a).   [1556] CA 2006, s 996(2)(b)(i).   [1557] CA 2006, s 996(2)(b)(ii).
[1558] CA 2006, s 996(2)(c).   [1559] CA 2006, s 996(2)(d).   [1560] CA 2006, s 996(2)(e).

an order of the court under Part 30 of the CA 2006 alters the company's constitution;[1561] or gives leave for the company to make any, or any specified, alterations to its constitution,[1562] the company must deliver a copy of the order to the registrar.

It must do so within 14 days from the making of the order, or such longer period as the court may allow.[1563]

If a company defaults in complying with this section, an offence is committed by the company;[1564] and every officer of the company who is in default.[1565] A person guilty of an offence under this section is liable on summary conviction to a fine not exceeding level 3 on the standard scale and, for continued contravention, a daily default fine not exceeding one-tenth of level 3 on the standard scale.[1566]

Supplementary provisions where company's constitution altered

7.53 Section 999 of the CA 2006 applies where an order under this Part alters a company's constitution.[1567]

If the order amends a company's articles;[1568] or any resolution or agreement to which Chapter 3 of Part 3 applies (resolution or agreement affecting a company's constitution),[1569] the copy of the order delivered to the registrar by the company under s 998 of the CA 2006 must be accompanied by a copy of the company's articles, or the resolution or agreement in question, as amended. Every copy of a company's articles issued by the company after the order is made must be accompanied by a copy of the order, unless the effect of the order has been incorporated into the articles by amendment.[1570]

If a company defaults in complying with this section an offence is committed by the company;[1571] and every officer of the company who is in default.[1572] A person guilty of an offence under this section is liable on summary conviction to a fine not exceeding level 3 on the standard scale.[1573]

Section 999 of the CA 2006 is a new section. It ensures that, if the court makes an order under Part 30 of the CA 2006 amending the company's articles, the updated articles must be registered and a copy of the court order supplied with any copies of the articles that are issued by the company, unless they already incorporate the amendments.

[1561] CA 2006, s 998(1)(a).   [1562] CA 2006, s 998(1)(b).   [1563] CA 2006, s 998(2).
[1564] CA 2006, s 998(3)(a).   [1565] CA 2006, s 998(3)(b).   [1566] CA 2006, s 998(4).
[1567] CA 2006, s 999(1).   [1568] CA 2006, s 999(2)(a).   [1569] CA 2006, s 999(2)(b).
[1570] CA 2006, s 999(3).   [1571] CA 2006, s 999(4)(a).   [1572] CA 2006, s 999(4)(b).
[1573] CA 2006, s 999(5).

Chapter 8

Directors: Appointment and Removal

Introduction

8.1 Chapter 1 of Part 10 of the CA 2006 is concerned with the appointment and removal of directors. It sets out the requirements to have directors; qualification for appointment; the register of directors; and the procedure for removal.

Part 10 of the CA 2006 also comprises provisions on directors' duties and specific duties and liabilities of directors considered in subsequent chapters. It replaces Part 10 of the CA 1985 (enforcement of fair dealing by directors), as well as the provisions relating to directors in Part 9 of the CA 1985 and the provisions relating to confidentiality orders in Part 25 of the CA 1985. The CA 2006 also introduces the statutory statement of directors' general duties to the company, following recommendations of the Law Commissions of England and Wales and Scotland, which were largely accepted by the Government.

Who is a director?

8.2 Section 250 of the CA 2006 defines a director as any person occupying the position of director, by whatever name called. This is the same as the definition that was contained in s 741(1) of the CA 1985. The CA 2006 does not attempt a more detailed definition of a director, because it is important to ensure that the term is applied to anybody who exercises real power within the company, particularly in relation to decision taking. The term 'director' includes:

(a) an executive director who has been properly appointed by the company;
(b) a non-executive director who has been properly appointed by the company;
(c) a de facto director (that is, a person who has assumed the status and functions of a company director even though he has not been properly appointed).

A 'shadow director' is defined by section 251(1) of the CA 2006 as 'a person in accordance with whose directions or instructions the directors of the company are accustomed to act. A person is not to be regarded as a shadow director by reason only that the directors act on advice given by him in a professional capacity'.[1574] This is the same as the definition previously contained in s 741(2) of the CA 1985.

Powers of directors

8.3 Part 10 of the CA 2006 does not generally directly give powers to the directors, but, under the model Articles of Association for private companies limited by shares, the directors' functions are to manage the company's business; and to exercise all the powers of the company for any purpose connected with managing the company's business.

Appointment of directors

Companies required to have directors

8.4 Section 154 of the CA 2006 sets out the requirement to have company directors. A private company must have at least one director.[1575] A public company must have at least two directors.[1576]

Section 154 of the CA 2006 replaces s 282 of the CA 1985.[1577] It distinguishes between private and public companies. It retains the requirement for a private company to have at least one director and requires all public companies to have at least two. There will no longer be an exception for public companies registered before 1 November 1929 (or before 1 January 1933 in Northern Ireland).

Companies required to have at least one director who is a natural person

8.5 Section 155 of the CA 2006 states that a company must have at least one director who is a natural person.[1578] This requirement will be met if the office of director is held by a natural person as a corporation sole, or otherwise by virtue of an office.[1579]

Section 155 of the CA 2006 is a new provision. It introduces a requirement

---

[1574] CA 2006, s 251(2).   [1575] CA 2006, s 154(1).   [1576] CA 2006, s 154(2).

[1577] CA 1985, s 282(1) stated that every company registered on or after 1 November 1929 (other than a private company) must have at least two directors. Every company registered before that date (other than a private company) must have at least one director: CA 1985, s 282(2). Every private company must have at least one director: CA 1985, s 282(3).

[1578] CA 2006, s 155(1).   [1579] CA 2006, s 155(2).

that every company have at least one director who is a natural person, that is, an individual. Subject to this requirement being satisfied, any legal person, including a company, can be a director, but one company cannot be sole director of another company.

Section 155(2) of the CA 2006 states that the only director may be a corporation sole (for example, the Archbishop of Canterbury), or someone appointed on the basis of some other appointment that they hold.

Direction requiring company to make appointment

8.6 The powers of the Secretary of State to make a direction requiring a company to make an appointment of director is governed by s 156 of the CA 2006. Where it appears to the Secretary of State that a company is in breach of s 154 of the CA 2006 (requirements as to the number of directors), or s 155 of the CA 2006 (requirement to have at least one director who is a natural person), the Secretary of State may give the company a direction under this section.[1580] The direction must specify the statutory requirement the company appears to be in breach of;[1581] what the company must do in order to comply with the direction;[1582] and the period within which it must do so.[1583] The period must not be less than one month or more than three months after the date on which the direction is given.[1584]

The direction must also inform the company of the consequences of failing to comply.[1585]

Where the company is in breach of ss 154 or 155 of the CA 2006, it must comply with the direction by making the necessary appointment or appointments;[1586] and giving notice of them under s 167 of the CA 2006[1587] before the end of the period specified in the direction.

If the company has already made the necessary appointment or appointments (or so far as it has done so), it must comply with the direction by giving notice of them under s 167 of the CA 2006 before the end of the period specified in the direction.[1588]

If the company fails to comply with a direction, an offence will be committed by the company;[1589] and every officer of the company who is in default.[1590] A shadow director will be treated as an officer of the company for the purposes of this section.[1591] A person guilty of an offence is liable on summary conviction to a fine not exceeding level 5 on the standard scale and, for continued contravention a daily default fine not exceeding one-tenth of level 5 on the standard scale.[1592]

[1580] CA 2006, s 156(1). [1581] CA 2006, s 156(2)(a). [1582] CA 2006, s 156(2)(b).
[1583] CA 2006, s 156(2)(c). [1584] CA 2006, s 156(2). [1585] CA 2006, s 156(3).
[1586] CA 2006, s 156(4)(a). [1587] CA 2006, s 156(4)(b). [1588] CA 2006, s 156(5).
[1589] CA 2006, s 156(6)(a). [1590] CA 2006, s 156(6)(b). [1591] CA 2006, s 156(6).
[1592] CA 2006, s 156(7).

Section 156 of the CA 2006 is a new provision, enabling enforcement of the existing requirement for a private company to have at least one director and a public company to have at least two directors, and the new requirement for every company to have at least one director who is an individual. Where it appears to the Secretary of State that one of these requirement is not met, the Secretary of State will be able to direct the company to comply by issuing a notice. It will be an offence not to comply.

Appointment

Minimum age for appointment as director

8.7 Section 157 of the CA 2006 sets out the requirements and eligibility for directorship. A person may not be appointed a director of a company unless he has attained the age of 16 years.[1593] This does not affect the validity of an appointment that is not to take effect until the person appointed attains that age.[1594]

Where the office of a director of a company is held by a corporation sole, or otherwise by virtue of another office, the appointment to that other office of a person who has not attained the age of 16 years, is not effective also to make him a director of the company until he attains the age of 16 years.[1595]

Any appointment made in contravention of s 157 of the CA 2006 is void.[1596]

However, nothing in s 157 of the CA 2006 affects any liability of a person under any provision of the Companies Acts, if he purports to act as director;[1597] or acts as shadow director[1598] although he could not, by virtue of s 157 of the CA 2006, be validly appointed as a director.

Section 157 of the CA 2006 is, however, subject to s 158 of the CA 2006 (power to provide for exceptions from minimum age requirement).[1599]

Section 157 of the CA 2006 is a new provision. It introduces a minimum age of 16 for a natural person to be a director. Section 157(2) of the CA 2006 states that prohibition will not prevent the appointment of a younger person, provided it is not to take effect until that person is 16 years old. Section 157(3) of the CA 2006 provides that the age limit applies even when the director's appointment is a consequence of some other appointment. This prohibition on under-age directors does not provide protection from criminal prosecution or civil liability, if he or she were to act as director, i.e. as de facto director, or if the company's directors usually act on that young person's instructions.

[1593] CA 2006, s 157(1).   [1594] CA 2006, s 157(2).   [1595] CA 2006, s 157(3).
[1596] CA 2006, s 157(4).   [1597] CA 2006, s 157(5)(a).   [1598] CA 2006, s 157(5)(b).
[1599] CA 2006, s 157(6).

Power to provide for exceptions from minimum age requirement

8.8 Section 158 of the CA 2006 provides for certain exceptions to s 157 of the CA 2006.

The Secretary of State may make provision by regulations for cases in which a person who has not attained the age of 16 years, may be appointed a director of a company.[1600]

The regulations must specify the circumstances in which, and any conditions subject to which, the appointment may be made.[1601] If the specified circumstances cease to obtain, or any specified conditions cease to be met, a person who was appointed by virtue of the regulations, and who has not since attained the age of 16 years, ceases to hold office.[1602]

The regulations may also make different provision for different parts of the United Kingdom. This is without prejudice to the general power to make different provision for different cases.[1603]

Any regulations made under s 158 of the CA 2006 are subject to negative resolution procedure.[1604]

Section 158 of the CA 2006 is a new provision. It provides for an exception from the prohibition in s 157 of the CA 2006 on anyone under 16 being appointed a director of a company. It provides a power for the Secretary of State to make regulations specifying circumstances in which a younger person may be a director. The regulations may differ for different parts of the United Kingdom.

Existing under-age directors

8.9 Section 159 of the CA 2006 is concerned with existing under-age directors. It applies where a person appointed a director of a company before s 157 of the CA 2006 (minimum age for appointment as director) comes into force, has not attained the age of 16 when that section comes into force;[1605] or the office of a director of a company is held by a corporation sole, or otherwise by virtue of another office, and the person appointed to that other office has not attained the age of 16 years when that section comes into force;[1606] and the matter is not one excepted from that section by regulations under s 158 of the CA 2006.[1607]

The effect is that the person ceases to be a director on s 157 of the CA 2006 coming into force.[1608]

The company must make the necessary consequential alteration in its register of directors, but need not give notice to the registrar of the change.[1609]

[1600] CA 2006, s 158(1). [1601] CA 2006, s 158(3). [1602] CA 2006, s 158(3).
[1603] CA 2006, s 158(4). [1604] CA 2006, s 158(5). [1605] CA 2006, s 159(1)(a).
[1606] CA 2006, s 159(1)(b). [1607] CA 2006, s 159(1). [1608] CA 2006, s 159(2).
[1609] CA 2006, s 159(3).

If it appears to the registrar (from other information) that a person has ceased by virtue of this section to be a director of a company, the registrar must note that fact on the register.[1610]

Section 159 of the CA 2006 is a transitional provision. Section 159(2) and (3) of the CA 2006 provides that where a person under 16 has been appointed as director (or holds the office of director by virtue of another office or is a corporation sole), prior to the prohibition on under-age directors coming into force, that person will cease to be a director when the prohibition in s 157 of the CA 2006 comes into force. Section 159(3) of the CA 2006 makes it the company's responsibility to amend its register of directors accordingly, but the company is not required to notify the registrar of the change. Section 159(4) of the CA 2006 gives the registrar power to amend the register without a notification by the company of the director's removal, but rather on the basis of information already held (i.e. the date of birth as provided when the appointment is notified).

Appointment of directors of public company to be voted on individually

8.10 Section 160 of the CA 2006 states that at a general meeting of a public company, a motion for the appointment of two or more persons as directors of the company by a single resolution, must not be made, unless a resolution that it should be so made has first been agreed to by the meeting without any vote being given against it.[1611]

A resolution moved in contravention of s 160 of the CA 2006 will be void, whether or not its being so moved was objected to at the time. But where a resolution so moved is passed, no provision for the automatic reappointment of retiring directors in default of another appointment applies.[1612]

For the purposes of s 160 of the CA 2006, a motion for approving a person's appointment, or for nominating a person for appointment, is treated as a motion for his appointment.[1613] It is further provided that nothing in s 160 of the CA 2006 applies to a resolution altering the company's articles.[1614]

Section 160 of the CA 2006 restates s 292 of the CA 1985: the appointment of each proposed director of a public company must be voted on individually, unless there is unanimous agreement to a block resolution. Without such consent, any appointment of a director that is not voted on individually is void. This section ensures that members can express their disapproval of any particular director without having to reject the entire board.

[1610] CA 2006, s 159(4).   [1611] CA 2006, s 160(1).   [1612] CA 2006, s 160(1).
[1613] CA 2006, s 160(3).   [1614] CA 2006, s 160(4).

Validity of acts of directors

8.11 The validity of acts of directors is governed by s 161 of the CA 2006. The acts of a person acting as a director are valid, notwithstanding that it is afterwards discovered that the following situations apply:

(a)   that there was a defect in his appointment;[1615]
(b)   that he was disqualified from holding office;[1616]
(c)   that he has ceased to hold office;[1617]
(d)   that he was not entitled to vote on the matter in question.[1618]

The above applies even if the resolution for his appointment is void under s 160 of the CA 2006.[1619]

Section 161 of the CA 2006, which replaces s 285 of the CA 1985,[1620] provides that a director's actions are valid even if his or her appointment is subsequently found to have been defective or void.

Register of directors

8.12 Section 162 of the CA 2006 deals with the register of directors. It states that every company must keep a register of directors.[1621] The register must contain the required particulars (see ss 163, 164 and 166 of the CA 2006) of each person who is a director of the company.[1622] The register must be kept available for inspection at the company's registered office;[1623] or at a place specified in regulations under s 1136 of the CA 2006.[1624]

The company must give notice to the registrar of the place at which the register is kept available for inspection;[1625] and of any change in that place,[1626] unless it has at all times been kept at the company's registered office.

The register must be open to the inspection of any member of the company without charge;[1627] and of any other person on payment of such fee as may be prescribed.[1628]

If a default is made in complying with s 162(1), (2) or (3) of the CA 2006, or if an inspection required under this section is refused, an offence will be committed by the company;[1629] and every officer of the company who is in default. A shadow director is treated as an officer of the company for the

---

[1615] CA 2006, s 161(1)(a).   [1616] CA 2006, s 161(1)(b).   [1617] CA 2006, s 161(1)(c).
[1618] CA 2006, s 161(1)(d).   [1619] CA 2006, s 160(2).
[1620] CA 1985, s 285 stated that the acts of a director or manager are valid notwithstanding any defect that may afterwards be discovered in his appointment or qualification; and this provision is not excluded by CA 1985, s 292(2) (void resolution to appoint).
[1621] CA 2006, s 162(1).   [1622] CA 2006, s 162(2).   [1623] CA 2006, s 162(3)(a).
[1624] CA 2006, s 162(3)(b).   [1625] CA 2006, s 162(4)(a).   [1626] CA 2006, s 162(4)(b).
[1627] CA 2006, s 162(5)(a).   [1628] CA 2006, s 162(5)(b).   [1629] CA 2006, s 162(6)(a).

purposes of this section.[1630] A person guilty of an offence is liable on summary conviction to a fine not exceeding level 5 on the standard scale and, for continued contravention, a daily default fine not exceeding one-tenth of level 5 on the standard scale.[1631]

Where there is a refusal of inspection of the register, the court may by order compel an immediate inspection of it.[1632]

Section 162 of the CA 2006 replaces part of s 288 of the CA 1985. It imposes on every company a requirement to keep a register of its directors (secretaries are dealt with in Part 12 of the CA 2006). This register need not contain particulars of shadow directors.

This section requires the register to be kept available for inspection either at the company's registered office, or at a place specified in regulations made under s 1136 of the CA 2006. It must be available for inspection by members (without charge) or the public (for a prescribed fee, set under powers provided under s 1137 of the CA 2006). Refusal to permit inspection is an offence. In addition, the court may compel immediate inspection if the company has refused.

Particulars of directors to be registered: individuals

8.13 Section 163 of the CA 2006 deals with particulars of directors (individual) that must be registered. A company's register of directors must contain the following particulars in the case of an individual:

- name and any former name;[1633]
- a service address;[1634]
- the country or state (or part of the United Kingdom) in which he is usually resident;[1635]
- nationality;[1636]
- business occupation (if any);[1637]
- date of birth.[1638]

The term 'name' means a person's Christian name (or other forename), and surname, except in the case of a peer;[1639] or an individual usually known by a title.[1640] In this case, the title may be stated instead of his Christian name (or other forename) and surname or in addition to either or both of them.[1641]

The term a 'former name' means a name by which the individual was

---

[1630] CA 2006, s 162(6)(b).   [1631] CA 2006, s 162(7).   [1632] CA 2006, s 162(8).
[1633] CA 2006, s 163(1)(a).   [1634] CA 2006, s 163(1)(b).   [1635] CA 2006, s 163(1)(c).
[1636] CA 2006, s 163(1)(d).   [1637] CA 2006, s 163(1)(e).   [1638] CA 2006, s 163(1)(f).
[1639] CA 2006, s 163(2)(a).   [1640] CA 2006, s 163(2)(b).   [1641] CA 2006, s 163(2).

formerly known for business purposes. Where a person is or was formerly known by more than one such name, each of them must be stated.[1642]

However, it is not necessary for the register to contain particulars of a former name in the following circumstances:

- in the case of a peer or an individual normally known by a British title, where the name is one by which the person was known previous to the adoption of or succession to the title;[1643]
- in the case of any person, where the former name was changed or disused before the person attained the age of 16 years;[1644] or has been changed or disused for 20 years or more.[1645]

A person's service address may be stated to be 'The company's registered office'.[1646]

Section 163 of the CA 2006 replaces s 289 of the CA 1985 so far as it applies to individuals. It specifies the particulars that must be entered on the register of directors for each director who is an individual (as opposed to a company or similar entity). One of the most significant changes is the requirement for companies to provide a service address for a director rather than (as in the of the CA 1985), the director's usual residential address.[1647] A director may give the company's registered office as his or her service address, however, this will not be apparent from the public record. Further, in fulfill-ment of a Government commitment given in March 1998, the particulars no longer include details of other directorships held. There are also changes to the requirement to provide the director's name. The requirement is now to include any name by which the individual is or was formerly known for business purposes. As recommended by the Company Law Review Group in its *Final Report*,[1648] there is no longer an exception for a married woman's former name. However, the section retains a protective provision relating to the former names of peers.

Particulars of directors to be registered: corporate directors and firms

8.14 Section 164 of the CA 2006 deals with the particulars of directors to be registered with respect to corporate directors and firms. A company's register of directors must contain the following particulars, in the case of a body corporate, or a firm that is a legal person under the law by which it is governed:

[1642] CA 2006, s 163(3).   [1643] CA 2006, s 163(4)(a).   [1644] CA 2006, s 163(4)(b)(i).
[1645] CA 2006, s 163(4)(b)(ii).   [1646] CA 2006, s 163(5).
[1647] See further Chapter 3 on company formation.
[1648] *Final Report*, para 11.38.

- corporate or firm name;[1649]
- registered or principal office;[1650]
- in the case of an EEA company to which the First Company Law Directive applies, particulars of: (i) the register in which the company file mentioned in Article 3 of that Directive is kept (including details of the relevant state);[1651] and (ii) the registration number in that register;[1652] and
- in any other case, particulars of the legal form of the company or firm and the law by which it is governed;[1653] and if applicable, the register in which it is entered (including details of the state), and the registration number in that register.[1654]

Section 164 of the CA 2006 replaces s 289(1)(b) of the CA 2006. It retains the requirement for the corporate or firm name and the registered or principal office to be recorded, where the director is either a body corporate or a firm that is a legal person. In addition, as recommended by the Company Law Review Group in its *Final Report*,[1655] it requires for EEA companies the register where the company is registered and its registration number; for all others, particulars of the legal form of the company or firm, the law by which it is governed, and if applicable where it is registered and its registration number.

Register of directors' residential addresses

8.15 Section 165 of the CA 2006 is concerned with register of directors' residential addresses. Every company is required to keep a register of directors' residential addresses.[1656] The register must state the usual residential address of each of the company's directors.[1657] If a director's service address (as stated in the company's register of directors) is his usual residential address, the register of directors' residential addresses need only contain an entry to that effect. However, this does not apply if his service address is stated to be 'The company's registered office'.[1658] If default is made in complying with this section, an offence will be committed by the company;[1659] and every officer of the company who is in default.[1660] A person guilty of an offence is liable on summary conviction to a fine not exceeding level 5 on the standard scale and, for continued contravention, a daily default fine not exceeding one-tenth of level 5 on the standard scale.[1661]

[1649] CA 2006, s 164(a).   [1650] CA 2006, s 164(b).   [1651] CA 2006, s 164(c)(i).
[1652] CA 2006, s 164(c)(ii).   [1653] CA 2006, s 164(d)(i).   [1654] CA 2006, s 164(d)(ii).
[1655] *Final Report*, para 11.38.   [1656] CA 2006, s 165(1).
[1657] CA 2006, s 165(2). See further Chapter 3 on company formation.
[1658] CA 2006, s 165(3).   [1659] CA 2006, s 165(4)(a).   [1660] CA 2006, s 165(4)(b).
[1661] CA 2006, s 165(5).

It is made clear that s 165 of the CA 2006 applies only to directors who are individuals, and not where the directors is a body corporate or a firm that is a legal person under the law by which it is governed.[1662]

This section is a new provision. It requires companies to keep a register of the usual residential addresses of directors who are individuals. As long as a director's service address is not the company's registered office, if his/her residential address is the same as his/her service address, then the register need only contain an entry making that clear. The register is not to be open to public inspection, but can be used in accordance with Chapter 8 of Part 10 of the CA 2006.

Particulars of directors to be registered: power to make regulations

8.16 Section 166 of the CA 2006 states that the Secretary of State may make provision by regulations amending s 163 of the CA 2006 (particulars of directors to be registered: individuals); s 164 of the CA 2006 (particulars of directors to be registered: corporate directors and firms); or s 165 of the CA 2006 (register of directors' residential addresses), so as to add to or remove items from the particulars required to be contained in a company's register of directors or register of directors' residential addresses.[1663] Any regulations under this section are subject to affirmative resolution procedure.[1664]

Section 166 of the CA 2006 is a new provision. It provides the Secretary of State with the power to make regulations that add or remove items from the particulars that have to be entered in a company's register of directors and register of directors' residential addresses.

Duty to notify registrar of changes

8.17 The duty to notify the registrar of changes is set out in s 167 of the CA 2006. A company must, within a period of 14 days from the occurrence of any change in its directors (that is, a person becoming or ceasing to be a director);[1665] or any change in the particulars contained in its register of directors or its register of directors' residential addresses,[1666] give notice to the registrar of the change and of the date on which it occurred. The notice of a person having become a director of the company must contain a statement of the particulars of the new director that are required to be included in the company's register of directors and its register of directors' residential addresses;[1667] and must be accompanied by a consent, by that person, to act in that capacity.[1668]

[1662] CA 2006, s 165(6).   [1663] CA 2006, s 166(1).   [1664] CA 2006, s 166(2).
[1665] CA 2006, s 167(1)(a).   [1666] CA 2006, s 167(1)(b).   [1667] CA 2006, s 167(2)(a).
[1668] CA 2006, s 167(2)(b).

Where a company gives notice of a change of a director's service address as stated in the company's register of directors;[1669] and the notice is not accompanied by notice of any resulting change in the particulars contained in the company's register of directors' residential addresses,[1670] the notice must be accompanied by a statement that no such change is required.

If a default is made in complying, an offence will be committed by the company;[1671] and every officer of the company who is in default.[1672] A shadow director will be treated as an officer of the company.[1673] A person guilty of an offence is liable on summary conviction to a fine not exceeding level 5 on the standard scale and, for continued contravention, a daily default fine not exceeding one-tenth of level 5 on the standard scale.[1674]

Section 167 of the CA 2006 replaces s 288(2) of the CA 1985 so far as it applies to directors. It retains the requirement that the appointment of a director, or a director's ceasing to hold office, and any change in an existing director's particulars be notified to the registrar within 14 days; default is an offence. It also requires a notice of appointment to be accompanied by the appointee's consent. This provision ensures that the public record is kept up to date. There is also a requirement to notify the registrar of changes to information in the register of directors' residential addresses. However, this information is not open to public inspection at Companies House.

Removal

Resolution to remove director

8.18 The removal of a director is governed by s 168 of the CA 2006. A company may by ordinary resolution, at a meeting, remove a director before the expiration of his period of office, notwithstanding anything in any agreement between it and him.[1675]

Special notice is required of a resolution to remove a director under this section, or to appoint somebody instead of a director so removed at the meeting at which he is removed.[1676]

A vacancy created by the removal of a director, which, if not filled at the meeting at which he is removed, may be filled as a casual vacancy.[1677]

A person appointed director in place of a person removed under s 168 of the CA 2006 is treated, for the purpose of determining the time at which he or any other director is to retire, as if he had been a director on the day on which the person in whose place he is appointed was last appointed a director.[1678]

[1669] CA 2006, s 167(3)(a).   [1670] CA 2006, s 167(3)(b).   [1671] CA 2006, s 167(4)(a).
[1672] CA 2006, s 167(4)(b).   [1673] CA 2006, s 167(4).   [1674] CA 2006, s 167(5).
[1675] CA 2006, s 168(1).   [1676] CA 2006, s 168(2).   [1677] CA 2006, s 168(3).
[1678] CA 2006, s 168(4).

However, s 168 of the CA 2006 is not to be taken as depriving a person removed under it of compensation or damages payable to him in respect of the termination of his appointment as director, or of any appointment terminating with that as director;[1679] or as derogating from any power to remove a director that may exist apart from s 168 of the CA 2006.[1680]

Section 168 of the CA 2006 replaces s 303 of the CA 1985. Section 168(1) of the CA 2006 provides that an ordinary resolution is sufficient to remove a director, but requires that it be a meeting so as to ensure the director's right to be heard.

Director's right to protest removal

8.19 Section 169 of the CA 2006 is concerned with a director's right to protest removal from office. It deals with a director's right to be heard and invokes the concept of natural justice and fairness.

On receipt of notice of an intended resolution to remove a director under s 168 of the CA 2006, the company must forthwith send a copy of the notice to the director concerned.[1681] The director (whether or not a member of the company) is entitled to be heard on the resolution at the meeting.[1682] Where notice is given of an intended resolution to remove a director under section 168 of the CA 2006, and the director concerned makes with respect to it, representations in writing to the company (not exceeding a reasonable length), and requests their notification to members of the company, the company must, unless the representations are received by it too late for it to do so in any notice of the resolution given to members of the company, state the fact of the representations having been made;[1683] and send a copy of the representations to every member of the company to whom notice of the meeting is sent (whether before or after receipt of the representations by the company).[1684]

If a copy of the representations is not sent as required under s 169(3) of the CA 2006, because received too late, or because of the company's default, the director may (without prejudice to his right to be heard orally) require that the representations shall be read out at the meeting.[1685]

Copies of the representations need not be sent out, and the representations need not be read out at the meeting if, on the application either of the company or of any other person who claims to be aggrieved, the court is satisfied that the rights conferred by s 169 of the CA 2006 are being abused.[1686]

The court may order the company's costs (in Scotland, expenses) on an application under s 169(5) of the CA 2006, to be paid in whole or in part by the director, notwithstanding that he is not a party to the application.[1687]

[1679] CA 2006, s 168(5)(a).   [1680] CA 2006, s 168(5)(b).   [1681] CA 2006, s 169(1).
[1682] CA 2006, s 169(2).   [1683] CA 2006, s 169(3)(a).   [1684] CA 2006, s 169(3)(b).
[1685] CA 2006, s 169(4).   [1686] CA 2006, s 169(5).   [1687] CA 2006, s 169(6).

Section 169 of the CA 2006 replaces s 304 of the CA 1985. The only main change is in s 169(5) of the CA 2006, where the court need no longer be satisfied that the rights conferred by this section are being abused to secure needless publicity for defamatory matter, so long as it is satisfied that they are being abused.

Chapter 9

Directors: General Duties

Introduction

9.1 Traditionally, in the United Kingdom, directors' duties have been fragmented comprising regulatory and self-regulatory mechanisms. The regulatory approach, which ensured that directors complied with their duties and obligations, had been random, embracing fiduciary duties, the common law duty and statutory duties imposed on directors under various legislation including the CA 1985; the Company Directors' Disqualification Act 1986; the Insolvency Act 1986; and the Financial Services and Markets Act 2000. Although not binding, the self-regulatory mechanisms such as the UK Listing Rules and City Code on Takeovers and Mergers, ensured that corporate control and power were exercised responsibly in the interests of shareholders and stakeholders. Legally directors are obliged to act in the best interests of the company. The law ensures that the controllers within the corporation have the authority to act and make decisions on the company's behalf under the powers vested in them by the company's constitution and the authority delegated by shareholders to directors to conduct the day-to-day management of the company; that there are established governance structures setting out the hierarchy of decision making within corporations. Those who have the power to make decisions must do so within the confines of the authority under the company's constitution. Although case law on directors' duties is well established in the form of fiduciary and common law duties, the legal effectiveness of the corporate governance system was hindered where directors were not fully appraised of their legal obligations owing to the fragmented nature of directors' duties, which made it difficult for directors to clearly find and understand the law that applied to them.

This chapter considers directors' general duties, which have now been codified under the CA 2006. It explains by way of a background the fiduciary and common law duties of directors as established by case law. This chapter then proceeds to analyse the relationship between the case law and codification of directors' general duties. It also includes Ministerial statements on duties of company directors issued by the DTI in June 2007.

Fiduciary Duties

9.2 This section considers a background to directors' fiduciary duties in order to understand their application to the new general statutory duties.

In order to restrict the potential for abuse of power within the corporation, directors in exercising their powers are subject to a number of controls and restrictions imposed by statute (principally under the Companies Acts, the Insolvency Act 1986 and the Company Directors' Disqualification Act 1986), and by equity as well as common law. In law, directors are fiduciaries and agree or undertake to act for, or on behalf of, or in the best interests of the company where they have been appointed. Although company law does not specify the company's main objective, it is implicit in the duties exercised by directors, that they must maximise shareholder welfare. The company's interests are synonymous with the interests of shareholders. Directors must, therefore, primarily exercise their duties towards profit maximisation in an ethical manner, balanced against the need for corporate survival and to consider the wider stakeholders of the corporation.

Company law has not adequately addressed the position of corporate philanthropy or gratuitous distributions to employees, nor consider the interests of wider potential claimants on the corporation in any of the fiduciary duties towards suppliers, customers, creditors or the wider public. Curiously in UK company law, there has never been a wide debate on the 'trusteeship' of directors, compared to the position in USA with debates between Berle and Dodd in the 1930s. It did not create a 'social law' that would address the needs of wider potential claimants on the corporation. Judicial attitudes towards corporate philanthropy and directors having regard to the interests of other stakeholders varied, and usually fell within the ambit of the *ultra vires* doctrine.

There was a little recognition in case law that a company had a corporate conscience – that it had some obligations towards other stakeholders. A company was not required to discharge any corporate social responsibilities in society nor to behave as a good corporate citizen in society. In the UK, there was some negative perception that giant corporations wielded wide control and power with a single-minded pursuit of profit maximation as their only objective. Such corporations were perceived as 'soulless' – devoid of any interest in the stakeholders on the corporation. The large dispersion of shareholding in these large corporations meant that directors had wide control to manage the affairs of the company, without much accountability to the shareholders. The passive, voiceless and 'absentee' shareholders including other stakeholders made little impact in such corporations on holding directors to account.

Traditionally, however, English company law has upheld the profit maximisation principle within the corporate governance system. In *North-West*

Transportation v Beatty,[1688] the claimant, Henry Beatty, sued the company's directors, and claimed an order to set aside the sale made to the company by James Hughes Beatty, who was one of the directors, of his steamer, *The United Empire*, of which he was the owner before she was sold. Sir Richard Baggallay stated that the resolution of a majority of the shareholders, duly adopted, upon any question coming under the pinnacle of the company's mandate was binding upon the majority, and consequently upon the company. Further, every shareholder had a right to vote upon any such question, although he might have a personal interest in the subject matter opposed to, or different from, the general or particular interests of the company.

In respect of fiduciary duties, directors have owed the following duties to the company whose assets they are appointed to manage.

Duty to act in good faith

9.2.1 In exercising each of the powers conferred upon them by a company's constitution, directors act not on their own account but for the benefit of the company on whose behalf they are appointed to act. As fiduciaries, directors must act at all times *bona fide* in what they consider (not what a court may consider) to be in the best interests of the company: *Re Smith & Fawcett*.[1689] This is a subjective test that reflects the court of equity's reluctance to interfere with or second-guess the commercial judgments of directors. The term 'company' would clearly include shareholders collectively as a group. This is illustrated by *Percival v Wright*,[1690] where Swinfen Eady J contended that directors of a company did not normally stand in a fiduciary position towards their shareholders individually. *Percival* was concerned with shareholders who offered to sell their shares to the company's directors and chairman at a price of £12.50 per share. The directors and chairman, however, negotiated a higher price with a third party for the sale of those shares. Swinfen Eady stated: 'The true rule is that a shareholder is fixed with knowledge of all the directors' powers, and has no more reason to assume that they are not negotiating a sale of the undertaking than to assume that they are not exercising any other power.' In this case, the directors were under no obligation to disclose the negotiations which had taken place between themselves and the third party. There was no question of unfair dealing. Further, the directors did not approach the shareholders with a view to purchasing their shares. Instead, the shareholders approached the directors and named the price at which they would be prepared to sell their shares. The directors did not take any initiative to buy the shares.

A number of basic obligations are in practice imposed upon directors, who seek to comply with their duty to act in good faith in the best interests of the

---

[1688] (1887) 12 App. Cas. 589.   [1689] [1942] Ch 304.   [1690] [1902] 2 Ch 421.

company: When taking any decision concerning the management of a company, directors must positively apply their minds to the question of what are the interests of the company. If they fail to carry out the task, the courts may intervene and impugn the decision: *Inland Revenue Commissioners v Richmond*.[1691] The belief held by directors that a particular decision is in the best interests of the company must be a belief that is held honestly. A director must independently apply his mind to the interests of the company and exercise his discretion in accordance with those interests. A director must not fetter his discretion.

It is fundamental that directors act primarily in the interests of the company as a legal entity, rather than in the interests of shareholders. However, the general rule is that the interests of the company are synonymous with the interests of shareholders, as a general body, both present and future: *Greenhalgh v Arderne Cinemas Ltd*.[1692] Further, directors are required to balance a long-term view against short-term interests of present members: *Gaiman v National Association for Mental Health*.[1693]

The courts will inquire into directors' decisions and not into what a reasonable director would have done in the circumstances. In *Greenhalgh*, Evershed MR stated that the expression '*bona fide* for the benefit of the company as a whole' did not mean the company as a commercial entity distinct from the corporators: 'it means the corporators as a general body. That is to say, a case may be taken of an individual hypothetical member and it may be asked whether what is proposed is, in the honest opinion of those who vote in its favour, for that person's benefit.'

The expression '*bona fide* for the benefit of the company as a whole' has been applied inconsistently in the context of altering Articles of Association. This inconsistency was highlighted in the Australian case of *Peter's American Delicacy Co Ltd v Heath*.[1694] Dixon J stated that reliance upon the general doctrine that powers shall be exercised *bona fide* and for no bye or sinister purpose brings its own difficulties. The power of alteration was not fiduciary. The shareholders were not trustees for one another, and unlike directors, they did not occupy any fiduciary position nor were they under any fiduciary duties. Shareholders voted in respect of their shares, which are property, and the right to vote is attached to the share itself as an incident of property to be enjoyed and exercised for the owner's personal advantage. Dixon J stated that reference to 'benefit as a whole' was a very general expression ruling out purposes foreign to the company's operations, affairs and organisation. The expression 'company as a whole' referred to a corporate entity comprising all the shareholders.

The concept of 'good faith' has, therefore, been treated in the abstract. It is

---

[1691] [2003] All ER 123.   [1692] [1951] Ch 286.   [1693] [1971] Ch 317.
[1694] (1939) 61 CLR 457.

based on the presumption that directors, like parties to commercial contracts, will perform their contractual obligations in good faith, otherwise a breach will be established. In the context of company law and corporate governance, the concept of 'good faith' has a broader meaning which encompasses not only issues that concern protecting the interests of the company's financial position, but also in protecting the community's interests. Traditionally, English law has treated the concept of good faith only in the context of directors performing their obligations towards shareholders of their company, which however requires modification. It is possible to apply the concept of good faith in relation to an acceptable corporate governance system by emphasising its role in protecting the interests of shareholders.

The duty to act in the best interests of the company as a whole includes the interests of creditors: *West Mercia Safety Wear Ltd v Dodd*,[1695] and employees: see previously s 309 of the CA 1985; *Parke v Daily News*.[1696] In some exceptional circumstances, it is possible for directors to act in the best interests of individual shareholders: *Allen v Hyatt*.[1697] In *Allen v Hyatt*, the directors undertook to act as agents of their shareholders in the sale of their shares. According to Viscount Haldane LC, directors presented themselves to individual shareholders as acting for them on the same footing as they were acting for the company itself, that is, as agents of the shareholders.

Coleman v Myers[1698] extended the agency approach established in the *Hyatt* case. It concerned a takeover bid whereby minority shareholders were compelled to sell their shares to the ultimate controller of the company. The Court of Appeal decided that a fiduciary duty was established between directors and shareholders in view of the 'special circumstances' that existed between them, namely: the company was a private company with shares held largely by members of one family; the other members of the family had habitually looked to the defendants for business advice; the information affecting the true value of the shares had been withheld from shareholders by the defendants. Woodhouse J stated: '. . . it is not the law that anyone holding the office as a director of a limited liability company is for that reason alone to be released from what would otherwise be regarded as fiduciary responsibility owed to those in a position of shareholders of the same company.'

In *Extrasure Travel Insurances Ltd v Scattergood*,[1699] the court stated that it was well established that a director owed his company a fiduciary duty to exercise his power (i) in what he, not the court, honestly believed to be in the company's best interests; and (ii) for the purposes for which those powers had been conferred on him. Fiduciary duties were concerned with concepts of honesty and loyalty, not with competence. Therefore, it was not sufficient for a company to prove that its directors had taken action that proved to be

---

[1695] [1988] BCLC 250. [1696] [1962] Ch 929. [1697] (1914) 30 TLR 444.
[1698] (1977) 2 NZLR 225. [1699] [2002] All ER 307.

damaging to the company, unless it could be shown that the directors had not honestly believed that the action was in the best interests of the company.

Duty to act for proper purposes

9.2.2 Directors must ensure that they act for a proper purpose: *Re Smith & Fawcett Ltd.*[1700] Where directors act for an improper or 'collateral', purpose the court will intervene and set aside the act in question. A duty not to act for improper purposes arises where directors have acted in breach of their contracted purposes, or in breach of purposes inherent in their duties. This can include situations where directors are forestalling a takeover in the belief that it would be contrary to the interests of the company, or issuing further shares to change the company's control structure.

In *Punt v Symons & Co Ltd*,[1701] in order to secure the passing of a special resolution, the directors had issued new shares to five additional shareholders. Byrne J held this to be an abuse of directors' powers. His Lordship stated that these shares were not issued *bona fide* for the general advantage of the company, but they were issued with the immediate object of controlling the holders of the greater number of shares in the company and of obtaining the necessary statutory majority for passing the special resolution, while at the same time, not conferring upon the minority the power to demand a poll. He stated: 'A power of the kind exercised by the directors in this case, is one which must be exercised for the benefit of the company; primarily it is given to them for the purpose of enabling them to raise capital when required for the purposes of the company.'

In *Hogg v Cramphorn*,[1702] the company's directors issued shares that carried special voting rights for the trustees of a scheme established for the benefit of the company's employees. The directors' aim was to prevent a takeover bid. They had acted in good faith throughout the transaction. Buckley J held that this was an improper purpose but that it could be ratified by shareholders at a general meeting. He stated:

> Unless a majority in a company is acting oppressively towards the minority, this court should not and will not itself interfere with the exercise by the majority of its constitutional rights or embark upon an inquiry into the respective merits of the views held or policies favoured by the majority and the minority. Nor will this court permit directors to exercise powers, which have been delegated to them by the company in circumstances which put the directors in a fiduciary position when exercising those powers, in such a way as to interfere with the exercise by the majority of its constitutional rights ... It is not, in my judgment, open to the

---

[1700] [1942] Ch 304.   [1701] [1903] 2 Ch 506.   [1702] [1967] Ch 254.

directors in such a case to say: 'we genuinely believe that what we seek to prevent the majority from doing will harm the company and, therefore, our act in arming ourselves or our party with sufficient shares to outvote the majority, is a conscientious exercise of our powers under the articles, which should not be interfered with.'

According to Buckley J, a majority of shareholders at a general meeting were entitled to pursue whatever course of action they chose within the company's powers, provided the majority did not unfairly oppress other members of the company.

The decision in *Hogg v Cramphorn* provokes further controversy in that it supported the view that an 'improper purpose' can be legitimised by means of a ratification initiated by shareholders at a general meeting. This is a disturbing phenomenon in that shareholders might thus indulge in ratifying improper purposes that would otherwise have been regarded as factors which formed the basis for illegal acts. Furthermore, the legitimisation process might be directed at disregarding the interests of the minority shareholders. Buckley J referred to the fiduciary position that directors hold in respect of the shareholders, but he seems to have limited it to majority shareholders only. The fiduciary position of a director demands that there be no discriminatory factors in protecting the interests of shareholders whether they are a majority or a minority. The act of disregarding the interests of the minority shareholders may in itself be regarded as an act for an improper purpose.

Judicial authorities in Australia and Canada rejected the *Hogg v Cramphorn* approach and decided that directors' decisions to use their powers to thwart a threatened takeover could be upheld by the courts. In *Harlowe's Nominees Pty Ltd v Woodside (Lakes Entrance) Oil Co*,[1703] and *Teck Corp Ltd v Millar*,[1704] the High Court of Australia and the Canadian Court respectively upheld directors' decisions to prevent a takeover. The issue of directors acting for improper purposes was reviewed by the Privy Council in *Howard Smith Ltd v Ampol Petroleum Ltd*,[1705] which also concerned attempts by directors to prevent a takeover. The court rejected as too narrow an approach the argument that the only valid purpose for which shares may be issued is to raise capital for the company. The law should not impose such limitations on directors' powers, as they should be assessed in the context of each particular case. Further, the test of '*bona fide* for the benefit of the company as a whole' did not serve a useful purpose when considering whether directors had acted for improper purposes. In Lord Wilberforce's opinion, it was:

 . . . necessary to start with a consideration of the power whose exercise is in question; in this case, a power to issue shares. Having ascertained, on a

---

[1703] (1968) 121 CLR 483.   [1704] (1972) 33 DLR 3(a) 288.   [1705] [1974] AC 821.

fair view, the nature of this power, and having defined as can best be done in the light of modern conditions, the awesome limits within which it may be exercised, it is then necessary for the court, if a particular exercise of it is to be challenged, to examine the substantial purpose for which it was exercised, and to reach a conclusion whether that purpose was proper or not. In so doing, it will necessarily give credit to the bona fide opinion of the directors, if such is found to exist, and will respect their judgement as to the matters of the management. Having done this, the ultimate conclusion has to be as to the side of a fairly broad line on which the case falls.

In determining whether directors have acted for improper purposes, the court will construe the powers conferred upon directors and the limitations placed upon them in the exercise of that power. The court will then consider the actual purpose for which the power was exercised. The court is entitled to:

... look at the situation objectively in order to estimate how critical or pressing, or substantial, or per contra, insubstantial an alleged require-ment may have been. If it finds that a particular requirement, though real, was not urgent or critical, at the relevant time, it may have reason to doubt or discount the assertions of individuals that they acted solely in order to deal with it, particularly when the action they took was unusual or even extreme.

The propriety or impropriety of purposes should be determined by referring to:

(a) the interests of shareholders whether they are a majority or a minority; and
(b) the interests of the company as a whole and also with reference to the parameters of power allowed to directors.

The various powers conferred upon directors by the constitution of a com-pany are capable of being exercised for a variety of purposes. The duty imposed upon directors to exercise those powers solely for a proper purpose envisages that each and every power is conferred to permit the directors to achieve certain limited ends: *Hogg v Cramphorn*.[1706] A proper purpose is one for which, on a true construction of the Articles of Association of the com-pany or the statutory provision conferring it, the power can be said to have been conferred. Any other purpose will be an improper purpose: *Howard Smith Ltd v Ampol Petroleum Ltd*.[1707]

[1706] [1967] Ch 254.   [1707] [1974] AC 821.

The no-conflict rule

9.2.3 Directors must not place themselves in a position where their personal interests may conflict with the duties they owe to the company of which they are directors: *Aberdeen Ryl Co v Blaikie Bros*.[1708] In addition, a director is not permitted to put himself in a position in which his duty to the company may conflict with any duty owed to another, for example, a second company of which he is a director. Where a director finds himself in a position of conflict of interest, he is bound to disregard his personal interests.

In order to avoid the possibility of conflict of interests, s 317 of the CA 1985 required directors of both public and private companies to disclose to the board of directors of both public and private companies any interest, direct or indirect, which they may have in a contract or purported contract or transaction or arrangement. The disclosure must be to the board of directors and not to a committee of the board: *Guinness v Saunders*.[1709]

Where a director does place himself in a position of conflict, any transaction with the director which is entered into by the company is voidable at the instance of the company: *Gardner v Parker*.[1710] The director is liable to account to the company for any profits he has made from his position.

In *Plus Group Ltd*[1711] the Court of Appeal stated that although the fiduciary duty of a director to his company was uniform and universal, there was no completely rigid rule that a director could not be involved in the business of another company that was in competition with a company of which he was a director. Every decision whether a fiduciary relationship existed in relation to the matter complained of was fact-specific, and in exceptional circumstances, where a director had been effectively excluded from the company, it was not a breach of fiduciary duty for him to work for a competing company.

The no-profit rule

9.2.4 A director is not entitled, unless expressly provided, to benefit from his position within the company. This is known as the 'no profit' rule and prevents a director from making a secret profit for himself from the use of corporate assets, information or opportunities: *Regal (Hastings) Ltd v Gulliver*;[1712] *Cook v Deeks*;[1713] *IDC v Cooley*.[1714] Where a director does so profit, he is liable to account to the company for any profits made. In *Cook v Deeks*, the company directors diverted a contract that belonged to the company for their own purposes. They were held liable to account to the company for the profits made from the contract. Lord Buckmaster stated that directors had a

---

[1708] (1854) 1 Macq 461. [1709] [1988] 1 WLR 863. [1710] [2003] All ER 346.
[1711] [2002] 2 BCLC. [1712] [1942] 1 All ER 378. [1713] [1916] 1 AC 554.
[1714] [1972] 1 WLR 443.

duty to protect the company's interests because of their position of authority and the knowledge they have acquired as a result of the transaction. Similarly, in *Regal (Hastings)*, Lord Russell decided that even where directors had acted *bona fide* throughout the transaction, they may be liable to account to the company for the profits made: 'The liability arises from the mere fact of a profit having, in the circumstances, been made. The profiteer, however honest and well-intentioned, cannot escape the risk of being called upon to account.'

The liability to account is a personal liability and is dependent upon a profit being made by the director: see *Gidman v Barron*,[1715] where a director had intentionally transferred business and income from a company to new companies. The court decided that the equitable remedy for a breach of fiduciary duty was restitution, which required the fiduciary to make account of the property that had been displaced: *Miller v Bain*.[1716] A director will not generally be liable on this basis, where the profit is made by a third party. It should be noted that where a profit is made by an individual or company associated with a director, that person or individual may incur liability for knowing receipt, while a director may be liable to pay the company damages for breach of fiduciary duty. Provided a director discloses the profit and shareholders ratify this, a director may retain the profit made: *Regal (Hastings)*.

The liability to pay damages for breach of duty will depend upon the company being able to show that it has suffered a loss by reason of the breach of duty. In *CMS Dolphin Ltd v Simonet*,[1717] the court stated that the underlying basis of the liability of a director who exploited after his resignation a maturing business opportunity of the company of which he had knowledge as a result of being a director, was that the opportunity was to be treated as if it was the company's property in relation to which the director had fiduciary duties. By seeking to exploit the opportunity after his resignation, the director was appropriating to himself that property and became a constructive trustee of the benefits of the abuse of the company's property. The director was liable to account to the company for the profits properly attributable to the breach of fiduciary duty, taking into account the expenses connected with those profits and a reasonable allowance for overheads together with a sum to take account of other benefits derived from those contracts. There must, however, be some reasonable connection between the breach of duty and the profits for which the fiduciary was accountable: *Canadian Aero Services Ltd v O'Malley*.[1718] In *Simonet*, the court further stated that a director remained liable to account for profits whether he exploited the opportunity personally, through a partnership or through a company controlled by him. The director remained liable notwithstanding that the profits were made by a company

[1715] [2003] All ER 182.   [1716] [2002] 1 BCLC 266.   [1717] [2001] 2 BCLC 704.
[1718] [1974] SCR 592

against which there was no effective remedy because, for reasons unconnected with the relevant contracts, it was insolvent. Where the director had placed the contract into a partnership he was fully accountable even if his partners were entitled to part of the profit and were ignorant of his breach of fiduciary duty. Where the business was put into a company that was established by directors who had wrongfully taken advantage of the corporate opportunity, the directors were equally liable to account for profits with the company formed by them to take advantage of those opportunities because they had participated in the breach of trust.

A duty not to fetter future discretion

9.2.5 Directors must not anticipate in advance as to how they will vote in the future. They must seek the company's consent before they can seek to fetter their future discretion. However, provided directors act *bona fide* and enter into a contract as to how they will vote at future board meetings, the courts will uphold such a contract. In *Thorby v Goldberg*,[1719] the Australian Court stated: 'There are many kinds of transaction in which the proper time for the exercise of the directors' discretion is the time of the negotiation of a contract and not the time at which the contract is to be performed . . . if at the former time they are bona fide of the opinion that it is in the best interests of the company that the transaction should be entered into and carried into effect, I can see no reason in law why they should not bind themselves to do whatever under the transaction is to be done by the board.'

In *Fulham Football Club Ltd v Cabra Estates plc*,[1720] the undertakings given by directors to the shareholders to support a planning application were held to confer substantial benefits on the company. The Court of Appeal held that the directors had not improperly fettered the future exercise of their discretion by giving those undertakings.

The duty not to fetter future discretion is subject to the condition that it does not run counter to the fiduciary duties that a director owes to the company, which includes a duty towards the majority as well as the minority shareholders.

Directors have a duty to protect the interests of the company because of their position of authority and the knowledge they have acquired as a result of the transaction. In *Regal (Hastings) Ltd v Gulliver*, Lord Russell decided that even where directors had acted *bona fide* throughout the transaction, they may be liable to account to the company for the profits they had made: 'The liability arises from the mere fact of a profit having, in the circumstances, been made. The profiteer, however honest and well-intentioned, cannot escape the risk of being called upon to account.'

[1719] (1964) 112 CLR 597.   [1720] [1994] 1 BCLC 363.

However, there are cases which have suggested that, provided the director has declared the contract and the company rejected the opportunity to pursue the contract, the director may keep the profits made from the contract: *Queensland Mines Ltd v Hudson*;[1721] *Island Export Finance Ltd v Umunna*;[1722] *Peso-Silver Mines Ltd v Cropper*.[1723]

Directors' duty of skill, care and diligence

9.2.6 At common law, a director owes the company a duty to act with reasonable skill, care and diligence. This is a lower standard of duty than the fiduciary duties imposed on directors.

These general rules were analysed in *Re City Equitable Fire Insurance Co Ltd*.[1724] Following this case, a director need not exhibit a greater degree of skill than 'may reasonably be expected of a person of his knowledge and experience'. Accordingly, the standard of skill to be expected of a director is to be determined by reference to his own personal qualities, and a director is not expected to exercise skill that he does not possess. In *Lagunas Nitrate Co v Lagunas Syndicate*,[1725] the Court of Appeal stated that: 'If directors act within their powers, if they act with such care as is reasonably to be expected from them, having regard to their knowledge and experience, and if they act honestly for the benefit of the company they represent, they discharge both their equitable as well as their legal duty to the company' (per Lindley MR).

It is also clear that the directors of a specific company are not required to be experts in the type of business that the company promotes, unless they are appointed in view of their specialist qualification. A director is not bound to bring any special qualifications to his office: *Re Brazilian Rubber Plantations & Estates Ltd*.[1726] The legal effect of this lower standard is that a director could undertake the management of a company in an industry of which he has no knowledge, without incurring responsibility for the mistakes that may result from such ignorance: *Overend, Gurney & Co v Gibb and Gibb*.[1727]

It has been suggested that the knowledge, skill and experience to be expected of a director at common law may be the same as that identified in s 214(4) of the Insolvency Act 1986 in relation to directors' liabilities for wrongful trading: *Norman v Theodore Goddard*;[1728] and *Re D'Jan of London Ltd*.[1729] Section 214(4) provides that the facts a director ought to know or ascertain, the conclusions he ought to reach and the steps he ought to take, are those that would otherwise be known or ascertained, reached or taken by a reasonably diligent person having both: the general knowledge, skill and experience that may reasonably be expected of a person carrying out the same

---

[1721] [1978] 52 ALJR 379.   [1722] [1986] BCLC 460.   [1723] (1966) 58 DLR (2d) 1.
[1724] [1925] Ch 407.   [1725] [1899] 2 Ch 392.   [1726] [1911] 1 Ch 425.
[1727] (1872) LR 5 HL 480.   [1728] [1992] BCC 14.   [1729] [1993] BCC 646.

functions as are carried out by that director in relation to the company; and the general knowledge, skill and experience of a particular director.

This approach continues the higher standard of expectation that a director has a particular knowledge, skill and experience of his own, while also applying to all directors an objective standard determined by reference to the function which the particular director carries out in relation to the company: *Re Produce Marketing Consortium Ltd (No 2)*;[1730] *Re Purpoint Ltd*;[1731] and *Re DKG Contractors Ltd*.[1732]

The position under the CA 2006

9.3 The position on directors' fiduciary and common law duties has now been partly codified and governed by the CA 2006.[1733]

Chapter 2 of Part 10 of the CA 2006 sets out the general duties of directors. It comprises 12 sections that apply to directors. The general duties of directors form a code of conduct, which sets out how directors are expected to behave – but it does not tell them in terms what to do. The duties set out in the CA 2006 address the possibility that a director may put his own or other interests ahead of those of the company; and the possibility that he may be negligent.

The general duties of directors are derived from equitable and common law rules. They are derived from case law although phrased differently.

The Law Commission of England and Wales and the Scottish Law Commission recommended that there should be a statutory statement of a director's main fiduciary duties, and the common law duty of care and skill in their joint report *Company Directors: Regulating Conflicts of Interests and Formulating a Statement of Duties*. The Company Law Review Group's main recommendations in respect of directors' general duties were summarised in Chapter 3 of the *Final Report*.

[1730] [1989] BCLC 520.   [1731] [1991] BCC 121.   [1732] [1990] BCC 903.

[1733] During the passage of the Companies Bill, Baroness Bottomley stated that there was real concern that the statutory code could be unworkable and counter productive. Directors may feel they will not be able to move without consulting lawyers as to whether they have complied with the legislation: see HL Debates, 11 Jan. 2006. during the same debates, Lord Patten argued that the statutory code approach would be inflexible, confusing, likely to lead to increase bureaucracy, and to lead more costs on to companies. He advocated a voluntary code structure rather than the statutory code. However, Lord Tunnicliffe remarked that the codification would clearly be valuable to all directors. However, one had to remember that there were two 'classes' of directors. There are those who are directors of large and quoted companies. In the case of large companies, the support of legal advice will be immediately available to them. The directors of quoted companies may be 'professional directors' and have a duty to ensure that they are well briefed on those duties. But the vast majority of directors in the UK were directors of small- and medium-sized enterprises. They may be family firms and would require a simple statement of their duties.

The Company Law Review Group recommended that there should be a statutory statement of directors' general duties, and that this should, with two exceptions set out below, be a codification of the current law. In particular, they wanted:

(a) to provide greater clarity on what was expected of directors, and make the law more accessible. In particular, they sought to address the key question: 'in whose interests should companies be run?' in a way which reflected modern business needs and wider expectations of responsible business behavior;

(b) to make development of the law in this area more predictable (but without hindering development of the law by the courts); and

(c) to correct what the Company Law Review Group saw as defects in the duties relating to conflicts of interest.

The Government in its two White Papers in 2002 and 2005 respectively on company law reform accepted these recommendations. However, there are two areas, both relating to the regulation of conflicts of interest, where the statutory statement departs from the law. First, under s 175 of the CA 2006, transactions or arrangements with the company do not have to be authorised by either the members or the board; instead interests in transactions or arrangements with the company must be declared under s 177 of the CA 2006 (in the case of proposed transactions), or under s 182 of the CA 2006 (in the case of existing transactions), unless an exception applies under those sections.

Second, s 175 of the CA 2006 also permits board authorisation of most conflicts of interest arising from third-party dealings by the director (for example, personal exploitation of corporate resources and opportunities). Such authorisation is effective only if the conflicted directors have not participated in taking the decision, or if the decision would have been valid even without the participation of the conflicted directors. Board authorisation of conflicts of interests will be the default position for private companies, but public companies will need to make provision in their constitutions to permit this. Board authorisation is not permitted in respect of the acceptance of benefits from third parties (s 176 of the CA 2006).

Both reforms implement recommendations of the Company Law Review Group, which noted that the basic principles in the current law relating to directors' conflicts of interest were very strict. They noted that in practice most companies permit a director to have an interest in a proposed transaction or arrangement with the company, provided that the interest is disclosed to his fellow directors. The statutory statement, therefore, reflects the current position in most companies. They also took the view that the current strict rule relating to conflicts of interest in respect of personal exploitation of corporate opportunities fettered entrepreneurial and business start-up activity by existing company directors. The statutory statement, therefore, provided for board authorisation of such conflicts.

These reforms are modified for charitable companies in England and Wales by s 181 of the CA 2006.

Codification of common law rules and equitable principles

9.4 According to the Explanatory Notes by the DTI, codification is not a matter of transposing wording taken from judgments into legislative propositions. Judgments are, of necessity, directed at particular cases. Even when they appear to state general principles, they will rarely be exhaustive. They will be the application of (perhaps unstated) general principles to particular facts. In the company law field, the principles being applied will frequently be taken from other areas of law, in particular trust and agency. It is important that these connections are not lost, and that company law may continue to reflect developments elsewhere, applying principles and concepts from other areas of law. Frequently, the courts may formulate the same idea in different ways. In contrast, legislation is formal. It is not easy to reconcile these approaches, but the provisions aim to balance precision against the need for continued flexibility and development. In particular:

- s 170(3) of the CA 2006 provides that the statutory duties are based on, and have effect in place of, certain common law rules and equitable principles;
- s 170(4) of the CA 2006 provides that the general duties should be interpreted and applied in the same way as common law rules and equitable principles. The courts should interpret and develop the general duties in a way that reflects the nature of the rules and principles they replace;
- s 170(4) of the CA 2006 also provides that when interpreting and applying the statutory duties, regard should be had to the common law rules and equitable principles that the general duties replace; thus developments in the law of trusts and agency should be reflected in the interpretation and application of duties;
- s 178 of the CA 2006 provides that the civil consequences of breach (or threatened breach) of the statutory duties are the same as would apply if the corresponding common law rule or equitable principle applied. It also makes clear that the statutory duties are to be regarded as fiduciary, with the exception of the duty to exercise reasonable care skill and diligence that is not under the present law regarded as a fiduciary duty, but a common law rule.

It should be noted that the statutory general duties do not cover all the duties that a director owes to the company. Many duties are imposed elsewhere in legislation, such as the duty to deliver accounts and reports to the registrar of companies (see, for example, s 441 of the CA 2006). Other duties under case law remain uncodified, such as any duty to consider the interest of creditors in times of threatened insolvency.[1734]

Duties owed to the company

9.5 Section 170(1) of the CA 2006 makes it clear that, as in the exiting law, the general duties are owed by a director to the company. It follows that, as now, only the company can enforce them. Part 11 of the CA 2006 (derivative claims and actions by members) describes the mechanism whereby members may be able to enforce the duties on behalf of the company.

Who are the duties owed by?

9.6 The duties are owed by every person who is a director of a company (as defined in s 250 of the CA 2006). They are owed by a de facto director in the same way and to the same extent they owed by a properly appointed director.

Certain aspects of the duty to avoid conflicts of interest and the duty not to accept benefits from third parties continue to apply even when a person ceases to be a director; it is important that a director cannot, for example, exploit an opportunity of which he became aware while managing the company's business without the necessary consent simply by resigning his position as director. The closing words of s 170(2) of the CA 2006 provide that the duties apply to a former director, subject to any necessary adaptations. This is to reflect that a former director is not in the same legal position as an actual director.

The statutory duties apply to shadow directors where, and to the extent that, the common law rules or equitable principles which they replace so apply (s 170(5) of the CA 2006). This means that where a common law rule or equitable principles currently applies to a shadow director, the statutory duty replacing that common law rule or equitable principle will apply to the shadow director (in place of that rule or principle). Where the rule or principle does not currently apply to a shadow director, the statutory duty replacing that rule of principle will not apply either.

The relationship between the general duties

9.7 Many of the general duties will frequently overlap. Taking a bribe from a third party would, for example, clearly fall within the duty not to accept benefits from third parties (s 176 of the CA 2006) but could also, depending on the facts, be characterised as a failure to promote the success of the

---

[1734] See, for example, *Walker v Wimborne* (1976) 50 ALJR 446; *Lonrho Ltd Shell Petroleum* [1980] 1 WLR 627.

company for the benefit of its members (s 172 of the CA 2006), or as an aspect of failing to exercise independent judgment (s 173 of the CA 2006).

The effect of the duties is cumulative, so that it is necessary to comply with every duty that applies in any given case. This principle is stated in s 179 of the CA 2006. One exception relates to the duty to avoid conflicts of interest (s 175 of the CA 2006). This particular duty does not apply to a conflict of interest in relation to a transaction or arrangement with the company. In such cases the duty to declare interests in proposed transactions or arrangements (s 177 of the CA 2006), or the requirement to declare interests in existing transactions or arrangements (s 182 of the CA 2006) will apply instead. Section 181 of the CA 2006 modifies these provisions for charitable companies in England and Wales.

The cumulative effect of the duties means that where more than one duty applies, the directors must comply with the applicable duty, and the duties must be read in this context. So, for example, the duty to promote the success of the company will not authorise the director to breach his duty when acting within his powers, even if he considers that it would be most likely to promote the success of the company.

As well as complying with all the duties, the directors must continue to comply with all other applicable laws. The duties do not require or authorise a director to breach any other prohibition or requirement imposed on him by law.

Relationship between the duties and the company's constitution

9.8 Under s 171 of the CA 2006, a director must act in accordance with the company's constitution.

Companies may, through their articles, go further than statutory duties by placing more onerous requirements on their directors (e.g. by requiring shareholder authorisation of the remuneration of the directors). The articles may not dilute the duties except to the extent that this is explicitly permitted by the sections:

- s 173 of the CA 2006 provides that a director will not be in breach of the duty to exercise independent judgment, if he has acted in a way that is authorised by the constitution;
- s 175 of the CA 2006 permits authorisation of some conflicts of interest by independent directors subject to the constitution;
- s 180(4)(a) of the CA 2006 preserves any rule of law enabling the company to give authority for anything that would otherwise be a breach of duty;
- s 180(4) (b) of the CA 2006 provides that a director will not be in breach of duty, if he acts in accordance with any provisions in the company's articles for dealing with conflicts of interest;

- s 232 of the CA 2006 places restrictions on the provisions that may be included in the company's articles. But nothing in that section prevents companies from including in their articles any such provisions as are currently lawful for dealing with conflicts of interest.

The company's constitution may also set out the propose of the company, especially in the case of an altruistic company that has purposes other than the benefit of the company's members. It is very important that directors understand the purposes of the company, so they are able to comply with their duty to promote the success of the company in s 172 of the CA 2006.

Relationship between the duties and the detailed rules requiring member approval of conflicts of interest

9.9 Under the provision in Chapter 4 of Part 10 of the CA 2006, the directors must sometimes obtain prior shareholder approval for the following types of transaction involving a director (or, in some cases, a person connected to a director): long services contracts; substantial property transactions; loans, quasi loans and credit transactions; and payments for loss of office.

Section 180 of the CA 2006 provides that:

- compliance with the general duties does not remove the need for member approval of such transactions: s 180(3) of the CA 2006;
- (subject to the exception set out below) the general duties apply even if the transactions also falls within Chapter 4 of Part 10 of the CA 2006 (because it is a long-service contract, substantial property transaction, loan, quasi loan, credit transaction or payment for loss of office). So, for example, the directors should only approve a loan to a director if they consider that it would promote the success of the company. This is so, even if the loan does not require the approval of members under Chapter 4 of Part 10 of the CA 2006 because it falls within a relevant exception, such as the exception of expenditure on company business in s 204 of the CA 2006;
- if the transaction falls within Chapter 4 of Part 10 of the CA 2006 (because it is a long-service contract, substantial property transaction, loan, quasi loan, credit transaction or payment for loss of office) and the approval of the member is obtained for the transaction in accordance with that Chapter, or an exception applies, so that approval is not necessary under that Chapter, and then the director does not need to comply with the duty to avoid conflicts of interest (s 175 of the CA 2006), or the duty not to accept benefits from third parties (s 176 of the CA 2006) in respect of that transaction. All other applicable duties will still apply. For example, a director would not be acting in breach of the duty to avoid conflicts of interests, if he failed to obtain authorisation from the

directors or the members for a loan from the company in respect of legal defence costs. Section 181 of the CA 2006 modifies this provision for charitable companies in England and Wales.

Relationship between the duties and the general law

9.10 Section 180(5) of the CA 2006 provides that the general duties have effect notwithstanding any enactment or rule of law, except where there is an express or implied exception to this rule. For example, s 247 of the CA 2006 provides that directors may make provision for employees on the cessation of transfer of a company's business, even if this would otherwise constitute a breach of the general duty to promote the success of the company.

Consequences of breach

9.11 Section 178 of the CA 2006 preserves the existing civil consequences of breach (or threatened breach) of any of the general duties. The remedies for breach of the general duties will be exactly the same as those that are currently available following a breach of the equitable principles and common law rules that the general duties replace.

Section 178(2) of the CA 2006 states that the duties are enforceable in the same way as any other fiduciary duty owed to a company by its directors (except for the duty to exercise reasonable care, skill and diligence, which is not considered to be a fiduciary duty). In the case of fiduciary duties the consequences of breach may include: damages or compensation where the company has suffered loss; restoration of the company's property; an account of profits made by the director; and rescission of a contract where the director failed to disclose an interest.

Scope and nature of general duties

9.12 Section 170 of the CA 2006 comprises five subsections setting out the scope and nature of the general duties (and their derivation). This section provides an answer to the question 'to whom directors owe the general duties'.[1735]

It states that the general duties specified in ss 171–177 of the CA 2006 are owed by a director of a company to the company.[1736] The effect of s 170(1) of the CA 2006 is that only the company can enforce directors' general duties, as the company will be the proper claimant in these circumstances. A separate regime for derivative claims and actions by shareholders to bring proceedings on behalf of the company is governed by Part 11 of the CA 2006. Part 11 sets

---

[1735] See further Chapter 26.   [1736] CA 2006, s 170(1).

out the mechanism that would allow shareholders to enforce duties on behalf of the company.[1737]

Section 170(2) of the CA 2006 considers the scope and the nature of the general duties where a person ceases to be a director of a company. It recognises that in some situations, there are some on-going obligations on a former director, although not necessarily the same degree of obligations as would apply to an existing director. These obligations are imposed on a former director owing to the position occupied while he was a director of a company, including the acquisition of knowledge, information and appointment that vested in the former director at the time he occupied the directorship position. A person who ceases to be a director continues to be subject to the following duties. First, to the duty in s 175 of the CA 2006 (duty to avoid conflicts of interest), as regards the exploitation of any property, information or opportunity of which he became aware at a time when he was a director.[1738] Second, the duty in s 176 of the CA 2006 (duty not to accept benefits from third parties) as regards things done or omitted by him before he ceased to be a director.[1739]

To that extent those duties apply to a former director as to a director, subject to any necessary adaptations.[1740]

For s 170(2) of the CA 2006 to apply, the director must have ceased to be a director of the company. The cessation of directorship may arise in various ways including retirement, resignation, disqualification or removal. This section recognises that there are on-going continuous obligations that should apply to a former director, and sets out the principles of company law derived from cases in this area.

The former director is subject to two continuous obligations under s 170(2) of the CA 2006. First, a duty to avoid conflict of interest. This requires the former director not to exploit any property, information or opportunity of which he became aware when he was a director. The term 'exploitation' is not defined, but suggests use of the property, information or opportunity for own personal benefit or for another person's benefit, and has wide scope. It is immaterial whether the company could take advantage of the property,

---

[1737] According to Lord Sainsbury, the duty to promote the success of the company answers one of the fundamental questions in company law: 'in whose interest should company run?' The answer is that directors should run the company for the benefit of its members collectively. However, directors will not be successful in promoting the success of the company if they focus on only the short-term financial bottom line. Successful companies see business prosperity and responsible business behaviour as two sides of the same coin. The CA 2006 adopts and approach known as 'enlightened shareholder value' under which a director must, in promoting the success of the company, have regard to factors such as the long-term consequences of business decisions and the impact of the company's activities on employees, the community and the environment: see HL Debates, 11 Jan 2006.

[1738] CA 2006, s 170(2)(a).   [1739] CA 2006, s 170(2)(b).   [1740] CA 2006, s 170(2).

information or opportunity.[1741] The property, information or opportunity are aspects that vested in or belonged to the company. For example, a third party wishes to enter into a lucrative joint venture with the company in respect of a product that would make the company highly profitable. One of the directors resigns and diverts the opportunity to another company he has set up.

The term 'property' is not defined, but is likely to be interpreted widely to include corporate property, as well use of corporate facilities and services that are used by a former director for benefit or gain – whether personally or for someone else.

This section does not define the term 'information', but not all types of information are likely to be protected as corporate information. A person who in the course of directorship, acquires information for enhancing his skills and experience is unlikely to be subject to a continuing obligation under s 170(2) of the CA 2006. However, confidential information, trade and business secrets that are exploited by the former director are likely to fall under the scope of continuous obligations of a former director under s 170(2) of the CA 2006.

The second continuous obligation on a former director, is a duty not to accept benefits from third parties as regards things done or omitted by him before he ceased to be a director. This is based on the duty imposed on directors under s 176 of the CA 2006 not to accept benefits from third parties.

There is no definition of 'benefits', and a wide interpretation is to be given to the term. It would include gratuitous benefits, pecuniary advantages, services performed, secret profits, favours provided, or any gains received. However, it is made clear that benefits received by a director from a person by whom his services (as director or otherwise) are provided to the company are not regarded as conferred by a third party.[1742]

The benefits must be received from third parties. The term 'third party' means a person other than the company, an associate body corporate, or a person acting on behalf of the company or an associate body corporate.[1743]

The duty not to accept benefits from third parties applies as regards 'things done or omitted by him' before a person ceased to be a director of the company. This refers to actions undertaken by the director, or lack of action in the form of omissions on the part of a director, while a director of the company, with respect to benefits received from third parties. For example, a director may have encouraged receipt of a third-party benefit, because a contract was awarded to that third party that would constitute the 'things done' by the director before he ceased his directorship. Alternatively, the director may have remained silent, or lack of inactivity on his part might have resulted in his accepting benefits from a third party, that is, the director took

---

[1741] See for example, CA 2006, s 175(2).   [1742] CA 2006, s 176(3).
[1743] See CA 2006, 176(2).

no steps to refuse the third-party benefit, which may constitute an 'omission' by him, while a director of the company.

The two continuous duties on a former director are subject to any 'necessary adaptations'. This recognises that the duties may not be too onerous on the former director as they apply to an existing director of a company.[1744] In some cases, a lower standard of application to the duties may be applied; or in other cases, a higher standard may be expected of a former director. This allows for flexibility to apply the duties by either extending or restricting the nature and scope of those duties, depending upon the circumstances of each case before the courts. This principle of flexibility could, for example, be applied in respect of the exploitation of information acquired by a former director. The information may not be so significant or material as to impose a duty of continuous obligation on a former director, such that the courts may hold that the former director had not exploited the information at issue. In other cases, the courts may hold that the former director had exploited the information (owing to the high level of sensitivity around the information) and is therefore, subject to the continuous obligation imposed by s 170(2) of the CA 2006.

The general duties are based on some of the common law rules and equitable principles, as they apply in relation to directors, and have effect in place of those rules and principles as regards the duties owed to a company by a director.[1745] The objective of s 170(3) of the CA 2006 is to make clear that the general duties partially codify only some of the common law and equitable principles as they apply to directors, based on established principles over the years set out in case law, while other duties remain uncodified, and will be subject to case law interpretation: for example, the duty to consider the interests of creditors in circumstances when insolvency is threatened. This duty will still continue to apply under case law rather than under the general statutory duties. The statutory codified duties, therefore, replace the common law rules and equitable principles as they apply to directors. The stating point will be to look at the applicable general duty or duties in issue, and apply to the facts in question.

The general duties must be interpreted and applied in the same way as common law rules or equitable principles, and regard will be had to the corresponding common law rules and equitable principles in interpreting and applying the general duties.[1746] This means that the courts will still have regard to previous applicable case law on equitable and common law duties

---

[1744] See Lord Goldsmith, who stated that the courts will need to take into account the fact that former directors are not in exactly the same position as current directors. The court would take into account the fact that the duties are being applied to former directors when interpreting and applying the duties. That means that the courts have more flexibility to take account of the fact that these are not current directors.

[1745] CA 2006, s 170(3).   [1746] CA 2006, s 170(4).

of directors, to assist in the statutory interpretation of the general duty provisions. This section emphasises the principle of equal application of the equitable and common law principles concerning directors towards the statutory interpretation of the general duties of directors. It requires the courts to comply with the following:[1747]

1   The general duties must be *interpreted* in the same way as the equitable and common law rules;
2   The general duties must be *applied* in the same manner as the equitable and common law principles; and
3   The courts must have regard to the *corresponding* equitable and common law rules in interpreting and applying the general duties.

However, s 170(4) of the CA 2006 allows for future flexibility, as company law borrows from various equitable and common law rules in its application to directors. It ensures that the duties are not frozen in time. This process of developing and expanding directors' duties will still continue, and the court may, for example, borrow from the law of trusts, or agency (as they have on various occasions) to impose duties on directors.[1748] This provision, therefore, takes account of new developments that may occur in law and the interpretation and applicability to the general duty of directors.

The general duties also apply to a shadow director where, and to the extent that the corresponding common law rules or equitable principles so apply.[1749]

Duty to act within powers

9.13 Section 171 of the CA 2006 imposes an obligation on a director of a company to undertake two important duties: first, a duty to act in accordance with the company's constitution;[1750] and second, a duty only to exercise powers for the purposes for which they are conferred.[1751]

The first duty codifies a director's fiduciary duty to comply with the company's constitution by acting in accordance with the company's constitution. The constitution is defined for the purpose of general duties in s 257 of the CA 2006. As well as the company's Articles of Association, it includes decisions taken in accordance with the company's articles; and other decisions taken by the members (or a class of them) if they can be regarded as

---

[1747] CA 2006, s 170(4). The effect of this provision is to specify that the company law system is moving from the common law and fiduciary principles to one of codifying the directors general duties. Not all the general duties correspond exactly to an existing rule or principle, although the relevant section of a directors' general duties is based on a particular rule or principle under case law.

[1748] See, for example, the use of trusts to impose obligations on directors under the trusteeship principle.

[1749] CA 2006, s 170(5).   [1750] CA 2006, s 171(a).   [1751] CA 2006, s 171(b).

decisions of the company, for example a decision taken by the informal unanimous consent of all the members.

Section 171 of the CA 2006 should also be considered in the light of s 40 of the CA 2006. This provides that directors must take account of limitations on their powers as set out in the company's constitution, as well as any resolution of the company or of any class of shareholders; or from any agreement between the members of the company or any class of shareholders. While this is not an issue for a third party, it is an internal matter between shareholders and directors, where directors will be held accountable for their actions. A breach of s 40 of the CA 2006 may also be a breach of s 171 of the CA 2006. If, for example, there are restrictions set out in the company's constitution (as widely defined), directors must observe such limitations or restrictions. The company's objects may be restricted to particular objects – a deviation from these objects will be a breach of a director's general duty to act in accordance with the company's constitution.

Section 171 of the CA 2006 also imposes a duty on a director only to exercise powers for the purposes for which they are conferred. The duty of directors to act within their powers codifies the current principle of law, under which a director should exercise his powers in accordance with the terms on which they were granted, and do so for a proper purpose (also known as the 'proper purposes' doctrine). What constitutes a proper purpose must be ascertained in the context of the specific situation under consideration. This duty codifies the 'proper purposes' doctrine in equity as applied to directors. It is a fiduciary duty that has been applied to directors who have abused the powers that have been granted to them. Directors must not use their powers for improper purposes for which were not intended.

Clearly, the courts will have regard to the case law in this area as an aid to interpreting and applying the statutory duty of directors to act within their powers. The court will consider (a) the nature of the power; (b) for what purpose the power was granted; and (c) whether there has been an abuse or misuse of that power.

Duty to promote the success of the company

9.14 Section 172(1) of the CA 2006 requires a director of a company to act in a way he considers, in good faith, would be most likely to promote the success of the company for the benefit of its members as a whole, and in doing so have regard (amongst other matters) to the following:

(a)   the likely consequences of any decision in the long term;[1752]
(b)   the interests of the company's employees;[1753]

[1752] CA 2006, s 172(1)(a).   [1753] CA 2006, s 172(1)(b).

(c) the need to foster the company's business relationships with suppliers, customers and others;[1754]

(d) the impact of the company's operations on the community and the environment;[1755]

(e) the desirability of the company maintaining a reputation for high standards of business conduct;[1756] and

(f) the need to act fairly as between members of the company.[1757]

Where or to the extent that the purposes of the company consist of or include purposes other than the benefit of its members, s 172(1) of the CA 2006 will apply as if the reference to promoting the success of the company for the benefit of its members were to achieving those purposes.[1758]

The duty imposed by s 172 of the CA 2006 will apply subject to any enactment or rule of law requiring directors, in certain circumstances, to consider or act in the interests of creditors of the company.[1759]

The duty to promote the success of the company codifies the current law fiduciary duty imposed on a director, and enshrines in statute what is commonly referred to as the principle of 'enlightened shareholder value'. The duty has two elements: first, a director must act in a way he or she considers, in good faith, would be most likely to promote the success of the company for the benefit of its members as a whole; and second, in doing so, the director must have regard *inter alia* to the factors listed in s 172(3) of the CA 2006.

The decision as to what will promote success, and what constitutes such success, is one for the director's good faith judgment.[1760] This ensures that business decisions on, for example, strategy and tactics are for the directors, and not subject to decision by the courts, subject to good faith. The term 'good faith' is not defined, but clearly a director's motive and intent will be taken into account in assessing this duty and the *bona fide* of the director is likely to be taken into account. Bad faith may apply where, for example, the director has acted illegally, fraudulently, or where an improper motive or intent is established and embraces a wide spectrum of such type of behaviour.

There is an obligation on a director not only to act in good faith, but also to consider what would most likely 'promote the success of the company'.

[1754] CA 2006, s 172(1)(c).   [1755] CA 2006, s 172(1)(d).   [1756] CA 2006, s 172(1)(e).
[1757] CA 2006, s 172(1)(f).   [1758] CA 2006, s 172(2).
[1759] CA 2006, s 172(3). See for example, *West Mercia Safety Ltd. v Dodd* [1998] BCLC 250.
[1760] There has been much debate in both Houses of Parliament as to what constitutes 'success'. According to Lord Freeman, directors of a successful company – and hence successful for the shareholders – should take into account the long-term. He contended: 'you cannot plan a successful company by looking at short-term gain and short-term popularity', HL Debates – Grand Committee, 6 Feb 2006.

The test is subjective. It requires the director in question (and not a reasonable nor a prudent director) to determine how to promote the success of the company. The words 'most likely' suggest that the director must project forward – address his visionary mind as to what will promote the success of the company. The term 'promote' is not defined but would suggest an enhancement or furtherance of the company's objectives, activities or success. There is no definition of 'success' but would most likely refer to long-term profit maximisation.

According to the Ministerial statements the Government sets out what may constitute 'success'. Lord Goldsmith stated that the starting point was that it was essentially for the members of the company to define the objective they wished to achieve. Success meant what the members collectively wanted the company to achieve. For a commercial company, success would usually mean 'long-term increase in value'. For certain companies, such as charities and community interest companies, it will mean the attainment of the objectives for which the company has been established.

Although for a commercial company, 'success' will normally mean long-term increase in value, the company's constitution and decisions made under it may also lay down the appropriate success model for the company. It was, therefore, essential for the members of a company to define the objectives they wished to achieve.

For most companies, 'success' would be measured in terms of profit maximisation. It is submitted, however, that companies can no longer entertain the single-minded obsession for profit maximisation. They must also have regard to their wider social responsibilities. Any decisions or actions taken by a director will have an impact on the company, and this provision ensures that a director promotes the success of the company by his actions or decisions, although this will be the overriding duty, whereas the factors will be subsidiary to this duty. It requires a director to be proactive in determining what will promote the company's success. It requires a positive action of thought on the part of the director, so that the consideration is based on a likelihood that his actions would promote the company's success.

It may be that afterwards it transpires that the director was mistaken in his business judgment – or that the action or the activity turns out to be a disaster or failure. It is not for the courts to second-guess directors' business judgments – judges are not business managers, nor is it their responsibility to preside over directors' business decisions, subject to good faith. It is submitted that the judges should simply consider the provision under s 172 of the CA 2006, and apply a natural and ordinary meaning to the facts at issue. The court must not substitute for what another prudent or reasonable director would have done in the circumstances – the test is to apply the wording of that section to the director in question, who is alleged to have breached the duty.

It is unclear, however, how promotion of success would be judged in certain circumstances. Take, for example, the position of a takeover of the company, where the existing management may cease to have any interest in taking the company forward. Another situation would be where the company is being wound up and will no longer exist.

In approaching of s 172 of the CA 2006, it is submitted that the director (i) must have acted in good faith; and (ii) he must ensure that his actions would be most likely to promote the success of the company. Section 172 of the CA 2006 then requires that the success of the company must be 'for the benefit of its members as a whole'. This is not defined under the CA 2006. However, according to case law, it refers to shareholders collectively, as a group, and not for the benefit of a single shareholder or a particular class of shareholders. The director must not treat various classes of shareholders differently. He must apply the principles of equity and fair treatment towards all the shareholders. He must not single out any particular shareholder for favourable or adverse treatment. He must not disadvantage minority shareholders or favour majority shareholders. The director's decision must be taken for the benefit of a collective group of shareholders.

In having regard to the factors listed in s 172(1) of the CA 2006, the duty to exercise reasonable care, skill and diligence (s 174 of the CA 2006) may apply. According to the Explanatory Notes, it will not be sufficient to pay lip service to the factors, and, in many cases, the directors will need to take action to comply with this aspect of the duty. At the same time, the duty does not require a director to do more than good faith, and the duty to exercise reasonable care, skill and diligence, would require, nor would it be possible for a director acting in good faith to be held liable for a process failure, which would not have affected his decision as to which course of action would best promote the success of the company.

The six factors

9.15 Section 172 of the CA 2006 proceeds to identify six factors to which a director must have regard in determining whether his actions would promote the interests of the company. It is made clear that in respect of every decision made, the directors must have regard, *inter alia*, to the six factors. The term 'have regard to' suggests to 'think about' – to address one's mind and consider the factors. It should be noted that the 'six factors' are subservient to the overriding duty of the directors to promote the success of the company.

No requirement for paper trail

9.15.1 One issue that has arisen under s 172 of the CA 2006 is whether the duty to promote the success of the company would in fact increase corporate bureaucracy, which could impede the effective operations of a company –

particularly one listed on the Stock Exchange.[1761] This could arise by way of companies having a regime or process in place to demonstrate that they have considered the six factors under s 172(1) of the CA 2006, in order to determine whether the action is likely to promote the success of the company. The company may adopt a procedure by formally documenting the process of considering the six factors in arriving at its decision. However, Lord Goldsmith, Attorney-General, stated: 'There is nothing in this Bill that says there is a need for a paper trail .... I do not agree that the effect of passing this Bill will be that the directors will be subject to a breach if they cannot demonstrate that they have considered every (factor).'[1762]

The courts should not, therefore, consider whether a process was in place, or have regard to a paper trail or minutes of directors' board meetings, to determine whether each of the six factors was considered by the directors. In large companies, speed in making decisions is of the essence, particularly on a day-to-day basis.

In some cases, decisions are delegated, which will make practically and logistically difficult for such companies to establish a formal process to consider each of the six factors on every occasion a decision is to be made.

It is submitted that a paper trail should not be required on every occasion as evidence of the directors' consideration of the six factors. In some cases it will matter – such as a takeover, merger or a redundancy – a situation that should be considered significant to the company. What should be required is to apply the best practice approach here. This would require companies fully ensuring directors are aware *inter alia* of their general duties including s 172(1) of the CA 2006.

A formal process for directors' decision making is usually taken with reference to background papers presented to directors, that should also identify the six factors and highlight only those factors that have an impact on the current decision to any negative statements concerning the six factors. The background papers will usually be prepared by a management team and the team's task must be to ensure all the factors were considered in the background papers to which the directors are to have regard.

In a single member company structure, the sole director will not need to go

---

[1761] According to Lord Sharman, it would be questionable whether CA 2006, s 172 will require senior directors to set up expensive and extensive internal procedures to create audit trails in respect of any authority that they delegate down the management chain: see HL Debates, 11 Jan 2006.

[1762] This is further supported by the then Secretary of State for Trade and Industry, Alistair Darling, who stated: 'I am concerned that we do not get ourselves into a situation where, whenever a company takes an individual decision, it has to go through legal hoops and a great deal of red tape, and establish almost an audit trail to ensure that it is covered.' HC Hansard Debates, 6 June 2006.

into such detail. It will be sufficient of the director had considered the factors in reaching a decision.

As part of best practice, (i) directors should have all the new statutory duties explained to them; (ii) those who are responsible for preparing briefing and background papers for the board should be aware of the general duties and the six factors; (iii) directors must direct their minds to the overriding duty to promote the success of the company and consider the six factors; (iv) directors should not set out in the board minutes that each of the six factors was considered in reaching their decision (unless a particular factor was important to the decision reached by the director) – but to keep the board minutes' brief of the decision reached. The minutes may still refer to promoting the success of the company with the words '. . . the board was of the view that this [whatever the action/event] promotes the success of the company in accordance with s 172 of the CA 2006.'

A failure by the directors to establish a formal process or record that all six factors or that any of them was considered, should not and must not be viewed as a breach of the directors' duty under s 172 of the CA 2006. The courts should have regard to the intention behind s 172 of the CA 2006: it does not require that a consideration of the six factors be documented or minuted, nor that a formal process be established for their consideration. This is clearly not the intention of s 172 of the CA 2006. Directors are only required to 'have regard' to the six factors – they should have thought about these factors and made a decision. This is a subjective and not an objective test.

Enhancing enlightened shareholder value

9.15.2 The principle of 'enlightened shareholder value' has its origins in the concept of corporate social responsibility – which is a generic term used to describe the need for directors to act in the interests of wider stakeholders, other than the shareholders. A corporation is perceived now to bear social responsibility. The activities of a company may have an impact on these potential claimants that could adversely affect them in some way. A corporation, therefore, has a 'soul'. It is a responsible corporation. It is a caring corporation. It is responsive to the needs of the local community, of suppliers, customers or employees. It is a soulful corporation – a corporation that feels and is sensitive to stakeholder responses to corporate activities.

The concept of corporate social responsibilities also maintains the principle of 'trusteeship' of directors towards the various stakeholders on the corporation. Although legally, directors are not trustees for the wider stakeholders in the true legal sense of the word, they are perceived as fiduciaries for these groups, in the sense of having a responsibility to consider the interests of these groups in society, and to discharge their responsibilities and obligations in a responsible manner.[1763] The concept of corporate social responsibilities also maintains the 'philanthropic principle'. Companies may, for example, provide donations, assist in the local community by providing services or facilities, secondments, or any other form of benefit to society in general. The concept of 'enlightened shareholder value' is, therefore, inextricably link to corporate social responsibilities. This is not exhaustive,

---

[1763] The concept of the trust, which has served as a useful method for imposing legal obligations and duties upon the legal owners of property, the trustees who hold property on behalf of others, and the beneficiaries of the trust. The concept of the trust has been applied by the courts in an analogous way to impose fiduciary duties upon directors towards some of the 'stakeholders' of the company. Indeed, this idea is germane in English law, and was originally revealed by Maitland when he stated that: 'It is a big affair our trust . . . the connection between trust and corporation is very ancient. It is at least four centuries old.' The concept of trusteeship has been a major feature in the legal development of corporate social responsibilities with particular reference to the fiduciary duties of directors, albeit employed sparingly. Wedderburn suggests that the trust and the corporation, although independent of one another 'have trodden paths that intertwine' in the history of the common law at least since the end of the fourteenth century. The concept of the trust was, from a practical standpoint, the creation of the Chancery courts, which developed rules and principles better known as 'equity'. This concept was developed essentially as a private jurisdiction based on the notions of conscience and justices It emerged as a result of the common law's failure to provide an effective remedy for breaches of duty by the trustees towards their beneficiaries. According to this concept, the assets of settlors (donors) would be held on trust by the trustees for the benefit of third parties, the *cestuis que trust*, who were usually known as the beneficiaries. This principle of equity imposed certain rights and obligations upon trustees to act in the best interests of their beneficiaries. A failure by the trustees to consider these interests was regarded as a potential breach of trust and hence unconscionable. The concept is so fundamental for the protection of interests of the beneficiaries that the 'settlor'; and the beneficiaries may sue the trustees for breaches of their 'fiduciary' duties. In the performance of their duties, trustees must act honestly and in good faith. They must also act with due care and diligence.

In *Bartlett v Barclays Bank*, Brightman J referred to 'the duty of a trustee . . . to conduct the business of the trust with the same care as an ordinary prudent man of business'. Some of the substantive duties of trustees include securing and preserving the trust assets and avoiding speculative risks and investments. Trustees must ensure that the proceeds of the trust are distributed to the beneficiaries in accordance with the trust instrument. They must act fairly and equitably as between the various beneficiaries. Equity demands that they are, therefore, required to maintain regular accounts and records, and provide full disclosure of information to the beneficiaries upon request. Trustees must not personally profit from the trust. The concept of the trust has, therefore, served as a useful method for imposing legal duties and obligations upon trustees who were given property to hold for the use and benefit of others. According to some commentators, the courts applied the trusteeship principle to directors, as they believed that directors' duties were similar to those of trustees: 'the origin of the concept of this extension to directors may be that in the earliest form of companies, the director was a trustee in the true sense'. It was sufficient for the courts to reason that, since directors had accepted an appointment that attached obligations towards stakeholders, they were trustees and therefore accountable to the company for any breaches of trust. Another explanation for the use of the trustee concept in company law has been that the deed of settlement of the earliest forms of companies usually constituted directors as trustees of their funds and

but highlights areas of particular importance that reflects wider expectations of responsible business behaviour, such as the interests of the company's employees, and the impact of the company's operations on the community and the environment.

During the passage of the Companies Bill, there had been much lobbying by two main organisations, namely the Trade Justice Movement and Corporate Responsibility Coalition (CORE) towards ensuring directors exercise

property. Directors would be held accountable to their companies and shareholders for a mismanagement of the trust fund.

Sealy, however, disagrees with these explanations. He argues that the cases do not establish that directors were trustees: 'The directors and the trustees seem unquestionably to have been treated as distinct working bodies, the deed making separate provision for the appointment of each group and for their respective functions, powers and duties.' He contends that the use of the trusteeship concept is not appropriate to impose duties upon directors, and that a higher standard of care should be imposed on them than would be applied to trustees: 'A trustee must be honest, and adhere strictly to the terms of the trust: the corresponding rules in company law are that a director must be honest, and act lawfully and within the terms of his own authority and the constitution of the company. To this limited extent the rules of equity have served some purpose. But whereas a trustee is properly held only to the layman's standard of honesty, a director . . . ought nowadays to be fixed with the professional man's standards of skill and care.' But such an argument questions the ethos upon which a trust is based. Whereas a director is an employee of a company, a trustee is not. Therefore, impartiality is necessarily presumed of a trustee, a presumption which may not be true of directors. Indeed, the courts have used the trusteeship principle as a deliberate analogy to impose duties upon directors, but they have also recognised that directors are not trustees in the true sense of the word. In *Re Forest of Dean Coal Mining Co*, Sir George Jessel MR stated: 'Directors have sometimes been called trustees, or commercial trustees, sometimes they have been called managing partners; it does not much matter what you call them as long as you understand what their true position is, which is really that they are commercial men managing a trading concern for the benefit of themselves and of all the other shareholders: they are bound to use fair and reasonable diligence in the management of their company's affairs, and to act honestly.' Bowen LJ in *Imperial Hydropathic Hotel Co v Hampson* expressed the view that: 'When persons who are directors of a company are from time to time spoken of by judges as agents, trustees or managing partners of the company, it is essential to recollect that such expressions are not used as exhaustive of the powers or responsibilities of those persons but only as indicating useful points of view from which they may for the moment and for the particular purpose be considered.' The courts also identified the extent and scope of the trusteeship concept as it applied to directors. In *Selangor United Rubber Estates Ltd v Cradock (No 3)*, for example, Ungoed Thomas J was of the opinion that: 'Directors are clearly not trustees identically with trustees of a will or various settlements . . . they have business to conduct and business functions to perform in a business manner, which are not normally at any rate associated with trustees of a will or marriage settlement.' However, Pennington argues that because there is a substantial volume of case law on directors' duties and powers, the courts are now less inclined to compare directors' duties with those of trustees. According to Gower: '. . . to describe directors as trustees seems today to be neither strictly correct nor invariably helpful. In truth, directors are agents of the company rather than the trustees of its property. But as agents they stand in a fiduciary relationship to their principal, the company. The duties of good faith which this fiduciary relationship imposes are virtually identical with those imposed on trustees, and to this extent the description "trustee" still has validity.'

their corporate social responsibilities to groups wider than just the share-holders,[1764] thereby ensuring that the company directors would have a duty not only to maximise profit, but also consider the impact of their business on people and the environment.[1765]

However, there has also been much debate in both Houses of Parliament and beyond as to just exactly what the six factors represent. According to Alistair Darling (then Secretary of State for Trade and Industry),[1766] the Bill (as it was then) recognised that to achieve sustainable success for the benefit of shareholders, directors were required to have regard to a wide range of factors. The statutory statement of directors' duties represented a code of conduct setting out how directors were expected to behave. This enshrined in statute the concept of 'enlightened shareholder value'. There was a recognition that directors would be more likely to achieve long-term sustainable success for the benefit of their shareholders if their companies paid attention to a wider range of matters. It was, therefore, important, that all companies recognised their obligations. It was not the intention of the Government that a director should be responsible to everybody in theory, but in fact to nobody. That would result in good directors, people acting in the best of faith, being unclear what they are supposed to do and to whom they were answerable. 'Bad directors' might use that term loosely and could easily play one side off against another.

Why only the six factors?

9.15.3 Another aspect for consideration has been why the particular 'six factors', and not any other factors? Related to this is whether the six factors are in any order of priority.

Guidance from the House of Common debates suggests that the six factors are not in any order of priority or precedence, and not one of the six factors

---

[1764] Both the Trade Justice Movement and CORE welcomed steps towards greater corporate social responsibility, but considered that the CA 2006 had not gone far enough to ensure that British business worked for people as well as profit. According to the Trade Justice Movement, in spite of calls from both business and civil society, the Government had failed to introduce a statutory standard for reporting, and it would continue to fall to groups like CORE and the Trade Justice Movement to scrutinise the transparency of business. The Government did, however, agree to review the situation in two years' time, and to introduce stricter legal standards if the reporting of social and environmental matters was not working. See Trade Justice Movement, Press Release, 10 November 2006.

[1765] According to the MP Patrick Hall, CA 2006, s 172 does not represent a 'pluralist approach' to corporate social responsibilities. A pluralist approach would allow the interests of all the company's stakeholders – its employees, the wider community, local residents and consumers – to be given the same priority as the interests of shareholders. The CA 2006 is one of enlightened shareholder value. It is not about a pluralist approach which means that the primary duty of directors is to promote the success of the company: See MC Debates 6 June 2006.

[1766] See HC Debates for 6 June 2006.

ranks higher than any other. All the six factors are given equal weight under the CA 2006 – but it may not be unreasonable to suppose that some of the factors may require the particular attention of directors, depending upon the facts, circumstances, events or situations that they encounter.

It is clear, however, that the list of six factors is applicable to all types and sizes of companies and does not distinguish between private and public companies. The six factors, however, may not be appropriate for all types of companies to take into account. For example, the director of a major plc and the sole director of a corner shop will not take into account the same factors when they make important decisions.

It should also be noted that the six factors are not an exhaustive list. Directors are also to have regard to 'other matters' that are not part of the six factors. This could include a wide spectrum of areas in which a company may be involved at any particular time – examples include (but are not limited to) takeovers; mergers; acquisitions; joint ventures; management buy-outs; as well as other matters that impact on the company's activities and operations. Apart from the six factors, therefore, directors must have regard to other matters that impact on the duty to promote their company's success.

Factor (a) – 'the likely consequence of any decision in the long term'

9.15.4 It is suggested that this factor requires directors to act positively and proactively in determining the likely consequence of any decision in the long term. The decision must not be reached on a short-term basis, as this will not be considered as promoting the success of the company. Directors will required to apply their minds to the likely future outcome or consequence in the long term of any decision they may make. Directors need not be certain of their decision as this factor does not require absolute certainty on the part of a director. They must ask themselves: 'What is likely to result from the decisions we make today in the long term?'

Take for example, a company that is established by the directors to specialise in the manufacture of spare parts for cars. The company has never engaged in any other activity. The directors then decide to embark on a new retail venture, specialising in the latest fashion accessories. They have never had any experience in this area of retail activity, nor are they prepared to hire any consultants or specialists to assist them. The 'likely consequence' of such a decision in the long term may lead to a disastrous business activity, that is likely to fail in the long term, and one that depletes shareholders' resources to the detriment of the company and may result in losses. This may be an extreme example, and the spectrum may be wide in determining, depending on the particular facts and circumstances, what may be the likely consequences of any decision in the long term. It is submitted that the courts should apply the ordinary and natural meaning to the words used in factor (a).

Factor (b) – 'the interests of the company's employees'

9.15.5 In requiring directors to have regard to the interest of employees, this provision replaces s 309 of the CA 1985.[1767]

Judicial attitudes towards directors considering the interests of employees have varied and the law has not been applied consistently, by the courts. Legal issues have arisen where a company has engaged in corporate philanthropy or gratuitous distributions of an altruistic nature towards, for example, its employees. Some cases have shown that the courts have viewed payments to employees with no great enthusiasm, and sometimes with outright hostility,[1768] whereas in other cases, the courts have permitted payments to employees as a recognition of directors taking account of employees' interests within the corporation.

In *Hampson v Price's Patent Candle Co*, where, as a matter of factory management policy, the directors had proposed to make one week's *ex gratia* payment (in addition to the usual wages) to their employees 'in recognition of the fact that their exertions have helped to make the company's profits larger than they have been for the last 16 years'. These payments were for employees who had 'worked there with good character throughout the year'. There was no express power in the memorandum to pay these gratuities. A majority of the shareholders had approved the payments, but the applicant, who was one

---

[1767] CA 1985, s 309 was concerned with directors to have regard to the interests of the company's employees. It stated that the matters to which the directors of the company were to have regard in the performance of their functions included the interests of the company's employees in general, as well as the interests of its members:s 309(1). Accordingly, the duty owed by directors by this section was owed by them to the company (and the company alone) and was enforceable in the same way as any other fiduciary duty owed to a company by its directors: s 309(2). Section 309 also applied to shadow directors: s 309(3). See too *Parke v Daily News* [1962] Ch 927.

[1768] According to Sealy: 'Perhaps the strongest factor influencing the judges, more especially in the Victorian period, has been the difficulty in reconciling notions of altruism with the capitalist ethic. It seems to have been accepted practically without question until only a decade ago that the sole purpose of any company was to make the greatest profits possible for its shareholders. Even today this approach is by no means dead, and most people would assume that this was at least a company's predominant purpose. A corporate gift which diminishes profits violates this philosophy, unless it can be justified on the ground that it is likely to bring a greater benefit in the long term.' However, Sealy suggests that the public and judicial perceptions on the 'shareholder money' approach have changed: Nowadays opinion has changed and there is general support for the view that 'responsible' companies ought not to neglect 'wider' interests such as those of their employees, clients and customers, the community, the environment and so on; but even so the 'shareholders' money' attitude can still influence questions such as the propriety of corporate gifts to charity or donations to political parties: 'why, it is asked, should company directors or even majority shareholders, decide where this benevolence is to be bestowed when there are likely to be other shareholders who would choose to do something quite different with their share of the money if it were paid out to them.' See Sealy, *Cases and Materials in Company Law* (1992) (5th edn) Chapter 3, pp 125–160.

of the dissentient shareholders, brought an action against the company. Hampson alleged that the company could not, under its constitution, authorise voluntary expenditure from the corporate funds. He contended that the resolution approving the payment was void and illegal and that the company should be restrained from making these payments. He also argued that the distribution of funds to the employees was beyond the scope of the directors' authority.

Jessel MR decided that the company's articles gave wide powers of management to its directors. They could, therefore, lawfully exercise all the powers of the company. In approving the payments, he reasoned:

> Can anything be more reasonable than that, when the employer has had a very good year through the exertions of the workmen employed by him, he should give them something more than their ordinary wages by encouraging them to exert themselves for the future?

The directors had clearly acted *bona fide* by seeking approval for the payment from their shareholders. The court would not interfere where directors had decided that the proposed payment to their employees would encourage them to work for the company's benefit. This was the 'best mode' of conducting the company's affairs as determined by the directors and 'no judge ought to give an opinion on matters of this kind, which he does not understand.' Jessel MR concluded that:

> ... the managers and directors of the company, whose business it is, and who ought to know how to conduct the business to the most advantage, ought to be allowed to judge whether what is about to be done is advantageous and reasonable or not.

In *Hutton v West Cork Railway Co*,[1769] an action was brought by the holder of a debenture stock who did not approve of a resolution by the company to make certain payments to the company's officers. The court was required to decide whether the sum of £1,050 could lawfully be paid by the company as compensation to its managing director and other officers for loss of their employment. It was also required to determine whether another sum of £1,500 could be paid to directors as remuneration for their past services in circumstances where the company was no longer a going concern. The railway company had sought to sell its undertaking to another company, but it had no express provisions in its articles for the payment of remuneration to its directors and had never previously made such payments. The Act authorising the transfer of business provided that, on completion of the transfer, the

---

[1769] (1883) 23 Ch D 654.

company would be dissolved except for the purposes of regulating its internal affairs and using the proceeds of the sale in the manner resolved by the company. The Court of Appeal held that a power to make these payments could not be implied after the company had ceased to be a going concern. The powers could be implied only as incidental to the company's business, but not where the company was moribund.

Cotton LJ distinguished this case from the *Taunton and Hampson*[1770] cases where payments were made by companies that were going concerns. In the present case, the company was no longer a going concern. The proposed payment of £1,050 to the company's directors was a gratuity, but without any prospect of it being in any way reasonably conducive to the company's benefit. His lordship considered that payment as *ultra vires*. The other proposed payment of £1,500 to the directors was not a reasonable sum as remuneration for their past services. It was instead 'a sum which might with reasonable generosity be paid to them taking into consideration the fact that they never received anything during the years when they carried on the railway'. This payment was also held to be beyond the company's powers and *ultra vires*.

Bowen LJ sympathised with the directors' dilemma, but felt that their interests must be balanced against the interests of the dissentient shareholders:

> They can only spend money which is not theirs but the company's, if they are spending it for purposes which are reasonably incidental to the carrying on of the business of the company.

Bowen LJ reasoned that *bona fide* could not be the sole test otherwise you might have a lunatic conducting the affairs of the company, and paying away its money with both hands in a matter perfectly *bona fide* yet perfectly irrational. The test was whether the payment was reasonably incidental to, and within the reasonable scope of, carrying on the company's business. In the absence of any express provisions in the company's articles, the payments to the directors would amount to a gratuity. Thus:

> A railway company, or the directors of the company, might send down all the porters at a railway station to have tea in the country at the expense of the company. Why should they not? It is for the directors to judge, provided it is a matter which is reasonably incidental to the carrying on of the business of the company; and a company which always treated its employees with Draconian severity, and never allowed them a single inch more than the strict letter of the bond, would soon find itself deserted – at all events, unless labour was very much more easy to obtain in the market than it often is . . .

[1770] See *Taunton v Royal Insurance Co.* (1864) 2 H&M 135.

> It is no charity sitting at the board of directors because . . . charity has
> no business to sit at the board of directors qua charity. The law does not
> say that there are to be no cakes and ale, but there are to be no cakes and
> ale except such as are required for the benefit of the company.

This statement by Bowen LJ clearly suggests that a company has the sole
authority to determine what would be regarded as being for the benefit of the
company in consideration of the 'interests of the employees'. However, where
the company had ceased to be a going concern it could not derive any benefit
from the gratuitous distribution. The company had a special and limited
business, and that business was to preside at its own funeral, to wind itself up
and to carry on its own internal affairs.

In *Parke v Daily News Ltd*,[1771] the defendant company was in the process of
selling its two main associated newspapers, which had incurred losses, to
Associated Newspapers. The directors of the *Daily News* had intended
to distribute the proceeds of the sale to the company's employees who were to
be made redundant, Before a meeting of *Daily News* shareholders could be
convened to approve the proposed payment to the employees, the plaintiff
brought an action against the company claiming that the proposed payment
was *ultra vires* the company.

Plowman J decided that the directors were not acting in the best interests
of their shareholders. The directors' decision was actuated by other motives,
predominant among which was 'a desire to treat the employees generously
beyond all legal entitlement'. In considering the directors' affidavits, which
provided substantive evidence that the employees had claims to consideration', which it was proper for the company to consider; Plowman J accepted:

> . . . the view that directors, in having regard to the question 'what is in the
> best interests of their company?' are entitled to take into account the
> interests of the employees, irrespective of any consequential benefit to
> the company, is one which may be widely held.

However, in answer to the affidavit of the *Daily News* accountant, that companies had an obligation to their employees, Plowman J replied: '. . . but no
authority to support that proposition as a proposition of law was cited to me.
I know of none, and in my judgment such is not the law'. The directors were
prompted by motives which, however laudable, and however enlightened
from the point of view of industrial relations, were such that the law would
not recognise them as sufficient justification for making the proposed payments to the employees. This was based on the reasoning that the *Daily News*
would cease to be a going concern after the business was sold to Associated
Newspapers.

[1771] [1962] Ch 927, noted by Wedderburn (1962) 21 Camb LJ 141.

Previously, s 309(1) of the CA 1985 provided that the matters to which the directors of the company were to have regard in the performance of their functions included the interests of the company's employees in general, as well as the interests of its members. Under s 309(2) of the CA 1985, the duty imposed by s 309 of the CA 1985 on the directors was owed by them to the company (and the company alone) and was enforceable in the same way as any other fiduciary duty owed to a company by its directors. Some commentators had viewed these provisions as 'mere window dressing', designed in practice to have little impact on the enforcement of the directors' duties. There was no enforcement mechanism for employees whose directors omitted to take account of their interests. The fiduciary duty was owed to the company and enforceable only in the same way as other duties owed to the company.

Under s 172(2)(b), the 'interests of the company's employees' should be interpreted widely. It would include issues such as the location of the company and re-location; redundancy; issues concerning takeovers and mergers; employee welfare; health and safety; security. The categories are wide and not exhaustive. however, this factor does not allow any enforcement mechanism for employees where directors fail to have regard to employees' interests.

Factor (c) – 'the need to foster the company's business relationship with suppliers, customers and others'

9.15.6 A company will have business dealings with various third parties. This factor provides for directors to address the requirement to foster the company's business relationship with suppliers, customers and others. The word 'foster' would suggest the need to promote growth or develop business relationships with such third parties. Developing such business relationships is vital for companies to ensure growth and success. A company cannot operate or function in a vacuum. Many businesses have regular dealings with their customers and/or suppliers, and in some cases, based on a contractual relationship. The list set out in factor (c) is not exhaustive and the category is not closed, as it includes 'others'. It is suggested that this may include lenders, creditors, professional advisers consultants, etc.[1772]

[1772] Although the traditional perception has been that directors do not have a fiduciary duty towards other groups in society, which include the claims of consumers, the community and suppliers, they have a moral duty in practice to consider the interests of these claimants. These claimants are a different category from those of shareholders, creditors and employees because they are not readily identifiable, but they may be so as parties to contracts. Consumer interest within the company structure has been described as, most controversial. This is because consumer discontent and an abuse of power by some companies in misleading and defrauding their consumers is suggested to have flowed from the unbridled power that companies have usurped in the marketplace. Nader, a leading champion of the rights of consumers in America, contended that 'consumers are being manipulated, defrauded and injured, not just by marginal business . . . but by US blue-chip firms.' In the UK, the Molony

Under this factor, there will be a duty, for example, not to mislead consumers or engage in illegal activities with suppliers. It may, for example, require companies to set out clearly for consumers in plain, intelligible language just exactly what are the products or services that consumers are purchasing. It may require companies to address clearly their business relationship with suppliers, such as terms of business or, paying invoices to suppliers on time.

This factor does not allow suppliers, consumers and others to bring proceedings where directors have failed to have regard to this factor.

Factor (d) – 'the impact of the company's operations on the community and the environment'

9.15.7 Directors are to have regard to the 'impact of the company's operations on the community and the environment.'

This factor has a number of implications. Take, for example, the situation where the community is living near a quarry, a coal mine or nuclear power station, or a chemical plant. Would this type of activity allow anyone from the local community the right to take the company to court because he/she did not like the activity of the company, even though it was legal and in compliance with all the health and safety regulations? Clearly, the applicant would lack the *locus standi* to enforce such a provision. It would not be possible to have a situation whereby essentially two groups of people are running the company – one being the directors and the other being people who do not like what the company is doing, and asking the courts to second-guess the company's decisions.

Another situation may involve the proposed closure of the company's operations in a particular part of the UK, where the local community is

Committee was alarmed at the lack of consumer protection and the inequality of bargaining position between companies and their consumers and the lack of information provided to consumers: 'Products are now being marketed in such manner that it is more difficult for consumers to judge their qualities adequately.' The CBI came to similar conclusions. It argued that the claims of consumers sometimes received neither the priority nor the attention they deserved. Faced with a large impersonal organisation, a revolution in the methods of marketing, changing standards of retail service and the technical complexity of many modern goods, has led to a feeling of frustration and perplexity among consumers. The CBI thought that companies should be under a duty not to mislead their consumers and to protect their interests: It is not the duty of boards of companies and their employees to protect their customers from their own willful ignorance or folly, nor to prevent them from spending their money as they please; but it is their duty not to mislead anyone and, if possible, to protect them from misleading themselves: There is recent evidence by an organisation New Consumer to suggest that consumers play an effective and influential role in shaping corporate policy on social issues such as environmental pollution and the quality of the products produced by companies: 'There is now evidence that consumers are realising the power of their economic vote which can be cast everyday.' Previously English company law did not directly recognise the interests of the consumers. To some extent, the obligations of consumers were covered by a wide range of legislation. However, company law cannot possibly cover the whole spectrum of consumerism.

heavily dependent upon local businesses for employment. The closure of a company branch could lead to redundancies and reflect poorly on the image of the company. In such circumstances, the directors must have regard to the impact the closure would have on the local community. It may mean finding alternative solutions to ensure survival of the company – ultimately the decision is for the directors to make, but directors must have regard to what they are doing, and how it will affect the community.[1773]

[1773] In some cases, judicial attitudes have been favourable towards companies engaging in philanthropic activities in their local communities. The case of *Evans v Brunner Mond* (1921) 1 Ch 359, is one of the first applications of this liberal approach. One of the companys objects in cl 3 of its memorandum stated that it could do 'all such business and things as may be incidental or conducive to the attainment of the above objects, or any of them'. The shareholders had passed a resolution authorising their directors to distribute £100,000 to various universities and scientific institutions in furtherance of scientific education and research. A dissentient shareholder sought an injunction to restrain the company from making this payment, claiming a declaration that the resolution was *ultra vires* the objects and powers of the company. The plaintiff's counsel argued that the donation was not within the company's objects and there was no direct benefit to the company. Counsel for the company argued, however, that the donation was reasonably incidental and conducive to the company's main objects because the company required persons equipped to undertake research work and the donation to the universities would assist the company in this respect. According to the evidence presented by the directors by way of affidavits, the company by its contribution wished to encourage a class of persons who would cultivate scientific study and research generally. According to the plaintiff's counsel, therefore, in the event of a donation being conducive to the company, it may be regarded as lawful.

Eve J construed the company's objects as permitting donations for the furtherance of scientific education and research. He appreciated the past practice by the courts of distinguishing between objects and powers but thought that it was not now necessary to distinguish between the two. It was merely sufficient to interpret the extent and scope of the company's objects. His Lordship concluded: 'The wide and general objects are to be construed as ancillary to the company's main purpose, and I apprehend that the act to be *intra vires* must be one which can fairly be regarded as incidental or conducive to the main or paramount purpose for which the company was formed.'

The liberal approach has also been applied in some American cases on corporate philanthropy. In *AP Smith Mfg v Barlow* (1953) 13NJ 145, the directors proposed to donate $1,500 to the Princeton University and a further contribution towards its maintenance. Some of the minority shareholders brought an action to prevent this distribution of corporate funds on the ground that the company's objects did not expressly permit such donations. Further, there was no implied power to make them. The company's president testified that he considered the payment as a good investment and that the public expected companies to aid philanthropic and benevolent institutions. He expressed the view that in contributing to the liberal arts institutions, companies 'were furthering self-interest' in ensuring the free flow of properly trained personnel for administrative and corporate employment. Jacobs J reviewed the historical literature on corporate social responsibilities and observed that the early corporate charters referred to services to the public in their recitals: 'The corporate object was the public one of managing and ordering the trade as well as the private one of profit for the members.' He upheld the validity of the donation because it was reasonably incidental to the company's objectives and benefited the company's reputation by establishing a closer relationship with local educational institutions. The court also upheld the donation on the general grounds of a company's wider obligations to the community. Jacobs J stated: 'Modern conditions require

Under s 172(2)(d) of the CA 2006, directors must also have regard to the environment. Any activities undertaken by the company must not harm the environment. For example, it should not pollute the atmosphere; or emit noxious fumes; or handle toxic chemicals without proper procedures and health and safety policies being in place.

The term 'operations' is not defined but would refer to activities or, procedures.

Although under separate legislation, the Corporate Manslaughter and Corporate Homicide Act 2007 will have significant implications for companies in terms of their operations and activities.[1774]

that corporations acknowledge and discharge social as well as private responsibilities as members of the communities within which they operate.' The liberal approach, therefore, justifies corporate philanthropy by referring to its role in contributing to the socio-economic health of the community.

[1774] The Act makes provision for a new criminal offence, which in England and Wales or Northern Ireland will be known as 'Corporate Manslaughter' (and as 'Corporate Homicide' in Scotland). The offence will apply to companies, unincorporated bodies, Government departments, similar institutions and police forces. Section 1 sets out 'the offence' and the type of organisations to whom the offence will apply. It provides that an 'organisation' is guilty of an offence if the way in which its activities are managed or organised results in the following two aspects: first, it causes a person's death. Second, it amounts to a gross breach of the relevant duty of care owed by the organisation to the deceased. The offence applies to a corporation; a department or body listed in Schedule 1; and the police force. A police force is to be treated as owing whatever duties of care it would owe if it were a body corporate. The term 'corporation' does not include a body sole but includes any body corporate wherever incorporated.

The new offence builds on the foundation of the common law offence of gross negligence manslaughter in England and Wales and Northern Ireland. Whereas the common law offence is contingent on the guilt of the individual(s) concerned, liability for the new offence will depend on a finding of gross negligence in the way in which the activities of the organisation are run. The offence will be committed where, in the particular circumstances, an organisation owes a duty to take responsibility for a person's safety, and the way in which the activities of the organisation have been managed or organised amounts to a gross breach of that duty and which causes that person's death. The activities that were managed or organised by senior management must be a substantial element of the gross breach.

The offence can be categorised as follows. First, the organisation must owe a relevant duty of care to the victim. Section 2 of the Act sets out the relevant duties of care. The organisation must be in breach of that duty of care as a result of the way in which the activities of the organisation were managed or organised. It should be noted that the offence is not concerned with hierarchical levels of management or sensitivity and does not attach blame to such hierarchy level. Instead, it is how the activity was managed within the organisation, which can be guilty of an offence only if the way in which its activities are managed or organised by its senior management is a 'substantial' element of the breach. The manner in which the organisation's activities were managed or organised must have caused the victim's death. In criminal law, the principles of causation will apply to determine whether the way in which the organisation's activities were managed or organised causes the victim's death. This need not be the sole cause of the death – but only a cause. However, intervening events could break the chain of causation in some circumstances. The management failure must amount to a 'gross' breach of duty of care. In determining what constitutes a gross breach of duty of care, s 1(4)(b) states that the conduct alleged to amount to a breach of that duty falls far below what could reasonably be expected of the organisation in the circumstances. The test reflects the current common law position of gross negligence/manslaughter. The jury must consider various factors in determining whether the test has been satisfied. It should be noted that liability will not arise where the management of an activity includes reasonable safeguards and death nevertheless occurs.

The new offence will apply to various types of organisations listed in s 1(2). It applies to a corporation. This refers to any body corporate, whether incorporated in the UK or elsewhere. It includes companies incorporated under company's legislation, as well as bodies incorporated under statute such as Non-Departmental Public Bodies and other bodies in the public sector, or by Royal Charter. The definition does not include a corporate sole which cover a number of individual offices in England and Wales and Northern Ireland.

The Act identifies who are the 'senior management' within the organisation. Section 1(4)(c) states that senior management in relation to an organisation means the persons who play 'significant' roles in the management of the whole or a substantial part of the organisation's activities. This covers both those in the direct chain of management including those in, for example, strategic or regulatory compliance roles. The definition applies to those who apply a significant role either in the making of decisions about how the whole or a substantial part of its activities are to be managed or organised; or the actual managing or organising of the whole or substantial part of those activities.

The Act also applies to the Crown and will apply to various Crown bodies and government departments. Although generally, Crown bodies do not have separate legal personality, but in the event that legal personality does not apply, then the application of the offence to corporations will also apply to Crown bodies. Where a separate legal personality does not apply then a mechanism is required to identify which Crown bodies are covered by the offence, and this is achieved by applying the offence to a list of government departments and other bodies set out in Schedule 1. An organisation that is guilty of corporate manslaughter or corporate homicide is liable on conviction on indictment to a fine.

The new offence will be liable only in the Crown Court in England and Wales and Northern Ireland and the High Court of Judiciary in Scotland. Proceedings will be before a jury. The penalty is an unlimited fine. However, s 9 sets out provisions for remedial orders. Section 2 elucidates on the concept of 'relevant duty of care' referred to in the offence. The offence will only apply in circumstances where an organisation owed a duty of care to the victim under the law of negligence. This mirrors the position at common law of gross negligence manslaughter.

The Act sets out the necessary relationship between the defendant organisation and the victim and sets out the broad scope of the offence. Section 2(1) categorises the following duties embracing the concept of 'relevant duty of care'. An organisation owes a duty to its employees or to other persons working for the organisation or performing services for it. This includes a duty by the employer to provide a safe system of work – a duty owed as occupier of the premises, which includes that owed by the occupier of buildings and land to people in or on, or potentially affected by the property. Although this is a duty owed at common law, in some cases, the duty has been superseded by legislation. It includes duties owed under the Occupiers' Liability Acts 1957 and 1984 and the Defective Premises Act 1972.

However, the common law continues to define by whom and to whom the duty is owed. In some circumstances, liability in the law of negligence has been superseded by statutory provision imposing strict liability, such as the liability of carriers under the Carriage of Air Act 1961. A duty owed in connection with: (i) the supply by the organisation of goods or services (whether for consideration or not); (ii) the carrying on by the organisation of any construction or maintenance operations; (iii) the carrying on by the organisation of any other activity on a commercial basis; (iv) the use or keeping by the organisation of any plant, vehicle or other things. The duty of care arises out of certain specific functions or activities performed by an organisation.

Factor (e) – 'the desirability of the company maintaining a reputation for high standards of business conduct'

9.15.8 Directors must have regard to the 'desirability of the company maintaining a reputation for high standards of business conduct.'

This factor is concerned with business ethics – the manner, behaviour and values of a company. The ethics may be enshrined in various forms ranging from mission statements, vision statements or even codes of conduct. In some cases, companies may also be affiliated to trade organisations to demonstrate high standards of business conduct.

The wording of factor (e) only requires a 'desirability' – this is voluntary and not an obligation for companies. If a company takes this voluntary approach, it should then 'maintain' a reputation for 'high standards' of business conduct. The term 'maintain' suggests regularising a specific standard and keeping up with such standard by, for example, frequent reviews or updates. Some companies now have international standards in place that regularise their systems and procedures as well as compliance standards. The standard is not an ordinary or reasonable one – but it is a high one. Some companies may prefer to demonstrate an appropriate approach to business conduct by drafting a code of conduct, which sets out the business conduct of companies ranging from its employees, to customers, suppliers and others, as a benchmark for regulating its business conduct. Other companies have specific codes of conduct on corporate social responsibilities or affiliated to trade associations.[1775]

[1775] The proposal for a code of conduct on corporate social responsibilities derives largely from the Conservative government's White Paper in 1973. It suggested that the wider social responsibilities of directors could be expressly identified in a Code of Conduct on Social Responsibilities supported by some external sanction and enforcement mechanisms.

According to the White Paper, the role of the proposed code would be to provide some 'positive guidance' that companies might require if they were safely to deviate from profit maximisation. It recommended that the code should be monitored by an independent organisation. Although the government initially suggested that the Panel on Take-Over and Mergers could undertake the role of enforcing the code, it eventually concluded that the Panel might not be the most appropriate institution in view of its connection with the London Stock Exchange. It stated that another organisation, similar to the Panel, ought to be established to exercise an independent judgment over those companies that were found to have breached the code.

The Code of Conduct recommended by the 1973 White Paper was in many ways loosely drafted, in that it was not articulate enough in putting forward its recommendations; nor did it explain certain expressions such as 'positive guidance'. Furthermore, the business community in the 1970s was not prepared for such a proposal and, therefore, it was never followed up. Indeed, in the same year, the CBI reported it was opposed to any form of mandatory code, whether of a social or moral kind, regulating companies and, emphasised that voluntary self-reform was still the best way forward for companies. It instead recommended a set of general 'principles' guiding corporate conduct, which could be voluntarily implemented by companies. According to the CBI, once these principles had gained general acceptance by

British companies, they could have 'a material effect' in helping to raise the general level of corporate behaviour.

But these principles were not aimed at providing specific rules prescribing the correct action to be pursued by directors in every situation. Where appropriate, directors could adapt the principles to suit their organisational structure.

Among the suggested principles were the following: Business today has to operate in a far wider context than ever before. It may be wise for boards to see that they have authority to allow for the wider judgments involved. Profit over the long term remains the principal yardstick by which the success or failure of a company should be judged. A company today is concerned with a wider range of matters than in years gone by. This requires the board to give increasing attention to relationships with employees, customers, suppliers, government, local authorities and the general public. However, the CBI did not propose any sanctions for breaches of these principles. It argued that 'no-one should be put on trial for an alleged offence that could not be precisely defined or tested by evidence. The business of private enterprise is capable of working out its own programme of self reform'.

This certainly confirms the attitudes that have been maintained by companies in England. Despite the conflict between the traditional notion of companies towards their business and the notion that was developing in England through the participation of various action groups, certain companies, of their own volition, did develop their own code of conduct. In other words, whereas formidable institutions such as the CBI were generally against a code of conduct, the case for a code was never entirely lost. Indeed, in May 1978, the Labour government issued a code of conduct for British companies that had interests in South Africa. The government urged companies to make every effort to promote best employment policies and practices recommended by the code.

The code, *inter alia*, required English companies in South Africa to ensure that all their employees, irrespective of racial or other distinction, were allowed to choose freely the type of organisation to represent their interests. Further, it encouraged employers to inform their employees that consultation and collective bargaining with organisations and employees' representatives were part of company policy. There were social provisions in the code on fringe benefits for employees. Paragraph 5A of the code required companies to 'concern themselves with the living conditions of their employees and families'. Employers were encouraged to do whatever was in their control to abolish any segregation at the workplace, in canteens, sports activities, education and training. The code also required parent companies to publish annually a detailed and fully documented report on the progress made in the application of the code. There were, however, no sanctions for breaches of this code.

The importance of codes of conduct has also been highlighted by several notable British studies. Melrose-Woodman and Kverndal conducted a study in 1976 to ascertain the degree of corporate commitment to codes and written policy statements. The survey revealed that most companies (66 per cent) supported the implementation of a code for various reasons, the most popular of which was to clarify and formalise corporate policy as a result of company growth and to provide guidelines and social objectives for managers. Companies also felt under a moral obligation to state expressly their particular philosophy on social responsibilities. Other companies had introduced a code to improve staff and customer relations, and a few had formulated a code owing to external pressures. The authors suggested it might be desirable for a code to have some sanctions attached to it. Woodman and Kverndal's findings were confirmed later in 1987 by the Institute of Business Ethics ('the Institute'), which conducted a survey based on 300 questionnaires sent to chief executives of the largest UK companies and 100 to the members of the Christian Association of Business Executives. A total of 142 responses were received, and 55 per cent of respondents stated that they had a written philosophy and/or a code of practice. Corporate philosophies were largely enshrined in a variety of policy documents including a short statement in the annual report; in information brochures provided to employees, shareholders and the public; or in the general staff handbook.

Factor (e) displays the characteristics of corporate social rectitude.[1776] This is concerned with the ethical aspects of corporate social behaviour – the need to adopt ethical values towards shareholders, creditors, employees and other persons having a legal interest in the company.

Factor (f) – 'the need to act fairly as between members of the company'

9.15.9 Directors must have regard to the need to act fairly as between members of the company. They must not act for the advantage of one group to the detriment of another. They must be transparent with all groups concerned, and not engage in partial disclosure of information to one group to the exclusion of another.

The key word here is 'fairly'. They must exercise impartial judgment and decisions affecting various groups of members. It requires them to exercise a degree of objectivity towards members and not to act as judge, jury and executioner to the prejudice of a group of members.[1777] The concept of

The survey found that chief executives and senior management were committed to their codes. Those companies that were members of professional associations emphasised the importance of their professional codes of conduct in assisting them to decide broader social issues. At least 20 per cent of the companies that did not have a code or a written statement of philosophy stated that they had intended to produce one. The results therefore demonstrate a high level of interest shown by English companies in formulating a code of conduct as part of their wider social responsibilities.

However, in view of the traditional attitudes maintained by companies, doubts still prevail as to whether a majority of companies would adopt codes of conduct themselves. From the perspective of corporate social responsibilities, the need for a national code is more particularly felt in respect of those companies that are involved in manufacturing. Moreover, companies in general should be subject to a national code by virtue of the concept of trusteeship.

[1776] See. S. Sheikh, *Corporate Social Responsibilities: Law and Practice* (1995).

[1777] English courts have recognised that directors may, in particular circumstances, owe fiduciary duties to individual shareholders based on the agency principle. This would apply, for example, where directors undertook to act as agents for their shareholders in the sale of their members' shares. Directors can also be under a fiduciary duty to individual shareholders in the law of tort to act with honesty and with due care. New Zealand has recognised the existence of a fiduciary duty of directors towards their shareholders that was not limited to the agency relationship. Their liability to individual shareholders can arise because of a failure by directors to disclose material information to their shareholders. In *Coleman v Myers*, the New Zealand Court of Appeal thought *Percival* was rightly decided on its particular facts but held that, in the case before it, a fiduciary relationship existed between the directors and the individual shareholders because of the 'special circumstances' identified by the court. The directors were liable to compensate the shareholders because the company was a private limited company with a substantial number of shares that were held by one family; the other members of the family frequently looked to the directors to provide them with business advice; the information affecting the true value of the shares had been withheld from the shareholders by their directors; and the directors had a high level of inside knowledge.

In the course of his judgment, Woodhouse J in the Court of Appeal referred to the *Percival*

fairness could also involve issues of natural justice – allowing groups a right to be heard, allowing representations, deliberating, consulting, getting feedback before making a decision.[1778]

Other aspects of s 172 of the CA 2006

9.15.10 Section 172(2) of the CA 2006 addresses the question of altruistic, or partly altruistic, companies. Examples of such companies include charitable companies and community interest companies, but it is possible for any company to have 'unselfish' objectives that prevail over the 'selfish' interests of members. Where the purpose of the company is something other than the benefits of its members, the directors must act in the way they consider, in good faith, would be likely to achieve that purpose. It is a matter for the good faith judgment of the director as to what those purposes are, and, where the company is partially for the benefit of its members and partly for other purposes, the extent to which other purposes apply in place of the benefit of the members. This section highlights that the main objective of a company may not be simply profit maximation. Directors could engage in other socially responsible objectives, such as corporate philanthropy, provided this was in good faith and likely to promote the success of the company.

Section 172(3) of the CA 2006 recognises that the duty to promote the success of the company is displaced when the company is insolvent. Section 214 of the Insolvency Act 1986 provides a mechanism under which the liquidator can require the directors to contribute towards the funds available to creditors in an insolvent winding up, where they ought to have recognised that the company had no reasonable prospect of avoiding insolvent liquidation, and then failed to take all reasonable steps to minimise the losses of creditors.

It has been suggested that the duty to promote the success of the company may also be modified by an obligation to have regard to the interests of creditors as the company nears insolvency. However, s 172(3) of the CA 2006 will leave the law to develop in this area.

decision and stated: 'In my opinion it is not the law that anybody holding the office of director of a limited liability company is for that reason alone to be released from what otherwise would be regarded as a fiduciary responsibility owed to those in the position of shareholders of the same company.'

[1778] In the context of takeovers and mergers see City Code on Takeover and Mergers. This provides *inter alia*, that the code is designed principally to ensure that shareholders are treated 'fairly' and not denied an opportunity to debate the merits of a takeover and that shareholders of the same class are afforded equivalent treatment by the offeror. General Principle 1 states that all holders of securities of an offeree company of the same class must be afforded equivalent treatment – moreover, if a person acquires control of a company, the other holders of securities must be protected.

Duty to exercise independent judgment

9.16 Section 173 of the CA 2006 is concerned with the duty to exercise independent judgment. A director of a company is required to exercise independent judgment.[1779] However, this duty will not be infringed by the director acting in accordance with an agreement duly entered into by the company that restricts the future exercise of discretion by its directors;[1780] or in a way authorised by the company's constitution.[1781]

This duty codifies the current principle of law under which directors must exercise their powers independently, without subordinating their powers to the will of others, whether by delegation or otherwise (unless authorised by or under the constitution to do so).

It provides that directors must not fetter the future exercise of their discretion unless they are acting in accordance with an agreement which has been duly entered into by the company; or in a way authorised by the company's constitution.

The duty does not confer a power on the directors to delegate, or prevent a director from exercising a power to delegate conferred by the company's constitution, provided that it is exercised in accordance with the company's constitution. Under the model Articles of Association for private companies limited by shares, the directors may delegate their functions in accordance with the articles.

The term exercising 'independent judgment' is not defined. However, it is suggested that it refers to a director's opinion not being fettered or limited, or restricted in any way. A director should be in a position to make up his own mind on the issue in question and not be influenced or prejudiced by any matter. However, s 173(2) of the CA 2006 identifies two situations in which the duty to exercise independent judgment may be restricted, but in which such duty will not be infringed. First, there will be no infringement by a director acting in accordance with an agreement entered into by the company that restricts the future exercise of discretion by its directors. Section 173 (2)(a) of the CA 2006 does not prescribe the terms of the 'agreement' to be in writing, but also suggests there could be an informal process or mechanism that has been entered into by the company that could constitute an 'agreement' (from conduct or actions) restricting the future exercise of discretion by its directors.

Second, the duty to exercise independent judgment will not be infringed by a director acting in a way authorised by the company's constitution. The term 'company's constitution' will be given a broad interpretation in accordance with s 257 of the CA 2006, to include not only a company's Articles of Association (see s 17 of the CA 2006), but also any resolution or other decision come to in accordance with the constitution; and any decision by the

---

[1779] CA 2006, s 173(1).   [1780] CA 2006, s 173(2)(a).   [1781] CA 2006, s 173(2)(b).

members of the company, or a class of members, that is treated by virtue of any enactment or rule of law as equivalent to a decision by the company.

Duty to exercise reasonable care, skill and diligence

9.17 Section 174 of the CA 2006 is concerned with the duty to exercise reasonable care, skill and diligence. It requires a director of a company to exercise reasonable care, skill and diligence.[1782] The test of 'care, skill and diligence' is set out in s 174(2) of the CA 2006. It means the care, skill and diligence that would be exercised by a reasonably diligent person with the general knowledge, skill and experience that may reasonably be expected of a person carrying out the functions carried out by the director in relation to the company (an objective test);[1783] and the general knowledge, skill and experience that the director has (a subjective test).[1784]

This duty codifies the director's common law duty to exercise reasonable care, skill and diligence. Traditionally, the courts did not require directors to exhibit a greater degree of skill than may reasonably be expected from a person with their knowledge and experience (a subjective test). More recently, the courts have stated that the common law standard now mirrors the tests set out in s 214 of the Insolvency Act 1986, which includes an objective assessment of a director's conduct. Section 174 of the CA 2006 is modeled on s 214 of the IA 1986.[1785] Section 214 of the IA 1986 is, however, concerned with 'wrongful trading'. It provides that a company's liquidator may in the course of a company's winding up, apply for an order that a director (as well as shadow director) make such contribution to the company's assets as the court thinks proper if certain conditions are met. The conditions are that (i) the company has gone into insolvent liquidation; (ii) the company has continued trading after a period of time before commencement of the winding up, when a director knew or ought to have concluded that there was no reasonable prospect that the company would avoid going into insolvent liquidation. There is a defence for a director if he can satisfy the court that, after a period of time was reached, he took every step with a view of minimising the potential loss to the company's creditors as he ought to have taken.

Section 214(4) of the IA 1986 states that the facts that a director of a company ought to know or the conclusions that he ought to reach, and the steps that he ought to take are those which would be known or ascertained, or reached or taken by a reasonably diligent person having both (a) the general knowledge, skill and experience that may reasonably be expected of a person carrying out the same functions as are carried out by that director in relation to the company; and (b) the general knowledge, skill and experience that

---

[1782] CA 2006, s 174(1).   [1783] CA 2006, s 174(2)(a).   [1784] CA 2006, s 174(2)(b).

[1785] See *Re Produce Marketing Consortium Ltd* (No. 2) [1989] BCLC 520; and *Re Mc Bacon Ltd* (No. 2) [1990] BCLC 607.

director has. This is the same test that will be applicable under s 174(2) of the CA 2006 – both a subjective and an objective test. The courts are likely to consider cases decided under s 214(4) of the IA 1986 for application to s 174(2) of the CA 2006, but only for the purposes of interpreting the test to be applied, as the two sections are clearly concerned with different areas of company law.

Duty to avoid conflicts of interest

9.18 Section 175 of the CA 2006 is concerned with a director's duty to avoid conflicts of interest. It imposes a duty on a director of a company to avoid a situation in which he has, or can have, a direct or indirect interest that conflicts, or possibly may conflict, with the interests of the company.[1786]

This applies in particular to the exploitation of any property, information or opportunity (and it is immaterial whether the company could take advantage of the property, information or opportunity).[1787]

This duty does not apply to a conflict of interest arising in relation to a transaction or arrangement with the company.[1788]

However, the duty to avoid conflicts of interest will not be infringed in two circumstances: first, if the situation cannot reasonably be regarded as likely to give rise to a conflict of interest;[1789] or second, if the matter has been authorised by the directors.[1790]

Authorisation may be given by the directors where the company is a private company and nothing in the company's constitution invalidates such authorisation, by the matter being proposed and authorised by the directors;[1791] or where the company is a public company and its constitution includes a provision enabling the directors to authorise the matter, by the matter being proposed to and authorised by them in accordance with the constitution.[1792]

The authorisation is effective only if any requirement as to the quorum at the meeting at which the matter is considered is met, without counting the director in question or any other interested director;[1793] and the matter was agreed to without their voting or would have been agreed to if their votes had not been counted.[1794]

Any reference in s 175 of the CA 2006 to a conflict of interest includes a conflict of interest and duty and a conflict of duties.[1795]

This duty replaces the fiduciary no-conflict rule applying to directors. Under the previous no-conflict rule, certain consequences flowed if directors placed themselves in a position where their personal interests or duties to other persons were liable to conflict with their duties to the company, unless

---

[1786] CA 2006, s 175(1).   [1787] CA 2006, s 175(2).   [1788] CA 2006, s 175(3).
[1789] CA 2006, s 175(4)(a).   [1790] CA 2006, s 175(4)(b).   [1791] CA 2006, s 175(5)(a).
[1792] CA 2006, s 175(5)(b).   [1793] CA 2006, s 175(6)(a).   [1794] CA 2006, s 175(6)(b).
[1795] CA 2006, s 175(7).

the company gave its consent. A conflict of interest may, in particular, arise when a director makes personal use of information, property or opportunities belonging to the company, or when a director enters into a contract with his company. Conflicts of interest may also arise whenever a director makes a profit in the course of being a director, in the matter of his directorship, without the knowledge and consent of his company.

This duty covers all conflicts, actual and potential, between the interests of the director and the interests of the company. This includes conflicts relating to the exploitation of the company's property, information or opportunity for personal purposes. The only conflicts not covered by this duty are those relating to transactions or arrangements with the company (interests in transactions or arrangements with the company, must be declared under s 177 of the CA 2006 in the case of proposed transactions, or under s 182 of the CA 2006 in the case of existing transactions, unless an exception applies under those sections).

Section 180(4) of the CA 2006 preserves the ability of the members of a company to authorise conflicts that would otherwise be a breach of this duty.

Under s 175(4)–(6) of the CA 2006, the duty is not also infringed if:

(a)   the situation cannot reasonably be regarded as likely to give rise to a conflict of interest – the test will be one of reasonableness;

(b)   in the case of a private company, unless its constitution prevents this, authorisation has been given by directors who are genuinely independent (in the sense that they have no direct or indirect interest in the transaction) – consideration should, therefore, be given to whether there are any restrictions or limitations in the company's constitution on the issue of authorisation;

(c)   similarly, in the case of a public company, but only if its constitution expressly permits this, authorisation has been given by the independent directors. Therefore, the company's constitution should be considered on the issue of express authorisation.

The law prior to 2006 was that in all cases, conflicts of interest must be authorised by the members of the company, unless some alternative procedure was properly provided. The Company Law Review Group was concerned that this strict requirement might stifle entrepreneurial activity; and, therefore, recommended that, in the case of a private company, it should be possible for conflicts to be authorised by independent directors, unless the company's constitution prevented this.

Under s 175(6) of the CA 2006, board authorisation is effective only if the conflicted directors have not participated in taking the decision, or if the decision would have been valid without the participation of the conflicted directors: the votes of the conflicted directors in favour of the decision are ignored, and the conflicted directors are not counted in the quorum.

Duty not to accept benefits from third parties

9.19 Section 176 of the CA 2006 is concerned with the duty of a director not to accept benefits from third parties. It states that a director of a company must not accept a benefit from a third party conferred by reason of his being a director;[1796] or his doing (or not doing) anything as director.[1797]

The term 'third party' means a person other than the company, an associated body corporate or a person acting on behalf of the company or an associate body corporate.[1798]

Benefits received by a director from a person whose services (as a director or otherwise) are provided to the company are not regarded as conferred by a third party.[1799]

This duty is not infringed if the acceptance of the benefit cannot reasonably be regarded as likely to give rise to a conflict of interest.[1800] Any reference to a conflict of interest includes a conflict of interest and duty and a conflict of duties.[1801]

Section 176 of the CA 2006 codifies the rule prohibiting the exploitation of the position of director for personal benefit. It is also based on the fiduciary duty of director not to make secret profits established under case law. It prohibits the acceptance of benefits (including bribes). The acceptance of a benefit giving rise to an actual or potential conflict of interest will fall within the duty to avoid conflicts of interest (s 175 of the CA 2006), as well as this duty. This specific duty dealing with benefits from third parties is not subject to any provision for board authorisation.

Any current ability of the members of a company to authorise the acceptance of benefits which would otherwise be a breach of this duty is preserved by s 180(4) of the CA 2006.

The duty is not infringed if the acceptance of the benefit cannot reasonably be regarded as likely to give rise to a conflict of interest. Benefits conferred by the company (and its holding company or subsidiaries) do not fall within this duty.

Duty to declare interest in proposed transaction or arrangement

9.20 Section 177 of the CA 2006 is concerned with a director's duty to declare interest in a proposed transaction or arrangement. It states that if a director of a company is in any way, directly or indirectly, interested in a proposed transaction or arrangement with the company, he must declare the nature and extent of that interest to the other directors.[1802] The declaration may (but need not) be made at a meeting of the directors;[1803] or by notice to

---

[1796] CA 2006, s 176(1)(a).   [1797] CA 2006, s 176(1)(b).   [1798] CA 2006, s 176(2).
[1799] CA 2006, s 176(3).   [1800] CA 2006, s 176(4).   [1801] CA 2006, s 176(5).
[1802] CA 2006, s 177(1).   [1803] CA 2006, s 177(2)(a).

the directors in accordance with s 184 of the CA 2006 (notice in writing) or s 185 of the CA 2006 (general notice).[1804]

If a declaration of interest under s 177 of the CA 2006 proves to be, or becomes, inaccurate or incomplete, a further declaration must be made.[1805] Any declaration required by s 177 of the CA 2006 must be made before the company enters into the transaction or arrangement.[1806]

Section 177 of the CA 2006 does not require declaration of an interest of which the director is not aware, or where the director is not aware of the transaction or arrangement in question. For this purpose, a director is treated as being aware of matters of which he ought reasonably to be aware.[1807]

A director does not need to declare an interest in the following circumstances:

- if it cannot reasonably be regarded as likely to give rise to a conflict of interest;[1808]
- if, or to the extent that, the other directors are already aware of it (and for this purpose the other directors are treated as aware of anything of which they ought reasonably to be aware);[1809] or
- if, or to the extent that, it concerns terms of his service contract that have been or are to be considered by a meeting of the directors;[1810] or by a committee of the directors appointed for the purpose under the company's constitution.[1811]

The equitable rule that directors may not have interest in transactions with the company unless the interest has been authorised by the members, is replaced by s 171 of the CA 2006. This section requires a director to disclose any interest, direct or indirect, that he has in relation to a proposed transaction or arrangement with the company. The director does not need to be party to the transaction for the duty to apply. An interest of another person in a contract may require the director to make a disclosure under this duty, if that other person's interest amounts to a direct or indirect interest on the part of the director.

Under the equitable rule, shareholder approval was required for transactions between a company and a director. Company articles often modified the equitable rule, requiring disclosure of the conflict instead. As proposed by the Company Law Review Group, shareholder approval for the transaction is not a requirement of the statutory duty. The members of the company may, however, still impose requirements for shareholder approval in the articles.

The duty requires directors to disclose their interest in any transaction

---

[1804] CA 2006, s 177(2)(b).   [1805] CA 2006, s 177(3).   [1806] CA 2006, s 177(4).
[1807] CA 2006, s 177(5).   [1808] CA 2006, s 177(6)(a).   [1809] CA 2006, s 177(6)(b).
[1810] CA 2006, s 177(6)(c)(i).   [1811] CA 2006, s 177(6)(c)(ii).

before the company enters into the transaction (s 177(4) of the CA 2006). The duty does not impose any rules on how the disclosure of interest must be made, but s 177(2) of the CA 2006 allows the disclosure at a meeting of the directors.

Disclosure to the members is not sufficient. The director must declare the nature and extent of his interest to the other directors. It is not enough for the director to merely state that he has an interest.

If after he has disclosed his interest, he becomes aware that the facts have changed, or for some other reason the earlier disclosure is no longer accurate or complete, the director must make a further declaration, correcting the earlier one (s 177(3) of the CA 2006). However, this is only necessary if the company has not yet entered into the transaction or arrangement at the time the director becomes aware of the inaccuracy or incompleteness of the earlier declaration (or ought reasonably to have become so aware).

As the duty requires disclosure to be made to the other directors, no disclosure is required where the company has only one director. There is no need to disclose anything the other directors already know about or ought reasonably to have known (s 177(6)(b)) of the CA 2006). A director will breach the duty if he fails to declare something he ought reasonably to have known, but the duty does not otherwise require a director to declare anything he does not know. Section 177(6)(c) of the CA 2006 makes special provision for service contracts that are considered by a meeting of the directors or a committee appointed for the purpose (such as a remuneration committee).

No declaration of interest is required if the director's interest in the transaction cannot reasonably be regarded as likely to give rise to a conflict of interest: (s 177 (6)(a) of the CA 2006).

Conflicted directors may, subject to the company's Articles of Association, participate in decision-taking relating to such transactions with the company.

Civil consequences of breach of general duties

9.21 Section 178 of the CA 2006 deals with the civil consequences of a breach of general duties. It states that the consequences of breach (or threatened breach) of ss 171–177 of the CA 2006 are the same as would apply if the corresponding common law rule or equitable principle applied.[1812] The duties in ss 171–177 of the CA 2006 (with the exception of s 174 of the CA 2006 (duty to exercise reasonable care, skill and diligence) are, accordingly, enforceable in the same way as any other fiduciary duty owed to the company by its directors.[1813]

[1812] CA 2006, s 178(1).   [1813] CA 2006, s 178(2).

Cases within more than one of the general duties

9.22 Section 179 of the CA 2006 provides that except as otherwise provided, more than one of the general duties may apply in any given case.

An action breach of director's duties under the Companies Act may embrace more than one duty that is the subject of legal action. This section states that a combination of directors' statutory duties may apply in any given situation. This would depend on the circumstances of the facts as to which of the duty or duties would apply to the director.

Consent, approval or authorisation by members

9.23 Section 180 of the CA 2006 provides that in a case where:

(a)   s 175 of the CA 2006 (duty to avoid conflicts of interest) is complied with by authorisation by the directors;[1814] or

(b)   s 177 of the CA 2006 (duty to declare interest in proposed transaction or arrangement) is complied with,[1815]

the transaction or arrangement is not liable to be set aside by virtue of any common law rule or equitable principle requiring the consent or approval of the members of the company.

This is without prejudice to any enactment, or provision of the company's constitution, requiring such consent or approval.[1816]

The application of the general duties is not affected by the fact that the case also falls within Chapter 4 of Part 10 of the CA 2006 (transactions requiring approval of members), except that where that Chapter applies and approval is given under that Chapter;[1817] or the matter is one as to which it is provided that approval is not needed, it is not necessary also to comply with s 175 of the CA 2006 (duty to avoid conflicts of interest) or s 176 of the CA 2006 (duty not to accept benefits from third parties).[1818]

Compliance with the general duties does not remove the need for approval under applicable provision of Chapter 4 of Part 10 of the CA 2006 (transactions requiring approval of members).[1819]

The general duties apply subject to any rule of law enabling the company to give authority, specifically or generally, for anything to be done (or omitted) by the directors, or any one of them, that would otherwise be a breach of duty;[1820] and where the company's articles contain provisions for dealing with

---

[1814] CA 2006, s 180(1)(a).   [1815] CA 2006, s 180(1)(b).   [1816] CA 2006, s 180(1).
[1817] CA 2006, s 180(2)(a).   [1818] CA 2006, s 180(2)(b).   [1819] CA 2006, s 180(3).
[1820] CA 2006, s 180(4)(a).

conflicts of interest, are not infringed by anything done (or omitted) by the directors, or any of them, in accordance with those provisions.[1821]

Otherwise, the general duties will apply (except as otherwise provided or the context otherwise requires) notwithstanding any enactment or rule of law.[1822]

Modification of provisions in relation to charitable companies

9.24 Section 181 of the CA 2006 modifies the provisions concerning directors' duties in respect of charitable companies. It states that in their application to a company that is a charity, the provisions of Chapter 2 of Part 10 of the CA 2006 have effect subject to this section.[1823]

Section 175 of the CA 2006 (duty to avoid conflicts of interest) will apply as if:

(a) for subs (3) (which disapplies the duty to avoid conflicts of interest in the case of a transaction or arrangement with the company) there were substituted:

> (3) This duty does not apply to a conflict of interest arising in relation to a transaction or arrangement with the company if or to the extent that the company's articles allow that duty to be so disapplied, which they may do only in relation to descriptions of transaction or arrangement specified in the company's articles;[1824]

(b) for subs (5) (which specifies how directors of a company may give authority under that section for a transaction or arrangement) there were substituted:

> (5) Authorisation may be given by the directors where the company's constitution includes provision enabling them to authorise the matter, by the matter being proposed to and authorised by them in accordance with the constitution.[1825]

Section 180(2)(b) of the CA 2006 (which disapplies certain duties under this Chapter in relation to cases excepted from requirement to obtain approval by members under Chapter 4) applies only if or to the extent that the company's articles allow those duties to be so disapplied, which they may do only in relation to descriptions of transaction or arrangement specified in the company's articles.[1826]

After s 26(5) of the Charities Act 1993 (c 10) (the power of Charity Commission to authorise dealings with charity property, etc) the following is inserted:

[1821] CA 2006, s 180(4)(b).   [1822] CA 2006, s 180(5).   [1823] CA 2006, s 181(1).
[1824] CA 2006, s 181(2)(a).   [1825] CA 2006, s 181(2)(b).   [1826] CA 2006, s 181(3).

(5A) In the case of a charity that is a company, an order under this section may authorise an act notwithstanding that it involves the breach of a duty imposed on a director of the company under Chapter 2 of Part 10 of the CA the CA 2006 (general duties of directors).[1827]

Section 181 of the CA 2006 does not extend to Scotland.[1828]

Section 181 of the CA 2006 reverses certain relaxations made to the no-conflict rule as it applies to directors of charitable companies in England and Wales and Northern Ireland.

Section 181(2)(a) of the CA 2006 replaces s 175(3) of the CA 1985, which excludes conflicts of interest arising out of transactions or arrangements with the company. The replacement excludes such conflicts of interest from the duty only if or to the extent that the charitable company's articles so allow. The articles must describe the transactions or arrangements that are to be so excluded from the duty.

Section 181(2)(b) of the CA 2006 replaces s 175(5) of the CA 1985, which allows authorisation for conflicts of interest to be given by the directors. The replacement only allows authorisation to be given by the directors where the charitable company's constitution expressly allows them to do so.

Section 181(3) of the CA 2006 restricts the application of s 180(2)(b) of the CA 1985 which disapplies ss 175 and 176 of the CA 2006 in relation to those matters expected from the requirement for member approval under Chapter 4 of Part 10 of the CA 2006. Section 180(2)(b) of the CA 2006 is restricted, so that it only applies if or to the extent that the charitable company's articles allow the duties in ss 175 and 176 of the CA 2006 to be disapplied. The articles must describe the transactions or arrangements that are to be excluded from those duties.

Section 181(4) of the CA 2006 amends the Charities Acts 1993 to give the Charity Commission the power to authorise acts that would otherwise be in breach of the general duties. This is necessary to preserve the current power of the Charity Commissioners to do so, in the light of the statutory statement of the general duties.

Ministerial statements concerning the duties of company directors

9.25 In June 2007, the DTI (now known as the Department for Business, Enterprise and Regulatory Reform) issued Ministerial Statements on the 'Duties of Company Directors'. According to Rt Hon Margaret Hodge, Minister of State for Industry and the Regions, Part 10 of the CA 2006 on directors' duties will continue to be seen as one of the most significant parts of the CA 2006. The publication by the DTI comprises a number of

---

[1827] CA 2006, s 181(4).   [1828] CA 2006, s 181(5).

Ministerial Statements on a range of directors' duties set out in Part 10. The Minister stated that there were two ways of looking at the statutory statement of director duties: on the one hand it simply codifies the existing law obligations of company directors; on the other hand – especially in s 172 of the CA 2006 (duty to promote the company's success) – it marked a radical departure in articulating the connection between what is good for the company and what is good for society at large.

According to the DTI, the statutory expression of the duties was essentially the same as the existing duties established by case law – the only major exception being the new procedures for dealing with conflicts of interest. The DTI has prepared high-level guidance for directors set out below, illustrating the way in which the codification maintains continuity with the existing law, for example, the advice on how the director has to live up to his position of trust is applicable to the pre-existing common law as well as to the new codification.

However, compared with most textbook definitions of the common law duties of directors, the new statutory statement captures a 'cultural change' in the way in which companies conduct their business. There was a time when business success in the interests of shareholders was thought to be in conflict with society's appreciation for people who work in the company or in supply chain companies, for the long-term well-being of the community and for the protection of the environment. The law was now based on a new approach. Pursuing the interest of the shareholders and embracing wider responsibilities were complementary purposes – not contradictory ones.

The DTI has set out the following '8 point guidance' for company directors:

1   Act in the company's best interests, taking everything you think relevant into account.
2   Obey the company's constitution and decisions taken under it.
3   Be honest, and remember that the company's property belongs to it and not to you or to its shareholders.
4   Be diligent, careful and well-informed about the company's affairs. If you have any special skills or experience, use them.
5   Make sure the company keeps records of your decisions.
6   Remember that you remain responsible for the work you give to others.
7   Avoid situations where your interests conflict with those of the company. When in doubt disclose potential conflicts quickly.
8   Seek external advice where necessary, particularly if the company is in financial difficulty.

It is submitted that this '8 point guidance' confuses the position for directors rather than clarifies it. Although this guidance is set out in plain English, it is difficult to see the clear relationship between this guidance and the statutory general duties of directors. Some of the provisions of this '8 point guidance' seem to relate back to the fiduciary and common law duties set out in case law, for example, 'act in the company's bests interests' rather than elucidate on the statutory general duties. Other guidance provisions bear no direct relationship to the statutory general duties.

The government had previously indicated that it would set out clear and plain guidance for directors in respect of their general statutory duties. However, what has emerged has been a collection of 'cut and paste' ministerial statements – being extracts from debates in UK Parliament, at various stages of the passage of the Companies Bill. It is difficult to see how this will assist directors, as the ministerial statements fall far short of what was envisaged in providing a clear guidance for directors. To this extent, the collection of Ministerial statements is disappointing.

The Ministerial statements are set out in the appendix to this chapter.

Appendix to Chapter 9
Ministerial Statements

Companies Act 2006 – Duties of directors

Collated Hansard extracts from debates on Companies Bill (originally Company Law Reform Bill)

Background

The law commissions and the Company Law Review concluded that a statutory statement of duties would be helpful . . . it is important that . . . flexibility and ability to note changing circumstances are not lost.

> *Lord Goldsmith, Lords Grand Committee, 6 February 2006, column 242*

First . . . the origins of the general duties [is] . . . that they are based in certain common law rules and equitable principles . . . the statutory statement replaces the common rule equitable principle . . . once the Act is passed, one will go to the statutory statement of duties to identify the duties to identify the duty the director owed.

> *Lord Goldsmith, Lords Grand Committee, 6 February 2006, column 243*

. . . the main purpose in codifying the general duties of directors is to make what is expected of directors clearer and to make the law more accessible to them and to others.

> *Lord Goldsmith, Lords Grand Committee, 6 February 2006, column 254*

We should remind ourselves that being a company director is a wonderful thing for the person who is a company director. But it is a position of great responsibility which involves running the affairs of a company for the benefit of other people. It is a heavy responsibility we should not water down.

> *Lord Goldsmith, Lords Grand Committee, 6 February 2006, column 291*

Interpretation by the courts

The courts should be left to interpret the words Parliament passes.

Lord Goldsmith, Lords Grand Committee, 6 February 2006, column 243

Although the duties in relation to directors have developed in a distinctive way, they are often manifestations of more general principles ... [it] is intended to enable the courts to continue to have regard to development in the common law rules and equitable principles applying to these other types of fiduciary relationships.

The advantage of that is it will enable the statutory duties to develop in line with relevant developments in the law as it applies elsewhere.

Lord Goldsmith, Lords Grand Committee, 6 February 2006, column 244

Effect of codification

One proposition [is] that the result of this codification will be increased litigation. That is not how we see it ... as in existing law, the general duties are owed by the director to the company. It follows that, as now, only the company can enforce them. Directors are liable to the company for loss to the company, and not more widely. It is quite rare for companies to sue their directors for breach of duty. That may well continue to be the position.

Lord Goldsmith, Lords Grand Committee, 6 February 2006, column 242

Effect of the provision of new duties

[On] the provision of new duties, we do not see why that should lead to increased litigation either. For example ... the need to have regard to the interests of employees as part of the main duty to promote the success of the company ... was part of case law before becoming statute. It is an important principle, and plays a crucial part in business decisions ... however ... there is not evidence of which we are aware that it has led to legalistic decision making by companies, or people turning away from bringing their talent to the world of enterprise. We have no reason to expect that there will be a greater degree of litigation on those duties than there is now.

Lord Goldsmith, Lords Grand Committee, 6 February 2006, column 243

Statement of general duties

The statement of general duties ... is not intended to be an exhaustive list of all the duties owed by a director to his company. The directors may owe a wide range of duties to their companies in addition to the general duties listed. Those are general, basic duties which it is seen as right and important to set out in this way. The statement that these are the general duties does not allow a director to escape any other obligation he has, including obligations under the Insolvency Act 1986.

Lord Goldsmith, Lords Grand Committee, 6 February 2006, column 249

Enlightened shareholder value

The Company Law Review considered and consulted on two main options. The first was 'enlightened shareholder value', under which a director must first act in the way that he or she considers, in good faith, would be most likely to promote the success of the company for its members . . . The Government agrees this is the right approach. It resolves any confusion in the mind of directors as to what that the interests of the company are, and prevents any inclination to identify those interests with their own. It also prevents confusion between the interests of those who depend on the company and those of the members.

Lord Goldsmith, Lords Grand Committee, 6 February 2006, column 255

For the first time, the Bill includes a statutory statement of directors' general duties. It provides a code of conduct that sets out how directors are expected to behave. That enshrines in statue what the law review called 'enlightened shareholder value'. It recognises that directors will be more likely to achieve long-term sustainable success for the benefit of their shareholders if their companies pay attention to a wider range of matters . . . Directors will be required to promote the success of the company in the collective best interest of the shareholders, but in doing so they will have to have regard to a wider range of factors, including the interests of employees and the environment.

Alistair Darling, Commons Second Reading, 6 June 2006, column 125

Duty to promote the success of the company

What is success? The starting point is that it is essentially for the members of the company to define the objective they wish to achieve. Success means what the members collectively want the company to achieve. For a commercial company, success will usually mean long-term increase in value. For certain companies, such as charities and community interest companies, it will mean the attainment of the objectives for which the company has been established.

Lord Goldsmith, Lords Grand Committee, 6 February 2006, column 255

. . . for a commercial company, success will normally mean long-term increase in value, but the company's constitution and decisions made under it may also lay down the appropriate success model for the company . . . it is essentially for the members of a company to define the objectives they wish to achieve. The normal way for that to be done – the traditional way – is that the members do it at the time the company is established. In the old style, it would have been set down in the company's memorandum. That is changing ... but the principle does not change that those who establish the company will start off by setting out what they hope to achieve. For most people who invest in companies, there is never any doubt about it – money. That is what they want. They want a long-term increase in the company. It is not a snap poll to be taken at any point in time.

Lord Goldsmith, Lords Grand Committee, 6 February 2006, column 258

... it is for the directors, by reference to those things we are talking about – the objective of the company – to judge and form a good faith judgment about what is to be regarded as success for the members as a whole .... they will need to look at the company's constitution, shareholder decisions and anything else that they consider relevant in helping them to reach that judgment ... the duty is to promote the success for the benefit of the members as a whole – that is, for the members as a collective body – not only to benefit the majority shareholders, or any particular shareholder or section of shareholders, still less the interests of directors who might happen to be shareholders themselves. That is an important statement of the way in which directors need to look at this judgment they have to make.

Lord Goldsmith, Lords Grand Committee, 6 February 2006, column 256

... we have included the words 'amongst other matters'. We want to be clear that the list of factors [for a director to have regard to] is not exhaustive.

Lord Goldsmith, Lords Grand Committee, 9 May 2006, column 846

The clause does not impose a requirement on directors to keep records, as some people have suggested, in any circumstances in which they would not have to do so now.

Margaret Hodge, Commons Committee, 11 July 2006, column 592

The Government believe that our enlightened shareholder value approach will be mutually beneficial to business and society. We do not, however, claim that the interests of the company and of its employees will always be identical; regrettably, it will sometimes be necessary, for example, to lay off staff. The drafting ... must therefore clearly point directors towards their overarching objective. We have made it clear that [the clause] will make a difference, and a very important difference.

The words 'have regard to' mean 'think about'; they are absolutely not about just ticking boxes. If 'thinking about' leads to the conclusion, as we believe it will in many cases, that the proper course is to act positively to achieve the objectives in the clause, that will be what the director's duty is. In other words 'have regard to' means 'give proper consideration to ...

Consideration of the factors will be an integral part of the duty to promote the success of the company for the benefit of its members as a whole. The clause makes it clear that a director is to have regard to the factors in fulfilling that duty. The decisions taken by a director and the weight given to the factors will continue to be a matter for his good faith judgment.

Margaret Hodge, Commons Report, 17 October 2006, column 789

Duty to exercise independent judgment

. . . the clause does not mean that a director has to form his judgment totally independently from anyone or anything. It does not actually mean that the director has to be independent himself. He can have an interest in the matter . . . It is the exercise of the judgment of a director that must be independent in the sense of it being his own judgment . . . The duty does not prevent a director from relying on the advice or work of others, but the final judgment must be his responsibility. He clearly cannot be expected to do everything himself. Indeed, in certain circumstances directors may be in breach of duty if they fail to take appropriate advice – for example, legal advice. As with all advice, slavish reliance is not acceptable, and the obtaining of outside advice does not absolve directors from exercising their judgment on the basis of such advice.

Lord Goldsmith, Lords Grand Committee, 6 February 2006, column 282

Standard of care owed by a director

. . . the standard of care which a director owes is enormously important . . . it is now accepted that the duty of care . . . is accurately stated in Section 214(4) of the Insolvency Act 1986 . . . Under the clause you take account both of the general knowledge, skills and experience that may be reasonably expected of a person carrying out those functions and the general knowledge, skills and experience that that director has. It is a cumulative requirement . . . I want to emphasise the point that it is not making a change from what is already the common law.

Lord Goldsmith, Lords Grand Committee, 6 February 2006, column 284

Duty to avoid conflicts of interest

. . . the law already recognises that potential conflicts in certain circumstances are to be avoided . . . there is currently no absolute rule prohibiting directors from holding multiple directorships or even from engaging in business that competes with the company of which they are a director, but obviously a tension results from that degree of tolerance and the fiduciary duties which the director owes. The solution to it is . . . there is no prohibition of a conflict or potential conflict as long as it is has been authorised by the directors in accordance with the requirements set out in [the Act].

Lord Goldsmith, Lords Grand Committee, 6 February 2006, column 288

. . . we do not say that this should happen just because in the mind of a director it is all right; there should be a process for the company, through its members or directors, to make that decision, and that is what these new regulations permit.

Lord Goldsmith, Lords Grand Committee, 6 February 2006, column 289

Following consultation, the Government have already adjusted the provision . . . to use instead the expression 'if the situation cannot reasonably be regarded as likely to give rise to a conflict of interest'. This introduces the concept of reasonableness which makes the situation easier from the point of view of a director and avoids a very harsh test, although it is still a heavy duty and intended to be.

Lord Goldsmith, Lords Grand Committee, 6 February 2006, column 293

So far as private companies are concerned, the default position is that the directors may authorise the matter unless there is a provision in the company's constitution saying otherwise. In the case of a public company . . . directors may authorise the matter only if the company's constitution includes provisions saying they can do so. It must follow that if the constitution does not do so, steps will have to be taken to amend it to that effect and the members of the company will be able to take a view about whether they think that is a good move.

Lord Goldsmith, Lords Grand Committee, 6 February 2006, column 294

. . . the authorisation has to be given without relying on the votes of directors seeking the authorisation or any other director with an interest in it . . . Those directors cannot count towards the quorum either . . . [and] any requirements under the common law for what is necessary for a valid authorisation remain in force . . . Finally, in general terms, the directors who are giving the authorisation will need to comply with the general duties imposed on them. Those will include, specifically, the general duty . . . to act in such a way that in good faith they consider that authorisation is the course of action most likely to promote the success of the company.

Lord Goldsmith, Lords Grand Committee, 9 February 2006, column 327

. . . the duty does not apply if the situation cannot reasonably be regarded as being likely to give rise to a conflict of interest. If the matter falls outside the ambit of the company's business, a real conflict of interest is unlikely.

Lord Goldsmith, Lords Grand Committee, 9 May 2006, column 864

. . . the company's articles may contain provisions for dealing with conflicts of interests, and directors will not be in breach of duty if they act in accordance with those provisions. Examples might include arrangements whereby the directors withdraw from any board meeting at which the matters relating to conflicts of interest are discussed ... our amendments will allow all the normal, perfectly acceptable, lawful ways in which companies and their directors deal with conflicts of interest to continue.

Lord Sainsbury of Turville, Lords Report, 23 May 2006, column 722

Duty not to accept benefits from third parties

... the purpose of the clause ... is to impose on a director a duty not to accept benefits from third parties. It applies only to benefits conferred because the director is a director of the company or because of something that the director does or doesn't do as director. The word 'benefit' ... includes benefits of any description, including non-financial benefits.

The clause codifies ... [the] long-standing rule, prohibiting the exploitation of the position of director for personal benefit. It does not apply to benefits that the director receives from the company, or from any associated company, or from any person acting on behalf of any of those companies ... I ... draw attention to the fact that benefits are prohibited by the duty only if their acceptance is likely to give rise to a conflict of interest.

Lord Goldsmith, Lords Grand Committee, 9 February 2006, column 330

Duty to declare interest in proposed transaction or arrangement

[This] clause ... is deliberately intended to apply only to proposed transactions ... if a company is told that a director has an interest in a proposed transaction, it can decide whether to enter into the transaction, on what terms and with what safeguards. [As for] 'a director is treated as being aware of matters he ought reasonably to be aware' ... I believe that the test is objective – that is, one judges objectively whether this is a matter of which the director ought to be aware reasonably.

Lord Goldsmith, Lords Grand Committee, 9 February 2006, column 334

Civil consequences of breach of general duties

... we take the view that the 'duty to exercise reasonable care, skill and diligence' is not a fiduciary duty. It may be owed by someone who is a fiduciary. But that is not the same thing. ... It is important to keep to the principle that these are enforceable in the same way as any other fiduciary duty owed to the company by its directors.

Lord Goldsmith, Lords Grand Committee, 9 February 2006, column 336

Consent, approval or authorisation by members

[The Bill] permitted director authorisation of what would otherwise be impermissible conflicts of interests [and] . . . required declarations of interest in proposed company transactions. In both those cases, the general duty no longer requires the consent of the members. The common law rules or principles that refer to the failure to have had a conflict of interest approved by the member of a company under certain circumstances need to be set aside . . . However . . . the company's constitution can reverse the change and can insist on certain steps being taken requiring the consent of the members in certain circumstances.

Lord Goldsmith, Lords Grand Committee, 9 February 2006, column 337

Indemnifying directors

. . . the starting point for our reform package was a principle . . . that companies should be prohibited from exempting directors from, or indemnifying them against, liability for negligence, default, breach of duty or breach of trust in relation to the company. However the reform package also recognised that companies should be permitted to indemnify directors in respect of third-party claims in most circumstances . . . There are four main possible exceptions to indemnification: criminal penalties; penalties imposed by regulatory bodies: costs incurred by the director in defending criminal proceedings in which he is convicted; and costs incurred by the director in defending civil proceedings brought by the company in which final judgment is given against him.

Lord Goldsmith, Lords Grand Committee, 9 February 2006, column 364

[The Companies (Audit, Investigations and Community Enterprise) Act 2004] . . . closed an important loophole concerning the indemnification of directors by third parties. It used to be the practice in some groups that one group company would indemnify the director of another group company . . . in effect to circumvent the rule that the company could not indemnify its own directors. We take the view that . . . continuing to make directors properly accountable for what they do in relation to the company . . . should stand.

Lord Goldsmith, Lords Grand Committee, 9 February 2006, column 366

It is also important to remember that at the same time as the loophole was closed, important reforms were introduced that permit all companies to indemnify directors against third-party claims, subject to . . . [certain] requirements. Although we agree that indemnification by a parent company of the directors is less likely to result in attempts at circumvention of the prohibition than indemnification by a wholly owned subsidiary company of the director of a holding company, we still believe there is scope for mischief.

We cannot . . . accept [any] amendment.

Lord Sainsbury of Turville, Lords Report, 23 May 2006, column 724

Shadow directors

The law is still developing. It would not be right for the general duties not to apply at all to a shadow directors, but the law may develop in such a way that some do and some don't. It is right to leave those areas, as now, to the courts . . .

Lord Goldsmith, Lords Grand Committee, 9 May 2006, column 828

Chapter 10

Directors: Specific Duties and Liabilities

Introduction

10.1 This chapter addresses the specific duties of directors and their liabilities under the CA 2006. It considers the provisions of Chapter 3 of Part 10 of the CA 2006 on declaration by directors of interest in existing transaction or arrangement. Chapter 4 of Part 10 of the CA 2006 deals with a company's transaction with directors requiring approval of members. In particular, it considers directors' long-term service contracts; substantial property transactions; loans to directors; credit transactions; and related arrangements as well as payment for loss of office. Chapter 5 of Part 10 of the CA 2006 is concerned with directors' service contracts; and Chapter 6 of Part 10 of the CA 2006 with contracts with sole members who are directors. Chapter 7 of Part 10 of the CA 2006 addresses directors' liabilities.

This chapter also addresses supplementary provisions in respect of directors' duties that are set out in Chapter 9 of the CA 2006.

Declaration of Interest

10.2 Chapter 3 of Part 10 of the CA 2006 addresses the issue of declaration of interest by a director in an existing transaction or arrangement. It comprises six sections. The pattern that is followed in these provisions is to set out first the nature of the specific duty, followed by any defences or exemptions, and then the offence.

Declaration of interest in existing transaction of arrangement

10.3 There is a specific obligation on a director to declare an interest in an existing transaction or arrangement. Section 182 of the CA 2006 provides that where a director of a company is in any way, directly or indirectly, interested in a transaction or arrangement that has been entered into by the company, he must declare the nature and extent of the interest to the other directors in accordance with this section.[1829] Section 182 of the CA 2006 does not apply if or to the extent that the interest has been declared under s 177 of the CA 2006 (duty to declare interest in proposed transaction or arrangement).

The declaration must be made by any of the following methods: at a meeting of the directors;[1830] or by notice in writing (see s 184 of the CA 2006);[1831] or by general notice (see s 185 of the CA 2006).[1832]

If a declaration of interest under this section proves to be, or becomes, inaccurate or incomplete, a further declaration must be made.[1833] Any declaration required by this section must be made as soon as is reasonably practicable. Failure to comply with this requirement does not affect the underlying duty to make the declaration.[1834]

Section 182 of the CA 2006 does not require a declaration of an interest of which the director is not aware, or where the director is not aware of the transaction or arrangement in question. For this purpose, a director is treated as being aware of matters of which he ought reasonably to be aware.[1835]

However, a director need not declare an interest under s 182 of the CA 2006 in the following circumstances:

- if it cannot reasonably be regarded as likely to give rise to a conflict of interest;[1836]
- if or to the extent that, the other directors are already aware of it (and for this purpose the other directors are treated as aware of anything of which they ought reasonably to be aware);[1837] or
- if, or to the extent that, it concerns terms of his service contract that have been or are to be considered by a meeting of the directors;[1838] or by a committee of the directors appointed for the purpose under the company's constitution.[1839]

Section 182 of the CA 2006 requires a director to declare the nature and any direct or indirect interest that he has in any transaction or arrangement entered into by the company. It replaces the provision made by s 317 of the CA 1985.[1840] Chapter 3 of Part 10 of the CA 2006 differs from the provisions of s 317 of the CA 2006 in a number of important respects. They include the following.

[1829] CA 2006, s 182(1).   [1830] CA 2006, s 182(2)(a).   [1831] CA 2006, s 182(2)(b).
[1832] CA 2006, s 182(2)(c).   [1833] CA 2006, s 182(3).   [1834] CA 2006, s 182(4).
[1835] CA 2006, s 182(5).   [1836] CA 2006, s 182(6)(a).   [1837] CA 2006, s 182(6)(b).
[1838] CA 2006, s 182(6)(c)(i).   [1839] CA 2006, s 182(6)(c)(ii).
[1840] CA 1985, s 317 provided that it was the duty of a director of a company who was in any way, whether directly or indirectly, interested in a contract or proposed contract with the company to declare the nature of his interest at a meeting of the directors of the company: CA 1985, s 317(1). In case of a proposed contract, the declaration must be made at the meeting of the directors at which the question of entering into the contract is firstly taken into consideration;

What should be declared?

10.3.1 Directors are required to declare any interest, direct or indirect, that they have in an existing transaction or arrangement entered into by the company. This section only applies to transactions or arrangements already entered into by the company. Section 177 of the CA 2006 (duty to declare interest) applies to the proposed transactions or arrangements with the company.

The director does not need to be party to the transaction with the company in order for a declaration to be required under s 182 of the CA 2006. For example, where the director's spouse enters into a transaction with the company, that may (but need not necessarily) give rise to an indirect interest on the part of the director in that transaction.

The declaration must be of the nature and extent of the director's direct and indirect interest.

If the director has declared his interest in accordance with s 177 of the CA 2006 at the time the transaction was proposed, and before it was entered into by the company, the director does not need to repeat that declaration, once the transaction becomes an existing transaction to which this section applies (see s 182(1) of the CA 2006).

Furthermore, a director need not declare any interest:

- that cannot reasonably be regarded as likely to give rise to a conflict of interest;
- that the other directors already know about, or ought reasonably to know about; or
- that concerns his service contract, considered (or to be considered) by a meeting of directors or by the relevant committee of directors.

A director is regarded as failing to make the declarations required by s 182 of the CA 2006, if he fails to declare something that he ought reasonably to have known. But the director is not otherwise expected by this section to declare things he does not know (see s 182(5) of the CA 2006).

When should the declaration be made?

10.3.2 The declaration should be made as soon as is reasonably practicable. But even if the declaration is not made as soon as it should have been, it must

or if the director was not at the date of that meeting interested in the proposed contract, at the next meeting of the directors held after he became so interested, and in a case where the director becomes interested in a contract after it is made, the declaration must be made at the first meeting of directors held after he becomes so interested: CA 1985, s 317(2). The remaining sections. 317(3)–317(9) of the CA 1985, address the procedural aspects of the declaration and applicability to shadow directors including failure to made the declaration.

still be made (see s 182(4) of the CA 2006). If after a declaration has been made, the director's interest in the transaction or arrangement changes, or the director realises that his interests were not as originally declared, the director must make another declaration of interest, correcting or updating the earlier one (see s 182(3) of the CA 2006).

How should the declaration be made?

10.3.3 The declaration of interest must be made to the other directors using one of the following three methods:

- at a meeting of the directors; or
- by notice in writing (in accordance with the requirements of s 184 of the CA 2006); or
- by general notice (in accordance with the requirement of s 185 of the CA 2006).

Offence of failure to declare interest

10.4 Section 183 of the CA 2006 is concerned with the offence of failure to declare interest. It states that a director who fails to comply with the requirements of s 182 of the CA 2006 (declaration of interest in existing transaction or arrangement) commits an offence.[1841] On conviction on indictment, the maximum liability is an unlimited fine.[1842] On summary conviction, the fine must not exceed the statutory maximum (currently £5,000).[1843] This section does not affect the validity of the transaction or impose any other civil consequences for a failure to make the declaration of interest required by s 182 of the CA 2006.

Declaration made by notice in writing

10.5 Section 184 of the CA 2006 applies to a declaration of interest made by notice in writing.[1844] The director must send the notice to the other directors.[1845] The notice must be sent in hard copy form or, if the recipient has agreed to receive it in electronic form, in an agreed electronic form.[1846] The notice may be sent by hand or by post;[1847] or if the recipient has agreed to receive it by electronic means, by agreed electronic means.[1848]

[1841] CA 2006, s 183(1).   [1842] CA 2006, s 183(2)(a).   [1843] CA 2006, s 183(2)(b).
[1844] CA 2006, s 184(1).   [1845] CA 2006, s 184(2).   [1846] CA 2006, s 184(3).
[1847] CA 2006, s 184(4)(a).
[1848] CA 2006, s 184(4)(b). CA 2006, s 248 states that every company must cause minutes of all proceedings at meetings of its directors to be recorded. The records must be kept for at least ten years from the date of the meeting.

Where a director declares an interest by notice in writing in accordance with s 184 of the CA 2006, the making of the declaration is deemed to form part of the proceedings at the next meeting of directors after the notice is given;[1849] and the provisions of s 248 of the CA 2006 (minutes of meetings of directors) apply as if the declaration had been made at the meeting.[1850]

Section 184 of the CA 2006 provides a new written procedure for the declaration of interest required by s 182 of the CA 2006. A written notice declaring the nature and extent of the director's interest must be sent to all the other directors. It may be sent in hard copy form or, if the recipient agrees, in electronic form. It may be posted, delivered by hand or by electronic means. When this is done, the notice is treated as forming part of the proceedings of the next meeting of the directors, and so should form part of the minutes of that meeting (see s 184(5) of the CA 2006).

General notice treated as sufficient declaration

10.6 Section 185 of the CA 2006 deals with the general notice aspects in respect of a declaration. General notice in accordance with s 184 of the CA 2006 is a sufficient declaration of interest in relation to the matters to which it relates.[1851]

General notice is notice given to the directors of the company to the effect that the director:

- has an interest (as member, officer, employee or otherwise) in a specified body corporate or firm, and is to be regarded as interested in any transaction or arrangement that may, after the date of the notice, be made with that body corporate or firm;[1852] or
- is connected with a specified person (other than a body corporate or firm), and is to be regarded as interested in any transaction or arrangement that may, after the date of the notice, be made with that person.[1853]

The notice must state the nature and extent of the director's interest in the body corporate or firm or, as the case may be, the nature of his connection with the person.[1854] However, general notice is not effective unless it is given at a meeting of directors;[1855] or the director takes reasonable steps to secure that it is brought up and read at the next meeting of the directors after it is given.[1856]

Section 185 of the CA 2006 replaces s 317(3) and (4) of the CA 2006. It enables a director to give a general notice of his interests. A general notice is a

---

[1849] CA 2006, s 184(5)(a).   [1850] CA 2006, s 184(5)(b).   [1851] CA 2006, s 185(1).
[1852] CA 2006, s 185(2)(a).   [1853] CA 2006, s 185(2)(b).   [1854] CA 2006, s 185(3).
[1855] CA 2006, s 185(4)(a).   [1856] CA 2006, s 185(4)(b).

declaration that the director is interested in another body corporate or firm, or that the director is connected with another person. If the company enters into a contract with the body corporate, firm or other person named in the general notice, the director does not need to declare any direct or indirect interest that he has in that contract, arising as a result of his interest in the body corporate or firm named in the general notice, or arising as a result of his connection to the person named in the general notice.

In order to be effective, the general notice must state the nature and extent of the director's interest in the body corporate or firm (for example, sole shareholder of the company) or the nature of his connection with the person (for example, spouse or other connected person as defined in s 253 of the CA 2006). The requirement to disclose the extent of the interest implements a recommendation of the English and Scottish Law Commissions.

Declaration of interest in case of company with sole director

10.7 Section 186(1) of the CA 2006 provides that where a declaration of interest under s 182 of the CA 2006 (duty to declare interest in existing transaction or arrangement) is required of a sole director of a company that is required to have more than one director, the following apply:

- the declaration must be recorded in writing;[1857]
- the making of the declaration is deemed to form part of the proceedings at the next meeting of the directors after the notice is given;[1858] and
- the provisions of s 248 of the CA 2006 (minutes of meetings of directors) apply as if the declaration had been made at that meeting.[1859]

However, nothing in s 186 of the CA 2006 affects the operation of s 231 of the CA 2006 (contract with sole member who is also a director: terms to be set out in writing or recorded in minutes).[1860]

Section 186 of the CA 2006 is a new provision. Where a company has only one director, it is not possible for the director to declare his interests to the other directors, because there are no other directors. Therefore, a sole director does not need to comply with s 182 of the CA 2006 (declaration of interest in existing transaction or arrangement).

Section 186 of the CA 2006 makes special provisions where the company has only one director, when it should in fact have more directors (for example, because it is a public company). In such a case, the sole director must record in writing the nature and extent of his interest in any transaction or arrangement that has been entered into by the company.

[1857] CA 2006, s 186(1)(a).   [1858] CA 2006, s 186(1)(b).   [1859] CA 2006, s 186(1)(c).
[1860] CA 2006, s 186(2).

Declaration of interest in existing transaction by shadow director

10.8 Section 187 of the CA 2006 applies in respect of a declaration of interest in existing transaction by a shadow director. The provisions of Chapter 3 of Part 10 of the CA 2006 relating to the duty under s 182 of the CA 2006 (duty to declare interest in existing transaction or arrangement) apply to a shadow director as to a director, but with adaptations.[1861] Section 182(2)(a) of the CA 2006 (declaration at meeting of directors) does not apply.[1862] In s 185 of the CA 2006 (general notice treated as sufficient declaration), subs (4) (notice to be given at or brought up and read at meeting of directors) does not apply.[1863] General notice by a shadow director is not effective unless given by notice in writing in accordance with s 184 of the CA 2006.

Section 187 of the CA 2006 replaces s 317(8) of the CA 2006. It extends Chapter 3 of Part 10 of the CA 2006 to shadow directors, so that a shadow director must also declare the nature and extent of his interest in any transaction or arrangement that has been entered into by the company, in accordance with s 182 of the CA 2006. The declaration must be made by notice in writing (s 184 of the CA 2006) or by general notice (s 185 of the CA 2006).

The declaration is not made at a meeting of the directors, as this is not appropriate in the case of a shadow director. If the shadow director makes the declaration by general notice, that notice be given in accordance with the notice in writing procedure set out in s 184 of the CA 2006. This means that a general notice by a shadow director must comply with both s 184 of the CA 2006, and the first three subsections of s 185 of the CA 2006.

Otherwise, apart from s 186 of the CA 2006 (declaration of interest in case of company with sole director), which is not relevant to a shadow director, all the other provisions of Chapter 3 apply to a shadow director, including the exemptions in s 182 of the CA 2006.

Chapters 4 and 5 of Part 10 of the CA 2006

10.9 Chapters 4 and 5 of Part 10 of the CA 2006 contain several provisions designed to deal with particular situations in which a director has a conflict of interest. They replace provisions of Part 10 of the CA 1985, but with a number of changes. The principal aim of the changes is: first, to improve accessibility and consistency. The English and Scottish Law Commissions commented that Part 10 of the CA 1985 'is widely perceived as being extremely detailed, fragmented, excessive and in some respects, defective,

---

[1861] CA 2006, s 187(1).   [1862] CA 2006, s 187(2).   [1863] CA 2006, s 187(3).

regulation of directors'; and second, to implement various recommendations of the Law Commissions and the Company Law Review Group.[1864]

Provisions regulating director's conflicts of interest fall into two main categories: first, requirements for disclosure to members; and second, requirements for member approval.

The four types of transaction requiring the approval of members (long-term service contracts; substantial property transactions; loans, quasi loans and credit transactions; and payments for loss of office) have been brought together within Chapter 4. Provisions for disclosure to members in respect of directors' service contracts are contained in Chapter 5

However, the requirements in Part 10 of the CA 1985 to disclose, and maintain a register of, share dealings by directors and their families are repealed.[1865]

Transactions with Directors Requiring Approval of Members

10.10 Chapter 4 of Part 10 of the CA 2006 sets out requirement for member approval in relation to four different types of transaction by a company:

- long-term service contracts;
- substantial property transactions;
- loans, quasi loans and credit transactions;
- payments for loss of office.

The rules relating to each type of transaction tend to adopt the following structure: they begin with the rule requiring approval, followed by exceptions to that rule, and the consequences of breaching that rule.

Alignment of provisions

10.11 The provisions of Chapter 4 have been aligned wherever appropriate, so as to achieve greater consistency of approach. Particular examples of alignment are mentioned below.

Criminal penalties

10.12 Chapter 4 no longer imposes any criminal penalties for a failure to comply with its requirements.

[1864] See in particular, section B of the Law of Commissions' joint report *Company Directors: Regulating Conflicts of Interests and Formulating a Statement of Duties*, Annex C of *Development and Framework*, Chapter 4 of *Completing the Structure* and Chapter 6 of the *Final Report*).

[1865] See CA 2006, s 1177.

Civil remedies

10.13 The civil consequences of a failure to comply with the requirements for member approval of substantial property and loans, quasi loans and credit transactions have been aligned.

Approval by holding company

10.14 Chapter 4 applies to long-term service contracts, substantial property transactions, loans, etc. and payments for loss of office by a company and involving either a director of a company, or a director of the company's holding company. In the latter case, the transaction must be approved by both the company and the holding company (unless an exception applies).

Transactions between a company and the director of a fellow subsidiary

10.15 Chapter 4 does not normally apply to transactions entered into by a company that is neither the company of which the person is a director nor a subsidiary of the company of which the person is a director. The two exceptions are s 218 of the CA 2006 (payment for loss of office in connection with transfer of undertaking); and s 219 of the CA 2006 (payment for loss of office in connection with share transfer), where member approval is required for such a payment by any person to a director.

Exception for wholly-owned subsidiary

10.16 Approval is never required under Chapter 4 on the part of the member of a wholly-owned subsidiary, or on the part of the members of an overseas company.

Shadow directors

10.17 Section 223 of the CA 2006 applies all the requirements of Chapter 4 to shadow directors (with a small modification in the case of payments for loss of office).

Approval required

10.18 Section 281(3) of the CA 2006 provides that the member approval required is an ordinary resolution, but the company's articles may impose a higher majority or even unanimity.

Where approval for a transaction or arrangement is required under more than one set of rules in Chapter 4, all relevant sets of rules should apply, unless otherwise provided (s 225 of the CA 2006). For example, if the matter involves both a loan and a substantial property transaction, approval should be required under s 190 of the CA 2006 and s 197 of the CA 2006, unless in each case a relevant exemption applies. Approval may be given for both purposes by a single resolution.

Memorandum with details of the transaction

10.19 In the case of long-term service contracts, loans, etc., and payments for loss of office, a memorandum setting out particulars about the transaction requiring approval of the members must be made available to the members.

If the approval is to be given by way of written resolution, the memorandum must be sent to the members able to vote on the written resolution no later than when the written resolution is sent to them. Section 224 of the CA 2006 provides that any accidental failure to send the memorandum to one or more members will not invalidate the approval given by the members, unless the company's articles state otherwise.

Service contracts

10.20 The first transaction considered under Chapter 4 of Part 10 of the CA 2006 is service contracts.

Directors' long-term service contracts: requirement of members' approval

10.21 Sections 188–189 of the CA 2006 are concerned with directors' service contracts. Section 188 of the CA 2006 deals with directors' long-term service contracts that require members' approval. It applies to a provision under which the 'guaranteed term' of a director's employment with the company of which he is a director;[1866] or where he is a director of a holding company within the group consisting of that company and its subsidiaries, is or may be longer than two years.[1867]

A company may not agree to such provision unless it has been approved by a resolution of the members of the company;[1868] and, in the case of a director of a holding company, by resolution of the members of that company.[1869]

The 'guaranteed term' of a director's employment is (a) the period (if any) during which the director's employment is to continue, or may be continued otherwise than at the instance of the company (whether under the original agreement or under a new agreement entered into in pursuance of it)[1870] and

[1866] CA 2006, s 188(1)(a).   [1867] CA 2006, s 188(1)(b).   [1868] CA 2006, s 188(2)(a).
[1869] CA 2006, s 188(2)(b).   [1870] CA 2006, s 188(3)(a)(i).

it cannot be terminated by the company by notice, or can be so terminated only in specified circumstances;[1871] or (b) in the case of employment terminable by the company by notice, the period of notice required to be given;[1872] or (c) in the case of employment having a period within para (a) and a period within para (b), the aggregate of those periods.

If more than six months before the end of the guaranteed term of a director's employment, the company enters into a further service contract (otherwise than in pursuance of a right conferred by or under the original contract on the other party to it), s 188 of the CA 2006 applies if there were added to the guaranteed term of the new contract the unexpired period of the guaranteed term of the original contract.[1873]

A resolution approving provision to which s 188 of the CA 2006 applies must not be passed unless a memorandum setting out the proposed contract incorporating the provision is made available to the members in the following circumstances:

(a)   in the case of a written resolution, by being sent or submitted to every eligible member at or before the time at which the proposed resolution is sent or submitted to him;[1874]
(b)   in the case of a resolution at a meeting, by being made available for inspection by members of the company both at the company's registered office for not less than 15 days ending with the date of the meeting;[1875] and at the meeting itself.[1876]

No approval is required under s 188 of the CA 2006 on the part of the members of a body corporate that is not a UK-registered company;[1877] or is a wholly-owned subsidiary of another body corporate.[1878]

The term 'employment' means any employment under a director's service contract.[1879]

Directors' long-term service contracts: civil consequences for contravention

10.22 Section 189 of the CA 2006 deals with the civil consequences for contravention of s 188 of the CA 2006. If a company agrees to a provision in contravention of s 188 of the CA 2006 (directors' long-term service contracts: requirement of members' approval), the provision will be void, to the extent of the contravention.[1880] Further, the contract is deemed to contain a term entitling the company to terminate at any time by giving reasonable notice.[1881]

[1871] CA 2006, s 188(3)(a)(ii).   [1872] CA 2006, s 188(3)(b).   [1873] CA 2006, s 188(4).
[1874] CA 2006, s 188(5)(a).   [1875] CA 2006, s 188(5)(b)(i).   [1876] CA 2006, s 188(5)(b)(ii).
[1877] CA 2006, s 188(6)(a).   [1878] CA 2006, s 188(6)(b).   [1879] CA 2006, s 188(7).
[1880] CA 2006, s 188(a).   [1881] CA 2006, s 189(b).

Sections 188 and 189 of the CA 2006 replace s 319 of the CA 1985[1882] and require member approval of long-term service contracts. In broad terms, these are contracts under which director is guaranteed at least two years of employment with the company of which he is a director, or with any subsidiary of that company.

A director's 'service contract' is defined in s 227 of the CA 2006 as including a contract of service, a contract for services, and a letter of appointment as director.

Failure to obtain approval allows the company to terminate the service contract at any time by giving reasonable notice. The purpose of s 188 of the CA 2006 is to limit the duration of a director's service contracts, as the long-term contract can make it too expensive for the members to remove a director using the procedure in s 168 of the CA 2006 (ordinary resolution to remove a director), while allowing the members to approve longer arrangements if they wish.

The length of service contract for which member approval is required has been reduced from those longer than five years to those longer than two years.

Substantial property transactions

10.23 Sections 190–196 of the CA 2006 are concerned with substantial property transactions.

Section 190 of the CA 2006 states that a company may not enter into an arrangement under which a director of the company or of its holding company, or a person connected with such a director, acquires or is to acquire from the company (directly or indirectly) a substantial non-cash asset;[1883] or where the company acquires or is to acquire a non-cash asset (directly or indirectly) from a director or a person so connected).[1884] Such non-cash assets may only be so acquired if the arrangement has been approved by a resolution of the members of the company, or is conditional on such approval being obtained. The term 'non-cash asset' is defined in s 191 of the CA 2006.

[1882] CA 1985, s 319(1) applied in respect of any term of an agreement whereby a director's employment with the company of which he is a director or, where he is the director of a holding company, his employment within the group is to continue, or may be continued, otherwise than at the instance of the company (whether under the original agreement or under a new agreement entered into in pursuance of it), for a period of more than five years during which the employment cannot be terminated by the company by notice; or can be so terminated only in specified circumstances.

[1883] CA 2006, s 190(1)(a).

[1884] CA 2006, s 190(1)(b).

If the director or connected person is a director of the company's holding company or a person connected with such a director, the arrangement must also have been approved by a resolution of the members of the holding company, or be conditional upon such approval being obtained.[1885]

A company will not be subject to any liability by reason of a failure to obtain the approval required.[1886]

However, approval will not be required from shareholders of a body corporate that is not a UK-registered company;[1887] or is a wholly owned subsidiary of another body corporate.[1888]

An arrangement involving more than one non-cash asset;[1889] or an arrangement that is one of a series involving non-cash assets,[1890] will be treated as if they involved a non-cash asset of a value equal to the aggregate value of all the non-cash assets involved in the arrangement or, as the case may be, the series.

Section 190(6) of the CA 2006 does not apply to a transaction so far as it relates to anything to which a director of a company is entitled under his service contract.[1891] It does not apply to payment for loss of office as defined in s 215 of the CA 2006 (payments requiring member's approval).[1892]

Meaning of 'substantial'

10.24 Section 191 of the CA 2006 sets out what is meant in s 190 of the CA 2006 (requirement of approval for substantial property transactions) by a 'substantial' non-cash asset.[1893] An asset is a substantial asset in relation to the company if its value exceeds 10 per cent of the company's assets value and is more than £5,000;[1894] or exceeds £100,000.[1895]

A company's 'asset value' at any time is the value of the company's net assets determined by reference to its most recent statutory accounts[1896] or if no statutory accounts have been prepared, the amount of the company's called-up share capital.[1897]

A company's 'statutory accounts' means its annual accounts prepared in accordance with Part 15 of the CA 2006 and its 'most recent' statutory accounts means those in relation to which the time for sending them out to members (see s 424 of the CA 2006) is most recent.[1898]

Whether an asset is a substantial asset must be determined as at the time the arrangement is entered into.[1899]

[1885] CA 2006, s 190(2).   [1886] CA 2006, s 190(3).   [1887] CA 2006, s 190(4)(a).
[1888] CA 2006, s 190(4)(b).   [1889] CA 2006, s 190(5)(a).   [1890] CA 2006, s 190(5)(b).
[1891] CA 2006, s 190(6)(a).   [1892] CA 2006, s 190(6)(b).   [1893] CA 2006, s 191(1).
[1894] CA 2006, s 191(2)(a).   [1895] CA 2006, s 191(2)(b).   [1896] CA 2006, s 191(3)(a).
[1897] CA 2006, s 191(3)(b).   [1898] CA 2006, s 191(4).   [1899] CA 2006, s 191(5).

Exception for transactions with members or other group companies

10.25 Section 192 of the CA 2006 is concerned with exception for transaction with member or other group companies. Approval will not be required under s 190 of the CA 2006 (requirement of members' approval for substantial property transactions) for a transaction between a company and a person in his character as a member of that company;[1900] or for a transaction between a holding company and its wholly-owned subsidiary;[1901] or two wholly-owned subsidiaries of the same holding company.[1902]

Exception in the case of company in winding up or administration

10.26 Section 193 of the CA 2006 applies to a company that is being a wound up (unless the winding up is a member's voluntary winding up);[1903] or that is in administration within the meaning of Schedule B1 to the Insolvency Act 1986 (c.45) or the Insolvency (Northern Ireland) Order 1989 (SI 1989/2405) (NI 19).[1904] In such circumstances, approval is not required under s 190 of the CA 2006 (requirement of member's approval for substantial property transactions) on the part of the members of a company;[1905] or for an arrangement entered into by a company.[1906]

Exceptions for transactions on recognised investment exchange

10.27 Section 194 of the CA 2006 deals with exceptions for transactions on recognised investment exchange. Approval is not required under s 190 of the CA 2006 (requirement of members' approval for substantial property transactions) for a transaction on a recognised investment exchange effected by a director, or a person connected with him, through the agency of a person who in relation to the transaction acts as an independent broker.[1907]

An 'independent broker' means a person who, independently of the director or any person connected with him, selects the person with whom the transaction is to be effected.[1908] A 'recognised investment exchange' has the same meaning as in Part 18 of the Financial Services and Markets Act 2000.[1909]

Property transactions: civil consequences of transaction

10.28 The CA 2006 sets out the civil consequences for breach of the substantial property transaction provisions.

[1900] CA 2006, s 192(a).   [1901] CA 2006, s 192(b)(i).   [1902] CA 2006, s 192(b)(ii).
[1903] CA 2006, s 193(1)(a).   [1904] CA 2006, s 193(1)(b).   [1905] CA 2006, s 193(2)(a).
[1906] CA 2006, s 193(2)(b).   [1907] CA 2006, s 194(1).   [1908] CA 2006, s 194(2)(a).
[1909] CA 2006, s 194(2)(b).

Section 195 of the CA 2006 applies where a company enters into an arrangement in contravention of s 190 of the CA 2006 (requirement of members' approval for substantial property transactions).[1910]

The arrangement and any transaction entered into in pursuance of the arrangement (whether by the company or any other person) is voidable at the instance of the company, unless any of the following exceptions apply. First, restitution of any money or other asset that was the subject matter of the arrangement or transaction is no longer possible.[1911] Second, the company has been indemnified by any other persons for the loss or damage suffered by it.[1912] Third, where rights are acquired in good faith, for value and without actual notice of the contravention by a person who is not a party to the arrangement or transaction would be affected by the avoidance.[1913]

Section 195(3) of the CA 2006 ensures that whether or not the arrangement or any such transaction has been avoided, each of the persons specified in s 195(4) of the CA 2006 is liable to account to the company for any gain that has been made directly or indirectly by the arrangement or transaction;[1914] and (jointly and severally with any other person so liable under s 195 of the CA 2006) to indemnify the company for any loss or damage resulting from the arrangement or transaction.[1915]

The persons who will be liable are:

(a)   any director of the company or of its holding company with whom the company entered into the arrangement in contravention of s 190 of the CA 2006;[1916]

(b)   any person with whom the company entered into the arrangement in contravention of that section who is connected with a director of the company or of its holding company;[1917]

(c)   the director of the company or of its holding company with whom any such person is connected;[1918] and

(d)   any other director of the company who authorised the arrangement or any transaction entered into in pursuance of such an arrangement.[1919]

However, ss 195(3) and (4) of the CA 2006 are subject to s 195(6) and (7) of the CA 2006.[1920] Section 195(6) of the CA 2006 states that in the case of an arrangement entered into by a company in contravention of s 190 of the CA 2006 with a person connected with a director of the company or of its holding company, that director is not liable by virtue of s 195(4)(c) of the CA 2006 if he shows that he took all reasonable steps to secure the company's compliance with that section.[1921]

[1910] CA 2006, s 195(1).   [1911] CA 2006, s 195(2)(a).   [1912] CA 2006, s 195(2)(b).
[1913] CA 2006, s 195(2)(c).   [1914] CA 2006, s 195(3)(a).   [1915] CA 2006, s 195(3)(b).
[1916] CA 2006, s 195(4)(a).   [1917] CA 2006, s 195(4)(b).   [1918] CA 2006, s 195(4)(c).
[1919] CA 2006, s 195(4)(d).   [1920] CA 2006, s 195(5).   [1921] CA 200, s 195(6).

In any case, a person so connected is not liable by virtue of s 195(4)(b) of the CA 2006;[1922] and a director is not liable under s 195(4)(d) of the CA 2006,[1923] if he shows that, at the time the arrangement was entered into, he did not know the relevant circumstances constituting the contravention.

Nothing in s 195 of the CA 2006 will be read as excluding the operation of any other enactment or rule of law by virtue of which the arrangement or transaction may be called into question or any liability to the company may arise.[1924]

Property transactions: effect of subsequent affirmation

10.29 Section 196 of the CA 2006 deals with property transactions and the effect of subsequent affirmation. Where a transaction or arrangement is entered into by a company in contravention of s 190 of the CA 2006 (requirement of members' approval) but, within a reasonable period, it is affirmed in the case of a contravention of s 190(1) of the CA 2006 by resolution of the members of the company;[1925] and in the case of a contravention of s 190(2) of the CA 2006 by resolution of the members of the holding company,[1926] the transaction or arrangement may no longer be avoided by s 195 of the CA 2006.

Sections 190–196 of the CA 2006 require member approval to substantial property transactions. These are transactions where the company buys or sells a non-cash asset (as defined in s 1163 of the CA 2006 to or from:

- a director of the company;
- a director of its holding company;
- a person connected with a director of the company; or
- a person connected with a director of its holding company.

Approval is only required where the value of the asset exceeds £100,000 or 10 per cent of the company's net assets (based on its last set of annual accounts, or called-up share capital if it has not yet produced any accounts). No approval is required if the value of the asset is less than £5,000.

These sections replace ss 320 and 322 of the CA 1985. The changes include:

- permitting a company to enter into a contract that is conditional on member approval (s 190(1) of the CA 2006). This implements a recommendation of the Law Commissions. In cases where the approval of the members of the holding company is also required, the company may enter into arrangements conditional on approval being obtained from the members of the holding company (s 190(2) of the CA 2006). The

---

[1922] CA 2006, s 195(7)(a).   [1923] CA 2006, s 195(7)(b).   [1924] CA 2006, s 195(8).
[1925] CA 2006, s 196(a).   [1926] CA 2006, s 196(b).

454 A Guide to the Companies Act 2006

company is not to be liable under the contract if member approval is not forthcoming (s 190(3) of the CA 2006);

- providing for the aggregation of non-cash assets forming part of an arrangement or series of arrangements for the purpose of determining whether the financial thresholds have been exceeded so that the member approval is required (s 190(5) of the CA 2006);
- excluding payments under directors' service contracts and payments for loss of office from the requirements of these sections (s 190(6) of the CA 2006). This implements a recommendation of the Law Commissions;
- raising the minimum value of what may be regarded as a substantial non-cash asset from £2,000 to £5,000 (s 191 of the CA 2006);
- providing an exception for transactions made by companies in administration (s 193 of the CA 2006). This implements a recommendation of the Law Commissions;
- not requiring the approval on the part of the members of a company that is in administration or is being wound up (unless it is a members' voluntary winding up) (s 193 of the CA 2006).

Loans, quasi loans and credit transactions

10.30 Sections 197–214 of the CA 2006 are concerned with loans, quasi loans and credit transactions.

Section 197 of the CA 2006 is concerned with loans to directors with reference to requirement of members' approval. A company may not make a loan to a director of the company or its holding company;[1927] or give a guarantee or provide security in connection with a loan or quasi loan made by any person to such a director,[1928] unless the transaction has been approved by a resolution of the members of the company.

If the director is a director of the company's holding company, the transaction must also have been approved by a resolution of the members of the holding company.[1929]

A resolution approving a transaction under s 197 of the CA 2006 must not be passed unless a memorandum setting out the matters in s 197(4) of the CA 2006 is made available to the members, in the following two circumstances. First, in the case of a written resolution, by being sent or submitted to every eligible member at or before the time at which the proposed resolution is sent or submitted to him;[1930] and second, in the case of a resolution at a meeting, by being made available for inspection by members of the company both at the company's registered office for not less than 15 days ending with the date of the meeting;[1931] and at the meeting itself.[1932]

[1927] CA 2006, s 197(1)(a).   [1928] CA 2006, s 197(1).   [1929] CA 2006, s 197(2).
[1930] CA 2006, s 197(3)(a).   [1931] CA 2006, s 197(3)(b)(i).   [1932] CA 2006, s 197(3)(b)(ii).

The matters that must be disclosed are:

(a)   the nature of the transaction;[1933]
(b)   the amount of the loan and the purpose for which it is required;[1934] and
(c)   the extent of the company's liability under any transaction connected with the loan.[1935]

However, no approval is required from the members of a body corporate that is not a UK-registered company;[1936] or from a company associated with a public company.[1937]

Quasi loans to directors: requirement of members' approval

10.31 Section 198 of the CA 2006 deals with 'quasi loans' to directors and the requirement for members' approval. It applies to a company if it is a public company;[1938] or a company associated with a public company.[1939] A company may not make a quasi loan to a director of the company or of its holding company;[1940] or give a guarantee or provide security in connection with a quasi loan made by any person to such a director,[1941] unless the transaction has been approved by a resolution of members of the company.

If the director is the director of the company's holding company, the transaction must also have been approved by a resolution of the members of the holding company.[1942]

A resolution approving a transaction must not be passed unless a memorandum setting out the matters set out in s 198(5) of the CA 2006 is made available to the members, in the following two circumstances. First, in the case of a written resolution, by being sent or submitted to every eligible member at or before the time at which the proposed resolution is sent or submitted to him.[1943] Second, in the case of a resolution at a meeting, by being made available for inspection by members of the company both at the company's registered office for not less than 15 days ending with the date of the meeting;[1944] and at the meeting itself.[1945]

In respect of s 198(4) of the CA 2006, the matters to be disclosed are the nature of the transaction;[1946] the amount of the quasi loan and the purpose for which it is required;[1947] and the extent of the company's liability under any transaction connected with the quasi loan.[1948]

[1933] CA 2006, s 197(4)(a).   [1934] CA 2006, s 197(4)(b).   [1935] CA 2006, s 197(4)(c).
[1936] CA 2006, s 197(5)(a).   [1937] CA 2006, s 197(5)(b).   [1938] CA 2006, s 198(1)(a).
[1939] CA 2006, s 198(1)(b).   [1940] CA 2006, s 198(2)(a).   [1941] CA 2006, s 198(2)(b).
[1942] CA 2006, s 198(3).   [1943] CA 2006, s 198(4)(a).   [1944] CA 2006, s 198(4)(b)(i).
[1945] CA 2006, s 198(4)(b)(ii).   [1946] CA 2006, s 198(5)(a).   [1947] CA 2006, s 198(5)(b).
[1948] CA 2006, s 198(5)(c).

However, no approval is required under s 198 of the CA 2006 on the part of the members of a body corporate that is not a UK-registered company;[1949] or is a wholly-owned subsidiary of another body corporate.[1950]

Meaning of 'quasi loan' and related expressions

10.32 Section 199 of the CA 2006 provides definitions of 'quasi loan' and related expressions.

A 'quasi loan' is defined as a transaction under which one party known as the creditor 'agrees to pay', or pays otherwise than in pursuance of an agreement; a sum for another person, known as 'the borrower', or agrees to reimburse, or reimburses otherwise than in pursuance of an agreement, expenditure incurred by another party for the borrower, on terms that the borrower (or a person on his behalf) will reimburse the creditor;[1951] or in circumstances giving rise to a liability, on the borrower to reimburse the creditor.[1952]

Any reference to the person to whom a quasi loan is made is a reference to the borrower.[1953]

The liabilities of the borrower under a quasi loan include the liabilities of any person who has agreed to reimburse the creditor on behalf of the borrower.[1954]

Loans or quasi loans to persons connected with directors: requirement of members' approval

10.33 Section 200 of the CA 2006 is concerned with loans or quasi loans to persons connected with directors with reference to requirement of members' approval.

It applies to a company if it is a public company;[1955] or a company associated with a public company.[1956] A company may not make a loan or quasi loan to a person connected with a director of the company or of its holding company;[1957] or give a guarantee or provide security in connection with a loan or quasi loan made by any person to a person connected with such a director,[1958] unless the transaction has been approved by a resolution of the members of the company.

If the connected person is a person connected with a director of the company's holding company, the transaction must also have been approved by a resolution of the members of the holding company.[1959]

[1949] CA 2006, s 198(6)(a).   [1950] CA 2006, s 198(6)(b).   [1951] CA 2006, s 199(1)(a).
[1952] CA 2006, s 199(1)(b).   [1953] CA 2006, s 199(2).   [1954] CA 2006, s 199(3).
[1955] CA 2006, s 200(1)(a).   [1956] CA 2006, s 200(1)(b).   [1957] CA 2006, s 200(2)(a).
[1958] CA 2006, s 200(2)(b).   [1959] CA 2006, s 200(3).

A resolution approving a transaction must not be passed unless a memorandum setting out the matters set out in s 198(5) of the CA 2006 is made available to the members, in the following two circumstances. First, in the case of a written resolution, by being sent or submitted to every eligible member at or before the time at which the proposed resolution is sent or submitted to him.[1960] Second, in the case of a resolution at a meeting, by being made available for inspection by members of the company both at the company's registered office for not less than 15 days ending with the date of the meeting;[1961] and at the meeting itself.[1962]

In respect of s 198(4) of the CA 2006, the matters to be disclosed are the nature of the transaction;[1963] the amount of the quasi loan and the purpose for which it is required;[1964] and the extent of the company's liability under any transaction connected with the quasi loan.[1965]

However, no approval is required under s 198 of the CA 2006 on the part of the members of a body corporate that is not a UK-registered company; or is a wholly-owned subsidiary of another body corporate.[1966]

Sections 197–214 of the CA 2006 require member approval for loans, quasi loans, credit transactions and related guarantees or security made by a company for a director of the company; or a director of its holding company.

In the case of a public company, or a private company associated with a public company, ss 197, 198, 200 and 201 of the CA 2006 require member approval for loans, quasi loans (as defined in s 199 of the CA 2006), credit transactions (as defined in s 202 of the CA 2006) and related guarantees or security made by the company for:

- a director of the company;
- a director of its holding company;
- a person connected with a director of the company; or
- a person connected with a director of its holding company.

Section 256 of the CA 2006 sets out what is meant by references to 'associated companies'. A holding company is associated with all its subsidiaries, and a subsidiary is associated with its holding company and all the other subsidiaries of its holding company.

Member approval is not required by these sections for the following:

- loans, quasi loans and credit transaction to meet expenditure on company business. The total value of transactions under this exception made in respect of a director and any person connected to him must not exceed £50,000 (s 204 of the CA 2006);

[1960] CA 2006, s 200(4)(a).   [1961] CA 2006, s 200(4)(b)(i).   [1962] CA 2006, s 200(4)(b)(ii).
[1963] CA 2006, s 200(5)(a).   [1964] CA 2006, s 200(5)(b).   [1965] CA 2006, s 299(5)(c).
[1966] CA 2006, s 200(6).

- money lent to fund a director's defence costs for legal proceedings in connection with any alleged negligence, default, breach of duty or breach of trust by him in relation to the company or an associated company (s 205 of the CA 2006) or in connection with regulatory action or investigation under the same circumstances (s 206 of the CA 2006);
- small loans and quasi loans, as long as the total value of such loans and quasi loans made in respect of a director and any person connected to him does not exceed £10,000 (s 207(1) of the CA 2006);
- small credit transactions, as long as the total value of such credit transaction made in respect of a director and any person connected to him does not exceed £15,000 (s 207(2) of the CA 2006);
- credit transactions made in the ordinary course of the company's business (s 207(3) of the CA 2006);
- intra-group transactions (s 208 of the CA 2006); and
- loans and quasi loans made by a money-lending company in the ordinary course of the company's business (as long as the requirements of s 209 of the CA 2006 are met).

These sections replace ss 330–342 of the CA 1985. The changes include:

- abolishing the prohibition on loans, quasi loans, etc. to directors and replacing it with a requirement for member approval. This implements the recommendation of the Company Law Review Group;
- abolishing the criminal penalty for breach;
- replacing the concept of relevant company in s 331 of the CA 1985 with 'associated company' as defined in s 256 of the CA 2006;
- removing some of the requirements that were imposed by s 337 of the CA 1985 on the exception for expenditure on company business (s 204 of the CA 2006);
- widening the exception for expenditure on company business to include directors of the company's holding company and connected persons (s 204 of the CA 2006);
- creating a new exception specifically for expenditure in connection with regulatory actions or investigations (s 206 of the CA 2006);
- restricting the exceptions for expenditure on defending legal or regulatory proceedings to proceedings in connection with any alleged negligence, default, breach of duty or breach of trust by the director in relation to the company or an associated company (ss 205 and 206 of the CA 2006);
- widening the exception for small loans to include small quasi loans (s 207(1) of the CA 2006) in place of the exception under s 332 of the CA 1985 for short-term quasi loans;
- widening the exception for small loans and quasi loans to include transactions with connected persons (s 207(1) of the CA 2006);

- widening the exception for 'home loans' to include those connected persons who are employees (s 209(3) of the CA 2006);
- raising the maximum amounts permitted under the exception for expenditure on company business (s 204 of the CA 2006), the exception for small loans and small quasi loans (s 207(1) of the CA 2006) and the exception for small credit transactions (s 207(2) of the CA 2006);
- widening the exceptions for intra-group transactions (s 208(1) of the CA 2006);
- abolishing the maximum amounts permitted under the exception for money-lending companies (s 209 of the CA 2006); and
- allowing affirmation of loans, quasi loans and credit transactions entered into by the company in line with the provision in respect of substantial property transactions.

Credit transactions

10.34 Sections 201–214 of the CA 2006 are concerned with credit transactions and related arrangements.

Credit transactions: requirement of members' approval

10.35 Section 201 of the CA 2006 deals with credit transactions and the requirement for members' approval. It applies to a company if it is a public company;[1967] or a company associated with a public company.[1968]

A company may not enter into a credit transaction as creditor for the benefit of a director of the company or of its holding company, or a person connected with such a director;[1969] or give a guarantee or provide security in connection with a credit transaction entered into by any person for the benefit of such a director, or a person connected with such a director,[1970] unless the credit transaction, the giving of the guarantee or the provision of security, (as the case may be) has been approved by a resolution of the members of the holding company.

If the director or connected person is a director of its holding company or a person connected with such a director, the transaction must also have been approved by a resolution of the members of the holding company.[1971]

A resolution approving a transaction under s 201 of the CA 2006 cannot be passed unless a memorandum setting out the matters in s 201(4) of the CA 2006 is made available to the members in the following two circumstances. First, in the case of a written resolution, by being sent or submitted to every eligible member at or before the time at which the proposed resolution is sent

---

[1967] CA 2006, s 201(1)(a).   [1968] CA 2006, s 201(1)(b).   [1969] CA 2006, s 201(2)(a).
[1970] CA 2006, s 201(2)(b).   [1971] CA 2006, s 201(3).

or submitted to him;[1972] second, in the case of a resolution at a meeting, by being made available for inspection by members of the company both at the company's registered office for not less than 15 days ending with the date of the meeting, and at the meeting itself.[1973]

The matters that must be disclosed are the nature of the transaction;[1974] the value of the transaction and the purpose for which the land, goods and services sold or otherwise disposed of, leased, hired or supplied under the credit transaction are supplied;[1975] and the extent of the company's liability under any transaction connected with the credit transaction.[1976]

However, no approval is required from the members of a body corporate that is not a UK-registered company;[1977] or is a wholly-owned subsidiary of another body corporate.[1978]

Meaning of credit transaction

10.36 The meaning of 'credit transaction' is set out in s 202 of the CA 2006. A 'credit transaction' is defined as a transaction under which one party known as 'the creditor' does any of the following: supplies any goods or sells any land under a hire-purchase agreement or a conditional sale agreement;[1979] or leases or hires any land or goods in return for periodical payments;[1980] or otherwise disposes of land or supplies goods or services on the undertaking that payment (whether in lump sum or instalments or by way of periodical payments or otherwise) is to be deferred.[1981]

Any reference to the person for whose benefit a credit transaction is entered into is to the person to whom goods, land or services are supplied, sold, leased, hired, or otherwise disposed of under the transaction.[1982]

A reference to a 'conditional sale agreement' has the same meaning as in the Consumer Credit Act 1974. The term 'services' means anything other than goods or land.[1983]

Related arrangements: requirement of members' approval

10.37 The related arrangements with particular reference to members' approval is governed by s 203 of the CA 2006. A company may not take part in an arrangement under which another person enters into a transaction that, if it had been entered into by the company, would have required approval under ss 197, 198, 200 or 201 of the CA 2006;[1984] and that person, in pursuance of the arrangement, obtains a benefit from the company or a body

---

[1972] CA 2006, s 201(4)(a).   [1973] CA 2006, s 201(4)(b).   [1974] CA 2006, s 201(5)(a).
[1975] CA 2006, s 201(5)(b).   [1976] CA 2006, s 201(5)(c).   [1977] CA 2006, s 201(6)(a).
[1978] CA 2006, s 201(6)(b).   [1979] CA 2006, s 202(1)(a).   [1980] CA 2006, s 202(1)(b).
[1981] CA 2006, s 202(1)(c).   [1982] CA 2006, s 202(2).   [1983] CA 2006, s 202(3).
[1984] CA 2006, s 203(1)(a)(i).

corporate associated with it;[1985] or arrange for the assignment to it, or assumption by it, of any rights, obligations or liabilities under a transaction that, if it had been entered into by the company, would have required such approval,[1986] unless the arrangement in question has been approved by a resolution of the members of the company.

If the director or connected person for whom the transaction is entered into is a director of its holding company or a person connected with such a director, the arrangement must also have been approved by a resolution of the members of the holding company.[1987]

A resolution approving an arrangement to which s 203 of the CA 2006 applies must not be passed unless a memorandum setting out the matters mentioned in s 203(4) of the CA 2006 is made available to members – in the case of a written resolution, by being sent or submitted to every eligible member at or before the time at which the proposed resolution is sent or submitted to him;[1988] in the case of a resolution at a meeting, by being made available for inspection by members of the company both at the company's registered office for not less than 15 days ending with the date of the meeting;[1989] and at the meeting itself.[1990]

The matters to be disclosed are the matters that would have to be disclosed if the company were seeking approval of the transaction to which the arrangement relates;[1991] the nature of the arrangement;[1992] and the extent of the company's liability under the arrangement or any transaction connected with it.[1993]

No approval is required on the part of the members of a body corporate that is not a UK-registered company;[1994] or is a wholly-owned subsidiary of another body corporate.[1995]

In determining whether a transaction is one that would have required approval under ss 197, 198, 200 or 201 of the CA 2006, if it had been entered into by the company, the transaction must be treated as having been entered into on the date of the arrangement.[1996]

Exception for expenditure on company business

10.38 Section 204 of the CA 2006 deals with exceptions for expenditure on company business. Approval is not required under ss 197, 198, 200 or 201 of the CA 2006 (requirement of members' approval for loans, etc.) for anything done by a company to provide a director of the company or of its holding company, or a person connected with any such director, with funds to meet

---

[1985] CA 2006, s 203(1)(a)(ii).   [1986] CA 2006, s 203(1)(b).   [1987] CA 2006, s 203(2).
[1988] CA 2006, s 203(3)(a).   [1989] CA 2006, s 203(3)(b)(i).   [1990] CA 2006, s 203(3)(b)(ii).
[1991] CA 2006, s 203(4)(a).   [1992] CA 2006, s 203(4)(b).   [1993] CA 2006, s 203(4)(c).
[1994] CA 2006, s 203(5)(a).   [1995] CA 2006, s 203(5)(b).   [1996] CA 2006, s 203(6).

expenditure incurred or to be incurred by him for the purposes of the company;[1997] or for the purpose of enabling him properly to perform his duties as an officer of the company;[1998] or to enable any such person to avoid incurring such expenditure.[1999]

Section 204 of the CA 2006 does not authorise a company to enter into a transaction if the aggregate of the value of the transaction in question,[2000] and the value of any other relevant transactions or arrangements, exceeds £50,000.[2001]

Exception for expenditure on defending proceedings, etc.

10.39 Section 205 of the CA 2006 is concerned with exceptions for expenditure on defending proceedings. Approval is not required under ss 197, 198, 200 or 201 of the CA 2006 (requirement of members' approval for loans, etc.) for anything done by a company to provide a director of the company or of its holding company with funds to meet expenditure incurred or to be incurred by him in defending any criminal or civil proceedings in connection with any alleged negligence, default, breach of duty or breach of trust by him in relation to the company or an associated company;[2002] or in connection with an application for relief (see subs (5));[2003] or to enable any such director to avoid incurring such expenditure,[2004] if it is done on the following terms.

The terms are:

(a)   that the loan is to be repaid, or (as the case may be) any liability of the company incurred under any transaction connected with the thing done is to be discharged, in the event of:

   (i)   the director being convicted in the proceedings;[2005]
   (ii)   judgment being given against him in the proceedings,[2006] or
   (iii) the court refusing to grant him relief on the application;[2007] and

(c)   that it is to be so repaid or discharged not later than:

   (i)   the date when the conviction becomes final;[2008]
   (ii)   the date when the judgment becomes final;[2009] or
   (iii) the date when the refusal of relief becomes final.[2010]

For this purpose a conviction, judgment or refusal of relief becomes final if

[1997] CA 2006, s 204(1)(a)(i).   [1998] CA 2006, s 204(1)(a)(ii).   [1999] CA 2006, s 204(1)(b).
[2000] CA 2006, s 204(2)(a).   [2001] CA 2006, s 204(2)(b).   [2002] CA 2006, s 205(1)(a)(i).
[2003] CA 2006, s 205(1)(a)(ii).   [2004] CA 2006, s 205(1)(b).   [2005] CA 2006, s 205(2)(a)(i).
[2006] CA 2006, s 205(2)(a)(ii).   [2007] CA 2006, s 205(2)(a)(iii).   [2008] CA 2006, s 205(b)(i).
[2009] CA 2006, s 205(b)(ii).   [2010] CA 2006, s 205(b)(iii).

not appealed against, at the end of the period for bringing an appeal;[2011] if appealed against, when the appeal (or any further appeal) is disposed of.[2012]

An appeal is disposed of if it is determined and the period for bringing any further appeal has ended;[2013] or if it is abandoned or otherwise ceases to have effect.[2014]

The reference in subs (1)(a)(ii) to an application for relief is to an application for relief under s 661(3) or (4) of the CA 2006 (power of court to grant relief in case of acquisition of shares by innocent nominee), or s 1157 of the CA 2006 (general power of court to grant relief in case of honest and reasonable conduct).[2015]

Exception for expenditure in connection with regulatory action or investigation

10.40 Section 206 of the CA 2006 deals with exceptions for expenditure in connection with regulatory actions or investigations. Approval is not required under ss 197, 198, 200 or 201 of the CA 2006 (requirement of members' approval for loans, etc.) for anything done by a company to provide a director of the company or of its holding company with funds to meet expenditure incurred or to be incurred by him in defending himself in an investigation by a regulatory authority;[2016] or against action proposed to be taken by a regulatory authority,[2017] in connection with any alleged negligence, default, breach of duty or breach of trust by him in relation to the company or an associated company; or to enable any such director to avoid incurring such expenditure.[2018]

Exceptions for minor and business transactions

10.41 Section 207 of the CA 2006 deals with exceptions for minor and business transactions. Approval is not required under ss 197, 198 or 200 of the CA 2006 for a company to make a loan or quasi loan, or to give a guarantee or provide security in connection with a loan or quasi loan, if the aggregate of the value of the transaction;[2019] and the value of any other relevant transactions or arrangements,[2020] does not exceed £10,000.

Approval is not required under s 201 of the CA 2006 for a company to enter into a credit transaction, or to give a guarantee or provide security in connection with a credit transaction, if the aggregate of the value of the

---

[2011] CA 2006, ss 205(3)(a).   [2012] CA 2006, s 205(3)(b).   [2013] CA 2006, s 205(4)(a).
[2014] CA 2006, s 205(4)(b).   [2015] CA 2006, s 205(5).   [2016] CA 2006, s 206(a)(i).
[2017] CA 2006, s 206(a)(ii).   [2018] CA 2006, s 206(b).   [2019] CA 2006, s 207(1)(a).
[2020] CA 2006, s 207(1)(b).

transaction (that is, of the credit transaction, guarantee or security),[2021] and the value of any other relevant transactions or arrangements[2022] does not exceed £15,000.

Approval is not required under s 201 of the CA 2006 for a company to enter into a credit transaction, or to give a guarantee or provide security in connection with a credit transaction, if the transaction is entered into by the company in the ordinary course of the company's business,[2023] and the value of the transaction is not greater, and the terms on which it is entered into are not more favourable, than it is reasonable to expect the company would have offered to, or in respect of, a person of the same financial standing but unconnected with the company.[2024]

Exceptions for intra-group transactions

10.42 Section 208 of the CA 2006 deals with exceptions for intra-group transactions. Approval is not required under ss 197, 198 or 200 of the CA 2006 for the making of a loan or quasi loan to an associated body corporate,[2025] or the giving of a guarantee or provision of security in connection with a loan or quasi loan made to an associated body corporate.[2026]

Approval is not required under s 201 of the CA 2006 to enter into a credit transaction as creditor for the benefit of an associated body corporate,[2027] or to give a guarantee or provide security in connection with a credit transaction entered into by any person for the benefit of an associated body corporate.[2028]

Exceptions for money-lending companies

10.43 Section 209 of the CA 2006 deals with exceptions for money-lending companies. Approval is not required under ss 197, 198 or 200 of the CA 2006 for the making of a loan or quasi loan, or the giving of a guarantee or provision of security in connection with a loan or quasi loan, by a money-lending company if the transaction (that is, the loan, quasi loan, guarantee or security) is entered into by the company in the ordinary course of the company's business,[2029] and the value of the transaction is not greater, and its terms are not more favourable, than it is reasonable to expect the company would have offered to a person of the same financial standing but unconnected with the company.[2030]

A 'money-lending company' means a company whose ordinary business includes the making of loans or quasi loans, or the giving of guarantees or provision of security in connection with loans or quasi loans.[2031]

[2021] CA 2006, s 207(2)(a).   [2022] CA 2006, s 207(2)(b).   [2023] CA 2006, s 207(3)(a).
[2024] CA 2006, s 207(3)(b).   [2025] CA 2006, s 208(1)(a).   [2026] CA 2006, s 208(1)(b).
[2027] CA 2006, s 208(2)(a).   [2028] CA 2006, s 208(2)(b).   [2029] CA 2006, s 208(1)(a).
[2030] CA 2006, s 208(1)(b).   [2031] CA 2006, s 209(2).

The condition specified in s 209(1)(b) of the CA 2006 does not of itself prevent a company from making a home loan to a director of the company or of its holding company;[2032] or to an employee of the company,[2033] if loans of that description are ordinarily made by the company to its employees and the terms of the loan in question are no more favourable than those on which such loans are ordinarily made.

For the purposes of s 209(3) of the CA 2006 a 'home loan' means a loan:

(a) for the purpose of facilitating the purchase, for use as the only or main residence of the person to whom the loan is made, of the whole or part of any dwelling-house together with any land to be occupied and enjoyed with it;[2034]

(b) for the purpose of improving a dwelling-house or part of a dwelling-house so used or any land occupied and enjoyed with it;[2035] or

(c) in substitution for any loan made by any person and falling within para (a) or (b).[2036]

Other relevant transactions or arrangements

10.44 Section 210 of the CA 2006 deals with other relevant transactions or arrangements. It applies for determining what are 'other relevant transactions or arrangements' for the purposes of any exception to ss 197, 198, 200 or 201 of the CA 2006. In the following provisions 'the relevant exception' means the exception for the purposes of which that falls to be determined.[2037]

Other relevant transactions or arrangements are those previously entered into, or entered into at the same time as the transaction or arrangement in question in relation to which the following conditions are met.[2038]

Where the transaction or arrangement in question is entered into for a director of the company entering into it,[2039] or for a person connected with such a director,[2040] the conditions are that the transaction or arrangement was (or is) entered into for that director, or a person connected with him, by virtue of the relevant exception by that company or by any of its subsidiaries.

Where the transaction or arrangement in question is entered into for a director of the holding company of the company entering into it,[2041] or for a person connected with such a director,[2042] the conditions are that the transaction or arrangement was (or is) entered into for that director, or a person connected with him, by virtue of the relevant exception by the holding company or by any of its subsidiaries.

[2032] CA 2006, s 209(3)(a).   [2033] CA 2006, s 209(3)(b).   [2034] CA 2006, s 209(4)(a).
[2035] CA 2006, s 209(4)(b).   [2036] CA 2006, s 209(4)(c).   [2037] CA 2006, s 210(1).
[2038] CA 2006, s 210(2).   [2039] CA 2006, s 210(3)(a).   [2040] CA 2006, s 210(3)(b).
[2041] CA 2006, s 210(4)(a).   [2042] CA 2006, s 210(4)(b).

A transaction or arrangement entered into by a company that at the time it was entered into was a subsidiary of the company entering into the transaction or arrangement in question,[2043] or was a subsidiary of that company's holding company,[2044] is not a relevant transaction or arrangement if, at the time the question arises whether the transaction or arrangement in question falls within a relevant exception, it is no longer such a subsidiary.

The value of transactions and arrangements

10.45 Section 211 of the CA 2006 deals with the value of transactions or arrangements. For the purposes of ss 197–214 of the CA 2006 (loans, etc.) the value of a transaction or arrangement is determined as follows,[2045] and the value of any other relevant transaction or arrangement is taken to be the value so determined reduced by any amount by which the liabilities of the person for whom the transaction or arrangement was made have been reduced.[2046]

The value of a loan is the amount of its principal.[2047]

The value of a quasi loan is the amount, or maximum amount, that the person to whom the quasi loan is made is liable to reimburse the creditor.[2048]

The value of a credit transaction is the price that it is reasonable to expect could be obtained for the goods, services or land to which the transaction relates if they had been supplied (at the time the transaction is entered into) in the ordinary course of business and on the same terms (apart from price) as they have been supplied, or are to be supplied, under the transaction in question.[2049]

The value of a guarantee or security is the amount guaranteed or secured.[2050]

The value of an arrangement to which s 203 of the CA 2006 (related arrangements) applies is the value of the transaction to which the arrangement relates.[2051]

If the value of a transaction or arrangement is not capable of being expressed as a specific sum of money, whether because the amount of any liability arising under the transaction or arrangement is unascertainable, or for any other reason,[2052] and whether or not any liability under the transaction or arrangement has been reduced,[2053] its value is deemed to exceed £50,000.

[2043] CA 2006, s 210(5)(a).   [2044] CA 2006, s 210(5)(b).   [2045] CA 2006, s 211(a).
[2046] CA 2006, s 211(1)(b).   [2047] CA 2006, s 211(2).   [2048] CA 2006, s 211(3).
[2049] CA 2006, s 211(4).   [2050] CA 2006, s 211(5).   [2051] CA 2006, s 211(6).
[2052] CA 2006, s 211(7)(a).   [2053] CA 2006, s 211(7)(b).

The person for whom a transaction or arrangement is entered into

10.46 Section 212 of the CA 2006 elaborates on the concept of 'the person for whom a transaction or arrangement is entered into'. For the purposes of ss 197–214 of the CA 2006 (loans, etc.) the person for whom a transaction or arrangement is entered into is:

(a) in the case of a loan or quasi loan, the person to whom it is made;[2054]
(b) in the case of a credit transaction, the person to whom goods, land or services are supplied, sold, hired, leased or otherwise disposed of under the transaction;[2055]
(c) in the case of a guarantee or security, the person for whom the transaction is made in connection with which the guarantee or security is entered into;[2056]
(d) in the case of an arrangement within s 203 of the CA 2006 (related arrangements), the person for whom the transaction is made to which the arrangement relates.[2057]

Loans, etc.: civil consequences of contravention

10.47 Section 213 of the CA 2006 deals with the civil consequences of contravention in respect of loans. It applies where a company enters into a transaction or arrangement in contravention of ss 197, 198, 200, 201 or 203 of the CA 2006 (requirement of members' approval for loans, etc.).[2058]

The transaction or arrangement is voidable at the instance of the company, unless:

(a) restitution of any money or any other asset that was the subject matter of the transaction or arrangement is no longer possible;[2059]
(b) the company has been indemnified for any loss or damage resulting from the transaction or arrangement;[2060] or
(c) rights acquired in good faith, for value and without actual notice of the contravention by a person who is not a party to the transaction or arrangement, would be affected by the avoidance.[2061]

Whether or not the transaction or arrangement has been avoided, each of the persons specified in s 213(4) of the CA 2006 is liable to account to the company for any gain that he has made directly or indirectly by the transaction or arrangement;[2062] and (jointly and severally with any other person so liable

---

[2054] CA 2006, s 212(a).   [2055] CA 2006, s 212(b).   [2056] CA 2006, s 212(c).
[2057] CA 2006, s 212(d).   [2058] CA 2006, s 213(1).   [2059] CA 2006, s 213(2)(a).
[2060] CA 2006, s 213(b).   [2061] CA 2006, s 213(c).   [2062] CA 2006, s 213(3)(a).

under this section) to indemnify the company for any loss or damage resulting from the transaction or arrangement.[2063]

The persons who are liable are:

(a)   any director of the company or of its holding company with whom the company entered into the transaction or arrangement in contravention of ss 197, 198, 201 or 203 of the CA 2006;[2064]

(b)   any person with whom the company entered into the transaction or arrangement in contravention of any of those sections who is connected with a director of the company or of its holding company;[2065]

(c)   the director of the company or of its holding company with whom any such person is connected;[2066] and

(d)   any other director of the company who authorised the transaction or arrangement.[2067]

Sections 213(3) and (4) of the CA 2006 are subject to the following two subsections.[2068]

In the case of a transaction or arrangement entered into by a company in contravention of ss. 200, 201 or 203 of the CA 2006 with a person connected with a director of the company or of its holding company, that director is not liable by virtue of s 213(4)(c) of the CA 2006 if he shows that he took all reasonable steps to secure the company's compliance with the section concerned.[2069]

In any case a person so connected is not liable by virtue of s 213(4)(b) of the CA 2006,[2070] and a director is not liable by virtue of s 213(4)(d) of the CA 2006,[2071] if he shows that, at the time the transaction or arrangement was entered into, he did not know the relevant circumstances constituting the contravention.

Nothing in s 213 of the CA 2006 is be read as excluding the operation of any other enactment or rule of law, by virtue of which the transaction or arrangement may be called into question or any liability to the company may arise.[2072]

Loans, etc.: effect of subsequent affirmation

10.48 Section 214 of the CA 2006 deals with loans and the effect of subsequent affirmation. Where a transaction or arrangement is entered into by a company in contravention of ss 197, 198, 200, 201 or 203 of the CA 2006 (requirement of members' approval for loans, etc.) but, within a reasonable

---

[2063] CA 2006, s 213(3)(b).   [2064] CA 2006, s 213(4)(a).   [2065] CA 2006, s 213(4)(b).
[2066] CA 2006, s 213(c).   [2067] CA 2006, s 213(d).   [2068] CA 2006, s 213(5).
[2069] CA 2006, s 213(6).   [2070] CA 2006, s 213(7)(a).   [2071] CA 2006, s 213(7)(b).
[2072] CA 2006, s 213(8).

period, it is affirmed, in the case of a contravention of the requirement for a resolution of the members of the company, by a resolution of the members of the company;[2073] and in the case of a contravention of the requirement for a resolution of the members of the company's holding company, by a resolution of the members of the holding company,[2074] the transaction or arrangement may no longer be avoided under s 213 of the CA 2006.

Payments for loss of office

10.49 Section 215 of the CA 2006 contains provisions dealing with payments for loss of office. The term 'payment for loss of office' means a payment made to a director or past director of a company:

(a)   by way of compensation for loss of office as director of the company;[2075]
(b)   by way of compensation for loss, while director of the company or in connection with his ceasing to be a director of it, of:

    (i)   any other office or employment in connection with the management of the affairs of the company;[2076] or
    (ii)   any office (as director or otherwise) or employment in connection with the management of the affairs of any subsidiary undertaking of the company;[2077]

(c)   as consideration for or in connection with his retirement from his office as director of the company;[2078] or
(d)   as consideration for or in connection with his retirement, while director of the company or in connection with his ceasing to be a director of it, from:

    (i)   any other office or employment in connection with the management of the affairs of the company;[2079] or
    (ii)   any office (as director or otherwise) or employment in connection with the management of the affairs of any subsidiary undertaking of the company.[2080]

The references to 'compensation' and 'consideration' include benefits otherwise than in cash and references in Chapter 4 of Part 10 of the CA 2006 to payment have a corresponding meaning.[2081]

    For the purposes of ss 217–221 of the CA 2006 (payments requiring members' approval) payment to a person connected with a director,[2082] or payment

---

[2073] CA 2006, s 214(a).   [2074] CA 2006, s 214(b).   [2075] CA 2006, s 215(1)(a).
[2076] CA 2006, s 215(1)(b)(i).   [2077] CA 2006, s 215(1)(b)(ii).   [2078] CA 2006, s 215(1)(c).
[2079] CA 2006, s 215(1)(d)(i).   [2080] CA 2006, s 215(1)(d)(ii).   [2081] CA 2006, s 215(2).
[2082] CA 2006, s 215(3)(a).

to any person at the direction of, or for the benefit of, a director or a person connected with him,[2083] is treated as payment to the director.

References in those sections to payment by a person include payment by another person at the direction of, or on behalf of, the person referred to.[2084]

These sections require member approval for payments for loss of office. These are payments made to a director (or former director) to compensate him for ceasing to be a director, or for losing any other office or employment with the company or with a subsidiary of the company. They also include payments made in connection with retirement. In the case of loss of employment or retirement from employment, the employment must relate to the management of the affairs of the company.

Member approval is required under s 217 of the CA 2006 if a company wishes to make a payment for loss of office to one of its directors; or a director of its holding company.

Member approval is also required if any person (including the company or anyone else) wishes to make a payment for loss of office to a director of the company in connection with the transfer of the whole or any part of the undertaking or the property of the company or of a subsidiary of the company (s 218 of the CA 2006).

In the case of a payment for loss of office to a director in connection with the transfer of shares in the company or in a subsidiary of the company resulting from a takeover bid, approval is required of the holders of the shares to which the bid relates and of any other holders of shares of the same class (s 219 of the CA 2006).

These sections replace ss 312–316 of the CA 1985. The changes include:

- extending the requirements to include payments to connected persons (s 215(3) of the CA 2006);
- extending the requirements to include payments to directors in respect of the loss of any office, or employment in connection with the management of the affairs of the company, and not merely loss of office as a director as such (s 215 of the CA 2006). This implements a recommendation of the Law Commissions;
- extending the requirements to include payments by a company to a director of its holding company (s 217(2) of the CA 2006);
- extending the requirements in connection with the transfer of the undertaking or property of the company to include transfers of the undertaking or property of a subsidiary (s 218(2) of the CA 2006);
- extending the requirements in connection with share transfers so as to include all transfers of shares in the company or in a subsidiary resulting from a takeover bid (s 219(1) of the CA 2006);

[2083] CA 2006, s 215(3)(b).   [2084] CA 2006, s 215(4).

- excluding the persons making the offer for shares in the company and any associate of them from voting on any resolution to approve a payment for loss of office in connection with a share transfer (s 219(4) of the CA 2006). This implements a recommendation of the Law Commissions;
- setting out the exception for payments in discharge of certain legal obligations (s 220 of the CA 2006);
- creating a new exception for small payments (s 221 of the CA 2006);
- clarifying the civil consequences of breach of these sections (s 222(1)–(3) of the CA 2006); and
- resolving conflicts between the remedies where more than one requirement of these sections is breached (s 222(4) and (5) of the CA 2006). For example, if the payment contravenes both s 217 and s 219 of the CA 2006, because it was a payment by a company to one of its directors and it was a payment in connection with a takeover bid, and none of the required member approvals have been obtained, then the payment is held on trust for the persons who have sold their shares as a result of the offer and not on trust for the company making the payment.

Amounts taken to be payments for loss of office

10.50 Section 216 of the CA 2006 sets out the basis for the amounts taken to be payments for loss of office. It applies where in connection with any such transfer as is mentioned in s 218 or s 219 of the CA 2006 (payment in connection with transfer of undertaking, property or shares) a director of the company:

(a) is to cease to hold office;[2085] or

(b) is to cease to be the holder of: (i) any other office or employment in connection with the management of the affairs of the company;[2086] or (ii) any office (as director or otherwise) or employment in connection with the management of the affairs of any subsidiary undertaking of the company.[2087]

If in connection with any such transfer:

(a) the price to be paid to the director for any shares in the company held by him is in excess of the price which could at the time have been obtained by other holders of like shares,[2088] or

any valuable consideration is given to the director by a person other than the company, (the excess or, as the case may be, the money value of the

---

[2085] CA 2006, s 216(1)(a).   [2086] CA 2006, s 216(1)(b)(i).   [2087] CA 2006, s 215(1)(b)(ii).
[2088] CA 2006, s 216(2)(a).

consideration is taken for the purposes of those sections to have been a payment for loss of office).[2089]

Payment by company: requirement of members' approval

10.51 Section 217 of the CA 2006 deals with the requirement for members' approval where payment is to be made by the company. A company may not make a payment for loss of office to a director of the company unless the payment has been approved by a resolution of the members of the company.[2090]

A company may not make a payment for loss of office to a director of its holding company unless the payment has been approved by a resolution of the members of each of those companies.[2091]

A resolution approving a payment to which this section applies must not be passed unless a memorandum setting out particulars of the proposed payment (including its amount) is made available to the members of the company whose approval is sought:

(a)   in the case of a written resolution, by being sent or submitted to every eligible member at or before the time at which the proposed resolution is sent or submitted to him;[2092]

(b)   in the case of a resolution at a meeting, by being made available for inspection by the members both (i) at the company's registered office for not less than 15 days ending with the date of the meeting,[2093] and (ii) at the meeting itself.[2094]

No approval is required under this section on the part of the members of a body corporate that is not a UK-registered company;[2095] or that is a wholly-owned subsidiary of another body corporate.[2096]

Payment in connection with transfer of undertaking, etc.: requirement of members' approval

10.52 Section 218 of the CA 2006 deals with payment in connection with transfer of undertaking with the requirement for members' approval. No payment for loss of office may be made by any person to a director of a company in connection with the transfer of the whole or any part of the undertaking or property of the company unless the payment has been approved by a resolution of the members of the company.[2097]

[2089] CA 2006, s 216(2)(b).   [2090] CA 2006, s 217(1).   [2091] CA 2006, s 217(2).
[2092] CA 2006, s 217(3)(a).   [2093] CA 2006, s 217(3)(b)(i).   [2094] CA 2006, s 217(3)(b)(ii).
[2095] CA 2006, s 217(4)(a).   [2096] CA 2006, s 217(4)(b).   [2097] CA 2006, s 218(1).

No payment for loss of office may be made by any person to a director of a company in connection with the transfer of the whole or any part of the undertaking or property of a subsidiary of the company, unless the payment has been approved by a resolution of the members of each of the companies.[2098]

A resolution approving a payment to which s 218 of the CA 2006 applies must not be passed unless a memorandum setting out particulars of the proposed payment (including its amount) is made available to the members of the company whose approval is sought:

(a)   in the case of a written resolution, by being sent or submitted to every eligible member at or before the time at which the proposed resolution is sent or submitted to him;[2099]

(b)   in the case of a resolution at a meeting, by being made available for inspection by the members both (i) at the company's registered office for not less than 15 days ending with the date of the meeting,[2100] and (ii) at the meeting itself.[2101]

No approval is required under this section on the part of the members of a body corporate that is not a UK-registered company;[2102] or that is a wholly-owned subsidiary of another body corporate.[2103]

A payment made in pursuance of an arrangement:

(a)   entered into as part of the agreement for the transfer in question, or within one year before or two years after that agreement;[2104] and

(b)   to which the company whose undertaking or property is transferred, or any person to whom the transfer is made, is privy,[2105]

is presumed, except in so far as the contrary is shown, to be a payment to which this section applies.

Payment in connection with share transfer: requirement of members' approval

10.53 Section 219 of the CA 2006 deals with payment in connection with share transfer and the requirement of members' approval. No payment for loss of office may be made by any person to a director of a company in connection with a transfer of shares in the company, or in a subsidiary of the company, resulting from a takeover bid unless the payment has been approved by a resolution of the relevant shareholders.[2106]

[2098] CA 2006, s 218(2).   [2099] CA 2006, s 218(3)(a).   [2100] CA 2006, s 218(3)(b)(i).
[2101] CA 2006, s 218(3)(b)(ii).   [2102] CA 2006, s 218((4)(a).   [2103] CA 2006, s 218(4)(b).
[2104] CA 2006, s 218(5)(a).   [2105] CA 2006, s 218(5)(b).   [2106] CA 2006, s 219(1).

The relevant shareholders are the holders of the shares to which the bid relates, and any holders of shares of the same class as any of those shares.[2107]

A resolution approving a payment to which this section applies must not be passed, unless a memorandum setting out particulars of the proposed payment (including its amount) is made available to the members of the company whose approval is sought:

(a)   in the case of a written resolution, by being sent or submitted to every eligible member at or before the time at which the proposed resolution is sent or submitted to him;[2108]

(b)   in the case of a resolution at a meeting, by being made available for inspection by the members both (i) at the company's registered office for not less than 15 days ending with the date of the meeting,[2109] and at the meeting itself.[2110]

Neither the person making the offer, nor any associate of his (as defined in s 988 of the CA 2006), is entitled to vote on the resolution, but:

(a)   where the resolution is proposed as a written resolution, they are entitled (if they would otherwise be so entitled) to be sent a copy of it;[2111] and

(b)   at any meeting to consider the resolution they are entitled (if they would otherwise be so entitled) to be given notice of the meeting, to attend and speak and if present (in person or by proxy) to count towards the quorum.[2112]

If at a meeting to consider the resolution a quorum is not present, and after the meeting has been adjourned to a later date a quorum is again not present, the payment is (for the purposes of this section) deemed to have been approved.[2113]

No approval is required under this section on the part of shareholders in a body corporate that is not a UK-registered company,[2114] or is a wholly-owned subsidiary of another body corporate.[2115]

A payment made in pursuance of an arrangement entered into as part of the agreement for the transfer in question, or between one year before or two years after that agreement;[2116] and to which the company whose shares are the subject of the bid, or any person to whom the transfer is made, is privy,[2117] is presumed, except in so far as the contrary is shown, to be a payment to which this section applies.

[2107] CA 2006, s 219(2).   [2108] CA 2006, s 219(3)(a).   [2109] CA 2006, s 219(3)(b)(i).
[2110] CA 2006, s 219(3)(b)(ii).   [2111] CA 2006, s 219(4)(a).   [2112] CA 2006, s 219(4)(b).
[2113] CA 2006, s 219(5).   [2114] CA 2006, s 219(6)(a).   [2115] CA 2006, s 219(6)(b).
[2116] CA 2006, s 219(7)(a).   [2117] CA 2006, s 219(7)(b).

Exception for payments in discharge of legal obligations, etc.

10.54 Section 220 of the CA 2006 deals with the exceptions for payments in discharge of legal obligations. Approval is not required under ss 217, 218 or 219 of the CA 2006 (payments requiring members' approval) for a payment made in good faith in the following circumstances:

(a)   in discharge of an existing legal obligation (as defined below);[2118]
(b)   by way of damages for breach of such an obligation;[2119]
(c)   by way of settlement or compromise of any claim arising in connection with the termination of a person's office or employment;[2120] or
(d)   by way of pension in respect of past services.[2121]

In relation to a payment within s 217 of the CA (payment by company) an existing legal obligation means an obligation of the company, or any body corporate associated with it, that was not entered into in connection with, or in consequence of, the event giving rise to the payment for loss of office.[2122]

In relation to a payment within s 218 or 219 of the CA 2006 (payment in connection with transfer of undertaking, property or shares) an existing legal obligation means an obligation of the person making the payment that was not entered into for the purposes of, in connection with, or in consequence of, the transfer in question.[2123]

In the case of a payment within both s 217 and s 218 of the CA 2006, or within both s 217 of the CA 2006 and s 219 of the CA 2006, s 220(2) of the CA 2006 above applies and not s 220(3) of the CA 2006.[2124]

A payment, part of which falls within s 220(1) of the CA 2006 above and part of which does not, is treated as if the parts were separate payments.[2125]

Exception for small payments

10.55 Section 221 of the CA 2006 deals with the exception for small payments. Approval is not required under ss 217, 218 or 219 of the CA 2006 (payments requiring members' approval) if the payment in question is made by the company or any of its subsidiaries;[2126] and the amount or value of the payment, together with the amount or value of any other relevant payments, does not exceed £200.[2127]

For this purpose 'other relevant payments' are payments for loss of office in relation to which the following conditions are met.[2128]

[2118] CA 2006, s 220(1)(a).   [2119] CA 2006, s 220(1)(b).   [2120] CA 2006, s 220(1)(c).
[2121] CA 200, s 220(1)(d).   [2122] CA 2006, s 220(2).   [2123] CA 2006, s 220(3).
[2124] CA 2006, s 220(4).   [2125] CA 2006, s 220(5).   [2126] CA 2006, s 221(1)(a).
[2127] CA 2006, s 221(1)(b).   [2128] CA 2006, s 221(2).

Where the payment in question is one to which s 217 of the CA 2006 (payment by company) applies, the conditions are that the other payment was or is paid:

(a) by the company making the payment in question or any of its subsidiaries;[2129]

(b) to the director to whom that payment is made;[2130] and

(c) in connection with the same event.[2131]

Where the payment in question is one to which s 218 or s 219 of the CA 2006 applies (payment in connection with transfer of undertaking, property or shares), the conditions are that the other payment was (or is) paid in connection with the same transfer to the director to whom the payment in question was made;[2132] and by the company making the payment or any of its subsidiaries.[2133]

Payments made without approval: civil consequences

10.56 Section 222 of the CA 2006 deals with the civil consequences for payments made without approval. If a payment is made in contravention of s 217 of the CA 2006 (payment by company) it is held by the recipient on trust for the company making the payment;[2134] and any director who authorised the payment is jointly and severally liable to indemnify the company that made the payment for any loss resulting from it.[2135]

If a payment is made in contravention of s 218 of the CA 2006 (payment in connection with transfer of undertaking, etc.), it is held by the recipient on trust for the company whose undertaking or property is or is proposed to be transferred.[2136]

If a payment is made in contravention of s 219 of the CA 2006 (payment in connection with share transfer) it is held by the recipient on trust for persons who have sold their shares as a result of the offer made;[2137] and the expenses incurred by the recipient in distributing that sum amongst those persons shall be borne by him and not retained out of that sum.[2138]

If a payment is in contravention of ss 217 and 218 of the CA 2006, s 222(2) of the CA 2006 of this section applies rather than s 222(1) of the CA 2006.[2139]

If a payment is in contravention of ss 217 and 219 of the CA 2006, s 222(3) of the CA 2006 of this section applies rather than s 222(1) of the CA 2006, unless the court directs otherwise.[2140]

[2129] CA 2006, s 221(3)(a).   [2130] CA 2006, s 221(3)(b).   [2131] CA 2006, s 221(3)(c).

[2132] CA 2006, s 221(4)(a).   [2133] CA 2006, s 221(4)(b).   [2134] CA 2006, s 222(1)(a).

[2135] CA 2006, s 222(1)(b).   [2136] CA 2006, s 222(2).   [2137] CA 2006, s 222(3)(a).

[2138] CA 2006, s 222(3)(b).   [2139] CA 2006, s 222(4).   [2140] CA 2006, s 222(5).

Supplementary

*Transactions requiring members' approval: application of provisions to
shadow directors*

10.57 Section 223 of the CA 2006 applies to shadow directors. For the
purposes of:

(a)   ss 188 and 189 of the CA 2006 (directors' service contracts);
(b)   ss 190 to 196 of the CA 2006 (property transactions);
(c)   ss 197 to 214 of the CA 2006 (loans etc); and
(d)   ss 215 to 222 of the CA 2006 (payments for loss of office),

a shadow director is treated as a director.[2141]

Any reference in those provisions to loss of office as a director does not
apply in relation to loss of a person's status as a shadow director.[2142]

*Approval by written resolution: accidental failure to send
memorandum*

10.58 Section 224 of the CA 2006 is concerned with approval by written
resolution in respect of accidental failure to send a memorandum. Where
approval under this Chapter is sought by written resolution;[2143] and a memorandum is required under this Chapter to be sent or submitted to every
eligible member before the resolution is passed,[2144] any accidental failure
to send or submit the memorandum to one or more members shall be
disregarded for the purpose of determining whether the requirement has
been met.

Section 224(1) of the CA 2006 applies subject to any provision of the
company's articles.[2145]

Cases where approval is required under more than one provision

10.59 Section 225 of the CA 2006 recognises that there may be circumstances
where approval is required under more than one provision. Approval may be
required under more than one provision of this Chapter.[2146]

If so, the requirements of each applicable provision must be met.[2147] This
does not require a separate resolution for the purposes of each provision.[2148]

[2141] CA 2006, s 223(1).   [2142] CA 2006, s 223(2).   [2143] CA 2006, s 224(1)(a).
[2144] CA 2006, s 224(1)(b).   [2145] CA 2006, s 224(2).   [2146] CA 2006, s 225(1).
[2147] CA 2006, s 225(2).   [2148] CA 2006, s 225(3).

Requirement of consent of Charity Commission: companies that are charities

10.60 Section 226 of the CA 2006 applies in respect of companies that are charities. For s 66 of the Charities Act 1993 (c 10) the following is substituted:

> 66. Consent of Commission required for approval, etc. by members of charitable companies
>
> Where a company is a charity:
>
> (a)   any approval given by the members of the company under any provision of Chapter 4 of Part 10 of the CA 2006 (transactions with directors requiring approval by members) listed in subsection (2) below, and
>
> (b)   any affirmation given by members of the company under ss 196 or 214 of that Act (affirmation of unapproved property transactions and loans),
>
> is ineffective without the prior written consent of the Commission.
> The provisions are:
>
> (a)   s 188 (directors' long-term service contracts);
> (b)   s 190 (substantial property transactions with directors, etc.);
> (c)   ss 197, 198 or 200 (loans and quasi loans to directors, etc.);
> (d)   s 201 (credit transactions for benefit of directors, etc.);
> (e)   s 203 (related arrangements);
> (f)   s 217 (payments to directors for loss of office);
> (g)   s 218 (payments to directors for loss of office: transfer of undertaking, etc.).
>
> Consent of Commission required for certain acts of charitable company
>
> A company that is a charity may not perform an act to which this section applies without the prior written consent of the Commission.
> This section applies to an act that:
>
> (a)   does not require approval under a listed provision of Chapter 4 of Part 10 of the CA 2006 (transactions with directors) by the members of the company, but
>
> (b)   would require such approval but for an exemption in the provision in question that disapplies the need for approval on the part of the members of a body corporate that is a wholly-owned subsidiary of another body corporate.
>
> The reference to a listed provision is a reference to a provision listed in s 66(2) above.
>   If a company acts in contravention of this section, the exemption referred to in subsection (2)(b) shall be treated as of no effect in relation to the act.

Directors' Service Contracts

Directors' service contracts

10.61 Section 227 of the CA 2006 applies to directors' service contracts. For the purposes of Part 10, Chapter 5 of the CA 2006, a director's 'service contract', in relation to a company, means a contract under which a director of the company undertakes personally to perform services (as director or otherwise) for the company, or for a subsidiary of the company;[2149] or services (as director or otherwise) that a director of the company undertakes personally to perform are made available by a third party to the company, or to a subsidiary of the company.[2150]

The provisions of Part 10 of the CA 2006 relating to directors' service contracts apply to the terms of a person's appointment as a director of a company. They are not restricted to contracts for the performance of services outside the scope of the ordinary duties of a director.[2151]

Section 227 of the CA 2006 is a new provision. It defines what is meant in Chapter 5 by references to a director's service contract. The term is used in ss 177, 182, 188 and 190 of the CA 2006 and in Chapter 5. It includes contracts of employment with the company, or with a subsidiary of the company. It also includes contracts for services and letters of appointment to the office of director. The contract may relate to services as a director or to any other services that a director undertakes personally to perform for the company or a subsidiary.

Copy of contract or memorandum of terms to be available for inspection

10.62 Section 228 of the CA 2006 deals with a copy of the contract or memorandum of terms of service contract being available for inspection. A company must keep available for inspection a copy of every director's service contract with the company or with a subsidiary of the company;[2152] or if the contract is not in writing, a written memorandum setting out the terms of the contract.[2153]

All the copies and memoranda must be kept available for inspection at the company's registered office;[2154] or a place specified in regulations under s 1136 of the CA 2006.[2155]

The copies and memoranda must be retained by the company for at least one year from the date of termination or expiry of the contract, and must be kept available for inspection during that time.[2156]

[2149] CA 2006, s 227(1)(a).   [2150] CA 2006, s 227(1)(b).   [2151] CA 2006, s 227(2).
[2152] CA 2006, s 228(1)(a).   [2153] CA 2006, s 228(1)(b).   [2154] CA 2006, s 228(2)(a).
[2155] CA 2006, s 228(2)(b).   [2156] CA 2006, s 228(3).

The company must give notice to the registrar of the place at which the copies and memoranda are kept available for inspection;[2157] and of any change in that place;[2158] unless they have at all times been kept at the company's registered office.

If default is made in complying with s 228(1), (2) or (3) of the CA 2006, or default is made for 14 days in complying with s 228(4) of the CA 2006, an offence is committed by every officer of the company who is in default.[2159] A person guilty of an offence under this section is liable on summary conviction to a fine not exceeding level 3 on the standard scale and, for continued contravention, a daily default fine not exceeding one-tenth of level 3 on the standard scale.[2160]

The provisions of this section apply to a variation of a director's service contract as they apply to the original contract.[2161]

Section 228 of the CA 2006 requires a company to keep available for inspection copies of every director's service contract entered into by the company or by a subsidiary of the company. If the contract is not in writing, the company must keep available for inspection a written memorandum of its terms. This section together with ss 229 and 230 of the CA 2006, replaces s 318 of the CA 1985.

Section 228(3) of the CA 2006 is a new provision. It requires service contracts to be retained and kept available for inspection by the company for at least one year after they have expired, but the subsection does not require the copies to be retained thereafter. As a result of the expanded definition of service contract in s 227 of the CA 2006, this section now applies to contracts for services and letters of appointment, as recommended by the Law Commissions.

As recommended by Law Commissions, the exemptions for contracts requiring a director to work outside the UK (s 318(5) of the CA 1985) and the exemptions for contracts with less than 12 months to run, (s 318(11) of the CA 1985) have not been retained.

Failure to comply with requirement of s 228 of the CA 2006 is a criminal offence, for which every officer of the company who is in default maybe held liable on summary conviction to a fine not exceeding level 3 on the standard scale (currently £1,000), or in case of continued contravention as a daily default fine not exceeding one-tenth of that. In a change from the previous position under s 318 of the CA 1985, the company will no longer be liable for the criminal offence.

[2157] CA 2006, s 228(4)(a).   [2158] CA 2006, s 228(4)(b).   [2159] CA 2006, s 228(5).
[2160] CA 2006, s 228(6).   [2161] CA 2006, s 228(7).

Right of members to inspect and request copy

10.63 The right of every member to inspect and request a copy of the service contract or memorandum is set out in s 229 of the CA 2006. Every copy or memorandum required to be kept under s 228 of the CA 2006 must be open to inspection by any member of the company without charge.[2162]

Any member of the company is entitled, on request and on payment of such fee as may be prescribed, to be provided with a copy of any such copy or memorandum. The copy must be provided within seven days of the request being received by the company.[2163]

If an inspection required under s 229(1) of the CA 2006 is refused, or default is made in complying with s 229(2) of the CA 2006, an offence is committed by every officer of the company who is in default.[2164] A person guilty of an offence under s 229 of the CA 2006 is liable on summary conviction to a fine not exceeding level 3 on the standard scale and, for continued contravention, a daily default fine not exceeding one-tenth of level 3 on the standard scale.[2165]

In the case of any such refusal or default the court may by order compel an immediate inspection or, as the case may be, direct that the copy required be sent to the person requiring it.[2166]

This section gives members a right to inspect without charge the copies of service contracts held by the company in accordance with s 228 of the CA 2006. Section 209(2) of the CA 2006 creates a new rights for members to request a copy of the service contracts on payment of a fee set by regulations under s 1137 of the CA 2006.

Section 229 of the CA 2006 gives members a right to inspect without charge the copies of service contracts held by the company in accordance with s 228 of the CA 2006. Section 229(2) of the CA 2006 creates a new right for members to request a copy of the service contracts on payment of a fee set by regulations under s 1137 of the CA 2006.

*Directors' service contracts: application of provisions to
shadow directors*

10.64 Section 230 of the CA 2006 states that a shadow director is treated as a director for the purposes of the provisions of this Chapter.

[2162] CA 2006, s 229(1).   [2163] CA 2006, s 229(2).   [2164] CA 2006, s 229(3).
[2165] CA 2006, s 229(4).   [2166] CA 2006, s 229(5).

Contract with Sole Members Who are Directors

Contract with sole member who is also a director

10.65 Section 231 of the CA 2006 applies to contracts with sole members who are directors. It applies where:

(a)   a limited company having only one member enters into a contract with the sole member;[2167]

(b)   the sole member is also a director of the company;[2168] and

(c)   the contract is not entered into in the ordinary course of the company's business.[2169]

The company must, unless the contract is in writing, ensure that the terms of the contract are either set out in a written memorandum;[2170] or recorded in the minutes of the first meeting of the directors of the company following the making of the contract.[2171]

If a company fails to comply with s 231 of the CA 2006 an offence is committed by every officer of the company who is in default.[2172] A person guilty of an offence under this section is liable on summary conviction to a fine not exceeding level 5 on the standard scale.[2173]

For the purposes of s 231 of the CA 2006, a shadow director is treated as a director.[2174]

Failure to comply with this section in relation to a contract does not affect the validity of the contract.[2175]

Nothing in s 231 of the CA 2006 is to be read as excluding the operation of any other enactment or rule of law applying to contracts between a company and a director of the company.[2176]

Under s 231 of the CA 2006, contracts entered into by limited company with its only member must be recorded in writing if the sole member is also a director or shadow director of the company. This does not apply to contracts entered into the ordinary course of the company's business. The purpose of this section is to ensure that records are kept in those cases where there is a high risk of the lines becoming blurred between where a person acts in his personal capacity and when he acts on behalf of the company. This may be of particular interest to a liquidator should the company become insolvent.

Section 231 of the CA 2006 replaces s 322B CA 1985, which implements article 5 of the 12th Company Law Directive 89/667/EEC. As the CA 2006 will permit public companies to have a single shareholder, this section applies to both private and public limited companies.

[2167] CA 2006, s 231(1)(a).   [2168] CA 2006, s 231(1)(b).   [2169] CA 2006, s 231(1)(c).
[2170] CA 2006, s 231(2)(a).   [2171] CA 2006, s 231(2)(b).   [2172] CA 2006, s 231(3).
[2173] CA 2006, s 231(4).   [2174] CA 2006, s 231(5).   [2175] CA 2006, s 231(6).
[2176] CA 2006, s 231(7).

A failure to record the contract in writing will not affect the validity of the contract (s 231(6) of the CA 2006) but other legislation or rules of law might do so (s 231(7) of the CA 2006).

If there is a breach of s 231 of the CA 2006, every officer of the company in default is liable on summary conviction to a fine not exceeding level 5 on the standard scale (currently £5,000). In a change from the current position under s 322B CA 1985, the company will no longer be liable under the criminal offence.

Directors' Liabilities

10.66 The sections in Chapter 7 of Part 10 of the CA 2006 (ss 232–239 of the CA 2006) deal with two matters: first, they restate ss 309A–309C of the CA 1985 (provisions relating to directors' liability). The only substantive changes to those sections are a new provision permitting companies to indemnify the directors of companies acting as trustees of occupational pension schemes (s 235 of the CA 2006), the creation of a right for members to request a copy of a qualifying third party indemnity provision (s 238(2) of the CA 2006), the removal of criminal liability on the part of the company for failures to comply with the requirements of s 237 of the CA 2006 (copy of qualifying indemnity provision to be available for inspection), provision for regulations to specify places in addition to the registered office where inspection may take place (s 237(3) of the CA 2006) and a requirement for all qualifying indemnity provisions to be retained by a company for at least one year after they have expired (s 237(4) of the CA 2006); and second, they introduce a substantive reform of the law on the ratification of acts giving rise to liability on the part of a director (s 239 of the CA 2006).

Provision protecting directors from liability

Provisions protecting directors from liability

10.67 Section 232 of the CA 2006 states that any provision that purports to exempt a director of a company (to any extent) from any liability that would otherwise attach to him in connection with any negligence, default, breach of duty or breach of trust in relation to the company, is void.[2177]

Any provision by which a company directly or indirectly provides an indemnity (to any extent) for a director of the company, or of an associated company, against any liability attaching to him in connection with any negligence, default, breach of duty or breach of trust in relation to the company of which he is a director is void, except as permitted by:

[2177] CA 2006, s 232(1).

(a)   s 233 of the CA 2006 (provision of insurance);[2178]
(b)   s 234 of the CA 2006 (qualifying third party indemnity provision);[2179] or
(c)   s 235 of the CA 2006 (qualifying pension scheme indemnity provision).[2180]

Section 232 of the CA 2006 applies to any provision, whether contained in a company's articles or in any contract with the company or otherwise.[2181]

Nothing in s 232 of the CA 2006 prevents a company's articles from making such provision as has previously been lawful for dealing with conflicts of interest.[2182]

Section 232 of the CA 2006 prohibits a company from exempting a director from, or indemnifying him against, any liability in connection with any negligence, default, breach of duty or breach of trust by him in relation to the company. Section 232(2) of the CA 2006 prohibits indemnification by an associated company as well as by his own company. 'Associated company' is defined in s 256 of the CA 2006 as, in effect, a company in the same group.

Any provision, whether in the company's articles, in a contract or otherwise, attempting to exempt or indemnify a director in breach of this section is void. But this does not apply to lawful provisions in the articles for dealing with conflicts of interest.

Provision of insurance

10.68 Section 233 of the CA 2006 states that (voidness of provisions for indemnifying directors) does not prevent a company from purchasing and maintaining for a director of the company, or of an associated company, insurance against any such liability as is mentioned in that subsection, as mentioned in that section.

Section 233 of the CA 2006 permits a company to purchase and maintain insurance for its directors, or the directors of an associated company, against any liability attaching to them in connection with any negligence, breach of duty or breach of trust by them in relation to the company of which they are a director.

Qualifying third party indemnity provision

10.69 Section 234 of the CA 2006 states that s 232(2) of the CA 2006 (voidness of provisions for indemnifying directors) does not apply to qualifying third party indemnity provisions.[2183]

Third party indemnity provision means provision for indemnity against

[2178] CA 2006, s 232(2)(a).   [2179] CA 2006, s 232(2)(b).   [2180] CA 2006, s 232(2)(c).
[2181] CA 2006, s 232(3).   [2182] CA 2006, s 232(4).   [2183] CA 2006, s 234(1).

liability incurred by the director to a person other than the company or an associated company.[2184]

Such provision is qualifying third party indemnity provision if the following requirements are met. The provision must not provide any indemnity against:

(a) any liability of the director to pay: (i) a fine imposed in criminal proceedings;[2185] or (ii) a sum payable to a regulatory authority by way of a penalty in respect of non-compliance with any requirement of a regulatory nature (however arising);[2186] or

(b) any liability incurred by the director: (i) in defending criminal proceedings in which he is convicted;[2187] or (ii) in defending civil proceedings brought by the company, or an associated company, in which judgment is given against him;[2188] or (iii) in connection with an application for relief (see s 234(6)CA 2006) in which the court refuses to grant him relief.[2189]

The references in s 234(3)(b) of the CA 2006 to a conviction, judgment or refusal of relief are to the final decision in the proceedings.[2190]

For this purpose:

(a) a conviction, judgment or refusal of relief becomes final: (i) if not appealed against, at the end of the period for bringing an appeal;[2191] or (ii) if appealed against, at the time when the appeal (or any further appeal) is disposed of;[2192] and

(b) an appeal is disposed of: (i) if it is determined and the period for bringing any further appeal has ended;[2193] or (ii) if it is abandoned or otherwise ceases to have effect.[2194]

The reference in s 234(3)(b)(iii) of the CA 2006 to an application for relief is to an application for relief under: s 661(3) or (4) of the CA 2006 (power of court to grant relief in case of acquisition of shares by an innocent nominee); or s 1157 of the CA 2006 (general power of court to grant relief in case of honest and reasonable conduct).[2195]

This section permits (but does not require) companies to indemnify directors in respect of proceedings brought by third parties (such as class actions in the US). It also permits (but does not require) companies to indemnify directors in respect of applications for relief from liability made under s 1157

[2184] CA 2006, s 234(2).   [2185] CA 2006, s 234(3)(a)(i).   [2186] CA 2006, s 234(3)(a)(ii).
[2187] CA 2006, s 234(3)(b)(i).   [2188] CA 2006, s 234(3)(b)(ii).
[2189] CA 2006, s 234(3)(b)(iii).   [2190] CA 2006, s 234(4).   [2191] CA 2006, s 234(5)(a)(i).
[2192] CA 2006, s 234(5)(a)(ii).   [2193] CA 2006, s 234(5)(b)(i).   [2194] CA 2006, s 234(5)(b)(ii).
[2195] CA 2006, s 234(6).

of the CA 2006 (general power of the court to grant relief in case of an honest and reasonable conduct) or under s 661(3) or (4) of the CA 2006 (power of court to grant relief in case of acquisition of shares by innocent nominee).

The indemnity may cover liability incurred by the director to any person other than the company or an associated company. This may include both the legal and financial costs of an adverse judgment. But the indemnity must not cover liabilities to the company or to any associated company (s 234(2) of the CA 2006).

Another condition is that the indemnity must not cover criminal fines, penalties imposed by regulatory bodies (such as Financial Services Authority), the defence costs of criminal proceedings where the director is found guilty, the defence costs of civil proceedings successfully brought against the director by the company or an associated company and the costs of successful applications by the director for relief (s 234(2) of the CA 2006).

Section 234(4) and (5) of the CA 2006 explain when legal proceedings will be considered to have concluded for the purpose of the conditions imposed by s 234(3) of the CA 2006.

An indemnity that complies with these conditions is described as a qualifying third party indemnity provision.

Qualifying pension scheme indemnity provisions

10.70 Section 235 of the CA 2006 states that s 232(2) of the CA 2006 (voidness of provisions for indemnifying directors) does not apply to qualifying pension scheme indemnity provision.[2196]

Pension scheme indemnity provision means provision indemnifying a director of a company that is a trustee of an occupational pension scheme, against liability incurred in connection with the company's activities as trustee of the scheme.[2197]

Such provision is qualifying pension scheme indemnity provision if the following requirements are met. The provision must not provide any indemnity against:

(a) any liability of the director to pay (i) a fine imposed in criminal proceedings,[2198] or (ii) a sum payable to a regulatory authority by way of a penalty in respect of non-compliance with any requirement of a regulatory nature (however arising);[2199] or
(b) any liability incurred by the director in defending criminal proceedings in which he is convicted.[2200]

[2196] CA 2006, s 235(1).   [2197] CA 2006, s 235(2).   [2198] CA 2006, s 235(3)(a)(i).
[2199] CA 2006, s 235(3)(a)(ii).   [2200] CA 2006, s 235(3)(b).

The reference in s 235(3)(b) of the CA 2006 to a conviction is to the final decision in the proceedings.[2201]

For this purpose:

(a)   a conviction becomes final (i) if not appealed against, at the end of the period for bringing an appeal,[2202] or (ii) if appealed against, at the time when the appeal (or any further appeal) is disposed of;[2203] and

(b)   an appeal is disposed of (i) if it is determined and the period for bringing any further appeal has ended;[2204] or (ii) if it is abandoned or otherwise ceases to have effect.[2205]

The term 'occupational pension scheme' means an occupational pension scheme as defined in s 150(5) of the Finance Act 2004 (c 12) that is established under a trust.[2206]

Section 235 of the CA 2006 permits (but does not require) companies to indemnify a director of a company acting a trustee of an occupational pension scheme against liability incurred in connection with the companies activities as trustee of the scheme. An indemnity that complies with the conditions set out in this section is described as a qualifying pension scheme indemnity provision.

Qualifying indemnity provision to be disclosed in directors' report

10.71 Section 236 of the CA 2006 requires disclosure in the directors' report of:

(a)   qualifying third party indemnity provision;[2207] and

(b)   qualifying pension scheme indemnity provision.[2208]

Such provision is referred to in this section as 'qualifying indemnity provision'.

If when a directors' report is approved any qualifying indemnity provision (whether made by the company or otherwise) is in force for the benefit of one or more directors of the company, the report must state that such provision is in force.[2209]

If at any time during the financial year to which a directors' report relates any such provision were in force for the benefit of one or more persons who were then directors of the company, the report must state that such provision was in force.[2210]

[2201] CA 2006, s 235(4).   [2202] CA 2006, s 235(5)(a)(i).   [2203] CA 2006, s 235(5)(a)(ii).
[2204] CA 2006, s 235(b)(i).   [2205] CA 2006, s 235(b)(ii).   [2206] CA 2006, s 235(6).
[2207] CA 2006, s 236(1)(a).   [2208] CA 2006, s 236(1)(b).   [2209] CA 2006, s 236(2).
[2210] CA 2006, s 236(3).

If when a directors' report is approved qualifying indemnity provision made by the company is in force for the benefit of one or more directors of an associated company, the report must state that such provision is in force.[2211]

If at any time during the financial year to which a directors' report relates any such provision was in force for the benefit of one or more persons who were then directors of an associated company, the report must state that such provision was in force.[2212]

If a qualifying indemnity provision is in force for the benefit of one or more directors or was in the previous year, this must be disclosed by the company in the director's report (as to the director's report, see Chapter 5 of Part 15 of the CA 2006). Where the director is of one company but the qualifying indemnity provision is provided by an associated company, then it must be disclosed in the director's report of both companies. Companies that choose not to indemnify directors will not have to make any disclosure.

Copy of qualifying indemnity provision to be available for inspection

10.72 Section 237 of the CA 2006 applies where qualifying indemnity provision is made for a director of a company, and applies to the company of which he is a director (whether the provision is made by that company or an associated company);[2213] and where the provision is made by an associated company, to that company.[2214]

That company or, as the case may be, each of them, must keep available for inspection a copy of the qualifying indemnity provision;[2215] or if the provision is not in writing, a written memorandum setting out its terms.[2216]

The copy or memorandum must be kept available for inspection at the company's registered office;[2217] or a place specified in regulations under s 1136 of the CA 2006.[2218]

The copy or memorandum must be retained by the company for at least one year from the date of termination or expiry of the provision and must be kept available for inspection during that time.[2219]

The company must give notice to the registrar of the place where the copy or memorandum is kept available for inspection;[2220] and of any change in that place,[2221] unless it has at all times been kept at the company's registered office.

If default is made in complying with s 237(2), (3) or (4) of the CA 2006, or default is made for 14 days in complying with s 237(5) of the CA 2006, an offence is committed by every officer of the company who is in default.[2222] A person guilty of an offence under s 237 of the CA 2006 is liable on summary conviction to a fine not exceeding level 3 on the standard scale and, for

[2211] CA 2006, s 236(4).   [2212] CA 2006, s 236(5).   [2213] CA 2006, s 237(1)(a).
[2214] CA 2006, s 237(1)(b).   [2215] CA 2006, s 237(2)(a).   [2216] CA 2006, s 237(2)(b).
[2217] CA 2006, s 237(3)(a).   [2218] CA 2006, s 237(3)(b).   [2219] CA 2006, s 237(4).
[2220] CA 2006, s 237(5)(a).   [2221] CA 2006, s 237(5)(b).   [2222] CA 2006, s 237(6).

continued contravention, a daily default fine not exceeding one-tenth of level 3 on the standard scale.[2223]

The provisions of s 237 of the CA 2006 apply to a variation of a qualifying indemnity provision as they apply to the original provision.[2224] The term 'qualifying indemnity provision' means qualifying third party indemnity provision;[2225] and qualifying pension scheme indemnity provision.[2226]

Section 237 of the CA 2006 requires a company to keep available for inspection copies of all the qualifying indemnity provisions it has made for its own directors, and also copies of all those it has made for directors of associated companies.

Section 237(4) of the CA 2006 is a new provision. It requires all indemnity provisions to be retained and made available for inspection for a further one-year period after they have expired or terminated. But the company is not required by this section to retain copies of the indemnity provision thereafter.

Section 237(6) of the CA 2006 makes a failure to comply with the requirements of this section a criminal offence. The maximum penalty that can be imposed on summary conviction is a fine not exceeding level 3 on the standard scale (currently £1,000), or in cases of continued contravention, a daily default fine not exceeding one-tenth of that. In a change from the previous position under s 309C CA 1985, the company will no longer be liable for the criminal offence.

Right of members to inspect and request copy

10.73 Section 238 of the CA 2006 states that every copy or memorandum required to be kept by a company under s 237 of the CA 2006 must be open to inspection by any member of the company without charge.[2227]

Any member of the company is entitled, on request and on payment of such fee as may be prescribed, to be provided with a copy of any such copy or memorandum. The copy must be provided within seven days after the request is received by the company.[2228]

If an inspection required under s 238(1) of the CA 2006 is refused, or default is made in complying with s 238(2) of the CA 2006, an offence is committed by every officer of the company who is in default.[2229] A person guilty of an offence under s 238 of the CA 2006 is liable on summary conviction to a fine not exceeding level 3 on the standard scale and, for continued contravention, a daily default fine not exceeding one-tenth of level 3 on the standard scale.[2230]

[2223] CA 2006, s 237(7).   [2224] CA 2006, s 237(8).   [2225] CA 2006, s 237(9)(a).
[2226] CA 2006, s 237(9)(b).   [2227] CA 2006, s 238(1).   [2228] CA 2006, s 238(2).
[2229] CA 2006, s 238(3).   [2230] CA 2006, s 238(4).

In the case of any such refusal or default the court may by order compel an immediate inspection or, as the case may be, direct that the copy required be sent to the person requiring it.[2231]

Section 238 of the CA 2006 gives members a right to inspect without charge the copies of the qualifying indemnity provisions (or where they are not in writing, the written memorandum of their terms) held by the company in accordance with s 237 of the CA 2006.

This section also creates a new right for members on payment of a fee to request a copy of the copy or memorandum held by the company. The fee will be set by regulations made under s 1137 of the CA 2006.

Ratification of acts giving rise to liability

Ratification of acts of directors

10.74 Section 239 of the CA 2006 applies to the ratification by a company of conduct by a director amounting to negligence, default, breach of duty or breach of trust in relation to the company.[2232]

The decision of the company to ratify such conduct must be made by resolution of the members of the company.[2233]

Where the resolution is proposed as a written resolution, neither the director (if a member of the company) nor any member connected with him is an eligible member.[2234]

Where the resolution is proposed at a meeting, it is passed only if the necessary majority is obtained disregarding votes in favour of the resolution by the director (if a member of the company) and any member connected with him.

This does not prevent the director or any such member from attending, being counted towards the quorum and taking part in the proceedings at any meeting at which the decision is considered.[2235]

For the purposes of s 239 of the CA 2006, the term 'conduct' includes acts and omissions;[2236] 'director' includes a former director;[2237] a shadow director is treated as a director;[2238] and in s 252 of the CA 2006 (meaning of 'connected person'), s 252(3) of the CA 2006 does not apply (exclusion of person who is himself a director).[2239]

Nothing in s 239 of the CA 2006 affects the validity of a decision taken by the unanimous consent of the members of the company;[2240] or any power of the directors to agree not to sue, or to settle or release a claim made by them on behalf of the company.[2241]

[2231] CA 2006, s 238(5).   [2232] CA 2006, s 239(1).   [2233] CA 2006, s 239(2).
[2234] CA 2006, s 239(3).   [2235] CA 2006, s 239(4).   [2236] CA 2006, s 239(5)(a).
[2237] CA 2006, s 239(5)(b).   [2238] CA 2006, s 239(5)(c).   [2239] CA 2006, s 239(5)(d).
[2240] CA 2006, s 239(6)(a).   [2241] CA 2006, s 239(6)(b).

This section does not affect any other enactment or rule of law imposing additional requirements for valid ratification, or any rule of law as to acts that are incapable of being ratified by the company.[2242]

Section 239 of the CA 2006 preserves the law previously under the CA 1985 on ratification of acts of directors, but with one significant change. Any decision by a company ratifying conduct by a director amounting to negligence, default, breach of duty or breach of trust in relation to the company, must be taken by the members, and without reliance on votes in favour by the director or any connected person. Section 252 of the CA 2006 defines what is meant by a person being connected with a director. For the purposes of this section it may also include fellow directors (s 239(5)(d) of the CA 2006).

If the ratification decision is taken by way of a written resolution (see Chapter 2 of Part 13 of the CA 2006) the director and his connected persons may not take part in the written resolution procedure (s 239(3) of the CA 2006). This means that the company does not need to send them a copy of the written resolution, and they are not counted when determining the number of votes required for the written resolution to be passed.

If the ratification decision is taken at a meeting, those people whose votes are to be disregarded may still attend the meeting, take part in the meeting and count towards the quorum for the meeting (if their membership gives them the right to do so).

Section 239(6) of the CA 2006 makes clear that nothing in this section changes the law on unanimous consent, so the restrictions imposed by this section as to who may vote will not apply when every member votes (informally or otherwise) in favour of the resolution. It also makes clear that nothing in this section removes any powers of the directors that they may have to manage the affairs of the company.

Section 239(7) of the CA 2006 explains that the requirements imposed by this section are in addition to any other limitations or restrictions imposed by the law as to what may or may not be ratified and when.

Supplementary Provisions

10.75 Chapter 9 to Part 10 of the CA 2006 sets out the supplementary provisions in respect of company directors.

Power to make provision for employees on cessation of transfer business

10.76 Section 247 of the CA 2006 provides that the powers of the directors of a company include (if they would not otherwise do so) power to make

---

[2242] CA 2006, s 239(7).

provision for the benefit of persons employed or formerly employed by the company, or any of its subsidiaries, in connection with the cessation or the transfer to any person of the whole or part of the undertaking of the company or that subsidiary.[2243]

This power given to the directors is exercisable notwithstanding the general duty imposed by s 172 of the CA 2006 (duty to promote the success of the company).[2244]

Where a company is a charity, the power conferred on directors to make provision for employees on cessation or transfer of business is exercisable notwithstanding any restrictions on the directors' powers (or the company's capacity) flowing from the objects of the company.[2245]

The power may only be exercised if sanctioned by a resolution of the company;[2246] or by a resolution of the directors,[2247] in accordance with the provisions below.

A resolution of the directors must be authorised by the company's articles;[2248] and is not sufficient sanction for payments to or for the benefit of directors, former directors or shadow directors.[2249] Any other requirements of the company's articles as to the exercise of the power conferred by this section must be complied with.[2250]

Section 247 of the CA 2006 confers on the power of directors to make provisions for the benefit of employees (including former employees) of the company or its subsidiaries on the cessation or transfer of the whole or part of the undertaking of the company or the subsidiary: s 247(1) of the CA 2006.

The directors may exercise this power, even if it will not promote the success of the company. The directors' general duty under s 172 of the CA 2006 act in the way they consider would be most likely to promote the success of the company for the benefit of its members as a whole, does not apply when the directors exercise this power to make provision for employees: s 247(2) of the CA 2006.

There are a number of conditions to the exercise of this power. It must be authorised by a resolution of the members or, if the articles of the company allow it, by the board of directors. The company's articles may also impose further conditions on its use: s 247(6) of the CA 2006.

Any payments made by the directors using the power conferred by this section must be made before the commencement of the winding up of the company and can only be made out of profits available for dividend. Section 187 of the Insolvency Act 1986 confers power to make provision for employees once the company has commenced winding up.

[2243] CA 2006, s 247(1).   [2244] CA 2006, s 247(2).   [2245] CA 2006, s 247(3).
[2246] CA 2006, s 247(4)(a).   [2247] CA 2006, s 247(4)(b).   [2248] CA 2006, s 247(5)(a).
[2249] CA 2006, s 247(5)(b).   [2250] CA 2006, s 247(6).

Section 247 of the CA 2006 replaces s 719 of the CA 1985. In a change from that section, the directors can no longer use the power conferred by this section to make payments to themselves or to former directors or to shadow directors, unless the payments are authorised by the members. The Company Law Review Group recommended that directors should be prevented from abusing the power by making excessive payments to themselves.

Records of meetings of directors

Minutes of directors meetings

10.77 Section 248 of the CA 2006 requires every company to cause minutes of all proceedings at meetings of its directors to be recorded.[2251] The records must be kept for at least ten years from the date of the meeting.[2252]

If a company fails to comply with s 248 of the CA 2006, an offence is committed by every officer of the company who is in default.[2253] A person guilty of an offence under this section will be liable on summary conviction to a fine not exceeding level 3 on the standard scale and, for continued contravention, a daily default fine not exceeding one-tenth of level 3 on the standard scale.[2254]

This section together with section 249 of the CA 2006, replaces the provisions of s 382 of the CA 1985 relating to records of meetings of directors. The requirement of s 382 of the CA 1985 relating to records of meetings of managers has not been retained. This clause required a company to record minutes of all meetings of its directors.

Section 248(2) of the CA 2006 is new. The minutes must be kept for at least ten years. Failure to make and keep minutes as required by s 249 of the CA 2006 is a criminal offence, applying to every officer of the company who is in default. In a change from s 382 of the CA 1985, liability for the offence will no longer fall on the company.

Part 37 of the CA 2006 makes provision as to the form in which company records (including minutes) may be kept and imposes a duty to take precautions against falsification.

Minutes as evidence

10.78 Section 249(1) of the CA 2006 provides that minutes recorded in accordance with s 248 of the CA 2006, if purporting to be authenticated by the chairman of the meeting or by the chairman of the next directors' meeting, are evidence (in Scotland, sufficient evidence) of the proceedings at the meeting.[2255]

[2251] CA 2006, s 248(1).   [2252] CA 2006, s 248(2).   [2253] CA 2006, s 248(3).
[2254] CA 2006, s 248(4).   [2255] CA 2006, s 249(1).

Where minutes have been made in accordance with that section of the proceedings of a meeting of directors, then, until the contrary is proved, the meeting is deemed duly held; and convened;[2256] and all proceedings at the meeting are deemed to have duly taken place;[2257] and all appointments at the meeting are deemed valid.[2258]

Section 249 of the CA 2006 makes provision in respect of the evidential value of the minutes of directors' meetings.

Meaning of 'director' and 'shadow director'

Director

10.79 Section 250 of the CA 2006 provides a definition of a 'director'. It states that in the Companies Acts, the term 'director' includes any person occupying the position of director, by whatever name called.

It restates s 741(1) of the CA 1985.

Shadow director

10.80 Section 251 of the CA 2006 provides a definition of a 'shadow director'. In the Companies Acts, the term 'shadow director', in relation to a company, means a person in accordance with whose directions or instructions the directors of the company are accustomed to act.[2259]

A person is not to be regarded as a shadow director by reason only that the directors act on advice given by him in a professional capacity.[2260]

A body corporate is not to be regarded as a shadow director of any of its subsidiary companies for the purposes of Chapter 2 (general duties of directors); or Chapter 4 (transactions requiring members' approval); or Chapter 6 (contract with sole member who is also a director), by reason only that the directors of the subsidiary are accustomed to act in accordance with its directions or instructions.[2261]

It restates s 741(2) of the CA 1985.

Other definitions

10.81 Sections 252–259 of the CA 2006 set out other definitions applicable under Part 10 of the CA 2006.

Persons connected with a director

10.82 Section 252 of the CA 2006 defines what is meant by references to a

[2256] CA 2006, s 249(2)(a).   [2257] CA 2006, s 249(2)(b).   [2258] CA 2006, s 249(2)(c).
[2259] CA 2006, s 251(1).   [2260] CA 2006, s 251(2).   [2261] CA 2006, s 251(3).

person being 'connected' with a director of a company (or a director being 'connected' with a person).[2262]

The following persons (and only those persons) are connected with a director of a company:

(a)   members of the director's family (see s 253 of the CA 2006);[2263]
(b)   a body corporate with which the director is connected (as defined in s 254 of the CA 2006);[2264]
(c)   a person acting in his capacity as trustee of a trust:

   (i)   the beneficiaries of which include the director or a person who by virtue of para (a) or (b) is connected with him,[2265] or
   (ii)   the terms of which confer a power on the trustees that may be exercised for the benefit of the director or any such person, other than a trust for the purposes of an employees' share scheme or a pension scheme;[2266]

(d)   a person acting in his capacity as partner:

   (i)   of the director,[2267] or
   (ii)   of a person who, by virtue of para (a), (b) or (c), is connected with that director;[2268]

(e)   a firm that is a legal person under the law by which it is governed and in which:

   (i)   the director is a partner;[2269] or
   (ii)   a partner is a person who, by virtue of para (a), (b) or (c) is connected with the director;[2270] or
   (iii) a partner is a firm in which the director is a partner or in which there is a partner who, by virtue of para (a), (b) or (c), is connected with the director.[2271]

References in the CA 2006 to a person connected with a director of a company do not include a person who is himself a director of the company.[2272]

This section sets out the definition of 'connected persons' that is used in many sections in Part 10 of the CA 2006 in relation to the regulation of directors.

This section, together with ss 236–238 of the CA 2006, replaces s 346 of the CA 1985.

[2262] CA 2006, s 252(1).   [2263] CA 2006, s 252(2)(a).   [2264] CA 2006, s 252(2)(b).
[2265] CA 2006, s 252(2)(c)(i).   [2266] CA 2006, s 252(2)(c)(ii).   [2267] CA 2006, s 252(2)(d)(i).
[2268] CA 2006, s 252(2)(d)(ii).   [2269] CA 2006, s 252(2)(e)(i).   [2270] CA 2006, s 252(2)(e)(ii).
[2271] CA 2006, s 252(2)(e)(iii).   [2272] CA 2006, s 252(3).

Members of a director's family

10.83 Section 253 of the CA 2006 defines what is meant by references to members of a director's family.[2273] The members of a director's family are:

(a)   the director's spouse or civil partner;[2274]
(b)   any other person (whether of a different sex or the same sex) with whom the director lives as partner in an enduring family relationship;[2275]
(c)   the director's children or step-children;[2276]
(d)   any children or step-children of a person within para (b) (and who are not children or step-children of the director) who live with the director and have not attained the age of 18;[2277]
(e)   the director's parents.[2278]

Section 253(2)(b) of the CA 2006 does not apply if the other person is the director's grandparent or grandchild, sister, brother, aunt or uncle, or nephew or niece.[2279]

Section 253 of the CA 2006 sets out those members of a director's family who fall within the definition of persons connected with the director. The list includes all those family members previously falling within the definition of connected person in s 346 of the CA 1985, and in addition it covers:

- the directors parents;
- children or step-children of the directors who are over 18 years old (those under 18 were already included under s 346 of the CA 1985);
- persons with whom the director lives as partner in an enduring family relationship; and
- children or step-children of the director's unmarried partner if they live with the director and are under 18 years of age.

This implements the Law Commission's recommendation that the definition of connected person be extended so as to include cohabitants, infant children of the cohabitant if they live with the director, adult children of the director and the director's parents. The recommendation that the definition be extended to siblings has not been implemented.

Director 'connected with' a body corporate

10.84 Section 254 of the CA 2006 defines what is meant by references to a director being 'connected with' a body corporate.[2280]

[2273] CA 2006, s 253(1).   [2274] CA 2006, s 253(2)(a).   [2275] CA 2006, s 253(2)(b).
[2276] CA 2006, s 253(2)(c).   [2277] CA 2006, s 253(2)(d).   [2278] CA 2006, s 253(2)(e).
[2279] CA 2006, s 253(3).   [2280] CA 2006, s 254(1).

A director is connected with a body corporate if, but only if, he and the persons connected with him together are interested in shares comprised in the equity share capital of that body corporate of a nominal value equal to at least 20 per cent of that share capital;[2281] or are entitled to exercise or control the exercise of more than 20 per cent of the voting power at any general meeting of that body.[2282]

Section 254 of the CA 2006 must be read together with Schedule 1 of the CA 2006. The rules set out in Schedule 1 (references to interest in shares or debentures) apply for the purposes of this section.[2283]

References in s 254 of the CA 2006 to voting power the exercise of which is controlled by a director include voting power whose exercise is controlled by a body corporate controlled by him.[2284]

Shares in a company held as treasury shares, and any voting rights attached to such shares, are disregarded for the purposes of s 254 of the CA 2006.[2285]

For the avoidance of circularity in the application of s 252 of the CA 2006 (meaning of 'connected person'):

(a)   a body corporate with which a director is connected is not treated for the purposes of this section as connected with him unless it is also connected with him by virtue of subs (2)(c) or (d) of that section (connection as trustee or partner);[2286] and

(b)   a trustee of a trust the beneficiaries of which include (or may include) a body corporate with which a director is connected is not treated for the purposes of this section as connected with a director by reason only of that fact.[2287]

Section 254 of the CA 2006 determines whether a company or other body corporate is a person connected with a director. Broadly speaking, the director, together with any other person connected with him, must be interested in 20 per cent of the equity share capital, or control (directly or indirectly through another body corporate controlled by them) more than 20 per cent of the voting power exercisable at any general meeting.

Schedule 1 contains the rules for determining whether a person is 'interested in shares' for this purpose.

Director 'controlling' a body corporate

10.85 Section 255 of the CA 2006 defines what is meant by references to a director 'controlling' a body corporate.[2288]

[2281] CA 2006, s 254(2)(a).   [2282] CA 2006, s 254(2)(b).   [2283] CA 2006, s 254(3).
[2284] CA 2006, s 254(4).   [2285] CA 2006, s 254(5).   [2286] CA 2006, s 254(6)(a).
[2287] CA 2006, s 254(6)(b).   [2288] CA 2006, s 255(1).

A director of a company is taken to control a body corporate if, but only if:

(a)   he or any person connected with him:

   (i)   is interested in any part of the equity share capital of that body;[2289] or

   (ii)   is entitled to exercise or control the exercise of any part of the voting power at any general meeting of that body,[2290] and

(b)   he, the persons connected with him and the other directors of that company, together:

   (i)   are interested in more than 50 per cent of that share capital;[2291] or

   (ii)   ˙ are entitled to exercise or control the exercise of more than 50 per cent of that voting power.[2292]

Section 255 of the CA 2006 must be read together with Schedule 1 of the CA 2006. The rules set out in Schedule 1 (references to interest in shares or debentures) apply for the purposes of s 238 of the CA 2006.[2293]

References in s 255 of the CA 2006 to voting power the exercise of which is controlled by a director include voting power whose exercise is controlled by a body corporate controlled by him.[2294]

Shares in a company held as treasury shares, and any voting rights attached to such shares, are disregarded for the purposes of s 255 of the CA 2006.[2295]

For the avoidance of circularity in the application of s 252 of the CA 2006 (meaning of 'connected person'):

(a)   a body corporate with which a director is connected is not treated for the purposes of this section as connected with him unless it is also connected with him by virtue of subs (2)(c) or (d) of that section (connection as trustee or partner);[2296] and

(b)   a trustee of a trust the beneficiaries of which include (or may include) a body corporate with which a director is connected is not treated for the purposes of this section as connected with a director by reason only of that fact.[2297]

Section 255 of the CA 2006 defines the circumstances in which a director is deemed to control a body for the purposes of s 254 of the CA 2006. These circumstances involve two cumulative hurdles. First, the director or any other person connected with him must be interested in the equity share capital or be entitled to control some part of the voting power exercisable at any general

---

[2289] CA 2006, s 255(2)(a)(i).   [2290] CA 2006, s 255(2)(a)(ii).   [2291] CA 2006, s 255(2)(b)(i).
[2292] CA 2006, s 255(2)(b)(ii).   [2293] CA 2006, s 255(3).   [2294] CA 2006, s 255(4).
[2295] CA 2006, s 255(5).   [2296] CA 2006, s 255(6)(a).   [2297] CA 2006, s 255(6)(b).

meeting. Secondly, the director, fellow directors and other persons connected with him must be interested in more than 50 per cent of the equity share capital or be entitled to control more than 50 per cent of the voting power exercisable at any general meeting.

Schedule 1 of the CA 2006 contains the rules for determining whether a person is 'interested in shares' for this purpose.

Associated bodies corporate

10.86 Section 256 of the CA 2006 states that bodies corporate are associated if one is a subsidiary of the other or both are subsidiaries of the same body corporate.[2298] Further, any references to an 'associated company' have a corresponding meaning.[2299]

This section explains what it means by references in this Part to associated bodies corporate. A holding company is associated with all its subsidiaries and a subsidiary is associated with its holding company and all the other subsidiaries of its holding company.

References to a company's constitution

10.87 Section 257 of the CA 2006 states that references to a company's constitution include any resolution or other decision reached in accordance with the constitution;[2300] and any decision by the members of the company, or a class of members, that is treated by virtue of any enactment or rule of law as equivalent to a decision by the company.[2301]

This is in addition to the matters mentioned in s 17 of the CA 2006 (general provisions as to matters contained in company's constitution).[2302]

Section 257 of the CA 2006 is a new provision. It makes provision as to the meaning of references to a company's constitution in Part 10 of the CA 2006.

The section is relevant to a number of provisions in Part 10 of the CA 2006, including the duty to act within powers (s 173 of the CA 2006) and the duty to exercise independent judgment (s 159 of the CA 2006).

General

10.88 Section 258–259 of the CA 2006 deals with general provisions of Part 10 of the CA 2006.

[2298] CA 2006, s 256(a).   [2299] CA 2006, s 256(b).   [2300] CA 2006, s 257(1)(a).
[2301] CA 2006, s 257(1)(b).   [2302] CA 2006, s 257(2).

Power to increase financial limits

10.89 Section 258 of the CA 2006 provides that the Secretary of State may by order substitute for any sum of money specified in Part 10 of the CA 2006 a larger sum specified in the order.[2303]

An order under s 258 of the CA 2006 is subject to negative resolution procedure.[2304]

An order does not have effect in relation to anything done or not done before it comes into force. Accordingly, proceedings in respect of any liability incurred before that time may be continued or instituted as if the order had not been made.[2305]

Section 258 of the CA 2006 gives power to the Secretary of State by order to increase financial limits in Part 10 of the CA 2006. All the financial limits appear in Chapter 4 (provisions regulating transactions with directors requiring approval of members). This section restates s 345 of the CA 1985.

Transactions under foreign law

10.90 Section 259 of the CA 2006 provides that it is immaterial whether the law that (apart from the CA 2006) governs an arrangement or transaction is the law of the United Kingdom, or a part of it, or not.

This section makes clear that the rules under Part 10 of the CA 2006 apply whether or not the proper law governing a transaction or arrangement is the law of a part of the UK.

This provision is necessary to prevent parties seeking to avoid the application of the rules as to approval of long-term service contracts, substantial property transactions and loans and similar transactions by choosing a foreign law. This section restates s 347 of the CA 1985.

[2303] CA 2006, s 258(1).   [2304] CA 2006, s 258(2).   [2305] CA 2006, s 258(3).

Chapter 11

Directors: Foreign Disqualification

Introduction

11.1 Part 40 of the CA 2006 governs the foreign disqualification of company directors. It addresses a gap in the law as it stood prior to 2006. Persons who have been disqualified from being a director, or from holding an equivalent position, or engaging in the management of a company in another State, are currently able to form a company in the United Kingdom, to appoint themselves a director of that company and then operate the company either in the United Kingdom or in the State where they have been disqualified. The provisions of Part 40 of the CA 2006 give the Secretary of State power to close the gap by making regulations to disqualify from being a director of a United Kingdom company, persons who have been disqualified in another State.

Part 40 is the first Part that is outside the company law provisions of the CA 2006. It does not, therefore, form part of the Companies Acts and is outside this regime. This is owing to the fact that the provisions of Part 40 are linked with those of the Company Directors' Disqualification Act 1986. The 1986 Act is not part of the Companies Acts because it has implications that extend beyond companies to other bodies (such as NHS Foundation trusts), and it also extends beyond persons covered by the Companies Acts to persons such as insolvency practitioners. The fact that Part 40 is not part of the Companies Acts has the consequence that the definitions in the earlier Parts of the CA 2006 do not apply – hence the need to define the term 'the court' in s 1183 of the CA 2006. Similarly, the definitions for Part 40 are not listed in Schedule 8 of the CA 2006.

Introductory

11.2 The introductory part comprises ss 1182 and 1183 of the CA 2006.

Persons subject to foreign restrictions

11.3 Section 1182 of the CA 2006 defines what is meant by references in Part 40 of the CA 2006 to a 'person being subject to foreign restrictions'.[2306]

A person is subject to foreign restrictions if under the law of a country or territory outside the United Kingdom he is, by reason of misconduct or unfitness, disqualified to any extent from acting in connection with the affairs of a company;[2307] or he is, by reason of misconduct or unfitness, required to obtain permission from a court or other authority,[2308] or to meet any other condition,[2309] before acting in connection with the affairs of a company, or he has, by reason of misconduct or unfitness, given undertakings to a court or other authority of a country or territory outside the United Kingdom not to act in connection with the affairs of a company,[2310] or restricting the extent to which, or the way in which, he may do so.[2311]

The references in s 1182(2) of the CA 2006 to 'acting in connection with the affairs of a company' are to doing any of the following: being a director of a company;[2312] or acting as receiver of a company's property;[2313] or being concerned or taking part in the promotion, formation or management of a company.[2314]

The term 'company' means a company incorporated or formed under the law of the country or territory in question;[2315] and in relation to such a company, 'director' means the holder of an office corresponding to that of director of a UK company; and 'receiver' includes any corresponding officer under the law of that country or territory.[2316]

Section 1182 of the CA 2006, therefore, has as the objective of defining what is meant by 'a person being subject to foreign restrictions'. Only persons falling in this category may be disqualified by regulations made under Part 40 of the CA 2006. This category is intended to include those who have been disqualified under (or otherwise fallen foul of) a foreign law equivalent to that in the Company Directors' Disqualification Act 1986.

Meaning of 'the court' and 'UK company'

11.4 Section 1183 of the CA 2006 sets out the meaning of the 'court' and 'UK company'. In Part 40 of the CA 2006, the term 'the court' means, in England and Wales, the High Court or a county court;[2317] in Scotland, the Court of Session or the sheriff court;[2318] in Northern Ireland, the High Court.[2319]

The term 'UK company' means a company registered under the CA 2006.

[2306] CA 2006, s 1182(a).   [2307] CA 2006, s 1182(a).   [2308] CA 2006, s 1182(b)(i).
[2309] CA 2006, s 1182(b)(ii).   [2310] CA 2006, s 1182(c)(i).   [2311] CA 2006, s 1182(c)(ii).
[2312] CA 2006, s 1182(3)(a).   [2313] CA 2006, s 1182(3)(b).   [2314] CA 2006, s 1182(3)(c).
[2315] CA 2006, s 1182(4)(a).   [2316] CA 2006, s 1182(4)(b).   [2317] CA 2006, s 1183(a).
[2318] CA 2006, s 1183(b).   [2319] CA 2006, s 1183(c).

Power to disqualify

11.5 Sections 1184–1186 of the CA 2006 are concerned with the power to disqualify.

Disqualification of persons subject to foreign restrictions

11.6 Section 1184 of the CA 2006 sets out the disqualification of persons subject to foreign restrictions. The Secretary of State may make provision by regulations disqualifying a person subject to foreign restrictions from being a director of a UK company;[2320] or acting as receiver of a UK company's property;[2321] or in any way, whether directly or indirectly, being concerned or taking part in the promotion, formation or management of a UK company.[2322]

The regulations may provide that a person subject to foreign restrictions is disqualified automatically by virtue of the regulations;[2323] or may be disqualified by order of the court on the application of the Secretary of State.[2324]

The regulations may provide that the Secretary of State may accept an undertaking (a 'disqualification undertaking') from a person subject to foreign restrictions that he will not do anything that would be in breach of a disqualification under s 1184(1) of the CA 2006.[2325]

The term a 'person disqualified under this Part' is a person disqualified as mentioned in s 1184(2)(a) or (b) of the CA 2006;[2326] or who has given and is subject to a disqualification undertaking;[2327] and references to a breach of a disqualification include a breach of a disqualification undertaking.[2328]

The regulations may provide for applications to the court by persons disqualified under this Part for permission to act in a way that would otherwise be in breach of the disqualification.[2329]

The regulations must provide that a person ceases to be disqualified under this Part on his ceasing to be subject to foreign restrictions.[2330]

Regulations under s 1184 of the CA 2006 are subject to an affirmative resolution procedure.[2331]

Section 1184 of the CA 2006 provides the power for the Secretary of State to make regulations disqualifying a person, subject to foreign restrictions, from being a director of a UK company, acting as a receiver of a UK company's property, or, in any way, taking part in the promotion, formation or management of a UK company.

[2320] CA 2006, s 1184(1)(a).   [2321] CA 2006, s 1184(1)(b).   [2322] CA 2006, s 1184(1)(c).
[2323] CA 2006, s 1184(2)(a).   [2324] CA 2006, s 1184(2)(b).   [2325] CA 2006, s 1184(3).
[2326] CA 2006, s 1184(4)(a)(i).   [2327] CA 2006, s 1184(a)(ii).   [2328] CA 2006, s 1184(b).
[2329] CA 2006, s 1184(5).   [2330] CA 2006, s 1184(6).   [2331] CA 2006, s 1184(7).

504 A Guide to the Companies Act 2006

Disqualification regulations: supplementary

11.7 Section 1185 of the CA 2006 sets out the supplementary aspects of disqualification regulations. Regulations under s 1184 of the CA 2006 may make different provision for different cases, and may in particular, distinguish between cases by reference to the conduct, on the basis of which the person became subject to foreign restrictions;[2332] the nature of the foreign restrictions;[2333] and the country or territory under whose law the foreign restrictions were imposed.[2334]

Regulations under s 1184(2)(b) or (5) of the CA 2006 (provision for applications to the court) must specify the grounds on which an application may be made;[2335] and may specify factors to which the court shall have regard in determining an application.[2336]

The regulations may, in particular, require the court to have regard to the following factors:

(a) whether the conduct on the basis of which the person became subject to foreign restrictions would, in relation to a UK company, have led a court to make a disqualification order on an application under the Company Directors' Disqualification Act 1986 (c 46) or the Company Directors' Disqualification (Northern Ireland) Order 2002 (SI 2002/3150 (NI 4));[2337]

(b) in a case in which the conduct on the basis of which the person became subject to foreign restrictions would not be unlawful in relation to a UK company, the fact that the person acted unlawfully under foreign law;[2338]

(c) whether the person's activities in relation to UK companies began after he became subject to foreign restrictions;[2339]

(d) whether the person's activities (or proposed activities) in relation to UK companies are undertaken (or are proposed to be undertaken) outside the United Kingdom.[2340]

Regulations under s 1184(3) of the CA 2006 (provision as to undertakings given to the Secretary of State) may include provisions allowing the Secretary of State, in determining whether to accept an undertaking, to take into account matters other than criminal convictions, notwithstanding that the person may be criminally liable in respect of those matters.[2341]

Regulations under s 1184(5) of the CA 2006 (provision for application to court for permission to act) may include provisions entitling the Secretary of State to be represented at the hearing of the application,[2342] and as to the

---

[2332] CA 2006, s 1185(1)(a).   [2333] CA 2006, s 1185(1)(b).   [2334] CA 2006, s 1185(1)(c).
[2335] CA 2006, s 1185(2)(a).   [2336] CA 2006, s 1185(2)(b).   [2337] CA 2006, s 1185(3)(a).
[2338] CA 2006, s 1185(3)(b).   [2339] CA 2006, s 1185(3)(c).   [2340] CA 2006, s 1185(3)(d).
[2341] CA 2006, s 1185(4).   [2342] CA 2006, s 1185(5)(a).

giving of evidence or the calling of witnesses by the Secretary of State at the hearing of the application.[2343]

Section 1185 of the CA 2006 states that the regulations under s 1184 of the CA 2006 may make different provision for different types of cases, and sets out examples. If the regulations provide for application to the court (either by the Secretary of State for a disqualification order under s 1184(2)(b) of the CA 2006, or by a disqualified person seeking relief under s 1184(5) of the CA 2006), the section requires the regulations to specify the grounds on which an application to the court may be made. It also allows the regulations to set out matters to which the court should have regard when considering the application.

Offence of breach of disqualification

11.8 Section 1186 of the CA 2006 sets out the offences of breach of disqualification. Regulations under s 1184 of the CA 2006 may provide that a person disqualified under this Part who acts in breach of the disqualification commits an offence.[2344]

The regulations may provide that a person guilty of such an offence is liable on conviction on indictment, to imprisonment for a term not exceeding two years or a fine (or both);[2345] on summary conviction in England and Wales, to imprisonment for a term not exceeding 12 months or to a fine not exceeding the statutory maximum (or both);[2346] in Scotland or Northern Ireland, to imprisonment for a term not exceeding six months, or to a fine not exceeding the statutory maximum (or both).[2347]

In relation to an offence committed before the commencement of s 154(1) Criminal Justice Act 2003 (c 44), for '12 months' in subs (2)(b)(i) substitute 'six months'.[2348]

This section provides that regulations made under s 1184 of the CA 2006, may provide that a person disqualified under this Part, who acts in breach of the disqualification, commits an offence.

Power to make persons liable for company's debts

Personal liability for debts of a company

11.9 Section 1187 of the CA 2006 deals with personal liability for debts of a company. The Secretary of State may provide by regulations that a person who, at a time when he is subject to foreign restrictions is a director of a UK

[2343] CA 2006, s 1185(5)(b).   [2344] CA 2006, s 1186(1).
[2345] CA 2006, s 1186(2)(a).   [2346] CA 2006, s 1186(2)(b)(i).
[2347] CA 2006, s 1186(2)(b)(ii).   [2348] CA 2006, s 1186(3).

company;[2349] or is involved in the management of a UK company,[2350] is personally responsible for all debts and other liabilities of the company incurred during that time.

A person who is personally responsible by virtue of s 1187 of the CA 2006 for debts and other liabilities of a company, is jointly and severally liable in respect of those debts and liabilities with the company;[2351] and any other person with such debts and liabilities (whether by virtue of this section or otherwise) is so liable.[2352]

For the purposes of s 1187 of the CA 2006, a person is involved in the management of a company if he is concerned, whether directly or indirectly, or takes part, in the management of the company.[2353]

The regulations may make different provision for different cases, and may in particular distinguish between cases by reference to the conduct on the basis of which the person became subject to foreign restrictions;[2354] the nature of the foreign restrictions;[2355] and the country or territory under whose law the foreign restrictions were imposed.[2356]

Regulations under s 1187 of the CA 2006 are subject to an affirmative resolution procedure.[2357]

Section 1187 of the CA 2006 provides for the Secretary of State to make regulations to the effect that a person disqualified under Part 40 of the CA 2006 who acts as a director of a UK company, or is involved in the management of a UK company, is personally responsible for all debts and liabilities of the company incurred during the time that he or she is subject to foreign restrictions.

Power to require statements to be sent to the registrar of companies

Statements from persons subject to foreign restrictions

11.10 Section 1188 of the CA 2006 states that the Secretary of State may make provision by regulations requiring a person who is subject to foreign restrictions;[2358] and is not disqualified under this Part,[2359] to send a statement to the registrar if he does anything that, if done by a person disqualified under this Part, would be in breach of the disqualification.

The statement must include such information as may be specified in the regulations relating to the person's activities in relation to UK companies;[2360] and the foreign restrictions to which the person is subject.[2361]

[2349] CA 2006, s 1187(1)(a).　　[2350] CA 2006, s 1187(1)(b).　　[2351] CA 2006, s 1187(2)(a).
[2352] CA 2006, s 1187(2)(b).　　[2353] CA 2006, s 1187(3).　　[2354] CA 2006, s 1187(4)(a).
[2355] CA 2006, s 1187(4)(b).　　[2356] CA 2006, s 1187(4)(c).　　[2357] CA 2006, s 1187(5).
[2358] CA 2006, s 1188(1)(a).　　[2359] CA 2006, s 1188(1)(b).　　[2360] CA 2006, s 1188(2)(a).
[2361] CA 2006, s 1188(2)(b).

The statement must be sent to the registrar within such period as may be specified in the regulations.[2362]

The regulations may make different provision for different cases, and may in particular distinguish between cases by reference to the conduct on the basis of which the person became subject to foreign restrictions;[2363] the nature of the foreign restrictions;[2364] and the country or territory under whose law the foreign restrictions were imposed.[2365]

Regulations under s 1188 of the CA 2006 are subject to an affirmative resolution procedure.[2366]

Statements from persons disqualified

11.11 Section 1189 of the CA 2006 states that the Secretary of State may make provision by regulations, requiring a statement or notice sent to the registrar of companies, under any of the provisions listed below that relate (wholly or partly) to a person who is a person disqualified under this Part;[2367] or is subject to a disqualification order or disqualification undertaking under the Company Directors' Disqualification Act 1986 (c 46) or the Company Directors Disqualification (Northern Ireland) Order 2002 (SI 2002/3150 (NI 4)),[2368] to be accompanied by an additional statement.

The provisions referred to above are s 12 of the CA 2006 (statement of a company's proposed officers);[2369] s 167(2) of the CA 2006 (notice of person having become director);[2370] and s 276 of the CA 2006 (notice of a person having become secretary or one of joint secretaries).[2371]

The additional statement is a statement that the person has obtained permission from a court, on an application under s 1184(5) of the CA 2006 or (as the case may be) for the purposes of s 1(1)(a) Company Directors Disqualification Act 1986 (c 46) or Article 3(1) of the Company Directors Disqualification (Northern Ireland) Order 2002 (SI 2002/3150 (NI 4)), to act in the capacity in question.[2372]

Regulations under this section are subject to affirmative resolution procedure.[2373]

Section 1189 of the CA 2006 provides the power for the Secretary of State to make provisions by regulation, that would require a disqualified director to provide an additional statement, explaining where he or she has received approval from the court to act in a capacity that would otherwise be a breach of the disqualification.

[2362] CA 2006, s 1188(3).

[2363] CA 2006, s 1188(4)(a).

[2364] CA 2006, s 1188(4)(b).

[2365] CA 2006, s 1188(4)(c).

[2366] CA 2006, s 1188(5).

[2367] CA 2006, s 1189(1)(a).

[2368] CA 2006, s 1189(1)(b).

[2369] CA 2006, s 1189(2)(a).

[2370] CA 2006, s 1189(2)(b).

[2371] CA 2006, s 1189(2)(c).

[2372] CA 2006, s 1189(3).

[2373] CA 2006, s 1189(4).

Statements: whether to be made public

11.12 Section 1190 of the CA 2006 states that regulations under s 1188 or s 1189 of the CA 2006 (statements required to be sent to registrar) may provide that a statement sent to the registrar of companies under the regulations is to be treated as a record relating to a company for the purposes of s 1080 of the CA 2006 (the companies register).[2374]

The regulations may make provision as to the circumstances in which such a statement is to be, or may be, withheld from public inspection;[2375] or removed from the register.[2376]

The regulations may, in particular, provide that a statement is not to be withheld from public inspection or removed from the register unless the person to whom it relates provides such information, and satisfies such other conditions as may be specified.[2377]

The regulations may provide that s 1081 of the CA 2006 (notice of removal of material from the register) does not apply, or applies with such modifications as may be specified, in the case of material removed from the register under the regulations.[2378]

The term 'specified' means specified in the regulations.[2379]

Section 1190 of the CA 2006 provides for regulations under ss 1188 and 1189 of the CA 2006 to state whether statements made under those regulations must be on the public register, and the circumstances in which they may be withheld from public inspection or removed from the register.

Offences

11.13 Section 1191 of the CA 2006 sets out the offences to be specified in the regulations. Regulations under s 1188 or s 1189 of the CA 2006 may provide that it is an offence for a person to fail to comply with a requirement under the regulations to send a statement to the registrar;[2380] or knowingly or recklessly to send a statement under the regulations to the registrar that is misleading, false or deceptive in a material particular.[2381]

The regulations may provide that a person guilty of such an offence is liable on conviction on indictment, to imprisonment for a term not exceeding two years or a fine (or both);[2382] on summary conviction in England and Wales, to imprisonment for a term not exceeding 12 months or to a fine not exceeding the statutory maximum (or both);[2383] in Scotland or Northern Ireland, to imprisonment for a term not exceeding six months, or to a fine not exceeding the statutory maximum (or both).[2384]

[2374] CA 2006, s 1190(1).   [2375] CA 2006, s 1190(2)(a).   [2376] CA 2006, s 1190(2)(b).
[2377] CA 2006, s 1190(3).   [2378] CA 2006, s 1190(4).   [2379] CA 2006, s 1190(5).
[2380] CA 2006, s 1191(1)(a).   [2381] CA 2006, s 1191(1)(b).   [2382] CA 2006, s 1191(2)(a).
[2383] CA 2006, s 1191(2)(b)(i).   [2384] CA 2006, s 1191(2)(b)(ii).

In relation to an offence committed before the commencement of s 154(1) Criminal Justice Act 2003 (c 44), for '12 months' in subs (2)(b)(i) substitute 'six months'.[2385]

Section 1,191 of the CA 2006 provides for regulations to apply criminal sanctions for a failure to comply with any requirements on statements under ss 1188 and 1189 of the CA 2006.

[2385] CA 2006, s 1191(3).

Chapter 12

Company Secretaries

Introduction

The position before CA 2006

12.1 Previously, the role of the company secretary was relegated to purely administrative matters. In *Barnett, Hoares & Co v South London Tramway Co*,[2386] Lord Esher MR stated that a secretary was a mere servant. His position was that he was to do what he was told, and that no person could assume that he had any authority to represent anything at all. However, over the years, company secretaries began to occupy an important position in the corporate governance structure. In *Panorama Developments (Guildford) Ltd v Fidelis Furnishing Fabrics Ltd*,[2387] Lord Denning stated that a company secretary was now considered to be an important person within the company. He was an officer of the company with extensive duties and responsibilities, especially with regard to the role played by the secretary in the day-to-day business of companies. The secretary was no longer a mere clerk. A secretary regularly made representations on behalf of the company and entered into contracts on its behalf, which came within the day-to-day running of the company's business. He was also regarded as having authority to do such things on behalf of the company. He was entitled to sign contracts connected with the administrative side of the company's affairs. All such matters were within the ostensible authority of the company secretary. The Combined Code of best practice also emphasised the important role played by a company secretary in a public company.[2388]

[2386] (1887) 18 QB D 815.

[2387] [1971] 2 QB 711.

[2388] See Combined Code, para A.5.3, which provides that all directors should have access to the advice and services of the company secretary, who is responsible to the board for ensuring that board procedures are complied with. Both the appointment and removal of the company secretary should be a matter for the board as a whole.

The position after CA 2006

12.2 The CA 2006 sets out a statutory basis for the company secretary. Part 12 of the CA 2006 is concerned with company secretaries and distinguishes between private and public secretaries in companies, including some common provisions applicable to both types of secretaries. This Part contains 11 sections. Under the CA 2006, the status of a company secretary in a private company has virtually diminished.

General

Private company not required to have a secretary

12.3 Section 270(1) of the CA 2006 states that a private company is not required to have a secretary. The references in the Companies Acts to a private company 'without a secretary' are to a private company that for the time being is taking advantage of the exemption in s 270(1) of the CA 2006. Further, references to a private company 'with a secretary' are to be construed accordingly.[2389]

In the case of a private company without a secretary, anything authorised or required to be given or sent to, or served on, the company by being sent to its secretary may be given or sent to, or served on, the company itself;[2390] and if addressed to the secretary will be treated as addressed to the company;[2391] and anything else required or authorised to be done by or to the secretary of the company may be done by or to a director;[2392] or a person authorised generally or specifically in that behalf by the directors.[2393]

Section 270 of the CA 2006 implements the Company Law Review Group's recommendation[2394] that the requirement for a private company to have a secretary be abolished. The section defines a private company 'without a secretary' for the purposes of the Companies Acts as a company which has taken advantage of the exemption provided by s 270(1) of the CA 2006, as opposed to one that normally has a secretary but for some reason (such as the death of the office holder) is without a secretary at a given time. Section 270(3) of the CA 2006 makes provision for private companies without a secretary.

Public company required to have a secretary

12.4 Section 271 of the CA 2006 states that a public company must have a secretary.

This section replaces s 283(1) of the CA 1985 insofar as it applies to public

---

[2389] CA 2006, s 270(2).   [2390] CA 2006, s 270(3)(a)(i).   [2391] CA 2006, s 270(3)(a)(ii).
[2392] CA 2006, s 270(3)(b)(i).   [2393] CA 2006, s 270(3)(b)(ii).   [2394] *Final Report*, para 4.7.

companies. It retains the requirement that a public company must have a secretary. The secretary may also be one of the directors.

Direction requiring public company to appoint secretary

12.5 Section 272(1) of the CA 2006 states that if it appears to the Secretary of State that a public company is in breach of s 271 of the CA 2006 (requirement to have a secretary), the Secretary of State may give the company a direction under this section.

The direction must state that the company appears to be in breach of that section, and specify what the company must do in order to comply with the direction;[2395] and the period within which it must do so.[2396] That period must be not less than one month or more than three months after the date on which the direction is given.

The direction must also inform the company of the consequences of failing to comply.[2397]

Where the company is in breach of s 271 of the CA 2006, it must comply with the direction by making the necessary appointment;[2398] and giving notice of it under s 276 of the CA 2006,[2399] before the end of the period specified in the direction.

If the company has already made the necessary appointment, it must comply with the direction by giving notice of it under s 276 of the CA 2006 before the end of the period specified in the direction.[2400]

If a company fails to comply with a direction under this section, an offence is committed by the company;[2401] and every officer of the company who is in default.[2402] For this purpose, a shadow director is treated as an officer of the company.[2403] A person guilty of an offence under this section is liable on summary conviction to a fine not exceeding level 5 on the standard scale and, for continued contravention, a daily default fine not exceeding one-tenth of level 5 on the standard scale.[2404]

Section 272 of the CA 2006 is a new provision, enabling enforcement of the continuing requirement for a public company to have a secretary. It does not apply to private companies. Where it appears that a public company does not have a secretary, the Secretary of State may give a direction to the company. The company must comply with the direction (by making the appropriate appointment and giving notice of it) within a period specified in the direction. The section provides for an offence for failure to comply with a direction.

[2395] CA 2006, s 272(2)(a). [2396] CA 2006, s 272(2)(b). [2397] CA 2006, s 272(3).
[2398] CA 2006, s 272(4)(a). [2399] CA 2006, s 272(4)(b). [2400] CA 2006, s 272(5).
[2401] CA 2006, s 272(6)(a). [2402] CA 2006, s 272(6)(b). [2403] CA 2006, s 272(6).
[2404] CA 2006, s 272(7).

Provisions applying to secretaries of public companies

Qualifications of secretaries of public companies

12.6 Section 273(1) of the CA 2006 states that it is the duty of the directors of a public company to take all reasonable steps to secure that the secretary (or each joint secretary) of the company is a person who appears to them to have the requisite knowledge and experience to discharge the functions of secretary of the company;[2405] and has one or more of the following qualifications.[2406]

The qualifications are:

(a) that he has held the office of secretary of a public company for at least three of the five years immediately preceding his appointment as secretary;[2407]

(b) that he is a member of any of the bodies specified in s 273(3) of the CA 2006;[2408]

(c) that he is a barrister, advocate or solicitor called or admitted in any part of the United Kingdom;[2409]

(d) that he is a person who, by virtue of his holding or having held any other position or his being a member of any other body, appears to the directors to be capable of discharging the functions of secretary of the company.[2410]

The bodies referred to in s 273(2)(b) of the CA 2006 are:

(a) the Institute of Chartered Accountants in England and Wales (ICAEW);[2411]

(b) the Institute of Chartered Accountants of Scotland (ICAS);[2412]

(c) the Association of Chartered Certified Accountants (ACCA;[2413]

(d) the Institute of Chartered Accountants in Ireland;[2414]

(e) the Institute of Chartered Secretaries and Administrators (ICSA);[2415]

(f) the Chartered Institute of Management Accountants;[2416]

(g) the Chartered Institute of Public Finance and Accountancy.[2417]

This section updates s 286 of the CA 1985. It makes it the duty of the directors of a public company to ensure that the secretary has both the necessary knowledge and experience and also one of the specified qualifications

[2405] CA 2006, s 273(1)(a).   [2406] CA 2006, s 273(1)(b).   [2407] CA 2006, s 273(2)(a).
[2408] CA 2006, s 273(2)(b).   [2409] CA 2006, s 273(2)(c).   [2410] CA 2006, s 273(2)(d).
[2411] CA 2006, s 273(3)(a).   [2412] CA 2006, s 273(3)(b).   [2413] CA 2006, s 273(3)(c).
[2414] CA 2006, s 273(3)(d).   [2415] CA 2006, s 273(3)(e).   [2416] CA 2006, s 273(3)(f).
[2417] CA 2006, s 273(3)(g).

listed in s 273(2) of the CA 2006. The qualifications specified in this section are the same as in the CA 1985 except that: (i) they do not include the qualification of having held the office of the company's secretary (or assistant or deputy secretary) on 22 December 1980; and (ii) in s 273(3)(f) of the CA 2006, 'Chartered Institute of Management Accountants' replaces 'Institute of Cost and Management Accountants', as the Institute changed its name in 1986.

There is no requirement for the company secretary to be natural person. (Compare the requirement in s 155 of the CA 2006 that a company must have at least one director who is a natural person.)

Provisions applying to private companies with a secretary and to public companies

Discharge of functions where office vacant or secretary unable to act

12.7 Section 274(1) of the CA 2006 provides that where in the case of any company the office of secretary is vacant, or there is for any other reason no secretary capable of acting, anything required or authorised to be done by or to the secretary may be done by or to an assistant or deputy secretary (if any);[2418] or, if there is no assistant or deputy secretary or none capable of acting, by or to any person authorised generally or specially in that behalf by the directors.[2419]

Section 274 of the CA 2006 replaces s 283(3) of the CA 1985. It provides for a situation where the office of secretary is vacant, or there is no secretary capable of acting for any other reason. In these circumstances, if the company has an assistant or deputy secretary, then that person may fill the position of secretary; if not, any person authorised by the directors may do so. This section differs from s 283(3) of the CA 1985 by permitting the directors to authorise any person to act as secretary, rather than only an officer of the company.

Duty to keep register of secretaries

12.8 Section 275(1) of the CA 2006 states that a public company must keep a register of its secretaries.

The register must contain the required particulars (see ss 277–279 of the CA 2006) of the person who is, or persons who are, the secretary or joint secretaries of the company.[2420]

The register must be kept available for inspection at the company's

---

[2418] CA 2006, s 274(a).   [2419] CA 2006, s 274(b).   [2420] CA 2006, s 275(2).

registered office;[2421] or at a place specified in regulations under s 1136 of the CA 2006.[2422]

The company must give notice to the registrar of the place at which the register is kept available for inspection;[2423] and of any change in that place, unless it has at all times been kept at the company's registered office[2424] unless it has at all times been kept at the company's registered office.

The register must be open to the inspection of any member of the company without charge.[2425] and of any other person on payment of such fee as may be prescribed.[2426]

If default is made in complying with s 275(1) or (2) of the CA 2006, or if default is made for 14 days in complying with s 275(4) of the CA 2006, or if an inspection required under s 275(5) of the CA 2006 is refused, an offence is committed by the company;[2427] and every officer of the company who is in default.[2428] For this purpose, a shadow director is treated as an officer of the company.[2429] A person guilty of an offence under this section is liable on summary conviction to a fine not exceeding level 5 on the standard scale and, for continued contravention, a daily default fine not exceeding one-tenth of level 5 on the standard scale.[2430]

In the case of a refusal of inspection of the register, the court may by order compel an immediate inspection of it.[2431]

Section 275 of the CA 2006 replaces the requirement in s 288 of the CA 1985. It requires every public company to keep a register of its secretaries containing specified details. Section 275(3) of the CA 2006 provides that the register must be kept available for inspection either at the company's registered office or at a place specified in regulations made under s 1136 of the CA 2006. Section 275(5)–(8) of the CA 2006 retains the public right of inspection, sanctions and means of enforcement of the right of inspection.

Duty to notify registrar of changes

12.9 Section 276(1) of the CA 2006 states that a company must, within a period of 14 days of a person becoming or ceasing to be its secretary or one of its joint secretaries;[2432] or the occurrence of any change in the particulars contained in its register of secretaries,[2433] give notice to the registrar of the change and of the date on which it occurred.

Notice of a person having become secretary, or one of joint secretaries, of the company must be accompanied by a consent by that person to act in the relevant capacity.[2434]

[2421] CA 2006, s 275(3)(a).   [2422] CA 2006, s 275(3)(b).   [2423] CA 2006, s 275(4)(a).
[2424] CA 2006, s 275(4)(b).   [2425] CA 2006, s 275(5)(a).   [2426] CA 2006, s 275(5)(b).
[2427] CA 2006, s 275(6)(a).   [2428] CA 2006, s 275(6)(b).   [2429] CA 2006, s 275(6).
[2430] CA 2006, s 275(7).   [2431] CA 2006, s 275(8).   [2432] CA 2006, s 276(1)(a).
[2433] CA 2006, s 276(1)(b).   [2434] CA 2006, s 276(2).

If default is made in complying, an offence is committed by every officer of the company who is in default. For this purpose a shadow director is treated as an officer of the company.[2435] A person guilty of an offence under this section is liable on summary conviction to a fine not exceeding level 5 on the standard scale and, for continued contravention, a daily default fine not exceeding one-tenth of level 5 on the standard scale.[2436]

Section 276 of the CA 2006 replaces the requirement in s 288(2) of the CA 1985. It requires notification to the registrar within 14 days of any change in the company's secretary or any change in the particulars contained in the register of secretaries. The consent of the person having become a secretary or joint secretary of a company must accompany the notice. Section 276 of the CA 2006 retains the existing sanction and ensures that the public record is kept up to date as regards the secretary of every public company.

Particulars of secretaries to be registered: individuals

12.10 Section 277(1) of the CA 2006 provides that a company's register of secretaries must contain the following particulars in the case of an individual: name and any former name;[2437] and address.[2438]

The term 'name' means a person's Christian name (or other forename) and surname, except that in the case of a peer,[2439] or an individual usually known by a title,[2440] the title may be stated instead of his Christian name (or other forename) and surname or in addition to either or both of them.

The term 'former name' means a name by which the individual was formerly known for business purposes. Where a person is or was formerly known by more than one such name, each of them must be stated.[2441]

It is not necessary for the register to contain particulars of a former name in the following cases: in the case of a peer or an individual normally known by a British title, where the name is one by which the person was known previous to the adoption of or succession to the title;[2442] in the case of any person, where the former name was changed or disused before the person attained the age of 16[2443] years; or has been changed or disused for 20 years or more.[2444]

The address required to be stated in the register is a service address. This may be stated to be 'The company's registered office'.[2445]

Section 277 of the CA 2006 replaces s 290 of the CA 1985 insofar as it applies to secretaries who are individuals. It requires a company to enter in its register of secretaries the name and address of any individual who is its secretary. The definition of name is the same as for directors (see s 163 of the

[2435] CA 2006, s 276(3).   [2436] CA 2006, s 276(4).   [2437] CA 2006, s 277(1)(a).
[2438] CA 2006, s 277(1)(b).   [2439] CA 2006, s 277(2)(a).   [2440] CA 2006, s 277(2)(b).
[2441] CA 2006, s 277(3).   [2442] CA 2006, s 277(4)(a).   [2443] CA 2006, s 277(4)(b)(i).
[2444] CA 2006, s 277(4)(b)(ii).   [2445] CA 2006, s 277(5).

CA 2006): in particular, the register must include any name used or in use for business purposes since the age of 16. The section retains an exception relating to the former names of peers but, as recommended by the Company Law Review Group, not that for the former names of married women. The address to be registered is a service address: this implements the Company Law Review Group recommendation[2446] that the requirement for home address for company secretaries be abolished.

Particulars of secretaries to be registered: corporate secretaries and firms

12.11 Section 278(1) of the CA 2006 states that a company's register of secretaries must contain the following particulars in the case of a body corporate, or a firm that is a legal person under the law by which it is governed:

(a) corporate or firm name;[2447]
(b) registered or principal office;[2448]
(c) in the case of an EEA company to which the First Company Law Directive applies, particulars of the register in which the company file mentioned in article 3 of that Directive is kept (including details of the relevant state);[2449] and the registration number in that register;[2450]
(d) in any other case, particulars of the legal form of the company or firm and the law by which it is governed;[2451] and if applicable, the register in which it is entered (including details of the state) and its registration number in that register.[2452]

If all the partners in a firm are joint secretaries, it is sufficient to state the particulars that would be required if the firm were a legal person and the firm had been appointed secretary.[2453]

Section 278 of the CA 2006 replaces s 290 of the CA 1985 insofar as it applies to secretaries who are not individuals. It sets out the details that must be registered where the secretary of a public company is either a body corporate, or a firm that is a legal person under the law by which it is governed. The requirements that apply in the case of an EEA company follow the recommendations of the Company Law Review Group.[2454]

The section also makes provision about the details that must be registered where all the partners in a firm are joint secretaries.

[2446] *Final Report*, para 11.46.   [2447] CA 2006, s 278(1)(a).   [2448] CA 2006, s 278(1)(b).
[2449] CA 2006, s 278(1)(c)(i).   [2450] CA 2006, s 278(1)(c)(ii).   [2451] CA 2006, s 278(1)(d)(i).
[2452] CA 2006, s 278(1)(d)(ii).   [2453] CA 2006, s 278(2).   [2454] *Final Report*, para 11.39.

Particulars of secretaries to be registered: power to make regulations

12.12 Section 279(1) of the CA 2006 provides that the Secretary of State may make provision by regulations amending s 277 of the CA 2006 (particulars of secretaries to be registered: individuals), or s 278 of the CA 2006 (particulars of secretaries to be registered: corporate secretaries and firms), so as to add to or remove items from the particulars required to be contained in a public company's register of secretaries.

Regulations under this section are subject to affirmative resolution procedure.[2455]

This section is a new provision. It provides a power for the Secretary of State to make regulations that add or remove items from the particulars that have to be entered in a company's register of secretaries. A similar power is provided by s 166 of the CA 2006 for directors' particulars.

Acts done by a person in a dual capacity

12.13 Section 280 of the CA 2006 provides that a provision requiring or authorising a thing to be done by or to a director and the secretary of a company, is not satisfied by its being done by or to the same person acting both as director and as, or in place of, the secretary.

This section replaces s 284 of the CA 1985.

[2455] CA 2006, s 279(2).

Registrar of Companies

Introduction

13.1 The registrar fulfils a vital function in company law and practice process. The CA 2006 modernises the position of the registrar. Although the CA 2006 restates a large part of the provisions of the CA 1985 in respect of the registrar of companies, it sets out new provisions that further expand and clarify the registrar's role.

A large part of the registrar's duties, functions and powers are set out in the CA 2006. However, they are further supplemented by regulations made by the Secretary of State.

The register kept at Companies House continues to be an important record of documents and materials lodged and recorded by the registrar. New provisions have been introduced by the CA 2006 in respect of the register, including the registrar's role to update the register. This chapter should be read together with the Companies (Registrar of Companies) Regulations 2008.

Overview

13.2 Part 35 of the CA 2006 is concerned with the registrar of companies. This Part replaces Part 24 of the CA 1985, which applied to the registrar of companies, has functions and offices, and set out the basic functions of the registrar of companies (these functions are currently carried out by Companies House in England and Wales, and in Scotland and by the equivalent registry in Northern Ireland). The new sections under Part 35 of the CA 2006 implement a number of recommendations proposed by the Company Law Review Group.

The registrar

13.3 Section 1060 of the CA 2006 ensures continuity of the registrar from his position under the CA 1985. It also expands on the role of the registrar previously set out in s 704 of the CA 1985, but also modernises the duties and functions of a registrar. It provides that there will continue to be a registrar for the three jurisdictions: for England and Wales;[2456] for Scotland;[2457] and for Northern Ireland.[2458] All registrars must be appointed by the Secretary of State.[2459]

The section also provides clarification on terminology so that in the Companies Acts, 'the registrar of companies' and the 'registrar' mean the registrar of companies for England and Wales, or Scotland or Northern Ireland, as the case may require.[2460] Further, references in the Companies Acts to registration in a particular part of the United Kingdom, are to registration for that part of the United Kingdom.[2461]

Section 1060 of the CA 2006 advances the approach of s 704 of the CA 1985 Act[2462] as to the appointment and status of the registrar of companies, but omits some of the more outdated aspects of that provision. It specifies that there shall continue to be a registrar for England and Wales, Scotland and Northern Ireland.

The registrar's functions

13.4 The registrar's functions are set out in s 1061 of the CA 2006. The registrar will continue to perform the functions conferred on him under the Companies Acts;[2463] and in other legislation as specified in the enactments listed in s 1061(2) of the CA 2006.[2464] The Secretary of State will additionally have power to confer on the registrar particular functions in relation to the

[2456] CA 2006, s 1060(1)(a).   [2457] CA 2006, s 1060(1)(b).   [2458] CA 2006, s 1060(1)(c).
[2459] CA 2006, s 1060(2).   [2460] CA 2006, s 1060(3).   [2461] CA 2006, s 1060(4).
[2462] CA 1985, s 704 was concerned with registration offices and provided, *inter alia*, that there would continue to be offices in England and Wales and Scotland and such other places as the Secretary of State thought fit. The Secretary of State had powers to appoint registrars, assistant registrars, clerks and servants and to make regulations with respect to their duties and to remove persons so appointed. The salaries of such persons were fixed by the registrar from funds provided by Parliament. Further, the Secretary of State could direct seals to be prepared for authentication of documents.
[2463] CA 2006, s 1061(a)(i). The references in the CA 2006 as to the functions of the registrar as to the functions set out in ss 1061(1)(a) and (b).
[2464] CA 2006, s 1061(a)(ii). The enactments are: the Joint Stock Companies Acts; the Newspaper Libel and Registration Act 1881; the Limited Partnerships Act 1907; the Industrial and Provident Societies Act 1965, s 53, or for Northern Ireland, the Industrial and Provident Societies Act (Northern Ireland) 1969, s 62; the Insolvency Act 1986, or for Northern Ireland, the Insolvency (Northern Ireland Order) 1989 (SI 1989/2405 (NI 19)); s 12 of the Statutory Water Companies Act 1991; the Housing Act 1996, ss 3, 4, 6, 63 and 64 and Schedule 1 or, for Northern Ireland, the Housing (Northern Ireland) Order 1992, (SI 1992/1725 (NI 15)), articles 3 and 16–32; the Commonwealth Development Corporation Act 1999, ss 24 and 26; the Financial Services and Markets Act 2000, Part 6 and s 366; the Limited Liability Partnerships Act 2000; the Insolvency Act 2000, s 14, or, for Northern Ireland, the Insolvency (Northern Ireland) Order 2002 (SI 2002/3152) (NI 6), Article 11; the Land Registration Act 2002, s 121; and CA 2006, s 1258.

registration of companies or other matters, as the Secretary of State may from time to time direct.[2465]

The registrar's official seal

13.5 Section 1062 of the CA 2006 states that the registrar must have an official seal for the authentication of documents in connection with the performance of the registrar's functions. It replaces s 704(4) of the CA 1985.[2466]

Fees payable to the registrar

13.6 The CA 2006 takes account of the fees that are payable to the registrar. The Secretary of State is empowered under s 1063 of the CA 2006 to set fees by regulations in relation to the performance of any function of the registrar;[2467] and in relation to the provision of services or facilities or the purposes incidental to, or otherwise connected with, the performance of any of her functions.[2468]

There is a list of fees that may be charged and includes the performance of a duty imposed on the registrar or the Secretary of State;[2469] the receipt of documents delivered to the registrar;[2470] and the inspection, or provision of copies, of documents kept by the registrar.[2471]

Further, the regulations may provide for the amount of the fees to be fixed by or determined under the regulations;[2472] provide for different fees to be payable in respect of the same matter in different circumstances;[2473] specify the person by whom any fee payable under the regulations is to be paid;[2474] and specify when and how fees are to be paid.[2475] Regulations under s 1063 of the CA 2006 are subject to negative resolution procedure.[2476]

In respect of the performance of functions or the provision of services or facilities for which fees are not provided for by regulations;[2477] or in circumstances other than those for which fees are provided for by regulations,[2478] the registrar may determine from time to time, what fees (if any) are chargeable. Any fees received by the registrar must be paid into the Consolidated Fund.[2479]

[2465] CA 2006, s 1061(b).

[2466] CA 1985, s 704(4) provided that the Secretary of State could direct a seal or seals to be prepared for the authentication of documents required for or in connection with the registration of companies; and any seal so prepared was referred to as the registrar's official seal.

[2467] CA 2006, s 1063(1)(a).   [2468] CA 2006, s 1063(1)(b).   [2469] CA 2006, s 1063(2)(a).
[2470] CA 2006, s 1063(2)(b).   [2471] CA 2006, s 1063(2)(c).   [2472] CA 2006, s 1063(3)(a).
[2473] CA 2006, s 1063(3)(b).   [2474] CA 2006, s 1063(3)(c).   [2475] CA 2006, s 1063(3)(d).
[2476] CA 2006, s 1063(4).   [2477] CA 2006, s 1063(5)(a).   [2478] CA 2006, s 1063(5)(b).

[2479] CA 2006, s 1063(6). CA 2006, s 1063(7) makes amendments to the Limited Partnerships Act 1907 amending s 16 (inspection of statements registered) and s 17 (power to make rules). The Limited Partnerships Act 1907, s 16(1) will now read: 'Any person may inspect the statements filed by the registrar in the register offices aforesaid . . .'. The Limited Partnerships Act 1907, s 17 will now read: 'The Board of Trade may make rules concerning any of the following matters . . .'.

Section 1,063 of the CA 2006 gives the Secretary of State power to set fees by regulations in relation to any function of the registrar, and in relation to the provision of services and facilities incidental to the registrar's functions. It replaces s 708 of the CA 1985, but is more specific on the types of matters for which fees may be charged, although this list is not exhaustive.

Previously under the CA 1985, and now under the CA 2006, fees relating to the normal statutory obligations of companies under companies legislation will be set by regulations made by the Secretary of State. It will also be possible for fees to be charged for any ad hoc and bespoke services which Companies House provides. Section 708(5) of the CA 1985 made clear that the registrar could determine fees for services for which there was no direct legal obligation. Section 1063(5) of the CA 2006 replaces this with a more general power for the registrar to determine fees, where no fee has been set in regulations by the Secretary of State. Such fees might relate, for example, to the introduction of new services (for example, those made possible by new technologies), which could not have been anticipated when the Secretary of State last made fees regulations; or for services such as seminars and road shows, which Companies House arranges.

Certificates of incorporation

13.7 Sections 1064 and 1065 of the CA 2006 address the position of certificates of incorporation.

Public notice of issue of certificate of incorporation

13.8 Section 1064 states that the registrar is required to publish notice of the issue by the registrar of any certificate of incorporation by the company in the Gazette;[2480] or alternatively in accordance with s 1116 of the CA 2006 (alternative means of giving public notice).[2481] The notice must state the name and registered number of the company and the date of issue of the certificate.[2482]

Section 1064 of the CA 2006 applies to a certificate of incorporation issued under s 80 of the CA 2006 (change of name);[2483] s 88 of the CA 2006 (Welsh companies);[2484] or any provision of Part 7 of the CA 2006 (re-registration),[2485] as well as to the certificate issued on a company's formation.

Section 1064 of the CA 2006 replaces s 711(1)(a) of the CA 1985 and provides for notice of the issue of certificates to be published in the Gazette. The publication must include the company's registered number as well as its name.

[2480] CA 2006, s 1064(1)(a).   [2481] CA 2006, s 1064(1)(b).   [2482] CA 2006, s 1064(2).
[2483] CA 2006, s 1064(3)(a).   [2484] CA 2006, s 1064(3)(b).   [2485] CA 2006, s 1064(3)(c)

Right to certificate of incorporation

13.9 Section 1065 of the CA 2006 provides for a right to a certificate of incorporation. Any person may require the registrar to provide him with a copy of any certificate of incorporation of a company, signed by the registrar or authenticated by the registrar's seal.

Section 1065 of the CA 2006 replaces s 710 of the CA 1985 (which allows any person to obtain a certificate of incorporation of a company). Sections 1064 and 1065 of the CA 2006 cover all certificates of incorporation (including, for example, certificates of incorporation on change of name).

Registered numbers

13.10 Sections 1066 and 1067 of the CA 2006 deal with the company's registered numbers.

Company's registered numbers

13.11 Section 1066 of the CA 2006 states that the registrar must allocate to every company a number that will be known as the company's registered number.[2486] Companies' registered numbers must be in such form, consisting of one or more sequences of figures or letters, as the registrar may determine.[2487] On adopting a new form of registered number, the registrar may make such changes of the existing registered numbers as appear necessary.[2488] A change of a company's registered number has effect from the date on which the company is notified by the registrar of the change.[2489] For a period of three years beginning with that date, any requirement to disclose the company's registered number imposed by regulations under s 82 or s 1051 of the CA 2006 (trading disclosures) is satisfied by the use of either the old number or the new.[2490]

The references in s 1066 of the CA 2006 to a 'company', includes an overseas company whose particulars have been registered under s 1046 of the CA 2006, other than the company that appears to the registrar not to be required to register particulars under that section.[2491]

Section 1066 of the CA 2006 replaces s 705 of the CA 1985 (rules on companies' registered numbers), without change of substance.

Registered numbers of branches of overseas company

13.12 Section 1067 of the CA 2006 states that the registrar is required to allocate to every branch of an overseas company whose particulars are registered under s 1046 of the CA 2006 (duty to register particulars) a number,

---

[2486] CA 2006, s 1066(1).   [2487] CA 2006, s 1066(2).   [2488] CA 2006, s 1066(3).
[2489] CA 2006, s 1066(4).   [2490] CA 2006, s 1066(5).   [2491] CA 2006, s 1066(6).

which will be known as the branch's registered number.[2492] Branches' registered numbers must be in such form, consisting of one or more sequences of figures or letters, as the registrar may determine.[2493] The registrar may on adopting a new form of registered number make such changes of existing registered numbers as appear necessary.[2494] A change of a branch's registered number applies from the date on which the company is notified by the registrar of the change.[2495] For a period of three years beginning with that date, any requirement to disclose the branch's registered number imposed by regulations under s 1051 of the CA 2006 (trading disclosures) is satisfied by the use of either the old number or the new.[2496]

Section 1067 of the CA 2006 replaces the provisions of s 705A of the CA 1985 that relate to registered numbers of branches of overseas companies.

Delivery of documents to the registrar

13.13 Sections 1068–1071 of the CA 2006 are concerned with delivery of documents to the registrar.

Registrar's requirements as to form, authentication and manner of delivery

13.14 Certain formalities are required to be complied with in respect of delivery of documents to the registrar. The registrar may impose requirements as to (i) the form; (ii) authentication; and (iii) manner of delivery of documents, required or authorised to be delivered to the registrar under any enactment.[2497]

With regards to the form of the document, the registrar may require the contents of the documents to be in a standard form.[2498] The registrar may also impose requirements for the purpose of enabling the document to be scanned or copied.[2499]

With reference to authentication, the registrar may require the document to be authenticated by a particular person, or a person of a particular description;[2500] specify the means of authentication;[2501] or require the document to contain or be accompanied by the name or registered number of the company to which it related (or both).[2502]

As regards the manner of delivery, the registrar may specify requirements as to the physical form of the document (for example, hard copy or electronic form);[2503] the means to be used for delivering the document (for example, by

[2492] CA 2006, s 1067(1).   [2493] CA 2006, s 1067(2).   [2494] CA 2006, s 1067(3).
[2495] CA 2006, s 1067(4).   [2496] CA 2006, s 1067(5).   [2497] CA 2006, s 1068 (1).
[2498] CA 2006, s 1068(2)(a).   [2499] CA 2006, s 1068(2)(b).   [2500] CA 2006, s 1068(3)(a).
[2501] CA 2006, s 1068(3)(b).   [2502] CA 2006, s 1068(3)(c).   [2503] CA 2006, s 1068(4)(a).

post or electronic means);[2504] the address to which the document is to be sent;[2505] in the case of a document to be delivered by electronic means, the hardware and software to be used, and technical specifications (for example, matters relating to protocol, security, anti-virus protection or encryption).[2506]

The registrar must secure that as from 1 January 2007, all documents subject to the Directive disclosure requirements (see s 1078 of the CA 2006), may be delivered to the registrar by electronic means.[2507]

However, the power conferred by s 1068 of the CA 2006 does not authorise the registrar to require documents to be delivered by electronic means.[2508] Any requirements imposed by s 1068 of the CA 2006 must not be inconsistent with requirements imposed by any enactment with respect to the form, authentication or manner of delivery of the document concerned.[2509]

The effect of s 1068 of the CA 2006 is to give the registrar power to make requirements about form, authentication and manner of delivery of documents, including the physical form and means of communication (for example electronic or hard copy by post), the format, and the address to which it is to be sent, and where appropriate, technical specifications. It should be noted that the power under this section does not allow the registrar to require documents to be delivered in electronic form.

Power to require delivery by electronic means

13.15 The CA 2006 contains provisions allowing for delivery of documents by electronic means. Under s 1069 of the CA 2006, the Secretary of State is empowered to make regulations requiring documents that are authorised or required to be delivered to the registrar, to be delivered by electronic means.[2510]

Any requirement to deliver documents by electronic means will be effective only if the registrar's rules have been published with respect to the detailed requirements for such delivery.[2511]

The regulations made under s 1069 of the CA 2006 are subject to affirmative resolution procedure.[2512]

The objective of s 1069 of the CA 2006 is that the Secretary of State, and not the registrar, will have a new power to provide for electronic-only delivery of classes of document. This power will only be exercisable by the Secretary of State in respect of classes of document that are authorised, or required to be delivered, and for which the registrar has published rules relating to electronic delivery. The regulations will specify precisely what should be the mechanism for the electronic communication.

[2504] CA 2006, s 1068(4)(b).   [2505] CA 2006, s 1068(4)(c).   [2506] CA 2006, s 1068(4)(d).
[2507] CA 2006, s 1068(5).   [2508] CA 2006, s 1068(6).   [2509] CA 2006, s 1068(7).
[2510] CA 2006, s 1069(1).   [2511] CA 2006, s 1069(2).   [2512] CA 2006, s 1069(3).

Agreement for delivery by electronic means

13.16 There is now power conferred on registrar to agree on documents to be delivered by electronic means only. Section 1070 of the CA 2006 addresses such agreement for delivery by electronic means. In future, this section may become known as the 'section 1070 Agreement'. It sets out the power of the registrar to make agreements with companies to deliver information to him only electronically. The registrar may agree with a company that documents relating to the company that are required or authorised to be delivered to the registrar, will be delivered by electronic means, except as provided in the agreement;[2513] and will conform to such requirements as may be specified in the agreement, or specified by the registrar in accordance with the agreement.[2514]

An agreement made under s 1070 of the CA 2006 may relate to all or any description of documents to be delivered to the registrar.[2515] Documents in relation to which an agreement is in force under s 1070 of the CA 2006, must be delivered only in accordance with the agreement.[2516]

The agreements could cover all documents (to the extent that electronic means of filing are available), or just selected documents. It is envisaged that the agreements will be in a standard form and contain detailed provisions for communications between the registrar and the company (including possible use of codes and encryption). The agreements do not need to be available to be entered into by everyone in the same form or at all.

Document not delivered until received

13.17 It is made clear under s 1071 of the CA 2006 that a document is not delivered to the registrar, until it is received by the registrar.[2517] Provision may be made by registrar's rules as to when a document is to be regarded as received.[2518]

Section 1071 of the CA 2006 ensures that 'delivery' obligations go beyond an obligation simply to send or post information to the registrar, and that the registrar may make rules governing what it is for a document to be 'received', (which might include, for example, setting out which offices of the registrar should receive a document).

Requirements for Proper Delivery

13.18 Sections 1072–1076 of the CA 2006 are concerned with requirements for proper delivery of documents to the registrar.

Section 1072 of the CA 2006 states that a document delivered to the

---

[2513] CA 2006, s 1070(1)(a).   [2514] CA 2006, s 1070(1)(b).   [2515] CA 2006, s 1070(2).
[2516] CA 2006, s 1070(3).   [2517] CA 2006, s 1071(1).   [2518] CA 2006, s 1071(2).

registrar will not be properly delivered, unless all the following requirements are met:[2519]

- The contents of the document;[2520]
- Form, authentication and manner of delivery;[2521]
- Any applicable requirements under s 1068 of the CA 2006 (registrar's requirements as to form, authentication and manner of delivery); s 1069 of the CA 2006 (power to require delivery by electronic means); or s 1070 of the CA 2006 (agreement for delivery by electronic means);[2522]
- Any requirements as to the language in which the document is drawn up and delivered, or as to its being accompanied on delivery by a certified translation into English;[2523]
- In so far as it consists of or includes names and addresses, any requirements as to permitted characters, letters or symbols, or to its being accompanied on delivery by a certificate as to the transliteration of any element;[2524]
- Any applicable requirements under s 1111 of the CA 2006 (registrar's requirements as to certification or verification);[2525]
- Any requirement of regulations under s 1082 of the CA 2006 (use of unique identifiers);[2526]
- Any requirements as regards payment of a fee of its receipt by the registrar.[2527]

A document that is not properly delivered, will be treated for the purposes of the provision requiring or authorising it to be delivered, as not having been delivered. This is, however, subject to s 1073 of the CA 2006 (power to accept documents not meeting requirements for proper delivery).[2528]

The effect of s 1072 of the CA 2006 is to set out various conditions that must be satisfied in order for a document to be properly delivered to the registrar as set out in s 1072(a)–(g) of the CA 2006. If these conditions are not satisfied, the document cannot, therefore, be regarded as 'properly' delivered.

Power to accept documents not meeting requirements for proper delivery

13.19 There are situations where the registrar may accept documents that do not meet the requirements for proper delivery, as an exception to s 1072 of the CA 2006. Section 1073 of the CA 2006 states that the registrar may

[2519] CA 2006, s 1072(1).   [2520] CA 2006, s 1072(1)(a)(i).   [2521] CA 2006, s 1072(1)(a)(ii).
[2522] CA 2006, s 1072(1)(b).   [2523] CA 2006, s 1072(1)(c).   [2524] CA 2006, s 1072(1)(d).
[2525] CA 2006, s 1072(1)(e).   [2526] CA 2006, s 1072(1)(f).   [2527] CA 2006, s 1072(1)(g).
[2528] CA 2006, s 1072(2).

accept (and register) a document that does not comply with the requirements for proper delivery.[2529] A document that is accepted by the registrar, is treated as received by the registrar for the purposes of s 1077 of the CA 2006 (public notice of receipt of certain documents).[2530] It will not be possible to make any objection to the legal consequences of a document's being accepted (or registered) by the registrar on the ground that the requirements for proper delivery were not met.[2531]

The acceptance of a document by the registrar does not affect the continuing obligation to comply with the requirements for proper delivery;[2532] or subject as follows, to any liability for failure to comply with those requirements.[2533]

It is made clear that for the purposes of s 453 of the CA 2006 (civil penalty for failure to file accounts and reports);[2534] and any enactment imposing a daily default fine for failure to deliver the document,[2535] the period after the document is accepted does not count as a period during which there is default in complying with the requirements for proper delivery.

However, if subsequently the registrar issues a notice under s 1094(4) of the CA 2006 in respect of the document (notice of administrative removal from the register);[2536] and the requirements for proper delivery are not complied with before the end of a period of 14 days after the issue of that notice,[2537] any subsequent period of default does not count for the purposes of those provisions.

It should be noted that acceptance by the registrar to register the document does not exempt the filer from any consequence attaching to failure to comply with the original requirements for delivery.

Documents containing unnecessary material

13.20 It is envisaged that there may be occasions where a document is delivered to the registrar that contains unnecessary material, owing to superfluous or irrelevant information being accompanied or provided with the document, for which there is no legal requirement or authorisation.

The position is governed by s 1074 of the CA 2006, and applies where a document delivered to the registrar contains unnecessary material.[2538] The term 'unnecessary material' means material that is not necessary in order to comply with any obligation under any enactment;[2539] and is not specifically authorised to be delivered to the registrar.[2540]

An obligation to deliver a document of a particular description, or conforming to certain requirements, is regarded as not extending to anything that

---

[2529] CA 2006, s 1073(1).   [2530] CA 2006, s 1077(2).   [2531] CA 2006, s 1073(3).
[2532] CA 2006, s 1073(4)(a).   [2533] CA 2006, s 1073(4)(b).   [2534] CA 2006, s 1073(5)(a).
[2535] CA 2006, s 1073(5)(b).   [2536] CA 2006, s 1073(6)(a).   [2537] CA 2006, s 1073(6)(b).
[2538] CA 2006, s 1074(1).   [2539] CA 2006, s 1074(2)(a).   [2540] CA 2006, s 1074(2)(b).

is not needed for a document of that description or, as the case may be, conforming to those requirements.[2541] The test is that if the unnecessary material cannot readily be separated from the rest of the document, the document as a whole will be treated as not meeting the requirements for proper delivery.[2542]

However, if the unnecessary material can readily be separated from the rest of the document, the registrar is given the option of either registering the document either with the omission of the unnecessary material, that is, excluding the unnecessary material and registering the remainder;[2543] or registering the remainder as delivered.[2544]

Informal correction of document

13.21 It may be possible, in certain circumstances, for the registrar to make an informal correction of the document. Under s 1075(1) of the CA 2006, a document delivered to the registrar may be corrected by the registrar, if it appears to the registrar to be incomplete or internally inconsistent. However, this power is exerciseable only on instructions;[2545] and if the company has given (and has not withdrawn) its consent to instructions being given.[2546]

The following conditions must be met as regards the instructions:

- The instructions must be given in response to an enquiry by the registrar;[2547]
- The registrar must be satisfied that the person giving the instructions is authorised to do so by the person by whom the document was delivered;[2548] or by the company to which the document relates;[2549]
- The instructions must meet any requirements of registrar's rules, as to the form and manner in which they are given, and authentication.[2550]

The company's consent to instructions being given (and any withdrawal of such consent), must be in a hard copy or electronic form;[2551] and must be notified to the registrar.[2552]

Section 1075 of the CA 2006 also applies in relation to documents delivered under Part 25 of the CA 2006 (company charges), by a person other than the company, as if the references to the company were to the company or the person by whom the document was delivered.[2553]

A document that is so corrected is treated for the purposes of any enactment relating to its delivery, as having been delivered when the correction was

---

[2541] CA 2006, s 1074(3).   [2542] CA 2006, s 1074(4).   [2543] CA 2006, s 1074(5)(a).
[2544] CA 2006, s 1074(5)(b).   [2545] CA 2006, s 1075(2)(a).   [2546] CA 2006, s 1075(2)(b).
[2547] CA 2006, s 1075(3)(a).   [2548] CA 2006, s 1075(3)(b)(i).
[2549] CA 2006, s 1075(3)(b)(ii).   [2550] CA 2006, s 1075(3)(c).
[2551] CA 2006, s 1075(4)(a).   [2552] CA 2006, s 1075(4)(b).   [2553] CA 2006, s 1075(5).

made.[2554] The power conferred by s 1075 of the CA 2006 is not exercisable, if the document has been registered under s 1073 of the CA 2006 (power to accept documents not meeting requirements for proper delivery).[2555]

Section 1075 of the CA 2006 is a new provision. It gives the registrar power to correct information by informal means, such as, for example, by taking revisions or supplementary information from the company over the telephone, but only in very limited circumstances. It can be used as an alternative to rejecting or removing information either on the grounds that it is incomplete (for example, empty fields within the documents); or on the grounds that it is internally inconsistent (e.g. the company number does not correspond to the company name).

This ability to make informal corrections would only apply where companies have informed the registrar that it should apply. The registrar will most likely initiate the correction, and be satisfied that the person is authorised to give the information sought. In order to be satisfied as to the authority of the person she is telephoning, the registrar would be able to provide for identification numbers or other checks on identity.

Replacement of document not meeting requirements for proper delivery

13.22 Section 1076 of the CA 2006 applies to replacing a document not meeting requirements for proper delivery. It is possible, subject to the registrar's discretion, for the registrar to accept a replacement for a document previously delivered that did not comply with the requirements for proper delivery;[2556] or contained unnecessary material within the meaning of s 1074 of the CA 2006.[2557]

A replacement document must not be accepted unless the registrar is satisfied that it is delivered by the person by whom the original document was delivered;[2558] or the company to which the original document relates; and that it complies with the requirements for proper delivery.[2559]

The power of the registrar to impose requirements as to the form and manner of delivery, includes power to impose requirements as to the identification of the original document, and the delivery of the replacement in a form and manner enabling it to be associated with the original.[2560]

However, s 1076 of the CA 2006 will not apply where the original document was delivered under Part 25 of the CA 2006 (company charges), but see ss 873 and 888 of the CA 2006 (rectification of register of charges).[2561]

The purpose of s 1076 of the CA 2006 is to set out how the registrar may

---

[2554] CA 2006, s 1075(6).   [2555] CA 2006, s 1075(7).   [2556] CA 2006, s 1076(1)(a).
[2557] CA 2006, s 1076(1)(b).   [2558] CA 2006, s 1076(2)(a).   [2559] CA 2006, s 1076(2)(b).
[2560] CA 2006, s 1076(3).   [2561] CA 2006, s 1076(4).

accept a replacement document that was not properly delivered in the first place. In essence, he must be satisfied that the replacement document is delivered by the original filer, or by the company to which the original documents relates, and that the replacement is 'properly delivered' (as defined by s 1072 of the CA 2006). It also allows the registrar to impose requirements that will ensure that the replacement can clearly be associated with a particular original.

Public notice of receipt of certain documents

13.23 In certain circumstances, the registrar is required to give public notice of receipt of documents that are subject to the 'Directive disclosure requirements' (see s 1078 of the CA 2006). Section 1077 of the CA 2006 sets out the requirements. The registrar is required to publish in the Gazette,[2562] or in accordance with s 1116 of the CA 2006 (alternative means of giving public notice),[2563] notice of receipt by the registrar of any document that, on receipt, is subject to the Directive disclosure requirements (see s 1078 of the CA 2006).

The notice must state the name and registered number of the company, the description of document, and the date of receipt.[2564] The registrar is not required to cause notice of the receipt of a document to be published before the date of incorporation of the company to which the document relates.[2565]

Section 1077 of the CA 2006 replaces s 711 of the CA 1985, which provides that certain notices must be published in the Gazette (that is London, Edinburgh or Belfast Gazette as appropriate), and sets out the documents to which that requirement relates. This list derives from Community legislation, principally the First Company Law Directive (68/151/EEC) as amended by Directive 2003/58/EC. Section 1077 of the CA 2006 states that notice of receipt of these documents must be published either in the Gazette, or by some other means as are set out in s 1116 of the CA 2006. Section 1078 of the CA 2006 lists the documents that are subject to the Directive disclosure requirements.

Documents subject to Directive disclosure requirements

13.24 The documents that are subject to the 'Directive disclosure requirements' are set out in s 1078 of the CA 2006. The requirements referred to are those of Article 3 of the First Company Law Directive (68/151/EEC), as amended, extended or applied.

The following applies in the case of every company.

[2562] CA 2006, s 1077(1)(a).   [2563] CA 2006, s 1077(1)(b).   [2564] CA 2006, s 1077(2).
[2565] CA 2006, s 1077(3).

Constitutional documents

(a)   The company's memorandum and articles.

(b)   Any amendment of the company's articles (including every resolution or agreement required to be embodied in or annexed to copies of the company's articles issued by the company).

(c)   After any amendment of the company's articles, the text of the articles as amended.

(d)   Any notice of a change of the company's name.

Directors

(a)   The statement of proposed officers required on formation of the company.

(b)   Notification of any change among the company's directors.

(c)   Notification of any change in the particulars of directors required to be delivered to the registrar.

Accounts, reports and returns

(a)   All documents required to be delivered to the registrar under s 441 of the CA 2006 (annual accounts and reports).

(b)   The company's annual return.

Registered office

Notification of any change of the company's registered office.

Winding up

(a)   Copy of any winding-up order in respect of the company.

(b)   Notice of the appointment of liquidators.

(c)   Order for the dissolution of a company on a winding up.

(d)   Return by a liquidator of the final meeting of a company on a winding up.

In the case of public company the following requirements apply.

Share capital

(a)   Any statement of capital and initial shareholdings.

(b)   Any return of allotment and the statement of capital accompanying it.

(c)   Copy of any resolution under s 570 or s 571 of the CA 2006 (disapplication of pre-emption rights).

(d)   Copy of any report under s 593 or s 599 of the CA 2006 as to the value of a non-cash asset.

(e)   Statement of capital accompanying notice given under s 625 of the CA 2006 (notice by company of redenomination of shares).

(f)   Statement of capital accompanying notice given under s 627 of the CA 2006 (notice by company of reduction of capital in connection with redenomination of shares).

(g)   Notice delivered under s 636 of the CA 2006 (notice of new name of class of shares) or s 637 of the CA 2006 (notice of variation of rights attached to shares).

(h)   Statement of capital accompanying order delivered under s 649 of the CA 2006 (order of court confirming reduction of capital).

(i)   Notification (under s 689 of the CA 2006) of the redemption of shares and the statement of capital accompanying it.

(j)   Statement of capital accompanying return delivered under s 708 of the CA 2006 (notice of cancellation of shares on purchase of own shares) or s 730 of the CA 2006 (notice of cancellation of shares held as treasury shares).

(k)   Any statement of compliance delivered under s 762 of the CA 2006 (statement that company meets conditions for issue of trading certificate).

Mergers and divisions

(a)   Copy of any draft of the terms of a scheme required to be delivered to the registrar under s 906 of the CA 2006 or s 921 of the CA 2006.

(b)   Copy of any order under s 899 of the CA 2006 or s 900 of the CA 2006 in respect of a compromise or arrangement to which Part 27 of the CA 2006 (mergers and divisions of public companies) applies.

Where a private company re-registers as a public company (see s 96 of the CA 2006), the last statement of capital relating to the company received by the registrar under any provision of the Companies Acts becomes subject to the Directive disclosure requirements;[2566] and s 1077 of the CA 2006 (public notice of receipt of certain documents) applies as if the statement had been received by the registrar when the re-registration takes effect.[2567]

In the case of an overseas company, such particulars, returns and other documents required to be delivered under Part 34 of the CA 2006 as may be specified by the Secretary of State by regulations.[2568]

Any regulations made under s 1078(5) of the CA 2006 are subject to negative resolution procedure.[2569]

[2566] CA 2006, s 1078(4)(a).   [2567] CA 2006, s 1078(4)(b).   [2568] CA 2006, s 1078(5).
[2569] CA 2006, s 1078(6).

Effect of failure to give public notice

13.25 Section 1079 of the CA 2006 addresses the effect of failure to give public notice. It states that a company is not entitled to rely against other persons on the happening of any event, unless the event has been officially notified at the material time;[2570] or the company shows that the person concerned knew of the event at the material time.[2571]

The events are:

(a) an amendment to the company's articles;[2572]
(b) a change among the company's directors;[2573]
(c) (as regards service of any document on the company) a change of the company's registered office;[2574]
(d) the making of a winding-up order in respect of the company;[2575] or
(e) the appointment of a liquidator in a voluntary winding-up of the company.[2576]

In the event the material time falls on or before the fifteenth day after the date of official notification;[2577] or where the fifteenth day was not a working day, on or before the next day that was a working day,[2578] then the company is not entitled to rely on the happening of the event as against a person who shows that he was unavoidably prevented from knowing of the event at that time.

The term 'official notification' means:

(a) In relation to an amendment of the company's articles, notification in accordance with s 1077 of the CA 2006 (public notice of receipt by registrar of certain documents) of the amendment and the amended text of the articles;[2579]
(b) In relation to anything else stated in a document subject to the Directive disclosure requirements, notification of that document in accordance with that section;[2580]
(c) In relation to the appointment of a liquidator in a voluntary winding up, notification of that event in accordance with s 109 Insolvency Act 1986 or Article 95 of the Insolvency (Northern Ireland) Order 1989 (SI 1989/2405 (NI 19)).[2581]

Section 1079 of the CA 2006 effectively replaces s 42 of the CA 1985 Act. It sets out how a company, in its dealings with third parties, may not rely on the consequences of certain events, which are set out in s 1079(2) of the CA

[2570] CA 2006, s 1079(1)(a).　[2571] CA 2006, s 1079(1)(b).　[2572] CA 2006, s 1079(2)(a).
[2573] CA 2006, s 1079(2)(b).　[2574] CA 2006, s 1079(2)(c).　[2575] CA 2006, s 1079(2)(d).
[2576] CA 2006, s 1079(2)(e).　[2577] CA 2006, s 1079(3)(a).　[2578] CA 2006, s 1079(3)(b).
[2579] CA 2006, s 1079(4)(a).　[2580] CA 2006, s 1079(4)(b).　[2581] CA 2006, s 1079(4)(c).

2006, unless notice of the event has duly appeared in the Gazette or been published in some other way provided for in s 1116 of the CA 2006.

The register

13.26 Sections 1080–1084 of the CA 2006 deal with the register.

The maintenance of the register is one of the important aspects of the Companies House. Section 1080 of the CA 2006 provides that the registrar must continue to keep records of the information contained in documents delivered to the registrar under any enactment;[2582] as well as certificates of incorporation issued by the registrar;[2583] and certificates issued by the registrar under s 869(5) or s 885(4) of the CA 2006 (certificates of registration of charge).[2584]

The records relating to companies are referred to collectively in the Companies Acts as 'the register'.[2585]

Any information deriving from documents that are subject to the Directive disclosure requirements (see s 1078 of the CA 2006), that are delivered to the registrar on or after 1 January 2007, must be kept by the registrar in electronic form.[2586] Subject to that, information contained in documents delivered to the registrar, may be recorded and kept in any form the registrar thinks fit, provided it is possible to inspect it and produce a copy of it. This is sufficient compliance with any duty of the registrar to keep, file or register the document or to record the information contained in it.[2587]

The records kept by the registrar must be such that, information relating to a company is associated with that company, in such manner as the registrar may determine, so as to enable all the information relating to the company to be retrieved.[2588]

The objective of s 1080 of the CA 2006 is to impose an obligation on the registrar to keep a record of the material the registrar receives. It gives him discretion as to the form in which the record is kept. This discretion will be subject to the terms of the amended First Company Law Directive (38/151/EEC), article 3.2 of which requires any documents and particulars it covers that are delivered on after 1 January 2007, to be retained in electronic form. The documents covered by this obligation are those already set out in s 1078 of the CA 2006.

Annotation of the register

13.27 It is important that the register is as useful and transparent a source of information as possible for users. Section 1081 of the CA 2006 sets out

---

[2582] CA 2006, s 1080(1)(a).   [2583] CA 2006, s 1080(1)(b).   [2584] CA 2006, s 1080(1)(c).
[2585] CA 2006, s 1080(2).   [2586] CA 2006, s 1080(3).   [2587] CA 2006, s 1080(4).
[2588] CA 2006, s 1080(5).

provisions for annotation of the register. The registrar must place a note in the register, recording the date on which a document is delivered to the registrar;[2589] if a document is corrected under s 1075 of the CA 2006, the nature and date of the correction;[2590] if a document is replaced (whether or not material derived from it is removed), the fact that it has been replaced and the date of delivery of the replacement;[2591] and if material is removed what was removed (giving a general description of its contents), under what power, and the date on which that was done.[2592]

The Secretary of State may make provision by regulations authorising or requiring the registrar to annotate the register in such other circumstances as may be specified in the regulations;[2593] and as to the contents of any such annotation.[2594] However, an annotation will not be required in the case of a document which by virtue of s 1072(2) of the CA 2006 (documents not meeting the requirements for proper delivery) is treated as not having been delivered.[2595]

A note may be removed by the registrar if it no longer serves any useful purpose.[2596]

Any duty or power of the registrar with respect to annotation of the register, is subject to the court's power under s 1097 of the CA 2006 (powers of court on ordering removal of material from the register), to direct that a note be removed from the register;[2597] or that no note shall be made of the removal of material that is subject to the court's order.[2598]

Notes placed in the register in accordance with s 1081(1) of the CA 2006, or in pursuance of regulations under s 1081(2) of the CA 2006, are part of the register for all purposes of the Companies Acts.[2599]

The regulations under s 1081 of the CA 2006 are subject to negative resolution procedure.[2600]

The object of s 1081 of the CA 2006 is to set out certain circumstances in which the registrar will be obliged to annotate the information on the register to gloss or provide supplementary information. Annotations must, for example, be provided to show the date of delivery of information; and in the event that information has been replaced, corrected or removed. This section implements a specific recommendation of the Company Law Review Group[2601] The court can dispense with the need for annotation in certain

---

[2589] CA 2006, s 1081(1)(a).   [2590] CA 2006, s 1081(1)(b).   [2591] CA 2006, s 1081(1)(c).

[2592] CA 2006, s 1081(1)(d).

[2593] CA 2006, s 1081(2)(a). See regulation 2 of the Companies (Registrar of Companies) Regulations 2008, which authorises the registrar to annotate the register where he believes that any material in the register is misleading or confusing. Any annotation must contain such information as the registrar believes necessary to remedy, so far as possible, the misleading or confusing nature of the material.

[2594] CA 2006, s 1081(2)(b).   [2595] CA 2006, s 1081(3).   [2596] CA 2006, s 1081(4).

[2597] CA 2006, s 1081(5)(a).   [2598] CA 2006, s 1081(5)(b).   [2599] CA 2006, s 1081(6).

[2600] CA 2006, s 1081(7).   [2601] *Final Report*, para 11.48.

circumstances. The Secretary of State has power to make provision by regulations extending the circumstances where the registrar can or should make annotations.

Allocation of unique identifiers

13.28 Section 1082 of the CA 2006 is concerned with the allocation of 'unique identifiers'. It is a new provision. The Secretary of State is empowered to make provision for the use, in connection with the register, of reference numbers known as 'unique identifiers', to identify each person who:

(a) is a director of a company;[2602]
(b) is secretary (or a joint secretary) of a company;[2603] or
(c) in the case of an overseas company whose particulars are registered under s 1046 of the CA 2006, holds any such position as may be specified for the purposes of this section by regulations under that section.[2604]

The regulations may provide that a unique identifier may be in such form, consisting of one or more sequences of letters or numbers, as the registrar may from time to time determine;[2605] make provision for the allocation of unique identifiers by the registrar;[2606] require there to be included, in any specified description of documents delivered to the registrar, as well as a statement of the person's name a statement of the person's unique identifier; or a statement that the person has not been allocated a unique identifier.[2607] The regulations may also enable the registrar to take steps where a person appears to have more than one unique identifier to discontinue the use of all but one of them.[2608]

The regulations may contain provision for the application of the scheme in relation to persons appointed, and documents registered, before the commencement of the CA 2006.[2609]

The regulations may make different provision for different descriptions of person and different descriptions of document.[2610]

Any regulations under s 1082 of the CA 2006 are subject to affirmative resolution procedure.[2611]

Section 1082 of the CA 2006 gives the Secretary of State a power to make regulations so that individuals, for example company directors, are allocated a unique identifier. This provision supports those that provide for the home addresses of directors no longer to be kept on the public record. The unique

---

[2602] CA 2006, s 1082(1)(a).
[2603] CA 2006, s 1082(1)(b).
[2604] CA 2006, s 1082(1)(c).
[2605] CA 2006, s 1082(2)(a).
[2606] CA 2006, s 1082(2)(b).
[2607] CA 2006, s 1082(2)(c).
[2608] CA 2006, s 1082(2)(d).
[2609] CA 2006, s 1082(3).
[2610] CA 2006, s 1082(4).
[2611] CA 2006, s 1082(5).

identifier will enable searchers to distinguish between different persons of the same name.

Preservation of original documents

13.29 Certain documents must be preserved by the registrar for a specific period of time. Section 1083 of the CA 2006 addresses the preservation of original documents. The originals of documents that are delivered to the registrar in hard copy form, must be kept for three years after they are received by the registrar. After this period, they may be destroyed, provided the information contained in them has been recorded in the register.[2612] This is subject to s 1087(3) of the CA 2006 (extent of obligation to retain material not available for public inspection).

The registrar is not under any obligation to keep the originals of documents delivered in electronic form, provided the information contained in them has been recorded in the register.[2613]

Section 1083 of the CA 2006 applies to documents held by the registrar when this section came into force as well as to documents subsequently received.[2614]

Section 1083 of the CA 2006 replaces s 707A(2) of the CA 1985, with the difference that the obligation on the registrar to keep the originals of documents received under the CA 2006 only applies for three years, whereas it was ten years under s 707A(2) of the CA 1985. It should also be noted that the obligation to retain originals does not extend to an original document provided electronically as long as the information itself has been placed on the register.

Records relating to companies that have been dissolved etc

13.30 The CA 2006 makes provision in respect of records of companies that have been dissolved. Section 1,084 of the CA 2006 applies in three circumstances where:

(a)   a company is dissolved;[2615] or
(b)   an overseas company ceases to have any connection with the United Kingdom, by virtue of which it is required to register particulars under s 1046 of the CA 2006;[2616] or
(c)   a credit or financial institution ceases to be within s 1050 of the CA 2006 (overseas institutions required to file accounts with the registrar).[2617]

The term 'company' includes a company provisionally or completely registered under the Joint Stock Companies Act 1844 (c 110).[2618]

[2612] CA 2006, s 1083(1).   [2613] CA 2006, s 1083(2).   [2614] CA 2006, s 1083(3).
[2615] CA 2006, s 1084(1)(a).   [2616] CA 2006, s 1084(1)(b).   [2617] CA 2006, s 1084(21)(c).
[2618] CA 2006, s 1084(4).

At any time after two years from the date on which it appears to the registrar that (a) the company has been dissolved;[2619] or (b) the overseas company has ceased to have any connection with the United Kingdom by virtue of which it is required to register particulars under s 1046 of the CA 2006;[2620] or (c) the credit or financial institution has ceased to be within s 1050 of the CA 2006 (overseas institutions required to file accounts with the registrar),[2621] the registrar may direct that records relating to the company or institution may be removed to the Public Record Office or, as the case may be, the Public Record Office of Northern Ireland.[2622]

The records in respect of which such a direction is given must be disposed of under the enactments relating to that Office and the rules made under them.[2623] Section 1084 of the CA 2006 does not extend to Scotland.[2624]

Section 1084 of the CA 2006 replaces ss 707(3) and (4) of the CA 1985. Records may be transferred to the Public Records Office two years after a company has been dissolved. It also makes equivalent provision for certain overseas companies which, for example, by ceasing to have any connection with the United Kingdom, are no longer caught by United Kingdom regulatory requirements.

Inspection of the register

13.31 Sections 1085–1092 of the CA 2006 are concerned with inspection of the register.

Section 1085 of the CA 2006 provides that there is a right for any person to inspect the register.[2625] The right of inspection extends to the originals of documents delivered to the registrar in hard copy form if, and only if, the record kept by the registrar of the contents of the document is illegible or unavailable. The period for which such originals are to be kept is limited by s 1083(1) of the CA 2006.[2626]

Section 1085 of the CA 2006 is, however, subject to s 1087 of the CA 2006 (material not available for public inspection).[2627]

The objective of this section makes it clear that any person may inspect the register. Searchers will, however, have a right to inspect the original of a hard copy document, only where the registrar still retains it, and where the public record kept by the registrar and derived from it is illegible or unavailable.

Right to copy of material on the register

13.32 Section 1086 of the CA 2006 is concerned with the right to copy material on the register. Any person may require a copy of any material on

---

[2619] CA 2006, s 1084(2)(a). [2620] CA 2006, s 1084(2)(b). [2621] CA 2006, s 1084(2)(c).
[2622] CA 2006, s 1084(2). [2623] CA 2006, s 1084(3). [2624] CA 2006, s 1084(5).
[2625] CA 2006, s 1085(1). [2626] CA 2006, s 1085(2). [2627] CA 2006, s 1085(3).

the register.[2628] The fee for any such copy of material derived from a document subject to the Directive disclosure requirements (see s 1078 of the CA 2006), whether in hard copy or electronic form, must not exceed the administrative cost of providing it.[2629]

Section 1086 of the CA 2006 is subject to s 1087 of the CA 2006 (material not available for public inspection).[2630]

Section 1086 of the CA 2006 makes clear that any person is entitled to a copy of material on the register. Consistent with the provisions of the amended First Company Law Directive (68/151/EEC), this section provides that the fee for a copy may not exceed the administrative cost of providing the service.

Material not available for public inspection

13.33 Section 1087 of the CA 2006 sets out certain circumstances where the material will not be available for public inspection. The following material will not be made available by the registrar for public inspection:[2631]

(a) the contents of any document sent to the registrar containing views expressed pursuant to s 56 of the CA 2006 (comments on proposal by company to use certain words or expressions in its company name);[2632]

(b) protected information within s 242(1) of the CA 2006 (directors' residential addresses: restriction on disclosure by registrar) or any corresponding provision of regulations under s 1046 of the CA 2006 (overseas companies);[2633]

(c) any application to the registrar under s 1024 of the CA 2006 (application for administrative restoration to the register) that has not yet been determined or was not successful;[2634]

(d) any document received by the registrar in connection with the giving or withdrawal of consent under s 1075 of the CA 2006 (informal correction of documents);[2635]

(e) any application or other document delivered to the registrar under s 1088 of the CA 2006 (application to make address unavailable for public inspection) and any address in respect of which such an application is successful;[2636]

(f) any application or other document delivered to the registrar under s 1095 of the CA 2006 (application for rectification of register);[2637]

(g) any court order under s 1096 of the CA 2006 (rectification of the register under court order) that the court has directed under s 1097 of

[2628] CA 2006, s 1086(1).   [2629] CA 2006, s 1086(2).   [2630] CA 2006, s 1086(3).
[2631] See CA 2006, s 1087(1).   [2632] CA 2006, s 1087(1)(a).   [2633] CA 2006, s 1087(1)(b).
[2634] CA 2006, s 1087(1)(c).   [2635] CA 2006, s 1087(1)(d).   [2636] CA 2006, s 1087(1)(e).
[2637] CA 2006, s 1087(1)(f).

the CA 2006 (powers of court on ordering removal of material from the register);[2638]

(h) the contents of any instrument creating or evidencing a charge and delivered to the registrar under s 860 of the CA 2006 (registration of company charges: England and Wales or Northern Ireland);[2639] or any certified copy of an instrument creating or evidencing a charge and delivered to the registrar under s 878 CA 2006 (registration of company charges: Scotland);[2640]

(i) any e-mail address, identification code or password deriving from a document delivered for the purpose of authorising or facilitating electronic filing procedures or providing information by telephone;[2641]

(j) the contents of any documents held by the registrar pending a decision of the Regulator of Community Interest Companies under s 36 or s 38 of the Companies (Audit, Investigations and Community Enterprise) Act 2004 (c 27) (decision on eligibility for registration as community interest company) and that the registrar is not later required to record;[2642]

(k) any other material excluded from public inspection by or under any other enactment.[2643]

A restriction applying by reference to material deriving from a particular description of document does not affect the availability for public inspection of the same information contained in material derived from another description of document in relation to which no such restriction applies.[2644]

The material to which s 1087 of the CA 2006 applies need not be retained by the registrar for longer than appears to the registrar reasonably necessary for the purposes for which the material was delivered to the registrar.[2645]

This section sets out a number of exceptions to the rights to inspect and copy material on the register. They include, for example, 'protected information', that is, information about directors' home addresses covered by Part 10, Chapter 8 of the CA 2006. This section makes clear that the fact that certain material (for example, an address) which has been placed on the register as a result of the filing of two or more different types of document, is confidential in one of those contexts, does not mean that it cannot be made public in its other context.

Application to registrar to make address unavailable for public inspection

13.34 Section 1088 of the CA 2006 deals with an application to the registrar to make an address unavailable for public inspection. The Secretary of State

---

[2638] CA 2006, s 1087(1)(g). [2639] CA 2006, s 1087(1)(h)(i).
[2640] CA 2006, s 1087(1)(h)(ii). [2641] CA 2006, s 1087(1)(i). [2642] CA 2006, s 1087(1)(j).
[2643] CA 2006, s 1087(1)(k). [2644] CA 2006, s 1087(2). [2645] CA 2006, s 1087(3).

may make provision by regulations requiring the registrar, on application, to make an address on the register unavailable for public inspection.[2646]

The regulations may make provision as to:

(a)   who may make an application;[2647]
(b)   the grounds on which an application may be made;[2648]
(c)   the information to be included in and documents to accompany an application;[2649]
(d)   the notice to be given of an application and of its outcome;[2650] and
(e)   how an application is to be determined.[2651]

Any provision under s 1088(2)(e) of the CA 2006 may in particular confer a discretion on the registrar;[2652] or provide for a question to be referred to a person other than the registrar for the purposes of determining the application.[2653]

An application must specify the address to be removed from the register and indicate where on the register it is.[2654]

The regulations may provide that an address is not to be made unavailable for public inspection under this section unless replaced by a service address;[2655] and that in such a case the application must specify a service address.[2656]

The regulations under this section are subject to affirmative resolution procedure.[2657]

Section 1088 of the CA 2006 is a new provision. It confers power on the Secretary of State to make regulations providing for applications to remove addresses from the public record held by Companies House. The regulations will set out the details of who can apply, and on what ground, and the procedure involved.

Form of application for inspection or copy

13.35 The CA 2006 addresses the form of application required for inspection of copy. This is set out in s 1089 of the CA 2006. The registrar may specify the form and manner in which application is to be made for inspection under s 1085 of the CA 2006;[2658] or a copy under s 1086 of the CA 2006.[2659]

As from 1 January 2007, applications in respect of documents subject to the Directive disclosure requirements, may be submitted to the registrar in hard copy or electronic form, as the applicant chooses. This does not affect

[2646] CA 2006, s 1088(1).   [2647] CA 2006, s 1088(2)(a).   [2648] CA 2006, s 1088(2)(b).
[2649] CA 2006, s 1088(2)(c).   [2650] CA 2006, s 1088(2)(d).   [2651] CA 2006, s 1088(2)(e).
[2652] CA 2006, s 1088(3)(a).   [2653] CA 2006, s 1088(3)(b).   [2654] CA 2006, s 1088(4).
[2655] CA 2006, s 1088(5)(a).   [2656] CA 2006, s 1088(5)(b).   [2657] CA 2006, s 1088(6).
[2658] CA 2006, s 1089(1)(a).   [2659] CA 2006, s 1089(1)(b).

the registrar's power under s 1089(1) of the CA 2006 to impose requirements in respect of other matters.[2660]

Form and manner in which copies to be provided

13.36 Section 1090 of the CA 2006 applies as regards the form and manner in which copies are to be provided under s 1086 of the CA 2006.[2661] As from 1 January 2007, copies of documents subject to the Directive disclosure requirements must be provided in hard copy or electronic form, as the applicant chooses.[2662]

This is subject to the following proviso. The registrar is not obliged by s 1090(2) of the CA 2006 to provide copies in electronic form of a document that was delivered to the registrar in hard copy form, if the document was delivered to the registrar on or before 31 December 1996;[2663] or the document was delivered to the registrar on or before 31 December 2006, and ten years or more elapsed between the date of delivery, and the date of receipt of the first application for a copy on or after 1 January 2007.[2664]

In any other case, the registrar may determine the form and manner in which copies are to be provided.[2665]

Certification of copies as accurate

13.37 Section 1091 of the CA 2006 states that copies provided under s 1086 of the CA 2006 in hard copy form must be certified as true copies, unless the applicant dispenses with such certification.[2666] Copies so provided in electronic form, must not be certified as true copies unless the applicant expressly requests such certification.[2667]

A copy provided under s 1086 of the CA 2006, certified by the registrar (whose official position it is unnecessary to prove) to be an accurate record of the contents of the original document, is in all legal proceedings admissible in evidence as of equal validity with the original document;[2668] and as evidence (in Scotland, sufficient evidence) of any fact stated in the original document of which direct oral evidence would be admissible.[2669]

The Secretary of State may make provision by regulations as to the manner in which such a certificate is to be provided in a case where the copy is provided in electronic form.[2670]

Except in the case of documents that are subject to the Directive disclosure requirements (see s 1078 of the CA 2006), copies provided by the registrar

---

[2660] CA 2006, s 1089(2). [2661] CA 2006, s 1090(1). [2662] CA 2006, s 1090(2).
[2663] CA 2006, s 1090(3)(a). [2664] CA 2006, s 1090(3)(b). [2665] CA 2006, s 1090(4).
[2666] CA 2006, s 1091(1). [2667] CA 2006, s 1091(2). [2668] CA 2006, s 1091(3)(a).
[2669] CA 2006, s 1091(3)(b). [2670] CA 2006, s 1901(4).

may, instead of being certified in writing to be an accurate record, be sealed with the registrar's official seal.[2671]

The effect of ss 1089–1091 of the CA 2006 is to enable the registrar to specify the form and manner in which applications for inspection of the register, or copies of material on it, must be made, and to determine the form and manner in which copies are provided. They are subject to important exemptions, arising from the amended First Company Law Directive (68/151/EEC), in respect of the documents listed at s 1078 of the CA 2006. Section 1089 of the CA 2006 states that applications must be capable of being submitted in hard copy or in electronic form, as the applicant chooses. Section 1090 of the CA 2006 states that the applicant is entitled to insist on receiving the copies themselves in hard copy or in electronic form (subject to an exception in respect of documents delivered before 1 January 2007).

Section 1091 of the CA 2006, again responding to provisions of the amended First Company Law Directive (68/151/EEC), makes clear that, unless the applicant chooses otherwise, copies of information provided in hard copy must be certified as true copies; but electronic copies must not be so certified. Section 1091(3) of the CA 2006 provides for the evidential status of certified hard copies in legal proceedings. The Secretary of State will have the power to prescribe by regulations methods of certification for copies provided by electronic means.

Issue of process for production of record kept by the registrar

13.38 Section 1092 of the CA 2006 deals with issue of process for production of records kept by the registrar. It states that no process for compelling the production of a record kept by the registrar, shall issue from any court except with the permission of the court.[2672] Any such process must bear on it a statement that it is issued with the permission of the court.[2673]

Section 1092 of the CA 2006 restates s 709(5) of the CA 1985 and provides that no one can take proceedings against the registrar for production of records, without first obtaining the permission of the court.

Correction or removal of material on the register

Registrar's notice to resolve inconsistency on the register

13.39 Section 1093 of the CA 2006 deals with the registrar's notice to resolve inconsistency on the register. Where it appears to the registrar that the information contained in a document delivered to the registrar, is inconsistent with other information on the register, the registrar may give notice to the

[2671] CA 2006, s 1901(5).   [2672] CA 2006, s 1092(1).   [2673] CA 2006, s 1092(2).

company to which the document relates stating in what respects the information contained in it appears to be inconsistent with other information on the register;[2674] and requiring the company to take steps to resolve the inconsistency.[2675]

The notice must state the date on which it is issued;[2676] and require the delivery to the registrar, within 14 days after that date, of such replacement or additional documents as may be required to resolve the inconsistency.[2677]

If the necessary documents are not delivered within the period specified, an offence is committed by the company;[2678] and every officer of the company who is in default.[2679] A person guilty of an offence under s 1093(3) of the CA 2006 is liable on summary conviction to a fine not exceeding level 5 on the standard scale and, for continued contravention, a daily default fine not exceeding one-tenth of level 5 on the standard scale.[2680]

Section 1093 of the CA 2006 enables the registrar to notify a company of an apparent inconsistency in the information on the register. An example might be where a document is received notifying the removal of a director, where there is no record of his appointment. In such circumstances, the registrar may give notice to the company requiring them to resolve the inconsistency within 14 days by providing additional or replacement documents. Failure to do so on the company's part will be an offence.

Administrative removal of material from the register

13.40 Section 1094 of the CA 2006 provides that the registrar may remove from the register anything that there was power, but no duty, to include.[2681]

This power is exercisable, in particular, so as to remove unnecessary material within the meaning of s 1074 of the CA 2006;[2682] and material derived from a document that has been replaced under s 1076 of the CA 2006 (replacement of document not meeting requirements for proper delivery), or s 1093 of the CA 2006 (notice to remedy inconsistency on the register).[2683]

Section 1094 of the CA 2006, however, does not authorise the removal from the register of:

(a) anything whose registration has had legal consequences in relation to the company as regards:

- its formation;[2684]
- a change of name;[2685]

[2674] CA 2006, s 1093(1)(a).   [2675] CA 2006, s 1093(1)(b).   [2676] CA 2006, s 1093(2)(a).
[2677] CA 2006, s 1093(2)(b).   [2678] CA 2006, s 1093(3)(a).   [2679] CA 2006, s 1093(3)(b).
[2680] CA 2006, s 1093(4).   [2681] CA 2006, s 1094(1).   [2682] CA 2006, s 1094(2)(a).
[2683] CA 2006, s 1094(2)(b).   [2684] CA 2006, s 1094(3)(a)(i).   [2685] CA 2006, s 1094(3)(a)(ii).

- its re-registration;[2686]
- its becoming or ceasing to be a community interest company;[2687]
- a reduction of capital;[2688]
- a change of registered office;[2689]
- the registration of a charge;[2690] or
- its dissolution;[2691]

(b) an address that is a person's registered address for the purposes of s 1140 of the CA 2006 (service of documents on directors, secretaries and others).[2692]

On or before removing any material under this section (otherwise than at the request of the company), the registrar must give notice to the person by whom the material was delivered (if the identity, and name and address of that person are known);[2693] or to the company to which the material relates (if notice cannot be given under para (a) and the identity of that company is known).[2694]

The notice must state what material the registrar proposes to remove, or has removed, and on what grounds;[2695] and state the date on which it is issued.[2696]

This section empowers the registrar to remove from the register information that he had a power, but no duty to enter. Under s 1094(4) of the CA 2006, the registrar will need to send a notice to the presenter of the information in question, or to the company to which the materials relates, on or before removing the material.

The registrar may not, however, be able to remove information from the register where registration has had legal consequences for the company as regards certain key events, as set out in s 1094(3) of the CA 2006, including, for example, its formation or a change of registered office.

Rectification of register on application to registrar

13.41 Section 1095 of the CA 2006 applies to rectification of register on application to registrar. The Secretary of State may make provision by regulations requiring the registrar, on application, to remove from the register material of a description specified in the regulations that derives from anything invalid or ineffective or that was done without the authority of the

---

[2686] CA 2006, s 1094(3)(a)(iii).   [2687] CA 2006, s 1094(3)(a)(iv).
[2688] CA 2006, s 1094(3)(a)(v).   [2689] CA 2006, s 1094(3)(a)(vi).
[2690] CA 2006, s 1094(3)(a)(vii).   [2691] CA 2006, s 1094(3)(a).
[2692] CA 2006, s 1094(3)(b).   [2693] CA 2006, s 1094(a).   [2694] CA 2006, s 1094(4)(b).
[2695] CA 2006, s 1094(5)(a).   [2696] CA 2006, s 1094(5)(b).

company;[2697] or is factually inaccurate, or is derived from something that is factually inaccurate or forged.[2698]

The regulations may make provision as to who may make an application;[2699] the information to be included in and documents to accompany an application;[2700] the notice to be given of an application and of its outcome;[2701] a period in which objections to an application may be made;[2702] and how an application is to be determined.[2703]

An application must specify what is to be removed from the register, and indicate where on the register it is;[2704] and be accompanied by a statement that the material specified in the application complies with this section and the regulations.[2705]

If no objections are made to the application, the registrar may accept the statement as sufficient evidence that the material specified in the application should be removed from the register.[2706]

Where anything is removed from the register under this section the registration of which had legal consequences as mentioned in s 1094(3) of the CA 2006, any person appearing to the court to have a sufficient interest may apply to the court for such consequential orders as appear just with respect to the legal effect (if any) to be accorded to the material by virtue of its having appeared on the register.[2707]

Any regulations under this section are subject to affirmative resolution procedure.[2708]

Section 1095 of the CA 2006 gives the Secretary of State a power to make regulations under which, following a successful application, the registrar may be required to remove certain kinds of material from the register. The procedure may only cover certain types of document. It will operate in respect of material that derives from something that is invalid or ineffective, or from something that was done without the authority of the company (this would cover forms filed without authority); and material that is factually inaccurate or forged or derives from something which is factually inaccurate or forged.

It should be noted that the registrar will only act as a result of an application and the regulations will specify such issues as who may make the application, what information will need to be provided with it, and so on. Where the material that is removed is of kind whose registration has had legal consequences, s 1095(5) of the CA 2006 provides that interested parties will have the right to go to court to obtain an order as to the material's legal effect.

[2697] CA 2006, s 1095(1)(a). See regulations 3 and 4 of the Companies (Registrar of Companies) Regulations 2008.
[2698] CA 2006, s 1095(1)(b).   [2699] CA 2006, s 1095(2)(a).   [2700] CA 2006, s 1095(2)(b).
[2701] CA 2006, s 1095(2)(c).   [2702] CA 2006, s 1095(2)(d).   [2703] CA 2006, s 1095(2)(e).
[2704] CA 2006, s 1095(3)(a).   [2705] CA 2006, s 1095(3)(b).   [2706] CA 2006, s 1095(4).
[2707] CA 2006, s 1095(5).   [2708] CA 2006, s 1095(6).

Rectification of the register under court order

13.42 Under s 1096 of the CA 2006, the registrar must remove from the register any material that derives from anything that the court has declared to be invalid or ineffective, or to have been done without the authority of the company;[2709] or that a court declares to be factually inaccurate, or to be derived from something that is factually inaccurate, or forged,[2710] and that the court directs should be removed from the register.

The court order must specify what is to be removed from the register and indicate where on the register it is.[2711] The court must not make an order for the removal from the register of anything the registration of which had legal consequences as mentioned in s 1094(3) of the CA 2006, unless satisfied that the presence of the material on the register has caused, or may cause, damage to the company;[2712] and that the company's interest in removing the material outweighs any interest of other persons in the material continuing to appear on the register.[2713]

Where in such a case the court does make an order for removal, it may make such consequential orders as appear just with respect to the legal effect (if any) to be accorded to the material by virtue of its having appeared on the register.[2714]

A copy of the court's order must be sent to the registrar for registration.[2715]

Section 1096 of the CA 2006 does not apply where the court has other, specific, powers to deal with the matter, for example, under the provisions of Part 15 of the CA 2006 relating to the revision of defective accounts and reports;[2716] or ss 873 or 888 of the CA 2006 (rectification of the register of charges).[2717]

Under s 1096 of the CA 2006, the registrar will also be required to remove material from the register where there is a court order to that effect. The court's rectification power will operate in the same circumstances as the registrar's power following regulations made under s 1094 of the CA 2006. However, the court's power will be of general application. For example, there will be not be a limit on the types of document covered. The court will be able to make an order to remove material from the register, where its presence on the register has caused damage or may cause damage to the company, and the company's interests in removing the material outweigh the interests of others in it continuing to be on the register. The court will be able to make such consequential orders as appear just regarding the period that the information was on the register, and the effect of the information being on the register during that period. The court's rectification power will not operate where the court has other rectification powers (e.g. in relation to accounts or charges).

[2709] CA 2006, s 1096(1)(a).   [2710] CA 2006, s 1096(1)(b).   [2711] CA 2006, s 1096(2).
[2712] CA 2006, s 1096(3)(a).   [2713] CA 2006, s 1096(3)(b).   [2714] CA 2006, s 1096(4).
[2715] CA 2006, s 1096(5).   [2716] CA 2006, s 1096(6)(a).   [2717] CA 2006, s 1096(6)(b).

Powers of the court on ordering removal of material from the register

13.43 Section 1097 of the CA 2006 is concerned with powers of court on ordering removal of material from the register. Where the court makes an order for the removal of anything from the register under s 1096 of the CA 2006 (rectification of the register), it may give directions.[2718] It may direct that any note on the register that is related to the material that is the subject of the court's order shall be removed from the register.[2719] It may direct that its order must not be available for public inspection as part of the register.[2720] It may direct that no note must be made on the register as a result of its order;[2721] or that any such note must be restricted to such matters as may be specified by the court.[2722]

The court must not give any direction under this section unless it is satisfied that the presence on the register of the note or, as the case may be, of an unrestricted note;[2723] or the availability for public inspection of the courts order,[2724] may cause damage to the company, and that the company's interest in non-disclosure outweighs any interest of other persons in disclosure.[2725]

Section 1097 of the CA 2006 provides that where a court decides that certain information should be removed from the public register, the court may also make directions as to annotations (removing notes that are already there, or directing that now new notes appear as a result of its order – or that notes appear in a restricted form), and as to whether its own order should be available for public inspection.

Public notice of removal of certain material from the register

13.44 Section 1098 of the CA 2006 deals with public notice of removal of certain material from the register. The registrar must publish in the Gazette;[2726] or in accordance with s 1116 of the CA 2006 (alternative means of giving public notice),[2727] notice of the removal from the register of any document subject to the Directive disclosure requirements (see s 1078 of the CA 2006) or of any material derived from such a document.

The notice must state the name and registered number of the company, the description of the document and the date of receipt.[2728]

Section 1098 of the CA 2006 provides for the registrar to give public notice that he has received certain documents relating to a company, in the Gazette, or through some other form of publication. It creates the corresponding obligation for him to give notice where he removes such material.

[2718] CA 2006, s 1097(1).   [2719] CA 2006, s 1097(2).   [2720] CA 2006, s 1097(3).
[2721] CA 2006, s 1097(4)(a).   [2722] CA 2006, s 1097(4)(b).   [2723] CA 2006, s 1097(5)(a)(i).
[2724] CA 2006, s 1097(5)(a)(ii).   [2725] CA 2006, s 1097(5)(b).
[2726] CA 2006, s 1098(1)(a).   [2727] CA 2006, s 1098(1)(b).   [2728] CA 2006, s 1098(2).

The registrar's index of company names

13.45 Sections 1099 to 1101 of the CA 2006 are concerned with the registrar's index of company names.

Section 1099 of the CA 2006 provides that the registrar of companies must keep an index of the names of the companies and other bodies. This is known as 'the registrar's index of company names'.[2729]

Section 1099 of the CA 2006 applies to UK-registered companies;[2730] any body to which any provision of the Companies Acts applies by virtue of regulations under s 1043 of the CA 2006 (unregistered companies);[2731] and overseas companies that have registered particulars with the registrar under s 1046 of the CA 2006, other than companies that appear to the registrar not to be required to do so.[2732]

Section 1099 of the CA 2006 also applies to limited partnerships registered in the United Kingdom;[2733] limited liability partnerships incorporated in the United Kingdom;[2734] European Economic Interest Groupings registered in the United Kingdom;[2735] open-ended investment companies authorised in the United Kingdom;[2736] societies registered under the Industrial and Provident Societies Act 1965 (c 12) or the Industrial and Provident Societies Act (Northern Ireland) 1969 (c 24 (NI)).[2737]

The Secretary of State may by order amend s 1099(3) of the CA 2006 by the addition of any description of a body;[2738] or by the deletion of any description of a body.[2739]

Any such order is subject to negative resolution procedure.[2740]

Section 1099 of the CA 2006 replaces and updates s 714 of the CA 1982. It provides for the registrar of companies to keep an index of the names not only of companies incorporated under Companies Acts, but also of business entities formed under other legislation, and overseas companies with a UK branch or place of business. It also provides power for regulations to update the categories of business entities that are included in the index.

Right to inspect index

13.46 There is a right granted to inspect the public index. Section 1100 of the CA 2006 states that any person may inspect the registrar's index of company names.

Section 1100 of the CA 2006 retains the public right to inspect the index (it can be searched online, without charge, at www.companieshouse.gov.uk). The index of company names is important, not only as the means of access to

---

[2729] CA 2006, s 1099(1).   [2730] CA 2006, s 1099(2)(a).   [2731] CA 2006, s 1099(2)(b).
[2732] CA 2006, s 1099(2)(c).   [2733] CA 2006, s 1099(3)(a).   [2734] CA 2006, s 1099(3)(b).
[2735] CA 2006, s 1099(3)(c).   [2736] CA 2006, s 1099(3)(d).   [2737] CA 2006, s 1099(3)(e).
[2738] CA 2006, s 1099(4)(a).   [2739] CA 2006, s 1099(4)(b).   [2740] CA 2006, s 1099(5).

the information on the public record of companies incorporated in Great Britain, but also as the list of names with which every proposed new name is compared, to ensure that the public is not confused by the simultaneous appearance on the register of two names that are very similar to that of an existing entity.

Power to amend enactments relating to bodies other than companies

13.47 Section 1101 of the CA 2006 deals with power to amend enactments relating to bodies other than companies. The Secretary of State may by regulations amend the enactments relating to any description of body for the time being within s 1099(3) of the CA 2006 (bodies other than companies whose names are to be entered in the registrar's index), so as to require the registrar to be provided with information as to the names of bodies registered, incorporated, authorised or otherwise regulated under those enactments;[2741] and make provision in relation to such bodies corresponding to that made by s 66 of the CA 2006 (company name not to be the same as another in the index), and ss 67 and 68 of the CA 2006 (power to direct change of company name in case of similarity to existing name).[2742]

Any regulations under this section are subject to affirmative resolution procedure.[2743]

Section 1101 of the CA 2006 provides power for the Secretary of State to amend the rules for the names that can be adopted by other business entities on the index of company names. This power is subject to affirmative resolution procedure. Each category of business entity was subject to its own rules, which include various safeguards to minimise the risk of public confusion. These rules differed from those that applied to companies in particular as regards the adoption of a name the same or very similar to one already on the index. This lack of reciprocity was a weakness of the existing system, which this section provided the power to address.

Language requirements: translation

13.48 Sections 1102–1107 of the CA 2006 deal with the language requirements with respect to translation.

Application of language requirements

13.49 Section 1102 of the CA 2006 states that the provisions listed below apply to all documents required to be delivered to the registrar under any

---

[2741] CA 2006, s 1101(1)(a).   [2742] CA 2006, s 1101(1)(b).   [2743] CA 2006, s 1101(2).

provision of the Companies Acts;[2744] or the Insolvency Act 1986 (c 45) or the Insolvency (Northern Ireland) Order 1989 (SI 1989/2405 (NI 19)).[2745]

The Secretary of State may make provision by regulations applying all or any of the listed provisions, with or without modifications, in relation to documents delivered to the registrar under any other enactment.[2746]

The provisions are s 1103 of the CA 2006 (documents to be drawn up and delivered in English); s 1104 of the CA 2006 (documents relating to Welsh companies); s 1105 of the CA 2006 (documents that may be drawn up and delivered in other languages); and s 1107 of the CA 2006 (certified translations).[2747]

Any regulations under this section are subject to negative resolution procedure.[2748]

Documents to be drawn up and delivered in English

13.50 Section 1103 of the CA 2006 states that the general rule is that all documents required to be delivered to the registrar must be drawn up and delivered in English.[2749]

This is subject to s 1104 of the CA 2006 (documents relating to Welsh companies) and s 1105 of the CA 2006 (documents that may be drawn up and delivered in other languages).[2750]

Sections 1102 and 1103 of the CA 2006 sets out language requirements in respect of the documents. Section 1103 of the CA 2006 sets out the general rule that all documents must be in English (subject to exceptions). Section 1102 of the CA 2006 provides that this general rule, and its exceptions, applies automatically to documents required under the Companies Acts and Insolvency Act 1986 (and its Northern Ireland equivalent).

There are, however, a variety of other pieces of legislation that may require companies, in certain circumstances, to supply material to the registrar. Depending on the nature of the particular requirement and its origin (for example, whether it responds to European law), it may or may not be appropriate to apply the language provisions of the CA 2006 unchanged to such material. Section 1102(2) of the CA 2006), therefore, enables the Secretary of State to make regulations to apply specified requirements to documents filed under other legislation.

Documents relating to Welsh companies

13.51 The CA 2006 envisages there will be documents relating to Welsh companies. Section 1104 of the CA 2006 addresses this position. Any documents

[2744] CA 2006, s 1102(1)(a).   [2745] CA 2006, s 1102(1)(b).   [2746] CA 2006, s 1102(2).
[2747] CA 2006, s 1102(3).   [2748] CA 2006, s 1102(4).   [2749] CA 2006, s 1103(1).
[2750] CA 2006, s 1103(2).

relating to a Welsh company may be drawn up and delivered to the registrar in Welsh.[2751]

On delivery to the registrar, any such document must be accompanied by a certified translation into English, unless it is of a description excepted from that requirement by regulations made by the Secretary of State;[2752] or in a form prescribed in Welsh (or partly in Welsh and partly in English) by virtue of s 26 of the Welsh Language Act 1993 (c 38).[2753]

Where a document is properly delivered to the registrar in Welsh without a certified translation into English, the registrar must obtain such a translation if the document is to be available for public inspection. The translation is treated as if delivered to the registrar in accordance with the same provision as the original.[2754]

A Welsh company may deliver to the registrar a certified translation into Welsh of any document in English that relates to the company and is or has been delivered to the registrar.[2755]

Section 1105 of the CA 2006 (which requires certified translations into English of documents delivered to the registrar in another language) does not apply to a document relating to a Welsh company that is drawn up and delivered in Welsh.[2756]

Section 1104 of the CA 2006 provides an exception to the general rule in s 1103 of the CA 2006: that documents relating to Welsh companies may be drawn up and filed in Welsh (and sometimes only in Welsh). It replaces, without any substantive change, s 710B of the CA 2006.

Documents that may be drawn up and delivered in other languages

13.52 Section 1105 of the CA 2006 deals with documents that may be drawn up and delivered in other languages. The documents may be drawn up and delivered to the registrar in a language other than English, but when delivered to the registrar they must be accompanied by a certified translation into English.[2757]

Section 1105 of the CA 2006 applies to:

(a) agreements required to be forwarded to the registrar under Chapter 3 of Part 3 of the CA 2006 (agreements affecting the company's constitution);[2758]

(b) documents required to be delivered under s 400(2)(e) or s 401(2)(f) of

---

[2751] CA 2006, s 1104(1).
[2752] CA 2006, s 1104(2)(a). See regulation 5 of the Companies (Registrar of Companies) Regulations 2008.
[2753] CA 2006, s 1104(2)(b). [2754] CA 2006, s 1104(3). [2755] CA 2006, s 1104(4).
[2756] CA 2006, s 1104(5). [2757] CA 2006, s 1105(1). [2758] CA 2006, s 1105(2)(a).

the CA 2006 (company included in accounts of larger group: required to deliver copy of group accounts);[2759]

(c)   instruments or copy instruments required to be delivered under Part 25 of the CA 2006 (company charges);[2760]

(d)   documents of any other description specified in regulations made by the Secretary of State.[2761]

Any regulations under this section are subject to negative resolution procedure.[2762]

Section 1105 of the CA 2006 sets out the circumstances in which documents may be drawn up and filed in other languages, but requires them to be accompanied by a certified translation into English. These documents are listed in s 1105(2) of the CA 2006 and include agreements affecting the company's constitution, documents relating to group accounts for companies in a group, and instruments relating to a company charges. For some companies, documents of these sorts may well originate in languages other than English, and there may be an interest in ensuring that the original version is registered with the registrar. Section 1105(2)(d) of the CA 2006 also allows the Secretary of State to extend the categories of documents to which this section applies.

Voluntary filing of transactions

13.53 Section 1106 of the CA 2006 deals with the voluntary filing of translations. A company may deliver to the registrar, one or more certified translations of any document relating to the company that is or has been delivered to the registrar.[2763]

The Secretary of State may by regulations specify the languages;[2764] and the descriptions of document,[2765] in relation to which this facility is available.

The regulations must provide that it is available as from 1 January 2007 in relation to all the official languages of the European Union;[2766] and in relation to all documents subject to the Directive disclosure requirements (see s 1078 of the CA 2006).[2767]

The power of the registrar to impose requirements as to the form and manner of delivery includes the power to impose requirements as to the identification of the original document and the delivery of the translation in a form and manner enabling it to be associated with the original.[2768]

[2759] CA 2006, s 1105(2)(b).   [2760] CA 2006, s 1105(2)(c).

[2761] CA 2006, s 1105(2)(d). See regulation 6 of the Companies (Registrar of Companies) Regulations 2008.

[2762] CA 2006, s 1105(3).   [2763] CA 2006, s 1106.   [2764] CA 2006, s 1106(2)(a).

[2765] CA 2006, s 1106(2)(b).   [2766] CA 2006, s 1106(3)(a).   [2767] CA 2006, s 1106(3)(b).

[2768] CA 2006, s 1106(4).

Any regulations under this section are subject to negative resolution procedure.[2769]

Section 1106 of the CA 2006 does not apply where the original document was delivered to the registrar before this section came into force.[2770]

The main objective of s 1106 of the CA 2006 is to implement aspects of the amended First Company Law Directive (68/151/EEC). It provides that companies may send the registrar certified transactions of documents relating to the company. Section 1106(2) of the CA 2006 enables the Secretary of State to set out in regulations those languages and documents in relation to which this facility is available. Section 1106(3) of the CA 2006 provides that these regulations must as a minimum, specify the official languages of the EU, and the documents covered by the amended First Company Law Directive (68/151/EEC) (see s 1078 of the CA 2006), to ensure compliance with that directive. However, other languages (and categories of document) may be covered by regulations.

Certified translations

13.54 Section 1107 of the CA 2007 is concerned with certified translations. The term 'certified translation' means a translation certified to be a correct translation.[2771]

In the case of any discrepancy between the original language version of a document and a certified translation, the company may not rely on the translation as against a third party;[2772] but a third party may rely on the translation unless the company shows that the third party had knowledge of the original.[2773] A 'third party' is defined as a person other than the company or the registrar.[2774]

Section 1107 of the CA 2006 provides that a 'certified translation' is one that has been certified in a manner prescribed by the registrar. It also provides that, where there is a discrepancy between an original and a translation, the company may not rely on the translation as against a third party, but the third party may rely on the translation (unless the company can show that the third party had knowledge of the original). This implements article 34a of the amended First Company Law Directive (68/151/EEC).

Language requirements: transliteration

13.55 Sections 1108–1110 of the CA 2006 are concerned with language requirements with regard to transliteration.

[2769] CA 2006, s 1106(5).   [2770] CA 2006, s 1106(6).   [2771] CA 2006, s 1107(1).
[2772] CA 2006, s 1107(2)(a).   [2773] CA 2006, s 1107(2)(b).   [2774] CA 2006, s 1107(3).

Transliteration of names and addresses: permitted characters

13.56 Section 1108 of the CA 2006 addresses the issue of transliteration of names and addresses, with particular reference to permitted characters. Names and addresses in a document delivered to the registrar must contain only letters, characters and symbols (including accents and other diacritical marks) that are permitted.[2775]

The Secretary of State may make provision by regulations as to the letters, characters and symbols (including accents and other diacritical marks) that are permitted;[2776] and permitting or requiring the delivery of documents in which names and addresses have not been transliterated into a permitted form.[2777]

Any regulations under this section are subject to negative resolution procedure.[2778]

Section 1108 of the CA 2006 is a new provision. It deals with the possibility that the name and address of a director or of an overseas company may use a character set (for example, that of Urdu or Japanese), which is different from those with which the bulk of Companies House's users are familiar. This section restricts the characters that are permitted for names and addresses in a document delivered to the registrar to those specified in regulations. The regulations, which are subject to negative resolution procedure, may also provide for names and addresses to be delivered in their original form.

Transliteration of names and addresses: voluntary transliteration into Roman characters

13.57 Section 1,109 of the CA 2006 states that where a name or address is or has been delivered to the registrar in a permitted form using other than Roman characters, the company may deliver to the registrar a transliteration into Roman characters.[2779]

The power of the registrar to impose requirements as to the form and manner of delivery includes the power to impose requirements as to the identification of the original document, and the delivery of the transliteration in a form and manner enabling it to be associated with the original.[2780]

Section 1109 of the CA 2006 is a new provision. It provides for the possibility that the Regulations made under s 1108 of the CA 2006 may permit letters and characters that are not drawn from the Roman alphabet, for example, Greek letters. The requirement for transliteration under that section, will not apply to names using such letters and characters. This section permits these names to be transliterated provided that certain requirements are met.

[2775] CA 2006, s 1108(1).   [2776] CA 2006, s 1108(2)(a).   [2777] CA 2006, s 1108(2)(b).
[2778] CA 2006, s 1108(3).   [2779] CA 2006, s 1109(1).   [2780] CA 2006, s 1109(2).

Transliteration of names and addresses: certification

13.58 The Secretary of State may make provision by regulations requiring the certification of transliterations and prescribing the form of certification.[2781] Different provision may be made for compulsory and voluntary transliterations.[2782]

Any regulations under this section are subject to negative resolution procedure.[2783]

Section 1110 of the CA 2006 is a new provision. It confers power on the Secretary of State to make regulations relating to transliteration of names and addresses. The regulations may distinguish between compulsory transliteration under s 1108 of the CA 2006 and voluntary transliteration under s 1109 of the CA 2006.

Supplementary provisions

13.59 Sections 1111–1120 of the CA 2006 are concerned with supplementary provisions to Part 35.

Registrar's requirements as to certification or verification

13.60 Section 1111 of the CA 2006 is concerned with the registrar's requirements as to certification or verification. Where a document required or authorised to be delivered to the registrar under any enactment is required to be certified as an accurate translation or transliteration;[2784] or to be certified as a correct copy or verified,[2785] the registrar may impose requirements as to the person, or description of person, by whom the certificate or verification is to be given.

The power conferred by s 1068 of the CA 2006 (registrar's requirements as to form, authentication and manner of delivery), is exercisable in relation to the certificate or verification as if it were a separate document.[2786]

Any requirements imposed under s 1111 of the CA 2006, must not be inconsistent with requirements imposed by any enactment with respect to the certification or verification of the document concerned.[2787]

Documents delivered to the registrar are sometimes required to be certified or verified in some way, such as for example, to the effect that they are an accurate translation. Section 1111 of the CA 2006 allows the registrar to impose requirements as to who must provide the relevant certification or verification. Section 1111(2) of the CA 2006 provides that the registrar's powers to specify requirements in relation to documents submitted to him

---

[2781] CA 2006, s 1110(1). [2782] CA 2006, s 1110(2). [2783] CA 2006, s 1110(3).
[2784] CA 2006, s 1111(1)(a). [2785] CA 2006, s 1111(1)(b). [2786] CA 2006, s 1111(2).
[2787] CA 2006, s 1111(3).

(s 1068 of the CA 2006), extends to the certification or verification as if it were a separate document.

General false statement offence

13.61 Section 1112 of the CA 2006 deals with the general false statement offence. This is a new provision. It states that it is an offence for a person knowingly or recklessly to deliver or cause to be delivered to the registrar, for any purpose of the Companies Acts, a document;[2788] or to make to the registrar, for any such purpose, a statement,[2789] that is misleading, false or deceptive in a material particular.

A person guilty of an offence under this section is liable on conviction on indictment, to imprisonment for a term not exceeding two years or a fine (or both);[2790] or on summary conviction in England and Wales, to imprisonment for a term not exceeding 12 months or to a fine not exceeding the statutory maximum (or both); in Scotland or Northern Ireland, to imprisonment for a term not exceeding six months, or to a fine not exceeding the statutory maximum (or both).[2791]

Section 1112 of the CA 2006 provides for a new offence of knowingly or recklessly delivering to the registrar information which is misleading, false or deceptive in a material particular. It responds to a recommendation of the Company Law Review Group.[2792] This new general offence makes it necessary to reproduce specific offences covering false information or false statements in respects of specific legislative requirements that were a feature of the CA 1985.

Enforcement of company's filing obligations

13.62 Section 1113 of the CA 2006 applies where a company has defaulted in complying with any obligation under the Companies Acts regarding delivering a document to the registrar;[2793] or giving notice to the registrar of any matter.[2794]

The registrar, or any member or creditor of the company, may give notice to the company requiring it to comply with the obligation.[2795]

If the company fails to make good the default within 14 days after service of the notice, the registrar, or any member or creditor of the company, may apply to the court for an order directing the company, and any specified officer of it, to make good the default within a specified time.[2796]

The court's order may provide that all costs (in Scotland, expenses) of or

---

[2788] CA 2006, s 1112(1)(a).   [2789] CA 2006, s 1112(1)(b).   [2790] CA 2006, s 1112(2)(a).
[2791] CA 2006, s 1112(2)(b).   [2792] *Final Report*, para 11.48.   [2793] CA 2006, s 1113(1)(a).
[2794] CA 2006, s 1113(1)(b).   [2795] CA 2006, s 1113(2).   [2796] CA 2006, s 1113(3).

incidental to the application are to be borne by the company or by any officers of it responsible for the default.[2797]

Section 1113 of the CA 2006 does not affect the operation of any enactment making it an offence, or imposing a civil penalty, for the default.[2798]

Section 1113 of the CA 2006 (which restates s 713 of the CA 1985) provides the mechanism for ensuring that companies can be compelled to comply with their obligations to file documents or give notices to the registrar. Where a company has defaulted on an obligation, the registrar himself, any member of the company, or any creditor, may serve a notice of the company requiring it to file. If the company continues the breach after 14 days, the applicant may apply to the court for an order requiring the company, or any specified officer of it, to make good the default. The court order may ensure that costs are borne by the company or its officers. Section 1113(5) of the CA 2006 provides that this process does not affect any offence or civil penalty arising from the company's failure to comply with the original requirement.

Application of provisions about documents and delivery

13.63 Section 1114 of the CA 2006 states that under Part 35 of the CA 2006, references to a 'document' means information recorded in any form;[2799] and references to delivering a document include forwarding, lodging, registering, sending, producing or submitting it or (in the case of a notice) giving it.[2800]

Except as otherwise provided, Part 35 of the CA 2006 applies in relation to the supply to the registrar of information otherwise than in documentary form as it applies in relation to the delivery of a document.[2801]

Section 1114 of the CA 2006, which replaces s 715A of the CA 1985, provides that 'document' means information recorded in any form, and that 'delivery' of a document includes forwarding, lodging, registering, producing or submitting it, or giving a notice. It also provides that requirements relating to 'documents' also apply (unless otherwise provided for) to information passed to the registrar in some other way. This caters for the possibility that information may not be 'recorded' in any form, for example (arguably) when it is sent via a website.

Supplementary provisions relating to electronic communications

13.64 Section 1115 of the CA 2006 states that the registrar's rules may require a company to give any necessary consent to the use of electronic means for communications by the registrar to the company, as a condition of making use of any facility to deliver material to the registrar by electronic means.[2802]

[2797] CA 2006, s 1113(4).   [2798] CA 2006, s 1113(5).   [2799] CA 2006, s 1114(1)(a).
[2800] CA 2006, s 1114(1)(b).   [2801] CA 2006, s 1114(2).   [2802] CA 2006, s 1115(1).

A document that is required to be signed by the registrar or authenticated by the registrar's seal must, if sent by electronic means, be authenticated in such manner as may be specified by registrar's rules.[2803]

Section 1115 of the CA 2006 (which replaces s 710A of the CA 1985) allows the registrar to require those who choose to file electronically, to accept electronic communications from the registrar. It also makes clear that, where a document is required to be 'signed' by the registrar, or authenticated by seal, he may determine by rules how it is to be authenticated when it is fact sent by electronic means.

Alternatives to publication in the Gazette

13.65 Section 1116 of the CA 2006 is concerned with alternative to publication in the Gazette. Any notices that would otherwise need to be published by the registrar in the Gazette, may instead be published by such means as may from time to time be approved by the registrar in accordance with regulations made by the Secretary of State.[2804]

The Secretary of State may make provision by regulations as to what alternative means may be approved.[2805]

The regulations may, in particular, require the use of electronic means;[2806] require the same means to be used for all notices or for all notices of specified descriptions;[2807] and whether the company is registered in England and Wales, Scotland or Northern Ireland;[2808] and impose conditions as to the manner in which access to the notices is to be made available.[2809]

Any regulations under s 1116 of the CA 2006 are subject to negative resolution procedure.[2810]

Before starting to publish notices by means approved under this section, the registrar must publish at least one notice to that effect in the Gazette.[2811]

Section 1116 of the CA 2006 does not prevent the registrar from giving public notice both in the Gazette, and by means approved under this section. In that case, the requirement of public notice is met when notice is first given by either means.[2812]

The registrar was required under the CA 1985 to publish certain statutory notices in the Gazette. The objective was to ensure that such notices were well-publicised and made available to all those who might wish to take notice of them. The Gazette is a long-established and well-understood mechanism for ensuring such publicity. However, it is possible that developments, in particular in electronic publishing, will mean over time that alternative mechanisms are equally or more appropriate as ways of meeting the underlying

---

[2803] CA 2006, s 1115(2).   [2804] CA 2006, s 1116(1).   [2805] CA 2006, s 1116(2).

[2806] CA 2006, s 1116(3)(a).   [2807] CA 2006, s 1116(3)(b)(i).

[2808] CA 2006, s 1116(3)(b)(ii).   [2809] CA 2006, s 1116(3)(c).   [2810] CA 2006, s 1116(4).

[2811] CA 2006, s 1116(5).   [2812] CA 2006, s 1116(6).

policy objective. The Company Law Review Group envisaged that the registrar should be able to make use of such mechanisms.[2813] This section, therefore, provides a power for the Secretary of State to specify alternative means which the registrar may then approve for use. To ensure that any such change is itself well-publicised in advance, s 1116(5) of the CA 2006 provides that the changes must themselves be announced in the Gazette.

Registrar's rules

13.66 Section 1117 of the CA 2006 is concerned with the registrar's rules. It states that where any provision of Part 35 of the CA 2006 enables the registrar to make provision, or impose requirements, as to any matter, the registrar may make such provision or impose such requirements by means of rules under this section. This is without prejudice to the making of such provision or the imposing of such requirements by other means.[2814]

The registrar's rules may make different provision for different cases;[2815] and may allow the registrar to disapply or modify any of the rules.[2816]

The registrar must publicise the rules in a manner appropriate to bring them to the notice of persons affected by them;[2817] and make copies of the rules available to the public (in hard copy or electronic form).[2818]

Other provisions in Part 35 of the CA 2006 enable the registrar to impose requirements in relation to certain matters. For example, s 1068 of the CA 2006 enables the registrar to specify the form, authentication and manner of delivery of documents to him: and s 1075 of the CA 2006 similarly enables her to determine the form and manner of any company instructions as to informal correction of the register. Section 1117 of the CA 2006 provides that the registrar may set out these requirements in registrar's rules. Such rules can make different provision for different cases, and may allow her to modify or disapply the rules. The registrar must publicise any such rules in a way designed to make sure that those who will need to know about them get to hear of them (which might in practice, for example, be by using the Companies House website); and must make copies of the rules publicly available.

Payments into the Consolidated Fund

13.67 Section 1118 of the CA 2006 states that nothing in the Companies Acts or any other enactment as to the payment of receipts into the Consolidated Fund, shall be read as affecting the operation in relation to the registrar of s 3(1) of the Government Trading Funds Act 1973.

[2813] *Final Report*, para 11.48.   [2814] CA 2006, s 1117(1).   [2815] CA 2006, s 1117(2)(a).
[2816] CA 2006, s 1117(2)(b).   [2817] CA 2006, s 1117(3)(a).   [2818] CA 2006, s 1117(3)(b).

Section 1118 of the CA 2006 ensures that nothing in this or other companies legislation that affects the continued operation in relation to the registrar of the Government Trading Funds Acts. The Companies House is and remains a Trading Fund.

Contracting out of registrar's functions

13.68 Section 1119 of the CA 2006 is concerned with contracting out of registrar's functions. It states that where by virtue of an order made under s 69 of the Deregulation and Contracting Out Act 1994, a person is authorised by the registrar to accept delivery of any class of documents that are under any enactment to be delivered to the registrar, the registrar may direct that documents of that class shall be delivered to a specified address of the authorised person. Any such direction must be printed and made available to the public (with or without payment).[2819]

A document of that class that is delivered to an address other than the specified address, is treated as not having been delivered.[2820]

The registrar's rules are not subordinate legislation for the purposes of s 71 of the Deregulation and Contracting Out Act 1994 (functions excluded from contracting out).[2821]

Section 1119 of the CA 2006 largely restates s 704(7) and (8) of the CA 1985. The Deregulation and Contracting Out Act 1994 envisages that some of the registrar's functions may be contracted out. Section 1119 of the CA 2006 provides for this possibility by stating that where a contractor is processing documents, the registrar can provide for them to be sent directly to the contractor.

The Deregulation and Contracting Out Act 1994 does not permit the function of making subordinate legislation to be delegated. Section 1119(3) of the CA 2006 provides that registrar's rules are not regarded as subordinate legislation for this purpose, permitting the contractor to make rules about form and manner of delivery, for example.

Application of Part to overseas companies

13.69 Section 1120 of the CA 2006 states that unless the context otherwise requires, Part 35 of the CA 2006 applies to an overseas company as they apply to a company as defined in s 1 of the CA 2006.

[2819] CA 2006, s 1119(1).   [2820] CA 2006, s 1119(2).   [2821] CA 2006, s 1119(3).

Resolutions and Meetings

Introduction

14.1 Part 13 of the CA 2006 is concerned with resolutions and meetings of a company, and comprises seven Chapters. Chapter 1 deals with general provisions about resolutions in their application to private and public companies, including various types of resolutions; Chapter 2 contains provisions on written resolutions; Chapter 3 addresses resolutions at meetings as well as procedures for meetings; Chapter 4 is concerned with public companies with specific reference to additional requirements for AGMs; Chapter 5 contains additional requirements for quoted companies; Chapter 6 deals with records of resolutions and meetings; and Chapter 7 contains supplemented provisions.

The provisions in Part 13 of the CA 2006 replace most of Chapter 4 of Part 11 of the CA 1985 Act on meetings and resolutions. The changes in the law derive principally from the Company Law Review Group's consultation on *Company General Meetings and Shareholder Communications* and recommendations from Chapter 2, 6 and 7 of their *Final Report*, together with two subsequent consultations; the *Modernising Company Law* White Paper of July 2002 and the *Company Law Reform* White Paper of March 2005.

In addition to implementing detailed policy changes, Part 13 of the CA 2006 implements two general changes. First, the law makes the 'elective' regime the default regime for private companies. This means, for example, that private companies will no longer need to 'elect' to dispense with the Annual General Meeting (AGM); they will not be required to hold an AGM in the first place. Second, the CA 1985 was drafted on the basis that the main mechanism in which shareholder decisions were taken was in general meetings. The new provisions proceed on the basis that in future, this will not be the case for many private companies. Private companies will not be required in future to hold general meetings; instead provision is made for new procedures for decisions to be taken by written resolution.

The law relating to decisions has been restated in a way that deals first with private companies. Additional layers of requirement for public and quoted companies holding general meetings follow in subsequent provisions. There are provisions at the end of Part 13 of the CA 2006 about record keeping. In general, where Part 13 of the CA 2006 imposes an obligation or confers a power, it will apply notwithstanding anything in the articles unless otherwise indicated.

General Provisions About Resolutions

14.2 Chapter 1 deals with general provisions about resolutions. It contains seven provisions and establishes the general nature of resolutions in their application to private and public companies. Chapter 1 also sets out the main resolutions applicable to companies depending upon the type of meeting proposed.

Resolutions

14.3 Section 281 of the CA 2006 is concerned with resolutions. It states that a resolution of the members (or of a class of members) of a private company must be passed either as a written resolution in accordance with Chapter 2 of Part 13 of the CA 2006;[2822] or at a meeting of the members (to which the provisions of Chapter 3 of Part 13 of the CA 2006 apply).[2823]

A resolution of the members (or of a class of members) of a public company must be passed at a meeting of the members (to which the provisions of Chapter 3 and, where relevant, Chapter 4 of Part 13 of the CA 2006 apply).[2824]

Where a provision of the Companies Acts requires a resolution of a company, or of the members (or a class of members) of a company;[2825] and does not specify what kind of resolution is required,[2826] what is required is an ordinary resolution unless the company's articles require a higher majority (or unanimity).

Nothing in Part 13 of the CA 2006 affects any enactment or rule of law as to things done otherwise than by passing a resolution;[2827] or circumstances in which a resolution is or is not treated as having been passed;[2828] or cases in which a person is precluded from alleging that a resolution has not been duly passed.[2829]

This section provides that members' resolutions can only be passed accordance with the provisions of Part 13 of the CA 2006. There is no equivalent in the CA 1985.

[2822] CA 2006, s 281(1)(a).   [2823] CA 2006, s 281(1)(b).   [2824] CA 2006, s 281(2).
[2825] CA 2006, s 281(3)(a).   [2826] CA 2006, s 281(3)(b).   [2827] CA 2006, s 281(4)(a).
[2828] CA 2006, s 281(4)(b).   [2829] CA 2006, s 281(4)(c).

Section 281(1) of the CA 2006 allows a private company to pass a resolution either as a written resolution or at a meeting of the members. Section 281(2) of the CA 2006 allows a public company to pass a resolution only at a meeting of the members. Section 281(3) of the CA 2006 ensures that where a resolution is required but the type of resolution is not specified, the default will be an ordinary resolution, unless the articles require a higher majority. When a provision specifies that an ordinary resolution is required, the articles will not be able to specify a higher majority. Section 281(4) of the CA 2006 preserves the common law 'unanimous consent' rule.

Ordinary resolutions

14.4 Section 282 of the CA 2006 is concerned with ordinary resolutions. An ordinary resolution of the members (or of a class of members) of a company means a resolution that is passed by a simple majority.[2830]

A written resolution is passed by a simple majority if it is passed by members representing a simple majority of the total voting rights of eligible members (see Chapter 2 to Part 13 of the CA 2006).[2831]

A resolution passed at a meeting on a show of hands is passed by a simple majority if it is passed by a simple majority of the members who, being entitled to do so, vote in person on the resolution;[2832] and the persons who vote on the resolution as duly appointed proxies of members entitled to vote on it.[2833]

A resolution passed on a poll taken at a meeting is passed by a simple majority if it is passed by members representing a simple majority of the total voting rights of members who (being entitled to do so) vote in person or by proxy on the resolution.[2834]

Anything that may be done by ordinary resolution may also be done by special resolution.[2835]

Section 282 of the CA 2006 provides a definition of an ordinary resolution, whether of the members generally or a class of the members, and whether as a written resolution or as a resolution passed at a meeting. A simple majority, namely over 50 per cent, is required.

Special resolutions

14.5 Section 283 of the CA 2006 is concerned with special resolutions. A special resolution of the members (or of a class of members) of a company means a resolution passed by a majority of not less than 75 per cent.[2836]

A written resolution is passed by a majority of not less than 75 per cent if it

---

[2830] CA 2006, s 282(1).   [2831] CA 2006, s 282(2).   [2832] CA 2006, s 282(3)(a).
[2833] CA 2006, s 282(3)(b).   [2834] CA 2006, s 282(4).   [2835] CA 2006, s 282(5).
[2836] CA 2006, s 283(1).

is passed by members representing not less than 75 per cent of the total voting rights of eligible members (see Chapter 2 of Part 13 of the CA 2006).[2837]

Where a resolution of a private company is passed as a written resolution, the resolution is not a special resolution unless it is stated that it was proposed as a special resolution;[2838] and if the resolution so stated, it may only be passed as a special resolution.[2839]

A resolution passed at a meeting on a show of hands is passed by a majority of not less than 75 per cent, if it is passed by not less than 75 per cent of the members who, being entitled to do so, vote in person on the resolution;[2840] and the persons who vote on the resolution as duly appointed proxies of members entitled to vote on it.[2841]

A resolution passed on a poll taken at a meeting is passed by a majority of not less than 75 per cent if it is passed by members representing not less than 75 per cent of the total voting rights of the members who (being entitled to do so) vote in person or by proxy on the resolution.[2842]

Where a resolution is passed at a meeting the resolution is not a special resolution, unless the notice of the meeting included the text of the resolution and specified the intention to propose the resolution as a special resolution;[2843] and if the notice of the meeting so specified, the resolution may only be passed as a special resolution.[2844]

Section 283 of the CA 2006 provides a definition of a special resolution, whether of the members generally or of a class of the members, and whether as a written resolution or as a resolution passed at a meeting. A 75 per cent majority is required. If a resolution is proposed as a special resolution, there is a requirement to say so, either in the written resolution text or in the meeting notice. Where a resolution is proposed as a special resolution, it can only be passed as such.

The main difference from the existing definition in s 378 of the CA 1985 is that there is no longer a requirement for 21 days' notice where a special resolution is to be passed at a meeting. The subject matter of s 378(3) of the CA 1985 is now dealt with in s 307(4)–(6) of the CA 2006 (notice required of general meeting), while the subject matter of s 378(4) and (6) of the CA 1985 is dealt with in ss 320 and 301 of the CA 2006 respectively.

Votes: general rules

14.6 Section 284 of the CA 2006 states that on a vote on a written resolution in the case of a company having a share capital, every member has one vote in

[2837] CA 2006, s 283(2).   [2838] CA 2006, s 283(3)(a).   [2839] CA 2006, s 283(3)(b).
[2840] CA 2006, s 283(4)(a).   [2841] CA 2006, s 283(4)(b).   [2842] CA 2006, s 283(5).
[2843] CA 2006, s 283(6)(a).   [2844] CA 2006, s 283(6)(b).

respect of each share or each £10 of the CA stock held by him;[2845] and in any other case, every member has one vote.[2846]

On a vote on a resolution on a show of hands at a meeting, every member present in person has one vote;[2847] and every proxy present who has been duly appointed by a member entitled to vote on the resolution has one vote.[2848]

On a vote on a resolution on a poll taken at a meeting in the case of a company having a share capital, every member has one vote in respect of each share or each £10 of the CA stock held by him;[2849] and in any other case, every member has one vote.[2850]

The provisions of s 284 of the CA 2006 apply subject to any provision of the company's articles.[2851]

Section 284 of the CA 2006 sets out the general rules on votes of members taken by written resolution, on a show of hands at a meeting or on a poll taken at a meeting. These are adapted from s 370 of the CA 1985 and the default regulations in Table A. Section 284(4) of the CA 2006 allows these general rules to be varied by the company's articles.

Votes: specific requirements

14.7 Section 285 of the CA 2006 deals with specific requirements on votes. Where a member entitled to vote on a resolution has appointed one proxy only, and the company's articles provide that the proxy has fewer votes in a vote on a resolution on a show of hands taken at a meeting than the member would have if he were present in person, the provision about how many votes the proxy has on a show of hands is void;[2852] and the proxy has the same number of votes on a show of hands as the member who appointed him would have if he were present at the meeting.[2853]

Where a member entitled to vote on a resolution has appointed more than one proxy, s 285(1) of the CA 2006 applies as if the references to the proxy were references to the proxies taken together.[2854]

In relation to a resolution required or authorised by an enactment, if a private company's articles provide that a member has a different number of votes in relation to a resolution when it is passed as a written resolution and when it is passed on a poll taken at a meeting, the provision about how many votes a member has in relation to the resolution passed on a poll is void;[2855] and a member has the same number of votes in relation to the resolution when it is passed on a poll as he has when it is passed as a written resolution.[2856]

[2845] CA 2006, s 284(1)(a).   [2846] CA 2006, s 284(1)(b).   [2847] CA 2006, s 284(2)(a).
[2848] CA 2006, s 284(2)(b).   [2849] CA 2006, s 284(3)(a).   [2850] CA 2006, s 284(3)(b).
[2851] CA 2006, s 284(4).   [2852] CA 2006, s 285(1)(a).   [2853] CA 2006, s 285(1)(b).
[2854] CA 2006, s 285(2).   [2855] CA 2006, s 285(3)(a).   [2856] CA 2006, s 285(3)(b).

Section 285 of the CA 2006 sets out specific requirements on votes of members, which the company's articles may not override. Section 285(1) and (2) of the CA 2006 provide for entitlement to vote where proxies have been appointed and ensure that the articles do not disadvantage a member voting by proxy or proxies. Section 285(3) of the CA 2006 makes new provision rights on written resolutions, reflecting the fact that they will no longer need to be passed unanimously. A member will have the same number of votes whether passing a resolution on a poll in a general meeting or on a written resolution.

Votes of joint holders of shares

14.8 Section 286 of the CA 2006 states that in the case of joint holders of shares of a company, only the vote of the senior holder who votes (and any proxies duly authorised by him) may be counted by the company.[2857]

The senior holder of a share is determined by the order in which the names of the joint holders appear in the register of members.[2858]

Section 286(1) and (2) of the CA 2006 apply subject to any provision of the company's articles.[2859]

Section 286 of the CA 2006 puts on a statutory footing what was default regulation under Article 55 of Table A on votes of joint holders of shares. The person whose vote counts is the 'senior' holder, the joint holder whose name appears first in the register of members.

Saving for provisions of articles as to determination of entitlement to vote

14.9 Section 287 of the CA 2006 states that nothing in Chapter 1 of Part 13 of the CA 2006 affects any provision of a company's articles requiring an objection to a person's entitlement to vote on a resolution to be made in accordance with the articles;[2860] and for the determination of any such objection to be final or conclusive;[2861] or the grounds on which such a determination may be questioned in legal proceedings.[2862]

Section 287 of the CA 2006 is a new provision to preserve the right for a company to require objections to votes to be made in accordance with procedures in their articles. If an objection is overruled, the decision will be final, except in cases of fraud and certain other kinds of misconduct detailed in case law where a court may intervene. This provision preserves the law prior to 2006. The provision ensures on the other hand, certainty for company by enabling the chairman to settle matters relating to the admissibility of votes

---

[2857] CA 2006, s 286(1).   [2858] CA 2006, s 286(2).   [2859] CA 2006, s 286(3).
[2860] CA 2006, s 287(a)(i).   [2861] CA 2006, s 287(a)(ii).   [2862] CA 2006, s 287(b).

in accordance with the articles and, on the other hand, sufficient remedies for members to challenge a decision if they have suffered unfair prejudice.

Written Resolutions

14.10 Chapter 2 of Part 13 of the CA 2006 is concerned with written resolutions. It comprises 13 sections.

The provisions of Chapter 2 replace the rules on written resolutions of private companies previously under the CA 1985. A key change (apparent from ss 282 and 283 of the CA 2006) is that where the statutory procedure under the CA 1985 required unanimity, the procedure in the CA 2006 does not. Accordingly, the sections in this Chapter are more detailed than those previously in ss 381A–381C of the CA 1985, and they set out the procedures for decisions taken outside of a general meeting framework. The use of the expression 'written resolution' does not mean that there is a requirement for 'writing' in the sense of hard copy.

General provision about written resolutions

14.11 Sections 288–289 of the CA 2006 set out the general provisions about written resolutions.

Written resolutions of private companies

14.12 Section 288 of the CA 2006 states that in the Companies Acts, a 'written resolution' means a resolution of a private company proposed and passed in accordance with Chapter 2 of Part 13 of the CA 2006.[2863]

The following may not be passed as a written resolution a resolution under s 168 of the CA 2006: removing a director before the expiration of his period of office;[2864] or a resolution under s 510 of the CA 2006 removing an auditor before the expiration of his term of office.[2865]

A resolution may be proposed as a written resolution by the directors of a private company (see s 291 of the CA 2006);[2866] or by the members of a private company (see ss 292–295 of the CA 2006).[2867]

References in enactments passed or made before Chapter 2 of Part 13 of the CA 2006 comes into force to a resolution of a company in general meeting,[2868] or a resolution of a meeting of a class of members of the company,[2869] apply as if they included references to a written resolution of the members, or of a class of members, of a private company (as appropriate).

A written resolution of a private company has effect as if passed (as the

---

[2863] CA 2006, s 288(1).   [2864] CA 2006, s 288(2)(a).   [2865] CA 2006, s 288(2)(b).
[2866] CA 2006, s 288(3)(a).   [2867] CA 2006, s 288(3)(b).   [2868] CA 2006, s 288(4)(a).
[2869] CA 2006, s 288(4)(b).

case may be) by the company in general meeting;[2870] or by a meeting of a class of members of the company,[2871] and references in enactments passed or made before this section comes into force to a meeting at which a resolution is passed or to members voting in favour of a resolution shall be construed accordingly.

Section 288 of the CA 2006 introduces the written resolution provisions in Chapter 2 of Part 13 of the CA 2006. They apply to private companies only. Section 288(2)(a) and (b) of the CA 2006 reproduces the two exceptions that were provided for in Part 1 of Schedule 15A of the CA 1985: a resolution to remove a director or an auditor before the expiration of his term of office may not be passed as a written resolution. These are the only two exceptions to a private company's right to pass resolutions using the written resolution procedure.

Eligible members

14.13 Section 289 of the CA 2006 states that in relation to a resolution proposed as a written resolution of a private company, the eligible members are the members who would have been entitled to vote on the resolution on the circulation date of the resolution (see s 290 of the CA 2006).[2872]

If the persons entitled to vote on a written resolution change during the course of the day that is the circulation date of the resolution, the eligible members are the persons entitled to vote on the resolution at the time that the first copy of the resolution is sent or submitted to a member for his agreement.[2873]

The eligibility of members to vote on a written resolution is fixed on the day the resolution is circulated. Section 289(2) of the CA 2006 ensures that the same shares cannot be voted more than once on the same written resolution. If the person entitled to vote changes during the course of that day, the eligible member is the person entitled to vote at the time that the first copy of the resolution is sent or submitted to a member for his agreement.

Circulation of written resolutions

14.14 Sections 290–295 of the CA 2006 are concerned with the circulation of written resolutions.

Circulation date

14.15 Section 290 of the CA 2006 addresses the circulation date in respect of written resolutions. References to the circulation date of a written resolution are to the date on which copies of it are sent or submitted to members in

---

[2870] CA 2006, s 288(5)(a).   [2871] CA 2006, s 288(5)(b).   [2872] CA 2006, s 289(1).
[2873] CA 2006, s 289(2).

accordance with Chapter 2 of Part 13 to the CA 2006 (or if copies are sent or submitted to members on different days, to the first of those days).

Section 290 of the CA 2006 ensures that the circulation date of a written resolution means the date on which copies are sent or submitted to members (or copies are sent on different days, the first of those days).

Circulation of written resolutions proposed by directors

14.16 Section 291 of the CA 2006 provides that the section applies to a resolution proposed as a written resolution by the directors of the company.[2874] The company must send or submit a copy of the resolution to every eligible member.[2875]

The company must do so (a) by sending copies at the same time (so far as reasonably practicable) to all eligible members in hard copy form, in electronic form or by means of a website;[2876] or (b) if it is possible to do so without undue delay, by submitting the same copy to each eligible member in turn (or different copies to each of a number of eligible members in turn),[2877] or by sending copies to some members in accordance with para (a), and submitting a copy or copies to other members in accordance with para (b).

The copy of the resolution must be accompanied by a statement informing the member how to signify agreement to the resolution (see s 296 of the CA 2006);[2878] and as to the date by which the resolution must be passed if it is not to lapse (see s 297 of the CA 2006).[2879]

In the event of default in complying with s 291 of the CA 2006, an offence is committed by every officer of the company who is in default.[2880] A person guilty of an offence under is liable on conviction on indictment, to a fine;[2881] on summary conviction, to a fine not exceeding the statutory maximum.[2882]

The validity of the resolution, if passed, is not affected by a failure to comply with s 291 of the CA 2006.[2883]

Section 291 of the CA 2006 provides for the circulation of written resolutions by directors of the company. A company must circulate a written resolution either by sending to all eligible members at the same time or, if it can be done without undue delay, submitting the same copy of the resolution to each eligible member in turn. The latter would allow companies to pass round a document or e-mail rather than sending out several copies.

[2874] CA 2006, s 291(1). [2875] CA 2006, s 291(2). [2876] CA 2006, s 291(3)(a).
[2877] CA 2006, s 291(3)(b). [2878] CA 2006, s 291(4)(a). [2879] CA 2006, s 291(4)(b).
[2880] CA 2006, s 291(5). [2881] CA 2006, s 291(6)(a). [2882] CA 2006, s 291(6)(b).
[2883] CA 2006, s 291(7).

Members' power to require circulation of written resolutions

14.17 Section 292 of the CA 2006 states that the members of a private company may require the company to circulate a resolution that may properly be moved and is proposed to be moved as a written resolution.[2884]

Any resolution may properly be moved as a written resolution unless it would, if passed, be ineffective (whether by reason of inconsistency with any enactment or the company's constitution or otherwise),[2885] or it is defamatory of any person,[2886] or it is frivolous or vexatious.[2887]

Where the members require a company to circulate a resolution they may require the company to circulate with it a statement of not more than 1,000 words on the subject matter of the resolution.[2888]

A company is required to circulate the resolution and any accompanying statement once it has received requests that it do so from members representing not less than the requisite percentage of the total voting rights of all members entitled to vote on the resolution.[2889]

The 'requisite percentage' is 5 per cent or such lower percentage as is specified for this purpose in the company's articles.[2890]

A request may be in hard copy form or in electronic form,[2891] and must identify the resolution and any accompanying statement,[2892] and must be authenticated by the person or persons making it.[2893]

Section 292 of the CA 2006 enables members to require a written resolution to be circulated. They may also require circulation of a statement about its subject matter. Like the members' right to require a resolution to be moved at an AGM, the percentage needed is 5 per cent of the total voting rights (or lower if specified in the company's articles). Section 292(2) of the CA 2006 specifies some limits on the kind of resolution that may be circulated in this way, designed to stop the power being abused.

Circulation of written resolution proposed by members

14.18 Section 293 of the CA 2006 states that a company that is required under s 292 of the CA 2006 to circulate a resolution must send or submit to every eligible member a copy of the resolution;[2894] and a copy of any accompanying statement.[2895] This is subject to s 294(2) of the CA 2006 (deposit or tender of sum in respect of expenses of circulation) and s 295 of the CA 2006 (application not to circulate members' statement).[2896]

The company must do so (a) by sending copies at the same time (so far as

---

[2884] CA 2006, s 292(1).   [2885] CA 2006, s 292(2)(a).   [2886] CA 2006, s 292(2)(b).
[2887] CA 2006, s 292(2)(c).   [2888] CA 2006, s 292(3).   [2889] CA 2006, s 292(4).
[2890] CA 2006, s 292(5).   [2891] CA 2006, s 292(6)(a).   [2892] CA 2006, s 292(6)(b).
[2893] CA 2006, s 292(6)(c).   [2894] CA 2006, s 293(1)(a).   [2895] CA 2006, s 293(1)(b).
[2896] CA 2006, s 293(1).

reasonably practicable) to all eligible members in hard copy form, in electronic form or by means of a website;[2897] or (b) if it is possible to do so without undue delay, by submitting the same copy to each eligible member in turn (or different copies to each of a number of eligible members in turn);[2898] or by sending copies to some members in accordance with para (a) and submitting a copy or copies to other members in accordance with para (b).

The company must send or submit the copies (or, if copies are sent or submitted to members on different days, the first of those copies) not more than 21 days after it becomes subject to the requirement under s 292 of the CA 2006 to circulate the resolution.[2899]

The copy of the resolution must be accompanied by guidance as to how to signify agreement to the resolution (see s 296 of the CA 2006),[2900] and the date by which the resolution must be passed if it is not to lapse (see s 297 of the CA 2006).[2901]

In the event of default in complying with, s 293 of the CA 2006 an offence is committed by every officer of the company who is in default.[2902] A person guilty of an offence under this section is liable on conviction on indictment, to a fine;[2903] or on summary conviction, to a fine not exceeding the statutory maximum.[2904]

The validity of the resolution, if passed, is not affected by a failure to comply with this section.[2905]

Section 293 of the CA 2006 specifies what a company has to do when it is required under s 292 of the CA 2006 to circulate a resolution and accompanying statement. It must circulate the resolution and statement by sending it to all eligible members at the same time or, if it can be done without undue delay, by submitting the same copy of the resolution and statement to each eligible member in turn, or a combination of these. These latter two points would allow companies to pass round a document or email rather than sending out several copies. Section 293(3) of the CA 2006 requires that the members' written resolution be circulated within 21 days of the company being requested to do so by those members, except that if the written resolution is circulated to members on different days, then the first copy should be dispatched not more than 21 days after the request to circulate the resolution.

Expenses of circulation

14.19 Section 294 of the CA 2006 is concerned with expenses of circulation of resolutions. The expenses of the company in complying with s 293 of the

---

[2897] CA 2006, s 293(2)(a).   [2898] CA 2006, s 293(2)(b).   [2899] CA 2006, s 293(3).
[2900] CA 2006, s 293(4)(a).   [2901] CA 2006, s 293(4)(b).   [2902] CA 2006, s 293(5).
[2903] CA 2006, s 293(6)(a).   [2904] CA 2006, s 293(6)(b).   [2905] CA 2006, s 293(7).

CA 2006 must be paid by the members who requested the circulation of the resolution, unless the company resolves otherwise.[2906]

Unless the company has previously so resolved, it is not bound to comply with s 293 of the CA 2006, unless there is deposited with or tendered to it a sum reasonably sufficient to meet its expenses in doing so.[2907]

Section 294 of the CA 2006 provides that the expenses of complying with s 293 of the CA 2006 are to be paid by the members who requested the circulation of the resolution unless the company resolves otherwise. The company can require the deposit of a sum to meet its expenses before it circulates the resolution, subject to any resolution to the contrary.

Application not to circulate members' statements

14.20 Section 295 of the CA 2006 states that a company is not required to circulate a member's statement under s 293 of the CA 2006 if, on an application by the company or another person who claims to be aggrieved, the court is satisfied that the rights conferred by s 292 of the CA 2006 and that section are being abused.[2908]

The court may order the members who requested the circulation of the statement to pay the whole or part of the company's costs (in Scotland, expenses) on such an application, even if they are not parties to the application.[2909]

Section 295 of the CA 2006 enables the court on application to relieve the company of an obligation to circulate a member's statement under s 293 of the CA 2006 if in the court's view the right to require circulation is being abused. This mirrors s 317 of the CA 2006 (application not to circulate a member's statement relating to resolutions to be passed in general meeting) in the context of general meetings.

Agreeing to written resolutions

14.21 Sections 296–297 are concerned with provisions for agreeing to written resolutions.

Procedure for signifying agreement to written resolution

14.22 Section 296 of the CA 2006 sets out the procedure for signifying agreements to written resolutions. A member signifies his agreement to a proposed written resolution when the company receives from him (or from someone acting on his behalf) an authenticated document identifying the

---

[2906] CA 2006, s 294(1).   [2907] CA 2006, s 294(2).   [2908] CA 2006, s 295(1).
[2909] CA 2006, s 295(2).

resolution to which it relates;[2910] and indicating his agreement to the resolution.[2911]

The document must be sent to the company in hard copy form or in electronic form.[2912] A member's agreement to a written resolution, once signified, may not be revoked.[2913]

A written resolution is passed when the required majority of eligible members have signified their agreement to it.[2914]

The objective of s 296 of the CA 2006 is that a member may signify agreement to a written resolution in hard copy or electronic form, although if the company does not permit electronic form communications, or is not deemed to do so by virtue of s 298 of the CA 2006 (sending documents relating to written resolutions by electronic means), the member will have to signify his consent in hard copy (see para 6 (conditions for use of communications in electronic form) of Schedule 4 of the CA 2006 – documents and information sent or supplied to a company).

Once a member has signified agreement to a written resolution, he cannot withdraw his agreement. This provides certainly for the company as to when the required majority of eligible needed to agree the resolution has been reached.

Period of agreeing to written resolution

14.23 Section 297 of the CA 2006 sets out the period for agreeing a written resolution. A proposed written resolution lapses if it is not passed before the end of the period specified for this purpose in the company's articles;[2915] or if none is specified, the period of 28 days beginning with the circulation date.[2916]

The agreement of a member to a written resolution is ineffective if signified after the expiry of that period.[2917]

Section 297 of the CA 2006 puts a time limit of 28 days for passing a written resolution, unless the company's articles specify a different period. This means that there will be a definite point when the company can say that a resolution with insufficient support has not been passed.

Supplementary

Sending documents relating to written resolutions by electronic means

14.24 Section 298 of the CA 2006 states that where a company has given an electronic address in any document containing or accompanying a proposed written resolution, it is deemed to have agreed that any document or

---

[2910] CA 2006, s 296(1)(a).   [2911] CA 2006, s 296(1)(b).   [2912] CA 2006, s 296(2).
[2913] CA 2006, s 296(3).   [2914] CA 2006, s 296(4).   [2915] CA 2006, s 297(1)(a).
[2916] CA 2006, s 297(1)(b).   [2917] CA 2006, s 297(2).

information relating to that resolution may be sent by electronic means to that address (subject to any conditions or limitations specified in the document).[2918]

The term 'electronic address' means any address or number used for the purposes of sending or receiving documents or information by electronic means.[2919]

Section 298 of the CA 2006 should be read together with the provisions about electronic communications to companies in Part 3 of Schedule 4 of the CA 2006 (communications in electronic form). Taken together, these provisions allow a member to communicate with the company by electronic means, where the company has given an electronic address in a document containing or accompanying a proposed written resolution.

Publication of written resolutions on website

14.25 Section 299 of the CA 2006 applies where a company sends a written resolution;[2920] or a statement relating to a written resolution,[2921] to a person by means of a website.

The resolution or statement is not validly sent for the purposes of Chapter 2 of Part 13 of the CA 2006 unless the resolution is available on the website throughout the period beginning with the circulation date and ending on the date on which the resolution lapses under s 297 of the CA 2006.[2922]

Section 299 of the CA 2006 should be read in conjunction with the provisions about communications by means of a website by a company other than a traded company under Part 4 (communications by means of a website) of Schedule 5 of the CA 2006 (communications by a company). Section 299 of the CA 2006, together with those provisions, allows a company, provided certain conditions are met, to publish written resolution on a website rather than send it to a member individually.

Relationship between this chapter and provisions of company's articles

14.26 Section 300 of the CA 2006 deals with the relationship between Chapter 2 of Part 13 of the CA 2006 and provisions of company's articles. A provision of the articles of a private company is void in so far as it would have the effect that a resolution that is required by or otherwise provided for in an enactment could not be proposed and passed as a written resolution.

This section ensures that the company's articles cannot remove the ability

---

[2918] CA 2006, s 298(1).   [2919] CA 2006, s 298(2).   [2920] CA 2006, s 299(1)(a).
[2921] CA 2006, s 299(1)(b).   [2922] CA 2006, s 299(2).

of a private company and its members to propose and pass a statutory resolution using the statutory written resolutions procedures of this Chapter.

Resolutions At Meetings

14.27 Chapter 3 of Part 13 of the CA 2006 is concerned with resolutions at meetings. It contains 35 sections on the practice and procedure of company meetings. It replaces ss 368–377, 379 and 381 of the CA 1985 and makes provision about resolutions passed in general meetings. The provisions apply equally to private and public companies.

The new provisions reflect the fact that private companies will no longer have to hold AGMs. For example, the provisions about circulation of statement in ss 376 and 377 of the CA 1985 have been separated from the provisions on circulation of resolutions prior to an AGM (which are in Chapter 4 of the CA 2006). The CA 2006 repeals s 367 of the CA 1985, which gave the Secretary of State a power to call a meeting where there was no AGM.

General provisions about resolutions at meetings

Resolutions at general meetings

14.28 Section 301 of the CA 2006 states that a resolution of the members of a company is validly passed at a general meeting if notice of the meeting and of the resolution is given,[2923] and the meeting is held and conducted,[2924] in accordance with the provisions of Chapter 2 of Part 13 of the CA 2006 (and, where relevant, Chapter 4 of Part 13 of the CA 2006) and the company's articles.

Section 301 of the CA 2006 is a general provision about the circumstances in which resolutions at meetings are validly passed. It extends to all resolutions the principle in s 378(6) of the CA 1985 relating to special resolutions: that passing a resolution in a meeting is not just a question of obtaining the right majority, but of using the correct procedures.

An important difference from the position under s 378(6) of the CA 1985 is that, under this section, a resolution must be passed in accordance with the relevant provisions of the CA 2006 and with any additional requirements imposed by the company's articles. So where there are mandatory provisions in the CA 2006 (like those proxies' rights to vote), these cannot be avoided by making alternative provision in the articles; and where provision is made about meetings in a company's articles, these must also be complied with.

[2923] CA 2006, s 301(1)(a).   [2924] CA 2006, s 301(1)(b).

Calling meetings

Directors' power to call general meetings

14.29 Section 302 of the CA 2006 deals with directors' power to call general meetings. The directors of a company may call a general meeting of the company.

This section puts into statute part of the default regulation at Article 37 of Table A, which allows the directors to call a general meeting. The company's articles will set out how the directors act collectively.

Members' power to require directors to call general meeting

14.30 Section 303 of the CA 2006 deals with members' power to require directors to call general meetings. The members of a company may require the directors to call a general meeting of the company.[2925]

The directors are required to call a general meeting once the company has received requests to do so from members, who hold at least the required percentage of such of the paid-up capital of the company as carries the right of voting at general meetings of the company (excluding any paid-up capital held as treasury shares);[2926] or in the case of a company not having a share capital, members who represent at least the required percentage of the total voting rights of all the members having a right to vote at general meetings.[2927]

The required percentage is 10 per cent unless, in the case of a private company, more than 12 months has elapsed since the end of the last general meeting called in pursuance of a requirement under this section;[2928] or in relation to which any members of the company had (by virtue of an enactment, the company's articles or otherwise) rights with respect to the circulation of a resolution no less extensive than they would have had if the meeting had been so called at their request,[2929] in which case the required percentage is 5 per cent.

A request must state the general nature of the business to be dealt with at the meeting;[2930] and may include the text of a resolution that may properly be moved and is intended to be moved at the meeting.[2931]

A resolution may properly be moved at a meeting unless it would, if passed, be ineffective (whether by reason of inconsistency with any enactment or the company's constitution or otherwise);[2932] or, it is defamatory of any person;[2933] or it is frivolous or vexatious.[2934]

[2925] CA 2006, s 303(1).   [2926] CA 2006, s 303(2)(a).   [2927] CA 2006, s 303(2)(b).
[2928] CA 2006, s 303(3)(a).   [2929] CA 2006, s 303(3)(b).   [2930] CA 2006, s 303(4)(a).
[2931] CA 2006, s 303(4).   [2932] CA 2006, s 303(5)(a).   [2933] CA 2006, s 303(5)(b).
[2934] CA 2006, s 303(5)(c).

A request may be in hard copy form or in electronic form,[2935] and must be authenticated by the person or persons making it.[2936]

Section 303 of the CA 2006 together with ss 304 and 305 of the CA 2006 make provision similar to that previously in s 368 of the CA 1985, requiring the directors to call a general meeting if requested by the members.

There are three main changes. First, there is a change in the threshold required for a meeting. For public companies, this remains members with voting rights holding at least 10 per cent of the paid-up capital. For private companies, the threshold is 5 per cent or 10 per cent of the paid-up capital (or, in a company with no share capital, 5 per cent or 10 per cent of the total voting rights) depending on when there was last a meeting in advance of which members had a right – equivalent to the right under this section – to circulate resolutions. The threshold is lower if there has been no such meeting in the preceding 12 months. Second, s 303(4)(b) of the CA 2006 extends the provisions of the CA 1985 by enabling members to include the text of a resolution to be moved at the requested meeting. For example, if the resolution would have no effect, then it cannot be properly moved. Third, requests in electronic form are permitted.

Directors' duty to call meetings required by members

14.31 Sections 304 of the CA 2006 is concerned with directors' duty to call meetings required by members. Directors required under s 303 of the CA 2006 to call a general meeting of the company must call a meeting within 21 days from the date on which they become subject to the requirement,[2937] and to be held on a date not more than 28 days after the date of the notice convening the meeting.[2938]

If the requests received by the company identify a resolution intended to be moved at the meeting, the notice of the meeting must include notice of the resolution.[2939]

The business that may be dealt with at the meeting includes a resolution of which notice is given in accordance with this section.[2940]

If the resolution is to be proposed as a special resolution, the directors are treated as not having duly called the meeting if they do not give the required notice of the resolution in accordance with s 283 of the CA 2006.[2941]

Section 304 of the CA 2006 sets time limits within which the directors must call and hold a meeting required by members. Section 304(2) of the CA 2006 requires that if the members' request identifies a resolution to be moved at the meeting, this should be included in the notice of the meeting.

[2935] CA 2006, s 303(6)(a).   [2936] CA 2006, s 303(6)(b).   [2937] CA 2006, s 304(1)(a).
[2938] CA 2006, s 304(1)(b).   [2939] CA 2006, s 304(2).   [2940] CA 2006, s 304(3).
[2941] CA 2006, s 304(4).

Power of members to call meeting at the company's expense

14.32 Section 305 of the CA 2006 addresses the power of members to call meeting at the company's expense. If the directors are required under s 303 of the CA 2006 to call a meeting,[2942] and do not do so in accordance with s 304 of the CA 2006,[2943] the members who requested the meeting, or any of them representing more than one-half of the total voting rights of all of them, may themselves call a general meeting.

Where the requests received by the company included the text of a resolution intended to be moved at the meeting, the notice of the meeting must include notice of the resolution.[2944]

The meeting must be called for a date not more than three months after the date on which the directors become subject to the requirement to call a meeting.[2945]

The meeting must be called in the same manner, as near as possible, as that in which meetings are required to be called by directors of the company.[2946]

The business that may be dealt with at the meeting includes a resolution of which notice is given in accordance with this section.[2947]

Any reasonable expenses incurred by the members requesting the meeting by reason of the failure of the directors duly to call a meeting must be reimbursed by the company.[2948]

Any sum so reimbursed shall be retained by the company out of any sums due or to become due from the company by way of fees or other remuneration in respect of their services to such of the directors as were in default.[2949]

Section 305 of the CA 2006 enables the members to call a meeting in the event that the directors fail to call a meeting on member's request. Section 305(6) and (7) of the CA 2006 provides for members to be reimbursed appropriately and for the directors to be penalised directly, by the reimbursement being taken out of the fees or other remuneration due to them.

Power of court to order meeting

14.33 Section 306 of the CA 2006 deals with the power of the court to order a meeting. It applies if for any reason it is impracticable to call a meeting of a company in any manner in which meetings of that company may be called;[2950] or to conduct the meeting in the manner prescribed by the company's articles or this Act.[2951]

The court may, either of its own motion or on the application of a director

[2942] CA 2006, s 305(1)(a).   [2943] CA 2006, s 305(1)(b).   [2944] CA 2006, s 305(2).
[2945] CA 2006, s 305(3).   [2946] CA 2006, s 305(4).   [2947] CA 2006, s 305(5).
[2948] CA 2006, s 305(6).   [2949] CA 2006, s 305(7).   [2950] CA 2006, s 306(1)(a).
[2951] CA 2006, s 306(1)(b).

of the company,[2952] or of a member of the company who would be entitled to vote at the meeting,[2953] order a meeting to be called, held and conducted in any manner the court thinks fit.

Where such an order is made, the court may give such ancillary or consequential directions as it thinks expedient.[2954] Such directions may include a direction that one member of the company present at the meeting be deemed to constitute a quorum.[2955]

A meeting called, held and conducted in accordance with an order under this section is deemed for all purposes to be a meeting of the company duly called, held and conducted.[2956]

Section 306 of the CA 2006 reproduces the effect of s 371 of the CA 1985 and gives the court power to order a meeting of the company and to direct the manner in which that meeting is called, held and conducted.

Notice of meetings

14.34 Sections 307–313 of the CA 2006 deal with the procedures for notice of meetings.

Notice required of general meeting

14.35 Section 307 of the CA 2006 states that a general meeting of a private company (other than an adjourned meeting) must be called by notice of at least 14 days.[2957]

A general meeting of a public company (other than an adjourned meeting) must be called by notice of, in the case of an annual general meeting, at least 21 days,[2958] and in any other case, at least 14 days.[2959]

The company's articles may require a longer period of notice than that specified in s 307(1) or (2) of the CA 2006.[2960]

A general meeting may be called by shorter notice than that otherwise required if shorter notice is agreed by the members.[2961]

The shorter notice must be agreed to by a majority in number of the members having a right to attend and vote at the meeting, being a majority who together hold not less than the requisite percentage in nominal value of the shares giving a right to attend and vote at the meeting (excluding any shares in the company held as treasury shares),[2962] or in the case of a company not having a share capital, together represent not less than the requisite percentage of the total voting rights at that meeting of all the members.[2963] This does not apply to an annual general meeting of a public company.[2964]

[2952] CA 2006, s 306(2)(a).   [2953] CA 2006, s 306(2)(b).   [2954] CA 2006, s 306(3).
[2955] CA 2006, s 306(4).   [2956] CA 2006, s 306(5).   [2957] CA 2006, s 307(1).
[2958] CA 2006, s 307(2)(a).   [2959] CA 2006, s 307(2)(b).   [2960] CA 2006, s 307(3).
[2961] CA 2006, s 307(4).   [2962] CA 2006, s 307(5)(a).   [2963] CA 2006, s 307(5)(b).
[2964] CA 2006, s 307(7). See instead CA 2006, s 337(2).

The requisite percentage is, in the case of a private company, 90 per cent or such higher percentage (not exceeding 95 per cent) as may be specified in the company's articles;[2965] or in the case of a public company, 95 per cent.[2966] This does not apply to an annual general meeting of a public company.[2967]

Section 307 of the CA 2006 replaces part of s 369 of the CA 1985. It retains the current minimum notice period requirement of 21 days for public company AGMs, with 14 days' notice required for all other general meetings (whether public or private company general meetings). A general meeting may be called on shorter notice if the requisite majority of members agree.

The key substantive change from the position under the CA 1985 is that the requisite majority required to agree a short notice period has been reduced for private companies from 95 per cent to 90 per cent of the voting rights, although the articles may specify up to 95 per cent if the company wishes. For public companies, the majority required to agree a short-notice period remains at 95 per cent of the voting rights.

Manner in which notice to be given

14.36 Section 308 of the CA 2006 deals with the manner in which notice is to be given. Notice of a general meeting of a company must be given in hard copy form,[2968] or in electronic form,[2969] or by means of a website (see s 309 of the CA 2006),[2970] or partly by one such means and partly by another.

Section 308 of the CA 2006 should be read in conjunction with the general requirement for different types of companies in sending and supplying information as set out in Part 37 and Schedule 5 of the CA 2006.

Publication of notice of meeting on website

14.37 Section 309 of the CA 2006 states that notice of a meeting is not validly given by a company by means of a website unless it is given in accordance with this section.[2971]

When the company notifies a member of the presence of the notice on the website the notification must state that it concerns a notice of a company meeting;[2972] specify the place, date and time of the meeting;[2973] and in the case of a public company, state whether the meeting will be an annual general meeting.[2974]

The notice must be available on the website throughout the period beginning with the date of that notification and ending with the conclusion of the meeting.[2975]

[2965] CA 2006, s 307(6)(a).   [2966] CA 2006, s 307(6)(b).   [2967] CA 2006, s 307(7).
[2968] CA 2006, s 308(a).   [2969] CA 2006, s 308(b).   [2970] CA 2006, s 308(c).
[2971] CA 2006, s 309(1).   [2972] CA 2006, s 309(2)(a).   [2973] CA 2006, s 309(2)(b).
[2974] CA 2006, s 309(2)(c).   [2975] CA 2006, s 309(3).

Section 309 of the CA 2006 contains some specific provisions on communications by means of a website and needs to be read with the general provisions on communications referred to above. The overall effect is similar to that of the website provisions in the s 369 of the CA 1985.

Persons entitled to receive notice of meetings

14.38 Section 310 of the CA 2006 deals with persons entitled to receive notice of meetings. Notice of a general meeting of a company must be sent to every member of the company,[2976] and every director.[2977]

In s 310(1) of the CA 2006, the reference to 'members' includes any person who is entitled to a share in consequence of the death or bankruptcy of a member, if the company has been notified of their entitlement.[2978]

In s 310(2) of the CA 2006, the reference to the 'bankruptcy of a member' includes the sequestration of the estate of a member;[2979] or a member's estate being the subject of a protected trust deed (within the meaning of the Bankruptcy (Scotland) Act 1985 (c 66)).[2980]

Section 310 of the CA 2006 applies subject to any enactment, and any provision of the company's articles.[2981]

Section 310 of the CA 2006 puts into statute part of Article 38 of Table A. The new provision ensures that notice of meetings must be sent to all members, directors and any person entitled to shares as a consequence of the death or bankruptcy (or the equivalent in Scots insolvency law) of a member. The provision is subject to any enactment and to any provision in the articles. This means that a company may, for example, make provision in its articles to stop sending notice of meeting to members for whom the company no longer has a valid address.

Contents of notices of meetings

14.39 Section 311 of the CA 2006 states that notice of a general meeting of a company must state the time and date of the meeting,[2982] and the place of the meeting.[2983]

Notice of a general meeting of a company must state the general nature of the business to be dealt with at the meeting. This subsection applies subject to any provision of the company's articles.[2984]

Section 311 of the CA 2006 puts into statute another part Article 38 of Table A. The new provision ensures that the notice of meeting must include the time, date and place of the meeting and, subject to the articles, the general nature of the business to be conducted at the meeting.

[2976] CA 2006, s 310(1)(a).   [2977] CA 2006, s 310(1)(b).   [2978] CA 2006, s 310(2).
[2979] CA 2006, s 310(3)(a).   [2980] CA 2006, s 310(3)(b).   [2981] CA 2006, s 310(4).
[2982] CA 2006, s 311(1)(a).   [2983] CA 2006, s 311(1)(b).   [2984] CA 2006, s 311(2).

Resolution requiring special notice

14.40 Section 312 of the CA 2006 states that where by any provision of the Companies Acts special notice is required of a resolution, the resolution is not effective unless notice of the intention to move it has been given to the company at least 28 days before the meeting at which it is moved.[2985]

The company must, where practicable, give its members notice of any such resolution in the same manner and at the same time as it gives notice of the meeting.[2986]

Where that is not practicable, the company must give its members notice at least 14 days before the meeting by advertisement in a newspaper having an appropriate circulation;[2987] or in any other manner allowed by the company's articles.[2988]

If, after notice of the intention to move such a resolution has been given to the company, a meeting is called for a date 28 days or less after the notice has been given, the notice is deemed to have been properly given, though not given within the time required.[2989]

Section 312 of the CA 2006 replaces s 379 of the CA 1985 setting out the requirements for special notice resolutions. It makes provision only in relation to resolutions passed at meetings. This is because the resolutions for which special notice is required are either resolutions that are not capable of being passed as written resolutions (in the case of ss 168 and 510 of the CA 2006, or in relation written resolutions have their own special procedure (see ss 514 and 515 of the CA 2006).

There is no change from the existing law, whereby at least 28 days' notice must be given to the company of the intention to move a resolution requiring special notice. Where it is not practicable for the company to give members notice of such resolution at the same time as it gives notice of a meeting at which the resolution is to be moved, the company must in the future give at least 14 days' notice either, by newspaper advertisement or by any other manner allowed by the articles.

Accidental failure to give notice of resolution or meeting

14.41 Section 313 of the CA 2006 addresses accidental failure to give notice of resolution or meeting. Where a company gives notice of a general meeting,[2990] or a resolution intended to be moved at a general meeting,[2991] any accidental failure to give notice to one or more persons shall be disregarded for the purpose of determining whether notice of the meeting or resolution (as the case may be) is duly given.

[2985] CA 2006, s 312(1).   [2986] CA 2006, s 312(2).   [2987] CA 2006, s 312(3)(a).
[2988] CA 2006, s 312(3)(b).   [2989] CA 2006, s 312(4).   [2990] CA 2006, s 313(1)(a).
[2991] CA 2006, s 313(1)(b).

Section 313(2) of the CA 2006 states that except in relation to notice given under s 304 of the CA 2006 (notice of meetings required by members), or s 305 of the CA 2006 (notice of meetings called by members), or s 322 of the CA 2006 (notice of resolutions at AGMs proposed by members), s 313(1) of the CA 2006 applies subject to any provision of the company's articles.

Section 313 of the CA 2006 expands on Article 39 of Table A. It contains the rule that an accidental failure to give notice of a resolution or a general meeting is generally disregarded. Under s 313(2) of the CA 2006, this rule can be altered by the articles in some but not all cases.

Members' statement

14.42 Sections 314–317 of the CA 2006 are concerned with members' statements.

Members' power to require circulation of statements

14.43 Particular provisions apply to members' statements. Section 314 of the CA 2006 applies to members' power to require circulation of statements. The members of a company may require the company to circulate, to members of the company entitled to receive notice of a general meeting, a statement of not more than 1,000 words with respect to a matter referred to in a proposed resolution to be dealt with at that meeting,[2992] or other business to be dealt with at that meeting.[2993]

A company is required to circulate a statement once it has received requests to do so from members representing at least 5 per cent of the total voting rights of all the members who have a relevant right to vote (excluding any voting rights attached to any shares in the company held as treasury shares);[2994] or at least 100 members who have a relevant right to vote and hold shares in the company on which there has been paid up an average sum, per member, of at least £100.[2995]

A 'relevant right to vote' means in relation to a statement with respect to a matter referred to in a proposed resolution, a right to vote on that resolution at the meeting to which the requests relate,[2996] and in relation to any other statement, a right to vote at the meeting to which the requests relate.[2997]

A request may be in hard copy form or in electronic form.[2998] It must identify the statement to be circulated;[2999] must be authenticated by the person or persons making it,[3000] and must be received by the company at least one week before the meeting to which it relates.[3001]

[2992] CA 2006, s 314(1)(a).   [2993] CA 2006, s 314(1)(b).   [2994] CA 2006, s 314(2)(a).
[2995] CA 2006, s 314(2)(b).   [2996] CA 2006, s 314(3)(a).   [2997] CA 2006, s 314(3)(b).
[2998] CA 2006, s 314(4)(a).   [2999] CA 2006, s 314(4)(b).   [3000] CA 2006, s 314(4)(c).
[3001] CA 2006, s 314(4)(d).

Section 314 of the CA 2006, together with s 315 of the CA 2006 replaces ss 376 and 377 of the CA 1985 and provides a right for members to require the company to circulate a statement of up to 1,000 words.

The key policy change is that where the statement relates to a resolution or other matter to be dealt with at a public company's AGM and is received before the company's financial year end, the shareholders are not required to cover the costs of circulating the statement. There are two other notable changes. The first is that the shares relied on to trigger the circulation of a statement must in each case carry rights to vote on the relevant resolution rather that just at the meeting. The second is that requests in electronic form are permitted.

Company's duty to circulate members' statement

14.44 Section 315 of the CA 2006 deals with the company's duty to circulate members' statements. A company that is required under s 314 of the CA 2006, to circulate a statement must send a copy of it to each member of the company entitled to receive notice of the meeting in the same manner as the notice of the meeting,[3002] and at the same time as, or as soon as reasonably practicable after, it gives notice of the meeting.[3003]

Section 315(1) applies subject to s 316(2) of the CA 2006 (deposit or tender of sum in respect of expenses of circulation) and s 317 of the CA 2006 (application not to circulate members' statement).[3004]

In the event of default in complying with this section, an offence is committed by every officer of the company who is in default.[3005] A person guilty of an offence under this section is liable on conviction on indictment, to a fine;[3006] on summary conviction, to a fine not exceeding the statutory maximum.[3007]

Section 315 of the CA 2006 replaces the remainder of ss 376 and 377 of the CA 1985 and specifies what the company is to do when it is required to circulate a members' statement. The statement must be circulated in the same manner as notice of the meeting and at the same time, or as soon as reasonably practicable, after the company gives notice of the meeting. Where the company fails to comply with the provisions of this section, an offence is committed by every officer of the company who is in default.

Expenses of circulating members' statements

14.45 Section 316 of the CA 2006 makes provision for the expenses of circulating a members' statement. The expenses of the company in complying with s 315 of the CA 2006 need not be paid by the members who requested the

---

[3002] CA 2006, s 315(1)(a).   [3003] CA 2006, s 315(1)(b).   [3004] CA 2006, s 315(2).
[3005] CA 2006, s 315(3).   [3006] CA 2006, s 315(4)(a).   [3007] CA 2006, s 315(4)(b).

circulation of the statement if the meeting to which the requests relate is an annual general meeting of a public company,[3008] and requests sufficient to require the company to circulate the statement are received before the end of the financial year preceding the meeting.[3009]

Otherwise the expenses of the company in complying with that section must be paid by the members who requested the circulation of the statement unless the company resolves otherwise;[3010] and unless the company has previously so resolved, it is not bound to comply with that section unless there is deposited with or tendered to it, not later than one week before the meeting, a sum reasonably sufficient to meet its expenses in doing so.[3011]

This section provides that the expenses of complying with s 315 of the CA 2006 need not be paid by the members if the meeting to which the request relates is a public company AGM, and a sufficient number of requests are received before the company's year end. Otherwise the company's expenses will have to be met by the members who requested the circulation of the statement, unless the company resolves otherwise. In this case, the members requesting the statement must deposit a sum to cover the company's costs (unless the company has resolved otherwise).

Application not to circulate members' statements

14.46 Section 317 of the CA 2006 is concerned with application not to circulate members' statements. A company is not required to circulate members' statements under s 315 of the CA 2006 if, on an application by the company or another person who claims to be aggrieved, the court is satisfied that the rights conferred by s 314 of the CA 2006 and that section are being abused.[3012]

The court may order the members who requested the circulation of the statement to pay the whole or part of the company's costs (in Scotland, expenses) on such an application, even if they are not parties to the application.[3013]

Section 317 of the CA 2006 replaces s 377(3) of the CA 1985. It enables the court on application to relieve the company of an obligation to circulate a members' statement if in its opinion the right to require circulation is being abused.

Procedure at meetings

14.47 Sections 318–323 of the CA 2006 are concerned with procedure at meetings.

[3008] CA 2006, s 316(1)(a).   [3009] CA 2006, s 316(1)(b).   [3010] CA 2006, s 316(2)(a).
[3011] CA 2006, s 316(2).   [3012] CA 2006, s 317(1).   [3013] CA 2006, s 317(2).

Quorum at meetings

14.48 Section 318 of the CA 2006 states that in the case of a company limited by shares or guarantee and having only one member, one qualifying person present at a meeting is a quorum.[3014]

In any other case, subject to the provisions of the company's articles, two qualifying persons present at a meeting are a quorum, unless each is a qualifying person only because he is authorised under s 323 of the CA 2006 to act as the representative of a corporation in relation to the meeting, and they are representatives of the same corporation;[3015] or each is a qualifying person only because he is appointed as proxy of a member in relation to the meeting, and they are proxies of the same member.[3016]

A 'qualifying person' is defined as an individual who is a member of the company;[3017] or a person authorised under s 323 of the CA 2006 (representation of corporations at meetings) to act as the representative of a corporation in relation to the meeting, or a person appointed as proxy of a member in relation to the meeting;[3018] or a person appointed as proxy of a member in relation to the meeting.[3019]

Section 318 of the CA 2006 replaces ss 370(4) and 370A of the CA 1985. It sets a quorum for a meeting of one 'qualifying person' in the case of a single member company and – as a default – 'two qualifying persons' in any other case. Section 318(2) and (3) of the CA 2006 ensure that a member, corporate representative or proxy present at the meeting may all be 'qualifying persons', but excludes the possibility of two or more corporate representatives or proxies of the same member comprising a quorum. Under these provisions, proxies and corporate representatives do not count towards a quorum in companies with more than one member.

Chairman of meeting

14.49 Section 319 of the CA 2006 addresses who may elect as chairman at meetings. A member may be elected to be the chairman of a general meeting by a resolution of the company passed at the meeting.[3020]

Section 319(1) of the CA 2006 is subject to any provision of the company's articles that states who may or may not be chairman.[3021]

Section 319 of the CA 2006 reproduces the effect of s 370(5) of the CA 1985 and provides a default provision, where the company's articles are silent to allow any member to be elected as chairman of general meeting by a resolution of the company passed at the meeting.

[3014] CA 2006, s 318(1).   [3015] CA 2006, s 318(2)(a).   [3016] CA 2006, s 318(2)(b).
[3017] CA 2006, s 318(3)(a).   [3018] CA 2006, s 318(3)(b).   [3019] CA 2006, s 318(3)(c).
[3020] CA 2006, s 319(1).   [3021] CA 2006, s 319(2).

Declaration by chairman on a show of hands

14.50 Section 320 of the CA 2006 deals with a declaration by the chairman on a show of hands. On a show of hands, a declaration by the chairman that the resolution has or has not been passed,[3022] or passed with a particular majority,[3023] is conclusive evidence of that fact without proof of the number or proportion of the votes recorded in favour of or against the resolution.

An entry in respect of such a declaration in minutes of the meeting recorded in accordance with s 355 of the CA 2006 is also conclusive evidence of that fact without such proof.[3024]

This section does not have effect if a poll is demanded in respect of the resolution (and the demand is not subsequently withdrawn).[3025]

Section 320 of the CA 2006 replaces s 378(4) of the CA 1985 and part of Article 47 of Table A. It ensures that the chairman's declaration of a vote taken on a show of hands is conclusive evidence of the resolution being passed or lost without further proof being provided, unless a poll is demanded on the resolution.

There are two main differences from s 378(4) of the CA 1985, both of which are drawn from Table A. First, if the demand for a poll is withdrawn, then the chairman's declaration will stand. Second, the minutes of the meeting also provide conclusive evidence of the chairman's declaration. This section is intended to provide certainty by preventing members from challenging a declaration of the chairman as to the votes cast on a resolution at a meeting otherwise than by calling a poll.

Right to demand a poll

14.51 Section 321 of the CA 2006 deals with who can demand a poll. A provision of a company's articles is void, insofar as it would have the effect of excluding the right to demand a poll at a general meeting on any question other than the election of the chairman of the meeting,[3026] or the adjournment of the meeting.[3027]

A provision of a company's articles is void, insofar as it would have the effect of making ineffective a demand for a poll on any such question which is made by not less than five members having the right to vote on the resolution;[3028] or by a member or members representing not less than 10 per cent of the total voting rights of all the members having the right to vote on the resolution (excluding any voting rights attached to any shares in the company held as treasury shares);[3029] or by a member or members holding shares in the company conferring a right to vote on the resolution, being shares on which

---

[3022] CA 2006, s 320(1)(a).   [3023] CA 2006, s 320(1)(b).   [3024] CA 2006, s 320(2).
[3025] CA 2006, s 320(3).   [3026] CA 2006, s 321(1)(a).   [3027] CA 2006, s 321(1)(b).
[3028] CA 2006, s 321(2)(a).   [3029] CA 2006, s 321(2)(b).

an aggregate sum has been paid up equal to not less than 10 per cent of the total sum paid up on all the shares conferring that right (excluding shares in the company conferring a right to vote on the resolution which are held as treasury shares).[3030]

Section 321 of the CA 2006 replaces s 373 of the CA 1985. It restricts companies' ability, through their articles, to exclude members' rights to call a poll. However, it allows articles to exclude the right to a poll on the election of the chairman of the meeting and the adjournment of the meeting. The section provides for three effective types of demands for a poll, including a demand made by at least five members with a right to vote on the resolution.

Voting on a poll

14.52 Section 322 of the CA 2006 deals with voting on a poll. On a poll taken at a general meeting of a company, a member entitled to more than one vote need not, if he votes, use all his votes or cast all the votes he uses in the same way.

This section replaces s 374 of the CA 1985. This provision recognises that a member may hold shares on behalf of third parties and allows the member to cast votes in different ways according to instructions from his clients. The reference to class meetings in s 374 of the CA 1985 is dealt with by s 334 of the CA 2006 (application to class meetings).

Representation of corporations at meetings

14.53 Section 323 of the CA 2006 states that if a corporation (whether or not a company within the meaning of this Act) is a member of a company, it may by resolution of its directors or other governing body authorise a person or persons to act as its representative or representatives at any meeting of the company.[3031]

Where the corporation authorises only one person, he is entitled to exercise the same powers on behalf of the corporation as the corporation could exercise if it were an individual member of the company.[3032]

Where the corporation authorises more than one person, any one of them is entitled to exercise the same powers on behalf of the corporation as the corporation could exercise if it were an individual member of the company.[3033]

Where the corporation authorises more than one person and more than one of them purports to exercise a power under s 323(3) of the CA 2006, if they purport to exercise the power in the same way,[3034] the power is treated as

---

[3030] CA 2006, s 321(2)(c).   [3031] CA 2006, s 232(1).   [3032] CA 2006, s 323(2).
[3033] CA 2006, s 323(3).   [3034] CA 2006, s 323(4)(a).

exercised in that way, or if they do not purport to exercise the power in the same way, the power is treated as not exercised.[3035]

Section 323 of the CA 2006 replaces s 375 of the CA 1985. It expressly provides for the appointment of multiple corporate representatives. This was possible under s 375 of the CA 1985, although the effect of appointing multiple representatives under the existing law was in some cases unclear. The new section spells out the position. Any one of the corporate representatives will be entitled to vote and exercise other powers on behalf of the member at meetings, but in the event that representatives' votes or other powers conflict, the corporation is deemed to have abstained from exercising its vote or power. If a corporation wishes to appoint people with different voting intentions or with authority to vote different blocks of shares, they should appoint proxies.

Proxies

14.54 Sections 324–331 of the CA 2006 deal with proxies.

Right to appoint proxies

14.55 Section 324 of the CA 2006 deals with the right to appoint proxies. A member of a company is entitled to appoint another person as his proxy to exercise all or any of his rights to attend, and to speak and vote at a meeting of the company.[3036]

In the case of a company having a share capital, a member may appoint more than one proxy in relation to a meeting, provided that each proxy is appointed to exercise the rights attached to a different share or shares held by him, or (as the case may be) to a different £10, or multiple of £10, of stock held by him.[3037]

Section 324 of the CA 2006 sets out new provisions for the appointment of proxies, expanding on the rights given under s 372 and Table A of the CA 1985. It sets out the existing rights given under s 372 and Table A of the CA 1985. It puts on a statutory footing certain rights that, under the CA 1985, are subject to the articles.

In future, members of both private and public companies will have the right to appoint more than one proxy. All proxies will be able to attend, to speak and vote at a meeting. As to voting rights of a proxy on a show of hands, see s 284(2)(b) and s 285 of the CA 2006. The effect of those sections is that the default position will be that, where a member appoints more than one proxy, each proxy will have a vote. The articles will be capable of restricting the number of votes of the proxies that they still have at least one vote between them.

[3035] CA 2006, s 323(4)(b). [3036] CA 2006, s 324(1). [3037] CA 2006, s 324(2).

Notice of meeting to contain a statement of rights

14.56 Section 325 of the CA 2006 deals with the requirement for a notice of a meeting to contain a statement of rights. In every notice calling a meeting of a company there must appear, with reasonable prominence, a statement informing the member of his rights under s 324 of the CA 2006,[3038] and any more extensive rights conferred by the company's articles to appoint more than one proxy.[3039]

Failure to comply with this section does not affect the validity of the meeting or of anything done at the meeting.[3040]

If this section is not complied with as respects any meeting, an offence is committed by every officer of the company who is in default.[3041] A person guilty of an offence under this section is liable on summary conviction to a fine not exceeding level 3 on the standard scale.[3042]

Section 325 of the CA 2006 replaces ss 372(3) and 372(4) of the CA 2006 with changes consequential on the extended rights to appoint proxies under s 324 of the CA 2006. The new provision requires every notice calling a meeting to contain a statement informing the member of his right to appoint one or more proxies and any more extensive rights conferred by the company's articles. Failure to include such a statement will not invalidate the meeting, but is an offence attracting a fine for every officer of the company found in default.

Company-sponsored invitations to appoint proxies

14.57 Section 326 of the CA 2006 deals with company-sponsored invitations to appoint proxies. If for the purposes of a meeting there are issued at the company's expense invitations to members to appoint as proxy a specified person or a number of specified persons, the invitations must be issued to all members entitled to vote at the meeting.[3043]

Section 326(1) of the CA 2006 is not contravened if there is issued to a member at his request a form of appointment naming the proxy or a list of persons willing to act as proxy,[3044] and the form or list is available on request to all members entitled to vote at the meeting.[3045]

If s 326(1) of the CA 2006 is contravened as respects a meeting, an offence is committed by every officer of the company who is in default.[3046] A person guilty of an offence under this section is liable on summary conviction to a fine not exceeding level 3 on the standard scale.[3047]

Section 326 of the CA 2006 reproduces the effect of s 372(6) of the CA

[3038] CA 2006, s 325(1)(a).   [3039] CA 2006, s 325(1)(b).   [3040] CA 2006, s 325(2).
[3041] CA 2006, s 325(3).   [3042] CA 2006, s 325(4).   [3043] CA 2006, s 326(1).
[3044] CA 2006, s 326(2)(a).   [3045] CA 2006, s 326(2)(b).   [3046] CA 2006, s 326(3).
[3047] CA 2006, s 326(4).

2006 and requires a company to ensure that if it invites members to appoint a particular person or persons as proxy, such an invitation must be issued to all members entitled to vote at the meeting. Section 326(2) of the CA 2006 lists two exceptions to the requirement. Failure to comply attracts a fine for every officer in default.

Notice required of appointment of a proxy, etc.

14.58 Section 327 of the CA 2006 deals with the notice required of the appointment of a proxy. It applies to the appointment of a proxy,[3048] and any document necessary to show the validity of, or otherwise relating to, the appointment of a proxy.[3049]

Any provision of the company's articles is void insofar as it would have the effect of requiring any such appointment or document to be received by the company or another person earlier than the following time: in the case of a meeting or adjourned meeting, 48 hours before the time for holding the meeting or adjourned meeting;[3050] or in the case of a poll taken more than 48 hours after it was demanded, 24 hours before the time appointed for the taking of the poll;[3051] or in the case of a poll taken not more than 48 hours after it was demanded, the time at which it was demanded.[3052]

In calculating the periods mentioned in s 327(2) of the CA 2006 no account shall be taken of any part of a day that is not a working day.[3053]

Section 327 of the CA 2006 replaces s 372(5) of the CA 1985. There are two changes. The first relates to the timing required for a notice of proxy appointment. The new provision ensures that weekends, Christmas Day, Good Friday and any holiday are excluded from the time counting towards the minimum 48-hour notice required to appoint proxies. This means, for example, that for a meeting to be held at 3:00 pm on a Tuesday after a bank holiday Monday, the cut-off point for proxy appointment will be 3:00 pm the previous Thursday, not 3:00 pm Sunday as under the CA 1985. The second change is that polls which are not taken immediately are covered by the rules as well as meetings and adjourned meetings.

Chairing meetings

14.59 Section 328 of the CA 2006 deals with chairing meetings. A proxy may be elected to be the chairman of a general meeting by a resolution of the company passed at the meeting.[3054]

Section 328(1) of the CA 2006 is subject to any provision of the company's articles that states who may or who may not be chairman.[3055]

[3048] CA 2006, s 327(1)(a).   [3049] CA 2006, s 327(1)(b).   [3050] CA 2006, s 327(2)(a).
[3051] CA 2006, s 327(2)(b).   [3052] CA 2006, s 327(2)(c).   [3053] CA 2006, s 327(3).
[3054] CA 2006, s 328(1).   [3055] CA 2006, s 328(2).

This section provides a default regulation subject to the articles that a proxy may be elected as chairman of a general meeting by resolution of the shareholders passed at the meeting.

Right of proxy to demand a poll

14.60 Section 329 of the CA 2006 governs the right to demand a poll. The appointment of a proxy to vote on a matter at a meeting of a company authorises the proxy to demand, or join in demanding, a poll on that matter.[3056]

In applying the provisions of s 321(2) of the CA 2006 (requirements for effective demand), (a) a demand by a proxy counts for the purposes of para (a), as a demand by the member; or (b) for the purposes of para (b), as a demand by a member representing the voting rights that the proxy is authorised to exercise; or (c) for the purposes of para (c), as a demand by a member holding the shares to which those rights are attached.[3057]

This section sets out the way in which a proxy may participate in a demand for a poll.

Notice required of termination of a proxy's authority

14.61 Section 330 of the CA 2006 sets out the notice required of termination of a proxy's authority. It applies to the notice required that the authority of a person to act as proxy is terminated ('notice of termination').[3058]

The termination of the authority of a person to act as proxy does not affect whether he counts in deciding whether there is a quorum at a meeting;[3059] or the validity of anything he does as chairman of a meeting;[3060] or the validity of a poll demanded by him at a meeting,[3061] unless the company receives notice of the termination before the commencement of the meeting.

The termination of the authority of a person to act as proxy does not affect the validity of a vote given by that person unless the company receives notice of the termination before the commencement of the meeting or adjourned meeting at which the vote is given;[3062] or in the case of a poll taken more than 48 hours after it is demanded, before the time appointed for taking the poll.[3063]

If the company's articles require or permit members to give notice of termination to a person other than the company, the references above to the company receiving notice have effect as if they were or (as the case may be) included a reference to that person.[3064]

[3056] CA 2006, s 329(1).   [3057] CA 2006, s 329(2).   [3058] CA 2006, s 330(1).
[3059] CA 2007, s 330(1)(a).   [3060] CA 2006, s 330(2)(b).   [3061] CA 2006, s 330(2)(c).
[3062] CA 2006, s 330(3)(a).   [3063] CA 2006, s 330(3)(b).   [3064] CA 2006, s 330(4).

Section 330(2) and (3) of the CA 2006 apply subject to any provision of the company's articles that has the effect of requiring notice of termination to be received by the company or another person at a time earlier than that specified in those subsections. This is subject to s 330(6) of the CA 2006(6).[3065]

Any provision of the company's articles is void in so far as it would have the effect of requiring notice of termination to be received by the company or another person earlier than the following time: in the case of a meeting or adjourned meeting, 48 hours before the time for holding the meeting or adjourned meeting;[3066] or in the case of a poll taken more than 48 hours after it was demanded, 24 hours before the time appointed for the taking of the poll;[3067] or in the case of a poll taken not more than 48 hours after it was demanded, the time at which it was demanded.[3068]

In calculating the periods mentioned in s 330(3)(b) and (6) of the CA 2006, no account shall be taken of any part of a day that is not a working day.[3069]

Section 330 of the CA 2006 provides a default regulation to replace Article 63 of Table A of the CA 1985. This ensures that, subject to the articles, an appointed proxy's actions at a meeting are valid unless notice of termination of the proxy's authority is given before the meeting starts. The company's articles may specify a longer advance notice period but this cannot be more than 48 hours in advance of the meeting (excluding weekends, Christmas Day, Good Friday and bank holidays).

Saving for more extensive rights conferred by articles

14.62 Section 331 of the CA 2006 deals with savings for more extensive rights conferred by articles. This section states that nothing in ss 324–330 of the CA 2006 (proxies) prevents a company's articles from conferring more extensive rights on members or proxies than are conferred by those sections.

This section makes clear that the company's articles confer more extensive rights than are provided for under the CA 2006 on members and their proxies.

Adjourned meetings

Resolution passed at adjourned meeting

14.63 Section 332 of the CA 2006 deals with resolution passed at adjourned meeting. Where a resolution is passed at an adjourned meeting of a company, the resolution is for all purposes to be treated as having been passed on the date on which it was in fact passed, and is not to be deemed passed on any earlier date.

[3065] CA 2006, s 330(5).   [3066] CA 2006, s 330(6)(a).   [3067] CA 2006, s 330(6)(b).
[3068] CA 2006, s 330(6)(c).   [3069] CA 2006, s 330(7).

Section 332 of the CA 2006 reproduces the effect of part s 381 of the CA 1985 as it applies to members' meetings. It ensures that a resolution of the members of the company passed at an adjourned meeting is treated as passed on that date and not on any earlier date. The reference to class meetings in s 381 of the CA 1985 is dealt with by s 334 of the CA 2006.

Electronic communications

Sending documents relating to meetings etc. in electronic form

14.64 Section 333 of the CA 2006 states that where a company has given an electronic address in a notice calling a meeting, it is deemed to have agreed that any document or information relating to proceedings at the meeting may be sent by electronic means to that address (subject to any conditions or limitations specified in the notice).[3070]

Where a company has given an electronic address in an instrument of proxy sent out by the company in relation to the meeting,[3071] or in an invitation to appoint a proxy issued by the company in relation to the meeting,[3072] it is deemed to have agreed that any document or information relating to proxies for that meeting may be sent by electronic means to that address (subject to any conditions or limitations specified in the notice).

In s 333(2), documents relating to proxies include the appointment of a proxy in relation to a meeting CA 2006,[3073] or any document necessary to show the validity of, or otherwise relating to, the appointment of a proxy;[3074] and notice of the termination of the authority of a proxy.[3075]

The term 'electronic address' means any address or number used for the purposes of sending or receiving documents or information by electronic means.[3076]

Section 333 of the CA 2006 should be read together with the provisions about electronic communications to companies in Part 3 of Schedule 4 of the CA 2006. Taken together, these provisions allow a member to communicate with the company by electronic means where the company has given an electronic address in a notice calling a meeting or in an instrument of proxy or proxy invitation.

Application to class meetings

14.65 Sections 334 and 335 of the CA 2006 deal with class meetings.

Section 334 of the CA 2006 states that the provisions of Chapter 3 of Part 13 of the CA 2006 apply (with necessary modifications) in relation to a

---

[3070] CA 2006, s 333(1).   [3071] CA 2006, s 333(2)(a).   [3072] CA 2006, s 333(2)(b).
[3073] CA 2006, s 333(3)(a).   [3074] CA 2006, s 333(3)(b).   [3075] CA 2006, s 333(3)(c).
[3076] CA 2006, s 333(4).

meeting of holders of a class of shares, as they apply in relation to a general meeting. This is subject to s 334(2) and (3) of the CA 2006.[3077]

The following provisions of Chapter 3 of the CA 2006 do not apply in relation to a meeting of holders of a class of shares, namely, ss 303–305 of the CA 2006 (members' power to require directors to call a general meeting);[3078] and s 306 (power of court to order a meeting).[3079]

The following provisions (in addition to those mentioned in s 334(2)) of the CA 2006 do not apply in relation to a meeting in connection with the variation of rights attached to a class of shares (a 'variation of class rights meeting'): s 318 of the CA 2006 (quorum),[3080] and s 321 of the CA 2006 (right to demand a poll).[3081]

The quorum for a variation of class rights meeting is for a meeting other than an adjourned meeting, two persons present holding at least one-third in nominal value of the issued shares of the class in question (excluding any shares of that class held as treasury shares);[3082] for an adjourned meeting, one person present holding shares of the class in question.[3083]

For the purposes of s 334(4) of the CA 2006, where a person is present by proxy or proxies, he is treated as holding only the shares in respect of which those proxies are authorised to exercise voting rights.[3084]

At a variation of class rights meeting, any holder of shares of the class in question present may demand a poll.[3085]

For the purposes of s 334 of the CA 2006, any amendment of a provision contained in a company's articles for the variation of the rights attached to a class of shares, or the insertion of any such provision into the articles, is itself to be treated as a variation of those rights;[3086] and references to the variation of rights attached to a class of shares include references to their abrogation.[3087]

This section applies the provisions of Chapter 3 to Part 13 of the CA 2006 with some modifications to meetings of classes of members of companies without a share capital.

Application to class meetings: companies without a share capital

14.66 Section 335 of the CA 2006 states that the provisions of Chapter 3 of Part 13 of the CA 2006 apply (with necessary modifications) in relation to a meeting of a class of members of a company without a share capital as they apply in relation to a general meeting. This is subject to s 335(2) and (3) of the CA 2006.[3088]

[3077] CA 2006, s 334(1).   [3078] CA 2006, s 334(2)(a).   [3079] CA 2006, s 334(2)(b).
[3080] CA 2006, s 334(3)(a).   [3081] CA 2006, s 334(3)(b).   [3082] CA 2006, s 334(4)(a).
[3083] CA 2006, s 334(4)(b).   [3084] CA 2006, s 335(5).   [3085] CA 2006, s 334(6).
[3086] CA 2006, s 334(7)(a).   [3087] CA 2006, s 334(7)(b).   [3088] CA 2006, s 335(1).

The following provisions of Chapter 3 of Part 13 of the CA 2006 do not apply in relation to a meeting of a class of members, namely, ss 303–305 of the CA 2006 (members' power to require directors to call a general meeting;[3089] and s 306 of the CA 2006 (power of court to order a meeting).[3090]

The following provisions (in addition to those mentioned in s 335(2) of the CA 2006) do not apply in relation to a meeting in connection with the variation of the rights of a class of members (a 'variation of class rights meeting'): s 318 of the CA 2006 (quorum),[3091] and s 321 of the CA 2006 (right to demand a poll).[3092]

The quorum for a variation of class rights meeting is for a meeting other than an adjourned meeting, two members of the class present (in person or by proxy) who together represent at least one-third of the voting rights of the class;[3093] for an adjourned meeting, one member of the class present (in person or by proxy).[3094]

At a variation of class rights meeting, any member present (in person or by proxy) may demand a poll.[3095]

For the purposes of s 335 of the CA 2006 any amendment of a provision contained in a company's articles for the variation of the rights of a class of members, or the insertion of any such provision into the articles, is itself to be treated as a variation of those rights,[3096] and references to the variation of rights of a class of members include references to their abrogation.[3097]

This section applies the provisions of Chapter 3 of Part 13 of the CA 2006 with some modifications to meetings of classes of members of companies without a share capital.

Public Companies: Additional Requirements For AGMs

14.67 The requirements for public companies relating to annual general meetings are set out under Chapter 4 to Part 13 of the CA 2006. The main substantive changes to the CA 1985 are, as the Company Law Review Group recommended, that private companies will no longer be required to hold an AGM. The provisions of this Chapter therefore do not apply to private companies; and public company AGMs must be held within six months of their financial year-end.

Public companies: annual general meeting

14.68 Section 336 of the CA 2006 deals with the AGM of the public companies. Every public company must hold a general meeting as its annual

---

[3089] CA 2006, s 335(2)(a).   [3090] CA 2006, s 335(2)(b).   [3091] CA 2006, s 335(3)(a).
[3092] CA 2006, s 335(3)(b).   [3093] CA 2006, s 335(4)(a).   [3094] CA 2006, s 335(4)(b).
[3095] CA 2006, s 335(5).   [3096] CA 2006, s 335(6)(a).   [3097] CA 2006, s 335(6)(b).

general meeting in each period of six months beginning with the day following its accounting reference date (in addition to any other meetings held during that period).[3098]

A company that fails to comply with s 336(1) of the CA 2006 as a result of giving notice under s 392 of the CA 2006 (alteration of accounting reference date) specifying a new accounting reference date,[3099] and stating that the current accounting reference period or the previous accounting reference period is to be shortened,[3100] shall be treated as if it had complied with s 336(1) of the CA 2006 if it holds a general meeting as its annual general meeting within three months of giving that notice.

If a company fails to comply with s 336(1) of the CA 2006, an offence is committed by every officer of the company who is in default.[3101] A person guilty of an offence under this section is liable on conviction on indictment, to a fine;[3102] or on summary conviction, to a fine not exceeding the statutory maximum.[3103]

Section 336 of CA 2006 replaces s 366 of CA 1985, but will apply only to public companies since private companies are no longer to be required to hold an AGM.

Where s 366 of the CA 1985 required an AGM to held each year and not more than 15 months after the previous AGM, a public company will now be required to hold an AGM within six months of its financial year end. This new requirement is intended to ensure that shareholders have more timely opportunity to hold the directors of a public company to account.

Public companies: notice of AGM

14.69 Section 337 of the CA 2006 states that a notice calling an annual general meeting of a public company must state that the meeting is an annual general meeting.[3104]

An annual general meeting may be called by shorter notice than that required by s 307(2) of the CA 2006 or by the company's articles (as the case may be), if all the members entitled to attend and vote at the meeting agree to the shorter notice.[3105]

Section 337 of the CA 2006 reproduces the effects of parts of s 369 of the CA 1985 Act relating to the AGM notice. The minimum notice period for recalling a public company AGM is 21 days, as set out under s 307 of the CA 2006 (notice required of a general meeting), or longer if provided for in the company's articles. An AGM may be called at shorter notice if all members of the company agree.

[3098] CA 2006, s 336(1).   [3099] CA 2006, s 336(2)(a).   [3100] CA 2006, s 336(2)(b).
[3101] CA 2006, s 336(3).   [3102] CA 2006, s 336(4)(a).   [3103] CA 2006, s 336(4)(b).
[3104] CA 2006, s 337(1).   [3105] CA 2006, s 337 (2).

Public companies: members' power to require circulation of resolutions for AGMs

14.70 Section 338 of the CA 2006 deals with members' power to require circulation of resolutions for AGMs. The members of a public company may require the company to give, to members of the company entitled to receive notice of the next annual general meeting, notice of a resolution that may properly be moved and is intended to be moved at that meeting.[3106]

A resolution may properly be moved at an annual general meeting unless it would, if passed, be ineffective (whether by reason of inconsistency with any enactment or the company's constitution or otherwise);[3107] or it is defamatory of any person;[3108] or it is frivolous or vexatious.[3109]

A company is required to give notice of a resolution once it has received requests that it do so from members representing at least 5 per cent of the total voting rights of all the members who have a right to vote on the resolution at the annual general meeting to which the requests relate (excluding any voting rights attached to any shares in the company held as treasury shares);[3110] or at least 100 members who have a right to vote on the resolution at the annual general meeting to which the requests relate and hold shares in the company on which there has been paid up an average sum, per member, of at least £100.[3111] See also s 153 of the CA 2006 (exercise of rights where shares held on behalf of others).

A request may be in hard copy form or in electronic form,[3112] and must identify the resolution of which notice is to be given,[3113] and must be authenticated by the person or persons making it,[3114] and must be received by the company not later than six weeks before the annual general meeting to which the requests relate;[3115] or if later, the time at which notice is given of that meeting.[3116]

Section 338 of the CA 2006, with s 339 of the CA 2006 (public companies: company's duty to circulate members' resolutions for AGMs), replaces ss 376 and 377 of the CA 1985 (to the extent that they relate to resolutions proposed by members to be moved at an AGM).

Members holding at least 5 per cent voting rights or at least 100 members holding an average of £100 paid-up capital have the right to propose a resolution for the AGM agenda and to require the company to circulate details of the resolution to all members. A change from the existing legislation is that the shares must in each case carry rights to vote on the relevant resolution.

The key policy change is that, if the members' request is received before the financial year end, then the members are not required to cover the cost of circulation.

[3106] CA 2006, s 338(1).   [3107] CA 2006, s 338(2)(a).   [3108] CA 2006, s 338(2)(b).
[3109] CA 2006, s 338(2)(c).   [3110] CA 2006, s 338(3)(a).   [3111] CA 2006, s 338(3)(b).
[3112] CA 2006, s 338(4)(a).   [3113] CA 2006, s 338(4)(b).   [3114] CA 2006, s 338(4)(c).
[3115] CA 2006, s 338(4)(d)(i).   [3116] CA 2006, s 338(4)(d)(ii).

Public companies: a company's duty to circulate members' resolutions for AGMs

14.71 Section 339 of the CA 2006 is concerned with a company's duty to circulate members' resolutions for AGMs in respect of public companies. A company that is required under s 338 of the CA 2006 to give notice of a resolution must send a copy of it to each member of the company entitled to receive notice of the annual general meeting in the same manner as a notice of the meeting,[3117] and at the same time as, or as soon as reasonably practicable after, it gives notice of the meeting.[3118]

Section 339(1) of the CA 2006, applies subject to s 340(2) of the CA 2006 (deposit or tender of sum in respect of expenses of circulation).[3119]

The business that may be dealt with at an annual general meeting includes a resolution, of which notice is given in accordance with this section.[3120]

In the event of default in complying with this section, an offence is committed by every officer of the company who is in default.[3121] A person guilty of an offence under this section is liable on conviction on indictment, to a fine;[3122] or on summary conviction, to a fine not exceeding the statutory maximum.[3123]

Section 339 of the CA 2006 replaces the remaining parts of ss 376 and 377 of the CA 1985 (to the extent that they relate to resolutions proposed by members to be moved at an AGM). It specifies what a company has to do when it is required to circulate a members' resolution for an AGM.

Public companies: expenses of circulating members' resolutions for AGM

14.72 Section 340 of the CA 2006 states that the expenses of the company in complying with s 339 of the CA 2006 need not be paid by the members who requested the circulation of the resolution, if requests sufficient to require the company to circulate it are received before the end of the financial year preceding the meeting.[3124]

Otherwise the expenses of the company in complying with that section must be paid by the members who requested the circulation of the resolution, unless the company resolves otherwise;[3125] and unless the company has previously so resolved, it is not bound to comply with that section unless there is deposited with or tendered to it, not later than six weeks before the annual general meeting to which the requests relate;[3126] or if later, the time at which notice is given of that meeting, a sum reasonably sufficient to meet its expenses in complying with that section.[3127]

[3117] CA 2006, s 339(1)(a).   [3118] CA 2006, s 339(1)(b).   [3119] CA 2006, s 339(2).
[3120] CA 2006, s 339(3).   [3121] CA 2006, s 339(4).   [3122] CA 2006, s 339(5)(a).
[3123] CA 2006, s 339(5)(b).   [3124] CA 2006, s 340(1).   [3125] CA 2006, s 340(2)(a).
[3126] CA 2006, s 340(2)(b)(i).   [3127] CA 2006, s 340(2)(b)(ii).

Section 340 of the CA 2006 provides that the expenses of complying with s 339 of the CA 2006 (public companies: a company's duty to circulate members' resolutions for AGMs) need not be paid by the members who requested the circulation of the resolution, if requests sufficient to require the company to circulate it are received before the company's year end. Otherwise, the company's expenses will have to be met by the members who requested the circulation of the resolution unless the company resolves otherwise. In this case, the members requesting the statement must deposit a sum to cover the company's costs (unless the company has resolved otherwise).

Additional Requirements For Quoted Companies

14.73 Chapter 5 to Part 13 of the CA 2006 imposes new requirements on quoted companies relating to the disclosure on a website of the results of polls at general meetings, and an independent report on a poll if a sufficient number of members demand one. These two measures were recommended by the Company Law Review Group.[3128]

Website publication of poll results

Results of poll to be made available on website

14.74 Section 341 of the CA 2006 provides that where a poll is taken at a general meeting of a quoted company, the company must ensure that the following information is made available on a website: the date of the meeting,[3129] the text of the resolution or, as the case may be, a description of the subject matter of the poll,[3130] the number of votes cast in favour,[3131] and the number of votes cast against.[3132]

The provisions of s 341(2) of the CA 2006 (requirements as to website availability) apply.[3133]

In the event of default in complying with this section (or with the requirements of s 353 of the CA 2006 as it applies for the purposes of this section), an offence is committed by every officer of the company who is in default.[3134] A person guilty of an offence under subs (3) is liable on summary conviction to a fine not exceeding level 3 on the standard scale.[3135]

Failure to comply with this section (or the requirements of s 353 of the CA 2006) does not affect the validity of the poll,[3136] or the resolution or other business (if passed or agreed to) to which the poll relates.[3137]

[3128] *Final Report*, para 6.39(ii) and (iv).   [3129] CA 2006, s 341(1)(a).
[3130] CA 2006, s 341(1)(b).   [3131] CA 2006, s 341(1)(c).   [3132] CA 2006, s 341(1)(d).
[3133] CA 2006, s 341(2).   [3134] CA 2006, s 341(3).   [3135] CA 2006, s 341(4).
[3136] CA 2006, s 341(5)(a).   [3137] CA 2006, s 341(5)(b).

Section 341 of the CA 2006 only applies to polls taken after this section comes into force.[3138]

Section 341 of the CA 2006 requires quoted companies to disclose on a website the results of all polls taken at a general meeting. Section 341 of the CA 2006 sets out the minimum information that must be disclosed. Companies may disclose additional information about the poll results if they wish. Section 341(4) of the CA 2006 imposes a penalty on every officer in default for non-compliance. Non-compliance however does not invalidate the poll, the resolution or other business to which the poll relates.

Section 353 of the CA 2006 (requirements as to website availability) sets out the requirements relating to website on which the poll results must be published.

Independent report on poll

Members' power to require independent reports on polls

14.75 Section 342 of the CA 2006 deals with members' powers to require independent reports on polls.

The members of a quoted company may require the directors to obtain an independent report on any poll taken, or to be taken, at a general meeting of the company.[3139]

The directors are required to obtain an independent report if they receive requests to do so from members representing not less than 5 per cent of the total voting rights of all the members who have a right to vote on the matter to which the poll relates (excluding any voting rights attached to any shares in the company held as treasury shares);[3140] or not less than 100 members who have a right to vote on the matter to which the poll relates and hold shares in the company on which there has been paid up an average sum, per member, of not less than £100.[3141] See also s 153 of the CA 2006 (exercise of rights where shares held on behalf of others).

Where the requests relate to more than one poll, s 342(2) of the CA 2006 must be satisfied in relation to each of them.[3142]

A request may be in hard copy or electronic form,[3143] must identify the poll or polls to which it relates,[3144] must be authenticated by the person or persons making it,[3145] and must be received by the company not later than one week after the date on which the poll is taken.[3146]

Section 342 of the CA 2006 gives members of a quoted company the right to require an independent report of any poll taken, or to be taken, at a

[3138] CA 2006, s 341(6).   [3139] CA 2006, s 342(1).   [3140] CA 2006, s 342(2)(a).

[3141] CA 2006, s 342(2)(b).   [3142] CA 2006, s 342(3).   [3143] CA 2006, s 342(4)(a).

[3144] CA 2006, s 342(4)(b).   [3145] CA 2006, s 342(4)(c).   [3146] CA 2006, s 342(4)(d).

general meeting. The minimum threshold required for the demand is the same
as that requiring the circulation of a resolution – that is members holding 5
per cent of the voting rights or 100 members holding on average £100 of the
CA paid-up capital. The members' request must be made within one week of
the meeting where the poll is taken. This allows members to decide after a
poll is taken whether they wish to require an independent report, for example
on a controversial resolution or where there appears to be a problem relating
to voting procedures. Members may make their request in advance of the
meeting if they wish, but unless the company's articles already require all
votes to be taken on a poll, members may need to take steps to ensure that a
poll is called.

Appointment of an independent assessor

14.76 Section 343 of the CA 2006 is concerned with the appointment of an
independent assessor.

Directors who are required under s 342 of the CA 2006 to obtain an
independent report on a poll, or polls, must appoint a person they consider to
be appropriate (an 'independent assessor') to prepare a report for the company on it, or on them.[3147]

The appointment must be made within one week after the company being
required to obtain the report.[3148]

The directors must not appoint a person who does not meet the independence requirement in s 344 of the CA 2006;[3149] or has another role in relation to
any poll on which he is to report (including, in particular, a role in connection
with collecting or counting votes or with the appointment of proxies).[3150]

In the event of a default in complying with this section, an offence is
committed by every officer of the company who is in default.[3151] A person
guilty of an offence under this section is liable on summary conviction to a
fine not exceeding level 5 on the standard scale.[3152]

If at the meeting no poll on which a report is required is taken, the directors are not required to obtain a report from the independent assessor;[3153]
and his appointment ceases (but without prejudice to any right to be paid for
work done before the appointment ceased).[3154]

Section 343 of the CA 2006 provides that the appointment of an independent assessor must be made within one week of the members' request. This
means that the appointment could be made either before or after the meeting
depending on when the members' request is made. The independent assessor
must be independent (sees 344 of the CA 2006) and must not be someone
already involved in the voting process for the company.

[3147] CA 2006, s 343(1).   [3148] CA 2006, s 343(2).   [3149] CA 2006, s 343(3)(a).
[3150] CA 2006, s 343(3)(b).   [3151] CA 2006, s 343(4).   [3152] CA 2006, s 343(5).
[3153] CA 2006, s 343(6)(a).   [3154] CA 2006, s 343(6)(b).

Independence requirement

14.77 Section 344 of the CA 2006 states that a person may not be appointed as an independent assessor if he is an officer or employee of the company;[3155] or a partner or employee of such a person, or a partnership of which such a person is a partner;[3156] or if he is an officer or employee of an associated undertaking of the company;[3157] or a partner or employee of such a person, or a partnership of which such a person is a partner;[3158] or if there exists between the person or an associate of his,[3159] and the company or an associated undertaking of the company,[3160] a connection of any such description as may be specified by regulations made by the Secretary of State.

An auditor of the company is not regarded as an officer or employee of the company for this purpose.[3161]

An associated undertaking is defined as as a parent undertaking or subsidiary undertaking of the company,[3162] or a subsidiary undertaking of a parent undertaking of the company; and 'associate' has the meaning given by s 345 of the CA 2006.[3163]

Regulations under this section are subject to negative resolution procedure.[3164]

Section 344 of the CA 2006 prevents a person acting as an independent assessor on a poll if he is too closely connected to the company or an associated undertaking of the company. The independence requirements are set out in s 344(1) of the CA 2006. They correspond to the independence requirements for an auditor (sees 1214 of the CA 2006). Section 344 of the CA 2006 allows, but does not require, an auditor to be appointed as an assessor.

Meaning of 'associate'

14.78 Section 345 of the CA 2006 defines 'associate' for the purposes of s 344 of the CA 2006 (independence requirement).[3165]

In relation to an individual, 'associate' means that individual's spouse or civil partner or minor child or step-child;[3166] or any body corporate of which that individual is a director;[3167] and any employee or partner of that individual.[3168]

In relation to a body corporate, 'associate' means any body corporate of which that body is a director;[3169] any body corporate in the same group as that body;[3170] and any employee or partner of that body or of any body corporate in the same group.[3171]

[3155] CA 2006, s 344(1)(a)(i). [3156] CA 2006, s 344(1)(a)(ii). [3157] CA 2006, s 344(1)(b)(i).
[3158] CA 2006, s 344(1)(b)(ii). [3159] CA 2006, s 344(1)(c)(i). [3160] CA 2006, s 344(1)(c)(ii).
[3161] CA 2006, s 344(2). [3162] CA 2006, s 344(3)(a). [3163] CA 2006, s 344(3)(b).
[3164] CA 2006, s 344(4). [3165] CA 2006, s 345(1). [3166] CA 2006, s 345(2)(a).
[3167] CA 2006, s 345(2)(b). [3168] CA 2006, s 345(2)(c). [3169] CA 2006, s 345(3)(a).
[3170] CA 2006, s 345(3)(b). [3171] CA 2006, s 345(3)(c).

In relation to a partnership that is a legal person under the law by which it is governed, 'associate' means any body corporate of which that partnership is a director;[3172] any employee of or partner in that partnership;[3173] and any person who is an associate of a partner in that partnership.[3174]

In relation to a partnership that is not a legal person under the law by which it is governed, 'associate' means any person who is an associate of any of the partners.[3175]

It is provided in this section, that in relation to a limited liability partnership, for 'director' read 'member'.[3176]

Section 345 of the CA 2006 defines 'associate' for the purpose of the independence requirements in s 344 of the CA 2006.

Effect of appointment of a partnership

14.79 Section 346 of the CA 2006 deals with the effect of appointment of a partnership. It applies where a partnership, which is not a legal person under the law by which it is governed, is appointed as an independent assessor.[3177]

Unless a contrary intention appears, the appointment is of the partnership as such and not of the partners.[3178]

Where the partnership ceases, the appointment is to be treated as extending to any partnership that succeeds to the practice of that partnership,[3179] or any other person who succeeds to that practice having previously carried it on in partnership.[3180]

For the purposes of s 346(3) of the CA 2006, a partnership is regarded as succeeding to the practice of another partnership only if the members of the successor partnership are substantially the same as those of the former partnership,[3181] and a partnership or other person is regarded as succeeding to the practice of a partnership only if it or he succeeds to the whole, or substantially the whole, of the business of the former partnership.[3182]

Where the partnership ceases and the appointment is not treated under s 346(3) of the CA 2006 as extending to any partnership or other person, the appointment may with the consent of the company be treated as extending to a partnership, or other person, who succeeds to the business of the former partnership;[3183] or such part of it as is agreed by the company is to be treated as comprising the appointment.[3184]

This section provides for where a partnership that is not a legal person is appointed as an independent assessor on a poll.

[3172] CA 2006, s 345(4)(a).   [3173] CA 2006, s 345(4)(b).   [3174] CA 2006, s 345(4)(c).
[3175] CA 2006, s 345(5).   [3176] CA 2006, s 345(6).   [3177] CA 2006, s 346(1).
[3178] CA 2006, s 346(2).   [3179] CA 2006, s 346(3)(a).   [3180] CA 2006, s 346(3)(b).
[3181] CA 2006, s 346(4)(a).   [3182] CA 2006, s 346(4)(b).   [3183] CA 2006, s 346(5)(a).
[3184] CA 2006, s 346(5)(b).

The independent assessor's report

14.80 Section 347 of the CA 2006 addresses the independent assessor's report.

The report of the independent assessor must state his opinion whether the procedures adopted in connection with the poll or polls were adequate;[3185] the votes cast (including proxy votes) were fairly and accurately recorded and counted;[3186] the validity of members' appointments of proxies was fairly assessed;[3187] the notice of the meeting complied with s 325 of the CA 2006 (notice of meeting to contain statement of rights to appoint proxy);[3188] and s 326 of the CA 2006 (company-sponsored invitations to appoint proxies) was complied with in relation to the meeting.[3189]

The report must give his reasons for the opinions stated.[3190]

If he is unable to form an opinion on any of those matters, the report must record that fact and state the reasons for it.[3191] The report must state the name of the independent assessor.[3192]

This section sets out the minimum information the independent assessor's must contain.

Rights of independent assessor: right to attend meeting, etc.

14.81 Section 348 of the CA 2006 deals with rights of independent assessor with particular reference to rights to attend meeting. Where an independent assessor has been appointed to report on a poll, he is entitled to attend the meeting at which the poll may be taken,[3193] and any subsequent proceedings in connection with the poll.[3194]

He is also entitled to be provided by the company with a copy of the notice of the meeting,[3195] and any other communication provided by the company in connection with the meeting to persons who have a right to vote on the matter to which the poll relates.[3196]

The rights conferred by s 348 of the CA 2006 are only to be exercised to the extent that the independent assessor considers necessary for the preparation of his report.[3197]

If the independent assessor is a firm, the right under s 348(1) of the CA 2006 to attend the meeting and any subsequent proceedings in connection with the poll is exercisable by an individual authorised by the firm in writing to act as its representative for that purpose.[3198]

Section 348 of the CA 2006 gives the independent assessor rights to attend

[3185] CA 2006, s 347(1)(a).   [3186] CA 2006, s 347(1)(b).   [3187] CA 2006, s 347(1)(c).
[3188] CA 2006, s 347(1)(d).   [3189] CA 2006, s 347(1)(e).   [3190] CA 2006, s 347(2).
[3191] CA 2006, s 347(3).   [3192] CA 2006, s 347(4).   [3193] CA 2006, s 348(1)(a).
[3194] CA 2006, s 348(1)(b).   [3195] CA 2006, s 348(2)(a).   [3196] CA 2006, s 348(2)(b).
[3197] CA 2006, s 348(3).   [3198] CA 2006, s 348(4).

the meeting at which the poll or polls may be taken, and to be provided with information relating to the meeting. He is to exercise these rights only to the extent he considers necessary for the preparation of his report.

Rights of independent assessor: right to information

14.82 Section 349 of the CA 2006 deals with the rights of independent assessor with particular reference to the right to information.

The independent assessor is entitled to access to the company's records relating to any poll on which he is to report;[3199] and the meeting at which the poll or polls may be, or were, taken.[3200]

The independent assessor may require anyone who at any material time was a director or secretary of the company;[3201] or an employee of the company,[3202] or a person holding or accountable for any of the company's records,[3203] or a member of the company,[3204] or an agent of the company,[3205] to provide him with information or explanations for the purpose of preparing his report.

The term 'agent' includes the company's bankers, solicitors and auditor.[3206]

A statement made by a person in response to a requirement under s 349 of the CA 2006 may not be used in evidence against him in criminal proceedings except proceedings for an offence under s 350 of the CA 2006 (offences relating to provision of information).[3207]

A person is not required by s 349 of the CA 2006 to disclose information in respect of which a claim to legal professional privilege (in Scotland, to confidentiality of communications) could be maintained in legal proceedings.[3208]

Section 349 of the CA 2006 gives the independent assessor the right to access company records relating to any poll on which he is to report and to the meeting at which the poll or polls may be taken.

Offences relating to provision of information

14.83 Section 350 of the CA 2006 addresses the offences and sanctions relating to provision of information.

A person who fails to comply with a requirement under s 349 of the CA 2006 without delay commits an offence unless it was not reasonably practicable for him to provide the required information or explanation.[3209] A person guilty of an offence under s 350(1) of the CA 2006 is liable on summary conviction to a fine not exceeding level 3 on the standard scale.[3210]

[3199] CA 2006, s 349(1)(a).   [3200] CA 2006, s 349(1)(b).   [3201] CA 2006, s 349(2)(a).
[3202] CA 2006, s 349(2)(b).   [3203] CA 2006, s 349(2)(c).   [3204] CA 2006, s 349(2)(d).
[3205] CA 2006, s 349(2)(e).   [3206] CA 2006, s 349(3).   [3207] CA 2006, s 349(4).
[3208] CA 2006, s 349(5).   [3209] CA 2006, s 350(1).   [3210] CA 2006, s 350(2).

A person commits an offence who knowingly or recklessly makes to an independent assessor a statement (oral or written) that conveys or purports to convey any information or explanations that the independent assessor requires, or is entitled to require, under s 349 of the CA 2006;[3211] which is misleading, false or deceptive in a material particular.[3212]

A person guilty of an offence under s 350(3) of the CA 2006 is liable on conviction on indictment, to imprisonment for a term not exceeding two years or a fine (or both);[3213] on summary conviction in England and Wales, to imprisonment for a term not exceeding 12 months or to a fine not exceeding the statutory maximum (or both);[3214] in Scotland or Northern Ireland, to imprisonment for a term not exceeding six months, or to a fine not exceeding the statutory maximum (or both).[3215]

Nothing in s 350 of the CA 2006 affects any right of an auditor to apply for an injunction (in Scotland, an interdict or an order for specific performance) to enforce any of his rights under s 348 or s 349 of the CA 2006.[3216]

Section 350 of the CA 2006 imposes a penalty on any person listed in s 349(2) of the CA 2006 (rights of an independent assessor: right to information) who fails to comply with the requirement to provide information or explanation relating to the poll on which the independent assessor is preparing a report.

Information to be made available on website

14.84 Section 351 of the CA 2006 states that where an independent assessor has been appointed to report on a poll, the company must ensure that the following information is made available on a website: the fact of his appointment;[3217] his identity;[3218] the text of the resolution or, as the case may be, a description of the subject matter of the poll to which his appointment relates,[3219] and a copy of a report by him which complies with s 347 of the CA 2006.[3220]

The provisions of s 353 of the CA 2006 (requirements as to website availability) apply.[3221]

In the event of default in complying with s 351 of the CA 2006 (or with the requirements of s 353 of the CA 2006 as it applies for the purposes of this section), an offence is committed by every officer of the company who is in default.[3222]

A person guilty of an offence under s 351(3) of the CA 2006 is liable on summary conviction to a fine not exceeding level 3 on the standard scale.[3223]

[3211] CA 2006, s 350(3)(a).   [3212] CA 2006, s 350(3)(b).   [3213] CA 2006, s 350(4)(a).
[3214] CA 2006, s 350(4)(1)(i).   [3215] CA 2006, s 350(4)(1)(ii).   [3216] CA 2006, s 350(5).
[3217] CA 2006, s 351(1)(a).   [3218] CA 2006, s 351(3)(b).   [3219] CA 2006, s 351(1)(c).
[3220] CA 2006, s 351(1)(d).   [3221] CA 2006, s 351(2).   [3222] CA 2006, s 351(3).
[3223] CA 2006, s 354(4).

Failure to comply with s 351 of the CA 2006 (or the requirements of s 353 of the CA 2006) does not affect the validity of the poll;[3224] or the resolution or other business (if passed or agreed to) to which the poll relates.[3225]

Section 351 of the CA 2006 requires the company to publish on a website the independent assessor's report of the poll or polls and sets out the minimum information relating to the assessor's appointment, his identity, the text of the resolution and the assessor's report that must be made available. Section 351(3) and (4) of the CA 2006 imposes a penalty on every officer in default for non-compliance with this requirement. Failure to comply, however, does not invalidate the poll or the resolution or other business to which the poll relates. Section 353 of the CA 2006 (requirements as to website availability) sets out the requirement relating to the website on which the independent report must be published.

Supplementary

Application of provision to class meetings

14.85 Section 352 of the CA 2006 deals with the application of provisions with the application of provisions to class meetings.

The provisions of s 341 of the CA 2006 (results of poll to be made available on website), and ss 342–351 (independent report on poll), apply (with any necessary modifications) in relation to a meeting of holders of a class of shares of a quoted company in connection with the variation of the rights attached to such shares as they apply in relation to a general meeting of the company.[3226]

For the purposes of s 352 of the CA 2006 any amendment of a provision contained in a company's articles for the variation of the rights attached to a class of shares, or the insertion of any such provision into the articles, is itself to be treated as a variation of those rights;[3227] and references to the variation of the attached to a class of shares include references to their abrogation.[3228]

This section applies the provisions of Chapter 5 of Part 13 of the CA 2006 to meetings of holders of a class of shares of a quoted company.

Requirements as to website availability

14.86 Section 353 of the CA 2006 deals with the requirements as to website availability. The following provisions apply for the purposes of s 341 of the CA 2006 (results of poll to be made available on website), and s 351 of the

[3224] CA 2006, s 354(5)(a).   [3225] CA 2006, s 351(5)(b).   [3226] CA 2006, s 352(1).
[3227] CA 2006, s 352(2)(a).   [3228] CA 2006, s 352(2)(b).

CA 2006 (report of an independent observer to be made available on website).[3229]

The information must be made available on a website that is maintained by or on behalf of the company,[3230] and identifies the company in question.[3231]

Access to the information on the website, and the ability to obtain a hard copy of the information from the website, must not be conditional on the payment of a fee or otherwise restricted.[3232]

The information must be made available as soon as reasonably practicable;[3233] and must be kept available throughout the period of two years beginning with the date on which it is first made available on a website in accordance with this section.[3234]

A failure to make information available on a website throughout the period specified in s 353(4)(b) of the CA 2006 is disregarded if the information is made available on the website for part of that period,[3235] and the failure is wholly attributable to circumstances that it would not be reasonable to have expected the company to prevent or avoid.[3236]

Section 353 of the CA 2006 sets out the minimum requirements that should apply to information to be published on a quoted company's website under s 341 of the CA 2006 (results of poll to be made available on website) and s 351 of the CA 2006 (information to be made available on website). The website on which the information is made available must be maintained by or on behalf of the quoted company, and must identify the company in question. This provides flexibility as to whether a website is the company's own or one operated by a website service provider. Information published on a website must be kept available for a minimum of two years. Section 353(5) of the CA 2006 provides a let-out when a company's failure to make the information available on a website for part of the period is wholly attributable to circumstances beyond the company's control.

Power to limit or extend the types of company to which provisions of this Chapter apply

14.87 Section 354 of the CA 2006 deals with the power to limit or extend the types of company to which provisions of Chapter 5 of Part 13 of the CA 2006 apply. The Secretary of State may by regulations limit the types of company to which some or all of the provisions of Chapter 5 of Part 13 of the CA 2006 apply;[3237] or extend some or all of the provisions of this Chapter to additional types of company.[3238]

[3229] CA 2006, s 353(1).   [3230] CA 2006, s 352(2)(a).   [3231] CA 2006, s 353(2)(b).
[3232] CA 2006, s 353(3).   [3233] CA 2006, s 353(4)(a).   [3234] CA 2006, s 353(4)(b).
[3235] CA 2006, s 353(5)(a).   [3236] CA 2006, s 353(5)(b).   [3237] CA 2006, s 354(1)(a).
[3238] CA 2006, s 354(1)(b).

Regulations under s 354 of the CA 2006 extending the application of any provision of Chapter 5 of Part 13 of the CA 2006 are subject to affirmative resolution procedure.[3239]

Any other regulations under this section are subject to negative resolution procedure.[3240]

Regulations under this section may amend the provisions of Chapter 5 of Part 13 of the CA 2006 (apart from this section);[3241] repeal and re-enact provisions of this Chapter with modifications of form or arrangement, whether or not they are modified in substance;[3242] contain such consequential, incidental and supplementary provisions (including provisions amending, repealing or revoking enactments) as the Secretary of State thinks fit.[3243]

At present the provisions of Chapter 5 of Part 13 of the CA 2006 apply to quoted companies as defined in s 385 of the CA 2006 (which replaces s 262 of the CA 1985). This section confers on the Secretary of State a power to make regulations to limit or extend the types of company to which the provisions of this Chapter apply. The Parliamentary procedure that will apply to such regulations depends on whether they extend or limit the application of the Chapter.

Records of Resolutions and Meetings

14.88 Chapter 6 of Part 13 of the CA 2006 is concerned with records of resolutions and meetings. It comprises 5 sections. The provisions replace ss 382, 382A, 382B and 383 of the CA 1985 relating to the records of company proceedings. They should be read in conjunction with the provisions of company records in Part 31 of the CA 2006. The main changes are the ten-year minimum period of keeping records (the CA 1985 envisaged that records would be retained forever); that meetings of directors are dealt with elsewhere (in Part 10 of the CA 2006); and that the new provisions apply to class meetings.

Records of resolutions and meetings, etc

14.89 Section 355 of the CA 2006 deals with records of resolutions and meetings. Every company must keep records comprising copies of all resolutions of members passed otherwise than at general meetings;[3244] and minutes of all proceedings of general meetings;[3245] and details provided to the company in accordance with s 357 of the CA 2006 (decisions of a sole member).[3246]

[3239] CA 2006, s 354(2).   [3240] CA 2006, s 354(3).   [3241] CA 2006, s 354(4)(a).
[3242] CA 2006, s 354(4)(b).   [3243] CA 2006, s 354(4)(c).   [3244] CA 2006, s 355(1)(a).
[3245] CA 2006, s 355(1)(b).   [3246] CA 2006, s 355(1)(c).

The records must be kept for at least ten years from the date of the resolution, meeting or decision (as appropriate).[3247]

If a company fails to comply with this section, an offence is committed by every officer of the company who is in default.[3248] A person guilty of an offence under this section is liable on summary conviction to a fine not exceeding level 3 on the standard scale and, for continued contravention, a daily default fine not exceeding one-tenth of level 3 on the standard scale.[3249]

Section 355 of the CA 2006 requires all companies to maintain records comprising: copies of all resolutions passed otherwise than at general meetings (which would include all written resolutions), minutes of all proceedings of general meetings, and details of decisions of a sole member taken in accordance with s 357 of the CA 2006 (records of decision by sole member). All records must be kept for a minimum of ten years. Section 355(3) and (4) of the CA 2006 imposes a penalty on every officer in default for non-compliance.

Records as evidence of resolutions, etc.

14.90 Section 356 of the CA 2006 addresses the issue of records as evidence of resolutions. Section 356 of the CA 2006 applies to the records kept in accordance with s 355 of the CA 2006.[3250]

The record of a resolution passed otherwise than at a general meeting, if purporting to be signed by a director of the company or by the company secretary, is evidence (in Scotland, sufficient evidence) of the passing of the resolution.[3251]

Where there is a record of a written resolution of a private company, the requirements of this Act with respect to the passing of the resolution are deemed to be complied with unless the contrary is proved.[3252]

The minutes of proceedings of a general meeting, if purporting to be signed by the chairman of that meeting or by the chairman of the next general meeting, are evidence (in Scotland, sufficient evidence) of the proceedings at the meeting.[3253]

Where there is a record of proceedings of a general meeting of a company, then, until the contrary is proved the meeting is deemed duly held and convened;[3254] all proceedings at the meeting are deemed to have duly taken place;[3255] and all appointments at the meeting are deemed valid.[3256]

Section 356 of the CA 2006 ensures that all records of resolutions or written resolutions and minutes of meetings, where signed off by a director or

---

[3247] CA 2006, s 355(2).   [3248] CA 2006, s 355(3).   [3249] CA 2006, s 355(4).
[3250] CA 2006, s 356(1).   [3251] CA 2006, s 356(2).   [3252] CA 2006, s 356(3).
[3253] CA 2006, s 356(4).   [3254] CA 2006, s 356(5)(a).   [3255] CA 2006, s 356(5)(b).
[3256] CA 2006, s 356(5)(c).

a company secretary or by the chairman in the case of a general, are the evidence of the passing of a resolution or the proceedings at the meeting. In legal proceedings, a litigant will have to accept that the records are accurate unless he can prove that they are not.

Records of decisions by sole member

14.91 Section 357 of the CA 2006 applies to a company limited by shares or by guarantee that has only one member.[3257]

Where the member takes any decision that may be taken by the company in general meeting,[3258] and has effect as if agreed by the company in general meeting,[3259] he must (unless that decision is taken by way of a written resolution) provide the company with details of that decision.

If a person fails to comply with this section he commits an offence.[3260] A person guilty of an offence under this section is liable on summary conviction to a fine not exceeding level 2 on the standard scale.[3261]

A failure to comply with this section does not affect the validity of any decision referred to in s 357(2) of the CA 2006.[3262]

Section 357 of the CA 2006 makes a provision for the recording of decisions of a company with only one member.

Inspection of records of resolution and meetings

14.92 Section 358 of the CA 2006 deals with inspection of records resolutions and meetings. The records of referred to in s 355 of the CA 2006 (records of resolutions, etc.) relating to the previous ten years must be kept available for inspection at the company's registered office;[3263] or at a place specified in regulations under s 1136 of the CA 2006.[3264]

The company must give notice to the registrar of the place at which the records are kept available for inspection;[3265] and of any change in that place,[3266] unless they at all times been kept at the company's registered office.

The records must be open to inspection of any member of the company without charge.[3267] Any member may require a copy of any of the records on payment of such free as may be prescribed.[3268]

If default is made for 14 days in complying with s 358(2) of the CA 2006 or an inspection required under s 358(3) of the CA 2006 is refused, or a copy requested under s 358(4) of the CA 2006 is not sent, an offence is committed by every officer of the company who is in default.[3269]

[3257] CA 2006, s 357(1).   [3258] CA 2006, s 357(2)(a).   [3259] CA 2006, s 357(2)(b).
[3260] CA 2006, s 357(3).   [3261] CA 2006, s 357(4).   [3262] CA 2006, s 357(5).
[3263] CA 2006, s 358(1)(a).   [3264] CA 2006, s 358(1)(b).   [3265] CA 2006, s 358(2)(a).
[3266] CA 2006, s 358(2)(b).   [3267] CA 2006, s 358(3).   [3268] CA 2006, s 358(4).
[3269] CA 2006, s 358(5).

A person guilty of an offence under this section is liable on summary conviction to a fine not exceeding level 3 on the standard scale and, for continued contravention, to a daily default fine not exceeding one-tenth of level 3 on the standard scale.[3270]

In a case in which an inspection required under s 358(3) of the CA 2006 is referred or a copy requested under s 358(4) of the CA 2006 is not sent; the court may by order compel an immediate inspection of the records or direct that the copies required be sent to the persons who requested them.[3271]

This section requires every company to keep its record available for inspection by members for ten years. Section 358(5) of the CA 2006 enables a member to seek a court order to compel the company to make the records available for inspection or to provide copies of the records.

Records of resolutions and meetings of classes of members

14.93 Section 359 of the CA 2006 deals with records of resolutions and meetings of classes of members. The provisions of Chapter 6 of Part 13 of the CA 2006 apply (with necessary modifications) in relation to resolutions and meetings of holders of a class of shares,[3272] and in the case of a company without a share capital, a class of members, as they apply in relation to resolutions of members generally and to general meetings.[3273]

This section applies the provisions of Chapter 6 to resolutions and meetings of holders of a class of shares in the case of a company with share capital or classes of members in the case of a company without a share capital.

Supplementary Provisions

14.94 Chapter 7 to Part 13 of the CA 2006 is concerned with supplementary provisions. It has two sections.

Computation of periods of notice, etc.: clear day rule

14.95 Section 360 of the CA 2006 deals with computation of periods of notices. It applies for the purposes of the following provisions of Part 13 of the CA 2006:

(a)   s 307(1) and (2) of the CA 2006 (notice required of general meeting);
(b)   s 312(1) and (3) of the CA 2006 (resolution requiring special notice);
(c)   s 314(4)(d) of the CA 2006 (request to circulate member's statement);

[3270] CA 2006, s 358(6).   [3271] CA 2006, s 358(7).   [3272] CA 2006, s 359(a).
[3273] CA 2006, s 359(b).

(d)   s 316(2)(b) of the CA 2006 (expenses of circulating statement to be deposited or tendered before meeting);

(e)   s 338(4)(d)(i) of the CA 2006 (request to circulate members resolution at AGM of public company); and

(f)   s 340(2)(b)(i) of the CA 2006 (expenses of circulating statement to be deposited or tendered before meeting).[3274]

Any reference in those provisions to a period of notice, or to a period before a meeting by which a request must be received or sum deposited or tendered, is to a period of the specified length excluding the day of the meeting;[3275] and the day on which the notice is given, the request received or the sum deposited or tendered.[3276]

Meaning of 'quoted company'

14.96 Section 361 of the CA 2006 states that in Part 13 of the CA 2006, the term 'quoted company' has the same meaning as in Part 15 (accounts and reports) of the CA 2006.

[3274] CA 2006, s 360(1).   [3275] CA 2006, s 360(2)(a).   [3276] CA 2006, s 360(2)(b).

Chapter 15

A Company's Share Capital

Introduction

15.1 Part 17 of the CA 2006 contains provisions dealing with a company's share capital. It replaces Part 4 and (in part) Part 5 of the CA 1985, and contains a mixture of new sections which replace corresponding provisions in the CA 1985, and sections that restate corresponding provisions in that Act. Sections 541, 543–544, 547–548, 552–553, 558, 561, 563–568, 570–572, 574–577, 579–582, 584–588, 590–605, 607–609, 611–616, 645–648, and 655–656 of the CA 2006 restate various provisions in the CA 1985, but do not make any changes to those provisions.

Part 17 comprises ten Chapters. Chapter 1 is concerned with shares and share capital of a company; Chapter 2 contains general provisions on allotment of shares; Chapter 3 is concerned with allotment of equity securities containing existing shareholders' right of pre-emption; Chapter 4 addresses public companies allotment, where the issue is not fully subscribed; Chapter 5 deals with payment for shares; Chapter 6 is concerned with independent valuation of non-cash consideration of public companies; Chapter 7 addresses share premiums; Chapter 8 applies to alteration of share capital; Chapter 9 deals with classes of shares and class rights; and Chapter 10 is concerned with reduction of share capital.

Shares and Share Capital of A Company

15.2 Chapter 1 addresses the issue of shares and share capital of a company. It comprises nine sections, providing definitions on terms used, and clarification of some of the concepts used in Part 17 of the CA 2006.

Shares

15.3 Section 540 of the CA 2006 is concerned with definitional aspects of the term 'shares'. In the Companies Acts, the term 'share', in relation to a company, means share in the company's share capital.[3277] A company's shares may no longer be converted into stock.[3278]

Stock created before the commencement of Part 17 of the CA 2006, may be reconverted into shares in accordance with s 620 of the CA 2006.[3279]

In the Companies Acts, references to shares include stock, except where a distinction between share and stock is express or implied;[3280] and references to a number of shares include an amount of stock where the context admits of the reference to shares being read as including stock.[3281]

As previously under the CA 1985, and now under the CA 2006, references to a 'share' in the Companies Acts includes stock. However, as recommended by the Company Law Review Group, it will now no longer be possible for a company to convert its shares into stock under s 540(2) of the CA 2006, but a company that has stock at the date that this provision comes into force will be able to reconvert its stock back into shares (see s 620 of the CA 2006).

Nature of shares

15.4 Section 541 of the CA 2006 governs the nature of shares. The shares or other interest of a member in a company are personal property (or, in Scotland, moveable property) and are not in the nature of real estate (or heritage).

Nominal value of shares

15.5 Section 542 of the CA 2006 sets out the nominal value of the shares. Shares in a limited company having a share capital must each have a fixed nominal value.[3282]

An allotment of a share that does not have a fixed nominal value is void.[3283]

Shares in a limited company having a share capital may be denominated in any currency, and different classes of shares may be denominated in different currencies. But see s 765 of the CA 2006 (initial authorised minimum share capital requirement for public company to be met by reference to share capital denominated in sterling or euros).[3284]

If a company purports to allot shares in contravention of s 542 of the CA 2006, an offence is committed by every officer of the company who is in default.[3285] A person guilty of an offence under s 542 of the CA 2006 is liable on conviction on indictment, to a fine;[3286] on summary conviction, to a fine not exceeding the statutory maximum.[3287]

[3277] CA 2006, s 540(1).   [3278] CA 2006, s 540(2).   [3279] CA 2006, s 540(3).
[3280] CA 2006, s 540(4)(a).   [3281] CA 2006, s 540(4)(b).   [3282] CA 2006, s 542(1).
[3283] CA 2006, s 542(2).   [3284] CA 2006, s 542(3).   [3285] CA 2006, s 542(4).
[3286] CA 2006, s 542(5)(a).   [3287] CA 2006, s 542(5)(b).

This is a new provision, which is required as a result of changes to requirements with respect to the Memorandum of Association: see s 8 of the CA 2006.

Previously under s 2(5)(a) of the CA 1985 (requirements with respect to the memorandum) there was a requirement that in the case of a company having a share capital, the memorandum of a limited company had to state the amount of the share capital with which the company proposed to be registered, and the division of that share capital into shares of a fixed amount. This capital figure as stated in the memorandum (known as the 'authorised share capital') acted as a ceiling on the amount of shares that a company may issue. Such authorised share capital could, however, be increased by ordinary resolution under s 121 of the CA 1985. The Company Law Review Group recommended that the requirement for a company to have an authorised share capital should be abolished,[3288] and so the CA 2006 does not require a company to state in its memorandum the amount of its share capital.

Section 542 of the CA 2006 is required as a consequence of the repeal of this requirement. It fulfils two main functions. First, it makes clear that the shares in a limited company having a share capital must have a fixed nominal value, e.g. 1p, £, $1 or 1 euro and therefore prevents a company from issuing shares of no par value (thereby implementing, for public companies, Article 8 of the Second Company Law Directive (77/91/EEC)). Second, it places in statute the common law rule, that shares may be denominated in any currency and that different classes of shares maybe be denominated in different currencies.

Where a company purports to allot shares without a fixed nominal value, every officer of the company who is in default commits an offence and is liable to a fine: s 542(2) of the CA 2006.

This section should be read together with s 9 of the CA 2006, which requires the application for registration of a company that is to be formed with a share capital, to include a 'statement of capital and initial shareholdings'. The contents of this statement are prescribed in s 10 of the CA 2006, and this includes a requirement to set out a total number of shares, and the aggregate nominal value of the shares, which are to be taken by the subscribers to the memorandum on formation.

Numbering of shares

15.6 Section 543 of the CA 2006 states that each share in a company having a share capital must be distinguished by its appropriate number, except in the following circumstances.[3289]

[3288] *Final Report*, para 10.6.   [3289] CA 2006, s 543(1).

If at any time all the issued shares in a company are fully paid up and rank *pari passu* for all purposes;[3290] or all the issued shares of a particular class in a company are fully paid up and rank *pari passu* for all purposes,[3291] none of those shares need thereafter have a distinguishing number so long as it remains fully paid up and ranks pari passu for all purposes with all shares of the same class for the time being issued and fully paid up.

Transferability of shares

15.7 Section 544 of the CA 2006 states that the shares or other interest of any member in a company are transferable in accordance with the company's articles.[3292]

This is subject to the Stock Transfer Act 1963 (c 18), or the Stock Transfer Act (Northern Ireland) 1963 (c 24 (NI)) (which enables securities of certain descriptions to be transferred by a simplified process);[3293] and regulations under Chapter 2 of Part 21 of the CA 2006 (which enable title to securities to be evidenced and transferred without a written instrument).[3294] See Part 21 of this Act generally as regards share transfers.[3295]

Companies having a share capital

15.8 Section 545 of the CA 2006 provides that references in the Companies Acts to a company having a share capital, are to a company that has power under its constitution to issue shares.

Section 545 of the CA 2006, and reference to the Companies Acts as defined by s 2 of the CA 2006, is a new provision.

Issued and allotted share capital

15.9 Section 546 of the CA 2006 states that the references in the Companies Acts to 'issued share capital' are to shares of a company that have been issued;[3296] and those to 'allotted share capital' are to shares of a company that have been allotted.[3297]

References in the Companies Acts to issued or allotted shares, or to issued or allotted share capital, include shares taken on the formation of the company by the subscribers to the company's memorandum.[3298]

[3290] CA 2006, s 543(2)(a).   [3291] CA 2006, s 543(2)(b).   [3292] CA 2006, s 544(1).
[3293] CA 2006, s 544(2)(a).   [3294] CA 2006, s 544(2)(b).   [3295] CA 2006, s 544(3).
[3296] CA 2006, s 546(1)(a).   [3297] CA 2006, s 546(1)(b).   [3298] CA 2006, s 546(2).

Share capital

15.10 Sections 547–548 of the CA 2006 defines a company's share capital.

Called-up share capital

15.11 Section 547 of the CA 2006 defines a company's called-up share capital. In the Companies Acts 'called-up share capital', in relation to a company, means so much of its share capital as equals the aggregate amount of the calls made on its shares (whether or not those calls have been paid), together with any share capital paid up without being called;[3299] and any share capital to be paid on a specified future date under the articles, the terms of allotment of the relevant shares or any other arrangements for payment of those shares;[3300] and 'uncalled share capital' is to be construed accordingly.

Equity share capital

15.12 Section 548 of the CA 2006 defines equity share capital. In the Companies Acts 'equity share capital', in relation to a company, means its issued share capital excluding any part of that capital that does not, either as respects dividends or as respects capital, carry any right to participate beyond a specified amount in a distribution.

Allotment of Shares: General Provisions

15.13 Chapter 2 of the CA 2006 sets out the provisions on allotment of shares. It comprises 11 sections.

Under the CA 1985, the directors of a company could only allot shares (or grant rights to subscribe for shares or to convert into shares), if they were authorised to do so by ordinary resolution of the company's members or by the Articles of Association.

Such an authority could be general (that it, it may give the directors a general authority to allot shares) or specific (that is, it may, for example, be restricted to allotment, an allotment of shares up to a specified value, or an allotment of shares on a particular class). In either case, the authority was required to state the 'maximum amount of relevant securities that may be allotted under it' and the date when the authority would expire, (which could not be more than five years from the date on which the authority is given). The authority could be renewed for further periods not exceeding five years.

There was also a relaxation for private companies from the requirement to state the date on which the authority would expire, and so such companies

---

[3299] CA 2006, s 547(a).   [3300] CA 2006, s 547(b).

could, by elective resolution under s 379A of the CA 1985, give such authority either for an indefinite period or a fixed period of the company's choice.

The CA 2006 removes for private companies the requirement for prior authorisation in certain circumstances (described in s 550 of the CA 2006). It also abolishes the concept of authorised share capital (see s 542 of the CA 2006) – a company's constitution will no longer have to contain a ceiling on the number of shares that the directors are authorised to allot.

Power of directors to allot shares

15.14 Sections 549–551 of the CA 2006 deal with the power of directors to allot shares.

Exercise by directors of power to allot shares, etc.

15.15 Section 549 CA 2006 states that the directors of a company must not exercise any power of the company to allot shares in the company;[3301] or to grant rights to subscribe for, or to convert any security into, shares in the company,[3302] except in accordance with s 550 of the CA 2006 (private company with a single class of shares) or s 551 of the CA 2006 (authorisation by a company).

Section 549(1) of the CA 2006 does not apply to the allotment of shares in pursuance of an employees' share scheme;[3303] or to the grant of a right to subscribe for, or to convert any security into, shares so allotted.[3304]

If this section applies in relation to the grant of a right to subscribe for, or to convert any security into, shares, it does not apply in relation to the allotment of shares pursuant to that right.[3305]

A director who knowingly contravenes, or permits or authorises a contravention of, this section commits an offence.[3306]

A person guilty of an offence under s 549 of the CA 2006 is liable on conviction on indictment, to a fine;[3307] and on summary conviction, to a fine not exceeding the statutory maximum.[3308]

Nothing in this section affects the validity of an allotment or other transaction.[3309]

Section 549 of the CA 2006 replaces s 80(1), (2), (9) and (10) of the CA 1985. It provides that the directors may not allot shares (or grant rights to subscribe for shares or to convert any security into shares), except in accordance with one of the following two classes.

Section 549(2) of the CA 2006 provides that directors may allot shares in

---

[3301] CA 2006, s 549(1)(a).   [3302] CA 2006, s 549(1)(b).   [3303] CA 2006, s 549(2)(a).
[3304] CA 2006, s 549(2)(b).   [3305] CA 2006, s 549(3).   [3306] CA 2006, s 549(4).
[3307] CA 2006, s 549(5)(a).   [3308] CA 2006, s 549(5)(b).   [3309] CA 2006, s 549(6).

pursuance of an employees' share without having to comply with one of the foregoing two subsections. This mirrors the current position (see s 80(2) of the CA 1985).

Similarly, where a right to subscribe for, or to convert any security into, shares already exists, then the directors may allot shares pursuant to that right without having to comply with one of the following two classes (see s 549(3) of the CA 2006).

A director who knowingly and willfully allots shares in contravention of the requirements imposed by this section commits an offence. Such an allotment is not, however, invalid.

Power of directors to allot shares, etc.: private company with only one class of shares

15.16 Section 550 of the CA 2006 is concerned with the power of directors to allot shares in respect of a private company with only one class of shares. Where a private company has only one class of shares, the directors may exercise any power of the company to allot shares of that class,[3310] or to grant rights to subscribe for or to convert any security into such shares,[3311] except to the extent that they are prohibited from doing so by the company's articles.

In line with the recommendations of the Company Law Review Group,[3312] s 550 of the CA 2006 empowers the directors to allot shares (or to grant rights to subscribe for or convert any security into shares), where the company is a private company that will have only one class after the proposed allotment and removes the previous requirement (contained in s 80 of the CA 1985) for the directors to have prior authority from the company's members for such an allotment of shares. In addition, it provides that the members may, if they wish, restrict or prohibit this power through the Articles of Association. The definition of 'classes of shares' is contained in s 808 of the CA 2006.

Powers of directors to allot shares, etc.: authorisation by company

15.17 Section 551 of the CA 2006 deals with the authorisation by the company to allow directors power to allot shares. The directors of a company may exercise a power of the company to allot shares in the company,[3313] or to grant rights to subscribe for or to convert any security into shares in the company,[3314] if they are authorised to do so by the company's articles or by resolution of the company.

Authorisation may be given for a particular exercise of the power or for its exercise generally, and may be unconditional or subject to conditions.[3315] The

---

[3310] CA 2006, s 550(a).   [3311] CA 2006, s 550(b).   [3312] *Final Report*, para 4.5.
[3313] CA 2006, s 551(1)(a).   [3314] CA 2006, s 551(1)(b).   [3315] CA 2006, s 551(2).

authorisation must state the maximum amount of shares that may be allotted under it,[3316] and specify the date on which it will expire, which must be not more than five years from (i) in the case of authorisation contained in the company's articles at the time of its original incorporation, the date of that incorporation;[3317] and (ii) in any other case, the date on which the resolution is passed by virtue of which the authorisation is given.[3318]

The authorisation may be renewed or further renewed by resolution of the company for a further period not exceeding five years,[3319] and be revoked or varied at any time by resolution of the company.[3320]

A resolution renewing authorisation must state (or restate) the maximum amount of shares that may be allotted under the authorisation or, as the case may be, the amount remaining to be allotted under it,[3321] and specify the date on which the renewed authorisation will expire.[3322]

In relation to rights to subscribe for or to convert any security into shares in the company, references in this section to the maximum amount of shares that may be allotted under the authorisation, are to the maximum amount of shares that may be allotted pursuant to the rights.[3323]

The directors may allot shares, or grant rights to subscribe for or to convert any security into shares, after authorisation has expired if the shares are allotted, or the rights are granted, in pursuance of an offer or agreement made by the company before the authorisation expired,[3324] and the authorisation allowed the company to make an offer or agreement that would or might require shares to be allotted, or rights to be granted, after the authorisation had expired.[3325]

A resolution of a company to give, vary, revoke or renew authorisation under this section may be an ordinary resolution, even though it amends the company's articles.[3326]

Chapter 3 of Part 3 of the CA 2006 (resolutions affecting a company's constitution) applies to a resolution under this section.[3327]

This section replaces s 80(3)–(8) of the CA 1985 and applies both to private companies that will have more than one class of shares after a proposed allotment, and to public companies. It provides that the directors may only allot shares (or grant rights to subscribe for shares or to convert any security into shares) if they have been given prior authorisation for the proposed allotment by ordinary resolution of the company's members or by the articles.

Section 551(2)–(5) of the CA 2006 sets out details of the way in which prior authorisation (or a renewal of such authorisation) may be given and, in particular, provides that the authority may not be given for a period of more

[3316] CA 2006, s 551(3)(a).   [3317] CA 2006, s 551(3)(b)(i).   [3318] CA 2006, s 551(3)(b)(ii).
[3319] CA 2006, s 551(4)(a).   [3320] CA 2006, s 551(4)(b).   [3321] CA 2006, s 551(5)(a).
[3322] CA 2006, s 551(5)(b).   [3323] CA 2006, s 551(6).   [3324] CA 2006, s 551(7)(a).
[3325] CA 2006, s 551(7)(b).   [3326] CA 2006, s 551(8).   [3327] CA 2006, s 551(9).

than five years. An authority given to the directors under this section, and any resolution of the company renewing such an authority, must state 'the maximum amount of shares' to be allotted pursuant to the authority. This mirrors the formulation of words used in s 80 of the CA 1985, and enables the members to limit the authority to a specific number of shares up to a given maximum nominal value.

Section 551(8) of the CA 2006 makes it clear that an ordinary resolution of the company's members will suffice for the purpose of giving authority to the directors, even where the effect of the resolution is to alter the company's Articles of Association (which would normally require a special resolution of the company's members).

Prohibition of commissions, discounts and allowances

General prohibition of commissions, discounts and allowances

15.18 Section 552 of the CA 2006 sets out the general prohibition of commissions, discounts and allowance. Except as permitted by s 553 of the CA 2006 (permitted commission), a company must not apply any of its shares or capital money, either directly or indirectly, in payment of any commission, discount or allowance to any person in consideration of his subscribing or agreeing to subscribe (whether absolutely or conditionally) for shares in the company,[3328] or procuring or agreeing to procure subscriptions (whether absolute or conditional) for shares in the company.[3329]

It is immaterial how the shares or money are so applied, whether by being added to the purchase money of property acquired by the company or to the contract price of work to be executed for the company, or being paid out of the nominal purchase money or contract price, or otherwise.[3330]

Nothing in s 552 of the CA 2006 affects the payment of such brokerage as has previously been lawful.[3331]

Permitted commission

15.19 Section 553 of the CA 2006 states that a company may, if the following conditions are satisfied, pay a commission to a person in consideration of his subscribing or agreeing to subscribe (whether absolutely or conditionally) for shares in the company, or procuring or agreeing to procure subscriptions (whether absolute or conditional) for shares in the company.[3332]

The conditions are that the payment of the commission is authorised by the company's articles;[3333] and the commission paid or agreed to be paid does

---

[3328] CA 2006, s 552(1)(a).   [3329] CA 2006, s 552(1)(b).   [3330] CA 2006, s 552(2).
[3331] CA 2006, s 552(3).   [3332] CA 2006, s 553(1).   [3333] CA 2006, s 553(2)(a).

not exceed (i) 10 per cent of the price at which the shares are issued,[3334] or (ii) the amount or rate authorised by the articles,[3335] whichever is the less.

A vendor to, or promoter of, or other person who receives payment in money or shares from, a company may apply any part of the money or shares so received in payment of any commission the payment of which directly by the company would be permitted by this section.[3336]

Registration of allotment

15.20 Section 554 of the CA 2006 is concerned with registration of allotment. A company must register an allotment of shares as soon as practicable and in any event within two months after the date of the allotment.[3337] This does not apply if the company has issued a share warrant in respect of the shares (see s 779 of the CA 2006).[3338]

If a company fails to comply with s 554 of the CA 2006, an offence is committed by the company,[3339] and every officer of the company who is in default.[3340] A person guilty of an offence under s 554 of the CA 2006 is liable on summary conviction to a fine not exceeding level 3 on the standard scale and, for continued contravention, a daily default fine not exceeding one-tenth of level 3 on the standard scale.[3341]

For the company's duties as to the issue of share certificates, etc., see Part 21 of the CA 2006 (certification and transfer of securities).[3342]

Section 554 of the CA 2006 is a new provision that requires the directors to register an allotment of shares as soon as practicable (but in any event within two months of the date of allotment). Whereas the CA 1985 imposed a duty on the company to issue certificates within two months after the allotment of its shares, it did not stipulate a timescale relating to the step which was anterior to this, namely the registration of the allotment.

Section 554(2) of the CA 2006 makes it clear that the requirement to register an allotment of shares does not apply if the company has issued a share warrant in respect of the shares in question (see s 779 of the CA 2006).

Where a company fails to comply with s 554 of the CA 2006, the company and every officer of the company who is in default commits an offence. The penalty for this offence is set out in s 554(4) of the CA 2006.

Return of an allotment

15.21 Sections 555–557 of the CA 2006 are concerned with provisions dealing with the return of an allotment.

[3334] CA 2006, s 553(2)(b)(i).   [3335] CA 2006, s 553(2)(b)(ii).   [3336] CA 2006, s 553(3).
[3337] CA 2006, s 554(1).   [3338] CA 2006, s 554(2).   [3339] CA 2006, s 554(3)(a).
[3340] CA 2006, s 554(3)(b).   [3341] CA 2006, s 554(4).   [3342] CA 2006, s 554(5).

Return of an allotment by limited company

15.22 Section 555 of the CA 2006 applies to a company limited by shares and to a company limited by guarantee and having a share capital.[3343] The company must, within one month of making an allotment of shares, deliver to the registrar for registration a return of the allotment.[3344]

The return must contain the prescribed information,[3345] and be accompanied by a statement of capital.[3346]

The statement of capital must state with respect to the company's share capital at the date to which the return is made up the total number of shares of the company,[3347] the aggregate nominal value of those shares,[3348] for each class of shares (i) prescribed particulars of the rights attached to the shares,[3349] (ii) the total number of shares of that class,[3350] and (iii) the aggregate nominal value of shares of that class,[3351] and the amount paid up and the amount (if any) unpaid on each share (whether on account of the nominal value of the share or by way of premium).[3352]

Section 555 of the CA 2006 replaces s 88 of the CA 1985. As previously under the CA 1985 and now under the CA 2006, within one month of an allotment of new shares in a limited company, the company is required to make a return of allotments to the registrar. This return must contain 'prescribed information' relating to the allotment (that is, prescribed by the Secretary of State by order or by regulations made under the CA 2006).

A return of allotments made under this section must be accompanied by a statement of capital. A statement of capital is in essence a 'snapshot' of a company's total subscribed capital at a particular point in time (in this context, the date to which the return of allotments is made up).

The requirement for a statement of capital when an allotment of new shares is made is new. It is based on a recommendation by the Company Law Review Group[3353] and for public companies, this implements a requirement in the Second Company Law Directive (77/91/EEC) which states:

> the statutes or instruments of incorporation of the company shall always give at least the following information . . . (e) when the company has no authorised capital, the amount of the subscribed capital.

'Statutes' and 'instruments of incorporation' equate to the articles and memorandum and the need to disclose information pertaining to the aggregate of a company's subscribed capital flows from the abolition of the requirement for a company to have an authorised share capital.

[3343] CA 2006, s 555(1).   [3344] CA 2006, s 555(2).   [3345] CA 2006, s 555(3)(a).
[3346] CA 2006, s 555(3)(b).   [3347] CA 2006, s 555(4)(a).   [3348] CA 2006, s 555(4)(b).
[3349] CA 2006, s 555(4)(c)(i).   [3350] CA 2006, s 555(4)(c)(ii).   [3351] CA 2006, s 555(4)(c)(iii).
[3352] CA 2006, s 555(5).   [3353] *Final Report*, para 7.30.

Whilst this Directive only applies to public companies, the requirement to provide a statement of capital, here and elsewhere in the CA 2006, has been extended to private companies limited by shares (and in certain cases to unlimited companies having a share capital, for example, where such companies make their annual return to the registrar). This will mean that the public register will contain up-to-date information on a company's share capital (the requirement for a statement of capital supplements existing provisions that require a company to give notice to the registrar when it amends its share capital in any way).

The information that will in future be set out in the statement of capital, includes prescribed particulars of the rights attached to each class of shares. Again this nformation will be prescribed in regulations or by order made under the Act. Such information was required to be filed under either s 123 of the CA 1985 (which relates to increases in authorised share capital) or s 128(1) and (2) of the CA 1985 (which relates to allotments of a new class of shares).

Currently, if shares are allotted as fully or partly paid up otherwise than in cash, the company must deliver the contract that it has with the allottee (or details of this contract if it is not in writing) to the registrar. Such a contract may contain commercially sensitive information, which the company would not normally want to disclose. This section does not reproduce this requirement. It should be noted, however, that, in prescribing the information that must be included in the return of allotments, the Secretary of State may require details of any consideration received in respect of shares that are allotted as fully or partly paid up otherwise than in cash.

Return of allotment by unlimited company allotting new class of shares

15.23 Section 556 of the CA 2006 applies to an unlimited company that allots shares of a class with rights that are not in all respects uniform with shares previously allotted.[3354] The company must, within one month of making such an allotment, deliver to the registrar for registration a return of the allotment.[3355]

The return must contain the prescribed particulars of the rights attached to the shares.[3356]

For the purposes of this section, shares are not to be treated as different from shares previously allotted, by reason only that the former do not carry the same rights to dividends as the latter during the 12 months immediately following the former's allotment.[3357]

Section 556 of the CA 2006 requires unlimited companies to make a return

---

[3354] CA 2006, s 556(1).   [3355] CA 2006, s 556(2).   [3356] CA 2006, s 556(3).
[3357] CA 2006, s 556(4).

of allotments to the registrar where the directors allot a new class of shares. This carries forward the provisions of s 128(1) and (2) of the CA 1985 as it applies to unlimited companies. The return must contain 'prescribed particulars of the rights attached to the shares', that is, such information as may be prescribed by the Secretary of State in regulations or by order made under the CA 2006.

Offence of failure to make a return

15.24 Section 557 of the CA 2006 deals with the offence of failure to make a return. If a company makes default in complying with s 555 of the CA 2006 (return of allotment of shares by a limited company), or s 556 of the CA 2006 (return of allotment of new class of shares by an unlimited company), an offence is committed by every officer of the company who is in default.[3358]

A person guilty of an offence under s 557 of the CA 2006 is liable on conviction on indictment, to a fine;[3359] and on summary conviction, to a fine not exceeding the statutory maximum and, for continued contravention, a daily default fine not exceeding one-tenth of the statutory maximum.[3360]

In the case of default in delivering to the registrar within one month of the allotment the return required by s 555 or s 556 of the CA 2006 any person liable for the default may apply to the court for relief,[3361] and the court, if satisfied (i) that the omission to deliver the document was accidental or due to inadvertence,[3362] or (ii) that it is just and equitable to grant relief,[3363] may make an order extending the time for delivery of the document for such period as the court thinks proper.

Section 557 of the CA 2006 replaces s 88(5) of the CA 2006 and (insofar as it relates to a requirement for an unlimited company to register particulars of an allotment of a new class of shares) s 128(5) of the CA 1985. Where a company fails to comply with the requirements to make a return of allotments to the registrar, every officer of the company who is in default commits an offence.

As previously under s 88(6) of the CA 1985, where there is a default in making a return of allotments within the specified time (one month after the allotment) a person who is liable for the default may apply to the court for relief (see s 557(3) of the CA 2006, which extends the right to apply for relief to a person liable under s 556 of the CA 2006).

[3358] CA 2006, s 557(1).   [3359] CA 2006, s 557(2)(a).   [3360] CA 2006, s 557(2)(b).
[3361] CA 2006, s 557(3)(a).   [3362] CA 2006, s 557(3)(b)(i).   [3363] CA 2006, s 557(3)(b)(ii).

Supplementary provisions

When shares are allotted

15.25 Section 558 of the CA 2006 states that for the purposes of the Companies Acts, shares in a company are taken to be allotted when a person acquires the unconditional right to be included in the company's register of members in respect of the shares.

Provisions about allotments not applicable to shares taken on formation

15.26 Section 559 of the CA 2006 provides that the provisions of Chapter 2 to Part 17 of the CA 2006 have no application in relation to the taking of shares by the subscribers to the memorandum on the formation of the company.

This provision replicates the effect of s 80(2)(a) of the CA 1985, and provides that the allotment provisions in Chapter 2 to Part 17 of the CA 2006 do not apply to the shares taken by the subscribers to the memorandum on the formation of a company. Such persons become members of the company of in respect of the shares that are taken by them by virtue of s 16 of the CA 2006 and provisions of the Act on share allotments do not apply to them.

Allotment of Equity Securities: Existing Shareholders' Right of Pre-Emption

15.27 Chapter 3 to Part 17 of the CA 2006 is concerned with the allotment of equity securities with reference to existing shareholders' rights of pre-emption.

Introductory

Meaning of 'equity securities' and related expressions

15.28 Section 560 of the CA 2006 defines equity securities and related expressions. The term 'equity securities' means ordinary shares in the company,[3364] or rights to subscribe for, or to convert securities into, ordinary shares in the company;[3365] the term 'ordinary shares' means shares other than shares which, as respects dividends and capital, carry a right to participate only up to a specified amount in a distribution.

The references in Chapter 3 to Part 17 of the CA 2006 to the allotment of equity securities, include the grant of a right to subscribe for, or to convert

---

[3364] CA 2006, s 560(1)(a).   [3365] CA 2006, s 560(1)(b).

any securities into, ordinary shares in the company,[3366] and the sale of ordinary shares in the company that immediately before the sale are held by the company as treasury shares.[3367]

Section 560 of the CA 2006 sets out a definition of 'equity securities' for the purposes of Chapter 3 of Part 17 of the CA 2006 (which is concerned with the allotment of equity securities and existing shareholders' right of pre-emption). It partially restates s 94(2), (3), (3A) and (5) of the CA 1985. The exception for shares taken by a subscriber to the memorandum and for bonus shares provided in s 94(2) of the CA 1985 is contained in ss 577 and 564 of the CA 2006. The exclusion of the allotment of shares pursuant to the grant of a right to subscribe for such shares contained in s 93(3) of the CA 1985 is contained in s 561(3) of the CA 2006.

Existing shareholders' right of pre-emption

Existing shareholders' right of pre-emption

15.29 Section 561 of the CA 2006 deals with existing shareholders right of pre-emption. A company must not allot equity securities to a person on any terms, unless it has made an offer to each person who holds ordinary shares in the company, to allot to him on the same or more favourable terms, a proportion of those securities that is as nearly as practicable equal to the proportion in nominal value held by him of the ordinary share capital of the company,[3368] and the period during which any such offer may be accepted has expired or the company has received notice of the acceptance or refusal of every offer so made.[3369]

Securities that a company has offered to allot to a holder of ordinary shares may be allotted to him, or anyone in whose favour he has renounced his right to their allotment, without contravening s 561(1)(b) of the CA 2006.[3370]

If s 561(1) of the CA 2006 applies in relation to the grant of such a right, it does not apply in relation to the allotment of shares in pursuance of that right.[3371]

Shares held by the company as treasury shares are disregarded for the purposes of this section, so that the company is not treated as a person who holds ordinary shares,[3372] and the shares are not treated as forming part of the ordinary share capital of the company.[3373]

This section is subject to ss 564–566 of the CA 2006 (exceptions to pre-emption rights),[3374] ss 567 and 568 of the CA 2006 (exclusion of rights of

---

[3366] CA 2006, s 560(2)(a).   [3367] CA 2006, s 560(2)(b).   [3368] CA 2006, s 561(1)(a).
[3369] CA 2006, s 561(1)(b).   [3370] CA 2006, s 561(2).   [3371] CA 2006, s 561(3).
[3372] CA 2006, s 561(4)(a).   [3373] CA 2006, s 561(4)(b).   [3374] CA 2006, s 561(5)(a).

pre-emption),[3375] ss 569–573 of the CA 2006 (disapplication of pre-emption rights),[3376] and s 576 of the CA 2006 (saving for certain older pre-emption procedures).[3377]

Subject to some exceptions, under s 89(1) of the CA 1985, a company that is proposing to allot equity securities (defined in s 560 of the CA 2006) must offer them to existing shareholders first (that is, on a pre-emptive basis). The basic principle (which is unchanged by the CA 2006) is that a shareholder should be able to protect his proportion of the total equity of a company by having the opportunity to subscribe for any new issue of equity securities. This is subject to various exceptions and s 561(5) of the CA 2006 provides a pointer to these exceptions.

Communication of pre-emption offers to shareholders

15.30 Section 562 of the CA 2006 applies as to the manner in which offers required by s 561 of the CA 2006 are to be made to holders of a company's shares.[3378]

The offer may be made in hard copy or electronic form.[3379]

If the holder has no registered address in an EEA State and has not given to the company an address in an EEA State for the service of notices on him,[3380] or is the holder of a share warrant,[3381] the offer may be made by causing it, or a notice specifying where a copy of it can be obtained or inspected, to be published in the Gazette.

The offer must state a period during which it may be accepted and the offer shall not be withdrawn before the end of that period.[3382]

The period must be a period of at least 21 days beginning in the case of an offer made in hard copy form, with the date on which the offer is sent or supplied;[3383] in the case of an offer made in electronic form, with the date on which the offer is sent;[3384] or in the case of an offer made by publication in the Gazette, with the date of publication.[3385]

The Secretary of State may by regulations made by statutory instrument reduce the period specified in s 562(5) of the CA 2006 (but not to less than 14 days),[3386] or increase that period.[3387]

A statutory instrument containing regulations made under subs (6) is subject to affirmative resolution procedure.[3388]

Section 562 of the CA 2006 replaces s 90(1), (5) and (6) of the CA 1985. Section 90(6) of the CA 1985 provides that where a company communicates a pre-emption offer to its existing shareholders, the offer must state a period of

---

[3375] CA 2006, s 561(5)(b).   [3376] CA 2006, s 561(5)(c).   [3377] CA 2006, s 561(5)(d).
[3378] CA 2006, s 562(1).   [3379] CA 2006, s 562(2).   [3380] CA 2006, s 562(3)(a).
[3381] CA 2006, s 562(3)(b).   [3382] CA 2006, s 562(4).   [3383] CA 2006, s 562(5)(a).
[3384] CA 2006, s 562(5)(b).   [3385] CA 2006, s 562(5)(c).   [3386] CA 2006, s 562(6)(a).
[3387] CA 2006, s 562(6)(b).   [3388] CA 2006, s 562(7).

not less than 21 days during which it may be accepted and it may not be withdrawn before the end of that period. This section contains a new provision that gives the Secretary of State the power to vary, in regulations made under the Act, the period of 21 days (but not so as to reduce it to fewer than 14 days) – see s 562(6) of the CA 2006.

It also updates the CA 1985 provision to ensure that the communications of pre-emption offers to shareholders continue to be compatible with EU law: in particular, in future companies will be required to give individual notice (which may be in hard copy or electronic form) to all shareholders who have a registered address in the EEA or who have given an address for service of notices in the EEA (under the CA 1985, a company is only required to give individual notice to shareholders who have given a service address in the UK). As now, where no relevant address for service has been provided, the company may discharge its obligation by causing notice of the offer to be published in the London, Edinburgh or Belfast Gazette as appropriate.

Liability of company and officers in case of contravention

15.31 Section 563 of the CA 2006 concerns the liability of company and officers in case of contravention. It applies where there is a contravention of s 561 of the CA 2006 (existing shareholders' right of pre-emption), or s 562 of the CA 2006 (communication of pre-emption offers to shareholders).[3389]

The company and every officer of it who knowingly authorised or permitted the contravention, are jointly and severally liable to compensate any person to whom an offer should have been made in accordance with those provisions for any loss, damage, costs or expenses that the person has sustained or incurred by reason of the contravention.[3390]

No proceedings to recover any such loss, damage, costs or expenses shall be commenced after the expiration of two years from the delivery to the registrar of companies of the return of allotment,[3391] or where equity securities other than shares are granted, from the date of the grant.[3392]

Exceptions to right of pre-emption

15.32 Sections 564–566 of the CA 2006 are concerned with exceptions to pre-emption.

Exception to pre-emption rights: bonus shares

15.33 Section 564 of the CA 2006 deals with exceptions to the right of pre-emption in respect of bonus shares. It states that s 561(1) of the CA 2006

[3389] CA 2006, s 563(1).   [3390] CA 2006, s 563(2).   [3391] CA 2006, s 563(3)(a).
[3392] CA 2006, s 563(3)(b).

(existing shareholders' right of pre-emption) does not apply in relation to the allotment of bonus shares.

Exception to pre-emption rights: issue for non-cash consideration

15.34 Section 565 of the CA 2006 states that s 561(1) of the CA 2006 (existing shareholders' right of pre-emption) does not apply to a particular allotment of equity securities if these are, or are to be, wholly or partly paid up otherwise than in cash.

Exception to pre-emption rights: securities held under employees' share scheme

15.35 Section 566 of the CA 2006 states that s 561 of the CA 2006 (existing shareholders' rights of pre-emption) does not apply to the allotment of securities that would, apart from any renunciation or assignment of the right to their allotment, be held under an employees' share scheme.

Exclusion of right of pre-emption

15.36 Sections 567–568 of the CA 2006 are concerned with exclusion of rights of pre-emption.

Exclusion of requirements by private companies

15.37 Section 567 of the CA 2006 states that all or any of the requirements of s 561 of the CA 2006 (existing shareholders' rights of pre-emption),[3393] or s 562 of the CA 2006 (communication of pre-emption offers to shareholders)[3394] may be excluded by provision contained in the articles of a private company.

They may be excluded generally in relation to the allotment by the company of equity securities,[3395] or in relation to allotments of a particular description.[3396]

Any requirement or authorisation contained in the articles of a private company that is inconsistent with either of those sections is treated for the purposes of this section as a provision excluding that section.[3397]

A provision to which s 568 of the CA 2006 applies (exclusion of pre-emption rights: corresponding rights conferred by articles) is not to be treated as inconsistent with s 561 of the CA 2006.[3398]

[3393] CA 2006, s 567(1)(a).   [3394] CA 2006, s 567(1)(b).   [3395] CA 2006, s 567(2)(a).
[3396] CA 2006, s 567(2)(b).   [3397] CA 2006, s 567(3).   [3398] CA 2006, s 567(4).

Exclusion of pre-emption rights: articles conferring corresponding rights

15.38 Section 568 of the CA 2006 deals with the exclusion of pre-emption rights with reference to articles conferring corresponding rights. The provisions of this section apply where, in a case in which s 561 of the CA 2006 (existing shareholders' right of pre-emption) would otherwise apply, a company's articles contain provision (a 'pre-emption provision') prohibiting the company from allotting ordinary shares of a particular class unless it has complied with the condition that it makes such an offer as is described in s 561(1) of the CA 2006 to each person who holds ordinary shares of that class,[3399] and in accordance with that provision (i) the company makes an offer to allot shares to such a holder,[3400] and (ii) he or anyone in whose favour he has renounced his right to their allotment accepts the offer.[3401]

In that case, s 561 of the CA 2006 does not apply to the allotment of those shares and the company may allot them accordingly.[3402]

The provisions of s 562 of the CA 2006 (communication of pre-emption offers to shareholders) apply in relation to offers made in pursuance of the pre-emption provision of the company's articles.[3403] This is subject to s 567 of the CA 2006 (exclusion of requirements by private companies).

If there is a contravention of the pre-emption provision of the company's articles, the company, and every officer of it who knowingly authorised or permitted the contravention, are jointly and severally liable to compensate any person to whom an offer should have been made under the provision for any loss, damage, costs or expenses which the person has sustained or incurred by reason of the contravention.[3404]

No proceedings to recover any such loss, damage, costs or expenses may be commenced after the expiration of two years from the delivery to the registrar of companies of the return of allotments,[3405] or where equity securities other than shares are granted, from the date of the grant.[3406]

Disapplication of pre-emption rights

15.39 Sections 569–573 of the CA 2006 deal with the disapplication of pre-emption rights.

[3399] CA 2006, s 568(1)(a).   [3400] CA 2006, s 568(1)(b)(i).   [3401] CA 2006, s 568(1)(b)(ii).
[3402] CA 2006, s 568(2).   [3403] CA 2006, s 568(3).   [3404] CA 2006, s 568(4).
[3405] CA 2006, s 568(5)(a).   [3406] CA 2006, s 568(5)(b).

Disapplication of pre-emption rights: private company with only one class of shares

15.40 Section 569 of the CA 2006 states that the directors of a private company that has only one class of shares may be given power by the articles, or by a special resolution of the company, to allot equity securities of that class as if s 561 of the CA 2006 (existing shareholders' right of pre-emption) did not apply to the allotment,[3407] or applied to the allotment with such modifications as the directors may determine.[3408]

Where the directors make an allotment under this section, the provisions of Chapter 3 to Part 17 of the CA 2006 apply accordingly.[3409]

Disapplication of pre-emption rights: directors acting under general authorisation

15.41 Section 570 of the CA 2006 states that where the directors of a company are generally authorised for the purposes of s 551 of the CA 2006 (powers of directors to allot shares, etc.: authorisation by company), they may be given power by the articles, or by a special resolution of the company, to allot equity securities pursuant to that authorisation as if s 561 of the CA 2006 (existing shareholders' right of pre-emption) did not apply to the allotment,[3410] or applied to the allotment with such modifications as the directors may determine.[3411]

Where the directors make an allotment under this section, the provisions of this Chapter have effect accordingly.[3412]

The power conferred by this section ceases to have effect when the authorisation to which it relates is revoked,[3413] or would (if not renewed) expire.[3414] But if the authorisation is renewed the power may also be renewed, for a period not longer than that for which the authorisation is renewed, by a special resolution of the company.

Notwithstanding that the power conferred by this section has expired, the directors may allot equity securities in pursuance of an offer or agreement previously made by the company, if the power enabled the company to make an offer or agreement that would or might require equity securities to be allotted after it expired.[3415]

Disapplication of pre-emption rights by special resolution

15.42 Section 571 of the CA 2006 applies to the disapplication of pre-emption rights by special resolution. Where the directors of a company are

---

[3407] CA 2006, s 569(1)(a).   [3408] CA 2006, s 569(1)(b).   [3409] CA 2006, s 569(2).
[3410] CA 2006, s 570(1)(a).   [3411] CA 2006, s 570(1)(b).   [3412] CA 2006, s 570(2).
[3413] CA 2006, s 570(3)(a).   [3414] CA 2006, s 570(3)(b).   [3415] CA 2006, s 570(4).

authorised for the purposes of s 551 of the CA 2006 (power of directors to allot shares, etc.: authorisation by company), whether generally or otherwise, the company may by special resolution resolve that s 561 of the CA 2006 (existing shareholders' right of pre-emption) does not apply to a specified allotment of equity securities to be made pursuant to that authorisation,[3416] or applies to such an allotment with such modifications as may be specified in the resolution.[3417]

Where such a resolution is passed the provisions of this Chapter have effect accordingly.[3418]

A special resolution under this section ceases to have effect when the authorisation to which it relates is revoked,[3419] or would (if not renewed) expire.[3420] But if the authorisation is renewed the resolution may also be renewed, for a period not longer than that for which the authorisation is renewed, by a special resolution of the company.

Notwithstanding that any such resolution has expired, the directors may allot equity securities in pursuance of an offer or agreement previously made by the company if the resolution enabled the company to make an offer or agreement that would or might require equity securities to be allotted after it expired.[3421]

A special resolution under this section, or a special resolution to renew such a resolution, must not be proposed unless it is recommended by the directors,[3422] and the directors have complied with the following provisions.[3423]

Before such a resolution is proposed, the directors must make a written statement setting out their reasons for making the recommendation,[3424] the amount to be paid to the company in respect of the equity securities to be allotted,[3425] and the directors' justification of that amount.[3426]

The directors statement must, if the resolution is proposed as a written resolution, be sent or submitted to every eligible member at or before the time at which the proposed resolution is sent or submitted to him;[3427] or if the resolution is proposed at a general meeting, be circulated to the members entitled to notice of the meeting with that notice.[3428]

Liability for false statements in directors' statement

15.43 Section 572 of the CA 2006 deals with liability for false statements in a directors' statement. It applies in relation to a directors' statement under s 571 of the CA 2006 (special resolution disapplying pre-emption rights) that is sent, submitted or circulated under s 571(7) of the CA 2006.[3429]

[3416] CA 2006, s 571(1)(a).   [3417] CA 2006, s 571(1)(b).   [3418] CA 2006, s 571(2).
[3419] CA 2006, s 571(3)(a).   [3420] CA 2006, s 571(3)(b).   [3421] CA 2006, s 571(4).
[3422] CA 2006, s 571(5)(a).   [3423] CA 2006, s 571(5)(b).   [3424] CA 2006, s 571(6)(a).
[3425] CA 2006, s 571(6)(b).   [3426] CA 2006, s 571(6)(c).   [3427] CA 2006, s 571(7)(a).
[3428] CA 2006, s 571(7)(b).   [3429] CA 2006, s 572(1).

A person who knowingly or recklessly authorises or permits the inclusion of any matter that is misleading, false or deceptive in a material particular in such a statement commits an offence.[3430]

A person guilty of an offence under s 572 of the CA 2006 is liable on conviction on indictment, to imprisonment for a term not exceeding two years or a fine (or both);[3431] on summary conviction (i) in England and Wales, to imprisonment for a term not exceeding 12 months or to a fine not exceeding the statutory maximum (or both);[3432] (ii) in Scotland or Northern Ireland, to imprisonment for a term not exceeding six months, or to a fine not exceeding the statutory maximum (or both).[3433]

Disapplication of pre-emption rights: sale of treasury shares

15.44 Section 573 of the CA 2006 applies in relation to a sale of shares that is an allotment of equity securities by virtue of s 560(2)(b) of the CA 2006 (sale of shares held by company as treasury shares).[3434]

The directors of a company may be given power by the articles, or by a special resolution of the company, to allot equity securities as if s 561 of the CA 2006 (existing shareholders' right of pre-emption) did not apply to the allotment,[3435] or applied to the allotment with such modifications as the directors may determine.[3436]

The provisions of s 570(2) and (4) of the CA 2006 apply in that case as they apply to a case within subs (1) of that section.[3437]

The company may by special resolution resolve that s 561 of the CA 2006 shall not apply to a specified allotment of securities,[3438] or shall apply to the allotment with such modifications as may be specified in the resolution.[3439]

The provisions of s 571(2) and (4)–(7) of the CA 2006 apply in that case as they apply to a case within s 571(1) of the CA 2006.[3440]

Sections 569–573 of the CA 2006 deal with the circumstances in which the statutory preemption requirements may be disapplied or modifed by a power under the articles or by special resolution in accordance with the detailed rules in these sections. The rules replace or restate equivalent provisions in s 95 of the CA 1985.

Section 569 of the CA 2006 is a new provision that sets out how members of a private company with only one class of shares may authorise the directors to allot shares without complying with the statutory pre-emption provisions.

Section 573 of the CA 2006 is concerned with the disapplication of pre-emption rights in connection with a sale of treasury shares. Generally

[3430] CA 2006, s 572(2).   [3431] CA 2006, s 572(3)(a).   [3432] CA 2006, s 572(3)(b)(i).
[3433] CA 2006, s 572(3)(b)(ii).   [3434] CA 2006, s 573(1).   [3435] CA 2006, s 573(2)(a).
[3436] CA 2006, s 573(2)(b).   [3437] CA 2006, s 573(3).   [3438] CA 2006, s 573(4)(a).
[3439] CA 2006, s 573(4)(b).   [3440] CA 2006, s 573(5).

speaking, where a company buys back its own shares, it is normally required to cancel those shares (see s 706(b) of the CA 2006). Certain companies (principally those which are listed or those whose shares are traded on the Alternative Investment Market and equivalent companies in the EEA) may however elect not to cancel shares that have been bought back but may hold the shares 'in treasury ... A share that is held in treasury may be sold at a future point in time, and this facility enables such companies to raise capital more quickly than they would otherwise be able to do, as the directors do not have to obtain prior authority from the company's members before selling treasury shares. However, the provisions of s 561 of the CA 2006 do apply to sales of treasury shares as they apply to allotments of shares (see s 560(2)(b) of the CA 2006).

This section applies to a sale of shares that have been held in treasury by the company. It replaces s 95(2A) of the CA 1985 and reproduces the effect of that section by enabling a company's members to give a general power to the directors (through the company's articles or by special resolution of the company's members) to sell such shares as if statutory pre-emption rights did not apply, or applied with modifications.

This section also permits the members to confer upon the directors (by special resolution) a specific power that enables them to sell treasury shares as if statutory preemption rights did not apply to a specifed sale, or applied with modifcations.

Supplementary

References to holder of shares in relation to offer

15.45 Section 574 of the CA 2006 states that in Chapter 3 to Part 17 of the CA 2006, in relation to an offer to allot securities required by s 561 of the CA 2006 (existing shareholders' right of pre-emption),[3441] or any provision to which s 568 of the CA 2006 applies (articles conferring corresponding rights), a reference (however expressed) to the holder of shares of any description is to whoever was the holder of shares of that description at the close of business on a date to be specified in the offer.[3442]

The specified date must fall within the period of 28 days immediately before the date of the offer.[3443]

Saving for other restrictions on offers or allotments

15.46 Section 575 of the CA 2006 states that the provisions of Chapter 3 to Part 17 of the CA 2006 are without prejudice to any other enactment by

---

[3441] CA 2006, s 574(1)(a).   [3442] CA 2006, s 574(1)(b).   [3443] CA 2006, s 574(2).

virtue of which a company is prohibited (whether generally or in specified circumstances) from offering or allotting equity securities to any person.[3444]

Where a company cannot by virtue of such an enactment offer or allot equity securities to a holder of ordinary shares of the company, those shares are disregarded for the purposes of s 561 of the CA 2006 (existing shareholders' right of pre-emption), so that the person is not treated as a person who holds ordinary shares,[3445] and the shares are not treated as forming part of the ordinary share capital of the company.[3446]

Saving for certain older pre-emption requirements

15.47 Section 576 of the CA 2006 applies to saving for certain other pre-emption requirements. In the case of a public company the provisions of this Chapter do not apply to an allotment of equity securities that are subject to a pre-emption requirement in relation to which s 96(1) of the CA 1985 (c 6) or Article 106(1) of the Companies (Northern Ireland) Order 1986 (SI 1986/1032 (NI 6)) applied immediately before the commencement of this Chapter.[3447]

In the case of a private company, a pre-emption requirement to which s 96(3) of the CA 1985 or Article 106(3) of the Companies (Northern Ireland) Order 1986 applied immediately before the commencement of this Chapter will have effect, so long as the company remains a private company, as if it were contained in the company's articles.[3448]

A pre-emption requirement to which s 96(4) of the CA 1985 or Article 106(4) of the Companies (Northern Ireland) Order 1986 applied immediately before the commencement of this section will be treated for the purposes of Chapter 3 to Part 17 of the CA 2006 as if it were contained in the company's articles.[3449]

Provisions about pre-emption not applicable to shares taken on formation

15.48 Sections 577 of the CA 2006 is concerned with provisions about pre-emptions not applicable to shares taken on formation. The provisions of Chapter 3 to Part 17 of the CA 2006 have no application in relation to the taking of shares by the subscribers to the memorandum on the formation of the company.

[3444] CA 2006, s 575(1).   [3445] CA 2006, s 575(2)(a).   [3446] CA 2006, s 575(2)(b).
[3447] CA 2006, s 576(1).   [3448] CA 2006, s 576(2).   [3449] CA 2006, s 576(3).

Public Companies: Allotment Where Issue is Not Fully Subscribed

15.49 Chapter 4 to Part 17 of the CA 2006 is concerned with public companies with regard to allotment where an issue is not fully subscribed.

Public companies: allotment where issue not fully subscribed

15.50 Section 578 of the CA 2006 states that no allotment will be made of shares of a public company offered for subscription, unless the issue is subscribed for in full,[3450] or the offer is made on terms that the shares subscribed for may be allotted (i) in any event,[3451] or (ii) if specified conditions are met (and those conditions are met).[3452]

If shares are prohibited from being allotted by s 578(1) of the CA 2006, and 40 days have elapsed after the first making of the offer, all money received from applicants for shares must be repaid to them forthwith, without interest.[3453]

If any of the money is not repaid within 48 days after the first making of the offer, the directors of the company are jointly and severally liable to repay it, with interest at the rate for the time being specified under s 17 of the Judgments Act 1838 (c 110) from the expiration of the forty-eighth day.[3454]

A director is not so liable if he proves that the default in the repayment of the money was not due to any misconduct or negligence on his part.

Section 578 of the CA 2006 applies in the case of shares offered as wholly or partly payable otherwise than in cash, as it applies in the case of shares offered for subscription.[3455]

In that case the references in s 578(1) of the CA 2006 to subscription are to be construed accordingly;[3456] references in s 578(2) and (3) of the CA 2006 to the repayment of money received from applicants for shares include (i) the return of any other consideration so received (including, if the case so requires, the release of the applicant from any undertaking),[3457] or (ii) if it is not reasonably practicable to return the consideration, the payment of money equal to its value at the time it was so received;[3458] and references to interest apply accordingly.[3459]

Any condition requiring or binding an applicant for shares to waive compliance with any requirement of this section is void.[3460]

The provisions of s 578 of the CA 2006 relate to the allotment of shares by public companies and apply where not all the shares offered are taken up. A public company must not allot shares following an offer to subscribe for

---

[3450] CA 2006, s 578(1)(a). [3451] CA 2006, s 578(1)(b)(i). [3452] CA 2006, s 578(1)(b)(ii).
[3453] CA 2006, s 578(2). [3454] CA 2006, s 578(3). [3455] CA 2006, s 578(4).
[3456] CA 2006, s 578(5)(a). [3457] CA 2006, s 578(5)(b)(i). [3458] CA 2006, s 578(5)(b)(ii).
[3459] CA 2006, s 578(5)(c). [3460] CA 2006, s 578(6).

shares, unless all the shares offered are taken up, or the offer is made on the basis that it will go ahead even if all the shares offered are not taken up or if other conditions specified in the offer are met. It is not possible for the terms of the offer to override the requirement of this section (s 578(6) of the CA 2006).

The purpose of this rule is to protect persons who apply for shares, by ensuring that if the increase in capital is not fully subscribed, the capital will be increased by the amount of the subscriptions received only if the conditions of the issue so provide (Article 28 of the Second Company Law Directive (77/91/EEC)).

If 40 days after first making the offer, the offer is unsuccessful because not enough shares have been applied for under the offer, any money or other consideration received from those that did apply for shares under the offer must be repaid or returned (subs (2)). Interest becomes payable after the expiration of the forty-eighth day after the offer was first made (s 578(3) of the CA 2006). The rate of interest will be as specified at the time under s 17 of the Judgments Act 1838 (currently 8 per cent). This is a change from s 84 of the CA 1985, which sets the interest rate at 5 per cent per annum.

The 40-day and 48-day time limits imposed by s 578(2) and (3) of the CA 2006 now run from the making of the offer rather than from the issue of any prospectus (as was the case under s 84 of the CA 1985) given that the requirement or otherwise for a prospectus is a matter of securities law.

The regulation of public offers, especially requirements relating to prospectuses, is generally a matter of securities law. Sections 82 and 83 of the CA 1985 are, therefore, not restated in the CA 2006.

Public companies: effect of irregular allotment where issue not fully subscribed

15.51 Section 579 of the CA 2006 states that an allotment made by a public company to an applicant in contravention of s 578 of the CA 2006 (public companies: allotment where issue not fully subscribed) is voidable at the instance of the applicant within one month after the date of the allotment, and not later.[3461] It is so voidable even if the company is in the course of being wound up.[3462]

A director of a public company who knowingly contravenes, or permits or authorises the contravention of, any provision of s 578 of the CA 2006 with respect to allotment is liable to compensate the company and the allottee respectively for any loss, damages, costs or expenses that the company or allottee may have sustained or incurred by the contravention.[3463]

[3461] CA 2006, s 579(1).   [3462] CA 2006, s 579(2).   [3463] CA 2006, s 579(3).

Proceedings to recover any such loss, damages, costs or expenses may not be brought more than two years after the date of the allotment.[3464]

Payment for Shares

15.52 Chapter 5 to Part 17 of the CA 2006 is concerned with the provisions dealing with payment for shares. It contains 13 provisions.

General rules

Shares not to be allotted at a discount

15.53 Section 580 of the CA 2006 addresses the rule that shares must not be allotted at a discount. A company's shares must not be allotted at a discount.[3465] If shares are allotted in contravention of this section, the allottee is liable to pay the company an amount equal to the amount of the discount, with interest at the appropriate rate.[3466]

Provision for different amounts to be paid on shares

15.54 Section 581 of the CA 2006 deals with the provision for different amounts to be paid on shares. A company, if so authorised by its articles, may make arrangements on the issue of shares for a difference between the shareholders in the amounts and times of payment of calls on their shares;[3467] accept from any member the whole or part of the amount remaining unpaid on any shares held by him, although no part of that amount has been called up;[3468] pay a dividend in proportion to the amount paid up on each share where a larger amount is paid up on some shares than on others.[3469]

General rule as to means of payment

15.55 Shares allotted by a company, and any premium on them, may be paid up in money or money's worth (including goodwill and know-how).[3470]

This section does not prevent a company from allotting bonus shares to its members,[3471] or from paying up, with sums available for the purpose, any amounts for the time being unpaid on any of its shares (whether on account of the nominal value of the shares or by way of premium).[3472]

Section 581 of the CA 2006 applies subject to the following provisions of Chapter 5 to Part 17 of the CA 2006 (additional rules for public companies).[3473]

[3464] CA 2006, s 579(4). [3465] CA 2006, s 580(1). [3466] CA 2006, s 580(2).
[3467] CA 2006, s 581(1)(a). [3468] CA 2006, s 581(1)(b). [3469] CA 2006, s 581(1)(c).
[3470] CA 2006, s 582(1). [3471] CA 2006, s 582(2)(a). [3472] CA 2006, s 582(2)(b).
[3473] CA 2006, s 582(3).

Meaning of payment in cash

15.56 Section 583 of the CA 2006 sets out the definition of payment in cash. The following provisions apply for the purposes of the Companies Acts.[3474]

A share in a company is deemed paid up (as to its nominal value or any premium on it) in cash, or allotted for cash, if the consideration received for the allotment or payment up is a cash consideration.[3475]

The term 'cash consideration' means cash received by the company,[3476] or a cheque received by the company in good faith, which the directors have no reason for suspecting will not be paid,[3477] or a release of a liability of the company for a liquidated sum,[3478] or an undertaking to pay cash to the company at a future date,[3479] or payment by any other means giving rise to a present or future entitlement (of the company or a person acting on the company's behalf) to a payment, or credit equivalent to payment, in cash.[3480]

The Secretary of State may by order provide that particular means of payment specified in the order are to be regarded as falling within s 583(3)(e) of the CA 2006.[3481]

In relation to the allotment or payment up of shares in a company, the payment of cash to a person other than the company,[3482] or an undertaking to pay cash to a person other than the company, counts as consideration other than cash.[3483] This does not apply for the purposes of Chapter 3 to Part 17 of the CA 2006 (allotment of equity securities: existing shareholders' right of pre-emption). For the purpose of determining whether a share is or is to be allotted for cash, or paid up in cash, 'cash' includes foreign currency.[3484]

An order under this section is subject to negative resolution procedure.[3485]

This section replaces s 738(2)–(4) of the CA 1985. It provides a defnition of 'payment in cash' for the purposes of the Companies Acts and is relevant to a number of provisions (for example, s 593 of the CA 2006 requires public companies to obtain an independent valuation of any non-cash consideration where it allots shares otherwise than for cash).

Section 583(3) of the CA 2006 provides a definition of 'cash consideration', which lists the items currently contained in s 738(2) of the CA 1985. It is generally accepted that certain forms of payment, in addition to those listed in s 583(3) of the CA 2006, constitute 'payment in cash', where shares in a company are deemed to be paid up or allotted for cash, for example an assured payment obligation under the CREST assured payment system, but this matter is not beyond doubt. (An assured payment obligation is the creation of an obligation to make payment to or for the account of the company in accordance with the rules and practices of the operator of a relevant

[3474] CA 2006, s 583(1).   [3475] CA 2006, s 583(2).   [3476] CA 2006, s 583(3)(a).
[3477] CA 2006, s 583(3)(b).   [3478] CA 2006, s 583(3)(c).   [3479] CA 2006, s 583(3)(d).
[3480] CA 2006, s 583(3)(e).   [3481] CA 2006, s 583(4).   [3482] CA 2006, s 583(5)(a).
[3483] CA 2006, s 583(5)(b).   [3484] CA 2006, s 583(6).   [3485] CA 2006, s 583(7).

system as defined by regulation 2(1) of the Uncertificated Securities Regulations 2001.) The power contained in s 583(4) of the CA 2006 will enable the Secretary of State to make provision for other forms of payment to be regarded as falling within the definition of 'payment in cash'. This will eradicate the uncertainty that currently surrounds certain forms of payment and will also 'future proof' the current definition should other settlement systems be developed in the future (or should other settlement systems within the EU be identified).

Additional rules for public companies

Public companies: shares taken by subscribers of memoranda

15.57 Section 584 of the CA 2006 deals with shares taken by subscribers of memoranda in respect of public companies. Shares taken by a subscriber to the memorandum of a public company in pursuance of an undertaking of his in the memorandum, and any premium on the shares, must be paid up in cash.

Public companies: must not accept undertaking to do work or perform services

15.58 Section 585 of the CA 2006 provides rules for public companies with prohibition against undertaking to do work or perform services. A public company must not accept at any time, in payment up of its shares or any premium on them, an undertaking given by any person that he or another should do work or perform services for the company or any other person.[3486]

If a public company accepts such an undertaking in payment up of its shares or any premium on them, the holder of the shares when they or the premium are treated as paid up (in whole or in part) by the undertaking is liable (a) to pay the company in respect of those shares an amount equal to their nominal value, together with the whole of any premium or, if the case so requires, such proportion of that amount as is treated as paid up by the undertaking;[3487] and (b) to pay interest at the appropriate rate on the amount payable under para (a).[3488]

The reference in s 585(2) of the CA 2006 to the holder of shares includes a person who has an unconditional right to be included in the company's register of members in respect of those shares,[3489] or to have an instrument of transfer of them executed in his favour.[3490]

[3486] CA 2006, s 585(1).   [3487] CA 2006, s 585(2)(a).   [3488] CA 2006, s 585(2)(b).
[3489] CA 2006, s 585(3)(a).   [3490] CA 2006, s 585(3)(b).

Public companies: shares must be at least one-quarter paid up

15.59 Section 586 of the CA 2006 states that a public company must not allot a share except as paid up at least as to one-quarter of its nominal value and the whole of any premium on it.[3491]

This does not apply to shares allotted in pursuance of an employees' share scheme.[3492]

If a company allots a share in contravention of this section the share is to be treated as if one-quarter of its nominal value, together with the whole of any premium on it, had been received,[3493] and the allottee is liable to pay the company the minimum amount that should have been received in respect of the share under s 586(1) of the CA 2006 (less the value of any consideration actually applied in payment up, to any extent, of the share and any premium on it), with interest at the appropriate rate.[3494]

Section 586(3) of the CA 2006 does not apply to the allotment of bonus shares, unless the allottee knew or ought to have known the shares were allotted in contravention of this section.[3495]

Public companies: payment by long-term undertaking

15.60 Section 587 of the CA 2006 applies to payment by long-term undertaking in respect of public companies. A public company must not allot shares as fully or partly paid up (as to their nominal value or any premium on them) otherwise than in cash if the consideration for the allotment is or includes an undertaking which is to be, or may be, performed more than five years after the date of the allotment.[3496]

If a company allots shares in contravention of s 587(1) of the CA 2006, the allottee is liable to pay the company an amount equal to the aggregate of their nominal value and the whole of any premium (or, if the case so requires, so much of that aggregate as is treated as paid up by the undertaking), with interest at the appropriate rate.[3497]

Where a contract for the allotment of shares does not contravene s 587(1) of the CA 2006, any variation of the contract that has the effect that the contract would have contravened the subsection, if the terms of the contract as varied had been its original terms, is void.[3498]

This applies also to the variation by a public company of the terms of a contract entered into before the company was re-registered as a public company.

Where a public company allots shares for a consideration which consists of or includes (in accordance with subs (1)) an undertaking that is to be

---

[3491] CA 2006, s 586(1).   [3492] CA 2006, s 586(2).   [3493] CA 2006, s 586(3)(a).
[3494] CA 2006, s 586(3)(b).   [3495] CA 2006, s 586(4).   [3496] CA 2006, s 587(1).
[3497] CA 2006, s 587(2).   [3498] CA 2006, s 587(3).

performed within five years of the allotment,[3499] and the undertaking is not performed within the period allowed by the contract for the allotment of the shares,[3500] the allottee is liable to pay the company, at the end of the period so allowed, an amount equal to the aggregate of the nominal value of the shares and the whole of any premium (or, if the case so requires, so much of that aggregate as is treated as paid up by the undertaking), with interest at the appropriate rate.

The references in s 587 of the CA 2006 to a contract for the allotment of shares include an ancillary contract relating to payment in respect of them.[3501]

Supplementary provisions

Liability of subsequent holders of shares

15.61 Section 588 of the CA 2006 states that if a person becomes a holder of shares in respect of which there has been a contravention of any provision of Chapter 5 to Part 17 of the CA 2006,[3502] and by virtue of that contravention another person is liable to pay any amount under the provision contravened,[3503] that person is also liable to pay that amount (jointly and severally with any other person so liable), subject as follows.

A person otherwise liable under s 587(1) of the CA 2006 is exempted from that liability if either he is a purchaser for value and, at the time of the purchase, he did not have actual notice of the contravention concerned,[3504] or he derived title to the shares (directly or indirectly) from a person who became a holder of them after the contravention and was not liable under s 588(1) of the CA 2006.[3505]

The references in s 588 of the CA 2006 to a holder, in relation to shares in a company, include any person who has an unconditional right to be included in the company's register of members in respect of those shares,[3506] or to have an instrument of transfer of the shares executed in his favour.[3507]

Section 588 of the CA 2006 applies in relation to a failure to carry out a term of a contract as mentioned in s 587(4) of the CA 2006 (public companies: payment by long-term undertakings) as it applies in relation to a contravention of a provision of Chapter 5 to Part 17 of the CA 2006.[3508]

Power of court to grant relief

15.62 Section 589 of the CA 2006 deals with the power of the court to grant interim relief. It applies in relation to liability under s 585(2) of the CA 2006

[3499] CA 2006, s 587(4)(a).　　[3500] CA 2006, s 587(4)(b).　　[3501] CA 2006, s 587(5).
[3502] CA 2006, s 588(1)(a).　　[3503] CA 2006, s 588(1)(b).　　[3504] CA 2006, s 588(2)(a).
[3505] CA 2006, s 588(2)(b).　　[3506] CA 2006, s 588(3)(a).　　[3507] CA 2006, s 588(3)(b).
[3508] CA 2006, s 588(4).

(liability of allottee in case of breach by public company of prohibition on accepting undertaking to do work or perform services), s 587(2) or (4) of the CA 2006 (liability of allottee in case of breach by public company of prohibition on payment by long-term undertaking), or s 588 of the CA 2006 (liability of subsequent holders of shares), as it applies in relation to a contravention of those sections.[3509]

A person who is subject to any such liability to a company in relation to payment in respect of shares in the company,[3510] or is subject to any such liability to a company by virtue of an undertaking given to it in, or in connection with, payment for shares in the company,[3511] may apply to the court to be exempted in whole or in part from the liability.

In the case of a liability within s 589(2)(a) of the CA 2006, the court may exempt the applicant from the liability only if and to the extent that it appears to the court just and equitable to do so having regard to (a) whether the applicant has paid, or is liable to pay, any amount in respect of (i) any other liability arising in relation to those shares under any provision of Chapter 5 or Chapter 6 to Part 17 of the CA 2006,[3512] or (ii) any liability arising by virtue of any undertaking given in or in connection with payment for those shares;[3513] (b) whether any person other than the applicant has paid or is likely to pay, whether in pursuance of any order of the court or otherwise, any such amount;[3514] (c) whether the applicant or any other person (i) has performed in whole or in part, or is likely so to perform any such undertaking,[3515] or (ii) has done or is likely to do any other thing in payment or part payment for the shares.[3516]

In the case of a liability within s 589(2)(b) of the CA 2006, the court may exempt the applicant from the liability only if and to the extent that it appears to the court just and equitable to do so having regard to whether the applicant has paid or is liable to pay any amount in respect of liability arising in relation to the shares under any provision of Chapter 5 or Chapter 6 of the CA 2006;[3517] or whether any person other than the applicant has paid or is likely to pay, whether in pursuance of any order of the court or otherwise, any such amount.[3518]

In determining whether it should exempt the applicant in whole or in part from any liability, the court must have regard to the following overriding principles (a) a company that has allotted shares should receive money or money's worth at least equal in value to the aggregate of the nominal value of those shares and the whole of any premium or, if the case so requires, so much of that aggregate as is treated as paid up;[3519] (b) subject to that, where a

[3509] CA 2006, s 589(1).   [3510] CA 2006, s 589(2)(a).   [3511] CA 2006, s 589(2)(b).
[3512] CA 2006, s 589(3)(a)(i).   [3513] CA 2006, s 589(3)(a)(ii).   [3514] CA 2006, s 589(3)(b).
[3515] CA 2006, s 589(3)(c)(i).   [3516] CA 2006, s 589(3)(c)(ii).   [3517] CA 2006, s 589(4)(a).
[3518] CA 2006, s 589(4)(b).   [3519] CA 2006, s 589(5)(a).

company would, if the court did not grant the exemption, have more than one remedy against a particular person, it should be for the company to decide which remedy it should remain entitled to pursue.[3520]

If a person brings proceedings against another ('the contributor') for a contribution in respect of liability to a company arising under any provision of Chapter 5 or Chapter 6 of the CA 2006 and it appears to the court that the contributor is liable to make such a contribution, the court may, if and to the extent that it appears to it just and equitable to do so having regard to the respective culpability (in respect of the liability to the company) of the contributor and the person bringing the proceedings exempt the contributor in whole or in part from his liability to make such a contribution,[3521] or order the contributor to make a larger contribution than, but for this subsection, he would be liable to make.[3522]

Section 589 restates s 113(1)–(7) of the CA 1985. It enables the court to grant relief to the applicant, from a liability to the company that has arisen as a result of a contravention of section 585, 587(2) or (4) or 588. There is a minor change in the restatement insofar as the matters to which the court must have regard in applying the just and equitable test in s 589(3) of the CA 2006 also apply where the liability relates to the payment of interest (under s 113(2)(b)) of the CA 1985 the court is not required to have regard to those matters in applying the just and equitable test).

Penalty for contravention of Chapter 5 to Part 17 of the CA 2006

15.63 Section 590 of the CA 2006 sets out the penalty for contravention of Chapter 5. If a company contravenes any of the provisions of this Chapter, an offence is committed by the company,[3523] and every officer of the company who is in default.[3524] A person guilty of an offence is liable on conviction on indictment, to a fine;[3525] on summary conviction, to a fine not exceeding the statutory maximum.[3526]

Enforceability of undertakings to do work, etc.

15.64 Section 591 of the CA 2006 sets out the enforceability of undertakings to do work. An undertaking given by any person, in or in connection with payment for shares in a company, to do work or perform services or to do any other thing, if it is enforceable by the company apart from Chapter 5, is so enforceable notwithstanding that there has been a contravention in relation to it of a provision of Chapter 5 or Chapter 6 to Part 17 of the CA 2006.[3527]

[3520] CA 2006, s 589(5)(b).   [3521] CA 2006, s 589(6)(a).   [3522] CA 2006, s 589(6)(b).
[3523] CA 2006, s 590(1)(a).   [3524] CA 2006, s 590(1)(b).   [3525] CA 2006, s 590(2)(a).
[3526] CA 2006, s 590(2)(b).   [3527] CA 2006, s 591(1).

This is without prejudice to s 589 of the CA 2006 (power of court to grant relief etc. in respect of liabilities).[3528]

The appropriate rate of interest

15.65 Section 592 of the CA 2006 sets out the appropriate rate of interest. For the purposes of Chapter 5 to Part 17 of the CA 2006 the 'appropriate rate' of interest is 5 per cent per annum or such other rate as may be specified by order made by the Secretary of State.[3529] An order under this section is subject to negative resolution procedure.[3530]

Public Companies: Independent Valuation of Non-Cash Considerations

Non-cash consideration for shares

15.66 Chapter 6 to Part 17 of the CA 2006 addresses the issue of independent valuation of non-cash consideration in respect of public companies.

Public company: valuation of non-cash consideration for shares

15.67 Section 593 of the CA 2006 considers the public company valuation of non-cash consideration for shares. A public company must not allot shares as fully or partly paid up (as to their nominal value or any premium on them) otherwise than in cash unless the consideration for the allotment has been independently valued in accordance with the provisions of this Chapter,[3531] the valuer's report has been made to the company during the six months immediately preceding the allotment of the shares[3532] and a copy of the report has been sent to the proposed allottee.[3533]

For this purpose the application of an amount standing to the credit of any of a company's reserve accounts,[3534] or its profit and loss account,[3535] in paying up (to any extent) shares allotted to members of the company, or premiums on shares so allotted, does not count as consideration for the allotment.

Accordingly, s 593(1) of the CA 2006 does not apply in that case.

If a company allots shares in contravention of s 593(1) of the CA 2006, and either the allottee has not received the valuer's report required to be sent to him,[3536] or there has been some other contravention of the requirements of this section or s 596 of the CA 2006 that the allottee knew or ought to have

[3528] CA 2006, s 591(2).   [3529] CA 2006, s 592(1).   [3530] CA 2006, s 592(2).
[3531] CA 2006, s 593(1)(a).   [3532] CA 2006, s 593(1)(b).   [3533] CA 2006, s 593(1)(c).
[3534] CA 2006, s 593(2)(a).   [3535] CA 2006, s 593(2)(b).   [3536] CA 2006, s 593(3)(a).

known amounted to a contravention,[3537] the allottee is liable to pay the company an amount equal to the aggregate of the nominal value of the shares and the whole of any premium (or, if the case so requires, so much of that aggregate as is treated as paid up by the consideration), with interest at the appropriate rate.

This section applies subject to s 594 of the CA 2006 (exception to valuation requirement: arrangement with another company), and s 595 of the CA 2006 (exception to valuation requirement: merger).[3538]

Exception to valuation requirement: arrangement with another company

15.68 Section 594 of the CA 2006 states that s 593 of the CA 2006 (valuation of non-cash consideration) does not apply to the allotment of shares by a company (company A) in connection with an arrangement to which this section applies.[3539]

This section applies to an arrangement for the allotment of shares in company A on terms that the whole or part of the consideration for the shares allotted is to be provided by the transfer to that company,[3540] or the cancellation,[3541] of all or some of the shares, or of all or some of the shares of a particular class, in another company (company B).

It is immaterial whether the arrangement provides for the issue to company A of shares, or shares of any particular class, in company B.[3542]

This section applies to an arrangement only if under the arrangement it is open to all the holders of the shares in company B (or, where the arrangement applies only to shares of a particular class, to all the holders of shares of that class) to take part in the arrangement.[3543]

In determining whether that is the case, the following shall be disregarded (a) shares held by or by a nominee of company A;[3544] (b) shares held by or by a nominee of a company which is (i) the holding company, or a subsidiary, of company A,[3545] or (ii) a subsidiary of such a holding company;[3546] (c) shares held as treasury shares by company B.[3547]

In s 594 of the CA 2006 the term 'arrangement' means any agreement, scheme or arrangement (including an arrangement sanctioned in accordance with Part 26 (arrangements and reconstructions),[3548] or s 110 of the CA the Insolvency Act 1986 (c 45) or Article 96 of the Insolvency (Northern Ireland) Order 1989 (SI 1989/2405 (NI 19)) (liquidator in winding up accepting shares

---

[3537] CA 2006, s 593(3)(b).   [3538] CA 2006, s 593(4).   [3539] CA 2006, s 594(1).
[3540] CA 2006, s 594(2)(a).   [3541] CA 2006, s 594(2)(b).   [3542] CA 2006, s 594(3).
[3543] CA 2006, s 594(4).   [3544] CA 2006, s 594(5)(a).   [3545] CA 2006, s 594(5)(b)(i).
[3546] CA 2006, s 594(5)(b)(ii).   [3547] CA 2006, s 594(5)(c).   [3548] CA 2006, s 594(6)(a)(i).

as consideration for sale of company property)).[3549] The term 'company', except in reference to company A, includes any body corporate.[3550]

Exception to valuation requirement: merger

Section 595 of the CA 2006 sets out another exception to a valuation requirement in respect of a merger. It states that s 593 of the CA 2006 (valuation of non-cash consideration) does not apply to the allotment of shares by a company in connection with a proposed merger with another company.[3551]

A proposed merger is where one of the companies proposes to acquire all the assets and liabilities of the other in exchange for the issue of shares or other securities of that one to shareholders of the other, with or without any cash payment to shareholders.[3552]

The term 'company', in reference to the other company, includes any body corporate.[3553]

Non-cash consideration for shares: requirements as to valuation and report

15.69 Section 596 of the CA 2006 applies to non-consideration for shares and requirements as to valuation and report. The provisions of ss 1150–1153 of the CA 2006 (general provisions as to independent valuation and report) apply to the valuation and report required by s 593 of the CA 2006 (public company: valuation of non-cash consideration for shares).[3554]

The valuer's report must state the nominal value of the shares to be wholly or partly paid for by the consideration in question;[3555] the amount of any premium payable on the shares;[3556] the description of the consideration and, as respects so much of the consideration as he himself has valued, a description of that part of the consideration, the method used to value it and the date of the valuation;[3557] the extent to which the nominal value of the shares and any premium are to be treated as paid up (i) by the consideration;[3558] (ii) in cash.[3559]

The valuer's report must contain or be accompanied by a note by him in the case of a valuation made by a person other than himself, that it appeared to himself reasonable to arrange for it to be so made or to accept a valuation so made,[3560] whoever made the valuation, that the method of valuation was reasonable in all the circumstances,[3561] that it appears to the valuer that there has been no material change in the value of the consideration in question

---

[3549] CA 2006, s 594(6)(a)(ii).   [3550] CA 2006, s 594(6)(b).   [3551] CA 2006, s 595(1).
[3552] CA 2006, s 595(2).   [3553] CA 2006, s 595(3).   [3554] CA 2006, s 596(1).
[3555] CA 2006, s 596(2)(a).   [3556] CA 2006, s 596(2)(b).   [3557] CA 2006, s 596(2)(c).
[3558] CA 2006, s 596(2)(d)(i).   [3559] CA 2006, s 596(2)(d)(ii).   [3560] CA 2006, s 596(3)(a).
[3561] CA 2006, s 596(3)(b).

since the valuation,[3562] and that, on the basis of the valuation, the value of the consideration, together with any cash by which the nominal value of the shares or any premium payable on them is to be paid up, is not less than so much of the aggregate of the nominal value and the whole of any such premium as is treated as paid up by the consideration and any such cash.[3563]

Where the consideration to be valued is accepted partly in payment up of the nominal value of the shares and any premium and partly for some other consideration given by the company, s 593 of the CA 2006 and the preceding provisions of this section apply as if references to the consideration accepted by the company included the proportion of that consideration that is properly attributable to the payment up of that value and any premium.[3564]

In such a case the valuer must carry out, or arrange for, such other valuations as will enable him to determine that proportion,[3565] and his report must state what valuations have been made under this subsection and also the reason for, and method and date of, any such valuation and any other matters which may be relevant to that determination.[3566]

Copy of report to be delivered to registrar

15.70 Section 597 of the CA 2006 provides for a copy of report to be delivered to the registrar. A company to which a report is made under s 593 of the CA 2006 as to the value of any consideration for which, or partly for which, it proposes to allot shares must deliver a copy of the report to the registrar for registration.[3567]

The copy must be delivered at the same time that the company files the return of the allotment of those shares under s 555 of the CA 2006 (return of allotment by a limited company).[3568]

If default is made in complying with s 597(1) or (2) of the CA 2006, an offence is committed by every officer of the company who is in default.[3569] A person guilty of an offence under this section is liable on conviction on indictment, to a fine;[3570] on summary conviction, to a fine not exceeding the statutory maximum and, for continued contravention, a daily default fine not exceeding one-tenth of the statutory maximum.[3571]

In the case of a default in delivering to the registrar any document as required by this section, any person liable for the default may apply to the court for relief.[3572]

The court, if satisfied that the omission to deliver the document was accidental or due to inadvertence, or that it is just and equitable to grant relief,[3573]

[3562] CA 2006, s 596(3)(c).   [3563] CA 2006, s 596(3)(d).   [3564] CA 2006, s 596(4).
[3565] CA 2006, s 596(5)(a).   [3566] CA 2006, s 596(5)(b).   [3567] CA 2006, s 597(1).
[3568] A 2006, s 597(2).   [3569] CA 2006, s 597(3).   [3570] CA 2006, s 597(4)(a).
[3571] CA 2006, s 597(4)(b).   [3572] CA 2006, s 597(5).   [3573] CA 2006, s 597(6)(a).

may make an order extending the time for delivery of the document for such period as the court thinks proper.[3574]

Transfer of non-cash assets in initial period

Public company: agreement for transfer of non-cash asset in initial period

15.71 Section 598 of the CA 2006 states that a public company formed as such must not enter into an agreement with a person who is a subscriber to the company's memorandum,[3575] for the transfer by him to the company, or another, before the end of the company's initial period of one or more non-cash assets,[3576] and under which the consideration for the transfer to be given by the company is at the time of the agreement equal in value to one-tenth or more of the company's issued share capital,[3577] unless the conditions referred to below have been complied with.

The company's 'initial period' means the period of two years beginning with the date of the company being issued with a certificate under s 761 of the CA 2006 (trading certificate).[3578]

The conditions are those specified in s 599 of the CA 2006 (requirement of independent valuation), and s 601 of the CA 2006 (requirement of approval by members).[3579]

Section 598 of the CA 2006 does not apply where it is part of the company's ordinary business to acquire, or arrange for other persons to acquire, assets of a particular description,[3580] and the agreement is entered into by the company in the ordinary course of that business.[3581]

Section 598 of the CA 2006 does not apply to an agreement entered into by the company under the supervision of the court or of an officer authorised by the court for the purpose.[3582]

Agreement for transfer of a non-cash asset: requirement of an independent valuation

15.72 Section 599 of the CA 2006 deals with an agreement for transfer of a non-cash asset and the requirement of an independent valuation. The following conditions must have been complied with, namely: the consideration to be received by the company, and any consideration other than cash to be given by the company, must have been independently valued in accordance with the provisions of Chapter 6 to Part 17 of the CA 2006;[3583] the valuer's report

[3574] CA 2006, s 597(6)(b).   [3575] CA 2006, s 598(1)(a).   [3576] CA 2006, s 598(1)(b).
[3577] CA 2006, s 598(1)(c).   [3578] CA 2006, s 598(2).   [3579] CA 2006, s 598(3).
[3580] CA 2006, s 598(4)(a).   [3581] CA 2006, s 598(4)(b).   [3582] CA 2006, s 598(5).
[3583] CA 2006, s 599(1)(a).

must have been made to the company during the six months immediately preceding the date of the agreement,[3584] and a copy of the report must have been sent to the other party to the proposed agreement not later than the date on which copies have to be circulated to members under s 601(3) of the CA 2006.[3585]

The reference in s 599(1)(a) of the CA 2006 to the consideration to be received by the company is to the asset to be transferred to it or, as the case may be, to the advantage to the company of the asset's transfer to another person.[3586]

The reference in s 599(1)(c) of the CA 2006 to the other party to the proposed agreement is to the person referred to in s 598(1)(a) of the CA 2006.[3587]

If he has received a copy of the report under s 601 of the CA 2006 in his capacity as a member of the company, it is not necessary to send another copy under this section.

Section 599 of the CA 2006 does not affect any requirement to value any consideration for purposes of s 593 of the CA 2006 (valuation of non-cash consideration for shares).[3588]

Agreement for transfer of non-cash asset: requirements as to valuation and report

15.73 Section 600 of the CA 2006 applies to an agreement for transfer of non-cash asset. it states that the provisions of ss 1150 to 1153 of the CA 2006 (general provisions as to an independent valuation and report) apply to the valuation and report required by s 599 of the CA 2006 (public company: transfer of a non-cash asset).[3589]

The valuer's report must state the consideration to be received by the company, describing the asset in question (specifying the amount to be received in cash) and the consideration to be given by the company (specifying the amount to be given in cash),[3590] and the method and date of valuation.[3591]

The valuer's report must contain or be accompanied by a note by him in the case of a valuation made by a person other than himself; that it appeared to himself reasonable to arrange for it to be so made or to accept a valuation so made;[3592] whoever made the valuation, that the method of valuation was reasonable in all the circumstances;[3593] that it appears to the valuer that there has been no material change in the value of the consideration in question since the valuation;[3594] and that, on the basis of the valuation, the value of the

[3584] CA 2006, s 599(1)(b). [3585] CA 2006, s 599(1)(c). [3586] CA 2006, s 599(2).
[3587] CA 2006, s 599(3). [3588] CA 2006, s 599(4). [3589] CA 2006, s 600(1).
[3590] CA 2006, s 600(2)(a). [3591] CA 2006, s 600(2)(b). [3592] CA 2006, s 600(3)(a).
[3593] CA 2006, s 600(3)(b). [3594] CA 2006, s 600(3)(c).

consideration to be received by the company is not less than the value of the consideration to be given by it.[3595]

Any reference in s 599 of the CA 2006 or this section to consideration given for the transfer of an asset includes consideration given partly for its transfer.[3596]

In such a case the value of any consideration partly so given is to be taken as the proportion of the consideration properly attributable to its transfer,[3597] the valuer must carry out or arrange for such valuations of anything else as will enable him to determine that proportion,[3598] and his report must state what valuations have been made for that purpose and also the reason for and method and date of any such valuation and any other matters that may be relevant to that determination.[3599]

Agreement for transfer of non-cash asset: requirement of approval by members

15.74 Section 601 of the CA 2006 applies to an agreement for transfer of non-cash assets with regards to the requirement of approval by members.

The following conditions must have been complied with, namely: the terms of the agreement must have been approved by an ordinary resolution of the company,[3600] the requirements of this section must have been complied with as respects the circulation to members of copies of the valuer's report under s 599 of the CA 2006,[3601] and a copy of the proposed resolution must have been sent to the other party to the proposed agreement.[3602]

The reference in s 601(1)(c) of the CA 2006 to the other party to the proposed agreement is to the person referred to in s 598(1)(a) of the CA 2006.[3603]

The requirements of this section as to the circulation of copies of the valuer's report are as follows: if the resolution is proposed as a written resolution, copies of the valuer's report must be sent or submitted to every eligible member at or before the time at which the proposed resolution is sent or submitted to him;[3604] if the resolution is proposed at a general meeting, copies of the valuer's report must be circulated to the members entitled to notice of the meeting not later than the date on which notice of the meeting is given.[3605]

Copy of resolution to be delivered to registrar

15.75 Section 602 of the CA 2006 applies to copy of the resolution that is to be delivered to the registrar. A company that has passed a resolution under

---

[3595] CA 2006, s 600(3)(d).   [3596] CA 2006, s 600(4).   [3597] CA 2006, s 600(5)(a).
[3598] CA 2006, s 600(5)(b).   [3599] CA 2006, s 600(5)(c).   [3600] CA 2006, s 601(1)(a).
[3601] CA 2006, s 601(1)(b).   [3602] CA 2006, s 601(1)(c).   [3603] CA 2006, s 601(2).
[3604] CA 2006, s 601(3)(a).   [3605] CA 2006, s 601(3)(b).

s 601 of the CA 2006 with respect to the transfer of an asset must, within 15 days of doing so, deliver to the registrar a copy of the resolution together with the valuer's report required by that section.[3606]

If a company fails to comply with s 602(1) of the CA 2006, an offence is committed by the company,[3607] and every officer of the company who is in default.[3608] A person guilty of an offence under s 602 of the CA 2006 is liable on summary conviction to a fine not exceeding level 3 on the standard scale and, for continued contravention, to a daily default fine not exceeding one-tenth of level 3 on the standard scale.[3609]

Adaptation of provisions in relation to a company re-registering as public

15.76 Section 603 of the CA 2006 deals with the adaptation of provisions in relation to a company re-registering as public. The provisions of ss 598–602 of the CA 2006 (public companies: transfer of non-cash assets) apply, with the following adaptations in relation to a company re-registered as a public company the reference in s 598(1)(a) of the CA 2006 to a person who is a subscriber to the company's memorandum shall be read as a reference to a person who is a member of the company on the date of re-registration;[3610] the reference in s 598(2) of the CA 2006 to the date of the company being issued with a certificate under s 761 of the CA 2006 (trading certificate) shall be read as a reference to the date of re-registration.[3611]

Agreement for transfer of non-cash asset: effect of contravention

15.77 Section 604 of the CA 2006 addresses the effect of a contravention in respect of an agreement to a transfer of a non-cash asset. It applies where a public company enters into an agreement in contravention of s 598 of the CA 2006 and either the other party to the agreement has not received the valuer's report required to be sent to him,[3612] or there has been some other contravention of the requirements of Chapter 6 to Part 17 of the CA 2006 that the other party to the agreement knew or ought to have known amounted to a contravention.[3613]

In those circumstances the company is entitled to recover from that person any consideration given by it under the agreement, or an amount equal to the value of the consideration at the time of the agreement,[3614] and the agreement, so far as not carried out, is void.[3615]

[3606] CA 2006, s 602(1).   [3607] CA 2006, s 602(2)(a).   [3608] CA 2006, s 602(2)(b).
[3609] CA 2006, s 602(3).   [3610] CA 2006, s 603(a).   [3611] CA 2006, s 603(b).
[3612] CA 2006, s 604(1)(a).   [3613] CA 2006, s 604(1)(b).   [3614] CA 2006, s 604(2)(a).
[3615] CA 2006, s 604(2)(b).

If the agreement is or includes an agreement for the allotment of shares in the company, then whether or not the agreement also contravenes s 593 of the CA 2006 (valuation of non-cash considerations for shares), this section does not apply to it insofar as it is for the allotment of shares,[3616] and the allottee is liable to pay the company an amount equal to the aggregate of the nominal value of the shares and the whole of any premium (or, if the case so requires, so much of that aggregate as is treated as paid up by the consideration), with interest at the appropriate rate.[3617]

Supplementary provisions

Liability of subsequent holders of shares

15.78 Section 605 of the CA 2006 deals with liability of subsequent holders of shares. If a person becomes a holder of shares in respect of which there has been a contravention of s 593 of the CA 2006 (public company: valuation of non-cash consideration for shares),[3618] and by virtue of that contravention another is liable to pay any amount under the provision contravened,[3619] that person is also liable to pay that amount (jointly and severally with any other person so liable), unless he is exempted from liability under s 605(3) of the CA 2006 below.

If a company enters into an agreement in contravention of s 598 of the CA 2006 (public company: agreement of transfer of a non-cash asset in the initial period) and the agreement is or includes an agreement for the allotment of shares in the company,[3620] a person becomes a holder of shares allotted under the agreement,[3621] and by virtue of the agreement and allotment under it another person is liable to pay an amount under s 604 of the CA 2006,[3622] the person who becomes the holder of the shares is also liable to pay that amount (jointly and severally with any other person so liable), unless he is exempted from liability under s 605(3) of the CA 2006 below.

This applies whether or not the agreement also contravenes s 593 of the CA 2006.

A person otherwise liable under s 605(1) or (2) of the CA 2006 is exempted from that liability if either he is a purchaser for value and, at the time of the purchase, he did not have actual notice of the contravention concerned,[3623] or he derived title to the shares (directly or indirectly) from a person who became a holder of them after the contravention and was not liable under s 605(1) or (2) of the CA 2006.[3624]

The references in s 605 of the CA 2006 to a holder, in relation to shares in a company, include any person who has an unconditional right to be included

---

[3616] CA 2006, s 604(3)(a).   [3617] CA 2006, s 604(3)(b).   [3618] CA 2006, s 605(1)(a).
[3619] CA 2006, s 605(1)(b).   [3620] CA 2006, s 605(2)(a).   [3621] CA 2006, s 605(2)(b).
[3622] CA 2006, s 605(2)(c).   [3623] CA 2006, s 605(3)(a).   [3624] CA 2006, s 605(3)(b).

in the company's register of members in respect of those shares,[3625] or to have an instrument of transfer of the shares executed in his favour.[3626]

Power of court to grant relief

15.79 Section 606 of the CA 2006 applies to power of court to grant relief. A person who is liable to a company under any provision of this Chapter in relation to payments in respect of any shares in the company,[3627] or is liable to a company by virtue of an undertaking given to it in, or in connection with, payment for any shares in the company,[3628] may apply to the court to be exempted in whole or in part from the liability.

In the case of a liability within s 606(1)(a) of the CA 2006, the court may exempt the applicant from the liability only if and to the extent that it appears to the court just and equitable to do so having regard to (a) whether the applicant has paid, or is liable to pay, any amount in respect of (i) any other liability arising in relation to those shares under any provision of this Chapter or Chapter 5,[3629] or (ii) any liability arising by virtue of any undertaking given in or in connection with payment for those shares;[3630] (b) whether any person other than the applicant has paid or is likely to pay, whether in pursuance of any order of the court or otherwise, any such amount;[3631] (c) whether the applicant or any other person (i) has performed in whole or in part, or is likely so to perform any such undertaking,[3632] or (ii) has done or is likely to do any other thing in payment or part payment for the shares.[3633]

In the case of a liability within s 606(1)(b) of the CA 2006, the court may exempt the applicant from the liability only if and to the extent that it appears to the court just and equitable to do so having regard to whether the applicant has paid or is liable to pay any amount in respect of liability arising in relation to the shares under any provision of this Chapter or Chapter 5;[3634] whether any person other than the applicant has paid or is likely to pay, whether in pursuance of any order of the court or otherwise, any such amount.[3635]

In determining whether it should exempt the applicant in whole or in part from any liability, the court must have regard to the following overriding principles, namely, that a company that has allotted shares should receive money or money's worth at least equal in value to the aggregate of the nominal value of those shares and the whole of any premium or, if the case so requires, so much of that aggregate as is treated as paid up;[3636] subject to this, that where such a company would, if the court did not grant the exemption,

---

[3625] CA 2006, s 605(4)(a).   [3626] CA 2006, s 605(4)(b).   [3627] CA 2006, s 606(1)(a).
[3628] CA 2006, s 606(1)(b).   [3629] CA 2006, s 606(2)(a)(i).   [3630] CA 2006, s 606(2)(a)(ii).
[3631] CA 2006, s 606(2)(b).   [3632] CA 2006, s 606(2)(c)(i).   [3633] CA 2006, s 606(2)(c)(ii).
[3634] CA 2006, s 606(3)(a).   [3635] CA 2006, s 606(3)(b).   [3636] CA 2006, s 606(4)(a).

have more than one remedy against a particular person, it should be for the company to decide which remedy it should remain entitled to pursue.[3637]

If a person brings proceedings against another ('the contributor') for a contribution in respect of liability to a company arising under any provision of this Chapter or Chapter 5 and it appears to the court that the contributor is liable to make such a contribution, the court may, if and to the extent that it appears to it just and equitable to do so having regard to the respective culpability (in respect of the liability to the company) of the contributor and the person bringing the proceedings, exempt the contributor in whole or in part from his liability to make such a contribution,[3638] or order the contributor to make a larger contribution than, but for this subsection, he would be liable to make.[3639]

Where a person is liable to a company under s 604(2) of the CA 2006 (agreement of transfer of a non-cash asset: effect of contravention), the court may, on application, exempt him in whole or in part from that liability if and to the extent that it appears to the court to be just and equitable to do so having regard to any benefit accruing to the company by virtue of anything done by him towards the carrying out of the agreement mentioned in that subsection.[3640]

Section 606 restates s 113(1)–(8) of the CA 1985. It enables the court to grant relief, to the applicant, from a liability to the company which has arisen (under any provision of Chapter 6 to Part 17 of the CA 2006) in relation to payment in respect of shares in a company or an undertaking given to the company in, or in connection with, payment for any shares in it. There is a minor change in the restatement insofar as the matters to which the court must have regard in applying the just and equitable test in s 606(2) of the CA 2006 also apply where the liability relates to the payment of interest (under s 113(2)(b)) of the CA 1985, the court is not required to have regard to those matters in applying the just and equitable test).

Penalty for contravention of Chapter 6 to Part 17 of the CA 2006

15.80 Section 607 of the CA 2006 sets out the penalty for contravention of Chapter 6 to Part 17 of the CA 2006. It applies where a company contravenes s 593 of the CA 2006 (public company allotting shares for a non-cash consideration), or s 598 of the CA 2006 (public company entering into an agreement for transfer of a non-cash asset).[3641]

An offence is committed by the company,[3642] and every officer of the company who is in default.[3643] A person guilty of an offence under this section is

---

[3637] CA 2006, s 606(4)(b).   [3638] CA 2006, s 606(5)(a).   [3639] CA 2006, s 606(5)(b).
[3640] CA 2006, s 606(6).   [3641] CA 2006, s 607(1).   [3642] CA 2006, s 607(2)(a).
[3643] CA 2006, s 607(2)(b).

liable on conviction on indictment, to a fine;[3644] on summary conviction, to a fine not exceeding the statutory maximum.[3645]

Enforceability of undertakings to do work etc

15.81 Section 608 of the CA 2006 applies to enforceability of undertakings to do work. An undertaking given by any person, in or in connection with payment for shares in a company, to do work or perform services or to do any other thing, if it is enforceable by the company apart from this Chapter, is so enforceable notwithstanding that there has been a contravention in relation to it of a provision of this Chapter or Chapter 5.[3646]

This is without prejudice to s 606 of the CA 2006 (power of court to grant relief etc. in respect of liabilities).[3647]

The appropriate rate of interest

15.82 Section 609 of the CA 2006 states that for the purposes of this Chapter the 'appropriate rate' of interest is 5 per cent per annum or such other rate as may be specified by order made by the Secretary of State.[3648] An order under this section is subject to negative resolution procedure.[3649]

Share premiums

15.83 Chapter 7 to Part 17 of the CA 2006 contains provisions on share premiums. Under s 130 of the CA 1985, where shares in a company were issued at a premium, (that is, at a price that was greater than their nominal value), an amount equal to the premium paid on those shares had to be transferred to a non-distributable reserve: the share premium account. This account could only be used in a limited number of circumstances described in s 130 of the CA 1985.

The share premium account

Application of share premiums

15.84 Section 610 of the CA 2006 deals with application of share premiums.

If a company issues shares at a premium, whether for cash or otherwise, a sum equal to the aggregate amount or value of the premiums on those shares must be transferred to an account called 'the share premium account'.[3650]

[3644] CA 2006, s 607(3)(a).   [3645] CA 2006, s 607(3)(b).   [3646] CA 2006, s 608(1).
[3647] CA 2006, s 608(2).   [3648] CA 2006, s 609(1).   [3649] CA 2006, s 609(2).
[3650] CA 2006, s 610(1).

Where, on issuing shares, a company has transferred a sum to the share premium account, it may use that sum to write off the expenses of the issue of those shares,[3651] or any commission paid on the issue of those shares.[3652]

The company may use the share premium account to pay up new shares to be allotted to members as fully paid bonus shares.[3653]

Subject to s 610(2) and (3) of the CA 2006, the provisions of the Companies Acts relating to the reduction of a company's share capital apply as if the share premium account were part of its paid up share capital.[3654]

Section 610 of the CA 2006 applies subject to[3655] s 611 of the CA 2006 (group reconstruction relief); s 612 of the CA 2006 (merger relief); and s 614 of the CA 2006 (power to make further provisions by regulations).

In Chapter 7, the term 'the issuing company' means the company issuing shares as mentioned in s 610(1) of the CA 2006 above.[3656]

In line with the recommendations of the Company Law Review Group,[3657] s 610 of the CA 2006 further restricts the application of the share premium account, and in the future, companies will not be able to use the share premium account to write off preliminary expenses (that is, expenses incurred in connection with the company's formation). Companies will continue to be able to use the share premium account to write off any expenses incurred, or commission paid, in connection with an issue of shares but the application of the share premium account in these circumstances will be limited so that the company will only be able to use the share premium account arising on a particular issue of shares to write off expenses incurred or commission paid in respect of that issue. As now, companies will also be able to use the share premium account to pay up new shares to be allotted to existing members as fully paid bonus shares.

A further change is that in future, companies will not be able to use the share premium account to write off any expenses incurred, commission paid or discount allowed in respect of an issue of debentures or in providing for the premium payable on a redemption of debentures.

Relief from requirements as to share premiums

Group reconstruction relief

15.85 Section 611 of the CA 2006 deals with group reconstruction relief. It applies where the issuing company (a) is a wholly-owned subsidiary of another company (the holding company),[3658] and (b) allots shares (i) to the holding company,[3659] or (ii) to another wholly-owned subsidiary of the

---

[3651] CA 2006, s 610(2)(a).   [3652] CA 2006, s 610(2)(b).   [3653] CA 2006, s 610(3).
[3654] CA 2006, s 610(4).   [3655] CA 2006, s 610(5).   [3656] CA 2006, s 610(6).
[3657] *Completing the Structure*, para 7.8.   [3658] CA 2006, s 611(1)(a).
[3659] CA 2006, s 611(1)(b)(i).

holding company,[3660] in consideration for the transfer to the issuing company of non-cash assets of a company (the transferor company) that is a member of the group of companies that comprises the holding company and all its wholly-owned subsidiaries.

Where the shares in the issuing company allotted in consideration for the transfer are issued at a premium, the issuing company is not required by s 610 of the CA 2006 to transfer any amount in excess of the minimum premium value to the share premium account.[3661]

The minimum premium value means the amount (if any) by which the base value of the consideration for the shares allotted exceeds the aggregate nominal value of the shares.[3662]

The base value of the consideration for the shares allotted is the amount by which the base value of the assets transferred exceeds the base value of any liabilities of the transferor company assumed by the issuing company as part of the consideration for the assets transferred.[3663]

For the purposes of this section (a) the base value of assets transferred is taken as (i) the cost of those assets to the transferor company,[3664] or (ii) if less, the amount at which those assets are stated in the transferor company's accounting records immediately before the transfer;[3665] (b) the base value of the liabilities assumed is taken as the amount at which they are stated in the transferor company's accounting records immediately before the transfer.[3666]

Merger relief

15.86 Section 612 of the CA 2006 applies where the issuing company has secured at least a 90 percent equity holding in another company in pursuance of an arrangement providing for the allotment of equity shares in the issuing company on terms that the consideration for the shares allotted is to be provided by the issue or transfer to the issuing company of equity shares in the other company,[3667] or by the cancellation of any such shares not held by the issuing company.[3668]

If the equity shares in the issuing company allotted in pursuance of the arrangement in consideration for the acquisition or cancellation of equity shares in the other company are issued at a premium, s 610 of the CA 2006 does not apply to the premiums on those shares.[3669]

Where the arrangement also provides for the allotment of any shares in the issuing company on terms that the consideration for those shares is to be provided by the issue or transfer to the issuing company of non-equity shares

[3660] CA 2006, s 611(1)(b)(ii).   [3661] CA 2006, s 611(2).   [3662] CA 2006, s 611(3).
[3663] CA 2006, s 611(4).   [3664] CA 2006, s 611(5)(a)(i).   [3665] CA 2006, s 611(5)(a)(ii).
[3666] CA 2006, s 611(5)(b).   [3667] CA 2006, s 612(1)(a).   [3668] CA 2006, s 612(1)(b).
[3669] CA 2006, s 612(2).

in the other company,[3670] or by the cancellation of any such shares in that company not held by the issuing company,[3671] relief under s 612(2) of the CA 2006 extends to any shares in the issuing company allotted on those terms in pursuance of the arrangement.

This section does not apply in a case falling within s 611 of the CA 2006 (group reconstruction relief).[3672]

Merger relief: meaning of 90 per cent equity holding

15.87 Section 613 of the CA 2006 states that the following provisions have effect to determine for the purposes of s 612 of the CA 2006 (merger relief) whether a company (company A) has secured at least a 90 per cent equity holding in another company (company B) in pursuance of such an arrangement as is mentioned in s 612(1) of the CA 2006.[3673]

Company A has secured at least a 90 per cent equity holding in company B if in consequence of an acquisition or cancellation of equity shares in company B (in pursuance of that arrangement) it holds equity shares in company B of an aggregate amount equal to 90 per cent or more of the nominal value of that company's equity share capital.[3674]

For this purpose it is immaterial whether any of those shares were acquired in pursuance of the arrangement;[3675] and shares in company B held by the company as treasury shares are excluded in determining the nominal value of company B's share capital.[3676]

Where the equity share capital of company B is divided into different classes of shares, company A is not regarded as having secured at least a 90 per cent equity holding in company B unless the requirements of s 613(2) of the CA 2006 are met in relation to each of those classes of shares taken separately.[3677]

For the purposes of this section, shares held by a company that is company A's holding company or subsidiary,[3678] or a subsidiary of company A's holding company,[3679] or its or their nominees,[3680] are treated as held by company A.

Power to make further provision by regulations

15.88 Section 614 of the CA 2006 considers the power to make further provisions by regulations. The Secretary of State may by regulations make such provision as he thinks appropriate for relieving companies from the requirements of s 610 of the CA 2006 (application of share premiums) in relation to

---

[3670] CA 2006, s 612(3)(a).   [3671] CA 2006, s 612(3)(b).   [3672] CA 2006, s 612(4).
[3673] CA 2006, s 613(1).   [3674] CA 2006, s 613(2).   [3675] CA 2006, s 613(3)(a).
[3676] CA 2006, s 613(3)(b).   [3677] CA 2006, s 613(4).   [3678] CA 2006, s 613(5)(a).
[3679] CA 2006, s 613(5)(b).   [3680] CA 2006, s 613(5)(c).

premiums other than cash premiums;[3681] for restricting or otherwise modifying any relief from those requirements provided by this Chapter.[3682]

Regulations under this section are subject to affirmative resolution procedure.[3683]

Relief may be reflected in company's balance sheet

15.89 Section 615 of the CA 2006 states that an amount corresponding to the amount representing the premiums, or part of the premiums, on shares issued by a company that by virtue of any relief under this Chapter is not included in the company's share premium account may also be disregarded in determining the amount at which any shares or other consideration provided for the shares issued is to be included in the company's balance sheet.

Alteration of Share Capital

15.90 Chapter 8 to Part 17 of the CA 2006 applies to alteration of share capital.

How share capital may be altered

Alteration of share capital of limited company

15.91 Section 617 of the CA 2006 states that a limited company having a share capital may not alter its share capital except in the following ways.[3684] The company may increase its share capital by allotting new shares in accordance with this Part,[3685] or reduce its share capital in accordance with Chapter 10 of the CA 2006.[3686]

The company may sub-divide or consolidate all or any of its share capital in accordance with s 618 of the CA 2006,[3687] or reconvert stock into shares in accordance with s 620 of the CA 2006.[3688]

The company may redenominate all or any of its shares in accordance with s 622 of the CA 2006, and may reduce its share capital in accordance with s 626 of the CA 2006 in connection with such a redenomination.[3689]

Section 617 of the CA 2006 does not affect the power of a company to purchase its own shares, or to redeem shares, in accordance with Part 18;[3690] or the power of a company to purchase its own shares in pursuance of an order of the court under s 98 of the CA 2006 (application to court to cancel resolution for re-registration as a private company),[3691] s 721(6) of the CA

[3681] CA 2006, s 614(1)(a).   [3682] CA 2006, s 614(1)(b).   [3683] CA 2006, s 614(2).
[3684] CA 2006, s 617(1).   [3685] CA 2006, s 617(2)(a).   [3686] CA 2006, s 617(2)(b).
[3687] CA 2006, s 617(3)(a).   [3688] CA 2006, s 617(3)(b).   [3689] CA 2006, s 617(4).
[3690] CA 2006, s 617(5)(a).   [3691] CA 2006, s 617(5)(b)(i)

2006 (powers of court on objection to redemption or purchase of shares out of capital),[3692] s 759 of the CA 2006 (remedial order in case of breach of prohibition of public offers by private company),[3693] or Part 30 of the CA 2006 (protection of members against unfair prejudice);[3694] the forfeiture of shares, or the acceptance of shares surrendered in lieu, in pursuance of the company's articles, for failure to pay any sum payable in respect of the shares;[3695] the cancellation of shares under s 662 of the CA 2006 (duty to cancel shares held by or for a public company);[3696] the power of a company to enter into a compromise or arrangement in accordance with Part 26 of the CA 2006 (arrangements and reconstructions),[3697] or to do anything required to comply with an order of the court on an application under that Part.[3698]

This section prohibits a limited company from altering its share capital except in the ways permitted under the CA 2006. It includes a signpost to a new provision which will enable companies limited by shares easily to convert (or 'redenominate') their share capital from one currency to another (see s 622 of the CA 2006).

Subdivision or consolidation of shares

Sub-division or consolidation of shares

15.92 Section 618 of the CA 2006 applies to subdivision or consolidation of shares.

A limited company having a share capital may sub-divide its shares, or any of them, into shares of a smaller nominal amount than its existing shares,[3699] or consolidate and divide all or any of its share capital into shares of a larger nominal amount than its existing shares.[3700]

In any sub-division, consolidation or division of shares under this section, the proportion between the amount paid and the amount (if any) unpaid on each resulting share must be the same as it was in the case of the share from which that share is derived.[3701]

A company may exercise a power conferred by this section only if its members have passed a resolution authorising it to do so.[3702]

A resolution under s 618(3) of the CA 2006 may authorise a company to exercise more than one of the powers conferred by this section;[3703] to exercise a power on more than one occasion;[3704] to exercise a power at a specified time or in specified circumstances.[3705]

[3692] CA 2006, s 617(2)(b)(ii).   [3693] CA 2006, s 617(5)(b)(iii).   [3694] CA 2006, s 617(5)(b)(iv).
[3695] CA 2006, s 617(5)(c).   [3696] CA 2006, s 617(5)(d).   [3697] CA 2006, s 617(5)(e)(i).
[3698] CA 2006, s 617(5)(e)(ii).   [3699] CA 2006, s 618(1)(a).   [3700] CA 2006, s 618(1)(b).
[3701] CA 2006, s 618(2).   [3702] CA 2006, s 618(3).   [3703] CA 2006, s 618(4)(a).
[3704] CA 2006, s 618(4)(b).   [3705] CA 2006, s 618(4)(c).

The company's articles may exclude or restrict the exercise of any power conferred by this section.[3706]

Consolidation of a company's share capital involves combining a number of shares into a new share of commensurate nominal value: for example, ten £1 shares may be combined to make one £10 share. Sub-division of a company's share capital involves dividing a share into a number of new shares with a smaller nominal value: for example, a £10 share may be sub-divided into ten £1 shares.

Section 618 of the CA 2006 replaces s 121(2)(b) and (d) of the CA 1985. It sets out the circumstances and manner in which a limited company may consolidate or sub-divide its share capital. Where shares in a company are sub-divided or consolidated, the proportion between the amount paid and the amount unpaid (if any) on the original share(s) must remain the same in relation to the share(s) resulting from the sub-division or consolidation. If, for example, £2 is unpaid on a £10 share that is subsequently sub-divided into ten £1 shares, there will now be 20p unpaid on each of those ten shares.

A company may exercise a power conferred on it under this section only if the members have passed a resolution authorising it to do so, which may be an ordinary resolution or a resolution requiring a higher majority (as the articles may require). Such a resolution may authorise a company to exercise more than one of the powers conferred on it under this section, for example, the resolution may authorise a sub-division of one class of the company's shares and a consolidation of another. It may also authorise the company to exercise a power conferred on it under this section on more than one occasion or at a specified time or in specified circumstances. This avoids the directors having to obtain authorisation from the company's members on each and every occasion that a company alters its share capital under this section (which may be inconvenient to the directors and members alike or impractical due to timing constraints).

The flexibility to pass a conditional resolution (that is, a resolution that will only take effect if certain conditions are met) given in s 618(4)(c) of the CA 2006 is necessary as a sub-division or consolidation of share capital (or any class of it) may form part of a wider re-organisation of a company's share capital, for example, a reduction of share capital following a redenomination of share capital. It may, therefore, not be appropriate, or necessary, for a company's share capital to be altered in this way if the reorganisation of share capital that the sub-division or consolidation is linked to does not go ahead.

Under the CA 1985 a company could only sub-divide or consolidate its share capital if it is authorised to do so by the company's article (see s 121 of the CA 1985). This restriction has not been retained.

[3706] CA 2006, s 618(5).

Notice to registrar of sub-division or consolidation

15.93 Section 619 of the CA 2006 deals with notice to registrar of sub-division or consolidation. If a company exercises the power conferred by s 618 of the CA 2006 (sub-division or consolidation of shares) it must within one month after doing so give notice to the registrar, specifying the shares affected.[3707]

The notice must be accompanied by a statement of capital.[3708]

The statement of capital must state with respect to the company's share capital immediately following the exercise of the power (a) the total number of shares of the company,[3709] (b) the aggregate nominal value of those shares,[3710] (c) for each class of shares (i) prescribed particulars of the rights attached to the shares,[3711] (ii) the total number of shares of that class,[3712] and (iii) the aggregate nominal value of shares of that class,[3713] and (d) the amount paid up and the amount (if any) unpaid on each share (whether on account of the nominal value of the share or by way of premium).[3714]

If default is made in complying with this section, an offence is committed by the company,[3715] and every officer of the company who is in default.[3716] A person guilty of an offence under s 619 of the CA 2006 is liable on summary conviction to a fine not exceeding level 3 on the standard scale and, for continued contravention, a daily default fine not exceeding one-tenth of level 3 on the standard scale.[3717]

The section replaces a similar requirement to notify the registrar contained in s 122(1)(a) and (d) of the CA 1985. Where a company sub-divides or consolidates its share capital under s 618 of the CA 2006, it will continue to be required to give notice of this alteration to its share capital to the registrar within one month. However, there is a new requirement to file a statement of capital (see s 619(2) and (3) of the CA 2006), which is in essence a 'snap-shot' of the company's total share capital at a particular point in time: in this case following the consolidation/sub-division.

For public companies, the requirement for a statement of capital is linked to the abolition of authorised share capital: it implements Article 2 of the Second Company Law Directive (77/91/EEC), which states:

> the statutes or instruments of incorporation of the company shall always give at least the following information . . . (c) when the company has no authorised capital, the amount of the subscribed capital. . .

The statement of capital will require the following information to be provided:

[3707] CA 2006, s 619(1).   [3708] CA 2006, s 619(2).   [3709] CA 2006, s 619(3)(a).
[3710] CA 2006, s 619(3)(b).   [3711] CA 2006, s 619(3)(c)(i).   [3712] CA 2006, s 619(3)(c)(ii).
[3713] CA 2006, s 619(3)(c)(iii).   [3714] CA 2006, s 619(3)(d).   [3715] CA 2006, s 619(4)(a).
[3716] CA 2006, s 619(4)(b).   [3717] CA 2006, s 619(5).

a) the total number of shares of the company,

b) the aggregate nominal value of those shares,

c) for each class of shares, prescribed particulars of the rights attached to the shares, the total number of shares of that class and the aggregate nominal value of shares of that class, and

d) the amount paid up and the amount (if any) unpaid on each share (whether on account of the nominal value of the share or by way of premium).

Whilst this Directive applies only to public companies it is important that the information on the public register is up-to-date. A statement of capital will, therefore, be required where it is proposed that a company formed under the Act will have a share capital on formation and, with limited exceptions (in particular, where there has been a variation of class rights which does not affect the company's aggregate subscribed capital) whenever a limited company makes an alteration to its share capital. A statement of capital is also called for in certain circumstances where an unlimited company having a share capital makes a return to the registrar (see, s 856 of the CA 2006).

In making a statement of capital, a company is required to provide 'prescribed particulars of the rights attached to the shares'. Here, and elsewhere in the Act where a statement of capital is called for, 'prescribed' means prescribed by the Secretary of State in regulations or by order made under the Act.

The power conferred on the Secretary of State under this section enables the Secretary of State to specify the particular detail of the information that he requires to be filed with the registrar by a company. A statutory instrument made pursuant to this power will not be subject to any form of Parliamentary scrutiny.

Criminal liability for any failure to comply with the procedural requirements as to notice is retained (see s 619(4) of the CA 2006). The penalty for this offence is set out in s 619(5) of the CA 2006.

Reconversion of stock into shares

Reconversion of stock into shares

15.94 Section 620 of the CA 2006 applies to reconversion of stock into shares. A limited company that has converted paid-up shares into stock (before the repeal by this Act of the power to do so) may reconvert that stock into paid-up shares of any nominal value.[3718]

[3718] CA 2006, s 620(1).

A company may exercise the power conferred by this section only if its members have passed an ordinary resolution authorising it to do so.[3719]

A resolution under s 620(2) of the CA 2006 may authorise a company to exercise the power conferred by this section on more than one occasion;[3720] at a specified time or in specified circumstances.[3721]

Stock cannot be issued directly by a company, but arises from a conversion of fully paid up shares into stock under s 121(2)(c) of the CA 1985. This ability to convert shares into stock has not been retained. A company that currently has stock may, however, wish to re-convert this stock back into fully paid shares, and this is permitted by the following section.

Section 620 of the CA 2006 replaces s 121(2)(c) of the CA 1985. It retains the ability to reconvert stock back into fully paid shares but removes the requirement for prior authorisation in the articles (currently a company may only re-convert stock back into shares if provision for this is made in its articles).

A re-conversion of stock into shares will require an ordinary resolution of the company's members. Such a resolution may give the directors power to convert stock into fully paid shares on more than one occasion; at a specified time; or only if certain conditions are met (see s 620(3) of the CA 2006). The flexibility to pass a conditional resolution (that is, a resolution that will only take effect if certain conditions are met) is necessary, as a reconversion of stock into shares may form part of a wider re-organisation of a company's share capital.

Notice to registrar of reconversion of stock into shares

15.95 Section 621 of the CA 2006 deals with a notice to the registrar of reconversion of stock into shares.

If a company exercises a power conferred by s 620 of the CA 2006 (reconversion of stock into shares) it must within one month after doing so give notice to the registrar, specifying the stock affected.[3722]

The notice must be accompanied by a statement of capital.[3723]

The statement of capital must state with respect to the company's share capital immediately following the exercise of the power (a) the total number of shares of the company,[3724] (b) the aggregate nominal value of those shares,[3725] (c) for each class of shares (i) prescribed particulars of the rights attached to the shares,[3726] (ii) the total number of shares of that class,[3727] and (iii) the aggregate nominal value of shares of that class,[3728] and (d) the

[3719] CA 2006, s 620(2).   [3720] CA 2006, s 620(3)(a).   [3721] CA 2006, s 620(3)(b).
[3722] CA 2006, s 621(1).   [3723] CA 2006, s 621(2).   [3724] CA 2006, s 621(3)(a).
[3725] CA 2006, s 621(3)(b).   [3726] CA 2006, s 621(3)(c)(i).   [3727] CA 2006, s 621(3)(c)(ii).
[3728] CA 2006, s 621(3)(c)(ii).

amount paid up and the amount (if any) unpaid on each share (whether on account of the nominal value of the share or by way of premium).[3729]

If default is made in complying with this section, an offence is committed by the company,[3730] and every officer of the company who is in default.[3731] A person guilty of an offence under s 621 of the CA 2006 is liable on summary conviction to a fine not exceeding level 3 on the standard scale and, for continued contravention, a daily default fine not exceeding one-tenth of level 3 on the standard scale.[3732]

Where a company re-converts stock into shares it must give notice of the alteration to its share capital to the registrar under the provisions in s 621 of the CA 2006. This requirement replaces a similar provision in s 122(1)(c) of the CA 1985.

A statement of capital is required. Criminal liability for any failure to comply with the procedural requirements as to notice is retained (see s 621(4) of the CA 2006). The penalty for this offence is set out in s 621(5) of the CA 2006.

Redenomination of share capital

Redenomination of share capital

15.96 Section 622 of the CA 2006 states that a limited company having a share capital may by resolution redenominate its share capital or any class of its share capital.[3733] The term 'redenominate' means convert shares from having a fixed nominal value in one currency to having a fixed nominal value in another currency.

The conversion must be made at an appropriate spot rate of exchange specified in the resolution.[3734]

The rate must be either a rate prevailing on a day specified in the resolution,[3735] or a rate determined by taking the average of rates prevailing on each consecutive day of a period specified in the resolution.[3736]

The day or period specified for the purposes of para (a) or (b) must be within the period of 28 days ending on the day before the resolution is passed.

A resolution under this section may specify conditions which must be met before the redenomination takes effect.[3737]

Redenomination in accordance with a resolution under this section takes effect on the day on which the resolution is passed,[3738] or on such later day as may be determined in accordance with the resolution.[3739] A resolution under this section lapses if the redenomination for which it provides has not taken

---

[3729] CA 2006, s 621(3)(d).   [3730] CA 2006, s 621(4)(a).   [3731] CA 2006, s 621(4)(b).
[3732] CA 2006, s 621(5).   [3733] CA 2006, s 622(1).   [3734] CA 2006, s 622(2).
[3735] CA 2006, s 622(3)(a).   [3736] CA 2006, s 622(3)(b).   [3737] CA 2006, s 622(4).
[3738] CA 2006, s 622(5)(a).   [3739] CA 2006, s 622(5)(b).

effect at the end of the period of 28 days beginning on the date on which it is passed.[3740]

A company's articles may prohibit or restrict the exercise of the power conferred by this section.[3741]

Chapter 3 of Part 3 of the CA 2006 (resolutions affecting a company's constitution) applies to a resolution under this section.[3742]

Where a public company applies for a trading certificate under s 117 of the CA 1985, it must satisfy a minimum share capital requirement (known as the 'authorised minimum'). There is a similar requirement where a private company re-registers as a public company under s 43 of the CA 1985. The authorised minimum is currently set at £50,000 and must be expressed in sterling. This implements Article 6 of the Second Company Law Directive (77/91/EEC) which requires that, in order that a company may be incorporated or obtain authorisation to commence business, a minimum capital shall be subscribed, the amount of which shall be not less than 25,000 ECU (expressed in the domestic currency of the Member State) Under s 763 of the CA 2006, in future the authorised minimum will be capable of being satisfied in sterling (£50,000) or the euro equivalent to the sterling amount. Subject to this change, the Act retains the effect of the CA 1985 provisions on the authorised minimum (see, for example, ss 91, 650 and 761 of the CA 2006).

Subject to the above qualification (and any restriction in a company's articles) a company is free to allot shares in any currency that it wishes (see s 542(3) of the CA 2006). It may also have its share capital made up of shares of a mixture of denominations, for example, one class of a company's shares may be denominated in sterling, whereas another class may be denominated in dollars, euros or some other currency of the company's choosing. What a company cannot currently do is easily redenominate its share capital (or any class of it) from one currency to another, for example, from dollars to sterling or vice versa. The current procedure involves cancelling existing shares under the court-approved procedure for capital reductions set out in s 135 of the CA 1985 or, in the case of private companies only, buying back or redeeming shares out of capital under s 171 of the CA 1985, and then issuing new shares in the desired currency.

Section 622 of the CA 2006 introduces a new procedure that will allow a company limited by shares to redenominate its share capital easily. This requires a resolution of the company's members. (Unlimited companies having a share capital are already free to redenominate their share capital as they see fit, and no change to the legislation is required in respect of such companies).

Section 622(2) of the CA 2006 of this section provides that the spot rate used when converting a company's share capital from one currency to

---

[3740] CA 2006, s 622(6).   [3741] CA 2006, s 622(7).   [3742] CA 2006, s 622(8).

another must be specified in the resolution to redenominate the company's share capital. There is a choice of spot rates and this is set out in s 622(3) of the CA 2006.

A company is free to pass a conditional resolution under this section (see s 622(4) of the CA 2006). A resolution will, however, lapse if the redenomination of share capital has not taken effect within 28 days of the date on which the resolution is passed (see s 622(6) of the CA 2006). Where a resolution lapses, the company will not be able to redenominate its capital unless it passes a new resolution and the redenomination is effected in accordance with the new resolution.

Section 622(7) of the CA 2006 makes it clear that, if it wishes, a company may restrict or prohibit a redenomination of its share capital by incorporating a provision to this effect in the company's articles.

It should be noted that this section does not make provision for the authorised minimum to continue to be denominated in sterling (or the euro equivalent). This means that once a public company has obtained a trading certificate under s 761 of the CA 2006 (or previously under s 117 of the CA 1985) or where a private company has re-registered as a public company, such a company is free, if it wishes, to redenominate all of its share capital, including the authorised minimum, into any currency of its choosing.

Calculation of new nominal values

15.97 Section 623 of the CA 2006 deals with calculation of nominal values. It provides that for each class of share, the new nominal value of each share is calculated as follows: step 1: take the aggregate of the old nominal values of all the shares of that class; step 2: translate that amount into the new currency at the rate of exchange specified in the resolution; step 3: divide that amount by the number of shares in the class.

This section explains how the new nominal value of a share which has been redenominated from one currency to another should be calculated.

Effect of redenomination

15.98 Section 624 of the CA 2006 deals with the effect of redomination. The redenomination of shares does not affect any rights or obligations of members under the company's constitution, or any restrictions affecting members under the company's constitution.

In particular, it does not affect entitlement to dividends (including entitlement to dividends in a particular currency), voting rights or any liability in respect of amounts unpaid on shares.[3743]

[3743] CA 2006, s 624(1).

For this purpose the company's constitution includes the terms on which any shares of the company are allotted or held.[3744]

Subject to s 624(1) of the CA 2006, references to the old nominal value of the shares in any agreement or statement, or in any deed, instrument or document, shall (unless the context otherwise requires) be read after the resolution takes effect as references to the new nominal value of the shares.[3745]

This section makes it clear that a redenomination of a company's share capital (or any class of it) does not affect any rights or obligations that the members may have under the company's constitution or any restrictions affecting members under the company's constitution. In particular, it does not affect entitlement to dividends, voting rights or any liability in respect of amounts unpaid on shares. If, for example, a dividend of 20p was declared on a £1 share prior to a redenomination of that share, and that £1 share is subsequently converted into a $1.5 share, the member who now owns a $1.5 share in the company will still be entitled to a 20p dividend (albeit that the company and the member in question may agree that the 20p dividend can be paid in cents – or indeed in some other currency). Similarly, where a company has issued partly paid shares, the member's liability to the company will remain in the currency in which the share was originally denominated.

Notice to registrar of redenomination

15.99 Section 625 of the CA 2006 states that if a limited company having a share capital redenominates any of its share capital, it must within one month after doing so give notice to the registrar, specifying the shares redenominated.[3746]

The notice must state the date on which the resolution was passed,[3747] and be accompanied by a statement of capital.[3748]

The statement of capital must state with respect to the company's share capital as redenominated by the resolution (a) the total number of shares of the company,[3749] (b) the aggregate nominal value of those shares,[3750] (c) for each class of shares (i) prescribed particulars of the rights attached to the shares,[3751] (ii) the total number of shares of that class,[3752] and (iii) the aggregate nominal value of shares of that class,[3753] and (d) the amount paid up and the amount (if any) unpaid on each share (whether on account of the nominal value of the share or by way of premium).[3754]

If default is made in complying with this section, an offence is committed by the company,[3755] and every officer of the company who is in default.[3756] A

[3744] CA 2006, s 624(2).   [3745] CA 2006, s 624(3).   [3746] CA 2006, s 625(1).
[3747] CA 2006, s 625(2)(a).   [3748] CA 2006, s 625(2)(b).   [3749] CA 2006, s 625(3)(a).
[3750] CA 2006, s 625(3)(b).   [3751] CA 2006, s 625(3)(c)(i).   [3752] CA 2006, s 625(3)(c)(ii).
[3753] CA 2006, s 625(3)(c)(iii).   [3754] CA 2006, s 625(3)(d).   [3755] CA 2006, s 625(4)(a).
[3756] CA 2006, s 625(4)(b).

person guilty of an offence under s 625 of the CA 2006 is liable on summary conviction to a fine not exceeding level 3 on the standard scale and, for continued contravention, a daily default fine not exceeding one-tenth of level 3 on the standard scale.[3757]

This section sets out the requirements as to notice where a company redenominates its share capital (or any class of it). Notice must be given to the registrar in accordance with s 625(1) and (2) of the CA 2006 and there is a requirement for a statement of capital.

A copy of the resolution to redenominate the company's share capital must be forwarded to the registrar within 15 days after it is passed notwithstanding that it may be an ordinary resolution (see s 622(8) of the CA 2006, which provides that Chapter 3 of Part 3 of the CA 2006 applies to the resolution and in particular s 30 of the CA 2006).

If a company fails to comply with the procedural requirements as to notice, the company and every officer of the company commits an offence. The penalty for this offence is set out in s 625(5) of the CA 2006.

Reduction of capital in connection with redenomination

15.100 Section 626 of the CA 2006 applies to reduction of capital in connection with redenomination. A limited company that passes a resolution redenominating some or all of its shares may, for the purpose of adjusting the nominal values of the redenominated shares to obtain values that are, in the opinion of the company, more suitable, reduce its share capital under this section.[3758]

A reduction of capital under this section requires a special resolution of the company.[3759] Any such resolution must be passed within three months of the resolution effecting the redenomination.[3760]

The amount by which a company's share capital is reduced under this section must not exceed 10 per cent of the nominal value of the company's allotted share capital immediately after the reduction.[3761]

A reduction of capital under this section does not extinguish or reduce any liability in respect of share capital not paid up.[3762]

Nothing in Chapter 10 applies to a reduction of capital under this section.[3763]

Following a redenomination of a company's share capital, it is likely that the company will be left with shares expressed in awkward fractions of the new currency, for example, 0.997 dollars or 1.01 euros. The company may therefore wish to renationalise the value of the shares affected (that is, alter the nominal value of these shares) to obtain share values in whole units of the

---

[3757] CA 2006, s 625(5).   [3758] CA 2006, s 626(1).   [3759] CA 2006, s 626(2).
[3760] CA 2006, s 626(3).   [3761] CA 2006, s 626(4).   [3762] CA 2006, s 626(5).
[3763] CA 2006, s 626(6).

new currency. It can do this in one of two ways: if the company has distributable reserves it may capitalise those reserves to increase the nominal value of the shares affected; alternatively, it may reduce its share capital using the procedure set out in s 626 of the CA 2006.

Section 626(4) CA 2006 provides that the amount by which a company can reduce its share capital using this new provision is capped at 10 per cent of the nominal value of the company's share capital immediately after the reduction. This 10 per cent cap is required by the Second Company Law Directive (77/91/EEC) and applies to any reduction of capital in a public company which is not approved by the court.

Where a company reduces its share capital under this section, the amount by which the company's share capital is reduced must be transferred to a new non-distributable reserve (see s 628 of the CA 2006).

Notice to registrar of reduction of capital in connection with redenomination

15.101 Section 627 of the CA 2006 deals with the notice to the registrar of a reduction of capital in connection with redenomination. A company that passes a resolution under s 626 of the CA 2006 (reduction of capital in connection with redenomination) must within 15 days after the resolution is passed give notice to the registrar stating the date of the resolution,[3764] and the date of the resolution under s 622 of the CA 2006 in connection with which it was passed.[3765]

This is in addition to the copies of the resolutions themselves that are required to be delivered to the registrar under Chapter 3 of Part 3 of the CA 2006.

The notice must be accompanied by a statement of capital.[3766] The statement of capital must state with respect to the company's share capital as reduced by the resolution (a) the total number of shares of the company,[3767] (b) the aggregate nominal value of those shares,[3768] (c) for each class of shares (i) prescribed particulars of the rights attached to the shares,[3769] (ii) the total number of shares of that class,[3770] and (iii) the aggregate nominal value of shares of that class,[3771] and (d) the amount paid up and the amount (if any) unpaid on each share (whether on account of the nominal value of the share or by way of premium).[3772]

The registrar must register the notice and the statement on receipt.[3773]

The reduction of capital is not effective until those documents are registered.[3774]

[3764] CA 2006, s 627(1)(a).   [3765] CA 2006, s 627(1)(b).   [3766] CA 2006, s 627(2).
[3767] CA 2006, s 627(3)(a).   [3768] CA 2006, s 627(3)(b).   [3769] CA 2006, s 627(3)(c)(i).
[3770] CA 2006, s 627(3)(c)(ii).   [3771] CA 2006, s 627(3)(c)(iii).   [3772] CA 2006, s 627(3)(d).
[3773] CA 2006, s 627(4).   [3774] CA 2006, s 627(5).

The company must also deliver to the registrar, within 15 days after the resolution is passed, a statement by the directors confirming that the reduction in share capital is in accordance with s 626(4) of the CA 2006 (reduction of capital not to exceed 10 per cent of nominal value of allotted shares immediately after reduction).[3775]

If a default is made in complying with this section, an offence is committed by the company,[3776] and every officer of the company who is in default.[3777] A person guilty of an offence under this section is liable on conviction on indictment to a fine,[3778] and on summary conviction to a fine not exceeding the statutory maximum.[3779]

This section sets out the requirements as to notice where a company reduces its share capital in connection with a redenomination of its share capital (that is, to renationalise the value of its shares). Notice must be given to the registrar in accordance with s 627(1)CA 2006. This notice must be accompanied by a statement of capital.

The resolution to reduce the share capital must be filed with the registrar in accordance with s 30 of the CA 2006.

The reduction of capital will not take effect until the documents that are required to be delivered to the registrar under s 627(1) and (2) of the CA 2006 are registered by the registrar (see s 627(5) of the CA 2006).

In addition to delivering the above documents to the registrar, within 15 days of the date that a resolution to reduce capital in connection with a redenomination is passed, under s 627(6) of the CA 2006 the company must also deliver to the registrar a statement made by the directors confirming that the reduction of share capital was made in accordance with s 626(4) of the CA 2006.

If a company fails to comply with the procedural requirements as to notice, the company and every officer of the company commits an offence. The penalty for this offence is set out in s 627(8) of the CA 2006. In addition, where the statement made by the directors under s 627(6) CA 2006 is misleading, false or deceptive in a material particular, the directors are liable to an offence under s 1112 of the CA 2006.

The redenomination reserve

15.102 Section 628 of the CA 2006 states that the amount by which a company's share capital is reduced under s 626 of the CA 2006 (reduction of capital in connection with redenomination) must be transferred to a reserve, called 'the redenomination reserve'.[3780]

[3775] CA 2006, s 627(6). [3776] CA 2006, s 627(7)(a). [3777] CA 2006, s 627(7)(b).
[3778] CA 2006, s 627(8)(a). [3779] CA 2006, s 627(8)(b). [3780] CA 2006, s 628(1).

The redenomination reserve may be applied by the company in paying up shares to be allotted to members as fully paid bonus shares.[3781]

Subject to that, the provisions of the CA 2006 relating to the reduction of a company's share capital apply as if the redenomination reserve were paid-up share capital of the company.[3782]

Where a company reduces its share capital under s 626 of the CA 2006, it must transfer an amount equal to the value of the reduction to a non-distributable reserve known as the redenomination reserve.

This section provides that amounts transferred to the redenomination reserve may be used by the company in paying up shares to be allotted to existing members as fully paid bonus shares. Subject to this, the provisions of the Companies Acts relating to the reduction of a company's share capital, apply to the redenomination reserve as if it were paid-up share capital. These provisions mirror those contained in s 733 of the CA 2006, (which restates s 170 of the CA 1985).

Classes of Shares and Class Rights

15.103 The term 'classes of shares' (or 'class rights') is not defined in the 1985 Act but at common law this term is normally used where the rights that attach to a particular share relate to matters such as voting rights, a right to dividends and a right to a return of capital when a company is wound up. Rights attach to a particular class of shares if the holders of shares in that class enjoy rights that are not enjoyed by the holders of shares in another class.

Introductory

Classes of shares

15.104 Section 629 of the CA 2006 applies to classes of shares. It states that for the purposes of the Companies Acts, shares are of one class if the rights attached to them are in all respects uniform.[3783]

For this purpose the rights attached to shares are not regarded as different from those attached to other shares by reason only that they do not carry the same rights to dividends in the 12 months immediately following their allotment.[3784]

Section 629 of the CA 2006 provides that for the purposes of the Act, shares are of one class if the rights attached to them are in all respects uniform. It reproduces the provision in s 128(2) of the CA 1985. It is

---

[3781] CA 2006, s 628(2).   [3782] CA 2006, s 628(3).   [3783] CA 2006, s 629(1).
[3784] CA 2006, s 629(2).

particularly relevant to the provisions of ss 550 and 569 of the CA 2006. This definition of 'classes of shares' also applies in determining the extent to which shares constitute different classes for the purposes of the statement of capital required to be filed under various provisions of the CA 2006.

Variations of class rights

Variations of class rights: companies having a share capital

15.105 Section 630 of the CA 2006 is concerned with the variations of the rights attached to a class of shares in a company having a share capital.[3785]

Rights attached to a class of a company's shares may only be varied in accordance with a provision in the company's articles for the variation of those rights,[3786] or where the company's articles contain no such provision, if the holders of shares of that class consent to the variation in accordance with this section.[3787]

This is without prejudice to any other restrictions on the variation of the rights.[3788]

The consent required for the purposes of this section on the part of the holders of a class of a company's shares is consent in writing from the holders of at least three-quarters in nominal value of the issued shares of that class (excluding any shares held as treasury shares),[3789] or a special resolution passed at a separate general meeting of the holders of that class sanctioning the variation.[3790]

Any amendment of a provision contained in a company's articles for the variation of the rights attached to a class of shares, or the insertion of any such provision into the articles, is itself to be treated as a variation of those rights.[3791]

In this section, and (except where the context otherwise requires) in any provision in a company's articles for the variation of the rights attached to a class of shares, references to the variation of those rights include references to their abrogation.[3792]

On variations of class rights the Company Law Review Group[3793] recommended that the current provisions should be retained with some simplification, and extended to companies without a share capital (see s 631 of the CA 2006).

Section 630 of the CA 2006 replaces s 125 of the CA 1985. It is concerned with the manner in which rights attached to a class of shares may be varied. Class rights typically cover matters such as voting rights, rights to dividends and rights to a return of capital on a winding up.

[3785] CA 2006, s 630(1).   [3786] CA 2006, s 630(2)(a).   [3787] CA 2006, s 630(2)(b).
[3788] CA 2006, s 630(3).   [3789] CA 2006, s 630(4)(a).   [3790] CA 2006, s 630(4)(b).
[3791] CA 2006, s 630(5).   [3792] CA 2006, s 630(6).   [3793] *Final Report*, para 7.28.

Currently class rights may be set out in the memorandum or articles or elsewhere, and provision may or may not be made for their alteration. Under the CA 2006 it will not be possible for class rights to be set out in the memorandum (see s 8) of the CA 2006 and where class rights attaching to shares in an existing company are specified in the memorandum these will be deemed, by virtue of s 28 of the CA 2006, to be a provision in the company's articles.

Class rights are 'attached to a class of shares' (see s 630(1) of the CA 2006). Where all the shares in a company fall within the one class, there are no class rights, only shareholder rights. What amounts to a class is not defined either in the current law or the CA 2006 (other than in s 629 of the CA 2006) and remains a matter for case law.

The current requirement for an extraordinary resolution where a company is proposing to vary the rights attached to a class of its shares is replaced with a requirement for a special resolution (see s 630(4)(b) of the CA 2006). The Act abolishes the concept of an extraordinary resolution. Special resolution is defined in s 283 of the CA 2006.

Section 630(2) and (4) of the CA 2006 provides that rights may be varied in accordance with the company's articles or, where the articles make no provision for a variation of class rights, if the holders of at least three-quarters in nominal value of the issued shares of that class consent in writing or a special resolution passed by the holders of that class sanctions the variation. This means that the articles may specify a less demanding procedure for a variation of class rights than the statutory scheme (for example, that the holders of 51 per cent by nominal value of the class consent in writing), or may permit a simple majority of the class at a class meeting.

The provisions of s 630 of the CA 2006 are expressed to be without prejudice to any other restriction on the variation of rights (see s 630(3) of the CA 2006). This has two important effects. First, if and to the extent that the company has adopted a more onerous regime in its articles for the variation of class rights, for example requiring a higher percentage than the statutory minimum, the company must comply with the more onerous regime. Second, if and to the extent that the company has protected class rights by making provision for the entrenchment of those rights in its articles (see s 22 of the CA 2006), that protection cannot be circumvented by changing the rights attached to a class of shares under this section.

Variation of class rights: companies without a share capital

15.106 Section 631 of the CA 2006 deals with variations of class rights in respect of companies without a share capital. This section is concerned with the variation of the rights of a class of members of a company where the company does not have a share capital.[3794]

[3794] CA 2006, s 631(1).

Rights of a class of members may only be varied in accordance with a provision in the company's articles for the variation of those rights,[3795] or where the company's articles contain no such provision, if the members of that class consent to the variation in accordance with this section.[3796]

This is without prejudice to any other restrictions on the variation of the rights.[3797]

The consent required for the purposes of this section on the part of the members of a class is consent in writing from at least three-quarters of the members of the class,[3798] or a special resolution passed at a separate general meeting of the members of that class sanctioning the variation.[3799]

Any amendment of a provision contained in a company's articles for the variation of the rights of a class of members, or the insertion of any such provision into the articles, is itself to be treated as a variation of those rights.[3800]

In this section, and (except where the context otherwise requires) in any provision in a company's articles for the variation of the rights of a class of members, references to the variation of those rights include references to their abrogation.[3801]

This section extends the statutory provisions on variation of class rights to companies without a share capital. Companies limited by guarantee (which since December 1980 cannot be formed with a share capital) may, for example, have different classes of members with different voting rights.

At present the question of how members' rights may be varied will depend to a large extent on whether provision has been made, either in the memorandum or articles, for their variation. Under the Act class rights may also be varied in accordance with this section, which contains new provisions, comparable to those for companies with a share capital. Thus there is a minimum requirement that class rights may be varied if three-quarters of that class consent in writing or a special resolution of those members sanctions the variation, unless the company has made provision for a less onerous regime to apply in its articles. Again, a company may also make provision, in its articles, for a more onerous regime to apply than that provided in this section, and where they do, the company must comply with the regime set out in the articles.

Variations of class rights: preserving court's powers under other provisions

15.107 Section 632 of the CA 2006 deals with variations of class rights with respect to preserving the court's power under other provisions. It states that

---

[3795] CA 2006, s 631(2)(a).　[3796] CA 2006, s 631(2)(b).　[3797] CA 2006, s 631(3).
[3798] CA 2006, s 631(4)(a).　[3799] CA 2006, s 631(4)(b).　[3800] CA 2006, s 631(5).
[3801] CA 2006, s 631(6).

nothing in s 630 or s 631 of the CA 2006 (variations of class rights) affects the power of the court under s 98 of the CA 2006 (application to cancel resolution for public company to be re-registered as private), Part 26 (arrangements and reconstructions), or Part 30 (protection of members against unfair prejudice) of the CA 2006.

Section 631 of the CA 2006 preserves the court's powers under various other provisions of the Act and substantially restates s 126 of the CA 1985.

Right to object to variations: companies having a share capital

15.108 Section 633 of the CA 2006 applies where the rights attached to any class of shares in a company are varied under s 630 of the CA 2006 (variations of class rights: companies having a share capital).[3802]

The holders of not less in the aggregate than 15 per cent of the issued shares of the class in question (being persons who did not consent to or vote in favour of the resolution for the variation) may apply to the court to have the variation cancelled.[3803] For this purpose, any of the company's share capital held as treasury shares is disregarded.

If such an application is made, the variation has no effect unless and until it is confirmed by the court.[3804]

Application to the court must be made within 21 days after the date on which the consent was given or the resolution was passed (as the case may be),[3805] and may be made on behalf of the shareholders entitled to make the application by such one or more of their number as they may appoint in writing for the purpose.[3806]

The court, after hearing the applicant and any other persons who apply to the court to be heard and appear to the court to be interested in the application, may, if satisfied, having regard to all the circumstances of the case, that the variation would unfairly prejudice the shareholders of the class represented by the applicant, disallow the variation, and shall if not so satisfied confirm it.

The decision of the court on any such application is final.[3807]

References in this section to the variation of the rights of holders of a class of shares include references to their abrogation.[3808]

Right to object to variations: companies without a share capital

15.109 Section 634 of the CA 2006 applies where the rights of any class of members of a company are varied under s 631 of the CA 2006 (variations of class rights: companies without a share capital).[3809]

[3802] CA 2006, s 633(1).   [3803] CA 2006, s 633(2).   [3804] CA 2006, s 633(3).
[3805] CA 2006, s 633(4)(a).   [3806] CA 2006, s 633(4)(b).   [3807] CA 2006, s 633(5).
[3808] CA 2006, s 633(6).   [3809] CA 2006, s 634(1).

Members amounting to not less than 15 per cent of the members of the class in question (being persons who did not consent to or vote in favour of the resolution for the variation) may apply to the court to have the variation cancelled.[3810]

If such an application is made, the variation has no effect unless and until it is confirmed by the court.[3811]

Application to the court must be made within 21 days after the date on which the consent was given or the resolution was passed (as the case may be) and may be made on behalf of the members entitled to make the application by such one or more of their number as they may appoint in writing for the purpose.[3812]

The court, after hearing the applicant and any other persons who apply to the court to be heard and appear to the court to be interested in the application, may, if satisfied, having regard to all the circumstances of the case, that the variation would unfairly prejudice the members of the class represented by the applicant, disallow the variation, and shall if not so satisfied confirm it.

The decision of the court on any such application is final.[3813]

References in this section to the variation of the rights of a class of members include references to their abrogation.[3814]

Section 633 of the CA 2006 replaces s 127 of the CA 1985 (which confers a right on shareholders to object to a variation of class rights). It sets out the procedure that must be followed where there is an objection to a variation of the rights attached to a class of a company's shares and enables shareholders holding not less in aggregate than 15 per cent of the issued shares of the class in question (being persons who did not consent to or vote in favour of the resolution approving the variation) to apply to the court for the variation to be cancelled.

Section 634 of the CA 2006 makes similar provision in respect of a variation of class rights in companies not having a share capital. This is a new provision, which enables members, amounting to not less than 15 per cent of the members of the class affected (being persons who did not consent to or vote in favour of the resolution approving the variation), to apply to the court to have the variation cancelled and gives the court the power to confirm the variation, or disallow it if the court is satisfied that it would unfairly prejudice the members in that class.

Copy of court order to be forwarded to the registrar

15.110 Section 635 of the CA 2006 provides for a copy of the court order to be forwarded to the registrar. The company must within 15 days after the

---

[3810] CA 2006, s 634(2).   [3811] CA 2006, s 634(3).   [3812] CA 2006, s 634(4).
[3813] CA 2006, s 634(5).   [3814] CA 2006, s 634(6).

making of an order by the court on an application under s 633 or s 634 of the CA 2006 (objection to variation of class rights) forward a copy of the order to the registrar.[3815]

If default is made in complying with s 635 of the CA 2006 an offence is committed by the company,[3816] and every officer of the company who is in default.[3817] A person guilty of an offence under this section is liable on summary conviction to a fine not exceeding level 3 on the standard scale and, for continued contravention, a daily default fine not exceeding one-tenth of level 3 on the standard scale.[3818]

Section 635 of the CA 2006 sets out the procedural requirements as to notice where the court has made an order on an application under s 633 or s 634 of the CA 2006. Where the court has made an order on application under these sections, the company must forward a copy of that order to the registrar within 15 days of the date on which the order is made. Where a company fails to comply with the provisions of this section, the company, and every officer of the company, who is in default, commits an offence (see s 635(2) and (3) of the CA 2006).

Matters to be notified to the registrar

Notice of name or other designations of classes of shares

15.111 Section 636 of the CA 2006 deals with notice of name or other designations of classes of shares. Where a company assigns a name or other designation, or a new name or other designation, to any class or description of its shares, it must within one month from doing so deliver to the registrar a notice giving particulars of the name or designation so assigned.[3819]

If default is made in complying with s 636 of the CA 2006, an offence is committed by the company,[3820] and every officer of the company who is in default.[3821] A person guilty of an offence under this section is liable on summary conviction to a fine not exceeding level 3 on the standard scale and, for continued contravention, a daily default fine not exceeding one-tenth of level 3 on the standard scale.[3822]

Notice of particulars of variation of rights attached to shares

15.112 Section 637 of the CA 2006 applies to notice of particulars of variations of rights attached to shares.

Where the rights attached to any shares of a company are varied, the

---

[3815] CA 2006, s 635(1).   [3816] CA 2006, s 635(2)(a).   [3817] CA 2006, s 635(2)(b).
[3818] CA 2006, s 635(3).   [3819] CA 2006, s 636(1).   [3820] CA 2006, s 636(2)(a).
[3821] CA 2006, s 636(2)(b).   [3822] CA 2006, s 636(3).

company must within one month from the date on which the variation is made deliver to the registrar a notice giving particulars of the variation.[3823]

If default is made in complying with this section, an offence is committed by the company,[3824] and every officer of the company who is in default.[3825]

A person guilty of an offence under s 637 of the CA 2006 is liable on summary conviction to a fine not exceeding level 3 on the standard scale and, for continued contravention, a daily default fine not exceeding one-tenth of level 3 on the standard scale.[3826]

Notice of new class of members

15.113 Section 638 of the CA 2006 deals with notice of new class of members. If a company not having a share capital creates a new class of members, the company must within one month from the date on which the new class is created deliver to the registrar a notice containing particulars of the rights attached to that class.[3827]

If default is made in complying with s 638 of the CA 2006, an offence is committed by the company,[3828] and every officer of the company who is in default.[3829] A person guilty of an offence under this section is liable on summary conviction to a fine not exceeding level 3 on the standard scale and, for continued contravention, a daily default fine not exceeding one-tenth of level 3 on the standard scale.[3830]

Notice of name or other designations of classes of members

15.114 Section 639 of the CA 2006 deals with notice of names or other designations of classes of members. Where a company not having a share capital assigns a name or other designation, or a new name or other designation, to any class of its members, it must within one month of doing so deliver to the registrar a notice giving particulars of the name or designation so assigned.[3831]

If default is made in complying with s 639 of the CA 2006, an offence is committed by the company,[3832] and every officer of the company who is in default.[3833] A person guilty of an offence under s 639 of the CA 2006 is liable on summary conviction to a fine not exceeding level 3 on the standard scale and, for continued contravention, a daily default fine not exceeding one-tenth of level 3 on the standard scale.[3834]

[3823] CA 2006, s 637(1). [3824] CA 2006, s 637(2)(a). [3825] CA 2006, s 637(2)(b).
[3826] CA 2006, s 637(3). [3827] CA 2006, s 638(1). [3828] CA 2006, s 638(2)(a).
[3829] CA 2006, s 638(2)(b). [3830] CA 2006, s 638(3). [3831] CA 2006, s 639(1).
[3832] CA 2006, s 639(2)(a). [3833] CA 2006, s 639(2)(b). [3834] CA 2006, s 639(3).

Notices of particulars of variations of class rights

15.115 Section 640 of the CA 2006 deals with notices of particulars of variations of class rights. If the rights of any class of members of a company not having a share capital are varied, the company must within one month of the date on which the variation is made deliver to the registrar a notice containing particulars of the variation.[3835]

If default is made in complying with s 640 of the CA 2006, an offence is committed by the company,[3836] and every officer of the company who is in default.[3837] A person guilty of an offence under s 640 of the CA 2006 is liable on summary conviction to a fine not exceeding level 3 on the standard scale and, for continued contravention, a daily default fine not exceeding one-tenth of level 3 on the standard scale.[3838]

Sections 636–640 of the CA 2006 replace various provisions in ss 128 and 129 of the CA 1985 that are concerned with notification to the registrar of the creation of, and variations to, rights attached to a class of a company's shares (s 128 of the CA 1985) or class rights of members (s 129 of the CA 1985).

Under the CA 2006, where a limited company creates a new class of shares, it will be required to provide details of the rights attached to the shares in the return of allotment and statement of capital required under s 555 of the CA 2006. There is a similar requirement in s 556 of the CA 2006 where an unlimited company allots a new class of share. Those provisions replace s 128 (1) and (2) of the CA 1985.

In addition, where a company varies the rights attached to any of its shares (or assigns a name or other designation, or a new name or other designation, to any class or description of its shares), it will in future be required to register particulars of the rights affected under s 637 (or s 636) of the CA 2006 irrespective of how the variation in rights was achieved. Currently companies are not required to provide this information if the rights attached to a particular share or class of shares are varied by an amendment to the company's memorandum or articles or by a special resolution or agreement of the company's members, which is required to be filed under s 380 of the CA 1985. Sections 638–640 of the CA 2006 make similar changes to the disclosure requirements that apply to companies limited by guarantee not having a share capital and unlimited companies not having a share capital that may, nevertheless, have different classes of members.

It should be noted, that, in contrast to other alterations to a company's share capital, there is no requirement in s 637 of the CA 2006 for a statement of capital. Such a requirement would be superfluous, as a variation of class rights will not result in a change to the aggregate amount of a company's subscribed capital.

[3835] CA 2006, s 640(1).   [3836] CA 2006, s 640(2)(a).   [3837] CA 2006, s 640(2)(b).
[3838] CA 2006, s 640(3).

Reduction of Share Capital

15.116 Chapter 10 is concerned with reduction of capital.

Introductory

Circumstances in which a company may reduce its share capital

15.117 Section 641 of the CA 2006 sets out the circumstances in which a company may reduce its share capital.

A limited company having a share capital may reduce its share capital in the case of a private company limited by shares, by special resolution supported by a solvency statement (see ss 642–644 of the CA 2006);[3839] in any case, by special resolution confirmed by the court (see ss 645–651 of the CA 2006).[3840]

A company may not reduce its capital under s 641(1)(a) of the CA 2006, if as a result of the reduction, there would no longer be any member of the company holding shares other than redeemable shares.[3841]

Subject to that, a company may reduce its share capital under this section in any way.[3842]

In particular, a company may extinguish or reduce the liability on any of its shares in respect of share capital not paid up,[3843] or either with or without extinguishing or reducing liability on any of its shares cancel any paid-up share capital that is lost or unrepresented by available assets,[3844] or repay any paid-up share capital in excess of the company's wants.[3845]

A special resolution under this section may not provide for a reduction of share capital to take effect later than the date on which the resolution has effect in accordance with this Chapter.[3846]

This Chapter (apart from s 641(5) of the CA 2006 above) applies subject to any provision of the company's articles restricting or prohibiting the reduction of the company's share capital.[3847]

This section replaces s 135(1) and (2) of the CA 1985. It sets out the circumstances and manner in which a company limited by shares may reduce its share capital. As recommended by the Company Law Review Group,[3848] in future a private company limited by shares will be able to reduce its share capital using a new solvency statement procedure for capital reductions (see s 642).

A company could only reduce its share capital under the previous s 135 of the CA 1985 if it was authorised to do so by its articles. In line with the

---

[3839] CA 2006, s 641(1)(a).   [3840] CA 2006, s 641(1)(b).   [3841] CA 2006, s 641(2).
[3842] CA 2006, s 641(3).   [3843] CA 2006, s 641(4)(a).   [3844] CA 2006, s 641(4)(b)(i).
[3845] CA 2006, s 641(4)(b)(ii).   [3846] CA 2006, s 641(5).   [3847] A 2006, s 641(6).
[3848] *Final Report*, para 10.6.

recommendations of the Company Law Review Group,[3849] the requirement for prior authorisation in the articles has not been retained but, if it wishes, a company may restrict or prohibit a reduction of capital by making provision to this effect in its articles (see s 641(6) of the CA 2006).

Section 641(1)(a) of the CA 2006 contains a signpost to a new provision, which will enable a private company limited by shares to reduce its share capital using the new solvency statement procedure (see above). In addition, private companies and public companies alike can still use the court-approved procedure for capital reductions – which is retained in s 641(1)(b) of the CA 2006.

In the case of a private company limited by shares that is proposing to use the new solvency statement procedure to effect a reduction of capital, the company may only reduce its share capital under s 641(1)(a) of the CA 2006 if it will have at least one member remaining after the proposed reduction (see s 641(2) of the CA 2006). That member need only hold one share in the company but that share must not be a redeemable share. The principle behind this requirement is that a private company limited by shares should not be capable of reducing its share capital to zero unless the reduction of capital is sanctioned by the court. This mirrors the previous equivalent provision in s 162(3) of the CA 1985, which applies to a purchase of own shares.

Both the solvency statement procedure for capital reductions and the court-approved procedure require a special resolution of the company's members. Under s 641(5) of the CA 2006 a special resolution to reduce a company's share capital may not provide for the proposed reduction to take effect on a date later than the date on which the resolution to reduce capital takes effect. Under the solvency statement procedure, a resolution to reduce capital will take effect when the documents referred to in s 644 of the CA 2006 have been registered by the registrar (see s 644(4) of the CA 2006). This would operate to prevent a company passing a resolution on, say, 1 January stating that the reduction is to take effect on 1 October. Under the court-approved procedure, the resolution will take effect on the registration of the court order and statement of capital or, in the context of a reduction forming part of a compromise or arrangement under Part 26 of the CA 2006, on delivery of those documents to the registrar (unless the court orders otherwise) (see s 649 of the CA 2006).

[3849] *Completing the Structure*, para 2.15

Private companies: reduction of capital supported by solvency statement

Reduction of capital supported by solvency statement

15.118 Section 642 of the CA 2006 sets out the nature of the solvency statement.

A resolution for reducing the share capital of a private company limited by shares is supported by a solvency statement, if the directors of the company make a statement of the solvency of the company in accordance with s 643 of the CA 2006 (a 'solvency statement') not more than 15 days before the date on which the resolution is passed,[3850] and the resolution and solvency statement are registered in accordance with s 644 of the CA 2006.[3851]

Where the resolution is proposed as a written resolution, a copy of the solvency statement must be sent or submitted to every eligible member at or before the time at which the proposed resolution is sent or submitted to him.[3852]

Where the resolution is proposed at a general meeting, a copy of the solvency statement must be made available for inspection by members of the company throughout that meeting.[3853]

The validity of a resolution is not affected by a failure to comply with s 642 (2) or (3) of the CA 2006.[3854]

This section sets out the conditions that must be satisfied in order for a private company limited by shares to reduce its share capital using the new solvency statement procedure.

The procedural requirements that the directors must follow when they propose a capital reduction using the solvency statement route are set out in s 642(1)–(3) of the CA 2006, which provides that the solvency statement made in connection with a reduction of capital by a private company cannot be made more than 15 days before the date on which the resolution to reduce capital is passed. It also provides that both the resolution and the solvency statement must be filed with the registrar in accordance with the provisions of s 644 of the CA 2006. The solvency statement must also be made available to the company's members when they vote on the resolution to reduce capital, and the procedure for providing a copy of the solvency statement to the members varies according to whether the resolution to reduce capital is proposed as a written resolution or at a meeting of the company's members (see s 642(2) and (3) of the CA 2006). Whilst a failure to observe these procedural requirements will not affect the validity of the resolution to reduce capital, if a solvency statement that has not been provided to the company's members in accordance with the provision of this section is subsequently filed with the

---

[3850] CA 2006, s 642(1)(a).   [3851] CA 2006, s 642(1)(b).   [3852] CA 2006, s 642(2).
[3853] CA 2006, s 642(3).   [3854] CA 2006, s 642(4).

registrar, every officer of the company who is in default commits an offence (see s 644 of the CA 2006).

Solvency statement

15.119 Section 643 of the CA 2006 sets out the nature of the solvency statement.

A solvency statement is a statement that each of the directors has formed the opinion, as regards the company's situation at the date of the statement, that there is no ground on which the company could then be found to be unable to pay (or otherwise discharge) its debts;[3855] and has also formed the opinion if it is intended to commence the winding up of the company within 12 months of that date, that the company will be able to pay (or otherwise discharge) its debts in full within 12 months of the commencement of the winding up;[3856] or in any other case, that the company will be able to pay (or otherwise discharge) its debts as they fall due during the year immediately following that date.[3857]

In forming those opinions, the directors must take into account all of the company's liabilities (including any contingent or prospective liabilities).[3858]

The solvency statement must be in the prescribed form and must state the date on which it is made,[3859] and the name of each director of the company.[3860]

If the directors make a solvency statement without having reasonable grounds for the opinions expressed in it, and the statement is delivered to the registrar, an offence is committed by every director who is in default.[3861] A person guilty of an offence under s 642(4) of the CA 2006 is liable on conviction on indictment, to imprisonment for a term not exceeding two years or a fine (or both);[3862] on summary conviction in England and Wales, to imprisonment for a term not exceeding 12 months or to a fine not exceeding the statutory maximum (or both);[3863] in Scotland or Northern Ireland, to imprisonment for a term not exceeding six months, or to a fine not exceeding the statutory maximum (or both).[3864]

A solvency statement made under s 643 of the CA 2006 must be made by all of the directors. If one or more of the directors is unable or unwilling to make this statement, the company will not be able to use the solvency statement procedure to effect a reduction of capital unless the dissenting director or directors resign (in which case the solvency statement must be made by all of the remaining directors).

The solvency statement must be in the 'prescribed form' and 'prescribed' in

---

[3855] CA 2006, s 643(1)(a).   [3856] CA 2006, s 643(1)(b)(i).   [3857] CA 2006, s 643(1)(b)(ii).
[3858] CA 2006, s 643(2).   [3859] CA 2006, s 643(3)(a).   [3860] CA 2006, s 643(3)(b).
[3861] CA 2006, s 643(4).   [3862] CA 2006, s 643(5)(a).   [3863] CA 2006, s 643(5)(b)(i).
[3864] CA 2006, s 643(5)(b)(ii).

this context means prescribed by the Secretary of State in regulations or by order made under the CA 2006.

The solvency statement must state the date on which it is made and the name of each director of the company, but there is no requirement that the directors must all be in the same location when they make this statement. The registrar will be able to make rules under s 1068 as to the form of the solvency statement.

In forming their opinions, the directors must take account of all the company's liabilities including contingent and prospective liabilities (see s 643(2) of the CA 2006). So, in circumstances where a company holds redeemable preference shares which, for the purposes of the accounting standards that applied to the company on the date that the directors made the solvency statement, are treated as liabilities, a proposed redemption or purchase of these shares in the relevant period should be treated as a contingent or prospective liability.

If the directors make a solvency statement without having reasonable grounds for the opinions expressed in it, and that statement is subsequently delivered to the registrar, every director who is in default commits an offence (see s 643(4) of the CA 2006). The penalty for this offence is set out in s 643(5) of the CA 2006.

Registration of resolution and supporting documents

15.120 Section 644 of the CA 2006 deals with registration of resolution and supporting documents.

Within 15 days after the resolution for reducing share capital is passed, the company must deliver to the registrar a copy of the solvency statement,[3865] and a statement of capital. This is in addition to the copy of the resolution itself that is required to be delivered to the registrar under Chapter 3 of Part 3.[3866]

The statement of capital must state with respect to the company's share capital as reduced by the resolution:

(a)   the total number of shares of the company,[3867]
(b)   the aggregate nominal value of those shares,[3868]
(c)   for each class of shares prescribed particulars of the rights attached to the shares,[3869] the total number of shares of that class,[3870] and the aggregate nominal value of shares of that class,[3871] and
(d)   the amount paid up and the amount (if any) unpaid on each share

---

[3865] CA 2006, s 644(1)(a).   [3866] CA 2006, s 644(1)(b).   [3867] CA 2006, s 644(2)(a).
[3868] CA 2006, s 644(2)(b).   [3869] CA 2006, s 644(2)(c)(i).   [3870] CA 2006, s 644(2)(c)(ii).
[3871] CA 2006, s 644(2)(c)(iii).

(whether on account of the nominal value of the share or by way of premium).[3872]

The registrar must register the documents delivered to him under s 644(1) of the CA 2006 on receipt.[3873]

The resolution does not take effect until those documents are registered.[3874]

The company must also deliver to the registrar, within 15 days after the resolution is passed, a statement by the directors confirming that the solvency statement was made not more than 15 days before the date on which the resolution was passed,[3875] and provided to members in accordance with s 642(2) or (3) of the CA 2006.[3876]

The validity of a resolution is not affected by a failure to deliver the documents required to be delivered to the registrar under s 644(1) of the CA 2006 within the time specified in that subsection,[3877] or a failure to comply with subs (5).[3878]

If the company delivers to the registrar a solvency statement that was not provided to members in accordance with s 642(2) or (3) of the CA 2006, an offence is committed by every officer of the company who is in default.[3879]

If default is made in complying with s 644 of the CA 2006, an offence is committed by the company,[3880] and every officer of the company who is in default.[3881] A person guilty of an offence under s 644(7) or (8) of the CA 2006 is liable on conviction on indictment, to a fine;[3882] on summary conviction, to a fine not exceeding the statutory maximum.[3883]

This section sets out the requirements as to delivery of the solvency statement and other key documents to the registrar. The resolution to reduce capital itself must be filed with the registrar within the same time period as currently applies – that is, within 15 days of the date that it is passed (see s 30 of the CA 2006) and it will not take effect until the solvency statement and statement of capital (see s 644(1) and (2) of the CA 2006) are registered by the registrar. As with all circumstances where the company makes an alteration to its subscribed capital, the company is required to deliver a statement of capital to the registrar.

In addition to making a solvency statement in accordance with s 643 of the CA 2006, the directors must also make a statement confirming that the solvency statement was made not more than 15 days before the date on which the resolution to reduce capital was passed and that this statement was provided to the company's members in accordance with s 642 of the CA 2006 (see s 644(5) of the CA 2006).

In addition to the new offences that are set out in s 643(4) of the CA 2006

[3872] CA 2006, s 644(2)(d).   [3873] CA 2006, s 644(3).   [3874] CA 2006, s 644(4).
[3875] CA 2006, s 644(5)(a).   [3876] CA 2006, s 644(5)(b).   [3877] CA 2006, s 644(6)(a).
[3878] CA 2006, s 644(6)(b).   [3879] CA 2006, s 644(7).   [3880] CA 2006, s 644(8)(a).
[3881] CA 2006, s 644(8)(b).   [3882] CA 2006, s 644(9)(a).   [3883] CA 2006, s 644(9)(b).

(directors making a solvency statement without reasonable grounds for the opinion expressed in it) and s 644(7) of the CA 2006 (company delivering a solvency statement that was not provided to members and to the registrar), where a company fails to. comply with any of the filing requirements under s 644 of the CA 2006, an offence is committed by the company and every officer of the company who is in default (see s 644(8) of the CA 2006). The penalty for this offence is set out s 644(9) of the CA 2006.

Reduction of capital confirmed by the court

Application to court for an order of confirmation

15.121 Section 645 of the CA 2006 deals with applications to court for an order of confirmation.

Where a company has passed a resolution for reducing share capital, it may apply to the court for an order confirming the reduction.[3884]

If the proposed reduction of capital involves either diminution of liability in respect of unpaid share capital,[3885] or the payment to a shareholder of any paid-up share capital,[3886] s 646 of the CA 2006 (creditors entitled to object to a reduction) applies unless the court directs otherwise.

The court may, if having regard to any special circumstances of the case it thinks proper to do so, direct that s 646 of the CA 2006 is not to apply as regards any class or classes of creditors.[3887]

The court may direct that s 646 of the CA 2006 is to apply in any other case.[3888]

Creditors entitled to object to a reduction

15.122 Section 646 of the CA 2006 deals with the creditors' entitlement to object to a reduction.

Where this section applies (see s 645(2) and (4) of the CA 2006), every creditor of the company who at the date fixed by the court is entitled to any debt or claim that, if that date were the commencement of the winding up of the company would be admissible in proof against the company, is entitled to object to the reduction of capital.[3889]

The court shall settle a list of creditors entitled to object.[3890]

For that purpose the court (a) shall ascertain, as far as possible without requiring an application from any creditor, the names of those creditors and the nature and amount of their debts or claims,[3891] and (b) may publish notices fixing a day or days within which creditors not entered on the list are

---

[3884] CA 2006, s 645(1).   [3885] CA 2006, s 645(2)(a).   [3886] CA 2006, s 645(2)(b).
[3887] CA 2006, s 645(3).   [3888] CA 2006, s 645(4).   [3889] CA 2006, s 646(1).
[3890] CA 2006, s 646(2).   [3891] CA 2006, s 646(3)(a).

to claim to be so entered or are to be excluded from the right of objecting to the reduction of capital.[3892]

If a creditor entered on the list whose debt or claim is not discharged or has not determined does not consent to the reduction, the court may, if it thinks fit, dispense with the consent of that creditor on the company securing payment of his debt or claim.[3893]

For this purpose the debt or claim must be secured by appropriating (as the court may direct) the following amount if the company admits the full amount of the debt or claim or, though not admitting it, is willing to provide for it, the full amount of the debt or claim;[3894] if the company does not admit, and is not willing to provide for, the full amount of the debt or claim, or if the amount is contingent or not ascertained, an amount fixed by the court after the like enquiry and adjudication as if the company were being wound up by the court.[3895]

Offences in connection with list of creditors

15.123 Section 647 of the CA 2006 deals with the offences in connection with listing creditors.

If an officer of the company (a) intentionally or recklessly (i) conceals the name of a creditor entitled to object to the reduction of capital,[3896] or (ii) misrepresents the nature or amount of the debt or claim of a creditor,[3897] or (b) is knowingly concerned in any such concealment or misrepresentation, he commits an offence.[3898] A person guilty of an offence under s 647 of the CA 2006 is liable (a) on conviction on indictment, to a fine;[3899] (b) on summary conviction, to a fine not exceeding the statutory maximum.[3900]

Court order confirming reduction

15.124 Section 648 of the CA 2006 deals with the court confirming reduction.

The court may make an order confirming the reduction of capital on such terms and conditions as it thinks fit.[3901]

The court must not confirm the reduction unless it is satisfied, with respect to every creditor of the company who is entitled to object to the reduction of capital that either his consent to the reduction has been obtained,[3902] or his debt or claim has been discharged, or has determined or has been secured.[3903]

Where the court confirms the reduction, it may order the company to publish (as the court directs) the reasons for reduction of capital, or such other information in regard to it as the court thinks expedient with a view to

---

[3892] CA 2006, s 646(3)(b).   [3893] CA 2006, s 646(4).   [3894] CA 2006, s 646(5)(a).
[3895] CA 2006, s 646(5)(b).   [3896] CA 2006, s 647(1)(a)(i).   [3897] CA 2006, s 647(1)(a)(ii).
[3898] CA 2006, s 647(1)(b).   [3899] CA 2006, s 647(2)(a).   [3900] CA 2006, s 647(2)(b).
[3901] CA 2006, s 648(1).   [3902] CA 2006, s 648(2)(a).   [3903] CA 2006, s 648(2)(b).

giving proper information to the public, and (if the court thinks fit) the causes that led to the reduction.[3904]

The court may, if for any special reason it thinks proper to do so, make an order directing that the company must, during such period (commencing on or at any time after the date of the order) as is specified in the order, add to its name as its last words the words 'and reduced'.

If such an order is made, those words are, until the end of the period specified in the order, deemed to be part of the company's name.[3905]

Registration of order and statement of capital

15.125 The registrar, on production of an order of the court confirming the reduction of a company's share capital and the delivery of a copy of the order and of a statement of capital (approved by the court), shall register the order and statement.

This is subject to s 650 of the CA 2006 (public company reducing capital below authorised minimum).[3906]

The statement of capital must state with respect to the company's share capital as altered by the order:

(a)   the total number of shares of the company,[3907]
(b)   the aggregate nominal value of those shares,[3908]
(c)   for each class of shares:

    (i)   prescribed particulars of the rights attached to the shares,[3909]
    (ii)   the total number of shares of that class,[3910] and
    (iii)   the aggregate nominal value of shares of that class,[3911] and

(d)   the amount paid up and the amount (if any) unpaid on each share (whether on account of the nominal value of the share or by way of premium).[3912]

The resolution for reducing share capital, as confirmed by the court's order, takes effect:

(a)   in the case of a reduction of share capital that forms part of a compromise or arrangement sanctioned by the court under Part 26 of the CA 2006 (arrangements and reconstructions):

    (i)   on delivery of the order and statement of capital to the registrar,[3913] or

---

[3904] CA 2006, s 648(3).   [3905] CA 2006, s 648(4).   [3906] CA 2006, s 649(1).
[3907] CA 2006, s 649(2)(a).   [3908] CA 2006, s 649(2)(b).   [3909] CA 2006, s 649(2)(c)(i).
[3910] CA 2006, s 649(2)(c)(ii).   [3911] CA 2006, s 649(2)(c)(iii).   [3912] CA 2006, s 649(2)(d).
[3913] CA 2006, s 649(3)(a)(i).

> (ii)   if the court so orders, on the registration of the order and state-
> ment of capital;[3914]
>
> (b)   in any other case, on the registration of the order and statement of
> capital.[3915]

Notice of the registration of the order and statement of capital must be published in such manner as the court may direct.[3916] The registrar must certify the registration of the order and statement of capital.[3917]

The certificate (a) must be signed by the registrar or authenticated by the registrar's official seal,[3918] and (b) is conclusive evidence that the requirements of this Act with respect to the reduction of share capital have been complied with,[3919] and that the company's share capital is as stated in the statement of capital.[3920]

These sections replace or restate various provisions in the CA 1985 that are concerned with reductions of capital confirmed by order of the court.

Sections 645 and 646 of the CA 2006 restate s 136 of the CA 1985, which is concerned with the procedure for making an application to court to confirm a reduction of capital (including the creditors' right to object). If, on such an application, an officer of the company intentionally or recklessly conceals a creditor or misrepresents the nature or amount of a debt owed by the company, or is knowingly concerned in any such concealment or misrepresentation he commits an offence (see s 647 of the CA 2006). As previously, the court may make an order confirming the reduction of capital on such terms and conditions as it thinks fit (see s 648 of the CA 2006 which restates s 137 of the CA 1985).

Section 649 of the CA 2006 replaces s 138(1)–(4) of the CA 1985. Under s 138 of the CA 1985, a resolution to reduce capital using the existing court-approved scheme took effect when the court order confirming the reduction and minute of the reduction are registered by the registrar. The minute (which must be approved by the court) set out key information regarding the company's share capital immediately after the reduction. Section 649 of the CA 2006 updates the CA 1985 provisions by replacing the previous requirement for a minute of the reduction with a statement of capital (see note on s 619 of the CA 2006). Like the minute confirming the reduction, this statement must be approved by the court.

In line with the Company Law Review Group[3921] recommendations, s 649(3)(a)(i) of the CA 2006 provides that a reduction of capital that forms part of a compromise or arrangement under Part 26 of the CA 2006, will take effect at the same time as other aspects of that compromise or arrangement:

[3914] CA 2006, s 649(3)(a)(ii).   [3915] CA 2006, s 649(3)(b).   [3916] CA 2006, s 649(4).
[3917] CA 2006, s 649(5).   [3918] CA 2006, s 649(6)(a).   [3919] CA 2006, s 649(6)(b)(i).
[3920] CA 2006, s 649(6)(b)(ii).   [3921] *Final Report*, para 13.11.

namely on delivery of the court order confirming the reduction (and state-ment of capital approved by the court) to the registrar (unless the court orders that it should take effect on the registration of these documents) (see new s 649(3)(a)(ii) of the CA 2006).

In all other cases, that is, where the reduction of capital does not form part of a compromise or scheme of arrangement under Part 26 of the CA 2006, where a company reduces its share capital using the court-approved pro-cedure the reduction will, as now, take effect on registration of the court order confirming the reduction (and statement of capital) by the registrar. Section 649(5) of the CA 2006 requires the registrar to certify the registration of the order and statement of capital. Section 649(6) of the CA 2006 restates s 138(4) of the CA 1985 in relation to such a certificate.

Public companies reducing capital below the authorised minimum

Public company reducing capital below the authorised minimum

15.126 Section 650 of the CA 2006 deals with public companies reducing share capital below the authorised minimum.

This section applies where the court makes an order confirming a reduction of a public company's capital that has the effect of bringing the nominal value of its allotted share capital below the authorised minimum.[3922]

The registrar must not register the order unless either the court so dir-ects,[3923] or the company is first re-registered as a private company.[3924] Section 650 of the CA 2006 provides an expedited procedure for re-registration in these circumstances.[3925]

Expedited procedure for re-registration as a private company

15.127 Section 651 of the CA 2006 sets out the expited procedure for re-registration as a private company.

The court may authorise the company to be re-registered as a private com-pany without its having passed the special resolution required by s 97 of the CA 2006.[3926] If it does so, the court must specify in the order the changes to the company's name and articles to be made in connection with the re-registration.[3927]

The company may then be re-registered as a private company if an application to that effect is delivered to the registrar together with a copy of the court's order,[3928] and notice of the company's name, and a copy of the company's articles, as altered by the court's order.[3929]

[3922] CA 2006, s 650(1).   [3923] CA 2006, s 650(2)(a).   [3924] CA 2006, s 650(2)(b).
[3925] CA 2006, s 650(3).   [3926] CA 2006, s 651(1).   [3927] CA 2006, s 651(2).
[3928] CA 2006, s 651(3)(a).   [3929] CA 2006, s 651(3)(b).

On receipt of such an application the registrar must issue a certificate of incorporation altered to meet the circumstances of the case.[3930]

The certificate must state that it is issued on re-registration and the date on which it is issued.[3931]

On the issue of the certificate the company by virtue of the issue of the certificate becomes a private company,[3932] and the changes in the company's name and articles take effect.[3933] The certificate is conclusive evidence that the requirements of this Act as to re-registration have been complied with.[3934]

This section, together with s 650 of the CA 2006, substantially restates s 139 of the CA 1985 and provides for the consequences where the court confirms the reduction by a public company of its share capital below the authorised minimum (defined in s 763 of the CA 2006): in particular they facilitate the re-registration of the company as private.

Section 651(3) of the CA 2006 replaces s 139(4) of the CA 1985. It introduces a requirement to send a copy of the court's order (that is, the order authorising the company to be so reregistered without its having passed a special resolution) to the registrar, together with an application for re-registration. The current requirement for the application to be signed by a director (or secretary) has not been retained.

Effect of reduction of capital

Liability of members following a reduction of capital

15.128 Section 652 of the CA 2006 sets out the liability of members following a reduction of capital.

Where a company's share capital is reduced, a member of the company (past or present) is not liable in respect of any share to any call or contribution exceeding in amount the difference (if any) between the nominal amount of the share as notified to the registrar in the statement of capital delivered under ss 644 or 649 of the CA 2006,[3935] or to the amount paid on the share or the reduced amount (if any) that is deemed to have been paid on it, as the case may be.[3936]

This is subject to s 653 of the CA 2006 (liability to creditor in case of omission from a list).[3937]

Nothing in this section affects the rights of the contributors among themselves.[3938]

[3930] CA 2006, s 651(4).   [3931] CA 2006, s 651(5).   [3932] CA 2006, s 651(6)(a).
[3933] CA 2006, s 651(6)(b).   [3934] CA 2006, s 651(7).   [3935] CA 2006, s 652(1)(a).
[3936] CA 2006, s 652(1)(b).   [3937] CA 2006, s 652(2).   [3938] CA 2006, s 652(3).

Liability to creditor in case of omission from a list of creditors

15.129 Section 653 of the CA 2006 sets out the liability to creditors in case of their omission from a list of creditors.

This section applies where, in the case of a reduction of capital confirmed by the court:

(a)   a creditor entitled to object to the reduction of share capital is by reason of his ignorance:

    (i)   of the proceedings for reduction of share capital,[3939] or
    (ii)   of their nature and effect with respect to his debt or claim,

    not entered on the list of creditors,[3940] and

(b)   after the reduction of capital the company is unable to pay the amount of his debt or claim.[3941]

Every person who was a member of the company at the date on which the resolution for reducing capital took effect under s 649(3) of the CA 2006 is liable to contribute for the payment of the debt or claim an amount not exceeding that which he would have been liable to contribute if the company had commenced to be wound up on the day before that date.[3942]

If the company is wound up, the court on the application of the creditor in question, and proof of ignorance as mentioned in s 653(1)(a) of the CA 2006 is supplied, may if it thinks fit:

(a)   settle accordingly a list of persons liable to contribute under this section,[3943] and

(b)   make and enforce calls and orders on them as if they were ordinary contributors in a winding up.[3944]

The reference in s 653(1)(b) of the CA 2006 to a company being unable to pay the amount of a debt or claim has the same meaning as in s 123 of the Insolvency Act 1986 (c 45) or Article 103 of the Insolvency (Northern Ireland) Order 1989 (SI 1989/2405 (NI 19)).[3945]

These sections restate s 140 of the CA 1985 (with the exception of references to the minute being replaced with references to the statement of capital), which is concerned with the liability of a company's members in respect of any amounts unpaid on its shares following a reduction of capital. As now, there are special rules where a creditor was omitted from the list of creditors settled by the court.

[3939] CA 2006, s 653(1)(a)(i).   [3940] CA 2006, s 653(1)(a)(ii).   [3941] CA 2006, s 653(1)(b).
[3942] CA 2006, s 653(2).   [3943] CA 2006, s 653(3)(a).   [3944] CA 2006, s 653(3)(b).
[3945] CA 2006, s 653(4).

Miscellaneous and supplementary provisions

15.130 Chapter 11 is concerned with miscellaneous and supplementary provisions.

Treatment of reserve arising from a reduction of capital

15.131 Section 654 of the CA 2006 sets out the treatment of a reserve arising from a reduction of capital.

A reserve arising from the reduction of a company's share capital is not distributable, subject to any provision made by order under this section.[3946]

The Secretary of State may by order specify cases in which the prohibition in s 654(1) of the CA 2006 does not apply,[3947] and the reserve is to be treated for the purposes of Part 23 of the CA 2006 (distributions) as a realised profit.[3948]

An order under this section is subject to affirmative resolution procedure.[3949]

This is a new provision which enables the Secretary of State, by order, to specify the circumstances in which a reserve arising from a reduction of capital will be distributable.

Whilst there is no requirement in the CA 2006 (or indeed CA 1985) to create a statutory reserve following such a reduction, we understand that it is usual for companies to create an accounting reserve in these circumstances to 'balance the books' (that is, the section relates to reserves that arise as a result of generally accepted accounting treatments). Currently, the question whether a reserve arising from a reduction of capital (which, for a limited company, may currently only be made pursuant to a court order) may be treated as a realised profit for the purposes of computing whether a company has sufficient distributable profits to make a distribution, is the subject of technical guidance issued by the Institutes of Chartered Accountants. The Act introduces a new procedure that enables private companies to reduce their share capital without going to court (see s 641 of the CA 2006), which is not on all fours with the court-approved route (in particular there is no requirement to settle a list of creditors or to provide security for the company's debts) and in the circumstances it is desirable to deal with the question of when amounts credited to such a reserve should be treated as a realised profit in statute. Owing to the technical nature of the rules that will need to be made this issue will be dealt with in secondary legislation. An order made under s 654 of the CA 2006 will however be subject to the affirmative resolution procedure – that is, the regulations will need to be approved by both Houses of Parliament.

[3946] CA 2006, s 654(1).   [3947] CA 2006, s 654(2)(a).   [3948] CA 2006, s 654(2)(b).
[3949] CA 2006, s 654(3).

Shares no bar to damages against acompany

15.132 Section 655 of the CA 2006 deals with the issue that shares are no bar to damages against the company.

A person is not debarred from obtaining damages or other compensation from a company by reason only of his holding or having held shares in the company or any right to apply or subscribe for shares or to be included in the company's register of members in respect of shares.

Public companies: duty of directors to call a meeting on serious loss of capital

15.133 Section 656 of the CA 2006 sets out in respect of public companies, a duty of directors to call a meeting on serious loss of capital.

Where the net assets of a public company are half or less of its called-up share capital, the directors must call a general meeting of the company to consider whether any, and if so what, steps should be taken to deal with the situation.[3950]

They must do so not later than 28 days from the earliest day on which that fact is known to a director of the company.[3951] The meeting must be convened for a date not later than 56 days from that day.[3952]

If there is a failure to convene a meeting as required by s 656 of the CA 2006, each of the directors of the company who knowingly authorises or permits the failure,[3953] or after the period during which the meeting should have been convened, knowingly authorises or permits the failure to continue, commits an offence.[3954] A person guilty of an offence under s 656 of the CA 2006 is liable on conviction on indictment, to a fine;[3955] on summary conviction, to a fine not exceeding the statutory maximum.[3956]

Nothing in this section authorises the consideration at a meeting convened in pursuance of s 1 of the CA 2006 of any matter that could not have been considered at that meeting apart from this section.[3957]

Section 656 of the CA 2006 restates s 142(1) and (3) of the CA 1985. It sets out the procedure that must be followed where the net assets of a public company fall below half (or less) of the company's called up share capital. Section 656(4) of the CA 2006 imposes a liability on any director who knowingly authorised or permitted a failure to all a meeting as required by this section.

[3950] CA 2006, s 656(1).   [3951] CA 2006, s 656(2).   [3952] CA 2006, s 656(3).
[3953] CA 2006, s 656(4)(a).   [3954] CA 2006, s 656(4)(b).   [3955] CA 2006, s 656(5)(a).
[3956] CA 2006, s 656(5)(b).   [3957] CA 2006, s 656(6).

General power to make further provisions by regulations

15.134 Section 657 of the CA 2006 sets out the general power to make further provisions by regulation.

The Secretary of State may by regulations modify the following provisions of this Part:[3958]

a)   ss 552 and 553 of the CA 2006 (prohibited commissions, discounts and allowances);
b)   Chapter 5 (payment for shares);
c)   Chapter 6 (public companies: independent valuation of non-cash considerations);
d)   Chapter 7 (share premiums);
e)   ss 622–628 of the CA 2006 (redenomination of share capital);
f)   Chapter 10 (reduction of capital); and
g)   s 656 of the CA 2006 (public companies: duty of directors to call a meeting on serious loss of capital).

The regulations may amend or repeal any of those provisions,[3959] or make such other provision as appears to the Secretary of State appropriate in place of any of those provisions.[3960]

Regulations under this section may make consequential amendments or repeals in other provisions of this Act, or in other enactments.[3961]

Regulations under this section are subject to affirmative resolution procedure.[3962]

This is a new provision which enables the Secretary of State, in regulations made under the CA 2006, to modify various provisions in Part 17 of the CA 2006 (see s 657(1) of the CA 2006).

Regulations made under this section rnay amend or repeal any of the specified provisions or make such other provision as appears to the Secretary of State appropriate in place of those provisions. This will enable the Secretary of State to future-proof the specified provisions in this Part of the CA 2006.

Regulations made pursuant to the power in this section are subject to the affirmative resolution procedure.

[3958] CA 2006, s 657(1).   [3959] CA 2006, s 657(2)(a).   [3960] CA 2006, s 657(2)(b).
[3961] CA 2006, s 657(3).   [3962] CA 2006, s 657(4).

Chapter 16

Certification and Transfer of Securities

Introduction

16.1 Part 21 of the CA 2006 sets out the provisions on the certification and transfer of securities. It is divided into two Chapters. Chapter 1 is concerned with general provisions on certification and transfer of securities. Chapter 2 deals with evidencing and transfer of title to securities without written instrument.

Under Part 21, ss 768–770, 772–779 and 781–782 of the CA 2006 restate the provisions in Part 5 of the CA 1985 (ss 183–189) relating to the certification and transfer of shares and other securities.

Certification And Transfer of Securities: General

Share certificates

Share certificate to be evidence of a title

16.2 Section 768 of the CA 2006 sets out the provisions on share certificate to be evidence of a title.

In the case of a company registered in England and Wales or Northern Ireland, a certificate under the common seal of the company specifying any shares held by a member is prima facie evidence of his title to the shares.[3963]

In the case of a company registered in Scotland, a certificate under the common seal of the company specifying any shares held by a member,[3964] or a certificate specifying any shares held by a member and subscribed by the company in accordance with the Requirements of Writing (Scotland) Act 1995 (c 7),[3965] is sufficient evidence, unless the contrary is shown, of his title to the shares.

[3963] CA 2006, s 768(1).   [3964] CA 2006, s 768(2)(a).   [3965] CA 2006, s 768(2)(b).

Issue of certificates, etc. on allotment

Duty of company as to issue of certificates, etc. on allotment

16.3 Section 769 of the CA 2006 sets out the duty of a company as to issue of certificates on allotment. A company must, within two months of the allotment of any of its shares, debentures or debenture stock, complete and have ready for delivery the certificates of the shares allotted,[3966] the debentures allotted,[3967] or the certificates of the debenture stock allotted.[3968]

Section 769(1) of the CA 2006 does not apply if the conditions of issue of the shares, debentures or debenture stock provide otherwise,[3969] or in the case of allotment to a financial institution (see s 778 of the CA 2006),[3970] or in the case of an allotment of shares if, following the allotment, the company has issued a share warrant in respect of the shares (see s 779 of the CA 2006).[3971]

If default is made in complying with s 769(1) of the CA 2006 an offence is committed by every officer of the company who is in default.[3972] A person guilty of an offence under s 769(3) of the CA 2006 is liable on summary conviction to a fine not exceeding level 3 on the standard scale and, for continued contravention, a daily default fine not exceeding one-tenth of level 3 on the standard scale.[3973]

Transfer of securities

Registration of transfers

16.4 Section 770 of the CA 2006 deals with the procedure for registration of a transfer. A company may not register a transfer of shares in or debentures of the company, unless a proper instrument of transfer has been delivered to it,[3974] or the transfer (i) is an exempt transfer within the Stock Transfer Act 1982 (c 41),[3975] or (ii) is in accordance with regulations under Chapter 2 of Part 20 of the CA 2006.[3976]

Section 770(1) of the CA 2006 does not affect any power of the company to register as shareholder or debenture holder, a person to whom the right to any shares in or debentures of the company has been transmitted by operation of law.[3977]

[3966] CA 2006, s 769(1)(a).   [3967] CA 2006, s 769(1)(b).   [3968] CA 2006, s 769(1)(c).
[3969] CA 2006, s 769(2)(a).   [3970] CA 2006, s 769(2)(b).   [3971] CA 2006, s 769(2)(c).
[3972] CA 2006, s 769(3).   [3973] CA 2006, s 769(4).   [3974] CA 2006, s 770(1)(a).
[3975] CA 2006, s 770(1)(b)(i).   [3976] CA 2006, s 770(1)(b)(ii).
[3977] CA 2006, s 770(2).

Procedure on transfer being lodged

16.5 Section 771 of the CA 2006 states that when a transfer of shares in or debentures of a company has been lodged with the company, the company must either register the transfer,[3978] or give the transferee notice of refusal to register the transfer, together with its reasons for the refusal,[3979] as soon as practicable and in any event, within two months after the date on which the transfer is lodged with it.

If the company refuses to register the transfer, it must provide the transferee with such further information about the reasons for the refusal as the transferee may reasonably request.[3980] This does not include copies of minutes of meetings of directors.

If a company fails to comply with this section, an offence is committed by the company,[3981] and every officer of the company who is in default.[3982] A person guilty of an offence under this section is liable on summary conviction to a fine not exceeding level 3 on the standard scale and, for continued contravention, a daily default fine not exceeding one-tenth of level 3 on the standard scale.[3983]

Section 771 of the CA 2006 does not apply in relation to a transfer of shares if the company has issued a share warrant in respect of the shares (see s 779);[3984] or in relation to the transmission of shares or debentures by operation of law.[3985]

Previously under s 183(5) of the CA 1985, if a company refused to register a transfer of shares (or debentures), it was required, within two months of receipt of the transfer, to send to the transferee notice of its refusal to register the transfer of shares. Such a refusal would not affect the transferee's beneficial interest in a share, for example, he would still be entitled to any dividend declared on that share, and a return of capital on winding up, but the transferee would not be able to exercise all of the rights of a member of the company, for example, he could not vote at meetings, until such time as the transfer was registered and his name was entered in the register of members.

Section 771 of the CA 2006 is a new provision that amends the law on the registration of transfers. As recommended by the Company Law Review Group,[3986] it requires the directors to either register a transfer of shares or debentures, or provide the transferee with reasons for their refusal to register.

In either case, this must be done as soon as practicable, but in any event within two months of the transfer being lodged with the company.

Under s 771(2) of the CA 2006, where the directors refuse to register the transfer of a share, the transferee is entitled to receive such information as he

[3978] CA 2006, s 771(1)(a).   [3979] CA 2006, s 771(1)(b).   [3980] CA 2006, s 771(2).
[3981] CA 2006, s 771(3)(a).   [3982] CA 2006, s 771(3)(b).   [3983] CA 2006, s 771(4).
[3984] CA 2006, s 771(4)(a).   [3985] CA 2006, s 771(4)(b).
[3986] *Final Report*, paras 7.44 and 7.45.

may reasonably require regarding the reasons for the directors' refusal to register the transfer. Such information does not extend to minutes of meetings of the directors.

Where a company fails to comply with this section, the company and every officer of the company who is in default commits an offence (see s 771(3) of the CA 2006).

Section 771(5) of the CA 2006 makes it clear that this section does not apply to a transfer of shares where the company has issued a share warrant in respect of the shares under s 779 of the CA 2006, or in relation to a transmission of shares by operation of the law (for example, where a bankrupt member's trustee in bankruptcy or a deceased member's personal representative becomes entitled to shares).

Transfer of shares on the application of a transferor

16.6 Section 772 of the CA 2006 deals with transfer of shares on the application of a transferor.

On the application of the transferor of any share or interest in a company, the company must enter in its register of members, the name of the transferee in the same manner and subject to the same conditions as if the application for the entry were made by the transferee.

Execution of share transfer by a personal representative

16.7 Section 773 of the CA 2006 deals with the execution of share transfer by a personal representative. An instrument of transfer of the share or other interest of a deceased member of a company may be made by his personal representative, although the personal representative is not himself a member of the company,[3987] and is as effective as if the personal representative had been such a member at the time of the execution of the instrument.[3988]

Evidence of grant of probate, etc.

16.8 Section 774 of the CA 2006 states that the production to a company of any document, that is by law sufficient evidence of the grant of probate of the will of a deceased person,[3989] or letters of administration of the estate of a deceased person,[3990] or confirmation as executor of a deceased person,[3991] will be accepted by the company as sufficient evidence of the grant.

[3987] CA 2006, s 773(a).   [3988] CA 2006, s 773(b).   [3989] CA 2006, s 774(a).
[3990] CA 2006, s 774(b).   [3991] CA 2006, s 774(c).

Certification of an instrument of transfer

16.9 Section 775 of the CA 2006 is concerned with certification of an instrument of transfer. The certification by a company of an instrument of transfer of any shares in, or debentures of, the company is to be taken as a representation by the company to any person acting on the faith of the certification, that there have been produced to the company such documents as on their face, show a prima facie title to the shares or debentures in the transferor named in the instrument.[3992]

The certification is not to be taken as a representation that the transferor has any title to the shares or debentures.[3993]

Where a person acts on the faith of false certification by a company made negligently, the company is under the same liability to him as if the certification had been made fraudulently.[3994]

Under s 775(4) of the CA 2006, an instrument of transfer is certificated if it bears the words 'certificate lodged' (or words to the like effect);[3995] the certification of an instrument of transfer is made by a company if (i) the person issuing the instrument is a person authorised to issue certificated instruments of transfer on the company's behalf,[3996] and (ii) the certification is signed by a person authorised to certificate transfers on the company's behalf or by an officer or employee either of the company or of a body corporate so authorised.[3997] Further, a certification is treated as signed by a person if (i) it purports to be authenticated by his signature or initials (whether handwritten or not),[3998] and (ii) it is not shown that the signature or initials was or were not placed there either by himself or by a person authorised to use the signature or initials for the purpose of certificating transfers on the company's behalf.[3999]

Issue of certificates, etc. on transfer

Duty of company as to the issue of certificates, etc. on transfer

16.10 Section 776 of the CA 200 states that a company must, within two months of the date on which a transfer of any of its shares, debentures or debenture stock is lodged with the company, complete and have ready for delivery the certificates of the shares transferred,[4000] the debentures transferred,[4001] or the certificates of the debenture stock transferred.[4002]

[3992] CA 2006, s 775(1).   [3993] CA 2006, s 775(2).   [3994] CA 2006, s 775(3).
[3995] CA 2006, s 775(4)(a).   [3996] CA 2006, s 775(4)(b)(i).   [3997] CA 2006, s 775(4)(b)(ii).
[3998] CA 2006, s 775(4)(c)(i).   [3999] CA 2006, s 775(4)(c)(ii).   [4000] CA 2006, s 776(1)(a).
[4001] CA 2006, s 776(1)(b).   [4002] CA 2006, s 776(1)(c).

708 A Guide to the Companies Act 2006

The term 'transfer' means a transfer duly stamped and otherwise valid,[4003] or an exempt transfer within the Stock Transfer Act 1982 (c 41),[4004] but does not include a transfer that the company is for any reason entitled to refuse to register and does not register.

Section 776(1) of the CA 2006, however, does not apply if the conditions of issue of the shares, debentures or debenture stock provide otherwise,[4005] or in the case of a transfer to a financial institution (see s 778 of the CA 2006),[4006] or in the case of a transfer of shares if, following the transfer, the company has issued a share warrant in respect of the shares (see s 779 of the CA 2006).[4007]

Section 776 (1) of the CA 2006 applies subject to s 777 of the CA 2006 (cases where the Stock Transfer Act 1982 applies).[4008]

If default is made in complying with s 777(1) of the CA 2006, an offence is committed by every officer of the company who is in default.[4009] A person guilty of an offence under this section is liable on summary conviction to a fine not exceeding level 3 on the standard scale and, for continued contravention, a daily default fine not exceeding one-tenth of level 3 on the standard scale.[4010]

Issue of certificates, etc.: cases within the Stock Transfer Act 1982

16.11 Section 777 of the CA 2006 states that s 776(1) of the CA 2006 (duty of company as to issue of certificates etc. on transfer) does not apply in the case of a transfer to a person where, by virtue of regulations under s 3 of the Stock Transfer Act 1982, he is not entitled to a certificate or other document of or evidencing title in respect of the securities transferred.[4011]

But if in such a case, the transferee subsequently becomes entitled to such a certificate or other document by virtue of any provision of those regulations,[4012] and gives notice in writing of that fact to the company,[4013] then s 776 of the CA 2006 (duty to the company as to issue of certificates, etc.) applies as if the reference in s 777(1) of the CA 2006 to the date of the lodging of the transfer were a reference to the date of the notice.

[4003] CA 2006, s 776(2)(a). [4004] CA 2006, s 776(2)(b). [4005] CA 2006, s 776(3)(a).
[4006] CA 2006, s 776(3)(b). [4007] CA 2006, s 776(3)(c). [4008] CA 2006, s 776(4).
[4009] CA 2006, s 776(5). [4010] CA 2006, s 776(6). [4011] CA 2006, s 777(1).
[4012] CA 2006, s 777(2)(a). [4013] CA 2006, s 777(2)(b).

Issue of certificates, etc. on allotment or transfer to a financial institution

Issue of certificates, etc.: allotment or transfer to a financial institution

16.12 Section 778 of the CA 2006 provides that a company of which shares or debentures are allotted to a financial institution,[4014] or of which debenture stock is allotted to a financial institution,[4015] or with which a transfer for transferring shares, debentures or debenture stock to a financial institution is lodged,[4016] is not required in consequence of that allotment or transfer to comply with s 769(1) or s 776(1) of the CA 2006 (duty of a company as to issue of certificates, etc.).

The term 'financial institution' means a recognised clearing house acting in relation to a recognised investment exchange,[4017] or a nominee of (i) a recognised clearing house acting in that way,[4018] or (ii) a recognised investment exchange,[4019] designated for the purposes of this section in the rules of the recognised investment exchange in question.

The expressions used in s 778(2) of the CA 2006 have the same meaning as in Part 18 of the Financial Services and Markets Act 2000 (c 8).[4020]

Share warrants

Issue and effect of share warrant to the bearer

16.13 Section 779 of the CA 2006 applies to the issue and effect of share warrant to the bearer. A company limited by shares may, if so authorised by its articles, issue with respect to any fully paid shares a warrant (a 'share warrant') stating that the bearer of the warrant is entitled to the shares specified in it.[4021]

A share warrant issued under the company's common seal or (in the case of a company registered in Scotland) subscribed in accordance with the Requirements of Writing (Scotland) Act 1995 (c 7), entitles the bearer to the shares specified in it and the shares may be transferred by delivery of the warrant.[4022]

A company that issues a share warrant may, if so authorised by its articles, provide (by coupons or otherwise) for the payment of the future dividends on the shares included in the warrant.[4023]

[4014] CA 2006, s 778(1)(a).   [4015] CA 2006, s 778(1)(b).   [4016] CA 2006, s 778(1)(c).
[4017] CA 2006, s 778(2)(a).   [4018] CA 2006, s 778(2)(b)(i).   [4019] CA 2006, s 778(2)(b)(ii).
[4020] CA 2006, s 778(3).   [4021] CA 2006, s 779(1).   [4022] CA 2006, s 779(2).
[4023] CA 2006, s 779(3).

Duty of company as to issue of certificates on the surrender of a
share warrant

16.14 Section 780 of the CA 2006 states that a company must, within two
months of the surrender of a share warrant for cancellation, complete and
have ready for delivery the certificates of the shares specified in the
warrant.[4024]

However, s 780(1) of the CA 2006 does not apply if the company's articles
provide otherwise.[4025]

If default is made in complying with s 780(1) of the CA 2006 an offence is
committed by every officer of the company who is in default.[4026] A person
guilty of an offence under s 780(3) of the CA 2006 is liable on summary
conviction to a fine not exceeding level 3 on the standard scale and, for
continued contravention, a daily default fine not exceeding one-tenth of level
3 on the standard scale.[4027]

Section 780 of the CA 2006 is a new provision. Its objective is to ensure
that a company must issue a share certificate where a share warrant is subsequently surrendered for cancellation. It gives a company two months from
the date of surrender to complete and have ready for delivery a certificate of
the shares specified in the warrant and failure to do so is a criminal offence:
see s 780(3) of the CA 2006. This requirement is, however, subject to any
contrary provisions in the company's articles, which may give the company
more or less time to deliver such certificates to the transferee: see s 780(2) of
the CA 2006.

Offences in connection with share warrants (Scotland)

16.15 Section 781 of the CA 2006 states that if in Scotland a person with
intent to defraud forges or alters, or offers, utters, disposes of, or puts off,[4028]
knowing the same to be forged or altered, any share warrant or coupon, or
any document purporting to be a share warrant or coupon issued in pursuance of this Act, or by means of any such forged or altered share warrant,
coupon or document (i) demands or endeavours to obtain or receive any
share or interest in a company under this Act,[4029] or (ii) demands or
endeavours to receive any dividend or money payment in respect of any such
share or interest,[4030] knowing the warrant, coupon or document to be forged
or altered, he commits an offence.

If in Scotland a person without lawful authority or excuse (of which the
onus of proof lies with him) (a) engraves or makes on any plate, wood, stone,
or other material, any share warrant or coupon purporting to be (i) a share

---

[4024] CA 2006, s 780(1).   [4025] CA 2006, s 780(2).   [4026] CA 2006, s 780(3).
[4027] CA 2006, s 780(4).   [4028] CA 2006, s 781(1)(a).   [4029] CA 2006, s 781(1)(b)(i).
[4030] CA 2006, s 781(1)(b)(ii).

warrant or coupon issued or made by any particular company in pursuance of this Act,[4031] or (ii) a blank share warrant or coupon so issued or made,[4032] or (iii) a part of such a share warrant or coupon,[4033] or (b) uses any such plate, wood, stone, or other material, for the making or printing of any such share warrant or coupon, or of any such blank share warrant or coupon or of any part of such a share warrant or coupon,[4034] or (c) knowingly has in his custody or possession any such plate, wood, stone, or other material,[4035] he commits an offence.

A person guilty of an offence under s 781(1) of the CA 2006 is liable on summary conviction to imprisonment for a term not exceeding six months, or to a fine not exceeding level 5 on the standard scale (or both).[4036]

A person guilty of an offence under s 781(2) of the CA 2006 is liable on conviction on indictment, to imprisonment for a term not exceeding seven years or a fine (or both);[4037] or on summary conviction, to imprisonment for a term not exceeding six months or a fine not exceeding the statutory maximum (or both).[4038]

Supplementary provisions

Issue of certificates, etc.: court order to make good default

16.16 Section 782 of the CA 2006 states that if a company on which a notice has been served requiring it to make good any default in complying with s 769(1) of the CA 2006 (duty of company as to issue of certificates, etc. on allotment),[4039] s 776(1) of the CA 2006 (duty of company as to issue of certificates, etc. on transfer),[4040] or s 780(1) of the CA 2006 (duty of company as to issue of certificates, etc. on surrender of share warrant),[4041] fails to make good the default within ten days after service of the notice, the person entitled to have the certificates or the debentures delivered to him may apply to the court.

The court may, on such an application, make an order directing the company and any officer of it, to make good the default within such time as may be specified in the order.[4042]

The order may provide that all costs (in Scotland, expenses) of and incidental to the application, are to be borne by the company or by an officer of it responsible for the default.[4043]

[4031] CA 2006, s 781(2)(a)(i).   [4032] CA 2006, s 781(2)(a)(ii).   [4033] CA 2006, s 781(2)(a)(iii).
[4034] CA 2006, s 781(2)(b).   [4035] CA 2006, s 781(2)(c).   [4036] CA 2006, s 781(3).
[4037] CA 2006, s 781(4)(a).   [4038] CA 2006, s 781(4)(b).   [4039] CA 2006, s 782(1)(a).
[4040] CA 2006, s 782(1)(b).   [4041] CA 2006, s 782(1)(c).   [4042] CA 2006, s 782(2).
[4043] CA 2006, s 782(3).

Evidencing And Transfer of Title To Securities Without Written Instrument

16.17 Chapter 2 to Part 21 of the CA 2006 sets out provisions concerning evidencing and transfer of the title to securities without written instrument.

Introductory

Scope of Chapter 2

16.18 Section 783 of the CA 2006 sets out definitions that are applied in Chapter 2. The term 'securities' means shares, debentures, debenture stock, loan stock, bonds, units of a collective investment scheme within the meaning of the Financial Services and Markets Act 2000 (c 8), and other securities of any description.[4044] The references to 'title to securities' include any legal or equitable interest in securities;[4045] the references to a 'transfer of title' include a transfer by way of security;[4046] and references to 'transfer without a written instrument' include, in relation to bearer securities, transfer without delivery.[4047]

Power to make regulations

16.19 Section 784 of the CA 2006 sets out the power of the Treasury and Secretary of State to make regulations. The power to make regulations under Chapter 2 is exercisable by the Treasury and the Secretary of State, either jointly or concurrently.[4048]

The references in Chapter 2 to the authority having power to make regulations shall accordingly be read as references to both or either of them, as the case may require.[4049]

The regulations under Chapter 2 are subject to affirmative resolution procedure.[4050]

Section 784 of the CA 2006 provides for the power to make regulations about the transfer of title to securities without written instrument to be exercisable by the Secretary of State or the Treasury. Responsibility for s 207 of the CA 1989 and the regulations made under it are passed from the Department of Trade and Industry to HM Treasury by virtue of article 2(1) of the Transfer of Functions (Financial Services) Order 1992 (SI 1992/1315) as part of a general transfer responsibility for financial services matters. Dual responsibility is considered more appropriate by the making of regulations under the new power, as the extension of paperless holding and transfer to

---

[4044] CA 2006, s 783(a).   [4045] CA 2006, s 783(b).   [4046] CA 2006, s 783(c).
[4047] CA 2006, s 783(d).   [4048] CA 2006, s 784(1).   [4049] CA 2006, s 784(2).
[4050] CA 2006, s 784(3).

new classes of shares or other securities involve matters that are part of company law. The exercise of the power will continue to be subject to the affirmative procedure.

Powers exercisable

Provision enabling procedures for evidencing and transferring title

16.20 Section 785 of the CA 2006 states that provisions may be made by regulations for enabling title to securities to be evidenced and transferred without a written instrument.[4051]

The regulations may make provision for procedures for recording and transferring title to securities,[4052] and for the regulation of those procedures and the persons responsible for or involved in their operation.[4053]

The regulations must contain such safeguards as appear to the authority making the regulations appropriate for the protection of investors and for ensuring that competition is not restricted, distorted or prevented.[4054]

The regulations may, for the purpose of enabling or facilitating the operation of the procedures provided for by the regulations, make provision with respect to the rights and obligations of persons in relation to securities dealt with under the procedures.[4055]

The regulations may include provision for the purpose of giving effect to the transmission of title to securities by operation of law;[4056] any restriction on the transfer of title to securities arising by virtue of the provisions of any enactment or instrument, court order or agreement;[4057] any power conferred by any such provision on a person to deal with securities on behalf of the person entitled.[4058]

The regulations may make provision with respect to the persons responsible for the operation of the procedures provided for by the regulations as to the consequences of their insolvency or incapacity,[4059] or as to the transfer from them to other persons of their functions in relation to those procedures.[4060]

Provision enabling or requiring arrangements to be adopted

16.21 Section 786 of the CA 2006 provides that regulations under Chapter 2 may make provision enabling the members of a company, or of any designated class of companies, to adopt, by ordinary resolution, arrangements

---

[4051] CA 2006, s 785(1).   [4052] CA 2006, s 785(2)(a).   [4053] CA 2006, s 785(2)(b).
[4054] CA 2006, s 785(3).   [4055] CA 2006, s 785(4).   [4056] CA 2006, s 785(5)(a).
[4057] CA 2006, s 785(5)(b).   [4058] CA 2006, s 785(5)(c).   [4059] CA 2006, s 785(6)(a).
[4060] CA 2006, s 785(6)(b).

under which title to securities is required to be evidenced or transferred (or both) without a written instrument;[4061] or requiring companies, or any designated class of companies, to adopt such arrangements.[4062]

The regulations may make such provision in respect of all securities issued by a company,[4063] or in respect of all securities of a specified description.[4064]

The arrangements provided for by regulations making such provision as is mentioned in s 786(1) of the CA 2006 must not be such that a person who, but for the arrangements, would be entitled to have his name entered in the company's register of members, ceases to be so entitled,[4065] and must be such that a person who, but for the arrangements, would be entitled to exercise any rights in respect of the securities continues to be able effectively to control the exercise of those rights.[4066]

The regulations may prohibit the issue of any certificate by the company in respect of the issue or transfer of securities;[4067] require the provision by the company to holders of securities of statements (at specified intervals or on specified occasions) of the securities held in their name,[4068] and make provision as to the matters of which any such certificate or statement is, or is not, evidence.[4069]

Under s 786 of the CA 2006, references to a 'designated class of companies' are to a class designated in the regulations or by order under s 787 of the CA 2006;[4070] and 'specified' means specified in the regulations.[4071]

Section 786 of the CA 2006 states that regulations under Chapter 2 may require, as well as permit, the paper-free holding and transfer of securities. The effect of s 786(1) and (2) of the CA 2006 is that regulations made under s 207 may enable members of companies or of designated classes of company, by ordinary resolution, to adopt a new form of paperless holding and transfer of shares and abandon paper-based forms of holding and transfer in relation to all existing and new securities of that company, or to specified types of securities. Alternatively, regulations made under s 207 may make the adoption of a form of paperless transfer and the abandonment of paper-based forms of transfer mandatory for all securities, or specified types of securities, issued by companies generally or by designated classes of company.

Regulations do not need to make it obligatory both to hold and to transfer securities in a paper-free way; the new arrangements could relate just to holding or just to transfer.

Section 786(3) of the CA 2006 is designed to protect the right of individual investors to continue to hold shares in their own names rather than through

---

[4061] CA 2006, s 786(1)(a).   [4062] CA 2006, s 786(1)(b).   [4063] CA 2006, s 786(2)(a).
[4064] CA 2006, s 786(2)(b).   [4065] CA 2006, s 786(3)(a).   [4066] CA 2006, s 786(3)(b).
[4067] CA 2006, s 786(4)(a).   [4068] CA 2006, s 786(4)(b).   [4069] CA 2006, s 786(4)(c).
[4070] CA 2006, s 786(5)(a).   [4071] CA 2006, s 786(5)(b).

nominees. It ensures that the new arrangements prescribed in the regulations will not mean that people who would have been entitled to have their names entered in the company's register of members will lose that entitlement; or people who are entitled to exercise rights in respect of securities will lose that right.

Section 786(4) of the CA 2006 provides that the regulations will be able to prohibit the issue of share certificates or certificates for other types of security. Holders of securities to which such prohibition applies will lose the option of continuing to hold certificates and transfer their shares by paper-based methods. It also ensures that such holders of securities are sent periodic statements of their holdings. Further, it makes provision about the evidential value of certificates or statements.

Provision enabling or requiring arrangements to be adopted: order-making powers

16.22 Section 787 of the CA 2006 states that the authority having power to make regulations under Chapter 2 may by order designate classes of companies for the purposes of s 786 of the CA 2006 (provision enabling or requiring arrangements to be adopted);[4072] provides that, in relation to securities of a specified description (i) in a designated class of companies,[4073] or (ii) in a specified company or class of companies,[4074] specified provisions of regulations made under Chapter 2 by virtue of that section either do not apply or apply subject to specified modifications.

In s 787(1) of the CA 2006, the term 'specified' means specified in the order.[4075]

An order under this section is subject to negative resolution procedure.[4076]

Section 787 of the CA 2006 provides additional flexibility by enabling ministers to designate, by order (subject to negative resolution procedure), companies or classes of company to which the regulations are to apply, or to modify the effect of the regulations (or disapply them) in relation to a designated class of companies or specified companies.

Supplementary

Provision that may be included in regulations

16.23 Section 788 of the CA 2006 states that regulations under Chapter 2 may modify or exclude any provision of any enactment or instrument, or any rule of law;[4077] apply, with such modifications as may be appropriate, the

---

[4072] CA 2006, s 787(1)(a).   [4073] CA 2006, s 787(1)(b)(i).   [4074] CA 2006, s 787(1)(b)(ii).
[4075] CA 2006, s 787(2).   [4076] CA 2006, s 787(3).   [4077] CA 2006, s 788(a).

provisions of any enactment or instrument (including provisions creating criminal offences);[4078] require the payment of fees, or enable persons to require the payment of fees, of such amounts as may be specified in the regulations or determined in accordance with them;[4079] empower the authority making the regulations to delegate to any person willing and able to discharge them any functions of the authority under the regulations.[4080]

Duty to consult

16.24 Section 789 of the CA 2006 applies to a duty to consult. Before making regulations under this Chapter,[4081] or any order under s 787 of the CA 2006,[4082] the authority having power to make regulations under this Chapter must carry out such consultation as appears to it to be appropriate.

Under s 789 of the CA 2006, Ministers will be obliged to consult such persons as they consider appropriate before making regulations or designating a class of companies by order under the new powers. This obligation reflects the breadth of the proposed new powers, as well as the technical nature of some of the regulations that could be made under it.

Resolutions to be forwarded to the registrar

16.25 Section 790 of the CA 2006 applies to resolutions to be forwarded to the registrar. Chapter 3 of Part 3 of the CA 2006 (resolutions affecting a company's constitution) applies to a resolution passed by virtue of regulations under this Chapter.

[4078] CA 2006, s 788(b).   [4079] CA 2006, s 788(c).   [4080] CA 2006, s 788(d).
[4081] CA 2006, s 789(a).   [4082] CA 2006, s 789(b).

Chapter 17

Information about Interests in a Company's Shares

Introduction

17.1 Part 22 of the CA 2006 is concerned with information about interests in a company's shares. The provisions of this Part concern a public company's right to investigate who has an interest in its shares. They replace equivalent provisions in Part 6 of the CA 1985. These are purely domestic provisions, and are not required by European Community law.

The automatic disclosure obligations previously contained in ss 198–211 of Part 6 of the CA 1985 are replaced by regulations under the Financial Services and Markets Act 2000, as amended by Part 43 of the CA 2006, in implementation of the Transparency Directive. In the regulations, a different concept of 'interest in voting rights' will be adopted in order to implement the Transparency Directive.

Part 22 of the CA 2006 re-enacts, with certain modifications, the disclosure obligations pursuant to a notice issued by the company previously contained in ss 212–219 of the CA 1985. There is no change to the definition of 'interest in shares' for this purpose.

The main changes to s 212 of the CA 1985 and related provisions are: first, making it clear that notices are not required to be in hard copy, and therefore can be given in electronic form (s 793 of the CA 2006 read in conjunction with the provisions in Part 37 of the CA 2006 on the sending or supplying of documents or information); second, providing for how information is to be entered on the register when the name of the present holder of the shares is not known or there is no present holder (s 808 of the CA 2006); third, removing the requirement on the company to verify third-party information supplied in response to a s 793 of the CA 2006 notice before putting it on the register (s 817 of the CA 2006); fourth, removing the requirement for a company to keep information on the register in relation to notices issued more than six years previously (s 816 of the CA 2006); and fifth, requiring a company to refuse a request to inspect the register if not satisfied that the request is made for a proper purpose (s 812 of the CA 2006).

Companies to which this Part applies

17.2 Section 791 of the CA 2006 states that Part 22 of the CA 2006 applies only to public companies.[4083]

Shares to which this Part applies

17.3 Section 792 of the CA 2006 states that references in Part 22 of the CA 2006 to a company's shares are to the company's issued shares of a class, carrying rights to vote in all circumstances at general meetings of the company (including any shares held as treasury shares).[4084]

The temporary suspension of voting rights in respect of any shares does not affect the application of Part 22 of the CA 2006 in relation to interests in those or any other shares.[4085]

Section 792 of the CA 2006 re-enacts in part the definition in s 198(2) of the CA 1985 of the type of shares concerning which a s 793 (CA 2006) notice may be issued, namely shares carrying the rights to vote in all circumstances at general meetings. However, shares held by a company 'in treasury' following a purchase of its own shares, (as an alternative to cancelling to such shares on purchase) are included in the definition.

Notice requiring information about interests in shares

Notice of company requiring information about interests in its shares

17.4 Under s 793 of the CA 2006, a public company may give notice to any person whom the company knows or has reasonable cause to believe to be interested in the company's shares,[4086] or to have been so interested at any time during the three years immediately preceding the date on which the notice is issued.[4087]

The notice may require the person to confirm that fact or (as the case may be) to state whether or not it is the case,[4088] and if he holds, or has during that time held, any such interest, to give such further information as may be required in accordance with the following provisions of this section.[4089]

The notice may require the person to whom it is addressed, to give particulars of his own present or past interest in the company's shares (held by him at any time during the three-year period mentioned in s 793(1)(b) of the CA 2006).[4090]

The notice may require the person to whom it is addressed, where his interest is a present interest and another interest in the shares subsists,[4091] or

[4083] See previously CA 1985, s 212.   [4084] CA 2006, s 792(1).   [4085] CA 2006, s 792(2).
[4086] CA 2006, s 793(1)(a).   [4087] CA 2006, s 793(1)(b).   [4088] CA 2006, s 793(2)(a).
[4089] CA 2006, s 793(2)(b).   [4090] CA 2006, s 793(3).   [4091] CA 2006, s 793(4)(a).

another interest in the shares subsisted during that three year period at a time when his interest subsisted,[4092] to give, so far as lies within his knowledge, such particulars with respect to that other interest as may be required by the notice.

The particulars referred to in s 793(3) and (4) of the CA 2006 include (a) the identity of persons interested in the shares in question,[4093] and (b) whether persons interested in the same shares are or were parties to (i) an agreement to which s 824 of the CA 2006 applies (certain share acquisition agreements),[4094] or (ii) an agreement or arrangement relating to the exercise of any rights conferred by the holding of the shares.[4095]

The notice may require the person to whom it is addressed, where his interest is a past interest, to give (so far as lies within his knowledge) particulars of the identity of the person who held that interest immediately upon his ceasing to hold it.[4096]

The information required by the notice must be given within such reasonable time as may be specified in the notice.[4097]

Section 793 of the CA 2006 re-enacts s 212(1)–(4) of the CA 1985. It allows a public company to issue a notice requiring a person whom it knows, or has reasonable cause to believe, has an interest in its shares (or to have had an interests in the previous three years) to confirm or deny the fact, and if the former, to disclose certain information about the interest, including information about any other person with an interest in the shares.

Section 783(3) and (4) of the CA 2006 enable the company to require details to be given of a person's past or present interest, and to provide details of any other interest subsisting in the shares of which he is aware. This provision allows the company to pursue information through a chain of nominees by requiring each in the chain to disclose the person for whom they are acting. Under s 783(6) of the CA 2006, where the addressee's interest is a past one, a company can ask for information concerning any person by whom the interest was acquired immediately subsequent to their interest. Particulars may also be required of any share acquisition agreements, or any agreement or arrangement as to how the rights attaching to those shares should be exercised (ss 824 and 825 of the CA 2006).

This section serves a different purpose to the automatic disclosure obligations previously contained in ss 198–211 of Part 6 of the CA 1985. It enables companies to discover the identity of those with voting rights (direct or indirect) that fall below the thresholds for automatic disclosure, and it also enables companies (and members of the company) to ascertain the underlying beneficial owners of shares.

[4092] CA 2006, s 793(4)(b).   [4093] CA 2006, s 793(5)(a).   [4094] CA 2006, s 793(5)(b)(i).
[4095] CA 2006, s 793(5)(b)(ii).   [4096] CA 2006, s 793(6).   [4097] CA 2006, s 793(7).

In contrast to s 212 of the CA 1985, the notice is not required to be in hard copy (under the general provisions on sending or supplying documents or information in Part 37 of the CA 2006). Notices, and response thereto, may be given in electronic form. A response must be given within a reasonable time. What is reasonable has not been defined so as to allow flexibility according to the circumstances, but if the time given is not reasonable, the company will not have served a valid notice.

Notice requiring information: order imposing restrictions on shares

17.5 Section 794 of the CA 2006 states that where a notice under s 793 of the CA 2006 (notice requiring information about interests in a company's shares) is served by a company on a person who is or was interested in shares in the company,[4098] and that person fails to give the company the information required by the notice within the time specified in it,[4099] the company may apply to the court for an order directing that the shares in question be subject to restrictions. For the effect of such an order see s 797 of the CA 2006.

If the court is satisfied that such an order may unfairly affect the rights of third parties in respect of the shares, the court may, for the purpose of protecting those rights and subject to such terms as it thinks fit, direct that such acts by such persons or descriptions of persons and for such purposes as may be set out in the order shall not constitute a breach of the restrictions.[4100]

On an application under this section the court may make an interim order.[4101] Any such order may be made unconditionally or on such terms as the court thinks fit.

Sections 798–802 of the CA 2006 make further provision about orders under this section.[4102]

Notice requiring information: offences

17.6 Section 795 of the CA 2006 states that a person who (a) fails to comply with a notice under s 793 of the CA 2006 (notice requiring information about interests in company's shares),[4103] or (b) in purported compliance with such a notice (i) makes a statement that he knows to be false in a material particular,[4104] or (ii) recklessly makes a statement that is false in a material particular,[4105] commits an offence.

A person does not commit an offence under s 795(1)(a) of the CA 2006 if he proves that the requirement to give information was frivolous or vexatious.[4106]

[4098] CA 2006, s 794(1)(a).   [4099] CA 2006, s 794(1)(b).   [4100] CA 2006, s 794(2).
[4101] CA 2006, s 794(3).   [4102] CA 2006, s 794(4).   [4103] CA 2006, s 795(1)(a).
[4104] CA 2006, s 795(1)(b)(i).   [4105] CA 2006, s 795(1)(b)(ii).   [4106] CA 2006, s 795(2).

A person guilty of an offence under s 795 of the CA 2006 is liable on conviction on indictment, to imprisonment for a term not exceeding two years or a fine (or both);[4107] on summary conviction in England and Wales, to imprisonment for a term not exceeding 12 months or to a fine not exceeding the statutory maximum (or both);[4108] in Scotland or Northern Ireland, to imprisonment for a term not exceeding six months, or to a fine not exceeding the statutory maximum (or both).[4109]

Sections 794 and 795 of the CA 2006 re-enact s 216(1)–(4) of the CA 1985. They specify the penalties for failure to provide information within the specified time when served with a notice under s 793 of the CA 2006. There are criminal penalties, (although a person does not commit an offence of he can show that the requirement to give information was frivolous or vexatious).

Additionally, application may be made to the court for a direction that the shares in question are to be subject to the restrictions specified in s 797 of the CA 2006.

Notice requiring information: persons exempted from obligation to comply

17.7 Section 796 of the CA 2006 states that a person is not obliged to comply with a notice under s 793 of the CA 2006 (notice requiring information about interests in company's shares) if he is for the time being exempted by the Secretary of State from the operation of that section.[4110]

The Secretary of State must not grant any such exemption unless he has consulted the Governor of the Bank of England,[4111] and he (the Secretary of State) is satisfied that, having regard to any undertaking given by the person in question with respect to any interest held or to be held by him in any shares, there are special reasons why that person should not be subject to the obligations imposed by that section.[4112]

This section re-enacts s 216(5) of the CA 1985. It provides that the Secretary of State may exempt a person from complying with a notice. The Secretary of State must consult the Governor of the Bank of England, and must be satisfied that there are special reasons for exempting the person (taking account of any undertaking given).

Orders imposing restrictions on shares

17.8 Sections 797–802 of the CA 2006 deal with provisions on orders imposing restrictions on shares.

[4107] CA 2006, s 795(3)(a).   [4108] CA 2006, s 795(3)(b)(i).   [4109] CA 2006, s 795(3)(b)(ii).
[4110] CA 2006, s 796(1).   [4111] CA 2006, s 796(2)(a).   [4112] CA 2006, s 796(2)(b).

Consequences of order imposing restrictions

17.9 Section 797 of the CA 2006 states that the effect of an order under s 794 of the CA 2006 that shares are subject to restrictions is as follows, namely: (a) any transfer of the shares is void;[4113] (b) no voting rights are exercisable in respect of the shares;[4114] (c) no further shares may be issued in right of the shares or in pursuance of an offer made to their holder;[4115] (d) except in a liquidation, no payment may be made of sums due from the company on the shares, whether in respect of capital or otherwise.[4116]

Where shares are subject to the restriction in s 797(1)(a) of the CA 2006, an agreement to transfer the shares is void.[4117]

This does not apply to an agreement to transfer the shares on the making of an order under s 800 of the CA 2006 made by virtue of s 979(3)(b) of the CA 2006 (removal of restrictions in case of court-approved transfer).

Where shares are subject to the restriction in s 797(1)(c) or (d) of the CA 2006, an agreement to transfer any right to be issued with other shares in right of those shares, or to receive any payment on them (otherwise than in a liquidation), is void.[4118]

This does not apply to an agreement to transfer any such right on the making of an order under s 800 of the CA 2006 made by virtue of s 797(3)(b) of the CA 2006 (removal of restrictions in case of court-approved transfer).

The provisions of s 797 of the CA 2006 are subject to any directions under s 794(2) of the CA 2006 or s 799(3) of the CA 2006 (directions for protection of third parties),[4119] and in the case of an interim order under s 794(3) of the CA 2006, to the terms of the order.[4120]

Penalty for attempted evasion of restrictions

17.10 Section 798 of the CA 2006 applies where shares are subject to restrictions by virtue of an order under s 794 of the CA 2006.[4121]

A person commits an offence if he (a) exercises or purports to exercise any right (i) to dispose of shares that to his knowledge, are for the time being subject to restrictions,[4122] or (ii) to dispose of any right to be issued with any such shares,[4123] or (b) votes in respect of any such shares (whether as holder or proxy), or appoints a proxy to vote in respect of them,[4124] or (c) being the holder of any such shares, fails to notify of their being subject to those restrictions a person whom he does not know to be aware of that fact but does know to be entitled (apart from the restrictions) to vote in respect of

[4113] CA 2006, s 797(1)(a).   [4114] CA 2006, s 797(1)(b).   [4115] CA 2006, s 797(1)(c).
[4116] CA 2006, s 797(1)(d).   [4117] CA 2006, s 797(2).   [4118] CA 2006, s 797(3).
[4119] CA 2006, s 797(4)(a).   [4120] CA 2006, s 797(4)(b).   [4121] CA 2006, s 798(1).
[4122] CA 2006, s 798(2)(a)(i).   [4123] CA 2006, s 798(2)(a)(ii).   [4124] CA 2006, s 798(2)(b).

those shares whether as holder or as proxy,[4125] or (d) being the holder of any such shares, or being entitled to a right to be issued with other shares in right of them, or to receive any payment on them (otherwise than in a liquidation), enters into an agreement that is void under s 797(2) or (3) of the CA 2006.[4126]

If shares in a company are issued in contravention of the restrictions, an offence is committed by the company,[4127] and every officer of the company who is in default.[4128] A person guilty of an offence under this section is liable on conviction on indictment, to a fine;[4129] on summary conviction, to a fine not exceeding the statutory maximum.[4130]

The provisions of s 798 of the CA 2006 are subject to any directions under s 794(2) of the CA 2006 (directions for protection of third parties); or ss 799 or 800 of the CA 2006 (relaxation or removal of restrictions),[4131] and in the case of an interim order under s 794(3) of the CA 2006, to the terms of the order.[4132]

Relaxation of restrictions

17.11 Section 799 of the CA 2006 deals with the relaxation of restrictions. An application may be made to the court on the ground that an order directing that shares, shall be subject to restrictions unfairly affects the rights of third parties in respect of the shares.[4133]

An application for an order under this section may be made by the company or by any person aggrieved.[4134]

If the court is satisfied that the application is well-founded, it may, for the purpose of protecting the rights of third parties in respect of the shares, and subject to such terms as it thinks fit, direct that such acts by such persons or descriptions of persons and for such purposes as may be set out in the order do not constitute a breach of the restrictions.[4135]

Removal of restrictions

17.12 Section 800 of the CA 2006 states that an application may be made to the court for an order directing that the shares shall cease to be subject to restrictions.[4136]

An application for an order under this section may be made by the company or by any person aggrieved.[4137]

The court must not make an order under this section, unless it is satisfied that the relevant facts about the shares have been disclosed to the company

[4125] CA 2006, s 798(2)(c).   [4126] CA 2006, s 798(2)(d).   [4127] CA 2006, s 798(3)(a).
[4128] CA 2006, s 798(3)(b).   [4129] CA 2006, s 798(4)(a).   [4130] CA 2006, s 798(4)(b).
[4131] CA 2006, s 798(5)(a).   [4132] CA 2006, s 798(5)(b).   [4133] CA 2006, s 799(1).
[4134] CA 2006, s 799(2).   [4135] CA 2006, s 799(3).   [4136] CA 2006, s 800(1).
[4137] CA 2006, s 800(2).

and no unfair advantage has accrued to any person as a result of the earlier failure to make that disclosure,[4138] or the shares are to be transferred for valuable consideration and the court approves the transfer.[4139]

An order under this section made by virtue of s 800(3)(b) of the CA 2006 may continue, in whole or in part, the restrictions mentioned in s 797(1)(c) and (d) of the CA 2006 (restrictions on issue of further shares or making of payments) so far as they relate to a right acquired or offer made before the transfer.[4140]

Where any restrictions continue in force under s 800(4) of the CA 2006 an application may be made under this section for an order directing that the shares shall cease to be subject to those restrictions,[4141] and s 800(3) of the CA 2006 does not apply in relation to the making of such an order.[4142]

Order for a sale of shares

17.13 Section 801 of the CA 2006 states that the court may order that the shares subject to restrictions be sold, subject to the court's approval as to the sale.[4143]

An application for an order under s 801 of the CA 2006 may only be made by the company.[4144]

Where the court has made an order under s 801 of the CA 2006, it may make such further order relating to the sale or transfer of the shares as it thinks fit.[4145]

An application for an order under s 801(3) of the CA 2006 may be made by the company,[4146] by the person appointed by or in pursuance of the order to effect the sale,[4147] or by any person interested in the shares.[4148]

On making an order under s 801(1) or (3) of the CA 2006, the court may order that the applicant's costs (in Scotland, expenses) be paid out of the proceeds of sale.[4149]

Application of proceeds of sale under court order

17.14 Section 802 of the CA 2006 states that where shares are sold in pursuance of an order of the court under s 801 of the CA 2006, the proceeds of the sale, less the costs of the sale, must be paid into court for the benefit of the persons who are beneficially interested in the shares.[4150]

A person who is beneficially interested in the shares may apply to the court for the whole or part of those proceeds to be paid to him.[4151]

[4138] CA 2006, s 800(3)(a).   [4139] CA 2006, s 800(3)(b).   [4140] CA 2006, s 800(4).
[4141] CA 2006, s 800(5)(a).   [4142] CA 2006, s 800(5)(b).   [4143] CA 2006, s 801(1).
[4144] CA 2006, s 801(2).   [4145] CA 2006, s 801(3).   [4146] CA 2006, s 801(4)(a).
[4147] CA 2006, s 801(4)(b).   [4148] CA 2006, s 801(4)(c).   [4149] CA 2006, s 801(5).
[4150] CA 2006, s 802(1).   [4151] CA 2006, s 802(2).

On such an application the court must order payment to the applicant of the whole of the proceeds of the sale together with any interest on them,[4152] or if another person had a beneficial interest in the shares at the time of their sale, such proportion of the proceeds and interest as the value of the applicant's interest in the shares bears to the total value of the shares.[4153] This is subject to the following qualification.

If the court has ordered under s 801(5) of the CA 2006 that the costs (in Scotland, expenses) of an applicant under that section are to be paid out of the proceeds of the sale, the applicant is entitled to payment of his costs (or expenses) out of those proceeds before any person interested in the shares receives any part of those proceeds.[4154]

Sections 797–802 of the CA 2006 restate Part 15 of the CA 1985 without any substantive change insofar as its provisions apply in relation to Part 22 of the CA 2006. They set out the effect of a court order made under s 794 of the CA 2006 imposing restrictions on shares and the penalties for attempted evasion of the restrictions. They also make provisions for the relaxation or removal of restrictions, or for an order for the sale of shares.

Power of members to require a company to act

17.15 Section 803 of the CA 2006 states that the members of a company may require it to exercise its powers under s 793 of the CA 2006 (notice requiring information about interests in shares).[4155]

A company is required to do so once it has received requests (to the same effect) from members of the company holding at least 10 per cent of such of the paid-up capital of the company as carries a right to vote at general meetings of the company (excluding any voting rights attached to any shares in the company held as treasury shares).[4156]

A request (a) may be in hard copy form or in electronic form,[4157] (b) must (i) state that the company is requested to exercise its powers under s 793 of the CA 2006,[4158] (ii) specify the manner in which the company is requested to act,[4159] and (iii) give reasonable grounds for requiring the company to exercise those powers in the manner specified,[4160] and (c) must be authenticated by the person or persons making it.[4161]

Section 803 of the CA 2006 re-enacts s 214(1) and (2) of the CA 1985. It requires a company to exercise its powers under s 793 of the CA 2006 on the request of members holding at least 10 per cent of such of the paid up capital of the company as carries the right to vote at general meetings (other than voting rights attached to shares held in treasury). This provision, which has

---

[4152] CA 2006, s 802(3)(a).   [4153] CA 2006, s 802(3)(b).   [4154] CA 2006, s 802(4).
[4155] CA 2006, s 803(1).   [4156] CA 2006, s 803(2).   [4157] CA 2006, s 803(3)(a).
[4158] CA 2006, s 803(3)(b)(i).   [4159] CA 2006, s 803(3)(b)(ii).
[4160] CA 2006, s 803(3)(b)(iii).   [4161] CA 2006, s 803(3)(c).

rarely been used under the CA 1985, recognises that members of a company may have a legitimate reason for wanting the company to exercise its statutory powers to demand information even if the management does not want to. For example, the members might want to act where they suspect that the directors are involved in building a holding from behind the shelter of nominees.

Provision is made as to the form and the procedure in relation to requests. Unlike s 214 of the CA 1985, the 10 per cent threshold may be met a series of requests from members that the company act, rather than one collective request. Those making a request must not only specify the manner in which they require the powers to be exercised, but must also give reasonable grounds for requiring the company to exercise the powers in the manner specified (s 803(3)(b)(ii) and (iii) of the CA 2006).

Duty of company to comply with requirement

17.16 Section 804 of the CA 2006 states that a company that is required under s 803 of the CA 2006 to exercise its powers under s 793 of the CA 2006 (notice requiring information about interests in a company's shares) must exercise those powers in the manner specified in the requests.[4162]

If default is made in complying with s 804(1) of the CA 2006, an offence is committed by every officer of the company who is in default.[4163] A person guilty of an offence under this section is liable on conviction on indictment, to a fine;[4164] and on summary conviction, to a fine not exceeding the statutory maximum.[4165]

This section re-enacts s 214(4) and (5) of the CA 1985. It specifies the criminal penalties arising if the company fails to act as required. In contrast to s 214 of the CA 1985, every officer in default is liable to fine, but the company itself is not.

Report to members on outcome of an investigation

17.17 Section 805 of the CA 2006 states that on the conclusion of an investigation carried out by a company in pursuance of a requirement under s 803 of the CA 2006 the company must cause a report of the information received in pursuance of the investigation to be prepared.

The report must be made available for inspection within a reasonable period (not more than 15 days) after the conclusion of the investigation.[4166]

Where a company undertakes an investigation in pursuance of a requirement under s 803,[4167] and the investigation is not concluded within three

---

[4162] CA 2006, s 804(1).   [4163] CA 2006, s 804(2).   [4164] CA 2006, s 804(3)(a).
[4165] CA 2006, s 804(3)(b).   [4166] CA 2006, s 805(1).   [4167] CA 2006, s 805(2)(a).

months after the date on which the company became subject to the require-ment,[4168] the company must cause to be prepared in respect of that period, and in respect of each succeeding period of three months ending before the conclusion of the investigation, an interim report of the information received during that period in pursuance of the investigation.

Each such report must be made available for inspection within a reasonable period (not more than 15 days) after the end of the period to which it relates.[4169]

The reports must be retained by the company for at least six years from the date on which they are first made available for inspection and must be kept available for inspection during that time at the company's registered office,[4170] or at a place specified in the regulations under s 1136 of the CA 2006.[4171]

The company must give notice to the registrar of the place at which the reports are kept available for inspection,[4172] and of any change in that place,[4173] unless they have at all times been kept at the company's registered office.

The company must within three days of making any report prepared under this section available for inspection, notify the members who made the requests under s 803 where the report is so available.[4174]

An investigation carried out by a company in pursuance of a requirement under s 803 of the CA 2006 is concluded when (a) the company has made all such inquiries as are necessary or expedient for the purposes of the require-ment,[4175] and (b) in the case of each such inquiry (i) a response has been received by the company,[4176] or (ii) the time allowed for a response has elapsed.[4177]

Section 805 of the CA 2006 re-enacts s 215 of the CA 1985. It specifies that on the conclusion of an investigation carried out by the company in pursu-ance of a member's request, it is the duty of the company to prepare a report of the information received. The report must be available at the company's registered office within a reasonable period (not exceeding 15 days) after the conclusion of the investigation. Where the company's investigation exceeds three months, it must make interim reports available at three monthly inter-vals. Those making the request must be notified of reports being available. In contrast to s 215 of the CA 2006, the report should be kept at the company's registered office or at a place specified in regulations made under s 1136 of the CA 2006.

[4168] CA 2006, s 805(2)(b).   [4169] CA 2006, s 805(3).   [4170] CA 2006, s 805(4)(a).
[4171] CA 2006, s 805(4)(b).   [4172] CA 2006, s 805(5)(a).   [4173] CA 2006, s 805(5)(b).
[4174] CA 2006, s 805(6).   [4175] CA 2006, s 805(7)(a).   [4176] CA 2006, s 805(7)(b)(i).
[4177] CA 2006, s 805(7)(b)(ii).

Report to members: offences

17.18 Section 806 of the CA 2006 states that if default is made for 14 days in complying with s 805(5) (notice to registrar of place at which reports made available for inspection) an offence is committed by the company,[4178] and every officer of the company who is in default.[4179] A person guilty of an offence under s 806(1) of the CA 2006 is liable on summary conviction to a fine not exceeding level 3 on the standard scale and, for continued contravention, a daily default fine not exceeding one-tenth of level 3 on the standard scale.[4180]

If a default is made in complying with any other provision of s 805 of the CA 2006 (report to members on outcome of investigation), an offence is committed by every officer of the company who is in default.[4181] A person guilty of an offence under s 806(3) of the CA 2006 is liable on conviction on indictment, to a fine;[4182] on summary conviction, to a fine not exceeding the statutory maximum.[4183]

Section 806 of the CA 2006 re-enacts s 215(8) of the CA 1985. It specifies the criminal penalties arising if the company fails to report as required on the outcome of the investigation under s 805 of the CA 2006. Unlike s 215 of the CA 1985, every officer in default was liable to a fine, but the company itself was not.

Right to inspect and request copy of reports

17.19 Section 807 of the CA 2006 states that any report prepared under s 805 of the CA 2006 must be open to inspection by any person without charge.[4184]

Any person is entitled, on request and on payment of such fee as may be prescribed, to be provided with a copy of any such report or any part of it.

The copy must be provided within ten days after the request is received by the company.[4185]

If an inspection required under s 807(1) of the CA 2006 is refused, or default is made in complying with s 807(2) of the CA 2006, an offence is committed by the company,[4186] and every officer of the company who is in default.[4187] A person guilty of an offence under this section is liable on summary conviction to a fine not exceeding level 3 on the standard scale and, for continued contravention, a daily default fine not exceeding one-tenth of level 3 on the standard scale.[4188]

In the case of any such refusal or default the court may by order compel an

---

[4178] CA 2006, s 806(1)(a).   [4179] CA 2006, s 806(1)(b).   [4180] CA 2006, s 806(2).
[4181] CA 2006, s 806(3).   [4182] CA 2006, s 806(4)(a).   [4183] CA 2006, s 806(4)(b).
[4184] CA 2006, s 807(1).   [4185] CA 2006, s 807(2).   [4186] CA 2006, s 807(3)(a).
[4187] CA 2006, s 807(3)(b).   [4188] CA 2006, s 807(4).

immediate inspection or, as the case may be, direct that the copy required be sent to the person requiring it.[4189]

Section 807 of the CA 2006 re-enacts provisions in s 219 of the CA 1985. It requires the company to allow reports to members to be inspected by anyone without charge. Any person can request a copy of the report, on payment of the prescribed fee. Section 807(3) and (5) of the CA 2006 specifies the criminal penalties arising if the company fails to disclose the report as required and make provision for the courts to compel disclosure.

Register of interests disclosed

17.20 Section 808 of the CA 2006 states that the company must keep a register of information received by it in pursuance of a requirement imposed under s 793 of the CA 2006 (notice requiring information about interests in company's shares).[4190]

A company which receives any such information must, within three days of its receipt, enter in the register the fact that the requirement was imposed and the date on which it was imposed,[4191] and the information received in pursuance of the requirement.[4192]

The information must be entered against the name of the present holder of the shares in question or, if there is no present holder or the present holder is not known, against the name of the person holding the interest.[4193]

The register must be made up so that the entries against the names entered in it appear in chronological order.[4194]

If default is made in complying with this section an offence is committed by the company,[4195] and every officer of the company who is in default.[4196] A person guilty of an offence under this section is liable on summary conviction to a fine not exceeding level 3 on the standard scale and, for continued contravention, a daily default fine not exceeding one-tenth of level 3 on the standard scale.[4197]

The company is not by virtue of anything done for the purposes of this section affected with notice of, or put upon inquiry as to, the rights of any person in relation to any shares.[4198]

The register that was required to be kept by s 211 of the CA 1985 covered all interests notified, whether under the automatic disclosure rules or in response to a notice served under s 212 of the CA 1985 (company investigations). The latter are currently kept as a separate part of the register of interests in shares. In future it will be for regulations made under the

---

[4189] CA 2006, s 807(5).   [4190] CA 2006, s 808(1).   [4191] CA 2006, s 808(2)(a).
[4192] CA 2006, s 808(2)(b).   [4193] CA 2006, s 808(3).   [4194] CA 2006, s 808(4).
[4195] CA 2006, s 808(5)(a).   [4196] CA 2006, s 808(5)(b).   [4197] CA 2006, s 808(6).
[4198] CA 2006, s 808(7).

Financial Services and Markets Act 2000 (as amended by Part 43 of the CA 2006) to make provisions as to how interests notified under the automatic disclosure rules will be made public.

This section provides that if, as a result of a s 793 of the CA 2006 investigation, the company receives information relating to the present interests held by any person in relevant shares, it must within three days enter in a register of interests the fact that the requirement (to disclose information under the notice) was imposed and the date on which it was imposed; and the information received in response to the notice under s 793 of the CA 2006.

Section 808 of the CA 2006 provides that the information must be entered against the name of the present holder of the shares in question (as under the CA 1985), or if the present holder is not known or there is no present holder, then against the name of the person holding the interest. Section 808(6) and (7) of the CA 2006 provides for criminal penalties for any default in complying with this section. Section 808(8) of the CA 2006 makes it clear that information that a company receives under this part, does not mean that the company needs to be concerned with the existence of any trust over the shares.

Register to be kept available for inspection

17.21 Section 809 of the CA 2006 states that the register kept under s 808 of the CA 2006 (register of interests disclosed) must be kept available for inspection at the company's registered office,[4199] or at a place specified in regulations under s 1136 of the CA 2006.[4200]

A company must give notice to the registrar of companies of the place where the register is kept available for inspection and of any change in that place.[4201]

No such notice is required if the register has at all times been kept available for inspection at the company's registered office.[4202]

If default is made in complying with s 809(1) of the CA 2006, or a company makes a default for 14 days in complying with s 809(2) of the CA 2006, an offence is committed by the company,[4203] and every officer of the company who is in default.[4204] A person guilty of an offence under s 810 of the CA 2006 is liable on summary conviction to a fine not exceeding level 3 on the standard scale and, for continued contravention, a daily default fine not exceeding one-tenth of level 3 on the standard scale.[4205]

[4199] CA 2006, s 809(1)(a).   [4200] CA 2006, s 809(1)(b).   [4201] CA 2006, s 809(2).
[4202] CA 2006, s 809(3).   [4203] CA 2006, s 809(4)(a).   [4204] CA 2006, s 809(4)(b).
[4205] CA 2006, s 809(5).

Associated index

17.22 Unless the register kept under s 808 of the CA 2006 (register of interests disclosed) is kept in such a form as constitutes an index, the company must keep an index of the names entered in it.[4206]

The company must make any necessary entry or alteration in the index within ten days after the date on which any entry or alteration is made in the register.[4207]

The index must contain, in respect of each name, a sufficient indication to enable the information entered against it to be readily found.[4208] The index must be at all times kept available for inspection at the same place as the register.[4209]

If a default is made in complying with this section, an offence is committed by the company,[4210] and every officer of the company who is in default.[4211] A person guilty of an offence under this section is liable on summary conviction to a fine not exceeding level 3 on the standard scale and, for continued contravention, a daily default fine not exceeding one-tenth of level 3 on the standard scale.[4212]

This sections re-enact s 211(6) and (8) (as applied by s 231(3) of the CA 1985). Section 809 of the CA 2006 provides that the register of interests disclosed must be kept available for inspection at the company's registered office or at the place specified in regulations made under s 1136 of the CA 2006. The company must advise the registrar where the register is kept (unless it has always been kept at the registered office). Section 809(4) and (5) of the CA 2006 provides for criminal penalties for any default in complying with this section.

Section 810 of the CA 2006 provides that the register should have an index unless it is in a form that itself constitutes an index (for example a searchable database).

Rights to inspect and require copy of entries

17.23 Section 811 of the CA 2006 states that the register required to be kept under s 808 of the CA 2006 (register of interests disclosed), and any associated index, must be open to inspection by any person without charge.[4213]

Any person is entitled, on request and on payment of such fee as may be prescribed, to be provided with a copy of any entry in the register.[4214]

A person seeking to exercise either of the rights conferred by this section must make a request to the company to that effect.[4215]

[4206] CA 2006, s 810(1).   [4207] CA 2006, s 810(2).   [4208] CA 2006, s 810(3).
[4209] CA 2006, s 810(4).   [4210] CA 2006, s 810(5)(a).   [4211] CA 2006, s 810(5)(b).
[4212] CA 2006, s 810(6).   [4213] CA 2006, s 811(1).   [4214] CA 2006, s 811(2).
[4215] CA 2006, s 811(3).

The request must contain the following information: (a) in the case of an individual, his name and address;[4216] (b) in the case of an organisation, the name and address of an individual responsible for making the request on behalf of the organisation;[4217] (c) the purpose for which the information is to be used;[4218] and (d) whether the information will be disclosed to any other person, and if so (i) where that person is an individual, his name and address,[4219] (ii) where that person is an organisation, the name and address of an individual responsible for receiving the information on its behalf,[4220] and (iii) the purpose for which the information is to be used by that person.[4221]

This section re-enacts s 219 of the CA 1985. It provides that the register and index must be open to inspection by any person without charge. For a prescribed fee, any person is entitled to a copy of any entry on the register. A person seeking access to the register under this section must provide the information specified in s 811(4) of the CA 2006, including his name and address and the purpose for which the information is to be used.

Court supervision of purpose for which rights may be exercised

17.24 Where a company receives a request under s 811 of the CA 2006 (register of interests disclosed: right to inspect and require copy), it must comply with the request if it is satisfied that it is made for a proper purpose,[4222] and refuse the request if it is not so satisfied.[4223]

If the company refuses the request, it must inform the person making the request, stating the reason why it is not satisfied.[4224] A person whose request is refused may apply to the court.[4225]

If an application is made to the court the person who made the request must notify the company,[4226] and the company must use its best endeavours to notify any persons whose details would be disclosed if the company were required to comply with the request.[4227]

If the court is not satisfied that the inspection or copy is sought for a proper purpose, it shall direct the company not to comply with the request.[4228]

If the court makes such a direction and it appears to the court that the company is or may be subject to other requests made for a similar purpose (whether made by the same person or different persons), it may direct that the company is not to comply with any such request.[4229] The order must contain such provision as appears to the court appropriate to identify the requests to which it applies.

If the court does not direct the company not to comply with the request,

---

[4216] CA 2006, s 811(4)(a).   [4217] CA 2006, s 811(4)(b).   [4218] CA 2006, s 811(4)(c).
[4219] CA 2006, s 811(4)(d)(i).   [4220] CA 2006, s 811(4)(d)(ii).
[4221] CA 2006, s 811(4)(d)(iii).   [4222] CA 2006, s 812(1)(a).   [4223] CA 2006, s 812(1)(b).
[4224] CA 2006, s 812(2).   [4225] CA 2006, s 812(3).   [4226] CA 2006, s 812(4)(a).
[4227] CA 2006, s 812(4)(b).   [4228] CA 2006, s 812(5).   [4229] CA 2006, s 812(6).

the company must comply with the request immediately upon the court giving its decision or, as the case may be, the proceedings being discontinued.[4230]

This section provides that the company must only allow the inspection of the register or the copy requested if satisfied that it is for a proper purpose. If it refuses, the person concerned may apply to the court for it to allow the inspection. If an application to the court is made, the person must notify the company, and the company must use its best endeavours to notify any persons whose details might be disclosed.

Register of interests disclosed: refusal of inspection or default in providing copy

17.25 Section 813 of the CA 2006 states that if an inspection required under s 811 of the CA 2006 (gister of interests disclosed: right to inspect and require copy) is refused or default is made in providing a copy required under that section, otherwise than in accordance with an order of the court, an offence is committed by the company,[4231] and every officer of the company who is in default.[4232] A person guilty of an offence under s 813 of the CA 2006 is liable on summary conviction to a fine not exceeding level 3 on the standard scale and, for continued contravention, a daily default fine not exceeding one-tenth of level 3 on the standard scale.[4233]

In the case of any such refusal or default the court may by order compel an immediate inspection or, as the case may be, direct that the copy required be sent to the person requesting it.[4234]

This section provides for court enforcement and criminal penalties for any default in complying with s 811 of the CA 2006.

Register of interests disclosed: offences in connection with request for or disclosure of information

17.26 Under s 814 of the CA 2006, it is an offence for a person knowingly or recklessly to make in a request under s 811 of the CA 2006 (register of interests disclosed: right to inspect or require copy) a statement that is misleading, false or deceptive in a material particular.[4235]

It is an offence for a person in possession of information obtained by exercise of either of the rights conferred by that section to do anything that results in the information being disclosed to another person,[4236] or to fail to do anything with the result that the information is disclosed to another

---

[4230] CA 2006, s 812(7).   [4231] CA 2006, s 813(1)(a).   [4232] CA 2006, s 813(1)(b).
[4233] CA 2006, s 813(2).   [4234] CA 2006, s 813(3).   [4235] CA 2006, s 814(1).
[4236] CA 2006, s 814(2)(a).

person,[4237] knowing, or having reason to suspect, that person may use the information for a purpose that is not a proper purpose.

A person guilty of an offence under s 814 of the CA 2006 is liable on conviction on indictment, to imprisonment for a term not exceeding two years or a fine (or both);[4238] and on summary conviction in England and Wales, to imprisonment for a term not exceeding 12 months or to a fine not exceeding the statutory maximum (or both);[4239] in Scotland or Northern Ireland, to imprisonment for a term not exceeding six months, or to a fine not exceeding the statutory maximum (or both).[4240]

Section 814 of the CA 2006 provides for criminal penalties for misleading, false or deceptive statements given when making a request under s 811 of the CA 2006. It also makes it a criminal offence for the person who receives information under s 811 of the CA 2006 to disclose it to another person, if he knows or has reason to suspect that it may be used for an improper purpose.

Entries not to be removed from register

17.27 Section 815 of the CA 2006 states that entries in the register kept under s 808 of the CA 2006 (register of interests disclosed) must not be deleted except in accordance with s 816 of the CA 2006 (old entries), or s 817 of the CA 2006 (incorrect entry relating to third party).[4241]

If an entry is deleted in contravention of s 815(1) of the CA 2006, the company must restore it as soon as reasonably practicable.[4242]

If a default is made in complying with s 815(1) or (2) of the CA 2006, an offence is committed by the company,[4243] and every officer of the company who is in default.[4244] A person guilty of an offence under s 815 of the CA 2006 is liable on summary conviction to a fine not exceeding level 3 on the standard scale and, for continued contravention of s 815 (2) of the CA 2006, a daily default fine not exceeding one-tenth of level 3 on the standard scale.[4245]

This section re-enacts s 218 of the CA 1985. It provides that entries can only be removed from the register in accordance with ss 816 and 817 of the CA 2006, and if wrongly deleted must be restored as soon as reasonably practicable. Section 815(3) and (4) of the CA 2006 provides for criminal penalties for any default in complying with this section.

Removal of entries from register: old entries

17.28 Section 816 of the CA 2006 states that a company may remove an entry from the register kept under s 808 of the CA 2006 (register of interests disclosed) if more than six years have elapsed since the entry was made.

[4237] CA 2006, s 814(2)(b).   [4238] CA 2006, s 814(3)(a).   [4239] CA 2006, s 814(3)(b)(i).
[4240] CA 2006, s 814(3)(b)(ii).   [4241] CA 2006, s 815(1).   [4242] CA 2006, s 815(2).
[4243] CA 2006, s 815(3)(a).   [4244] CA 2006, s 815(3)(b).   [4245] CA 2006, s 815(4).

Section 271(1) of the CA 1985 provided that a company may remove an entry against a person's name from the register of interests in shares if more that six years have elapsed since the date of the entry being made, and either the entry recorded the fact that the person in question had ceased to have an interest notifiable under Part 6 in the company's relevant share capital (in which case the person's name will also be removed from the register); or the entry has been superseded by a later entry against the same person's name.

By contrast, s 816 of the CA 2006 simply provides that a company is not required to keep information on the register if more than six years have elapsed since the entry was made.

Removal of entries from register: incorrect entry relating to a third party

17.29 Section 817 of the CA 2006 applies where in pursuance of an obligation imposed by a notice under s 793 of the CA 2006 (notice requiring information about interests in company's shares) a person gives to a company the name and address of another person as being interested in shares in the company.[4246]

That other person may apply to the company for the removal of the entry from the register.[4247]

If the company is satisfied that the information in pursuance of which the entry was made is incorrect, it shall remove the entry.[4248]

If an application under s 817(3) of the CA 2006 is refused, the applicant may apply to the court for an order directing the company to remove the entry in question from the register. The court may make such an order if it thinks fit.[4249]

This section re-enacts s 217 of the CA 1985 but does not include the requirement for the company to verify information relating to third parties supplied in response to a s 793 of the CA 2006 notice. However, the third party retains the right to apply to have his name removed from the register if the information is incorrect. Section 817(4) of the CA 2006 provides for the courts to enforce removal of incorrect information.

Adjustment of entry relating to share acquisition agreement

17.30 Section 818 of the CA 2006 states that if a person who is identified in the register kept by a company under s 808 of the CA 2006 (register of interests disclosed) as being a party to an agreement to which s 824 of the CA 2006 applies (certain share acquisition agreements) ceases to be a party to the

---

[4246] CA 2006, s 817(1).   [4247] CA 2006, s 817(2).   [4248] CA 2006, s 817(3).
[4249] CA 2006, s 817(4).

agreement, he may apply to the company for the inclusion of that information in the register.[4250]

If the company is satisfied that he has ceased to be a party to the agreement, it must record that information (if not already recorded) in every place where his name appears in the register as a party to the agreement.[4251]

If an application under this section is refused (otherwise than on the ground that the information has already been recorded), the applicant may apply to the court for an order directing the company to include the information in question in the register. The court may make such an order if it thinks fit.[4252]

Section 818 of the CA 2006 re-enacts s 217(4) and (5) of the CA 1985. It provides that a person identified in the register as being party to a s 824 (CA 2006) share acquisition agreement (this may include a concert party agreement) may when he ceases to be party to the agreement, request that the register should be amended to record that information. Such entries may appear in several places on the register, as each member of the concert party is required in their individual notification to identify the other members of the concert party. If the company refuses an application, the court may order the company to comply if it thinks fit.

Duty of company ceasing to be public company

17.31 Section 819 of the CA 2006 states that if a company ceases to be a public company, it must continue to keep any register kept under s 808 of the CA 2006 (register of interests disclosed), and any associated index, until the end of a period of six years after it ceased to be such a company.[4253]

If default is made in complying with s 819 of the CA 2006, an offence is committed by the company,[4254] and every officer of the company who is in default.[4255] A person guilty of an offence under s 819 of the CA 2006 is liable on summary conviction to a fine not exceeding level 3 on the standard scale and, for continued contravention, a daily default fine not exceeding one-tenth of level 3 on the standard scale.[4256]

This section re-enacts provisions in s 211(7) and (10) of the CA 1985. It provides that a company ceasing to be a public company must continue to keep any register it has kept under s 808 of the CA 2006 and any associated index for six years after it ceases to be a public company.

[4250] CA 2006, s 818(1).   [4251] CA 2006, s 818(2).   [4252] CA 2006, s 818(3).
[4253] CA 2006, s 819(1).   [4254] CA 2006, s 819(2)(a).   [4255] CA 2006, s 819(2)(b).
[4256] CA 2006, s 819(3).

Meaning of interest in shares

Interest in shares: general

17.32 Section 820 of the CA 2006 applies to determine for the purposes of Part 22 of the CA 2006 whether a person has an interest in shares.[4257]

In Part 22 of the CA 2006, a reference to an interest in shares includes an interest of any kind whatsoever in the shares,[4258] and any restraints or restrictions to which the exercise of any right attached to the interest is or may be subject shall be disregarded.[4259]

Where an interest in shares is comprised in property held on trust, every beneficiary of the trust is treated as having an interest in the shares.[4260]

A person is treated as having an interest in shares if (a) he enters into a contract to acquire them,[4261] or (b) not being the registered holder, he is entitled (i) to exercise any right conferred by the holding of the shares,[4262] or (ii) to control the exercise of any such right.[4263]

For the purposes of s 820(4)(b) of the CA 2006 a person is entitled to exercise or control the exercise of a right conferred by the holding of shares if he has a right (whether subject to conditions or not) the exercise of which would make him so entitled,[4264] or is under an obligation (whether subject to conditions or not) the fulfillment of which would make him so entitled.[4265]

A person is treated as having an interest in shares if he has a right to call for delivery of the shares to himself or to his order,[4266] or he has a right to acquire an interest in shares or is under an obligation to take an interest in shares.[4267] This applies whether the right or obligation is conditional or absolute.

Persons having a joint interest are treated as each having that interest.[4268]

It is immaterial that shares in which a person has an interest are unidentifiable.[4269]

This section re-enacts the definition of 'interests in shares' in s 208 of the CA 1985 (as applied by s 212(5) of the CA 1985) for the purposes of Part 22 of the CA 2006. An 'interest in shares' is widely defined as an interest of any kind whatsoever in the shares and includes beneficial ownership as well as direct ownership. The courts have described this wide definition as being designed 'to counter the limitless ingenuity of persons who prefer to conceal their interest behind trusts and corporate entities': *re TR Technology Investment Trust plc*.[4270]

[4257] CA 2006, s 820(1). [4258] CA 2006, s 820(2)(a). [4259] CA 2006, s 820(2)(b).
[4260] CA 2006, s 820(3). [4261] CA 2006, s 820(4)(a). [4262] CA 2006, s 820(4)(b)(i).
[4263] CA 2006, s 820(4)(b)(ii). [4264] CA 2006, s 820(5)(a). [4265] CA 2006, s 820(5)(b).
[4266] CA 2006, s 820(6)(a). [4267] CA 2006, s 820(6)(b). [4268] CA 2006, s 820(7).
[4269] CA 2006, s 820(8). [4270] [1988] BCLC 256 at 261.

Interest in shares: right to subscribe for shares

17.33 Section 821 of the CA 2006 states that s 793 of the CA 2006 (notice by a company requiring information about interests in its shares) applies in relation to a person who has, or previously had, or is or was entitled to acquire, a right to subscribe for shares in the company as it applies in relation to a person who is or was interested in shares in that company.[4271]

The references in that section to an interest in shares shall be read accordingly.[4272]

This section re-enacts s 212(6) of the CA 1985. It provides that a notice under s 793 of the CA 2006 applies in relation to rights to subscribe for shares.

Interest in shares: family interests

17.34 Section 822 of the CA 2006 states that for the purposes of Part 22 of the CA 2006, a person is taken to be interested in shares in which his spouse or civil partner,[4273] or any infant child or step-child of his,[4274] is interested.

In relation to Scotland 'infant' means a person under the age of 18 years.[4275]

Interest in shares: corporate interests

17.35 Section 823 of the CA 2006 states that for the purposes of Part 22 of the CA 2006, a person is taken to be interested in shares if a body corporate is interested in them and the body or its directors are accustomed to act in accordance with his directions or instructions,[4276] or he is entitled to exercise or control the exercise of one-third or more of the voting power at general meetings of the body.[4277]

A person is treated as entitled to exercise or control the exercise of voting power if another body corporate is entitled to exercise or control the exercise of that voting power,[4278] and he is entitled to exercise or control the exercise of one-third or more of the voting power at general meetings of that body corporate.[4279]

A person is treated as entitled to exercise or control the exercise of voting power if he has a right (whether or not subject to conditions) the exercise of which would make him so entitled,[4280] or he is under an obligation (whether or not subject to conditions) the fulfillment of which would make him so entitled.[4281]

[4271] CA 2006, s 821(1).   [4272] CA 2006, s 821(2).   [4273] CA 2006, s 822(1)(a).
[4274] CA 2006, s 822(1)(b).   [4275] CA 2006, s 822(2).   [4276] CA 2006, s 823(1)(a).
[4277] CA 2006, s 823(1)(b).   [4278] CA 2006, s 823(2)(a).   [4279] CA 2006, s 823(2)(b).
[4280] CA 2006, s 823(3)(a).   [4281] CA 2006, s 823(3)(b).

These sections re-enact s 203 of the CA 1985. They provide for certain family interests to be attributed to persons for the purpose of disclosure, as well as certain interests held indirectly through a corporate body.

Interest in shares: agreement to acquire interests in a particular company

17.36 Section 824 of the CA 2006 states that for the purposes of Part 22 of the CA 2006, an interest in shares may arise from an agreement between two or more persons that includes provision for the acquisition by any one or more of them of interests in shares of a particular public company (the 'target company' for that agreement).[4282]

Section 824 of the CA 2006 applies to such an agreement if the agreement includes provisions imposing obligations or restrictions on any one or more of the parties to it with respect to their use, retention or disposal of their interests in the shares of the target company acquired in pursuance of the agreement (whether or not together with any other interests of theirs in the company's shares to which the agreement relates),[4283] and an interest in the target company's shares is in fact acquired by any of the parties in pursuance of the agreement.[4284]

The reference in s 824(2) of the CA 2006 to the use of interests in shares in the target company is to the exercise of any rights or of any control or influence arising from those interests (including the right to enter into an agreement for the exercise, or for control of the exercise, of any of those rights by another person).[4285]

Once an interest in shares in the target company has been acquired in pursuance of the agreement, this section continues to apply to the agreement so long as the agreement continues to include provisions of any description mentioned in s 824(2) of the CA 2006.[4286]

This applies irrespective of (a) whether or not any further acquisitions of interests in the company's shares take place in pursuance of the agreement;[4287] (b) any change in the persons who are for the time being parties to it;[4288] (c) any variation of the agreement.[4289]

The references in this subsection to the agreement include any agreement having effect (whether directly or indirectly) in a substitution for the original agreement.

Under s 824 of the CA 2006, the term 'agreement' includes any agreement or arrangement;[4290] and references to provisions of an agreement include undertakings, expectations or understandings operative under an

---

[4282] CA 2006, s 824(1).   [4283] CA 2006, s 824(2)(a).   [4284] CA 2006, s 824(2)(b).
[4285] CA 2006, s 824(3).   [4286] CA 2006, s 824(4).   [4287] CA 2006, s 824(4)(a).
[4288] CA 2006, s 824(4)(b).   [4289] CA 2006, s 824(4)(c).   [4290] CA 2006, s 824(5).

arrangement;[4291] and any provision whether express or implied and whether absolute or not.[4292] The references elsewhere in Part 22 of the CA 2006 to an agreement to which this section applies have a corresponding meaning.

Section 824 of the CA 2006 does not apply to an agreement that is not legally binding, unless it involves mutuality in the undertakings, expectations or understandings of the parties to it;[4293] or to an agreement to underwrite or sub-underwrite an offer of shares in a company, provided the agreement is confined to that purpose and any matters incidental to it.[4294]

This section re-enacts s 204 of the CA 1985 concerning the obligation to give details of certain share acquisition arrangements in response to a notice under s 793 of the CA 2006. It covers any agreement or arrangement, whether or not legally binding, that involves undertakings, expectations or understandings that interests in shares will be acquired and that they will be subject to relevant restrictions while the agreement subsists. This may include groups of persons acting in concerts to prepare the way for a takeover offer for the company or to support a pending takeover offer.

Extent of obligation in case of share acquisition agreement

17.37 Section 825 of the CA 2006 states that for the purposes of Part 22 of the CA 2006, each party to an agreement to which s 824 of the CA 2006 applies is treated as interested in all shares in the target company in which any other party to the agreement is interested, apart from the agreement (whether or not the interest of the other party was acquired, or includes any interest that was acquired, in pursuance of the agreement).[4295]

For those purposes, the interest of a party to such an agreement in shares in the target company, is an interest apart from the agreement if he is interested in those shares otherwise than by virtue of the application of s 824 of the CA 2006 (and this section) in relation to the agreement.[4296]

Accordingly, any such interest of the person (apart from the agreement) includes for those purposes any interest treated as his under ss 822 or 823 of the CA 2006 (family or corporate interests) or by the application of s 824 of the CA 2006 (and this section) in relation to any other agreement with respect to shares in the target company to which he is a party.[4297]

A notification with respect to his interest in shares in the target company made to the company under Part 22 of the CA 2006 by a person who is for the time being a party to an agreement to which s 824 of the CA 2006 applies, must state that the person making the notification is a party to such an agreement,[4298] and include the names and (so far as known to him) the

---

[4291] CA 2006, s 824(5)(i).   [4292] CA 2006, s 824(5)(b)(ii).   [4293] CA 2006, s 824(6)(a).
[4294] CA 2006, s 824(6)(b).   [4295] CA 2006, s 825(1).   [4296] CA 2006, s 825(2).
[4297] CA 2006, s 825(3).   [4298] CA 2006, s 825(4)(a).

addresses of the other parties to the agreement, identifying them as such,[4299] and state whether or not any of the shares to which the notification relates are shares in which he is interested by virtue of s 824 of the CA 2006 (and this section) and, if so, the number of those shares.[4300]

This section re-enacts s 205 of the CA 2006. Section 825(1) of the CA 2005 provides that one person's interest in a concert party agreement is to be attributed to another. Section 825(2) and (3) of the CA 2006 explains what an interest apart from the concert party is, and s 825(4) of the CA 2006 concerns the mechanics of notification of an interest in a concert party agreement.

Other supplementary provisions

Information protected from wider disclosure

17.38 Section 826 of the CA 2006 states that information in respect of which a company is for the time being entitled to any exemption conferred by regulations under s 409(3) of the CA 2006 (information about related undertakings to be given in notes to accounts: exemption where disclosure harmful to company's business) must not be included in a report under s 805 of the CA 2006 (report to members on outcome of investigation),[4301] and must not be made available under s 811 of the CA 2006 (right to inspect and request copy of entries).[4302]

Where any such information is omitted from a report under s 805 of the CA 2006, that fact must be stated in the report.[4303]

Section 826 of the CA 2006 re-enacts provisions in s 211(9) of the CA 1985 (as applied by s 213(3) of the CA 1985 and s 215(4) of the CA 1985). Under s 409 of the CA 2006, the Secretary of State may make regulations exempting a company from the need to disclose information relating to related undertakings in notes to its accounts. The Secretary of State must agree that the information need not be disclosed. Where advantage is taken of this exemption, the fact must be stated in the company's annual accounts. This section provides that this name information must not be included in a s 805 of the CA 2006 report, (though its omission must be noted in the report), and must not be available for inspection under s 811 of the CA 2006.

Reckoning of periods for fulfilling obligations

17.39 Section 827 of the CA 2006 states that where the period allowed by any provision of Part 22 of the CA 2006 for fulfilling an obligation is expressed as a number of days, any day that is not a working day shall be disregarded in reckoning that period.

[4299] CA 2006, s 825(4)(b).   [4300] CA 2006, s 825(4)(c).   [4301] CA 2006, s 826(1)(a).
[4302] CA 2006, s 826(1)(b).   [4303] CA 2006, s 826(2).

This provision re-enacts the provision of s 220(2) of the CA 1985 concerning the calculation of periods in the Part expressed as a number of working days (as defined in s 1173 of the CA 2006). In contrast to s 220(2) of the CA 1985, the definition of 'working days' excludes bank holidays only in the part of the UK where the company is registered.

Power to make further provision by regulations

17.40 Section 828 of the CA 2006 states that the Secretary of State may by regulations amend the definition of shares to which Part 22 of the CA 2006 applies (s 792 of the CA 2006),[4304] the provisions as to notice by a company requiring information about interests in its shares (s 793 of the CA 2006),[4305] and the provisions as to what is taken to be an interest in shares (ss 820 and 821 of the CA 2006).[4306]

The regulations may amend, repeal or replace those provisions and make such other consequential amendments or repeals of provisions of Part 22 of the CA 2006 as appear to the Secretary of State to be appropriate.[4307]

The regulations under this section are subject to affirmative resolution procedure.[4308]

This section re-enacts s 210A of the CA 1985. It confers on the Secretary of State the power to make regulations to amend the definition of shares to which this Part applies (s 828(1)(a) of the CA 2006 re-enacting s 210A(1)(a) of the CA 1985. Power is also conferred on the Secreetary of State to amend the provisions in s 793 of the CA 2006 as to notice by a company requiring information about interests in its shares, (s 828(1)(b) of the CA 2006 re-enacting s 210A(1)(e)) of the CA 1985, and the provisions as to what is to be taken to be an interest in shares, (s 828(1)(c) of the CA 2006 re-enacting section 210A (1)(d)) of the CA 1985.

[4304] CA 2006, s 828(1)(a).   [4305] CA 2006, s 828(1)(b).   [4306] CA 2006, s 828(1)(c).
[4307] CA 2006, s 828(2).   [4308] CA 2006, s 828(3).

Chapter 18

Distributions

Introduction

18.1 Part 23 of the CA 2006 is concerned with distributions. It restates the provisions on distributions in Part 8 of the CA 1985. The only substantive change is to the rules on distributions in kind, and the new provisions are governed by ss 845, 846 and 851 of the CA 2006.

Part 23 comprises three Chapters. Chapter 1 addresses the restrictions on when distributions may be made. It sets out the meaning of distributions and some general rules. Chapter 2 sets out the justification of distribution by reference to accounts. Chapter 3 contains the supplementary provisions.

Restrictions On When Distributions May Be Made

18.2 Chapter 1 sets out the restrictions on when distributions may be made, with some introductory and general rules including definitions.

Introductory

Meaning of 'distribution'

18.3 Section 829 of the CA 2006 sets out the definition of 'distribution'. It means every description of distribution of a company's assets to its members, whether in cash or otherwise, subject to the following exceptions.[4309]

The following are not distributions for the purposes of Part 23 of the CA 2006, namely: (a) an issue of shares as fully or partly paid bonus shares;[4310] (b) the reduction of share capital (i) by extinguishing or reducing the liability of any of the members on any of the company's shares in respect of share capital not paid up,[4311] or (ii) by repaying paid-up share capital;[4312] (c) the

---

[4309] CA 2006, s 829(1).   [4310] CA 2006, s 829(2)(a).   [4311] CA 2006, s 829(2)(b)(i).
[4312] CA 2006, s 829(2)(b)(ii).

redemption or purchase of any of the company's own shares out of capital (including the proceeds of any fresh issue of shares) or out of unrealised profits in accordance with Chapter 3, 4 or 5 of Part 18 of the CA 2006;[4313] (d) a distribution of assets to members of the company on its winding up.[4314]

General rules

18.4 Sections 830–831 of the CA 2006 set out the general rules applicable to distributions.

Distributions to be made only out of profits available for the purpose

18.5 Section 830 of the CA 2006 deals with distributions to be made only out of profits available for the purpose. A company may only make a distribution out of profits available for the purpose.[4315]

A company's profits available for distribution are its accumulated, realised profits, so far as not previously utilised by distribution or capitalisation, less its accumulated, realised losses, so far as not previously written off in a reduction or reorganisation of capital duly made.[4316]

Section 830(2) of the CA 2006 applies subject to ss 832 and 835 of the CA 2006 (investment companies etc.: distributions out of accumulated revenue profits).

Net asset restriction on distributions by public companies

18.6 Section 831 of the CA 2006 states that a public company may only make a distribution if the amount of its net assets is not less than the aggregate of its called-up share capital and undistributable reserves,[4317] and if, and to the extent that, the distribution does not reduce the amount of those assets to less than that aggregate.[4318]

The term a company's 'net assets' means the aggregate of the company's assets less the aggregate of its liabilities.[4319]

'Liabilities' here includes (a) where the relevant accounts are Companies Act accounts, provisions of a kind specified for the purposes of this subsection by regulations under s 396 of the CA 2006;[4320] (b) where the relevant accounts are IAS accounts, provisions of any kind.[4321]

A company's undistributable reserves are (a) its share premium account;[4322] (b) its capital redemption reserve;[4323] (c) the amount by which its accumulated, unrealised profits (so far as not previously utilised by capitalisation)

[4313] CA 2006, s 829(2)(c).   [4314] CA 2006, s 829(2)(d).   [4315] CA 2006, s 830(1).
[4316] CA 2006, s 830(2).   [4317] CA 2006, s 831(1)(a).   [4318] CA 2006, s 831(1)(b).
[4319] CA 2006, s 831(2).   [4320] CA 2006, s 831(3)(a).   [4321] CA 2006, s 831(3)(b)
[4322] CA 2006, s 831(4)(a).   [4323] CA 2006, s 831(4)(b).

exceed its accumulated, unrealised losses (so far as not previously written off in a reduction or reorganisation of capital duly made);[4324] (d) any other reserve that the company is prohibited from distributing (i) by any enactment (other than one contained in Part 23 of the CA 2006),[4325] or (ii) by its articles.[4326]

The reference in para (c) to capitalisation does not include a transfer of profits of the company to its capital redemption reserve.

A public company must not include any uncalled share capital as an asset in any accounts relevant for purposes of this section.[4327]

Section 831(1) of the CA 2006 applies subject to ss 832 and 835 of the CA 2006 (investment companies, etc.: distributions out of accumulated revenue profits).[4328]

Distributions by investment companies

Distributions by investment companies out of accumulated revenue profits

18.7 Section 832 of the CA 2006 sets out the distributions by investment companies out of accumulated revenue profits. An investment company may make a distribution out of its accumulated, realised revenue profits if the following conditions are met.[4329]

It may make such a distribution only if, and to the extent that, its accumulated, realised revenue profits, so far as not previously utilised by a distribution or capitalisation, exceed its accumulated revenue losses (whether realised or unrealised), so far as not previously written off in a reduction or reorganisation of capital duly made.[4330]

It may make such a distribution only if the amount of its assets is at least equal to one-and-a-half times the aggregate of its liabilities to creditors,[4331] and if, and to the extent that, the distribution does not reduce that amount to less than one-and-a-half times that aggregate.[4332]

For this purpose, a company's liabilities to creditors include in the case of Companies Act accounts, provisions of a kind specified for the purposes of this subsection by regulations under s 396 of the CA 2006;[4333] in the case of IAS accounts, provisions for liabilities to creditors.[4334]

The following conditions must also be met, namely: (a) the company's shares must be listed on a recognised UK investment exchange;[4335] (b) during the relevant period it must not have (i) distributed any capital profits otherwise than by way of the redemption or purchase of any of the company's own

---

[4324] CA 2006, s 831(4)(c).   [4325] CA 2006, s 831(4)(d)(i).   [4326] CA 2006, s 831(4)(d)(ii).

[4327] CA 2006, s 831(5).   [4328] CA 2006, s 831(6).   [4329] CA 2006, s 832(1).

[4330] CA 2006, s 832(2).   [4331] CA 2006, s 832(3)(a).   [4332] CA 2006, s 832(3)(b).

[4333] CA 2006, s 832(4)(a).   [4334] CA 2006, s 832(4)(b).   [4335] CA 2006, s 832(5)(a).

shares in accordance with Chapter 3 or 4 of Part 18 of the CA 2006,[4336] or (ii) applied any unrealised profits or any capital profits (realised or unrealised) in paying up debentures or amounts unpaid on its issued shares;[4337] (c) it must have given notice to the registrar under s 833(1) of the CA 2006 (notice of intention to carry on business as an investment company) (i) before the beginning of the relevant period,[4338] or (ii) as soon as reasonably practicable after the date of its incorporation.[4339]

For the purposes of s 832 of the CA 2006, the term 'recognised UK investment exchange' means a recognised investment exchange within the meaning of Part 18 of the Financial Services and Markets Act 2000 (c 8), other than an overseas investment exchange within the meaning of that Part;[4340] and the 'relevant period' is the period beginning with (i) the first day of the accounting reference period immediately preceding that in which the proposed distribution is to be made,[4341] or (ii) where the distribution is to be made in the company's first accounting reference period, the first day of that period,[4342] and ending with the date of the distribution.

The company must not include any uncalled share capital as an asset in any accounts relevant for purposes of this section.[4343]

Meaning of 'investment company'

18.8 Section 833 of the CA 2006 sets out the meaning of investment company. Under Part 23 of the CA 2006 an 'investment company' means a public company that has given notice (which has not been revoked) to the registrar of its intention to carry on business as an investment company,[4344] and since the date of that notice has complied with the following requirements.[4345]

Those requirements are: (a) that the business of the company consists of investing its funds mainly in securities, with the aim of spreading investment risk and giving members of the company the benefit of the results of the management of its funds;[4346] (b) that the condition in s 834 of the CA 2006 is met as regards holdings in other companies;[4347] (c) that distribution of the company's capital profits is prohibited by its articles;[4348] (d) that the company has not retained, otherwise than in compliance with this Part, in respect of any accounting reference period more than 15 per cent of the income it derives from securities.[4349]

Section 833(2)(c) of the CA 2006 does not require an investment company to be prohibited by its articles from redeeming or purchasing its own shares in

---

[4336] CA 2006, s 832(5)(b)(i).   [4337] CA 2006, s 832(5)(b)(ii).   [4338] CA 2006, s 832(5)(c)(i).
[4339] CA 2006, s 832(5)(c)(ii).   [4340] CA 2006, s 832(6)(a).   [4341] CA 2006, s 832(6)(b)(i).
[4342] CA 2006, s 832(6)(b)(ii).   [4343] CA 2006, s 832(7).   [4344] CA 2006, s 833(1)(a).
[4345] CA 2006, s 833(1)(b).   [4346] CA 2006, s 833(2)(a).   [4347] CA 2006, s 833(2)(b).
[4348] CA 2006, s 833(2)(c).   [4349] CA 2006, s 833(2)(d).

accordance with Chapter 3 or 4 of Part 18 of the CA 2006 out of its capital profits.[4350]

Notice to the registrar under this section may be revoked at any time by the company on giving notice to the registrar that it no longer wishes to be an investment company within the meaning of this section.[4351] On giving such a notice, the company ceases to be such a company.[4352]

Investment company: condition as to holdings in other companies

18.9 Section 834 of the CA 2006 deals with the investment company with reference as to conditions regarding holdings in other companies. The condition referred to in s 833(2)(b) of the CA 2006 (requirements to be complied with by investment company) is that none of the company's holdings in companies (other than those that are for the time being investment companies) represents more than 15 per cent by value of the company's investments.[4353]

For this purpose (a) holdings in companies that (i) are members of a group (whether or not including the investing company),[4354] and (ii) are not for the time being investment companies,[4355] are treated as holdings in a single company; and (b) where the investing company is a member of a group, money owed to it by another member of the group (i) is treated as a security of the latter held by the investing company,[4356] and (ii) is accordingly treated as, or as part of, the holding of the investing company in the company owing the money.[4357]

The condition does not apply to a holding in a company acquired before 6th April 1965 that on that date represented not more than 25 per cent by value of the investing company's investments,[4358] or to a holding in a company that, when it was acquired, represented not more than 15 per cent by value of the investing company's investments,[4359] so long as no addition is made to the holding.

For the purposes of s 834(3) of the CA 2006, (a) the term 'holding' means the shares or securities (whether or one class or more than one class) held in any one company;[4360] (b) an addition is made to a holding whenever the investing company acquires shares or securities of that one company, otherwise than by being allotted shares or securities without becoming liable to give any consideration, and if an addition is made to a holding that holding is acquired when the addition or latest addition is made to the holding;[4361] and (c) where in connection with a scheme of reconstruction a company issues

---

[4350] CA 2006, s 833(3). [4351] CA 2006, s 833(4). [4352] CA 2006, s 833(5).
[4353] CA 2006, s 834(1). [4354] CA 2006, s 834(2)(a)(i). [4355] CA 2006, s 834(2)(a)(ii).
[4356] CA 2006, s 834(2)(b)(i). [4357] CA 2006, s 834(2)(b)(ii). [4358] CA 2006, s 834(3)(a).
[4359] CA 2006, s 834(3)(b). [4360] CA 2006, s 834(4)(a). [4361] CA 2006, s 834(4)(b).

shares or securities to persons holding shares or securities in a second company in respect of and in proportion to (or as nearly as may be in proportion to) their holdings in the second company, without those persons becoming liable to give any consideration, a holding of the shares or securities in the second company and a corresponding holding of the shares or securities so issued shall be regarded as the same holding.[4362]

Under s 834 of the CA 2006, the terms 'company' and 'shares' are to be construed in accordance with ss 99 and 288 of the Taxation of Chargeable Gains Act 1992 (c 12); the term 'group' means a company and all companies that are its 51 per cent subsidiaries (within the meaning of s 838 of the Income and Corporation Taxes Act 1988 (c 1)); and the term 'scheme of reconstruction' has the same meaning as in s 136 of the Taxation of Chargeable Gains Act 1992.[4363]

Power to extend provisions relating to investment companies

18.10 Section 835 of the CA 2006 applies to power to extend provisions relating to investment companies. It states that the Secretary of State may by regulations extend the provisions of ss 832–834 of the CA 2006 (distributions by investment companies out of accumulated profits), with or without modifications, to other companies whose principal business consists of investing their funds in securities, land or other assets with the aim of spreading investment risk and giving their members the benefit of the results of the management of the assets.[4364]

Any regulations under s 835 of the CA 2006 are subject to affirmative resolution procedure.[4365]

Justification of Distribution By Reference To Accounts

18.11 Chapter 2 of Part 23 applies to justification of distribution by reference to accounts.

Section 836 of the CA 2006 states that whether a distribution may be made by a company without contravening Part 23 of the CA 2006 is determined by reference to the following items as stated in the relevant accounts (a) profits, losses, assets and liabilities;[4366] (b) provisions of the following kinds (i) where the relevant accounts are Companies Act accounts, provisions of a kind specified for the purposes of this subsection by regulations under s 396;[4367] (ii) where the relevant accounts are IAS accounts, provisions of any kind;[4368] (c) share capital and reserves (including undistributable reserves).[4369]

[4362] CA 2006, s 834(4)(c).   [4363] CA 2006, s 834(5).   [4364] CA 2006, s 835(1).
[4365] CA 2006, s 835(2).   [4366] CA 2006, s 836(1)(a).   [4367] CA 2006, s 836(1)(b)(i).
[4368] CA 2006, s 836(1)(b)(ii).   [4369] CA 2006, s 836(1)(c).

The relevant accounts are the company's last annual accounts, except that where the distribution would be found to contravene Part 23 of the CA 2006 by reference to the company's last annual accounts, it may be justified by reference to interim accounts,[4370] and where the distribution is proposed to be declared during the company's first accounting reference period, or before any accounts have been circulated in respect of that period, it may be justified by reference to initial accounts.[4371]

The requirements of s 837 of the CA 2006 (as regards the company's last annual accounts), s 838 of the CA 2006 (as regards interim accounts), and s 839 of the CA 2006 (as regards initial accounts), must be complied with, as and where applicable.[4372]

If any applicable requirement of those sections is not complied with, the accounts may not be relied on for the purposes of Part 23 of the CA 2006, and the distribution is accordingly treated as contravening this Part.[4373]

Requirements applicable in relation to relevant accounts

Requirements where last annual accounts used

18.12 Section 837 of the CA 2006 provides that the company's last annual accounts means the company's individual accounts that were last circulated to members in accordance with s 423 of the CA 2006 (duty to circulate copies of annual accounts and reports),[4374] or if in accordance with s 426 of the CA 2006 the company provided a summary financial statement instead, that formed the basis of that statement.[4375]

The accounts must have been properly prepared in accordance with the CA 2006, or have been so prepared subject only to matters that are not material for determining (by reference to the items mentioned in s 836(1)) of the CA 2006 whether the distribution would contravene Part 23 of the CA 2006.[4376]

Unless the company is exempt from audit and the directors take advantage of that exemption, the auditor must have made his report on the accounts.[4377]

If that report was qualified (a) the auditor must have stated in writing (either at the time of his report or subsequently) whether in his opinion the matters in respect of which his report is qualified are material for determining whether a distribution would contravene Part 23 of the CA 2006,[4378] and (b) a copy of that statement must (i) in the case of a private company, have been circulated to members in accordance with s 423 of the CA 2006,[4379] or (ii) in the case of a public company, have been laid before the company in general meeting.[4380]

[4370] CA 2006, s 836(2)(a).　　[4371] CA 2006, s 836(2)(b).　　[4372] CA 2006, s 836(3).
[4373] CA 2006, s 836(4).　　[4374] CA 2006, s 837(1)(a).　　[4375] CA 2006, s 837(1)(b).
[4376] CA 2006, s 837(2).　　[4377] CA 2006, s 837(3).　　[4378] CA 2006, s 837(4)(a).
[4379] CA 2006, s 837(4)(b)(i).　　[4380] CA 2006, s 837(4)(b)(ii).

An auditor's statement is sufficient for the purposes of a distribution, if it relates to distributions of a description that includes the distribution in question, even if at the time of the statement it had not been proposed.[4381]

Requirements where interim accounts used

18.13 Section 838 of the CA 2006 provides that interim accounts must be accounts that enable a reasonable judgment to be made as to the amounts of the items mentioned in s 836(1) of the CA 2006.[4382]

Where interim accounts are prepared for a proposed distribution by a public company, the following requirements apply.[4383]

The accounts must have been properly prepared, or have been so prepared subject to matters that are not material for determining (by reference to the items mentioned in s 836(1)) of the CA 2006 whether the distribution would contravene Part 23 of the CA 2006.[4384]

The term 'properly prepared' means prepared in accordance with ss 395–397 of the CA 2006 (requirements for individual company accounts), applying those requirements with such modifications as are necessary because the accounts are prepared otherwise than in respect of an accounting reference period.[4385]

The balance sheet comprised in the accounts must have been signed in accordance with s 414 of the CA 2006.[4386]

A copy of the accounts must have been delivered to the registrar. Any requirement of Part 35 of the CA 2006 as to the delivery of a certified translation into English of any document forming part of the accounts must also have been met.[4387]

Requirements where initial accounts used

18.14 Section 839 of the CA 2006 sets out the requirements where initial accounts are used. Initial accounts must be accounts that enable a reasonable judgment to be made as to the amounts of the items mentioned in s 836(1) of the CA 2006.[4388]

Where initial accounts are prepared for a proposed distribution by a public company, the following requirements apply.[4389]

The accounts must have been properly prepared, or have been so prepared subject to matters that are not material for determining (by reference to the items mentioned in s 836(1) of the CA 2006) whether the distribution would contravene Part 23 of the CA 2006.[4390]

[4381] CA 2006, s 837(5).   [4382] CA 2006, s 838(1).   [4383] CA 2006, s 838(2).
[4384] CA 2006, s 838(3).   [4385] CA 2006, s 838(4).   [4386] CA 2006, s 838(5).
[4387] CA 2006, s 838(6).   [4388] CA 2006, s 839(1).   [4389] CA 2006, s 839(2).
[4390] CA 2006, s 839(3).

The term 'properly prepared' means prepared in accordance with ss 395–397 of the CA 2006 (requirements for individual company accounts), applying those requirements with such modifications as are necessary because the accounts are prepared otherwise than in respect of an accounting reference period.[4391]

The company's auditor must have made a report stating whether, in his opinion, the accounts have been properly prepared.[4392]

If that report was qualified (a) the auditor must have stated in writing (either at the time of his report or subsequently) whether in his opinion the matters in respect of which his report is qualified are material for determining whether a distribution would contravene Part 23 of the CA 2006,[4393] and (b) a copy of that statement must (i) in the case of a private company, have been circulated to members in accordance with s 423 of the CA 2006,[4394] or (ii) in the case of a public company, have been laid before the company in general meeting.[4395]

A copy of the accounts, of the auditor's report and of any auditor's statement must have been delivered to the registrar.

Any requirement of Part 35 of the CA 2006 as to the delivery of a certified translation into English of any of those documents must also have been met.[4396]

Application of provisions to successive distributions, etc.

Successive distributions etc. by reference to the same accounts

18.15 Section 840 of the CA 2006 states that in determining whether a proposed distribution may be made by a company in a case where one or more previous distributions have been made in pursuance of a determination made by reference to the same relevant accounts,[4397] or relevant financial assistance has been given, or other relevant payments have been made, since those accounts were prepared,[4398] the provisions of Part 23 of the CA 2006 apply as if the amount of the proposed distribution was increased by the amount of the previous distributions, financial assistance and other payments.

The financial assistance and other payments that are relevant for this purpose are: (a) financial assistance lawfully given by the company out of its distributable profits;[4399] (b) financial assistance given by the company in contravention of s 678 or s 679 of the CA 2006 (prohibited financial assistance) in a case where the giving of that assistance reduces the company's net assets or increases its net liabilities;[4400] (c) payments made by the company in respect

---

[4391] CA 2006, s 839(4).   [4392] CA 2006, s 839(5).   [4393] CA 2006, s 839(6)(a).
[4394] CA 2006, s 839(6)(b)(i).   [4395] CA 2006, s 839(6)(b)(ii).   [4396] CA 2006, s 839(7).
[4397] CA 2006, s 840(1)(a).   [4398] CA 2006, s 840(1)(b).   [4399] CA 2006, s 840(2)(a).
[4400] CA 2006, s 840(2)(b).

of the purchase by it of shares in the company, except a payment lawfully made otherwise than out of distributable profits;[4401] (d) payments of any description specified in s 705 of the CA 2006 (payments apart from purchase price of shares to be made out of distributable profits).[4402]

The term 'financial assistance' has the same meaning as in Chapter 2 of Part 18 of the CA 2006 (see s 677 of the CA 2006).[4403]

For the purpose of applying s 840(2)(b) of the CA 2006 in relation to any financial assistance, the terms 'net assets' means the amount by which the aggregate amount of the company's assets exceeds the aggregate amount of its liabilities,[4404] and 'net liabilities' means the amount by which the aggregate amount of the company's liabilities exceeds the aggregate amount of its assets,[4405] taking the amount of the assets and liabilities to be as stated in the company's accounting records immediately before the financial assistance is given.

For this purpose a company's liabilities include any amount retained as reasonably necessary for the purposes of providing for any liability the nature of which is clearly defined,[4406] and which is either likely to be incurred or certain to be incurred but uncertain as to the amount or as to the date on which it will arise.[4407]

Supplementary Provisions

18.16 Chapter 3 of Part 23 of the CA 2006 sets out supplementary provisions governing distributions.

Accounting matters

Realised losses and profits and revaluation of fixed assets

18.17 Section 841 of the CA 2006 states that the following provisions have effect for the purposes of Part 23 of the CA 2006.[4408]

The following are treated as realised losses, namely, in the case of Companies Acts accounts, provisions of a kind specified for the purposes of this paragraph by regulations under s 396 of the CA 2006 (except revaluation provisions);[4409] in the case of IAS accounts, provisions of any kind (except revaluation provisions).[4410]

The term 'revaluation provision' means a provision in respect of a diminution in value of a fixed asset appearing on a revaluation of all the fixed assets of the company, or of all of its fixed assets other than goodwill.[4411]

[4401] CA 2006, s 840(2)(c).   [4402] CA 2006, s 840(2)(d).   [4403] CA 2006, s 840(3).
[4404] CA 2006, s 840(4)(a).   [4405] CA 2006, s 840(4)(b).   [4406] CA 2006, s 840(5)(a).
[4407] CA 2006, s 840(5)(b).   [4408] CA 2006, s 841(1).   [4409] CA 2006, s 841(2)(a).
[4410] CA 2006, s 841(2)(b).   [4411] CA 2006, s 841(3).

For the purpose of s 841(2) and (3) of the CA 2006, any consideration by the directors of the value at a particular time of a fixed asset is treated as a revaluation provided the directors are satisfied that the aggregate value at that time of the fixed assets of the company that have not actually been revalued is not less than the aggregate amount at which they are then stated in the company's accounts,[4412] and it is stated in a note to the accounts (i) that the directors have considered the value of some or all of the fixed assets of the company without actually revaluing them,[4413] (ii) that they are satisfied that the aggregate value of those assets at the time of their consideration was not less than the aggregate amount at which they were then stated in the company's accounts,[4414] and (iii) that accordingly, by virtue of this subsection, amounts are stated in the accounts on the basis that a revaluation of fixed assets of the company is treated as having taken place at that time.[4415]

Where on the revaluation of a fixed asset, an unrealised profit is shown to have been made,[4416] and on or after the revaluation, a sum is written off or retained for depreciation of that asset over a period,[4417] an amount equal to the amount by which that sum exceeds the sum which would have been so written off or retained for the depreciation of that asset over that period, if that profit had not been made, is treated as a realised profit made over that period.

Determination of profit or loss in respect of an asset where records are incomplete

18.18 In determining for the purposes of Part 23 of the CA 2006, whether a company has made a profit or loss in respect of an asset, where there is no record of the original cost of the asset, or a record cannot be obtained without unreasonable expense or delay, its cost is taken to be the value ascribed to it in the earliest available record of its value made on or after its acquisition by the company.

Realised profits and losses of long-term insurance business

18.19 Section 843 of the CA 2006 states that the provisions of this section apply for the purposes of Part 23 of the CA 2006 as it applies in relation to an authorised insurance company carrying on long-term business.[4418]

An amount included in the relevant part of the company's balance sheet that represents a surplus in the fund or funds maintained by it in respect of its long-term business,[4419] and has not been allocated to policy holders or, as the

---

[4412] CA 2006, s 841(4)(a). [4413] CA 2006, s 841(4)(b)(i). [4414] CA 2006, s 841(4)(b)(ii).
[4415] CA 2006, s 841(4)(b)(iii). [4416] CA 2006, s 841(5)(a). [4417] CA 2006, s 841(5)(b).
[4418] CA 2006, s 843(1). [4419] CA 2006, s 843(2)(a).

case may be, carried forward unappropriated in accordance with asset identification rules made under s 142(2) of the Financial Services and Markets Act 2000 (c 8),[4420] is treated as a realised profit.

For the purposes of s 843(2) of the CA 2006, the relevant part of the balance sheet is the part of the balance sheet that represents accumulated profit or loss;[4421] a surplus in the fund or funds maintained by the company in respect of its long-term business means an excess of the assets representing that fund or those funds over the liabilities of the company attributable to its long-term business, as shown by an actuarial investigation.[4422]

A deficit in the fund or funds maintained by the company in respect of its long-term business is treated as a realised loss.

For this purpose a deficit in any such fund or funds means an excess of the liabilities of the company attributable to its long-term business over the assets representing that fund or those funds, as shown by an actuarial investigation.[4423]

Subject to s 843(2) and (4) of the CA 2006, any profit or loss arising in the company's long-term business is to be left out of account.[4424]

The term an 'actuarial investigation' means an investigation made into the financial condition of an authorised insurance company in respect of its long-term business carried out once in every period of 12 months in accordance with rules made under Part 10 of the Financial Services and Markets Act 2000,[4425] or carried out in accordance with a requirement imposed under s 166 of that Act, by an actuary appointed as actuary to the company.[4426]

The term 'long-term business' means business that consists of effecting or carrying out contracts of long-term insurance. This definition must be read with s 22 of the Financial Services and Markets Act 2000, any relevant order under that section and Schedule 2 to that Act.[4427]

Treatment of development costs

18.20 Section 844 of the CA 2006 states that where development costs are shown or included as an asset in a company's accounts, any amount shown or included in respect of those costs is treated for the purposes of s 830 of the CA 2006 (distributions to be made out of profits available for the purpose) as a realised loss,[4428] and for the purposes of s 832 of the CA 2006 (distributions by investment companies out of accumulated revenue profits) as a realised revenue loss.[4429]

This is subject to the following exceptions.

[4420] CA 2006, s 843(2)(b).   [4421] CA 2006, s 843(3)(a).   [4422] CA 2006, s 843(3)(b).
[4423] CA 2006, s 843(4).   [4424] CA 2006, s 843(5).   [4425] CA 2006, s 843(6)(a).
[4426] CA 2006, s 843(6)(b).   [4427] CA 2006, s 843(7).   [4428] CA 2006, s 844(1)(a).
[4429] CA 2006, s 844(1)(b).

Section 844(1) of the CA 2006 does not apply to any part of that amount representing an unrealised profit made on revaluation of those costs.[4430]

Section 844(1) of the CA 2006 does not apply if (a) there are special circumstances in the company's case justifying the directors in deciding that the amount there mentioned is not to be treated as required by s 844(1) of the CA 2006;[4431] (b) it is stated (i) in the case of Companies Act accounts, in the note required by regulations under s 396 of the CA 2006 as to the reasons for showing development costs as an asset,[4432] or (ii) in the case of IAS accounts, in any note to the accounts,[4433] that the amount is not to be so treated; and (c) the note explains the circumstances relied upon to justify the decision of the directors to that effect.[4434]

Distributions in kind

Distributions in kind: determination of amounts

18.21 Section 845 of the CA 2006 applies for determining the amount of a distribution consisting of or including, or treated as arising in consequence of, the sale, transfer or other disposition by a company of a non-cash asset where at the time of the distribution the company has profits available for distribution,[4435] and if the amount of the distribution were to be determined in accordance with this section, the company could make the distribution without contravening Part 23 of the CA 2006.[4436]

The amount of the distribution (or the relevant part of it) is taken to be in a case where the amount or value of the consideration for the disposition is not less than the book value of the asset, zero;[4437] in any other case, the amount by which the book value of the asset exceeds the amount or value of any consideration for the disposition.[4438]

For the purposes of s 845(1)(a) of the CA 2006, the company's profits available for distribution are treated as increased by the amount (if any) by which the amount or value of any consideration for the disposition exceeds the book value of the asset.[4439]

The term 'book value', in relation to an asset, means the amount at which the asset is stated in the relevant accounts,[4440] or where the asset is not stated in those accounts at any amount, zero.[4441]

The provisions of Chapter 2 of Part 23 of the CA 2006 (justification of distribution by reference to accounts) apply subject to this section.[4442]

[4430] CA 2006, s 844(2).   [4431] CA 2006, s 844(3)(a).   [4432] CA 2006, s 844(3)(b)(i).
[4433] CA 2006, s 844(3)(b)(ii).   [4434] CA 2006, s 844(3)(c).   [4435] CA 2006, s 845(1)(a).
[4436] CA 2006, s 845(1)(b).   [4437] CA 2006, s 845(2)(a).   [4438] CA 2006, s 845(2)(b).
[4439] CA 2006, s 845(3).   [4440] CA 2006, s 845(4)(a).   [4441] CA 2006, s 845(4)(b).
[4442] CA 2006, s 845(5).

Distributions in kind: treatment of unrealised profits

18.22 Section 846 of the CA 2006 applies where a company makes a distribution consisting of or including, or treated as arising in consequence of, the sale, transfer or other disposition by the company of a non-cash asset,[4443] and any part of the amount at which that asset is stated in the relevant accounts represents an unrealised profit.[4444]

That profit is treated as a realised profit for the purpose of determining the lawfulness of the distribution in accordance with this Part (whether before or after the distribution takes place),[4445] and for the purpose of the application, in relation to anything done with a view to or in connection with the making of the distribution, of any provision of regulations under s 396 of the CA 2006 under which only realised profits are to be included in or transferred to the profit and loss account.[4446]

In *Capital Maintenance: Other Issues*,[4447] the Company Law Review Group explored the difficulties created by the decision in *Aveling Barford Ltd v Perion Ltd*[4448] and made a number of suggestions as to how these difficulties might be overcome. Section 845 of the CA 2006 is a new provision that removes doubts to which the decision in this case has given rise: in particular, when a transfer of an asset to a member amounts to a distribution. The concern behind this section is that, following the decision in *Aveling Barford*, it is unclear when intra-group transfers of assets can be conducted by reference to the asset's book value rather than its market value (which will frequently be higher than the book value).

The decision in *Aveling Barford* concerned the sale of a property by a company (which had no distributable profits) at a considerable undervalue to another company controlled by the company's ultimate sole beneficial shareholder. The transaction was held to be void as an unauthorised return of capital. Whilst this case decided nothing about a situation where a company that has distributable profits makes an intra-group transfer of assets at book value, there was a concern that, as such a transfer of an asset at book value may have an element of undervalue, the transaction would constitute a distribution, thereby requiring the company to have distributable profits sufficient to cover the difference in value. The result has been that companies are often required either to abandon a transfer or to structure it in a more complex way, for example, having the assets revalued and then sold (or distributed under s 276 of the CA 1985) so that the distributable reserves are increased by the 'realised profit' arising on the sale/distribution followed by a capital contribution of the asset to the relevant group member.

[4443] CA 2006, s 846(1)(a).   [4444] CA 2006, s 846(1)(b).   [4445] CA 2006, s 846(2)(a).
[4446] CA 2006, s 846(2)(b).   [4447] See paras 24–43.   [4448] [1989] BCLC 626.

Section 845 of the CA 2006 does not disturb the position in the *Aveling Barford* case such that where a company which does not have distributable profits makes a distribution by way of a transfer of assets at an undervalue, this will be an unlawful distribution contrary to Part 23 of the CA 2006.

It clarifies, however, the position where a company does have distributable profits and provides that where the conditions referred to in s 845(1)(a) and (b) of the CA 2006 are amounts of any distribution consisting of or arising from the sale, a transfer or other disposition by a company of a non-cash asset to a member of the company should be calculated by reference to the value at which that asset is included in the company's accounts, that is, its 'book value'. Thus, if an asset is transferred for a consideration not less than its book value, the amount of the distribution is zero, but if the asset is transferred for a consideration less than its book value, the amount of the distribution is equal to that shortfall (which will therefore need to be covered by distributable profits) – see s 845(2)(a) and (b) of the CA 2006. This avoids the potential need for many companies to carry out asset revaluations requiring professional advice, and incurring fees to advisors prior to making a distribution of a non-cash asset.

The conditions that must be satisfied for s 845(2)(a) and (b) of the CA 2006 to apply are that at the time of the disposition of the asset, the company must have profits available for distribution, and that if the amount of such a distribution were to be determined in accordance with this section, it could be made without contravening any of the provisions of Part 23 of the CA 2006 (for example, ss 830 and 831 of the CA 2006).

Under s 845(3) of the CA 2006, in determining whether a company has profits available for distribution (as defined in s 830 of the CA 2006), a company may treat any profit that would arise on the proposed disposition of the non-cash asset, (that is, the amount (if any) by which the consideration received exceeds the book value of the asset) as increasing its distributable profits.

Section 846 of the CA 2006 replaces s 276 of the CA 1985, which applies where a company *makes a distribution of or including a non-cash asset*, and allows a company that has revalued assets showing an unrealised profit in the accounts, to treat that profit as a realised profit where the distribution is one of, or including, a non-cash asset. Section 846 of the CA 2006 tracks the drafting of s 845 of the CA 2006, so that it applies not only where the company makes a distribution consisting of or including a non-cash asset, but also where a company makes a distribution arising from the sale, transfer or other disposition by it of a non-cash asset, in other words in the same circumstances that are described in s 845 of the CA 2006.

758 A Guide to the Companies Act 2006

Consequences of unlawful distribution

Consequences of unlawful distribution

18.23 Section 847 of the CA 2006 applies where a distribution, or part of one, made by a company to one of its members is made in contravention of Part 23 of the CA 2006.[4449]

If at the time of the distribution, the member knows or has reasonable grounds for believing that it is so made, he is liable to repay it (or that part of it, as the case may be) to the company,[4450] or in the case of a distribution made otherwise than in cash, to pay the company a sum equal to the value of the distribution (or part) at that time.[4451]

This is without prejudice to any obligation imposed apart from this section on a member of a company to repay a distribution unlawfully made to him.[4452]

Section 847 of the CA 2006 does not apply in relation to financial assistance given by a company in contravention of ss 678 or 679 of the CA 2006,[4453] or any payment made by a company in respect of the redemption or purchase by the company of shares in itself.[4454]

Other matters

Preserving certain older provisions in articles

18.24 Section 848 of the CA 2006 sets out to preserve certain older provisions in articles. Where immediately before the relevant date a company was authorised by a provision of its articles to apply its unrealised profits in paying up in full or in part unissued shares to be allotted to members of the company as fully or partly paid bonus shares, that provision continues (subject to any alteration of the articles) as authority for those profits to be so applied after that date.[4455]

For this purpose the relevant date for companies registered in Great Britain, is 22 December 1980;[4456] and for companies registered in Northern Ireland, 1 July 1983.[4457]

Restriction on application of unrealised profits

18.25 Section 849 of the CA 2006 states that a company must not apply an unrealised profit in paying up debentures or any amounts unpaid on its issued shares.

[4449] CA 2006, s 847(1).   [4450] CA 2006, s 847(2)(a).   [4451] CA 2006, s 847(2)(b).
[4452] CA 2006, s 847(3).   [4453] CA 2006, s 847(4)(a).   [4454] CA 2006, s 847(4)(b).
[4455] CA 2006, s 848(1).   [4456] CA 2006, s 848(2)(a).   [4457] CA 2006, s 848(2)(b).

Treatment of certain older profits or losses

18.26 Section 850 of the CA 2006 applies to the treatment of certain older profits or losses. It states that where the directors of a company are, after making all reasonable enquiries, unable to determine whether a particular profit made before the relevant date is realised or unrealised, they may treat the profit as realised.[4458]

Where the directors of a company, after making all reasonable enquiries, are unable to determine whether a particular loss made before the relevant date is realised or unrealised, they may treat the loss as unrealised.[4459]

The relevant date is for companies registered in Great Britain, 22 December 1980;[4460] and for companies registered in Northern Ireland, 1 July 1983.[4461]

Application of rules of law restricting distributions

18.27 Section 851 of the CA 2006: except as provided in this section, the provisions of this Part are without prejudice to any rule of law restricting the sums out of which, or the cases in which, a distribution may be made.[4462]

For the purposes of any rule of law requiring distributions to be paid out of profits or restricting the return of capital to members, s 845 of the CA 2006 (distributions in kind: determination of amounts) applies to determine the amount of any distribution or return of capital consisting of or including, or treated as arising in consequence of the sale, transfer or other disposition by a company of a non-cash asset;[4463] and s 846 of the CA 2006 (distributions in kind: treatment of unrealised profits) applies as it applies for the purposes of Part 23 of the CA 2006.[4464]

The references to distributions are to amounts regarded as distributions for the purposes of any such rule of law as referred to in s 851(1) of the CA 2006.[4465]

Section 851 of the CA 2006 is a new provision that preserves the existing common law rules on unlawful distributions (see s 851(1) of the CA 2006) – which continue to be an essential component in determining what amounts to an unlawful distribution.

Section 851(2) of the CA 2006 makes an exception to this: in particular, it provides that the lawfulness and amount of distributions in kind are established by the statutory rules in ss 845 and 846 of the CA 2006 and not by any applicable common law rules.

[4458] CA 2006, s 850(1).   [4459] CA 2006, s 850(2).   [4460] CA 2006, s 850(3)(a).
[4461] CA 2006, s 850(3)(b).   [4462] CA 2006, s 851(1).   [4463] CA 2006, s 851(2)(a).
[4464] CA 2006, s 851(2)(b).   [4465] CA 2006, s 851(3).

Saving for other restrictions on distributions

18.28 Section 852 of the CA 2006 states that the provisions of Part 23 of the CA 2006 are without prejudice to any enactment, or any provision of a company's articles, restricting the sums out of which, or the cases in which, a distribution may be made.

Minor definitions

18.29 Under s 853 of the CA 2006, the following provisions apply for the purposes of Part 23 of the CA 2006.[4466]

The references to profit or losses of any description are to profits or losses of that description made at any time;[4467] and except where the context otherwise requires, are to profits or losses of a revenue or capital character.[4468]

The term 'capitalisation', in relation to a company's profits, means any of the following operations (whenever carried out) applying the profits in wholly or partly paying up unissued shares in the company to be allotted to members of the company as fully or partly paid bonus shares;[4469] or transferring the profits to capital redemption reserve.[4470]

The references to 'realised profits' and 'realised losses', in relation to a company's accounts, are to such profits or losses of the company as fall to be treated as realised in accordance with principles generally accepted at the time when the accounts are prepared, with respect to the determination for accounting purposes of realised profits or losses.

Section 853(4) of the CA 2006 is without prejudice to the construction of any other expression (where appropriate) by reference to accepted accounting principles or practice;[4471] or any specific provision for the treatment of profits or losses of any description as realised.[4472]

The term 'fixed assets' means assets of a company which are intended for use on a continuing basis in the company's activities.[4473]

[4466] CA 2006, s 853(1).   [4467] CA 2006, s 853(2)(a).   [4468] CA 2006, s 853(2)(b).
[4469] CA 2006, s 853(3)(a).   [4470] CA 2006, s 853(3)(b).   [4471] CA 2006, s 853(5)(a).
[4472] CA 2006, s 853(5)(b).   [4473] CA 2006, s 853(6).

Acquisition by Limited Company of its Own Shares

Introduction

19.1 Part 18 of the CA 2006 is concerned with acquisition by a limited company of its own shares. The sections on financial assistance replace various provisions in Chapters 6 and 7 of Part 5 of the CA 1985, and make substantive changes to some of those provisions. Sections 658–659, 662, 666–677, 680–683, 687, 691, 693, 695–701, 704–706, 710–713, 716–719, 721–726, 728–729, 731 and 733 of the CA 2006 restate various provisions of the CA 1985, but do not make any changes to those provisions.

General Provisions

Introductory

General rule against limited company acquiring its own shares

19.2 Section 658 of the CA 2006 sets out the general rule against a limited company acquiring its own shares. A limited company must not acquire its own shares, whether by purchase, subscription or otherwise, except in accordance with the provisions of Part 18 of the CA 2006.[4474]

If a company purports to act in contravention of this section an offence is committed by the company,[4475] and every officer of the company who is in default,[4476] and the purported acquisition is void.[4477] A person guilty of an offence under s 658 of the CA 2006 is liable on conviction on indictment, to imprisonment for a term not exceeding two years or a fine (or both);[4478] on summary conviction in England and Wales, to imprisonment for a term not exceeding 12 months or a fine not exceeding the statutory maximum (or both);[4479] in Scotland or Northern Ireland, to imprisonment for a term not

---

[4474] CA 2006, s 658(1). [4475] CA 2006, s 658(2)(a)(i). [4476] CA 2006, s 658(2)(a)(ii).
[4477] CA 2006, s 658(2)(b). [4478] CA 2006, s 658(3)(a). [4479] CA 2006, s 658(3)(b)(i).

exceeding six months or a fine not exceeding the statutory maximum (or both).[4480]

Exceptions to general rule

19.3 Section 659 of the CA 2006 provides exceptions to the general rule. A limited company may acquire any of its own fully paid shares otherwise than for valuable consideration.[4481]

Section 658 of the CA 2006 does not prohibit the following: (a) the acquisition of shares in a reduction of capital duly made;[4482] (b) the purchase of shares in pursuance of an order of the court under (i) s 98 of the CA 2006 (application to court to cancel a resolution for re-registration as a private company),[4483] (ii) s 721(6) of the CA 2006 (powers of court on objection to a redemption or purchase of shares out of capital),[4484] (iii) s 759 of the CA 2006 (remedial order in case of a breach of prohibition of public offers by a private company),[4485] or (iv) Part 30 of the CA 2006 (protection of members against unfair prejudice);[4486] (c) the forfeiture of shares, or the acceptance of shares surrendered in lieu, in pursuance of the company's articles, for failure to pay any sum payable in respect of the shares.[4487]

Shares held by company's nominee

Treatment of shares held by nominee

19.4 Section 660 of the CA 2006 deals with the treatment of shares held by a nominee. It applies where shares in a limited company are taken by a subscriber to the memorandum as a nominee of the company,[4488] are issued to a nominee of the company,[4489] or are acquired by a nominee of the company, partly paid up, from a third person.[4490]

For all purposes, the shares are to be treated as held by the nominee on his own account,[4491] and the company is to be regarded as having no beneficial interest in them.[4492]

Section 660 of the CA 2006 does not apply: (a) to shares acquired otherwise than by subscription by a nominee of a public company, where (i) a person acquires shares in the company with financial assistance given to him, directly or indirectly, by the company for the purpose of or in connection with the acquisition,[4493] and (ii) the company has a beneficial interest in the

---

[4480] CA 2006, s 658(3)(b)(ii).   [4481] CA 2006, s 659(1).   [4482] CA 2006, s 659(2)(a).
[4483] CA 2006, s 659(2)(b)(i).   [4484] CA 2006, s 659(2)(b)(ii).
[4485] CA 2006, s 659(2)(b)(iii).   [4486] CA 2006, s 659(2)(b)(iv).   [4487] CA 2006, s 659(3).
[4488] CA 2006, s 660(1)(a).   [4489] CA 2006, s 660(1)(b).   [4490] CA 2006, s 660(1)(c).
[4491] CA 2006, s 660(2)(a).   [4492] CA 2006, s 660(2)(b).   [4493] CA 2006, s 660(3)(a)(i).

shares;[4494] (b) to shares acquired by a nominee of the company when the company has no beneficial interest in the shares.[4495]

Liability of others where nominee fails to make a payment in respect of shares

19.5 Section 661 of the CA 2006 sets out the liability of others where a nominee fails to make a payment in respect of shares. It applies where shares in a limited company (a) are taken by a subscriber to the memorandum as nominee of the company;[4496] (b) are issued to a nominee of the company;[4497] or (c) are acquired by a nominee of the company, partly paid up, from a third person.[4498]

If the nominee, having been called on to pay any amount for the purposes of paying up, or paying any premium on, the shares, fails to pay that amount within 21 days from being called on to do so, then in the case of shares that he agreed to take as subscriber to the memorandum, the other subscribers to the memorandum,[4499] and in any other case, the directors of the company when the shares were issued to or acquired by him,[4500] are jointly and severally liable with him to pay that amount.

If in proceedings for the recovery of an amount under s 661(2) of the CA 2006, it appears to the court that the subscriber or director has acted honestly and reasonably,[4501] and having regard to all the circumstances of the case, ought fairly to be relieved from liability,[4502] the court may relieve him, either wholly or in part, from his liability on such terms as the court thinks fit.

If a subscriber to a company's memorandum or a director of a company has reason to apprehend that a claim will or might be made for the recovery of any such amount from him he may apply to the court for relief,[4503] and the court has the same power to relieve him as it would have had in proceedings for recovery of that amount.[4504]

Section 661 of the CA 2006 does not apply to shares acquired by a nominee of the company when the company has no beneficial interest in the shares.[4505]

Sections 660 and 661 of the CA 2006 restate ss 144 and 145(1) of the CA 1985, but with the clarification that they apply to shares taken by a subscriber to the memorandum as nominee of the company.

[4494] CA 2006, s 660(3)(a)(ii). [4495] CA 2006, s 660(3)(b). [4496] CA 2006, s 661(1)(a).
[4497] CA 2006, s 661(1)(b). [4498] CA 2006, s 661(10)(c). [4499] CA 2006, s 661(2)(a).
[4500] CA 2006, s 661(2)(b). [4501] CA 2006, s 661(3)(a). [4502] CA 2006, s 661(3)(b).
[4503] CA 2006, s 661(4)(a). [4504] CA 2006, s 661(4)(b). [4505] CA 2006, s 661(5).

Shares held by or for a public company

Duty to cancel shares in a public company held by or for the company

19.6 Section 662 of the CA 2006 deals with the duty to cancel shares in a public company held by or for the company. It applies in the case of a public company (a) where shares in the company are forfeited, or surrendered to the company in lieu of forfeiture, in pursuance of the articles, for failure to pay any sum payable in respect of the shares;[4506] (b) where shares in the company are surrendered to the company in pursuance of s 102C(1)(b) of the Building Societies Act 1986 (c 53);[4507] (c) where shares in the company are acquired by it (otherwise than in accordance with this Part or Part of the 30 of the CA 2006 (protection of members against unfair prejudice)) and the company has a beneficial interest in the shares;[4508] (d) where a nominee of the company acquires shares in the company from a third party without financial assistance being given directly or indirectly by the company and the company has a beneficial interest in the shares;[4509] or (e) where a person acquires shares in the company, with financial assistance given to him, directly or indirectly, by the company for the purpose of or in connection with the acquisition, and the company has a beneficial interest in the shares.[4510]

Unless the shares or any interest of the company in them are previously disposed of, the company must cancel the shares and diminish the amount of the company's share capital by the nominal value of the shares cancelled,[4511] and where the effect is that the nominal value of the company's allotted share capital is brought below the authorised minimum, apply for re-registration as a private company, stating the effect of the cancellation.[4512]

It must do so no later than (a) in a case within s 662(1)(a) or (b) of the CA 2006, three years from the date of the forfeiture or surrender;[4513] (b) in a case within s 662(1)(c) or (d) of the CA 2006, three years from the date of acquisition;[4514] and (c) in a case within s 662(1)(e) of the CA 2006, one year from the date of acquisition.[4515]

The directors of the company may take any steps necessary to enable the company to comply with s 662 of the CA 2006, and may do so without complying with the provisions of Chapter 10 of Part 17 of the CA 2006 (reduction of capital).[4516] See also s 664 of the CA 2006 (re-registration as private company in consequence of cancellation).

Neither the company nor, in a case within s 662(1)(d) or (e) of the CA 2006, the nominee or other shareholder may exercise any voting rights in respect of the shares.[4517] Any purported exercise of those rights is void.[4518]

[4506] CA 2006, s 662(1)(a).   [4507] CA 2006, s 662(1)(b).   [4508] CA 2006, s 662(1)(c).
[4509] CA 2006, s 662(1)(d).   [4510] CA 2006, s 662(1)(e).   [4511] CA 2006, s 662(2)(a).
[4512] CA 2006, s 662(2)(b).   [4513] CA 2006, s 662(3)(a).   [4514] CA 2006, s 662(3)(b).
[4515] CA 2006, s 662(3)(c).   [4516] CA 2006, s 662(4).   [4517] CA 2006, s 662(5).
[4518] CA 2006, s 662(6).

Notice of cancellation of shares

19.7 Section 663 of the CA 2006 states that where a company cancels shares in order to comply with s 662 of the CA 2006, it must within one month after the shares are cancelled give notice to the registrar, specifying the shares cancelled.[4519]

The notice must be accompanied by a statement of capital.[4520]

The statement of capital must state with respect to the company's share capital immediately following the cancellation (a) the total number of shares of the company;[4521] (b) the aggregate nominal value of those shares;[4522] (c) for each class of shares (i) prescribed particulars of the rights attached to the shares,[4523] (ii) the total number of shares of that class,[4524] and (iii) the aggregate nominal value of shares of that class;[4525] and (d) the amount paid up and the amount (if any) unpaid on each share (whether on account of the nominal value of the share or by way of premium).[4526]

If a default is made in complying with this section, an offence is committed by the company,[4527] and every officer of the company who is in default.[4528] A person guilty of an offence under s 663 of the CA 2006 is liable on summary conviction to a fine not exceeding level 3 on the standard scale and, for continued contravention, a daily default fine not exceeding one-tenth of level 3 on the standard scale.[4529]

Section 663 of the CA 2006 restates s 122(1)(f) and (2) of the CA 1985 and Schedule 24 of the CA 1985. Section 663(2) and (3) of the CA 2006 update the current notice requirements to require a company that has cancelled shares in order to comply with s 662 of the CA 2006 to provide the registrar with a statement of capital at the time of giving notice of the cancellation.

Re-registration as a private company in consequence of a cancellation

19.8 Section 664 of the CA 2006 sets out the provisions dealing with re-registration as a private company in consequence of a cancellation. Where a company is obliged to re-register as a private company in order to comply with s 662 of the CA 2006, the directors may resolve that the company should be so re-registered.[4530] Chapter 3 of Part 3 of the CA 2006 (resolutions affecting a company's constitution) applies to any such resolution.

The resolution may make such changes in the company's name,[4531] and in the company's articles,[4532] as are necessary in connection with its becoming a private company.

[4519] CA 2006, s 663(1).   [4520] CA 2006, s 663(2).   [4521] CA 2006, s 663(3)(a).
[4522] CA 2006, s 663(3)(b).   [4523] CA 2006, s 663(3)(c)(i).   [4524] CA 2006, s 663(3)(c)(ii).
[4525] CA 2006, s 663(3)(d).   [4526] CA 2006, s 663(3)(c)(iii).   [4527] CA 2006, s 663(4)(a).
[4528] CA 2006, s 663(4)(b).   [4529] CA 2006, s 663(5).   [4530] CA 2006, s 664(1).
[4531] CA 2006, s 664(2)(a).   [4532] CA 2006, s 664(2)(b).

The application for re-registration must contain a statement of the company's proposed name on re-registration.[4533]

The application must be accompanied by a copy of the resolution (unless a copy has already been forwarded under Chapter 3 of Part 3 of the CA 2006),[4534] a copy of the company's articles as amended by the resolution,[4535] and a statement of compliance.[4536]

The statement of compliance required is a statement that the requirements of this section as to re-registration as a private company have been complied with.[4537] The registrar may accept the statement of compliance as sufficient evidence that the company is entitled to be re-registered as a private company.[4538]

Section 664 of the CA 2006 replaces s 147(2) and (3) of the CA 1985. These provisions have been updated to reflect the fact that as of 2006, it is not possible to alter the memorandum, and that key information of a type which was previously in the memorandum is now in the articles. The resolution to re-register as a private company in consequence of a duty to cancel shares, however, still needs to be filed with the registrar under Chapter 3 of Part 3 of the CA 2006.

There is also a new requirement in s 664(3) of the CA 2006, for the application for re-registration to be accompanied by a statement of the company's proposed name on re-registration. Section 664(5) and (6) of the CA 2006 is also new. Consistent with the approach taken where a company is formed as a private company under the CA 2006 (see s 9 of the CA 2006), where a public company applies to re-register as private under this section, the application for re-registration must be accompanied by a statement of compliance.

Issue of certificate of incorporation on re-registration

19.9 Section 665 of the CA 2006 sets out the issue of certificate of incorporation on re-registration. If on an application under s 664 of the CA 2006, the registrar is satisfied that the company is entitled to be re-registered as a private company, the company shall be re-registered accordingly.[4539]

The registrar must issue a certificate of incorporation altered to meet the circumstances of the case.[4540] The certificate must state that it is issued on re-registration and the date on which it is issued.[4541]

On the issue of the certificate the company by virtue of the issue of the certificate becomes a private company,[4542] and the changes in the company's name and articles take effect.[4543]

[4533] CA 2006, s 664(3).   [4534] CA 2006, s 664(4)(a).   [4535] CA 2006, s 664(4)(b).
[4536] CA 2006, s 664(4)(c).   [4537] CA 2006, s 664(5).   [4538] CA 2006, s 664(6).
[4539] CA 2006, s 665(1).   [4540] CA 2006, s 665(2).   [4541] CA 2006, s 665(3).
[4542] CA 2006, s 665(4)(a).   [4543] CA 2006, s 665(4)(b).

The certificate is conclusive evidence that the requirements of the CA 2006 as to re-registration have been complied with.[4544]

Section 665 of the CA 2006 replaces s 147(4)(a) of the CA 1985 and restates s 147(4) and (4)(b) of the CA 1985. This provision was updated to reflect the fact that now companies are not capable of altering, and do not need to alter their memoranda. Section 665(3) of the CA 2006 is new. Consistent with the approach taken in Part 7 of the CA 2006, a certificate of incorporation issued on the re-registration of a company under s 664 of the CA 2006 needs to specify that it is being issued on the re-registration of the company and the date on which it is issued.

Effect of failure to re-register

19.10 Section 666 of the CA 2006 deals with the effect of failure to re-register. If a public company that is required by s 662 of the CA 2006 to apply to be re-registered as a private company fails to do so before the end of the period specified in s 662(3) of the CA 2006, Chapter 1 of Part 20 of the CA 2006 (prohibition of public offers by private company) applies to it as if it were a private company.[4545]

Subject to that, the company continues to be treated as a public company until it is so re-registered.[4546]

Offence in case of failure to cancel shares or re-register

19.11 Section 667 of the CA 2006 applies to offence in cases of failure to cancel shares or re-register.

It applies where a company, when required to do by s 662 of the CA 2006 fails to cancel any shares,[4547] or fails to make an application for re-registration as a private company,[4548] within the time specified in s 662(3) of the CA 2006.

An offence is committed by the company,[4549] and every officer of the company who is in default.[4550] A person guilty of an offence under this section is liable on summary conviction to a fine not exceeding level 3 on the standard scale and, for continued contravention, a daily default fine not exceeding one-tenth of level 3 on the standard scale.[4551]

Application of provisions to a company re-registering as a public company

19.12 Section 668 of the CA 2006 applies where, after shares in a private company: (a) are forfeited in pursuance of the company's articles or are

---

[4544] CA 2006, s 665(5). [4545] CA 2006, s 666(1). [4546] CA 2006, s 666(2).
[4547] CA 2006, s 667(1)(a). [4548] CA 2006, s 667(1)(b). [4549] CA 2006, s 667(2)(a).
[4550] CA 2006, s 667(2)(b). [4551] CA 2006, s 667(3).

surrendered to the company in lieu of forfeiture;[4552] (b) are acquired by the company (otherwise than by any of the methods permitted by this Part or Part 30 of the CA 2006 (protection of members against unfair prejudice)), the company having a beneficial interest in the shares;[4553] (c) are acquired by a nominee of the company from a third party without financial assistance being given directly or indirectly by the company, the company having a beneficial interest in the shares;[4554] or (d) are acquired by a person with financial assistance given to him, directly or indirectly, by the company for the purpose of or in connection with the acquisition, the company having a beneficial interest in the shares,[4555] the company is re-registered as a public company.

In that case the provisions of ss 662–667 of the CA 2006 apply to the company as if it had been a public company at the time of the forfeiture, surrender or acquisition, subject to the following modification.[4556]

The modification is that the period specified in s 662(3)(a), (b) or (c) of the CA 2006 (period for complying with obligations under that section) runs from the date of the re-registration of the company as a public company.[4557]

Transfer to reserve on acquisition of shares by public company or nominee

19.13 Section 669 of the CA 2006 deals with the transfer to reserve on acquisition of shares by a public company or nominee. Where a public company, or a nominee of a public company, acquires shares in the company,[4558] and those shares are shown in a balance sheet of the company as an asset,[4559] an amount equal to the value of the shares must be transferred out of profits available for dividend to a reserve fund, and is not then available for distribution.

Section 669(1) of the CA 2006 applies to an interest in shares as it applies to shares.[4560] As it so applies, the reference to the value of the shares shall be read as a reference to the value to the company of its interest in the shares.[4561]

Charges of public company on own shares

Public companies: general rule against lien or charge on own shares

19.14 Section 670 of the CA 2006 sets out the rule against lien or charge on own shares in respect of public companies. A lien or other charge of a public company on its own shares (whether taken expressly or otherwise) is void, except as permitted by this section.[4562]

[4552] CA 2006, s 668(1)(a).   [4553] CA 2006, s 668(1)(b).   [4554] CA 2006, s 668(1)(c).
[4555] CA 2006, s 668(1)(d).   [4556] CA 2006, s 668(2).   [4557] CA 2006, s 668(3).
[4558] CA 2006, s 669(1)(a).   [4559] CA 2006, s 669(1)(b).   [4560] CA 2006, s 669(2).
[4561] CA 2006, s 669(2).   [4562] CA 2006, s 670(1).

In the case of any description of company, a charge is permitted if the shares are not fully paid up and the charge is for an amount payable in respect of the shares.[4563]

In the case of a company whose ordinary business includes the lending of money,[4564] or consists of the provision of credit or the bailment (in Scotland, hiring) of goods under a hire-purchase agreement, or both,[4565] a charge is permitted (whether the shares are fully paid or not) if it arises in connection with a transaction entered into by the company in the ordinary course of that business.

In the case of a company that has been re-registered as a public company, a charge is permitted if it was in existence immediately before the application for re-registration.[4566]

Supplementary provisions

Interests to be disregarded in determining whether a company has beneficial interest

19.15 Section 671 of the CA 2006 states that in determining for the purposes of Chapter 1 of Part 22 of the CA 2006 whether a company has a beneficial interest in shares, there must be disregarded any such interest as is mentioned in s 672 of the CA 2006 (residual interest under pension scheme or employees' share scheme), s 673 of the CA 2006 (employer's charges and other rights of recovery), or s 674 of the CA 2006 (rights as personal representative or trustee).

Residual interest under a pension scheme or employees' share scheme

19.16 Section 672 of the CA 2006 sets out the residual interest under a pension scheme or employees' share scheme. Where the shares are held on trust for the purposes of a pension scheme or employees' share scheme, there shall be disregarded any residual interest of the company that has not vested in possession.[4567]

The term 'residual interest' means a right of the company to receive any of the trust property in the event of all the liabilities arising under the scheme having been satisfied or provided for,[4568] or the company ceasing to participate in the scheme,[4569] or the trust property at any time exceeding what is necessary for satisfying the liabilities arising or expected to arise under the scheme.[4570]

In s 672(2) of the CA 2006, the reference to a right includes a right

---

[4563] CA 2006, s 670(2).   [4564] CA 2006, s 670(3)(a).   [4565] CA 2006, s 670(3)(b).
[4566] CA 2006, s 670(4).   [4567] CA 2006, s 672(1).   [4568] CA 2006, s 672(2)(a).
[4569] CA 2006, s 672(2)(b).   [4570] CA 2006, s 672(2)(c).

dependent on the exercise of a discretion vested by the scheme in the trustee or another person,[4571] and the reference to liabilities arising under a scheme includes liabilities that have resulted, or may result, from the exercise of any such discretion.[4572]

For the purposes of this section a residual interest vests in possession in a case within s 672(2)(a) of the CA 2006, on the occurrence of the event mentioned there (whether or not the amount of the property receivable pursuant to the right is ascertained);[4573] or in a case within s 672(2)(b) or (c) of the CA 2006, when the company becomes entitled to require the trustee to transfer to it any of the property receivable pursuant to that right.[4574]

Where by virtue of this section shares are exempt from ss 660 or 661 of the CA 2006 (shares held by the company's nominee) at the time they are taken, issued or acquired but the residual interest in question vests in possession before they are disposed of or fully paid up, those sections apply to the shares as if they had been taken, issued or acquired on the date on which that interest vests in possession.[4575]

Where by virtue of this section shares are exempt from ss 662–668 of the CA 2006 (shares held by or for a public company) at the time they are acquired but the residual interest in question vests in possession before they are disposed of, those sections apply to the shares as if they had been acquired on the date on which the interest vests in possession.[4576]

Employer's charges and other rights of recovery

19.17 Section 673 of the CA 2006 sets out the employer's charges and other rights of recovery. Where the shares are held on trust for the purposes of a pension scheme there shall be disregarded (a) any charge or lien on, or set-off against, any benefit or other right or interest under the scheme for the purpose of enabling the employer or former employer of a member of the scheme to obtain the discharge of a monetary obligation due to him from the member;[4577] (b) any right to receive from the trustee of the scheme, or as trustee of the scheme to retain, an amount that can be recovered or retained (i) under s 61 of the Pension Schemes Act 1993 (c 48), or otherwise, as reimbursement or partial reimbursement for any contributions equivalent premium paid in connection with the scheme under Part 3 of that Act,[4578] or (ii) under s 57 of the Pension Schemes (Northern Ireland) Act 1993 (c 49), or otherwise, as reimbursement or partial reimbursement for any contributions equivalent premium paid in connection with the scheme under Part 3 of that Act.[4579]

[4571] CA 2006, s 672(3)(a).   [4572] CA 2006, s 672(3)(b).   [4573] CA 2006, s 672(4)(a).
[4574] CA 2006, s 672(4)(b).   [4575] CA 2006, s 672(5).   [4576] CA 2006, s 672(6).
[4577] CA 2006, s 673(1)(a).   [4578] CA 2006, s 673(1)(b)(i).   [4579] CA 2006, s 673(1)(b)(ii).

Where the shares are held on trust for the purposes of an employees' share scheme, there shall be disregarded any charge or lien on, or set-off against, any benefit or other right or interest under the scheme for the purpose of enabling the employer or former employer of a member of the scheme to obtain the discharge of a monetary obligation due to him from the member.[4580]

Rights as personal representative or trustee

19.18 Section 674 of the CA 2006 deals with the rights as personal representative or trustee. Where the company is a personal representative or trustee, there shall be disregarded any rights that the company has in that capacity including, in particular, any right to recover its expenses or be remunerated out of the estate or trust property,[4581] and any right to be indemnified out of that property for any liability incurred by reason of any act or omission of the company in the performance of its duties as personal representative or trustee.[4582]

Meaning of 'pension scheme'

19.19 Section 675 of the CA 2006 defines the term pension scheme. It means a scheme for the provision of benefits consisting of or including relevant benefits for or in respect of employees or former employees.[4583]

In s 675(1) of the CA 2006, the term 'relevant benefits' means any pension, lump sum, gratuity or other like benefit given or to be given on retirement or on death or in anticipation of retirement or, in connection with past service, after retirement or death.[4584]

Application of provisions to directors

19.20 Section 676 of the CA 2006 states that for the purposes of Chapter 1 of Part 18 of the CA 2006 references to 'employer' and 'employee', in the context of a pension scheme or employees' share scheme, shall be read as if a director of a company were employed by it.

Financial Assistance for Purchase of Own Shares

19.21 Chapter 2 of Part 18 of the CA 2006 addresses the financial assistance for purchase of own shares. The sections on financial assistance replace Chapter 6 of Part 5 of the CA 1985, which contains a prohibition of giving

---

[4580] CA 2006, s 673(2).   [4581] CA 2006, s 674(a).   [4582] CA 2006, s 674(b).
[4583] CA 2006, s 675(1).   [4584] CA 2006, s 675(2).

financial assistance (broadly defined) by a company or any its subsidiaries for the purpose of the acquisition of shares in itself. There are exceptions that apply to all companies, contained in s 153 of the CA 1985, and a relaxation of the general rule for private companies in ss 155–158 of the CA 1985.

As recommended by the Company Law Review Group,[4585] the CA 2006 abolishes the prohibition on giving financial assistance by a private company for the purchase of shares in itself and, as a consequence, the relaxations for a private company for the purchase of shares in itself. As a consequence, the relaxations for private companies (sometimes referred to as the 'whitewash' procedure) are no longer required. The provisions in ss 155–158 of the CA 1985 have therefore been repealed and are not carried forward in the CA 2006.

Introductory

Meaning of 'financial assistance'

19.22 Section 677 of the CA 2006 sets out the definition of financial assistance. In Chapter 2 of Part 18 of the CA 2006, the term 'financial assistance' means (a) financial assistance given by way of gift;[4586] (b) financial assistance given (i) by way of guarantee, security or indemnity (other than an indemnity in respect of the indemnifier's own neglect or default),[4587] or (ii) by way of release or waiver;[4588] (c) financial assistance given (i) by way of a loan or any other agreement under which any of the obligations of the person giving the assistance are to be fulfilled at a time when in accordance with the agreement any obligation of another party to the agreement remains unfulfilled,[4589] or (ii) by way of the novation of, or the assignment (in Scotland, assignation) of rights arising under, a loan or such other agreement;[4590] or (d) any other financial assistance given by a company where: (i) the net assets of the company are reduced to a material extent by the giving of the assistance,[4591] or (ii) the company has no net assets.[4592]

The term 'net assets' here means the aggregate amount of the company's assets less the aggregate amount of its liabilities.[4593]

For this purpose a company's liabilities include where the company draws up Companies Act individual accounts, any provision of a kind specified for the purposes of this subsection by regulations under s 396 of the CA 2006;[4594] and, where the company draws up IAS individual accounts, any provision made in those accounts.[4595]

[4585] *Final Report*, para 10.6. [4586] CA 2006, s 677(1)(a). [4587] CA 2006, s 677(1)(b)(i).
[4588] CA 2006, s 677(1)(b)(ii). [4589] CA 2006, s 677(1)(c)(i). [4590] CA 2006, s 677(1)(c)(ii).
[4591] CA 2006, s 677(1)(d)(i). [4592] CA 2006, s 677(1)(d)(ii). [4593] CA 2006, s 677(2).
[4594] CA 2006, s 677(3)(a). [4595] CA 2006, s 677(3)(b).

Circumstances in which financial assistance prohibited

Assistance for acquisition of shares in a public company

19.23 Section 678 of the CA 2006 deals with assistance in the acquisition of shares in a public company. Where a person is acquiring or proposing to acquire shares in a public company, it is not lawful for that company, or a company that is a subsidiary of that company, to give financial assistance directly or indirectly for the purpose of the acquisition before or at the same time as the acquisition takes place.[4596]

Section 678(1) of the CA 2006 does not prohibit a company from giving financial assistance for the acquisition of shares in it or its holding company if the company's principal purpose in giving the assistance is not to give it for the purpose of any such acquisition;[4597] or the giving of the assistance for that purpose is only an incidental part of some larger purpose of the company,[4598] and the assistance is given in good faith in the interests of the company.

Where a person has acquired shares in a company,[4599] and a liability has been incurred (by that or another person) for the purpose of the acquisition,[4600] it is not lawful for that company, or a company that is a subsidiary of that company, to give financial assistance directly or indirectly for the purpose of reducing or discharging the liability if, at the time the assistance is given, the company in which the shares were acquired is a public company.

Section 678(3) of the CA 2006 does not prohibit a company from giving financial assistance if the company's principal purpose in giving the assistance is not to reduce or discharge any liability incurred by a person for the purpose of the acquisition of shares in the company or its holding company;[4601] or the reduction or discharge of any such liability is only an incidental part of some larger purpose of the company,[4602] and the assistance is given in good faith in the interests of the company.

This section applies subject to ss 681 and 682 of the CA 2006 (unconditional and conditional exceptions to prohibition).[4603]

Section 678 of the CA 2006 replaces s 151 (1) and (2) of the CA 1985 and restates s 153(1) and (2) of the CA 1985. The key change is that the prohibition on private companies providing financial assistance for a purchase of own shares is not carried forward.

The general prohibition on the giving of financial assistance by a public company is required by the Second Company Law Directive (77/91/EEC) and this prohibition is retained in amended s 151(1). As under the CA 1985, the prohibition extends to post-acquisition assistance (see s 678(3) of the CA 2006).

[4596] CA 2006, s 678(1).   [4597] CA 2006, s 678(2)(a).   [4598] CA 2006, s 678(2)(b).
[4599] CA 2006, s 678(3)(a).   [4600] CA 2006, s 678(3)(b).   [4601] CA 2006, s 678(4)(a).
[4602] CA 2006, s 678(4)(b).   [4603] CA 2006, s 678(5).

The prohibition on the giving of post-acquisition assistance only applies if the company in which the shares were acquired is a public company at the time that the assistance is given (see s 678(3) of the CA 2006). It follows that where a company has re-registered as a private company since the shares were acquired and is a private company at the time the post-acquisition assistance is given, the prohibition in this section will not apply. However, if at the time the shares were acquired the company was a private company, but at the time the post-acquisition assistance is given it has re-registered as a public company, the prohibition will apply.

The provisions of s 153(1) and (2) of the CA 1985 are retained in s 678(2) and (4) of the CA 2006, which carries forward the current exemption from the prohibition on the giving of financial assistance: namely, that such assistance is not prohibited if the principal purpose of the assistance is not to give it for the purpose of an acquisition of shares, or where this assistance is incidental to some other larger purpose of the company and (in either case) where the assistance is given in good faith in the interests of the company. As before, in these circumstances no offence is committed by the company or its officers (see s 680 of the CA 2006). The changes introduced by s 678 of the CA 2006 also give statutory effect to the decision in *Arab Bank plc v Mercantile Holdings Ltd*:[4604] namely, that the statutory prohibition on a company giving financial assistance for the purpose of acquiring its own shares or shares in its holding company does not apply to the giving of assistance by a subsidiary incorporated in an overseas jurisdiction.

In *Arab Bank*, Millett J considered the geographical scope of s 151 of the CA 1985 and concluded that this had inadvertently been altered during the consolidation of UK companies legislation in 1985. In particular, the CA 1985 appears to go further than the CA 1980 and, in interpreting the current provision, Millett J applied the presumption that, in the absence of a contrary intention, s 151 of the CA 1985 could not have extra-territorial effect. The difficulty with the CA 1985 provision arises as a result of how the prohibition is framed: in particular, the prohibition applies 'to the company or any of its subsidiaries', and 'subsidiary', as defined in s 736 of the CA 1985, includes foreign companies. The prohibition in the Act is restricted to UK public companies and their UK subsidiaries as a result of the definition of 'company in s 1. Subsection (1) of that section makes it clear that, unless the context otherwise requires, 'company' means a company that is formed and registered under the Act or a former UK Companies Act.

[4604] [1994] 2 All ER 74.

*Assistance by a public company in the acquisition of shares in its
private holding company*

19.24 Section 679 of the CA 2006 states that where a person is acquiring or
proposing to acquire shares in a private company, it is not lawful for a public
company that is a subsidiary of that company to give financial assistance
directly or indirectly for the purpose of the acquisition before or at the same
time as the acquisition takes place.[4605]

Section 679(1) of the CA 2006 does not prohibit a company from giving
financial assistance for the acquisition of shares in its holding company if
the company's principal purpose in giving the assistance is not to give it for
the purpose of any such acquisition,[4606] or the giving of the assistance for
that purpose is only an incidental part of some larger purpose of the
company,[4607] and the assistance is given in good faith in the interests of the
company.

Where a person has acquired shares in a private company,[4608] and a liability
has been incurred (by that or another person) for the purpose of the acquisition,[4609] it is not lawful for a public company that is a subsidiary of that
company to give financial assistance directly or indirectly for the purpose of
reducing or discharging the liability.

Section 679(3) of the CA 2006 does not prohibit a company from giving
financial assistance if the company's principal purpose in giving the assistance is not to reduce or discharge any liability incurred by a person for the
purpose of the acquisition of shares in its holding company,[4610] or the reduction or discharge of any such liability is only an incidental part of some larger
purpose of the company,[4611] and the assistance is given in good faith in the
interests of the company.

Section 679 of the CA 2006 applies subject to ss 681 and 682 of the CA
2006 (unconditional and conditional exceptions to prohibition).[4612]

Section 679 of the CA 2006 replaces ss 151(1) and (2) and 153(1) and (2) of
the CA 1985.

Like section 678, s 679 of the CA 2006 does not carry forward the prohibition on private companies providing financial assistance for the purchase of
its own shares, but the current prohibition on the giving of financial assistance by a public company subsidiary for the purpose of an acquisition of
shares in its private holding company is retained. Section 679 of the CA 2006
also retains the prohibition on the giving of post-acquisition assistance by a
public company subsidiary.

[4605] CA 2006, s 679(1).   [4606] CA 2006, s 679(2)(a).   [4607] CA 2006, s 679(2)(b).
[4608] CA 2006, s 679(3)(a).   [4609] CA 2006, s 679(3)(b).   [4610] CA 2006, s 679(4)(a).
[4611] CA 2006, s 679(4)(b).   [4612] CA 2006, s 679(5).

Prohibited financial assistance is an offence

19.25 Section 680 of the CA 2006 states that if a company contravenes s 678(1) or (3) of the CA 2006 or s 679(1) or (3) of the CA 2006 (prohibited financial assistance) an offence is committed by the company,[4613] and every officer of the company who is in default.[4614] A person guilty of an offence under this section is liable on conviction on indictment, to imprisonment for a term not exceeding two years or a fine (or both);[4615] on summary conviction in England and Wales, to imprisonment for a term not exceeding 12 months or to a fine not exceeding the statutory maximum (or both);[4616] in Scotland or Northern Ireland, to imprisonment for a term not exceeding six months, or to a fine not exceeding the statutory maximum (or both).[4617]

Exceptions from prohibition

Unconditional exceptions

19.26 Section 681 of the CA 2006 states that neither s 678 nor s 679 of the CA 2006 prohibits a transaction to which this section applies.[4618]

Those transactions are: (a) a distribution of the company's assets by way of (i) a dividend lawfully made,[4619] or (ii) a distribution in the course of a company's winding up;[4620] (b) an allotment of bonus shares;[4621] (c) a reduction of capital under the CA, Part 17 to Chapter 10 of the CA 2006;[4622] (d) a redemption of shares under Chapter 3 to Part 18 of the CA 2006 or a purchase of shares under Chapter 4 to Part 18 of the CA 2006;[4623] (e) anything done in pursuance of an order of the court under Part 26 of the CA 2006 (order sanctioning compromise or arrangement with members or creditors);[4624] (f) anything done under an arrangement made in pursuance of s 110 of the CA the Insolvency Act 1986 (c 45) or Article 96 of the Insolvency (Northern Ireland) Order 1989 (SI 1989/2405 (NI 19)) (liquidator in winding up accepting shares as consideration for sale of company's property);[4625] (g) anything done under an arrangement made between a company and its creditors that is binding on the creditors by virtue of Part 1 of the Insolvency Act 1986 or Part 2 of the Insolvency (Northern Ireland) Order 1989 (SI 1989/2405 (NI 19)).[4626]

[4613] CA 2006, s 680(1)(a).   [4614] CA 2006, s 680(1)(b).   [4615] CA 2006, s 680(2)(a).

[4616] CA 2006, s 680(2)(b)(i).   [4617] CA 2006, s 680(2)(b)(ii).   [4618] CA 2006, s 681(1).

[4619] CA 2006, s 681(2)(a)(i).   [4620] CA 2006, s 681(2)(a)(ii).   [4621] CA 2006, s 681(2)(b).

[4622] CA 2006, s 681(2)(c).   [4623] CA 2006, s 681(2)(d).   [4624] CA 2006, s 681(2)(e).

[4625] CA 2006, s 681(2)(f).   [4626] CA 2006, s 681(2)(g).

Conditional exceptions

19.27 Section 682 of the CA 2006 states that neither s 678 nor s 679 of the CA 2006 prohibits a transaction to which this section applies (a) if the company giving the assistance is a private company;[4627] or (b) if the company giving the assistance is a public company and (i) the company has net assets that are not reduced by the giving of the assistance,[4628] or (ii) to the extent that those assets are so reduced, the assistance is provided out of distributable profits.[4629]

The transactions to which this section applies are (a) where the lending of money is part of the ordinary business of the company, the lending of money in the ordinary course of the company's business;[4630] (b) the provision by the company, in good faith in the interests of the company or its holding company, of financial assistance for the purposes of an employees' share scheme;[4631] (c) the provision of financial assistance by the company for the purposes of or in connection with anything done by the company (or another company in the same group) for the purpose of enabling or facilitating transactions in shares in the first-mentioned company or its holding company between, and involving the acquisition of beneficial ownership of those shares by (i) bona fide employees or former employees of that company (or another company in the same group),[4632] or (ii) spouses or civil partners, widows, widowers or surviving civil partners, or minor children or step-children of any such employees or former employees;[4633] (d) the making by the company of loans to persons (other than directors) employed in good faith by the company with a view to enabling those persons to acquire fully paid shares in the company or its holding company to be held by them by way of beneficial ownership.[4634]

The term 'net assets' refers to the amount by which the aggregate of the company's assets exceeds the aggregate of its liabilities.[4635]

For this purpose the amount of both assets and liabilities shall be taken to be as stated in the company's accounting records immediately before the financial assistance is given,[4636] and 'liabilities' includes any amount retained as reasonably necessary for the purpose of providing for a liability the nature of which is clearly defined and that is either likely to be incurred or certain to be incurred but uncertain as to the amount, or as to the date on which it will arise.[4637]

For the purposes of s 679(2)(c) of the CA 2006, a company is in the same group as another company if it is a holding company or subsidiary of that company or a subsidiary of a holding company of that company.[4638]

[4627] CA 2006, s 682(1)(a).   [4628] CA 2006, s 682(1)(b)(i).   [4629] CA 2006, s 682(1)(b)(ii).
[4630] CA 2006, s 682(2)(a).   [4631] CA 2006, s 682(2)(b).   [4632] CA 2006, s 682(2)(c)(i).
[4633] CA 2006, s 682(2)(c)(ii).   [4634] CA 2006, s 682(2)(d).   [4635] CA 2006, s 682(3).
[4636] CA 2006, s 682(4)(a).   [4637] CA 2006, s 682(4)(b).   [4638] CA 2006, s 682(5).

Supplementary

Definitions for this Chapter

19.28 Section 683 of the CA 2006 sets out various definitions to Chapter 2. The term 'distributable profits', in relation to the giving of any financial assistance (a) means those profits out of which the company could lawfully make a distribution equal in value to that assistance;[4639] and (b) includes, in a case where the financial assistance consists of or includes, or is treated as arising in consequence of, the sale, transfer or other disposition of a non-cash asset, any profit that, if the company were to make a distribution of that character would be available for that purpose (see s 846 of the CA 2006);[4640] and 'distribution' has the same meaning as in Part 23 of the CA 2006 (distributions) (see s 829 of the CA 2006).

In Chapter 2 to Part 18 of the CA 2006, a reference to a person incurring a liability includes his changing his financial position by making an agreement or arrangement (whether enforceable or unenforceable, and whether made on his own account or with any other person) or by any other means,[4641] and a reference to a company giving financial assistance for the purposes of reducing or discharging a liability incurred by a person for the purpose of the acquisition of shares includes its giving such assistance for the purpose of wholly or partly restoring his financial position to what it was before the acquisition took place.[4642]

Redeemable Shares

19.29 Chapter 3 to Part 18 of the CA 2006 is concerned with redeemable shares. Under s 159 of the CA 1985, a company that was limited by shares, or limited by guarantee and having a share capital, could, if authorised to do so by its articles, issue shares that could be redeemed at a future point in time at the option of the company or the shareholder. The provisions of s 159 of the CA 1985 are carried forward in the following sections but there are changes to the ways in which companies may issue redeemable shares and redeem such shares.

Power of a limited company to issue redeemable shares

19.30 Section 684 of the CA 2006 states that a limited company having a share capital may issue shares that are to be redeemed or are liable to be redeemed at the option of the company or the shareholder (redeemable shares), subject to the following provisions.[4643]

[4639] CA 2006, s 683(1)(a).   [4640] CA 2006, s 683(1)(b).   [4641] CA 2006, s 683(2)(a).
[4642] CA 2006, s 683(2)(b).   [4643] CA 2006, s 684(1).

The articles of a private limited company may exclude or restrict the issue of redeemable shares.[4644]

A public limited company may only issue redeemable shares if it is authorised to do so by its articles.[4645]

No redeemable shares may be issued at a time when there are no issued shares of the company that are not redeemable.[4646]

Section 684 of the CA 2006 replaces s 159(1) of the CA 1985 and restates s 159(2) of the CA 1985.

For private companies only, it removes the requirement for prior authorisation in the company's articles for a proposed allotment of redeemable shares. If they wish, the members may, however, restrict or prohibit the authority given to a company by this section, by including a provision to this effect in the company's articles (see s 684(2) of the CA 2006).

Terms and manner of a redemption

19.31 Section 685 of the CA 2006 is concerned with the terms and manner of a redemption. The directors of a limited company may determine the terms, conditions and manner of a redemption of shares if they are authorised to do so by the company's articles,[4647] or by a resolution of the company.[4648]

A resolution under s 685(1)(b) of the CA 2006 may be an ordinary resolution, even though it amends the company's articles.[4649]

Where the directors are authorised under s 685(1) of the CA 2006 to determine the terms, conditions and manner of redemption of shares they must do so before the shares are allotted,[4650] and any obligation of the company to state in a statement of capital the rights attached to the shares extends to the terms, conditions and manner of redemption.[4651]

Where the directors are not so authorised, the terms, conditions and manner of redemption of any redeemable shares must be stated in the company's articles.[4652]

Section 685 of the CA 2006 replaces s 160(3) of the CA 1985 (which provided that the terms and manner of redemption must be set out in the company's articles) and s 159A of the CA 1985 (also entitled 'terms and manner of redemption'), which was inserted into the CA 1985 by s 133 of the CA 1989 and remains uncommenced.

As recommended by the Company Law Review Group,[4653] s 685 of the CA 2006 enables the directors of both private and public companies alike to determine the terms, conditions and manner of a redemption of redeemable shares. The power conferred on the directors by this section requires prior

---

[4644] CA 2006, s 684(2).   [4645] CA 2006, s 684(3).   [4646] CA 2006, s 684(4).
[4647] CA 2006, s 685(1)(a).   [4648] CA 2006, s 685(1)(b).   [4649] CA 2006, s 685(2).
[4650] CA 2006, s 685(3)(a).   [4651] CA 2006, s 685(3)(b).   [4652] CA 2006, s 685(4).
[4653] *Final Report*, para 4.5.

authorisation by the company's members, either by resolution of the company or through the articles (see s 685(1) of the CA 2006). As recommended by the Company Law Review Group,[4654] the terms and conditions of redemption will have to be stated in the statement of capital required to be filed under s 555 of the CA 2006. If the directors are not authorised to set the terms of the redemption, then they must be set out in the company's articles (see s 685(4) of the CA 2006).

Where the directors exercise this power they must do so before the shares in question are allotted (see s 685(3) of the CA 2006).

Payment for redeemable shares

19.32 Section 686 of the CA 2006 states that redeemable shares in a limited company may not be redeemed unless they are fully paid.[4655] The terms of redemption of shares in a limited company may provide that the amount payable on redemption may, by agreement between the company and the holder of the shares, be paid on a date later than the redemption date.[4656]

Unless redeemed in accordance with a provision authorised by s 686(2) of the CA 2006, the shares must be paid for on redemption.[4657]

This section replaces s 159(3) of the CA 1985 (which required that where a company issued redeemable shares, the terms of redemption must provide for payment on redemption). It removes the requirement, in s 159(3) of the CA 1985, that the terms of redemption must provide for payment on redemption. This means that the terms of redemption may provide for the company and the holder of the shares to agree that payment may be made on a date later than the redemption date.

Financing of redemption

19.33 Section 687 of the CA 2006 states that a private limited company may redeem redeemable shares out of capital in accordance with Chapter 5 to Part 18 of the CA 2006.[4658]

Subject to that, redeemable shares in a limited company may only be redeemed out of distributable profits of the company,[4659] or the proceeds of a fresh issue of shares made for the purposes of the redemption.[4660]

Any premium payable on redemption of shares in a limited company must be paid out of distributable profits of the company, subject to the following provision.[4661]

If the redeemable shares were issued at a premium, any premium payable on their redemption may be paid out of the proceeds of a fresh issue of shares

---

[4654] *Final Report*, para 7.30.   [4655] CA 2006, s 686(1).   [4656] CA 2006, s 686(2).
[4657] CA 2006, s 686(3).   [4658] CA 2006, s 687(1).   [4659] CA 2006, s 687(2)(a).
[4660] CA 2006, s 687(2)(b).   [4661] CA 2006, s 687(3).

made for the purposes of the redemption, up to an amount equal to the aggregate of the premiums received by the company on the issue of the shares redeemed,[4662] or the current amount of the company's share premium account (including any sum transferred to that account in respect of premiums on the new shares),[4663] whichever is the less.

The amount of the company's share premium account is reduced by a sum corresponding (or by sums in the aggregate corresponding) to the amount of any payment made under s 687(4) of the CA 2006.[4664]

This section is subject to s 735(4) of the CA 2006 (terms of redemption enforceable in a winding up).[4665]

Redeemed shares treated as cancelled

19.34 Section 678 of the CA 2006 provides that where shares in a limited company are redeemed the shares are treated as cancelled,[4666] and the amount of the company's issued share capital is diminished accordingly by the nominal value of the shares redeemed.[4667]

This section restates s 160(4) of the CA 1985 but with the exception of the reference to the impact of the redemption on the authorised share capital of the company, the concept of which is not replicated under the Act.

Notice to registrar of a redemption

19.35 Under s 689 of the CA 2006, if a limited company redeems any redeemable shares it must within one month after doing so give notice to the registrar, specifying the shares redeemed.[4668]

The notice must be accompanied by a statement of capital.[4669]

The statement of capital must state with respect to the company's share capital immediately following the redemption (a) the total number of shares of the company;[4670] (b) the aggregate nominal value of those shares;[4671] (c) for each class of shares (i) prescribed particulars of the rights attached to the shares,[4672] (ii) the total number of shares of that class,[4673] and (iii) the aggregate nominal value of shares of that class;[4674] and (d) the amount paid up and the amount (if any) unpaid on each share (whether on account of the nominal value of the share or by way of premium).[4675]

If default is made in complying with this section, an offence is committed by the company,[4676] and every officer of the company who is in default.[4677] A

[4662] CA 2006, s 687(4)(a).   [4663] CA 2006, s 687(4)(b).   [4664] CA 2006, s 687(5).
[4665] CA 2006, s 687(6).   [4666] CA 2006, s 688(a).   [4667] CA 2006, s 688(b).
[4668] CA 2006, s 689(1).   [4669] CA 2006, s 689(2).   [4670] CA 2006, s 689(3)(a).
[4671] CA 2006, s 689(3)(b).   [4672] CA 2006, s 689(3)(c)(i).   [4673] CA 2006, s 689(3)(c)(ii).
[4674] CA 2006, s 689(3)(c)(iii).   [4675] CA 2006, s 689(3)(d).   [4676] CA 2006, s 689(4)(a).
[4677] CA 2006, s 689(4)(b).

person guilty of an offence under this section is liable on summary conviction to a fine not exceeding level 3 on the standard scale and, for continued contravention, a daily default fine not exceeding one-tenth of level 3 on the standard scale.[4678]

This section restates ss 122(1)(e) and 122(2) of the CA 1985 and Schedule 24 of the CA 1985 but there is a new requirement for a statement of capital where a company gives notice to the registrar of a redemption of redeemable shares (see s 689(2) and (3) of the CA 2006).

Purchase Of Own Shares

19.36 Chapter 4 to Part 18 of the CA 2006 is concerned with purchase of own shares. Section 162 of the CA 1985 enabled a company limited by shares or limited by guarantee and having a share capital to purchase its own shares, provided it was authorised to do so by the articles. It was common for members to give authority for such a purchase of own shares through the articles, see, for example, regulation 35 of the CA 1985, Table A.

General provisions

Power of a limited company to purchase its own shares

19.37 Section 690 of the CA 2006 is concerned with power of a limited company to purchase its own shares. A limited company having a share capital may purchase its own shares (including any redeemable shares), subject to the following provisions of Chapter 5 to Part 18 of the CA 2006,[4679] and any restriction or prohibition in the company's articles.[4680]

A limited company may not purchase its own shares if as a result of the purchase there would no longer be any issued shares of the company other than redeemable shares or shares held as treasury shares.[4681]

This section replaces s 162(1) of the CA 1985 and restates s 162(3) of the CA 1985.

In line with the recommendations of the Company Law Review Group,[4682] s 690 of the CA 2006 removes the requirement for prior authorisation in a company's articles for a purchase of its own shares (including any redeemable shares) by the company but makes it clear that, if they wish, the members may restrict or prohibit a purchase of the company's own shares by including a provision to this effect in the company's articles.

[4678] CA 2006, s 689(5).   [4679] CA 2006, s 690(1)(a).   [4680] CA 2006, s 690(1)(b).
[4681] CA 2006, s 690(2).   [4682] *Completing the Structure*, para 2.15.

Payment for purchase of a company's own shares

19.38 Section 691 of the CA 2006 states that a limited company may not purchase its own shares unless they are fully paid.[4683]

Where a limited company purchases its own shares, the shares must be paid for on purchase.[4684]

Financing of the purchase of a company's own shares

19.39 Section 692 of the CA 2006 provides that a private limited company may purchase its own shares out of capital in accordance with Chapter 5 to Part 18 of the CA 2006.[4685]

Subject to that (a) a limited company may only purchase its own shares out of (i) distributable profits of the company,[4686] or (ii) the proceeds of a fresh issue of shares made for the purpose of financing the purchase;[4687] and (b) any premium payable on the purchase by a limited company of its own shares must be paid out of the distributable profits of the company, subject to s 693(3) of the CA 2006.[4688]

If the shares to be purchased were issued at a premium, any premium payable on their purchase by the company may be paid out of the proceeds of a fresh issue of shares made for the purpose of financing the purchase, up to an amount equal to the aggregate of the premiums received by the company on the issue of the shares purchased,[4689] or the current amount of the company's share premium account (including any sum transferred to that account in respect of premiums on the new shares),[4690] whichever is the less.

The amount of the company's share premium account is reduced by a sum corresponding (or by sums in the aggregate corresponding) to the amount of any payment made under s 692(3) of the CA 2006.[4691]

Section 692 of the CA 2006 applies subject to s 735(4) of the CA 2006 (terms of purchase enforceable in a winding up).[4692]

This section restates, the provisions of ss 160(1) and (2) and 162(2) of the CA 1985 on a redemption of own shares that are applicable to a purchase of own shares, and makes such adaptations to those provisions as are necessary to ensure that the restated provisions work in this context.

[4683] CA 2006, s 691(1).   [4684] CA 2006, s 691(2).   [4685] CA 2006, s 692(1).
[4686] CA 2006, s 692(2)(a)(i).   [4687] CA 2006, s 692(2)(a)(ii).   [4688] CA 2006, s 692(2)(b).
[4689] CA 2006, s 692(3)(a).   [4690] CA 2006, s 692(3)(b).   [4691] CA 2006, s 692(4).
[4692] CA 2006, s 692(5).

Authority for the purchase of a company's own shares

Authority for the purchase of a company's own shares

19.40 Section 693 of the CA 2006 sets out the authority for the purchase of a company'sown shares. A limited company may only purchase its own shares by an off-market purchase, in pursuance of a contract approved in advance in accordance with s 694 of the CA 2006;[4693] or by a market purchase, authorised in accordance with s 701 of the CA 2006.[4694]

A purchase is 'off-market' if the shares either are purchased otherwise than on a recognised investment exchange,[4695] or are purchased on a recognised investment exchange but are not subject to a marketing arrangement on the exchange.[4696]

For this purpose a company's shares are subject to a marketing arrangement on a recognised investment exchange if (a) they are listed under Part 6 of the Financial Services and Markets Act 2000 (c 8);[4697] or (b) the company has been afforded facilities for dealings in the shares to take place on the exchange (i) without prior permission for individual transactions from the authority governing that investment exchange,[4698] and (ii) without limit as to the time during which those facilities are to be available.[4699]

A purchase is a 'market purchase' if it is made on a recognised investment exchange and is not an off-market purchase by virtue of s 693(2)(b) of the CA 2006.[4700]

The term 'recognised investment exchange' means a recognised investment exchange (within the meaning of Part 18 of the Financial Services and Markets Act 2000) other than an overseas exchange (within the meaning of that Part).[4701]

Authority for an off-market purchase

Authority for an off-market purchase

19.41 Section 694 of the CA 2006 states that a company may only make an off-market purchase of its own shares in pursuance of a contract approved prior to the purchase in accordance with this section.[4702]

Either the terms of the contract must be authorised by a special resolution of the company before the contract is entered into,[4703] or the contract must provide that no shares may be purchased in pursuance of the contract until its terms have been authorised by a special resolution of the company.[4704]

[4693] CA 2006, s 693(1)(a).　[4694] CA 2006, s 693(1)(b).　[4695] CA 2006, s 693(2)(a).
[4696] CA 2006, s 693(2)(b).　[4697] CA 2006, s 693(3)(a).　[4698] CA 2006, s 693(3)(b)(i).
[4699] CA 2006, s 693(3)(b)(ii).　[4700] CA 2006, s 693(4).　[4701] CA 2006, s 693(5).
[4702] CA 2006, s 694(1).　[4703] CA 2006, s 694(2)(a).　[4704] CA 2006, s 694(2)(b).

The contract may be a contract, entered into by the company and relating to shares in the company, which does not amount to a contract to purchase the shares but under which the company may (subject to any conditions) become entitled or obliged to purchase the shares.[4705]

The authority conferred by a resolution under this section may be varied, revoked or from time to time renewed by a special resolution of the company.[4706]

In the case of a public company a resolution conferring, varying or renewing authority must specify a date on which the authority is to expire, which must not be later than 18 months after the date on which the resolution is passed.[4707]

A resolution conferring, varying, revoking or renewing authority under this section is subject to s 695[4708] of the CA 2006 (the exercise of voting rights), and s 696 of the CA 2006 (disclosure of details of a contract).

Section 694 of the CA 2006 replaces ss 164(2) and 165(2) of the CA 1985 and restates ss 164(1), (3) and (4) and 165(1) of the CA 1985.

Under CA 1985, a company could only enter into a contract for an off-market purchase of shares if the shareholders approved the contract by special resolution before the contract is entered into. An off-market purchase of shares is a purchase that is not conducted through a recognised investment exchange (for example, the London Stock Market).

Section 694 of the CA 2006 enables a company to enter into a contract for an off-market purchase of its own shares conditional on the contract being approved by the shareholders. This will save companies valuable time as it will be possible for the directors to negotiate and agree the terms of a contract for an off-market purchase of shares ahead of seeking shareholder approval. If, however, the shareholders do not subsequently pass a special resolution approving the contract, the company may not purchase the shares in question and the contract will lapse.

Resolution authorising an off-market purchase: the exercise of voting rights

19.42 Section 694 of the CA 2006 applies to a resolution to confer, vary, revoke or renew authority for the purposes of s 694 of the CA 2006 (authority for an off-market purchase of a company's own shares).[4709]

Where the resolution is proposed as a written resolution, a member who holds shares to which the resolution relates is not an eligible member.[4710]

Where the resolution is proposed at a meeting of the company, it is not effective if any member of the company holding shares to which the

---

[4705] CA 2006, s 694(3).   [4706] CA 2006, s 694(4).   [4707] CA 2006, s 694(5).
[4708] CA 2006, s 694(6).   [4709] CA 2006, s 695(1).   [4710] CA 2006, s 695(2).

resolution relates exercises the voting rights carried by any of those shares in voting on the resolution,[4711] and the resolution would not have been passed if he had not done so.[4712]

For this purpose, a member who holds shares to which the resolution relates is regarded as exercising the voting rights carried by those shares, not only if he votes in respect of them on a poll on the question whether the resolution shall be passed, but also if he votes on the resolution otherwise than on a poll;[4713] any member of the company may demand a poll on that question;[4714] a vote and a demand for a poll by a person as proxy for a member are the same respectively as a vote and a demand by the member.[4715]

Resolution authorising an off-market purchase: disclosure of details of a contract

19.43 Section 696 of the CA 2006 applies in relation to a resolution to confer, vary, revoke or renew authority for the purposes of s 694 of the CA 2006 (authority for off-market purchase of a company's own shares).[4716]

A copy of the contract (if it is in writing) or a memorandum setting out its terms (if it is not) must be made available to members (a) in the case of a written resolution, by being sent or submitted to every eligible member at or before the time at which the proposed resolution is sent or submitted to him;[4717] (b) in the case of a resolution at a meeting, by being made available for inspection by members of the company both (i) at the company's registered office for not less than 15 days ending with the date of the meeting,[4718] and (ii) at the meeting itself.[4719]

A memorandum of contract terms so made available must include the names of the members holding shares to which the contract relates.[4720]

A copy of the contract so made available must have annexed to it a written memorandum specifying such of those names as do not appear in the contract itself.[4721]

The resolution is not validly passed if the requirements of this section are not complied with.[4722]

Variation of contract for off-market purchase

19.44 Section 697 of the CA 2006 states that a company may only agree to a variation of a contract authorised under s 694 of the CA 2006 (authority for

[4711] CA 2006, s 695(3)(a).   [4712] CA 2006, s 695(3)(b).   [4713] CA 2006, s 695(4)(a).
[4714] CA 2006, s 695(4)(b).   [4715] CA 2006, s 695(4)(c).   [4716] CA 2006, s 696(1).
[4717] CA 2006, s 696(2)(a).   [4718] CA 2006, s 696(2)(b)(i).   [4719] CA 2006, s 696(2)(b)(ii).
[4720] CA 2006, s 696(3).   [4721] CA 2006, s 696(4).   [4722] CA 2006, s 696(5).

off-market purchase) if the variation is approved in advance in accordance with this section.[4723]

The terms of the variation must be authorised by a special resolution of the company before it is agreed to.[4724]

That authority may be varied, revoked or from time to time renewed by a special resolution of the company.[4725]

In the case of a public company a resolution conferring, varying or renewing authority must specify a date on which the authority is to expire, which must not be later than 18 months after the date on which the resolution is passed.[4726]

A resolution conferring, varying, revoking or renewing authority under this section is subject to ss 698 of the CA 2006 (exercise of voting rights), and 699 of the CA 2006 (disclosure of details of variation).[4727]

Resolution authorising variation: exercise of voting rights

19.45 Section 698 of the CA 2006 applies to a resolution to confer, vary, revoke or renew authority for the purposes of s 697 of the CA 2006 (variation of contract for off-market purchase of own shares).[4728]

Where the resolution is proposed as a written resolution, a member who holds shares to which the resolution relates is not an eligible member.[4729]

Where the resolution is proposed at a meeting of the company, it is not effective if any member of the company holding shares to which the resolution relates exercises the voting rights carried by any of those shares in voting on the resolution,[4730] and the resolution would not have been passed if he had not done so.[4731]

For this purpose (a) a member who holds shares to which the resolution relates is regarded as exercising the voting rights carried by those shares not only if he votes in respect of them on a poll on the question whether the resolution shall be passed, but also if he votes on the resolution otherwise than on a poll;[4732] (b) any member of the company may demand a poll on that question;[4733] (c) a vote and a demand for a poll by a person as proxy for a member are the same respectively as a vote and a demand by the member.[4734]

Resolution authorising a variation: disclosure of details of a variation

19.46 Section 699 of the CA 2006 applies in relation to a resolution under s 697 of the CA 2006 (variation of a contract for off-market purchase of own shares).[4735]

[4723] CA 2006, s 697(1). [4724] CA 2006, s 697(2). [4725] CA 2006, s 697(3).
[4726] CA 2006, s 697(4). [4727] CA 2006, s 697(5). [4728] CA 2006, s 698(1).
[4729] CA 2006, s 698(2). [4730] CA 2006, s 698(3)(a). [4731] CA 2006, s 698(3)(b).
[4732] CA 2006, s 698(4)(a). [4733] CA 2006, s 698(4)(b). [4734] CA 2006, s 698(4)(c).
[4735] CA 2006, s 699(1).

A copy of the proposed variation (if it is in writing) or a written memorandum giving details of the proposed variation (if it is not) must be made available to members (a) in the case of a written resolution, by being sent or submitted to every eligible member at or before the time at which the proposed resolution is sent or submitted to him;[4736] (b) in the case of a resolution at a meeting, by being made available for inspection by members of the company both (i) at the company's registered office for not less than 15 days ending with the date of the meeting,[4737] and (ii) at the meeting itself.[4738]

There must also be made available as mentioned in s 699(2) of the CA 2006 a copy of the original contract or, as the case may be, a memorandum of its terms, together with any variations previously made.[4739]

A memorandum of the proposed variation so made available must include the names of the members holding shares to which the variation relates.[4740]

A copy of the proposed variation so made available must have annexed to it a written memorandum specifying such of those names as do not appear in the variation itself.[4741]

The resolution is not validly passed if the requirements of this section are not complied with.[4742]

Release of a company's rights under contract for an off-market purchase

19.47 Section 700 of the CA 2006 states that an agreement by a company to release its rights under a contract approved under s 694 of the CA 2006 (authorisation of an off-market purchase) is void unless the terms of the release agreement are approved in advance in accordance with this section.[4743]

The terms of the proposed agreement must be authorised by a special resolution of the company before the agreement is entered into.[4744] That authority may be varied, revoked or from time to time renewed by a special resolution of the company.[4745]

In the case of a public company a resolution conferring, varying or renewing authority must specify a date on which the authority is to expire, which must not be later than 18 months after the date on which the resolution is passed.[4746]

The provisions of ss 698 of the CA 2006 (exercise of voting rights), and 699 of the CA 2006 (disclosure of details of variation), apply to a resolution authorising a proposed release agreement as they apply to a resolution authorising a proposed variation.[4747]

[4736] CA 2006, s 699(2)(a).   [4737] CA 2006, s 699(2)(b)(i).   [4738] CA 2006, s 699(2)(b)(ii).
[4739] CA 2006, s 699(3).   [4740] CA 2006, s 699(4).   [4741] CA 2006, s 699(5).
[4742] CA 2006, s 699(6).   [4743] CA 2006, s 700(1).   [4744] CA 2006, s 700(2).
[4745] CA 2006, s 700(3).   [4746] CA 2006, s 700(4).   [4747] CA 2006, s 700(5).

Authority for a market purchase

Authority for a market purchase

19.48 Under s 701 of the CA 2006, a company may only make a market purchase of its own shares if the purchase has first been authorised by a resolution of the company.[4748]

That authority may be general or limited to the purchase of shares of a particular class or description,[4749] and may be unconditional or subject to conditions.[4750]

The authority must specify the maximum number of shares authorised to be acquired,[4751] and determine both the maximum and minimum prices that may be paid for the shares.[4752]

The authority may be varied, revoked or from time to time renewed by a resolution of the company.[4753]

A resolution conferring, varying or renewing authority must specify a date on which it is to expire, which must not be later than 18 months after the date on which the resolution is passed.[4754]

A company may make a purchase of its own shares after the expiry of the time limit specified if (a) the contract of purchase was concluded before the authority expired;[4755] and (b) the terms of the authority permitted the company to make a contract of purchase that would or might be executed wholly or partly after its expiration.[4756]

A resolution to confer or vary authority under this section may determine either or both the maximum and minimum price for purchase by specifying a particular sum,[4757] or providing a basis or formula for calculating the amount of the price (but without reference to any person's discretion or opinion).[4758]

Chapter 3 of Part 3 of the CA 2006 (resolutions affecting a company's constitution) applies to a resolution under this section.[4759]

Supplementary provisions

Copy of contract or memorandum to be available for inspection

19.49 Section 702 of the CA 2006 applies where a company has entered into a contract approved under s 694 of the CA 2006 (authorisation of contract for an off-market purchase),[4760] or a contract for a purchase authorised under s 701 of the CA 2006 (authorisation of a market purchase).[4761]

[4748] CA 2006, s 701(1).   [4749] CA 2006, s 701(2)(a).   [4750] CA 2006, s 701(2)(b).
[4751] CA 2006, s 701(3)(a).   [4752] CA 2006, s 701(3)(b).   [4753] CA 2006, s 701(4).
[4754] CA 2006, s 701(5).   [4755] CA 2006, s 701(6)(a).   [4756] CA 2006, s 701(6)(b).
[4757] CA 2006, s 701(7)(a).   [4758] CA 2006, s 701(7)(b).   [4759] CA 2006, s 701(8).
[4760] CA 2006, s 702(1)(a).   [4761] CA 2006, s 702(1)(b).

The company must keep available for inspection a copy of the contract,[4762] or if the contract is not in writing, a written memorandum setting out its terms.[4763]

The copy or memorandum must be kept available for inspection from the conclusion of the contract until the end of the period of ten years beginning with the date on which the purchase of all the shares in pursuance of the contract is completed,[4764] or the date on which the contract otherwise determines.[4765]

The copy or memorandum must be kept available for inspection at the company's registered office,[4766] or at a place specified in regulations under s 1136 of the CA 2006.[4767]

The company must give notice to the registrar of the place at which the copy or memorandum is kept available for inspection,[4768] and of any change in that place,[4769] unless it has at all times been kept at the company's registered office.

Every copy or memorandum required to be kept under this section must be kept open to inspection without charge by any member of the company,[4770] and in the case of a public company, by any other person.[4771]

The provisions of this section apply to a variation of a contract as they apply to the original contract.[4772]

Section 702 of the CA 2006 replaces s 169(4) and (9) of the CA 1985. Under the CA 1985, where a company enters into a contract for a purchase of own shares it must make available for inspection a copy of the relevant contract or a memorandum of its terms at the company's registered office for a period of ten years. Section 702(4) of the CA 2006 alters the current requirements by providing that the contract may, alternatively, be kept available for inspection at a place specified in regulations made under section 1136. If the company is a private company, the contract must be available for inspection by any of its members; otherwise it must be open to inspection by anyone. If default is made an offence is committed by the company and every officer in default.

Section 702(5) of the CA 2006 is a new provision that requires companies to give notice to the registrar of the place where the contract is kept available for inspection. This is consequential on the choice conferred on companies under s 702(4) of the CA 2006 as to where such documents are kept.

Enforcement of right to inspect a copy or memorandum

19.50 Section 703 of the CA 2006 states that if a default is made in complying with s 702(2), (3) or (4) of the CA 2006, or default is made for 14 days in

---

[4762] CA 2006, s 702(2)(a).   [4763] CA 2006, s 702(2)(b).   [4764] CA 2006, s 702(3)(a).
[4765] CA 2006, s 702(3)(b).   [4766] CA 2006, s 702(4)(a).   [4767] CA 2006, s 702(4)(b).
[4768] CA 2006, s 702(5)(a).   [4769] CA 2006, s 702(5)(b).   [4770] CA 2006, s 702(6)(a).
[4771] CA 2006, s 702(6)(b).   [4772] CA 2006, s 702(7).

complying with s 702(5) of the CA 2006, or an inspection required under s 702(6) of the CA 2006 is refused, an offence is committed by the company,[4773] and every officer of the company who is in default.[4774] A person guilty of an offence under this section is liable on summary conviction to a fine not exceeding level 3 on the standard scale and, for continued contravention, a daily default fine not exceeding one-tenth of level 3 on the standard scale.[4775]

In the case of refusal of an inspection required under s 702(6) of the CA 2006 the court may by order compel an immediate inspection.[4776]

This section replaces s 169(7) of the CA 1985 and Schedule 24 of the CA 1985. It retains the existing offences for failing to keep available/allow inspection of the contract/memorandum as required under s 702 of the CA 2006, but with the addition of a new offence for failure to notify the registrar of the place where such documentation is kept. It also restates s 169(8) of the CA 1985.

No assignment of a company's right to purchase its own shares

19.51 Section 704 of the CA 2006 provides that the rights of a company under a contract authorised under s 694 of the CA 2006 (authority for an off-market purchase),[4777] or s 701 of the CA 2006 (authority for a market purchase)[4778] are not capable of being assigned.

Payments apart from purchase price to be made out of distributable profits

19.52 Under s 705 of the CA 2006, a payment made by a company in consideration of (a) acquiring any right with respect to the purchase of its own shares in pursuance of a contingent purchase contract approved under s 694 of the CA 2006 (authorisation of an off-market purchase),[4779] (b) the variation of any contract approved under that section,[4780] or (c) the release of any of the company's obligations with respect to the purchase of any of its own shares under a contract (i) approved under s 694,[4781] or (ii) authorised under s 701 of the CA 2006 (authorisation of a market purchase),[4782] must be made out of the company's distributable profits.

If this requirement is not met in relation to a contract, then (a) in a case within s 705 (1)(a) of the CA 2006, no purchase by the company of its own shares in pursuance of that contract may be made under this Chapter;[4783] (b) in a case within s 705(1)(b) of the CA 2006, no such purchase following the

---

[4773] CA 2006, s 703(1)(a).   [4774] CA 2006, s 703(1)(b).   [4775] CA 2006, s 703(2).
[4776] CA 2006, s 703(3).   [4777] CA 2006, s 704(a).   [4778] CA 2006, s 704(b).
[4779] CA 2006, s 705(1)(a).   [4780] CA 2006, s 705(1)(b).   [4781] CA 2006, s 705(1)(c)(i).
[4782] CA 2006, s 705(1)(c)(ii).   [4783] CA 2006, s 705(2)(a).

variation may be made under this Chapter;[4784] (c) in a case within s 705(1)(c) of the CA 2006, the purported release is void.[4785]

Treatment of shares purchased

19.53 Section 706 of the CA 2006 states that where a limited company makes a purchase of its own shares in accordance with this Chapter, then (a) if s 724 of the CA 2006 (treasury shares) applies, the shares may be held and dealt with in accordance with Chapter 6;[4786] (b) if that section does not apply (i) the shares are treated as cancelled,[4787] and (ii) the amount of the company's issued share capital is diminished accordingly by the nominal value of the shares cancelled.[4788]

Return to registrar of purchase of own shares

19.54 Section 707 of the CA 2006 states that where a company purchases shares under this Chapter, it must deliver a return to the registrar within the period of 28 days beginning with the date on which the shares are delivered to it.[4789]

The return must distinguish (a) shares in relation to which s 724 of the CA 2006 (treasury shares) applies and shares in relation to which that section does not apply;[4790] and (b) shares in relation to which that section applies (i) that are cancelled forthwith (under s 729 of the CA 2006 (cancellation of treasury shares)),[4791] and (ii) that are not so cancelled.[4792]

The return must state, with respect to shares of each class purchased the number and nominal value of the shares,[4793] and the date on which they were delivered to the company.[4794]

In the case of a public company the return must also state the aggregate amount paid by the company for the shares,[4795] and the maximum and minimum prices paid in respect of shares of each class purchased.[4796]

Particulars of shares delivered to the company on different dates and under different contracts may be included in a single return.[4797]

In such a case the amount required to be stated under s 707(4)(a) of the CA 2006 is the aggregate amount paid by the company for all the shares to which the return relates.

If default is made in complying with s 707 of the CA 2006 an offence is committed by every officer of the company who is in default.[4798] A person guilty of an offence under s 707 of the CA 2006 is liable on conviction on

---

[4784] CA 2006, s 705(2)(b).   [4785] CA 2006, s 705(2)(c).   [4786] CA 2006, s 706(a).
[4787] CA 2006, s 706(b)(i).   [4788] CA 2006, s 706(b)(ii).   [4789] CA 2006, s 707(1).
[4790] CA 2006, s 707(2)(a).   [4791] CA 2006, s 707(2)(b)(i).   [4792] CA 2006, s 707(2)(b)(ii).
[4793] CA 2006, s 707(3)(a).   [4794] CA 2006, s 707(3)(b).   [4795] CA 2006, s 707(4)(a).
[4796] CA 2006, s 707(4)(b).   [4797] CA 2006, s 707(5).   [4798] CA 2006, s 707(6).

indictment, to a fine;[4799] and on summary conviction to a fine not exceeding the statutory maximum and, for continued contravention, a daily default fine not exceeding one-tenth of the statutory maximum.[4800]

Section 707 of the CA 2006 replaces s 169(1), (1A) and (1B) of the CA 1985 and restates s 169(2), (3) and (6) of the CA 1985 and Schedule 24 of the CA 1985. It requires a company to make a return to the registrar within 28 days of a purchase of its own shares stating, amongst other things, the number and nominal value of the shares purchased. The return must indicate whether the shares are of a type that could be held in treasury (see s 724 of the CA 2006), and, if so, whether the shares were cancelled forthwith or whether they are being held in treasury.

Notice to registrar of a cancellation of shares

19.55 Section 708 of the CA 2006 states that if on the purchase by a company of any of its own shares in accordance with this Part (a) s 724 of the CA 2006 (treasury shares) does not apply (so that the shares are treated as cancelled);[4801] or (b) that section applies but the shares are cancelled forthwith (under s 729 of the CA 2006 (cancellation of treasury shares)),[4802] the company must give notice of cancellation to the registrar, within the period of 28 days beginning with the date on which the shares are delivered to it, specifying the shares cancelled.

The notice must be accompanied by a statement of capital.[4803]

The statement of capital must state with respect to the company's share capital immediately following the cancellation (a) the total number of shares of the company;[4804] (b) the aggregate nominal value of those shares;[4805] (c) for each class of shares (i) prescribed particulars of the rights attached to the shares,[4806] (ii) the total number of shares of that class,[4807] and (iii) the aggregate nominal value of shares of that class;[4808] and (d) the amount paid up and the amount (if any) unpaid on each share (whether on account of the nominal value of the share or by way of premium).[4809]

If default is made in complying with this section, an offence is committed by the company,[4810] and every officer of the company who is in default.[4811] A person guilty of an offence under s 708 of the CA 2006 is liable on summary conviction to a fine not exceeding level 3 on the standard scale and, for continued contravention, a daily default fine not exceeding one-tenth of level 3 on the standard scale.[4812]

[4799] CA 2006, s 707(7)(a).   [4800] CA 2006, s 707(7)(b).   [4801] CA 2006, s 708(1)(a).
[4802] CA 2006, s 708(1)(b).   [4803] CA 2006, s 708(2).   [4804] CA 2006, s 708(3)(a).
[4805] CA 2006, s 708(3)(b).   [4806] CA 2006, s 708(3)(c)(i).   [4807] CA 2006, s 708(3)(c)(ii).
[4808] CA 2006, s 708(3)(c)(iii).   [4809] CA 2006, s 708(3)(d).   [4810] CA 2006, s 708(4)(a).
[4811] CA 2006, s 708(4)(b).   [4812] CA 2006, s 708(5).

This section replaces ss 169(1), (1A) and (1B) of the CA 1985 and restates s 169(6) of the CA 1985 Act and Schedule 24 of the CA 1985. It updates the notice requirements so as to require that where shares are cancelled forthwith following a purchase (either in circumstances where the shares are treated as automatically cancelled or where treasury shares are cancelled) the company has to notify the registrar of such cancellation and provide the registrar with a statement of capital.

As before, where a company fails to comply with the procedural requirements as to notice, the company, and every officer of the company who is in default, commits an offence (see s 708(4) of the CA 2006).

Redemption or Purchase By Private Company Out of Capital

19.56 Chapter 5 to Part 18 of the CA 2006 is concerned with the redemption or purchase by private company out of capital.

Sections 171–177 of the CA 1985 provided a statutory scheme for the redemption or purchase of own shares out of capital. This scheme was available to private companies only, and the facility to redeem or purchase shares out of capital is carried forward in the following sections under the CA 2006.

Introductory

Power of private limited company to redeem or purchase own shares out of capital

19.57 Under s 709 of the CA 2006, a private limited company may in accordance with Chapter 5, but subject to any restriction or prohibition in the company's articles, make a payment in respect of the redemption or purchase of its own shares otherwise than out of distributable profits or the proceeds of a fresh issue of shares.[4813]

The references in Chapter 5 to payment out of capital are to any payment so made, whether or not it would be regarded apart from this section as a payment out of capital.[4814]

This section replaces s 171(1) of the CA 1985 and restates s 171(2) of the CA 1985. It removes the current requirement for prior authorisation in the articles where a private company makes a payment out of capital in respect of a redemption or purchase of its own shares. If they wish, the members may, however, restrict or prohibit such a payment by including a provision to this effect in the company's articles.

[4813] CA 2006, s 709(1).   [4814] CA 2006, s 709(2).

The permissible capital payment

The permissible capital payment

19.58 Section 710 of the CA 2006 states that the payment that may, in accordance with Chapter 5, be made by a company out of capital in respect of the redemption or purchase of its own shares is such amount as, after applying for that purpose any available profits of the company,[4815] and the proceeds of any fresh issue of shares made for the purposes of the redemption or purchase,[4816] is required to meet the price of redemption or purchase.

That is referred to in Chapter 5 as 'the permissible capital payment' for the shares.[4817]

Available profits

19.59 Under s 711 of the CA 2006, for the purposes of Chapter 5, the available profits of the company, in relation to the redemption or purchase of any shares, are the profits of the company that are available for distribution (within the meaning of Part 23 of the CA 2006).[4818]

But the question whether a company has any profits so available, and the amount of any such profits, shall be determined in accordance with s 712 of the CA 2006 instead of in accordance with ss 836–842 of the CA 2006 in that Part.[4819]

Determination of available profits

19.60 Section 712 of the CA 2006 states that the available profits of the company are determined as follows.[4820]

First, determine the profits of the company by reference to the following items as stated in the relevant accounts (a) profits, losses, assets and liabilities;[4821] (b) provisions of the following kinds (i) where the relevant accounts are Companies Act accounts, provisions of a kind specified for the purposes of this subsection by regulations under s 396 of the CA 2006,[4822] (ii) where the relevant accounts are IAS accounts, provisions of any kind;[4823] (c) share capital and reserves (including undistributable reserves).[4824]

Second, reduce the amount so determined by the amount of any distribution lawfully made by the company,[4825] and any other relevant payment lawfully made by the company out of distributable profits,[4826] after the date of the relevant accounts and before the end of the relevant period.

[4815] CA 2006, s 710(1)(a). [4816] CA 2006, s 710(1)(b). [4817] CA 2006, s 710(2).
[4818] CA 2006, s 711(1). [4819] CA 2006, s 711(2). [4820] CA 2006, s 712(1).
[4821] CA 2006, s 712(2)(a). [4822] CA 2006, s 712(2)(b)(i). [4823] CA 2006, s 712(2)(b)(ii).
[4824] CA 2006, s 712(2)(c). [4825] CA 2006, s 712(3)(a). [4826] CA 2006, s 712(3)(b).

The term 'other relevant payment lawfully made' includes (a) financial assistance lawfully given out of distributable profits in accordance with Chapter 2;[4827] (b) payments lawfully made out of distributable profits in respect of the purchase by the company of any shares in the company;[4828] and (c) payments of any description specified in s 705 of the CA 2006 (payments other than purchase price to be made out of distributable profits) lawfully made by the company.[4829]

The resulting figure is the amount of available profits.[4830]

The term 'the relevant accounts' are any accounts that are prepared as at a date within the relevant period,[4831] and are such as to enable a reasonable judgment to be made as to the amounts of the items mentioned in s 712(2) of the CA 2006.[4832]

The term 'the relevant period' means the period of three months ending with the date on which the directors' statement is made in accordance with s 714 of the CA 2006.[4833]

Requirements for payments out of capital

Requirements for payments out of capital

19.61 Section 713 of the CA 2006 states that a payment out of capital by a private company for the redemption or purchase of its own shares is not lawful unless the requirements of the following sections are met, namely: s 714 of the CA 2006 (directors' statement and auditor's report); s 716 of the CA 2006 (approval by special resolution); s 719 of the CA 2006 (public notice of proposed payment); and s 720 of the CA 2006 (directors' statement and auditor's report to be available for inspection).[4834]

This is subject to any order of the court under s 721 of the CA 2006 (power of the court to extend the period for compliance on application by persons objecting to a payment).[4835]

Directors' statement and auditor's report

19.62 Section 714 of the CA 2006 states that the company's directors must make a statement in accordance with this section.[4836]

The statement must specify the amount of the permissible capital payment for the shares in question.[4837]

It must state that, having made full inquiry into the affairs and prospects of the company, the directors have formed the opinion (a) as regards its initial

---

[4827] CA 2006, s 712(4)(a).   [4828] CA 2006, s 712(4)(b).   [4829] CA 2006, s 712(4)(c).
[4830] CA 2006, s 712(5).   [4831] CA 2006, s 712(6)(a).   [4832] CA 2006, s 712(6)(b).
[4833] CA 2006, s 712(7).   [4834] CA 2006, s 713(1).   [4835] CA 2006, s 713(2).
[4836] CA 2006, s 714(1).   [4837] CA 2006, s 714(2).

situation immediately following the date on which the payment out of capital is proposed to be made, that there will be no grounds on which the company could then be found unable to pay its debts;[4838] and (b) as regards its prospects for the year immediately following that date, that having regard to (i) their intentions with respect to the management of the company's business during that year,[4839] and (ii) the amount and character of the financial resources that will in their view be available to the company during that year,[4840] the company will be able to continue to carry on business as a going concern (and will accordingly be able to pay its debts as they fall due) throughout that year.

In forming their opinion for the purposes of s 714(3)(a) of the CA 2006, the directors must take into account all of the company's liabilities (including any contingent or prospective liabilities).[4841]

The directors' statement must be in the prescribed form and must contain such information with respect to the nature of the company's business as may be prescribed.[4842]

It must in addition have annexed to it a report addressed to the directors by the company's auditor stating that he has inquired into the company's state of affairs,[4843] the amount specified in the statement as the permissible capital payment for the shares in question is in his view properly determined in accordance with ss 710–712 of the CA 2006,[4844] and he is not aware of anything to indicate that the opinion expressed by the directors in their statement as to any of the matters mentioned in s 714(3) of the CA 2006 above is unreasonable in all the circumstances.[4845]

Section 714 of the CA 2006 replaces s 173(3)–(5) of the CA 1985.

Under the CA 1985, before a private company could make a payment out of capital in respect of a purchase of own shares, the directors must have made a full enquiry into the affairs and prospects of the company and were required, under s 173 of the CA 1985, to make a statutory declaration confirming that: as regards the company's situation immediately after the date on which the payment out of capital is made, there will be no grounds on which the company could then be found unable to pay its debts; and as regards the company's prospects for the year immediately following that date, the company will be able to continue to carry on business as a going concern and be able to pay its debts as they fall due in the year immediately following the date on which the payment out of capital is made. In forming their opinion on the company's solvency and prospects, the directors must take into account the same liabilities (including contingent and prospective liabilities) as would be relevant under s 122 of the Insolvency Act 1986 (winding up by the court) to the question whether a company is unable to pay its debts.

[4838] CA 2006, s 714(3)(a).   [4839] CA 2006, s 714(3)(b)(i).   [4840] CA 2006, s 714(3)(b)(ii).
[4841] CA 2006, s 714(4).   [4842] CA 2006, s 714(5).   [4843] CA 2006, s 714(6)(a).
[4844] CA 2006, s 714(6)(b).   [4845] CA 2006, s 714(6)(c).

Consistent with the approach taken in respect of reductions of capital using the new solvency statement procedure (see ss 642 and 643 of the CA 2006 and in particular s 643(2) of the CA 2006, this section requires a private company limited by shares that wishes to use this statutory scheme for a purchase or redemption of shares to take account of all contingent and prospective liabilities, not just those that are relevant for the purposes of s 122 of the Insolvency Act 1986 (see s 714(4) of the CA 2006).

Again, to achieve consistency with the approach taken elsewhere in the CA 2006, the current requirement for a statutory declaration is replaced with a requirement for a simple statement. In contrast to a statutory declaration, the directors' statement does not need to be sworn before a solicitor or Commissioner of Oaths.

Directors' statement: offence if no reasonable grounds for an opinion

19.63 If the directors make a statement under s 714 of the CA 2006 without having reasonable grounds for the opinion expressed in it, an offence is committed by every director who is in default.[4846] A person guilty of an offence under this section is liable on conviction on indictment, to imprisonment for a term not exceeding two years or a fine (or both);[4847] on summary conviction in England and Wales, to imprisonment for a term not exceeding 12 months or a fine not exceeding the statutory maximum (or both);[4848] in Scotland or Northern Ireland, to imprisonment for a term not exceeding six months or a fine not exceeding the statutory maximum (or both).[4849]

Section 715 of the CA 2006 restates s 173(6) of the CA 1985 and Schedule 24 of the CA 1985 (but substitutes the reference to 'declaration' with 'statement'). The offence that was contained in s 173(6) of the CA 1985 (offence of making a declaration without reasonable grounds) is replaced with an offence of making a statement under s 714 of the CA 2006 without having reasonable grounds for the opinion expressed in it. As before, the offence is committed by every director of the company who is in default.

Payment to be approved by special resolution

19.64 Section 716 of the CA 2006 states that the payment out of capital must be approved by a special resolution of the company.[4850]

The resolution must be passed on, or within the week immediately following, the date on which the directors make the statement required by s 714.[4851]

[4846] CA 2006, s 715(1).   [4847] CA 2006, s 715(2)(a).   [4848] CA 2006, s 715(2)(b)(i).
[4849] CA 2006, s 715(2)(b)(ii).   [4850] CA 2006, s 716(1).   [4851] CA 2006, s 716(2).

A resolution under this section is subject to s 717 of the CA 2006 (exercise of voting rights), and s 718 of the CA 2006 (disclosure of directors' statement and auditors' report).[4852]

Resolution authorising payment: exercise of voting rights

19.65 Section 717 of the CA 2006 applies to a resolution under s 716 of the CA 2006 (authority for payment out of capital for a redemption or purchase of own shares).[4853]

Where the resolution is proposed as a written resolution, a member who holds shares to which the resolution relates is not an eligible member.[4854]

Where the resolution is proposed at a meeting of the company, it is not effective if any member of the company holding shares to which the resolution relates exercises the voting rights carried by any of those shares in voting on the resolution,[4855] and the resolution would not have been passed if he had not done so.[4856]

For this purpose (a) a member who holds shares to which the resolution relates is regarded as exercising the voting rights carried by those shares, not only if he votes in respect of them on a poll on the question whether the resolution shall be passed, but also if he votes on the resolution otherwise than on a poll;[4857] (b) any member of the company may demand a poll on that question;[4858] (c) a vote and a demand for a poll by a person as proxy for a member are the same respectively as a vote and a demand by the member.[4859]

Resolution authorising payment: disclosure of a directors' statement and an auditor's report

19.66 Section 718 of the CA 2006 applies to a resolution under s 716 of the CA 2006 (resolution authorising a payment out of capital for a redemption or purchase of own shares).[4860]

A copy of the directors' statement and auditor's report under s 714 of the CA 2006 must be made available to members in the case of a written resolution, by being sent or submitted to every eligible member at or before the time at which the proposed resolution is sent or submitted to him;[4861] in the case of a resolution at a meeting, by being made available for inspection by members of the company at the meeting.[4862]

The resolution is ineffective if this requirement is not complied with.[4863]

[4852] CA 2006, s 716(3).   [4853] CA 2006, s 717(1).   [4854] CA 2006, s 717(2).
[4855] CA 2006, s 717(3)(a).   [4856] CA 2006, s 717(3)(b).   [4857] CA 2006, s 717(4)(a).
[4858] CA 2006, s 717(4)(b).   [4859] CA 2006, s 717(4)(c).   [4860] CA 2006, s 718(1).
[4861] CA 2006, s 718(2)(a).   [4862] CA 2006, s 718(2)(b).   [4863] CA 2006, s 718(3).

Public notice of proposed payment

19.67 Section 719 of the CA 2006 states that within the week immediately following the date of the resolution under s 716 of the CA 2006 the company must cause to be published in the Gazette a notice (a) stating that the company has approved a payment out of capital for the purpose of acquiring its own shares by redemption or purchase or both (as the case may be);[4864] (b) specifying (i) the amount of the permissible capital payment for the shares in question,[4865] and (ii) the date of the resolution;[4866] (c) stating where the directors' statement and auditor's report required by s 714 of the CA 2006 are available for inspection;[4867] and (d) stating that any creditor of the company may at any time within the five weeks immediately following the date of the resolution apply to the court under s 721 of the CA 2006 for an order preventing the payment.[4868]

Within the week immediately following the date of the resolution the company must also either cause a notice to the same effect as that required by s 719(1) of the CA 2006 to be published in an appropriate national newspaper,[4869] or give notice in writing to that effect to each of its creditors.[4870]

The term 'an appropriate national newspaper' means a newspaper circulating throughout the part of the United Kingdom in which the company is registered.[4871]

Not later than the day on which the company first publishes the notice required by s 719(1) of the CA 2006,[4872] or if earlier, first publishes or gives the notice required by s 719(2) of the CA 2006, the company must deliver to the registrar a copy of the directors' statement and auditor's report required by s 714 of the CA 2006.[4873]

Directors' statement and auditor's report to be available
for inspection

19.68 Section 720 of the CA 2006 provides that the directors' statement and auditor's report must be kept available for inspection throughout the period (a) beginning with the day on which the company (i) first publishes the notice required by s 719(1) of the CA 2006,[4874] or (ii) if earlier, first publishes or gives the notice required by s 719(2) of the CA 2006;[4875] and (b) ending five weeks after the date of the resolution for payment out of capital.[4876]

They must be kept available for inspection at the company's registered

---

[4864] CA 2006, s 719(1)(a).   [4865] CA 2006, s 719(1)(b)(i).   [4866] CA 2006, s 719(1)(b)(ii).
[4867] CA 2006, s 719(1)(c).   [4868] CA 2006, s 719(1)(d).   [4869] CA 2006, s 719(2)(a).
[4870] CA 2006, s 719(2)(b).   [4871] CA 2006, s 719(3).   [4872] CA 2006, s 719(4)(a).
[4873] CA 2006, s 719(4)(b).   [4874] CA 2006, s 720(1)(a)(i).   [4875] CA 2006, s 720(1)(a)(ii).
[4876] CA 2006, s 720(1)(b).

office,[4877] or at a place specified in regulations under s 1136 of the CA 2006.[4878]

The company must give notice to the registrar of the place at which the statement and report are kept available for inspection,[4879] and of any change in that place,[4880] unless they have at all times been kept at the company's registered office.

They must be open to the inspection of any member or creditor of the company without charge.[4881]

If a default is made for 14 days in complying with s 720(3) of the CA 2006, or an inspection under s 720(4) of the CA 2006 is refused, an offence is committed by the company,[4882] and every officer of the company who is in default.[4883] A person guilty of an offence under this section is liable on summary conviction to a fine not exceeding level 3 on the standard scale and, for continued contravention, a daily default fine not exceeding one-tenth of level 3 on the standard scale.[4884]

In the case of a refusal of an inspection required by subs (4), the court may by order compel an immediate inspection.[4885]

Section 720 of the CA 2006 replaces s 175(6)(a) and (7) of the CA 1985 and restates s 175(4), (6)(b), and (8) of the CA 1985 and Schedule 24 of the CA 1985. Section 720(2) of the CA 2006 alters the requirement, contained in s 175(6)(a) of the CA 1985, by providing that the directors' statement and auditor's report may, alternatively, be kept available for inspection at a place specified in regulations made under s 1136 of the CA 2006. There is a new requirement (in s 720(3) of the CA 2006) for the company to give notice to the registrar of the place where the statement and report are kept available for inspection and of any change to that place. This change is consequential on the change introduced by s 720(2) of the CA 2006.

Section 720(5) of the CA 2006 provides that if the company fails to give such notice to the registrar within 14 days or an inspection of the statement and report are refused, the company and every officer in default commit an offence.

Objection to payment by members or creditors

Application to court to cancel resolution

19.69 Section 721 of the CA 2006 states that where a private company passes a special resolution approving a payment out of capital for the redemption or purchase of any of its shares any member of the company (other than one

---

[4877] CA 2006, s 720(2)(a).   [4878] CA 2006, s 720(2)(b).   [4879] CA 2006, s 720(3)(a).
[4880] CA 2006, s 720(3)(b).   [4881] CA 2006, s 720(4).   [4882] CA 2006, s 720(5)(a).
[4883] CA 2006, s 720(5)(b).   [4884] CA 2006, s 720(6).   [4885] CA 2006, s 720(7).

who consented to or voted in favour of the resolution),[4886] and any creditor of the company,[4887] may apply to the court for a cancellation of the resolution.

The application must be made within five weeks after the passing of the resolution,[4888] and may be made on behalf of the persons entitled to make it by such one or more of their number as they may appoint in writing for the purpose.[4889]

On an application under this section the court may if it thinks fit (a) adjourn the proceedings in order that an arrangement may be made to the satisfaction of the court (i) for the purchase of the interests of dissentient members,[4890] or (ii) for the protection of dissentient creditors;[4891] and (b) give such directions and make such orders as it thinks expedient for facilitating or carrying into effect any such arrangement.[4892]

Subject to that, the court must make an order either cancelling or confirming the resolution, and may do so on such terms and conditions as it thinks fit.[4893]

If the court confirms the resolution, it may by order alter or extend any date or period of time specified in the resolution,[4894] or in any provision of this Chapter applying to the redemption or purchase to which the resolution relates.[4895]

The court's order may, if the court thinks fit, provide for the purchase by the company of the shares of any of its members and for the reduction accordingly of the company's capital,[4896] and make any alteration in the company's articles that may be required in consequence of that provision.[4897]

The court's order may, if the court thinks fit, require the company not to make any, or any specified, amendments of its articles without the leave of the court.[4898]

Notice to registrar of a court application or order

19.70 Under s 722 of the CA 2006, on making an application under s 721 of the CA 2006 (application to court to cancel a resolution) the applicants, or the person making the application on their behalf, must immediately give notice to the registrar.[4899]

This is without prejudice to any provision of rules of court as to service of a notice of the application.

On being served with notice of any such application, the company must immediately give notice to the registrar.[4900]

[4886] CA 2006, s 721(1)(a).   [4887] CA 2006, s 721(1)(b).   [4888] CA 2006, s 721(2)(a).
[4889] CA 2006, s 721(2)(b).   [4890] CA 2006, s 721(3)(a)(i).   [4891] CA 2006, s 721(3)(a)(ii).
[4892] CA 2006, s 721(3)(b).   [4893] CA 2006, s 721(4).   [4894] CA 2006, s 721(5)(a).
[4895] CA 2006, s 721(5)(b).   [4896] CA 2006, s 721(6)(a).   [4897] CA 2006, s 721(6)(b).
[4898] CA 2006, s 721(7).   [4899] CA 2006, s 722(1).   [4900] CA 2006, s 722(2).

Within 15 days of the making of the court's order on the application, or such longer period as the court may at any time direct, the company must deliver to the registrar a copy of the order.[4901]

If a company fails to comply with s 722(2) or (3) of the CA 2006, an offence is committed by the company,[4902] and every officer of the company who is in default.[4903] A person guilty of an offence under this section is liable on summary conviction to a fine not exceeding level 3 on the standard scale and, for continued contravention, a daily default fine not exceeding one-tenth of level 3 on the standard scale.[4904]

Supplementary provisions

When a payment out of capital is to be made

19.71 Section 723 of the CA 2006 states that a payment out of capital must be made no earlier than five weeks after the date on which the resolution under s 716 of the CA 2006 is passed,[4905] and no more than seven weeks after that date.[4906]

This is subject to any exercise of the court's powers under s 721(5) of the CA 2006 (power to alter or extend time where a resolution is confirmed after objection).[4907]

Treasury Shares

19.72 Chapter 6 to Part 18 of the CA 2006 is concerned with treasury shares.

Where a company buys back its own shares, it is normally required to cancel those shares. Certain companies (principally those that are listed or those that are traded on the Alternative Investment Market and equivalent companies in the EEA) may elect not to cancel shares that have been bought back but may hold the shares 'in treasury'. A share that is held in treasury may be sold at a future point in time and this facility enables such companies to raise capital more quickly than they would otherwise be able to, as the directors do not have to obtain prior authority from the company's members before selling treasury shares.

Treasury shares

19.73 Section 724 of the CA 2006 applies where a limited company makes a purchase of its own shares in accordance with Chapter 4 to Part 18 of the CA

[4901] CA 2006, s 722(3).   [4902] CA 2006, s 722(4)(a).   [4903] CA 2006, s 722(4)(b).
[4904] CA 2006, s 722(5).   [4905] CA 2006, s 723(1)(a).   [4906] CA 2006, s 723(1)(b).
[4907] CA 2006, s 723(2).

2006,[4908] the purchase is made out of distributable profits,[4909] and the shares are qualifying shares.[4910]

The term 'qualifying shares' means shares that (a) are included in the official list in accordance with the provisions of Part 6 of the Financial Services and Markets Act 2000 (c 8);[4911] (b) are traded on the market known as the Alternative Investment Market established under the rules of London Stock Exchange plc;[4912] (c) are officially listed in an EEA State;[4913] or (d) are traded on a regulated market.[4914]

In para (a) 'the official list' has the meaning given in s 103(1) of the Financial Services and Markets Act 2000.

Where this section applies the company may hold the shares (or any of them),[4915] or deal with any of them, at any time, in accordance with ss 727 or 729 of the CA 2006.[4916]

Where shares are held by the company, the company must be entered in its register of members as the member holding the shares.[4917]

In the Companies Acts, references to a company holding shares as treasury shares are to the company holding shares that were (or are treated as having been) purchased by it in circumstances in which this section applies,[4918] and have been held by the company continuously since they were so purchased (or treated as purchased).[4919]

Treasury shares: maximum holdings

19.74 Section 725 of the CA 2006 states that where a company has shares of only one class, the aggregate nominal value of shares held as treasury shares must not at any time exceed 10 per cent of the nominal value of the issued share capital of the company at that time.[4920]

Where the share capital of a company is divided into shares of different classes, the aggregate nominal value of the shares of any class held as treasury shares must not at any time exceed 10 per cent of the nominal value of the issued share capital of the shares of that class at that time.[4921]

If s 725(1) or (2) of the CA 2006 is contravened by a company, the company must dispose of or cancel the excess shares, in accordance with ss 727 or 729 of the CA 2006, before the end of the period of 12 months beginning with the date on which that contravention occurs.[4922]

'Excess shares' means such number of the shares held by the company as treasury shares at the time in question as resulted in the limit being exceeded.

Where a company purchases qualifying shares out of distributable profits

---

[4908] CA 2006, s 724(1)(a).   [4909] CA 2006, s 724(1)(b).   [4910] CA 2006, s 724(1)(c).
[4911] CA 2006, s 724(2)(a).   [4912] CA 2006, s 724(2)(b).   [4913] CA 2006, s 724(2)(c).
[4914] CA 2006, s 724(2)(d).   [4915] CA 2006, s 724(3)(a).   [4916] CA 2006, s 724(3)(b).
[4917] CA 2006, s 724(4).   [4918] CA 2006, s 724(5)(a).   [4919] CA 2006, s 724(5)(b).
[4920] CA 2006, s 725(1).   [4921] CA 2006, s 725(2).   [4922] CA 2006, s 725(3).

in accordance with s 724 of the CA 2006, a contravention by the company of s 725(1) or (2) of the CA 2006 above does not render the acquisition void under s 658 of the CA 2006 (general rule against a limited company acquiring its own shares).[4923]

Treasury shares: exercise of rights

19.75 Section 726 of the CA 2006 applies where shares are held by a company as treasury shares.[4924]

The company must not exercise any right in respect of the treasury shares, and any purported exercise of such a right is void.[4925] This applies, in particular, to any right to attend or vote at meetings.

No dividend may be paid, and no other distribution (whether in cash or otherwise) of the company's assets (including any distribution of assets to members on a winding up) may be made to the company, in respect of the treasury shares.[4926]

Nothing in s 726 of the CA 2006 prevents an allotment of shares as fully paid bonus shares in respect of the treasury shares,[4927] or the payment of any amount payable on the redemption of the treasury shares (if they are redeemable shares).[4928]

Shares allotted as fully paid bonus shares in respect of the treasury shares are treated as if purchased by the company, at the time they were allotted, in circumstances in which s 724(1) of the CA 2006 (treasury shares) applied.[4929]

Treasury shares: disposal

19.76 Section 727 of the CA 2006 states that where shares are held as treasury shares, the company may at any time sell the shares (or any of them) for a cash consideration,[4930] or transfer the shares (or any of them) for the purposes of or pursuant to an employees' share scheme.[4931]

In s 727(1)(a) of the CA 2006 'cash consideration' means (a) of the cash received by the company;[4932] or (b) a cheque received by the company in good faith that the directors have no reason to suspect will not be paid;[4933] or (c) a release of a liability of the company for a liquidated sum;[4934] or (d) an undertaking to pay cash to the company on or before a date not more than 90 days after the date on which the company agrees to sell the shares;[4935] or (e) payment by any other means giving rise to a present or future entitlement (of the

---

[4923] CA 2006, s 725(4).   [4924] CA 2006, s 726(1).   [4925] CA 2006, s 726(2).
[4926] CA 2006, s 726(3).   [4927] CA 2006, s 726(4)(a).   [4928] CA 2006, s 726(4)(b).
[4929] CA 2006, s 726(5).   [4930] CA 2006, s 727(1)(a).   [4931] CA 2006, s 727(1)(b).
[4932] CA 2006, s 727(2)(a).   [4933] CA 2006, s 727(2)(b).   [4934] CA 2006, s 727(2)(c).
[4935] CA 2006, s 727(2)(d).

company or a person acting on the company's behalf) to a payment, or credit equivalent to payment, in cash.[4936]

For this purpose, the term 'cash' includes foreign currency.

The Secretary of State may by order provide that the particular means of payment specified in the order is to be regarded as falling within s 727(2)(e) of the CA 2006.[4937]

If the company receives a notice under s 979 of the CA 2006 (takeover offers: right of offeror to buy out minority shareholders) that a person desires to acquire shares held by the company as treasury shares, the company must not sell or transfer the shares to which the notice relates, except to that person.[4938]

An order under this section is subject to negative resolution procedure.[4939]

Section 727 of the CA 2006 replaces s 162D(2) of the CA 1985 and restates s 162D(1)(a) and (b) and 162D(3) of the CA 1985. It defines (in s 727(2) of the CA 2006) what is meant by 'cash consideration', where treasury shares are sold, and this mirrors, in part, the definition in s 583 of the CA 2006 (which restates s 738(2)–(4) of the CA 1985 and defines when a share is deemed to be paid up or allotted for cash).

Section 727(2)(e), (3) and (5) of the CA 2006 are new. They enable the Secretary of State to specify, by order, what, in addition to the items specifically referred to in s 727(2) of the CA 2006, constitutes 'cash consideration' for the purposes of s 727(1)(a) of the CA 2006.

The power to make further provision in respect of what constitutes 'cash consideration' for the purposes of a sale of treasury shares (that is, in addition to those already specified in s 727(2) of the CA 2006) is intended to *remove* uncertainties surrounding other methods of settlement, for example, the CREST settlement system, and will also act as a future proofing mechanism in the event that new methods of settlement are developed or identified.

Treasury shares: notice of disposal

19.77 Under s 728 of the CA 2006, where shares held by a company as treasury shares are sold,[4940] or are transferred for the purposes of an employees' share scheme,[4941] the company must deliver a return to the registrar not later than 28 days after the shares are disposed of.

The return must state with respect to shares of each class disposed of the number and nominal value of the shares,[4942] and the date on which they were disposed of.[4943]

[4936] CA 2006, s 727(2)(e).   [4937] CA 2006, s 727(3).   [4938] CA 2006, s 727(4).

[4939] CA 2006, s 727(5).   [4940] CA 2006, s 728(1)(a).   [4941] CA 2006, s 728(1)(b).

[4942] CA 2006, s 728(2)(a).   [4943] CA 2006, s 728(2)(b).

Particulars of shares disposed of on different dates may be included in a single return.[4944]

If default is made in complying with this section an offence is committed by every officer of the company who is in default.[4945] A person guilty of an offence under this section is liable on conviction on indictment, to a fine;[4946] and on summary conviction, to a fine not exceeding the statutory maximum and, for continued contravention, a daily default fine not exceeding one-tenth of the statutory maximum.[4947]

Treasury shares: cancellation

19.78 Section 729 of the CA 2006 states that where shares are held as treasury shares, the company may at any time cancel the shares (or any of them).[4948]

If shares held as treasury shares cease to be qualifying shares, the company must forthwith cancel the shares.[4949]

For this purpose shares are not to be regarded as ceasing to be qualifying shares by virtue only of (a) the suspension of their listing in accordance with the applicable rules in the EEA State in which the shares are officially listed;[4950] or (b) the suspension of their trading in accordance with (i) in the case of shares traded on the market known as the Alternative Investment Market, the rules of London Stock Exchange plc,[4951] and (ii) in any other case, the rules of the regulated market on which they are traded.[4952]

If company cancels shares held as treasury shares, the amount of the company's share capital is reduced accordingly by the nominal amount of the shares cancelled.[4953]

The directors may take any steps required to enable the company to cancel its shares under this section without complying with the provisions of Chapter 10 to Part 17 of the CA 2006 (reduction of share capital).[4954]

Treasury shares: notice of cancellation

19.79 Section 730 of the CA 2006 states that where shares held by a company as treasury shares are cancelled, the company must deliver a return to the registrar not later than 28 days after the shares are cancelled.[4955] This does not apply to shares that are cancelled forthwith on their acquisition by the company (see s 708 of the CA 2006).

The return must state with respect to shares of each class cancelled, the

---

[4944] CA 2006, s 728(3). [4945] CA 2006, s 728(4). [4946] CA 2006, s 728(5)(a).
[4947] CA 2006, s 728(5)(b). [4948] CA 2006, s 729(1). [4949] CA 2006, s 729(2).
[4950] CA 2006, s 729(3)(a). [4951] CA 2006, s 729(3)(b)(i). [4952] CA 2006, s 729(3)(b)(ii).
[4953] CA 2006, s 729(4). [4954] CA 2006, s 729(5). [4955] CA 2006, s 730(1).

number and nominal value of the shares,[4956] and the date on which they were cancelled.[4957]

Particulars of shares cancelled on different dates may be included in a single return.[4958]

The notice must be accompanied by a statement of capital.[4959] The statement of capital must state with respect to the company's share capital immediately following the cancellation (a) the total number of shares of the company;[4960] (b) the aggregate nominal value of those shares;[4961] (c) for each class of shares (i) prescribed particulars of the rights attached to the shares,[4962] (ii) the total number of shares of that class,[4963] and (iii) the aggregate nominal value of shares of that class;[4964] and (d) the amount paid up and the amount (if any) unpaid on each share (whether on account of the nominal value of the share or by way of premium).[4965]

If a default is made in complying with this section, an offence is committed by the company,[4966] and every officer of the company who is in default.[4967] A person guilty of an offence under s 730 of the CA 2006 is liable on summary conviction to a fine not exceeding level 3 on the standard scale and, for continued contravention, a daily default fine not exceeding one-tenth of level 3 on the standard scale.[4968]

This section restates ss 169A(1)(b)(i), and (2)–(4) of the CA 1985 and Schedule 24 of the CA 1985. Where a company cancels shares that it has held in treasury it is required to give notice of this to the registrar within 28 days of the cancellation. The provision has, however, been updated to require companies to file a statement of capital in these circumstances.

Treasury shares: treatment of proceeds of a sale

19.80 Section 731 of the CA 2006 states that where shares held as treasury shares are sold, the proceeds of the sale must be dealt with in accordance with this section.[4969]

If the proceeds of sale are equal to or less than the purchase price paid by the company for the shares, the proceeds are treated for the purposes of Part 23 of the CA 2006 (distributions) as a realised profit of the company.[4970]

If the proceeds of sale exceed the purchase price paid by the company, an amount equal to the purchase price paid is treated as a realised profit of the company for the purposes of that Part,[4971] and the excess must be transferred to the company's share premium account.[4972]

[4956] CA 2006, s 730(2)(a).   [4957] CA 2006, s 730(2)(b).   [4958] CA 2006, s 730(3).
[4959] CA 2006, s 730(4).   [4960] CA 2006, s 730(5)(a).   [4961] CA 2006, s 730(5)(b).
[4962] CA 2006, s 730(5)(c)(i).   [4963] CA 2006, s 730(5)(c)(ii).
[4964] CA 2006, s 730(5)(c)(iii).   [4965] CA 2006, s 730(5)(d).   [4966] CA 2006, s 730(6)(a).
[4967] CA 2006, s 730(6)(b).   [4968] CA 2006, s 730(7).   [4969] CA 2006, s 731(1).
[4970] CA 2006, s 731(2).   [4971] CA 2006, s 731(3)(a).   [4972] CA 2006, s 731(3)(b).

For the purposes of s 731 of the CA 2006, the purchase price paid by the company must be determined by the application of a weighted average price method,[4973] and if the shares were allotted to the company as fully paid bonus shares, the purchase price paid for them is treated as nil.[4974]

Treasury shares: offences

19.81 Section 732 of the CA 2006 states that if a company contravenes any of the provisions of this Chapter (except s 730 of the CA 2006 (notice of cancellation)), an offence is committed by the company,[4975] and every officer of the company who is in default.[4976] A person guilty of an offence under this section is liable on conviction on indictment, to a fine;[4977] on summary conviction to a fine not exceeding the statutory maximum.[4978]

Section 732 of the CA 2006 replaces s 162G of the CA 1985. It renders both the company and every officer in default liable to an offence for any contravention of the provisions of this Chapter.

Supplementary Provisions

19.82 Chapter 7 to Part 18 of the CA 2006 sets out the supplementary provisions.

The capital redemption reserve

19.83 Section 733 of the CA 2006 states that in the following circumstances a company must transfer amounts to a reserve, called the 'capital redemption reserve'.[4979]

Where under this Part shares of a limited company are redeemed or purchased wholly out of the company's profits, the amount by which the company's issued share capital is diminished in accordance with s 688(b) of the CA 2006 (on the cancellation of shares redeemed),[4980] or s 706(b)(ii) of the CA 2006 (on the cancellation of shares purchased),[4981] must be transferred to the capital redemption reserve.

If the shares are redeemed or purchased wholly or partly out of the proceeds of a fresh issue,[4982] and the aggregate amount of the proceeds is less than the aggregate nominal value of the shares redeemed or purchased,[4983] the amount of the difference must be transferred to the capital redemption reserve. This does not apply in the case of a private company if, in addition to

---

[4973] CA 2006, s 731(4)(a).　　[4974] CA 2006, s 731(4)(b).　　[4975] CA 2006, s 732(1)(a).
[4976] CA 2006, s 732(1)(b).　　[4977] CA 2006, s 732(2)(a).　　[4978] CA 2006, s 732(2)(b).
[4979] CA 2006, s 733(1).　　[4980] CA 2006, s 733(2)(a).　　[4981] CA 2006, s 733(2)(b).
[4982] CA 2006, s 733(3)(a).　　[4983] CA 2006, s 733(3)(b).

810   A Guide to the Companies Act 2006

the proceeds of the fresh issue, the company applies a payment out of capital under Chapter 5 in making the redemption or purchase.

The amount by which a company's share capital is diminished in accordance with s 729(4) of the CA 2006 (on the cancellation of shares held as treasury shares) must be transferred to the capital redemption reserve.[4984]

The company may use the capital redemption reserve to pay up new shares to be allotted to members as fully paid bonus shares.[4985]

Subject to that, the provisions of the Companies Acts relating to the reduction of a company's share capital apply as if the capital redemption reserve were part of its paid up share capital.[4986]

Accounting consequences of payment out of capital

19.84 Section 734 of the CA 2006 applies where a payment out of capital is made in accordance with Chapter 5 (redemption or purchase of own shares by private company out of capital).[4987]

If the permissible capital payment is less than the nominal amount of the shares redeemed or purchased, the amount of the difference must be transferred to the company's capital redemption reserve.[4988]

If the permissible capital payment is greater than the nominal amount of the shares redeemed or purchased the amount of any capital redemption reserve, share premium account or fully paid share capital of the company,[4989] and any amount representing unrealised profits of the company for the time being standing to the credit of any revaluation reserve maintained by the company, may be reduced by a sum not exceeding (or by sums not in total exceeding) the amount by which the permissible capital payment exceeds the nominal amount of the shares.[4990]

Where the proceeds of a fresh issue are applied by the company in making a redemption or purchase of its own shares in addition to a payment out of capital under this Chapter, the references in s 734(2) and (3) of the CA 2006 to the permissible capital payment are to be read as referring to the aggregate of that payment and those proceeds.[4991]

Effect of a company's failure to redeem or purchase

19.85 Section 735 of the CA 2006 applies where a company issues shares on terms that they are or are liable to be redeemed,[4992] or agrees to purchase any of its shares.[4993]

[4984] CA 2006, s 733(4).   [4985] CA 2006, s 733(5).   [4986] CA 2006, s 733(6).
[4987] CA 2006, s 734(1).   [4988] CA 2006, s 734(2).   [4989] CA 2006, s 734(3)(a).
[4990] CA 2006, s 734(3)(b).   [4991] CA 2006, s 734(4).   [4992] CA 2006, s 735(1)(a).
[4993] CA 2006, s 735(1)(b).

The company is not liable in damages in respect of any failure on its part to redeem or purchase any of the shares.[4994]

This is without prejudice to any right of the holder of the shares other than his right to sue the company for damages in respect of its failure.

The court shall not grant an order for specific performance of the terms of redemption or purchase if the company shows that it is unable to meet the costs of redeeming or purchasing the shares in question out of distributable profits.[4995]

If the company is wound up and at the commencement of the winding up any of the shares have not been redeemed or purchased, the terms of redemption or purchase may be enforced against the company.[4996]

When shares are redeemed or purchased under this subsection, they are treated as cancelled.

Section 735(4) of the CA 2006 does not apply if (a) the terms provided for the redemption or purchase to take place at a date later than that of the commencement of the winding up;[4997] or (b) during the period (i) beginning with the date on which the redemption or purchase was to have taken place,[4998] and (ii) ending with the commencement of the winding up, the company could not at any time have lawfully made a distribution equal in value to the price at which the shares were to have been redeemed or purchased.[4999]

There shall be paid, in priority to any amount that the company is liable under s 735(4) of the CA 2006 to pay in respect of any shares, all other debts and liabilities of the company (other than any due to members in their character as such),[5000] and if other shares carry rights (whether as to capital or as to income) that are preferred to the rights as to capital attaching to the first-mentioned shares, any amount due in satisfaction of those preferred rights. Subject to that, any such amount shall be paid in priority to any amounts due to members in satisfaction of their rights (whether as to capital or income) as members.[5001]

Meaning of 'distributable profits'

19.86 Section 736 of the CA 2006 sets out the definition of distributable profits. In this Part (except in Chapter 2 (financial assistance): see s 683 of the CA 2006) 'distributable profits', in relation to the making of any payment by a company, means profits out of which the company could lawfully make a distribution (within the meaning given by s 830 of the CA 2006) equal in value to the payment.

[4994] CA 2006, s 735(2).   [4995] CA 2006, s 735(3).   [4996] CA 2006, s 735(4).
[4997] CA 2006, s 735(5)(a).   [4998] CA 2006, s 735(5)(b)(i).   [4999] CA 2006, s 735(5)(b)(ii).
[5000] CA 2006, s 735(6)(a).   [5001] CA 2006, s 735(6)(b).

General power to make further provision by regulations

19.87 Section 737 of the CA 2006 provides that the Secretary of State may by regulations modify the provisions of this Part.[5002]

The regulations may amend or repeal any of the provisions of this Part,[5003] or make such other provision as appears to the Secretary of State appropriate in place of any of the provisions of this Part.[5004]

Regulations under this section may make consequential amendments or repeals in other provisions of this Act, or in other enactments.[5005]

The regulations under this section are subject to affirmative resolution procedure.[5006]

Section 737 of the CA 2006 is a new provision that enables the Secretary of State, by regulations, to modify the provisions of Part 18 of the CA 2006 (see s 737(1) of the CA 2006).

Regulations made under this section may amend or repeal any of the provisions in this Part or make such other provision as appears to the Secretary of State appropriate in place of those provisions.

The power to make regulations in this section will enable the Secretary of State to 'future-proof' the provisions in Part 18 – which are primarily concerned with the maintenance of capital. This is desirable, as many of these provisions are derived from EU law and may require amendment in the relatively near future (subject in part to the outcome of a fundamental study into alternatives to the current capital maintenance regime that is being carried out at EU level).

Regulations made pursuant to the power in this section are subject to the affirmative resolution procedure, which means that they must be approved by both Houses of Parliament.

[5002] CA 2006, s 737(1).   [5003] CA 2006, s 737(2)(a).   [5004] CA 2006, s 737(2)(b).
[5005] CA 2006, s 737(3).   [5006] CA 2006, s 737(4).

Chapter 20

Debentures

Introduction

20.1 Part 19 of the CA 2006 sets out the provisions on debentures. It restates the provisions of the CA 1985 relating to debentures. Sections 739–740, 742 and 749–754 of the CA 2006 make no change to the law.

General provisions

20.2 Sections 738–742 of the CA 2006 are concerned with general provisions on debentures.

Meaning of 'debenture'

20.3 Section 738 of the CA 2006 defines a debenture. It states that in the Companies Acts, the term 'debenture' includes debenture stock, bonds and any other securities of a company, whether or not constituting a charge on the assets of the company.

Perpetual debentures

20.4 Section 739 of the CA 2006 states that a condition contained in debentures, or in a deed for securing debentures, is not invalid by reason only that the debentures are made (a) irredeemable;[5007] or (b) redeemable only (i) on the happening of a contingency (however remote),[5008] or (ii) on the expiration of a period (however long),[5009] any rule of equity to the contrary notwithstanding.

Section 739(1) of the CA 2006 applies to debentures whenever issued and to deeds whenever executed.[5010]

[5007] CA 2006, s 739(1)(a).   [5008] CA 2006, s 739(1)(b)(i).   [5009] CA 2006, s 739(1)(b)(ii).
[5010] CA 2006, s 739(2).

Enforcement of contract to subscribe for debentures

20.5 Section 740 of the CA 2006 states that a contract with a company to take up and pay for debentures of the company, may be enforced by an order for specific performance.

Registration of allotment of debentures

20.6 Section 741 of the CA 2006 is concerned with registration of allotment of debentures. A company must register an allotment of debentures as soon as practicable, and in any event within two months after the date of the allotment.[5011]

If a company fails to comply with s 741 of the CA 2006, an offence is committed by the company,[5012] and every officer of the company who is in default.[5013] A person guilty of an offence under this section is liable on summary conviction to a fine not exceeding level 3 on the standard scale and, for continued contravention, a daily default fine not exceeding one-tenth of level 3 on the standard scale.[5014]

For the duties of the company as to the issue of the debentures, or certificates of debenture stock, see Part 21 of the CA 2006 (certification and transfer of securities)[5015]

Section 741 of the CA 2006 is a new provision, which obliges a company to register an allotment of debentures as soon as practicable, but in any event within two months after their allotment. It completes the picture as regards the previous requirement in s 185(1) of the CA 1985 (which is restated in s 769(1) of the CA 2006), which obliges a company to complete and deliver certificates for debentures within two months after their allotment.

Debentures to bearer (Scotland)

20.7 Section 742 of the CA 2006 deals with debentures to bearer (Scotland). It provides that notwithstanding anything in the statute of the Scots Parliament of 1696, Chapter 25, debentures to bearers issued in Scotland are valid and binding according to their terms.

Register of debenture holders

20.8 Sections 743–748 of the CA 2006 are concerned with the register of debenture holders.

[5011] CA 2006, s 741(1).   [5012] CA 2006, s 741(2)(a).   [5013] CA 2006, s 741(2)(b).
[5014] CA 2006, s 741(3).   [5015] CA 2006, s 741(4).

Register of debenture holders

20.9 Section 743 of the CA 2006 deals with the register of debenture holders. Any register of debenture holders of a company that is kept by the company, must be kept available for inspection at the company's registered office,[5016] or at a place specified in regulations under s 1136 of the CA 2006.[5017]

A company must give notice to the registrar of the place where any such register is kept available for inspection and of any change in that place.[5018] No such notice is required if the register has, at all times since it came into existence, been kept available for inspection at the company's registered office.[5019]

If a company makes a default for 14 days in complying with s 743(2) of the CA 2006, an offence is committed by the company,[5020] and every officer of the company who is in default.[5021] A person guilty of an offence under s 743 of the CA 2006 is liable on summary conviction to a fine not exceeding level 3 on the standard scale and, for continued contravention, a daily default fine not exceeding one-tenth of level 3 on the standard scale.[5022]

References in s 743 of the CA 2006 to a 'register of debenture holders' include a duplicate of a register of debenture holders that is kept outside the United Kingdom,[5023] or of any part of such a register.[5024]

Section 743 of the CA 2006 replaces s 190 of the CA 1985. There is no requirement for a company to keep a register of debenture holders but if such a register is kept, then it (or any duplicate) must be kept available for inspection at either the company's registered office or a place permitted under regulations made under s 1136 of the CA 2006. (This is the same as for the obligatory registers of members: see s 114 of the CA 2006.)

Register of debenture holders: the right to inspect and require copy

20.10 Section 744 of the CA 2006 states that every register of debenture holders of a company must, except when duly closed, be open to the inspection of the registered holder of any such debentures, or any holder of shares in the company, without charge,[5025] and of any other person on payment of such fee as may be prescribed.[5026]

Any person may require a copy of the register, or any part of it, on payment of such fee as may be prescribed.[5027]

A person seeking to exercise either of the rights conferred by s 744 of the CA 2006 must make a request to the company to that effect.[5028]

[5016] CA 2006, s 743(1)(a).   [5017] CA 2006, s 743(1)(b).   [5018] CA 2006, s 743(2).
[5019] CA 2006, s 743(3).   [5020] CA 2006, s 743(4)(a).   [5021] CA 2006, s 743(4)(b).
[5022] CA 2006, s 743(5).   [5023] CA 2006, s 743(6)(a).   [5024] CA 2006, s 743(6)(b).
[5025] CA 2006, s 744(1)(a).   [5026] CA 2006, s 744(1)(b).   [5027] CA 2006, s 744(2).
[5028] CA 2006, s 744(3).

The request must contain the following information:

(a)   in the case of an individual, his name and address;[5029]
(b)   in the case of an organisation, the name and address of an individual responsible for making the request on behalf of the organisation;[5030]
(c)   the purpose for which the information is to be used;[5031] and
(d)   whether the information will be disclosed to any other person, and if so (i) where that person is an individual, his name and address,[5032] (ii) where that person is an organisation, the name and address of an individual responsible for receiving the information on its behalf,[5033] and (iii) the purpose for which the information is to be used by that person.[5034]

Under s 744 of the CA 2006, a register is 'duly closed' if it is closed in accordance with provision contained in the articles or in the debentures,[5035] or in the case of debenture stock in the stock certificates,[5036] or in the trust deed or other document securing the debentures or debenture stock.[5037]

The total period for which a register is closed in any year must not exceed 30 days.

The references in s 744 of the CA 2006 to a register of debenture holders include a duplicate of a register of debenture holders that is kept outside the United Kingdom,[5038] or of any part of such a register.[5039]

Section 744 of the CA 2006 replaces part of s 191 of the CA 1985. It modifies the existing right of public access to any register of debenture holders kept by a company. The changes mirror similar requirements in Part 8 of the CA 2006 relating to the register of members. Section 744(3) and (4) of the CA 2006 requires those seeking to inspect or to be provided with a copy of the register, to provide their names and addresses, the purpose for which the information will be used, and, if the access is sought on behalf of others, similar information for them.

Register of debenture holders: response to request for inspection or copy

20.11 Section 745 of the CA 2006 states that where a company receives a request under s 744 of the CA 2006 (register of debenture holders: right to inspect and require copy), it must within five working days either comply with the request,[5040] or apply to the court.[5041]

[5029] CA 2006, s 744(4)(a).   [5030] CA 2006, s 744(4)(b).   [5031] CA 2006, s 744(4)(c).
[5032] CA 2006, s 744(4)(d)(i).   [5033] CA 2006, s 744(4)(d)(ii).
[5034] CA 2006, s 744(4)(d)(iii).   [5035] CA 2006, s 744(5)(a).   [5036] CA 2006, s 744(5)(b).
[5037] CA 2006, s 744(5)(c).   [5038] CA 2006, s 744(6)(a).   [5039] CA 2006, s 744(6)(b).
[5040] CA 2006, s 745(1)(a).   [5041] CA 2006, s 745(1)(b).

If it applies to the court it must notify the person making the request.[5042]

If on an application under s 745 of the CA 2006, the court is satisfied that the inspection or copy is not sought for a proper purpose, it must direct the company not to comply with the request,[5043] and it may further order that the company's costs (in Scotland, expenses) on the application be paid in whole or in part by the person who made the request, even if he is not a party to the application.[5044]

If the court makes such a direction and it appears to the court that the company is or may be subject to other requests made for a similar purpose (whether made by the same person or different persons), it may direct that the company is not to comply with any such request.[5045]

The order must contain such provision as appears to the court appropriate to identify the requests to which it applies.

If on an application under s 745 of the CA 2006 the court does not direct the company not to comply with the request, the company must comply with the request immediately upon the court giving its decision or, as the case may be, the proceedings being discontinued.[5046]

Section 745 of the CA 2006 is a new provision. It provides a procedure by which the company can refer the matter to the court, if it considers the request is not for a proper purpose. It specifies a five-day period within which the company must either comply with the request, or apply to the court for relief from the obligation. If the company opts for the latter, then s 745(3), (4) and (5) of the CA 2006 applies. Under s 745(3) of the CA 2006, if the court is satisfied that the access to the register of debenture holders is not sought for a proper purpose, it will require the company not to comply with the obligation to meet the request, and may require that the person who made the request pay the company's costs. Under s 745(4) of the CA 2006, the court may also require the company not to comply with other requests made for similar purposes. If the court does not make an order under s 745(3) of the CA 2006, or the proceedings are discontinued, then, under s 745(5) of the CA 2006, the company must immediately comply with the request.

Register of debenture holders: refusal of inspection or default in providing copy

20.12 Section 746 of the CA 2006 deals with the register of debenture holders in respect of a refusal of inspection or a default in providing copy. If an inspection required under s 744 of the CA 2006 (register of debenture holders: right to inspect and require copy) is refused, or default is made in providing a copy required under that section, otherwise than in accordance with an

---

[5042] CA 2006, s 745(2).   [5043] CA 2006, s 745(3)(a).   [5044] CA 2006, s 745(3)(b).
[5045] CA 2006, s 745(4).   [5046] CA 2006, s 745(5).

order of the court, an offence is committed by the company,[5047] and every officer of the company who is in default.[5048]

A person guilty of an offence under s 746 of the CA 2006 is liable on summary conviction to a fine not exceeding level 3 on the standard scale and, for continued contravention, a daily default fine not exceeding one-tenth of level 3 on the standard scale.[5049]

In the case of any such refusal or default, the court may by order compel an immediate inspection or, as the case may be, direct that the copy required be sent to the person requesting it.[5050]

Section 746 of the CA 2006 retains the existing sanctions under s 191 of the CA 1985 for failure to comply with a request. They do not apply if the court has directed that the company need not comply with the request.

Register of debenture holders: offences in connection with a request for or disclosure of information

20.13 Section 747 of the CA 2006 states that it is an offence for a person knowingly or recklessly to make in a request under s 744 of the CA 2006 (register of debenture holders: right to inspect and require copy) a statement that is misleading, false or deceptive in a material particular.[5051]

It is an offence for a person in possession of information obtained by exercise of either of the rights conferred by that section to do anything that results in the information being disclosed to another person,[5052] or to fail to do anything with the result that the information is disclosed to another person,[5053] knowing, or having reason to suspect, that person may use the information for a purpose that is not a proper purpose.

A person guilty of an offence under s 747 of the CA 2006 is liable on conviction on indictment, to imprisonment for a term not exceeding two years or a fine (or both);[5054] or on summary conviction in England and Wales, to imprisonment for a term not exceeding 12 months or to a fine not exceeding the statutory maximum (or both);[5055] in Scotland or Northern Ireland, to imprisonment for a term not exceeding six months, or to a fine not exceeding the statutory maximum (or both).[5056]

Section 747 of the CA 2006 is a new provision. It creates two offences. First, in relation to the new requirement in s 744 of the CA 2006 to provide information in a request for access, it is an offence knowingly or recklessly to make a statement that is misleading, false or deceptive in a material particular. Second, it is an offence for a person having obtained information

---

[5047] CA 2006, s 746(1)(a).   [5048] CA 2006, s 746(1)(b).   [5049] CA 2006, s 746(2).
[5050] CA 2006, s 746(3).   [5051] CA 2006, s 747(1).   [5052] CA 2006, s 747(2)(a).
[5053] CA 2006, s 747(2)(b).   [5054] CA 2006, s 747(3)(a).   [5055] CA 2006, s 747(3)(b)(i).
[5056] CA 2006, s 747(3)(b)(ii).

pursuant to an exercise of the rights in s 744 of the CA 2006, to do anything or fail to do anything that results in that information being disclosed to another person knowing, or having reason to suspect that the other person may use the information for a purpose that is not a proper purpose.

Time limit for claims arising from entry in the register

20.14 Section 748 of the CA 2006 sets out the time limit for claims arising from an entry in the register. Liability incurred by a company from the making or deletion of an entry in the register of debenture holders,[5057] or from a failure to make or delete any such entry,[5058] is not enforceable more than ten years after the date on which the entry was made or deleted or, as the case may be, the failure first occurred.

This is without prejudice to any lesser period of limitation (and, in Scotland, to any rule that the obligation giving rise to the liability prescribes before the expiry of that period).[5059]

Section 748 of the CA 2006 replaces s 191(7) of the CA 1985. It amends the existing time limit for claims arising from errors in the register from 20 years to ten years. This mirrors equivalent provisions applicable to the register of members (see s 128 of the CA 1985).

Supplementary provisions

20.15 Sections 749–754 of the CA 2006 are concerned with supplementary provisions to debentures.

Right of debenture holder to copies of deeds

20.16 Section 749 of the CA 2006 deals with the right of debenture holders to copies of deeds. Any holder of debentures of a company is entitled, on request and on payment of such fee as may be prescribed, to be provided with a copy of any trust deed for securing the debentures.[5060]

If default is made in complying with this section, an offence is committed by every officer of the company who is in default.[5061] A person guilty of an offence under s 749 of the CA 2006 is liable on summary conviction to a fine not exceeding level 3 on the standard scale and, for continued contravention, a daily default fine not exceeding one-tenth of level 3 on the standard scale.[5062]

In the case of any such default the court may direct that the copy required be sent to the person requiring it.[5063]

[5057] CA 2006, s 748(1)(a).   [5058] CA 2006, s 748(1)(b).   [5059] CA 2006, s 748(2).
[5060] CA 2006, s 749(1).   [5061] CA 2006, s 749(2).   [5062] CA 2006, s 749(3).
[5063] CA 2006, s 749(4).

Liability of trustees of debentures

20.17 Section 750 of the CA 2006 is concerned with the liability of trustees of debentures. It states that any provision contained in a trust deed for securing an issue of debentures,[5064] or any contract with the holders of debentures secured by a trust deed,[5065] is void insofar as it would have the effect of exempting a trustee of the deed from, or indemnifying him against, liability for a breach of trust where he fails to show the degree of care and diligence required of him as a trustee, having regard to the provisions of the trust deed conferring on him any powers, authorities or discretions.

Section 750(1) of the CA 2006 does not invalidate: (a) a release otherwise validly given in respect of anything done or omitted to be done by a trustee before the giving of the release;[5066] (b) any provision enabling such a release to be given (i) on being agreed to by a majority of not less than 75 per cent in value of the debenture holders present and voting in person or, where proxies are permitted, by proxy at a meeting summoned for the purpose,[5067] and (ii) either with respect to specific acts or omissions or on the trustee dying or ceasing to act.[5068]

Section 750 of the CA 2006 is subject to s 751 of the CA 2006 (preserving certain older provisions).[5069]

Liability of trustees of debentures: preserving certain older provisions

20.18 Section 751 of the CA 2006 sets out the liability of trustees of debentures while preserving for certain older provisions. It states that s 750 of the CA 2006 (liability of trustees of debentures) does not operate (a) to invalidate any provision in force on the relevant date so long as any person (i) then entitled to the benefit of the provision,[5070] or (ii) afterwards given the benefit of the provision under s 751(3) of the CA 2006 below,[5071] remains a trustee of the deed in question; or (b) to deprive any person of any exemption or right to be indemnified in respect of anything done or omitted to be done by him while any such provision was in force.[5072]

The relevant date for this purpose is 1 July 1948 in a case where s 192 of the CA 1985 (c 6) applied immediately before the commencement of this section;[5073] or 1 July 1961 in a case where Article 201 of the Companies (Northern Ireland) Order 1986 (SI 1986/1032 (NI 6)) then applied.[5074]

While any trustee of a trust deed remains entitled to the benefit of a provision saved by s 751(1) of the CA 2006 above, the benefit of that provision may be given either to all trustees of the deed, present and future,[5075] or to any

---

[5064] CA 2006, s 750(1)(a). [5065] CA 2006, s 750(1)(b). [5066] CA 2006, s 750(2)(a).
[5067] CA 2006, s 750(2)(b)(i). [5068] CA 2006, s 750(2)(b)(ii). [5069] CA 2006, s 750(3).
[5070] CA 2006, s 751(1)(a)(i). [5071] CA 2006, s 751(1)(a)(ii). [5072] CA 2006, s 751(1)(b).
[5073] CA 2006, s 751(2)(a). [5074] CA 2006, s 751(2)(b). [5075] CA 2006, s 751(3)(a).

named trustees or proposed trustees of it,[5076] by a resolution passed by a majority of not less than 75 per cent in value of the debenture holders present in person or, where proxies are permitted, by proxy at a meeting summoned for the purpose.

A meeting for that purpose must be summoned in accordance with the provisions of the deed or, if the deed makes no provision for summoning meetings, in a manner approved by the court.[5077]

Power to re-issue redeemed debentures

20.19 Section 752 of the CA 2006 deals with the power to re-issue redeemed debentures. Where a company has redeemed debentures previously issued, then unless provision to the contrary (express or implied) is contained in the company's articles or in any contract made by the company,[5078] or the company has, by passing a resolution to that effect or by some other act, manifested its intention that the debentures shall be cancelled,[5079] the company may re-issue the debentures, either by re-issuing the same debentures or by issuing new debentures in their place. This subsection is deemed always to have had effect.

On a re-issue of redeemed debentures, the person entitled to the debentures has (and is deemed always to have had) the same priorities as if the debentures had never been redeemed.[5080]

The re-issue of a debenture or the issue of another debenture in its place under this section is treated as the issue of a new debenture for the purposes of stamp duty.[5081]

It is not so treated for the purposes of any provision limiting the amount or number of debentures to be issued.

A person lending money on the security of a debenture re-issued under this section that appears to be duly stamped may give the debenture in evidence in any proceedings for enforcing his security without payment of the stamp duty or any penalty in respect of it, unless he had notice (or, but for his negligence, might have discovered) that the debenture was not duly stamped.[5082]

In that case the company is liable to pay the proper stamp duty and penalty.

Deposit of debentures to secure advances

20.20 Section 753 of the CA 2006 states that where a company has deposited any of its debentures to secure advances from time to time on current accounts or otherwise, the debentures are not treated as redeemed by reason

[5076] CA 2006, s 751(3)(b).   [5077] CA 2006, s 751(4).   [5078] CA 2006, s 752(1)(a).
[5079] CA 2006, s 752(1)(b).   [5080] CA 2006, s 752(2).   [5081] CA 2006, s 752(3).
[5082] CA 2006, s 752(4).

only of the company's account having ceased to be in debit while the debentures remained so deposited.

Priorities where debentures secured by a floating charge

20.21 Section 754 of the CA 2006 applies where debentures of a company registered in England and Wales or Northern Ireland are secured by a charge that, as created, was a floating charge.[5083]

If possession is taken, by or on behalf of the holders of the debentures, of any property comprised in or subject to the charge, and the company is not at that time in the course of being wound up, the company's preferential debts shall be paid out of assets coming into the hands of the persons taking possession in priority to any claims for principal or interest in respect of the debentures.[5084]

The term 'preferential debts' means the categories of debts listed in Schedule 6 to the Insolvency Act 1986 (c 45) or Schedule 4 to the Insolvency (Northern Ireland) Order 1989 (SI 1989/2405 (NI 19)).[5085] For the purposes of those Schedules 'the relevant date' is the date of possession being taken as mentioned in s 754(2) of the CA 2006.

Payments under s 754 of the CA 2006 must be recouped, as far as may be, out of the assets of the company available for payment of general creditors.[5086]

[5083] CA 2006, s 754(1).   [5084] CA 2006, s 754(2).   [5085] CA 2006, s 754(3).
[5086] CA 2006, s 754(4).

Company Charges

Introduction

21.1 Part 25 of the CA 2006 is concerned with company charges. This Part of the CA 2006 provides a scheme for the registration of charges created by a company. Part 12 of the CA 1985 was prospectively repealed and replaced by the CA 1989, but these amendments and repeals were never brought into force, and they are now also being repealed (see Schedule 16 of the CA 2006).

Chapters 1 and 2 of Part 25 of the CA 2006 restate Part 12 of the CA 1985, with a few changes. The principal differences between the restated provisions under the CA 2006 and those of the CA 1985 are set out in this chapter. Three aspects should be noted. First, changes have been made to provisions in Part 25 as a result of other provisions in the CA 2006. So, for example, references to a statutory declaration in ss 403 and 419 of the CA 1985 are replaced by references to a statement in ss 872 and 887 of the CA 2006.

Second, changes have been made to ss 408 and 423 of the CA 1985 (now ss 877 and 892 of the CA 2006 respectively) to enable a company to keep its instruments creating charges and its register of charges in a place other than its registered office, bringing these provisions into line with provisions elsewhere in the CA 2006 relating to availability of documents for inspection.

Third, the provisions relating to charges created by an overseas company in ss 409 and 424 of the CA 1985 have not been restated. Instead s 1052 of the CA 2006 provides a new regulation-making power for the Secretary of State to make provision about the registration of charges over property in the United Kingdom of an overseas company that has registered its particulars with the registrar under s 1046 of the CA 2006.

There are no longer to be daily default fines for the offences under Part 25 of the CA 2006 of failure to register a new charge under ss 860 or 878 of the CA 2006 (compare ss 399 and 415 of the CA 1985) and failure to register an existing charge over acquired property under ss 862 or 880 of the CA 2006 (compare ss 400 and 416 of the CA 1985).

Part 25 of the CA 2006 comprises three Chapters. Chapter 1 is concerned with companies registered in England and Wales or in Northern Ireland. Chapter 2 addresses company charges in Scotland and considers a consultation document issued by the Department of Trade and Industry in May 2007. Chapter 3 deals with the powers of the Secretary of State.

Companies registered in England and Wales or in Northern Ireland

Requirement to register company charges

Charges created by a company

21.2 Chapter 1 is concerned with companies registered in England and Wales and Northern Ireland.

Section 860 of the CA 2006 states that a company that creates a charge to which this section applies must deliver the prescribed particulars of the charge, together with the instrument (if any) by which the charge is created or evidenced, to the registrar for registration before the end of the period allowed for registration.[5087]

Registration of a charge to which this section applies may instead be effected on the application of a person interested in it.[5088]

Where registration is effected on the application of some person other than the company, that person is entitled to recover from the company the amount of any fees properly paid by him to the registrar on registration.[5089]

If a company fails to comply with s 860(1) of the CA 2006, an offence is committed by the company,[5090] and every officer of it who is in default.[5091] A person guilty of an offence under this section is liable on conviction on indictment, to a fine;[5092] on summary conviction, to a fine not exceeding the statutory maximum.[5093]

Section 860(4) of the CA 2006 does not apply if registration of the charge has been effected on the application of some other person.[5094]

Section 860 of the CA 2006 applies to the following charges:

(a)   a charge on land or any interest in land, other than a charge for any rent or other periodical sum issuing out of land;[5095]

(b)   a charge created or evidenced by an instrument which, if executed by an individual, would require registration as a bill of sale;[5096]

(c)   a charge for the purposes of securing any issue of debentures;[5097]

[5087] CA 2006, s 860(1). See the Companies (Prescribed Particulars of Company Charges) Regulations 2007 – particularly regulations 2 and 3.
[5088] CA 2006, s 860(2).   [5089] CA 2006, s 860(3).   [5090] CA 2006, s 860(4)(a).
[5091] CA 2006, s 860(4)(b).   [5092] CA 2006, s 860(5)(a).   [5093] CA 2006, s 860(5)(b).
[5094] CA 2006, s 860(6).   [5095] CA 2006, s 860(7)(a).   [5096] CA 2006, s 860(7)(b).
[5097] CA 2006, s 860(7)(c).

(d)   a charge on uncalled share capital of the company;[5098]
(e)   a charge on calls made but not paid;[5099]
(f)   a charge on book debts of the company;[5100]
(g)   a floating charge on the company's property or undertaking;[5101]
(h)   a charge on a ship or aircraft, or any share in a ship;[5102]
(i)   a charge on goodwill or on any intellectual property.[5103]

Charges that have to be registered: supplementar

21.3 Section 861 of the CA 2006 states that the holding of debentures entitling the holder to a charge on land is not, for the purposes of s 860(7)(a) of the CA 2006, an interest in the land.[5104]

It is immaterial for the purposes of Chapter 1 to Part 25 of the CA 2006 where land subject to a charge is situated.[5105]

The deposit by way of security of a negotiable instrument given to secure the payment of book debts is not, for the purposes of s 860(7)(f) of the CA 2006, a charge on those book debts.[5106]

For the purposes of s 860(7)(i) of the CA 2006, the term 'intellectual property' means any patent, trade mark, registered design, copyright or design right;[5107] any licence under or in respect of any such right.[5108]

In Chapter 1 to Part 25 of the CA 2006, the term 'charge' includes mortgage, and 'company' means a company registered in England and Wales or in Northern Ireland.[5109]

Charges existing on property acquired

21.4 Section 862 of the CA 2006 applies where a company acquires property which is subject to a charge of a kind that would, if it had been created by the company after the acquisition of the property, have been required to be registered under Chapter 1 to Part 25 of the CA 2006.[5110]

The company must deliver the prescribed particulars of the charge, together with a certified copy of the instrument (if any) by which the charge is created or evidenced, to the registrar for registration.[5111]

Section 862(2) of the CA 2006 must be complied with before the end of the period allowed for registration.[5112]

If default is made in complying with this section, an offence is committed by the company,[5113] and every officer of it who is in default.[5114] A person

---

[5098] CA 2006, s 860(7)(d).   [5099] CA 2006, s 860(7)(e).   [5100] CA 2006, s 860(7)(f).
[5101] CA 2006, s 860(7)(g).   [5102] CA 2006, s 860(7)(h).   [5103] CA 2006, s 860(7)(i).
[5104] CA 2006, s 861(1).   [5105] CA 2006, s 861(2).   [5106] CA 2006, s 861(3).
[5107] CA 2006, s 861(4)(a).   [5108] CA 2006, s 861(4)(b).   [5109] CA 2006, s 861(5).
[5110] CA 2006, s 862(1).   [5111] CA 2006, s 862(2).   [5112] CA 2006, s 862(3).
[5113] CA 2006, s 862(4)(a).   [5114] CA 2006, s 862(4)(b).

guilty of an offence under this section is liable on conviction on indictment, to a fine;[5115] on summary conviction, to a fine not exceeding the statutory maximum.[5116]

Special rules about debentures

21.5 Sections 863–865 of the CA 2006 deal with special rules applicable to debentures.

Charge in series of debentures

21.6 Section 863 of the CA 2006 states that where a series of debentures containing, or giving by reference to another instrument, any charge to the benefit of which debenture holders of that series are entitled *pari passu* is created by a company, it is for the purposes of s 860(1) of the CA 2006 sufficient if the required particulars, together with the deed containing the charge (or, if there is no such deed, one of the debentures of the series), are delivered to the registrar before the end of the period allowed for registration.[5117]

The following are the required particulars: (a) the total amount secured by the whole series;[5118] and (b) the dates of the resolutions authorising the issue of the series and the date of the covering deed (if any) by which the series is created or defined;[5119] and (c) a general description of the property charged;[5120] and (d) the names of the trustees (if any) for the debenture holders.[5121]

Particulars of the date and amount of each issue of debentures of a series of the kind mentioned in s 863(1) of the CA 2006 must be sent to the registrar for entry in the register of charges.[5122]

Failure to comply with s 863(3) of the CA 2006 does not affect the validity of the debentures issued.[5123]

Section 860(2)–(6) of the CA 2006 applies for the purposes of this section as it apply for the purposes of that section, but as if references to the registration of a charge were references to the registration of a series of debentures.[5124]

Additional registration requirements for commission, etc. in relation to debentures

21.7 Section 864 of the CA 2006 states that where any commission, allowance or discount has been paid or made either directly or indirectly by a

[5115] CA 2006, s 862(5)(a).   [5116] CA 2006, s 862(5)(b).   [5117] CA 2006, s 863(1).
[5118] CA 2006, s 863(2)(a).   [5119] CA 2006, s 863(2)(b).   [5120] CA 2006, s 863(2)(c).
[5121] CA 2006, s 863(2)(d).   [5122] CA 2006, s 863(3).   [5123] CA 2006, s 863(4).
[5124] CA 2006, s 863(5).

company to a person, in consideration of his subscribing or agreeing to subscribe, whether absolutely or conditionally, for debentures in a company,[5125] or procuring or agreeing to procure subscriptions, whether absolute or conditional, for such debentures,[5126] the particulars required to be sent for registration under s 860 of the CA 2006 must include particulars as to the amount or percentage rate of the commission, discount or allowance so paid or made.

The deposit of debentures as security for a debt of the company is not, for the purposes of this section, treated as the issue of debentures at a discount.[5127]

Failure to comply with this section does not affect the validity of the debentures issued.[5128]

Endorsement of certificates on debentures

21.8 Section 865 of the CA 2006 states that the company shall cause a copy of every certificate of registration given under s 869 of the CA 2006 to be endorsed on every debenture or certificate of debenture stock that is issued by the company, and the payment of which is secured by the charge so registered.[5129]

However, this does not require a company to cause a certificate of registration of any charge so given to be endorsed on any debenture or certificate of debenture stock issued by the company before the charge was created.[5130]

If a person knowingly and willfully authorises, or permits the delivery of a debenture or certificate of debenture stock, which under this section is required to have endorsed on it a copy of a certificate of registration, without the copy being so endorsed upon it, he commits an offence.[5131] A person guilty of an offence under this section is liable on summary conviction to a fine not exceeding level 3 on the standard scale.[5132]

Charges in other jurisdictions

21.9 Sections 866–867 of the CA 2006 deal with charges in other jurisdictions.

Charges created in, or over property in, jurisdictions outside the United Kingdom

21.10 Section 866 of the CA 2006 states that where a charge is created outside the United Kingdom comprising property situated outside the United

---

[5125] CA 2006, s 864(1)(a).   [5126] CA 2006, s 864(1)(b).   [5127] CA 2006, s 864(2).
[5128] CA 2006, s 864(3).   [5129] CA 2006, s 865(1).   [5130] CA 2006, s 865(2).
[5131] CA 2006, s 865(3).   [5132] CA 2006, s 865(4).

Kingdom, the delivery to the registrar of a verified copy of the instrument by which the charge is created or evidenced has the same effect for the purposes of this Chapter as the delivery of the instrument itself.[5133]

Where a charge is created in the United Kingdom, but comprises property outside the United Kingdom, the instrument creating or purporting to create the charge may be sent for registration under s 860 of the CA 2006, even if further proceedings may be necessary to make the charge valid or effectual according to the law of the country in which the property is situated.[5134]

Charges created in, or over property in, another United Kingdom jurisdiction

21.11 Section 867 of the CA 2006 states that s 867(2) of the CA 2006 applies where a charge comprises property situated in a part of the United Kingdom other than the part in which the company is registered,[5135] and registration in that other part is necessary to make the charge valid or effectual under the law of that part of the United Kingdom.[5136]

The delivery to the registrar of a verified copy of the instrument by which the charge is created or evidenced, together with a certificate stating that the charge was presented for registration in that other part of the United Kingdom on the date on which it was so presented has, for the purposes of this Chapter, the same effect as the delivery of the instrument itself.[5137]

Orders charging land: Northern Ireland

Northern Ireland: registration of certain charges, etc. affecting land

21.12 Section 868 of the CA 2006 states that where a charge imposed by an order under Article 46 of the 1981 Order,[5138] or notice of such a charge is registered in the Land Registry against registered land[5139] or any estate in registered land of a company, the Registrar of Titles[5140] shall as soon as may be cause two copies of the order made under Article 46 of that Order or of any notice under Article 48 of that Order to be delivered to the registrar.[5141]

[5133] CA 2006, s 866(1).　　[5134] CA 2006, s 866(2).　　[5135] CA 2006, s 867(1)(a).

[5136] CA 2006, s 867(1)(b).　　[5137] CA 2006, s 867(2).

[5138] This means the Judgments Enforcement (Northern Ireland) Order 1981 (SI 1981) 226 (NI 6).

[5139] This has the same meaning as in the Registration of Deeds Acts. The Registration of Deeds means the Registration of Deeds Act (Northern Ireland) 1970 and every statutory provision for the time being in force amending that Act or otherwise relating to Part 3 the registry of deeds, or the registration of deeds, orders or other instruments or documents in such registry.

[5140] This has the same meaning as in the Land Registration Act (Northern Ireland) 1970, Part 3. Also for unregistered land.

[5141] CA 2006, s 868(1).

Where a charge imposed by an order under Article 46 of the 1981 Order is registered in the Registry of Deeds[5142] against any unregistered land[5143] or estate in land of a company, the Registrar of Deeds shall as soon as may be cause two copies of the order to be delivered to the registrar.[5144]

On delivery of copies under this section, the registrar shall register one of them in accordance with s 869 of the CA 2006,[5145] and not later than seven days from that date of delivery, cause the other copy together with a certificate of registration under section 869(5) to be sent to the company against which judgment was given.[5146]

Where a charge to which s 868(1) or (2) of the CA 2006 applies is vacated, the Registrar of Titles or, as the case may be, the Registrar of Deeds[5147] shall cause a certified copy of the certificate of satisfaction lodged under Article 132(1) of the 1981 Order to be delivered to the registrar for entry of a memorandum of satisfaction in accordance with s 872 of the CA 2006.[5148]

The register of charges

21.13 Sections 869–873 of the CA 2006 govern the register of charges.

Register of charges to be kept by the registrar

21.14 Section 869 of the CA 2006 states that the registrar shall keep, with respect to each company, a register of all the charges requiring registration under Chapter 1 to Part 25 of the CA 2006.[5149]

In the case of a charge to the benefit of which holders of a series of debentures are entitled, the registrar must enter in the register the required particulars specified in s 863(2) of the CA 2006.[5150]

In the case of a charge imposed by the Enforcement of Judgments Office under Article 46 of the Judgments Enforcement (Northern Ireland) Order 1981, the registrar must enter in the register the date on which the charge became effective.[5151]

In the case of any other charge, the registrar must enter in the register the following particulars: (a) if it is a charge created by a company, the date of its creation and, if it is a charge which was existing on property acquired by the company, the date of the acquisition,[5152] (b) the amount secured by the

[5142] This has the same meaning as in Part 3 of the Land Registration Act (Northern Ireland) 1970.
[5143] This is to be construed in accordance with s 1 of the Land Registration Act (Northern Ireland) 1970 (c 18).
[5144] CA 2006, s 868(2).   [5145] CA 2006, s 868(3)(a).   [5146] CA 2006, s 868(3)(b).
[5147] This means the registrar appointed under the Registration of Deeds Act (Northern Ireland) 1970 (c 25).
[5148] CA 2006, s 868(4).   [5149] CA 2006, s 869(1).   [5150] CA 2006, s 869(2).
[5151] CA 2006, s 869(3).   [5152] CA 2006, s 869(4)(a).

charge,[5153] (c) short particulars of the property charged,[5154] and (d) the persons entitled to the charge.[5155]

The registrar must give a certificate of the registration of any charge registered in pursuance of this Chapter, stating the amount secured by the charge.[5156]

The certificate must be signed by the registrar or authenticated by the registrar's official seal,[5157] and is conclusive evidence that the requirements of this Chapter as to registration have been satisfied.[5158]

The register kept in pursuance of this section must be open to inspection by any person.[5159]

The period allowed for registration

21.15 Section 870 of the CA 2006 states that the period allowed for registration of a charge created by a company is 21 days, beginning with the day after the day on which the charge is created,[5160] or if the charge is created outside the United Kingdom, 21 days beginning with the day after the day on which the instrument by which the charge is created or evidenced (or a copy of it) could, allowing postage/delivery time (and if despatched with due diligence) have been received in the United Kingdom.[5161]

The period allowed for registration of a charge to which property acquired by a company is subject is 21 days, beginning with the day after the day on which the acquisition is completed,[5162] or if the property is situated and the charge was created outside the United Kingdom, 21 days beginning with the day after the day on which the instrument by which the charge is created or evidenced (or a copy of it) could, allowing postage/delivery time (and if despatched with due diligence) have been received in the United Kingdom.[5163]

The period allowed for registration of particulars of a series of debentures as a result of s 863 is if there is a deed containing the charge mentioned in s 863(1) of the CA 2006, 21 days beginning with the day after the day on which that deed is executed,[5164] or if there is no such deed, 21 days beginning with the day after the day on which the first debenture of the series is executed.[5165]

Registration of enforcement of security

21.16 Section 871 of the CA 2006 states that if a person obtains an order for the appointment of a receiver or manager of a company's property, or appoints such a receiver or manager under powers contained in an

---

[5153] CA 2006, s 869(4)(b).   [5154] CA 2006, s 869(4)(c).   [5155] CA 2006, s 869(4)(d).
[5156] CA 2006, s 869(5).   [5157] CA 2006, s 869(6)(a).   [5158] CA 2006, s 869(6)(b).
[5159] CA 2006, s 869(7).   [5160] CA 2006, s 870(1)(a).   [5161] CA 2006, s 870(1)(b).
[5162] CA 2006, s 870(2)(a).   [5163] CA 2006, s 870(2)(b).   [5164] CA 2006, s 870(3)(a).
[5165] CA 2006, s 870(3)(b).

instrument, he must within seven days of the order or of the appointment under those powers, give notice of the fact to the registrar.[5166]

Where a person appointed receiver or manager of a company's property under powers contained in an instrument ceases to act as such a receiver or manager, he must, on so ceasing, give the registrar notice to that effect.[5167]

The registrar must enter a fact of which he is given notice under this section in the register of charges.[5168]

A person who makes a default in complying with the requirements of this section commits an offence.[5169] A person guilty of an offence under this section is liable on summary conviction to a fine not exceeding level 3 on the standard scale and, for continued contravention, a daily default fine not exceeding one-tenth of level 3 on the standard scale.[5170]

Entries of satisfaction and release

21.17 Section 872(2) of the CA 2006 applies if a statement is delivered to the registrar verifying with respect to a registered charge that the debt for which the charge was given has been paid or satisfied in whole or in part,[5171] or that part of the property or undertaking charged has been released from the charge or has ceased to form part of the company's property or undertaking.[5172]

The registrar may enter on the register a memorandum of satisfaction in whole or in part, or of the fact that part of the property or undertaking has been released from the charge or has ceased to form part of the company's property or undertaking (as the case may be).[5173]

Where the registrar enters a memorandum of satisfaction in whole, the registrar shall if required send the company a copy of it.[5174]

Rectification of the register of charges

21.18 Section 873 of the CA 2006 states that s 873(2) of the CA 2006 applies if the court is satisfied (a) that the failure to register a charge before the end of the period allowed for registration, or the omission or mis-statement of any particular with respect to any such charge or in a memorandum of satisfaction (i) was accidental or due to inadvertence or to some other sufficient cause,[5175] or (ii) is not of a nature to prejudice the position of creditors or shareholders of the company;[5176] or (b) that on other grounds it is just and equitable to grant relief.[5177]

The court may, on the application of the company or a person interested,

---

[5166] CA 2006, s 871(1).   [5167] CA 2006, s 871(2).   [5168] CA 2006, s 871(3).
[5169] CA 2006, s 871(4).   [5170] CA 2006, s 871(5).   [5171] CA 2006, s 872(1)(a).
[5172] CA 2006, s 872(1)(b).   [5173] CA 2006, s 872(2).   [5174] CA 2006, s 872(3).
[5175] CA 2006, s 873(1)(a)(i).   [5176] CA 2006, s 873(1)(a)(ii).   [5177] CA 2006, s 873(1)(b).

and on such terms and conditions as seem to the court just and expedient, order that the period allowed for registration shall be extended or, as the case may be, that the omission or mis-statement shall be rectified.[5178]

Avoidance of certain charges

Consequence of a failure to register charges created by a company

21.19 Section 874 of the CA 2006 states that if a company creates a charge to which s 860 of the CA 2006 applies, the charge is void (so far as any security on the company's property or undertaking is conferred by it) against a liquidator of the company,[5179] an administrator of the company,[5180] and a creditor of the company,[5181] unless that section is complied with.

Section 874(1) of the CA 2006 is subject to the provisions of Chapter 1 to Part 25 of the CA 2006.[5182]

Section 874(1) of the CA 2006 is without prejudice to any contract or obligation for repayment of the money secured by the charge; and when a charge becomes void under this section, the money secured by it immediately becomes payable.[5183]

Companies' records and registers

Companies to keep copies of instruments creating charges

21.20 Section 875 of the CA 2006 states that a company must keep available for inspection a copy of every instrument creating a charge requiring registration under Chapter 1 to Part 25 of the CA 2006, including any document delivered to the company under s 868(3)(b) of the CA 2006 (Northern Ireland: orders imposing charges affecting land).[5184]

In the case of a series of uniform debentures, a copy of one of the debentures of the series is sufficient.[5185]

Company's register of charges

21.21 Section 876 of the CA 2006 is concerned with a company's register of charges. It provides that every limited company must keep available for inspection a register of charges and enter in it all charges specifically affecting property of the company,[5186] and all floating charges on the whole or part of the company's property or undertaking.[5187]

[5178] CA 2006, s 873(2).   [5179] CA 2006, s 874(1)(a).   [5180] CA 2006, s 874(1)(b).
[5181] CA 2006, s 874(1)(c).   [5182] CA 2006, s 874(2).   [5183] CA 2006, s 874(3).
[5184] CA 2006, s 875(1).   [5185] CA 2006, s 875(2).   [5186] CA 2006, s 876(1)(a).
[5187] CA 2006, s 876(1)(b).

The entry shall in each case give a short description of the property charged, the amount of the charge and, except in the cases of securities to bearer, the names of the persons entitled to it.[5188]

If an officer of the company knowingly and willfully authorises or permits the omission of an entry required to be made in pursuance of this section, he commits an offence.[5189] A person guilty of an offence under this section is liable on conviction on indictment, to a fine;[5190] on summary conviction, to a fine not exceeding the statutory maximum.[5191]

Instruments creating charges, and register of charges to be available for inspection

21.22 Section 877 of the CA 2006 applies to documents required to be kept available for inspection under s 875 of the CA 2006 (copies of instruments creating charges),[5192] and a company's register of charges kept in pursuance of s 876 of the CA 2006.[5193]

The documents and register must be kept available for inspection at the company's registered office,[5194] or at a place specified in regulations under s 1136 of the CA 2006.[5195]

The company must give notice to the registrar of the place at which the documents and register are kept available for inspection,[5196] and of any change in that place,[5197] unless they have at all times been kept at the company's registered office.

The documents and register shall be open to the inspection of any creditor or member of the company without charge,[5198] and of any other person on payment of such fee as may be prescribed.[5199]

If default is made for 14 days in complying with s 877(3) of the CA 2006 or an inspection required under s 877(4) of the CA 2006 is refused, an offence is committed by the company,[5200] and every officer of the company who is in default.[5201] A person guilty of an offence under this section is liable on summary conviction to a fine not exceeding level 3 on the standard scale and, for continued contravention, a daily default fine not exceeding one-tenth of level 3 on the standard scale.[5202]

If an inspection required under s 877(4) of the CA 2006 is refused the court may by order compel an immediate inspection.[5203]

[5188] CA 2006, s 876(2). [5189] CA 2006, s 876(3). [5190] CA 2006, s 876(4)(a).
[5191] CA 2006, s 876(4)(b). [5192] CA 2006, s 877(1)(a). [5193] CA 2006, s 877(1)(b).
[5194] CA 2006, s 877(2)(a). [5195] CA 2006, s 877(2)(b). [5196] CA 2006, s 877(3)(a).
[5197] CA 2006, s 877(3)(b). [5198] CA 2006, s 877(4)(a). [5199] CA 2006, s 877(4)(b).
[5200] CA 2006, s 877(5)(a). [5201] CA 2006, s 877(5)(b). [5202] CA 2006, s 877(6).
[5203] CA 2006, s 877(7).

Companies Registered in Scotland

21.23 Chapter 2 to Part 25 of the CA 2006 is concerned with companies registered in Scotland.

Charges requiring registration

Charges created by a company

21.24 Section 878 of the CA 2006 states that a company that creates a charge to which this section applies must deliver the prescribed particulars of the charge, together with a copy certified as a correct copy of the instrument (if any) by which the charge is created or evidenced, to the registrar for registration before the end of the period allowed for registration.[5204]

Registration of a charge to which this section applies may instead be effected on the application of a person interested in it.[5205]

Where registration is effected on the application of some person other than the company, that person is entitled to recover from the company the amount of any fees properly paid by him to the registrar on the registration.[5206]

If a company fails to comply with s 878(1) of the CA 2006, an offence is committed by the company,[5207] and every officer of the company who is in default.[5208] A person guilty of an offence under this section is liable on conviction on indictment, to a fine;[5209] on summary conviction, to a fine not exceeding the statutory maximum.[5210]

Section 878(4) of the CA 2006 does not apply if registration of the charge has been effected on the application of some other person.[5211]

Section 878 of the CA 2006 applies to the following charges:

(a) a charge on land or any interest in such land, other than a charge for any rent or other periodical sum payable in respect of the land;[5212]

(b) a security over incorporeal moveable property of any of the following categories:

    (i) goodwill;[5213]

    (ii) a patent or a licence under a patent;[5214]

    (iii) a trademark;[5215]

    (iv) a copyright or a licence under a copyright;[5216]

    (v) a registered design or a licence in respect of such a design;[5217]

    (vi) a design right or a licence under a design right;[5218]

[5204] CA 2006, s 878(1).   [5205] CA 2006, s 878(2).   [5206] CA 2006, s 878(3).
[5207] CA 2006, s 878(4)(a).   [5208] CA 2006, s 878(4)(b).   [5209] CA 2006, s 878(5)(a).
[5210] CA 2006, s 878(5)(b).   [5211] CA 2006, s 878(6).   [5212] CA 2006, s 878(7)(a).
[5213] CA 2006, s 878(7)(b)(i).   [5214] CA 2006, s 878(7)(b)(ii).   [5215] CA 2006, s 878(7)(b)(iii).
[5216] CA 2006, s 878(7)(b)(iv).   [5217] CA 2006, s 878(7)(b)(v).   [5218] CA 2006, s 878(7)(b)(vi).

(vii) the book debts (whether book debts of the company or assigned to it);[5219] and

(viii) uncalled share capital of the company or calls made but not paid;[5220]

(c) a security over a ship or aircraft or any share in a ship;[5221]

(d) a floating charge.[5222]

Charges that have to be registered: supplementary

21.25 Under s 879 of the CA 2006, a charge on land, for the purposes of s 878(7)(a) of the CA 2006, includes a charge created by a heritable security within the meaning of s 9(8) of the Conveyancing and Feudal Reform (Scotland) Act 1970 (c 35).[5223]

The holding of debentures entitling the holder to a charge on land is not, for the purposes of s 878(7)(a) of the CA 2006, deemed to be an interest in land.[5224]

It is immaterial for the purposes of Chapter 2 to Part 25 of the CA 2006 where land subject to a charge is situated.[5225]

The deposit by way of security of a negotiable instrument given to secure the payment of book debts is not, for the purposes of s 878(7)(b)(vii) of the CA 2006, to be treated as a charge on those book debts.[5226]

The references in Chapter 2 to Part 25 of the CA 2006 to the date of the creation of a charge are in the case of a floating charge, the date on which the instrument creating the floating charge was executed by the company creating the charge,[5227] and in any other case, the date on which the right of the person entitled to the benefit of the charge was constituted as a real right.[5228]

In Chapter 2, the term 'company' means an incorporated company registered in Scotland.[5229]

Duty to register charges existing on property acquired

21.26 Section 880 of the CA 2006 states that s 880(2) of the CA 2006 applies where a company acquires any property that is subject to a charge of any kind as would, if it had been created by the company after the acquisition of the property, have been required to be registered under this Chapter.[5230]

The company must deliver the prescribed particulars of the charge, together with a copy (certified to be a correct copy) of the instrument (if any)

[5219] CA 2006, s 878(7)(b)(vii).   [5220] CA 2006, s 878(7)(b)(viii).

[5221] CA 2006, s 878(7)(c).   [5222] CA 2006, s 878(7)(d).   [5223] CA 2006, s 879(1).

[5224] CA 2006, s 879(2).   [5225] CA 2006, s 879(3).   [5226] CA 2006, s 879(4).

[5227] CA 2006, s 879(5)(a).   [5228] CA 2006, s 879(5)(b).   [5229] CA 2006, s 879(6).

[5230] CA 2006, s 880(1).

by which the charge was created or is evidenced, to the registrar for registration before the end of the period allowed for registration.[5231]

If default is made in complying with this section, an offence is committed by the company,[5232] and every officer of it who is in default.[5233] A person guilty of an offence under this section is liable on conviction on indictment, to a fine;[5234] on summary conviction, to a fine not exceeding the statutory maximum.[5235]

Charge by way of ex facie absolute disposition, etc.

21.27 Section 881 of the CA 2006 states that for the avoidance of doubt, it is hereby declared that, in the case of a charge created by way of an ex facie absolute disposition or assignation qualified by a back letter or other agreement, or by a standard security qualified by an agreement, compliance with s 878(1) of the CA 2006 does not of itself render the charge unavailable as security for indebtedness incurred after the date of compliance.[5236]

Where the amount secured by a charge so created is purported to be increased by a further back letter or agreement, a further charge is held to have been created by the *ex facie* absolute disposition or assignation or (as the case may be) by the standard security, as qualified by the further back letter or agreement.[5237]

In that case, the provisions of Chapter 2 to Part 25 of the CA 2006 apply to the further charge as if references in this Chapter (other than in this section) to a charge were references to the further charge,[5238] and references to the date of the creation of a charge were references to the date on which the further back letter or agreement was executed.[5239]

DTI consultation document: 'Registration of Scottish Floating Charges'

21.28 In May 2007, the DTI issued a consultation document on '*Registration of Scottish Floating Charges*' with a view to seeking comments from interest parties on the Government's proposal to use its powers under the CA 2006 so that floating charges were registered in the Scottish Register of Floating Charges as having been registered with the Registrar of Companies. Assuming the Government approves this proposal, the effect will be that there will not be a double registration that would otherwise apply to all floating charges granted under Scots law regardless of whether the grantor company is registered in Scotland, and this would apply once the relevant provisions

[5231] CA 2006, s 880(2).   [5232] CA 2006, s 880(3)(a).   [5233] CA 2006, s 880(3)(b).
[5234] CA 2006, s 880(4)(a).   [5235] CA 2006, s 880(4)(b).   [5236] CA 2006, s 881(1).
[5237] CA 2006, s 881(2).   [5238] CA 2006, s 881(3)(a).   [5239] CA 2006, s 881(3)(b).

of the Bankruptcy and Diligence, etc. (Scotland) Act 2007 come into force.[5240]

Special rules about debentures

Charges in a series of debentures

21.29 Section 882 of the CA 2006 states that where a series of debentures containing, or giving by reference to any other instrument any charge to the benefit of which the debenture-holders of that series are entitled *pari passu*, is created by a company, it is sufficient for purposes of s 878 of the CA 2006 if the required particulars, together with a copy of the deed containing the charge (or, if there is no such deed, of one of the debentures of the series) are delivered to the registrar before the end of the period allowed for registration.[5241]

The following are the required particulars:

(a) the total amount secured by the whole series;[5242]
(b) the dates of the resolutions authorising the issue of the series and the date of the covering deed (if any) by which the security is created or defined;[5243]
(c) a general description of the property charged;[5244]
(d) the names of the trustees (if any) for the debenture-holders;[5245] and
(e) in the case of a floating charge, a statement of any provisions of the charge and of any instrument relating to it that prohibit or restrict or regulate the power of the company to grant further securities ranking in

---

[5240] The Bankruptcy and Diligence, etc. (Scotland) Act 2007 provides that under Scots law, a floating charge is created only on its registration in the register of floating charges established by that Act. The effect would have been that a UK company would have to register a floating charge created under Scots law under the 2007 Act and the CA 2006. The Government is committed to the principles recommended by Philip Hampton, namely the fourth principle, 'business should not have to unnecessary information, nor give the same piece of information twice'. See *Reducing Administrative Burdens; Effective Inspection and Enforcement (2005)*. CA 2006, Part 25 (the 2006 Act) generally restates those provisions in the CA 1985 that provide schemes for the registration of company charges by UK companies. Part 25 does not change the current schemes and provides firstly, the power to make provision allowing a charge registered in a special register (such as the Register of Floating Charges) to be treated as if it had been registered with the Registrar (the multiple registration power); and secondly, a general power to amend the provisions in Part 25 of the 2006 Act.

Under Schedule 5 of the Scotland Act 1998, floating charges (and their registration) are a devolved matter. The 2007 Act provides for the establishment in Scotland of a new register to be called the Register of Floating Charges (ROFC). The register will be set up and maintained by the Keeper of the Registers of Scotland.

[5241] CA 2006, s 882(1).   [5242] CA 2006, s 882(2)(a).   [5243] CA 2006, s 882(2)(b).
[5244] CA 2006, s 882(2)(c).   [5245] CA 2006, s 882(2)(d).

priority to, or *pari passu* with, the floating charge, or that vary or other-wise regulate the order of ranking of the floating charge in relation to subsisting securities.[5246]

Where more than one issue is made of debentures in the series, particulars of the date and amount of each issue of debentures of the series must be sent to the registrar for entry in the register of charges.[5247]

Failure to comply with s 882(3) of the CA 2006 does not affect the validity of any of those debentures.[5248]

Section 878(2)–(6) of the CA 2006 applies for the purposes of this section as it applies for the purposes of that section but as if for the reference to the registration of the charge there were substituted a reference to the registration of the series of debentures.[5249]

Additional registration requirement for commission, etc. in relation to debentures

21.30 Section 883 of the CA 2006 states that where any commission, allow-ance or discount has been paid or made either directly or indirectly by a company to a person in consideration of his subscribing or agreeing to sub-scribe, whether absolutely or conditionally, for debentures in a company,[5250] or procuring or agreeing to procure subscriptions, whether absolute or con-ditional, for such debentures,[5251] the particulars required to be sent for regis-tration under s 878 of the CA 2006 shall include particulars as to the amount or percentage rate of the commission, discount or allowance so paid or made.

The deposit of debentures as security for a debt of the company is not, for the purposes of this section, treated as the issue of debentures at a discount.[5252]

Failure to comply with this section does not affect the validity of the debentures issued.[5253]

Charges on property outside the United Kingdom

Charges on property outside the United Kingdom

21.31 Under s 884 of the CA 2006, where a charge is created in the United Kingdom, but comprises property outside the United Kingdom, the copy of the instrument creating or purporting to create the charge may be sent for registration under s 878 of the CA 2006, even if further proceedings may

---

[5246] CA 2006, s 882(2)(e).   [5247] CA 2006, s 882(3).   [5248] CA 2006, s 882(4).
[5249] CA 2006, s 882(5).   [5250] CA 2006, s 883(1)(a).   [5251] CA 2006, s 883(1)(b).
[5252] CA 2006, s 883(2).   [5253] CA 2006, s 883(3).

be necessary to make the charge valid or effectual, according to the law of the country in which the property is situated.

The register of charges

Register of charges to be kept by the registrar

21.32 Section 885 of the CA 2006 states that the registrar shall keep, with respect to each company, a register of all the charges requiring registration under Chapter 2 to Part 25 of the CA 2006.[5254]

In the case of a charge to the benefit of which holders of a series of debentures are entitled, the registrar shall enter in the register the required particulars specified in s 882(2) of the CA 2006.[5255]

In the case of any other charge, the registrar shall enter in the register the following particulars:

(a)   if it is a charge created by a company, the date of its creation and, if it is a charge that existed on property acquired by the company, the date of the acquisition;[5256]
(b)   the amount secured by the charge;[5257]
(c)   short particulars of the property charged;[5258]
(d)   the persons entitled to the charge;[5259] and
(e)   in the case of a floating charge, a statement of any of the provisions of the charge and of any instrument relating to it that prohibit or restrict or regulate the company's power to grant further securities ranking in priority to, or *pari passu* with, the floating charge, or that vary or otherwise regulate the order of ranking of the floating charge in relation to subsisting securities.[5260]

The registrar shall give a certificate of the registration of any charge registered in pursuance of Chapter 2 to Part 25 of the CA 2006, stating the name of the company and the person first-named in the charge among those entitled to the benefit of the charge, (or, in the case of a series of debentures, the name of the holder of the first such debenture issued),[5261] and the amount secured by the charge.[5262]

The certificate must be signed by the registrar or authenticated by the registrar's official seal,[5263] and is conclusive evidence that the requirements of Chapter 2 to Part 25 of the CA 2006 as to registration have been satisfied.[5264]

[5254] CA 2006, s 885(1).   [5255] CA 2006, s 885(2).   [5256] CA 2006, s 885(3)(a).
[5257] CA 2006, s 885(3)(b).   [5258] CA 2006, s 885(3)(c).   [5259] CA 2006, s 885(3)(d).
[5260] CA 2006, s 885(3)(e).   [5261] CA 2006, s 885(4)(a).   [5262] CA 2006, s 885(4)(b).
[5263] CA 2006, s 885(5)(a).   [5264] CA 2006, s 885(5)(b).

The register kept in pursuance of this section shall be open to inspection by any person.[5265]

The period allowed for registration

21.33 Section 886 of the CA 2006 provides that the period allowed for registration of a charge created by a company is 21 days beginning with the day after the day on which the charge is created,[5266] or if the charge is created outside the United Kingdom, 21 days beginning with the day after the day on which a copy of the instrument by which the charge is created or evidenced could, allowing postage/delivery time (and if despatched with due diligence) have been received in the United Kingdom.[5267]

The period allowed for registration of a charge to which property acquired by a company is subject is 21 days beginning with the day after the day on which the transaction is settled,[5268] or if the property is situated and the charge was created outside the United Kingdom, 21 days beginning with the day after the day on which a copy of the instrument by which the charge is created or evidenced could, in due course of post (and if despatched with due diligence) have been received in the United Kingdom.[5269]

The period allowed for the registration of the particulars of a series of debentures as a result of s 882 of the CA 2006 is if there is a deed containing the charge mentioned in s 882(1) of the CA 2006, 21 days beginning with the day after the day on which that deed is executed,[5270] or if there is no such deed, 21 days beginning with the day after the day on which the first debenture of the series is executed.[5271]

Entries of satisfaction and relief

21.34 Section 887 of the CA 2006 states that s 887(2) of the CA 2006 applies if a statement is delivered to the registrar verifying with respect to any registered charge, that the debt for which the charge was given has been paid or satisfied in whole or in part,[5272] or that part of the property charged has been released from the charge or has ceased to form part of the company's property.[5273]

If the charge is a floating charge, the statement must be accompanied by either (a) a statement by the creditor entitled to the benefit of the charge, or a person authorised by him for the purpose, verifying that the statement mentioned in s 887(1) of the CA 2006 is correct,[5274] or (b) a direction obtained from the court, on the ground that the statement by the creditor mentioned in

[5265] CA 2006, s 885(6).   [5266] CA 2006, s 886(1)(a).   [5267] CA 2006, s 886(1)(b).
[5268] CA 2006, s 886(2)(a).   [5269] CA 2006, s 886(2)(b).   [5270] CA 2006, s 886(3)(a).
[5271] CA 2006, s 886(3)(b).   [5272] CA 2006, s 887(1)(a).   [5273] CA 2006, s 887(1)(b).
[5274] CA 2006, s 887(2)(a).

para (a) could not be readily obtained, dispensing with the need for that statement.[5275]

The registrar may enter on the register a memorandum of satisfaction (in whole or in part) regarding the fact contained in the statement mentioned in s 887(1) of the CA 2006.[5276]

Where the registrar enters a memorandum of satisfaction in whole, he shall, if required, furnish the company with a copy of the memorandum.[5277]

Nothing in this section requires the company to submit particulars with respect to the entry in the register of a memorandum of satisfaction where the company, having created a floating charge over all or any part of its property, disposes of part of the property subject to the floating charge.[5278]

Rectification of the register of charges

21.35 Section 888 of the CA 2006 states that s 888(2) of the CA 2006 applies if the court is satisfied (a) that the failure to register a charge before the end of the period allowed for registration, or the omission or mis-statement of any particular with respect to any such charge or in a memorandum of satisfaction (i) was accidental or due to inadvertence or to some other sufficient cause,[5279] or (ii) is not of a nature to prejudice the position of creditors or shareholders of the company;[5280] or (b) that on other grounds it is just and equitable to grant relief.[5281]

The court may, on the application of the company or a person interested, and on such terms and conditions as seem to the court just and expedient, order that the period allowed for registration shall be extended or, as the case may be, that the omission or mis-statement shall be rectified.[5282]

Avoidance of certain charges

Charges void unless registered

21.36 Section 889 of the CA 2006 states that if a company creates a charge to which s 878 of the CA 2006 applies, the charge is void (so far as any security on the company's property or any part of it is conferred by the charge) against the liquidator of the company,[5283] an administrator of the company,[5284] and any creditor of the company[5285] unless that section is complied with.

Section 889(1) of the CA 2006 is without prejudice to any contract or obligation for repayment of the money secured by the charge; and when a

[5275] CA 2006, s 887(2)(b). [5276] CA 2006, s 887(3). [5277] CA 2006, s 887(4).
[5278] CA 2006, s 887(5). [5279] CA 2006, s 888(1)(a)(i). [5280] CA 2006, s 888(1)(a)(ii).
[5281] CA 2006, s 888(1)(b). [5282] CA 2006, s 888(2). [5283] CA 2006, s 889(1)(a).
[5284] CA 2006, s 889(1)(b). [5285] CA 2006, s 889(1)(c).

charge becomes void under this section the money secured by it immediately becomes payable.[5286]

Companies' records and registers

Copies of instruments creating charges to be kept by the company

21.37 Section 890 of the CA 2006 states that every company shall cause a copy of every instrument creating a charge requiring registration under Chapter 2 to Part 25 of the CA 2006 to be kept available for inspection.[5287]

In the case of a series of uniform debentures, a copy of one debenture of the series is sufficient.[5288]

Company's register of charges

21.38 Section 891 of the CA 2006 states that every company shall keep available for inspection a register of charges and enter in it all charges specifically affecting the property of the company, and all floating charges on any property of the company.[5289]

There shall be given in each case a short description of the property charged, the amount of the charge and, except in the case of securities to the bearer, the names of the persons entitled to it.[5290]

If an officer of the company knowingly and wilfully authorises or permits the omission of an entry required to be made in pursuance of this section, he commits an offence.[5291] A person guilty of an offence under this section is liable on conviction on indictment, to a fine;[5292] and on summary conviction, to a fine not exceeding the statutory maximum.[5293]

Instruments creating charges and the register of charges to be available for inspection

21.39 Section 892 of the CA 2006 applies to documents required to be kept available for inspection under s 890 of the CA 2006 (copies of instruments creating charges),[5294] and a company's register of charges kept in pursuance of s 891 of the CA 2006.[5295]

The documents and register must be kept available for inspection at the company's registered office,[5296] or at a place specified in regulations under s 1136 of the CA 2006.[5297]

[5286] CA 2006, s 889(2).   [5287] CA 2006, s 890(1).   [5288] CA 2006, s 890(1).
[5289] CA 2006, s 891(1).   [5290] CA 2006, s 891(2).   [5291] CA 2006, s 891(3).
[5292] CA 2006, s 891(4)(a).   [5293] CA 2006, s 891(4)(b).   [5294] CA 2006, s 892(1)(a).
[5295] CA 2006, s 892(1)(b).   [5296] CA 2006, s 892(2)(a).   [5297] CA 2006, s 892(2)(b).

The company must give notice to the registrar of the place at which the documents and register are kept available for inspection,[5298] and of any change in that place,[5299] unless they have at all times been kept at the company's registered office.

The documents and register shall be open to the inspection of any creditor or member of the company without charge,[5300] and of any other person on payment of such fee as may be prescribed.[5301]

If a default is made for 14 days in complying with s 892(3) of the CA 2006 or an inspection required under s 892(4) of the CA 2006 is refused, an offence is committed by the company,[5302] and every officer of the company who is in default.[5303] A person guilty of an offence under this section is liable on summary conviction to a fine not exceeding level 3 on the standard scale and, for continued contravention, a daily default fine not exceeding one-tenth of level 3 on the standard scale.[5304]

If an inspection required under s 892(4) of the CA 2006 is refused the court may by order compel an immediate inspection.[5305]

Powers of the Secretary of State

21.40 Chapter 3 to Part 25 of the CA 2006 sets out the powers of the Secretary of State in respect of company charges. It comprises two sections.

Power to make provision for the effect of registration in special register

21.41 Under s 893 of the CA 2006, the term a 'special register' means a register, other than the register of charges kept under Part 25 of the CA 2006, in which a charge to which Chapter 1 or Chapter 2 to Part 25 of the CA 2006 applies is required or authorised to be registered.[5306]

The Secretary of State may by order make provision for facilitating the making of information-sharing arrangements between the person responsible for maintaining a special register (the responsible person) and the registrar that meet the requirement in s 893(4) of the CA 2006.

'Information-sharing arrangements' are arrangements to share and make use of information held by the registrar or by the responsible person.[5307]

If the Secretary of State is satisfied that appropriate information-sharing arrangements have been made, he may by order provide that: (a) the registrar is authorised not to register a charge of a specified description under Chapter 1 or Chapter 2 to Part 25 of the CA 2006;[5308] (b) a charge of a specified description that is registered in the special register within a specified period is

---

[5298] CA 2006, s 892(3)(a).   [5299] CA 2006, s 892(3)(b).   [5300] CA 2006, s 892(4)(a).

[5301] CA 2006, s 892(4)(b).   [5302] CA 2006, s 892(5)(a).   [5303] CA 2006, s 892(5)(b).

[5304] CA 2006, s 892(6).   [5305] CA 2006, s 892(7).   [5306] CA 2006, s 893(1).

[5307] CA 2006, s 893(2).   [5308] CA 2006, s 893(3)(a).

to be treated as if it had been registered (and certified by the registrar as registered) in accordance with the requirements of Chapter 1 or, as the case may be, Chapter 2 to Part 25 of the CA 2006;[5309] and (c) the other provisions of Chapter 1 or, as the case may be, Chapter 2 to Part 25 of the CA 2006 apply to a charge so treated with specified modifications.[5310]

The information-sharing arrangements must ensure that persons inspecting the register of charges are made aware, in a manner appropriate to the inspection, of the existence of charges in the special register that are treated in accordance with provision so made,[5311] and are able to obtain information from the special register about any such charge.[5312]

An order under this section may (a) modify any enactment or rule of law that would otherwise restrict or prevent the responsible person from entering into or giving effect to information-sharing arrangements;[5313] (b) authorise the responsible person to require information to be provided to him for the purposes of the arrangements;[5314] (c) make provision about (i) the charging by the responsible person of fees in connection with the arrangements and the destination of such fees (including provision modifying any enactment that would otherwise apply in relation to fees payable to the responsible person),[5315] and (ii) the making of payments under the arrangements by the registrar to the responsible person;[5316] (d) require the registrar to make copies of the arrangements available to the public (in hard copy or electronic form).[5317]

The term 'specified' means specified in an order under this section.[5318]

A description of charge may be specified, in particular, by reference to one or more of the following: (a) the type of company by which it is created;[5319] (b) what form of charge it is;[5320] (c) the description of assets over which it is granted;[5321] (d) the length of the period between the date of its registration in the special register and the date of its creation.[5322]

Provision may be made under this section relating to registers maintained under the law of a country or territory outside the United Kingdom.[5323]

An order under this section is subject to negative resolution procedure.[5324]

This is a new provision, which provides power for the Secretary of State to make an order providing that, if a charge is registered in another register (for example, the register of floating charges to be established under the Bankruptcy and Diligence, etc. (Scotland) Bill), then the registrar may not register it, but it will be treated as if it had been registered in accordance with the requirements of Part 25 of the CA 2006. The power may only be exercised if

[5309] CA 2006, s 893(3)(b).   [5310] CA 2006, s 893(3)(c).   [5311] CA 2006, s 893(4)(a).
[5312] CA 2006, s 893(4)(b).   [5313] CA 2006, s 893(5)(a).   [5314] CA 2006, s 893(5)(b).
[5315] CA 2006, s 893(5)(c)(i).   [5316] CA 2006, s 893(5)(c)(ii).   [5317] CA 2006, s 893(5)(d).
[5318] CA 2006, s 893(6).   [5319] CA 2006, s 893(7)(a).   [5320] CA 2006, s 893(7)(b).
[5321] CA 2006, s 893(7)(c).   [5322] CA 2006, s 893(7)(d).   [5323] CA 2006, s 893(8).
[5324] CA 2006, s 893(9).

appropriate information-sharing arrangements have been made between the registrar and the person responsible for the other register. This is to ensure that a person searching the register will have access to information about charges registered in the other register.

General power to make amendments to this Part

21.42 Section 894 of the CA 2006 states that the Secretary of State may by regulations under this section amend Part 25 of the CA 2006, by altering, adding or repealing provisions,[5325] make consequential amendments or repeals in this Act or any other enactment (whether passed or made before or after this Act).[5326]

Regulations under this section are subject to affirmative resolution procedure.[5327]

This is a new provision providing the Secretary of State with a power to amend the provisions of Part 25 of the CA 2006.

[5325] CA 2006, s 894(1)(a).   [5326] CA 2006, s 894(1)(b).   [5327] CA 2006, s 894(2).

Chapter 22

Accounts and Reports

Introduction

22.1 Part 15 of the CA 2006 contains provisions dealing with accounts and reports as they apply to companies. It comprises 12 Chapters. Chapter 1 is a general introduction; Chapter 2 is about accounting records; Chapter 3 deals with a company's financial year; Chapter 4 addresses the annual accounts; Chapter 5 is on the directors' report; Chapter 6 considers directors' remuneration reports in respect of quoted companies; Chapter 7 deals with the publication of accounts and reports; Chapter 8 is concerned with laying of accounts and reports before the general meeting for public companies; Chapter 9 considers members' approval of directors' remuneration reports for quoted companies; Chapter 10 is on filing of accounts and reports; Chapter 11 is on the revision of defective accounts and reports; and Chapter 12 contains supplementary provisions.

The sections of Part 15 of the CA 2006 replace the provisions of Part 7 of the CA 1985 relating to accounts and reports. The provisions of Part 7 of the CA 1985 relating to audit are replaced by provisions in Part 16 of the CA 2006.

The sections have been re-arranged and redrafted to make it easier for companies of whatever size to find the requirements relevant to them. Previously, in Part 7 of the CA 1985 the sections applying to small companies were generally expressed as modifications of the sections applying to large companies. The sections under Part 15 of the CA 2006 proceed on the opposite basis: where provisions do not apply to all kinds of company, provisions applying to small companies appear before the provisions applying to other companies.

A further change under the CA 2006 is to enable the Secretary of State to replace the detailed Schedules of Part 7 of the CA 1985 by regulations. This will give more flexibility to arrange the material currently in Schedules to make it easier to follow for different types of company. It is unnecessary and undesirable to have parallel and duplicative regimes on the detail for different types of company in primary legislation, but this could be done in parallel sets of regulations for different sizes and types of company.

The main substantive changes in Part 15 of the CA 2006 to consider are first, a reduction in the time limit for private companies to file their accounts from ten months to nine months after the year end (s 442 of the CA 2006). Second, a reduction in the time limit for public companies to lay full financial statements before the company in general meetings the file them from seven months to six months after the year end (s 442 of the CA 2006). Third, new requirements for quoted companies to publish their annual accounts and reports and preliminary results on a website (s 430 of the CA 2006); and fourth, replacement of the general power of the Secretary of State to alter accounting requirements in s 257 of the CA 1985 by a general power of amendment by regulations (s 468 of the CA 2006) and more specific powers in relation to specific sections.

Chapter 1 to Part 15 of the CA 2006 provides a general introduction to accounts and report. It comprises six sections.

Introduction

Scheme of this Part

22.2 Section 380 of the CA 2006 sets out the scheme for the operation of Part 15 of the CA 2006. The requirements of Part 15 of the CA 2006 as to accounts and reports apply in relation to each financial year of a company.[5328]

In certain respects different provisions apply to different kinds of company.[5329]

The main distinctions for this purpose are between companies subject to the small companies regime (see s 381 of the CA 2006) and companies that are not subject to that regime;[5330] and between quoted companies (see s 385 of the CA 2006) and companies that are not quoted.[5331]

Where provisions do not apply to all kinds of company (a) provisions applying to companies subject to the small companies regime appear before the provisions applying to other companies;[5332] (b) provisions applying to private companies appear before the provisions applying to public companies;[5333] and (c) provisions applying to quoted companies appear after the provisions applying to other companies.[5334]

This introductory section in Chapter 1 indicates the main way in which the structure of Part 15 of the CA 2006 differs from that of Part 7 of the CA 1985; provisions relating to small companies are set out before provisions

[5328] CA 2006, s 380(1).   [5329] CA 2006, s 380(2).   [5330] CA 2006, s 380(3)(a).
[5331] CA 2006, s 380(3)(b).   [5332] CA 2006, s 380(4)(a).   [5333] CA 2006, s 380(4)(b).
[5334] CA 2006, s 380(4)(c).

relating to larger companies: provisions applying to private companies appear before those applying to public companies; and provisions applying to quoted companies appear after those applying to other companies.

Companies subject to the small companies regime

22.3 Section 381 of the CA 2006 is concerned with companies subject to the small companies regime. The small companies regime for accounts and reports applies to a company for a financial year in relation to which the company qualifies as small (see ss 382 and 383 of the CA 2006);[5335] and is not excluded from the regime (see s 386 of the CA 2006).[5336]

Companies qualifying as small: general

22.4 A company qualifies as small in relation to a financial year if the qualifying conditions are met in that year.[5337]
  A company is qualified as small in relation to a subsequent financial year:

(a)   if the qualifying conditions are met in that year and the preceding financial year;[5338]
(b)   if the qualifying conditions are met in that year and the company qualified as small in relation to the preceding financial year;[5339] or
(c)   if the qualifying conditions were met in the preceding financial year and the company qualified as small in relation to that year.[5340]

The qualifying conditions are met by a company in a year in which it satisfies two or more of the following requirements:[5341]

(a)   turnover: not more than £5.6 million;
(b)   balance sheet total: not more than £2.8 million;
(c)   number of employees: not more than 50;

For a period that is a company's financial year, but not in fact a year, the maximum figures for turnover must be proportionately adjusted.[5342]
  The balance sheet total means the aggregate of the amounts shown as assets in the company's balance sheet.[5343]
  The number of employees means the average number of persons employed by the company in the year, determined as follows:

(a)   find for each month in the financial year the number of persons

---

[5335] CA 2006, s 381(a).   [5336] CA 2006, s 381(b).   [5337] CA 2006, s 382(1).
[5338] CA 2006, s 382(2)(a).   [5339] CA 2006, s 382(2)(b).   [5340] CA 2006, s 382(2)(c).
[5341] CA 2006, s 382(3).   [5342] CA 2006, s 382(4).   [5343] CA 2006, s 382(5).

employed under contracts of service by the company in that month (whether throughout the month or not);[5344]

(b)   add together the monthly totals;[5345] and

(c)   divide by the number of months in the financial year.[5346]

Section 382 of the CA 2006 is subject to s 383 of the CA 2006 (companies qualifying as small: parent companies).[5347]

Companies qualifying as small: parent companies

22.5 Section 383 of the CA 2006 deals with companies qualifying as small in respect of parent companies.

A parent company qualifies as a small company in relation to a financial year only if the group headed by it qualifies as a small group.[5348]

A group qualifies as small in relation to a financial year if the qualifying conditions are met in that year.[5349]

A group qualifies as small in relation to a subsequent financial year of the parent company:

(a)   if the qualifying conditions are met in that year and the preceding financial year;[5350]

(b)   if the qualifying conditions are met in that year and the group qualified as small in relation to the preceding financial year;[5351]

(c)   if the qualifying conditions are met in the preceding financial year and the group qualified as small in relation to that year.[5352]

The qualifying conditions are met by a group in a year in which it satisfies two or more of the following requirements:[5353]

(a)   aggregate turnover: not more than £5.6 million net (or £6.72 million gross);

(b)   aggregate balance sheet total: not more than £2.8 million net (or £3.36 million gross);

(c)   aggregate number of employees: not more than 50.

The aggregate figures are ascertained by aggregating the relevant figures determined in accordance with s 382 of the CA 2006 for each member of the group.[5354]

In relation to the aggregate figures for turnover and balance sheet total:

[5344] CA 2006, s 382(6)(a).   [5345] CA 2006, s 382(6)(b).   [5346] CA 2006, s 382(6)(c).
[5347] CA 2006, s 382(7).   [5348] CA 2006, s 383(1).   [5349] CA 2006, s 383(2).
[5350] CA 2006, s 383(3)(a).   [5351] CA 2006, s 383(3)(b).   [5352] CA 2006, s 383(3)(c).
[5353] CA 2006, s 383(4).   [5354] CA 2006, s 383(5).

'net' means after any set-offs and other adjustments made to eliminate group transactions:

(a)   in the case of Companies Act accounts, in accordance with regulations under s 404 of the CA 2006;[5355]
(b)   in the case of IAS accounts, in accordance with international accounting standards;[5356]

and the term 'gross' means without those set-offs and other adjustments.[5357]

A company may satisfy the relevant requirements on the basis of either the net or the gross figure.

The figures for each subsidiary undertaking shall be those included in its individual accounts for the relevant financial year, that is, if its financial year ends with that of the parent company, that financial year,[5358] and if not, its financial year ending last before the end of the financial year of the parent company.[5359]

If those figures cannot be obtained without disproportionate expense or undue delay, the latest available figures shall be taken.

Companies excluded from the small companies regime

22.6 Section 384 of the CA 2006 applies to companies excluded from the small companies regime.

The small companies regime does not apply to a company that is, or was at any time within the financial year to which the accounts relate:

(a)   a public company;[5360]
(b)   a company that (i) is an authorised insurance company, a banking company, a e-money issuer, an ISD investment firm or a UCITS Management company;[5361] or (ii) carries on insurance market activity;[5362] or
(c)   a member of an ineligible group.[5363]

A group is ineligible if any of its members is:

(a)   a public company;[5364]
(b)   a body corporate (other than a company) whose shares are admitted to trading on a regulated market in an EEA State;[5365]
(c)   a person (other than a small company) who has permission under Part 4

[5355] CA 2006, s 383(6)(a).   [5356] CA 2006, s 383(6)(b).   [5357] CA 2006, s 383(6).
[5358] CA 2006, s 383(7)(a).   [5359] CA 2006, s 383(7)(b).   [5360] CA 2006, s 384(1)(a).
[5361] CA 2006, s 384(1)(b)(i).   [5362] CA 2006, s 384(1)(b)(ii).   [5363] CA 2006, s 384(1)(c).
[5364] CA 2006, s 384(2)(a).   [5365] CA 2006, s 384(2)(b).

of the Financial Services and Markets Act 2000 to carry on a regulated activity;[5366]

(d)   a small company that is an authorised insurance company, an e-money issuer, an ISD investment firm or an UCITS management company;[5367] or

(e)   carries on insurance market activity.[5368]

Sections 381–384 of the CA 2006 set out which companies, parent companies or groups fall within the small companies regime – that is, those qualify as small companies or groups and are not excluded from the regime for one of the reasons set out in s 386 of the CA 2006.

With two small changes, the conditions for qualifications as a small company are unchanged from the CA 1985 regime (ss 247, 247A and 249 of the CA 1985). Firstly, s 382(5) of the CA 2006 now contains a generalised definition of a balance sheet total for both Companies Act and IAS individual accounts. Secondly, whereas s 247A(2) of the CA 1985 provided that a group was ineligible if any of its members was a body corporate having power to offer its shares or debentures to the public, the reference in s 384(2)(b) of the CA 2006 is now to a body corporate whose securities are admitted to trading on a regulated market in an EEA state. The definition of 'regulated market' is to be found in s 1173 of the CA 2006. This reflects changes made by the Accounts Modernisation Directive (2003/51/EEC).

Quoted and unquoted companies

22.7 Section 385 of the CA 2006 is concerned with quoted and unquoted companies. For the purposes of Part 15 to the CA 2006, a company is a quoted company in relation to a financial year if it is a quoted company immediately before the end of the accounting reference period by reference to which that financial year was determined.[5369]

A 'quoted company' means a company whose equity share capital:

(a)   has been included in the official list in accordance with the provisions of Part 6 of the Financial Services and Markets Act 2000;[5370]

(b)   is officially listed in an EEA State;[5371] or

(c)   is admitted to dealing on either the New York Stock Exchange or the exchange known as Nasdaq.[5372]

In para (a) 'the official list' has the meaning given by s 103(1) of the Financial Services and Markets Act 2000.

[5366] CA 2006, s 384(2)(c).   [5367] CA 2006, s 384(2)(d).   [5368] CA 2006, s 384(2)(e).
[5369] CA 2006, s 385(1).   [5370] CA 2006, s 385(2)(a).   [5371] CA 2006, s 385(2)(b).
[5372] CA 2006, s 385(2)(c).

An 'unquoted company' means a company that is not a quoted company.[5373]

The Secretary of State may by regulations amend or replace the provisions of s 385 (1)–(2) of the CA 2006, so as to limit or extend the application of some or all of the provisions of Part 15 that are expressed to apply to quoted companies.[5374]

Regulations under s 385 of the CA 2006 extending the application of any such provision of Part 15 of the CA 2006 are subject to affirmative resolution procedure.[5375]

Any other regulations under s 385 of the CA 2006 are subject to negative resolution procedure.[5376]

The definitions of quoted and unquoted company in s 385 of the CA 2006 are equivalent to the definition of a 'quoted company' in s 262 of the CA 1985. A power is conferred to amend the definition of a 'quoted company' by regulations. If the regulations extend the application of Part 15 of the CA 2006 then they will be subject to affirmative resolution procedure. Otherwise they are subject to negative resolution procedure.

Accounting Records

22.8 Chapter 2 of Part 15 to the CA 2006 is concerned with accounting records. It comprises four sections.

Duty to keep accounting records

22.9 Section 386 of the CA 2006 deals with a duty to keep accounting records. Every company must keep adequate accounting records.[5377]

The term 'adequate accounting records' means records that are sufficient:

(a)   to show and explain the company's transactions;[5378]
(b)   to disclose with reasonable accuracy, at any time, the financial position of the company at that time;[5379] and
(c)   to enable the directors to ensure that any accounts required to be prepared comply with the requirements of this Act (and, where applicable, of Article 4 of the IAS Regulation).[5380]

Accounting records must, in particular, contain entries from day to day of all sums of money received and expended by the company and the matters in

[5373] CA 2006, s 385(3).   [5374] CA 2006, s 385(4).   [5375] CA 2006, s 385(5).
[5376] CA 2006, s 385(6).   [5377] CA 2006, s 386(1).   [5378] CA 2006, s 386(2)(a).
[5379] CA 2006, s 386(2)(b).   [5380] CA 2006, s 386(2)(c).

respect of which the receipt and expenditure takes place,[5381] and a record of the assets and liabilities of the company.[5382]

If the company's business involves dealing in goods, the accounting records must contain (a) statements of stock held by the company at the end of each financial year of the company;[5383] (b) all statements of stocktakings from which any statement of stock as is mentioned in para (a) has been or is to be prepared;[5384] (c) and except in the case of goods sold by way of ordinary retail trade, statements of all goods sold and purchased, showing the goods and the buyers and sellers in sufficient detail to enable all these to be identified.[5385]

A parent company that has a subsidiary undertaking in relation to which the above requirements do not apply must take reasonable steps to ensure that the undertaking keeps such accounting records as to enable the directors of the parent company to ensure that any accounts required to be prepared under Part 15 of the CA 2006 comply with the requirements of this Act (and, where applicable, of Article 4 of the IAS Regulation).[5386]

Duty to keep accounting records: offence

22.10 Section 387 of the CA 2006 is concerned with the duty to keep accounting records with respect to offences and sanctions.

If a company fails to comply with any provision of s 386 of the CA 2006 (duty to keep accounting records), an offence is committed by every officer of the company who is in default.[5387]

It is a defence for a person charged with such an offence to show that he acted honestly, and that in the circumstances in which the company's business was carried on the default was excusable.[5388]

A person guilty of an offence under s 387 of the CA 2006 is liable on conviction on indictment, to imprisonment for a term not exceeding two years or a fine (or both);[5389] or on summary conviction in England and Wales, to imprisonment for a term not exceeding 12 months or to a fine not exceeding the statutory maximum (or both);[5390] or in Scotland or Northern Ireland, to imprisonment for a term not exceeding six months, or to a fine not exceeding the statutory maximum (or both).[5391]

Where and how long records to be kept

22.11 Section 388 of the CA 2006 deals with where and how long records are kept. A company's accounting records must be kept at its registered office or

[5381] CA 2006, s 386(3)(a).   [5382] CA 2006, s 384(3)(b).   [5383] CA 2006, s 386(4)(a).
[5384] CA 2006, s 386(4)(b).   [5385] CA 2006, s 386(4)(c).   [5386] CA 2006, s 386(5).
[5387] CA 2006, s 387(1).   [5388] CA 2006, s 387(2).   [5389] CA 2006, s 387(3)(a).
[5390] CA 2006, s 387(3)(b)(i).   [5391] CA 2006, s 387(3)(b)(ii).

such other place as the directors think fit,[5392] and must at all times be open to inspection by the company's officers.[5393]

If accounting records are kept at a place outside the United Kingdom, accounts and returns with respect to the business dealt with in the accounting records so kept must be sent to, and kept at, a place in the United Kingdom, and must at all times be open to such inspection.[5394]

The accounts and returns to be sent to the United Kingdom must be such as to disclose with reasonable accuracy the financial position of the business in question at intervals of not more than six months,[5395] and enable the directors to ensure that the accounts required to be prepared under Part 15 of the CA 2006 comply with the requirements of this Act (and, where applicable, of Article 4 of the IAS Regulation).[5396]

Accounting records that a company is required by s 386 of the CA 2006 to keep must be preserved by it in the case of a private company, for three years from the date on which they are made;[5397] in the case of a public company, for six years from the date on which they are made.[5398]

Section 388(4) of the CA 2006 is subject to any provision contained in rules made under s 411 of the Insolvency Act 1986 (c 45) (company insolvency rules) or Article 359 of the Insolvency (Northern Ireland) Order 1989 (SI 1989/2405 (NI 19)).[5399]

Where and how long records to be kept: offences and sanctions

22.12 Section 389 of the CA 2006 deals with where and for how long records are to be kept, with particular reference to the offences and sanctions. If a company fails to comply with any provision of s 388(1)–(3) of the CA 2006 (requirements as to the keeping of accounting records), an offence is committed by every officer of the company who is in default.[5400]

However, it is a defence for a person charged with such an offence to show that he acted honestly and that in the circumstances in which the company's business was carried on the default was excusable.[5401]

An officer of a company commits an offence if he fails to take all reasonable steps for securing compliance by the company with s 389(4) of the CA 2006 of that section (period for which records are to be preserved),[5402] or intentionally causes any default by the company under that subsection.[5403]

A person guilty of an offence is liable on conviction on indictment, to imprisonment for a term not exceeding two years or a fine (or both);[5404] or on summary conviction in England and Wales, to imprisonment for a term not

---

[5392] CA 2006, s 388(1)(a).   [5393] CA 2006, s 388(1)(b).   [5394] CA 2006, s 388(2).
[5395] CA 2006, s 388(3)(a).   [5396] CA 2006, s 388(3)(b).   [5397] CA 2006, s 388(4)(a).
[5398] CA 2006, s 388(4)(b).   [5399] CA 2006, s 388(5).   [5400] CA 2006, s 389(1).
[5401] CA 2006, s 389(2).   [5402] CA 2006, s 389(3)(a).   [5403] CA 2006, s 389(3)(b).
[5404] CA 2006, s 389(4)(a).

exceeding 12 months or to a fine not exceeding the statutory maximum (or both);[5405] or in Scotland or Northern Ireland, to imprisonment for a term not exceeding six months, or to a fine not exceeding the statutory maximum (or both).[5406]

Sections 386–389 of the CA 2006 (accounting records) set out the general duty to accounting records and specify where and for how long records are to be kept. They replace equivalent provisions in ss 221 and 222 of the CA 1985. Their purpose is to ensure that businesses have the right information to make informed decisions and to prepare accounts which comply with the Companies Act and, where relevant, with International Accounting Standards. 'Accounting records' is a broad term and includes, for example, bank statements, purchases orders, sales and purchase invoices, whilst a more sophisticated business may have integrated records, which it holds electronically.

Section 387 of the CA 2006 creates a criminal offence for every officer of a company who is in default, where the company has failed to keep adequate accounting records under s 386 of the CA 2006. The section replicates the existing penalties under s 221(5) of the CA 1985 (imprisonment or a fine).

Section 389 of the CA 2006 makes similar provision in relation to failure to comply with s 388 of the CA 2006, replacing s 222(4) and (6) of the CA 1985.

A Company's Financial Year

22.13 Chapter 3 of Part 15 to the CA 2006 addresses a company's financial year. It comprises three sections.

A company's financial year

22.14 Section 390 of the CA 2006 states that a company's financial year is determined as follows.[5407]

Its first financial year begins with the first day of its first accounting reference period,[5408] and ends with the last day of that period or such other date, not more than seven days before or after the end of that period, as the directors may determine.[5409]

Subsequent financial years begin with the day immediately following the end of the company's previous financial year,[5410] and end with the last day of its next accounting reference period or such other date, not more than seven days before or after the end of that period, as the directors may determine.[5411]

In relation to an undertaking that is not a company, references in the CA

[5405] CA 2006, s 389(4)(b)(i).   [5406] CA 2006, s 389(4)(b)(ii).   [5407] CA 2006, s 390(1).
[5408] CA 2006, s 390(2)(a).   [5409] CA 2006, s 390(2)(b).   [5410] CA 2006, s 390(3)(a).
[5411] CA 2006, s 390(3)(b).

2006 to its financial year are to any period in respect of which a profit and loss account of the undertaking is required to be made up (by its constitution or by the law under which it is established), whether that period is a year or not.[5412]

The directors of a parent company must secure that, except where in their opinion there are good reasons against it, the financial year of each of its subsidiary undertakings coincides with the company's own financial year.[5413]

Section 390 of the CA 2006 replaces s 223 of the CA 1985. A company's financial year is the period for which its accounts and reports must be prepared. A company's financial year is the same as its accounting reference period (see s 391 of the CA 2006), subject to the directors' decision to alter the last day of the period by plus or minus seven days.

Accounting reference periods and accounting reference date

22.15 Section 391 of the CA 2006 deals with accounting reference periods and the accounting reference date. A company's accounting reference periods are determined according to its accounting reference date in each calendar year.[5414]

The accounting reference date of a company incorporated in Great Britain before 1 April 1996 is:

(a) the date specified by notice to the registrar in accordance with s 224(2) of the CA 1985 (c 6) (notice specifying accounting reference date given within nine months of incorporation);[5415] or

(b) failing such notice (i) in the case of a company incorporated before 1 April 1990, 31 March,[5416] and (ii) in the case of a company incorporated on or after 1 April 1990, the last day of the month in which the anniversary of its incorporation falls.[5417]

The accounting reference date of a company incorporated in Northern Ireland before 22 August 1997 is:

(a) the date specified by notice to the registrar in accordance with article 232(2) of the Companies (Northern Ireland) Order 1986 (SI 1986/1032 (NI 6)) (notice specifying accounting reference date given within nine months of incorporation);[5418] or

(b) failing such notice (i) in the case of a company incorporated before the coming into operation of Article 5 of the Companies (Northern

---

[5412] CA 2006, s 390(4).   [5413] CA 2006, s 390(5).   [5414] CA 2006, s 391(1).
[5415] CA 2006, s 391(2)(a).   [5416] CA 2006, s 391(2)(b)(i).   [5417] CA 2006, s 391(2)(b)(ii).
[5418] CA 2006, s 391(3)(a).

Ireland) Order 1990 (SI 1990/593 (NI 5)), 31 March,[5419] and (ii) in the case of a company incorporated after the coming into operation of that Article, the last day of the month in which the anniversary of its incorporation falls.[5420]

The accounting reference date of a company incorporated:

(a)   in Great Britain on or after 1 April 1996 and before the commencement of this Act;[5421]
(b)   in Northern Ireland on or after 22 August 1997 and before the commencement of this Act;[5422] or
(c)   after the commencement of this Act, is the last day of the month in which the anniversary of its incorporation falls.[5423]

A company's first accounting reference period is the period of more than six months, but not more than 18 months, beginning with the date of its incorporation and ending with its accounting reference date.[5424]

Its subsequent accounting reference periods are successive periods of 12 months beginning immediately after the end of the previous accounting reference period and ending with its accounting reference date.[5425]

Section 392 of the CA 2006 has effect subject to the provisions of s 374 of the CLRA (alteration of accounting reference date).[5426]

Alteration of accounting reference date

22.16 Section 392 of the CA 2006 deals with alteration of the accounting reference date. A company may by notice given to the registrar specify a new accounting reference date having effect in relation to the company's current accounting reference period and subsequent periods;[5427] or the company's previous accounting reference period and subsequent periods.[5428]

A company's 'previous accounting reference period' means the one immediately preceding its current accounting reference period.

The notice must state whether the current or previous accounting reference period is to be shortened, so as to come to an end on the first occasion on which the new accounting reference date falls or fell after the beginning of the period;[5429] or is to be extended, so as to come to an end on the second occasion on which that date falls or fell after the beginning of the period.[5430]

A notice extending a company's current or previous accounting reference period is not effective if given less than five years after the end of an earlier

---

[5419] CA 2006, s 391(3)(b)(i).   [5420] CA 2006, s 391(3)(b)(ii).   [5421] CA 2006, s 391(4)(a).
[5422] CA 2006, s 391(4)(b).   [5423] CA 2006, s 391(4)(c).   [5424] CA 2006, s 391(5).
[5425] CA 2006, s 391(6).   [5426] CA 2006, s 391(7).   [5427] CA 2006, s 392(1)(a).
[5428] CA 2006, s 392(1)(b).   [5429] CA 2006, s 392(2)(a).   [5430] CA 2006, s 392(2)(b).

accounting reference period of the company that was extended under this section.[5431] This does not apply:

(a) to a notice given by a company that is a subsidiary undertaking or parent undertaking of another EEA undertaking if the new accounting reference date coincides with that of the other EEA undertaking or, where that undertaking is not a company, with the last day of its financial year;[5432] or

(b) where the company is in administration under Part 2 of the Insolvency Act 1986 (c 45) or Part 3 of the Insolvency (Northern Ireland) Order 1989 (SI 1989/2405 (NI 19));[5433] or

(c) where the Secretary of State directs that it should not apply, which he may do with respect to a notice that has been given or that may be given.[5434]

A notice under this section may not be given in respect of a previous accounting reference period if the period for filing accounts and reports for the financial year determined by reference to that accounting reference period has already expired.[5435]

An accounting reference period may not be extended so as to exceed 18 months and a notice under this section is ineffective if the current or previous accounting reference period as extended in accordance with the notice would exceed that limit.

This does not apply where the company is in administration under Part 2 of the Insolvency Act 1986 or Part 3 of the Insolvency (Northern Ireland) Order 1989 (SI 1989/2405 (NI 19)).[5436]

Under s 392 of the CA 2006, 'EEA undertaking' means an undertaking established under the law of any part of the United Kingdom or the law of any other EEA State.[5437]

Sections 391 and 392 of the CA 2006, replace ss 224 and 225 of the CA 1985. Section 391(2) and (3) of the CA 2006 preserves the accounting reference dates of companies incorporated before 1 April 1996 (in the case of GB companies), and before 22 August 1997 (in the case of Northern Irish companies). Otherwise, a company's accounting reference date is the last day of the month in which the anniversary of its incorporation falls. Its first accounting period is a period of more than six months but not more than 18 months beginning with the date of incorporation and ending with the accounting reference date unless the company changes its accounting reference date, (the date on which the accounting reference period ends) in

[5431] CA 2006, s 392(3).   [5432] CA 2006, s 392(3)(a).   [5433] CA 2006, s 392(3)(b).
[5434] CA 2006, s 392(3)(c).   [5435] CA 2006, s 392(4).   [5436] CA 2006, s 392(5).
[5437] CA 2006, s 392(6).

accordance with s 392 of the CA 2006. Subsequent accounting reference periods (financial years) are successive periods of 12 months, again subject to any alteration of the accounting reference date.

Section 392(4) of the CA 2006 provides that a company cannot change its accounting reference date if the period allowed for delivering accounts and reports to the registrar for that period has already expired. Under the corresponding provision in the CA 1985, the company could change the date 'if the period allowed for laying and delivering accounts and reports in relation to that period has already expired'. Under the CA 2006, only public companies are obliged to lay accounts at a general meeting (see s 437 of the CA 2006).

Annual Accounts

22.17 Chapter 4 deals with the annual accounts of the company. It contains 22 sections dealing with general aspects, individual accounts and group accounts.

General

Accounts to give a true and fair view

22.18 Section 393 of the CA 2006 addresses the fact that the accounts must give true and fair view. The directors of a company must not approve accounts for the purposes of Chapter 3 of Part 15 of the CA 2006 unless they are satisfied that they give a true and fair view of the assets, liabilities, financial position and profit or loss in the case of the company's individual accounts, of the company;[5438] in the case of the company's group accounts, of the undertakings included in the constitution as a whole, so far as concerns members of the company.[5439]

The auditor of a company in carrying out his functions under the CA 2006 in relation to the company's annual accounts must have regard to the directors' duty under s 393(1) of the CA 2006.[5440]

Section 393(1) of the CA 2006 introduces an overarching obligation on directors (the preparers of accounts) not to approve accounts, unless they give a true and fair view of the financial position of the company and, in the case of group accounts, the group. This provision reflects the underlying legal duty already expressed in Community law.

Section 393(2) of the CA 2006, in addition, places a requirement on auditors to take this overarching duty to give a true and fair view in consideration when giving an opinion on the accounts. This requirement supplements the functions of an auditor set out in s 485 of the CA 2006.

[5438] CA 2006, s 393(1)(a).   [5439] CA 2006, s 393(1)(b).   [5440] CA 2006, s 393(2).

Individual accounts

22.19 Sections 394–397 of the CA 2006 apply to individual accounts.

Duty to prepare individual accounts

22.20 Section 394 of the CA 2006 deals with the duty to prepare individual accounts. The directors of every company must prepare accounts for the company for each of its financial years. Those accounts are referred to as the company's 'individual accounts'.

Individual accounts: applicable accounting framework

22.21 Section 395 of the CA 2006 applies to individual accounts with reference to the applicable accounting framework. A company's individual accounts may be prepared in accordance with s 396 of the CA 2006 (Companies Act individual accounts);[5441] or in accordance with international accounting standards (IAS individual accounts).[5442]

This is subject to the following provisions of this section and to s 407 of the CA 2006 (consistency of financial reporting within group).

The individual accounts of a company that is a charity must be Companies Act individual accounts.[5443]

After the first financial year in which the directors of a company prepare IAS individual accounts (the first IAS year), all subsequent individual accounts of the company must be prepared in accordance with international accounting standards unless there is a relevant change of circumstance.[5444]

There is a relevant change of circumstance if, at any time during or after the first IAS year:

(a)   the company becomes a subsidiary undertaking of another undertaking that does not prepare IAS individual accounts;[5445]

(b)   the company ceases to be a company with securities admitted to trading on a regulated market in an EEA State;[5446] or

(c)   a parent undertaking of the company ceases to be an undertaking with securities admitted to trading on a regulated market in an EEA State.[5447]

If, having changed to preparing Companies Act individual accounts following a relevant change of circumstance, the directors again prepare IAS individual accounts for the company, s 395(3) and (4) of the CA 2006 applies

[5441] CA 2006, s 395(1)(a).   [5442] CA 2006, s 395(1)(b).   [5443] CA 2006, s 395(2).
[5444] CA 2006, s 395(3).   [5445] CA 2006, s 395(4)(a).   [5446] CA 2006, s 395(4)(b).
[5447] CA 2006, s 395(4)(c).

again as if the first financial year for which such accounts are again prepared were the first IAS year.[5448]

Companies Act individual accounts

22.22 Section 396 of the CA 2006 addresses the Companies Act individual accounts. The Companies Act individual accounts must comprise a balance sheet as at the last day of the financial year;[5449] and a profit and loss account.[5450]

The accounts must in the case of the balance sheet, give a true and fair view of the state of affairs of the company as at the end of the financial year;[5451] and in the case of the profit and loss account, give a true and fair view of the profit or loss of the company for the financial year.[5452]

The accounts must comply with provision made by the Secretary of State by regulations as to the form and content of the balance sheet and profit and loss account;[5453] and additional information to be provided by way of notes to the accounts.[5454]

If compliance with the regulations, and any other provision made by or under the CA 2006 as to the matters to be included in a company's individual accounts or in notes to those accounts, would not be sufficient to give a true and fair view, the necessary additional information must be given in the accounts or in a note to them.[5455]

If in special circumstances compliance with any of those provisions is inconsistent with the requirement to give a true and fair view, the directors must depart from that provision to the extent necessary to give a true and fair view.

Particulars of any such departure, the reasons for it and its effect must be given in a note to the accounts.[5456]

IAS individual accounts

22.23 Section 397 of the CA 2006 deals with IAS individual accounts. Where the directors of a company prepare IAS individual accounts, they must state in the notes to the accounts that the accounts have been prepared in accordance with international accounting standards.

Sections 394–397 of the CA 2006, which replace s 226, 226A and 226B CA 1985, concern the duty of the directors to prepare individual accounts. The

---

[5448] CA 2006, s 395(5).   [5449] CA 2006, s 396(1)(a).   [5450] CA 2006, s 396(1)(b).
[5451] CA 2006, s 396(2)(a).   [5452] CA 2006, s 396(2)(b).
[5453] CA 2006, s 396(3)(a). See the Small Companies and Groups (Accounts and Directors' Report) Regulations 2008, and the Large and Medium-sized Companies and Groups (Accounts and Reports) Regulations 2008.
[5454] CA 2006, s 396(3)(b).   [5455] CA 2006, s 396(4).   [5456] CA 2006, s 396(5).

individual accounts may either be prepared under the CA 2006 (Companies Act individual accounts) or (unless the company is a charity) in accordance with international accounting standards adopted under the IAS Regulation (IAS individual accounts). The terms 'IAS Regulation' and 'international accounting standards' are defined in s 474 of the CA 2006. Once a company has switched to IAS individual accounts, all subsequent individual accounts must be prepared in accordance with IAS, unless there is a relevant change of circumstance (see s 395(3)–(5) of the CA 2006).

The provisions concerning the form and content of Companies Act accounts currently to be found in the Schedule to Part 7 of the CA 1985 will in future be contained in regulations to be made by the Secretary of State (section 396(3) of the CA 2006). The Parliamentary procedure for such regulation is set out in s 473 of the CA 2006.

Group accounts: small companies

Option to prepare group accounts

22.24 Section 398 of the CA 2006 deals with group accounts with respect to small companies. If at the end of a financial year, a company subject to the small companies regime is a parent company, the directors, as well as preparing individual accounts for the year, may prepare consolidated accounts for the group for the year.

Section 398 of the CA 2006 provides that a company that is subject to the small companies regime and is a parent company is not obliged to prepare group accounts in addition to its individual accounts, (restating s 248 of the CA 1985), but it may opt to do so.

The exemption in s 248 of the CA 1985 from the preparation of group accounts by parent companies heading medium-sized groups has been abolished, following the substantial increase in the financial threshold for medium sized groups in 2004.

Group accounts: other companies

22.25 The sections relating to group accounts have been reorganised to make them easier to follow.

Sections 399–402 of the CA 2006 re-enact ss 227(1) and (8), 228, 228A and 229(5) of the CA 1985. Section 399 of the CA 2006 concerns the requirements and exemptions from the requirement in relation to group accounts. Parent companies not subject to the small companies regime have a duty to prepare consolidated accounts unless exempt from having to do so under ss 400–402 of the CA 2006. Section 400 of the CA 2006 provides an exemption from preparing group accounts for companies included in EEA group accounts of a larger group. Section 401 of the CA 2006 provides such an exemption for companies included in non-EEA group accounts of a larger group, and s 402 of the CA 2006 provides an exemption when all the company's subsidiary undertakings could be excluded from consolidation in Companies Act group accounts, (see s 405 of the CA 2006).

Duty to prepare group accounts

22.26 Section 399 of the CA 2006 deals with the duty to prepare group accounts. It applies to companies that are not subject to the small companies regime.[5457]

If at the end of a financial year the company is a parent company the directors, as well as preparing individual accounts for the year, must prepare consolidated accounts for the group for the year unless the company is exempt from that requirement.[5458]

There are exemptions under s 400 of the CA 2006 (company included in EEA accounts of a larger group); s 401 of the CA 2006 (company included in non-EEA accounts of a larger group); and s 402 of the CA 2006 (company none of whose subsidiary undertakings need be included in the consolidation).[5459]

A company to which this section applies but which is exempt from the requirement to prepare group accounts may do so.[5460]

Exemption for company included in EEA group accounts of a larger group

22.27 Section 400 of the CA 2006 applies to exemptions for a company included in the EEA group accounts of a larger group. A company is exempt from the requirement to prepare group accounts if it is itself a subsidiary undertaking and its immediate parent undertaking is established under the law of an EEA State, in the following cases:

(a) where the company is a wholly-owned subsidiary of that parent undertaking;[5461]

(b) where that parent undertaking holds more than 50 per cent of the allotted shares in the company and notice requesting the preparation of group accounts has not been served on the company by shareholders holding in aggregate (i) more than half of the remaining allotted shares in the company,[5462] or (ii) 5 per cent of the total allotted shares in the company.[5463]

Such notice must be served not later than six months after the end of the financial year before that to which it relates.

[5457] CA 2006, s 399(1).   [5458] CA 2006, s 399(2).   [5459] CA 2006, s 399(3).
[5460] CA 2006, s 399(4).   [5461] CA 2006, s 400(1)(a).   [5462] CA 2006, s 400(1)(b)(i).
[5463] CA 2006, s 400(1)(b)(ii).

Exemption is conditional upon compliance with all of the following conditions:

(a)   the company must be included in consolidated accounts for a larger group drawn up to the same date, or to an earlier date in the same financial year, by a parent undertaking established under the law of an EEA State;[5464]

(b)   those accounts must be drawn up and audited, and that parent undertaking's annual report must be drawn up, according to that law (i) in accordance with the provisions of the Seventh Directive (83/349/EEC) (as modified, where relevant, by the provisions of the Bank Accounts Directive (86/635/EEC) or the Insurance Accounts Directive (91/674/EEC)),[5465] or (ii) in accordance with international accounting standards;[5466]

(c)   the company must disclose in its individual accounts that it is exempt from the obligation to prepare and deliver group accounts;[5467]

(d)   the company must state in its individual accounts the name of the parent undertaking that draws up the group accounts referred to above and (i) if it is incorporated outside the United Kingdom, the country in which it is incorporated,[5468] or (ii) if it is unincorporated, the address of its principal place of business;[5469]

(e)   the company must deliver to the registrar, within the period for filing its accounts and reports for the financial year in question, copies of (i) those group accounts,[5470] and (ii) the parent undertaking's annual report, together with the auditor's report on them;[5471]

(f)   any requirement of Part 35 of this Act as to the delivery to the registrar of a certified translation into English must be met in relation to any document comprised in the accounts and reports delivered in accordance with para (e).[5472]

For the purposes of s 400(1)(b) of the CA 2006 shares held by a wholly-owned subsidiary of the parent undertaking, or held on behalf of the parent undertaking or a wholly-owned subsidiary, shall be attributed to the parent undertaking.[5473]

The exemption does not apply to a company any of whose securities are admitted to trading on a regulated market in an EEA State.[5474]

Shares held by directors of a company for the purpose of complying with any share qualification requirement shall be disregarded in determining for

[5464] CA 2006, s 400(2)(a).   [5465] CA 2006, s 400(2)(b)(i).   [5466] CA 2006, s 400(2)(b)(ii).
[5467] CA 2006, s 400(2)(c).   [5468] CA 2006, s 400(2)(d)(i).   [5469] CA 2006, s 400(2)(d)(ii).
[5470] CA 2006, s 400(2)(e)(i).   [5471] CA 2006, s 400(2)(e)(ii).   [5472] CA 2006, s 400(2)(f).
[5473] CA 2006, s 400(3).   [5474] CA 2006, s 400(4).

the purposes of this section whether the company is a wholly-owned subsidiary.[5475]

In s 400(4) of the CA 2006, the term 'securities' includes:

(a)   shares and stock;[5476]
(b)   debentures, including debenture stock, loan stock, bonds, certificates of deposit and other instruments creating or acknowledging indebtedness;[5477]
(c)   warrants or other instruments entitling the holder to subscribe for securities falling within para (a) or (b);[5478] and
(d)   certificates or other instruments that confer (i) property rights in respect of a security falling within para (a), (b) or (c),[5479] (ii) any right to acquire, dispose of, underwrite or convert a security, being a right to which the holder would be entitled if he held any such security to which the certificate or other instrument relates,[5480] or (iii) a contractual right (other than an option) to acquire any such security otherwise than by subscription.[5481]

Exemption for a company included in non-EEA group accounts of a larger group

22.28 Section 401 of the CA 2006 deals with exemption for a company included in non-EEA group accounts of a larger group. A company is exempt from the requirement to prepare group accounts if it is itself a subsidiary undertaking and its parent undertaking is not established under the law of an EEA State, in the following cases:

(a)   where the company is a wholly-owned subsidiary of that parent undertaking;[5482]
(b)   where that parent undertaking holds more than 50 per cent of the allotted shares in the company and notice requesting the preparation of group accounts has not been served on the company by shareholders holding in aggregate (i) more than half of the remaining allotted shares in the company,[5483] or (ii) 5 per cent of the total allotted shares in the company.[5484]

Such notice must be served not later than six months after the end of the financial year before that to which it relates.

[5475] CA 2006, s 400(5).   [5476] CA 2006, s 400(6)(a).   [5477] CA 2006, s 400(6)(b).
[5478] CA 2006, s 400(6)(c).   [5479] CA 2006, s 400(6)(d)(i).   [5480] CA 2006, s 400(6)(d)(ii).
[5481] CA 2006, s 400(6)(d)(iii).   [5482] CA 2006, s 401(1)(a).   [5483] CA 2006, s 401(1)(b)(i).
[5484] CA 2006, s 401(1)(b)(ii).

Exemption is conditional upon compliance with all of the following conditions:

(a)   the company and all of its subsidiary undertakings must be included in consolidated accounts for a larger group drawn up to the same date, or to an earlier date in the same financial year, by a parent undertaking;[5485]

(b)   those accounts and, where appropriate, the group's annual report, must be drawn up (i) in accordance with the provisions of the Seventh Directive (83/349/EEC) (as modified, where relevant, by the provisions of the Bank Accounts Directive (86/635/EEC) or the Insurance Accounts Directive (91/674/EEC)),[5486] or (ii) in a manner equivalent to consolidated accounts and consolidated annual reports so drawn up;[5487]

(c)   the consolidated accounts must be audited by one or more persons authorised to audit accounts under the law under which the parent undertaking that draws them up is established;[5488]

(d)   the company must disclose in its individual accounts that it is exempt from the obligation to prepare and deliver group accounts;[5489]

(e)   the company must state in its individual accounts the name of the parent undertaking that draws up the group accounts referred to above and (i) if it is incorporated outside the United Kingdom, the country in which it is incorporated,[5490] or (ii) if it is unincorporated, the address of its principal place of business;[5491]

(f)   the company must deliver to the registrar, within the period for filing its accounts and reports for the financial year in question, copies of (i) the group accounts,[5492] and (ii) where appropriate, the consolidated annual report, together with the auditor's report on them;[5493]

(g)   any requirement of Part 35 of the CA 2006 as to the delivery to the registrar of a certified translation into English must be met in relation to any document comprised in the accounts and reports delivered in accordance with para (f).[5494]

For the purposes of s 401(1)(b) of the CA 2006, shares held by a wholly-owned subsidiary of the parent undertaking, or held on behalf of the parent undertaking or a wholly-owned subsidiary, are attributed to the parent undertaking.[5495]

The exemption does not apply to a company any of whose securities are admitted to trading on a regulated market in an EEA State.[5496]

Shares held by directors of a company for the purpose of complying with any share qualification requirement shall be disregarded in determining for

[5485] CA 2006, s 401(2)(a).   [5486] CA 2006, s 401(2)(b)(i).   [5487] CA 2006, s 401(2)(b)(ii).
[5488] CA 2006, s 401(2)(c).   [5489] CA 2006, s 401(2)(d).   [5490] CA 2006, s 401(2)(e)(i).
[5491] CA 2006, s 401(2)(e)(ii).   [5492] CA 2006, s 401(2)(f)(i).   [5493] CA 2006, s 401(2)(f)(ii).
[5494] CA 2006, s 401(2)(g).   [5495] CA 2006, s 401(3).   [5496] CA 2006, s 401(4).

the purposes of this section whether the company is a wholly-owned subsidiary.[5497]

In s 401(4) of the CA 2006, the term 'securities' includes:

(a)   shares and stock;[5498]
(b)   debentures, including debenture stock, loan stock, bonds, certificates of deposit and other instruments creating or acknowledging indebtedness;[5499]
(c)   warrants or other instruments entitling the holder to subscribe for securities falling within para (a) or (b);[5500] and
(d)   certificates or other instruments that confer (i) property rights in respect of a security falling within para (a), (b) or (c),[5501] (ii) any right to acquire, dispose of, underwrite or convert a security, being a right to which the holder would be entitled if he held any such security to which the certificate or other instrument relates,[5502] or (iii) a contractual right (other than an option) to acquire any such security otherwise than by subscription.[5503]

Exemption if no subsidiary undertakings need be included in the consolidation

22.29 Section 402 of the CA 2006 provides that a parent company is exempt from the requirement to prepare group accounts if under s 405 of the CA 2006 all of its subsidiary undertakings could be excluded from consolidation in Companies Act group accounts.

Group accounts: general

22.30 Sections 403–408 of the CA 2006 deals with general aspects of group accounts.

Group accounts: applicable accounting framework

22.31 Section 403 of the CA 2006 deals with the applicable accounting framework for group accounts.

The group accounts of certain parent companies are required by Article 4 of the IAS Regulation to be prepared in accordance with international accounting standards (IAS group accounts).[5504]

The group accounts of other companies may be prepared in accordance

---

[5497] CA 2006, s 401(5).   [5498] CA 2006, s 401(6)(a).   [5499] CA 2006, s 401(6)(b).
[5500] CA 2006, s 401(6)(c).   [5501] CA 2006, s 401(6)(d)(i).   [5502] CA 2006, s 401(6)(d)(ii).
[5503] CA 2006, s 401(6)(d)(iii).   [5504] CA 2006, s 403(1).

with s 404 of the CA 2006 (Companies Act group accounts),[5505] or in accordance with international accounting standards (IAS group accounts).[5506]

This is subject to the following provisions of this section.

The group accounts of a parent company that is a charity must be Companies Act group accounts.[5507]

After the first financial year in which the directors of a parent company prepare IAS group accounts (the first IAS year), all subsequent group accounts of the company must be prepared in accordance with international accounting standards unless there is a relevant change of circumstance.[5508]

There is a relevant change of circumstance if, at any time during or after the first IAS year:

(a)   the company becomes a subsidiary undertaking of another undertaking that does not prepare IAS group accounts;[5509]
(b)   the company ceases to be a company with securities admitted to trading on a regulated market in an EEA State;[5510] or
(c)   a parent undertaking of the company ceases to be an undertaking with securities admitted to trading on a regulated market in an EEA State.[5511]

If, having changed to preparing Companies Act group accounts following a relevant change of circumstance, the directors again prepare IAS group accounts for the company, s 403(4) and (5) of the CA 2006 applies again as if the first financial year for which such accounts are again prepared were the first IAS year.[5512]

Section 403 of the CA 2006 replaces s 227(2)–(7) of the CA 1985. Parent companies whose securities are publicly traded must prepare group accounts in accordance with the IAS Regulation. Other parent companies (with the exception of charitable companies) have the choice whether to prepare group accounts under the Companies Act (Companies Act group accounts) or in accordance with adopted international accounting standards (IAS group accounts). Once a company has switched to IAS group accounts all subsequent group accounts must be prepared in accordance with IAS unless there is a relevant change of circumstance, (see s 403(4)–(6) of the CA 2006).

Companies Act group accounts

22.32 Section 404 of the CA 2006 is concerned with group accounts. Companies Act group accounts must comprise a consolidated balance sheet dealing with the state of affairs of the parent company and its subsidiary

[5505] CA 2006, s 403(2)(a).   [5506] CA 2006, s 403(2)(b).   [5507] CA 2006, s 403(3).
[5508] CA 2006, s 403(4).   [5509] CA 2006, s 403(5)(a).   [5510] CA 2006, s 403(5)(b).
[5511] CA 2006, s 403(5)(c).   [5512] CA 2006, s 403(6).

undertakings,[5513] and a consolidated profit and loss account dealing with the profit or loss of the parent company and its subsidiary undertakings.[5514]

The accounts must give a true and fair view of the state of affairs as at the end of the financial year, and the profit or loss for the financial year, of the undertakings included in the consolidation as a whole, so far as concerns members of the company.[5515]

The accounts must comply with provisions made by the Secretary of State by regulations as to the form and content of the consolidated balance sheet and consolidated profit and loss account,[5516] and additional information to be provided by way of notes to the accounts.[5517]

If compliance with the regulations, and any other provision made by or under this Act as to the matters to be included in a company's group accounts or in notes to those accounts, would not be sufficient to give a true and fair view, the necessary additional information must be given in the accounts or in a note to them.[5518]

If in special circumstances compliance with any of those provisions is inconsistent with the requirement to give a true and fair view, the directors must depart from that provision to the extent necessary to give a true and fair view.[5519]

Particulars of any such departure, the reasons for it and its effect must be given in a note to the accounts.

For companies preparing Companies Act group accounts, s 404 of the CA 2006 gives the Secretary of State power to make provision by regulations as to the form and content of the consolidated balance sheet and consolidated profit and loss account and additional information to be provided by way of notes to the accounts. The regulations replace the requirements contained in Schedule 4A of the CA 1985. These regulations are subject to the Parliamentary procedure in s 473 of the CA 2006.

Companies Act group accounts: subsidiary undertakings included in the consolidation

22.33 Section 405 of the CA 2006 deals with company group accounts with particular references to the subsidiary undertakings included in the consolidation. Where a parent company prepares Companies Act group accounts, all the subsidiary undertakings of the company must be included in the consolidation, subject to the following exceptions.[5520]

A subsidiary undertaking may be excluded from consolidation if its inclusion is not material for the purpose of giving a true and fair view (but two or

---

[5513] CA 2006, s 404(1)(a).   [5514] CA 2006, s 404(1)(b).   [5515] CA 2006, s 404(2).
[5516] CA 2006, s 404(3)(a).   [5517] CA 2006, s 404(3)(b).   [5518] CA 2006, s 404(4).
[5519] CA 2006, s 404(5).   [5520] CA 2006, s 405(1).

more undertakings may be excluded only if they are not material taken together).[5521]

A subsidiary undertaking may be excluded from consolidation where:

(a)   severe long-term restrictions substantially hinder the exercise of the rights of the parent company over the assets or management of that undertaking;[5522] or

(b)   information necessary for the preparation of group accounts cannot be obtained without disproportionate expense or undue delay;[5523] or

(c)   the interest of the parent company is held exclusively with a view to subsequent resale.[5524]

The reference in s 405(3)(a) of the CA 2006 to the rights of the parent company and the reference in s 405(3)(c) of the CA 2006 to the interest of the parent company are, respectively, to rights and interests held by or attributed to the company for the purposes of the definition of 'parent undertaking' (see s 1162 of the CA 2006) in the absence of which it would not be the parent company.[5525]

Section 405 of the CA 2006 replaces s 229 of the CA 1985. It requires all subsidiary undertakings to be included in the consolidated accounts subject to certain permitted exclusions.

IAS group accounts

22.34 Section 406 of the CA 2006 states that where the directors of a company prepare IAS group accounts, they must state in the notes to those accounts that the accounts have been prepared in accordance with international accounting standards.

Section 406 of the CA 2006 re-enacts s 227B CA 2006. A company may opt or may be required to prepare group accounts in accordance with international accounting standards. This section provides that where it does so, this must be stated in the notes to the accounts.

Consistency of financial reporting within the group

22.35 Section 407 of the CA 2006 deals with consistency of financial reporting within the group. The directors of a parent company must ensure that the individual accounts of the parent company,[5526] and each of its subsidiary undertakings,[5527] are all prepared using the same financial reporting

---

[5521] CA 2006, s 405(2). [5522] CA 2006, s 405(3)(a). [5523] CA 2006, s 405(3)(b).
[5524] CA 2006, s 405(3)(c). [5525] CA 2006, s 405(4). [5526] CA 2006, s 407(1)(a).
[5527] CA 2006, s 407(1)(b).

framework, except to the extent that in their opinion there are good reasons for not doing so.

Section 407(1) of the CA 2006 does not apply if the directors do not prepare group accounts for the parent company.[5528]

Section 407(1) of the CA 2006 only applies to the accounts of subsidiary undertakings that are required to be prepared under this Part.[5529]

Section 407(1) of the CA 2006 does not require accounts of undertakings that are charities to be prepared using the same financial reporting framework as accounts of undertakings that are not charities.[5530]

Section 407(1)(a) of the CA 2006 does not apply where the directors of a parent company prepare IAS group accounts and IAS individual accounts.[5531]

Section 407 of the CA 2006 re-enacts s 227C of the CA 1985. If the parent company prepares both the consolidated and individual accounts under IAS, it is not required to ensure that all its subsidiary undertakings also use IAS. However, it must ensure that its individual accounts and those of all its subsidiary undertakings use the same financial reporting framework, unless there are good reasons for not doing so.

Individual profit and loss account where group accounts prepared

22.36 Section 408 of the CA 2006 deals with individual profit and loss account where group accounts are prepared. It applies where a company prepares group accounts in accordance with this Act,[5532] and the notes to the company's individual balance sheet show the company's profit or loss for the financial year determined in accordance with this Act.[5533]

The profit and loss account need not contain the information specified in s 411 of the CA 2006 (information about employee numbers and costs).[5534]

The company's individual profit and loss account must be approved in accordance with s 414(1) of the CA 2006 (approval by directors) but may be omitted from the company's annual accounts for the purposes of the other provisions of the Companies Acts.[5535]

The exemption conferred by this section is conditional upon its being disclosed in the company's annual accounts that the exemption applies.[5536]

Section 408 of the CA 2006 replaces s 230 of the CA 1985. A parent company that prepares group accounts and that meets the criteria in subs (1)(a) and (b) may, subject to the profit and loss account being approved by the directors, dispense with the inclusion of a profit and loss account in the company's account, for example when delivered to the registrar. The profit and loss account may also omit the information on employee numbers and

---

[5528] CA 2006, s 407(2).   [5529] CA 2006, s 407(3).   [5530] CA 2006, s 407(4).
[5531] CA 2006, s 407(5).   [5532] CA 2006, s 408(1)(a).   [5533] CA 2006, s 408(1)(b).
[5534] CA 2006, s 408(2).   [5535] CA 2006, s 407(3).   [5536] CA 2006, s 408(4).

cost required by s 411 of the CA 2006. The exemption provided for in s 230(2) of the CA 1985 for certain information required by provisions of Schedule 4 of the CA 1985, will be provided for in regulations under s 396 of the CA 2006.

Information to be given in notes to the accounts

Information about related undertakings

22.37 Section 409 of the CA 2006 deals with information about related undertakings. The Secretary of State may make provision by regulations requiring information about related undertakings to be given in notes to a company's annual accounts.[5537]

The regulations may make different provision according to whether or not the company prepares group accounts;[5538] and may specify the descriptions of undertaking in relation to which they apply, and make different provision in relation to different descriptions of related undertaking.[5539]

The regulations may provide that information need not be disclosed with respect to an undertaking that is established under the law of a country outside the United Kingdom;[5540] or carries on business outside the United Kingdom,[5541] if the following conditions are met. The conditions are:

(a)   that in the opinion of the directors of the company the disclosures would be seriously prejudicial to the business of:

 (i)   that undertaking;[5542]
 (ii)   the Company;[5543]
 (iii)   any of the company's subsidiary undertakings; or[5544]
 (iv)   any other undertaking which is included in the consolidation;[5545]

(b)   that the Secretary of State agrees that the information need not be disclosed.[5546]

Where advantage is taken of any such exemption, that fact must be stated in a note to the company's annual accounts.[5547]

Section 409 of the CA 2006 replaces s 231(1)–(4) of the CA 1985. The requirement to disclose information about related undertakings in the notes to a company's annual accounts applies whether or not the company has to produce group accounts but there are different disclosure requirements in each case. This section gives the Secretary of State a new power to make

[5537] CA 2006, s 409(1).   [5538] CA 2006, s 409(2)(a).   [5539] CA 2006, s 409(2)(b).
[5540] CA 2006, s 409(3)(a).   [5541] CA 2006, s 409(3)(b).   [5542] CA 2006, s 409(4)(a)(i).
[5543] CA 2006, s 409(4)(a)(ii).   [5544] CA 2006, s 409(4)(a)(iii).
[5545] CA 2006, s 409(4)(a)(iv).   [5546] CA 2006, s 409(4)(b).   [5547] CA 2006, s 409(5).

regulations requiring information about related undertakings to be given in notes to a company's annual accounts. These regulations are subject to the Parliamentary procedure in s 473 of the CA 2006. The regulations replace the provisions of Schedule 5 to the CA 1985.

Section 409(3) of the CA 2006 enables regulations under the section to make provision corresponding to s 231(3) of the CA 1985 authorising the omission from the notes to the accounts of information in respect of undertakings established outside the UK, or carrying on business outside the UK where the directors consider that disclosure would be seriously prejudicial to the business of that undertaking, or to the business of the company or any of its subsidiary undertakings. The Secretary of State must agree to the omission. This exemption is sought by a very small number of companies each year.

Information about related undertakings: alternative compliance

22.38 Section 410 of the CA 2006 addresses the information about related undertakings with specific reference to alternative compliance. It applies where the directors of a company are of the opinion that the number of undertakings in respect of which the company is required to disclose information under any provision of regulations under s 409 of the CA 2006 (related undertakings) is such that compliance with that provision would result in information of excessive length being given in notes to the company's annual accounts.[5548]

The information need only be given in respect of the undertakings whose results or financial position, in the opinion of the directors, principally affected the figures shown in the company's annual accounts;[5549] and where the company prepares group accounts, undertakings excluded from consolidation under s 405(3) of the CA 2006 (undertakings excluded on ground other than maternity).[5550]

If advantage is taken of s 410(2) of the CA 2006 there must be included in the notes to the company's annual accounts a statement that the information is given only with respect to such undertakings as are mentioned in that subsection;[5551] and the full information (both that which is disclosed in the notes to the accounts and that which is not) must be annexed to the company's next annual return.[5552]

The term 'next annual return' means that next delivered to the registrar after the accounts in question have been approved under s 414 of the CA 2006.

If a company fails to comply with s 410(3)(b) of the CA 2006, an offence is committed by the company,[5553] and every officer of the company who is in

---

[5548] CA 2006, s 410(1).   [5549] CA 2006, s 410(2)(a).   [5550] CA 2006, s 410(2)(b).
[5551] CA 2006, s 410(3)(a).   [5552] CA 2006, s 410(3)(b).   [5553] CA 2006, s 410(4)(a).

default.[5554] A person guilty of an offence under s 410(4) of the CA 2006 is liable on summary conviction to a fine not exceeding level 3 on the standard scale and, for continued contravention, a daily default fine not exceeding one-tenth of level 3 on the standard scale.[5555]

Section 410 of the CA 2006 replaces s 231(5)–(7) of the CA 1985. Where there are numerous related undertakings and the directors believe that full disclosure would result in information of excessive length in the notes to the accounts, they may give more limited information. As a minimum this must include information in s 410(2)(a) and (b) of the CA 2006. Section 410(3) of the CA 2006 provides that the full information on the related undertakings must be submitted with the next annual return.

Information about employee numbers and costs

22.39 Section 411 of the CA 2006 deals with information about employee numbers and costs. In the case of a company not subject to the small companies regime, the following information with respect to the employees of the company must be given in notes to the company's annual accounts the average number of persons employed by the company in the financial year;[5556] and the average number of persons so employed within each category of persons employed by the company.[5557]

The categories by reference to which the number required to be disclosed by s 411(1)(b) of the CA 2006 is to be determined must be such as the directors may select having regard to the manner in which the company's activities are organised.[5558]

The average number required by s 411(1)(a) or (b) of the CA 2006 is determined by dividing the relevant annual number by the number of months in the financial year.[5559]

The relevant annual number is determined by ascertaining for each month in the financial year (a) for the purposes of s 411(1)(a) of the CA 2006, the number of persons employed under contracts of service by the company in that month (whether throughout the month or not);[5560] (b) for the purposes of s 411(1)(b) of the CA 2006, the number of persons in the category in question of persons so employed;[5561] and adding together all the monthly numbers.

In respect of all persons employed by the company during the financial year who are taken into account in determining the relevant annual number for the purposes of s 411(1)(a) of the CA 2006 there must also be stated the aggregate amounts respectively of:

[5554] CA 2006, s 410(4)(b).   [5555] CA 2006, s 410(5).   [5556] CA 2006, s 411(1)(a).
[5557] CA 2006, s 411(1)(b).   [5558] CA 2006, s 411(2).   [5559] CA 2006, s 411(3).
[5560] CA 2006, s 411(4)(a).   [5561] CA 2006, s 411(4)(b).

(a) wages and salaries paid or payable in respect of that year to those persons;[5562]

(b) social security costs incurred by the company on their behalf;[5563] and

(c) other pension costs so incurred.[5564]

This does not apply insofar as those amounts, or any of them, are stated elsewhere in the company's accounts.

In s 411(5) of the CA 2006 the term 'pension costs' includes any costs incurred by the company in respect of:

(a) any pension scheme established for the purpose of providing pensions for persons currently or formerly employed by the company;[5565]

(b) any sums set aside for the future payment of pensions directly by the company to current or former employees;[5566] and

(c) any pensions paid directly to such persons without having first been set aside.[5567]

The term 'social security costs' means any contributions by the company to any state social security or pension scheme, fund or arrangement.

Where the company prepares group accounts, this section applies as if the undertakings included in the consolidation were a single company.[5568]

Section 411 of the CA 2006 replaces s 231A of the CA 1985 concerning particulars of staff. Section 231A was inserted by the CA 1985 (International Accounting Standards and Other Accounting Amendments) Regulations 2004 (SI 2004/2947) re-enacting provisions previously in the Schedules to the 1985 Act so that they continued to apply both to companies preparing Companies Act accounts and to those preparing IAS accounts.

Information about directors' benefits: remuneration

22.40 Section 412 of the CA 2006 deals with information about directors' benefits with particular reference to remuneration. The Secretary of State may make provision by regulations requiring information to be given in notes to a company's annual accounts about directors' remuneration.[5569]

The matters about which information may be required include:

(a) gains made by directors on the exercise of share options;[5570]

[5562] CA 2006, s 411(5)(a).   [5563] CA 2006, s 411(5)(b).   [5564] CA 2006, s 411(5)(c).
[5565] CA 2006, s 411(6)(a).   [5566] CA 2006, s 411(6)(b).   [5567] CA 2006, s 411(6)(c).
[5568] CA 2006, s 411(7).   [5569] CA 2006, s 412(1).   [5570] CA 2006, s 412(2)(a).

(b)   benefits received or receivable by directors under long-term incentive schemes;[5571]
(c)   payments for loss of office (as defined in s 215 of the CA 2006);[5572]
(d)   benefits receivable, and contributions for the purpose of providing benefits, in respect of past services of a person as director or in any other capacity while director;[5573]
(e)   consideration paid to or receivable by third parties for making available the services of a person as director or in any other capacity while director.[5574]

Without prejudice to the generality of s 412(1) of the CA 2006, regulations under this section may make any such provision as was made immediately before the commencement of this Part by Part 1 of Schedule 6 to the CA 1985 (c 6).[5575]

For the purposes of this section, and regulations made under it, amounts paid to or receivable by a person connected with a director;[5576] or a body corporate controlled by a director,[5577] are treated as paid to or receivable by the director.

The expressions 'connected with' and 'controlled by' in this subsection have the same meaning as in Part 10 of the CA 2006 (company directors).

It is the duty of any director of a company,[5578] and any person who is or has at any time in the preceding five years been a director of the company,[5579] to give notice to the company of such matters relating to himself as may be necessary for the purposes of regulations under this section.

A person who makes a default in complying with s 412(5) of the CA 2006 commits an offence and is liable on summary conviction to a fine not exceeding level 3 on the standard scale.[5580]

This section, together with s 413 of the CA 2006, replaces s 232 of the CA 1985. Section 232 of the CA 1985, with Schedules 6 and 7A, provided for disclosure of specified information on directors' remuneration in notes to a company's annual accounts.

Section 412 of the CA 2006 gives the Secretary of State a new power to make provision by regulations requiring information about directors' remuneration to be given in notes to a company's annual accounts. Regulations under this section are subject to the Parliamentary procedure in s 473 of the CA 2006.

[5571] CA 2006, s 412(2)(b).   [5572] CA 2006, s 412(2)(c).   [5573] CA 2006, s 412(2)(d).
[5574] CA 2006, s 412(2)(e).   [5575] CA 2006, s 412(3).   [5576] CA 2006, s 412(4)(a).
[5577] CA 2006, s 412(4)(b).   [5578] CA 2006, s 412(5)(a).   [5579] CA 2006, s 412(5)(b).
[5580] CA 2006, s 412(6).

Information about directors' benefits: advances, credit and guarantees

22.41 Section 413 of the CA 2006 deals with information about directors' benefits with specific reference to advances, credit and guarantees. In the case of a company that does not prepare group accounts, details of advances and credits granted by the company to its directors;[5581] and guarantees of any kind entered into by the company on behalf of its directors, must be shown in the notes to its individual accounts.[5582]

In the case of a parent company that prepares group accounts, details of advances and credits granted to the directors of the parent company, by that company or by any of its subsidiary undertakings;[5583] and guarantees of any kind entered into on behalf of the directors of the parent company, by that company or by any of its subsidiary undertakings, must be shown in the notes to the group accounts.[5584]

The details required of an advance or credit are:

(a)   its amount;[5585]
(b)   an indication of the interest rate;[5586]
(c)   its main conditions;[5587] and
(d)   any amounts repaid.[5588]

The details required of a guarantee are:

(a)   its main terms;[5589]
(b)   the amount of the maximum liability that may be incurred by the company (or its subsidiary);[5590] and
(c)   any amount paid and any liability incurred by the company (or its subsidiary) for the purpose of fulfilling the guarantee (including any loss incurred by reason of enforcement of the guarantee).[5591]

There must also be stated in the notes to the accounts the totals:

(a)   of amounts stated under subs (3)(a) of the CA 2006;[5592]
(b)   of amounts stated under subs (3)(d) of the CA 2006;[5593]
(c)   of amounts stated under subs (4)(b) of the CA 2006;[5594] and
(d)   of amounts stated under subs (4)(c) of the CA 2006.[5595]

References in s 413 of the CA 2006 to the directors of a company are to the

---

[5581] CA 2006, s 413(1)(a).   [5582] CA 2006, s 413(1)(b).   [5583] CA 2006, s 413(2)(a).
[5584] CA 2006, s 413(2)(b).   [5585] CA 2006, s 413(3)(a).   [5586] CA 2006, s 413(3)(b).
[5587] CA 2006, s 413(3)(c).   [5588] CA 2006, s 413(3)(d).   [5589] CA 2006, s 413(4)(a).
[5590] CA 2006, s 413(4)(b).   [5591] CA 2006, s 413(4)(c).   [5592] CA 2006, s 413(5)(a).
[5593] CA 2006, s 413(5)(b).   [5594] CA 2006, s 413(5)(c).   [5595] CA 2006, s 413(5)(d).

persons who were directors at any time in the financial year to which the accounts relate.[5596]

The requirements of this section apply in relation to every advance, credit or guarantee subsisting at any time in the financial year to which the accounts relate whenever it was entered into;[5597] whether or not the person concerned was a director of the company in question at the time it was entered into;[5598] and in the case of an advance, credit or guarantee involving a subsidiary undertaking of that company, whether or not that undertaking was such a subsidiary undertaking at the time it was entered into.[5599]

Banking companies and the holding companies of credit institutions need only state the details required by subss (3)(a) and (4)(b).[5600]

Section 413 of the CA 2006 replaces s 232 of the CA 1985 as regards the disclosure of advances, credit and guarantees. Under s 232 of the CA 1985, information on the following areas had to be given in notes to a company's annual accounts: details of loans, quasi loans, credit transactions and related guarantees and security between a company and its directors or persons connected with its directors; and details of any other transactions or arrangements in which a director, indirectly or directly has a material interest.

This can be seen as an extension of the internal disclosure of directors' interests required by s 317 of the CA 1985.

Section 413 of the CA 2006 sets out the new disclosure requirements in respect of (a) advances and credits granted by the company to its directors, and (b) guarantees of any kind entered into by the company on behalf of its directors. The wording of the clause is much closer to that of articles 43(1)(13) and 34(13) of the Fourth (780660/EEC) and Seventh (89/349/EEC) Company Law Directives.

The powers under s 396(3)(b) of the CA 2006 (Companies Act individual accounts) and s 404(3)(b) (Companies Act group accounts) will be used to require the disclosure of information about certain party transactions in the notes to Companies Act accounts.

Companies will no longer be required to disclose transactions made between the company and officers other than directors.

Under s 413(8) of the CA 2006 banks and the holding companies of credit institutions need only state (i) the amount of an advance or credit, and (ii) in relation to guarantee, the amount of the maximum liability that may be incurred by the company (or its subsidiary). In the light of the simplified disclosure regime for advances, credit and guarantees, ss 343 and 344 of the CA 1985, which make special provision for financial institutions, are repealed.

[5596] CA 2006, s 413(6).   [5597] CA 2006, s 413(7)(a).   [5598] CA 2006, s 413(7)(b).
[5599] CA 2006, s 413(7)(c).   [5600] CA 2006, s 413(8).

Approval and signing of accounts

22.42 Section 414 of the CA 2006 deals with the approval and signing of accounts. A company's annual accounts must be approved by the board of directors and signed on behalf of the board by a director of the company.[5601] The signature must be on the company's balance sheet.[5602]

If the accounts are prepared in accordance with the provisions applicable to companies subject to the small companies regime, the balance sheet must contain a statement to that effect in a prominent position above the signature.[5603]

If annual accounts are approved that do not comply with the requirements of this Act (and, where applicable, of Article 4 of the IAS Regulation), every director of the company who knew that they did not comply, or was reckless as to whether they complied;[5604] and failed to take reasonable steps to secure compliance with those requirements or, as the case may be, to prevent the accounts from being approved, commits an offence.[5605] A person guilty of an offence under this section is liable on conviction on indictment, to a fine;[5606] on summary conviction, to a fine not exceeding the statutory maximum.[5607]

Section 414 of the CA 2006 replaces s 233 of the CA 1985. It provides that a company's annual accounts (its individual accounts and any group accounts) must be approved by the board of directors and the balance sheet must be signed.

Section 414(3) of the CA 2006, which requires the balance sheet of accounts prepared in accordance with the small companies regime to carry a statement to that effect, re-enacts ss 246(8) and 248A(5) of the CA 1985.

Sections 414(4) and (5) of the CA 2006 re-enact the criminal offence previously in s 233 of the CA 1985 for approval of accounts that did not comply with the requirements of the Companies Act or where applicable, of Article 4 of the IAS Regulation.

Section 233(4) of the CA 1985, which required that a director of the company should sign the copy of the balance sheet delivered to the registrar, has not been reproduced. This requirement would have hampered developments in the electronic delivery of accounts.

[5601] CA 2006, s 414(1).   [5602] CA 2006, s 414(2).   [5603] CA 2006, s 414(3).
[5604] CA 2006, s 414(4)(a).   [5605] CA 2006, s 414(4)(b).   [5606] CA 2006, s 414(5).
[5607] CA 2006, s 414(6).

Directors' Report

22.43 Chapter 5 addresses the directors' report. It comprises five sections.

Duty to prepare directors' report

22.44 The directors of a company must prepare a directors' report for each financial year of the company.[5608]

For a financial year in which the company is a parent company;[5609] and the directors of the company prepare group accounts,[5610] the directors' report must be a consolidated report (group directors' report) relating to the company and its subsidiary undertakings included in the consolidation.

A group directors' report may, where appropriate, give greater emphasis to the matters that are significant to the company and its subsidiary undertakings included in the consolidation, taken as a whole.[5611]

In the case of a failure to comply with the requirement to prepare a directors' report, an offence is committed by every person who was a director of the company immediately before the end of the period for filing accounts and reports for the financial year in question;[5612] and failed to take all reasonable steps for securing compliance with that requirement.[5613] A person guilty of an offence under this section is liable on conviction on indictment, to a fine; or on summary conviction, to a fine not exceeding the statutory maximum.[5614]

Contents of directors' report: general

22.45 Section 416 of the CA 2006 sets out the general contents of directors' reports. The directors' report for a financial year must state the names of the persons who, at any time during the financial year, were directors of the company;[5615] and the principal activities of the company in the course of the year.[5616]

In relation to a group directors' report s 416(1)(b) of the CA 2006 has effect as if the reference to the company was to the company and its subsidiary undertakings included in the consolidation.[5617]

Except in the case of a company subject to the small companies regime, the report must state the amount (if any) that the directors recommend should be paid by way of dividend.[5618]

The Secretary of State may make provision by regulations as to other matters that must be disclosed in a directors' report.

Without prejudice to the generality of this power, the regulations may

---

[5608] CA 2006, s 415(1).   [5609] CA 2006, s 415(2)(a).   [5610] CA 2006, s 415(2)(b).
[5611] CA 2006, s 415(3).   [5612] CA 2006, s 415(4)(a).   [5613] CA 2006, s 415(4)(b).
[5614] CA 2006, s 415(5).   [5615] CA 2006, s 416(1)(a).   [5616] CA 2006, s 416(1)(b).
[5617] CA 2006, s 416(2).   [5618] CA 2006, s 416(3).

make any such provision as was formerly made by Schedule 7 of the CA 1985.[5619]

Content of directors' report: business review

22.46 Section 417 of the CA 2006 deals with the contents of the directors' report with specific reference to the business review.

Unless the company is subject to the small companies' regime, the directors' report must contain a business review.[5620]

The purpose of the business review is to inform members of the company and help them assess how the directors have performed their duty under s 172 of the CA 2006 (duty to promote the success of the company).[5621]

The business review must contain a fair review of the company's business;[5622] and a description of the principal risks and uncertainties facing the company.[5623]

The review required is a balanced and comprehensive analysis of the development and performance of the company's business during the financial year;[5624] and the position of the company's business at the end of that year,[5625] consistent with the size and complexity of the business.

In the case of a quoted company the business review must, to the extent necessary for an understanding of the development, performance or position of the company's business, include:

(a) the main trends and factors likely to affect the future development, performance and position of the company's business;[5626] and

(b) information about (i) environmental matters (including the impact of the company's business on the environment),[5627] (ii) the company's employees,[5628] and (iii) social and community issues, including information about any policies of the company in relation to those matters and the effectiveness of those policies;[5629] and (c) subject to s 417(11) of the CA 2006, information about persons with whom the company has contractual or other arrangements that are essential to the business of the company.[5630]

If the review does not contain information of each kind mentioned in paras (b)(i), (ii), (iii) and (c), it must state which of those kinds of information it does not contain.[5631]

The review must, to the extent necessary for an understanding of the

[5619] CA 2006, s 416(4). [5620] CA 2006, s 417(1). [5621] CA 2006, s 417(2).
[5622] CA 2006, s 417(3)(a). [5623] CA 2006, s 417(3)(b). [5624] CA 2006, s 417(4)(a).
[5625] CA 2006, s 417(4)(b). [5626] CA 2006, s 417(5)(a). [5627] CA 2006, s 417(5)(b)(i).
[5628] CA 2006, s 417(5)(b)(ii). [5629] CA 2006, s 417(5)(b)(iii). [5630] CA 2006, s 417(5)(c).
[5631] CA 2006, s 417(5).

development, performance or position of the company's business, include analysis using financial key performance indicators;[5632] and where appropriate, analysis using other key performance indicators, including information relating to environmental matters and employee matters.[5633]

'Key performance indicators' means factors by reference to which the development, performance or position of the company's business can be measured effectively.[5634]

Where a company qualifies as medium-sized in relation to a financial year (see ss 465–487 of the CA 2006), the directors' report for the year need not comply with the requirements of s 417(6) of the CA 2006 so far as they relate to non-financial information.[5635]

The review must, where appropriate, include references to, and additional explanations of, amounts included in the company's annual accounts.[5636]

In relation to a group directors' report, this section has effect as if the references to the company were references to the company and its subsidiary undertakings included in the consolidation.[5637]

Nothing in this section requires the disclosure of information about impending developments or matters in the course of negotiation if the disclosure would, in the opinion of the directors, be seriously prejudicial to the interests of the company.[5638]

Nothing in s 417(5)(c) of the CA 2006 requires the disclosure of information about a person if the disclosure would, in the opinion of the directors, be seriously prejudicial to that person and contrary to the public interest.[5639]

Contents of directors' report statement as to disclosure to auditors

22.47 Section 418 of the CA 2006 deals with contents of the directors' report with specific reference to the statement as to disclosure to auditors.

Section 418 of the CA 2006 applies to a company unless it is exempt for the financial year in question from the requirements of Part 16 as to the audit of accounts;[5640] and the directors take advantage of that exemption.[5641]

The directors' report must contain a statement to the effect that, in the case of each of the persons who are directors at the time the report is approved so far as the director is aware, there is no relevant audit information of which the company's auditor is unaware;[5642] and he has taken all the steps that he ought to have taken as a director in order to make himself aware of any relevant audit information and to establish that the company's auditor is aware of that information.[5643]

[5632] CA 2006, s 417(6)(a).   [5633] CA 2006, s 417(6)(b).   [5634] CA 2006, s 417(6).
[5635] CA 2006, s 417(7).   [5636] CA 2006, s 417(8).   [5637] CA 2006, s 417(9).
[5638] CA 2006, s 417(10).   [5639] CA 2006, s 417(11).   [5640] CA 2006, s 418(1)(a).
[5641] CA 2006, s 418(1)(b).   [5642] CA 2006, s 418(2)(a).   [5643] CA 2006, s 418(2)(b).

The term 'relevant audit information' means information needed by the company's auditor in connection with preparing his report.[5644]

A director is regarded as having taken all the steps that he ought to have taken as a director in order to do the things mentioned in s 418(2)(b) of the CA 2006 if he has made such enquiries of his fellow directors and of the company's auditors for that purpose;[5645] and he has taken all the steps that he ought to have taken as a director in order to make himself aware of any relevant audit information and to establish that the company's auditor is aware of that information.[5646]

Where a directors' report containing the statement required by this section is approved but the statement is false, every director of the company who knew that the statement was false, or was reckless as to whether it was false;[5647] and failed to take reasonable steps to prevent the report from being approved,[5648] commits an offence. A person guilty of an offence under s 418(5) of the CA 2006 is liable on conviction on indictment, to imprisonment for a term not exceeding two years or a fine (or both);[5649] on summary conviction in England and Wales, to imprisonment for a term not exceeding 12 months or to a fine not exceeding the statutory maximum (or both);[5650] in Scotland or Northern Ireland, to imprisonment for a term not exceeding six months, or to a fine not exceeding the statutory maximum (or both).[5651]

Approval and signing of a directors' report

22.48 Section 419 of the CA 2006 applies to the approval and signing of a directors' report. The directors' report must be approved by the board of directors and signed on behalf of the board by a director or the secretary of the company.[5652]

If the report is prepared in accordance with the small companies regime, it must contain a statement to that effect in a prominent position above the signature.[5653]

If a directors' report is approved that does not comply with the reyuqire-ments of this Act, every director of the company who knew that it did not comply, or was reckless as to whether it complied,[5654] and failed to take rea-sonable steps to secure compliance with those requirements or, as the case may be, to prevent the report from being approved,[5655] commits an offence. A person guilty of an offence under this section is liable on conviction of indictment, to a fine;[5656] on summary conviction, to a fine not exceeding the statutory maximum.[5657]

[5644] CA 2006, s 418(3).   [5645] CA 2006, s 418(4)(a).   [5646] CA 2006, s 418(4)(b).
[5647] CA 2006, s 418(5)(a).   [5648] CA 2006, s 418(5)(b).   [5649] CA 2006, s 418(6)(a).
[5650] CA 2006, s 418(6)(b)(i).   [5651] CA 2006, s 418(6)(b)(ii).   [5652] CA 2006, s 419(1).
[5653] CA 2006, s 419(2).   [5654] CA 2006, s 419(3)(a).   [5655] CA 2006, s 419(3)(b).
[5656] CA 2006, s 419(4)(a).   [5657] CA 2006, s 419(4)(b).

Sections 415–419 of the CA 2006 concern the duty to prepare a directors' report, its content, approval and signature. They replace ss 234, 234ZZA, 234ZZB, 234A, 246 (4)(a) and 246A(2A) and 246(8) of the CA 1985.

Section 416(4) of the CA 2006 gives the Secretary of State power to make provisions by regulations as to other matters that must be disclosed in the directors' report. These regulations replace the provision formerly made by Schedule 7 of the CA 1985. The regulations are subject to the Parliamentary procedure in s 473 of the CA 2006.

Section 417 of the CA 2006 provides for what must be contained in the business review element of a directors' report. All companies, other than small companies, will need to produce a business review, as required by the EU Accounts Modernisation Directive (2003/51/EEC). Section 417(2) of the CA 2006 sets out the purpose of the review, that is, to inform members of the company and help them assess how the directors have performed their duty under s 172 of the CA 2006 (duty to promote the success of the company). Section 417(3), (4), (6) and (8) of the CA 2006 specifies the content of the review. Section 417(5) of the CA 2006 specifies information that quoted companies in particular must include in their review where necessary for an understanding of the company's business. Where directors of quoted companies have nothing to report on environmental, employee, social and community matters or essential contractual or other arrangements, their review must say so. Section 417(7) of the CA 2006 exempts medium-sized companies from reporting non-financial key performance indicators – an exemption allowed by the EU directive. Section 417(9) of the CA 2006 provides that where a directors' report is a group report, all references in s 417 of the CA 2006 to the company are to be read as references to the company and its consolidated subsidiary undertakings. Section 417(10) of the CA 2006 enables directors to omit from the business review information about impending developments or matters in the course of negotiation where in their opinion disclosure would be seriously prejudicial to the interests of the company. Section 417(11) of the CA 2006 enables directors to omit from the business review information about a third party otherwise required by s 417(5)(c) of the CA 2006 (essential contractual or other arrangements) where in the directors' opinion it would be seriously prejudicial to that third party and contrary to the public interest.

Quoted Companies: Directors' Remuneration Report

22.49 Chapter 6 of Part 15 to CA 2006 is concerned, solely with quoted companies with directors' remuneration. It contains three sections.

Duty to prepare a directors' remuneration report

22.50 Section 420 of the CA 2006 deals with the duty of directors to prepare a directors' remuneration report. The directors of a quoted company must prepare a directors' remuneration report for each financial year of the company.[5658]

In the case of failure to comply with the requirement to prepare a directors' remuneration report, every person who was a director of the company immediately before the end of the period for filing accounts and reports for the financial year in question;[5659] and failed to take all reasonable steps for securing compliance with that requirement,[5660] commits an offence. A person guilty of an offence under this section is liable on conviction on indictment, to a fine;[5661] or on summary conviction, to a fine not exceeding the statutory maximum.[5662]

Contents of directors' remuneration report

22.51 Section 421 of the CA 2006 deals with the contents of a directors' remuneration report. The Secretary of State may make provision by regulations as to:

(a) the information that must be contained in a directors' remuneration report;[5663]

(b) how information is to be set out in the report;[5664] and

(c) what is to be the auditable part of the report.[5665]

Without prejudice to the generality of this power, the regulations may make any such provision as was made, immediately before the commencement of this Part, by Schedule 7A of the CA 1985 (c 6).[5666]

It is the duty of any director of a company;[5667] and any person who is or has at any time in the preceding five years been a director of the company,[5668] to give notice to the company of such matters relating to himself as may be necessary for the purposes of regulations under this section. A person who makes default in complying with s 421(3) of the CA 2006 commits an offence and is liable on summary conviction to a fine not exceeding level 3 on the standard scale.[5669]

[5658] CA 2006, s 420(1). [5659] CA 2006, s 420(2)(a). [5660] CA 2006, s 420(2)(b). [5661] CA 2006, s 420(3)(a). [5662] CA 2006, s 420(3)(b). [5663] CA 2006, s 421(1)(a). [5664] CA 2006, s 421(1)(b). [5665] CA 2006, s 421(1)(c). [5666] CA 2006, s 421(2). [5667] CA 2006, s 421(3)(a). [5668] CA 2006, s 421(3)(b). [5669] CA 2006, s 421(4).

Approval and signing of a directors' remuneration report

22.52 Section 422 of the CA 2006 deals with approval and signing of a directors' remuneration report.

The directors' remuneration report must be approved by the board of directors and signed on behalf of the board by a director or the secretary of the company.[5670]

If a directors' remuneration report is approved that does not comply with the requirements of this Act, every director of the company who knew that it did not comply, or was reckless as to whether it complied;[5671] and failed to take reasonable steps to secure compliance with those requirements or, as the case may be, to prevent the report from being approved,[5672] commits an offence. A person guilty of an offence under this section is liable on conviction on indictment, to a fine;[5673] or on summary conviction, to a fine not exceeding the statutory maximum.[5674]

Sections 420–422 of the CA 2006 replace ss 242AA and 234B of the CA 1985. These sections, which were inserted into the Act by the Directors' Remuneration Report Regulations 2002 (SI 2002/1988), require quoted companies to publish a report on directors' remuneration as part of the company's annual reporting cycle; and disclose within the report details of individual directors' remuneration packages, the company's remuneration policy, and the role of the board and remuneration committee in this area.

Section 421 of the CA 2006 gives the Secretary of State power to make provision by regulations as to the information that must be contained in a directors' remuneration report and how it should be set out. These matters were previously set out in Schedule 7A of the CA 1985 and regulations made under this s 421 of the CA 2006 replace the provision in Schedule 7A. The regulations will also specify the extent to which the directors' remuneration report should be subject to audit. Regulations under s 421 of the CA 2006 are subject to the Parliamentary procedure in s 473 of the CA 2006.

Publication of Accounts and Reports

22.53 Chapter 7 of Part 15 of the CA 2006 is concerned with publication of the accounts and reports. It has 14 sections.

Duty to circulate copies of annual accounts and reports

22.54 Section 423 of the CA 2006 deals with the duty to circulate copies of annual accounts and reports. Every company must send a copy of its annual

---

[5670] CA 2006, s 422(1).   [5671] CA 2006, s 422(2)(a).   [5672] CA 2006, s 422(2)(b).
[5673] CA 2006, s 422(3)(a).   [5674] CA 2006, s 422(3)(b).

accounts and reports for each financial year to every member of the company,[5675] and every holder of the company's debentures,[5676] and every person who is entitled to receive notice of general meetings.[5677]

Copies need not be sent to a person for whom the company does not have a current address.[5678]

A company has a 'current address' for a person if an address has been notified to the company by the person as one at which documents may be sent to him;[5679] and the company has no reason to believe that documents sent to him at that address will not reach him.[5680]

In the case of a company not having a share capital, copies need not be sent to anyone who is not entitled to receive notices of general meetings of the company.[5681]

Where copies are sent out over a period of days, references in the Companies Acts to the day on which copies are sent out shall be read as references to the last day of that period.[5682]

Section 423 of the CA 2006 has effect subject to s 426 of the CA 2006 (option to provide a summary financial statement).[5683]

Section 423 of the CA 2006 replaces s 238 of the CA 1985. Section 423(1) of the CA 2006 provides that a company must send a copy of its annual accounts and reports (as defined in s 471 of the CA 2006 and including any relevant auditor's report) to specified persons.

Section 423(2) of the CA 2006 restricts the general obligation of companies to send copies of accounts and reports. The obligation will in future be to send the accounts and reports only to persons for whom they have a current address. This is to avoid companies having to send copies of the annual accounts and reports to addresses from which correspondence has previously been returned marked not known at this address (or its electronic equivalent). General provisions about how to supply copies to joint holders are in Part 6 of Schedule 5 of the CA 2006.

Time allowed for sending out copies of accounts and reports

22.55 Section 424 of the CA 2006 deals with the time allowed for sending out copies of accounts and reports. The time allowed for sending out copies of the company's annual accounts and reports is as follows.[5684]

A private company must comply with s 423 of the CA 2006 not later than the end of the period for filing accounts and reports;[5685] or if earlier, the date on which it actually delivers its accounts and reports to the registrar.[5686]

[5675] CA 2006, s 423(1)(a).   [5676] CA 2006, s 423(1)(b).   [5677] CA 2006, s 423(1)(c).
[5678] CA 2006, s 423(2).   [5679] CA 2006, s 423(3)(a).   [5680] CA 2006, s 423(3)(b).
[5681] CA 2006, s 423(4).   [5682] CA 2006, s 423(5).   [5683] CA 2006, s 423(6).
[5684] CA 2006, s 424(1).   [5685] CA 2006, s 424(2)(a).   [5686] CA 2006, s 424(2)(b).

A public company must comply with s 423. not later than 21 days before the relevant accounts meeting.[5687]

If in the case of a public company copies are sent out later than is required by s 424(3) of the CA 2006, they shall, despite that, be deemed to have been duly sent if it is so agreed by all the members entitled to attend and vote at the relevant accounts meeting.[5688]

Whether the time allowed is that for a private company or a public company is determined by reference to the company's status immediately before the end of the accounting reference period by reference to which the financial year for the accounts in question was determined.[5689]

In s 424 of the CA 2006 the 'relevant accounts meeting' means the accounts meeting of the company at which the accounts and reports in question are to be laid.[5690]

Section 424 of the CA 2006 makes changes to the time for distributing accounts for both private and public companies. Private companies (unless they opted out of the requirement) were previously required to lay their accounts at a general meeting and to send their accounts and reports to members 21 days before that meeting. They are no longer required to hold any general meeting and the requirement now is to send out their accounts and reports no later than the earlier of the date of actual delivery to the registrar or the deadline for delivery (see s 442 of the CA 2006 for the time limits for filing). Public companies must still send the annual accounts and reports out at least 21 days before the general meetings at which the accounts and reports are to be laid, defined as the 'relevant accounts meeting').

Default in sending out copies of accounts and reports: offences

22.56 Section 425 of the CA 2006 sets out the default in sending out copies of accounts and reports with offences and sanctions.

If default is made in complying with ss 423 or 424 of the CA 2006, an offence is committed by the company,[5691] and every officer of the company,[5692] who is in default. A person guilty of an offence under this section is liable on conviction on indictment, to a fine;[5693] or on summary conviction, to a fine not exceeding the statutory maximum.[5694]

There is no change to these offences that were previously contained in s 238(5) of the CA 1985.

Option to provide a summary financial statement

22.57 Section 426 of the CA 2006 deals with the option to provide a summary financial statement. A company may in such cases as may be specified

---

[5687] CA 2006, s 424(3).   [5688] CA 2006, s 424(4).   [5689] CA 2006, s 424(5).
[5690] CA 2006, s 424(6).   [5691] CA 2006, s 425(1)(a).   [5692] CA 2006, s 425(1)(b).
[5693] CA 2006, s 425(2)(a).   [5694] CA 2006, s 425(2)(b).

by regulations made by the Secretary of State,[5695] and provided any conditions so specified are complied with,[5696] provide a summary financial statement instead of copies of the accounts and reports required to be sent in accordance with s 423 of the CA 2006.

Copies of those reports and accounts must, however, be sent to any person entitled to be sent them in accordance with that section and with who wishes to receive them.[5697]

The Secretary of State may make provision by regulations as to the manner in which it is to be ascertained, whether before or after a person becomes entitled to be sent a copy of those accounts and reports, whether he wishes to receive them.[5698]

A summary financial statement must comply with the requirements of s 427 of the CA 2006 (form and contents of summary financial statement: unquoted companies), or s 428 of the CA 2006 (form and contents of summary financial statement: quoted companies).[5699]

Section 426 of the CA 2006 applies to copies of accounts and reports required to be sent out by virtue of s 146 of the CA 2006 to a person nominated to enjoy information rights as it applies to copies of accounts and reports required to be sent out in accordance with s 423 of the CA 2006 to a member of the company.[5700]

Regulations under this section are subject to negative resolution procedure.[5701]

Form and contents of summary financial statement: unquoted companies

22.58 Section 427 of the CA 2006 deals with form and contents of summary financial statements with respect to unquoted companies. A summary financial statement by a company that is not a quoted company must be derived from the company's annual accounts,[5702] and be prepared in accordance with this section and regulations made under it.[5703]

The summary financial statement must be in such a form, and contain such information, as the Secretary of State may specify by regulations. The regulations may require the statement to include information derived from the directors' report.[5704]

Nothing in this section or regulations made under it prevents a company from including in a summary financial statement additional information derived from the company's annual accounts or the directors' report.[5705]

The summary financial statement must:

[5695] CA 2006, s 426(1)(a).   [5696] CA 2006, s 426(1)(b).   [5697] CA 2006, s 426(2).
[5698] CA 2006, s 426(3). See the Companies (Summary Financial Statement) Regulations 2008.
[5699] CA 2006, s 426(4).   [5700] CA 2006, s 426(5).   [5701] CA 2006, s 426(6).
[5702] CA 2006, s 427(1)(a).   [5703] CA 2006, s 427(1)(b).   [5704] CA 2006, s 427(2).
[5705] CA 2006, s 427(3).

(a)   state that it is only a summary of information derived from the company's annual accounts;[5706]

(b)   state whether it contains additional information derived from the directors' report and, if so, that it does not contain the full text of that report;[5707]

(c)   state how a person entitled to them can obtain a full copy of the company's annual accounts and the directors' report;[5708]

(d)   contain a statement by the company's auditor of his opinion as to whether the summary financial statement:

  (i)   is consistent with the company's annual accounts and, where information derived from the directors' report is included in the statement, with that report;[5709] and

  (ii)   complies with the requirements of this section and regulations made under it;[5710]

(e)   state whether the auditor's report on the annual accounts was unqualified or qualified and, if it was qualified, set out the report in full together with any further material needed to understand the qualification;[5711]

(f)   state whether, in that report, the auditor's statement under s 496 of the CA 2006 (whether directors' report consistent with accounts) was qualified or unqualified and, if it was qualified, set out the qualified statement in full together with any further material needed to understand the qualification;[5712]

(g)   state whether that auditor's report contained a statement under (i) s 498(2)(a) of the CA 2006 (accounting records or returns inadequate or accounts not agreeing with records and returns),[5713] or (ii) s 498(3) of the CA 2006 (failure to obtain necessary information and explanations),[5714] and if so, set out the statement in full.

Regulations under this section may provide that any specified material may, instead of being included in the summary financial statement, be sent separately at the same time as the statement.[5715]

Regulations under this section are subject to negative resolution procedure.[5716]

Form and contents of a summary financial statement:
quoted companies

22.59 Section 428 of the CA 2006 sets out the form and contents of a summary financial statement in respect of quoted companies. A summary

---

[5706] CA 2006, s 427(4)(a).   [5707] CA 2006, s 427(4)(b).   [5708] CA 2006, s 427(4)(c).
[5709] CA 2006, s 427(4)(d)(i).   [5710] CA 2006, s 427(4)(d)(ii).   [5711] CA 2006, s 427(4)(e).
[5712] CA 2006, s 427(4)(f).   [5713] CA 2006, s 427(4)(g)(i).   [5714] CA 2006, s 427(4)(g)(ii).
[5715] CA 2006, s 427(5).   [5716] CA 2006, s 427(6).

financial statement by a quoted company must be derived from the company's annual accounts and the directors' remuneration report,[5717] and be prepared in accordance with this section and regulations made under it.[5718]

The summary financial statement must be in such form, and contain such information, as the Secretary of State may specify by regulations. The regulations may require the statement to include information derived from the directors' report.[5719]

Nothing in this section or regulations made under it prevents a company from including in a summary financial statement additional information derived from the company's annual accounts, the directors' remuneration report or the directors' report.

The summary financial statement must:

(a) state that it is only a summary of information derived from the company's annual accounts and the directors' remuneration report;[5720]

(b) state whether it contains additional information derived from the directors' report and, if so, that it does not contain the full text of that report;[5721]

(c) state how a person entitled to them can obtain a full copy of the company's annual accounts, the directors' remuneration report or the directors' report;[5722]

(d) contain a statement by the company's auditor of his opinion as to whether the summary financial statement (i) is consistent with the company's annual accounts and the directors' remuneration report and, where information derived from the directors' report is included in the statement, with that report,[5723] and (ii) complies with the requirements of this section and regulations made under it;[5724]

(e) state whether the auditor's report on the annual accounts and the auditable part of the directors' remuneration report was unqualified or qualified and, if it was qualified, set out the report in full together with any further material needed to understand the qualification;[5725]

(f) state whether that auditor's report contained a statement under (i) s 492(2) of the CA 2006 (accounting records or returns inadequate or accounts or directors' remuneration report not agreeing with records and returns),[5726] or (ii) s 493(3) of the CA 2006 (failure to obtain necessary information and explanations), and if so, set out the statement in full;[5727]

(g) state whether, in that report, the auditor's statement under s 496 of the

---

[5717] CA 2006, s 428(1)(a). [5718] CA 2006, s 428(1)(b). [5719] CA 2006, s 428(2).
[5720] CA 2006, s 428(4)(a). [5721] CA 2006, s 428(4)(b). [5722] CA 2006, s 428(4)(c).
[5723] CA 2006, s 428(4)(d)(i). [5724] CA 2006, s 428(4)(d)(ii). [5725] CA 2006, s 428(4)(e).
[5726] CA 2006, s 428(4)(f)(i). [5727] CA 2006, s 428(4)(f)(ii).

CA 2006 whether directors' report consistent with accounts) was qualified or unqualified and, if it was qualified, set out the qualified statement in full together with any further material needed to understand the qualification.[5728]

Regulations under this section may provide that any specified material may, instead of being included in the summary financial statement, be sent separately at the same time as the statement.

Regulations under this section are subject to negative resolution procedure.[5729]

Default in sending out copies of accounts and reports: offences

22.60 Section 429 sets out the offences and sanctions in respect of the summary financial statement.

If a default is made in complying with any provision of ss 426, 427 or 428 of the CA 2006, or of regulations under any of those sections, an offence is committed by the company,[5730] and every officer of the company who is in default.[5731] A person guilty of an offence under this section is liable on summary conviction to a fine not exceeding level 3 on the standard scale.[5732]

Sections 426–429 of the CA 2006 restate s 251 of the CA 1985. All companies have the option under s 426 of the CA 2006 to provide summary financial statements instead of copies of the full accounts and reports. This section reproduces the power for the Secretary of State to make provisions by regulations as to the circumstances in which a company may send out summary financial statements; and as to the manner in which it is to be ascertained whether a person wishes to receive a copy of the full accounts and reports.

It also makes new provision for persons nominated to enjoy information rights under s 146 of the CA 2006 (indirect investors) to be able to be provided with summary financial statements rather than the full accounts and reports.

Section 427 of the CA 2006 sets out the form and content requirement for summary financial statements prepared by unquoted companies, whilst s 428 of the CA 2006 sets out the form and content requirements for summary financial statements prepared by quoted companies. In both cases, the Secretary of State may make regulations as to the form and content of summary financial statements. There is also a new power for regulations to provide that specified material be sent separately at the same time as the summary financial statements instead of being included in it. This is to cover the

---

[5728] CA 2006, s 428(4)(g).   [5729] CA 2006, s 428(6).   [5730] CA 2006, s 429(1)(a).
[5731] CA 2006, s 429(1)(b).   [5732] CA 2006, s 429(2).

requirements of the Takeovers Directive as to necessary explanatory material (see s 992 of the CA 2006) as in the CA 1985, these powers are subject to the negative resolution procedure. Section 429 of the CA 2006 restates the existing offences in CA 1985.

Quoted companies as to website publication

Quoted companies: annual accounts and reports to be made available on website

22.61 Section 430 of the CA 2006 deals with quoted companies, with particular reference to annual accounts and reports to be made available on websites. A quoted company must ensure that its annual accounts and reports are made available on a website,[5733] and remain so available until the annual accounts and reports for the company's next financial year are made available in accordance with this section.[5734]

The annual accounts and reports must be made available on a website that is maintained by or on behalf of the company[5735] and indentifies the company in question.[5736]

Access to the annual accounts and reports on the website, and the ability to obtain a hard copy of the annual accounts and reports from the website, must not be conditional on the payment of a fee,[5737] or otherwise restricted, except so far as necessary to comply with any enactment or regulatory requirement (in the United Kingdom or elsewhere).[5738]

The annual accounts and reports must be made available as soon as reasonably practicable,[5739] and must be kept available throughout the period specified in s 430(1)(b) of the CA 2006.[5740]

Failure to make the annual accounts and reports available on a website throughout that period is disregarded if the annual accounts and reports are made available on the website for part of that period,[5741] and the failure is wholly attribute to circumstances that it would not be reasonable to have expected the company to prevent or avoid.[5742]

In the event of default in complying with this section, an offence is committed by every officer of the company who is in default.[5743] A person guilty of an offence under s 430(6) of the CA 2006 is liable on summary conviction to a fine not exceeding level 3 n the standard scale.[5744]

Section 430 of the CA 2006 introduces a new requirement on quoted companies (as defined in s 385) to put the full annual accounts and reports on a

[5733] CA 2006, s 430(1)(a).   [5734] CA 2006, s 430(1)(b).   [5735] CA 2006, s 430(2)(a).
[5736] CA 2006, s 430(2)(b).   [5737] CA 2006, s 430(3)(a).   [5738] CA 2006, s 430(3)(b).
[5739] CA 2006, s 430(4)(a).   [5740] CA 2006, s 430(4)(b).   [5741] CA 2006, s 430(5)(a).
[5742] CA 2006, s 430(5)(b).   [5743] CA 2006, s 430(6).   [5744] CA 2006, s 430(7).

website. A quoted company will still have to send the full accounts and reports to its members under s 423 of the CA 2006.

The annual accounts and reports must be made available as soon as is reasonably practicable on a website that is maintained by or on behalf of the company, and that identifies the company in question. Access to the website must be available to all members of the public and not just to members, and there must be continuous access to the website without charge. Access to the information on the website and the ability to obtain a hard copy of the information from the website may be restricted by the company where necessary to comply with any atatutory or regulatory requirement (for example, of an overseas regulator).

The annual accounts and report for a financial year must remain available until the acconts and reports for the next financial year are published on the website.

Right of member or debenture holder to demand copies of accounts and reports

Right of member or debenture holder to demand copies of accounts and reports: unquoted companies

22.62 Section 431 of the CA 2006 sets out the right of members or debenture holders to copies of accounts and reports in respect of unquoted companies. A member of, or holder of debentures of, an unquoted company is entitled to be provided, on demand and without charge, with a copy of:

(a)   the company's last annual accounts;[5745]
(b)   the last directors' report;[5746] and
(c)   the auditor's report on those accounts (including the statement on that report);[5747]

The entitlement under this section is to a single copy of those documents, but that is in addition to any copy to which a person may be entitled under s 423 of the CA 2006.[5748]

If a demand made under this section is not complied with within seven days of receipt by the company,[5749] an offence is committed by the company, and every officer of the company who is in default.[5750] A person guilty of an offence under s 431 of the CA 2006 is liable on summary conviction to a fine not exceeding level 3 on the standard scale and, for continued contravention,

---

[5745] CA 2006, s 431(1)(a).   [5746] CA 2006, s 431(1)(b).   [5747] CA 2006, s 431(1)(c).
[5748] CA 2006, s 431(2).   [5749] CA 2006, s 431(3)(a).   [5750] CA 2006, s 431(3)(b).

a daily default fine not exceeding one-tenth of level 3 on the standard scale.[5751]

Right of member or debenture holder to demand copies of accounts and reports: quoted companies

22.63 Section 432 of the CA 2006 sets out the right of members or debenture holders to copies of accounts and reports in respect of quoted companies. A member of, or holder of debentures of, a quoted company is entitled to be provided, on demand and without charge, with a copy of:

(a)   the company's last annual accounts;[5752]
(b)   the last directors' report;[5753]
(c)   the auditor's report on those accounts (including the statement on that report).[5754]

The entitlement under this section is to a single copy of those documents, but that is in addition to any copy to which a person may be entitled under s 423 of the CA 2006.[5755]

If a demand made under this section is not complied with within seven days of receipt by the company, an offence is committed by the company,[5756] and every officer of the company who is in default.[5757]

A person guilty of an offence under s 432 of the CA 2006 is liable on summary conviction to a fine not exceeding level 3 on the standard scale and, for continued contravention, a daily default fine not exceeding one-tenth of level 3 on the standard scale.[5758]

Sections 431 and 432 of the CA 2006 re-enact s 239 of the CA 1985 and entitle a member or debenture holder to a copy of the company's last annual accounts and reports without charge. Section 431 of the CA 2006 lists the documents to which members or debenture holders of unquoted companies are entitled, while s 432 of the CA 2006 lists those to which members or debenture holders of quoted companies are entitled.

Requirements in connection with publication of accounts and reports

Name of signatory to be stated in published copies of accounts and reports

22.64 Section 433 of the CA 2006 deals with the name of the signatory to be stated in published copies of accounts and reports. Every copy of a document

---

[5751] CA 2006, s 431(4).   [5752] CA 2006, s 432(1)(a).   [5753] CA 2006, s 432(1)(b).
[5754] CA 2006, s 432(1)(c).   [5755] CA 2006, s 432(2).   [5756] CA 2006, s 432(3)(a).
[5757] CA 2006, s 432(3)(b).   [5758] CA 2006, s 432(4).

to which this section applies that is published by or on behalf of the company must state the name of the person who signed it on behalf of the board.[5759]

In the case of an unquoted company, this section applies to copies of the company's balance sheet,[5760] and the directors' report.[5761]

In the case of a quoted company, this section applies to copies of the company's balance sheet;[5762] the directors' remuneration report;[5763] and the directors' report.[5764]

If a copy is published without the required statement of the signatory's name, an offence is committed by the company,[5765] and every officer of the company who is in default.[5766] A person guilty of an offence under s 433 of the CA 2006 is liable on summary conviction to a fine not exceeding level 3 on the standard scale.[5767]

Requirements in connection with the publication of statutory accounts

22.65 Section 434 of the CA 2006 deals with requirements in connection with the publication of statutory accounts. If a company publishes any of its statutory accounts, they must be accompanied by the auditor's report on those accounts (unless the company is exempt from audit and the directors have taken advantage of that exemption).[5768]

A company that prepares statutory group accounts for a financial year must not publish its statutory individual accounts for that year without also publishing with them its statutory group accounts.[5769]

A company's 'statutory accounts' are its accounts for a financial year as required to be delivered to the registrar under s 441 of the CA 2006.[5770]

If a company contravenes any provision of this section, an offence is committed by the company,[5771] and every officer of the company who is in default.[5772] A person guilty of an offence under s 434 of the CA 2006 is liable on summary conviction to a fine not exceeding level 3 on the standard scale.[5773]

This section does not apply in relation to the provision by a company of a summary financial statement (see s 426 of the CA 2006).[5774]

[5759] CA 2006, s 433(1).   [5760] CA 2006, s 433(2)(a).   [5761] CA 2006, s 433(2)(b).
[5762] CA 2006, s 433(3)(a).   [5763] CA 2006, s 433(3)(b).   [5764] CA 2006, s 433(3)(c).
[5765] CA 2006, s 433(4)(a).   [5766] CA 2006, s 433(4)(b).   [5767] CA 2006, s 433(5).
[5768] CA 2006, s 434(1).   [5769] CA 2006, s 434(2).   [5770] CA 2006, s 434(3).
[5771] CA 2006, s 434(4)(a).   [5772] CA 2006, s 434(4)(b).   [5773] CA 2006, s 434(5).
[5774] CA 2006, s 434(6).

Requirements in connection with the publication of non-statutory accounts

22.66 Section 434 of the CA 2006 deals with requirements in connection with the publication of statutory accounts. If a company publishes non-statutory accounts, it must publish with them a statement indicating:

(a) that they are not the company's statutory accounts;[5775]

(b) whether the statutory accounts dealing with any financial year with which the non-statutory accounts purport to deal have been delivered to the registrar;[5776] and

(c) whether an auditor's report has been made on the company's statutory accounts for any such financial year, and if so whether the report (i) was qualified or unqualified, or included a reference to any matters to which the auditor drew attention by way of emphasis without qualifying the report,[5777] or (ii) contained a statement under s 498(2) of the CA 2006 (accounting records or returns inadequate or accounts or directors' remuneration report not agreeing with records and returns), or s 498(2) of the CA 2006 (failure to obtain necessary information and explanations).[5778]

The company must not publish with non-statutory accounts the auditor's report on the company's statutory accounts.[5779]

References in this section to the publication by a company of 'non-statutory accounts' are to the publication of any balance sheet or profit and loss account relating to, or purporting to deal with, a financial year of the company;[5780] or an account in any form purporting to be a balance sheet or profit and loss account for the group headed by the company relating to, or purporting to deal with, a financial year of the company.[5781]

In s 435(3)(b) of the CA 2006, 'a group headed by the company' means a group consisting of the company and any other undertaking (regardless of whether it is a subsidiary undertaking of the company) other than a parent undertaking of the company.[5782]

If a company contravenes any provision of this section, an offence is committed by the company,[5783] and every officer of the company who is in default.[5784] A person guilty of an offence under this section is liable on summary conviction to a fine not exceeding level 3 on the standard scale.[5785]

Section 435 of the CA 2006 does not apply in relation to the provision by a company of a summary financial statement (see s 426 of the CA 2006).[5786]

[5775] CA 2006, s 435(1)(a).   [5776] CA 2006, s 435(1)(b).   [5777] CA 2006, s 435(1)(c)(i).

[5778] CA 2006, s 435(1)(c)(ii).   [5779] CA 2006, s 435(2).   [5780] CA 2006, s 435(3)(a).

[5781] CA 2006, s 435(3)(b).   [5782] CA 2006, s 435(4).   [5783] CA 2006, s 435(5)(a).

[5784] CA 2006, s 435(5)(b).   [5785] CA 2006, s 435(6).   [5786] CA 2006, s 435(7).

Meaning of 'publication' in relation to accounts and reports

22.67 Section 436 of the CA 2006 deals with the meaning of 'publication' in relation to accounts and reports. This section applies for the purposes of s 433 of the CA 2006 (name of signatory to be stated in published copies of accounts and reports), and s 434 of the CA 2006 (requirements in connection with the publication of statutory accounts), and s 435 of the CA 2006 (requirements in connection with the publication of non-statutory accounts).[5787]

For the purposes of those sections a company is regarded as publishing a document if it publishes, issues or circulates it or otherwise makes it available for public inspection in a manner calculated to invite members of the public generally, or any class of members of the public, to read it.[5788]

Section 433 of the CA 2006 bring together provisions scattered throughout Part 7 of the CA 1985 (in ss 233(3) and (6)(a), 234A(2) and (4)(a), 234C(2) and (4)(a)) concerning statements of the name of the signatory in published accounts and reports. In the case of unquoted companies, every copy of the balance sheet and directors' report that is published by or on behalf of the company must state the name of the director who signed it on behalf of the board. For quoted companies this applies to copies of the balance sheet, directors' remuneration report, and directors' report.

Sections 434 and 435 of the CA 2006 re-enact s 240 of the CA 1985 concerning requirements in connection with the publication of statutory or non-statutory accounts. The term 'publication' is defined in s 436 of the CA 2006.

Public Companies: Laying of Accounts and Reports before a General Meeting

22.68 Chapter 8 addresses the laying of accounts and reports before a general meeting in respect of public companies. It comprises two sections.

Public companies: laying of accounts and reports before a general meeting

22.69 Section 437 of the CA 2006 deals with the laying of acconts and reports before a general meeting for public companies. The directors of a public company must lay before the company in general meeting copies of its annual accounts and reports.[5789]

This section must be complied with not later than the end of the period for filing the accounts and reports in question.[5790]

[5787] CA 2006, s 436(1).   [5788] CA 2006, s 436(2).   [5789] CA 2006, s 437(1).
[5790] CA 2006, s 437(2).

In the Companies Acts, 'accounts meeting', in relation to a public company, means a general meeting of the company at which the company's annual accounts and reports are (or are to be) laid in accordance with this section.[5791]

Public companies: offence of failure to lay accounts and reports

22.70 Section 438 of the CA 2006 is concerned with the offence for public companies of failure to lay accounts and reports. If the requirements of s 437 of the CA 2006 (public companies: laying of accounts and reports before a general meeting) are not complied with before the end of the period allowed, every person who immediately before the end of that period was a director of the company commits an offence.[5792]

It is a defence for a person charged with such an offence to prove that he took all reasonable steps for securing that those requirements would be complied with before the end of that period.[5793]

It is not a defence to prove that the documents in question were not in fact prepared as required by this Part.[5794]

A person guilty of an offence under this section is liable on summary conviction to a fine not exceeding level 5 on the standard scale and, for continued contravention, a daily default fine not exceeding one-tenth of level 5 on the standard scale.[5795]

Sections 437 and 438 of the CA 2006 re-enact s 241 of the CA 1985 on the laying of accounts and reports before the company in a general meeting, but restrict its application to public companies.

Under the CA 2006, private companies are under no statutory obligation to hold an AGM or to lay accounts and reports in a general meeting. There is no statutory link for them between the accounts and AGMs (although such a link might be provided for in the company's articles). Any AGM that a private company may hold pursuant to its articles will not be a statutory meeting. Public companies will still be required to hold AGMs and they must now hold them within six months of the end of the accounting reference period.

Quoted Companies: Members' Approval of the Directors' Remuneration Report

22.71 Chapter 9 addresses members' approval of the directors' remuneration report in respect of quoted companies. It comprises two sections.

[5791] CA 2006, s 437(3).   [5792] CA 2006, s 438(1).   [5793] CA 2006, s 438(2).
[5794] CA 2006, s 438(3).   [5795] CA 2006, s 438(4).

Quoted companies: members' approval of directors'
remuneration report

22.72 Section 439 of the CA 2006 deals with members' approval of directors' remuneration report for quoted companies. A quoted company must, prior to the accounts meeting, give to the members of the company entitled to be sent notice of the meeting notice of the intention to move at the meeting, as an ordinary resolution, a resolution approving the directors' remuneration report for the financial year.[5796]

The notice may be given in any manner permitted for service on the members of notice of the meeting.[5797]

The business that may be dealt with at the accounts meeting includes the resolution. This is so notwithstanding any default in complying with s 439(1) or (2) of the CA 2006.[5798]

The existing directors must ensure that the resolution is put to the vote of the meeting.[5799]

No entitlement of a person to remuneration is made conditional on the resolution being passed by reason only of the provision made by this section.[5800]

The term 'the accounts meeting' means the general meeting of the company before which the company's annual accounts for the financial year are to be laid; and 'existing director' means a person who is a director of the company immediately before that meeting.[5801]

Quoted companies: offences in connection with the procedure
for approval

22.73 Section 440 of the CA 2006 deals with the offences in connection with the procedure for approval for quoted companies. In the event of default in complying with s 423(1) of the CA 2006 (notice to be given of resolution for the approval of directors' remuneration report), an offence is committed by every officer of the company who is in default.[5802]

If the resolution is not put to the vote of the accounts meeting, an offence is committed by each existing director.[5803]

It is a defence for a person charged with an offence under s 440(2) of the CA 2006 to prove that he took all reasonable steps for securing that the resolution was put to the vote of the meeting.[5804]

A person guilty of an offence under this section is liable on summary conviction to a fine not exceeding level 3 on the standard scale.[5805]

[5796] CA 2006, s 439(1).   [5797] CA 2006, s 439(2).   [5798] CA 2006, s 439(3).
[5799] CA 2006, s 439(4).   [5800] CA 2006, s 439(5).   [5801] CA 2006, s 439(6).
[5802] CA 2006, s 440(1).   [5803] CA 2006, s 440(2).   [5804] CA 2006, s 440(3).
[5805] CA 2006, s 440(4).

The term 'the accounts meeting' means the general meeting of the company before which the company's annual accounts for the financial year are to be laid; and 'existing director' means a person who is a director of the company immediately before that meeting.[5806]

Sections 439 and 440 of the CA 2006 restate the requirement under s 241A of the CA 1985 that a quoted company circulate a resolution approving the directors' remuneration report for the preceding financial year to its shareholders prior to its general meeting.

The vote is advisory: as such, it does not require directors to amend contractual entitlements, nor to amend their remuneration policy, but the result of the vote will send a very strong signal to directors about the level of support among shareholders for the board's remuneration policy. In practice, directors will wish to take notice of the views of the company's members and to respond appropriately.

All 'existing directors' (that is persons who, immediately before the general meeting, are directors of the company) have a responsibility to ensure that the resolution is put to the vote of the meeting. As such, the requirement does not apply to past directors (even if they served on the board or as members of the remuneration committee in the current financial year), but does apply to 'existing directors' who were, for whatever reason, not present at the general meeting.

Filing of Accounts and Reports

22.74 Chapter 10 is concerned with the filing of accounts and reports. It comprises 13 sections.

Duty to file accounts and reports

Duty to file accounts and reports with the registrar

22.75 Section 441 of the CA 2006 is concerned with the duty to file accounts and reports with the registrar.

The directors of a company must deliver to the registrar for each financial year the accounts and reports required by s 444 of the CA 2006 (filing obligations of companies subject to the small companies regime); s 445 of the CA 2006 (filing obligations of medium-sized companies); s 444 of the CA 2006 (filing obligations of unquoted companies); or s 447 of the CA 2006 (filing obligations of quoted companies).[5807]

This is subject to s 448 of the CA 2006 (unlimited companies exempt from filing obligations).[5808]

[5806] CA 2006, s 440(5).   [5807] CA 2006, s 441(1).   [5808] CA 2006, s 441(2).

Period allowed for filing accounts

22.76 Section 442 of the CA 2006 specifies the period allowed for the directors of a company to comply with their obligation under s 441 of the CA 2006 to deliver accounts and reports for a financial year to the registrar. This is referred to in the Companies Acts as the 'period for filing' those accounts and reports.[5809]

The period is, for a private company, nine months after the end of the relevant accounting reference period;[5810] and for a public company, six months after the end of that period.[5811]

This is subject to the following provisions of this section.

If the relevant accounting reference period is the company's first and is a period of more than 12 months, the period is nine months or six months, as the case may be, from the first anniversary of the incorporation of the company,[5812] or three months after the end of the accounting reference period, whichever last expires.[5813]

If the relevant accounting reference period is treated as shortened by virtue of a notice given by the company under s 392 of the CA 2006 (alteration of an accounting reference date), the period is that applicable in accordance with the above provisions,[5814] or three months from the date of the notice under that section, whichever last expires.[5815]

If for any special reason the Secretary of State thinks fit he may, on an application made before the expiry of the period otherwise allowed, by notice in writing to a company extend that period by such further period as may be specified in the notice.[5816]

Whether the period allowed is that for a private company or a public company is determined by reference to the company's status immediately before the end of the relevant accounting reference period.[5817]

In this section 'the relevant accounting reference period' means the accounting reference period by reference to which the financial year for the accounts in question was determined.[5818]

Calculation of period allowed

22.77 Section 443 of the CA 2006 applies for the purposes of calculating the period for filing a company's accounts and reports, which is expressed as a specified number of months from a specified date or after the end of a specified previous period.[5819]

[5809] CA 2006, s 442(1). [5810] CA 2006, s 442(2)(a). [5811] CA 2006, s 442(2)(b).
[5812] CA 2006, s 442(3)(a). [5813] CA 2006, s 442(3)(b). [5814] CA 2006, s 442(4)(a).
[5815] CA 2006, s 442(4)(b). [5816] CA 2006, s 442(5). [5817] CA 2006, s 442(6).
[5818] CA 2006, s 442(7). [5819] CA 2006, s 443(1).

Subject to the following provisions, the period ends with the date in the appropriate month corresponding to the specified date or the last day of the specified previous period.[5820]

If the specified date, or the last day of the specified previous period, is the last day of a month, the period ends with the last day of the appropriate month (whether or not that is the corresponding date).[5821]

If (a) the specified date, or the last day of the specified previous period, is not the last day of a month but is the 29th or 30th,[5822] and (b) the appropriate month is February,[5823] the period ends with the last day of February.

The term 'appropriate month' means the month that is the specified number of months after the month in which the specified date, or the end of the specified previous period, falls.

Sections 441–443 of the CA 2006 cover the general duty to file accounts and reports with the registrar of companies, and the period allowed for filing accounts.

Section 442 of the CA 2006 reduces the period for filing accounts from ten months to nine months for private companies and from seven months to six months for public companies. These periods are calculated from the end of the relevant accounting reference period. The timetable for delivering accounts to the registrar was last amended in 1976. The periods have been reduced to reflect improvements in technology and the increased rates at which information becomes out of date. Filing timescales in other countries are generally less generous that in the UK.

Under s 442(6) of the CA 2006, whether a company is private or public for the purpose of its filing obligations is determined by its status immediately before the end of the relevant accounting period.

Section 443 of the CA 2006 is a new provision defining how to calculate the periods allowed for filing accounts and reports. In general this is the same date the relevant number of months later. So, for example, if the end of the accounting reference period is 5 June, six months from then is 5 December. However, as months of are unequal length, there can be confusion as to whether six months from, say, 30 June is 30 of December (exactly six months later) or 31 December (the end of the sixth month). Under the rule laid down in this section, six months from 30 June will be 31 December. This reverses the 'corresponding date rule' laid down by the House of Lords in *Dodds v Walker*.[5824]

[5820] CA 2006, s 443(2).   [5821] CA 2006, s 443(3).   [5822] CA 2006, s 443(4)(a).
[5823] CA 2006, s 443(4)(b).   [5824] [1981] 1 WLR 1027.

Filing obligations of different descriptions of company

Filing obligations of companies subject to the small companies regime

22.78 Section 444 of the CA 2006 deals with the filing obligation of companies subject to the small companies regime. The directors of a company subject to the small companies regime:

(a) must deliver to the registrar for each financial year a copy of a balance sheet drawn up as at the last day of that year;[5825] and

(b) may also deliver to the registrar (i) a copy of the company's profit and loss account for that year,[5826] and (ii) a copy of the directors' report for that year.[5827]

The directors must also deliver to the registrar a copy of the auditor's report on those accounts (and on the directors' report). This does not apply if the company is exempt from an audit and the directors have taken advantage of that exemption.

The copies of accounts and reports delivered to the registrar must be copies of the company's annual accounts and reports, except that where the company prepares Companies Act accounts the directors may deliver to the registrar a copy of a balance sheet drawn up in accordance with regulations made by the Secretary of State,[5828] and there may be omitted from the copy of the profit and loss account delivered to the registrar such items as may be specified by the regulations. These are referred to in this Part as 'abbreviated accounts'.[5829]

If abbreviated accounts are delivered to the registrar the obligation to deliver a copy of the auditor's report on the accounts is to deliver a copy of the special auditor's report required by s 449 of the CA 2006.[5830]

Where the directors of a company subject to the small companies regime deliver to the registrar IAS accounts, or Companies Act accounts that are not abbreviated accounts, and in accordance with this section do not deliver to the registrar a copy of the company's profit and loss account,[5831] or do not deliver to the registrar a copy of the directors' report, the copy of the balance sheet delivered to the registrar must contain in a prominent position a statement that the company's annual accounts and reports have been delivered in accordance with the provisions applicable to companies subject to the small companies regime.[5832]

The copies of the balance sheet and any directors' report delivered to the registrar under this section must state the name of the person who signed it on behalf of the board.[5833]

[5825] CA 2006, s 444(1)(a).   [5826] CA 2006, s 444(1)(b)(i).   [5827] CA 2006, s 444(1)(b)(ii).
[5828] CA 2006, s 444(3)(a).   [5829] CA 2006, s 444(3)(b).   [5830] CA 2006, s 444(4).
[5831] CA 2006, s 444(5).   [5832] CA 2006, s 444(5)(b).   [5833] CA 2006, s 444(6).

The copy of the auditor's report delivered to the registrar under this section must state the name of the auditor and (where the auditor is a firm) the name of the person who signed it as senior statutory auditor,[5834] or if the conditions in s 506 of the CA 2006 (circumstances in which names may be omitted) are met, state that a resolution has been passed and notified to the Secretary of State in accordance with that section.[5835]

Filing obligations of medium-sized companies

22.79 Section 445 of the CA 2006 deals with filing obligations of medium-sized companies. The directors of a company that qualifies as a medium-sized company in relation to a financial year (see ss 465–467 of the CA 2006) must deliver to the registrar a copy of the company's annual accounts;[5836] and the directors' report.[5837]

They must also deliver to the registrar a copy of the auditor's report on those accounts (and on the directors' report). This does not apply if the company is exempt from audit and the directors have taken advantage of that exemption.[5838]

Where the company prepares Companies Act accounts, the directors may deliver to the registrar a copy of the company's annual accounts for the financial year that includes a profit and loss account in which items are combined in accordance with regulations made by the Secretary of State;[5839] and that does not contain items whose omission is authorised by the regulations.[5840]

These are referred to in this Part as 'abbreviated accounts'.

If abbreviated accounts are delivered to the registrar the obligation to deliver a copy of the auditor's report on the accounts is to deliver a copy of the special auditor's report required by s 449 of the CA 2006.[5841]

The copies of the balance sheet and directors' report delivered to the registrar under this section must state the name of the person who signed it on behalf of the board.[5842]

The copy of the auditor's report delivered to the registrar under this section must state the name of the auditor and (where the auditor is a firm) the name of the person who signed it as senior statutory auditor;[5843] or if the conditions in s 506 of the CA 2006 (circumstances in which names may be omitted) are met, state that a resolution has been passed and notified to the Secretary of State in accordance with that section.[5844]

Section 445 of the CA 2006 does not apply to companies within s 444 of the CA 2006 (filing obligations).

[5834] CA 2006, s 444(7)(a). [5835] CA 2006, s 444(7)(b). [5836] CA 2006, s 445(1)(a).
[5837] CA 2006, s 445(1)(b). [5838] CA 2006, s 445(2). [5839] CA 2006, s 445(3)(a).
[5840] CA 2006, s 445(3)(b). [5841] CA 2006, s 445(4). [5842] CA 2006, s 445(5).
[5843] CA 2006, s 445(6)(a). [5844] CA 2006, s 445(6)(b).

Filing obligations of unquoted companies

22.80 Section 446 of the CA 2006 is concerned with the filing obligations of unquoted companies. The directors of an unquoted company must deliver to the registrar for each financial year of the company a copy of the company's annual accounts;[5845] and the directors' report.[5846]

The directors must also deliver to the registrar a copy of the auditor's report on those accounts (and the directors' report). This does not apply if the company is exempt from audit and the directors have taken advantage of that exemption.[5847]

The copies of the balance sheet and directors' report delivered to the registrar under this section must state the name of the person who signed it on behalf of the board.[5848]

The copy of the auditor's report delivered to the registrar under this section must state the name of the auditor and (where the auditor is a firm) the name of the person who signed it as senior statutory auditor;[5849] or if the conditions in s 506 of the CA 2006 (circumstances in which names may be omitted) are met, state that a resolution has been passed and notified to the Secretary of State in accordance with that section.[5850]

This section does not apply to companies within s 444 of the CA 2006 (filing obligations of companies subject to the small companies regime);[5851] or s 445 of the CA 2006 (filing obligations of medium-sized companies).[5852]

Filing obligations of quoted companies

22.81 Section 447 of the CA 2006 deals with the filing obligations of quoted companies. The directors of a quoted company must deliver to the registrar for each financial year of the company a copy of:

(a)   the company's annual accounts;[5853]
(b)   the directors' remuneration report;[5854] and
(c)   the directors' report.[5855]

They must also deliver a copy of the auditor's report on those accounts (and on the directors' remuneration report and the directors' report).[5856]

The copies of the balance sheet, the directors' remuneration report and the directors' report delivered to the registrar under this section must state the name of the person who signed it on behalf of the board.[5857]

[5845] CA 2006, s 446(1)(a).   [5846] CA 2006, s 446(1)(b).   [5847] CA 2006, s 446(2).
[5848] CA 2006, s 446(3).   [5849] CA 2006, s 446(4)(a).   [5850] CA 2006, s 446(4)(b).
[5851] CA 2006, s 446(5)(a).   [5852] CA 2006, s 446(5)(b).   [5853] CA 2006, s 447(1)(a).
[5854] CA 2006, s 447(1)(b).   [5855] CA 2006, s 447(1)(c).   [5856] CA 2006, s 447(2).
[5857] CA 2006, s 447(3).

The copy of the auditor's report delivered to the registrar under this section must state the name of the auditor and (where the auditor is a firm) the name of the person who signed it as senior statutory auditor;[5858] or if the conditions in s 506 of the CA 2006 (circumstances in which names may be omitted) are met, state that a resolution has been passed and notified to the Secretary of State in accordance with that section.[5859]

Unlimited companies exempt from the obligation to file accounts

22.82 Section 448 of the CA 2006 deals with unlimited companies being exempt from the obligation to file accounts. The directors of an unlimited company are not required to deliver accounts and reports to the registrar in respect of a financial year if the following conditions are met.[5860]

The conditions are that at no time during the relevant accounting reference period:

(a)   has the company been, to its knowledge, a subsidiary undertaking of an undertaking that was then limited;[5861] or

(b)   have there been, to its knowledge, exercisable by or on behalf of two or more undertakings that were then limited, rights which if exercisable by one of them would have made the company a subsidiary undertaking of it;[5862] or

(c)   has the company been a parent company of an undertaking that was then limited.[5863]

The references above to an undertaking being limited at a particular time are to an undertaking (under whatever law established) the liability of whose members is at that time limited.

The exemption conferred by this section does not apply if the company is a banking or insurance company or the parent company of a banking or insurance group;[5864] or the company is a qualifying company within the meaning of the Partnerships and Unlimited Companies (Accounts) Regulations 1993 (SI 1993/1820).[5865]

Where a company is exempt by virtue of this section from the obligation to deliver accounts:

(a)   s 434(3) of the CA 2006 (requirements in connection with publication of statutory accounts: meaning of 'statutory accounts') has effect with the substitution for the words 'as required to be delivered to the registrar

---

[5858] CA 2006, s 447(4)(a).   [5859] CA 2006, s 447(4)(b).   [5860] CA 2006, s 448(1).
[5861] CA 2006, s 448(2)(a).   [5862] CA 2006, s 448(2)(b).   [5863] CA 2006, s 448(2)(c).
[5864] CA 2006, s 448(3)(a).   [5865] CA 2006, s 448(3)(b).

under section 441' of the words 'as prepared in accordance with this Part and approved by the board of directors';[5866] and

(b)   s 435(1)(b) of the CA 2006 (requirements in connection with publication of non-statutory accounts: statement whether statutory accounts delivered) has effect with the substitution for the words 'whether statutory accounts . . . have been delivered to the registrar' of the words 'that the company is exempt from the requirement to deliver statutory accounts'.[5867]

In this section the 'relevant accounting reference period', in relation to a financial year, means the accounting reference period by reference to which that financial year was determined.[5868]

Sections 444–448 of the CA 2006 concern the filing obligation of different sizes of company. They structure the provisions in ss 242, 246, 246A and 254 of the CA 1985 to make clearer what companies have to do.

Section 444 of the CA 2006 concerns the filing obligations of companies subject to the small companies regime (previously s 246(1) and (5)–(7) of the CA 1985). Such companies may file abbreviated accounts, and this section gives the Secretary of State the power to make regulations concerning abbreviated accounts for such companies. Under subs (5), small companies filing a full balance sheet with the registrar (whether prepared in accordance with international accounting standards or under CA 2006), but omitting a copy of the profit and loss account and/or the directors' report, must include a statement on the balance sheet that they are delivered in accordance with the small companies regime. Section 444(7) of the CA 2006 requires the filed copy of the audit report to state the name of the auditor and, if there is one, of the senior statutory auditor, unless they are taking advantage of the exemption in s 506 of the CA 2006, in which case they must state that they are doing so.

Section 445 of the CA 2006 restates provisions in s 246A of the CA 1985 permitting medium-sized companies (as defined in s 465 of the CA 2006) to file abbreviated accounts and gives the Secretary of State the power to make regulations concerning abbreviated accounts for such companies.

Section 446 of the CA 2006 concerns the filing obligations of unquoted companies.

Section 447 of the CA 2006 concerns the filing obligations of quoted companies. This is a restatement of s 242 of the CA 1985. Section 447(3) of the CA 2006 provides for the copies of all the accounting documents including the balance sheet to state the name of the person who signed the documents.

Section 448 of the CA 2006 replaces s 254 of the CA 1985. It exempts

---

[5866] CA 2006, s 448(4)(a).   [5867] CA 2006, s 448(4)(b).   [5868] CA 2006, s 448(5).

unlimited companies from the obligation of filing accounts. There are limitations on the exemption set out in s 448(2) and (3) of the CA 2006.

Requirements where abbreviated accounts delivered

Special auditor's report where abbreviated accounts delivered

22.83 Section 449 of the CA 2006 deals with the special auditors' report where abbreviated accounts are delivered. Section 449 of the CA 2006 applies where the directors of a company deliver abbreviated accounts to the registrar;[5869] and the company is not exempt from audit (or the directors have not taken advantage of any such exemption).[5870]

The directors must also deliver to the registrar a copy of a special report of the company's auditor stating that in his opinion the company is entitled to deliver abbreviated accounts in accordance with the section in question;[5871] and the abbreviated accounts to be delivered are properly prepared in accordance with regulations under that section.[5872]

The auditor's report on the company's annual accounts need not be delivered, but:

(a) if that report was qualified, the special report must set out that report in full together with any further material necessary to understand the qualification;[5873] and

(b) if that report contained a statement under (i) s 498(2)(a) or (b) of the CA 2006 (accounts, records or returns inadequate or accounts not agreeing with records and returns),[5874] or (ii) s 498(3) of the CA 2006 (failure to obtain necessary information and explanations), the special report must set out that statement in full.[5875]

The provisions of ss 503–506 of the CA 2006 (signature of auditor's report), and ss 507–509 of the CA 2006 (offences in connection with auditor's report), apply to a special report under this section as they apply to an auditor's report on the company's annual accounts prepared under Part 16 of the CA 2006.[5876]

If abbreviated accounts are delivered to the registrar, the references in ss 434 or 435 of the CA 2006 (requirements in connection with publication of accounts) to the auditor's report on the company's annual accounts shall be read as references to the special auditor's report required by this section.[5877]

[5869] CA 2006, s 449(1)(a).   [5870] CA 2006, s 449(1)(b).   [5871] CA 2006, s 449(2)(a).
[5872] CA 2006, s 449(2)(b).   [5873] CA 2006, s 449(3)(a).   [5874] CA 2006, s 449(3)(b)(i).
[5875] CA 2006, s 449(3)(b)(ii).   [5876] CA 2006, s 449(4).   [5877] CA 2006, s 449(5).

Approval and signing of abbreviated accounts

22.84 Section 450 of the CA 2006 deals with the approval and signing of abbreviated accounts. Abbreviated accounts must be approved by the board of directors and signed on behalf of the board by a director of the company.[5878] The signature must be on the balance sheet.[5879]

The balance sheet must contain in a prominent position above the signature a statement to the effect that it is prepared in accordance with the special provisions of this Act relating (as the case may be) to companies subject to the small companies regime or to medium-sized companies.[5880]

If abbreviated accounts are approved that do not comply with the requirements of regulations under the relevant section, every director of the company who knew that they did not comply, or was reckless as to whether they complied;[5881] and failed to take reasonable steps to prevent them from being approved, commits an offence.[5882] A person guilty of an offence under s 450(4) of the CA 2006 is liable on conviction on indictment, to a fine;[5883] on summary conviction, to a fine not exceeding the statutory maximum.[5884]

Section 449 of the CA 2006 replaces the provision in s 247B of the CA 1985 requiring a special auditor's report required by s 495 of the CA 2006, where a company delivers abbreviated accounts to the registrar of companies. There is no requirement for the special auditor's accounts where the company is entitled to exemption from audit and has taken advantage of that exemption.

Section 450 of the CA 2006 replaces s 246(7) and (8) and 246A(4) of the CA 1985 concerning the approval and signing of abbreviated accounts.

Failure to file accounts and reports

Defaults in filing accounts and reports: offences

22.85 Section 451 of the CA 2006 sets out the offences for defaults in filing accounts and reports. If the requirements of s 441 of the CA 2006 (duty to file accounts and reports) are not complied with in relation to a company's accounts and reports for a financial year before the end of the period for filing those accounts and reports, every person who immediately before the end of that period was a director of the company commits an offence.[5885]

It is a defence for a person charged with such an offence to prove that he took all reasonable steps for securing that those requirements would be complied with before the end of that period.[5886]

[5878] CA 2006, s 450(1). [5879] CA 2006, s 450(2). [5880] CA 2006, s 450(3).
[5881] CA 2006, s 450(4)(a). [5882] CA 2006, s 450(4)(b). [5883] CA 2006, s 450(5)(a).
[5884] CA 2006, s 450(5)(b). [5885] CA 2006, s 451(1). [5886] CA 2006, s 451(2).

It is not a defence to prove that the documents in question were not in fact prepared as required by this Part.[5887]

A person guilty of an offence under s 451 of the CA 2006 is liable on summary conviction to a fine not exceeding level 5 on the standard scale and, for continued contravention, a daily default fine not exceeding one-tenth of level 5 on the standard scale.[5888]

Default in filing accounts and reports: court order

22.86 Section 452 of the CA 2006 deals with defaults in filing accounts and reports with particular reference to court order. If:

(a) the requirements of s 441 of the CA 2006 (duty to file accounts and reports) are not complied with in relation to a company's accounts and reports for a financial year before the end of the period for filing those accounts and reports;[5889] and

(b) the directors of the company fail to make good the default within 14 days after the service of a notice on them requiring compliance,[5890]

the court may, on the application of any member or creditor of the company or of the registrar, make an order directing the directors (or any of them) to make good the default within such time as may be specified in the order.

The court's order may provide that all costs (in Scotland, expenses) of and incidental to the application are to be borne by the directors.[5891]

Civil penalty for failure to file accounts and reports

22.87 Section 453 of the CA 2006 deals with the civil penalty for the failure to file accounts and reports. Where the requirements of s 441 of the CA 2006 are not complied with in relation to a company's accounts and reports for a financial year before the end of the period for filing those accounts and reports, the company is liable to a civil penalty.

This is in addition to any liability of the directors under s 451 of the CA 2006.[5892]

The amount of the penalty shall be determined in accordance with regulations made by the Secretary of State by reference to the length of the period between the end of the period for filing the accounts and reports in question and the day on which the requirements are complied with;[5893] and whether the company is a private or public company.[5894]

[5887] CA 2006, s 451(3).   [5888] CA 2006, s 451(4).   [5889] CA 2006, s 452(1)(a).
[5890] CA 2006, s 452(1)(b).   [5891] CA 2006, s 452(2).   [5892] CA 2006, s 453(1).
[5893] CA 2006, s 453(2)(a).   [5894] CA 2006, s 453(2)(b).

The penalty may be recovered by the registrar and is to be paid into the Consolidated Fund.[5895]

It is not a defence in proceedings under this section to prove that the documents in question were not in fact prepared as required by this Part.[5896]

Regulations under this section having the effect of increasing the penalty payable in any case are subject to affirmative resolution procedure.

Otherwise, the regulations are subject to negative resolution procedure.[5897]

Sections 451 and 453 of the CA 2006 re-enact sanctions in ss 242(2)–(5) of the CA 1985 for failing to file accounts and reports within the required periods.

Section 453 of the CA 2006, which provides a civil penalty for failure to file accounts, restates s 242A of the CA 1985 with one change. Rather than setting out the table of penalties on the legislation, s 453(2) of the CA 2006 provides for the Secretary of State to make regulations specifying both the relevant periods and the amounts of the penalties. Regulations that have the effect of increasing the penalty will be subject to the affirmative resolution procedure. Otherwise, they will be subject to the negative resolution procedure.

Revision of Defective Accounts and Reports

22.88 Chapter 11 of Part 15 to CA 2006 is concerned with the revision of defective accounts and reports.

Voluntary revision of accounts, etc.

22.89 Section 454 of the CA 2006 deals with voluntary revision of accounts. If it appears to the directors of a company that:

(a)   the company's annual accounts;[5898]
(b)   the directors' remuneration report or the directors' report;[5899] or
(c)   a summary financial statement of the company,[5900]

did not comply with the requirements of this Act (or, where applicable, of Article 4 of the IAS Regulation), they may prepare revised accounts or a revised report or statement.

Where copies of the previous accounts or report have been sent out to members, delivered to the registrar or (in the case of a public company) laid before the company in a general meeting, the revisions must be confined to the correction of those respects in which the previous accounts or report did

---

[5895] CA 2006, s 453(3).   [5896] CA 2006, s 453(4).   [5897] CA 2006, s 453(5).
[5898] CA 2006, s 454(1)(a).   [5899] CA 2006, s 454(1)(b).   [5900] CA 2006, s 454(1)(c).

not comply with the requirements of this Act (or, where applicable, of Article 4 of the IAS Regulation),[5901] and the making of any necessary consequential alterations.[5902]

The Secretary of State may make provision by regulations as to the application of the provisions of this Act in relation to:

(a)   revised annual accounts;[5903]
(b)   a revised directors' remuneration report or directors' report;[5904] or
(c)   a revised summary financial statement.[5905]

The regulations may, in particular:

(a)   make different provision according to whether the previous accounts, report or statement are replaced or are supplemented by a document indicating the corrections to be made;[5906]
(b)   make provision with respect to the functions of the company's auditor or independent examiner in relation to the revised accounts, report or statement;[5907]
(c)   require the directors to take such steps as may be specified in the regulations where the previous accounts or report have been (i) sent out to members and others under s 423 of the CA 2006,[5908] (ii) laid before the company in general meeting,[5909] or (iii) delivered to the registrar,[5910] or where a summary financial statement containing information derived from the previous accounts or report has been sent to members under s 426 of the CA 2006;
(d)   apply the provisions of this Act (including those creating criminal offences) subject to such additions, exceptions and modifications as are specified in the regulations.[5911]

Regulations under this section are subject to negative resolution procedure.[5912]

Section 454 of the CA 2006 restates s 245 of the CA 1985 providing for the voluntary revision of defective accounts and reports and summary of financial statement. It replicates the existing power for the Secretary of State to make provisions in regulations as to the application of the provisions of this Act to revised annual accounts and reports and financial statements. Regulations under this section are subject to negative resolution procedure, which is consistent with the existing powers.

[5901] CA 2006, s 454(2)(a).   [5902] CA 2006, s 454(2)(b).
[5903] CA 2006, s 454(3)(a). See the Companies (Revision of Defective Accounts and Reports) Regulations 2008.
[5904] CA 2006, s 454(3)(b).   [5905] CA 2006, s 454(3)(c).   [5906] CA 2006, s 454(4)(a).
[5907] CA 2006, s 454(4)(b).   [5908] CA 2006, s 454(4)(c)(i).   [5909] CA 2006, s 454(4)(c)(ii).
[5910] CA 2006, s 454(4)(c)(iii).   [5911] CA 2006, s 454(4)(d).   [5912] CA 2006, s 454(5).

Secretary of State's notice in respect of accounts and reports

22.90 Section 455 of the CA 2006 deals with the Secretary of State's notice in respect of accounts or reports.

This section applies where copies of a company's annual accounts or the directors' report have been sent out under s 423 of the CA 2006,[5913] or a copy of a company's annual accounts or directors' report has been delivered to the registrar or (in the case of a public company) laid before the company in a general meeting, and it appears to the Secretary of State that there is, or may be, a question whether the accounts or report comply with the requirements of this Act (or, where applicable, of Article 4 of the IAS Regulation).[5914]

The Secretary of State may give notice to the directors of the company indicating the respects in which it appears that such a question arises or may arise.[5915]

The notice must specify a period of not less than one month for the directors to give an explanation of the accounts or report, or prepare revised accounts or a revised report.[5916]

If at the end of the specified period, or such longer period as the Secretary of State may allow, it appears to the Secretary of State that the directors have not given a satisfactory explanation of the accounts or report,[5917] or revised the accounts or report so as to comply with the requirements of this Act (or, where applicable, of Article 4 of the IAS Regulation),[5918] the Secretary of State may apply to the court.

The provisions of this section apply equally to revised annual accounts and revised directors' reports, in which case they have effect as if the references to revised accounts or reports were references to further revised accounts or reports.[5919]

Section 455 of the CA 2006 re-enacts s 245A of the CA 1985. It concerns the Secretary of State's duty to give notice to the directors of a company if there is a question as to whether the accounts comply with the Companies Act or the IAS Regulation (Regulation (EC) 1606/2002 on the application of international accounting standards).

Application to court

Application to court in respect of defective accounts or reports

22.91 Section 456 of the CA 2006 is concerned with application to court in respect of defective accounts or reports. An application may be made to the court by the Secretary of State, after having complied with s 455 of the CA

[5913] CA 2006, s 455(1)(a).   [5914] CA 2006, s 455(1)(b).   [5915] CA 2006, s 455(2).
[5916] CA 2006, s 455(3).   [5917] CA 2006, s 455(4)(a).   [5918] CA 2006, s 455(4)(b).
[5919] CA 2006, s 455(5).

2006;[5920] or by a person authorised by the Secretary of State for the purposes of this section,[5921] for a declaration (in Scotland, a declarator) that the annual accounts of a company do not comply, or a directors' report does not comply, with the requirements of this Act (or, where applicable, of Article 4 of the IAS Regulation) and for an order requiring the directors of the company to prepare revised accounts or a revised report.

Notice of the application, together with a general statement of the matters at issue in the proceedings, shall be given by the applicant to the registrar for registration.[5922]

If the court orders the preparation of revised accounts, it may give directions as to:

(a)   the auditing of the accounts;[5923]
(b)   the revision of any directors' remuneration report, directors' report or summary financial statement;[5924] and
(c)   the taking of steps by the directors to bring the making of the order to the notice of persons likely to rely on the previous accounts,[5925] and such other matters as the court thinks fit.

If the court orders the preparation of a revised directors' report it may give directions as to:

(a)   the review of the report by the auditors;[5926]
(b)   the revision of any summary financial statement;[5927]
(c)   the taking of steps by the directors to bring the making of the order to the notice of persons likely to rely on the previous report;[5928] and
(d)   such other matters as the court thinks fit.[5929]

If the court finds that the accounts or report did not comply with the requirements of this Act (or, where applicable, of Article 4 of the IAS Regulation) it may order that all or part of:

(a)   the costs (in Scotland, expenses) of and incidental to the application;[5930] and
(b)   any reasonable expenses incurred by the company in connection with or in consequence of the preparation of revised accounts or a revised report,[5931]

are to be borne by such of the directors as were party to the approval of the

---

[5920] CA 2006, s 456(1)(a).   [5921] CA 2006, s 456(1)(b).   [5922] CA 2006, s 456(2).
[5923] CA 2006, s 456(3)(a).   [5924] CA 2006, s 456(3)(b).   [5925] CA 2006, s 456(3)(c).
[5926] CA 2006, s 456(4)(a).   [5927] CA 2006, s 456(4)(b).   [5928] CA 2006, s 456(4)(c).
[5929] CA 2006, s 456(4)(d).   [5930] CA 2006, s 456(5)(a).   [5931] CA 2006, s 456(5)(b).

defective accounts or report. For this purpose every director of the company at the time of the approval of the accounts or report shall be taken to have been a party to the approval unless he shows that he took all reasonable steps to prevent that approval.

Where the court makes an order under s 456(5) of the CA 2006 it shall have regard to whether the directors party to the approval of the defective accounts or report knew or ought to have known that the accounts or report did not comply with the requirements of this Act (or, where applicable, of Article 4 of the IAS Regulation), and it may exclude one or more directors from the order, or order the payment of different amounts by different directors.[5932]

On the conclusion of proceedings on an application under this section, the applicant must send to the registrar for registration a copy of the court order or, as the case may be, give notice to the registrar that the application has failed or been withdrawn.[5933]

The provisions of this section apply equally to revised annual accounts and revised directors' reports, in which case they have effect as if the references to revised accounts or reports were references to further revised accounts or reports.[5934]

Other persons authorised to apply to the court

22.92 Section 457 of the CA 2006 deals with other persons authorised to apply to the court.

The Secretary of State may by order (an authorisation order) authorise for the purposes of s 456 of the CA 2006 any person appearing to him:

(a)   to have an interest in, and to have satisfactory procedures directed to securing, compliance by companies with the requirements of this Act (or, where applicable, of Article 4 of the IAS Regulation) relating to accounts and directors' reports;[5935]

(b)   to have satisfactory procedures for receiving and investigating complaints about companies' annual accounts and directors' reports;[5936] and

(c)   otherwise to be a fit and proper person to be authorised.[5937]

A person may be authorised generally or in respect of particular classes of case, and different persons may be authorised in respect of different classes of case.[5938]

The Secretary of State may refuse to authorise a person if he considers that

---

[5932] CA 2006, s 456(6).   [5933] CA 2006, s 456(7).   [5934] CA 2006, s 456(8).
[5935] CA 2006, s 457(1)(a).   [5936] CA 2006, s 457(1)(b).   [5937] CA 2006, s 457(1)(c).
[5938] CA 2006, s 457(2).

his authorisation is unnecessary having regard to the fact that there are one or more other persons who have been or are likely to be authorised.[5939]

If the authorised person is an unincorporated association, proceedings brought in, or in connection with, the exercise of any function by the association as an authorised person may be brought by or against the association in the name of a body corporate whose constitution provides for the establishment of the association.[5940]

An authorisation order may contain such requirements or other provisions relating to the exercise of functions by the authorised person as appear to the Secretary of State to be appropriate.

No such order is to be made unless it appears to the Secretary of State that the person would, if authorised, exercise his functions as an authorised person in accordance with the provisions proposed.[5941]

Where authorisation is revoked, the revoking order may make such provision as the Secretary of State thinks fit with respect to pending proceedings.[5942]

An order under this section is subject to negative resolution procedure.[5943]

Disclosure of information by tax authorities

22.93 Section 458 of the CA 2006 applies to disclosure of information by tax authorities. The Commissioners for Her Majesty's Revenue and Customs may disclose information to a person authorised under s 457 of the CA 2006 for the purpose of facilitating the taking of steps by that person to discover whether there are grounds for an application to the court under s 440 (application in respect of defective accounts, etc.),[5944] or a decision by the authorised person whether to make such an application.[5945]

This section applies despite any statutory or other restriction on the disclosure of information.

Provided that, in the case of personal data within the meaning of the Data Protection Act 1998 (c 29), information is not to be disclosed in contravention of that Act.[5946]

Information disclosed to an authorised person under this section:

(a) may not be used except in or in connection with (i) taking steps to discover whether there are grounds for an application to the court under s 456 of the CA 2006,[5947] or (ii) deciding whether or not to make such an application,[5948] or in, or in connection with, proceedings on such an application; and

---

[5939] CA 2006, s 457(3).   [5940] CA 2006, s 457(4).   [5941] CA 2006, s 457(5).
[5942] CA 2006, s 457(6).   [5943] CA 2006, s 457(7).   [5944] CA 2006, s 458(1)(a).
[5945] CA 2006, s 458(1)(b).   [5946] CA 2006, s 458(2).   [5947] CA 2006, s 458(3)(a)(i).
[5948] CA 2006, s 458(3)(a)(ii).

(b) must not be further disclosed except (i) to the person to whom the information relates,[5949] or (ii) in, or in connection with, proceedings on any such application to the court.[5950]

A person who contravenes s 458(3) of the CA 2006 commits an offence unless he did not know, and had no reason to suspect, that the information had been disclosed under this section,[5951] or he took all reasonable steps and exercised all due diligence to avoid the commission of the offence.[5952]

A person guilty of an offence under s 453(4) of the CA 2006 is liable on conviction on indictment, to imprisonment for a term not exceeding two years or a fine (or both);[5953] or on summary conviction in England and Wales, to imprisonment for a term not exceeding 12 months or to a fine not exceeding the statutory maximum (or both);[5954] in Scotland or Northern Ireland, to imprisonment for a term not exceeding six months, or to a fine not exceeding the statutory maximum (or both).[5955]

Sections 456 and 457 of the CA 2006 concern applications to the court in respect of defective accounts and reports. They re-enact ss 245B and 245C of the CA 1985. Section 457 of the CA 2006 gives the Secretary of State the power to authorise a person for the purpose of s 456 of the CA 2006 to apply to the courts to require the directors of companies to prepare revised accounts and reports where the original accounts and reports were defective. Authorisation is subject to the negative resolution procedure, which corresponds to the existing provision. The body known as the Financial Reporting Review Panel (FRRP) is the only authorised person under this provision to date (the Companies (Defective Accounts) (Authorised Person) Order 2005: SI 2005/699).

Section 458 of the CA 2006 re-enacts ss 245D and E of the CA 1985. It provides for the disclosure of information by the Commissioners for Her Majesty's Revenue and Customs to a person authorised under s 457 of the CA 2006 (currently FRRP) to apply to the court in respect of defective accounts and reports. The provision contains the important limitations, including criminal offences for use of disclosure of information other than for permitted purposes. Section 458(5)(b)(ii) of the CA 2006 increases the term of imprisonment from three months to sex months for a person convicted on summary of conviction in Scotland or Northern Ireland for an offence of unlawful disclosure. Subsection (2) provides that personal data may not be disclosed in contravention of the Data Protection Act 1998.

[5949] CA 2006, s 458(3)(b)(i).   [5950] CA 2006, s 458(3)(b)(ii).   [5951] CA 2006, s 458(4)(a).
[5952] CA 2006, s 458(4)(b).   [5953] CA 2006, s 458(5)(a).   [5954] CA 2006, s 458(5)(b)(i).
[5955] CA 2006, s 458(5)(b)(ii).

*Power of an authorised person to require documents, information
and explanations*

22.94 Section 459 of the CA 2006 deals with the power of an authorised person to require documents, information and explanations. It applies where it appears to a person who is authorised under s 457 of the CA 2006 that there is, or may be, a question whether a company's annual accounts or directors' report comply with the requirements of this Act (or, where applicable, of Article 4 of the IAS Regulation).[5956]

The authorised person may require any of the persons mentioned in s 459(3) of the CA 2006 to produce any document, or to provide him with any information or explanations, that he may reasonably require for the purpose of discovering whether there are grounds for an application to the court under s 456 of the CA 2006,[5957] or deciding whether to make such an application.[5958]

Those persons are:

(a) the company;[5959]

(b) any officer, employee, or auditor of the company;[5960]

(c) any persons who fell within para (b) at a time to which the document or information required by the authorised person relates.[5961]

If a person fails to comply with such a requirement, the authorised person may apply to the court.[5962]

If it appears to the court that the person has failed to comply with a requirement under s 459(2) of the CA 2006, it may order the person to take such steps as it directs for securing that the documents are produced or the information or explanations are provided.[5963]

A statement made by a person in response to a requirement under s 459(2) of the CA 2006 or an order under s 459(5) of the CA 2006 may not be used in evidence against him in any criminal proceedings.[5964]

Nothing in this section compels any person to disclose documents or information in respect of which a claim to legal professional privilege (in Scotland, to confidentiality of communications) could be maintained in legal proceedings.[5965]

The term 'document' includes information recorded in any form.[5966]

Section 459 of the CA 2006 re-enacts s 245F of the CA 1985. Section 459(1)–(3) of the CA 2006 provide the FRRP (as the person authorised under s 457 of the CA 2006) with a statutory power to require a company and its

---

[5956] CA 2006, s 459(1).   [5957] CA 2006, s 459(2)(a).   [5958] CA 2006, s 459(2)(b).
[5959] CA 2006, s 459(3)(a).   [5960] CA 2006, s 459(3)(b).   [5961] CA 2006, s 459(3)(c).
[5962] CA 2006, s 459(4).   [5963] CA 2006, s 459(5).   [5964] CA 2006, s 459(6).
[5965] CA 2006, s 459(7).   [5966] CA 2006, s 459(8).

officers, employees and auditors to provide documents and information. Where a person refuses to provide information or documents to the FRRP, the FRRP may apply to the court for an order. The court makes an order requiring disclosure. Failure to comply with such an order would be contempt of court.

Restrictions on disclosure of information obtained under compulsory powers

22.95 Section 460 of the CA 2006 applies to restrictions on disclosure of information obtained under compulsory powers. It applies to information (in whatever form) obtained in pursuance of a requirement or order under s 459 of the CA 2006 (power of authorised person to require documents, etc.) that relates to the private affairs of an individual or to any particular business.[5967]

No such information may, during the lifetime of that individual or so long as that business continues to be carried on, be disclosed without the consent of that individual or the person for the time being carrying on that business.[5968]

This does not apply to disclosure permitted by s 464 of the CA 2006 (permitted disclosure of information obtained under compulsory powers),[5969] or to the disclosure of information that is or has been available to the public from another source.[5970]

A person who discloses information in contravention of this section commits an offence, unless he did not know, and had no reason to suspect, that the information had been disclosed under s 459 of the CA 2006,[5971] or he took all reasonable steps and exercised all due diligence to avoid the commission of the offence.[5972]

A person guilty of an offence under s 460 of the CA 2006 is liable on conviction on indictment, to imprisonment for a term not exceeding two years or a fine (or both);[5973] on summary conviction in England and Wales, to imprisonment for a term not exceeding 12 months or to a fine not exceeding the statutory maximum (or both);[5974] in Scotland or Northern Ireland, to imprisonment for a term not exceeding six months, or to a fine not exceeding the statutory maximum (or both).[5975]

Section 460 of the CA 2006 re-enacts s 245G of the CA 2006. It ensures that information obtained by the FRRP under the powers in s 459 of the CA 2006 is subject to restrictions on onward disclosure. Information may not be disclosed by the FRRP without the consent of the individual business in question, except for the purpose of carrying out its functions, or unless it is

---

[5967] CA 2006, s 460(1).   [5968] CA 2006, s 460(2).   [5969] CA 2006, s 460(3)(a).
[5970] CA 2006, s 460(3)(b).   [5971] CA 2006, s 460(4)(a).   [5972] CA 2006, s 460(4)(b).
[5973] CA 2006, s 460(5)(a).   [5974] CA 2006, s 460(5)(b)(i).   [5975] CA 2006, s 460(5)(b)(ii).

disclosed to specified persons or for specified purposes set out in s 461 of the CA 2006.

Permitted disclosure of information obtained under compulsory powers

22.96 Section 461 of the CA 2006 applies to permitted disclosure of information obtained under compulsory powers. The prohibition in s 460 of the CA 2006 of the disclosure of information obtained in pursuance of a requirement or order under s 459 of the CA 2006 (power of an authorised person to require documents, etc.) that relates to the private affairs of an individual or to any particular business has effect subject to the following exceptions.[5976]

It does not apply to the disclosure of information for the purpose of facilitating the carrying out by the authorised person of his functions under s 456 of the CA 2006.[5977]

It does not apply to disclosure to:

(a) the Secretary of State;[5978]
(b) the Department of Enterprise, Trade and Investment for Northern Ireland;[5979]
(c) the Treasury;[5980]
(d) the Bank of England;[5981]
(e) the Financial Services Authority;[5982] or
(f) the Commissioners for Her Majesty's Revenue and Customs.[5983]

It does not apply to disclosure:

(a) for the purpose of assisting a body designated by an order under s 46 of the CA 1989 (c 40) (delegation of functions of the Secretary of State) to exercise its functions under Part 2 of that Act;[5984]
(b) with a view to the institution of, or otherwise for the purposes of, disciplinary proceedings relating to the performance by an accountant or auditor of his professional duties;[5985]
(c) for the purpose of enabling or assisting the Secretary of State or the Treasury to exercise any of their functions under any of the following (i) the Companies Acts,[5986] (ii) Part 15 of the Criminal Justice Act 1993 (c 36) (insider dealing);[5987] (iii) the Insolvency Act 1986 (c 45) or the Insolvency (Northern Ireland) Order 1989 (SI 1989/2405 (NI 19)),[5988]

[5976] CA 2006, s 461(1).   [5977] CA 2006, s 461(2).   [5978] CA 2006, s 461(3)(a).
[5979] CA 2006, s 461(3)(b).   [5980] CA 2006, s 461(3)(c).   [5981] CA 2006, s 461(3)(d).
[5982] CA 2006, s 461(3)(e).   [5983] CA 2006, s 461(3)(f).   [5984] CA 2006, s 461(4)(a).
[5985] CA 2006, s 461(4)(b).   [5986] CA 2006, s 461(4)(c)(i).   [5987] CA 2006, s 461(4)(c)(ii).
[5988] CA 2006, s 461(4)(c)(iii).

(iv) the Company Directors' Disqualification Act 1986 (c 46) or the Company Directors' Disqualification (Northern Ireland) Order 2002 (SI 2002/3150 (NI 4)),[5989] (v) the Financial Services and Markets Act 2000 (c 8);[5990]

(d) for the purpose of enabling or assisting the Department of Enterprise, Trade and Investment for Northern Ireland to exercise any powers conferred on it by the enactments relating to companies, directors' disqualification or insolvency;[5991]

(e) for the purpose of enabling or assisting the Bank of England to exercise its functions;[5992]

(f) for the purpose of enabling or assisting the Commissioners for Her Majesty's Revenue and Customs to exercise their functions;[5993]

(g) for the purpose of enabling or assisting the Financial Services Authority to exercise its functions under any of the following:

  (i) legislation relating to friendly societies or to industrial and provident societies,[5994]
  (ii) the Building Societies Act 1986 (c 53),[5995]
  (iii) Part 7 of the CA 1989 (c 40),[5996]
  (iv) the Financial Services and Markets Act 2000,[5997] or

(h) in pursuance of any Community obligation.[5998]

It does not apply to disclosure to a body exercising functions of a public nature under legislation in any country or territory outside the United Kingdom that appear to the authorised person to be similar to his functions under s 456 of the CA 2006 for the purpose of enabling or assisting that body to exercise those functions.[5999]

In determining whether to disclose information to a body in accordance with subs (6), the authorised person must have regard to the following considerations:

(a) whether the use that the body is likely to make of the information is sufficiently important to justify making the disclosure;[6000]

(b) whether the body has adequate arrangements to prevent the information from being used or further disclosed other than:

  (i) for the purposes of carrying out the functions mentioned in that subsection,[6001] or

---

[5989] CA 2006, s 461(4)(c)(iv).   [5990] CA 2006, s 461(4)(c)(v).   [5991] CA 2006, s 461(4)(d).
[5992] CA 2006, s 461(4)(e).   [5993] CA 2006, s 461(4)(f).   [5994] CA 2006, s 461(4)(g)(i).
[5995] CA 2006, s 461(4)(g)(ii).   [5996] CA 2006, s 461(4)(g)(iii).
[5997] CA 2006, s 461(4)(g)(iv).   [5998] CA 2006, s 461(4)(h).   [5999] CA 2006, s 461(5).
[6000] CA 2006, s 461(6)(a).   [6001] CA 2006, s 461(6)(b)(i).

(ii)   for other purposes substantially similar to those for which information disclosed to the authorised person could be used or further disclosed.[6002]

Section 461 of the CA 2006 restates s 245G(3) of, and Schedule 7B to, the CA 1985. It sets out the disclosures of information obtained by the authorised person under s 459 of the CA 2006 that are permitted. Section 461(3) of the CA 2006 lists the specified persons to whom disclosures are permitted and s 461(4) of the CA 2006 lists the specified purposes for which disclosure may be made. Section 461(5) and (6) of the CA 2006 set out the circumstances in which a disclosure to an overseas regulatory authority is permitted. Section 461(7) of the CA 2006 provides that nothing in the section authorises a disclosure in contravention of the Data Protection Act 1998.

Power to amend categories of permitted disclosure

22.97 Section 462 of the CA 2006 deals with the power to amend categories of permitted disclosure. The Secretary of State may by order amend s 445(3), (4) and (5) of the CA 2006.[6003]

An order under this section must not:

(a)   amend subs (3) of that section (UK public authorities) by specifying a person unless the person exercises functions of a public nature (whether or not he exercises any other function);[6004]
(b)   amend subs (4) of that section (purposes for which disclosure permitted) by adding or modifying a description of disclosure unless the purpose for which the disclosure is permitted is likely to facilitate the exercise of a function of a public nature;[6005]
(c)   amend subs (5) of that section (overseas regulatory authorities) so as to have the effect of permitting disclosures to be made to a body other than one that exercises the functions of a public nature in a country or territory outside the United Kingdom.[6006]

An order under this section is subject to negative resolution procedure.[6007]

Section 462 of the CA 2006 re-enacts s 245G(4) of the CA 1985. It gives the Secretary of State the power to amend the disclosure provisions relating to information obtained by the authorised person. As under the law prior to 2006, an order under the section is subject to the negative resolution procedure.

[6002] CA 2006, s 461(4)(b)(ii).   [6003] CA 2006, s 462(1).   [6004] CA 2006, s 462(2)(a).
[6005] CA 2006, s 462(2)(b).   [6006] CA 2006, s 462(2)(c).   [6007] CA 2006, s 462(3).

Supplementary Provisions

22.98 Chapter 12 deals with the supplementary provisions to Part 15 of the CA 2006.

Liability for false or misleading statements in reports

22.99 Section 463 of the CA 2006 applies to liability for false or misleading statements in reports. The reports to which this section applies are:

(a)   the directors' report;[6008]
(b)   the directors' remuneration report;[6009] and
(c)   a summary financial statement so far as it is derived from either of those reports.[6010]

A director of a company is liable to compensate the company for any loss suffered by it as a result of any untrue or misleading statement in a report to which this section applies;[6011] or the omission from a report to which this section applies of anything required to be included in it.[6012]

He is so liable only if he knew the statement to be untrue or misleading or was reckless as to whether it was untrue or misleading,[6013] or he knew the omission to be dishonest concealment of a material fact.[6014]

No person shall be subject to any liability to a person other than the company resulting from reliance, by that person or another, on information in a report to which this section applies.[6015]

The reference in s 463(4) of the CA 2006 to a person being subject to a liability includes a reference to another person being entitled as against him to be granted any civil remedy or to rescind or repudiate an agreement.[6016]

This section does not affect liability for a civil penalty,[6017] or liability for a criminal offence.[6018]

Section 463 of the CA 2006 is concerned with the extent of directors' liability in relation to the statutory narrative reporting requirements under this Part of CA 2006 (accounts and reports). Subsection (1) specifies that the liability provision applies to statements made in the directors' report (which includes the business review under s 417 of the CA 2006), the directors' remuneration report (under s 420 of the CA 2006) or summary financial statements derived from them. The section limits directors' liability to the company only in respect of loss suffered by it as a result of any untrue or misleading statement in a report, or the omission from a report of anything

---

[6008] CA 2006, s 463(1)(a).   [6009] CA 2006, s 463(1)(b).   [6010] CA 2006, s 463(1)(c).
[6011] CA 2006, s 463(2)(a).   [6012] CA 2006, s 463(2)(b).   [6013] CA 2006, s 463(3)(a).
[6014] CA 2006, s 463(3)(b).   [6015] CA 2006, s 463(4).   [6016] CA 2006, s 463(5).
[6017] CA 2006, s 463(6)(a).   [6018] CA 2006, s 463(6)(b).

required to be included. Section 463(3) of the CA 2006 specifies that a director will only be liable in certain circumstances – that is, if an untrue or misleading statement is made deliberately or recklessly, or an omission amounts to dishonest concealment of a material fact. Section 463(4) of the CA 2006 ensures that third parties, such as auditors, will remain liable to the company for negligence in preparing their own report. Section 463(6) of the CA 2006 ensures that these liability provisions do not affect any liability for a civil penalty or for a criminal offence.

Accounting standards

22.100 Section 464 of the CA 2006 states that in this Part 'accounting standards' means statements of standard accounting practice issued by such body or bodies as may be prescribed by regulations.[6019]

References in this Part to accounting standards applicable to a company's annual accounts are to such standards as are, in accordance with their terms, relevant to the company's circumstances and to the accounts.[6020]

Regulations under this section may contain such transitional and other supplementary and incidental provisions as appear to the Secretary of State to be appropriate.[6021]

This section re-enacts s 256 of the CA 1985.

Companies qualifying as medium-sized: general

22.101 Section 465 of the CA 2006 deals with the general aspects of companies qualifying as medium-sized.

A company qualifies as medium-sized in relation to a financial year if the qualifying conditions are met in that year.[6022]

A company qualifies as medium-sized in relation to a subsequent financial year:

(a) if the qualifying conditions are met in that year and he preceding financial year;[6023] or

(b) if the qualifying conditions are met in that year and the company qualified as medium-sized in relation to the preceding financial year;[6024] or

(c) if the qualifying conditions are not met in relation to the financial year in question but it qualified under para (b) in relation to the previous financial year.[6025]

[6019] CA 2006, s 464(1).   [6020] CA 2006, s 464(2).   [6021] CA 2006, s 464(3).
[6022] CA 2006, s 465(1).   [6023] CA 2006, s 465(2)(a).   [6024] CA 2006, s 465(2)(b).
[6025] CA 2006, s 465(2)(c).

The qualifying conditions are met by a company in a year in which it satisfies two or more of the following requirements:[6026]

1	Turnover	Not more than £22.8 million
2	Balance sheet total	Not more than £11.4 million
3	Number of employees	Not more than 250

For a period that is a company's financial year but not in fact a year the maximum figures for turnover must be proportionately adjusted.[6027]

The balance sheet total means the aggregate of the amounts shown as assets in the company's balance sheet.[6028]

The number of employees means the average number of persons employed by the company in the year, determined as follows:

(a) find for each month in the financial year the number of persons employed under contracts of service by the company in that month (whether throughout the month or not);[6029]

(b) add together the monthly totals;[6030] and

(c) divide by the number of months in the financial year.[6031]

This section is subject to s 466 of the CA 2006 (companies qualifying as medium-sized: parent companies).[6032]

Companies qualifying as medium-sized: parent companies

22.102 Section 466 of the CA 2006 deals with companies qualifying as medium-sized with respect ot parent companies. A parent company qualifies as a medium-sized company in relation to a financial year only if the group headed by it qualifies as a medium-sized group.[6033]

A group qualifies as medium-sized in relation to the parent company's first financial year if the qualifying conditions are met in that year.[6034]

A group qualifies as medium-sized in relation to a subsequent financial year of the parent company:

(a) if the qualifying conditions are met in that year and the preceding financial year;[6035] or

(b) if the qualifying conditions are met in that year and the group qualified as medium-sized in relation to the preceding financial year;[6036] or

---

[6026] CA 2006, s 465(3).   [6027] CA 2006, s 465(4).   [6028] CA 2006, s 465(5).
[6029] CA 2006, s 465(6)(a).   [6030] CA 2006, s 465(6)(b).   [6031] CA 2006, s 465(6)(c).
[6032] CA 2006, s 465(7).   [6033] CA 2006, s 466(1).   [6034] CA 2006, s 466(2).
[6035] CA 2006, s 466(3)(a).   [6036] CA 2006, s 466(3)(b).

(c)   if the qualifying conditions were met in the preceding financial year and the group qualified as medium-sized in relation to that year.[6037]

The qualifying conditions are met by a group in a year in which it satisfies two or more of the following requirements:[6038]

1	Aggregate turnover	Not more than £22.8 million net (or £27.36 million gross)
2	Aggregate balance sheet total	Not more than £11.4 million net (or £13.68 million gross)
3	Aggregate number of employees	Not more than 250

The aggregate figures are ascertained by aggregating the relevant figures determined in accordance with s 465 of the CA 2006 for each member of the group.[6039]

In relation to the aggregate figures for turnover and balance sheet total the term 'net' means after any set-offs and other adjustments made to eliminate group transactions: (a) in the case of Companies Act accounts, in accordance with regulations under s 404 of the CA 2006;[6040] (b) in the case of IAS accounts, in accordance with international accounting standards;[6041] and 'gross' means without those set-offs and other adjustments.

A company may satisfy the relevant requirements on the basis of either the net or the gross figure.

The figures for each subsidiary undertaking shall be those included in its individual accounts for the relevant financial year, that is if its financial year ends with that of the parent company, that financial year,[6042] and if not, its financial year ending last before the end of the financial year of the parent company.[6043]

If those figures cannot be obtained without disproportionate expense or undue delay, the latest available figures shall be taken.

Companies excluded from being treated as medium-sized

22.103 Section 467 of the CA 2006 deals with general powers to make further provision about accounts and reports. A company is not entitled to take advantage of any of the provisions of this Part relating to companies qualifying as medium-sized if it was at any time within the financial year in question:

(a)   a public company;[6044]

[6037] CA 2006, s 466(3)(c).   [6038] CA 2006, s 466(4).   [6039] CA 2006, s 466(5).
[6040] CA 2006, s 466(6)(a).   [6041] CA 2006, s 466(6)(b).   [6042] CA 2006, s 466(7)(a).
[6043] CA 2006, s 466(7)(b).   [6044] CA 2006, s 467(1)(a).

(b)   a company that (i) has permission under Part 4 of the Financial Services and Markets Act 2000 (c 8) to carry on a regulated activity,[6045] or (ii) carries on insurance market activity;[6046] or

(c)   a member of an ineligible group.[6047]

A group is ineligible if any of its members is:

(a)   a public company;[6048]
(b)   a body corporate (other than a company) whose shares are admitted to trading on a regulated market;[6049] or
(c)   a person (other than a small comapny) who has permission under Part 4 of the Financial Services and Markets Act 2000 to carry on a regulated activity;[6050]
(d)   a small company that is an authorise insurance company, a banking company, an e-money issuer, an ISD investment firm or a UCITS Management Company;[6051] or
(e)   carries on insurance market activity.[6052]

Medium-sized companies benefit from certain limited accounting and reporting exemptions. For example, s 417(7) of the CA 2006 exempts medium-sized companies from disclosing certain non-financial information in their directors' reports.

Sections 465–467 of the CA 2006 set out which companies or parent companies qualify as medium-sized. The conditions for qualification as a medium-sized company have been separated from those relating to small companies to make them easier to follow but they are otherwise unchanged from the current regime (ss 247, 247A and 249 of the CA 1985), save that, as in the case of the definition of small companies, the definition of balance sheet total in s 465(5) of the CA 2006 has been generalised.

General power to make further provision about accounts and reports

22.104 Section 468 of the CA 2006 deals with the general power to make further provision about accounts and reports. The Secretary of State may make provision by regulations about:

(a)   the accounts and reports that companies are required to prepare;[6053]

[6045] CA 2006, s 467(1)(b)(i).   [6046] CA 2006, s 467(1)(b)(ii).   [6047] CA 2006, s 467(1)(c).
[6048] CA 2006, s 467(2)(a).   [6049] CA 2006, s 467(2)(b).   [6050] CA 2006, s 467(2)(c).
[6051] CA 2006, s 467(2)(d).   [6052] CA 2006, s 467(2)(e).
[6053] CA 2006, s 468(1)(a). See the Companies Act 2006 (Accounts and Reports) (Amendment) Regulations 2008.

(b)   the categories of companies required to prepare accounts and reports of any description;[6054]

(c)   the form and content of the accounts and reports that companies are required to prepare;[6055]

(d)   the obligations of companies and others as regards (i) the approval of accounts and reports,[6056] (ii) the sending of accounts and reports to members and others,[6057] (iii) the laying of accounts and reports before the company in general meeting,[6058] (iv) the delivery of copies of accounts and reports to the registrar,[6059] and (v) the publication of accounts and reports.[6060]

The regulations may amend this Part by adding, altering or repealing provisions.[6061]

But they must not amend (other than consequentially) s 392 of the CA 2006 (accounts to give a true and fair view);[6062] or the provisions of Chapter 11 of the CA 2006 (revision of defective accounts and reports).[6063]

The regulations may create criminal offences in cases corresponding to those in which an offence is created by an existing provision of this Part. The maximum penalty for any such offence may not be greater than is provided in relation to an offence under the existing provision.[6064]

The regulations may provide for civil penalties in circumstances corresponding to those within s 453(1) of the CA 2006 (civil penalty for a failure to file accounts and reports).

The provisions of s 453(2)–(5) of the CA 2006 apply in relation to any such penalty.[6065]

Section 468 of the CA 2006 gives the Secretary of State a general power to amend Part 15 of the CA 2006 by regulations in the areas specified in s 468(1)(a)–(d) of the CA 2006. This power, together with a number of specific powers in Part 15 of the CA 2006 to enable the form and contents of accounts and reports to be prescribed by regulations, replaces a wider general power in s 257 of the CA 1985.

Section 468(3) of the CA 2006 provides that the general power may not be used to amend the provisions of s 393 of the CA 2006 (accounts to give a true and fair view) or Chapter 11 of the CA 2006 (revision of defective accounts and reports) other than consequentially.

Section 468(4) and (5) of the CA 2006 enable regulations under the section to create criminal offences or provide for civil penalties in circumstances corresponding to those in Part 15 of the CA 2006. The regulations are subject to the Parliamentary procedure in s 473 of the CA 2006.

[6054] CA 2006, s 468(1)(b).   [6055] CA 2006, s 468(1)(c).   [6056] CA 2006, s 468(1)(d)(i).
[6057] CA 2006, s 468(1)(d)(ii).   [6058] CA 2006, s 468(1)(d)(iii).
[6059] CA 2006, s 468(1)(d)(iv).   [6060] CA 2006, s 468(1)(d)(v).   [6061] CA 2006, s 468(2).
[6062] CA 2006, s 468(3)(a).   [6063] CA 2006, s 468(3)(b).   [6064] CA 2006, s 468(4).
[6065] CA 2006, s 468(5).

Other Supplementary Provisions

Preparation and filing of accounts in euros

22.105 Section 469 of the CA 2006 deals with the preparation and filing of accounts in euros. The amounts set out in the annual accounts of a company may also be shown in the same accounts translated into euros.[6066]

When complying with s 441 of the CA 2006 (duty to file accounts and reports), the directors of a company may deliver to the registrar an additional copy of the company's annual accounts in which the amounts have been translated into euros.[6067]

In both cases the amounts must have been translated at the exchange rate prevailing on the date to which the balance sheet is made up,[6068] and that rate must be disclosed in the notes to the accounts.[6069]

For the purposes of ss 434 and 435 of the CA 2006 (requirements in connection with published accounts) any additional copy of the company's annual accounts delivered to the registrar under s 469(2) of the CA 2006 shall be treated as statutory accounts of the company.

In the case of such a copy, references in those sections to the auditor's report on the company's annual accounts shall be read as references to the auditor's report on the annual accounts of which it is a copy.[6070]

Section 469 of the CA 2006 re-enacts s 242B of the CA 1985, replacing references to ECUs with references to euros. It enables companies to show the amounts in their annual accounts additionally in euros, and to deliver to the registrar an additional copy of their accounts translated into euros.

Power to apply provisions to banking partnerships

22.106 Section 470 of the CA 2006 deals with the power to apply provisions to banking partnerships. The Secretary of State may by regulations apply to banking partnerships, subject to such exceptions, adaptations and modifications as he considers appropriate, the provisions of this Part (and of regulations made under this Part) applying to banking companies.[6071]

A 'banking partnership' means a partnership that has permission under Part 4 of the Financial Services and Markets Act 2000 (c 8). But a partnership is not a banking partnership if it has permission to accept deposits only for the purpose of carrying on another regulated activity in accordance with that permission.[6072]

Expressions used in this section that are also used in the provisions regulating activities under the Financial Services and Markets Act 2000 have the

---

[6066] CA 2006, s 469(1).   [6067] CA 2006, s 469(2).   [6068] CA 2006, s 469(3)(a).
[6069] CA 2006, s 469(3)(b).   [6070] CA 2006, s 469(4).   [6071] CA 2006, s 470(1).
[6072] CA 2006, s 470(2).

same meaning here as they do in those provisions. See s 22 of that Act, orders made under that section and Schedule 2 to that Act.[6073]

Regulations under this section are subject to affirmative resolution procedure.[6074]

Section 470 of the CA 2006 re-enacts s 255D of the CA 1985. It gives the Secretary of State the power to apply the accounting and reporting provisions of CA 2006 that apply to banking companies, to banking partnerships. As under the current law, the regulations are subject to the affirmative resolution procedure.

Meaning of 'annual accounts' and related expressions

22.107 In this Part, a company's 'annual accounts', in relation to a financial year, means the company's individual accounts for that year (see s 394 of the CA 2006),[6075] and any group accounts prepared by the company for that year (see ss 398 and 399 of the CA 2006).[6076]

This is subject to s 408 of the CA 2006 (option to omit individual profit and loss account from annual accounts where information given in group accounts).

In the case of an unquoted company, its 'annual accounts and reports' for a financial year are its annual accounts,[6077] the directors' report,[6078] and the auditor's report on those accounts and the directors' report (unless the company is exempt from audit).[6079]

In the case of a quoted company, its 'annual accounts and reports' for a financial year are:

(a)   its annual accounts;[6080]
(b)   the directors' remuneration report;[6081]
(c)   the directors' report;[6082] and
(d)   the auditor's report on those accounts, on the auditable part of the directors' remuneration report and on the directors' report.[6083]

Section 471 of the CA 2006 provides a definition of the terms 'annual accounts' and 'annual accounts and reports' for the purpose of this Part, the meaning being different for unquoted and quoted companies.

[6073] CA 2006, s 470(3).   [6074] CA 2006, s 470(4).   [6075] CA 2006, s 471(1)(a).
[6076] CA 2006, s 471(1)(b).   [6077] CA 2006, s 471(2)(a).   [6078] CA 2006, s 471(2)(b).
[6079] CA 2006, s 471(2)(c).   [6080] CA 2006, s 471(3)(a).   [6081] CA 2006, s 471(3)(b).
[6082] CA 2006, s 471(3)(c).   [6083] CA 2006, s 471(3)(d).

Notes to the accounts

22.108 Section 472 of the CA 2006 states that information required by this Part to be given in notes to a company's annual accounts may be contained in the accounts or in a separate document annexed to the accounts.[6084]

References in this Part to a company's annual accounts, or to a balance sheet or profit and loss account, include notes to the accounts giving information that is required by any provision of this Act or international accounting standards, and required or allowed by any such provision to be given in a note to company accounts.[6085]

Section 472 of the CA 2006 re-enacts s 261 of the CA 1985.

Parliamentary procedure for certain regulations under this Part

22.109 Section 473 of the CA 2006 deals with the Parliamentary procedure for certain regulations under Part 15 of the CA 2006. This section applies to regulations under the following provisions of this Part:[6086]

s 396 of the CA 2006 (Companies Act individual accounts);
s 404 of the CA 2006 (Companies Act group accounts);
s 409 of the CA 2006 (information about related undertakings);
s 412 of the CA 2006 (information about directors' benefits: remuneration, pensions and compensation for loss of office);
s 416 of the CA 2006 (contents of directors' report: general);
s 421 of the CA 2006 (contents of directors' remuneration report);
s 444 of the CA 2006 (filing obligations of companies subject to the small companies regime);
s 445 of the CA 2006 (filing obligations of medium-sized companies);
s 468 of the CA 2006 (general powers to make further provision about accounts and reports).

Any such regulations may make consequential amendments or repeals in other provisions of this Act, or in other enactments.[6087]

Regulations that:

(a)   restrict the classes of company that have the benefit of any exemption, exception or special provision;[6088]

(b)   require additional matter to be included in a document of any class;[6089] or

(c)   otherwise render the requirements of this Part more onerous,

[6084] CA 2006, s 472(1).   [6085] CA 2006, s 472(2).   [6086] CA 2006, s 473(1).
[6087] CA 2006, s 473(2).   [6088] CA 2006, s 473(3)(a).   [6089] CA 2006, s 473(3)(b).

are subject to affirmative resolution procedure.[6090] Otherwise, the regulations are subject to negative resolution procedure.[6091]

Section 473 of the CA 2006 specifies the Parliamentary procedure that must be followed in connection with regulations made under the various provisions of this Part that replace the requirements as to the form and content of accounts and reports currently contained in Schedules to Part 7 of the CA 1985.

The section follows s 257 of the CA 1985 in requiring affirmative resolution procedure for regulations that add to the documents required to be prepared by companies, restrict the exemptions available to particular classes or types of company, add to the information to be included in any particular document or otherwise make the requirements more onerous. Other regulations are subject to negative resolution procedure.

Minor definitions

22.110 Section 474 of the CA 2006 sets out the minor definitions used in Part 15 of the CA 2006.

- 'group' means a parent undertaking and its subsidiary undertakings;
- 'IAS Regulation' means EC Regulation No 1606/2002 of the European Parliament and of the Council of 19 July 2002 on the application of international accounting standards;
- 'included in the consolidation', in relation to group accounts, or 'included in consolidated group accounts', means that the undertaking is included in the accounts by the method of full (and not proportional) consolidation, and references to an undertaking excluded from consolidation shall be construed accordingly;
- 'insurance market activity' has the meaning given in s 316(3) of the Financial Services and Markets Act 2000 (c 8);
- 'international accounting standards' means the international accounting standards, within the meaning of the IAS Regulation, adopted from time to time by the European Commission in accordance with that Regulation;
- 'listing rules' has the same meaning as in Part 6 of the Financial Services and Markets Act 2000 (see s 73A of that Act);
- 'profit and loss account', in relation to a company that prepares IAS accounts, includes an income statement or other equivalent financial statement required to be prepared according to international accounting standards;
- 'regulated activity' has the meaning given in s 22 of the Financial

---

[6090] CA 2006, s 473(3)(c).   [6091] CA 2006, s 473(4).

Services and Markets Act 2000, except that it does not include activities of the kind specified in any of the following provisions of the Financial Services and Markets Act 2000 (Regulated Activities) Order 2001:

(a) article 25A (arranging regulated mortgage contracts);

(b) article 39A (assisting administration and performance of a contract of insurance);

(c) article 53A (advising on regulated mortgage contracts);

(d) article 21 (dealing as agent), article 25 (arranging deals in investments) or article 53 (advising on investments) where the activity concerns relevant investments that are not contractually based investments (within the meaning of article 3 of that Order);

- 'turnover', in relation to a company, means the amounts derived from the provision of goods and services falling within the company's ordinary activities, after deduction of:

(a) trade discounts;

(b) value added tax; and

(c) any other taxes based on the amounts so derived.

In the case of an undertaking not trading for profit, any reference in this Part to a profit and loss account is to an income and expenditure account.

References to profit and loss and, in relation to group accounts, to a consolidated profit and loss account, shall be construed accordingly.

This section contains other definitions for the purposes of this Part.

Chapter 23

Auditors

Introduction

23.1 Part 16 of the CA 2006 brings together various provisions on the audit of companies from the CA 1985. It also introduces a number of significant changes to the law on auditing. Much of the law in this area reflects EU Company Law Directives, including parts of the Fourth (78/660/EEC), Seventh (83/349/EEC), and Eighth (84/253/EEC) Directives, and of the recently adopted Audit Directive (2006/43/EC), which will replace the Eighth Directive.

Part 16 of the CA 2006 comprises seven Chapters dealing with a requirement for audited accounts; appointment of auditors; the functions of auditors; the removal and resignation of auditors; quoted companies' rights of members to raise audit concerns at the accounts meeting; auditors' liability; and supplementary provisions.

Chapter 1 of the CA 2006 comprises ten sections. It restates the existing requirement under s 235(1) of the CA 1985 for companies to produce audited accounts, and the existing exemptions, in ss 249A–249E of the CA 1985.

The only change from the existing law in Chapter 1 is the removal of special rules for the audit of the accounts of small charitable companies (see s 1175 of the CA 2006), and new provisions disapplying the requirement for audit in relation to certain companies in the public sector audited by public sector auditors.

Audit

Requirement for audited accounts

23.2 Section 475 of the CA 2006 deals with the requirement for audited accounts. A company's annual accounts for a financial year must be audited in accordance with Part 16 of the CA 2006 unless the company is exempt from audit under s 477 of the CA 2006 (small companies) or s 480 of the CA

2006 (dormant companies);[6092] or exempt from the requirements of Part 16 of the CA 2006 under s 482 of the CA 2006 (non-profit-making companies subject to public sector audit).[6093]

A company is not entitled to any such exemption, unless its balance sheet contains a statement by the directors to that effect.[6094]

A company is not entitled to exemption under s 475(1)(a) of the CA 2006, unless its balance sheet contains a statement by the directors to the effect that the members have not required the company to obtain an audit of its accounts for the year in question in accordance with s 476 of the CA 2006;[6095] and the directors acknowledge their responsibilities for complying with the requirements of the CA 2006 with respect to accounting records and the preparation of accounts.[6096]

The statement required by s 475(2) or (3) of the CA 2006 must appear on the balance sheet above the signature required by s 414 of the CA 2006.

Section 475 of the CA 2006 restates the basic requirement for accounts to be audited, unless the company is exempt. The obligation is expressed as a duty on the company to have its accounts audited, whereas s 235 of the CA 1985 expressed it as a duty on the auditor to audit the accounts.

It is expressly stated that directors must state in the balance sheet if they are taking advantage of an exemption. Unless the company is subject to a public sector audit, the statement must say that the members have not required an audit, and that the directors take responsibility for producing compliant accounts.

Right of members to require audit

23.3 Members are provided with a right to require an audit under s 476 of the CA 2006. The members of a company that would otherwise be entitled to exemption from audit under any of the provisions mentioned in s 475(1)(a) of the CA 2006, may by notice under s 476 of the CA 2006 require it to obtain an audit of its accounts for a financial year.[6097]

The notice must be given by members holding not less in total than 10 per cent in nominal value of the company's issued share capital, or any class of it;[6098] or if the company does not have a share capital, not less than 10 per cent in number of the members of the company.[6099]

The notice may not be given before the financial year to which it relates and must be given not later than one month before the end of that year.[6100]

Section 476 of the CA 2006 restates the right of shareholders to require an audit, even if the company qualifies for one of the audit exemptions.

[6092] CA 2006, s 475(1)(a).   [6093] CA 2006, s 475(1)(b).   [6094] CA 2006, s 475(2).
[6095] CA 2006, s 475(3)(a).   [6096] CA 2006, s 475(3)(b).   [6097] CA 2006, s 476(1).
[6098] CA 2006, s 476(2)(a).   [6099] CA 2006, s 476(2)(b).   [6100] CA 2006, s 476(3).

Exemption from audit: small companies

Small companies: conditions for exemption from audit

23.4 Section 477 of the CA 2006 applies to small companies exemption. A company that meets the following conditions in respect of a financial year is exempt from the requirements of the CA 2006 relating to the audit of accounts for that year.[6101]

The conditions are:

(a) that the company qualifies as a small company in relation to that year;[6102]

(b) that its turnover in that year is not more than £5.6 million;[6103] and

(c) that its balance sheet total for that year is not more than £2.8 million.[6104]

For a period that is a company's financial year but not in fact a year the maximum figures for turnover or gross income must be proportionately adjusted.[6105]

For the purposes of s 477(4) of the CA 2006, whether a company qualifies as a small company shall be determined in accordance with s 382(1)–(6) of the CA 2006;[6106] and the term 'balance sheet total' has the same meaning as in that section.[6107]

Section 477 of the CA 2006 applies subject to s 475(2) and (3) of the CA 2006 (requirements as to statements to be contained in the balance sheet), s 476 of the CA 2006 (right of members to require an audit); s 478 of the CA 2006 (companies excluded from small companies exemption); and s 479 of the CA 2006 (availability of small companies exemption in the case of a group company).

Companies excluded from small companies exemption

23.5 Section 478 of the CA 2006 sets out those companies excluded from the small companies exemption. A company is not entitled to the exemption conferred by s 477 of the CA 2006 (small companies) if it was at any time within the financial year in question:

(a) a public company;[6108]

(b) a company that (i) is an authorised insurance company, a banking company, an e-money issuer, an ISD investment firm or a UCITS management company,[6109] or (ii) carries on insurance market activity;[6110] or

---

[6101] CA 2006, s 477(1).   [6102] CA 2006, s 477(2)(a).   [6103] CA 2006, s 477(2)(b).
[6104] CA 2006, s 477(2)(c).   [6105] CA 2006, s 477(3).   [6106] CA 2006, s 477(4)(a).
[6107] CA 2006, s 477(4)(b).   [6108] CA 2006, s 478(a).   [6109] CA 2006, s 478(b)(i).
[6110] CA 2006, s 478(b)(ii).

(c)   a special register body as defined in s 117(1) of the Trade Union and Labour Relations (Consolidation) Act 1992 (c 52) or an employers' association as defined in s 122 of that Act or Article 4 of the Industrial Relations (Northern Ireland) Order 1992 (SI 1992/807 (NI 5)).[6111]

Availability of small companies exemption in case of a group company

23.6 Section 479 of the CA 2006 deals with the availability of companies exemption in case of a group company. A company is not entitled to the exemption conferred by s 477 of the CA 2006 (small companies) in respect of a financial year during any part of which it was a group company unless the conditions specified in s 479(2) of the CA 2006 below are met,[6112] or s 479(3) of the CA 2006 applies.[6113]

The conditions are:

(a)   that the group (i) qualifies as a small group in relation to that financial year,[6114] and (ii) was not at any time in that year an ineligible group;[6115]
(b)   that the group's aggregate turnover in that year is not more than £2.8 million net (or £3.36 million gross);[6116] and
(c)   that the group's aggregate balance sheet total for that year is not more than £2.8 million net (or £3.36 million gross).[6117]

A company is not excluded by s 479(1) of the CA 2006 if, throughout the whole of the period or periods during the financial year when it was a group company, it was both a subsidiary undertaking and dormant.[6118]

The term 'group company' means a company that is a parent company or a subsidiary undertaking,[6119] and 'the group', in relation to a group company, means that company, together with all its associated undertakings.[6120]

For this purpose undertakings are associated if one is a subsidiary undertaking of the other or both are subsidiary undertakings of a third undertaking.

Under s 479 of the CA 2006, (a) whether a group qualifies as small shall be determined in accordance with s 383 of the CA 2006 (companies qualifying as small: parent companies);[6121] (b) 'ineligible group' has the meaning given by s 384(2) and (3) of the CA 2006;[6122] (c) a group's aggregate turnover and aggregate balance sheet total shall be determined as for the purposes of s 383

[6111] CA 2006, s 478(c).   [6112] CA 2006, s 479(1)(a).   [6113] CA 2006, s 479(1)(b).
[6114] CA 2006, s 479(2)(a)(i).   [6115] CA 2006, s 479(2)(a)(ii).   [6116] CA 2006, s 479(2)(b).
[6117] CA 2006, s 479(2)(c).   [6118] CA 2006, s 479(3).   [6119] CA 2006, s 479(4)(a).
[6120] CA 2006, s 479(4)(b).   [6121] CA 2006, s 479(5)(a).   [6122] CA 2006, s 479(5)(b).

of the CA 2006;[6123] (d) 'net' and 'gross' have the same meaning as in that section.[6124]

A company may meet any relevant requirement on the basis of either the gross or the net figure.[6125]

The provisions mentioned in s 479(5) of the CA 2006 apply for the purposes of this section as if all the bodies corporate in the group were companies.[6126]

Sections 477–479 of the CA 2006 restate the exemption from audit for small companies. Section 477 of the CA 2006 provides that a company must not only meet the general small company criteria in s 382 of the CA 2006, but its turnover and balance sheet totals must fall below £5.6 million and £2.8 million respectively.

Section 478 of the CA 2006 excludes from the exemption various categories of company including public companies and some financial services companies. Section 479 of the CA 2006 sets out the conditions for a company in a group qualifying for a small company exemption.

Exemption from audit: dormant companies

Dormant companies: conditions for exemption from audit

23.7 Section 480 of the CA 2006 deals with dormant companies with conditions for exemption from audit. A company is exempt from the requirements of this Act relating to the audit of accounts in respect of a financial year if it has been dormant since its formation;[6127] or it has been dormant since the end of the previous financial year and the following conditions are met.[6128]

The conditions are that the company (a) as regards its individual accounts for the financial year in question (i) is entitled to prepare accounts in accordance with the small companies regime (see ss 381–384 of the CA 2006),[6129] or (ii) would be so entitled but for having been a public company or a member of an ineligible group,[6130] and (b) is not required to prepare group accounts for that year.[6131]

Section 480 of the CA 2006 applies subject to:

(a) s 475(2) and (3) of the CA 2006 (requirements as to statements to be contained in balance sheet);
(b) s 460 of the CA 2006 (right of members to require audit); and
(c) s 481 of the CA 2006 (companies excluded from dormant companies exemption).

[6123] CA 2006, s 479(5)(c).   [6124] CA 2006, s 479(5)(d).   [6125] CA 2006, s 479(5)(e).
[6126] CA 2006, s 479(6).   [6127] CA 2006, s 480(1)(a).   [6128] CA 2006, s 480(1)(b).
[6129] CA 2006, s 480(2)(a)(i).   [6130] CA 2006, s 480(2)(a)(ii).   [6131] CA 2006, s 480(2)(b).

Companies excluded from dormant companies exemption

23.8 Section 481 of the CA 2006 applies to companies excluded from dormant companies exemption. A company is not entitled to the exemption conferred by s 480 of the CA 2006 (dormant companies) if it was at any time within the financial year in question a company that is an authorised insurance company, a banking company, an e-money issuer, an ISD Investment firm or a UCITS Management company;[6132] or carries on insurance market activity.[6133]

Sections 480 and 481 of the CA 2006 restate the exemptions from audit available to dormant companies. 'Dormant' is defined in s 1169 of the CA 2006. Certain financial services companies are excluded from using the exemption even if they are dormant.

Companies subject to public sector audit

23.9 Sections 482 and 483 of the CA 2006, the only wholly new provisions in this Chapter, are intended to enable a public sector auditor to audit non-commercial, public sector bodies that happen to be constituted as companies.

Non-profit-making companies subject to public sector audit

23.10 Section 482 of the CA 2006 states that the requirements of this Part as to the audit of accounts do not apply to a company for a financial year if it is non-profit-making and its accounts:

(a)   are subject to audit (i) by the Comptroller and Auditor General by virtue of an order under s 25(6) of the Government Resources and Accounts Act 2000 (c 20),[6134] or (ii) by the Auditor General for Wales by virtue of s 96, or an order under s 144 of the Government of Wales Act 1998 (c 38);[6135]

(b)   are accounts (i) in relation to which s 21 of the Public Finance and Accountability (Scotland) Act 2000 (asp 1) (audit of accounts: Auditor General for Scotland) applies,[6136] or (ii) that are subject to audit by the Auditor General for Scotland by virtue of an order under s 483 (Scottish public sector companies: audit by Auditor General for Scotland);[6137] or

(c)   are subject to audit by the Comptroller and Auditor General for Northern Ireland by virtue of an order under Article 5(3) of the Audit and Accountability (Northern Ireland) Order 2003 (SI 2003/418 (NI 5)).[6138]

In the case of a company that is a parent company or a subsidiary

---

[6132] CA 2006, s 481(a).   [6133] CA 2006, s 481(b).   [6134] CA 2006, s 482(1)(a)(i).
[6135] CA 2006, s 482(1)(a)(ii).   [6136] CA 2006, s 482(1)(b)(i).   [6137] CA 2006, s 482(1)(b)(ii).
[6138] CA 2006, s 482(1)(c).

undertaking, s 482(1) of the CA 2006 applies only if every group undertaking is non-profit-making.[6139] In this section 'non-profit-making' has the same meaning as in Article 48 of the Treaty establishing the European Community.[6140]

Section 482 of the CA 2006 applies subject to s 475(2) of the CA 2006 (balance sheet to contain statement that a company is entitled to exemption under this section).[6141]

Section 482 of the CA 2006 exempts from Companies Act audit any non-departmental public body that is a company and is non-profit-making, if it has been made subject by order to a public sector audit.

A UK body may be subject to public sector audit by virtue of an order made under the Government Resources and Accounts Act 2000. The body in question will then be audited by the National Audit Office on behalf of the UK Comptroller and Auditor General. Under the Audit and Accountability (Northern Ireland) Order 2003, an order can make a body subject to audit by the Comptroller and Audit General for Northern Ireland. Alternatively, under s 96 of the Government of Wales Act 1998, an order can make a body subject to audit by the Auditor General for Wales.

Some Scottish bodies are subject to public sector audit by the Auditor General for Scotland (AGS) under statute, namely the Public Finance and Accountability (Scotland) Act 2000.

The companies exempted by this section are not subject to the Fourth Company Law Directive: the Directive is based on Article 44(2)(g) (formerly 54(3)(g) of the EC Treaty and Article 48 of the Treaty excludes from the scope of Article 44 undertakings that are non-profit-making. That is why subs (3) gives 'non-profit-making' the same meaning as in the Treaty.

Section 482(2) of the CA 2006 clarifies that a group company can benefit from this exemption, only if every company in the group is non-profit-making. The effect of s 482(4) of the CA 2006 is that the exemption is not available unless the balance sheet contains the statement that the company is entitled to it.

Scottish public sector companies: audit by Auditor General for Scotland

23.11 Section 483 of the CA 2006 states that the Scottish Ministers may by order provide for the accounts of a company having its registered office in Scotland to be audited by the Auditor General for Scotland.[6142]

An order under s 483(1) of the CA 2006 may be made in relation to a company only if it appears to the Scottish Ministers that the company

---

[6139] CA 2006, s 482(2).   [6140] CA 2006, s 482(3).   [6141] CA 2006, s 482(4).
[6142] CA 2006, s 482(4).

exercises in or as regards Scotland functions of a public nature none of which relate to reserved matters (within the meaning of the Scotland Act 1998 (c 46)),[6143] or is entirely or substantially funded from a body having accounts falling within para (a) or (b) of subs (3).[6144]

Those accounts are accounts in relation to which s 21 of the Public Finance and Accountability (Scotland) Act 2000 (asp 1) (audit of accounts: Auditor General for Scotland) applies,[6145] and accounts that are subject to audit by the Auditor General for Scotland by virtue of an order under this section.[6146]

An order under s 483(1) of the CA 2006 may make such supplementary or consequential provision (including provision amending an enactment) as the Scottish Ministers think expedient.[6147]

An order under s 483(1) of the CA 2006 will not be made unless a draft of the statutory instrument containing it has been laid before, and approved by resolution of, the Scottish Parliament.[6148]

Section 483 of the CA 2006 confers a new power on Scottish Ministers to provide that a company should have its account audited by the Auditor General for Scotland (AGS).

This is available for companies depending on their functions or their funding. The Scottish Ministers can designate a company under this power if its functions are public functions that are all covered by the Scottish Parliament's responsibilities, or if the company receives all or most of its funding from a public body already audited by the AGS. In the latter case, the funding body may be audited by the AGS because it is covered by the Public Finance and Accountability (Scotland) Act 2000 or because it is itself a company that Scottish Ministers have made auditable by the AGS by a previous order under this section.

If an order is made under this section providing that a company should have a public sector audit by the AGS, and that if that company is non-profit-making, then it will benefit from audit in the preceding section.

General power of amendment by regulation

General power of amendment by regulations

23.12 Section 484 of the CA 2006 deals with the general power of amendment by regulations.

The Secretary of State may by regulations amend this Chapter by adding, altering or repealing provisions.[6149]

The regulations may make consequential amendments or repeals in other provisions of this Act, or in other enactments.[6150]

[6143] CA 2006, s 483(2)(a).   [6144] CA 2006, s 483(2)(b).   [6145] CA 2006, s 483(3)(a).
[6146] CA 2006, s 483(3)(b).   [6147] CA 2006, s 483(4).   [6148] CA 2006, s 483(5).
[6149] CA 2006, s 484(1).   [6150] CA 2006, s 484(2).

Regulations under this section imposing new requirements, or rendering existing requirements more onerous, are subject to affirmative resolution procedure.[6151] Other regulations under this section are subject to negative resolution procedure.[6152]

This section provides a power for the Secretary of State to change the provisions of this Chapter. Taken together with s 468 of the CA 2006, it broadly restates the power in s 257 of the CA 1985. Section 484(2) of the CA 2006 enables the regulations to make consequential changes to other legislation. The power is subject to affirmative resolution if it is extending the requirement for audit, or otherwise making requirements more onerous; and to negative resolution otherwise.

Appointment of Auditors

23.13 Chapter 2 of Part 16 of the CA 2006 addresses the appointment of auditors. It comprises ten sections.

Chapter 2 broadly restates the existing law in ss 384–388A of the CA 1985 on the way in which shareholders appoint a company's auditors, with some minor changes (as explained below). The provisions are reorganised to deal with private and public companies separately. The Chapter also restates the rules in ss 390A and 390B of the CA 1985 on auditors' remuneration and the disclosure required of services provided by auditors. It introduces a new power for the Secretary of State to require disclosure of the terms of audit appointments. The provisions dealing with appointment of auditors distinguish between appointments by private and public companies.

Private companies

23.14 Sections 485–488 of the CA 2006 restate the law on the appointment of auditors of private companies, providing that auditors are generally to be appointed by shareholders by ordinary resolution. For any financial year, this will generally be done within 28 days of the circulation to a company's shareholders of the accounts for the previous year.

There are two changes: firstly, that an auditor's term of office will typically run from the end of the 28-day period following circulation of the accounts until the end of the corresponding period the following year. This will apply even if the auditor is appointed at a meeting where the company's accounts are laid. The second change is that an auditor is now deemed to be re-appointed unless the company decides otherwise.

[6151] CA 2006, s 484(3).
[6152] CA 2006, s 484(4).

Appointment of auditors of private company: general

23.15 Section 485 of the CA 2006 applies to the appointment of auditors of private companies and contains general provisions. An auditor or auditors of a private company must be appointed for each financial year of the company, unless the directors reasonably resolve otherwise on the ground that audited accounts are unlikely to be required.[6153]

For each financial year for which an auditor or auditors is or are to be appointed (other than the company's first financial year), the appointment must be made before the end of the period of 28 days beginning with the end of the time allowed for sending out copies of the company's annual accounts and reports for the previous financial year (see s 424 of the CA 2006),[6154] or if earlier, the day on which copies of the company's annual accounts and reports for the previous financial year are sent out under s 423 of the CA 2006.[6155]

This is the 'period for appointing auditors'.

The directors may appoint an auditor or auditors of the company at any time before the company's first period for appointing auditors,[6156] or following a period during which the company (being exempt from audit) did not have any auditor, at any time before the company's next period for appointing auditors,[6157] or to fill a casual vacancy in the office of auditor.[6158]

The members may appoint an auditor or auditors by ordinary resolution during a period for appointing auditors,[6159] or if the company should have appointed an auditor or auditors during a period for appointing auditors but failed to do so,[6160] or where the directors had power to appoint under s 485(3) of the CA 2006 but have failed to make an appointment.[6161]

An auditor or auditors of a private company may only be appointed in accordance with this section,[6162] or in accordance with s 476 of the CA 2006 (default power of Secretary of State).[6163]

This is without prejudice to any deemed re-appointment under s 487 of the CA 2006.

Section 485 of the CA 2006 provides for a private company's obligation to appoint an auditor, unless it is taking advantage of an exemption from audit. The appointment is to be done the shareholders by ordinary resolution, except that the directors can appoint the company's first auditor (or the first after a period of audit exemption), and can fill a casual vacancy.

[6153] CA 2006, s 485(1).   [6154] CA 2006, s 485(2)(a).   [6155] CA 2006, s 485(2)(b).
[6156] CA 2006, s 485(3)(a).   [6157] CA 2006, s 485(3)(b).   [6158] CA 2006, s 485(3)(c).
[6159] CA 2006, s 485(4)(a).   [6160] CA 2006, s 485(4)(b).   [6161] CA 2006, s 485(4)(c).
[6162] CA 2006, s 485(5)(a).   [6163] CA 2006, s 485(5)(b).

Appointment of auditors of a private company: default power of the Secretary of State

23.16 Section 486 of the CA 2006 applies to the appointment of auditors of a private company with reference to the default power of the Secretary of State. If a private company fails to appoint an auditor or auditors in accordance with s 485 of the CA 2006, the Secretary of State may appoint one or more persons to fill the vacancy.[6164]

Where s 485(2) of the CA 2006 applies and the company fails to make the necessary appointment before the end of the period for appointing auditors, the company must within one week of the end of that period give notice to the Secretary of State of his power having become exercisable.[6165]

If a company fails to give the notice required by this section, an offence is committed by the company,[6166] and every officer of the company who is in default.[6167] A person guilty of an offence under s 486 of the CA 2006 is liable on summary conviction to a fine not exceeding level 3 on the standard scale and, for continued contravention, a daily default fine not exceeding one-tenth of level 3 on the standard scale.[6168]

Section 486 of the CA 2006 provides for the obligation on a company to inform the Secretary of State if it has failed to appoint an auditor within 28 days of circulation of its accounts. The Secretary of State has power to appoint an auditor in those circumstances. It derives from s 387 of the CA 1985.

Term of office of auditors of a private company

23.17 Section 487 of the CA 2006 deals with the term of office of auditors of a private company. An auditor or auditors of a private company hold office in accordance with the terms of their appointment, subject to the requirements that they do not take office until any previous auditor or auditors cease to hold office,[6169] and they cease to hold office at the end of the next period for appointing auditors unless re-appointed.[6170]

Where no auditor has been appointed by the end of the next period for appointing auditors, any auditor in office immediately before that time is deemed to be re-appointed at that time, unless:

(a)   he was appointed by the directors;[6171] or
(b)   the company's articles require actual re-appointment;[6172] or

---

[6164] CA 2006, s 486(1).   [6165] CA 2006, s 486(2).   [6166] CA 2006, s 486(3)(a).
[6167] CA 2006, s 486(3)(b).   [6168] CA 2006, s 486(4).   [6169] CA 2006, s 487(1)(a).
[6170] CA 2006, s 487(1)(b).   [6171] CA 2006, s 487(2)(a).   [6172] CA 2006, s 487(2)(b).

(c)   the deemed re-appointment is prevented by the members under s 488 of the CA 2006;[6173] or

(d)   the members have resolved that he should not be re-appointed;[6174] or

(e)   the directors have resolved that no auditor or auditors should be appointed for the financial year in question.[6175]

This is without prejudice to the provisions of Part 16 of the CA 2006 as to removal and resignation of auditors.[6176]

No account will be taken of any loss of the opportunity of deemed re-appointment under this section in ascertaining the amount of any compensation or damages payable to an auditor on his ceasing to hold office for any reason.[6177]

Section 487 of the CA 2006 provides that the end of the term of office of the auditor of a private company is to be the end of the 28-day period for appointing auditors. At the end of his term an auditor will automatically be deemed to be re-appointed except in five cases. First, if he was appointed by the directors; second, if the company's articles require actual re-appointment; third, if the members have given notice to the company under s 488 of the CA 2006; fourth, if there has been a resolution that the auditor should not be reappointed; or fifth, if the directors decide that they do not need auditors for the following year.

When there is a change of auditor, the term of office of the incoming auditor does not begin before the end of the previous auditor's term. This means that a new auditor's term will typically begin immediately after the end of the 28-day period for appointing auditors.

Prevention by members of deemed re-appointment of an auditor

23.18 Section 488 of the CA 2006 deals with the prevention by members of the deemed reappointment of an auditor. An auditor of a private company is not deemed to be re-appointed under s 487(2) of the CA 2006 if the company has received notices under this section from members who hold at least the requisite percentage of the total voting rights of all members who would be entitled to vote, on a resolution that the auditor should not be re-appointed.[6178]

The 'requisite percentage' is 5 per cent, or such lower percentage as is specified for this purpose in the company's articles.[6179]

A notice under this section (a) may be in hard copy or electronic form;[6180]

[6173] CA 2006, s 487(2)(c).   [6174] CA 2006, s 487(2)(d).   [6175] CA 2006, s 487(2)(e).
[6176] CA 2006, s 487(3).   [6177] CA 2006, s 487(4).   [6178] CA 2006, s 488(1).
[6179] CA 2006, s 488(2).   [6180] CA 2006, s 488(3)(a).

(b) must be authenticated by the person or persons giving it;[6181] and (c) must be received by the company before the end of the accounting reference period immediately preceding the time when the deemed re-appointment would have effect.[6182]

Section 488 of the CA 2006 enables members with at least 5 per cent of the voting rights in a private company to give notice that the auditor of the company should not be automatically re-appointed. The company's articles can enable members to do this with less than 5 per cent of the voting rights, but cannot increase the required percentage.

Section 488(3) of the CA 2006 provides that the deadline for such a notice excluding the re-appointment of an auditor is the end of the financial year the accounts for which he is auditing.

Public companies

23.19 Sections 489 and 491 of the CA 2006 deal with the appointment of auditors of public companies. They restate the law on the appointment of auditors of public companies, providing that auditors are generally to be appointed by shareholders by ordinary resolution in the general meeting before which the company's accounts are laid.

Appointment of auditors of a public company: general

23.20 Section 489 of the CA 2006 applies to the appointment of auditors of a public company with general application provisions. An auditor or auditors of a public company must be appointed for each financial year of the company, unless the directors reasonably resolve otherwise on the ground that audited accounts are unlikely to be required.[6183]

For each financial year for which an auditor or auditors is or are to be appointed (other than the company's first financial year), the appointment must be made before the end of the accounts meeting of the company at which the company's annual accounts and reports for the previous financial year are laid.[6184]

The directors may appoint an auditor or auditors of the company at any time before the company's first accounts meeting;[6185] or following a period during which the company (being exempt from audit) did not have any auditor, at any time before the company's next accounts meeting;[6186] or to fill a casual vacancy in the office of auditor.[6187]

The members may appoint an auditor or auditors by ordinary resolution at an accounts meeting;[6188] or if the company should have appointed an auditor

---

[6181] CA 2006, s 488(3)(b).   [6182] CA 2006, s 488(3)(c).   [6183] CA 2006, s 489(1).
[6184] CA 2006, s 489(2).   [6185] CA 2006, s 489(3)(a).   [6186] CA 2006, s 489(3)(b).
[6187] CA 2006, s 489(3)(c).   [6188] CA 2006, s 489(4)(a).

or auditors at an accounts meeting but failed to do so;[6189] or where the directors had power to appoint under s 489(3) of the CA 2006 but have failed to make an appointment.[6190]

An auditor or auditors of a public company may only be appointed in accordance with this section;[6191] or in accordance with s 490 of the CA 2006 (default power of Secretary of State).[6192]

Section 489 of the CA 2006 restates a public company's obligation to appoint auditors, unless it is taking advantage of an exemption from audit. This is to be done by the shareholders by ordinary resolution, normally at the general meeting at which the accounts are laid. The directors can appoint the company's first auditors (or the first after a period of audit exemption), and can fill a casual vacancy.

Appointment of auditors of a public company: default power of the Secretary of State

23.21 Section 490 of the CA 2006 deals with the appointment of auditors of public company with respect to the default power of the Secretary of State. If a public company fails to appoint an auditor or auditors in accordance with s 489 of the CA 2006, the Secretary of State may appoint one or more persons to fill the vacancy.[6193]

Where s 489(2) of the CA 2006 applies and the company fails to make the necessary appointment before the end of the accounts meeting, the company must within one week of the end of that meeting give notice to the Secretary of State of his power having become exercisable.[6194]

If a company fails to give the notice required by this section, an offence is committed by the company,[6195] and every officer of the company who is in default.[6196] A person guilty of an offence under this section is liable on summary conviction to a fine not exceeding level 3 on the standard scale and, for continued contravention, a daily default fine not exceeding one-tenth of level 3 on the standard scale.[6197]

Section 490 of the CA 2006 restates the obligation of a company to inform the Secretary of State if it has failed to appoint an auditor at the general meeting that considers the previous year's accounts: and the Secretary of State's power to appoint an auditor in those circumstances.

Term of office of auditors of a public company

23.22 Section 491 of the CA 2006 applies to the term of office of auditors of a public company. The auditor or auditors of a public company hold office in

---

[6189] CA 2006, s 489(4)(b).   [6190] CA 2006, s 489(4)(c).   [6191] CA 2006, s 489(5)(a).
[6192] CA 2006, s 489(5)(b).   [6193] CA 2006, s 490(1).   [6194] CA 2006, s 490(2).
[6195] CA 2006, s 490(3)(a).   [6196] CA 2006, s 490(3)(b).   [6197] CA 2006, s 490(4).

accordance with the terms of their appointment, subject to the requirements that they do not take office until the previous auditor or auditors have ceased to hold office,[6198] and they cease to hold office at the conclusion of the accounts meeting next following their appointment, unless re-appointed.[6199]

This is without prejudice to the provisions of Part 16 of the CA 2006 as to the removal and resignation of auditors.[6200]

Section 491 of the CA 2006 restates that an auditor of a public company holds office until the end of the meeting at which the accounts they are auditing are laid, unless re-appointed. Where there is a change of auditor, the term of office of the incoming auditor does not begin before the end of the previous auditor's term. This means that a new auditor's term will typically begin immediately after the end of the accounts meeting.

General provisions

23.23 Sections 492–494 of the CA 2006 contains general provisions that apply to both private and public companies.

Fixing of an auditor's remuneration

23.24 Section 492 of the CA 2006 applies to the fixing of auditors' remuneration. The remuneration of an auditor appointed by the members of a company must be fixed by the members by ordinary resolution or in such manner as the members may by ordinary resolution determine.[6201]

The remuneration of an auditor appointed by the directors of a company must be fixed by the directors.[6202]

The remuneration of an auditor appointed by the Secretary of State must be fixed by the Secretary of State.[6203]

The term 'remuneration' includes sums paid in respect of expenses.[6204] This section applies in relation to benefits in kind as to payments of money.[6205]

Section 492 of the CA 2006 restates the provision that it is the members of a company, by ordinary resolution, who determine the auditor's remuneration, or decide the method by which it should be determined. If the auditor was appointed by someone other than the members, then it will be the directors or the Secretary of State as appropriate who will determine his remuneration.

[6198] CA 2006, s 491(1)(a).   [6199] CA 2006, s 491(1)(b).   [6200] CA 2006, s 491(2).
[6201] CA 2006, s 492(1).   [6202] CA 2006, s 492(2).   [6203] CA 2006, s 492(3).
[6204] CA 2006, s 492(4).   [6205] CA 2006, s 492(5).

Disclosure of the terms of an audit appointment

23.25 Section 493 of the CA 2006 deals with the disclosure of the terms of an audit appointment. The Secretary of State may make provision by regulations for securing the disclosure of the terms on which a company's auditor is appointed, remunerated or performs his duties.

Nothing in the following provisions of this section affects the generality of this power.[6206]

The regulations may:

(a)   require disclosure of a copy of any terms that are in writing;[6207] and a written memorandum setting out any terms that are not in writing;[6208]
(b)   require disclosure to be at such times, in such places and by such means as are specified in the regulations;[6209]
(c)   require the place and means of disclosure to be stated (i) in a note to the company's annual accounts (in the case of its individual accounts) or in such manner as is specified in the regulations (in the case of group accounts),[6210] (ii) in the directors' report,[6211] or (iii) in the auditor's report on the company's annual accounts.[6212]

The provisions of this section apply to a variation of the terms mentioned in s 493(1) of the CA 2006 as they apply to the original terms.[6213]

Regulations under this section are subject to affirmative resolution procedure.[6214]

Section 493 of the CA 2006 creates a new power for the Secretary of State to require companies to disclose information about the terms on which they engage their auditors. Section 493(2) of the CA 2006 provides some examples of the detailed requirements that the Secretary of State could specify in regulations. Section 493(3) of the CA 2006 provides that regulations can require disclosure of changes in terms as well as the term of appointment. Section 493(4) of the CA 2006 specifies that the regulations are to be made by affirmative resolution procedure.

Disclosure of services provided by an auditor or associates and related remuneration

23.26 Section 494 of the CA 2006 deals with the disclosure of services by an auditor or associates and related remuneration.

The Secretary of State may make provision by regulations for securing the disclosure of the nature of any services provided for a company by the

---

[6206] CA 2006, s 493(1).   [6207] CA 2006, s 493(2)(a)(i).   [6208] CA 2006, s 493(2)(a)(ii).
[6209] CA 2006, s 493(2)(b).   [6210] CA 2006, s 493(2)(c)(i).   [6211] CA 2006, s 493(2)(c)(ii).
[6212] CA 2006, s 493(2)(c)(iii).   [6213] CA 2006, s 493(3).   [6214] CA 2006, s 493(4).

company's auditor (whether in his capacity as auditor or otherwise) or by his associates;[6215] and the amount of any remuneration received or receivable by a company's auditor, or his associates, in respect of any such services.[6216]

Nothing in the following provisions of this section affects the generality of this power.

The regulations may provide:

(a) for disclosure of the nature of any services provided to be made by reference to any class or description of services specified in the regulations (or any combination of services, however described);[6217]

(b) for the disclosure of amounts of remuneration received or receivable in respect of services of any class or description specified in the regulations (or any combination of services, however described);[6218]

(c) for the disclosure of separate amounts so received or receivable by the company's auditor or any of his associates, or of aggregate amounts so received or receivable by all or any of those persons.[6219]

The regulations may:

(a) provide that 'remuneration' includes sums paid in respect of expenses;[6220]

(b) apply to benefits in kind as well as to payments of money, and require the disclosure of the nature of any such benefits and their estimated money value;[6221]

(c) apply to services provided for the associates of a company as well as to those provided for a company;[6222]

(d) define 'associate' in relation to an auditor and a company respectively.[6223]

The regulations may provide that any disclosure required by the regulations is to be made:

(a) in a note to the company's annual accounts (in the case of its individual accounts) or in such manner as is specified in the regulations (in the case of group accounts);[6224]

(b) in the directors' report;[6225] or

(c) in the auditor's report on the company's annual accounts.[6226]

If the regulations provide that any such disclosure is to be made as mentioned

---

[6215] CA 2006, s 494(1)(a). See the Companies (Disclosure of Auditor Remuneration and Limited Liability Agreements) Regulations 2007.
[6216] CA 2006, s 494(1)(b).   [6217] CA 2006, s 494(2)(a).   [6218] CA 2006, s 494(2)(b).
[6219] CA 2006, s 494(2)(c).   [6220] CA 2006, s 494(3)(a).   [6221] CA 2006, s 494(3)(b).
[6222] CA 2006, s 494(3)(c).   [6223] CA 2006, s 494(3)(d).   [6224] CA 2006, s 494(4)(a).
[6225] CA 2006, s 494(4)(b).   [6226] CA 2006, s 494(4)(c).

in s 494(4)(a) or (b) of the CA 2006, the regulations may require the auditor to supply the directors of the company with any information necessary to enable the disclosure to be made.[6227]

Regulations under this section are subject to negative resolution procedure.[6228]

Section 474 of the CA 2006 restates that the existing power of the Secretary of State, in s 390B of the CA 1985, to require disclosure of details of all the services supplied to a company by its auditor, and the remuneration involved. Section 494(2)–(4) of the CA 2006 gives some illustrations of the detailed requirements that the Secretary of State can specify in regulations: s 494(2) of the CA 2006 relates to the level of disaggregation of different services and remuneration and between the auditor and his associates; s 494(3) of the CA 2006 lists of some definitional issues that can be covered in regulations; and s 494(4) of the CA 2006 provides examples of where the information should be disclosed.

Under s 494(4) of the CA 2006, the regulations might require disclosure in a document compiled by the company rather than by the auditor; s 494(5) of the CA 2006 provides that, if so, the regulations can require the auditor to supply the directors with the information to be disclosed, for example about the auditor's associates.

Section 494(6) of the CA 2006 specifies that the regulations are to be made by negative resolution procedure.

Functions of Auditors

23.27 Chapter 3 of Part 16 of the CA 2006 applies to the functions of auditors. It comprises 15 sections. It addresses the auditor's report; duties and rights of auditors; the signature on the auditor's report and offences in connection with auditors' report.

Auditor's report

Auditor's report on a company's annual accounts

23.28 Section 495 of the CA 2006 applies to an auditor's report on a company's annual accounts. A company's auditor must make a report to the company's members on all annual accounts of the company of which copies are, during his tenure of office (a) in the case of a private company, to be sent out to members under s 423 of the CA 2006;[6229] (b) in the case of a public company, to be laid before the company in general meeting under s 437 of the CA 2006.[6230]

[6227] CA 2006, s 494(5).   [6228] CA 2006, s 494(6).   [6229] CA 2006, s 495(1)(a).
[6230] CA 2006, s 495(1)(b).

The auditor's report must include an introduction identifying the annual accounts that are the subject of the audit, and the financial reporting framework that has been applied in their preparation,[6231] and a description of the scope of the audit identifying the auditing standards in accordance with which the audit was conducted.[6232]

The report must state clearly whether, in the auditor's opinion, the annual accounts:

(a) give a true and fair view (i) in the case of an individual balance sheet, of the state of affairs of the company as at the end of the financial year,[6233] (ii) in the case of an individual profit and loss account, of the profit or loss of the company for the financial year,[6234] (iii) in the case of group accounts, of the state of affairs as at the end of the financial year and of the profit or loss for the financial year of the undertakings included in the consolidation as a whole, so far as concerns members of the company;[6235]

(b) have been properly prepared in accordance with the relevant financial reporting framework;[6236] and

(c) have been prepared in accordance with the requirements of this Act (and, where applicable, Article 4 of the IAS Regulation).[6237]

Expressions used in s 495(3) of the CA 2006 that are defined for the purposes of Part 15 of the CA 2006 (see s 474 of the CA 2006) have the same meaning as in that Part.

The auditor's report must be either unqualified or qualified,[6238] and must include reference to any matters to which the auditor wishes to draw attention by way of emphasis without qualifying the report.[6239]

Auditor's report on the directors' report

23.29 Section 496 of the CA 2006 deals with auditors' reports on directors' reports. It states that auditor must state in his report on the company's annual accounts whether in his opinion the information given in the directors' report for the financial year for which the accounts are prepared is consistent with those accounts.

[6231] CA 2006, s 495(2)(a).   [6232] CA 2006, s 495(2)(b).   [6233] CA 2006, s 495(3)(a)(i).
[6234] CA 2006, s 495(3)(a)(ii).   [6235] CA 2006, s 495(3)(a)(iii).   [6236] CA 2006, s 495(3)(b).
[6237] CA 2006, s 495(3)(c).   [6238] CA 2006, s 495(4)(a).   [6239] CA 2006, s 495(4)(b).

Auditor's report on the auditable part of directors'
remuneration report

23.30 Section 497 of the CA 2006 deals with the auditor's report and the liable part of the directors' remuneration report. If the company is a quoted company, the auditor, in his report on the company's annual accounts for the financial year, must report to the company's members on the auditable part of the directors' remuneration report,[6240] and state whether in his opinion that part of the directors' remuneration report has been properly prepared in accordance with this Act.[6241]

The term 'the auditable part' of a directors' remuneration report is the part identified as such by regulations under s 421 of the CA 2006.[6242]

Sections 495–497 of the CA 2006 restate, with modifications, s 235 of the CA 1985, on what the auditor should include in his report on the accounts.

Section 495 of the CA 2006 imposes the basic duty to produce an audit report and requires that it should set out the way the auditor has approached the audit. Section 495(3) of the CA 2006 requires the auditor in his report to state his opinion on three overlapping matters: (i) whether the accounts provide a true and fair view, (ii) whether they comply with the appropriate reporting framework, and (iii) whether the accounts comply with the requirements in Part 15 of the CA 2006 (and, where applicable, with article 4 of the IAS Regulation (Regulation (EC) 1606/2002 on the application of international accounting standards)). Section 495(4) of the CA 2006 requires the audit report to be either qualified or unqualified, though it is open to the auditor to draw attention to aspects of his audit without qualifying the report.

Sections 496–497 of the CA 2006 restate the law on what the auditor should include in relation to the directors' report and the directors' remuneration report.

Duties and rights of auditors

23.31 Sections 498–502 of the CA 2006 apply to the duties and rights of auditors.

Duties of an auditor

23.32 Section 498 of the CA 2006 deals with the duties of auditors. A company's auditor, in preparing his report, must carry out such investigations as will enable him to form an opinion as to (a) whether adequate accounting records have been kept by the company and returns adequate for their audit

---

[6240] CA 2006, s 497(1)(a).   [6241] CA 2006, s 497(1)(b).   [6242] CA 2006, s 497(2).

have been received from branches not visited by him;[6243] and (b) whether the company's individual accounts are in agreement with the accounting records and returns;[6244] and (c) in the case of a quoted company, whether the auditable part of the company's directors' remuneration report is in agreement with the accounting records and returns.[6245]

If the auditor is of opinion (a) that adequate accounting records have not been kept, or that returns adequate for their audit have not been received from branches not visited by him;[6246] or (b) that the company's individual accounts are not in agreement with the accounting records and returns;[6247] or (c) in the case of a quoted company, that the auditable part of its directors' remuneration report is not in agreement with the accounting records and returns,[6248] the auditor must state that fact in his report.

If the auditor fails to obtain all the information and explanations that, to the best of his knowledge and belief, are necessary for the purposes of his audit, he shall state that fact in his report.[6249]

If the requirements of regulations under s 412 of the CA 2006 (disclosure of directors' benefits: remuneration, pensions and compensation for loss of office) are not complied with in the annual accounts,[6250] or in the case of a quoted company, the requirements of regulations under s 421 of the CA 2006 as to information forming the auditable part of the directors' remuneration report are not complied with in that report,[6251] the auditor must include in his report, so far as he is reasonably able to do so, a statement giving the required particulars.

If the directors of the company have prepared accounts and reports in accordance with the small companies regime and in the auditor's opinion they were not entitled so to do, the auditor shall state that fact in his report.[6252]

Auditor's general right to information

23.33 Section 499 of the CA 2006 deals with the auditors' general right to information. An auditor of a company has a right of access at all times to the company's books, accounts and vouchers (in whatever form they are held),[6253] and may require any of the following persons to provide him with such information or explanations as he thinks necessary for the performance of his duties as auditor.[6254]

[6243] CA 2006, s 498(1)(a).   [6244] CA 2006, s 498(1)(b).   [6245] CA 2006, s 498(1)(c).
[6246] CA 2006, s 498(2)(a).   [6247] CA 2006, s 498(2)(b).   [6248] CA 2006, s 498(2)(c).
[6249] CA 2006, s 498(3).   [6250] CA 2006, s 498(4)(a).   [6251] CA 2006, s 498(4)(b).
[6252] CA 2006, s 498(5).   [6253] CA 2006, s 499(1)(a).   [6254] CA 2006, s 499(1)(b).

Those persons are:

(a)   any officer or employee of the company;[6255]
(b)   any person holding or accountable for any of the company's books, accounts or vouchers;[6256]
(c)   any subsidiary undertaking of the company that is a body corporate incorporated in the United Kingdom;[6257]
(d)   any officer, employee or auditor of any such subsidiary undertaking or any person holding or accountable for any books, accounts or vouchers of any such subsidiary undertaking;[6258]
(e)   any person who fell within any of paras (a)–(d) at a time to which the information or explanations required by the auditor relates or relate.[6259]

A statement made by a person in response to a requirement under this section may not be used in evidence against him in criminal proceedings except proceedings for an offence under s 501 of the CA 2006.[6260]

Nothing in this section compels a person to disclose information in respect of which a claim to legal professional privilege (in Scotland, to confidentiality of communications) could be maintained in legal proceedings.[6261]

Auditor's right to information from overseas subsidiaries

23.34 Section 500 of the CA 2006 applies to the auditor's right to information from overseas subsidiaries.

Where a parent company has a subsidiary undertaking that is not a body corporate incorporated in the United Kingdom, the auditor of the parent company may require it to obtain from any of the following persons such information or explanations as he may reasonably require for the purposes of his duties as auditor.[6262]

Those persons are:

(a)   the undertaking;[6263]
(b)   any officer, employee or auditor of the undertaking;[6264]
(c)   any person holding or accountable for any of the undertaking's books, accounts or vouchers;[6265]
(d)   any person who fell within para (b) or (c) at a time to which the information or explanations relates or relate.[6266]

If so required, the parent company must take all such steps as are reasonably

---

[6255] CA 2006, s 499(2)(a).   [6256] CA 2006, s 499(2)(b).   [6257] CA 2006, s 499(2)(c).
[6258] CA 2006, s 499(2)(d).   [6259] CA 2006, s 499(2)(e).   [6260] CA 2006, s 499(3).
[6261] CA 2006, s 499(4).   [6262] CA 2006, s 500(1).   [6263] CA 2006, s 500(2)(a).
[6264] CA 2006, s 500(2)(b).   [6265] CA 2006, s 500(2)(c).   [6266] CA 2006, s 500(2)(d).

open to it to obtain the information or explanations from the person concerned.[6267]

A statement made by a person in response to a requirement under this section may not be used in evidence against him in criminal proceedings except proceedings for an offence under s 501 of the CA 2006.[6268]

Nothing in this section compels a person to disclose information in respect of which a claim to legal professional privilege (in Scotland, to confidentiality of communications) could be maintained in legal proceedings.[6269]

Auditor's rights to information: offences

23.35 Section 501 of the CA 2006 deals with offences and sanctions in respect of auditors' rights to information. A person commits an offence who knowingly or recklessly makes to an auditor of a company a statement (oral or written) that conveys or purports to convey any information or explanations that the auditor requires, or is entitled to require, under s 499 of the CA 2006,[6270] and is misleading, false or deceptive in a material particular.[6271]

A person guilty of an offence under s 501(1) of the CA 2006 is liable on conviction on indictment, to imprisonment for a term not exceeding two years or a fine (or both);[6272] and on summary conviction in England and Wales, to imprisonment for a term not exceeding 12 months or to a fine not exceeding the statutory maximum (or both);[6273] in Scotland or Northern Ireland, to imprisonment for a term not exceeding six months or to a fine not exceeding the statutory maximum (or both).[6274]

A person who fails to comply with a requirement under s 499 of the CA 2006 without delay commits an offence unless it was not reasonably practicable for him to provide the required information or explanations.[6275]

If a parent company fails to comply with s 500 of the CA 2006, an offence is committed by the company,[6276] and every officer of the company who is in default.[6277] A person guilty of an offence under s 501(3) or (4) of the CA 2006 is liable on summary conviction to a fine not exceeding level 3 on the standard scale.[6278]

Nothing in this section affects any right of an auditor to apply for an injunction (in Scotland, an interdict or an order for specific performance) to enforce any of his rights under ss 499 or 500 of the CA 2006.[6279]

[6267] CA 2006, s 500(3).   [6268] CA 2006, s 500(4).   [6269] CA 2006, s 500(5).
[6270] CA 2006, s 501(1)(a).   [6271] CA 2006, s 501(1)(b).   [6272] CA 2006, s 501(2)(a).
[6273] CA 2006, s 501(2)(b)(i).   [6274] CA 2006, s 501(2)(b)(ii).   [6275] CA 2006, s 501(3).
[6276] CA 2006, s 501(4)(a).   [6277] CA 2006, s 501(4)(b).   [6278] CA 2006, s 501(5).
[6279] CA 2006, s 501(6).

Auditor's rights in relation to resolutions and meetings

23.36 Section 502 of the CA 2006 deals with auditors' rights in relation to resolutions and meetings. In relation to a written resolution proposed to be agreed to by a private company, the company's auditor is entitled to receive all such communications relating to the resolution as, by virtue of any provision of Chapter 2 of Part 13 of the CA 2006, are required to be supplied to a member of the company.[6280]

A company's auditor is entitled to receive all notices of, and other communications relating to, any general meeting that a member of the company is entitled to receive,[6281] and to attend any general meeting of the company,[6282] and to be heard at any general meeting that he attends on any part of the business of the meeting that concerns him as auditor.[6283]

Where the auditor is a firm, the right to attend or be heard at a meeting is exercisable by an individual authorised by the firm in writing to act as its representative at the meeting.[6284]

Sections 498–502 of the CA 2006 bring together and restate the existing law on the auditor's duties (currently in s 237 of the CA 1985) in investigating, forming an opinion and making his report; and on the auditor's rights (ss 389A–390 of the CA 1985) to be provided with appropriate information.

Section 498 of the CA 2006 lists areas where an auditor must investigate and report on any problems: the companies accounting records, and whether there is consistency between these and (i) the accounts and (ii) – where there is one – the appropriate part of the directors' remuneration report. The auditor is also to report if he has not been able to get all the information he needs. If possible, he is to make good any gaps in the information relating to payment to directors. And he is report if he believes that the company is taking advantage of the small companies accounts regime without being entitled to do so.

Section 499 of the CA 2006 restates the auditor's right to obtain information and explanations from the company and its UK subsidiaries and from appropriate associated individuals.

Section 500 of the CA 2006 sets out the corresponding right to require the company to obtain information or explanations from any subsidiaries that are incorporated in the UK.

Section 501 of the CA 2006 sets out offences for those who supply inaccurate information to auditors or fail to respond to auditors' requests for information without delay.

Section 502 of the CA 2006 requires a private company to send to its auditors all the information about any written resolutions that it sends to its shareholders. It also gives the auditor of any company – public or private – the right to attend any general meetings it may have, and to be allowed to

---

[6280] CA 2006, s 502(1).   [6281] CA 2006, s 502(2)(a).   [6282] CA 2006, s 502(2)(b).
[6283] CA 2006, s 502(2)(c).   [6284] CA 2006, s 502(3).

speak on anything relevant to the audit. The auditor must also receive all communications relating to general meetings.

Signature of auditor's report

23.37 Section 503 of the CA 2006 deals with the signatory auditor's report. The auditor's report must state the name of the auditor and be signed and dated.[6285]

Where the auditor is an individual, the report must be signed by him.[6286]

Where the auditor is a firm, the report must be signed by the senior statutory auditor in his own name, for and on behalf of the auditor.[6287]

Section 503 of the CA 2006 specifies who must sign the audit report submitted to a company by its auditor. The report must state the name of the audit firm, or if an individual has been appointed an auditor, his name. This is as currently required by s 236 of the CA 1985.

For cases where the auditor is a firm, the section then makes a change from the CA 1985 by requiring the signature of an individual, the 'senior statutory auditor', as defined in s 504 of the CA 2006 to sign the report in his own name on behalf of the firm. This implements a new requirement of the Audit Directive (2006/43/EC). If the auditor is an individual, he must sign as under the CA 1985.

Senior statutory auditor

23.38 Section 504 of the CA 2006 of the CA 2006 deals with senior statutory auditors. The senior statutory auditor means the individual identified by the firm as senior statutory auditor in relation to the audit in accordance with standards issued by the European Commission,[6288] or if there is no applicable standard so issued, any relevant guidance issued by the Secretary of State,[6289] or a body appointed by order of the Secretary of State.[6290]

The person identified as senior statutory auditor must be eligible for appointment as auditor of the company in question (see Chapter 2 of Part 42 of the CA 2006).[6291]

The senior statutory auditor is not, by reason of being named or identified as senior statutory auditor or by reason of his having signed the auditor's report, subject to any civil liability to which he would not otherwise be subject.[6292]

An order appointing a body for the purpose of s 504(1)(b)(ii) of the CA 2006 is subject to negative resolution procedure.[6293]

Section 504 of the CA 2006 defines a new term, the 'senior statutory

---

[6285] CA 2006, s 503(1).   [6286] CA 2006, s 503(2).   [6287] CA 2006, s 503(3).
[6288] CA 2006, s 504(1)(a).   [6289] CA 2006, s 504(1)(b)(i).   [6290] CA 2006, s 504(1)(b)(ii).
[6291] CA 2006, s 504(2).   [6292] CA 2006, s 504(3).   [6293] CA 2006, s 504(4).

auditor', for the individual who will be asked to sign his name to an audit report carried out by a firm. The firm will identify this individual according to standards to be issued by the European Commission, or if there are no standards, to guidance issued either by the Secretary of State or by a body appointed by him by an order subject to negative resolution.

Section 504(2) of the CA 2006 specifies that to be eligible to be a senior statutory auditor of a company, an individual must be eligible himself to be appointed as auditor of the company.

Section 504(3) of the CA 2006 ensures that nomination of any individual as senior statutory auditor will not affect his exposure to liability in any way.

Name of auditor, etc. to be stated in published copies of auditor's report

23.39 Section 505 of the CA 2006 deals with name of auditor to be stated in published copies of the auditor's report. Every copy of the auditor's report that is published by or on behalf of the company must state the name of the auditor and (where the auditor is a firm) the name of the person who signed it as senior statutory auditor,[6294] or if the conditions in s 506 of the CA 2006 (circumstances in which names may be omitted) are met, state that a resolution has been passed and notified to the Secretary of State in accordance with that section.[6295]

A company is regarded as publishing the report if it publishes, issues or circulates it or otherwise makes it available for public inspection in a manner calculated to invite members of the public generally, or any class of members of the public, to read it.[6296]

If a copy of the auditor's report is published without the statement required by this section, an offence is committed by the company, and every officer of the company who is in default.[6297] A person guilty of an offence under this section is liable on summary conviction to a fine not exceeding level 3 on the standard scale.[6298]

Section 505 of the CA 2006 requires a company to ensure that the copies of its auditor's report it sends out include the name of the auditor and of the senior statutory auditor if there is one, or to say that it is taking advantage of the exemption in the following section.

Section 505(2) of the CA 2006 provides that this includes copies circulated to shareholders, as well as any others that would be expected to be seen by members of the public. It does not, however, cover copies sent to the registrar: these are dealt with by ss 444(7), 445(6), 446(4) and 447(4) of the CA 2006.

[6294] CA 2006, s 505(1)(a).   [6295] CA 2006, s 505(1)(b).   [6296] CA 2006, s 505(2).
[6297] CA 2006, s 505(3).   [6298] CA 2006, s 505(4).

Section 505(3) and (4) of the CA 2006 restate the offence, currently in s 236 of the CA 1985, of not including the auditor's name – and now also the senior statutory auditor's name – as required.

Circumstances in which names may be omitted

23.40 Section 506 of the CA 2006 deals with the circumstances in which names may be omitted. The auditor's name and, where the auditor is a firm, the name of the person who signed the report as senior statutory auditor, may be omitted from published copies of the report,[6299] and the copy of the report delivered to the registrar under Chapter 10 to Part 15 of the CA 2006 (filing of accounts and reports),[6300] if the following conditions are met.

The conditions are that the company:

(a) considering on reasonable grounds that statement of the name would create or be likely to create a serious risk that the auditor or senior statutory auditor, or any other person, would be subject to violence or intimidation, has resolved that the name should not be stated;[6301] and

(b) has given notice of the resolution to the Secretary of State, stating (i) the name and registered number of the company,[6302] (ii) the financial year of the company to which the report relates,[6303] and (iii) the name of the auditor and (where the auditor is a firm) the name of the person who signed the report as senior statutory auditor.[6304]

Section 506 of the CA 2006 provides an exemption from the requirements to include the names of the auditor in both the published and filed copies of the audit report. This is available if the company passes a resolution not to reveal the names because it considers on reasonable grounds that revealing them would lead to a serious risk of violence or intimidation. It is also a condition of using the exemption that the company must inform the Secretary of State, giving details of the name of the auditor, and of the senior auditor, if there is one.

Offences in connection with the auditor's report

23.41 Section 507 of the CA 2006 deals with the offences in connection with the auditor's report. A person to whom this section applies commits an offence if he knowingly or recklessly causes a report under s 495 of the CA 2006 (auditor's report on a company's annual accounts) to include any matter that is misleading, false or deceptive in a material particular.[6305]

[6299] CA 2006, s 506(1)(a).   [6300] CA 2006, s 506(1)(b).   [6301] CA 2006, s 506(2)(a).
[6302] CA 2006, s 506(2)(b)(i).   [6303] CA 2006, s 506(2)(b)(ii).
[6304] CA 2006, s 506(2)(b)(iii).   [6305] CA 2006, s 507(1).

A person to whom this section applies commits an offence if he knowingly or recklessly causes such a report to omit a statement required by:

(a)   s 492(2)(b) of the CA 2006 (statement that a company's accounts do not agree with accounting records and returns);[6306]

(b)   s 492(3) of the CA 2006 (statement that necessary information and explanations are not obtained);[6307] or

(c)   s 498(5) of the CA 2006 (statement that directors wrongly took advantage of exemption from the obligation to prepare group accounts).[6308]

Section 507 of the CA 2006 applies where the auditor is an individual, to that individual and any employee or agent of his who is eligible for appointment as auditor of the company;[6309] or where the auditor is a firm, any director, member, employee or agent of the firm who is eligible for appointment as auditor of the company.[6310]

A person guilty of an offence under this section is liable on conviction on indictment, to a fine;[6311] on summary conviction, to a fine not exceeding the statutory maximum.[6312]

Section 507 of the CA 2006 creates a new criminal offence in relation to inaccurate auditors' reports. The offence consists of knowingly or recklessly causing a report to include anything that is misleading, false or deceptive; or omitting a required statement of a problem with the accounts or audit.

Section 507(1) of the CA 2006 sets out the offence of commission, and s 507(2) of the CA 2006 that of omission. The items whose omission can be an offence are listed in paras (a)–(c) of s 507(2) of the CA 2006: statements about inadequate accounting records not being properly reflected in the accounts, and about the auditor having been unable to obtain all necessary information and explanations, and about the directors wrongly claiming the company is exempt from the requirement of group accounts.

Section 507(3) of the CA 2006 defines the individuals potentially caught by the offence as the auditor, if a sole practitioner, or his employees or agents; or the directors, members, employees and agents of an audit firm. But the offence only applies to such an individual if he is an accountant who would be qualified to act as an auditor of the company in his own right.

Section 507(4) of the CA 2006 sets out the maximum penalty as an unlimited fine.

[6306] CA 2006, s 507(2)(a).   [6307] CA 2006, s 507(2)(b).   [6308] CA 2006, s 507(2)(c).
[6309] CA 2006, s 507(3)(a).   [6310] CA 2006, s 507(3)(b).   [6311] CA 2006, s 507(4)(a).
[6312] CA 2006, s 507(4)(b).

*Guidance for regulatory and prosecuting authorities: England, Wales
and Northern Ireland*

23.42 Section 508 of the CA 2006 deals with guidance for regulatory and
persecuting authorities in England, Wales and Northern Ireland. The
Secretary of State may issue guidance for the purpose of helping relevant
regulatory and prosecuting authorities to determine how they should carry
out their functions in cases where behaviour occurs that:

(a)   appears to involve the commission of an offence under s 507 of the CA
      2006 (offences in connection with the auditor's report);[6313] and
(b)   has been, is being or may be investigated pursuant to arrangements (i)
      under para 15 of Schedule 10 to the CA 2006 (investigation of com-
      plaints against auditors and supervisory bodies),[6314] or (ii) of a kind
      mentioned in para 24 of that Schedule (independent investigation for
      disciplinary purposes of public interest cases).[6315]

The Secretary of State must obtain the consent of the Attorney General
before issuing any such guidance.[6316]
   The term 'relevant regulatory and prosecuting authorities' means:

(a)   supervisory bodies within the meaning of Part 42 of the CA 2006;[6317]
(b)   bodies to which the Secretary of State may make grants under s 16(1) of
      the Companies (Audit, Investigations and Community Enterprise) Act
      2004 (c 27) (bodies concerned with accounting standards, etc.);[6318]
(c)   the Director of the Serious Fraud Office (SFO);[6319]
(d)   the Director of Public Prosecutions or the Director of Public Prosecu-
      tions for Northern Ireland;[6320] and
(e)   the Secretary of State.[6321]

This section does not apply to Scotland.
   Section 508 of the CA 2006 enables the Secretary of State to issue guidance
about handling matters where the same auditor's report could give rise both
to disciplinary proceedings by a regulatory body and to prosecution for the
new offence. Section 508(2) of the CA 2006 requires the Secretary of State to
obtain the Attorney's General agreement to any guidance.
   Section 508(3) of the CA 2006 lists the regulatory and prosecuting authorities that the guidance would be intended to help. The list comprises the
accountancy supervisory bodies, recipients of grants under s 16 of the
Companies (Audit, Investigations and Community Enterprise) Act 2004

[6313] CA 2006, s 508(1)(a). [6314] CA 2006, s 508(1)(b)(i). [6315] CA 2006, s 508(1)(b)(ii).
[6316] CA 2006, s 508(2). [6317] CA 2006, s 508(3)(a). [6318] CA 2006, s 508(3)(b).
[6319] CA 2006, s 508(3)(c). [6320] CA 2006, s 508(3)(d). [6321] CA 2006, s 508(3)(e).

(currently the Financial Reporting Council and its subsidiaries), the Director of the Serious Fraud Office and the Director of Public Prosecutions, as well as the Secretary of State himself. Under s 508(4) of the CA 2006, the Secretary of State's guidance is limited to England, Wales and Northern Ireland.

It is likely that one of the most important aspects of the guidance would be to enable prosecutors to decide not to prosecute in a particular case that would be better handled in disciplinary proceedings.

Guidance for regulatory authorities: Scotland

23.43 Section 509 of the CA 2006 deals with guidance for regulatory authorities in Scotland. The Lord Advocate may issue guidance for the purpose of helping relevant regulatory authorities to determine how they should carry out their functions in cases where behaviour occurs that:

(a)   appears to involve the commission of an offence under s 507 of the CA 2006 (offences in connection with an auditor's report);[6322] and

(b)   has been, is being or may be investigated pursuant to arrangements (i) under para 15 of Schedule 10 to the CA 2006 (investigations of complaints against auditors and supervisory bodies),[6323] or (ii) of a kind mentioned in para 24 of that Schedule (independent investigations for disciplinary purposes of public interest cases).[6324]

The Lord Advocate must consult the Secretary of State before issuing any such guidance.[6325]

The term 'relevant regulatory authorities' means:

(a)   supervisory bodies within the meaning of Part 42 of the CA 2006;[6326]

(b)   bodies to which the Secretary of State may make grants under s 16(1) of the Companies (Audit, Investigations and Community Enterprise) Act 2004 (bodies concerned with accounting standards, etc.);[6327] and

(c)   the Secretary of State.[6328]

This section applies only to Scotland.[6329]

Section 509 of the CA 2006 enables the Lord Advocate to issue guidance about handling matters in Scotland where the same auditor's report and could give rise both to disciplinary proceedings by a regulatory body and to prosecution of the new offence. Section 509(2) of the CA 2006 requires the Lord Advocate to consult the Secretary of State before issuing guidance.

Section 509(3) of the CA 2006 lists the regulatory bodies that the guidance

---

[6322] CA 2006, s 509(1)(a).   [6323] CA 2006, s 509(1)(b)(i).   [6324] CA 2006, s 509(1)(b)(ii).
[6325] CA 2006, s 509(2).   [6326] CA 2006, s 509(3)(a).   [6327] CA 2006, s 509(3)(b).
[6328] CA 2006, s 509(3)(c).   [6329] CA 2006, s 509(4).

in intended to help. The list comprises the accountancy supervisory bodies, recipients of grants under s 16 of the C(AICE) Act 2004 (currently the Financial Reporting Council and its Subsidiaries), and the Secretary of State.

Removal, Resignation, etc. of Auditors

23.44 Chapter 4 of Part 16 of the CA 2006 applies to the removal and resignation of auditors. It comprises 17 sections. This Chapter restates the law on the ways in which auditors can cease to hold office. The old provisions were in ss 388 and 391–394A of the CA 1985.

There are some changes to the law resulting from the changes elsewhere in the CA 2006, making it easier to pass written resolutions. There are also changes in the requirements when auditors leave office: increasing the range of cases in which there is a requirement for a statement explaining why they are leaving, and requiring copies of any statement to be sent to shareholders and to appropriate regulators.

Resolutions removing auditors from office

23.45 Section 510 of the CA 2006 deals with the resolution for removing auditors from office. The members of a company may by ordinary resolution at any time remove an auditor from office at any time.[6330]

This power is exercisable only by ordinary resolution at a meeting;[6331] and in accordance with s 511 of the CA 2006 (special notice of a resolution to remove auditor).[6332]

Nothing in this section is to be taken as depriving the person removed of compensation or damages payable to him in respect of the termination of his appointment as auditor,[6333] or of any appointment terminating with that as auditor.[6334]

An auditor may not be removed from office before the expiration of his term of office except by resolution under this section.[6335]

Section 510 of the CA 2006 restates the law on the ways on which the auditors can cease to hold office. The provisions were previously in s 388 and ss 391–394A of the CA 1985. There are some changes to the law under elsewhere under the CA 2006 relating to written resolutions of private companies. There are also changes in the requirements when auditors leave office: increasing the range of cases in which there is a requirement for a statement explaining why they are leaving, and for copies of any statement to be sent to shareholders and to appropriate regulators.

[6330] CA 2006, s 510(1).   [6331] CA 2006, s 510(2)(a).   [6332] CA 2006, s 510(2)(b).
[6333] CA 2006, s 510(3)(a).   [6334] CA 2006, s 510(3)(b).   [6335] CA 2006, s 510(4).

Special notice required for resolution removing an auditor from office

23.46 Section 511 of the CA 2006 deals with the special notice required for a resolution to remove an auditor from office. Special notice is required for a resolution at a general meeting of a company removing an auditor from office.[6336]

On receipt of notice of such an intended resolution, the company must immediately send a copy of it to the person proposed to be removed.[6337]

The auditor proposed to be removed may make with respect to the intended resolution representations in writing to the company (not exceeding a reasonable length) and request their notification to members of the company.[6338]

The company must (unless the representations are received by it too late for it to do so) in any notice of the resolution given to members of the company, state the fact of the representations having been made,[6339] and send a copy of the representations to every member of the company to whom notice of the meeting is or has been sent.[6340]

If a copy of any such representations is not sent out as required because received too late or because of the company's default, the auditor may (without prejudice to his right to be heard orally) require that the representations be read out at the meeting.[6341]

Copies of the representations need not be sent out and the representations need not be read at the meeting if, on the application either of the company or of any other person claiming to be aggrieved, the court is satisfied that the auditor is using the provisions of this section to secure needless publicity for defamatory matter.[6342]

The court may order the company's costs (in Scotland, expenses) on the application to be paid in whole or in part by the auditor, notwithstanding that he is not a party to the application.[6343]

Section 511 of the CA 2006 restates the requirement that a resolution to dismiss an auditor needs special notice (i.e. 28 days before the general meeting, as defined in s 312 of the CA 2006). The company must send a copy to the auditor it is proposed to dismiss and then he has the right to make the statement of his case. The company then has to circulate his statement to the shareholders (or if time does not allow, the statement can be read out at the meeting).

Section 511(6) of the CA 2006 provides protection if the auditor it is proposed to dismiss abuses his right to have a statement circulated to secure needless publicity for defamatory material. It enables the company, or any one else who is aggrieved, to apply to the court, and the court can then

---

[6336] CA 2006, s 511(1).   [6337] CA 2006, s 511(2).   [6338] CA 2006, s 511(3).
[6339] CA 2006, s 511(4)(a).   [6340] CA 2006, s 511(4)(b).   [6341] CA 2006, s 511(5).
[6342] CA 2006, s 511(6).   [6343] CA 2006, s 512(4)(a).

determine whether the auditor is using the provision in that way, in which case the company is not obliged to circulate the statement. The court can order the auditor to pay some or all of the costs of the proceedings.

Notice to the registrar of resolution removing the auditor from office

23.47 Section 512 of the CA 2006 deals with the notice to the registrar of the resolution removing auditor from office.

Where a resolution is passed under s 510 of the CA 2006 (resolution removing the auditor from office), the company must give notice of that fact to the registrar within 14 days.[6344]

If a company fails to give the notice required by this section, an offence is committed by the company,[6345] and every officer of it who is in default.[6346] A person guilty of an offence under this section is liable on summary conviction to a fine not exceeding level 3 on the standard scale and, for continued contravention, a daily default fine not exceeding one-tenth of level 3 on the standard scale.[6347]

Section 511 of the CA 2006 restates the obligation on a company that has decided to dismiss its auditor to inform the registrar within 14 days.

Rights of an auditor who has been removed from office

23.48 Section 513 of the CA 2006 applies to the rights of auditors who have been removed from office. An auditor who has been removed by resolution under s 510 of the CA 2006 has, notwithstanding his removal, the rights conferred by s 502(2) of the CA 2006 in relation to any general meeting of the company at which his term of office would otherwise have expired,[6348] or at which it is proposed to fill the vacancy caused by his removal.[6349]

In such a case the references in that section to matters concerning the auditor as auditor shall be construed as references to matters concerning him as a former auditor.[6350]

Section 513 of the CA 2006 restates the right of a dismissed auditor to attend appropriate meetings, namely any meeting at which his term of office would have expired (i.e. a public company's accounts meeting), or any meeting at which it is proposed to replace him.

Failure to re-appoint auditor: special procedure required for written resolution

23.49 Section 514 of the CA 2006 applies where a resolution is proposed as a written resolution of a private company whose effect would be to appoint a

---

[6344] CA 2006, s 512(1).   [6345] CA 2006, s 512(2)(a).   [6346] CA 2006, s 512(2)(b).
[6347] CA 2006, s 512(3).   [6348] CA 2006, s 513(1)(a).   [6349] CA 2006, s 513(1)(b).
[6350] CA 2006, s 513(2).

person as auditor in place of a person (the outgoing auditor) whose term of office has expired, or is to expire, at the end of the period for appointing auditors.[6351]

The following provisions apply if no period for appointing auditors has ended since the outgoing auditor ceased to hold office,[6352] or such a period has ended and an auditor or auditors should have been appointed but were not.[6353]

The company must send a copy of the proposed resolution to the person proposed to be appointed and to the outgoing auditor.[6354]

The outgoing auditor may, within 14 days of receiving the notice, make with respect to the proposed resolution representations in writing to the company (not exceeding a reasonable length) and request their circulation to members of the company.[6355]

The company must circulate the representations together with the copy or copies of the resolution circulated in accordance with s 291 of the CA 2006 (resolution proposed by directors) or s 293 of the CA 2006 (resolution proposed by members).[6356]

Where s 515(5) of the CA 2006 applies (a) the period allowed under s 293(3) of the CA 2006 for service of copies of the proposed resolution is 28 days instead of 21 days;[6357] and (b) the provisions of s 293(5) and (6) of the CA 2006 (offences) apply in relation to a failure to comply with that subsection as in relation to a default in complying with that section.[6358]

Copies of the representations need not be circulated if, on the application either of the company or of any other person claiming to be aggrieved, the court is satisfied that the auditor is using the provisions of this section to secure needless publicity for defamatory matter.

The court may order the company's costs (in Scotland, expenses) on the application to be paid in whole or in part by the auditor, notwithstanding that he is not a party to the application.[6359]

If any requirement of this section is not complied with, the resolution is ineffective.[6360]

Section 514 of the CA 2006 sets out procedure for changing auditor from one financial year to the next by written resolution (a procedure only available to private companies). This may be done (i) during the term of office of the outgoing auditor, or (ii) afterwards, if no replacement has been appointed. But case (ii) will arise only if there is no automatic deemed re-appointment for one of the five reasons in s 487(2) of the CA 2006.

Section 514(3) of the CA 2006 provides that the company must first send a copy of the proposed resolution both to the outgoing auditor and to his

---

[6351] CA 2006, s 514(1).   [6352] CA 2006, s 514(2)(a).   [6353] CA 2006, s 514(2)(b).
[6354] CA 2006, s 514(3).   [6355] CA 2006, s 514(4).   [6356] CA 2006, s 514(5).
[6357] CA 2006, s 514(6)(a).   [6358] CA 2006, s 514(6)(b).   [6359] CA 2006, s 514(7).
[6360] CA 2006, s 514(8).

proposed replacement; and s 514(4) of the CA 2006 provides that the former then has 14 days to make a statement setting out his views. Section 514(5) of the CA 2006 then provides that the company should send to its shareholders, the resolution together with any statement from the outgoing auditor. Section 514(6) of the CA 2006 specifies how the general rules on written resolutions are to apply in this case.

Section 514(7) of the CA 2006 provides if the outgoing auditor abuses his right to have a statement circulated, to ensure needless publicity for defamatory material. It enables the company, or anyone else who is aggrieved by the statement, apply to the court and the court can then determine whether the auditor is using the provision in that way, in which case the company is not obliged to circulate the auditor's representations. The court can order the auditor to pay some or all the costs of the proceedings.

Section 514(8) of the CA 2006 provides that failure to comply with the rules in this clause will make the resolution ineffective.

Failure to re-appoint auditor: special notice required for resolution at a general meeting

23.50 Section 515 of the CA 2006 deals with failure to re-appoint an auditor with respect to the special notice required for a resolution at a general meeting. It applies to a resolution at a general meeting of a company whose effect would be to appoint a person as auditor in place of a person (the outgoing auditor) whose term of office has ended, or is to end in the case of a private company, at the end of the period for appointing auditors;[6361] or in the case of a public company, at the end of the next accounts meeting.[6362]

Special notice is required of such a resolution if:

(a) in the case of a private company (i) no period for appointing auditors has ended since the outgoing auditor ceased to hold office,[6363] or (ii) such a period has ended and an auditor or auditors should have been appointed but were not;[6364]

(b) in the case of a public company (i) there has been no accounts meeting of the company since the outgoing auditor ceased to hold office,[6365] or (ii) there has been an accounts meeting at which an auditor or auditors should have been appointed but were not.[6366]

On receipt of notice of such an intended resolution the company shall forthwith send a copy of it to the person proposed to be appointed and to the outgoing auditor.[6367]

[6361] CA 2006, s 515(1)(a).   [6362] CA 2006, s 515(1)(b).   [6363] CA 2006, s 515(2)(a)(i).
[6364] CA 2006, s 515(2)(a)(ii).   [6365] CA 2006, s 515(2)(b)(i).   [6366] CA 2006, s 515(2)(b)(ii).
[6367] CA 2006, s 515(3).

The outgoing auditor may make with respect to the intended resolution representations in writing to the company (not exceeding a reasonable length) and request their notification to members of the company.[6368]

The company must (unless the representations are received by it too late for it to do so) in any notice of the resolution given to members of the company, state the fact of the representations having been made,[6369] and send a copy of the representations to every member of the company to whom notice of the meeting is or has been sent.[6370]

If a copy of any such representations is not sent out as required because received too late or because of the company's default, the outgoing auditor may (without prejudice to his right to be heard orally) require that the representations be read out at the meeting.[6371]

Copies of the representations need not be sent out and the representations need not be read at the meeting if, on the application either of the company or of any other person claiming to be aggrieved, the court is satisfied that the auditor is using the provisions of this section to secure needless publicity for defamatory matter.

The court may order the company's costs (in Scotland, expenses) on the application to be paid in whole or in part by the outgoing auditor, notwithstanding that he is not a party to the application.[6372]

Section 515 of the CA 2006 sets out the procedure for changing auditor between one financial year and the next at a general meeting. This may be done by resolution at the meeting, but special notice is required if no deadline for appointing auditors has passed since the outgoing auditor left, or if the deadline has passed when an auditor should have been appointed without one being appointed. So, for example, if a public company chooses not to re-appoint an auditor at its accounts meeting, but later (before the next accounts meeting) changes its mind, it would need to give special notice of a general meeting appointing replacement auditors.

Section 515(3) of the CA 2006 provides that immediately it receives a proposed resolution for changing the auditor, the company should send a copy of it both to the outgoing auditor and to his proposed replacement; and s 515(4) of the CA 2006 provides that the former may then send the company a written statement setting out his views. Section 515(5) and (6) of the CA 2006 provides that the company should send its shareholders any statement from the outgoing auditor, and that if it is received too late for this it should be read out at the meeting.

Section 515(7) of the CA 2006 provides protection if the outgoing auditor abuses his right to have representations circulated, e.g. by providing defamatory material to be published. It enables the company, or someone else, to

---

[6368] CA 2006, s 515(4).   [6369] CA 2006, s 515(5)(a).   [6370] CA 2006, s 515(5)(b).
[6371] CA 2006, s 515(6).   [6372] CA 2006, s 515(7).

apply to the court and the court can then determine whether the right is being abused, in which case the company is not obliged to circulate the auditor's representations, nor need they be read out at the meeting. The court can order the auditor to pay some or all the costs of the proceedings.

Resignation of an auditor

23.51 Section 516 of the CA 2006 deals with the resignation of auditor. An auditor of a company may resign his office by depositing a notice in writing to that effect at the company's registered office.[6373]

The notice is not effective unless it is accompanied by the statement required by s 519 of the CA 2006.[6374]

An effective notice of resignation operates to bring the auditor's term of office to an end as of the date on which the notice is deposited or on such later date as may be specified in it.[6375]

Section 516 of the CA 2006 restates the right of an auditor to resign by written notice to the company. His resignation is effective from the date it is delivered to the company's registered office, or from a latter date specified in it. To be effective, it must be accompanied by the statement required by s 519 of the CA 2006.

Notice to registrar of resignation of an auditor

23.52 Section 517 of the CA 2006 deals with notice to the registrar of the resignation of an auditor. Where an auditor resigns the company must within 14 days of the deposit of a notice of resignation send a copy of the notice to the registrar of companies.[6376]

If a default is made in complying with this section, an offence is committed by the company,[6377] and every officer of the company who is in default.[6378] A person guilty of an offence under this section is liable on conviction on indictment, to a fine and, for continued contravention, a daily default fine not exceeding one-tenth of the statutory maximum;[6379] and on summary conviction, to a fine not exceeding the statutory maximum and, for continued contravention, a daily default fine not exceeding one-tenth of the statutory maximum.[6380]

This section restates the obligation on a company whose auditor resigns to inform the registrar. Default in complying is an offence.

[6373] CA 2006, s 516(1).   [6374] CA 2006, s 516(2).   [6375] CA 2006, s 516(3).
[6376] CA 2006, s 517(1).   [6377] CA 2006, s 517(2)(a).   [6378] CA 2006, s 517(2)(b).
[6379] CA 2006, s 517(3)(a).   [6380] CA 2006, s 517(3)(b).

Rights of a resigning auditor

23.53 Section 518 of the CA 2006 applies where an auditor's notice of resignation is accompanied by a statement of the circumstances connected with his resignation (see s 519 of the CA 2006).[6381]

He may deposit with the notice a signed requisition calling on the directors of the company forthwith duly to convene a general meeting of the company for the purpose of receiving and considering such explanation of the circumstances connected with his resignation as he may wish to place before the meeting.[6382]

He may request the company to circulate to its members before the meeting convened on his requisition,[6383] or before any general meeting at which his term of office would otherwise have expired or at which it is proposed to fill the vacancy caused by his resignation,[6384] a statement in writing (not exceeding a reasonable length) of the circumstances connected with his resignation.

The company must (unless the statement is received too late for it to comply) in any notice of the meeting given to members of the company, state the fact of the statement having been made,[6385] and send a copy of the statement to every member of the company to whom notice of the meeting is or has been sent.[6386]

The directors must within 21 days from the date of the deposit of a requisition under this section proceed duly to convene a meeting for a day not more than 28 days after the date on which the notice convening the meeting is given.[6387]

If default is made in complying with s 518(5) of the CA 2006, every director who failed to take all reasonable steps to secure that a meeting was convened commits an offence.[6388] A person guilty of an offence under this section is liable on conviction on indictment, to a fine;[6389] and on summary conviction to a fine not exceeding the statutory maximum.[6390]

If a copy of the statement mentioned above is not sent out as required because received too late or because of the company's default, the auditor may (without prejudice to his right to be heard orally) require that the statement be read out at the meeting.[6391]

Copies of a statement need not be sent out and the statement need not be read out at the meeting if, on the application either of the company or of any other person who claims to be aggrieved, the court is satisfied that the auditor is using the provisions of this section to secure needless publicity for defamatory matter.

[6381] CA 2006, s 518(1).   [6382] CA 2006, s 518(2).   [6383] CA 2006, s 518(3)(a).
[6384] CA 2006, s 518(3)(b).   [6385] CA 2006, s 518(4)(a).   [6386] CA 2006, s 518(4)(b).
[6387] CA 2006, s 518(5).   [6388] CA 2006, s 518(6).   [6389] CA 2006, s 518(7)(a).
[6390] CA 2006, s 518(7)(b).   [6391] CA 2006, s 518(8).

The court may order the company's costs (in Scotland, expenses) on such an application to be paid in whole or in part by the auditor, notwithstanding that he is not a party to the application.[6392]

An auditor who has resigned has, notwithstanding his resignation, the rights conferred by s 502(2) of the CA 2006 in relation to any such general meeting of the company as is mentioned in s 518(3)(a) or (b) of the CA 2006 above.

In such a case the references in that section to matters concerning the auditor as auditor shall be construed as references to matters concerning him as a former auditor.[6393]

Section 518 of the CA 2006 restates the right of an auditor who resigns to require the directors to convene a general meeting of the company so that it can consider his explanation of the circumstances that led to his decision to resign. The auditor can ask the company to send out a written explanation either in advance of that meeting if he has requested one, or before the next general meeting.

The directors have 21 days to send out a notice convening a meeting once a resigning auditor has asked for it and it must be held within 28 days of the notice.

Section 518(9) of the CA 2006 provides protection if the resigning auditor abuses his right to have an explanatory statement circulated, e.g. requesting defamatory material to be published. It enables the company, or someone else, to apply to the court and the court can determine whether the right is being abused, in which case the company is not obliged to circulate the statement. The court can order the auditor to pay some or all of the costs of the proceedings.

Statement by auditor to be deposited with the company

23.54 Section 519 of the CA 2006 deals with the statement by auditor to be deposited with company. Where an auditor of an unquoted company ceases for any reason to hold office, he must deposit at the company's registered office a statement of the circumstances connected with his ceasing to hold office, unless he considers that there are no circumstances in connection with his ceasing to hold office that need to be brought to the attention of members or creditors of the company.[6394]

If he considers that there are no circumstances in connection with his ceasing to hold office that need to be brought to the attention of members or creditors of the company, he must deposit at the company's registered office a statement to that effect.[6395]

[6392] CA 2006, s 518(9).   [6393] CA 2006, s 518(10).   [6394] CA 2006, s 519(1).
[6395] CA 2006, s 519(2).

Where an auditor of a quoted company ceases for any reason to hold office, he must deposit at the company's registered office a statement of the circumstances connected with his ceasing to hold office.[6396]

The statement required by this section must be deposited:

(a) in the case of resignation, along with the notice of resignation;[6397]

(b) in the case of failure to seek re-appointment, not less than 14 days before the end of the time allowed for next appointing an auditor;[6398]

(c) in any other case, not later than the end of the period of 14 days beginning with the date on which he ceases to hold office.[6399]

A person ceasing to hold office as auditor who fails to comply with this section commits an offence.[6400]

In proceedings for such an offence it is a defence for the person charged to show that he took all reasonable steps and exercised all due diligence to avoid the commission of the offence.[6401]

A person guilty of an offence under this section is liable on conviction on indictment, to a fine;[6402] on summary conviction, to a fine not exceeding the statutory maximum.[6403]

Section 519 of the CA 2006 requires a departing auditor to make a statement when he stops being the auditor of a company and to deposit it with the company. For quoted companies, this statement should explain the circumstances surrounding his departure. For other public companies and all private companies, it should be explain the circumstances unless the auditor thinks that there is no need for them to be brought to the attention of the shareholders or creditors. In that case, the statement should state that there are no such circumstances.

This reverses the position under s 394 of the CA 1985, where auditors were only required to make a statement if they considered there were relevant circumstances, and provides that auditors leaving quoted companies will now always be required to make a statement of the circumstances.

Section 519(4) of the CA 2006 sets out the deadline for depositing such a statement with the company, namely, if the auditor is resigning, the statement should accompany the resignation letter; or if the auditor is deciding not to seek re-appointment, the statement should be deposited at least 14 days before the end of the time allowed for appointing the next auditor; or in any other case, no more than 14 days after the date on which he stops being the auditor.

[6396] CA 2006, s 519(3).   [6397] CA 2006, s 519(4)(a).   [6398] CA 2006, s 519(4)(b).
[6399] CA 2006, s 519(4)(c).   [6400] CA 2006, s 519(5).   [6401] CA 2006, s 519(6).
[6402] CA 2006, s 519(7)(a).   [6403] CA 2006, s 519(7)(b).

Company's duties in relation to statement

23.55 Section 520 of the CA 2006 deals with company's duties in relation to the statement. It applies where the statement deposited under s 519 of the CA 2006 states the circumstances connected with the auditor's ceasing to hold office.[6404]

The company must within 14 days of the deposit of the statement either send a copy of it to every person who under s 423 of the CA 2006 is entitled to be sent copies of the accounts,[6405] or apply to the court.[6406]

If it applies to the court, the company must notify the auditor of the application.[6407]

If the court is satisfied that the auditor is using the provisions of s 519 of the CA 2006 to secure needless publicity for defamatory matter it must direct that copies of the statement need not be sent out,[6408] and it may further order the company's costs (in Scotland, expenses) on the application to be paid in whole or in part by the auditor, even if he is not a party to the application.

The company must within 14 days of the court's decision send to the persons mentioned in s 520(2)(a) of the CA 2006 a statement setting out the effect of the order.[6409]

If no such direction is made the company must send copies of the statement to the persons mentioned in s 520(2)(a) of the CA 2006 within 14 days of the court's decision or, as the case may be, of the discontinuance of the proceedings.[6410]

In the event of a default in complying with this section an offence is committed by every officer of the company who is in default.[6411]

In proceedings for such an offence it is a defence for the person charged to show that he took all reasonable steps and exercised all due diligence to avoid the commission of the offence.[6412]

A person guilty of an offence under this section is liable on conviction on indictment, to a fine;[6413] on summary conviction, to a fine not exceeding the statutory maximum.[6414]

Unless the departing auditor's statement says that there are no circumstances to be brought to the attention of shareholders and creditors, this clause obliges the company to circulate the statement to everyone to whom it needs to send the annual accounts. The company must do this within 14 days of receiving it.

If the company does not want to circulate the statement, e.g. because it appears to be defamatory, it can apply to the court, and if the court decides that the departing auditor is abusing his rights, then the company need not

[6404] CA 2006, s 520(1).　　[6405] CA 2006, s 520(2)(a).　　[6406] CA 2006, s 520(2)(b).
[6407] CA 2006, s 520(3).　　[6408] CA 2006, s 520(4)(a).　　[6409] CA 2006, s 520(4)(b).
[6410] CA 2006, s 520(5).　　[6411] CA 2006, s 520(6).　　[6412] CA 2006, s 520(7).
[6413] CA 2006, s 520(8)(a).　　[6414] CA 2006, s 520(8)(b).

circulate the statement, but instead must send an account of the court decision to those to whom have sent the statement. In the event of a successful application, the court can order the auditor to pay some or all of the costs.

In the event of unsuccessful application, the company must circulate the statement within 14 days of the end of the court proceedings.

Copy of statement to be sent to the registrar

23.56 Section 521 of the CA 2006 deals with a copy of the statement to be sent to the registrar. Unless within 21 days beginning with the day on which he deposited the statement under s 519 of the CA 2006 the auditor receives notice of an application to the court under s 520 of the CA 2006, he must within a further seven days send a copy of the statement to the registrar.[6415]

If an application to the court is made under s 520 of the CA of the 2006 and the auditor subsequently receives notice under s 520(5) of the CA 2006, he must within seven days of receiving the notice send a copy of the statement to the registrar.[6416]

An auditor who fails to comply with s 521(1) or (2) of the CA 2006 commits an offence.[6417]

In proceedings for such an offence it is a defence for the person charged to show that he took all reasonable steps and exercised all due diligence to avoid the commission of the offence.[6418]

A person guilty of an offence under this section is liable on conviction on indictment, to a fine;[6419] on summary conviction, to a fine not exceeding the statutory maximum.[6420]

Section 521 of the CA 2006 provides that the departing auditor must send a copy of his statement to the registrar, normally within 28 days of depositing it with the company.

The auditor is not required to send it to the registrar if within 21 days of depositing it he hears that the company has applied to the court. But if the company lets him know that its application was unsuccessful, then he must send it to the registrar within seven days of being told.

Copy of statement to be sent to the appropriate audit authority

23.57 Section 522 of the CA 2006 deals with a copy of the statement to be sent to the appropriate audit authority.

Where in the case of a major audit, an auditor ceases for any reason to hold office,[6421] or in the case of an audit that is not a major audit, an auditor

---

[6415] CA 2006, s 521(1).   [6416] CA 2006, s 521(2).   [6417] CA 2006, s 521(3).
[6418] CA 2006, s 521(4).   [6419] CA 2006, s 521(5)(a).   [6420] CA 2006, s 521(5)(b).
[6421] CA 2006, s 522(1)(a).

ceases to hold office before the end of his term of office,[6422] the auditor ceasing to hold office must notify the appropriate audit authority.

The notice must inform the appropriate audit authority that he has ceased to hold office,[6423] and be accompanied by a copy of the statement deposited by him at the company's registered office in accordance with s 519 of the CA 2006.[6424]

If the statement so deposited is to the effect that he considers that there are no circumstances in connection with his ceasing to hold office that need to be brought to the attention of members or creditors of the company, the notice must also be accompanied by a statement of the reasons for his ceasing to hold office.[6425]

The auditor must comply with this section (a) in the case of a major audit, at the same time as he deposits a statement at the company's registered office in accordance with s 519 of the CA 2006;[6426] (b) in the case of an audit that is not a major audit, at such time (not being earlier than the time mentioned in para (a)) as the appropriate audit authority may require.[6427]

A person ceasing to hold office as auditor who fails to comply with this section commits an offence.[6428] If that person is a firm an offence is committed by the firm,[6429] and every officer of the firm who is in default.[6430]

In proceedings for an offence under this section it is a defence for the person charged to show that he took all reasonable steps and exercised all due diligence to avoid the commission of the offence.[6431]

A person guilty of an offence under this section is liable on conviction on indictment, to a fine;[6432] on summary conviction, to a fine not exceeding the statutory maximum.[6433]

Section 522 of the CA 2006 introduces a new obligation on departing auditors to send copies of their leaving statements to an appropriate audit authority as defined in s 525 of the CA 2006. It contains different rules depending on whether the company the auditor is leaving is classified as a 'major audit', as defined in s 525 of the CA 2006.

In relation to major audits, the departing auditor should always send a copy of his statement to the appropriate audit authority. He should do this at the same time as he deposits his statement with the company under s 519 of the CA 2006.

In relation to other audits, the departing auditor is required to send his statement to the appropriate audit authority only if he is leaving before the end of his term of office, meaning only if he has resigned or has been dismissed.

[6422] CA 2006, s 522(1)(b).   [6423] CA 2006, s 522(2)(a).   [6424] CA 2006, s 522(2)(b).
[6425] CA 2006, s 522(3).   [6426] CA 2006, s 522(4)(a).   [6427] CA 2006, s 522(4)(b).
[6428] CA 2006, s 522(5).   [6429] CA 2006, s 522(6)(a).   [6430] CA 2006, s 522(6)(b).
[6431] CA 2006, s 522(7).   [6432] CA 2006, s 522(8)(a).   [6433] CA 2006, s 522(8)(b).

Section 522 (3) of the CA 2006 provides that where the auditor's statement to the company said that there were no circumstances that needed to be brought to the attention of shareholders and creditors, that statement must have attached to it a statement of the auditor's reasons for leaving when sending to the audit authority.

Section 522(5)–(8) of the CA 2006 sets out the offence of failure to comply with these requirements and the maximum penalties.

Duty of company to notify the appropriate audit authority

23.58 Section 523 of the CA 2006 applies to the duty of a company to notify the appropriate audit authority. Where an auditor ceases to hold office before the end of his term of office, the company must notify the appropriate audit authority.[6434]

The notice must:

(a)   inform the appropriate audit authority that the auditor has ceased to hold office;[6435] and

(b)   be accompanied by (i) a statement by the company of the reasons for his ceasing to hold office,[6436] or (ii) if the copy of the statement deposited by the auditor at the company's registered office in accordance with s 519 of the CA 2006 contains a statement of circumstances in connection with his ceasing to hold office that need to be brought to the attention of members or creditors of the company, a copy of that statement.[6437]

The company must give notice under this section not later than 14 days after the date on which the auditor's statement is deposited at the company's registered office in accordance with s 519 of the CA 2006.[6438]

If a company fails to comply with this section, an offence is committed by the company,[6439] and every officer of the company who is in default.[6440]

In proceedings for such an offence it is a defence for the person charged to show that he took all reasonable steps and exercised all due diligence to avoid the commission of the offence.[6441]

A person guilty of an offence under this section is liable on conviction on indictment, to a fine;[6442] on summary conviction, to a fine not exceeding the statutory maximum.[6443]

Section 523 of the CA 2006 introduces a new duty on a company to notify the appropriate audit authority whenever an auditor leaves office before the end of his term, that is when he has resigned or is dismissed. The company

---

[6434] CA 2006, s 523(1).   [6435] CA 2006, s 523(2)(a).   [6436] CA 2006, s 523(2)(b)(i).
[6437] CA 2006, s 523(2)(b)(ii).   [6438] CA 2006, s 523(3).   [6439] CA 2006, s 523(4)(a).
[6440] CA 2006, s 523(4)(b).   [6441] CA 2006, s 523(5).   [6442] CA 2006, s 523(6)(a).
[6443] CA 2006, s 523(6)(b).

has the choice of sending in the statement of circumstances made by the auditor under s 519 of the CA 2006, or of sending in its own statement of the reasons. Section 523(3) of the CA 2006 sets out the deadline for notification as 14 days after the auditor has deposited his statement with the company. Section 523(4)–(6) of the CA 2006 sets out the offence of failure to comply with this requirement, and the maximum penalty applies.

Information to be given to accounting authorities

23.59 Section 524 of the CA 2006 deals with information to be given to accounting authorities. The appropriate audit authority on receiving notice under ss 522 or 523 of the CA 2006 of an auditor's ceasing to hold office must inform the accounting authorities,[6444] and may if it thinks fit forward to those authorities a copy of the statement or statements accompanying the notice.[6445]

The accounting authorities are the Secretary of State,[6446] and any person authorised by the Secretary of State for the purposes of s 456 of the CA 2006 (revision of defective accounts: persons authorised to apply to court).[6447]

If either of the accounting authorities is also the appropriate audit authority it is only necessary to comply with this section as regards any other accounting authority.[6448]

If the court has made an order under s 520(4) of the CA 2006 directing that copies of the statement need not be sent out by the company, ss 460 and 461 of the CA 2006 (restriction on further disclosure) apply in relation to the copies sent to the accounting authorities as they apply to information obtained under s 459 of the CA 2006 (power to require documents, etc.).[6449]

Section 524 of the CA 2006 sets out the duty of audit authorities to give the accounting authorities information about departing auditors and if they think it right to do so, to pass on the statements that they receive from departing auditors under s 522 of the CA 2006 as from companies under s 523 of the CA 2006. The accounting authorities are the Secretary of State or anyone the Secretary of State has authorised under Part 15 to apply to the court in respect of the revision of defective accounts. At present this is the Financial Reporting Review Panel, part of the Financial Reporting Council organisation.

Section 524(3) of the CA 2006 deals with situations where the same body is both an audit authority and an accounting authority.

If an accounting authority receives a statement that the court has determined need not be circulated to members, then s 524(4) of the CA 2006 provides that it must treat the statement as confidential, in the same way that

---

[6444] CA 2006, s 524(1)(a). [6445] CA 2006, s 524(1)(b). [6446] CA 2006, s 524(2)(a).
[6447] CA 2006, s 524(2)(b). [6448] CA 2006, s 524(3). [6449] CA 2006, s 524(4).

authorities have to treat information obtained under compulsory powers under Part 15 of the CA 2006.

Meaning of 'appropriate audit authority' and 'major audit'

23.60 Section 525 of the CA 2006 deals with the meaning of 'appropriate audit authority' and 'major audit'. In ss 522, 523 and 524 of the CA 2006 'appropriate audit authority' means in the case of a major audit, the Secretary of State;[6450] or if the Secretary of State has delegated functions under s 1252 of the CA 2006, to a body whose functions include receiving the notice in question, that body;[6451] in the case of an audit that is not a major audit, the relevant supervisory body.[6452]

The term 'supervisory body' has the same meaning as in Part 42 of the CA 2006 (statutory auditors) (s 1213).[6453]

In s 522 of the CA 2006 and this section, 'major audit' means a statutory audit conducted in respect of a company any of whose securities have been admitted to the official list (within the meaning of Part 6 of the Financial Services and Markets Act 2000 (c 8)),[6454] or any other person in whose financial condition there is a major public interest.[6455]

In determining whether an audit is a major audit within s 525(2)(b) of the CA 2006, regard shall be had to any guidance issued by any of the authorities mentioned in s 525(1) of the CA 2006.[6456]

Section 525 of the CA 2006 defines two terms used in connection with the duty to inform the audit authority when an auditor leaves office namely 'appropriate audit authority' and 'major audit'. The former means the Secretary of State, or the body to whom he has delegated functions in relation to the supervision of statutory auditors under Part 42 of the CA 2006, currently the Professional Oversight Board, part of the Financial Reporting Council organisation.

A major audit is defined as meaning the audit of a listed company where there is a major public interest. Whether there is a major public interest is to be determined by reference to guidance issued by any of the audit authorities. In practice, this will generally be guidance issued by the Financial Reporting Council.

Effects of casual vacancies

23.61 Section 526 of the CA 2006 deals with the effect of casual vacancies. If an auditor ceases to hold office for any reason, any surviving or continuing auditor or auditors may continue to act.

[6450] CA 2006, s 525(1)(a)(i).   [6451] CA 2006, s 525(1)(a)(ii).   [6452] CA 2006, s 525(1)(b)(i).
[6453] CA 2006, s 525(1)(b)(ii).   [6454] CA 2006, s 525(2)(a).   [6455] CA 2006, s 525(2)(b).
[6456] CA 2006, s 525(3)(i).

This section applies when one out of two or more joint auditors ceases to be an auditor of the company. It enables the remaining auditors to continue in office. It restates s 388(2) of the CA 1985.

Quoted Companies: Right of Members to Raise Audit Concerns at an Accounts Meeting

23.62 Chapter 5 of Part 16 of the CA 2006 introduces the right of members to raise audit concerns at accounts meetings for quoted companies. All shareholders in a company limited by shares are members. It comprises five sections.

Members' power to require website publication of audit concerns

23.63 Section 527 of the CA 2006 deals with members' power to require website publication of audit concerns. The members of a quoted company may require the company to publish on a website a statement setting out any matter relating to the audit of the company's accounts (including the auditor's report and the conduct of the audit) that are to be laid before the following accounts meeting,[6457] or any circumstances connected with an auditor of the company ceasing to hold office since the previous accounts meeting, that the members propose to raise at the next accounts meeting of the company.[6458]

A company is required to do so once it has received requests to that effect from members representing at least 5 per cent of the total voting rights of all the members who have a relevant right to vote (excluding any voting rights attached to any shares in the company held as treasury shares),[6459] or at least 100 members who have a relevant right to vote and hold shares in the company on which there has been paid up an average sum, per member, of at least £100.[6460]

Under s 527(2) of the CA 2006 a 'relevant right to vote' means a right to vote at the accounts meeting.[6461]

A request (a) may be sent to the company in hard copy or electronic form;[6462] (b) must identify the statement to which it relates;[6463] (c) must be authenticated by the person or persons making it;[6464] and (d) must be received by the company at least one week before the meeting to which it relates.[6465]

A quoted company is not required to place on a website a statement under this section if, on an application by the company or another person who claims to be aggrieved, the court is satisfied that the rights conferred by this section are being abused.[6466]

[6457] CA 2006, s 527(1)(a).   [6458] CA 2006, s 527(1)(b).   [6459] CA 2006, s 527(2)(a).
[6460] CA 2006, s 527(2)(b).   [6461] CA 2006, s 527(3).   [6462] CA 2006, s 527(4)(a).
[6463] CA 2006, s 527(4)(b).   [6464] CA 2006, s 527(4)(c).   [6465] CA 2006, s 527(4)(d).
[6466] CA 2006, s 527(5).

The court may order the members requesting website publication to pay the whole or part of the company's costs (in Scotland, expenses) on such an application, even if they are not parties to the application.[6467]

Section 527 of the CA 2006 creates a new right whereby members of a quoted company – if they have a large enough holding in the company, or there are enough of them – can ask the company to publish on a website a statement raising questions about the accounts, or about the departure of an auditor, that they propose to bring up at the next meeting where the accounts are to be discussed.

Section 527(2) of the CA 2006 specifies the thresholds the members have to meet, which are the same as for shareholders who want to ask a company to circulate a statement under s 314 of the CA 2006; they must either have 5 per cent of the total voting rights, or there must be at least 100 of them, holding shares on which there has been paid up an average sum per member of at least £100.

Section 527(4) of the CA 2006 sets out the mechanics of transmitting the request to the company: it may be in hard copy or electronic.

Section 527(5) of the CA 2006 protects the company if members abuse the new right, for example, by requesting a defamatory statement to be published. It enables the company, or someone else as the auditor, to apply to the court and the court can then determine whether the right is being abused, in which case the company is not obliged to publish the statement. Section 527(6) of the CA 2006 provides that the court can order the shareholders who requested publication to pay some or all of the costs of the proceedings.

Requirements as to website availability

23.64 Section 528 of the CA 2006 deals with requirements as to website availability. The following provisions apply for the purposes of s 527 of the CA 2006 (website publication of members' statements of audit concerns).[6468]

The information must be made available on a website that is maintained by or on behalf of the company,[6469] and identifies the company in question.[6470]

Access to information on the website, and the ability to obtain a hard copy of the information from the website, must not be conditional on the payment of a fee or otherwise restricted.[6471]

The statement must be made available within three working days of the company being required to publish it on a website,[6472] and must be kept available until after the meeting to which it relates.[6473]

A failure to make information available on a website throughout the period specified in s 528(4)(b) of the CA 2006 is disregarded if the information is

---

[6467] CA 2006, s 527(6).   [6468] CA 2006, s 528(1).   [6469] CA 2006, s 528(2)(a).
[6470] CA 2006, s 528(2)(b).   [6471] CA 2006, s 528(3).   [6472] CA 2006, s 528(4)(a).
[6473] CA 2006, s 528(4)(b).

made available on the website for part of that period,[6474] and the failure is wholly attributable to circumstances that it would not be reasonable to have expected the company to prevent or avoid.[6475]

This section sets out the requirements that the company must meet in making the shareholders' statement available on a website, in the same way as s 353 of the CA 2006.

Subsection (4) requires the company to get the statement onto a website within three days of receiving it, and to keep it available at least until after the meeting to which it relates.

Website publication: a company's supplementary duties

23.65 Section 529 of the CA 2006 deals with website publication with respect to the company's supplementary duties. A quoted company must in the notice it gives of the accounts meeting draw attention to the possibility of a statement being placed on a website in pursuance of members' requests under s 527 of the CA 2006,[6476] and the effect of the following provisions of this section.[6477]

A company may not require the members requesting website publication to pay its expenses in complying with that section or s 528 of the CA 2006 (requirements in connection with website publication).[6478]

Where a company is required to place a statement on a website under s 527 of the CA 2006 it must forward the statement to the company's auditor not later than the time when it makes the statement available on the website.[6479]

The business that may be dealt with at the accounts meeting includes any statement that the company has been required under s 527 of the CA 2006 to publish on a website.[6480]

Section 529 of the CA 2006 requires quoted companies to draw attention to the possibility of a website statement in the notice of the accounts meeting. It also specifies that the costs of publication are to be borne by the company.

Section 529(3) of the CA 2006 requires the company to forward the statement to the auditor at the same time as it puts it on a website. Section 529(4) of the CA 2006 provides that – regardless of a company's articles – a statement under this chapter can be dealt with at the accounts meeting.

Website publication: offences

23.66 Section 530 of the CA 2006 deals with the offences and sanctions in respect of website publication. In the event of a default in complying with s 528 of the CA 2006 (requirements as to website publication),[6481] or s 529 of

---

[6474] CA 2006, s 528(5)(a).   [6475] CA 2006, s 528(5)(b).   [6476] CA 2006, s 529(1)(a).
[6477] CA 2006, s 529(1)(b).   [6478] CA 2006, s 529(2).   [6479] CA 2006, s 529(3).
[6480] CA 2006, s 529(4).   [6481] CA 2006, s 530(1)(a).

the CA 2006 (companies' supplementary duties in relation to a request for website publication),[6482] an offence is committed by every officer of the company who is in default.

A person guilty of an offence under s 530 of the CA 2006 is liable on conviction on indictment, to a fine;[6483] on summary conviction, to a fine not exceeding the statutory maximum.[6484]

This section provides for offences when a company fails to comply with either of the preceding two clauses, with maximum penalties of an unlimited fine.

Meaning of 'quoted company'

23.67 Section 531 of the CA 2006 sets out the meaning of 'quoted company'. For the purposes of this Chapter, a company is a quoted company if it is a quoted company in accordance with s 385 of the CA 2006 (quoted and unquoted companies for the purposes of Part 15 of the CA 2006) in relation to the financial year to which the accounts to be laid at the following accounts meeting relate.[6485]

The provisions of s 385(4)–(6) of the CA 2006 (power to amend definition by regulations) apply in relation to the provisions of this Chapter as in relation to the provisions of that Part.[6486]

This section defines the phrase 'quoted company' for the purposes of Chapter 5 of Part 16 as being the same definition in s 385 of the CA 2006 in Part 15, and the power in Part 15 to amend the definition also applies in this Chapter.

Auditors' Liability

23.68 Chapter 6 sets out the auditors' liability. It comprises seven sections.

This Chapter will make it possible for auditors to limit liability by agreement with a company, but the agreement will not be effective if it is not fair and reasonable.

It achieves this by defining the 'liability limitation agreement' – contractual limitation of an auditor's liability to a company, requiring member agreement – as a new exception to the general prohibition, restated here, on a company indemnifying its auditor. The court will be able to set aside such a limitation as ineffective if it purports to limit liability to an amount that is not fair and reasonable in all the circumstances.

[6482] CA 2006, s 530(1)(b).   [6483] CA 2006, s 530(2)(a).   [6484] CA 2006, s 530(2)(b).
[6485] CA 2006, s 531(1).   [6486] CA 2006, s 531(2).

Voidness of provisions protecting auditors from liability

23.69 Section 532 of the CA 2006 applies to the voidness of provisions protecting auditors from liability. It applies to any provision:

(a) for exempting an auditor of a company (to any extent) from any liability that would otherwise attach to him in connection with any negligence, default, breach of duty or breach of trust in relation to the company occurring in the course of the audit of accounts;[6487] or

(b) by which a company directly or indirectly provides indemnity (to any extent) for an auditor of the company, or of an associated company, against any liability attaching to him in connection with any negligence, default, breach of duty or breach of trust in relation to the company of which he is auditor occurring in the course of the audit of accounts.[6488]

Any such provision is void, except as permitted by s 532 of the CA 2006 (indemnity for costs of successfully defending proceedings),[6489] or ss 534–536 of the CA 2006 (liability limitation agreements).[6490]

This section applies to any provision, whether contained in a company's articles or in any contract with the company or otherwise.[6491]

Companies are associated if one is a subsidiary of the other or both are subsidiaries of the same body corporate.[6492]

Section 532 of the CA 2006 restates the general prohibition, previously in s 310 of the CA 1985, against a company indemnifying its auditor against claims by the company in the case of negligence or other default. Any such indemnities are void and unenforceable except where permitted by ss 533–536 of the CA 2006.

Indemnity for costs of successfully defending proceedings

23.70 Section 533 of the CA 2006 deals with indemnity for costs of successfully defending proceedings.

It states that section 532 of the CA 2006 (general voidness of provisions protecting auditors from liability) does not prevent a company from indemnifying an auditor against any liability incurred by him in defending proceedings (whether civil or criminal) in which judgment is given in his favour or he is acquitted,[6493] or in connection with an application under s 1157 of the CA 2006 (power of court to grant relief in case of honest and reasonable conduct) in which relief is granted to him by the court.[6494]

Section 533 of the CA 2006 contains the current exception from the

---

[6487] CA 2006, s 532(1)(a).   [6488] CA 2006, s 532(1)(b).   [6489] CA 2006, s 532(2)(a).
[6490] CA 2006, s 532(2)(b).   [6491] CA 2006, s 532(3).   [6492] CA 2006, s 532(4).
[6493] CA 2006, s 533(a).   [6494] CA 2006, s 533(b).

prohibition in s 532 of the CA 2006 allowing the company to indemnify the auditor against the costs of successfully defending himself against a claim, though it does not repeat the current exception that allows the company to buy insurance for its auditor.

Liability limitation agreements

23.71 Section 534 of the CA 2006 sets out the provisions dealing with limitation liability agreements. A 'liability limitation agreement' is an agreement that purports to limit the amount of a liability owed to a company by its auditor in respect of any negligence, default, breach of duty or breach of trust, occurring in the course of the audit of accounts, of which the auditor may be guilty in relation to the company.[6495]

Section 532 of the CA 2006 (general voidness of provisions protecting auditors from liability) does not affect the validity of a liability limitation agreement that complies with s 535 of the CA 2006 (terms of a liability limitation agreement) and of any regulations under that section,[6496] and is authorised by the members of the company (see s 536 of the CA 2006).[6497]

Such an agreement (a) is effective to the extent provided by s 537 of the CA 2006;[6498] and (b) is not subject (i) in England and Wales or Northern Ireland, to s 2(2) or 3(2)(a) of the Unfair Contract Terms Act 1977 (c 50),[6499] (ii) in Scotland, to s 16(1)(b) or 17(1)(a) of that Act.[6500]

Section 534 of the CA 2006 defines a 'liability limitation agreement' as an agreement that seeks to limit the liability of an auditor to a company whose accounts he audits. The agreement can cover liability for negligence, default, breach of duty or breach of trust by the auditor.

Section 534(2) of the CA 2006 provides that such an agreement is immune from the general voidness of such agreements under s 532 of the CA 2006, provided that the agreement has been authorised by the members of the company, in the way specified in s 536 of the CA 2006. Section 534(3) of the CA 2006 provides that the agreement's effect may be limited under s 536 of the CA 2006, which contains the specific test of fairness and reasonableness, and that certain provisions of the Unfair Contracts Terms Act 1977 accordingly do not apply.

Terms of liability limitation agreement

23.72 Section 535 of the CA 2006 sets out what should be the terms of the liability limitation agreement. A liability limitation agreement must not apply in respect of acts or omissions occurring in the course of the audit of

---

[6495] CA 2006, s 534(1).   [6496] CA 2006, s 534(2)(a).   [6497] CA 2006, s 534(2)(b).
[6498] CA 2006, s 534(3)(a).   [6499] CA 2006, s 534(3)(b)(i).   [6500] CA 2006, s 534(3)(b)(ii).

accounts for more than one financial year,[6501] and must specify the financial year in relation to which it applies.[6502]

The Secretary of State may by regulations require liability limitation agreements to contain specified provisions or provisions of a specified description;[6503] and prohibit liability limitation agreements from containing specified provisions or provisions of a specified description.[6504]

The term 'specified' here means specified in the regulations.

Without prejudice to the generality of the power conferred by s 535(2) of the CA 2006, that power may be exercised with a view to preventing adverse effects on competition.[6505]

Subject to the preceding provisions of this section, it is immaterial how a liability limitation agreement is framed. In particular, the limit on the amount of the auditor's liability need not be a sum of money, or a formula, specified in the agreement.[6506]

Regulations under this section are subject to negative resolution procedure.[6507]

Section 535 of the CA 2006 contains rules about the terms of a liability limitation agreement. An agreement must relate to the audit of a specified financial year, and the limitation may be expressed in any terms, not necessarily as a fixed financial amount or formula.

Section 535(2) of the CA 2006 confers on the Secretary of State a power to make regulations (subject to negative resolution) prescribing or proscribing specified provisions or descriptions of provisions; and s 535(3) of the CA 2006 provides that the power may be used to prevent adverse effects on competition.

Authorisation of an agreement by members of the company

23.73 Section 536 of the CA 2006 deals with the authorisation of an agreement by members of the company.

A liability limitation agreement is authorised by the members of the company if it has been authorised under this section and that authorisation has not been withdrawn.[6508]

A liability limitation agreement between a private company and its auditor may be authorised (a) by the company passing a resolution, before it enters into the agreement, waiving the need for approval;[6509] (b) by the company passing a resolution, before it enters into the agreement, approving the agreement's principal terms;[6510] or (c) by the company passing a resolution, after it enters into the agreement, approving the agreement.[6511]

[6501] CA 2006, s 535(1)(a). [6502] CA 2006, s 535(1)(b). [6503] CA 2006, s 535(2)(a).
[6504] CA 2006, s 535(2)(b). [6505] CA 2006, s 535(3). [6506] CA 2006, s 535(4).
[6507] CA 2006, s 535(5). [6508] CA 2006, s 536(1). [6509] CA 2006, s 536(2)(a).
[6510] CA 2006, s 536(2)(b). [6511] CA 2006, s 536(2)(c).

A liability limitation agreement between a public company and its auditor may be authorised by the company passing a resolution in general meeting, before it enters into the agreement, approving the agreement's principal terms,[6512] or by the company passing a resolution in general meeting, after it enters into the agreement, approving the agreement.[6513]

The 'principal terms' of an agreement are terms specifying, or relevant to the determination of (a) the kind (or kinds) of acts or omissions covered;[6514] (b) the financial year to which the agreement relates;[6515] or (c) the limit to which the auditor's liability is subject.[6516]

Authorisation under this section may be withdrawn by the company passing an ordinary resolution to that effect (a) at any time before the company enters into the agreement;[6517] or (b) if the company has already entered into the agreement, before the beginning of the financial year to which the agreement relates. Paragraph (b) applies notwithstanding anything in the agreement.[6518]

Section 536 of the CA 2006 specifies the way in which the company is to give approval to a liability limitation agreement, without which the approval agreement will not be effective.

The members of a private company can pass a resolution waiving the need for approval. The members in a private or public company can pass a resolution before an agreement is signed approving its principal terms, or can approve the agreement after it is signed. The resolution may be am ordinary resolution unless a higher threshold is set in the company's articles.

Section 536(5) of the CA 2006 specifies what the principal terms of a liability limitation agreement are for this purpose, namely the terms that specify, or enable one to determine, (i) the sorts of faults by the auditor that are covered, (ii) the financial year in relation to which those faults are covered, and (iii) the limit on the auditor's liability.

Section 536(6) of the CA 2006 provides that members, by passing an ordinary resolution, can withdraw their approval of a liability limitation agreement at any time before the agreement is entered into. If the company has already entered into the agreement, approval can be withdrawn, by ordinary resolution, only before the start of the financial year to which the agreement relates.

Effect of a liability agreement

23.74 Section 537 of the CA 2006 deals with the effect of a liability agreement.

A liability limitation agreement is not effective to limit the auditor's liability to less than such amount as is fair and reasonable in all the circumstances of the case having regard (in particular) to (a) the auditor's respon-

---

[6512] CA 2006, s 536(3)(a).   [6513] CA 2006, s 536(3)(b).   [6514] CA 2006, s 536(4)(a).
[6515] CA 2006, s 536(4)(b).   [6516] CA 2006, s 536(4)(c).   [6517] CA 2006, s 536(5)(a).
[6518] CA 2006, s 536(5)(b).

sibilities under this Part;[6519] (b) the nature and purpose of the auditor's contractual obligations to the company;[6520] and (c) the professional standards expected of him.[6521]

A liability limitation agreement that purports to limit the auditor's liability to less than the amount mentioned in s 537(1) of the CA 2006 shall have effect as if it limited his liability to that amount.[6522]

In determining what is fair and reasonable in all the circumstances of the case no account is to be taken of matters arising after the loss or damage in question has been incurred,[6523] or matters (whenever arising) affecting the possibility of recovering compensation from other persons liable in respect of the same loss or damage.[6524]

Section 537 of the CA 2006 provides that a liability limitation agreement will not be effective to limit an auditor's liability if the limitation would result in the company recovering an amount that was less that what was fair and reasonable, in all the circumstances of the case, having to the auditor's responsibilities, the auditor's contractual obligations, and the standards expected of the auditor. If a court decides that a liability limitation agreement would limit the auditor's liability to an excessive degree, the agreement will have effect as if it limited liability to the amount that the court determines is fair and reasonable.

Section 537(3) of the CA 2006 provides that in assessing what is fair and reasonable, the court should not take into account circumstances arising after the loss or damage in question has been incurred. Nor should it take into account the chances of the company successfully claiming compensation from any other people responsible for the loss or damage.

Disclosure of agreement by a company

23.75 Section 538 of the CA 2006 deals with the disclosure of agreement by a company. A company that has entered into a liability limitation agreement must make such disclosure in connection with the agreement as the Secretary of State may require by regulations.[6525]

The regulations may provide, in particular, that any disclosure required by the regulations shall be made in a note to the company's annual accounts (in the case of its individual accounts) or in such manner as is specified in the regulations (in the case of group accounts),[6526] or in the directors' report.[6527]

Regulations under this section are subject to negative resolution procedure.[6528]

Section 538 of the CA 2006 requires a company to disclose any liability limitation agreement they have made with their auditor. The Secretary of

[6519] CA 2006. s 537(1)(a).   [6520] CA 2006, s 537(1)(b).   [6521] CA 2006, s 537(1)(c).
[6522] CA 2006, s 537(2).   [6523] CA 2006, s 537(3)(a).   [6524] CA 2006, s 537(3)(b).
[6525] CA 2006, s 538(1).   [6526] CA 2006, s 537(2)(a).   [6527] CA 2006, s 537(2)(b).
[6528] CA 2006, s 537(3).

990 A Guide to the Companies Act 2006

State will produce regulations giving detailed requirements for this disclosure, through secondary legislation subject to negative resolution.

Section 538(2) of the CA 2006 provides that the regulations may require this disclosure to be in a company's annual accounts, or in the directors' report. Regulation 8 of the Companies (Disclosure of Auditor Remuneration and Liability Limitation Agreements) Regulations 2007 provides that a company which has entered into a limited liability agreement must disclose (i) its principal terms; and (ii) the date of the resolution approving the agreement or the agreement's principal terms or, in the case of a private company, the date of the resolution waiving the need for such approval, in the note to the company's annual accounts for the financial year to which the agreement relates.

Minor definitions

23.76 Section 539 of the CA 2006 deals with minor definitions used in Part 16 of the CA 2006:

- 'insurance market activity' has the meaning given in s 316(3) of the Financial Services and Markets Act 2000 (c 8);
- 'qualified', in relation to an auditor's report (or a statement contained in an auditor's report), means that the report or statement does not state the auditor's unqualified opinion that the accounts have been properly prepared in accordance with this Act or, in the case of an undertaking not required to prepare accounts in accordance with this Act, under any corresponding legislation under which it is required to prepare accounts; 'regulated activity' has the meaning given in s 22 of the Financial Services and Markets Act 2000, except that it does not include activities of the kind specified in any of the following provisions of the Financial Services and Markets Act 2000 (Regulated Activities) Order 2001:
  - (a) article 25A (arranging regulated mortgage contracts);
  - (b) article 39A (assisting administration and performance of a contract of insurance);
  - (c) article 53A (advising on regulated mortgage contracts); or
  - (d) article 21 (dealing as agent), article 25 (arranging deals in investments) or article 53 (advising on investments) where the activity concerns relevant investments that are not contractually based investments (within the meaning of article 3 of that Order);
- 'turnover', in relation to a company, means the amounts derived from the provision of goods and services falling within the company's ordinary activities, after deduction of:
  - (a) trade discounts;
  - (b) value added tax; and
  - (c) any other taxes based on the amounts so derived.

Chapter 24

Statutory Auditors

Introduction

24.1 Part 42 of the CA 2006 sets out the position of statutory auditors. It comprises six Chapters. Chapter 1 provides an introductory framework to Part 42. Chapter 2 contains provisions on individuals and firms. Chapter 3 deals with Auditors General. Chapter 4 is concerned with the register of auditors. Chapter 5 addresses the registered third country auditors. Chapter 6 contains supplementary and general provisions to Part 42.

The objectives of Part 42 are first, to replace Part 2 of the CA 1989 and equivalent Northern Ireland provisions, by restating those provisions with some modifications. Second, to extend the category of auditors that are subject to regulation, and to make provision for the registration and regulation of auditors (whether based in the UK or not) who audit companies that are incorporated outside the EU, but listed in the UK. Third, to provide that the Comptroller and Auditor General and the regional Auditors General are eligible to be appointed to perform statutory audits, and to provide a mechanism for the regulation and supervision of their functions as statutory auditor.

Many of the provisions in Part 42 of the CA 2006 implement obligations contained in the Eighth Company Law Directive on Audit.[6529] The provisions relating to Auditors General implement recommendations contained in Lord Sharman's report, *Holding to Account: The Review of Audit and Accountability for Central Government* published in 2001.[6530]

[6529] (2006/43/EC) published 9 June 2006.

[6530] The Sharman Report made a number of recommendations aimed at strengthening existing audit and accountability arrangements in Central Government. The Government's response to the Sharman Report was issued in March 2002, and it accepted that the Comptroller and Auditor-General should be responsible for validating the systems used in reporting to Public Service Agreement targets; audit all non-department public bodies; and have statutory access to all bodies receiving grants from, or who contract with bodies he audits, as well as to other bodies, such as registered social landlords and train operating companies.

Introductory Aspects

24.2 Chapter 1 sets out the introductory aspects to statutory auditors. This Chapter comprises three sections that set out the main purposes of Part 42. It provides a definition of the term 'statutory auditor', and an overview of eligibility for appointment as a statutory auditor.

Part 2 of the CA 1989 regulated only the auditors of companies. Section 1210(1) of the CA 2006 defines the meaning of statutory auditor more broadly. Persons within paras (1)(a)–(g) are 'statutory auditors'. This list includes those persons who audit companies (as required under Part 16 of the CA 2006), and those who audit building societies, insurers and banks. In addition, the Secretary of State has a power to add auditors of other persons to this list. Section 1211 of the CA 2006 cross-refers the eligibility for appointment as a statutory auditor to the requirements contained in Chapter 2 or Chapter 3 of Part 42 of the CA 2006.

Main purposes of Part

24.3 Section 1209 of the CA 2006 sets out the main objectives of Part 42. The main purposes of this Part are two-fold. First, the supervision and qualification aspect, namely to secure that only persons who are properly supervised and appropriately qualified are appointed as statutory auditors;[6531] and second, the ethics aspect, to secure that audits by persons so appointed are carried out properly, with integrity and with a proper degree of independence.[6532]

Meaning of 'statutory auditor', etc.

24.4 Section 1210 of the CA 2006 sets out the definition of 'statutory auditor' for Part 42. The term 'statutory auditor' means:

(a) a person appointed as auditor under Part 16 of the CA 2006;[6533]

(b) a person appointed as auditor under s 77 of or Schedule 11 to the Building Societies Act 1986 (c 53);[6534]

(c) a person appointed as auditor of an insurer that is a friendly society under s 72 of or Schedule 14 to the Friendly Societies Act 1992 (c 40);[6535]

(d) a person appointed as auditor of an insurer that is an industrial and provident society under s 4 of the Friendly and Industrial and Provident Societies Act 1968 (c 55) or under s 38 of the Industrial and Provident Societies Act (Northern Ireland) 1969 (c 24 (NI));[6536]

[6531] CA 2006, s 1209(a).   [6532] CA 2006, s 1209(b).   [6533] CA 2006, s 1210(1)(a).
[6534] CA 2006, s 1210(1)(b).   [6535] CA 2006, s 1210(1)(c).   [6536] CA 2006, s 1210(1)(d).

(e) a person appointed as auditor for the purposes of reg 3 of the Insurance Accounts Directive (Lloyds Syndicate and Aggregate Accounts) Regulations 2004 (SI 2004/3219) or appointed to report on the 'aggregate accounts' within the meaning of those Regulations;[6537]

(f) a person appointed as auditor of an insurer for the purposes of reg 3 of the Insurance Accounts Directive (Miscellaneous Insurance Undertakings) Regulations 1993 (SI 1993/3245);[6538]

(g) a person appointed as auditor of a bank for the purposes of reg 4 of the Bank Accounts Directive (Miscellaneous Banks) Regulations 1991 (SI 1991/2704);[6539] and

(h) a person appointed as auditor of a prescribed person under a prescribed enactment authorising or requiring the appointment.[6540]

Section 1210 of the CA 2006 states that the expressions 'statutory audit' and 'statutory audit work' are to be construed accordingly.

The term 'audited person' means the person in respect of whom a statutory audit is conducted.[6541]

In s 1210(1) of the CA 2006 the following are the defined terms:[6542]

• 'bank' means a person who:

 (a) is a credit institution within the meaning given by Article 4.1(a) of Directive 2006/48/EC of the European Parliament and of the Council relating to the taking up and pursuit of the business of credit institutions; and

 (b) is a company or firm as defined in Article 48 of the Treaty establishing the European Community.

• 'friendly society' means a friendly society within the meaning of the Friendly Societies Act 1992 (c 40);

• 'industrial and provident society' means:

 (a) a society registered under the Industrial and Provident Societies Act 1965 (c 12) or a society deemed by virtue of section 4 of that Act to be so registered, or

 (b) a society registered under the Industrial and Provident Societies Act (Northern Ireland) 1969 or a society deemed by virtue of s 4 of that Act to be so registered.

• 'insurer' means a person who is an insurance undertaking within the meaning given by Article 2.1 of Council Directive 1991/674/EEC on the annual accounts and consolidated accounts of insurance undertakings;

[6537] CA 2006, s 1210(1)(e). [6538] CA 2006, s 1210(1)(f). [6539] CA 2006, s 1210(1)(g).
[6540] CA 2006, s 1210(1)(h). [6541] CA 2006, s 1210(2). [6542] CA 2006, s 1210(3).

- 'prescribed' means prescribed, or of a description prescribed, by order made by the Secretary of State for the purposes of subs(1)(h).

An order under s 1210 of the CA 2006 is subject to negative resolution procedure.[6543]

Eligibility for appointment as a statutory auditor: overview

24.5 Section 1211 of the CA 2006 sets out a general overview of the eligibility of an appointment as a statutory auditor. It states that a person is eligible for appointment as a statutory auditor only if the person is so eligible by virtue of Chapter 2 (individuals and firms);[6544] or by virtue of Chapter 3 (Comptroller and Auditor General, etc.).[6545]

Individuals and Firms

24.6 Chapter 2 sets out the eligibility for appointment as statutory auditor for individuals and firms.

Eligibility for appointment

Individuals and firms: eligibility for appointment as a statutory auditor

24.7 Section 1212 of the CA 2006 sets out the appointment criteria for individuals and firms. An individual or firm is eligible for appointment as a statutory auditor, if the individual or firm is a member of a recognised supervisory body,[6546] and is eligible for appointment under the rules of that body.[6547]

In the cases to which s 1222 of the CA 2006 applies (individuals retaining only CA 1967 authorisation), a person's eligibility for appointment as a statutory auditor is restricted as mentioned in that section.[6548]

Effect of ineligibility

24.8 Section 1213 of the CA 2006 considers the effect of ineligibility. No person may act as statutory auditor of an audited person, if he is ineligible for appointment as a statutory auditor.[6549]

If at any time during his term of office a statutory auditor becomes ineligible for appointment as a statutory auditor, he must immediately resign

---

[6543] CA 2006, s 1210(4).   [6544] CA 2006, s 1211(1)(a).   [6545] CA 2006, s 1211(1)(b).
[6546] CA 2006, s 1212(1)(a).   [6547] CA 2006, s 1212(1)(b).   [6548] CA 2006, s 1212(2).
[6549] CA 2006, s 1213(1).

his office (with immediate effect),[6550] and give notice in writing to the audited person that he has resigned by reason of his becoming ineligible for appointment.[6551]

A person is guilty of an offence if he acts as a statutory auditor in contravention of s 1213(1) of the CA 2006,[6552] or he fails to give the notice mentioned in para (b) of s 1213(2) of the CA 2006 in accordance with that subsection.[6553]

A person guilty of an offence under s 1213(3) of the CA 2006 is liable on conviction on indictment, to a fine;[6554] on summary conviction, to a fine not exceeding the statutory maximum.[6555]

A person is guilty of an offence if he has been convicted of an offence under s 1213(3)(a) of the CA 2006 or this subsection,[6556] and he continues to act as a statutory auditor in contravention of s 1213(1) of the CA 2006 after the conviction.[6557]

A person is guilty of an offence if he has been convicted of an offence under s 1213(3)(b) of the CA 2006 or this subsection,[6558] and he continues, after the conviction, to fail to give the notice mentioned in s 1213(2)(b) of the CA 2006.[6559]

A person guilty of an offence under s 1213(5) or (6) of the CA 2006 is liable on conviction on indictment, to a fine;[6560] on summary conviction, to a fine not exceeding one-tenth of the statutory maximum for each day on which the act or the failure continues.[6561]

In proceedings against a person for an offence under this section it is a defence for him to show that he did not know and had no reason to believe that he was, or had become, ineligible for appointment as a statutory auditor.[6562]

Sections 1212 and 1213 of the CA 2006 are restatements of ss 25 and 28 of the CA 1989 adapted so as to apply in relation to statutory auditors. The sections provide that for a person or firm (defined in s 1261 of the CA 2006) to be eligible for appointment as a statutory auditor, the person must be a member of a recognised supervisory body and be eligible for appointment under the rules of that body. Section 1217(2) of the CA 2006 clarifies that references to such members include references to persons who are not members but who are subject to the body's rules (s 1214 and Schedule 10 of the CA 2006 address the recognition of supervisory bodies, and lay down the requirements they must meet to be recognised).

Section 1213 of the CA 2006 provides that no person may act as a statutory auditor if he is ineligible. It specifies that, on becoming ineligible, the

---

[6550] CA 2006, s 1213(2)(a).   [6551] CA 2006, s 1213(2)(b).   [6552] CA 2006, s 1213(3)(a).
[6553] CA 2006, s 1213(3)(b).   [6554] CA 2006, s 1213(4)(a).   [6555] CA 2006, s 1213(4)(b).
[6556] CA 2006, s 1213(5)(a).   [6557] CA 2006, s 1213(5)(b).   [6558] CA 2006, s 1213(6)(a).
[6559] CA 2006, s 1213(6)(b).   [6560] CA 2006, s 1213(7)(a).   [6561] CA 2006, s 1213(7)(b).
[6562] CA 2006, s 1213(8).

auditor must resign his office and give notice in writing. Failure to comply with this requirement is an offence, conviction of which can result in a fine (s 1213(3) and (4) of the CA 2006). If the auditor continues to act as a statutory auditor after conviction (s 1213(5) of the CA 2006), or continues to fail to give notice that he is ineligible for appointment as a statutory auditor (s 1213(6) of the CA 2006), he commits a further offence for which a daily fine may be imposed after conviction (s 1213(7) of the CA 2006). Section 1213(8) of the CA 2006 provides a defense if the person did not know or had no reason to believe that he was, or had become, ineligible.

Independence requirement

24.9 Section 1214 of the CA 2006 sets out the independence requirement. A person may not act as statutory auditor of an audited person if one or more of s 1214(2), (3) and (4) of the CA 2006 apply to him.[6563]

Section 1214(2) of the CA 2006 applies if the person is an officer or employee of the audited person,[6564] or a partner or employee of such a person, or a partnership of which such a person is a partner.[6565]

Section 1214(3) of the CA 2006 applies if the person is an officer or employee of an associated undertaking of the audited person,[6566] or a partner or employee of such a person, or a partnership of which such a person is a partner.[6567]

Section 1214(5) of the CA 2006 applies if there exists, between the person or an associate of his,[6568] and the audited person or an associated undertaking of the audited person,[6569] a connection of any such description as may be specified by regulations made by the Secretary of State.

An auditor of an audited person is not to be regarded as an officer or employee of the person for the purposes of s 1214(2) and (3) of the CA 2006.[6570]

The term 'associated undertaking', in relation to an audited person, means a parent undertaking or subsidiary undertaking of the audited person,[6571] or a subsidiary undertaking of a parent undertaking of the audited person.[6572]

Regulations under s 1214(4) of the CA 2006 are subject to negative resolution procedure.[6573]

Section 1214 of the CA 2006 restates s 27 of the CA 2006 1985 and indicates circumstances where a person may not act as a statutory auditor on grounds of lack of independence. Under s 1214(2) of the CA 2006 this includes persons who are officers or employees of the audited entity, or the partner or employee of such a person. Under 1214(3) of the CA 2006, this

---

[6563] CA 2006, s 1214(1).   [6564] CA 2006, s 1214(2)(a).   [6565] CA 2006, s 1214(2)(b).
[6566] CA 2006, s 1214(3)(a).   [6567] CA 2006, s 1214(3)(b).   [6568] CA 2006, s 1214(4)(a).
[6569] CA 2006, s 1214(4)(b).   [6570] CA 2006, s 1214(5).   [6571] CA 2006, s 1214(6)(a).
[6572] CA 2006, s 1214(6)(b).   [6573] CA 2006, s 1214(7).

includes where the person is an officer or employee of a subsidiary of the audited entity. Section 1214(4) of the CA 2006 allows the Secretary of State to make regulations regarding other connections between the audited entity and the statutory auditor by virtue of which a person will be regarded as lacking independence.

Effect of lack of independence

24.10 Section 1215 of the CA 2006 sets out the effect of lack of independence. If at any time during his term of office a statutory auditor becomes prohibited from acting by s 1214(1) of the CA 2006, he must immediately resign his office (with immediate effect),[6574] and give notice in writing to the audited person that he has resigned by reason of his lack of independence.[6575]

A person is guilty of an offence if he acts as a statutory auditor in contravention of s 1214(1) of the CA 2006,[6576] or he fails to give the notice mentioned in para (b) of s 1215(1) of the CA 2006.[6577] A person guilty of an offence under s 1215(2) of the CA 2006 is liable on conviction on indictment, to a fine;[6578] and on summary conviction, to a fine not exceeding the statutory maximum.[6579]

A person is guilty of an offence if he has been convicted of an offence under s 1215(2)(a) of the CA 2006 or this subsection,[6580] and he continues to act as a statutory auditor in contravention of s 1214(1) of the CA 2006 after the conviction.[6581]

A person is guilty of an offence if he has been convicted of an offence under s 1215(2)(b) of the CA 2006 or this subsection,[6582] and after the conviction, he continues to fail to give the notice mentioned in s 1215(1)(b) of the CA 2006.[6583] A person guilty of an offence under s 1215(4) or (5) of the CA 2006 is liable on conviction on indictment, to a fine;[6584] on summary conviction, to a fine not exceeding one-tenth of the statutory maximum for each day on which the act or the failure continues.[6585]

In proceedings against a person for an offence under this section it is a defence for him to show that he did not know and had no reason to believe that he was, or had become, prohibited from acting as statutory auditor of the audited person by s 1214(1) of the CA 2006.[6586]

Section 1215 of the CA 2006 sets out the consequences of the prohibition from acting as a statutory auditor on grounds of lack of independence, as defined in s 1214 of the CA 2006. They replicate the effect of ineligibility as explained for s 1213 of the CA 2006.

[6574] CA 2006, s 1215(1)(a). [6575] CA 2006, s 1215(1)(b). [6576] CA 2006, s 1215(2)(a).
[6577] CA 2006, s 1215(2)(b). [6578] CA 2006, s 1215(3)(a). [6579] CA 2006, s 1215(3)(b).
[6580] CA 2006, s 1215(4)(a). [6581] CA 2006, s 1215(4)(b). [6582] CA 2006, s 1215(5)(a).
[6583] CA 2006, s 1215(5)(b). [6584] CA 2006, s 1215(6)(a). [6585] CA 2006, s 1215(6)(b).
[6586] CA 2006, s 1215(7).

Effect of appointment of a partnership

24.11 Section 1,216 of the CA 2006 applies where a partnership constituted under the law of England and Wales,[6587] or Northern Ireland,[6588] or any other country or territory in which a partnership is not a legal person,[6589]is by virtue of Chapter 2 to Part 42 of the CA 2006 appointed as statutory auditor of an audited person.

Unless a contrary intention appears, the appointment is an appointment of the partnership as such and not of the partners.[6590]

Where the partnership ceases, the appointment is to be treated as extending to any appropriate partnership that succeeds to the practice of that partnership,[6591] or any other appropriate person who succeeds to that practice having previously carried it on in partnership.[6592]

For the purposes of s 1216(3) of the CA 2006, a partnership is to be regarded as succeeding to the practice of another partnership, only if the members of the successor partnership are substantially the same as those of the former partnership,[6593] and a partnership or other person is to be regarded as succeeding to the practice of a partnership only if it or he succeeds to the whole or substantially the whole of the business of the former partnership.[6594]

Where the partnership ceases and the appointment is not treated under s 1216(3) of the CA 2006 as extending to any partnership or other person, the appointment may with the consent of the audited person be treated as extending to an appropriate partnership, or other appropriate person, who succeeds to the business of the former partnership,[6595] or such part of it as is agreed by the audited person is to be treated as comprising the appointment.[6596]

A partnership or other person is 'appropriate' if it or he is eligible for appointment as a statutory auditor by virtue of Chapter 2 to Part 42 of the CA 2006,[6597] and is not prohibited by s 1214(1) of the CA 2006 from acting as statutory auditor of the audited person.[6598]

Section 1216 of the CA 2006 is a restatement of s 26 of the CA 1989. The effect of the section is to ensure that when a partnership constituted in England and Wales, Northern Ireland or any other country or territory in which a partnership is not legal person, is appointed as a statutory auditor under this Part, the appointment may continue even if a partner leaves the partnership. For a partnership or other person to be considered as appropriate for the appointment to continue, they must be eligible for appointment as

[6587] CA 2006, s 1216(1)(a).   [6588] CA 2006, s 1216(1)(b).   [6589] CA 2006, s 1216(1)(c).
[6590] CA 2006, s 1216(2).   [6591] CA 2006, s 1216(3)(a).   [6592] CA 2006, s 1216(3)(b).
[6593] CA 2006, s 1216(4)(a).   [6594] CA 2006, s 1216(4)(b).   [6595] CA 2006, s 1216(5)(a).
[6596] CA 2006, s 1216(5)(b).   [6597] CA 2006, s 1216(6)(a).   [6598] CA 2006, s 1216(6)(b).

a statutory and not be prohibited (as indicated in s 1214(1) of the CA 2006). Without this provision, the appointment would cease every time the membership of the partnership changed.

Supervisory bodies

24.12 Section 1217 of the CA 2006 deals with supervisory bodies. The term 'supervisory body' means a body established in the United Kingdom (whether a body corporate or an unincorporated association) that maintains and enforces rules as to the eligibility of persons for appointment as a statutory auditor,[6599] and the conduct of statutory audit work,[6600] which are binding on persons seeking appointment or acting as a statutory auditor either because they are members of that body or because they are otherwise subject to its control.

In this Part references to the members of a supervisory body are to the persons who, whether or not members of the body, are subject to its rules in seeking appointment or acting as a statutory auditor.[6601]

In this Part references to the rules of a supervisory body are to the rules (whether or not laid down by the body itself) that the body has power to enforce and that are relevant for the purposes of this Part. This includes rules relating to the admission or expulsion of members of the body, so far as relevant for the purposes of this Part.[6602]

Schedule 10 to the CA 2006 applies with respect to the recognition of supervisory bodies for the purposes of this Part.[6603]

Section 1217 of the CA 2006 restates s 30 of the CA 1989 and defines a supervisory body as a body established in the UK that maintains and enforces rules regarding the eligibility persons appointed as statutory auditors and the conduct of statutory audit work. Section 1217(4) of the CA 2006 introduces Schedule 10 to the CA 2006, which specifies the requirements that supervisory bodies must meet in order to be recognised, and the process for doing so.

Schedule 10 on recognised supervisory bodies restates provisions in Schedule 11 of the CA 1989. Paragraph 1 identifies the steps a body is required to take to become recognised by the Secretary of State. Paragraph 3 specifies the steps that the Secretary of State is required to take if the recognition of the body is revoked. Paragraph 5 provides that recognition (and revocation) orders are not statutory instruments. Paragraph 4 is a transitional provision that allows bodies recognised under CA 1989 or the Companies (Northern Ireland) Order 1990 to continue to be recognised.

Under Part 2 of Schedule 10, paras 6 and 7 require a recognised body to

---

[6599] CA 2006, s 1217(1)(a).   [6600] CA 2006, s 1217(1)(b).   [6601] CA 2006, s 1217(2).
[6602] CA 2006, s 1217(3).   [6603] CA 2006, s 1217(4).

ensure that persons eligible for appointment as a statutory auditor hold appropriate qualifications (as defined in s 1219 of the CA 2006). They require a firm that is statutory auditor to be controlled by qualified persons. Paragraphs 8–11 require the bodies to have rules and practices ensuring that auditors are fit and proper, that professional integrity and independence is maintained, that technical standards for audits are assured and that there are procedures for maintaining appropriate levels of competence. Paragraphs 12–16 specify the requirements for monitoring, enforcement, discipline and investigation of complaints.

Under Part 3, paras 21–27 specify the arrangements with independent bodies that recognised supervisory bodies must enter into in order to meet the requirements of this Schedule described above.

Exemption from liability for damages

24.13 Section 1218 of the CA 2006 deals with exemptions from liability for damages. It states that no person within s 1218(2) of the CA 2006 is to be liable in damages for anything done or omitted in the discharge or purported discharge of functions to which this subsection applies.[6604]

The persons within this subsection are (a) any recognised supervisory body;[6605] (b) any officer or employee of a recognised supervisory body;[6606] and (c) any member of the governing body of a recognised supervisory body.[6607]

Section 1218(1) of the CA 2006 applies to the functions of a recognised supervisory body so far as relating to, or to matters arising out of, any of the following: (a) rules, practices, powers and arrangements of the body to which the requirements of Part 2 of Schedule 10 to the CA 2006 apply;[6608] (b) the obligations with which para 20 of that Schedule requires the body to comply;[6609] (c) any guidance issued by the body;[6610] (d) the obligations imposed on the body by or by virtue of this Part.[6611]

The reference in s 1218(3)(c) of the CA 2006 to guidance issued by a recognised supervisory body is a reference to any guidance or recommendation that is issued or made by it to all or any class of its members or persons seeking to become members,[6612] and relevant for the purposes of this Part,[6613] including any guidance or recommendation relating to the admission or expulsion of members of the body, so far as relevant for the purposes of this Part.

Section 1218(1) of the CA 2006 does not apply if the act or omission is shown to have been in bad faith,[6614] or so as to prevent an award of damages in respect of the act or omission on the ground that it was unlawful as a result

---

[6604] CA 2006, s 1218(1).   [6605] CA 2006, s 1218(2)(a).   [6606] CA 2006, s 1218(2)(b).
[6607] CA 2006, s 1218(2)(c).   [6608] CA 2006, s 1218(3)(a).   [6609] CA 2006, s 1218(3)(b).
[6610] CA 2006, s 1218(3)(c).   [6611] CA 2006, s 1218(3)(d).   [6612] CA 2006, s 1218(4)(a).
[6613] CA 2006, s 1218(4)(b).   [6614] CA 2006, s 1218(5)(a).

of s 6(1) of the Human Rights Act 1998 (c 42) (acts of public authorities incompatible with Convention rights).[6615]

This section is restatement of s 48 of the CA 1989. It sets out those bodies and individuals that are exempt from liability for damages arising from the discharge or claimed discharge of supervisory functions as specified in this Part of the CA 2006 (these include the effects of rules, practices, powers and arrangements of the body). It applies to recognised supervisory bodies (see s 1217 of the CA 2006 and Schedule 10 to the CA 2006) and their officers, employees and members of their governing bodies. The exemption does not apply if they have acted in bad faith, or if it would prevent an award of damages because the act was unlawful under the Human Rights Act.

Professional qualifications

Appropriate qualifications

24.14 Section 1219 of the CA 2006 sets out the appropriate qualifications for statutory auditors. A person holds an appropriate qualification for the purposes of this Chapter if and only if:

(a) he holds a recognised professional qualification obtained in the United Kingdom;[6616]

(b) immediately before the commencement of this Chapter, he (i) held an appropriate qualification for the purposes of Part 2 of the CA 1989 (c 40) (eligibility for appointment as company auditor) by virtue of section 31(1)(a) or (c) of that Act,[6617] or (ii) was treated as holding an appropriate qualification for those purposes by virtue of s 31(2), (3) or (4) of that Act;[6618]

(c) immediately before the commencement of this Chapter, he (i) held an appropriate qualification for the purposes of Part III of the Companies (Northern Ireland) Order 1990 (SI 1990/593 (NI 5)) by virtue of Article 34(1)(a) or (c) of that Order,[6619] or (ii) was treated as holding an appropriate qualification for those purposes by virtue of Article 34(2), (3) or (4) of that Order;[6620]

(d) he is within subs (2);[6621]

(e) he has been authorised to practise the profession of statutory auditor pursuant to the European Communities (Recognition of Professional Qualifications) (First General System) Regulations 2005 (SI 2005/18) and has fulfilled any requirements imposed pursuant to regulation 6 of those Regulations;[6622] or

---

[6615] CA 2006, s 1218(5)(b). [6616] CA 2006, s 1219(1)(a). [6617] CA 2006, s 1219(1)(b)(i).
[6618] CA 2006, s 1219(1)(b)(ii). [6619] CA 2006, s 1219(1)(c)(i).
[6620] CA 2006, s 1219(1)(c)(ii). [6621] CA 2006, s 1219(1)(d). [6622] CA 2006, s 1219(1)(e).

(f)   subject to any direction under s 1221(5), he is regarded for the purposes of this Chapter as holding an approved overseas qualification.[6623]

A person is within this subsection if:

(a)   before 1 January 1990, he began a course of study or practical training leading to a professional qualification in accountancy offered by a body established in the United Kingdom;[6624]
(b)   he obtained that qualification on or after 1 January 1990 and before 1 January 1996;[6625] and
(c)   the Secretary of State approves his qualification as an appropriate qualification for the purposes of this Chapter.[6626]

The Secretary of State may approve a qualification under s 1219(2)(c) of the CA 2006 only if he is satisfied that, at the time the qualification was awarded, the body concerned had adequate arrangements to ensure that the qualification was awarded only to persons educated and trained to a standard equivalent to that required, at that time, in the case of a recognised professional qualification under Part 2 of the CA 1989 (c 40) (eligibility for appointment as company auditor).[6627]

Section 1219 of the CA 2006 restates s 31 of the CA 1989. It provides that a person holds an appropriate qualification if he holds a professional qualification obtained in the UK which is recognised in accordance with s 1220 and Schedule 11 of the CA 2006. Qualifications recognised under Part 2 of the CA 1989 or the Companies (Northern Ireland) Order 1990 will continue to be recognised.

Persons whose qualifications from other EU Member States are recognised under the European Communities (Recognition of Professional Qualifications) (First General System) Regulations 2005 as qualifications to practise as statutory auditors are also considered to hold an appropriate qualification. So too are overseas qualifications from non-EU countries if approved under s 1221 of the CA 2006. Section 1219(2) of the CA 2006 restates a transitional provision from CA 1989 for those persons who have begun a course of study in accountancy before 1 January 1990 and obtained a qualification between 1 January 1990 and 1 January 1996, enabling them to apply to the Secretary of State for approval for their qualification. The transitional provisions contained in s 31(2) and (3) of the CA 1989 have not been restated.

[6623] CA 2006, s 1219(1)(f).   [6624] CA 2006, s 1219(2)(a).   [6625] CA 2006, s 1219(2)(b).
[6626] CA 2006, s 1219(2)(c).   [6627] CA 2006, s 1219(2)(d).

Qualifying bodies and recognised professional qualifications

24.15 Section 1220 of the CA 2006 deals with qualifying bodies and recognised professional qualifications. The term 'qualifying body' means a body established in the United Kingdom (whether a body corporate or an unincorporated association) that offers a professional qualification in accountancy.[6628]

In this Part, references to the rules of a qualifying body are to the rules (whether or not laid down by the body itself) that the body has power to enforce and that are relevant for the purposes of this Part.

This includes, so far as so relevant, rules relating to admission to or expulsion from a course of study leading to a qualification,[6629] or the award or deprivation of a qualification,[6630] or the approval of a person for the purposes of giving practical training or the withdrawal of such approval.[6631]

Schedule 11 of the CA 2006 applies with respect to the recognition for the purposes of this Part of a professional qualification offered by a qualifying body.[6632]

This section is a restatement of s 32 of the CA 1989. It defines the term 'qualifying body' as a body that offers a professional qualification in accountancy and introduces Schedule 11 of the CA 2006, which sets out the requirements that qualifying bodies must impose. Only a qualification recognised in accordance with these provisions can be considered a recognised professional within the meaning of s 1219(1)(a) of the CA 2006.

Schedule 11: Recognised Professional Qualifications

Part 1: Grant and revocation of recognition of a professional qualification

Paragraph 1: Application for recognition of professional qualification

This Schedule restates provisions in Schedule 12 of the CA 1989. Paragraph 1 identifies the steps a body is required to take for a qualification it offers to be recognised by the Secretary of State. Paragraph 3 specifies the steps that the Secretary of State is required to take if the recognition is revoked. Paragraph 5 provides that recognition (and revocation) orders are not statutory instruments. Paragraph 4 is a transitional provision that allows qualifications recognised under the CA 1989 or the Companies (Northern Ireland) Order 1990 to continue to be recognised.

[6628] CA 2006, s 1220(1). [6629] CA 2006, s 1220(2)(a). [6630] CA 2006, s 1220(2)(b).
[6631] CA 2006, s 1220(2)(c). [6632] CA 2006, s 1220(3).

Part 2: Requirements for recognition of a professional qualification

Paragraph 6 sets the minimum academic standards that a person must have attained before he can attempt the professional qualification. Paragraph 7 requires that the qualification is restricted to persons who have either completed a relevant academic course or have seven years' professional experience. Paragraph 8 requires that an examination must be passed (part of which has to be in writing) for the person to achieve the qualification. This examination must be in subjects of knowledge prescribed by the Secretary of State; or a university or equivalent level examination; or by practical demonstration of knowledge to examination or diploma level that is recognised by the Secretary of State. Paragraph 9 requires persons to carry out at least three years' practical training.

Approval of overseas qualifications

24.16 Section 1221 of the CA 2006 sets out the approval of overseas qualifications. The Secretary of State may declare that the following are to be regarded for the purposes of this Chapter as holding an approved overseas qualification, namely, persons who are qualified to audit accounts under the law of a specified foreign country,[6633] or persons who hold a specified professional qualification in accountancy obtained in a specified foreign country.[6634]

A declaration under s 1221(1)(b) of the CA 2006 may be expressed to be subject to the satisfaction of any specified requirement or requirements.[6635]

The Secretary of State may make a declaration under s 1221(1) of the CA 2006 only if he is satisfied that in the case of a declaration under s 1221(1)(a) of the CA 2006, the fact that the persons in question are qualified to audit accounts under the law of the specified foreign country,[6636] or in the case of a declaration under s 1221(1)(b) of the CA 2006, the specified professional qualification taken with any requirement or requirements to be specified under s 1221(2) of the CA 2006,[6637] affords an assurance of professional competence equivalent to that afforded by a recognised professional qualification.

The Secretary of State may make a declaration under s 1221(1) of the CA 2006 only if he is satisfied that the treatment that the persons who are the subject of the declaration will receive as a result of it is comparable to the treatment which is, or is likely to be, afforded in the specified foreign country or a part of it, in the case of a declaration under s 1221(1)(a) of the CA 2006, to some or all persons who are eligible to be appointed as a statutory auditor,[6638] and in the case of a declaration under s 1221(1)(b) of the CA

[6633] CA 2006, s 1221(1)(a).   [6634] CA 2006, s 1221(1)(b).   [6635] CA 2006, s 1221(2).
[6636] CA 2006, s 1221(3)(a).   [6637] CA 2006, s 1221(3)(b).   [6638] CA 2006, s 1221(4)(a).

2006, to some or all persons who hold a corresponding recognised professional qualification.[6639]

The Secretary of State may direct that persons holding an approved overseas qualification are not to be treated as holding an appropriate qualification for the purposes of this Chapter unless they hold such additional educational qualifications as the Secretary of State may specify for the purpose of ensuring that such persons have an adequate knowledge of the law and practice in the United Kingdom relevant to the audit of accounts.[6640]

The Secretary of State may give different directions in relation to different approved overseas qualifications.[6641]

The Secretary of State may, if he thinks fit, having regard to the considerations mentioned in s 1221(3) and (4) of the CA 2006, withdraw a declaration under s 1221(1) of the CA 2006 in relation to persons becoming qualified to audit accounts under the law of the specified foreign country after such date as he may specify,[6642] or persons obtaining the specified professional qualification after such date as he may specify.[6643]

The Secretary of State may, if he thinks fit, having regard to the considerations mentioned in s 1221(3) and (4) of the CA 2006, vary or revoke a requirement specified under s 1221(2) of the CA 2006 from such date as he may specify.[6644]

The term 'foreign country', in relation to any time, means a country or territory that, at that time, is not a 'relevant State' within the meaning of the European Communities (Recognition of Professional Qualifications) (First General System) Regulations 2005 (SI 2005/18) or part of such a State.[6645]

This section restates s 33 of the CA 1989 as regards the approval of overseas qualifications from non-EU countries. It sets out the conditions that will need to be satisfied, relating to the assurance of professional competence. The section provides for approval of all those in a specified country who are qualified to audit accounts, or only those who hold specified qualifications in that country. In the case of the latter, the Secretary of State may specify any additional requirements to be satisfied. The section allows the Secretary of State to recognise an overseas qualification only if there is comparability of treatment in the country in question.

Eligibility of individuals retaining only 1967 Act authorisation

24.17 Section 1222 of the CA 2006 sets out the eligibility of individuals retaining only the CA 1967 authorisation. A person whose only appropriate qualification is based on his retention of an authorisation originally granted by the Board of Trade or the Secretary of State under s 13(1) of the CA 1967

[6639] CA 2006, s 1221(4)(b).   [6640] CA 2006, s 1221(5).   [6641] CA 2006, s 1221(6).
[6642] CA 2006, s 1221(7)(a).   [6643] CA 2006, s 1221(7)(b).   [6644] CA 2006, s 1221(8).
[6645] CA 2006, s 1221(9).

(c 81), is eligible only for appointment as auditor of an unquoted company.[6646]

A company is 'unquoted' if, at the time of the person's appointment, neither the company, nor any parent undertaking of which it is a subsidiary undertaking, is a quoted company within the meaning of s 385(2) of the CA 2006.[6647]

References to a person eligible for appointment as a statutory auditor by virtue of this Part in enactments relating to eligibility for appointment as auditor of a person other than a company do not include a person to whom this section applies.[6648]

This section restates s 34 of the CA 1989. Prior to the CA 1967, auditors of an unquoted company were exempt from the statutory qualification requirements placed on other company auditors. The CA 1967 abolished this exemption, but allowed an auditor with sufficient practical experience, to apply to the Secretary of State for authorisation to practice. Past authorisations will continue to be valid by virtue of the transitional provision in s 1219(1)(b) of the CA 2006. Section 1222 of the CA 2006 provides that auditors authorised under the CA 1967 may not be treated as statutory auditors for any purpose other than to perform the statutory audit of an unquoted company (as defined in s 385(2) of the CA 2006).

Information

Matters to be notified to the Secretary of State

24.18 Section 1223 of the CA 2006 states that the Secretary of State may require a recognised supervisory body or a recognised qualifying body to notify him immediately of the occurrence of such events as he may specify in writing and to give him such information in respect of those events as is so specified;[6649] and to give him, at such times or in respect of such periods as he may specify in writing, such information as is so specified.[6650]

The notices and information required to be given must be such as the Secretary of State may reasonably require for the exercise of his functions under this Part.[6651]

The Secretary of State may require information given under this section to be given in a specified form or verified in a specified manner.[6652]

Any notice or information required to be given under this section must be given in writing unless the Secretary of State specifies or approves some other manner.[6653]

[6646] CA 2006, s 1222(1).   [6647] CA 2006, s 1222(2).   [6648] CA 2006, s 1222(3).
[6649] CA 2006, s 1223(1)(a).   [6650] CA 2006, s 1223(1)(b).   [6651] CA 2006, s 1223(2).
[6652] CA 2006, s 1223(3).   [6653] CA 2006, s 1223(4).

Section 1223 of the CA 2006 is a restatement of s 37 of the CA 1989 and allows the Secretary of State to identify events that must be notified to him if they occur. It requires that recognised supervisory and qualifying bodies must provide information, either in writing or some other specified manner, that is reasonably required for the Secretary of State to carry out his functions – this might include annual reports, notifications of rule or bye-law changes. This information might relate to specific time periods or specific occurrences.

The Secretary of State's power to call for information

24.19 Section 1224 of the CA 2006 deals with the Secretary of State's power to call for information. It states that the Secretary of State may by notice in writing, require a person within s 1224(2) of the CA 2006 to give him such information as he may reasonably require for the exercise of his functions under this Part.[6654]

The persons within this subsection are any recognised supervisory body,[6655] any recognised qualifying body,[6656] and any person eligible for appointment as a statutory auditor by virtue of this Chapter.[6657]

The Secretary of State may require that any information that he requires under this section is to be given within such reasonable time and verified in such manner as he may specify.[6658]

This section restates s 38 of the CA 1989. It provides the Secretary of State with the power to require information from a recognised supervisory body, a recognised qualifying body or an individual statutory auditor. For example, as a result of a report provided under s 1223 of the CA 2006, the Secretary of State may request further information on a specific point to clarify if a recognised supervisory body is complying with the requirements in Schedule 10 to the CA 2006. The Secretary of State can specify the time period in which this information has to be provided.

Enforcement

Compliance orders

24.20 Section 1225 of the CA 2006 sets out the compliance orders. If at any time it appears to the Secretary of State (a) in the case of a recognised supervisory body, that any requirement of Schedule 10 to the CA 2006 is not satisfied;[6659] (b) in the case of a recognised professional qualification, that any requirement of Schedule 11 to the CA 2006 is not satisfied;[6660] or (c) that a recognised supervisory body or a recognised qualifying body has failed to

---

[6654] CA 2006, s 1224(1). [6655] CA 2006, s 1224(2)(a). [6656] CA 2006, s 1224(2)(b).
[6657] CA 2006, s 1224(2)(c). [6658] CA 2006, s 1224(3). [6659] CA 2006, s 1225(1)(a).
[6660] CA 2006, s 1225(1)(b).

comply with an obligation to which it is subject under or by virtue of this Part, he may, instead of revoking the relevant recognition order, make an application to the court under this section.[6661]

If on an application under this section the court decides that the requirement in question is not satisfied or, as the case may be, that the body has failed to comply with the obligation in question, it may order the body to take such steps as the court directs for securing that the requirement is satisfied or that the obligation is complied with.[6662]

In this section 'the court' means the High Court or, in Scotland, the Court of Session.[6663]

Section 1225 of the CA 2006 is a restatement of s 39 of the CA 1989. If a recognised supervisory or qualifying body fails to meet the requirements in Schedule 10 or 11 to the CA 2006 respectively, or it fails to comply with another requirement contained in this Part of the Act, then the Secretary of State may apply to the court for an order to make the body comply. The ultimate sanction for non-compliance by a body would be revocation of their status as a recognised body under Schedule 10 or 11 to the CA 2006.

Auditors General

Eligibility for appointment

Auditors General: eligibility for appointment as a statutory auditor

24.21 Section 1226 of the CA 2006 is concerned with the Auditors General's eligibility for appointment as a statutory auditor. The term 'Auditor General' means the following:

(a)   the Comptroller and Auditor General;[6664]
(b)   the Auditor General for Scotland;[6665]
(c)   the Auditor General for Wales;[6666] or
(d)   the Comptroller and Auditor General for Northern Ireland.[6667]

An Auditor General is eligible for appointment as a statutory auditor.[6668]

Section 1226 of the CA 2006 is subject to any suspension notice having effect under s 1234 of the CA 2006 (notices suspending eligibility for appointment as a statutory auditor).[6669]

Section 1226(1) of the CA 2006 defines an 'Auditor General' for the purposes of this Part as the Comptroller and Auditor General, the Auditor

[6661] CA 2006, s 1225(1)(c).   [6662] CA 2006, s 1225(2).   [6663] CA 2006, s 1225(3).
[6664] CA 2006, s 1226(1)(a).   [6665] CA 2006, s 1226(1)(b).   [6666] CA 2006, s 1226(1)(c).
[6667] CA 2006, s 1226(1)(d).   [6668] CA 2006, s 1226(2).   [6669] CA 2006, s 1226(3).

General for Scotland, the Auditor General for Northern Ireland. Section 1226(2) and (3) of the CA 2006 explains that an Auditor General is eligible for appointment as a statutory auditor, unless his eligibility has been suspended by the Independent Supervisor under s 1234 of the CA 2006.

Conduct of audits

Individuals responsible for audit work on behalf of Auditors General

24.22 Section 1227 of the CA 2006 states that an Auditor General must secure that each individual responsible for statutory audit work on behalf of that Auditor General is eligible for appointment as a statutory auditor by virtue of Chapter 2 to Part 42 of the CA 2006.

This section provides that an Auditor General must ensure that the individuals within his charge, who are carrying out statutory audits on the Auditor General's behalf, are in their own right, eligible for appointment as a statutory auditor by virtue of the qualifications and requirements that are set out in Chapter 2 to Part 42 of the CA 2006.

The Independent Supervisor

Appointment of the Independent Supervisor

24.23 Section 1228 of the CA 2006 deals with the appointment of the Independent Supervisor. The Secretary of State must appoint a body (the Independent Supervisor) to discharge the function mentioned in s 1229(1) of the CA 2006 (the supervision function).[6670]

An appointment under this section must be made by order.[6671]

The order has the effect of making the body appointed under s 1228(1) of the CA 2006 designated under s 5 of the Freedom of Information Act 2000 (c 36) (further powers to designate public authorities).[6672]

A body may be appointed under this section only if it is a body corporate or an unincorporated association that appears to the Secretary of State to be willing and able to discharge the supervision function,[6673] and to have arrangements in place relating to the discharge of that function which are such as to be likely to ensure that the conditions in s 1228(5) of the CA 2006 are met.[6674]

The conditions are that the supervision function will be exercised effectively,[6675] and where the order is to contain any requirements or other provisions specified under s 1228(6) of the CA 2006, that that function will be exercised in accordance with any such requirements or provisions.[6676]

[6670] CA 2006, s 1228(1). [6671] CA 2006, s 1228(2). [6672] CA 2006, s 1228(3).
[6673] CA 2006, s 1228(4)(a). [6674] CA 2006, s 1228(4)(b). [6675] CA 2006, s 1228(5)(a).
[6676] CA 2006, s 1228(5)(b).

An order under this section may contain such requirements or other provisions relating to the exercise of the supervision function by the Independent Supervisor, as appear to the Secretary of State to be appropriate.[6677]

An order under this section is subject to negative resolution procedure.[6678]

Section 1228(1) and (3) of the CA 2006 provides that the Secretary of State must appoint a body to be the Independent Supervisor of Auditors General, in respect of the exercise of statutory audit functions. Section 1228(2) of the CA 2006 provides for the appointment of the Independent Supervisor to have the effect of making it subject to the obligations of the Freedom of Information Act 2000. Section 1228(4), (5) and (6) of the CA 2006 provides for the appointment a body or unincorporated association that is willing to carry out the function, that has arrangements in place that will ensure the supervision is carried out effectively, and that will exercise such functions and requirements that may be laid down in the Secretary of State's order appointing it. The appointed Independent Supervisor must perform its function on a UK-wide basis for all four Auditors General in accordance with s 1229(1) of the CA 2006.

Supervision of Auditors General

Supervision of Auditors General by the Independent Supervisor

24.24 Section 1229 of the CA 2006 deals with the supervision of Auditors General by the Independent Supervisor. The Independent Supervisor must supervise the performance by each Auditor General of his functions as a statutory auditor.[6679]

The Independent Supervisor must discharge that duty by entering into supervision arrangements with one or more bodies,[6680] and overseeing the effective operation of any supervision arrangements entered into by it.[6681]

The term 'supervision arrangements' describes arrangements entered into by the Independent Supervisor with a body, for the purposes of this section, in accordance with which the body does one or more of the following:

(a)   determines standards relating to professional integrity and independence, which must be applied by an Auditor General in statutory audit work;[6682]

(b)   determines technical standards, which must be applied by an Auditor General in statutory audit work and the manner in which those standards are to be applied in practice;[6683]

[6677] CA 2006, s 1228(6).   [6678] CA 2006, s 1228(7).   [6679] CA 2006, s 1229(1).
[6680] CA 2006, s 1229(2)(a).   [6681] CA 2006, s 1229(2)(b).   [6682] CA 2006, s 1229(3)(a).
[6683] CA 2006, s 1229(3)(b).

(c)   monitors the performance of statutory audits carried out by an Auditor General;[6684]
(d)   investigates any matter arising from the performance by an Auditor General of a statutory audit;[6685]
(e)   holds disciplinary hearings in respect of an Auditor General that appear to be desirable following the conclusion of such investigations;[6686]
(f)   decides whether (and, if so, what) disciplinary action should be taken against an Auditor General to whom such a hearing related.[6687]

The Independent Supervisor may enter into supervision arrangements with a body despite any relationship that may exist between the Independent Supervisor and that body.[6688]

The Independent Supervisor must notify each Auditor General in writing of any supervision arrangements that it enters into under this section.[6689]

Supervision arrangements within s 1229(3)(f) of the CA 2006 may, in particular, provide for the payment by an Auditor General of a fine to any person.[6690]

Any fine received by the Independent Supervisor under supervision arrangements is to be paid into the Consolidated Fund.[6691]

Section 1229 of the CA 2006 sets out the framework for the supervision arrangements to be carried out by the Independent Supervisor. Section 1229(2) of the CA 2006 provides that the Independent Supervisor must establish arrangements with one or more third parties to carry out aspects of the supervisory function. Section 1229(3) of the CA 2006 provides that the arrangements with a third party cover standards on professional integrity and independence, as well as the technical standards for statutory audit work; monitoring performance; investigating matters arising form that perform-ance; and as necessary holding disciplinary hearings and deciding whether any disciplinary action should be taken. Section 1229(6) and (7) of the CA 2006 makes provisions relating to the payment of fines under the disciplinary arrangements.

Duties of Auditors General in relation to supervision arrangements

24.25 Section 1230 of the CA 2006 states that each Auditor General must (a) comply with any standards of the kind mentioned in s 1229(3)(a) or (b) of the CA 2006 determined under the supervision arrangements;[6692] (b) take such steps as may be reasonably required of that Auditor General to enable his performance of statutory audits to be monitored by means of inspections

---

[6684] CA 2006, s 1229(3)(c).   [6685] CA 2006, s 1229(3)(d).   [6686] CA 2006, s 1229(3)(e).
[6687] CA 2006, s 1229(3)(f).   [6688] CA 2006, s 1229(4).   [6689] CA 2006, s 1229(5).
[6690] CA 2006, s 1229(6).   [6691] CA 2006, s 1229(7).   [6692] CA 2006, s 1230(1)(a).

carried out under the supervision arrangements;[6693] and (c) comply with any decision of the kind mentioned in s 1229(3)(f) of the CA 2006 made under the supervision arrangements.[6694]

Each Auditor General must pay to the body or bodies with which the Independent Supervisor enters into the supervision arrangements, such proportion of the costs incurred by the body or bodies for the purposes of the arrangements as the Independent Supervisor may notify to him in writing.[6695]

Expenditure under s 1230(2) of the CA 2006 is in the case of expenditure of the Comptroller and Auditor General, to be regarded as expenditure of the National Audit Office for the purposes of section 4(1) of the National Audit Act 1983 (c 44);[6696] and in the case of expenditure of the Comptroller and Auditor General for Northern Ireland, to be regarded as expenditure of the Northern Ireland Audit Office for the purposes of Article 6(1) of the Audit (Northern Ireland) Order 1987 (SI 1987/460 (NI 5)).[6697]

The term 'the supervision arrangements' means the arrangements entered into under s 1229 of the CA 2006.[6698]

Section 1230(1) of the CA 2006 makes it a duty for the Auditor General to comply with the standards set by, as well as the monitoring arrangements and decisions of, the independent supervision arrangements. It also provides in s 1230(2) of the CA 2006 for each Auditor General to pay the proportion of the costs of the independent supervisory arrangements that may be notified to the Auditor General in writing. Section 1230(3) of the CA 2006 provides that the payment of such costs is to be regarded as expenditure of the National Audit Office in the case of the Comptroller and Auditor General, and as expenditure of the Northern Ireland Audit Office in the case of the Comptroller and Auditor General for Northern Ireland. In the case of the Auditor General for Scotland, under s 13 of the Public Finance and Accountability (Scotland) Act 2000 (asp 1) the expenses of the Auditor General are to be paid by Audit Scotland. In the case of the Auditor General for Wales, under s 93 of the Government of Wales Act 1998 the expenses of the General are to be met by the Assembly.

Reporting requirement

Reports by the Independent Supervisor

24.26 Section 1231 of the CA 2006 deals with reports by the independent supervisor. The Independent Supervisor must, at least once in each calendar year, prepare a report on the discharge of its functions.[6699]

[6693] CA 2006, s 1230(1)(b).   [6694] CA 2006, s 1230(1)(c).   [6695] CA 2006, s 1230(2).
[6696] CA 2006, s 1230(3)(a).   [6697] CA 2006, s 1230(3)(b).   [6698] CA 2006, s 1230(4).
[6699] CA 2006, s 1231(1).

The Independent Supervisor must give a copy of each report prepared under s 1231(1) of the CA 2006 to:

(a)   the Secretary of State;[6700]
(b)   the First Minister in Scotland;[6701]
(c)   the First Minister and the deputy First Minister in Northern Ireland;[6702]
(d)   the Assembly First Secretary in Wales.[6703]

The Secretary of State must lay before each House of Parliament a copy of each report received by him under s 1231(2)(a) of the CA 2006.[6704]

In relation to a calendar year during which an appointment of a body as the Independent Supervisor is made or revoked by an order under s 1228 of the CA 2006, this section applies with such modifications as may be specified in the order.[6705]

This section provides that the Independent Supervisor must provide at least one report each calendar year to the Secretary of State and to the First Minister in Scotland, the First Minister and the Deputy First Minister in Northern Ireland and the Assembly First Minister in Wales. The Secretary of State must then lay the report before each House of Parliament.

Information

Matters to be notified to the Independent Supervisor

24.27 Section 1232 of the CA 2006 sets out the matters to be notified to the Independent Supervisor.

The Independent Supervisor may require an Auditor General to notify the Independent Supervisor immediately of the occurrence of such events as it may specify in writing and to give him such information in respect of those events as is so specified;[6706] to give the Independent Supervisor, at such times or in respect of such periods as it may specify in writing, such information as is so specified.[6707]

The notices and information required to be given must be such as the Independent Supervisor may reasonably require for the exercise of the functions conferred on it by or by virtue of this Part.[6708]

The Independent Supervisor may require information given under this section to be given in a specified form or verified in a specified manner.[6709]

Any notice or information required to be given under this section must be

---

[6700] CA 2006, s 1231(2)(a).   [6701] CA 2006, s 1231(2)(b).   [6702] CA 2006, s 1231(2)(c).
[6703] CA 2006, s 1231(2)(d).   [6704] CA 2006, s 1231(3).   [6705] CA 2006, s 1231(1).
[6706] CA 2006, s 1232(1)(a).   [6707] CA 2006, s 1232(1)(b).   [6708] CA 2006, s 1232(2).
[6709] CA 2006, s 1232(3).

given in writing unless the Independent Supervisor specifies or approves some other manner.[6710]

Section 1232 of the CA 2006 makes it a legal requirement for an Auditor General to notify the Independent Supervisor in writing of events that the Independent Supervisor may specify and is consistent with the requirement for other statutory auditors as contained in s 1223 of the CA 2006.

The Independent Supervisor's power to call for information

24.28 Section 1233 of the CA 2006 deals with the Independent Supervisor's power to call for information. The Independent Supervisor may by notice in writing require an Auditor General to give it such information as it may reasonably require for the exercise of the functions conferred on it by or by virtue of this Part.[6711]

The Independent Supervisor may require that any information that it requires under this section is to be given within such reasonable time and verified in such manner as it may specify.[6712]

Section 1233 of the CA 2006 makes provision enabling the Independent Supervisor to require an Auditor General to provide information. It enables the Independent Supervisor to specify the period within which the information must be provided and how the information must be verified. This section is consistent with the requirement for other statutory auditors as contained in s 1224 of the CA 2006.

Enforcement

Suspension notices

24.29 Section 1234 of the CA 2006 is concerned with suspension notices. The Independent Supervisor may issue a notice (a suspension notice) suspending an Auditor General's eligibility for appointment as a statutory auditor in relation to all persons, or any specified person or persons, indefinitely or until a date specified in the notice;[6713] or a notice amending or revoking a suspension notice previously issued to an Auditor General.[6714]

In determining whether it is appropriate to issue a notice under s 1234(1) of the CA 2006, the Independent Supervisor must have regard to the Auditor General's performance of the obligations imposed on him by or by virtue of this Part,[6715] and the Auditor General's performance of his functions as a statutory auditor.[6716]

[6710] CA 2006, s 1232(4).   [6711] CA 2006, s 1233(1).   [6712] CA 2006, s 1233(2).
[6713] CA 2006, s 1234(1)(a).   [6714] CA 2006 s 1234(1)(b).   [6715] CA 2006, s 1234(2)(a).
[6716] CA 2006, s 1234(2)(b).

A notice under s 1234(1) of the CA 2006 must be in writing,[6717] and state the date on which it takes effect (which must be after the period of three months beginning with the date on which it is issued).[6718]

Before issuing a notice under s 1234(1) of the CA 2006, the Independent Supervisor must (a) give written notice of its intention to do so to the Auditor General;[6719] and (b) publish the notice mentioned in para (a) in such manner as it thinks appropriate for bringing it to the attention of any other persons who are likely to be affected.[6720]

A notice under s 1234(4) of the CA 2006 must state the reasons for which the Independent Supervisor proposes to act,[6721] and give particulars of the rights conferred by s 1234(6) of the CA 2006.[6722]

A person within s 1234(7) of the CA 2006 may, within the period of three months beginning with the date of service or publication of the notice under s 1234(4) of the CA 2006 or such longer period as the Independent Supervisor may allow, make written representations to the Independent Supervisor and, if desired, oral representations to a person appointed for that purpose by the Independent Supervisor.[6723]

The persons within this subsection are the Auditor General,[6724] and any other person who appears to the Independent Supervisor to be affected.[6725]

The Independent Supervisor must have regard to any representations made in accordance with s 1234(6) of the CA 2006 in determining whether to issue a notice under subs (1),[6726] and the terms of any such notice.[6727]

If in any case the Independent Supervisor considers it appropriate to do so in the public interest it may issue a notice under s 1234(1) of the CA 2006, without regard to the restriction in s 1234(3)(b) of the CA 2006, even if no notice has been given or published under s 1234(4) of the CA 2006,[6728] or the period of time for making representations in pursuance of such a notice has not expired.[6729]

On issuing a notice under s 1234(1) of the CA 2006, the Independent Supervisor must give a copy of the notice to the Auditor General,[6730] and publish the notice in such manner as it thinks appropriate for bringing it to the attention of persons likely to be affected.[6731]

The term 'specified' means specified in, or of a description specified in, the suspension notice in question.[6732]

Section 1234 of the CA 2006 provides the Independent Supervisor with the power to suspend an Auditor General's eligibility for appointment as a statutory auditor if, for example, he falls short of the standards laid down for

---

[6717] CA 2006, s 1234(3)(a).
[6718] CA 2006, s 1234(3)(b).
[6719] CA 2006, s 1234(4)(a).
[6720] CA 2006, s 1234(4)(b).
[6721] CA 2006, s 1234(5)(a).
[6722] CA 2006, s 1234(5)(b).
[6723] CA 2006, s 1234(6).
[6724] CA 2006, s 1234(7)(a).
[6725] CA 2006, s 1234(7)(b).
[6726] CA 2006, s 1234(8)(a).
[6727] CA 2006, s 1234(8)(b).
[6728] CA 2006, s 1234(9)(a).
[6729] CA 2006, s 1234(9)(b).
[6730] CA 2006, s 1234(10)(a).
[6731] CA 2006, s 1234(10)(b).
[6732] CA 2006, s 1234(11).

performance of statutory audit work. It also sets out the provisions as to how the suspension will be effected, the considerations pertaining to the decision to suspend, the reasons for such a decision and so on. It provides for a process leading up to the issuing of a suspension notice, including the hearing of representations from the Auditor General in question.

Effect of suspension notices

24.30 Section 1234 of the CA 2006 sets out the effect of suspension notices. An Auditor General must not act as a statutory auditor at any time when a suspension notice issued to him in respect of the audited person has effect.[6733]

If at any time during an Auditor General's term of office as a statutory auditor a suspension notice issued to him in respect of the audited person takes effect, he must immediately resign his office (with immediate effect),[6734] and give notice in writing to the audited person that he has resigned by reason of his becoming ineligible for appointment.[6735]

A suspension notice does not make an Auditor General ineligible for appointment as a statutory auditor for the purposes of s 1213 of the CA 2006 (effect of ineligibility: criminal offences).[6736]

Section 1235 of the CA 2006 provides that an Auditor General must not act as a statutory auditor of a particular person if he is suspended in relation to that person. If the suspension starts during his term of office, the Auditor General must resign as a statutory auditor immediately, and tell the audited person that he has resigned. Section 1235(3) of the CA 2006 makes it clear that the criminal offences in s 1213 of the CA 2006 (ineligibility for appointment as a statutory auditor) do not apply to an Auditor General who is ineligible by virtue of a suspension notice.

Compliance orders

24.31 Section 1236 of the CA 2006 sets out the compliance orders. If at any time it appears to the Independent Supervisor that an Auditor General has failed to comply with an obligation imposed on him by or by virtue of this Part, the Independent Supervisor may make an application to the court under this section.[6737]

If on an application under this section the court decides that the Auditor General has failed to comply with the obligation in question, it may order the Auditor General to take such steps as the court directs for securing that the obligation is complied with.[6738]

[6733] CA 2006, s 1235(1).   [6734] CA 2006, s 1235(2)(a).   [6735] CA 2006, s 1235(2)(b).
[6736] CA 2006, s 1235(3).   [6737] CA 2006, s 1236(1).   [6738] CA 2006, s 1236(2).

In this section 'the court' means the High Court or, in Scotland, the Court of Session.[6739]

Section 1236 of the CA 2006 provides the power for the Independent Supervisor to take an Auditor General to court if he fails to comply with any obligation by or by virtue of this Part of the CA 2006. The court may direct the Auditor General to take such steps as it thinks fit to ensure compliance.

Proceedings

Proceedings involving the Independent Supervisor

24.32 Section 1237 of the CA 2006 sets out the proceedings involving the Independent Supervisor. If the Independent Supervisor is an unincorporated association, any relevant proceedings may be brought by or against it in the name of any body corporate whose constitution provides for the establishment of the body.[6740]

The term 'relevant proceedings' means proceedings brought in or in connection with the exercise of any function by the body as the Independent Supervisor.[6741]

Where an appointment under s 1228 of the CA 2006 is revoked, the revoking order may make such provision as the Secretary of State thinks fit with respect to pending proceedings.[6742]

This section provides that where the Independent Supervisor is an unincorporated association, it may take proceedings in the name of the body corporate under which it is constituted.

Grants

Grants to the Independent Supervisor

24.33 Section 1238 of the CA 2006 deals with grants to the Independent Supervisor. It states that in s 16 of the Companies (Audit, Investigations and Community Enterprise) Act 2004 (c 27) (grants to bodies concerned with accounting standards, etc.), after subs (2)(k) insert:

(ka) exercising functions of the Independent Supervisor appointed under Chapter 3 of Part 42 of the CA 2006;

Section 1238 of the CA 2006 amends s 16(2) of the C(AICE) Act 2004. The effect of the amendment is that the body that carries out the functions of the

[6739] CA 2006, s 1236(3).   [6740] CA 2006, s 1237(1).   [6741] CA 2006, s 1237(2).
[6742] CA 2006, s 1237(3).

Independent Supervisor is eligible for grants from the Secretary of State under s 16 of that Act meet the expenditure of the body and any subsidiary. It also means that the body may be exempt from liability in damages under s 18 of that Act.

The Register of Auditors, etc.

24.34 Chapter 4 deals with the register of auditors. It comprises two sections.

The register of auditors

24.35 Section 1239 of the CA 2006 states that the Secretary of State must make regulations requiring the keeping of a register of the persons eligible for appointment as a statutory auditor,[6743] and third country auditors (see Chapter 5 to Part 42 of the CA 2006) who apply to be registered in the specified manner and in relation to whom specified requirements are met.[6744]

The regulations must require each person's entry in the register to contain the following:

(a)   his name and address;[6745]

(b)   in the case of an individual eligible for appointment as a statutory auditor, the specified information relating to any firm on whose behalf he is responsible for statutory audit work;[6746]

(c)   in the case of a firm eligible for appointment as a statutory auditor, the specified information relating to the individuals responsible for statutory audit work on its behalf;[6747]

(d)   in the case of an individual or firm eligible for appointment as a statutory auditor by virtue of Chapter 2, the name of the relevant supervisory body;[6748] and

(e)   in the case of a firm eligible for appointment as a statutory auditor by virtue of Chapter 2 or a third country auditor, the information mentioned in s 1239(3) of the CA 2006,[6749]

and may require each person's entry to contain other specified information.

The information referred to in s 1239(2)(e) of the CA 2006 is:

(a)   in relation to a body corporate, except where para (b) applies, the name and address of each person who is a director of the body or holds any shares in it;[6750]

[6743] CA 2006, s 1239(1)(a).   [6744] CA 2006, s 1239(1)(b).   [6745] CA 2006, s 1239(2)(a).

[6746] CA 2006, s 1239(2)(b).   [6747] CA 2006, s 1239(2)(c).   [6748] CA 2006, s 1239(2)(d).

[6749] CA 2006, s 1239(2)(e).   [6750] CA 2006, s 1239(3)(a).

(b) in relation to a limited liability partnership, the name and address of each member of the partnership;[6751]

(c) in relation to a corporation sole, the name and address of the individual for the time being holding the office by the name of which he is the corporation sole;[6752]

(d) in relation to a partnership, the name and address of each partner.[6753]

The regulations may provide that different parts of the register are to be kept by different persons.[6754]

The regulations may impose such obligations as the Secretary of State thinks fit on:

(a) recognised supervisory bodies;[6755]

(b) any body designated by order under s 1252 of the CA 2006 (delegation of Secretary of State's functions);[6756]

(c) persons eligible for appointment as a statutory auditor;[6757]

(d) third country auditors;[6758]

(e) any person with whom arrangements are made by one or more recognised supervisory bodies, or by any body designated by order under s 1252 of the CA 2006, with respect to the keeping of the register,[6759] or

(f) the Independent Supervisor appointed under s 1228 of the CA 2006.[6760]

The regulations may include (a) provision requiring that specified entries in the register be open to inspection at times and places specified or determined in accordance with the regulations;[6761] (b) provision enabling a person to require a certified copy of specified entries in the register;[6762] (c) provision authorising the charging of fees for inspection, or the provision of copies, of such reasonable amount as may be specified or determined in accordance with the regulations.[6763]

The Secretary of State may direct in writing that the requirements imposed by the regulations in accordance with s 1239(2)(e) and (3) of the CA 2006, or such of those requirements as are specified in the direction, are not to apply, in whole or in part, in relation to a particular registered third country auditor or class of registered third country auditors.[6764]

The obligations imposed by regulations under this section on such persons as are mentioned in s 1239(5)(b) or (e) of the CA 2006 are enforceable on the application of the Secretary of State by injunction or, in Scotland, by an order under s 45 of the Court of Session Act 1988 (c 36).[6765]

[6751] CA 2006, s 1239(3)(b).   [6752] CA 2006, s 1239(3)(c).   [6753] CA 2006, s 1239(3)(d).
[6754] CA 2006, s 1239(4).   [6755] CA 2006, s 1239(5)(a).   [6756] CA 2006, s 1239(5)(b).
[6757] CA 2006, s 1239(5)(c).   [6758] CA 2006, s 1239(5)(d).   [6759] CA 2006, s 1239(5)(e).
[6760] CA 2006, s 1239(5)(f).   [6761] CA 2006, s 1239(6)(a).   [6762] CA 2006, s 1239(6)(b).
[6763] CA 2006, s 1239(6)(c).   [6764] CA 2006, s 1239(7).   [6765] CA 2006, s 1239(8).

The term 'specified' means specified by regulations under this section.[6766]

Regulations under this section are subject to negative resolution procedure.[6767]

Section 1239 of the CA 2006 restates s 35 of the CA 1989 but extends the provision to cover other statutory auditors (as defined in s 1210 of the CA 2006) and third country auditors (as defined in s 1241 of the CA 2006). It requires the Secretary of State to make regulations that require the keeping of a register of those persons eligible to be a statutory auditor and registered third country auditors. Section 1239(2) of the CA 2006 sets out the information that must be included on the register and includes the name and address, and the name of the relevant supervisory body for the person. If an individual auditor works for a firm that is a statutory auditor, both must be entered separately on the register and cross-referenced. In s 1239(3)CA 2006 additional information, namely the name and address of directors, members or partners, is required from bodies corporate (including limited liability partnerships), corporations sole and partnerships. The section allows for certain parts of the register to be kept by different persons, for example an oversight body may keep the information regarding third country auditors, whilst the recognised supervisory bodies may keep information regarding other statutory auditors. Section 1239(6) of the CA 2006 confers a power to provide that information in the register or a certified copy of it, is to be made available to the public upon request. A charge for access to this information is permitted. Section 1239(7) of the CA 2006 allows the Secretary of State to disapply some or all of the requirements of s 1239(e) and (3) of the CA 2006 in relation to third country auditors (for example, if they are already subject to equivalent supervision in their home country.

Information to be made available to public

24.36 Section 1240 of the CA 2006 deals with the information to be made available to the public. The Secretary of State may make regulations requiring a person eligible for appointment as a statutory auditor, or a member of a specified class of such persons, to keep and make available to the public specified information, including information regarding:

(a)   the person's ownership and governance;[6768]
(b)   the person's internal controls with respect to the quality and independence of its audit work;[6769]
(c)   the person's turnover;[6770] and
(d)   the audited persons of whom the person has acted as statutory auditor.[6771]

[6766] CA 2006, s 1239(9).   [6767] CA 2006, s 1239(10).   [6768] CA 2006, s 1240(1)(a).
[6769] CA 2006, s 1240(1)(b).   [6770] CA 2006, s 1240(1)(c).   [6771] CA 2006, s 1240(1)(d).

The regulations under this section may impose such obligations as the Secretary of State thinks fit on persons eligible for appointment as a statutory auditor;[6772] and may require the information to be made available to the public in a specified manner.[6773]

The term 'specified' means specified by regulations under this section.[6774]

Regulations under this section are subject to negative resolution procedure.[6775]

This new provision gives the Secretary of State the power to make regulations placing an obligation on statutory auditors to make information regarding their ownership, governance, internal controls with respect to the quality and independence of their audit work, turnover and names of persons for whom the person has acted as statutory auditor, available to the public. Any such obligations are additional to those referred to in s 1239 of the CA 2006.

Registered Third Country Auditors

24.37 Chapter 5 is concerned with registered third country auditors.

Introductory

Meaning of 'third country auditor', 'registered third country auditor', etc.

24.38 Section 1241 of the CA 2006 sets out the definitions. The term 'third country auditor' means the auditor of the accounts of a traded non-Community company, and the expressions 'third country audit' and 'third country audit work' are to be construed accordingly; and 'registered third country auditor' means a third country auditor who is entered in the register kept in accordance with regulations under s 1239(1) of the CA 2006.[6776]

In s 1241(1) of the CA 2006, the term 'traded Non-Community Company' means a body corporate:

(a) that is incorporated or formed under the law of a country or territory which is not a member State or part of a member State;[6777]

(b) whose transferable securities are admitted to trading on a regulated market situated or operating in the United Kingdom;[6778] and

(c) that has not been excluded, or is not of a description of bodies corporate that has been excluded, from this definition by an order made by the Secretary of State.[6779]

[6772] CA 2006, s 1240(2)(a).   [6773] CA 2006, s 1240(2)(b).   [6774] CA 2006, s 1240(3).
[6775] CA 2006, s 1240(4).   [6776] CA 2006, s 1241(1).   [6777] CA 2006, s 1241(2)(a).
[6778] CA 2006, s 1241(2)(b).   [6779] CA 2006, s 1241(2)(c).

For this purpose, the term 'regulated market' has the meaning given by Article 4.1(14) of Directive 2004/39/EC of the European Parliament and of the Council on markets in financial instruments; and 'transferable securities' has the meaning given by Article 4.1(18) of that Directive.[6780]

An order under this section is subject to negative resolution procedure.[6781]

This is a new provision that sets out the definition of a third country auditor and a registered third country auditor. The section provides that a third country auditor is an auditor (whether based in the UK or not) of the accounts of a company incorporated or formed in a non-EU country, whose shares are admitted for trading on a UK market such as the London Stock Exchange.

Duties

Duties of registered third country auditors

24.39 Section 1242 of the CA 2006 sets out the duties of registered third country auditors. A registered third country auditor must participate in arrangements within para 1 of Schedule 12 of the CA 2006 (arrangements for the independent monitoring of audits of traded non-Community companies),[6782] and arrangements within para 2 of that Schedule (arrangements for independent investigation for disciplinary purposes of public interest cases).[6783]

A registered third country auditor must take such steps as may be reasonably required to enable its performance of third country audits to be monitored by means of inspections carried out under the arrangements mentioned in s 1242(1)(a) of the CA 2006,[6784] and comply with any decision as to disciplinary action to be taken against it made under the arrangements mentioned in s 1242(1)(b) of the CA 2006.[6785]

Schedule 12 makes further provision with respect to the arrangements in which registered third country auditors are required to participate.[6786]

The Secretary of State may direct in writing that s 1242(1)–(3) of the CA 2006 are not to apply, in whole or in part, in relation to a particular registered third country auditor or class of registered third country auditors.[6787]

Section 1242(1)–(3) of the CA 2006 require registered third country auditors to be subject to systems of independent monitoring and discipline in the UK in accordance with Schedule 12. These provisions are similar to supervision arrangements for statutory auditors contained in s 1212(1) of the CA 2006 (membership of a Recognised Supervisory Body) and s 1217 of the CA 2006 (Supervisory Bodies) and Schedule 10 of the CA 2006. Section

[6780] CA 2006, s 1241(3).   [6781] CA 2006, s 1241(4).   [6782] CA 2006, s 1242(1)(a).
[6783] CA 2006, s 1242(1)(b).   [6784] CA 2006, s 1242(2)(a).   [6785] CA 2006, s 1242(2)(b).
[6786] CA 2006, s 1242(3).   [6787] CA 2006, s 1242(4).

1242(4) of the CA 2006 empowers the Secretary of State to disapply the requirements in s 1242(1)–(3) of the CA 2006. For example, he may disapply the requirements if satisfied that the third country auditor is already subject to equivalent supervision arrangements in his home country.

Schedule 12: Arrangements in which registered third country auditors are required to participate

The requirements in this Schedule are new. They describe the independent monitoring and investigation arrangements which third country auditors must participate in.

Information

Matters to be notified to the Secretary of State

24.40 Section 1243 of the CA 2006 deals with matters to be notified to the Secretary of State. The Secretary of State may require a registered third country auditor to notify him immediately of the occurrence of such events as he may specify in writing and to give him such information in respect of those events as is so specified;[6788] and to give him, at such times or in respect of such periods as he may specify in writing, such information as is so specified.[6789]

The notices and information required to be given must be such as the Secretary of State may reasonably require for the exercise of his functions under this Part.[6790]

The Secretary of State may require information given under this section to be given in a specified form or verified in a specified manner.[6791]

Any notice or information required to be given under this section must be given in writing unless the Secretary of State specifies or approves some other manner.[6792]

The Secretary of State's power to call for information

24.41 Section 1244 of the CA 2006 sets out the Secretary of State's power to call for information. The Secretary of State may by notice in writing require a registered third country auditor to give him such information as he may reasonably require for the exercise of his functions under this Part.[6793]

The Secretary of State may require that any information which he requires under this section is to be given within such reasonable time and verified in such manner as he may specify.[6794]

[6788] CA 2006, s 1243(1)(a).   [6789] CA 2006, s 1243(1)(b).   [6790] CA 2006, s 1243(2).
[6791] CA 2006, s 1243(3).   [6792] CA 2006, s 1243(4).   [6793] CA 2006, s 1244(1).
[6794] CA 2006, s 1244(2).

Sections 1243 and 1244 of the CA 2006 replicate for registered third country auditors the requirements in ss 1243 and 1244 of the CA 2006 for the notification of information that might reasonably be required for the Secretary to carry out his functions.

Enforcement

Compliance orders

24.42 Section 1245 of the CA 2006 states that if at any time it appears to the Secretary of State that a registered third country auditor has failed to comply with an obligation imposed on him by or by virtue of this Part, the Secretary of State may make an application to the court under this section.[6795]

If on an application under this section the court decides that the auditor has failed to comply with the obligation in question, it may order the auditor to take such steps as the court directs for securing that the obligation is complied with.[6796]

In this section 'the court' means the High Court or, in Scotland, the Court of Session.[6797]

Removal of third country auditors from the register of auditors

24.43 Section 1246 of the CA 2006 deals with removal of third country auditors form the register of auditors. The Secretary of State may, by regulations, confer on the person keeping the register in accordance with regulations under s 1239(1) of the CA 2006 power to remove a third country auditor from the register.[6798]

Regulations under this section must require the person keeping the register, in determining whether to remove a third country auditor from the register, to have regard to the auditor's compliance with obligations imposed on him by or by virtue of this Part.[6799]

Where provision is made under s 1239(4) of the CA 2006 (different parts of the register to be kept by different persons), references in this section to the person keeping the register are to the person keeping that part of the register which relates to third country auditors.[6800]

Regulations under this section are subject to negative resolution procedure.[6801]

The provisions in s 1245 of the CA 2006 enable the Secretary of State to apply to the court for an order to make a registered third country auditor comply with its obligations under the Part. The provisions in s 1246 of the

---

[6795] CA 2006, s 1245(1).   [6796] CA 2006, s 1245(2).   [6797] CA 2006, s 1245(3).
[6798] CA 2006, s 1246(1).   [6799] CA 2006, s 1246(2).   [6800] CA 2006, s 1246(3).
[6801] CA 2006, s 1246(4).

CA 2006 empower the Secretary of State to make provision as to the removal of the third country auditors from the register of auditors in certain circumstances. In doing so, regard must be had to whether the third country auditor has complied with his obligation under this Part.

Grants to bodies concerned with arrangements under Schedule 12

24.44 Section 1247 of the CA 2006 is concerned with grants to bodies concerned with arrangements under Schedule 12 of the CA 2006. It states that in s 16 of the Companies (Audit, Investigations and Community Enterprise) Act 2004 (c 27) (grants to bodies concerned with accounting standards etc), after subs (2)(ka) (inserted by s 1238) insert:

> (kb) establishing, maintaining or carrying out arrangements within paragraph 1 or 2 of Schedule 12 to the Companies Act 2006; . . .

This section amends s 16(2) of the C(AICE) Act 2004. The effect of the amendment is that the body that carries out the monitoring and investigation functions in relation to third country auditors is eligible for grants from the Secretary of State under s 16 of that Act. It also means that the body may be exempt form liability in damages under s 18 of that Act.

Supplementary and General

24.45 Chapter 6 sets out the supplementary and general provisions of Part 42 of the CA 2006.

Power to require second company audit

Secretary of State's power to require second audit of a company

24.46 Section 1248 of the CA 2006 deals with the Secretary of State's power to require the second audit of a company. It applies where a person appointed as statutory auditor of a company was not an appropriate person for any part of the period during which the audit was conducted.[6802]

The Secretary of State may direct the company concerned to retain an appropriate person to conduct a second audit of the relevant accounts,[6803] or to review the first audit and to report (giving his reasons) whether a second audit is needed.[6804]

For the purposes of s 1248(1) and (2) of the CA 2006, a person is termed 'appropriate' if he is eligible for appointment as a statutory auditor or, if the

---

[6802] CA 2006, s 1248(1).   [6803] CA 2006, s 1248(2)(a).   [6804] CA 2006, s 1248(2)(b).

person is an Auditor General, for appointment as statutory auditor of the company,[6805] and is not prohibited by s 1214(1) of the CA 2006 (independence requirement) from acting as statutory auditor of the company.[6806]

The Secretary of State must send a copy of a direction under s 1248(2) of the CA 2006 to the registrar of companies.[6807]

The company is guilty of an offence if it fails to comply with a direction under s 1248(2) of the CA 2006 within the period of 21 days beginning with the date on which it is given,[6808] or it has been convicted of a previous offence under this subsection and the failure to comply with the direction which led to the conviction continues after the conviction.[6809]

The company must send a copy of a report under s 1248(2)(b) of the CA 2006 to the registrar of companies,[6810] and if the report states that a second audit is needed, take such steps as are necessary for the carrying out of that audit.[6811]

The company is guilty of an offence if (a) it fails to send a copy of a report under s 1248(2)(b) of the CA 2006 to the registrar within the period of 21 days beginning with the date on which it receives it;[6812] (b) in a case within s 1248(6)(b) of the CA 2006, it fails to take the steps mentioned immediately it receives the report;[6813] or (c) it has been convicted of a previous offence under this subsection; and the failure to send a copy of the report, or take the steps that led to the conviction, continues after the conviction.[6814]

A company guilty of an offence under this section is liable on summary conviction in a case within s 1248(5)(a) or (7)(a) or (b) of the CA 2006, to a fine not exceeding level 5 on the standard scale,[6815] and in a case within s 1248(5)(b) or (7)(c) of the CA 2006, to a fine not exceeding one-tenth of level 5 on the standard scale for each day on which the failure continues.[6816]

The term 'registrar of companies' has the meaning given by s 1060 of the CA 2006.[6817]

Supplementary provision about second audits

24.47 Section 1249 of the CA 2006 states that if a person accepts an appointment, or continues to act, as statutory auditor of a company at a time when he knows he is not an appropriate person, the company may recover from him any costs incurred by it in complying with the requirements of s 1248 of the CA 2006.[6818]

For this purpose, 'appropriate' is to be construed in accordance with s 1248(3) of the CA 2006.

[6805] CA 2006, s 1248(3)(a).   [6806] CA 2006, s 1248(3)(b).   [6807] CA 2006, s 1248(4).
[6808] CA 2006, s 1248(5)(a).   [6809] CA 2006, s 1248(5)(b).   [6810] CA 2006, s 1248(6)(a).
[6811] CA 2006, s 1248(6)(b).   [6812] CA 2006, s 1248(7)(a).   [6813] CA 2006, s 1248(7)(b).
[6814] CA 2006, s 1248(7)(c).   [6815] CA 2006, s 1248(8)(a).   [6816] CA 2006, s 1248(8)(b).
[6817] CA 2006, s 1248(9).   [6818] CA 2006, s 1249(1).

Where a second audit is carried out under s 1248 of the CA 2006, any statutory or other provision applying in relation to the first audit applies also, in so far as practicable, in relation to the second audit.[6819]

A direction under s 1248(2) of the CA 2006 is, on the application of the Secretary of State, enforceable by injunction or, in Scotland, by an order under s 45 of the Court of Session Act 1988 (c 36).[6820]

Sections 1248 and 1249 of the CA 2006 restates that s 29 of the CA 1989 empowering the Secretary of State to require a second audit of a company in circumstances where the person appointed as statutory auditor was not eligible for appointment or was not independent of the company audited. Section 1248(2) of the CA 2006 permits the Secretary of State to direct either that a second audit is performed or that a review of the first audit is carried out (which will inform whether a second audit is required). Section 1248(5)–(8) of the CA 2006 sets out the criminal sanctions on the company should it fail to comply with that order. Section 1249 of the CA 2006 allows the audited person to recover the costs of the second audit from the first auditor, if the first auditor knew when he acted that he was not eligible or not independent.

False and misleading statements

Misleading, false and deceptive statements

24.48 Section 1250 of the CA 2006 states that a person is guilty of an offence if for the purposes of or in connection with any application under this Part, or in purported compliance with any requirement imposed on him by or by virtue of this Part, he knowingly or recklessly furnishes information which is misleading, false or deceptive in a material particular.[6821]

It is an offence for a person whose name does not appear on the register of auditors kept under regulations under s 1239 of the CA 2006 in an entry made under s 1239(1)(a) of the CA 2006 to describe himself as a registered auditor or so to hold himself out as to indicate, or be reasonably understood to indicate, that he is a registered auditor.[6822]

It is an offence for a person whose name does not appear on the register of auditors kept under regulations under that section in an entry made under s 1239(1)(b) of the CA 2006 to describe himself as a registered third country auditor or so to hold himself out as to indicate, or be reasonably understood to indicate, that he is a registered third country auditor.[6823]

It is an offence for a body that is not a recognised supervisory body or a recognised qualifying body to describe itself as so recognised or so to describe

---

[6819] CA 2006, s 1249(2).   [6820] CA 2006, s 1249(3).   [6821] CA 2006, s 1250(1).
[6822] CA 2006, s 1250(2).   [6823] CA 2006, s 1250(3).

itself or hold itself out as to indicate, or be reasonably understood to indicate, that it is so recognised.[6824]

A person guilty of an offence under s 1250(1) of the CA 2006 is liable on conviction on indictment, to imprisonment for a term not exceeding two years or to a fine (or both);[6825] and on summary conviction in England and Wales, to imprisonment for a term not exceeding 12 months or to a fine not exceeding the statutory maximum (or both),[6826] in Scotland or Northern Ireland, to imprisonment for a term not exceeding six months or to a fine not exceeding the statutory maximum (or both).[6827]

In relation to an offence committed before the commencement of s 154(1) of the Criminal Justice Act 2003 (c 44), for '12 months' in para (b)(i) substitute 'six months'.

Subject to s 1250(7) of the CA 2006, a person guilty of an offence under s 1250(2), (3) or (4) of the CA 2006 is liable on summary conviction in England and Wales, to imprisonment for a term not exceeding 51 weeks or to a fine not exceeding level 5 on the standard scale (or both),[6828] in Scotland or Northern Ireland, to imprisonment for a term not exceeding six months or to a fine not exceeding level 5 on the standard scale (or both).[6829]

In relation to an offence committed before the commencement of s 281(5) of the Criminal Justice Act 2003, for '51 weeks' in para (a) substitute 'six months'.

Where a contravention of s 1250(2), (3) or (4) of the CA 2006 involves a public display of the offending description, the maximum fine that may be imposed is an amount equal to level 5 on the standard scale multiplied by the number of days for which the display has continued.[6830]

It is a defence for a person charged with an offence under s 1250(2), (3) or (4) of the CA 2006 to show that he took all reasonable precautions and exercised all due diligence to avoid the commission of the offence.[6831]

This section is a restatement of the offences in s 41 of the CA 1989 but also extends these offences to third country auditors. Section 1250(1) of the CA 2006 sets out offences in respect to persons who provide information that they know to be misleading, false or deceptive. Section 1250(2) of the CA 2006 makes it an offence for a person to hold himself out as a registered auditor where he is not registered as such in accordance with s 1239 of the CA 2006. Section 1250(3) of the CA 2006 makes a similar provision for third country auditors. Section 1250(4) of the CA 2006 makes it an offence for either a supervisory or qualifying body to hold itself out as recognised when it is not so recognised. Section 1250(8) of the CA 2006 provides a defence if the person took all reasonable precautions and exercised due diligence to avoid committing the offence.

[6824] CA 2006, s 1250(4).   [6825] CA 2006, s 1250(5)(a).   [6826] CA 2006, s 1250(5)(b)(i).
[6827] CA 2006, s 1250(5)(b)(ii).   [6828] CA 2006, s 1250(6)(a).
[6829] CA 2006, s 1250(6)(b).   [6830] CA 2006, s 1250(7).   [6831] CA 2006, s 1250(8).

Fees

24.49 Section 1251 of the CA 2006 sets out the fees. An applicant for a recognition order under this Part must pay such fee in respect of his application as the Secretary of State may by regulations prescribe; and no application is to be regarded as duly made unless this subsection is complied with.[6832]

The Secretary of State may by regulations prescribe periodical fees to be paid by:

(a) every recognised supervisory body;[6833]
(b) every recognised qualifying body;[6834]
(c) every Auditor General;[6835] and
(d) every registered third country auditor.[6836]

Fees received by the Secretary of State by virtue of this Part are to be paid into the Consolidated Fund.[6837]

Regulations under this section are subject to negative resolution procedure.[6838]

This provision is based on s 45 of the CA 1989 and extends the powers of the Secretary of State to make regulations to prescribe periodical fees that must be paid by the Auditors General and registered third country auditors as well as recognised supervisory bodies and recognised qualifying bodies.

Delegation of the Secretary of State's functions

Delegation of the Secretary of State's functions

24.50 Section 1252 of the CA 2006 deals with the delegation of the Secretary of State's functions. The Secretary of State may make an order under this section (a delegation order) for the purpose of enabling functions of the Secretary of State under this Part to be exercised by a body designated by the order.[6839]

The body designated by a delegation order may be either a body corporate that is established by the order,[6840] or subject to s 1253 of the CA 2006, a body (whether a body corporate or an unincorporated association) that is already in existence (an existing body).[6841]

A delegation order has the effect of making the body designated by the order designated under s 5 of the Freedom of Information Act 2000 (c 36) (further powers to designate public authorities).[6842]

[6832] CA 2006, s 1251(1).   [6833] CA 2006, s 1251(2)(a).   [6834] CA 2006, s 1251(2)(b).
[6835] CA 2006, s 1251(2)(c).   [6836] CA 2006, s 1251(2)(d).   [6837] CA 2006, s 1251(3).
[6838] CA 2006, s 1251(4).   [6839] CA 2006, s 1252(1).   [6840] CA 2006, s 1252(2)(a).
[6841] CA 2006, s 1252(2)(b).   [6842] CA 2006, s 1252(3).

A delegation order has the effect of transferring to the body designated by it all functions of the Secretary of State under this Part (a) subject to such exceptions and reservations as may be specified in the order;[6843] and (b) except (i) his functions in relation to the body itself,[6844] and (ii) his functions under s 1228 of the CA 2006 (appointment of an Independent Supervisor).[6845]

A delegation order may confer on the body designated by it such other functions supplementary or incidental to those transferred as appear to the Secretary of State to be appropriate.[6846]

Any transfer of functions under the following provisions must be subject to the reservation that the functions remain exercisable concurrently by the Secretary of State, namely: (a) s 1224 of the CA 2006 (power to call for information from recognised bodies etc);[6847] (b) s 1244 of the CA 2006 (power to call for information from registered third country auditors);[6848] (c) s 1254 of the CA 2006 (directions to comply with international obligations).[6849]

Any transfer of the function of refusing to make a declaration under s 1221(1) of the CA 2006 (approval of overseas qualifications) on the grounds referred to in s 1221(4) of the CA 2006 (lack of comparable treatment),[6850] or the function of withdrawing such a declaration under s 1221(7) of the CA 2006 on those grounds,[6851] must be subject to the reservation that the function is exercisable only with the consent of the Secretary of State.

A delegation order may be amended or, if it appears to the Secretary of State that it is no longer in the public interest that the order should remain in force, revoked by a further order under this section.[6852]

Where functions are transferred or resumed, the Secretary of State may by order confer or, as the case may be, take away such other functions supplementary or incidental to those transferred or resumed as appear to him to be appropriate.[6853]

Where a delegation order is made, Schedule 13 of the CA 2006 applies with respect to:

(a) the status of the body designated by the order in exercising functions of the Secretary of State under this Part;[6854]
(b) the constitution and proceedings of the body where it is established by the order;[6855]
(c) the exercise by the body of certain functions transferred to it;[6856] and
(d) other supplementary matters.[6857]

[6843] CA 2006, s 1252(4)(a).   [6844] CA 2006, s 1252(4)(b)(i).
[6845] CA 2006, s 1252(4)(b)(ii).   [6846] CA 2006, s 1252(5).   [6847] CA 2006, s 1252(6)(a).
[6848] CA 2006, s 1252(6)(b).   [6849] CA 2006, s 1252(6)(c).   [6850] CA 2006, s 1252(7)(a).
[6851] CA 2006, s 1252(7)(b).   [6852] CA 2006, s 1252(8).   [6853] CA 2006, s 1252(9).
[6854] CA 2006, s 1252(10)(a).   [6855] CA 2006, s 1252(10)(b).
[6856] CA 2006, s 1252(10)(c).   [6857] CA 2006, s 1252(10)(d).

An order under this section which has the effect of transferring or resuming any functions is subject to affirmative resolution procedure.[6858]

Any other order under this section is subject to negative resolution procedure.[6859]

Delegation of functions to an existing body

24.51 Section 1253 of the CA 2006 deals with delegation of functions to an existing body. The Secretary of State's power to make a delegation order under s 1252 of the CA 2006 that designates an existing body is exercisable in accordance with this section.[6860]

The Secretary of State may make such a delegation order if it appears to him that the body is able and willing to exercise the functions that would be transferred by the order,[6861] and the body has arrangements in place relating to the exercise of those functions that are such as to be likely to ensure that the conditions in s 1253(3) of the CA 2006 are met.[6862]

The conditions are that the functions in question will be exercised effectively,[6863] and where the delegation order is to contain any requirements or other provisions specified under s 1253(4) of the CA 2006, that those functions will be exercised in accordance with any such requirements or provisions.[6864]

The delegation order may contain such requirements or other provision relating to the exercise of the functions by the designated body as appear to the Secretary of State to be appropriate.[6865]

An existing body may be designated by a delegation order under s 1252 of the CA 2006,[6866] and may accordingly exercise functions of the Secretary of State in pursuance of the order,[6867] despite any involvement of the body in the exercise of any functions under arrangements within paras 21, 22, 23(1) or 24(1) of Schedule 10 or para 1 or 2 of Schedule 12 of the CA 2006.

Sections 1252 and 1253 of the CA 2006 replace ss 46 and 46A of the CA 1989 as amended by ss 3–5 of the C(AICE) Act 2004 and empower the Secretary of State to establish a body, or appoint an existing body, to exercise his functions relating to statutory auditors and the recognition of bodies that supervise auditors and/or provide professional qualifications. To do so, the Secretary of State must make a delegation order that is in accordance with Schedule 13 of the CA 2006. However, s 1252(6) of the CA 2006 provides that some delegated functions must remain exercisable concurrently by the Secretary of State: namely the power to call for information (ss 1224 and 1244 of the CA 2006) and the power to issue directions to comply with

[6858] CA 2006, s 1252(11).   [6859] CA 2006, s 1252(12).   [6860] CA 2006, s 1253(1).
[6861] CA 2006, s 1253(2)(a).   [6862] CA 2006, s 1253(2)(b).   [6863] CA 2006, s 1253(3)(a).
[6864] CA 2006, s 1253(3)(b).   [6865] CA 2006, s 1253(4).   [6866] CA 2006, s 1253(5)(a).
[6867] CA 2006, s 1253(5)(b).

international obligations (s 1254 of the CA 2006). Section 1252(7) of the CA 2006 also provides that certain delegated functions concerning the approval of overseas qualifications (s 1221 of the CA 2006) can be exercised only with the consent of the Secretary of State. Section 1252(3) of the CA 2006 provides for the appointment of the delegation of the body to have the effect of making it subject to the obligations of the Freedom of Information Act 2000. The Professional Oversight Board is currently appointed under s 46 of the CA 1989 to exercise the Secretary of State's functions.

Section 1253 of the CA 2006 specifies the conditions for delegating functions to an existing body. It ensures that an existing body is not precluded from exercising any delegated function on the basis of its involvement with the monitoring, investigation or disciplinary arrangements that are set out in Schedule 10 to the CA 2006.

Schedule 13: Supplementary provisions with respect to delegation order

This Schedule restates the provisions of Schedule 13 of the CA 1989. Paragraph 2 provides that the delegated body is not to be regarded as acting on behalf of the Crown. Paragraphs 7–9 provide for the delegated body to exercise any legislative functions by instrument in writing and not by statutory instrument. Instrument must be made available to the public and the Secretary of State may require the body to consult prior to the making of regulations. Paragraph 10 requires the delegated body to report annually to the Secretary of State on the performance of its functions.

International obligations

Directions to comply with international obligations

24.52 Section 1254 of the CA 2006 sets out the directions to comply with international obligations. If it appears to the Secretary of State (a) that any action proposed to be taken by a recognised supervisory body or a recognised qualifying body, or a body designated by order under s 1252 of the CA 2006, would be incompatible with Community obligations or any other international obligations of the United Kingdom;[6868] or (b) that any action which that body has power to take is required for the purpose of implementing any such obligations,[6869] he may direct the body not to take or, as the case may be, to take the action in question.

A direction may include such supplementary or incidental requirements as the Secretary of State thinks necessary or expedient.[6870]

[6868] CA 2006, s 1254(1)(a).   [6869] CA 2006, s 1254(1)(b).   [6870] CA 2006, s 1254(2).

A direction under this section given to a body designated by order under s 1252 of the CA 2006 is enforceable on the application of the Secretary of State by injunction or, in Scotland, by an order under s 45 of the Court of Session Act 1988 (c 36).[6871]

This provision restates s 40 of the CA 1989 and empowers the Secretary of State to direct recognised supervisory or qualifying bodies, or any body delegated under s 1252 of the CA 2006, to comply with Community or other international obligations. If the body fails to comply with the direction, the Secretary of State can apply to the court for his direction to be enforced.

General provision relating to offences

Offences by bodies corporate, partnerships and unincorporated associations

24.53 Section 1255 of the CA 2006 sets out the offences by bodies corporate, partnerships and unincorporated associations. Where an offence under this Part committed by a body corporate is proved to have been committed with the consent or connivance of, or to be attributable to any neglect on the part of, an officer of the body, or a person purporting to act in any such capacity, he as well as the body corporate is guilty of the offence and liable to be proceeded against and punished accordingly.[6872]

Where an offence under this Part committed by a partnership is proved to have been committed with the consent or connivance of, or to be attributable to any neglect on the part of, a partner, he as well as the partnership is guilty of the offence and liable to be proceeded against and punished accordingly.[6873]

Where an offence under this Part committed by an unincorporated association (other than a partnership) is proved to have been committed with the consent or connivance of, or to be attributable to any neglect on the part of, any officer of the association or any member of its governing body, he as well as the association is guilty of the offence and liable to be proceeded against and punished accordingly.[6874]

This provision restates s 42 of the CA 1989 and deals with offences committed by bodies corporate, partnerships and other unincorporated associations. Where an offence committed by such a body is committed with the consent or connivance of, or is attributable to the neglect of, an officer (in the case of a body corporate), a partner (in the case of a partnership) or an officer or a member (in the case of an unincorporated association), that officer, partner or member is also guilty of the offence.

[6871] CA 2006, s 1254(3). [6872] CA 2006, s 1255(1). [6873] CA 2006, s 1255(2).
[6874] CA 2006, s 1256(1).

Time limits for prosecution of offences

24.54 Section 1256 of the CA 2006 sets out the time limits for prosecution of offences. An information relating to an offence under this Part which is triable by a magistrates' court in England and Wales may be so tried if it is laid at any time within the period of 12 months beginning with the date on which evidence sufficient in the opinion of the Director of Public Prosecutions or the Secretary of State to justify the proceedings comes to his knowledge.[6875]

Proceedings in Scotland for an offence under this Part may be commenced at any time within the period of 12 months beginning with the date on which evidence sufficient in the Lord Advocate's opinion to justify proceedings came to his knowledge or, where such evidence was reported to him by the Secretary of State, within the period of 12 months beginning with the date on which it came to the knowledge of the Secretary of State.[6876]

For the purposes of s 1256(2) of the CA 2006, proceedings are to be deemed to be commenced on the date on which a warrant to apprehend or cite the accused is granted, if the warrant is executed without undue delay.[6877]

A complaint charging an offence under this Part, which is triable by a magistrates' court in Northern Ireland, may be so tried if it is made at any time within the period of 12 months beginning with the date on which evidence sufficient in the opinion of the Director of Public Prosecutions for Northern Ireland or the Secretary of State to justify the proceedings comes to his knowledge.[6878]

This section does not authorise (a) in the case of proceedings in England and Wales, the trial of an information laid;[6879] (b) in the case of proceedings in Scotland, the commencement of proceedings;[6880] or (c) in the case of proceedings in Northern Ireland, the trial of a complaint made,[6881] more than three years after the commission of the offence.

For the purposes of this section a certificate of the Director of Public Prosecutions, the Lord Advocate, the Director of Public Prosecutions for Northern Ireland or the Secretary of State as to the date on which such evidence as is referred to above came to his knowledge is conclusive evidence.[6882] Nothing in this section affects proceedings within the time limits prescribed by s 127(1) of the Magistrates' Courts Act 1980 (c 43), s 331 of the Criminal Procedure (Scotland) Act 1975 or Article 19 of the Magistrates' Courts (Northern Ireland) Order 1981 (SI 1981/1675 (NI 26)) (the usual time limits for criminal proceedings).[6883]

This provision restates s 43 of the CA 1989 and sets a 12-month time limit for the prosecution of offences within each of the jurisdictions. Section 1256(1)–(4) of the CA 2006 states that the date on which knowledge of

[6875] CA 2006, s 1256(1).   [6876] CA 2006, s 1256(2).   [6877] CA 2006, s 1256(3).
[6878] CA 2006, s 1256(4).   [6879] CA 2006, s 1256(5)(a).   [6880] CA 2006, s 1256(5)(b).
[6881] CA 2006, s 1256(5)(c).   [6882] CA 2006, s 1256(6).   [6883] CA 2006, s 1256(7).

sufficient evidence of the offence becomes known to either the Secretary of State or Director of Public Prosecutions (for England and Wales), the Lord Advocate (for Scotland) or Director of Public Prosecutions for Northern Ireland is taken as the date from which the 12-month time limit commences. In any event, the prosecution may not be commenced if three years have passed since the date on which the offence was committed.

Jurisdiction and procedure in respect of offences

24.55 Section 1257 of the CA 2006 sets out the jurisdiction and procedure in respect of offences. Summary proceedings for an offence under this Part may, without prejudice to any jurisdiction exercisable apart from this section, be taken against a body corporate or unincorporated association at any place at which it has a place of business,[6884] and against an individual at any place where he is for the time being.

Proceedings for an offence alleged to have been committed under this Part by an unincorporated association must be brought in the name of the association (and not in that of any of its members), and for the purposes of any such proceedings, any rules of court relating to the service of documents apply as in relation to a body corporate.[6885]

Section 33 of the Criminal Justice Act 1925 (c 86) and Schedule 3 to the Magistrates' Courts Act 1980 (c 43) (procedure on charge of offence against a corporation) apply in a case in which an unincorporated association is charged in England and Wales with an offence under this Part as they apply in the case of a corporation.[6886]

Section 18 of the Criminal Justice Act (Northern Ireland) 1945 (c 15 (NI)) and Article 166 and Schedule 4 to the Magistrates' Courts (Northern Ireland) Order 1981 (SI 1981/1675 (NI 26)) (procedure on charge of offence against a corporation) apply in a case in which an unincorporated association is charged in Northern Ireland with an offence under this Part as they apply in the case of a corporation.[6887]

In relation to proceedings on indictment in Scotland for an offence alleged to have been committed under this Part by an unincorporated association, s 70 of the Criminal Procedure (Scotland) Act 1995 (proceedings on indictment against bodies corporate) applies as if the association were a body corporate.[6888]

A fine imposed on an unincorporated association on its conviction of such an offence must be paid out of the funds of the association.[6889]

This provision restates s 44 of the CA 1989 and deals with jurisdiction and procedure in respect of offences. It specifies that the jurisdiction is that in

---

[6884] CA 2006, s 1257(1).   [6885] CA 2006, s 1257(2).   [6886] CA 2006, s 1257(3).
[6887] CA 2006, s 1257(4).   [6888] CA 2006, s 1257(5).   [6889] CA 2006, s 1257(6).

which a body corporate or unincorporated association has its place of business or, in the case of an individual, where he is located. It also provides for an unincorporated association to be treated in the same way as a body corporate.

Notices, etc.

Service of notices

24.56 Section 1258 of the CA 2006 deals with services of notices. It applies in relation to any notice, direction or other document required or authorised by or by virtue of this Part to be given to or served on any person other than the Secretary of State.[6890]

Any such document may be given to or served on the person in question:

(a)   by delivering it to him;[6891]
(b)   by leaving it at his proper address;[6892] or
(c)   by sending it by post to him at that address.[6893]

Any such document may:

(a)   in the case of a body corporate, be given to or served on an officer of that body;[6894]
(b)   in the case of a partnership, be given to or served on any partner;[6895]
(c)   in the case of an unincorporated association other than a partnership, be given to or served on any member of the governing body of that association.[6896]

For the purposes of s 1258 of the CA 2006 and s 7 of the Interpretation Act 1978 (c 30) (service of documents by post) in its application to this section, the proper address of any person is his last known address (whether of his residence or of a place where he carries on business or is employed) and also:

(a)   in the case of a person who is eligible under the rules of a recognised supervisory body for appointment as a statutory auditor and who does not have a place of business in the United Kingdom, the address of that body;[6897]
(b)   in the case of a body corporate or an officer of that body, the address of the registered or principal office of that body in the United Kingdom;[6898]

[6890] CA 2006, s 1258(1).   [6891] CA 2006, s 1258(2)(a).   [6892] CA 2006, s 1258(2)(b).
[6893] CA 2006, s 1258(2)(c).   [6894] CA 2006, s 1258(3)(a).   [6895] CA 2006, s 1258(3)(b).
[6896] CA 2006, s 1258(3)(c).   [6897] CA 2006, s 1258(4)(a).   [6898] CA 2006, s 1258(4)(b).

(c)   in the case of an unincorporated association other than a partnership or a member of its governing body, its principal office in the United Kingdom.[6899]

This provision restates s 49 of the CA 1989 and states how notices and other documents may be served under this Part of the CA 2006 on any person other than the Secretary of State. The three permitted methods of service are: delivery to the person, leaving the documents at the person's address, or sending it by post to the person's address.

Documents in electronic form

24.57 Section 1259 of the CA 2006 applies where (a) s 1258 of the CA 2006 authorises the giving or sending of a notice, direction or other document by its delivery to a particular person (the recipient);[6900] and (b) the notice, direction or other document is transmitted to the recipient (i) by means of an electronic communications network,[6901] or (ii) by other means but in a form that requires the use of apparatus by the recipient to render it intelligible.[6902]

The transmission has effect for the purposes of this Part as a delivery of the notice, direction or other document to the recipient, but only if the recipient has indicated to the person making the transmission his willingness to receive the notice, direction or other document in the form and manner used.[6903]

An indication to a person for the purposes of s 1258(2) of the CA 2006:

(a)   must be given to the person in such manner as he may require;[6904]
(b)   may be a general indication or an indication that is limited to notices, directions or other documents of a particular description;[6905]
(c)   must state the address to be used;[6906]
(d)   must be accompanied by such other information as the person requires for the making of the transmission;[6907] and
(e)   may be modified or withdrawn at any time by a notice given to the person in such manner as he may require.[6908]

The term 'electronic communications network' has the same meaning as in the Communications Act 2003 (c 21).[6909]

This is a new provision to allow delivery of notices, directions or other documents in electronic form. It allows the use of e-communications where existing provisions in this Part impose requirements on the giving or sending

---

[6899] CA 2006, s 1258(4)(c).
[6900] CA 2006, s 1259(1)(a).
[6901] CA 2006, s 1259(1)(b)(i).
[6902] CA 2006, s 1259(1)(b)(ii).
[6903] CA 2006, s 1259(2).
[6904] CA 2006, s 1259(3)(a).
[6905] CA 2006, s 1259(3)(b).
[6906] CA 2006, s 1259(3)(c).
[6907] CA 2006, s 1259(3)(d).
[6908] CA 2006, s 1259(3)(e).
[6909] CA 2006, s 1259(4).

of notices, directions or other documents, provide the recipient indicates he is prepared to accept this form of delivery.

Interpretation

Meaning of 'associate'

24.58 Section 1260 of the CA 2006 defines an 'associate', and provides that 'associate', in relation to a person, is to be construed as follows.[6910]
In relation to an individual, the term 'associate' means:

(a)   that individual's spouse, civil partner or minor child or step-child;[6911]
(b)   any body corporate of which that individual is a director;[6912] and
(c)   any employee or partner of that individual.[6913]

In relation to a body corporate, the term 'associate' means:

(a)   any body corporate of which that body is a director;[6914]
(b)   any body corporate in the same group as that body;[6915] and
(c)   any employee or partner of that body or of any body corporate in the same group.[6916]

In relation to a partnership constituted under the law of Scotland, or any other country or territory in which a partnership is a legal person, the term 'associate' means:

(a)   any body corporate of which that partnership is a director;[6917]
(b)   any employee of or partner in that partnership;[6918] and
(c)   any person who is an associate of a partner in that partnership.[6919]

In relation to a partnership constituted under the law of England and Wales or Northern Ireland, or the law of any other country or territory in which a partnership is not a legal person, 'associate' means any person who is an associate of any of the partners.[6920]
In s 1260(2)(b), (3)(a) and (4)(a) of the CA 2006, in the case of a body corporate which is a limited liability partnership, 'director' is to be read as 'member'.[6921]
This provision restates s 52 of the CA 1989 and defines the meaning of 'associate'. This definition is particularly relevant for the independence requirement for statutory auditors set out in s 1214 of the CA 2006.

[6910] CA 2006, s 1260(1).   [6911] CA 2006, s 1260(2)(a).   [6912] CA 2006, s 1260(2)(b).
[6913] CA 2006, s 1260(2)(c).   [6914] CA 2006, s 1260(3)(a).   [6915] CA 2006, s 1260(3)(b).
[6916] CA 2006, s 1260(3)(c).   [6917] CA 2006, s 1260(4)(a).   [6918] CA 2006, s 1260(4)(b).
[6919] CA 2006, s 1260(4)(c).   [6920] CA 2006, s 1260(5).   [6921] CA 2006, s 1260(6).

Minor definitions

24.59 In this Part, unless a contrary intention appears:

- 'address' means:

  (a) in relation to an individual, his usual residential or business address;

  (b) in relation to a firm, its registered or principal office in the United Kingdom;

- 'company' means any company or other body the accounts of which must be audited in accordance with Part 16;
- 'director', in relation to a body corporate, includes any person occupying in relation to it the position of a director (by whatever name called) and any person in accordance with whose directions or instructions (not being advice given in a professional capacity) the directors of the body are accustomed to act;
- 'firm' means any entity, whether or not a legal person, which is not an individual and includes a body corporate, a corporation sole and a partnership or other unincorporated association;
- 'group', in relation to a body corporate, means the body corporate, any other body corporate that is its holding company or subsidiary and any other body corporate that is a subsidiary of that holding company;
- 'holding company' and 'subsidiary' are to be read in accordance with s 1159 and Schedule 6;
- 'officer', in relation to a body corporate, includes a director, a manager, a secretary or, where the affairs of the body are managed by its members, a member;
- 'parent undertaking' and 'subsidiary undertaking' are to be read in accordance with s 1162 and Schedule 7 of the CA 2006.

For the purposes of this Part a body is to be regarded as 'established in the United Kingdom' if and only if:

(a) it is incorporated or formed under the law of the United Kingdom or a part of the United Kingdom; or

(b) its central management and control are exercised in the United Kingdom; and any reference to a qualification 'obtained in the United Kingdom' is to a qualification obtained from such a body.

The Secretary of State may by regulations make such modifications of this Part as appear to him to be necessary or appropriate for the purposes of its application in relation to any firm, or description of firm, that is not a body corporate or a partnership.

Regulations under subs (3) are subject to negative resolution procedure.

This provision is a restatement of s 53 of the CA 1989 with certain extra definitions. Subsection (3) empowers the Secretary of State, by regulations, to make amendments to this Part that are needed in relation to the application of the Part to a 'firm' (as defined by subs (1)) that is not a partnership or body corporate.

Chapter 25

Derivative Claims and Proceedings

Introduction

25.1 Part 11 of the CA 2006 is a new part dealing with derivative claims and proceedings by the members and was in force on 1 October 2007 (also known as the "Part II procedure". Section 170 of the CA 2006 (scope and nature of general duties) states that the directors' general duties are owed to the company rather than to individual members, or third parties such as employees or consumer groups. As was previously the case under the CA 1985, only the company could enforce directors' statutory duties – particularly under s 309 of the CA 1985. Section 309 of the CA 1985 provided that directors were to have regard to the interests of the company's employees.[6922] However, the duty imposed by that section was owed by the directors to the company (and the company alone), and was enforceable in the same way as any other fiduciary duty owed to a company by its directors. Employees did not have any *locus standi* to bring any proceedings.

There are three main mechanisms available to a company to take legal action against a director or a former director of a company for breach of duty. First, the board of directors may decide to commence proceedings. Second, if the liquidator or administrator following the commencement of a formal insolvency procedure, such as liquidation or administration, decides to commence proceedings. Third, where a derivative claim or action is brought by one or more members to enforce a right vested not in himself, but the company. Part 11 of the CA 2006 is, therefore, concerned with the third aspect of legal action.

The Chapter also considers new rules and a Practice Direction in connection with derivative claims.

[6922] See too *Parke v Daily Newspaper* [1967] Ch 927.

The Position Before the CA 2006

25.2 In England and Wales, it is possible under common law for a member to bring an action, in certain circumstances, on behalf of the company of which he is a member. This is known as a derivative claim. A member may bring such an action to enforce liability for a breach by one of the directors of his duties to the company.

The law relating to the ability of a member to bring proceedings on behalf of the company was not set out in any statute but governed by case law. The general principle which is commonly known as the 'rule in *Foss v Harbottle*',[6923] is that it is for the company itself to bring proceedings where a wrong has been done to the company. However, where there has been conduct amounting to a 'fraud on the minority', an exception may be made to the rule, so that a minority shareholder may bring an action to enforce the company's rights, where, for example, there has been an expropriation of company property or dishonest behaviour by a director, and the company is improperly prevented from bringing proceedings against the director by the majority shareholders, perhaps because the delinquent director controls the majority of the votes.[6924]

Under the existing law, where a wrong has been effectively ratified by the company, this will be a complete bar to a derivative claim. Additionally, if a wrong is capable of being ratified, then even if there has been no formal ratification, it may not be possible for a minority shareholder to bring a derivative claim.

The position in Northern Ireland in this area is the same as for England and Wales.

Under Scots law, a member's right to raise an action is conferred by substantive law. A member has title as a matter of substantive law to raise proceedings in respect of a director's breach of duty to obtain a remedy for the company. The action is raised in the name of the member, but the remedy is obtained for the company and the rights that the member can enforce against a director or third party are those of the company.

The member's right arises where the action claimed of is fraudulent or *ultra vires*, and so cannot be validated by a majority of members of the company. This remedy is not available if the majority of members acting in good faith, have validated or may validate the act complained of.

Two rules of substantive law apply to actions brought by the member to protect the company's interests, as well as to actions brought to protect the shareholder's personal interests, such as enforcement of rights in the Articles

---

[6923] (1843) 2 Hare 461. See too *Edwards v Halliwell* [1950] 2 All ER 1064. See too *Burland v Earle* (1902) AC 83 per Lord Davey.

[6924] As exceptions to the rule in *Foss v Harbottle*, see *Prudential Assurance Co. Ltd v Newman Industries Ltd (No 2)* [1982] Ch 204; *Eastmanco (Kilner House) Ltd v Greater London Council* [1982] 1 All ER 437; *Smith v Croft (No 2)* [1988] Ch 114.

of Association.[6925] First, the directors of the company owe duties to the company and not to the members. Second, the court will not interfere in matters of internal management that may be sanctioned by a majority of the members. The effect of these rules is similar to the first two strands of the rule in *Foss v Harbottle*.

The Position Under the CA 2006

25.3 Part 11 comprises two Chapters. Chapter 1 deals with derivative claims in England and Wales and Northern Ireland. Chapter 1 comprises five sections, and Chapter 2 also comprises five sections. The sections in Part 11 do not formulate a substantive rule to replace the rule in *Foss v Harbottle*, but instead reflect the recommendation of the Law Commission that there should be a new derivative procedure with more modern, flexible and accessible criteria for determining whether a shareholder can pursue an action.[6926] In line with the recommendations of the Law Commission, the derivative claim will be available for breach of the duty to exercise reasonable care, skill and diligence, even if the director has not benefited personally. It will not be necessary for the applicant to show that the wrongdoing directors control the majority of the company's shares. The rule in *Foss v Harbottle* still survives after the CA 2006.

The provisions in Chapter 1 of Part 11 of the CA 2006 introduce a two-stage procedure for permission to continue a derivative action by an applicant and widens the circumstances (which were previously restrictive) in which derivative claims may be brought. At the first stage, the applicant will be required to show on a claim form and on application by the shareholder, a *prima facie* case for permission to continue a derivative action, and the court will be required to consider the issue on the basis of the evidence filed by the applicant only, without requiring evidence from the defendant. The company will be a defendant in these proceedings. The shareholder is required to notify the company of the action – usually by sending a copy of the claim form and of the application notice. At this stage, the courts must dismiss the application if the applicant cannot establish a *prima facie* case. At the second stage, but before the substantive action, the court may require evidence to be provided by the company. The sections set out a list of the matters that the court must take into account in considering whether to give permission and the circumstances in which the court is bound to refuse permission. The sections in Part 11 of the CA 2006 will be supplemented by amended Civil Procedure Rules. (see para 25.15 on Consultation Letter by Her Majesty's Courts Service).

[6925] See now, for example, CA 2006, s 33(1), which states that the provisions of a company's constitution bind the company and its members to the same extent as if there were covenants on the part of the company and of each member to observe those provisions.

[6926] See Law Commission Report, *Shareholder Remedies*, para 6.15.

Derivative claims in England and Wales and Northern Ireland

Derivative claims

25.4 Chapter 1 of Part 11 of the CA 2006 sets out the nature of a derivative claims, and applies to proceedings in England and Wales or Northern Ireland by a member of a company, in respect of a cause of action vested in the company;[6927] and seeking relief on behalf of the company. This is referred to in as a 'derivative claim'.

A derivative claim may only be brought under Chapter 1 of Part 11 of the CA 2006;[6928] or in pursuance of an order of the court in proceedings under s 994 of the CA 2006 (proceedings for protection of members against unfair prejudice).[6929]

A derivative claim under Chapter 1 may be brought only in respect of a cause of action arising from an actual or proposed act or omission involving negligence, default, breach of duty or breach of trust by a director of the company. As such, a derivative claim may be brought in respect of an alleged breach of any of the general duties of directors in Chapter 2 of Part 10 of the CA 2006, including a duty to exercise reasonable care, skill and diligence (see s 174 of the CA 2006).[6930] The cause of action may be against the director or another person (or both).[6931] Derivative claims against third parties would be permitted only in very narrow circumstances, where the damage suffered by the company arose from an act involving a breach of duty on the part of the director, for example, for knowing receipt of money or property transferred in breach of trust, or for knowing assistance in a breach of trust. It is immaterial whether the cause of action arose before or after the person seeking to bring or continue the derivative claim became a member of the company.[6932] Therefore, a derivative claim may be brought by a member in respect of wrongs committed prior to his becoming a member. This reflects the fact that the rights being enforced are those of the member, and is the position at common law.

Under Chapter 1, the term 'director' includes a former director;[6933] and a shadow director is treated as a director.[6934]

The references to a 'member of a company' include a person who is not a member, but to whom shares in the company have been transferred or

---

[6927] CA 2006, s 260(1)(a).   [6928] CA 2006, s 260(2)(a).

[6929] CA 2006, s 260(2)(b). See further Chapter 7.

[6930] CA 2006, s 174(1) concerns a duty on a director of a company to exercise reasonable care, skill and diligence. The test of care, skill and diligence is one that would be exercised by a reasonably diligent person with the general knowledge, skill and experience that may reasonably be expected of a person carrying out the functions carried out by the director in relation to the company; and the general knowledge, skill and experience that the director has.

[6931] CA 2006, s 260(3).   [6932] CA 2006, s 260(4).   [6933] CA 2006, s 260(5)(a).

[6934] CA 2006, s 260(5)(b).

transmitted by operation of law.[6935] This would apply where, for example, a trustee in bankruptcy or personal representative of a deceased's member's estate acquires an interest in a share as a result of the bankruptcy or death of a member.

Section 260(1) of the CA 2006 provides a definition of a 'derivative claim'. It comprises three aspects: (i) the action is brought by a member of the company; (ii) the cause of action is vested in the company; and (iii) the relief is sought on the company's behalf.

Application for permission to continue derivative claim

25.5 A member of a company who brings a derivative claim under Chapter 1 of Part 11 of the CA 2006, must apply to the court for permission (in Northern Ireland, leave) to continue it.[6936] If it appears to the court that the application and the evidence filed by the applicant in support of it do not disclose a *prima facie* case for giving permission (or leave), the court must dismiss the application;[6937] and may make any consequential order it considers appropriate.[6938]

If the application is not dismissed under s 261(2) of the CA 2006, the court may give directions as to the evidence to be provided by the company;[6939] and may adjourn the proceedings to enable the evidence to be obtained.[6940]

On hearing the application, the court may order any of the following: (i) give permission (or leave) to continue the claim on such terms as it thinks fit;[6941] or (ii) refuse permission (or leave) and dismiss the claim;[6942] or (iii) adjourn the proceedings on the application and give such directions as it thinks fit.[6943]

Under s 261 of the CA 2006, once proceedings have been brought, the member is required to apply to the court for permission to continue the claim. This reflects the current procedure in England and Wales under the Civil Procedure Rules. The applicant must establish a *prima facie* case for the grant of permission, and the court will consider the issue on the basis of his evidence alone (based on the papers and documents submitted by the shareholder applicant) without requiring evidence to be filed by the defendant but this does not prevent the company or its directors from voluntary submitting evidence, but the company will not normally be allowed any costs relating to such submission. The court must dismiss the application at this stage if what is filed does not show a *prima facie* case, and it may make any consequential order that it considers appropriate, such as a costs order or a civil restraint order against the applicant. If the application is not dismissed, the court may

---

[6935] CA 2006, s 260(5)(c). [6936] CA 2006, s 261(1). [6937] CA 2006, s 261(2)(a).
[6938] CA 2006, s 261(2)(b). [6939] CA 2006, s 261(3)(a). [6940] CA 2006, s 261(3)(b).
[6941] CA 2006, s 261(4)(a). [6942] CA 2006, s 261(4)(b). [6943] CA 2006, s 261(4)(c).

direct the company to provide evidence and, on hearing the application, may grant permission, refuse permission and dismiss the claim, or adjourn the proceedings and give such directions as it thinks fit. This will enable the courts to dismiss unmeritorious claims at an early stage without involving the defendants or the company.

Application for permission to continue claim as a derivative claim

25.6 Section 262 of the CA 2006 applies where a company has brought a claim;[6944] and the cause of action on which the claim is based could be pursued as a derivative claim under Chapter 1 of Part 11 of the CA 2006.[6945]

A member of the company may apply to the court for permission (in Northern Ireland, leave) to continue the claim as a derivative claim on the ground that (a) the manner in which the company commenced or continued the claim amounts to an abuse of the process of the court;[6946] (b) the company has failed to prosecute the claim diligently;[6947] and (c) it is appropriate for the member to continue the claim as a derivative claim.[6948]

If it appears to the court that the application and the evidence filed by the applicant in support of it do not disclose a *prima facie* case for giving permission (or leave), the court must dismiss the application;[6949] and may make any consequential order it considers appropriate.[6950]

If the application is not dismissed under s 262(3) of the CA 2006, the court may give directions as to the evidence to be provided by the company;[6951] and may adjourn the proceedings to enable the evidence to be obtained.[6952]

On hearing the application, the court may order any of the following: (a) give permission (or leave) to continue the claim as a derivative claim on such terms as it thinks fit;[6953] (b) refuse permission (or leave) and dismiss the application;[6954] or (c) adjourn the proceedings on the application and give such directions as it thinks fit.[6955]

Section 262 of the CA 2006 deals with the possibility that, where a company has brought a claim and the cause of action on which the claim is based could be pursued by a member as a derivative action, the manner in which the company commenced or continued the claim may amount to an abuse of process (as where the company brought the claim with a view to preventing a member bringing a derivative claim). The company may fail to prosecute the claim diligently; and it may be appropriate for a member to continue the claim as a derivative claim. In these circumstances, a member may apply to the court to continue the claim as a derivative action.

[6944] CA 2006, s 262(1)(a).   [6945] CA 2006, s 262(1)(b).   [6946] CA 2006, s 262(2)(a).
[6947] CA 2006, s 262(2)(b).   [6948] CA 2006, s 262(2)(c).   [6949] CA 2006, s 262(3)(a).
[6950] CA 2006, s 262(3)(b).   [6951] CA 2006, s 262(4)(a).   [6952] CA 2006, s 262(4)(b).
[6953] CA 2006, s 262(5)(a).   [6954] CA 2006, s 262(5)(b).   [6955] CA 2006, s 262(5)(c).

Whether permission to be given

25.7 Section 263 of the CA 2006 applies where a member of a company applies for permission (in Northern Ireland, leave) under ss 261 or 262 of the CA 2006.[6956] This will usually be a full hearing of the shareholder's application with both the shareholder and the company making submissions. It sets out the criteria that must be taken into account by the court in considering whether to give permission to continue a derivative claim.

Permission (or leave) must be refused if the court is satisfied in the following circumstances that a person acting in accordance with s 172 of the CA 2006 (duty to promote the success of the company) would not seek to continue the claim;[6957] or where the cause of action arises from an act or omission that is yet to occur, that the act or omission has been authorised by the company;[6958] or where the cause of action arises from an act or omission that has already occurred, that the act or omission was authorised by the company before it occurred, or has been ratified by the company since it occurred.[6959]

It should be noted that s 180(4) of the CA 2006 preserves any rule of law enabling the company to give authority for anything that would otherwise be a breach of duty. Section 239 of the CA 2006 preserves the current law on ratification of acts of directors, but with one major change. Any decision by a company to ratify conduct by a director amounting to negligence, default, breach of duty or breach of trust in relation to the company must be taken by the members, and without reliance on votes in favour by the director or any connected person.

The court must have regard to particular criteria that it must take into account in considering whether or not to grant permission for the derivative claim to be continued. In considering whether to give permission (or leave) the court must take into account, in particular:

(a)   whether the member is acting in good faith in seeking to continue the claim;[6960]
(b)   the importance that a person acting in accordance with s 172 of the CA 2006 (duty to promote the success of the company) would attach to continuing it;[6961]
(c)   where the cause of action results from an act or omission that is yet to occur, whether the act or omission could be, and in the circumstances would be likely to be authorised by the company before it occurs, or ratified by the company after it occurs;[6962]
(d)   where the cause of action arises from an act or omission that has already occurred, whether the act or omission could be, and in the circumstances would be likely to be, ratified by the company;[6963]

[6956] CA 2006, s 263(1).   [6957] CA 2006, s 263(2)(a).   [6958] CA 2006, s 263(2)(b).
[6959] CA 2006, s 263(2)(c).   [6960] CA 2006, s 263(3)(a).   [6961] CA 2006, s 263(3)(b).
[6962] CA 2006, s 263(3)(c).   [6963] CA 2006, s 263(3)(d).

(e)   whether the company has decided not to pursue the claim;[6964]

(f)   whether the act or omission in respect of which the claim is brought gives rise to a cause of action that the member could pursue in his own right rather than on behalf of the company.[6965]

In considering whether to give permission (or leave) the court shall have particular regard to any evidence before it as to the views of members of the company who have no personal interest, direct or indirect, in the matter.[6966] The latter may be characterised as independent or disassociated members.

The Secretary of State may by regulations amend s 263(2) of the CA 2006 so as to alter or add to the circumstances in which permission (or leave) is to be refused;[6967] and amend s 263(3) of the CA 2006 so as to alter or add to the matters that the court is required to take into account in considering whether to give permission (or leave).[6968] Section 263(5) of the CA 2006 empowers the Secretary of State to make regulations with regard to the criteria to which the court must have regard in determining whether to grant leave to continue a derivative claim, and where leave of the court must be refused. Before making any such regulations the Secretary of State must consult such persons as he considers appropriate.[6969] The power reflects a recommendation by the Law Commission in its 1997 report on *Shareholder Remedies* in respect of similar shareholder actions in Scotland. The Regulations under this section are subject to affirmative resolution procedure.[6970]

The objective of the s 263 of the CA 2006 is to set out the criteria that must be taken into account by the court in considering whether to give permission to continue a derivative claim.

Application for permission to continue derivative claim brought by another member

25.8 Section 264 of the CA 2006 is concerned with an application for permission to continue a derivative claim brought by another member. It applies where a member of a company (the claimant) has brought a derivative claim;[6971] or has continued as a derivative claim brought by the company;[6972] or has continued a derivative claim under this section.[6973]

Another member of the company (the applicant) may apply to the court for permission (in Northern Ireland, leave) to continue the claim on the ground that the manner in which the proceedings have been commenced or continued by the claimant amounts to an abuse of the process of the court;[6974]

[6964] CA 2006, s 263(3)(e).   [6965] CA 2006, s 263(3)(f).   [6966] CA 2006, s 263(4).
[6967] CA 2006, s 263(5)(a).   [6968] CA 2006, s 263(5)(b).   [6969] CA 2006, s 263(6).
[6970] CA 2006, s 263(7).   [6971] CA 2006, s 264(1)(a).   [6972] CA 2006, s 264(1)(b).
[6973] CA 2006, s,264(1)(c).   [6974] CA 2006, s 264(2)(a).

the claimant has failed to prosecute the claim diligently;[6975] and it is appropriate for the applicant to continue the claim as a derivative claim.[6976]

If it appears to the court that the application and the evidence filed by the applicant in support of it do not disclose a *prima facie* case for giving permission (or leave), the court must dismiss the application;[6977] and may make any consequential order it considers appropriate.[6978]

If the application is not dismissed under s 264(3) of the CA 2006, the court may give directions as to the evidence to be provided by the company;[6979] and may adjourn the proceedings to enable the evidence to be obtained.[6980]

On hearing the application, the court may order any of the following give permission (or leave) to continue the claim on such terms as it thinks fit;[6981] refuse permission (or leave) and dismiss the application;[6982] or adjourn the proceedings on the application and give such directions as it thinks fit.[6983]

Section 264 of the CA 2006 addresses the possibility that, where the court has already decided that there is an appropriate case for a derivative claim, and a member has commenced or continued a claim the manner in which the member commenced or continued the claim may amount to an abuse of the court (as where a member brought the claim with a view to preventing another member from bringing the claim); the member may fail to prosecute the claim diligently; it may be appropriate for another member to continue the claim, as where, for example, the member who brought the claim is very ill.

In the above circumstances, another member may apply to the court to continue the claim as a derivative action.

Derivative Proceedings In Scotland

25.9 Chapter 2 of Part 11 is concerned with derivative proceedings in Scotland. Sections 265–269 of the CA 2006 seek to ensure maximum consistency between the position in England and Wales and Northern Ireland and the position in Scotland – although the sections reflect the different procedural requirements that apply where proceedings are commenced in the Scottish courts, in particular the fact that the leave of court must be obtained before derivative proceedings may be raised. They also put the rights of the member to raise actions on behalf of the company on a statutory footing.

The sections relating to proceedings in England and Wales and Northern Ireland assume that there is already a right to bring such proceedings in England and Wales and Northern Ireland – they, therefore, regulate the proceedings rather than confer the right to bring them.

[6975] CA 2006, s 264(2)(b). [6976] CA 2006, s 264(2)(c). [6977] CA 2006, s 264(3)(a).
[6978] CA 2006, s 264(3)(b). [6979] CA 2006, s 264(4)(a). [6980] CA 2006, s 264(4)(b).
[6981] CA 2006, s 264(5). [6982] CA 2006, s 264(5)(b). [6983] CA 2006, s 264(5)(c).

Section 265 of the CA 2006 differs from s 260 in its approach in that it confers the right to bring the proceedings in the first place, and then the sections that follow s 265 regulate the proceedings. By contrast, the sections relating to proceedings in England and Wales and Northern Ireland assume that there is already a right to bring such proceedings in England and Wales and Northern Ireland; they therefore regulate the proceedings rather than confer the right to bring them.

Derivative proceedings

25.10 Under s 265(1) of the CA 2006, in Scotland, a member of a company may raise proceedings in respect of an act or omission specified in s 265 (3) of the CA 2006 in order to protect the interests of the company and obtain a remedy on its behalf.

A member of a company may raise such proceedings only under s 265(1) of the CA 2006.[6984]

The act or omission referred to in s 265(1) of the CA 2006 is any actual or proposed act or omission involving negligence, default, breach of duty or breach of trust by a director of the company.[6985]

Proceedings may be raised under s 265(1) of the CA 2006 against (either or both) the director referred to in s 265(3) of the CA 2006;[6986] or another person.[6987]

It is immaterial whether the act or omission in respect of which the proceedings are to be raised or, in the case of continuing proceedings under ss 267 or 269 of the CA 2006, are raised, arose before or after the person seeking to raise or continue them became a member of the company.[6988]

Section 265 of the CA 2006 does not affect any right of a member of a company to raise proceedings in respect of an act or omission specified in s 265(3) of the CA 2006 in order to protect his own interests and obtain a remedy on his own behalf;[6989] or the court's power to make an order under section 996(2)(c) or anything done under such an order.[6990]

In this Chapter, proceedings raised under s 265(1) of the CA 2006 are referred to as 'derivative proceedings'.[6991] Further, the act or omission in respect of which they are raised is referred to as the 'cause of action'.[6992] The term 'director' includes a former director.[6993] The references to a director include a shadow director;[6994] and references to a member of a company include a person who is not a member but to whom shares in the company have been transferred or transmitted by operation of law.[6995]

[6984] CA 2006, s 265(2).   [6985] CA 2006, s 265(3).   [6986] CA 2006, s 265(4)(a).
[6987] CA 2006, s 265(4)(b).   [6988] CA 2006, s 265(5).   [6989] CA 2006, s 265(6)(a).
[6990] CA 2006, s 265(6)(b).   [6991] CA 2006, s 265(7)(a).   [6992] CA 2006, s 265(7)(b).
[6993] CA 2006, s 265(7)(c).   [6994] CA 2006, s 265(7)(d).   [6995] CA 2006, s 265(7)(e).

Requirement for leave and notice

25.11 Section 266 of the CA 2006 states that derivative proceedings may be raised by a member of a company only with the leave of the court.[6996]

An application for leave must specify the cause of action;[6997] and summarise the facts on which the derivative proceedings are to be based.[6998]

If it appears to the court that the application and the evidence produced by the applicant in support of it do not disclose a *prima facie* case for granting it, the court must refuse the application;[6999] and may make any consequential order it considers appropriate.[7000]

If the application is not refused under s 266(3) of the CA 2006 the applicant must serve the application on the company;[7001] the court may make an order requiring evidence to be produced by the company, and may adjourn the proceedings on the application to enable the evidence to be obtained;[7002] and the company is entitled to take part in the further proceedings on the application.[7003]

On hearing the application, the court may order any of the following, namely, grant the application on such terms as it thinks fit;[7004] refuse the application;[7005] or adjourn the proceedings on the application and make such order as to further procedure as it thinks fit.[7006]

Application to continue proceedings as derivative proceedings

25.12 Section 267 of the CA 2006 applies where a company has raised proceedings;[7007] and the proceedings are in respect of an act or omission that could be the basis for derivative proceedings.[7008]

A member of the company may apply to the court to be substituted for the company in the proceedings, and for the proceedings to continue in consequence as derivative proceedings, on the ground that the manner in which the company commenced or continued the proceedings amounts to an abuse of the process of the court;[7009] the company has failed to prosecute the proceedings diligently;[7010] and it is appropriate for the member to be substituted for the company in the proceedings.[7011]

If it appears to the court that the application and the evidence produced by the applicant in support of it do not disclose a *prima facie* case for granting it, the court must refuse the application;[7012] and may make any consequential order it considers appropriate.[7013]

[6996] CA 2006, s 266(1).   [6997] CA 2006, s 266(2)(a).   [6998] CA 2006, s 266(2)(b).

[6999] CA 2006, s 266(3)(a).   [7000] CA 2006, s 266(3)(b).   [7001] CA 2006, s 266(4)(a).

[7002] CA 2006, s 266(4)(b).   [7003] CA 2006, s 266(4)(c).   [7004] CA 2006, s 266(5)(a).

[7005] CA 2006, s 266(5)(b).   [7006] CA 2006, s 266(5)(c).   [7007] CA 2006, s 267(1)(a).

[7008] CA 2006, s 267(1)(b).   [7009] CA 2007, s 267(2)(a).   [7010] CA 2006, s 267(2)(b).

[7011] CA 2006, s 267(2)(c).   [7012] CA 2006, s 267(3)(a).   [7013] CA 2006, s 267(3)(b).

If the application is not refused under s 266(3) of the CA 2006: (a) the applicant must serve the application on the company;[7014] (b) the court may make an order requiring evidence to be produced by the company, and may adjourn the proceedings on the application to enable the evidence to be obtained;[7015] and (c) the company is entitled to take part in the further proceedings on the application.[7016]

On hearing the application, the court may order any of the following, namely, grant the application on such terms as it thinks fit;[7017] refuse the application;[7018] or adjourn the proceedings on the application and make such order as to further procedure as it thinks fit.[7019]

Granting of leave

25.13 Section 268 of the CA 2006 states that the court must refuse leave to raise derivative proceedings or an application under s 267 of the CA 2006 if satisfied that a person acting in accordance with s 172 of the CA 2006 (duty to promote the success of the company) would not seek to raise or continue the proceedings (as the case may be);[7020] or where the cause of action is an act or omission that is yet to occur, that the act or omission has been authorised by the company;[7021] or where the cause of action is an act or omission that has already occurred, that the act or omission was authorised by the company before it occurred, or has been ratified by the company since it occurred.[7022]

In considering whether to grant leave to raise derivative proceedings or an application under s 267 of the CA 2006, the court must take into account, in particular: (a) whether the member is acting in good faith in seeking to raise or continue the proceedings (as the case may be);[7023] (b) the importance that a person acting in accordance with s 172 of the CA 2006 (duty to promote the success of the company) would attach to raising or continuing them (as the case may be);[7024] (c) where the cause of action is an act or omission that is yet to occur, whether the act or omission could be, and in the circumstances would be likely to be (i) authorised by the company before it occurs, or (ii) ratified by the company after it occurs;[7025] (d) where the cause of action is an act or omission that has already occurred, whether the act or omission could be, and in the circumstances would be likely to be, ratified by the company;[7026] (e) whether the company has decided not to raise proceedings in respect of the same cause of action or to persist in the proceedings (as the case may

---

[7014] CA 2006, s 267(4)(a).   [7015] CA 2006, s 267(4)(b).   [7016] CA 2006, s 267(4)(c).
[7017] CA 2006, s 267(5)(a).   [7018] CA 2006, s 267(5)(b).   [7019] CA 2006, s 267(5)(c).
[7020] CA 2006, s 268(1)(a).   [7021] CA 2006, s 268(1)(b).   [7022] CA 2006, s 268(1)(c).
[7023] CA 2006, s 268(2)(a).   [7024] CA 2006, s 268(2)(b).   [7025] CA 2006, s 268(2)(c).
[7026] CA 2006, s 268(2)(d).

be);[7027] (f) whether the cause of action is one which the member could pursue in his own right rather than on behalf of the company.[7028]

In considering whether to grant leave to raise derivative proceedings or an application under s 267 of the CA 2006, the court shall have particular regard to any evidence before it as to the views of members of the company who have no personal interest, direct or indirect, in the matter.[7029]

The Secretary of State may by regulations amend s 268(1) of the CA 2006 so as to alter or add to the circumstances in which leave or an application is to be refused;[7030] amend s 268(2) of the CA 2006 so as to alter or add to the matters that the court is required to take into account in considering whether to grant leave or an application.[7031]

Before making any such regulations, the Secretary of State must consult such persons as he considers appropriate.[7032]

Regulations under this section are subject to affirmative resolution procedure.[7033]

Section 268(4)–(6) of the CA 2006 confers on the Secretary of State a parallel power to that in s 263 of the CA 2006 to make regulations with regard to the criteria to which the court must have regard in determining whether to grant leave to continue a derivative claim and where leave of court must be refused.

Application by member to be substituted for member pursuing derivative proceedings

25.14 Section 269 of the CA 2006 applies where a member of a company (the claimant) has raised derivative proceedings;[7034] has continued as derivative proceedings raised by the company;[7035] or has continued derivative proceedings under this section.[7036]

Another member of the company (the applicant) may apply to the court to be substituted for the claimant in the action on the ground that: (a) the manner in which the proceedings have been commenced or continued by the claimant amounts to an abuse of the process of the court;[7037] (b) the claimant has failed to prosecute the proceedings diligently;[7038] and (c) it is appropriate for the applicant to be substituted for the claimant in the proceedings.

If it appears to the court that the application and the evidence produced by the applicant in support of it do not disclose a *prima facie* case for granting it, the court (a) must refuse the application;[7039] and (b) may make any consequential order it considers appropriate.[7040]

[7027] CA 2006, s 268(2)(e).   [7028] CA 2006, s 268(2)(f).   [7029] CA 2006, s 268(3).
[7030] CA 2006, s 268(4)(a).   [7031] CA 2006, s 268(4)(b).   [7032] CA 2006, s 268(5).
[7033] CA 2006, s 268(6).   [7034] CA 2006, s 269(1)(a).   [7035] CA 2006, s 269(1)(b).
[7036] CA 2006, s 269(1)(c).   [7037] CA 2006, s 269(2)(a).   [7038] CA 2006, s 269(2)(b).
[7039] CA 2006, s 269(3)(a).   [7040] CA 2006, s 269(3)(b).

If the application is not refused under s 269(3) of the CA 2006: (a) the applicant must serve the application on the company;[7041] (b) the court (i) may make an order requiring evidence to be produced by the company, and (ii) may adjourn the proceedings on the application to enable the evidence to be obtained;[7042] and (c) the company is entitled to take part in the further proceedings on the application.[7043]

On hearing the application, the court may grant the application on such terms as it thinks fit;[7044] refuse the application;[7045] or adjourn the proceedings on the application and make such order as to further procedure as it thinks fit.[7046]

Consultation Letter – Her Majesty's Courts Service

25.15 On 23 May 2007, Her Majesty's Courts Services (a division of the Ministry of Justice, on behalf of the Civil Procedure Rule Committee, a Non-Departmental Public Body), issued a consultation letter on derivative claims under the CA 2006, seeking comments about changes to the substantive law on derivative claims contained in the CA 2006. The letter states that in England and Wales, it is already possible as a matter of common law for a member of a company to bring an action, in certain circumstances, on behalf of the company – this is termed a derivative claim. A member may bring such an action to enforce liability for breach by one of the directors of his duty to the company. The Civil Procedure Rules 1998 (the Rule) currently provides for derivative claims in Part 19 rule 19.9. That rule also covers derivative claims against an incorporated body that is not a company, or against a trade union. A trade union, although not incorporated in the full sense, has quasi-corporate status under s 10 of the Trade Union and Labour Relations (Consolidation) Act 1992, and can sue and be sued in its corporate name.

As a result of the consultation, new rules and a Practice Direction supplementing the new rules have been prepared. These are set out at the end of this section.

The rules must be read in conjunction with ss 260–264 of the CA 2006. The rules are intended to give procedural effect to those sections.

The CA 2006 requires a person seeking to bring a derivative claim to obtain the permission of the court to do so. Both the existing and proposed rules basically apply to the application for that permission – if permission is granted the claim proceeds in the same way as any other claim. The Act provides in s 261(2) of the CA 2006 for the court to dismiss an application 'on the papers' alone, without the company being required to file any evidence, and the new rules make appropriate provision. The new rules provide for that decision to be reconsidered at an oral hearing if the claimant so requests.

[7041] CA 2006, s 269(4)(a).   [7042] CA 2006, s 269(4)(b).   [7043] CA 2006, s 269(4)(c).
[7044] CA 2006, s 269(5)(a).   [7045] CA 2006, s 269(5)(b).   [7046] CA 2006, s 269(5)(c).

Until the court has decided, on the evidence filed by the claimant, whether or not there is a *prima facie* case, the company is not required to be involved in any way, although it must be notified (except if the court orders otherwise, in exceptional circumstances). However, if the court is unable to dismiss the application on the basis that the claimant's evidence discloses no prima facie case, the court will hold a hearing at which the defendant company can make representations. If the court grants permission to continue the claim, it may do so on terms, and can make appropriate consequential orders. Of course the court also has all the case management powers already available under the Rules.

It is intended that permission applications, if brought in the High Court, will be assigned to the Chancery Division in common with all other company matters. If brought in a county court, a permission application would be heard by a circuit judge.

The requirement for permission also applies if a claim that a company has already brought is to be taken over by a member and continued as a derivative claim, or if an existing derivative claim is to be taken over by another member of the company concerned.

The rules also applied to derivative claims against incorporated bodies of other kinds. It was proposed that the procedural aspects of the new Act provisions should apply to such derivative claims. This was proposed to be effected by a specific rule for such claims that would simply incorporate by reference the relevant Act provisions and the relevant provisions of the rules that applied to companies. It should be noted that derivative claims against bodies other than companies are extremely rare.

A provision of the new practice direction states that if the court grants permission to continue a derivative claim, it may impose a condition that the claim is not to be settled, discontinued or compromised without the permission of the court. This is intended to discourage the development in England and Wales of so-called 'greenmail' claims, where a person buys shares in a company and brings a claim that is settled on terms that include a purchase of the claimant's shares at a price above their market value.

Because the sections of the CA 2006 that deal with derivative claims were to come into effect in October 2007, because the relevant sections of the CA 2006 had already been extensively debated in Parliament, and because the rules are procedural only and create no substantive rights, the Rule Committee decided that the four-week period for consultation allowed by the need to make the rules before the CA 2006 provisions come into force was sufficient.

Derivative claims – how commenced

Below is the new rule on derivative claims:

19.9 (1) This rule applies to a derivative claim, whether under Chapter I of Part I1 of the CA 2006 or otherwise. It does not apply to a claim made following an order under section 994 of that Act.

(2) A derivative claim must be commenced by claim form.

(3) The company, body corporate or trade union concerned must be made a defendant to the claim.

(4) After the issue of the claim form, the claimant must not take any further step in the proceedings without the permission of the court, other than:

(a)   notifying the company, body corporate or trade union in accordance with rule 19.9A(4); or

(b)   making an urgent application for interim relief.

Derivative claims under Chapter I of Part I I of the Companies Act 2006 – applications for permission

19.9A. (1) In this rule, 'derivative claim' means a derivative claim under Chapter I of Part II of the CA 2006.

(2) The claim form for a derivative claim must be accompanied by an application notice under Part 23 for permission to continue the claim.

(3) The claimant must file with the application notice the written evidence on which the claimant relies in support of the permission application.

(4) Subject to sub-para (6), the claimant must notify the company concerned of the claim and application for permission by sending to the company, at its principal office, as soon as reasonably practicable after issue:

(a)   a copy of the claim form and the application notice;

(b)   a copy of the evidence fled by the claimant in support of the application for permission; and

(c)   the form of notice set out in the practice direction supplementing this rule.

(5) The notification and documents required by sub-para (4) may be sent to the company in any way that would constitute service of the documents on the company.

(6) If notifying the company of the application would be likely to frustrate some part of the relief sought, the court may, on application by the claimant, order that the company need not be notified for such period after the issue of the claim form as the court directs.

(7) An application under sub-para (6) may be made without notice.

(8) After the applicant has notified the company of the claim in accordance with para (4), the applicant must file a witness statement with the court as confirmation that the applicant has notified the company as required.

(9) If the court dismisses the permission application without a hearing, the claimant may ask for the decision to be reconsidered at a hearing, but must make the request to the court within seven days of being served with notice of the decision.

(In the case of a derivative claim involving a company, the court must dismiss the permission application if no *prima facie* case for the grant of permission is made out on the evidence fled by the applicant-see section 261(2) of the CA 2006. (This applies to other derivative claims by virtue of rule 199C(5).) Otherwise, the court will give directions for the hearing of the application.)

Derivative claims under Chapter I of Part 11 of the Companies Act 2006 – members of companies taking over claims by companies or other members

19.9B. (1) This rule applies in the circumstances described in section 262(1) or 264(1) of the CA 2006 ('the Act').

(Section 262(1) relates to a claim that has already been made by a company and is now sought to be taken over and continued by a member as a derivative claim under Chapter I of Part 11 of the Act; section 264(1) relates to a derivative claim (under that Chapter) already brought by a member of a company that is now sought to be taken over by another member of the company.)

(2) The application for permission must be made by application notice in accordance with Part 23.

(3) Rule 19.9A (except for paras (1) and (2) of that rule) applies to an application under this rule.

(4) For that application, references in that rule to the claimant are to be read as references to the person who seeks to take over the claim.

Derivative claims-other bodies corporate and trade unions

19.9C. (1) This rule applies where:

(a) either

    (i)   a body corporate that is not a company, or

    (ii) a trade union, is alleged to be entitled to a remedy; and

(b) either

    (i)   a claim is made by one or more of its members for it to be given that remedy; or

    (ii) a member of the body corporate or trade union seeks to take over or continue a claim already brought, by the body corporate or trade union or one or more of its members, for it to be given that remedy.

(2) The member who brings, or seeks to take over, the claim must apply to the court for permission to continue the claim.

(3) The application for permission must be made by application notice in accordance with Part 23.

(4) The court will apply to applications falling within this rule the procedure for applications in relation to companies in section 261, section 262 or sections 264(3), (4) and (5) (as the case requires) of the CA 2006.

(5) Rule 19.9A (except for paras (1) and (2) of that rule) applies to an application under this rule.

(6) In the application of a provision of the Act or rule 19.9A, references in the Act provision or the rule to a company are to be read as references to the body corporate or trade union.

Derivative claims arising in the course of other proceedings

19.9D. If a derivative claim (except such a claim in pursuance of an order under s 994 of the CA 2006) arises in the course of other proceedings:

(a)   in the case of a derivative claim under Chapter 1 of Part II of that Act, rule 19.9A or 19.9B applies, as the case requires; and

(b)   in any other case, rule 19.9C applies.

Derivative claims-incidental matters

19.9E. (1) The court may order the company, body corporate or trade union concerned to indemnify the claimant against liability for costs incurred in the permission application
or in the derivative claim or both.

(2) Once permission has been given to continue a derivative claim, the court may order that the claim may not be discontinued, settled or compromised without the permission of the court.

Practice Direction-derivative claims

This Practice Direction supplements Part 19

Below is the Practice Direction in respect of derivative claims:

Application of this Practice Direction

1. This Practice Direction applies to (i) derivative claims (whether under Chapter 1 of Part 11 of the CA 2006 or otherwise, and (ii) applications for permission to continue or take over such claims but excluding claims in pursuance of an order under s 994 of the CA 2006).

Claim form

2. (1) A claim form in relation to a derivative claim must be headed 'Derivative claim'.

(2) If the claimant seeks an order that the defendant company or other body concerned indemnify the claimant against liability for costs incurred in the permission application or the claim, this should be stated in the permission application or claim form or both, as the case requires.

Application for order delaying notice

3. If the applicant seeks an order under rule 19.9A(7) delaying notice to the defendant company or other body concerned, the applicant must also set out in the application notice a statement of the reasons for the application, and file with it written evidence in support.

Form to be sent to defendant company or other body

4. The form required by rule 19.9A(4)(a) to be sent to the defendant company or other body is set out at the end of this Practice Direction. There are separate versions of the form for claims involving a company, and claims involving a body corporate of another kind or a trade union.

Early intervention by the company

5. The decision whether the claimant's evidence discloses a *prima facie* case will normally be made without submissions from or in the case of an oral hearing to reconsider such a decision reached pursuant to rule 19.9A(9) attendance by the company. If without invitation from the court the company volunteers a submission or attendance, the company will not normally be allowed any costs of that submission or attendance. (Sections 261, 262 and 264 CA 2006 contain provisions about disclosing a *prima facie* case in applications to continue a derivative claim.)

Hearing of applications, etc.

6. If a claim or application to which this Practice Direction applies is made in a county court it will be decided by a circuit judge, and if made in the High Court it will be assigned to the Chancery Division and decided by a High Court judge.

Discontinuance of derivative claim

7. As a condition of granting permission to continue or take over a derivative claim, the court may order that the claim is not to be

discontinued, settled or compromised without the court's permission. Such a condition may be appropriate where any future proposal to discontinue or settle would not come to the attention of members of beneficiaries who might have an interest in taking over the claim.

The forms

For claims involving a company:

> CA 2006, section 261 or 263 or 264;
> Civil Procedure Rules 1998, rule 19.9A(4)(c).

Notice in relation to derivative claim

To {name of company etc} ('the company') (or as appropriate) in relation to a claim by {claimant}.
    Attached to this notice are:

- a copy of the claim form to which this notice relates;
- an application under rule 19.9A of the Civil Procedure Rules 1998 for permission to continue the claim; and
- copies of the evidence to be relied on by the claimant in obtaining permission to continue the claim.

The claim is a derivative claim. The claimant must obtain the permission of the court under section 261 of the Companies Act 2006 to continue the claim. A brief summary of the procedure follows.
    The court will make its initial decision on the basis of the documents filed by the claimant (copies are attached to this notice) and at present the company does not need to acknowledge service, file a defence or become involved in any other way unless it chooses to do so. If the court considers that the documents do not disclose a prima facie case, it will dismiss the action. It may then make consequential orders. If it does not dismiss the application at that stage, the court will adjourn the application to allow the company to obtain and file evidence and be heard on the application.
    The factors that the court must take into account are set out in section 263 of the Act. A copy of sections 263(1)–(4) of the Act is attached.
    For claims involving a body corporate that is not a company, or a trade union:

> Civil Procedure Rules 1998, rule 19.9A(4)(c)

Notice in relation to derivative claim

To {name of body corporate etc} ('the corporation') (or as appropriate) in relation to a claim by {claimant}.

Attached to this notice are:

- a copy of the claim form to which this notice relates;
- an application under rule 19.9A of the Civil Procedure Rules 1998 for permission to continue the claim; and
- copies of the evidence to be relied on by the claimant in obtaining permission to continue the claim.

The claim is a derivative claim. The claimant must obtain the permission of the court under the Civil Procedure Rules 1998 to continue the claim. A brief summary of the procedure follows.

The court will make its initial decision on the basis of the documents filed by the claimant (copies are attached to this notice) and at present the [corporation] does not need to acknowledge service, file a defence or become involved in any other way unless it chooses to do so. If the court considers that the documents do not disclose a *prima facie* case, it will dismiss the action. It may then make consequential orders. If it does not dismiss the application at that stage, the court will adjourn the application to allow the corporation to obtain and file evidence and be heard on the application.

Chapter 26

Arrangements and Reconstructions

Introduction

26.1 Part 26 of the CA 2006 is concerned with arrangements and reconstructions. The provisions of this Part enable companies to apply to the court for an order sanctioning an arrangement or reconstruction agreed with a majority of members or creditors. They restate ss 425–427 of the CA 1985.[7047] In addition to drafting changes resulting from the re-arrangement of the provisions, there are two major changes considered under ss 899(2) and 901 of the CA 2006.

Application of Part 26 of the CA 2006

26.2 Section 895 of the CA 2006 is concerned with the application of Part 26 of the CA 2006. The provisions of Part 26 of the CA 2006 apply where a compromise or arrangement is proposed between a company and its creditors;[7048] or any class of them, or its members, or any class of them.[7049]

In Part 26 of the CA 2006, the term 'arrangement' includes a reorganisation of the company's share capital by the consolidation of shares of different classes, or by the division of shares into shares of different classes, or by both of those methods;[7050] and the term 'company' (a) in s 900 of the CA 2006 (powers of court to facilitate reconstruction or amalgamation) means a company within the meaning of the CA 2006,[7051] and (b) elsewhere in Part 26 of the CA 2006 means any company liable to be wound up under the Insolvency Act 1986 (c 45) or the Insolvency (Northern Ireland) Order 1989 (SI 1989/2405 (NI 19)).[7052]

[7047] CA 1985, s 425 was concerned with power of the company to compromise with creditors and members. CA 1985, s 426 addressed the information as to compromise to be circulated. CA 1985, s 427 applied to provisions for facilitating company reconstruction or amalgamation.
[7048] CA 2006, s 895(1)(a).   [7049] CA 2006, s 895(1)(b).   [7050] CA 2006, s 895(2).
[7051] CA 2006, s 895(2)(a).   [7052] CA 2006, s 895(2)(b).

The provisions of Part 26 of the CA 2006 apply subject to Part 27 of the CA 2006 (mergers and divisions of public companies) where that Part applies (see ss 902 and 903 of the CA 2006).[7053]

Meeting of creditors or members

Court order for holding of a meeting

26.3 Section 896 of the CA 2006 deals with the court order for holding a meeting. The court may, on an application under this section, order a meeting of the creditors or class of creditors, or of the members of the company or class of members (as the case may be), to be summoned in such manner as the court directs.[7054]

An application under s 896 of the CA 2006 may be made by the company,[7055] or any creditor or member of the company,[7056] or if the company is being wound up or an administration order is in force in relation to it, the liquidator or administrator.[7057]

Statement to be circulated or made available

26.4 Section 897 of the CA 2006 applies to the statement to be circulated or made available. Where a meeting is summoned under s 896 of the CA 2006 (a) every notice summoning the meeting that is sent to a creditor or member must be accompanied by a statement complying with this section;[7058] and (b) every notice summoning the meeting that is given by advertisement must either (i) include such a statement,[7059] or (ii) state where and how creditors or members entitled to attend the meeting may obtain copies of such a statement.[7060]

The statement must (a) explain the effect of the compromise or arrangement;[7061] and (b) in particular, state (i) any material interests of the directors of the company (whether as directors or as members or as creditors of the company or otherwise),[7062] and (ii) the effect on those interests of the compromise or arrangement, in so far as it is different from the effect on the like interests of other persons.[7063]

Where the compromise or arrangement affects the rights of debenture holders of the company, the statement must give the like explanation as respects the trustees of any deed for securing the issue of the debentures as it is required to give as respects the company's directors.[7064]

[7053] CA 2006, s 895(3). [7054] CA 2006, s 896(1). [7055] CA 2006, s 896(2)(a).
[7056] CA 2006, s 896(2)(b). [7057] CA 2006, s 896(2)(c). [7058] CA 2006, s 897(1)(a).
[7059] CA 2006, s 897(1)(b)(i). [7060] CA 2006, s 897(1)(b)(ii). [7061] CA 2006, s 897(2)(a).
[7062] CA 2006, s 897(2)(b)(i). [7063] CA 2006, s 897(2)(b)(ii). [7064] CA 2006, s 897(3).

Where a notice given by advertisement states that copies of an explanatory statement can be obtained by creditors or members entitled to attend the meeting, every such creditor or member is entitled, on making application in the manner indicated by the notice, to be provided by the company with a copy of the statement free of charge.[7065]

If a company makes default in complying with any requirement of this section, an offence is committed by the company,[7066] and every officer of the company who is in default.[7067] This is subject to s 897(7) of the CA 2006 below.

The following are treated as officers of the company, namely, a liquidator or administrator of the company,[7068] and a trustee of a deed for securing the issue of debentures of the company.[7069]

A person is not guilty of an offence under s 897 of the CA 2006, if he shows that the default was due to the refusal of a director or trustee for debenture holders to supply the necessary particulars of his interests.[7070]

A person guilty of an offence under s 897 of the CA 2006 is liable on conviction on indictment, to a fine;[7071] and on summary conviction, to a fine not exceeding the statutory maximum.[7072]

Duty of directors and trustees to provide information

26.5 Section 898 of the CA 2006 deals with the duty of directors and trustees to provide information. It is the duty of any director of the company,[7073] and any trustee for its debenture holders,[7074] to give notice to the company of such matters relating to himself as may be necessary for the purposes of s 897 of the CA 2006 (explanatory statement to be circulated or made available).

Any person who makes default in complying with this section commits an offence.[7075] A person guilty of an offence under s 897 of the CA 2006 is liable on summary conviction to a fine not exceeding level 3 on the standard scale.[7076]

Court sanction for compromise or arrangement

26.6 Section 899 of the CA 2006 deals with the court's sanction for a compromise or arrangement. If a majority in number representing 75 per cent in value of the creditors or class of creditors or members or class of members (as the case may be), present and voting either in person or by proxy at the meeting summoned under s 896 of the CA 2006, agree a compromise or

---

[7065] CA 2006, s 897(4). [7066] CA 2006, s 897(5)(a). [7067] CA 2006, s 897(5)(b).
[7068] CA 2006, s 897(6)(a). [7069] CA 2006, s 897(6)(b). [7070] CA 2006, s 897(7).
[7071] CA 2006, s 897(8)(a). [7072] CA 2006, s 897(8)(b). [7073] CA 2006, s 898(1)(a).
[7074] CA 2006, s 898(1)(b). [7075] CA 2006, s 898(2). [7076] CA 2006, s 898(3).

arrangement, the court may, on an application under this section, sanction the compromise or arrangement.[7077]

An application under this section may be made by the company,[7078] or any creditor or member of the company,[7079] or if the company is being wound up, or an administration order is in force in relation it, the liquidator or administrator.[7080]

A compromise or agreement sanctioned by the court is binding on all creditors or the class of creditors or on the members or class of members (as the case may be),[7081] and the company or, in the case of a company in the course of being wound up, the liquidator and contributories of the company.[7082]

The court's order has no effect until a copy of it has been delivered to the registrar.[7083]

Section 899(2) of the CA 2006 makes clear that the persons who may apply for a court order sanctioning a compromise or arrangement are the same as those who may apply to the court for an order for a meeting (under s 896(2) of the CA 2006).

Reconstructions and amalgamations

Powers of court to facilitate reconstruction or amalgamation

26.7 Section 900 of the CA 2006 deals with the power of the court to facilitate reconstructions and amalgamations. It applies where application is made to the court under s 899 of the CA 2006 to sanction a compromise or arrangement, and it is shown that the compromise or arrangement is proposed for the purposes of, or in connection with, a scheme for the reconstruction of any company or companies, or the amalgamation of any two or more companies,[7084] and under the scheme the whole or any part of the undertaking or the property of any company concerned in the scheme (the transferor company) is to be transferred to another company (the transferee company).[7085]

The court may, either by the order sanctioning the compromise or arrangement or by a subsequent order, make provision for all or any of the following matters:

(a) the transfer to the transferee company of the whole or any part of the undertaking and of the property or liabilities of any transferor company;[7086]

[7077] CA 2006, s 899(1).   [7078] CA 2006, s 899(2)(a).   [7079] CA 2006, s 899(2)(b).
[7080] CA 2006, s 899(2)(c).   [7081] CA 2006, s 899(3)(a).   [7082] CA 2006, s 899(3)(b).
[7083] CA 2006, s 899(4).   [7084] CA 2006, s 900(1)(a).   [7085] CA 2006, s 900(1)(b).
[7086] CA 2006, s 900(2)(a).

(b)   the allotting or appropriation by the transferee company of any shares, debentures, policies or other like interests in that company that, under the compromise or arrangement, are to be allotted or appropriated by that company to or for any person;[7087]

(c)   the continuation by or against the transferee company of any legal proceedings pending by or against any transferor company;[7088]

(d)   the dissolution, without winding up, of any transferor company;[7089]

(e)   the provision to be made for any persons who, within such time and in such manner as the court directs, dissent from the compromise or arrangement;[7090]

(f)   such incidental, consequential and supplemental matters as are necessary to secure that the reconstruction or amalgamation is fully and effectively carried out.[7091]

If an order under s 900 of the CA 2006 provides for the transfer of property or liabilities, the property is by virtue of the order transferred to, and vests in, the transferee company,[7092] and the liabilities are, by virtue of the order, transferred to and become liabilities of that company.[7093]

The property (if the order so directs) vests freed from any charge that is by virtue of the compromise or arrangement to cease to have effect.[7094]

The term 'property' includes property, rights and powers of every description; and the term 'liabilities' includes duties.[7095]

Every company in relation to which an order is made under this section must cause a copy of the order to be delivered to the registrar within seven days after its making.[7096]

If default is made in complying with s 900(6) of the CA 2006, an offence is committed by the company,[7097] and every officer of the company who is in default.[7098] A person guilty of an offence under s 900(7) of the CA 2006 is liable on summary conviction to a fine not exceeding level 3 on the standard scale and, for continued contravention, a daily default fine not exceeding one-tenth of level 3 on the standard scale.[7099]

Obligations of company with respect to articles, etc.

26.8 Section 901 of the CA 2006 deals with obligations of company with respect to articles. It applies to any order under s 899 of the CA 2006 (order sanctioning a compromise or arrangement),[7100] and to any order under s 900

[7087] CA 2006, s 900(2)(b).   [7088] CA 2006, s 900(2)(c).   [7089] CA 2006, s 900(2)(d).
[7090] CA 2006, s 900(2)(e).   [7091] CA 2006, s 900(2)(f).   [7092] CA 2006, s 900(3)(a).
[7093] CA 2006, s 900(3)(b).   [7094] CA 2006, s 900(4).   [7095] CA 2006, s 900(5).
[7096] CA 2006, s 900(6).   [7097] CA 2006, s 900(7)(a).   [7098] CA 2006, s 900(7)(b).
[7099] CA 2006, s 900(8).   [7100] CA 2006, s 901(1)(a).

of the CA 2006 (order facilitating reconstruction or amalgamation) that alters the company's constitution.[7101]

If the order amends the company's articles,[7102] or any resolution or agreement to which Chapter 3 of Part 3 of the CA 2006 applies (resolution or agreement affecting a company's constitution),[7103] the copy of the order delivered to the registrar by the company under s 899(4) of the CA 2006 or s 900(6) of the CA 2006 must be accompanied by a copy of the company's articles, or the resolution or agreement in question, as amended.

Every copy of the company's articles issued by the company after the order is made must be accompanied by a copy of the order, unless the effect of the order has been incorporated into the articles by amendment.[7104]

Under s 901 of the CA 2006, references to the effect of the order include the effect of the compromise or arrangement to which the order relates;[7105] and in the case of a company not having articles, references to its articles shall be read as references to the instrument constituting the company or defining its constitution.[7106]

If a company makes default in complying with this section an offence is committed by the company,[7107] and every officer of the company who is in default.[7108] A person guilty of an offence under this section is liable on summary conviction to a fine not exceeding level 3 on the standard scale.[7109]

Section 901 of the CA 2006 requires a company to deliver to the registrar a court order that alters the company's constitution. It also requires that every copy of the company's articles subsequently issued must be accompanied by a copy of the order, unless the effect of the order has been incorporated into the articles by amendment. These changes are included for consistency with other provisions in the CA 2006 concerning such orders.

[7101] CA 2006, s 901(1)(b). [7102] CA 2006, s 901(2)(a). [7103] CA 2006, s 901(2)(b).
[7104] CA 2006, s 901(3). [7105] CA 2006, s 901(4)(a). [7106] CA 2006, s 901(4)(b).
[7107] CA 2006, s 901(5)(a). [7108] CA 2006, s 901(5)(b). [7109] CA 2006, s 901(6).

Chapter 27

Mergers and Divisions of Public Companies

Introduction

27.1 Part 27 of the CA 2006 is concerned with mergers and divisions of public companies. The provisions of this Part enable a public company, under certain conditions, to apply to the court for an order under Part 26 of the CA 2006, sanctioning an arrangement or reconstruction that concerns the merger or division of a public company. They implement the Third Council Directive 78/855/EEC concerning mergers of public limited liability companies, and the Sixth Council Directive 82/891/EEC concerning the division of public limited liability companies.

The provisions of Part 27 of the CA 2006 restate s 427A and Schedule 15B of the CA 1985. The opportunity has been taken to put the provisions in a form more closely corresponding to that of the Directives. Chapters 2 and 3 deal separately with mergers and divisions, and the provisions within those Chapters broadly follow the order of the provisions of the relevant Directive.

The independence requirements for experts and valuers in ss 936 and 937 of the CA 2006 are new, and correspond to the new independence requirements for a statutory auditor (see s 1214 of the CA 2006). They include a new power for the Secretary of State to define a disallowed connection for the purposes of determining whether a person is sufficiently independent to be an expert or valuer under this Part. This is consistent with the approach taken in ss 344 and 1151 of the CA 2006.

Part 27 contains four Chapters. Chapter 1 is introductory and sets out the application of Part 27. Chapter 2 deals with the issue of merger and the merging companies. Chapter 3 is concerned with the aspect of division and companies involved in a division. Chapter 4 deals with supplementary provisions.

Introductory

27.2 Chapter 1 is concerned with the introductory aspects to Part 27 of the CA 2006 with reference to the applicability of Part 27 of the CA 2006 and its relationship with other Parts of the CA 2006.

Application of this Part

27.3 Part 27 of the CA 2006 applies where (a) a compromise or arrangement is proposed between a public company and (i) its creditors or any class of them,[7110] or (ii) its members or any class of them,[7111] for the purposes of, or in connection with, a scheme for the reconstruction of any company or companies or the amalgamation of any two or more companies; (b) the scheme involves (i) a merger (as defined in s 904 of the CA 2006),[7112] or (ii) a division (as defined in s 919 of the CA 2006);[7113] and (c) the consideration for the transfer (or each of the transfers) is envisaged to be shares in the transferee company (or one or more of the transferee companies) receivable by members of the transferor company (or transferor companies), with or without any cash payment to members.[7114]

In Part 27 of the CA 2006, the term a 'new company' means a company formed for the purposes of, or in connection with, the scheme,[7115] and an 'existing company' means a company other than one formed for the purposes of, or in connection with, the scheme.[7116]

Part 27 of the CA 2006 does not apply where the company in respect of which the compromise or arrangement is proposed is being wound up.[7117]

Relationship of Part 27 to Part 26 of the CA 2006

27.4 Section 903 of the CA 2006 establishes the relationship between Parts 27 and 26 of the CA 2006.

The court must not sanction the compromise or arrangement under Part 26 of the CA 2006 (arrangements and reconstructions), unless the relevant requirements of this Part have been complied with.[7118]

The requirements applicable to a merger are specified in ss 905–914 of the CA 2006.[7119]

Certain of those requirements, and certain general requirements of Part 26 of the CA 2006, are modified or excluded by the provisions of ss 915–918 of the CA 2006.[7120]

The requirements applicable to a division are specified in ss 920–930 of the CA 2006.

Certain of those requirements, and certain general requirements of Part 26 of the CA 2006, are modified or excluded by the provisions of ss 931–934 of the CA 2006.[7121]

[7110] CA 2006, s 902(1)(a)(i).   [7111] CA 2006, s 902(1)(a)(ii).   [7112] CA 2006, s 902(1)(b)(i).
[7113] CA 2006, s 902(1)(b)(ii).   [7114] CA 2006, s 902(1)(c).   [7115] CA 2006, s 902(2)(a).
[7116] CA 2006, s 902(2)(b).   [7117] CA 2006, s 902(3).   [7118] CA 2006, s 903(1).
[7119] CA 2006, s 903(2).   [7120] CA 2006, s 903(3).   [7121] CA 2006, s 903(3).

Mergers

27.5 Chapter 2 deals with the specific aspects of mergers.

Introductory

Mergers and merging companies

27.6 Section 904 of the CA 2006 is concerned with mergers and merging companies. The scheme involves a merger where under the scheme (a) the undertaking, property and liabilities of one or more public companies, including the company in respect of which the compromise or arrangement is proposed, are to be transferred to another existing public company (a merger by absorption);[7122] or (b) the undertaking, property and liabilities of two or more public companies, including the company in respect of which the compromise or arrangement is proposed, are to be transferred to a new company, whether or not a public company, (a merger by formation of a new company).[7123]

The term 'the merging companies' applies (a) in relation to a merger by absorption, to the transferor and transferee companies;[7124] (b) in relation to a merger by formation of a new company, to the transferor companies.[7125]

Requirements applicable to mergers

Draft terms of the scheme (merger)

27.7 Section 905 of the CA 2006 sets out the draft terms of the scheme. A draft of the proposed terms of the scheme must be drawn up and adopted by the directors of the merging companies.[7126]

The draft terms must give particulars of at least the following matters:

(a) in respect of each transferor company and the transferee company (i) its name,[7127] (ii) the address of its registered office,[7128] and (iii) whether it is a company limited by shares or a company limited by guarantee and having a share capital;[7129]

(b) the number of shares in the transferee company to be allotted to members of a transferor company for a given number of their shares (the share exchange ratio) and the amount of any cash payment;[7130]

(c) the terms relating to the allotment of shares in the transferee company;[7131]

[7122] CA 2006, s 904(1)(a).   [7123] CA 2006, s 904(1)(b).   [7124] CA 2006, s 904(2)(a).
[7125] CA 2006, s 904(2)(b).   [7126] CA 2006, s 905(1).   [7127] CA 2006, s 905(2)(a)(i).
[7128] CA 2006, s 905(2)(a)(ii).   [7129] CA 2006, s 905(2)(a)(iii).   [7130] CA 2006, s 905(2)(b).
[7131] CA 2006, s 905(2)(c).

(d)   the date from which the holding of shares in the transferee company will entitle the holders to participate in profits, and any special conditions affecting that entitlement;[7132]

(e)   the date from which the transactions of a transferor company are to be treated for accounting purposes as being those of the transferee company;[7133]

(f)   any rights or restrictions attaching to shares or other securities in the transferee company to be allotted under the scheme to the holders of shares or other securities in a transferor company to which any special rights or restrictions attach, or the measures proposed concerning them;[7134]

(g)   any amount of benefit paid or given or intended to be paid or given (i) to any of the experts referred to in s 909 of the CA 2006 (expert's report),[7135] or (ii) to any director of a merging company,[7136] and the consideration for the payment of benefit.

The requirements in s 905(2)(b), (c) and (d) of the CA 2006 are subject to s 915 of the CA 2006 (circumstances in which certain particulars not required).[7137]

Publication of draft terms (merger)

27.8 Section 906 of the CA 2006 deals with publication of draft terms. The directors of each of the merging companies must deliver a copy of the draft terms to the registrar.[7138]

The registrar must publish in the Gazette a notice of receipt by him from that company of a copy of the draft terms.[7139] That notice must be published at least one month before the date of any meeting of that company summoned for the purpose of approving the scheme.[7140]

Approval of members of merging companies

27.9 Section 907 of the CA 2006 is concerned with approval of members of merging companies. The scheme must be approved by a majority in number, representing 75 per cent, in value, of each class of members of each of the merging companies, present and voting either in person or by proxy at a meeting.[7141]

This requirement is subject to ss 916, 917 and 918 of the CA 2006 (circumstances in which meetings of members not required).[7142]

[7132] CA 2006, s 905(2)(d).   [7133] CA 2006, s 905(2)(e).   [7134] CA 2006, s 905(2)(f).
[7135] CA 2006, s 905(2)(g)(i).   [7136] CA 2006, s 905(2)(g)(ii).   [7137] CA 2006, s 905(3).
[7138] CA 2006, s 906(1).   [7139] CA 2006, s 906(2).   [7140] CA 2006, s 906(3).
[7141] CA 2006, s 907(1).   [7142] CA 2006, s 907(2).

Directors' explanatory report (merger)

27.10 The directors of each of the merging companies must draw up and adopt a report.[7143]

The report must consist of (a) the statement required by s 897 of the CA 2006 (statement explaining effect of compromise or arrangement);[7144] and (b) insofar as that statement does not deal with the following matters, a further statement (i) setting out the legal and economic grounds for the draft terms, and in particular for the share exchange ratio,[7145] and (ii) specifying any special valuation difficulties.[7146]

The requirement in this section is subject to s 915 of the CA 2006 (circumstances in which reports are not required).[7147]

Expert's report (merger)

27.11 Section 909 of the CA 2006 is concerned with the expert's report. An expert's report must be drawn up on behalf of each of the merging companies.[7148]

The report required is a written report on the draft terms to the members of the company.[7149]

The court may on the joint application of all the merging companies approve the appointment of a joint expert to draw up a single report on behalf of all those companies.

If no such appointment is made, there must be a separate expert's report to the members of each merging company drawn up by a separate expert appointed on behalf of that company.[7150]

The expert must be a person who is eligible for appointment as a statutory auditor (see s 1212),[7151] and meets the independence requirement in s 936.[7152]

The expert's report must (a) indicate the method or methods used to arrive at the share exchange ratio;[7153] (b) give an opinion as to whether the method or methods used are reasonable in all the circumstances of the case, indicate the values arrived at using each such method and (if there is more than one method) give an opinion on the relative importance attributed to such methods in arriving at the value decided on;[7154] (c) describe any special valuation difficulties that have arisen;[7155] (d) state whether in the expert's opinion the share exchange ratio is reasonable;[7156] and (e) in the case of a valuation made by a person other than himself (see s 935 of the CA 2006), state that it appeared to him reasonable to arrange for it to be so made or to accept a valuation so made.[7157]

[7143] CA 2006, s 908(1).   [7144] CA 2006, s 908(2)(a).   [7145] CA 2006, s 908(2)(b)(i).
[7146] CA 2006, s 908(2)(b)(ii).   [7147] CA 2006, s 908(3).   [7148] CA 2006, s 909(1).
[7149] CA 2006, s 909(2).   [7150] CA 2006, s 909(3).   [7151] CA 2006, s 909(4)(a).
[7152] CA 2006, s 909(4)(b).   [7153] CA 2006, s 909(5)(a).   [7154] CA 2006, s 909(5)(b).
[7155] CA 2006, s 909(5)(c).   [7156] CA 2006, s 909(5)(d).   [7157] CA 2006, s 909(5)(e).

The expert (or each of them) has the right of access to all such documents of all the merging companies,[7158] and the right to require from the companies' officers all such information,[7159] as he thinks necessary for the purposes of making his report.

The requirement in this section is subject to s 915 of the CA 2006 (circumstances in which reports not required).[7160]

Supplementary accounting statement (merger)

27.12 Section 910 of the CA 2006 deals with the supplementary accounting statement. If the last annual accounts of any of the merging companies relate to a financial year ending more than seven months before the first meeting of the company summoned for the purposes of approving the scheme, the directors of that company must prepare a supplementary accounting statement.[7161]

That statement must consist of a balance sheet dealing with the state of affairs of the company as at a date not more than three months before the draft terms were adopted by the directors,[7162] and where the company would be required under s 399 of the CA 2006 to prepare group accounts if that date were the last day of a financial year, a consolidated balance sheet dealing with the state of affairs of the company and the undertakings that would be included in such a consolidation.[7163]

The requirements of this Act (and where relevant Article 4 of the IAS Regulation) as to the balance sheet forming part of a company's annual accounts, and the matters to be included in notes to it, apply to the balance sheet required for an accounting statement under this section, with such modifications as are necessary by reason of its being prepared otherwise than as at the last day of a financial year.[7164]

The provisions of s 414 of the CA 2006 as to the approval and signing of accounts apply to the balance sheet required for an accounting statement under this section.[7165]

Inspection of documents (merger)

27.13 Section 911 of the CA 2006 states that the members of each of the merging companies must be able, during the period specified below, to inspect at the registered office of that company copies of the documents listed below relating to that company and every other merging company,[7166] and to obtain copies of those documents or any part of them on request free of charge.[7167]

[7158] CA 2006, s 909(6)(a).   [7159] CA 2006, s 909(6)(b).   [7160] CA 2006, s 909(7).
[7161] CA 2006, s 910(1).   [7162] CA 2006, s 910(2)(a).   [7163] CA 2006, s 910(2)(b).
[7164] CA 2006, s 910(3).   [7165] CA 2006, s 910(4).   [7166] CA 2006, s 911(1)(a).
[7167] CA 2006, s 911(1)(b).

The period referred to above is the period beginning one month before,[7168] and ending on the date of,[7169] the first meeting of the members, or any class of members, of the company for the purposes of approving the scheme.

The documents referred to above are:

(a)   the draft terms;[7170]
(b)   the directors' explanatory report;[7171]
(c)   the expert's report;[7172]
(d)   the company's annual accounts and reports for the last three financial years ending on or before the first meeting of the members, or any class of members, of the company summoned for the purposes of approving the scheme;[7173] and
(e)   any supplementary accounting statement required by s 910 of the CA 2006.[7174]

The requirements of s 911(3)(b) and (c) of the CA 2006 are subject to s 915 of the CA 2006 (circumstances in which reports not required).[7175]

Approval of articles of the new transferee company (merger)

27.14 Section 912 of the CA 2006 applies to the approval of articles of the new transferee company. In the case of a merger by formation of a new company, the articles of the transferee company, or a draft of them, must be approved by ordinary resolution of the transferor company or, as the case may be, each of the transferor companies.

Protection of holders of securities to which special rights are attached (merger)

27.15 Section 913 of the CA 2006 states that the scheme must provide that where any securities of a transferor company (other than shares) to which special rights are attached are held by a person otherwise than as a member or creditor of the company, that person is to receive rights in the transferee company of equivalent value.[7176]

Section 913(1) of the CA 2006 does not apply if the holder has agreed otherwise,[7177] or the holder is, or under the scheme is to be, entitled to have the securities purchased by the transferee company on terms that the court considers reasonable.[7178]

[7168] CA 2006, s 911(2)(a).   [7169] CA 2006, s 911(2)(b).   [7170] CA 2006, s 911(3)(a).
[7171] CA 2006, s 911(3)(b).   [7172] CA 2006, s 911(3)(c).   [7173] CA 2006, s 911(3)(d).
[7174] CA 2006, s 911(3)(e).   [7175] CA 2006, s 911(4).   [7176] CA 2006, s 913(1).
[7177] CA 2006, s 913(2)(a).   [7178] CA 2006, s 913(2)(b).

No allotment of shares to the transferor company or its
nominee (merger)

27.16 Section 914 of the CA 2006 states that there are no allotment shares to a transferor company or its nominee.

The scheme must not provide for shares in the transferee company to be allotted to a transferor company (or its nominee) in respect of shares in the transferor company held by it (or its nominee).

Exceptions where shares of transferor company are held by a transferee company

Circumstances in which certain particulars and reports are not
required (merger)

27.17 Section 915 of the CA 2006 applies in the case of a merger by absorption, where all of the relevant securities of the transferor company (or, if there is more than one transferor company, of each of them) are held by or on behalf of the transferee company.[7179]

The draft terms of the scheme need not give the particulars mentioned in s 905(2)(b), (c) or (d) of the CA 2006 (particulars relating to the allotment of shares to members of the transferor company).[7180]

Section 897 of the CA 2006 (explanatory statement to be circulated or made available) does not apply.[7181]

The requirements of the following sections do not apply: s 908 of the CA 2006 (directors' explanatory report), and s 909 of the CA 2006 (expert's report).[7182]

The requirements of s 911 of the CA 2006 (inspection of documents), so far as relating to any document required to be drawn up under the provisions mentioned in s 915(3) of the CA 2006 above, do not apply.[7183]

The term 'relevant securities, in relation to a company, means shares or other securities carrying the right to vote at general meetings of the company.[7184]

Circumstances in which a meeting of members of transferee company
is not required (merger)

27.18 Section 916 of the CA 2006 applies in the case of a merger by absorption where 90 per cent or more (but not all) of the relevant securities of the

---

[7179] CA 2006, s 915(1).   [7180] CA 2006, s 915(2).   [7181] CA 2006, s 915(3).
[7182] CA 2006, s 915(4).   [7183] CA 2006, s 915(5).   [7184] CA 2006, s 915(6).

transferor company (or, if there is more than one transferor company, of each of them) are held by or on behalf of the transferee company.[7185]

It is not necessary for the scheme to be approved at a meeting of the members, or any class of members, of the transferee company if the court is satisfied that the following conditions have been complied with.[7186]

The first condition is that at least one month before a meeting of members (or a class of members) of the transferor company called to agree the scheme, the registrar should have published a notice of the draft terms of the invitation from the transferor company to the transferee company.[7187]

The second condition is that the members of the transferee company were able during the period beginning one month before, and ending on, that date to inspect at the registered office of the transferee company copies of the documents listed in s 911(3)(a), (d) and (e) of the CA 2006 relating to that company and the transferor company (or, if there is more than one transferor company, each of them),[7188] and to obtain copies of those documents or any part of them on request free of charge.[7189]

The third condition is that one or more members of the transferee company, who together held not less than 5 per cent of the paid-up capital of the company that carried the right to vote at general meetings of the company (excluding any shares in the company held as treasury shares) would have been able, during that period, to require a meeting of each class of members to be called for the purpose of deciding whether or not to agree to the scheme,[7190] and no such requirement was made.[7191]

The term 'relevant securities', in relation to a company, means shares or other securities carrying the right to vote at general meetings of the company.[7192]

Circumstances in which no meetings required (merger)

27.19 Section 917 of the CA 2006 applies in the case of a merger by absorption where all of the relevant securities of the transferor company (or, if there is more than one transferor company, of each of them) are held by or on behalf of the transferee company.[7193]

It is not necessary for the scheme to be approved at a meeting of the members, or any class of members, of any of the merging companies if the court is satisfied that the following conditions have been complied with.[7194]

The first condition is that publication of a notice by the registrar of receipt of the draft terms took place in respect of all the merging companies at least one month before the date of the court's order.[7195]

[7185] CA 2006, s 916(1).   [7186] CA 2006, s 916(2).   [7187] CA 2006, s 916(3).
[7188] CA 2006, s 916(4)(a).   [7189] CA 2006, s 916(4)(b).   [7190] CA 2006, s 916(5)(a).
[7191] CA 2006, s 916(5)(b).   [7192] CA 2006, s 916(6).   [7193] CA 2006, s 917(1).
[7194] CA 2006, s 917(2).   [7195] CA 2006, s 917(3).

The second condition is that the members of the transferee company were able during the period beginning one month before, and ending on, that date to inspect at the registered office of that company copies of the documents listed in s 911(3) of the CA 2006 relating to that company and the transferor company (or, if there is more than one transferor company, each of them),[7196] and to obtain copies of those documents or any part of them on request free of charge.[7197]

The third condition is that one or more members of the transferee company, who together held not less than 5 per cent of the paid-up capital of the company that carried the right to vote at general meetings of the company (excluding any shares in the company held as treasury shares) would have been able, during that period, to require a meeting of each class of members to be called for the purpose of deciding whether or not to agree to the scheme,[7198] and no such requirement was made.[7199]

The term 'relevant securities', in relation to a company, means shares or other securities carrying the right to vote at general meetings of the company.[7200]

Other exceptions

Other circumstances in which a meeting of members of a transferee company is not required (merger)

27.20 Section 918 of the CA 2006 states that in the case of any merger by absorption, it is not necessary for the scheme to be approved by the members of the transferee company if the court is satisfied that the following conditions have been complied with.[7201]

The first condition is that the publication of a notice of receipt of the draft terms by the registrar took place in respect of that company at least one month before the date of the first meeting of members, or any class of members, of the transferor company (or, if there is more than one transferor company, any of them) summoned for the purposes of agreeing to the scheme.[7202]

The second condition is that the members of that company were able during the period beginning one month before, and ending on, the date of any such meeting to inspect at the registered office of that company copies of the documents specified in s 911(3) of the CA 2006 relating to that company and the transferor company (or, if there is more than one transferor company, each of them),[7203] and to obtain copies of those documents or any part of them on request free of charge.[7204]

[7196] CA 2006, s 917(4)(a).   [7197] CA 2006, s 917(4)(b).   [7198] CA 2006, s 917(5)(a).
[7199] CA 2006, s 917(5)(b).   [7200] CA 2006, s 917(6).   [7201] CA 2006, s 918(1).
[7202] CA 2006, s 918(2).   [7203] CA 2006, s 918(3)(a).   [7204] CA 2006, s 918(3)(b).

The third condition is that one or more members of that company, who together held not less than 5 per cent of the paid-up capital of the company that carried the right to vote at general meetings of the company (excluding any shares in the company held as treasury shares) would have been able, during that period, to require a meeting of each class of members to be called for the purpose of deciding whether or not to agree to the scheme,[7205] and no such requirement was made.[7206]

Division

Introductory

27.21 Chapter 3 is concerned with the issue of division.

Divisions and companies involved in a division

27.22 Section 919 of the CA 2006 states that the scheme involves a division where under the scheme the undertaking, property and liabilities of the company in respect of which the compromise or arrangement is proposed are to be divided among and transferred to two or more companies, each of which is either an existing public company,[7207] or a new company (whether or not a public company).[7208]

References in this Part to the companies involved in the division are to the transferor company and any existing transferee companies.[7209]

Requirements to be complied with in case of division

Draft terms of scheme (division)

27.23 Section 920 of the CA 2006 sets out the draft terms of scheme. A draft of the proposed terms of the scheme must be drawn up and adopted by the directors of each of the companies involved in the division.[7210]

The draft terms must give particulars of at least the following matters:

(a) in respect of the transferor company and each transferee company (i) its name,[7211] (ii) the address of its registered office,[7212] and (iii) whether it is a company limited by shares or a company limited by guarantee and having a share capital;[7213]

(b) the number of shares in a transferee company to be allotted to members

[7205] CA 2006, s 918(4)(a).   [7206] CA 2006, s 918(4)(b).   [7207] CA 2006, s 919(1)(a).
[7208] CA 2006, s 919(1)(b).   [7209] CA 2006, s 919(2).   [7210] CA 2006, s 920(1).
[7211] CA 2006. s 920(2)(a)(i).   [7212] CA 2006, s 920(2)(a)(ii).
[7213] CA 2006, s 920(2)(a)(iii).

of the transferor company for a given number of their shares (the share exchange ratio) and the amount of any cash payment;[7214]

(c) the terms relating to the allotment of shares in a transferee company;[7215]

(d) the date from which the holding of shares in a transferee company will entitle the holders to participate in profits, and any special conditions affecting that entitlement;[7216]

(e) the date from which the transactions of the transferor company are to be treated for accounting purposes as being those of a transferee company;[7217]

(f) any rights or restrictions attaching to shares or other securities in a transferee company to be allotted under the scheme to the holders of shares or other securities in the transferor company to which any special rights or restrictions attach, or the measures proposed concerning them;[7218]

(g) any amount of benefit paid or given or intended to be paid or given (i) to any of the experts referred to in s 924 of the CA 2006 (expert's report),[7219] or (ii) to any director of a company involved in the division,[7220] and the consideration for the payment of benefit.

The draft terms must also: (a) give particulars of the property and liabilities to be transferred (to the extent that these are known to the transferor company) and their allocation among the transferee companies;[7221] (b) make provision for the allocation among and transfer to the transferee companies of any other property and liabilities that the transferor company has acquired or may subsequently acquire;[7222] and (c) specify the allocation to members of the transferor company of shares in the transferee companies and the criteria upon which that allocation is based.[7223]

Publication of draft terms (division)

27.24 Section 921 of the CA 2006 sets out the publication of draft terms. The directors of each company involved in the division must deliver a copy of the draft terms to the registrar.[7224]

The registrar must publish in the Gazette notice of receipt by him from that company of a copy of the draft terms.[7225] That notice must be published at least one month before the date of any meeting of that company summoned for the purposes of approving the scheme.[7226]

[7214] CA 2006, s 920(2)(b).   [7215] CA 2006, s 920(2)(c).   [7216] CA 2006, s 920(2)(d).
[7217] CA 2006, s 920(2)(e).   [7218] CA 2006, s 920(2)(f).   [7219] CA 2006, s 920(2)(g)(i).
[7220] CA 2006, s 920(2)(g)(ii).   [7221] CA 2006, s 920(3)(a).   [7222] CA 2006, s 920(3)(b).
[7223] CA 2006, s 920(3)(c).   [7224] CA 2006, s 921(1).   [7225] CA 2006, s 921(2).
[7226] CA 2006, s 921(3).

The requirements in this section are subject to s 934 of the CA 2006 (power of the court to exclude certain requirements).[7227]

Approval of members of companies involved in the division

27.25 Section 922 of the CA 2006 sets out the approval members of companies involved in the division. The compromise or arrangement must be approved by a majority in number, representing 75 per cent in value, of each class of members of each of the companies involved in the division, present and voting either in person or by proxy at a meeting.[7228]

This requirement is subject to ss 931 and 932 of the CA 2006 (circumstances in which a meeting of members not required).[7229]

Directors' explanatory report (division)

27.26 Section 923 of the CA 2006 deals with the directors' explanatory report. The directors of the transferor and each existing transferee company must draw up and adopt a report.[7230]

The report must consist of (a) the statement required by s 897 of the CA 2006 (statement explaining the effect of the compromise or arrangement),[7231] and (b) insofar as that statement does not deal with the following matters, a further statement (i) setting out the legal and economic grounds for the draft terms, and in particular for the share exchange ratio and for the criteria on which the allocation to the members of the transferor company of shares in the transferee companies was based,[7232] and (ii) specifying any special valuation difficulties.[7233]

The report must also state (a) whether a report has been made to any transferee company under s 593 of the CA 2006 (valuation of non-cash consideration for shares),[7234] and (b) if so, whether that report has been delivered to the registrar of companies.[7235]

The requirement in this section is subject to s 933 of the CA 2006 (agreement to dispense with reports etc).[7236]

Expert's report (division)

27.27 Section 924 of the CA 2006 sets out the expert's report. An expert's report must be drawn up on behalf of each company involved in the division.[7237]

[7227] CA 2006, s 921(4).   [7228] CA 2006, s 922(1).   [7229] CA 2006, s 922(2).
[7230] CA 2006, s 923(1).   [7231] CA 2006, s 923(2)(a).   [7232] CA 2006, s 923(2)(b)(i).
[7233] CA 2006, s 923(2)(b)(ii).   [7234] CA 2006, s 923(3)(a).   [7235] CA 2006, s 923(3)(b).
[7236] CA 2006, s 923(4).   [7237] CA 2006, s 924(1).

The report required is a written report on the draft terms to the members of the company.[7238]

The court may on the joint application of the companies involved in the division approve the appointment of a joint expert to draw up a single report on behalf of all those companies.

If no such appointment is made, there must be a separate expert's report to the members of each company involved in the division drawn up by a separate expert appointed on behalf of that company.[7239]

The expert must be a person who is eligible for appointment as a statutory auditor (see s 1212) of the CA 2006,[7240] and meets the independence requirement in s 936 of the CA 2006.[7241]

The expert's report must:

(a)   indicate the method or methods used to arrive at the share exchange ratio;[7242]
(b)   give an opinion as to whether the method or methods used are reasonable in all the circumstances of the case, indicate the values arrived at using each such method and (if there is more than one method) give an opinion on the relative importance attributed to such methods in arriving at the value decided on;[7243]
(c)   describe any special valuation difficulties that have arisen;[7244]
(d)   state whether in the expert's opinion the share exchange ratio is reasonable;[7245] and
(e)   in the case of a valuation made by a person other than himself (see s 935 of the CA 2006), state that it appeared to him reasonable to arrange for it to be so made or to accept a valuation so made.[7246]

The expert (or each of them) has the right of access to all such documents of the companies involved in the division,[7247] and the right to require from the companies' officers all such information[7248] as he thinks necessary for the purposes of making his report.

The requirement in this section is subject to s 933 of the CA 2006 (agreement to dispense with reports, etc.).[7249]

Supplementary accounting statement (division)

27.28 Section 925 of the CA 2006 deals with the supplementary accounting statement. If the last annual accounts of a company involved in the division relate to a financial year ending more than seven months before the first

---

[7238] CA 2006, s 924(2).   [7239] CA 2006, s 924(3).   [7240] CA 2006, s 924(4)(a).
[7241] CA 2006, s 924(4)(b).   [7242] CA 2006, s 924(5)(a).   [7243] CA 2006 s 924(5)(b).
[7244] CA 2006, s 924(5)(c).   [7245] CA 2006, s 924(5)(d).   [7246] CA 2006, s 924(5)(e).
[7247] CA 2006, s 924(6)(a).   [7248] CA 2006, s 924(6)(b).   [7249] CA 2006, s 924(7).

meeting of the company summoned for the purposes of approving the scheme, the directors of that company must prepare a supplementary accounting statement.[7250]

That statement must consist of a balance sheet dealing with the state of affairs of the company as at a date not more than three months before the draft terms were adopted by the directors,[7251] and where the company would be required under s 399 of the CA 2006 to prepare group accounts if that date were the last day of a financial year, a consolidated balance sheet dealing with the state of affairs of the company and the undertakings that would be included in such a consolidation.[7252]

The requirements of this Act (and where relevant Article 4 of the IAS Regulation) as to the balance sheet forming part of a company's annual accounts, and the matters to be included in notes to it, apply to the balance sheet required for an accounting statement under this section, with such modifications as are necessary by reason of its being prepared otherwise than as at the last day of a financial year.[7253]

The provisions of s 414 of the CA 2006 as to the approval and signing of accounts apply to the balance sheet required for an accounting statement under this section.[7254]

The requirement in this section is subject to s 933 of the CA 2006 (agreement to dispense with reports, etc.).[7255]

Inspection of documents (division)

27.29 Section 926 of the CA 2006 is concerned with the inspection of documents. The members of each company involved in the division must be able, during the period specified below, to inspect at the registered office of that company copies of the documents listed below relating to that company and every other company involved in the division,[7256] and to obtain copies of those documents or any part of them on request free of charge.[7257]

The period referred to above is the period beginning one month before,[7258] and ending on the date of,[7259] the first meeting of the members, or any class of members, of the company for the purposes of approving the scheme.

The documents referred to above are:

(a)   the draft terms;[7260]
(b)   the directors' explanatory report;[7261]
(c)   the expert's report;[7262]

[7250] CA 2006, s 925(1).   [7251] CA 2006, s 925(2)(a).   [7252] CA 2006, s 925(2)(b).
[7253] CA 2006, s 925(3).   [7254] CA 2006, s 925(4).   [7255] CA 2006, s 925(5).
[7256] CA 2006, s 926(1)(a).   [7257] CA 2006, s 926(1)(b).   [7258] CA 2006, s 926(2)(a).
[7259] CA 2006, s 926(2)(b).   [7260] CA 2006, s 926(3)(a).   [7261] CA 2006, s 926(3)(b).
[7262] CA 2006, s 926(3)(c).

(d) the company's annual accounts and reports for the last three financial years ending on or before the first meeting of the members, or any class of members, of the company summoned for the purposes of approving the scheme;[7263] and

(e) any supplementary accounting statement required by s 925 of the CA 2006.[7264]

The requirements in s 926(3)(b), (c) and (e) of the CA 2006 are subject to s 933 of the CA 2006 (agreement to dispense with reports, etc.) and s 934 of the CA 2006 (power of the court to exclude certain requirements).[7265]

Reports on material changes in the assets of the transferor company (division)

27.30 Section 927 of the CA 2006 deals with the report on material changes in the assets of the transferor company. The directors of the transferor company must report to every meeting of the members, or any class of members, of that company summoned for the purpose of agreeing to the scheme,[7266] and to the directors of each existing transferee company,[7267] any material changes in the property and liabilities of the transferor company between the date when the draft terms were adopted and the date of the meeting in question.

The directors of each existing transferee company must in turn report those matters to every meeting of the members, or any class of members, of that company summoned for the purpose of agreeing to the scheme,[7268] or send a report of those matters to every member entitled to receive notice of such a meeting.[7269]

The requirement in this section is subject to s 933 of the CA 2006 (agreement to dispense with reports, etc.).[7270]

Approval of articles of the new transferee company (division)

27.31 Section 928 of the CA 2006 concerns approval of the articles of a new transferee company. The articles of every new transferee company, or a draft of them, must be approved by ordinary resolution of the transferor company.

[7263] CA 2006, s 926(3)(d).   [7264] CA 2006, s 926(3)(e).   [7265] CA 2006, s 926(4).
[7266] CA 2006, s 927(1)(a).   [7267] CA 2006, s 927(1)(b).   [7268] CA 2006, s 927(2)(a).
[7269] CA 2006, s 927(2)(b).   [7270] CA 2006, s 927(3).

Protection of holders of securities to which special rights are attached (division)

27.32 Section 929 of the CA 2006 deals with the protection of holders of securities to which special rights are attached. The scheme must provide that where any securities of the transferor company (other than shares) to which special rights are attached are held by a person otherwise than as a member or creditor of the company, that person is to receive rights in a transferee company of equivalent value.[7271]

Section 929(1) of the CA 2006 does not apply if the holder has agreed otherwise,[7272] or the holder is, or under the scheme is to be, entitled to have the securities purchased by a transferee company on terms that the court considers reasonable.[7273]

No allotment of shares to the transferor company or its nominee (division)

27.33 Section 930 of the CA 2006 states that there is no allotment of shares to a transferor company or its nominee. The scheme must not provide for shares in a transferee company to be allotted to the transferor company (or its nominee) in respect of shares in the transferor company held by it (or its nominee).

Exceptions where the shares of a transferor company are held by transferee company

Circumstances in which meeting of members of transferor company not required (division)

27.34 Section 931 of the CA 2006 applies in the case of a division where all of the shares or other securities of the transferor company carrying the right to vote at general meetings of the company are held by or on behalf of one or more existing transferee companies.[7274]

It is not necessary for the scheme to be approved by a meeting of the members, or any class of members, of the transferor company if the court is satisfied that the following conditions have been complied with.[7275]

The first condition is that publication of notice of receipt of the draft terms by the registrar took place in respect of all the companies involved in the division at least one month before the date of the court's order.[7276]

The second condition is that the members of every company involved in the division were able during the period beginning one month before, and

---

[7271] CA 2006, s 929(1).   [7272] CA 2006, s 929(2)(a).   [7273] CA 2006, s 929(2)(b).
[7274] CA 2006, s 931(1).   [7275] CA 2006, s 931(2).   [7276] CA 2006, s 931(3).

ending on, that date to inspect at the registered office of their company copies of the documents listed in s 926(3) of the CA 2006 relating to every company involved in the division,[7277] and to obtain copies of those documents or any part of them on request free of charge.[7278]

The third condition is that one or more members of the transferor company, who together held not less than 5 per cent of the paid-up capital of the company (excluding any shares in the company held as treasury shares) would have been able, during that period, to require a meeting of each class of members to be called for the purpose of deciding whether or not to agree to the scheme,[7279] and no such requirement was made.[7280]

The fourth condition is that the directors of the transferor company have sent to every member who would have been entitled to receive notice of a meeting to agree to the scheme (had any such meeting been called),[7281] and to the directors of every existing transferee company,[7282] a report of any material change in the property and liabilities of the transferor company between the date when the terms were adopted by the directors and the date one month before the date of the court's order.

Other exceptions

Circumstances in which a meeting of members of the transferee company not required (division)

27.35 Section 932 of the CA 2006 deals with circumstances in which a meeting of members of the transferee company is not required. In the case of a division, it is not necessary for the scheme to be approved by the members of a transferee company if the court is satisfied that the following conditions have been complied with in relation to that company.[7283]

The first condition is that publication of notice of receipt of the draft terms by the registrar took place in respect of that company at least one month before the date of the first meeting of members of the transferor company summoned for the purpose of agreeing to the scheme.[7284]

The second condition is that the members of that company were able during the period beginning one month before, and ending on, that date to inspect at the registered office of that company copies of the documents specified in s 926(3) of the CA 2006 relating to that company and every other company involved in the division,[7285] and to obtain copies of those documents or any part of them on request free of charge.[7286]

[7277] CA 2006, s 931(4)(a). [7278] CA 2006, s 931(4)(b). [7279] CA 2006, s 931(5)(a).
[7280] CA 2006, s 931(5)(b). [7281] CA 2006, s 931(6)(a). [7282] CA 2006, s 931(6)(b).
[7283] CA 2006, s 932(1). [7284] CA 2006, s 932(2). [7285] CA 2006, s 932(3)(a).
[7286] CA 2006, s 932(3)(b).

The third condition is that one or more members of that company, who together held not less than 5 per cent of the paid-up capital of the company which carried the right to vote at general meetings of the company (excluding any shares in the company held as treasury shares) would have been able, during that period, to require a meeting of each class of members to be called for the purpose of deciding whether or not to agree to the scheme,[7287] and no such requirement was made.[7288]

The first and second conditions above are subject to s 934 of the CA 2006 (power of court to exclude certain requirements).[7289]

Agreement to dispense with reports, etc. (division)

27.36 Section 933 of the CA 2006 sets out the agreement to dispense with reports. If all members holding shares in, and all persons holding other securities of, the companies involved in the division, being shares or securities that carry a right to vote in general meetings of the company in question, so agree, the following requirements do not apply.[7290]

The requirements that may be dispensed with under this section are (a) the requirements of (i) s 923 of the CA 2006 (directors' explanatory report),[7291] (ii) s 924 of the CA 2006 (expert's report),[7292] (iii) s 925 of the CA 2006 (supplementary accounting statement),[7293] and (iv) s 927 of the CA 2006 (report on material changes in assets of the transferor company);[7294] and (b) the requirements of s 926 of the CA 2006 (inspection of documents) so far as relating to any document required to be drawn up under the provisions mentioned in para (a)(i), (ii) or (iii) above.[7295]

For the purposes of s 933 of the CA 2006, the members, or holders of other securities, of a company,[7296] and whether shares or other securities carry a right to vote in general meetings of the company,[7297] are determined as at the date of the application to the court under s 896 of the CA 2006.

Power of the court to exclude certain requirements (division)

27.37 Section 934 of the CA 2006 is concerned with the power of the court to exclude certain requirements. In the case of a division, the court may by order direct that (a) in relation to any company involved in the division, the requirements of (i) s 921 of the CA 2006 (publication of draft terms),[7298] and (ii) s 926 of the CA 2006 (inspection of documents),[7299] do not apply, and (b) in relation to an existing transferee company, s 932 of the CA 2006

[7287] CA 2006, s 932(4)(a).   [7288] CA 2006, s 932(4)(b).   [7289] CA 2006, s 932(5).
[7290] CA 2006, s 933(1).   [7291] CA 2006, s 933(2)(a)(i).   [7292] CA 2006, s 933(2)(a)(ii).
[7293] CA 2006, s 933(2)(a)(iii).   [7294] CA 2006, s 933(2)(a)(iv).   [7295] CA 2006, s 933(2)(b).
[7296] CA 2006, s 933(3)(a).   [7297] CA 2006, s 933(3)(b).   [7298] CA 2006, s 934(1)(a)(i).
[7299] CA 2006, s 934(1)(a)(ii).

(circumstances in which a meeting of members of the transferee company not required) has effect with the omission of the first and second conditions specified in that section,[7300] if the court is satisfied that the following conditions will be fulfilled in relation to that company.

The first condition is that the members of that company will have received, or will have been able to obtain free of charge, copies of the documents listed in s 926 of the CA 2006 in time to examine them before the date of the first meeting of the members, or any class of members, of that company summoned for the purposes of agreeing to the scheme,[7301] or in the case of an existing transferee company where in the circumstances described in s 932 of the CA 2006 no meeting is held, in time to require a meeting as mentioned in s 932(4) of the CA 2006.[7302]

The second condition is that the creditors of that company will have received or will have been able to obtain free of charge copies of the draft terms in time to examine them before the date of the first meeting of the members, or any class of members, of the company summoned for the purpose of agreeing to the scheme,[7303] or in the circumstances mentioned in s 934(2)(b) of the CA 2006 above, at the same time as the members of the company.[7304]

The third condition is that no prejudice would be caused to the members or creditors of the transferor company or any transferee company by making the order in question.[7305]

Supplementary Provisions

27.38 Chapter 4 sets out the supplementary provisions.

Expert's report and related matters

Expert's report: valuation by another person

27.39 Section 935 of the CA 2006 sets out the expert's reports in respect of valuation by another person. Where it appears to an expert (a) that a valuation is reasonably necessary to enable him to draw up his report;[7306] and (b) that it is reasonable for that valuation, or part of it, to be made by (or for him to accept a valuation made by) another person who (i) appears to him to have the requisite knowledge and experience to make the valuation or that part of it,[7307] and (ii) meets the independence requirement in s 936 of the CA 2006,[7308] he may arrange for or accept such a valuation, together with a report that will enable him to make his own report under s 909 or 924 of the CA 2006.

[7300] CA 2006, s 934(1)(b).   [7301] CA 2006, s 934(2)(a).   [7302] CA 2006, s 934(2)(b).
[7303] CA 2006, s 934(3)(a).   [7304] CA 2006, s 934(3)(b).   [7305] CA 2006, s 934(4).
[7306] CA 2006, s 935(1)(a).   [7307] CA 2006, s 935(1)(b)(i).   [7308] CA 2006, s 935(1)(b)(ii).

Where any valuation is made by a person other than the expert himself, the latter's report must state that fact and must also state the former's name and what knowledge and experience he has to carry out the valuation,[7309] and describe so much of the undertaking, property and liabilities as was valued by the other person, and the method used to value them, and specify the date of the valuation.[7310]

Experts and valuers: independence requirement

27.40 Section 936 of the CA 2006 is concerned with experts and valuers with particular references to the independence requirement. A person meets the independence requirement for the purposes of s 909 or 924 of the CA 2006 (expert's report) or s 935 of the CA 2006 (valuation by another person) only if:

(a) he is not (i) an officer or employee of any of the companies concerned in the scheme,[7311] or (ii) a partner or employee of such a person, or a partnership of which such a person is a partner;[7312]

(b) he is not (i) an officer or employee of an associated undertaking of any of the companies concerned in the scheme,[7313] or (ii) a partner or employee of such a person, or a partnership of which such a person is a partner;[7314] and

(c) there does not exist between (i) the person or an associate of his,[7315] and (ii) any of the companies concerned in the scheme or an associated undertaking of such a company,[7316] a connection of any such description as may be specified by regulations made by the Secretary of State.

An auditor of a company is not regarded as an officer or employee of the company for this purpose.[7317]

The term the 'companies concerned in the scheme' means every transferor and existing transferee company;[7318] and 'associated undertaking', in relation to a company, means (i) a parent undertaking or subsidiary undertaking of the company,[7319] or (ii) a subsidiary undertaking of a parent undertaking of the company;[7320] and the term 'associate' has the meaning given by s 937 of the CA 2006.[7321]

27.41 Regulations under this section are subject to negative resolution procedure.[7322]

[7309] CA 2006, s 935(2)(a). [7310] CA 2006, s 935(2)(b). [7311] CA 2006, s 936(1)(a)(i).
[7312] CA 2006, s 936(1)(a)(ii). [7313] CA 2006, s 936(1)(b)(i).
[7314] CA 2006, s 936(1)(b)(ii). [7315] CA 2006, s 936(1)(c)(i). [7316] CA 2006, s 936(1)(c)(ii).
[7317] CA 2006, s 936(2). [7318] CA 2006, s 936(3)(a). [7319] CA 2006, s 936(3)(b)(i).
[7320] CA 2006, s 936(3)(b)(ii). [7321] CA 2006, s 936(3)(c). [7322] CA 2006, s 936(4).

Experts and valuers: meaning of 'associate'

27.42 Section 937 of the CA 2006 defines 'associate' for the purposes of s 936 of the CA 2006 (experts and valuers: independence requirement).[7323]
In relation to an individual, 'associate' means:

(a)   that individual's spouse or civil partner or minor child or step-child;[7324]
(b)   any body corporate of which that individual is a director;[7325] and
(c)   any employee or partner of that individual.[7326]

In relation to a body corporate, 'associate' means:

(a)   any body corporate of which that body is a director;[7327]
(b)   any body corporate in the same group as that body;[7328] and
(c)   any employee or partner of that body or of any body corporate in the same group.[7329]

In relation to a partnership that is a legal person under the law by which it is governed, 'associate' means:

(a)   any body corporate of which that partnership is a director;[7330]
(b)   any employee of or partner in that partnership;[7331] and
(c)   any person who is an associate of a partner in that partnership.[7332]

In relation to a partnership that is not a legal person under the law by which it is governed, 'associate' means any person who is an associate of any of the partners.[7333]
In this section, in relation to a limited liability partnership, for 'director' it should read 'member'.[7334]

Powers of the court

Power of the court to summon a meeting of members or creditors of an existing transferee company

27.43 Section 938 of the CA 2006 states that the court may order a meeting of the members of an existing transferee company, or any class of them,[7335] or

---

[7323] CA 2006, s 937(1).   [7324] CA 2006, s 937(2)(a).   [7325] CA 2006, s 937(2)(b).
[7326] CA 2006, s 937(2)(c).   [7327] CA 2006, s 937(3)(a).   [7328] CA 2006, s 937(3)(b).
[7329] CA 2006, s 937(3)(c).   [7330] CA 2006, s 937(4)(a).   [7331] CA 2006, s 937(4)(b).
[7332] CA 2006, s 937(4)(c).   [7333] CA 2006, s 937(5).   [7334] CA 2006, s 937(6).
[7335] CA 2006, s 938(1)(a).

the creditors of an existing transferee company, or any class of them,[7336] to be summoned in such manner as the court directs.

An application for such an order may be made by the company concerned,[7337] or a member or creditor of the company,[7338] or if an administration order is in force in relation to the company, the administrator.[7339]

Court to fix a date for the transfer of an undertaking, etc. of a transferor company

27.44 Section 939 of the CA 2006 states that where the court sanctions the compromise or arrangement, it must in the order sanctioning the compromise or arrangement,[7340] or in a subsequent order under s 900 of the CA 2006 (powers of court to facilitate a reconstruction or amalgamation),[7341] fix a date on which the transfer (or transfers) to the transferee company (or transferee companies) of the undertaking, property[7342] and liabilities of the transferor company is (or are) to take place.

Any such order that provides for the dissolution of the transferor company must fix the same date for the dissolution.[7343]

If it is necessary for the transferor company to take steps to ensure that the undertaking, property and liabilities are fully transferred, the court must fix a date, not later than six months after the date fixed under s 939(1) of the CA 2006, by which such steps must be taken.[7344]

In that case, the court may postpone the dissolution of the transferor company until that date.[7345]

The court may postpone or further postpone the date fixed under s 939(3) of the CA 2006 if it is satisfied that the steps mentioned cannot be completed by the date (or latest date) fixed under that subsection.[7346]

Liability of transferee companies

Liability of transferee companies for each other's defaults

27.45 Section 940 of the CA 2006 sets out the liability of transferee companies for each other's defaults. In the case of a division, each transferee company is jointly and severally liable for any liability transferred to any other transferee company under the scheme to the extent that the other company has made a default in satisfying that liability.[7347] This is subject to the following provisions.

[7336] CA 2006, s 938(1)(b).   [7337] CA 2006, s 938(2)(a).   [7338] CA 2006, s 938(2)(b).
[7339] CA 2006, s 938(2)(c).   [7340] CA 2006, s 939(1)(a).   [7341] CA 2006, s 939(1)(b).
[7342] The term 'property' includes property, rights and powers of energy description.
[7343] CA 2006, s 939(2).   [7344] CA 2006, s 939(3).   [7345] CA 2006, s 939(4).
[7346] CA 2006, s 939(5).   [7347] CA 2006, s 940(1).

If a majority in number representing 75 per cent in value of the creditors or any class of creditors of the transferor company, present and voting either in person or by proxy at a meeting summoned for the purposes of agreeing to the scheme, so agree, s 940(1) of the CA 2006 does not apply in relation to the liabilities[7348] owed to the creditors or that class of creditors.[7349]

A transferee company is not liable under this section for an amount greater than the net value transferred to it under the scheme.

The 'net value transferred' is the value at the time of the transfer of the property transferred to it under the scheme, less the amount at that date of the liabilities so transferred.[7350]

[7348] The term 'liabilities' includes duties: CA 2006, s 941.
[7349] CA 2006, s 940(2).   [7350] CA 2006, s 940(3).

Chapter 28

Takeovers

Introduction

28.1 The takeover provisions are governed by Part 28 of the CA 2006. This Part implements the European Directive on Takeover Bids (2004/25/EC, the Takeovers Directive) which was adopted on 21 April 2004 and had to be implemented by 20 May 2006. It also contains a few minor amendments to the existing law not required by the Directive.

Background

28.2 With the exception of Chapter 3 to Part 28 of the CA 2006 which restates with amendments Part 13A of the CA 1985, the provisions set out in Part 28 of the CA 2006 are new.

The principal body of provisions emerged from the consultation document, *Company Law–Implementation of the European Directive on Takeover Bids*.[7351] Additionally, the Company Law Review Group considered issues related to 'squeeze-out' and 'sell-out' concerning the problems of, and for, residual minority shareholders following a successful takeover bid) in Chapter 11 and Annex B of *Completing the Structure*, and presented their conclusions in Chapter 13 of the *Final Report*. Certain provisions in Part 28 of the CA 2006 have been developed in the light of these conclusions.

Overview of part 28

28.3 Part 28 is divided into four Chapters. Chapter 1 deals with matters related to the Takeover Panel and its takeover regulatory functions. Chapter 2 concerns matters related to barriers to takeovers. Chapter 3 contains provisions relating to 'squeeze-out' and 'sell-out' concepts designed to address the problems of, and for, residual minority shareholders following a successful

---

[7351] Department of Trade and Industry, January 2005.

takeover bid; and Chapter 4 amends the provisions in Part 7 of the CA 1985 on the content of annual reports of companies traded on a regulated market.

It is intended that certain provisions of Part 28 of the CA 2006 will be extended to unregistered companies with shares traded on a regulated market. This will be achieved by the regulation that is necessary to ensure compliance with the Takeovers Directive.

The Takeover Panel

28.4 Chapter 1 sets out the position of the Takeover Panel.

The position before the Companies Act 2006

28.5 Since 1968, takeover regulation in the UK has been overseen by the Panel on Takeovers and Mergers (the Panel), which administered rules and principles contained in the non-statutory City Code on Takeovers and Mergers. In order to bring UK takeover regulation within the requirements laid down in the Takeovers Directive, Chapter 1 places it within a statutory framework.

The position under the Companies Act 2006

28.6 Under the CA 2006, the Panel will supervise takeover activity and similar types of transactions. The Panel will retain considerable autonomy to provide for its own constitution and appointment procedures. However, a minimum constitutional structure is laid down, providing for the Panel to make arrangements for carrying out its functions and, in particular, to function through committees, sub-committees, officers and members of staff. It is envisaged that the Panel will continue to carry out its day-to-day activities through its Executive. Provisions underpinning the funding of the Panel's regulatory activities are also included.

Additionally, the Panel is placed under an obligation to make statutory rules giving effect to certain articles of the Directive and is given a statutory rule-making power to make rules in relation to takeover activity and similar types of transactions, reflecting the current field of activity over which the existing Code lays down rules.

Sections 945, 951, 955, 956 and 961 of the CA 2006 are intended to limit litigation by: (a) channelling parties to take decisions of the Panel (including the Panel's Hearings Committee and the independent Takeover Appeal Board) before having recourse to the courts; (b) excluding new rights of action for breach of statutory duty; (c) protecting concluded transactions from challenge for breach of the Panel's rules; and (d) exempting the Panel and its individual members, officers and staff from liability in damages for things done in, or in connection with, the discharge of the regulatory functions of the Panel.

The CA 2006 does not affect the availability of judicial review by the courts. In the takeovers field, in the *Datafin* case (*R v Panel on Takeovers, ex parte Datafin plc*)[7352] the Court of Appeal concluded that generally the courts should limit themselves only to reviewing the Panel's decision-making processes after the bid has been concluded.

The CA 2006 confers on the Panel powers to make rulings and directions and to enforce these through the courts, to obtain information and documents from those involved in regulated activities and to impose sanctions on those who transgress its rules.

The Panel and its rules

The Panel

28.7 Section 942 of the CA 2006 sets out the basis for the Panel on Takeovers and Mergers. It states that the body known as the Panel on Takeovers and Mergers (the Panel) is to have the functions conferred on it by or under this Chapter.[7353]

The Panel may do anything that it considers necessary or expedient for the purposes of, or in connection with, its functions.[7354]

The Panel may make arrangements for any of its functions to be discharged by a committee or sub-committee of the Panel;[7355] or an officer or member of staff of the Panel, or a person acting as such.[7356] This is however, subject to ss 943(4) and (5) of the CA 2006.

The objective of s 942 of the CA 2006 is to confer on the Panel the takeover regulatory functions set out in Chapter 1. The Panel is empowered to do anything that it considers necessary or expedient in relation to its prescribed functions and it may also make arrangements for such functions to be carried out on its behalf by a committee or sub-committee of the Panel or an officer or member of staff of the Panel or a person acting as such.

It should be noted that Chapter 1 does not confer on the Panel the states of statutory body.

The Panel will remain an unincorporated body, as constituted from time to time, and, as such, having rights and obligations under the common law. Those rights and obligations will be supplemented by the provisions set out in the CA 2006.

[7352] [1987] QB 815.   [7353] CA 2006, s 942(1).   [7354] CA 2006, s 942(2).
[7355] CA 2006, s 942(3).   [7356] CA 2006, s 942(3)(b).

Rules

28.8 Section 943 of the CA 2006 sets out the basis of the rules by the Panel. The Panel must make rules giving effect to Articles 3.1, 4.2, 5, 6.1–6.3, 7–9 and 13 of the Takeovers Directive.[7357]

The rules made by the Panel may also make other provision (a) for or in connection with the regulation of (i) takeover bids,[7358] (ii) merger transactions,[7359] and (iii) transactions (not falling within sub-para (i) or (ii)) that have or may have, directly or indirectly, an effect on the ownership or control of companies;[7360] (b) for or in connection with the regulation of things done in consequence of, or otherwise in relation to, any such bid or transaction;[7361] (c) about cases where (i) any such bid or transaction is, or has been, contemplated or apprehended,[7362] or (ii) an announcement is made denying that any such bid or transaction is intended.[7363]

The provision that may be made under s 943(2) of the CA 2006 includes, in particular, provision for a matter that is, or is similar to, a matter provided for by the Panel in the City Code on Takeovers and Mergers as it had effect immediately before the passing of this Act.[7364]

In relation to rules made by virtue of s 957 of the CA 2006 (fees and charges), functions under this section may be discharged either by the Panel itself or by a committee of the Panel (but not otherwise).[7365]

In relation to rules of any other description, the Panel must discharge its functions under this section by a committee of the Panel.[7366]

Section 1 of the CA 2006 (meaning of the term 'company') does not apply for the purposes of this section.[7367]

The term 'takeover bid' includes a takeover bid within the meaning of the Takeovers Directive.[7368] The term 'the Takeovers Directive' means Directive 2004/25/EC of the European Parliament and of the Council.[7369]

A reference to rules in the following provisions of this Chapter is to rules under this section.[7370]

Further provisions about rules

28.9 Section 944 of the CA 2006 states that the rules may make different provisions for different purposes.[7371] They may make provision subject to exceptions or exemptions;[7372] contain incidental, supplemental, consequential or transitional provisions;[7373] authorise the Panel to dispense with or modify

---

[7357] CA 2006, s 943(1).   [7358] CA 2006, s 943(2)(a)(i).   [7359] CA 2006, s 943(2)(a)(ii).
[7360] CA 2006, s 943(2)(a)(iii).   [7361] CA 2006, s 943(2)(b).   [7362] CA 2006, s 943(2)(c)(i).
[7363] CA 2006, s 943(2)(c)(ii).   [7364] CA 2006, s 943(3).   [7365] CA 2006, s 943(4).
[7366] CA 2006, s 943(5).   [7367] CA 2006, s 943(6).   [7368] CA 2006, s 943(7).
[7369] CA 2006, s 943(8).   [7370] CA 2006, s 943(9).   [7371] CA 2006, s 944(1)(a).
[7372] CA 2006. s 944(1)(b).   [7373] CA 2006, s 944(1)(c).

the application of rules in particular cases and by reference to any circumstances.[7374] In the latter case, the rules must require the Panel to give reasons for dispensing or modifying the application of rules.[7375]

Rules must be made by an instrument in writing.[7376] Immediately after an instrument containing rules is made, the text must be made available to the public, with or without payment, in whatever way the Panel thinks appropriate.[7377]

A person is not to be taken to have contravened a rule if he shows that at the time of the alleged contravention the text of the rule had not been made available as required by s 944(3) of the CA 2006.[7378]

The production of a printed copy of an instrument purporting to be made by the Panel on which is endorsed a certificate signed by an officer of the Panel authorised by it for that purpose and stating (a) that the instrument was made by the Panel;[7379] (b) that the copy is a true copy of the instrument;[7380] and (c) that on a specified date the text of the instrument was made available to the public as required by s 944(3) of the CA 2006,[7381] is evidence (or in Scotland sufficient evidence) of the facts stated in the certificate.

A certificate purporting to be signed as mentioned in s 943(5) of the CA 2006 is to be treated as having been properly signed unless the contrary is shown.[7382]

A person who wishes in any legal proceedings to rely on an instrument by which rules are made may require the Panel to endorse a copy of the instrument with a certificate of the kind mentioned in s 943(5) of the CA 2006.[7383]

Under ss 943 and 944 of the CA 2006, the Panel is given the power to make rules in relation to takeover regulation. The rule-making power is broadly drawn to ensure that the Panel can continue to make rules on the range of matters that were previously regulated by the City Code on Takeovers and Mergers. The following provisions are included. First, the Panel is placed under an obligation to make rules as required by specified Articles of the Takeovers Directive. These are the general principles (Article 3.1 of the Directive), jurisdictional rules (Article 4.2), matters related to the protection of minority shareholders, mandatory bid and equitable price (Article 5), contents of the bid documentation (Article 6.1–6.3), time allowed for acceptance of a bid and publication of a bid (Articles 7 and 8), obligations of the management of the target company (Article 9) and other rules applicable to the conduct of bids (Article 13). In making rules in relation to these Articles, the Panel will be entitled to exercise Member State options where these are provided for in the Directive. The Panel's rules will not, however, deal with certain matters contained in the Directive such as squeeze-out and sell-out

---

[7374] CA 2006, s 944(1)(d).   [7375] CA 2006, s 944(1).   [7376] CA 2006, s 944(2).
[7377] CA 2006, s 944(3).   [7378] CA 2006, s 944(4).   [7379] CA 2006, s 944(5)(a).
[7380] CA 2006, s 944(5)(b).   [7381] CA 2006, s 944(5)(c).   [7382] CA 2006, s 944(6).
[7383] CA 2006, s 944(7).

(Articles 15 and 16), information to be published by companies in their annual report (Article 10) and barriers to takeovers (Article 11), which are more appropriately dealt with in company legislation (and are the subject of further provision at Chapters 2 and 3 of Part 28 of the CA 2006).

Second, the Panel is permitted to make rules on takeover bids (including, but not limited to, those that are the subject of the Directive), mergers and other transactions affecting the ownership or control of companies. The power is designed to be broad enough to cover the existing scope of the Code and sufficiently flexible to take account of future market developments. Types of matters currently covered by the Code but not covered by the Directive include the takeovers of companies not traded on a regulated market and transactions involving a change of control of a like nature to takeovers.

When making rules under this section, the Panel must do so by a committee of the Panel, except in the case of rules for fees and charges under s 957 of the CA 2006, which must be made either by a committee of the Panel or by the Panel itself.

The further provisions abut rules that may be made by the Panel under s 944 of the CA 2006 include the power to grant derogations and waivers, which by virtue of s 943(1) of the CA 2006 must respect the general principles laid down in Article 3.1 of the Directive.

Section 944(2)–(7) of the CA 2006 makes provision as to the form, public availability and verifications of rules made by the Panel.

Rulings

28.10 Section 945 of the CA 2006 applies to rulings. It empowers the Panel to give rulings on the interpretation, application or effect of rules.[7384]

To the extent and in the circumstances specified in the rules, and subject to any review or appeal, a ruling has binding effect.[7385]

This section enables the Panel, including (by virtue of s 942(3)) of the CA 2006, its Executive, to make rulings on the interpretation, application or effect of the rules made by the Panel.

To the extent and in the circumstances specified in the rules, a ruling of the Panel has binding effect unless reviewed by the Hearings Committee or successfully appealed to the Appeal Board in accordance with rules made under s 951 of the CA 2006. It is envisaged that the rules made under ss 943 and 944 of the CA 2006 will deal with matters such as notice to parties and proper representation of persons who might be bound by a Panel ruling.

[7384] CA 2006, s 945(1).   [7385] CA 2006, s 945(2).

Directions

28.11 Section 946 of the CA 2006 deals with Panel directions. The Panel rules may contain provision conferring power on the Panel to give any direction that appears to the Panel to be necessary in order to restrain a person from acting (or continuing to act) in breach of rules;[7386] or to restrain a person from doing (or continuing to do) a particular thing, pending determination of whether that or any other conduct of his is or would be a breach of rules;[7387] or otherwise to secure compliance with rules.[7388]

This section allows the Panel to make provision in its rules for it to give a direction preventing a person from breaching the rules (including on an interim basis whilst a matter is awaiting determination by the Panel) or otherwise to ensure compliance with the rules.

Information

Power to require documents and information

28.12 Section 947 of the CA 2006 states that the Panel may by notice in writing require a person to produce any documents that are specified or described in the notice;[7389] and to provide, in the form and manner specified in the notice, such information as may be specified or described in the notice.[7390]

A requirement under s 947(1) of the CA 2006 must be complied with at a place specified in the notice,[7391] and before the end of such reasonable period as may be so specified.[7392]

Section 947 of the CA 2006 applies only to documents and information reasonably required in connection with the exercise by the Panel of its functions.[7393]

The Panel may require any document produced to be authenticated,[7394] or any information provided (whether in a document or otherwise) to be verified,[7395] in such manner as it may reasonably require.

The Panel may authorise a person to exercise any of its powers under this section.[7396]

A person exercising a power by virtue of s 947(5) of the CA 2006 must, if required to do so, produce evidence of his authority to exercise the power.[7397]

The production of a document in pursuance of this section does not affect any lien that a person has on the document.[7398]

[7386] CA 2006, s 946(a). [7387] CA 2006, s 946(b). [7388] CA 2006, s 946(c).
[7389] CA 2006, s 947(1)(a). [7390] CA 2006, s 947(1)(b). [7391] CA 2006, s 947(2)(a).
[7392] CA 2006, s 947(2)(b). [7393] CA 2006, s 947(3). [7394] CA 2006, s 947(4)(a).
[7395] CA 2006, s 947(4)(b). [7396] CA 2006, s 947(5). [7397] CA 2006, s 947(6).
[7398] CA 2006, s 947(7).

The Panel may take copies of or extracts from a document produced in pursuance of this section.[7399]

The term 'production of a document' includes a reference to the production of a hard copy of information recorded otherwise than in hard copy form,[7400] or information in a form from which a hard copy can be readily obtained.[7401]

A person is not required by this section to disclose documents or information in respect of which a claim to legal professional privilege (in Scotland, to confidentiality of communications) could be maintained in legal proceedings.[7402]

The Panel has historically had no formal power to require persons involved in takeover activity to provide it with the information the Panel requires to carry out its functions. Persons authorised under the Financial Services and Markets Act 2000 are required by the rules of the Financial Services Authority to provide information and assistance to the Panel. In relation to others, the Panel has relied on the voluntary co-operation of market participants to provide explanations and documents that are not publicly available.

This section enables the Panel to require the production of such documents and information as it may reasonably require in the exercise of its functions. The Panel may also authorise a person to exercise the power under the section on its behalf, for example, if the Panel were to appoint a law or accountancy firm to help it collect and analyse documents.

Section 947(7) of the CA 2006 provides that a lien on a document is not affected by the production of that document in compliance with a requirement imposed by the panel or someone authorised on its behalf. A lien is a legal right to keep possession of a document belonging to someone else until a claim is satisfied – for example, a claim for payment of professional fees. This subsection does not entitle a professional to refuse to hand over a document to the Panel, but preserves his rights over those documents.

The section provides that the Panel may require the production of information in hard copy where it is held in some other form (for instance, electronically on a floppy disk).

The Panel may not compel the production of documents which would be protected form disclosure in legal proceedings on the ground of legal professional privilege or confidentiality of communications.

Restrictions on disclosure

28.13 Section 948 of the CA 2006 applies to restrictions on disclosure. It applies to information (in whatever form) relating to the private affairs of an

---

[7399] CA 2006, s 947(8).   [7400] CA 2006, s 947(9)(a).   [7401] CA 2006, s 947(9)(b).
[7402] CA 2006, s 947(10).

individual,[7403] or relating to any particular business[7404] that is provided to the Panel in connection with the exercise of its functions.

No such information may, during the lifetime of the individual or so long as the business continues to be carried on, be disclosed without the consent of that individual or (as the case may be) the person for the time being carrying on that business.[7405] This does not apply to any disclosure of information that has been authorised by the Panel and is made for the purpose of facilitating the carrying out by the Panel of any of its functions,[7406] is made to a person specified in Part 1 of Schedule 2,[7407] is of a description specified in Part 2 of that Schedule,[7408] or is made in accordance with Part 3 of that Schedule.[7409]

The Secretary of State may amend Schedule 2 by order subject to negative resolution procedure.[7410]

An order must made under s 948(4) of the CA 2006 must not:

(a)   amend Part 1 of Schedule 2 by specifying a person unless the person exercisesfunctions of a public nature (whether or not he exercises any other function);[7411]

(b)   amend Part 2 of Schedule 2 by adding or modifying a description of disclosure unless the purpose for which the disclosure is permitted is likely to facilitate the exercise of a function of a public nature;[7412]

(c)   amend Part 3 of Schedule 2 so as to have the effect of permitting disclosures to be made to a body other than one that exercises functions of a public nature in a country or territory outside the United Kingdom.[7413]

Section 948(2) of the CA 2006 does not apply to the disclosure by an authority within s 948(7) of the CA 2006 of information disclosed to it by the Panel in reliance on s 948(3) of the CA 2006;[7414] or to the disclosure of such information by anyone who has obtained it directly or indirectly from an authority within s 948(7) of the CA 2006.[7415]

The authorities within this subsection are the Financial Services Authority;[7416] an authority designated as a supervisory authority for the purposes of Article 4.1 of the Takeovers Directive;[7417] any other person or body that exercises functions of a public nature, under legislation in an EEA State other than the United Kingdom, which are similar to the Panel's functions or those of the Financial Services Authority.[7418]

Section 948 of the CA 2006 does not prohibit the disclosure of information

---

[7403] CA 2006, s 948(2)(a).   [7404] CA 2006, s 948(2)(b).   [7405] CA 2006, s 948(3)(a).
[7406] CA 2006, s 948(3)(b).   [7407] CA 2006, s 948(3)(c).   [7408] CA 2006, s 948(3)(d).
[7409] CA 2006, s 948(3)(e).   [7410] CA 2006, s 948(4).   [7411] CA 2006, s 948(5)(a).
[7412] CA 2006, s 948(5)(b).   [7413] CA 2006, s 948(5)(c).   [7414] CA 2006, s 948(6)(a).
[7415] CA 2006, s 948(6)(b).   [7416] CA 2006, s 948(7)(a).   [7417] CA 2006, s 948(7)(b).
[7418] CA 2006, s 948(7)(c).

if the information is or has been available to the public from any other source.[7419]

Section 948 of the CA 2006 does not authorise the making of a disclosure in contravention of the Data Protection Act 1998 (c 29).[7420]

Offence of disclosure in contravention of section 948

28.14 Section 949 of the CA 2006 sets out the offence of disclosures that is in contravention of s 948 of the CA 2006. A person who discloses information in contravention of s 948 of the CA 2006 is guilty of an offence, unless he did not know, and had no reason to suspect, that the information had been provided as mentioned in s 948(1) of the CA 2006,[7421] or he took all reasonable steps and exercised all due diligence to avoid the commission of the offence.[7422]

A person guilty of an offence under this section is liable on conviction on indictment, to imprisonment for a term not exceeding two years or a fine (or both);[7423] and on summary conviction in England and Wales, to imprisonment for a term not exceeding 12 months or to a fine not exceeding the statutory maximum (or both);[7424] in Scotland or Northern Ireland, to imprisonment for a term not exceeding six months, or to a fine not exceeding the statutory maximum (or both).[7425]

Where a company or other body corporate commits an offence under this section, an offence is also committed by every officer of the company or other body corporate who is in default.[7426]

Sections 948 and 949 of the CA 2006 provide that information obtained by the Panel in the course of its functions will be subject to restrictions on onward disclosure. Aside from the desirability of such provisions so that those providing information to the Panel can do so knowing that it will not be subject to improper further disclosure, these provisions also meet a requirement under Article 4.3 of the Directive: Member States shall ensure that information provided to those employed, or formerly employed, by takeover supervisory authorities shall not be further divulged: 'to any person or authority except under provisions laid down by law'. Section 948 of the CA 2006, accordingly, prescribes the conditions under which such information can be released.

Information concerning the private affairs of an individual or a business provided to the Panel in connection with its functions may not be disclosed during the individual's lifetime or while the business is carried on without the consent of the individual or business in question except for the purpose of

[7419] CA 2006, s 948(8).   [7420] CA 2006, s 948(9).   [7421] CA 2006, s 949(1)(a).
[7422] CA 2006, s 949(1)(b).   [7423] CA 2006, s 949(2)(a).   [7424] CA 2006, s 949(2)(b)(i).
[7425] CA 2006, s 949(2)(b)(ii).   [7426] CA 2006, s 949(3).

carrying out the Panel's functions or unless it is disclosed to a person or for a purpose set out in Schedule 2 of the CA 2006.

Schedule 2 sets out the 'gateways' for disclosure of information obtained by the Panel in the exercise of its functions that is permitted under s 948 of the CA 2006, including the circumstances in which a disclosure to an overseas regulatory authority is permitted. Under s 948(4) and (5) of the CA 2006, the Secretary of State has the power to amend the Schedule, but only to specify persons exercising functions of a public nature or descriptions of disclosure, where the purpose for which the disclosure is permitted is likely to assist in the exercise of a function of a public nature.[7427]

Section 948(6)(a) of the CA 2006 provides that certain authorities mentioned in s 948(7) of the CA 2006 are not bound by the restrictions on disclosure imposed by s 948(2) of the CA 2006. These bodies are those other takeover supervisory authorities and financial services regulators with which the Panel has a duty to co-operate. Section 948(6)(b) of the CA 2006 provides that persons or bodies obtaining information from those authorities (whether directly or indirectly) are also not bound by the restrictions on disclosure imposed by s 948(2) of the CA 2006. These provisions are necessary to implement fully Article 4.4 of the Directive. Those bodies mentioned in s 948(7) of the CA 2006, and persons and bodies receiving information from them, will themselves be subject to restrictions on disclosure that will mirror those imposed by s 948 of the CA 2006, and so information originating from the Panel will still be protected from improper further disclosure.

Section 949 of the CA 2006 makes it an offence to disclose information in contravention of s 948 of the CA 2006. A person guilty of such an offence is liable on conviction on indictment to two years' imprisonment or a fine or both; and on summary conviction to 12 months' imprisonment (six months in Scotland and Northern Ireland) or a fine or both. Section 949(1) of the CA 2006 provides a person with a defence if he can prove that he did not know, and had no reason to suspect, that the information in question had been provided to the Panel in the exercise of its function; or that he took reasonable steps to prevent wrongful disclosure.

[7427] The specified persons are set out in CA 2006, Schedule 2 of Part 1, namely: the Secretary of State; the Department of Enterprise, Trade and Investment for Northern Ireland; the Treasury; the Bank of England; the Financial Services Authority; the Commissioners for Her Majesty's Revenue and Customs; the Lord Advocate; the Director of Public Prosecutions; the Director of Public Prosecutions for Northern Ireland; a constable; a procurator fiscal; and the Scottish Ministers. Part 2 sets out the specified descriptions of disclosure. Part 3 sets out overseas regulatory bodies.

Co-operation

Panel's duty of co-operation

28.15 Section 950 of the CA 2006 states that the Panel must take such steps as it considers appropriate to co-operate with the Financial Services Authority;[7428] an authority designated as a supervisory authority for the purposes of Article 4.1 of the Takeovers Directive;[7429] any other person or body that exercises functions of a public nature, under legislation in any country or territory outside the United Kingdom, that appears to the Panel to be similar to its own functions or those of the Financial Services Authority.[7430]

The nature of co-operation may include the sharing of information that the Panel is not prevented from disclosing.[7431]

Article 4.4 of the Directive requires that takeover supervisory authorities and financial services regulators provide reasonable assistance to other such authorities within the EEA for the purposes of the Directive. This section is designed to give effect to this requirement by obliging the Panel to co-operate with overseas takeover and financial services regulatory authorities.

The form and manner of co-operation will be as the Panel considers appropriate in the light of the circumstances (in particular, its power to require documents and information may be exercised to support such an authority) and may include sharing information that the panel is not prevented from disclosing. The section mirrors similar co-operation obligations imposed on the Financial Services Authority by s 354 of the Financial Services and Markets Act 2000.

Hearings and appeals

Hearings and appeals

28.16 Section 951 of the CA 2006 states that the rules must provide for a decision of the Panel to be subject to review by a committee of the Panel (the Hearings Committee) at the instance of such persons affected by the decision as are specified in the rules.[7432]

The rules may also confer other functions on the Hearings Committee.[7433]

The rules must provide for there to be a right of appeal against a decision of the Hearings Committee to an independent tribunal (the Takeover Appeal Board) in such circumstances and subject to such conditions as are specified in the rules.[7434]

The rules may contain provisions as to matters of procedure in relation to

---

[7428] CA 2006, s 950(1)(a).   [7429] CA 2006, s 950(1)(b).   [7430] CA 2006, s 950(1)(c).
[7431] CA 2006, s 950(2).   [7432] CA 2006, s 951(1).   [7433] CA 2006, s 951(2).
[7434] CA 2006, s 951(3).

proceedings before the Hearings Committee (including provisions imposing time limits);[7435] provisions about evidence in such proceedings;[7436] provisions as to the powers of the Hearings Committee dealing with matters referred to it;[7437] provisions about the enforcement of decisions of the Hearings Committee and the Takeover Appeal Board.[7438]

The rules must contain provisions requiring the Panel, when acting in relation to any proceedings before the Hearings Committee or the Takeover Appeal Board, to do so by an officer or member of staff of the Panel (or a person acting as such);[7439] preventing a person who is or has been a member of the committee mentioned in s 943(5) of the CA 2006 from being a member of the Hearings Committee or the Takeover Appeal Board;[7440] and preventing a person who is a member of the committee mentioned in s 943(5) of the CA 2006, of the Hearings Committee or of the Takeover Appeal Board from acting as mentioned in para (a) above.[7441]

Section 951 of the CA 2006 ensures that proper procedures for review of and appeal against decisions taken by the Panel in connection with its regulatory functions are provided. Section 951(1) of the CA 2006 requires that the rules made by the Panel provide for a decision of the Panel to be subject to review by a Hearings Committee when requested by affected persons specified in the rules. Section 951(3) of the CA 2006 provides for a right of appeal, as provided for in rules, to an independent tribunal (the Takeover Appeal Board) against a decision of the Hearings Committee. The rules may make provisions in relation to the Hearings Committee as to procedural matters, evidence and the powers of the Committee. Further, rules may contain provisions related to the enforcement of decisions of the Hearings Committee and the Takeover Appeal Board.

Section 951 of the CA 2006 also requires the rules to provide that when appearing before the Hearings Committee or the Takeover Appeal Board, the Board, the Panel must act through an officer or member or staff of the Panel (who must not be member of the rule-making committee referred to in s 943(5) of the CA 2006, the Hearings Committee or the Appeal Board); and that no person who is, or has been, a member of the rule-making committee can be a member of the Hearing committee or the Takeover Appeal Board.

The general rules of natural justice will preclude a person who had taken part in a decision from later considering a review or appeal in relation to that decision.

This approach is designed to ensure a clear and transparent division of responsibilities between the various organs of the Panel in its executive, judicial and rule-making roles.

[7435] CA 2006, s 951(4)(a).   [7436] CA 2006, s 951(4)(b).   [7437] CA 2006, s 951(4)(c).
[7438] CA 2006, s 951(4)(d).   [7439] CA 2006, s 951(5)(a).   [7440] CA 2006, s 951(5)(b).
[7441] CA 2006, s 951(5)(c).

Contravention of rules, etc.

Sanctions

28.17 Section 952 of the CA 2006 sets out sanctions for the contravention of rules. The rules may contain provisions conferring power on the Panel to impose sanctions on a person who has acted in breach of rules,[7442] or failed to comply with a direction given by virtue of s 946 of the CA 2006.[7443]

Section 952(3) of the CA 2006 applies where rules made by virtue of s 952(1) of the CA 2006 confer power on the Panel to impose a sanction of a kind not provided for by the City Code on Takeovers and Mergers as it had effect immediately before the passing of this Act.[7444]

The Panel must prepare a statement (a policy statement) of its policy with respect to the imposition of the sanction in question,[7445] and where the sanction is in the nature of a financial penalty, the amount of the penalty that may be imposed.[7446] An element of the policy must be that, in making a decision about any such matter, the Panel has regard to the factors mentioned in s 952(4) of the CA 2006.

The factors are (a) the seriousness of the breach or failure in question in relation to the nature of the rule or direction contravened;[7447](b) the extent to which the breach or failure was deliberate or reckless;[7448] and (c) whether the person on whom the sanction is to be imposed is an individual.[7449]

The Panel may at any time revise a policy statement.[7450]

The Panel must prepare a draft of any proposed policy statement (or revised policy statement) and consult such persons about the draft as the Panel considers appropriate.[7451]

The Panel must publish, in whatever way it considers appropriate, any policy statement (or revised policy statement) that it prepares.[7452]

In exercising, or deciding whether to exercise, its power to impose a sanction within s 952(2) of the CA 2006 in the case of any particular breach or failure, the Panel must have regard to any relevant policy statement published and in force at the time when the breach or failure occurred.[7453]

This section confers on the Panel the power to make rules for imposing sanctions for breach of its rules or directors given under s 946 of the CA 2006. The Panel's previous sanctions regime, which was set out in the Introduction to the City Code on Takeovers and Mergers and which is expected to remain in the CA 2006, provided for private and public statements of censure of persons in breach of the Code.

Particularly flagrant breaches may lead to the Panel publishing a statement

[7442] CA 2006, s 952(1)(a).   [7443] CA 2006, s 952(1)(b).   [7444] CA 2006, s 952(2).
[7445] CA 2006, s 952(3)(a).   [7446] CA 2006, s 952(3)(b).   [7447] CA 2006, s 952(4)(a).
[7448] CA 2006, s 952(4)(b).   [7449] CA 2006, s 952(4)(c).   [7450] CA 2006, s 952(5).
[7451] CA 2006, s 952(6).   [7452] CA 2006, s 952(7).   [7453] CA 2006, s 952(8).

indicating that the offender is someone who is not likely to comply. The rules of the Financial Services Authority and certain professional organisations contain provisions obliging their members, in certain circumstances, not to act for somebody in such a statement. This is referred to as 'cold-shouldering'. The term in question, cover transactions in relevant securities requiring disclosure under rule 8 of the Code. Under s 952 of the CA 2006, it will continue to be possible, in the case of the transactions that are subject to the Panel rules, for the Panel to issue 'cold-shouldering' statements in appropriate cases. (The Panel will also be able to pass information concerning breaches of rules to other regulatory authorities and professional bodies by virtue of the statutory 'gateways' set out at s 948 of the CA 2006 and Schedule 2 of the CA 2006).

Should future rules made by the Panel confer a power on the Panel to impose a sanction of a kind not contained in the City Code on Takeovers and Mergers as it had effect immediately before the passing of CA 2006, the Panel must prepare a policy statement in respect of the sanction. The policy statement must set out the policy of the Panel with regard to imposition of the sanction and, for financial penalties, the penalty that may be imposed. An element of the policy must be that the Panel, in making a decision about any such matter, has regard to the seriousness of the breach or failure, the extent to which the breach or failure was deliberate or reckless and whether the person on whom the sanction is to be imposed is an individual.

Failure to comply with rules about bid documentation

28.18 Section 953 of the CA 2006 deals with the failure to comply with rules about bid documentation. Section 953 of the CA 2006 applies where a take-over bid is made for a company that has securities carrying voting rights admitted to trading on a regulated market in the United Kingdom.[7454]

Where an offer document published in respect of the bid does not comply with offer document rules, an offence is committed by the person making the bid,[7455] and where the person making the bid is a body of persons, by any director, officer or member of that body who caused the document to be published.[7456]

A person commits an offence under s 953(2) of the CA 2006 only if he knew that the offer document did not comply, or was reckless as to whether it complied,[7457] and he failed to take all reasonable steps to secure that it did comply.[7458]

Where a response document published in respect of the bid does not comply with response document rules, an offence is committed by any director or

---

[7454] CA 2006, s 953(1).   [7455] CA 2006, s 953(2)(a).   [7456] CA 2006, s 953(2)(b).
[7457] CA 2006, s 953(3)(a).   [7458] CA 2006, s 953(3)(b).

other officer of the company referred to in s 953(1) of the CA 2006 who knew that the response document did not comply, or was reckless as to whether it complied,[7459] and failed to take all reasonable steps to secure that it did comply.[7460]

Where an offence is committed under s 953(2)(b) or (4) of the CA 2006 by a company or other body corporate (the relevant body), s 953(2)(b) of the CA 2006 has effect as if the reference to a director, officer or member of the person making the bid included a reference to a director, officer or member of the relevant body;[7461] s 953(4) of the CA 2006 has effect as if the reference to a director or other officer of the company referred to in s 953(1) of the CA 2006 included a reference to a director, officer or member of the relevant body.[7462]

A person guilty of an offence under this section is liable on conviction on indictment, to a fine;[7463] on summary conviction, to a fine not exceeding the statutory maximum.[7464]

Section 953 of the CA 2006 does not effect any power of the Panel in relation to the enforcement of its rules.[7465]

Section 1 of the CA 2006 (meaning of 'company') does not apply for the purposes of this section.[7466]

The following are defined terms:

- 'designated' means designated in rules;
- 'offer document' means a document required to be published by rules giving effect to Article 6.2 of the Takeovers Directive;
- 'offer document rules' means rules designated as rules that give effect to Article 6.3 of that Directive;
- 'response document' means a document required to be published by rules giving effect to Article 9.5 of that Directive;
- 'response document rules' means rules designated as rules that give effect to the first sentence of Article 9.5 of that Directive;
- 'securities' means shares or debentures;
- 'takeover bid' has the same meaning as in that Directive;
- 'voting rights' means rights to vote at general meetings of the company in question, including rights that arise only in certain circumstances.[7467]

Section 953 of the CA 2006 creates new offences in relation to takeover bid documentation (i.e. offer documents prepared by the bidder and documents in response to the bid prepared by the board of the target company). Provisions related to bid documentation are laid down in particular by Articles 6.3 and 9.5 of the Directive, which are to be implemented by rules that the Panel

---

[7459] CA 2006, s 953(4)(a).   [7460] CA 2006, s 953(4)(b).   [7461] CA 2006, s 953(5)(a).
[7462] CA 2006, s 953(5)(b).   [7463] CA 2006, s 953(6)(a).   [7464] CA 2006, s 953(6)(b).
[7465] CA 2006, s 953(7).   [7466] CA 2006, s 953(8).   [7467] CA 2006, s 953(9).

is obliged to make under s 943 of the CA 2006. Consequently, in each case an offence will be committed where the document in question does not comply with rules designated by the Takeover Panel as giving effect to those provisions. The offence relating to offer documents may be committed by the bidder and any of its directors, officers or members who caused the offer document to be published. The offence relating to response documents may be committed by directors or other officers of the target company. Where either offence is committed by a corporate body (for instance, a corporate director), provisions are also included dealing with the liability of directors, officers or members of that body. In each case, an offence will be committed only where the relevant person knew that the document did not comply (or was reckless as to whether it did so) and failed to take all reasonable steps to ensure that it did comply.

A person guilty of an offence under this provision is liable on conviction to a fine (on summary conviction limited to the statutory maximum).

Compensation

28.19 Section 954 of the CA 2006 sets out the provisions on compensation. The rules may confer power on the Panel to order a person to pay such compensation as it thinks just and reasonable if he is in breach of a rule the effect of which is to require the payment of money.[7468]

The rules made by virtue of this section may include provision for the payment of interest (including compound interest).[7469]

Section 954 of the CA 2006 confers on the Panel the power to make rules providing for financial redress (together with interest (including compound interest)) in consequence of a breach of rules that require monetary payments to be made (for instance, a payment by the bidder to shareholders of any difference between the price actually paid and any higher price for shares that the bidder should have paid under the rules).

Enforcement by the court

28.20 Section 955 of the CA 2006 deals with enforcement by the court. If, on the application of the Panel, the court is satisfied that there is a reasonable likelihood that a person will contravene a rule-based requirement,[7470] or that a person has contravened a rule-based requirement or a disclosure requirement,[7471] the court may make any order it thinks fit to secure compliance with the requirement.

[7468] CA 2006, s 954(1).　　[7469] CA 2006, s 954(2).　　[7470] CA 2006, s 955(1)(a).
[7471] CA 2006, s 955(1)(b).

The term 'the court' means the High Court or, in Scotland, the Court of Session.[7472]

Except as provided by s 955(1) of the CA 2006, no person has a right to seek an injunction,[7473] or in Scotland, has title or interest to seek an interdict or an order for specific performance,[7474] to prevent a person from contravening (or continuing to contravene) a rule-based requirement or a disclosure requirement.

The following are defined terms:[7475]

- 'contravene' includes failure to comply;
- 'disclosure requirement' means a requirement imposed under s 947 of the CA 2006;
- 'rule-based requirement' means a requirement imposed by or under rules.

Section 955 of the CA 2006 provides a mechanism by which the Panel may, if necessary, apply to the court in order to enforce Panel rule-based requirements as well as requests for documents and information under s 947 of the CA 2006. The Panel may apply to the court either where there is reasonable likelihood that a person will contravene a requirement imposed by or under the rules, or where a person has failed to comply with such a requirement or with a requirement imposed under s 947 of the CA 2006.

It is expected that in accordance with usual practice, the court will not, in exercising its jurisdiction under this section, rehear the matter substantively, or examine the issues giving rise to the ruling or, as the case may be, the request for documents or information except where on 'judicial review principles' there has been an error of law or procedure.

The court is given a broad discretion as the order it may make to secure compliance with the requirement; but aside from the power granted to the Panel by this section, there is no right to seek injunction (or interdict) to prevent a person contravening, or continuing to contravene, a rule-based requirement or disclosure requirement.

No action for breach of a statutory duty, etc.

28.21 Section 956 of the CA 2006 states that there is no action for breach of statutory duty. Contravention of a rule-based requirement or a disclosure requirement does not give rise to any right of action for breach of statutory duty.[7476]

Contravention of a rule-based requirement does not make any transaction

---

[7472] CA 2006, s 955(2).   [7473] CA 2006, s 955(3)(a).   [7474] CA 2006, s 955(3)(b).
[7475] CA 2006, s 955(4).   [7476] CA 2006, s 956(1).

void or unenforceable or (subject to any provision made by rules) affect the validity of any other thing.[7477]

The following are defined terms:

* 'contravention' includes failure to comply;[7478]
* 'disclosure requirement'; and
* 'rule-based requirement' have the same meaning as in's 955 of the CA 2006.[7479]

Compliance with the rules made by the Panel is a matter solely for the Panel. Section 956 of the CA 2006 deals with two important aspects. First, it excludes new rights of action for breach of statutory duty for contraventions of requirements imposed by or under rules or a requirement imposed under s 947 of the CA 2006; and in order to ensure certainty, it provides that transactions are not made void or unenforceable or (subject to any provision of the rules) affect the validity of any other thing. As previously, transactions will be capable of being set aside or unraveled in cases of, for example, misrepresentation or fraud.

Funding

Fees and charges

28.22 Section 957 of the CA 2006 deals with fees and charges.

The rules may provide for fees or charges to be payable to the Panel for the purpose of meeting any part of its expenses.[7480]

A reference in this section or s 958 of the CA 2006 to expenses of the Panel is to any expenses that have been or are to be incurred by the Panel in, or in connection with, the discharge of its functions, including in particular payments in respect of the expenses of the Takeover Appeal Board;[7481] the cost of repaying the principal of, and of paying any interest on, any money borrowed by the Panel;[7482] the cost of maintaining adequate reserves.[7483]

Section 957 of the CA 2006 enables the Panel to make rules for the payment of fees or changes to the Panel for the purposes of meeting the Panel's expenses incurred in exercising its functions. Such fees and charges may be imposed to meet expenses of the Takeover Appeal Board; the cost of repaying capital and paying interest on loans; and the cost of maintaining adequate reserves. The rules under this section must be made by the Panel itself or by a committee of the panel (s 943(4)) of the CA 2006.

[7477] CA 2006, s 956(2).   [7478] CA 2006, s 956(3)(a).   [7479] CA 2006, s 956(3)(b).
[7480] CA 2006, s 957(1).   [7481] CA 2006, s 957(2)(a).   [7482] CA 2006, s 957(2)(b).
[7483] CA 2006, s 957(2)(c).

Levy

28.23 Section 958 of the CA 2006 states that for the purpose of meeting any part of the expenses of the Panel, the Secretary of State may by regulations provide for a levy to be payable to the Panel by specified persons or bodies, or persons or bodies of a specified description,[7484] or on transactions, of a specified description, in securities on specified markets.[7485]

The term 'specified' means specified in the regulations.[7486]

The power to specify (or to specify descriptions of) persons or bodies must be exercised in such a way that the levy is payable only by persons or bodies that appear to the Secretary of State to be capable of being directly affected by the exercise of any of the functions of the Panel;[7487] or otherwise to have a substantial interest in the exercise of any of those functions.[7488]

The regulations under this section may in particular specify the rate of the levy and the period in respect of which it is payable at that rate;[7489] make provision as to the times when, and the manner in which, payments are to be made in respect of the levy.[7490]

In determining the rate of the levy payable in respect of a particular period, the Secretary of State must take into account any other income received or expected by the Panel in respect of that period;[7491] and may take into account estimated as well as actual expenses of the Panel in respect of that period.[7492]

The Panel must keep proper accounts in respect of any amounts of levy received by virtue of this section;[7493] prepare, in relation to each period in respect of which any such amounts are received, a statement of account relating to those amounts in such form and manner as is specified in the regulations.[7494] Those accounts must be audited, and the statement certified, by persons appointed by the Secretary of State.[7495]

The regulations under this section are subject to affirmative resolution procedure if subs (7) applies to them;[7496] otherwise, are subject to negative resolution procedure.[7497]

Section 958 of the CA 2006 applies to the first regulations under this section;[7498] and any other regulations under this section that would result in a change in the persons or bodies by whom, or the transactions on which, the levy is payable.[7499]

If a draft of an instrument containing regulations under this section would, apart from this subsection, be treated for the purposes of the Standing Orders of either House of Parliament as a hybrid instrument, it is to proceed in that House as if it were not such an instrument.[7500]

[7484] CA 2006, s 958(1)(a).   [7485] CA 2006, s 958(1)(b).   [7486] CA 2006, s 958(1).
[7487] CA 2006, s 958(2)(a).   [7488] CA 2006, s 958(2)(b).   [7489] CA 2006, s 958(3)(a).
[7490] CA 2006, s 958(3)(b).   [7491] CA 2006, s 958(4)(a).   [7492] CA 2006, s 958(4)(b).
[7493] CA 2006, s 958(5)(a).   [7494] CA 2006, s 958(5)(b).   [7495] CA 2006, s 958(5).
[7496] CA 2006, s 958(6)(a).   [7497] CA 2006, s 958(6)(b).   [7498] CA 2006, s 958(7)(a).
[7499] CA 2006, s 958(7)(b).   [7500] CA 2006, s 958(8).

Section 958 of the CA 2006 gives the Secretary of State the power to make regulations imposing a levy for meeting the costs of the Panel. In determining the appropriate rate of the levy, the Secretary of State must take account of other income received, or expected to be received, by the Panel (which would include fees and charges under s 957 of the CA 2006) and may take account of estimated as well as actual costs of the Panel.

It is anticipated that a levy would only be imposed if the existing voluntary levy funding arrangements (contributions collected by members' firms of the London Stock Exchange and Ofex currently set a flat rate charge of £1 on contract notes on all chargeable transactions with a consideration in excess of (£10,000)) were no longer viable. The categories of persons or bodies to which the levy would apply may include only those capable of being directly affected by the exercise of the Panel's functions or otherwise having a substantial interest in the exercise of those functions.

The first regulations made in respect of the levy power – and any further regulations that change the persons or bodies by whom, or the transactions on which, the levy is payable – will be subject to the affirmative resolution procedure in both Houses of Parliament (but a draft of an instrument containing such regulations will not be treated as being hybrid even if otherwise it would be). Any other subsequent regulations will be subject to the negative resolution procedure.

Recovery of fees, charges or levy

28.24 Section 959 of the CA 2006 applies to the recovery of fees, charges or levy. An amount payable by any person or body by any person or body virtue of ss 957 or 958 of the CA 2006 (as a consequence of fees and charges imposed by the Panel or as a result of any levy fixed by the Secretary of State) will constitute a debt owed by that person to the Panel and be recoverable by the Panel as a debt.

Miscellaneous and supplementary

Panel as a party to proceedings

28.25 Section 960 of the CA 2006 provides that a Panel can be a party to proceedings. The Panel is capable (despite being an unincorporated body) of bringing proceedings under Chapter 1 to Part 28 of the CA 2006 in its own name;[7501] and of bringing or defending any other proceedings in its own name.[7502]

Notwithstanding its incorporated status, the Panel may in its own

---

[7501] CA 2006, s 960(1)(a).   [7502] CA 2006, s 960(1)(b).

name bring proceedings under this Chapter and bring or defend other proceedings.

Exemption from liability in damages

28.26 Section 961 of the CA 2006 deals with exemption from liability in damages. Neither the Panel, nor any person within s 961(2) of the CA 2006, is to be liable in damages for anything done (or omitted to be done) in, or in connection with, the discharge or purported discharge of the Panel's functions.[7503]

A person is within this subsection if he is (or is acting as) a member, officer or member of staff of the Panel,[7504] or he is a person authorised under s 947(5) of the CA 2006.[7505]

Section 961(1) of the CA 2006 does not apply if the act or omission is shown to have been in bad faith,[7506] or so as to prevent an award of damages in respect of the act or omission on the ground that it was unlawful as a result of s 6(1) of the Human Rights Act 1998 (c 42) (acts of public authorities incompatible with Convention rights).[7507]

Section 961 of the CA 2006 confers limited immunity on the Panel and those involved in carrying out its regulatory activities. The immunity provisions are consistent with those recently extended to the Financial Services Authority and the Financial Reporting Council in the exercise of their duties under financial services and company's legislation.

The section exempts the Panel, its members, officers and staff (which would include secondees), and persons authorised under s 947(5) of the CA 2006 by the Panel to exercise its powers in relation to documents and information, from liability in damages for things done or omitted in relation to the Panel's regulatory activities. (The Takeover Appeal Board benefits from a common law immunity on account of its exercise of judicial functions.)

Section 961(3) of the CA 2006 sets out the circumstances where the exemption will not apply, namely where the act or omission was in bad faith, or where it was unlawful under s 6(1) of the Human Rights Act 1998.

Privilege against self-incrimination

28.27 A statement made by a person in response to a requirement under s 947(1) of the CA 2006;[7508] or an order made by the court under s 947(1) of the CA 2006 to secure compliance with such a requirement,[7509] may not be used against him in criminal proceedings in which he is charged with an offence to which this subsection applies.

[7503] CA 2006, s 961(1).   [7504] CA 2006, s 961(2)(a).   [7505] CA 2006, s 961(2)(b).
[7506] CA 2006, s 961(3)(a).   [7507] CA 2006, s 961(3)(b).   [7508] CA 2006, s 962(1)(a).
[7509] CA 2006, s 962(1)(b).

Section 962(1) of the CA 2006 applies to any offence other than an offence under one of the following provisions (which concern false statements made otherwise than on oath), namely: s 5 of the Perjury Act 1911 (c. 6);[7510] s 44(2) of the Criminal Law (Consolidation) (Scotland) Act 1995 (c. 39);[7511] and Article 10 of the CA the Perjury (Northern Ireland) Order 1979 (SI 1979/ 1714 (NI 19)).[7512]

Section 962 of the CA 2006 provides that a statement made by a person to the Panel, or to a person authorised to act on its behalf, in compliance with a requirement to provide information under s 947 of the CA 2006 (or a court order made to secure compliance with such a requirement under s 955 of the CA 2006) cannot be used against that person in most types of criminal proceedings. Such statements can, however, be used in proceedings for offences of making false statements otherwise than on oath under s 5 of the Perjury Act 1911 and its Scottish and Northern Irish equivalents. These offences exist to deter and punish the making of false statements and it would not be possible to prosecute such offences if the false statements themselves could not be used in evidence against those by whom they were made.

Annual reports

28.28 Section 963 of the CA 2006 deals with annual reports for the Panel. After the end of each financial year the Panel must publish a report.[7513]

The report must set out how the Panel's functions were discharged in the year in question.[7514] It must include the Panel's accounts for that year;[7515] and mention any matters that the Panel considers to be of relevance to the discharge of its functions.[7516]

Consistent with the Panel's existing practice, the Panel will be required to publish an annual report containing annual accounts, setting out how the Panel's functions were discharged and including other matters considered by the panel to be relevant. Annual reports published by the Panel are available on the Panel's website.

Amendments to the Financial Services and Markets Act 2000

28.29 Section 964 of the CA 2006 amends parts of the FSMA 2000.[7517]

Section 143 of the FSMA 2000 (power to make rules endorsing the City Code on Takeovers and Mergers, etc.) is repealed.[7518]

In s 144 of the FSMA 2000 (power to make price establishing rules), for subs (7) the following is substituted:

[7510] CA 2006, s 962(2)(a).   [7511] CA 2006, s 962(2)(b).   [7512] CA 2006, s 962(2)(c).
[7513] CA 2006, s 963(1).   [7514] CA 2006, s 963(2)(a).   [7515] CA 2006, s 963(2)(b).
[7516] CA 2006, s 963(2)(c).   [7517] CA 2006, s 964(1).   [7518] CA 2006, s 964(2).

(7) 'Consultation procedures' means procedures designed to provide an opportunity for persons likely to be affected by alterations to those provisions to make representations about proposed alterations to any of those provisions.[7519]

In s 349 of the FSMA 2000 (exceptions from restrictions on disclosure of confidential information), after subs (3) the following is inserted:

(3A) Section 348 does not apply to –

(a) the disclosure by a recipient to which subsection (3B) applies of confidential information disclosed to it by the Authority in reliance on subsection (1);
(b) the disclosure of such information by a person obtaining it directly or indirectly from a recipient to which subsection (3B) applies.

(3B) This subsection applies to –

(a) the Panel on Takeovers and Mergers;
(b) an authority designated as a supervisory authority for the purposes of Article 4.1 of the Takeovers Directive;
(c) any other person or body that exercises public functions, under legislation in an EEA State other than the United Kingdom, that are similar to the Authority's functions or those of the Panel on Takeovers and Mergers.[7520]

In s 354 of the FSMA 2000 (Financial Services Authority's duty to co-operate with others), after subs (1) the following is inserted:

(1A) The Authority must take such steps as it considers appropriate to co-operate with –

(a) the Panel on Takeovers and Mergers;
(b) an authority designated as a supervisory authority for the purposes of Article 4.1 of the Takeovers Directive;
(c) any other person or body that exercises functions of a public nature, under legislation in any country or territory outside the United Kingdom, that appear to the Authority to be similar to those of the Panel on Takeovers and Mergers.[7521]

In s 417(1) FSMA 2000 (definitions), insert at the appropriate place:

[7519] CA 2006, s 964(3).   [7520] CA 2006, s 964(4).   [7521] CA 2006, s 964(5).

Takeovers Directive means Directive 2004/25/EC of the European Parliament and of the Council.[7522]

Section 964 of the CA 2006 repeals s 143 of the FSMA 2000, which, by endorsing the City Code on Takeovers and Mergers, provided a mechanism for the Financial Services Authority to bring disciplinary and enforcement action against authorised persons for misconduct in relation to the Code.[7523] Given that the Code would be replaced by rules that have legal force as a consequence of CA 2006, it was considered that there was no longer a need to maintain s 143 of the FSMA 2000.

This will not, however, preclude the Panel from reporting breaches of the Code by authorised persons in relation to takeover bids to the Financial Services Authority, as at present, and any such breaches will still be taken into account by the FSA, for example, in assessing whether such persons are fit and proper to be authorised for business of that kind or have otherwise complied with their regulatory obligations (for example, whether they are meeting proper standards of market conduct).

A consequential amendment is made by s 964(3) of the CA 2006 to preserve the definition of 'consultation procedures', previously at s 143(7) of the FSMA 2000 for the purposes of the provisions on s 144 of FSMA relating to price establishing rules. Additionally, consistent with the requirements of Article 4.4 of the Directive as regards the duties of takeover of regulatory and financial services authorities within the EU to co-operate with each other, the disclosure and regulatory co-operation obligations of the Financial Services Authority under ss 349 and 354 of the FSMA 2000 are amended to include co-operation with relevant authorities referred to by the Directive and to remove restrictions on disclosure to such authorities. These duties reflect the disclosure and co-operation provisions in ss 948 and 950 of the CA 2006 (including provisions related to the rules on disclosure that apply where information is passed to other takeover supervisory authorities and financial services regulators described in relation to s 948(6)) of the CA 2006.

[7522] CA 2006, s 964(6).

[7523] FSMA 2000, s 143 confers a power on the Authority to make rules endorsing the City Code on Takeovers and Mergers and the Substantial Acquisition Rules (SARs), or particular provisions of them. The section provides a mechanism enabling the Authority to exercise its disciplinary powers over authorised persons fos a breach of the endorsed provisions of the Takeover Code or SARs. The arrangements are designed to ensure that an adviser will cease to act where the Takeover Code or SARs have been breached. Before making the rules that endorse the Takeover Code or the SARS, the Authority must follow the usual procedures set out in the FSMA, s 155 for consulting on a draft of the proposed rules.

Power to extend provisions to the Isle of Man and Channel Islands

28.30 Section 965 of the CA 2006 deals with the power to extend provisions to the Isle of Man and the Channel Islands. Her Majesty may by Order in Council direct that any of the provisions of this Chapter extend, with such modifications as may be specified in the Order, to the Isle of Man or any of the Channel Islands.

This allows any provisions of Chapters 1 and 2 to Part 28 of CA 2006 to be extended to the Isle of Man or any of the Channel Islands by Order in Council, with any specified modifications.

Impediments to Takeovers

28.31 Chapter 2 to Part 28 of the CA 2006 addresses the impediments to takeovers. It comprises eight sections.

Summary and background

28.32 Article 11 of the Takeovers Directive seeks to override, in certain circumstances relating to a takeover, a number of defensive devices that may be adopted by companies prior to the bid, such as: different share structures under which minority shareholders may exercise disproportionate voting rights; restrictions on the transfer of shares in company articles or in contractual agreements; and limitations on share ownership.

There are currently no restrictions on the ways in which UK companies that are admitted to trading on a regulated market can structure their share capital and control. However, market pressure brought to bear, in particular, by institutional investors, has ensured that there are now few UK listed companies with different voting structures.

As permitted by Article 12 of the Directive, it has been decided not to apply the provisions of Article 11 in all cases but instead to include in ss 966–972 of the CA 2006 provision for companies with voting shares traded on a regulated market to opt in to its provisions should they choose to do so.

Opting in and opting out

28.33 Section 966 of the CA 2006 deals with the concept of 'opting-in' and 'opting-out'. A company may by special resolution (an 'opting-in resolution') opt in for the purposes of Chapter 2 to Part 28 of the CA 2006 if the following three conditions are met in relation to the company.[7524]

The first condition is that the company has voting shares admitted to trading on a regulated market.[7525]

[7524] CA 2006, s 966(1).   [7525] CA 2006, s 966(2).

The second condition is that the company's Articles of Association do not contain any such restrictions as are mentioned in Article 11 of the Takeovers Directive,[7526] or if they do contain any such restrictions, provide for the restrictions not to apply at a time when, or in circumstances in which, they would be disapplied by that Article,[7527] and those articles do not contain any other provision that would be incompatible with that Article.[7528]

The third condition is that no shares conferring special rights in the company are held by a minister,[7529] a nominee of, or any other person acting on behalf of, a minister,[7530] or a company directly or indirectly controlled by a minister,[7531] and no such rights are exercisable by or on behalf of a minister under any enactment.[7532]

A company may revoke an opting-in resolution by a further special resolution (an 'opting-out resolution').[7533]

For the purposes of s 966(3) of the CA 2006, a reference in Article 11 of the Takeovers Directive to Article 7(1) or 9 of that Directive is to be read as referring to rules under s 643(1) of the CA 2006 giving effect to the relevant Article.[7534]

In s 966(4) of the CA 2006, the term 'minister' means the holder of an office in Her Majesty's Government in the United Kingdom;[7535] the Scottish Ministers;[7536] a Minister within the meaning given by s 7(3) of the Northern Ireland Act 1998 (c 47);[7537] and for the purposes of that subsection, 'minister' also includes an officer in the Treasury, the Board of Trade, the Defence Council and the National Assembly for Wales.

The Secretary of State may by order subject to negative resolution procedure provide that s 966(4) of the CA 2006 applies in relation to a specified person or body that exercises functions of a public nature as it applies in relation to a minister.[7538]

Further provisions about opting-in and opting-out resolutions

28.34 Section 967 of the CA 2006 deals with further provision for opting-in resolutions. An opting-in resolution or an opting-out resolution must specify the date from which it is to have effect (the effective date).[7539]

The effective date of an opting-in resolution may not be earlier than the date on which the resolution is passed.[7540]

The second and third conditions in s 966 of the CA 2006 must be met at the

[7526] CA 2006, s 966(2)(a)(i).   [7527] CA 2006, s 966(2)(a)(ii).   [7528] CA 2006, s 966(2)(b).
[7529] CA 2006, s 966(4)(a)(i).   [7530] CA 2006, s 966(4)(a)(ii).
[7531] CA 2006, s 966(4)(a)(iii).   [7532] CA 2006, s 966(4)(b).   [7533] CA 2006, s 966(5).
[7534] CA 2006, s 966(6).   [7535] CA 2006, s 966(7)(a).   [7536] CA 2006, s 966(7)(b).
[7537] CA 2006, s 966(7)(c).   [7538] CA 2006, s 966(8).   [7539] CA 2006, s 967(1).
[7540] CA 2006, s 967(2).

time when an opting-in resolution is passed, but the first one does not need to be met until the effective date.[7541]

An opting-in resolution passed before the time when voting shares of the company are admitted to trading on a regulated market complies with the requirement in s 967(1) of the CA 2006 if, instead of specifying a particular date, it provides for the resolution to have effect from that time.[7542]

An opting-in resolution passed before the commencement of this section complies with the requirement in s 967(1) of the CA 2006 if, instead of specifying a particular date, it provides for the resolution to have effect from that commencement.[7543]

The effective date of an opting-out resolution may not be earlier than the first anniversary of the date on which a copy of the opting-in resolution was forwarded to the registrar.[7544]

Where a company has passed an opting-in resolution, any alteration of its Articles of Association that would prevent the second condition in s 966 of the CA 2006 from being met is of no effect until the effective date of an opting-out resolution passed by the company.[7545]

Consequences of opting in

28.35 Sections 968 and 969 of the CA 2006 deal with the consequences of opting in.

Effect on contractual restrictions

28.36 Section 968 of the CA 2006 deals with the effect on contractual restrictions. The following provisions will apply where a takeover bid is made for an opted-in company.[7546]

An agreement to which this section applies is invalid insofar as it places any restriction on the transfer to the offeror, or at his direction to another person, of shares in the company during the offer period;[7547] on the transfer to any person of shares in the company at a time during the offer period when the offeror holds shares amounting to not less than 75 per cent in value of all the voting shares in the company;[7548] on rights to vote at a general meeting of the company which decides whether to take any action that might result in the frustration of the bid;[7549] on rights to vote at a general meeting of the company that is the first such meeting to be held after the end of the offer period,[7550] and is held at a time when the offeror holds shares amounting to not less than 75 per cent in value of all the voting shares in the company.[7551]

[7541] CA 2006, s 967(3).   [7542] CA 2006, s 967(4).   [7543] CA 2006, s 967(5).
[7544] CA 2006, s 967(6).   [7545] CA 2006, s 967(7).   [7546] CA 2006, s 968(1).
[7547] CA 2006, s 968(2)(a).   [7548] CA 2006, s 968(2)(b).   [7549] CA 2006, s 968(2)(c).
[7550] CA 2006, s 968(2)(d)(i).   [7551] CA 2006, s 968(2)(d)(ii).

Section 968 of the CA 2006 applies to an agreement entered into between a person holding shares in the company and another such person on or after 21 April 2004,[7552] or entered into at any time between such a person and the company, and it applies to such an agreement even if the law applicable to the agreement (apart from this section) is not the law of a part of the United Kingdom.[7553]

The reference in s 968(2)(c) of the CA 2006 to rights to vote at a general meeting of the company that decides whether to take any action that might result in the frustration of the bid includes a reference to rights to vote on a written resolution concerned with that question.[7554]

For the purposes of s 968(2)(c) of the CA 2006, action that might result in the frustration of a bid is any action of that kind specified in rules under s 943(1) of the CA 2006 giving effect to Article 9 of the Takeovers Directive.[7555]

If a person suffers loss as a result of any act or omission that would (but for this section) be a breach of an agreement to which this section applies, he is entitled to compensation, of such amount as the court considers just and equitable, from any person who would (but for this section) be liable to him for committing or inducing the breach.[7556]

The term 'court' means the High Court or, in Scotland, the Court of Session.[7557]

A reference in this section to voting shares in the company does not include debentures,[7558] or shares that, under the company's Articles of Association, do not normally carry rights to vote at its general meetings (for example, shares carrying rights to vote that, under those articles, arise only where specified pecuniary advantages are not provided).[7559]

Section 968 of the CA 2006 provides that agreements entered into between shareholders in the company on or after 21 April 2004 (the date on which the Takeovers Directive was adopted), and agreements entered into between a shareholder and the company before as well as on or after that date, are invalid in so far as they impose any of the restrictions set out in s 968(2) of the CA 2006.

Those restrictions relate both to the bid period and to the time following a takeover bid when the bidder holds 75 per cent or more in value of all the voting shares in the company. Types of restrictions overridden are those imposing restrictions on the transfer of shares and on rights to vote at general meetings of the company to decide on action to frustrate the bid and at the first meeting to be held after the end of the offer period. For the purposes of determining when the bidder holds 75 per cent or more in value of all the voting shares in the company, both debentures and shares that do not

[7552] CA 2006, s 968(3)(a).   [7553] CA 2006, s 968(3)(b).   [7554] CA 2006, s 968(4).
[7555] CA 2006, s 968(5).   [7556] CA 2006, s 968(6)   [7557] CA 2006, s 968(7).
[7558] CA 2006, s 968(8)(a).   [7559] CA 2006, s 968(8)(b).

normally carry rights to vote at general meeting (such as preference shares) held by the bidder are to be disregarded (see s 968(8) of the CA 2006).

The provisions related to the types of contractual agreements to which override will apply (including the date at which such contracts were entered into) and the restrictions that are made invalid are designed to replicate the provisions of Article 11 of the Directive.

Section 968(6) of the CA 2006 provides that a person who suffers loss as a result of a contractual agreement being overridden can apply to the court for compensation. It is expected that, in the first instance, such compensation will be offered by the bidder in making the takeover offer. Where, however, the compensation offered by the bidder is not acceptable to the person whose rights are being overridden, there is a right to apply to the court. The court will award compensation to the person who suffers loss on a just and equitable basis to be paid any person (which could include the bidder or the other party to the contract that has been overridden) who would have been liable to him for committing or inducing the breach of contract that would have been committed had the restriction in question not been made invalid by this section.

Power of offeror to require a general meeting to be called

28.37 Section 969 of the CA 2006 states that where a takeover bid is made for an opted-in company, the offeror may by making a request to the directors of the company require them to call a general meeting of the company if, at the date at which the request is made, he holds shares amounting to not less than 75 per cent in value of all the voting shares in the company.[7560]

The reference in s 969(1) of the CA 2006 to voting shares in the company does not include debentures,[7561] or shares that, under the company's Articles of Association, do not normally carry rights to vote at its general meetings (for example, shares carrying rights to vote that, under those articles, arise only where specified pecuniary advantages are not provided).[7562]

Sections 303–305 of the CA 2006 (members' power to require general meetings to be called) apply as they would do if s 969(1) of the CA 2006 above were substituted for subss (1) and (2) of s 303 of the CA 2006, and with any other necessary modifications.[7563]

[7560] CA 2006, s 969(1).   [7561] CA 2006, s 969(2)(a).   [7562] CA 2006, s 969(2)(b).
[7563] CA 2006, s 969(3).

Supplementary

Communication of decisions

28.38 Section 970 of the CA 2006 deals with the communication of decisions. A company that has passed an opting-in resolution or an opting-out resolution must notify the Panel on Takeovers and Mergers,[7564] and where the company has voting shares admitted to trading on a regulated market in an EEA State other than the United Kingdom,[7565] has requested such admission, the authority designated by that state as the supervisory authority for the purposes of Article 4.1 of the Takeovers Directive.[7566]

Notification must be given within 15 days after the resolution is passed and, if any admission or request such as is mentioned in s 970(1)(b) of the CA 2006 occurs at a later time, within 15 days after that time.[7567]

If a company fails to comply with s 970 of the CA 2006, an offence is committed by the company, and every officer of it who is in default.[7568]

A person guilty of an offence under s 970 of the CA 2006 is liable on summary conviction to a fine not exceeding level 3 on the standard scale and, for continued contravention, a daily default fine not exceeding one-tenth of level 3 on the standard scale.[7569]

Section 970 of the CA 2006 provides that a company may pass a special resolution opting in to Article 11 (an opting-in resolution) provided that three conditions are met. First, it has voting shares admitted to trading on a regulated market (it is not considered necessary to extend this provision to other types of companies which are not covered by the Directive). Second, the company's Articles of Association do not contain restrictions as are mentioned in Article 11 (or other provisions which would be incompatible with Article 11) or, if they do contain those restrictions, the restrictions will not apply in circumstances related to a takeover bid as described by Article 11. Article 11 relates to both the takeover bid period and the time following the bid when the bidder has acquired 75 per cent or more of the company's capital carrying voting rights. It provides that restrictions both on the rights to transfer shares and on voting rights that are contained in the articles of the company should not apply. It also provides that, in certain circumstances, shares carrying multiple voting rights shall only have one vote and extraordinary rights of shareholders concerning the appointment or removal of board members should be disapplied. Third, no shares are held by a minister conferring special rights in the company and no such special rights are provided for in law. The Directive expressly provides that Article 11 does not apply to shares held by Member States conferring special rights on the Member State that are compatible with the Treaty, or to special rights

---

[7564] CA 2006, s 970(1)(a).   [7565] CA 2006, s 970(1)(b)(i).   [7566] CA 2006, s 970(1)(b)(ii).
[7567] CA 2006, s 970(2).   [7568] CA 2006, s 970(3).   [7569] CA 2006, s 970(4).

provided for in national law which are compatible with the Treaty. The UK Government holds a number of so-called 'golden shares' in formerly publicly-owned business that has been privatised to ensure that essential public interests considerations are protected. This provision will exclude all such companies where the Government holds the beneficial ownership of a golden share (since holdings by nominees and subsidiaries are also covered). The concept of Minister is broadly defined in CA 2006 to include Scottish Ministers and Northern Ireland Ministers under s 7(3) of the Northern Ireland Act 1998. Under s 966(8) of the CA 2006, a power is provided to the Secretary of State by the negative resolution procedure to apply the provision in s 966 of the CA 2006 (Minister holding golden shares) to persons or bodies exercising functions of a public nature as it applies in relation to a minister.

Section 966(5) of the CA 2006 enables a company to revoke an opting-in resolution by means of a further special resolution (an opting-out resolution).

Section 967 of the CA 2006 sets down provisions relating to the date that the opting-in and opting-out resolutions will take effect. Generally, this will be the date stated in the resolution.

Section 970 of the CA 2006 requires companies, within 15 days of an opting-in or opting-out resolution being passed, to notify the Panel and any other takeover supervisory authority in a Member State in which the company has shares admitted to trading on a regulated market or has requested such admission. Where a company fails to comply with this requirement, the company and every officer in default will be guilty of an offence and be liable in summary conviction to a fine not exceeding level 3 on the standard scale (and to a daily default fine for continued contravention).

Transitory provisions

28.39 Section 972 of the CA 2006 states that where a takeover bid is made for an opted-in company, s 368 of the CA 1985 (extraordinary general meeting on members' requisition) and s 378 of that Act (extraordinary and special resolutions) had effect as follows until their repeal by this Act.[7570]

Section 368 of the CA 1985 applied as if a members' requisition included a requisition of a person who was the offeror in relation to the takeover bid,[7571] and held at the date of the deposit of the requisition shares amounting to not less than 75 per cent in value of all the voting shares in the company.[7572]

In relation to a general meeting of the company that was the first such meeting to be held after the end of the offer period,[7573] and was held at a time when the offeror held shares amounting to not less than 75 per cent in value of all the voting shares in the company, s 378(2) of the CA 1985 (meaning of

---

[7570] CA 2006, s 972(1).   [7571] CA 2006, s 972(2)(a).   [7572] CA 2006, s 972(2)(b).
[7573] CA 2006, s 972(3)(a).

special resolution) had effect as if '14 days' notice' were substituted for '21 days' notice'.[7574]

A reference in this section to voting shares in the company does not include debentures,[7575] or shares that, under the company's Articles of Association, do not normally carry rights to vote at its general meetings (for example, shares carrying rights to vote that, under those articles, arise only where specified pecuniary advantages are not provided).[7576]

Section 969 of the CA 2006 provides the bidder with the special right to require the directors of an opted-in company to call a general meeting of the company when he holds 75 per cent in value of all the voting shares in the company (excluding debentures and shares that do not normally carry rights to vote at a general meeting (such as preference shares)). Section 969(3) of the CA 2006 applies ss 303–305 of the CA 2006, which deal with the calling of meetings, following such a request (with the necessary modifications). But in case those sections were not enacted by the time s 969 of the CA 2006 came into force, s 972 of the CA 2006 would make the same sort of adaptations in relation to the equivalent provisions of the CA 1985. In particular, s 972(3) of the CA 2006 would alter the application of s 378(2) of the CA 1985 so that a special resolution could still be passed at a general meeting called at only 14 days' notice (normally at least 21 days' notice would have to be given of the meeting for it to be able to pass a special resolution).

Power to extend provisions to the Isle of Man and Channel Islands

28.40 Section 973 of the CA 2006 states that Her Majesty may by Order in Council direct that any of the provisions of this Chapter extend, with such modifications as may be specified in the Order, to the Isle of Man or any of the Channel Islands.

Interpretation of Chapter

28.41 The following are defined terms for Chapter 2:

- 'company' means:
  - (a) a company within the meaning of this Act; or
  - (b) an unregistered company within the meaning of s 718 of the CA 1985 (c 6).

- 'offeror' and 'takeover bid' have the same meaning as in the Takeovers Directive; 'offer period', in relation to a takeover bid, means the time allowed for acceptance of the bid by:

[7574] CA 2006, s 972(3)(b).   [7575] CA 2006, s 972(4)(a).   [7576] CA 2006, s 972(4)(b).

(a) rules under s 643(1) of the CA 2006 giving effect to Article 7(1) of the Takeovers Directive; or

(b) where the rules giving effect to that Article which apply to the bid are those of an EEA State other than the United Kingdom, those rules.

- 'opted-in company' means a company in relation to which:

(a) an opting-in resolution has effect; and

(b) the conditions in s 666(2) and (4) of the CA 2006 continue to be met.

- 'opting-in resolution' has the meaning given by s 666(1);
- 'opting-out resolution' has the meaning given by s 666(5);
- 'the Takeovers Directive' means Directive 2004/25/EC of the European Parliament and of the Council;
- 'voting rights' means rights to vote at general meetings of the company in question, including rights that arise only in certain circumstances;
- 'voting shares' means shares carrying voting rights.

For the purposes of this Chapter:

(a) securities of a company are treated as shares in the company if they are convertible into or entitle the holder to subscribe for such shares;

(b) debentures issued by a company are treated as shares in the company if they carry voting rights.

'Squeeze-out' and 'sell-out'

28.42 Chapter 3 of Part 28 of the CA 2006 is concerned with the concepts of 'squeeze-out' and 'sell-out' in the context of takeover offers. The concepts of 'squeeze-out' and 'sell-out' are designed to address the problems of, and for, residual minority shareholders following a successful takeover bid. Squeeze-out rights enable a successful bidder to compulsorily purchase the shares of remaining minority shareholders who have not accepted the bid. Sell-out rights enable minority shareholders, in the wake of such a bid, to require the majority shareholder to purchase their shares. Because they involve the compulsory purchase or acquisition of shares against the will of the holder of the shares or the acquirer, high thresholds apply to the exercising of such rights and there are protective rules on the price that must be paid for the shares concerned.

Squeeze-out and sell-out provisions have been a feature of national company law for many years (and were previously contained in Part 13A (Takeover Offers) of the 1985 Act). Articles 15 and 16 of the Takeovers Directive, however, introduce EU-wide rules requiring all Member States to put appropriate provisions in place for the first time. The provisions at ss 974–991 of the Act restate Part 13A of the CA 1985 in a clearer form. However, in doing so they also make important changes to reflect the need to ensure compliance with the Directive and the decision to accept some recommendations of the Company Law Review Group.

The rules laid down in the Directive in relation to squeeze-out and sell-out are broadly consistent with provisions of Part 13A (ss 428–430F) of the CA 1985. The restated and amended provisions will apply equally to all companies and all bids within the ambit of Part 13A of the CA 1985, regardless of whether or not the Directive is required to be applied to such companies and bids.

The following changes are made in implementation of the Directive. First, calculation of the squeeze-out threshold (s 979 of the CA 2006) – there is a dual test imposed: in order to acquire the minority shareholder's shares, the bidder must have acquired both 90 per cent of the shares to which the offer relates, and 90 per cent of the voting rights carried by those shares. Where the offer relates to shares of different classes, acquire the remaining shares in a class, the bidder must have acquired 90 per cent of the shares of that class to which the offer relates, and 90 per cent of the voting rights carried by those shares. Under s 429 of the CA 1985, in each case only the first limb of that test applied.

Second, calculation of the sell-out threshold (s 983 of the CA 2006) – mirroring the change to be made in relation to the squeeze-out threshold, a dual test is similarly imposed in relation to the sell-out threshold, so that a minority shareholder may force a bidder to acquire his shares (i) when the bidder holds 90 per cent of the shares in the company, and 90 per cent of the voting rights attached to those shares, or (ii) when the bidder holds 90 per cent of the shares in the class to which the minority shareholder's shares belong, and 90 per cent of the voting rights attached to those shares. Under s 430A of the CA 1985, the test was that the bidder should have acquired 90 per cent of all shares in the company (or in the class concerned).

Third, a revised period during which squeeze-out and sell-out rights may be exercised (s 980(2) of the CA 2006) – the Directive provides (Articles 15.4 and 16.3) that squeeze-out and sell-out rights must be exercisable within a three-month period following the time allowed for acceptance of the bid. Section 429(3) of the CA 1985 provided that squeeze-out could be exercised within a period of four months beginning with the date of the offer and had to be exercised within two months of reaching the 90 per cent threshold. Accordingly, the rule provided by the Directive is substituted for the rule in the CA 1985. An exception to this rule is provided where takeover bids are not subject to the Directive, for instance takeovers of most private companies. In these cases, the squeeze-out notices must be given within six months of the date of the offer if this is earlier than the period ending three months after the end of the offer. This is intended to prevent offerors in such circumstances continually extending the offer period. A change is also made as regards the period during which sell-out may be exercisable so that this period is to be either three months from the end of the offer or, if later, three months from the notice given to the shareholder of his right to exercise sell-out rights (s 984(2) of the CA 2006). An extended period during which the sell-out right can be exercised where notice of such a right is only given after the end of the offer period is consistent with provisions of the Directive allowing more stringent provisions to be put in place (in this case to ensure the proper protection of minority shareholders).

Fourth, the court will no longer be able to reduce the consideration in relation to squeeze-out or sell-out following a takeover bid to below the consideration offered in the bid (which the Takeovers Directive presumes to be fair in all cases). Again utilising provisions of the Directive, which allow more stringent provisions to be included to protect minority shareholders, minority shareholders will continue to be able to apply to the court to request that consideration higher than that offered in the bid be paid in exceptional circumstances (s 986(4) of the CA 2006).

In most instances, it is considered that the first and second changes above will make no practical difference as the percentage of total capital-carrying voting rights in a company (or class of shares) and the percentage of voting rights will normally be the same. The provisions about voting rights will not apply where the shares being squeezed out or sold out are non-voting shares.

The Company Law Review Group also considered the issue of squeeze-out and sell-out and the scope for improving the provisions in the CA 1985. Its *Final Report*[7577] made a number of recommendations in relation to the reform of the squeeze-out and sell-out regime. Some of these recommendations are closely related to implementation of the Takeovers Directive. For instance, the Company Law Review Group questioned whether, in calculating the relevant squeeze-out and sell-out thresholds, only shares that had been unconditionally acquired should be taken into account or whether shares acquired subject to contract should also be included.

In implementing the Takeovers Directive, the opportunity is being taken to adopt recommendations of the Company Law Review Group, whether or not related to implementation of the Directive, except to the extent that they are not consistent with Articles 15 and 16 of the Directive or are no longer appropriate as a consequence of the Directive. The recommendations made by the Company Law Review Group were implemented by Chapter 3 of Part 28 of the CA 2006.

[7577] Chapter 13, pp 282–300.

Meaning of 'takeover offer'

28.43 Section 974 of the CA 2006 defines a 'takeover offer'. Section 974 of the CA 2006 states that for the purposes of this Chapter an offer to acquire shares in a company is a 'takeover offer' if the following two conditions are satisfied in relation to the offer.[7578]

The first condition is that it is an offer to acquire all the shares in a company,[7579] or where there is more than one class of shares in a company, all the shares of one or more classes,[7580] other than shares that at the date of the offer are already held by the offeror.

Section 975 of the CA 2006 contains provisions supplementing this subsection.

The second condition is that the terms of the offer are the same in relation to all the shares to which the offer relates,[7581] or where the shares to which the offer relates include shares of different classes, in relation to all the shares of each class.[7582]

Section 976 of the CA 2006 contains provisions treating this condition as satisfied in certain circumstances.

In s 974(1)–(3) of the CA 2006 the term 'shares' means shares, other than relevant treasury shares, that have been allotted on the date of the offer (but see s 974(5) of the CA 2006).[7583]

A takeover offer may include among the shares to which it relates all or any shares that are allotted after the date of the offer but before a specified date;[7584] all or any relevant treasury shares that cease to be held as treasury shares before a specified date;[7585] all or any other relevant treasury shares.[7586]

The term 'relevant treasury shares' means shares that are held by the company as treasury shares on the date of the offer,[7587] or become shares held by the company as treasury shares after that date but before a specified date.[7588] The term 'specified date' means a date specified in or determined in accordance with the terms of the offer.[7589]

Where the terms of an offer make provision for their revision and for acceptances on the previous terms to be treated as acceptances on the revised terms, then, if the terms of the offer are revised in accordance with that provision, the revision is not to be regarded for the purposes of this Chapter as the making of a fresh offer,[7590] and references in this Chapter to the date of the offer are accordingly to be read as references to the date of the original offer.[7591]

In order to be a takeover offer for the purposes of Part 13A of the CA

[7578] CA 2006, s 974(1).   [7579] CA 2006, s 974(2)(a).   [7580] CA 2006, s 974(2)(b).
[7581] CA 2006, s 974(3)(a).   [7582] CA 2006, s 974(3)(b).   [7583] CA 2006, s 974(4).
[7584] CA 2006, s 974(5)(a).   [7585] CA 2006, s 974(5)(b).   [7586] CA 2006, s 974(5)(c).
[7587] CA 2006, s 974(6)(a).   [7588] CA 2006, s 974(6)(b).   [7589] CA 2006, s 974(6).
[7590] CA 2006, s 974(7)(a).   [7591] CA 2006, s 974(7)(b).

1985, an offer to acquire shares had to be on terms that were the same in relation to all the shares to which the offer related. One problem with the CA 1985 legislation was how to treat any variations in value between shares of the same class that were attributable to the fact that some of the shares, because they were allotted later, do not yet carry a dividend. Section 976(2) of the CA 2006 rectifies this problem by providing that, even if the offeror offers to pay more for shares that carry a dividend than for those in the same class that do not, the offer will be treated as being made on the same terms in relation to those shares.

To deal with issues arising from an increasingly globalised market in shares and different legislative regimes outside the EEA, it is made clear that an offer is not prevented from being a takeover offer for the purposes of Chapter 3 of Part 28 of the CA 2006 merely because there are some offerees who will be unable to accept it (for instance, where the offeree cannot accept the offer because of restrictions on the cross-border transfer of cash or securities in the country in which the offeree resides). It is also provided that an offer can still be a takeover offer for the purposes of the squeeze-out and sell-out provisions if a shareholder has no registered address in the UK and the offer is not communicated to him to avoid contravening the law of another country as long as either the offer itself is published in the Gazette or a notice is published in the Gazette stating that a copy of the offer document can be obtained from a place in the EEA or on a website.

Shares already held by the offeror, etc.

28.44 Section 975 of the CA 2006 deals with shares already held by offerors. The reference in s 974(2) of the CA 2006 to shares already held by the offeror includes a reference to shares that he has contracted to acquire, whether unconditionally or subject to conditions being met.[7592]

This is subject to s 975(2) of the CA 2006.

The reference in s 974(2) of the CA 2006 to shares already held by the offeror does not include a reference to shares that are the subject of a contract (a) intended to secure that the holder of the shares will accept the offer when it is made;[7593] and (b) entered into (i) by deed and for no consideration,[7594] (ii) for consideration of negligible value,[7595] or (iii) for consideration consisting of a promise by the offeror to make the offer.[7596]

In relation to Scotland, this section applies as if the words 'by deed and' in subs (2)(b)(i) were omitted.[7597]

The condition in s 974(2) of the CA 2006 is treated as satisfied where the offer does not extend to shares that associates of the offeror hold or have

---

[7592] CA 2006, s 975(1).   [7593] CA 2006, s 975(2)(a).   [7594] CA 2006, s 975(2)(b)(i).
[7595] CA 2006, s 975(2)(b)(ii).   [7596] CA 2006, s 975(2)(b)(iii).   [7597] CA 2006, s 975(3).

contracted to acquire (whether unconditionally or subject to conditions being met),[7598] and the condition would be satisfied if the offer did extend to those shares.[7599]

For further provision about such shares, see s 977(2)) of the CA 2006.

Clarificatory amendments are made on this issue. Section 428(5) of the CA 1985 dealt with the offeror's position at the start of the bid, for the purpose of determining which shares could not be counted towards the achievement of the 90 per cent threshold (at which point shares may be compulsorily purchased). It was unclear as to whether the phrase 'contracted to acquire' in s 428(5) of the CA 1985 covered conditional as well as unconditional contracts. It is, therefore, clarified that, in ascertaining the offeror's position at the start of the bid, the shares he has conditionally contracted to acquire (other than those subject to irrevocable undertakings, as under the CA 1985) should be treated as being shares already held by the offeror. This means that only shares that the offeror has either acquired or unconditionally contracted to acquire will count towards the 90 per cent total needed to exercise squeeze-out. Consequential changes are also made to the provisions on joint offers and associates of the offeror to bring these into line with the above.

Under the CA 1985, the registered holder of shares could give an irrevocable undertaking to accept a takeover bid, and if he did this for no consideration or only in exchange for a promise to make the bid, his shares were still treated for the purposes of squeeze-out as included within the offer. This is extended to include undertakings given for only negligible consideration and undertakings the effect of which is to require the registered holder to accept the offer (where the undertaking is given by a person who is not the registered holder of the shares but can contract to bind the registered holder, such as the manager of shared held by a bare nominee). ('Irrevocable undertakings' are contractual agreements entered into by a bidder usually with major shareholder(s) of a proposed target company. Such agreements aim to give the bidder certainty – he will know that support for the offer can be guaranteed from shareholders party to the contract – so that his bid has a greater prospect of success. Such undertakings would normally prevent the giver of the undertaking from selling their shares or exercising voting rights to prevent the takeover from becoming successful.)

Cases where offer is treated as being on the same terms

28.45 Section 976 of the CA 2006 deals with cases where offers are treated as being on same terms. The condition in s 974(3) of the CA 2006 (terms of offer to be the same for all shares or all shares of particular classes) is treated as satisfied where s 976(2) or (3) of the CA 2006 below applies.[7600]

[7598] CA 2006, s 975(4)(a).   [7599] CA 2006, s 975(4)(b).   [7600] CA 2006, s 976(1).

Section 976(2) of the CA 2006 applies where:

(a) shares carry an entitlement to a particular dividend that other shares of the same class, by reason of being allotted later, do not carry;[7601]
(b) there is a difference in the value of consideration offered for the shares allotted earlier as against that offered for those allotted later;[7602]
(c) that difference merely reflects the difference in entitlement to the dividend;[7603] and
(d) the condition in s 974(3) of the CA 2006 would be satisfied but for that difference.[7604]

Section 976(3) of the CA 2006 applies where:

(a) the law of a country or territory outside the United Kingdom (i) precludes an offer of consideration in the form, or any of the forms, specified in the terms of the offer (the specified form),[7605] or (ii) precludes it except after compliance by the offeror with conditions with which he is unable to comply or which he regards as unduly onerous;[7606]
(b) the persons to whom an offer of consideration in the specified form is precluded are able to receive consideration in another form that is of substantially equivalent value;[7607] and
(c) the condition in s 974(3) of the CA 2006 would be satisfied but for the fact that an offer of consideration in the specified form to those persons is precluded.[7608]

Shares to which an offer relates

28.46 Section 977 of the CA 2006 deals with shares to which an offer relates. Where a takeover offer is made and, during the period beginning with the date of the offer and ending when the offer can no longer be accepted, the offeror acquires or unconditionally contracts to acquire any of the shares to which the offer relates,[7609] but does not do so by virtue of acceptances of the offer,[7610] those shares are treated for the purposes of this Chapter as excluded from those to which the offer relates.

For the purposes of this Chapter, shares that an associate of the offeror holds or has contracted to acquire, whether at the date of the offer or subsequently, are not treated as shares to which the offer relates, even if the offer extends to such shares.

[7601] CA 2006, s 976(2)(a). [7602] CA 2006, s 976(2)(b). [7603] CA 2006, s 976(2)(c).
[7604] CA 2006, s 976(2)(d). [7605] CA 2006, s 976(3)(a)(i). [7606] CA 2006, s 976(3)(a)(ii).
[7607] CA 2006, s 976(3)(b). [7608] CA 2006, s 976(3)(c). [7609] CA 2006, s 977(1)(a).
[7610] CA 2006, s 977(1)(b).

The term 'contracted' means contracted unconditionally or subject to conditions being met.[7611]

This section is subject to s 979(8) and (9) of the CA 2006.[7612]

Effect of the impossibility, etc. of communicating or accepting an offer

28.47 Section 978 of the CA 2006 deals with the effect of the impossibility of communicating or accepting offer. Where there are holders of shares in a company to whom an offer to acquire shares in the company is not communicated, that does not prevent the offer from being a takeover offer for the purposes of this Chapter if:

(a) those shareholders have no registered address in the United Kingdom;[7613]

(b) the offer was not communicated to those shareholders in order not to contravene the law of a country or territory outside the United Kingdom;[7614] and

(c) either (i) the offer is published in the Gazette,[7615] or (ii) the offer can be inspected, or a copy of it obtained, at a place in an EEA State or on a website, and a notice is published in the Gazette specifying the address of that place or website.[7616]

Where an offer is made to acquire shares in a company and there are persons for whom, by reason of the law of a country or territory outside the United Kingdom, it is impossible to accept the offer, or more difficult to do so, that does not prevent the offer from being a takeover offer for the purposes of this Chapter.[7617]

It is not to be inferred (a) that an offer that is not communicated to every holder of shares in the company cannot be a takeover offer for the purposes of this Chapter unless the requirements of paras (a)–(c) of s 978(1) of the CA 2006 are met;[7618] or (b) that an offer that is impossible, or more difficult, for certain persons to accept cannot be a takeover offer for those purposes unless the reason for the impossibility or difficulty is the one mentioned in s 978(2) of the CA 2006.[7619]

Section 979 of the CA 2006 deals with the right of the offeror to buy out a minority shareholder. It states that s 979(2) of the CA 2006 applies in a case where a takeover offer does not relate to shares of different classes.[7620]

If the offeror has, by virtue of acceptances of the offer, acquired or

---

[7611] CA 2006, s 977(2).   [7612] CA 2006, s 977(3).   [7613] CA 2006, s 978(1)(a).
[7614] CA 2006, s 978(1)(b).   [7615] CA 2006, s 978(1)(c)(i).   [7616] CA 2006, s 978(1)(c)(ii).
[7617] CA 2006, s 978(2).   [7618] CA 2006, s 978(3)(a).   [7619] CA 2006, s 978(3)(b).
[7620] CA 2006, s 979(1).

unconditionally contracted to acquire not less than 90 per cent; in value of the shares to which the offer relates,[7621] and in a case where the shares to which the offer relates are voting shares, not less than 90 per cent; of the voting rights carried by those shares,[7622] he may give notice to the holder of any shares to which the offer relates that the offeror has not acquired or unconditionally contracted to acquire, that he desires to acquire those shares.

Section 979(4) of the CA 2006 applies in a case where a takeover offer relates to shares of different classes.[7623]

If the offeror has, by virtue of acceptances of the offer, acquired or unconditionally contracted to acquire not less than 90 per cent in value of the shares of any class to which the offer relates,[7624] and in a case where the shares of that class are voting shares, not less than 90 per cent of the voting rights carried by those shares,[7625] he may give notice to the holder of any shares of that class to which the offer relates that the offeror has not acquired or unconditionally contracted to acquire, that he desires to acquire those shares.

In the case of a takeover offer that includes among the shares to which it relates shares that are allotted after the date of the offer,[7626] or relevant treasury shares (within the meaning of s 974 of the CA 2006) that cease to be held as treasury shares after the date of the offer,[7627] the offeror's entitlement to give a notice under s 979(2) or (4) of the CA 2006 on any particular date shall be determined as if the shares to which the offer relates did not include any allotted, or ceasing to be held as treasury shares, on or after that date.

Section 979(7) of the CA 2006 applies where the requirements for the giving of a notice under s 979(2) or (4) of the CA 2006 are satisfied,[7628] and there are shares in the company that the offeror, or an associate of his, has contracted to acquire subject to conditions being met, and in relation to which the contract has not become unconditional.[7629]

The offeror's entitlement to give a notice under s 979(2) or (4) of the CA 2006 will be determined as if the shares to which the offer relates included shares falling within para (b) of s 979(6) of the CA 2006,[7630] and in relation to shares falling within that paragraph, the words 'by virtue of acceptances of the offer' in s 979(2) or (4) of the CA 2006 were omitted.[7631]

Where (a) a takeover offer is made;[7632] (b) during the period beginning with the date of the offer and ending when the offer can no longer be accepted, the offeror (i) acquires or unconditionally contracts to acquire any of the shares to which the offer relates,[7633] but (ii) does not do so by virtue of acceptances of the offer,[7634] and (c) s 979(10) of the CA 2006 applies,[7635] then for the purposes of this section those shares are not excluded by s 977(1) of the CA

[7621] CA 2006, s 979(2)(a).
[7622] CA 2006, s 979(2)(b).
[7623] CA 2006, s 979(3).
[7624] CA 2006, s 979(4)(a).
[7625] CA 2006, s 979(4)(b).
[7626] CA 2006, s 979(5)(a).
[7627] CA 2006, s 979(5)(b).
[7628] CA 2006, s 979(6)(a).
[7629] CA 2006, s 979(6)(b).
[7630] CA 2006, s 979(7)(a).
[7631] CA 2006, s 979(7)(b).
[7632] CA 2006, s 979(8)(a).
[7633] CA 2006, s 979(8)(b)(i).
[7634] CA 2006, s 979(8)(b)(ii).
[7635] CA 2006, s 979(8)(c).

2006 from those to which the offer relates, and the offeror is treated as having acquired or contracted to acquire them by virtue of acceptances of the offer.

Where (a) a takeover offer is made;[7636] (b) during the period beginning with the date of the offer and ending when the offer can no longer be accepted, an associate of the offeror acquires or unconditionally contracts to acquire any of the shares to which the offer relates;[7637] and (c) s 979(10) of the CA 2006 applies,[7638] then for the purposes of this section those shares are not excluded by section 977(2) from those to which the offer relates.

Section 979(1) of the CA 2006 applies if (a) at the time the shares are acquired or contracted to be acquired as mentioned in s 979(8) or (9) of the CA 2006 (as the case may be), the value of the consideration for which they are acquired or contracted to be acquired (the acquisition consideration) does not exceed the value of the consideration specified in the terms of the offer,[7639] or (b) those terms are subsequently revised so that when the revision is announced the value of the acquisition consideration, at the time mentioned in para (a), no longer exceeds the value of the consideration specified in those terms.[7640]

Where an offeror makes an offer for all the target company's allotted shares and all or any shares subsequently allotted, it is provided that (a) in deciding whether the offeror has reached the 90 per cent threshold for the purposes of s 979 of the CA 2006, the offeror need only bring into the calculation shares that are actually in issue (i.e. allotted) at the relevant time; (b) if the offeror serves squeeze-out notices and more shares are subsequently allotted that take the percentage of acceptances then received below 90 per cent, that will not invalidate squeeze-out notices already served; and (c) if the offeror wishes to serve further squeeze-out notices, he must have at least 90 per cent acceptances of shares (or shares in a class) then in issue and subject to the offer at the time he sends the notices out.

Further provision about notices given under section 979 of the CA 2006

28.48 Section 980 of the CA 2006 deals with further provision about notices given under s 979 of the CA 2006. A notice under s 979 of the CA 2006 must be given in the prescribed manner.[7641]

No notice may be given under s 979(2) or (4) of the CA 2006 after the end of the period of three months beginning with the day after the last day on which the offer can be accepted,[7642] or the period of six months beginning with the date of the offer, where that period ends earlier and the offer is one to which s 980(3) of the CA 2006 below applies.[7643]

[7636] CA 2006, s 979(9)(a).   [7637] CA 2006, s 979(9)(b).   [7638] CA 2006, s 979(9)(c).
[7639] CA 2006, s 979(10)(a).   [7640] CA 2006, s 979(10)(b).   [7641] CA 2006, s 980(1).
[7642] CA 2006, s 980(2)(a).   [7643] CA 2006, s 980(2)(b).

Section 980(3) of the CA 2006 applies to an offer if the time allowed for acceptance of the offer is not governed by rules under s 943(1) of the CA 2006 that give effect to Article 7 of the Takeovers Directive.[7644]

In this subsection 'the Takeovers Directive' has the same meaning as in s 943 of the CA 2006.

At the time when the offeror first gives a notice under s 979 of the CA 2006 in relation to an offer, he must send to the company a copy of the notice,[7645] and a statutory declaration by him in the prescribed form, stating that the conditions for the giving of the notice are satisfied.[7646]

Where the offeror is a company (whether or not a company within the meaning of this Act) the statutory declaration must be signed by a director.[7647]

A person commits an offence if he fails to send a copy of a notice or a statutory declaration as required by s 980(4) of the CA 2006,[7648] or he makes such a declaration for the purposes of that subsection knowing it to be false or without having reasonable grounds for believing it to be true.[7649]

It is a defence for a person charged with an offence for failing to send a copy of a notice as required by s 980(4) of the CA 2006 to prove that he took reasonable steps for securing compliance with that subsection.[7650]

A person guilty of an offence under s 980 of the CA 2006 is liable on conviction on indictment, to imprisonment for a term not exceeding two years or a fine (or both);[7651] and on summary conviction in England and Wales, to imprisonment for a term not exceeding 12 months or to a fine not exceeding the statutory maximum (or both) and, for continued contravention, a daily default fine not exceeding one-fiftieth of the statutory maximum;[7652] in Scotland or Northern Ireland, to imprisonment for a term not exceeding six months, or to a fine not exceeding the statutory maximum (or both) and, for continued contravention, a daily default fine not exceeding one-fiftieth of the statutory maximum.[7653]

Effect of notice under section 979 of the CA 2006

28.49 Section 981 of the CA 2006 deals with effect of notice under s 979 of the CA 2006. It states that subject to s 986 of the CA 2006 (applications to the court), this section applies where the offeror gives a shareholder a notice under s 979 of the CA 2006.[7654]

The offeror is entitled and bound to acquire the shares to which the notice relates on the terms of the offer.[7655]

Where the terms of an offer are such as to give the shareholder a choice of

---

[7644] CA 2006, s 980(3).   [7645] CA 2006, s 980(4)(a).   [7646] CA 2006, s 980(4)(b).
[7647] CA 2006, s 980(5).   [7648] CA 2006, s 980(6)(a).   [7649] CA 2006, s 980(6)(b).
[7650] CA 2006, s 980(7).   [7651] CA 2006, s 980(8)(a).   [7652] CA 2006, s 980(8)(b)(i).
[7653] CA 2006, s 980(8)(b)(ii).   [7654] CA 2006, s 981(1).   [7655] CA 2006, s 981(2).

consideration, the notice must give particulars of the choice and state that the shareholder may, within six weeks from the date of the notice, indicate his choice by a written communication sent to the offeror at an address specified in the notice,[7656] and that the consideration specified in the offer will apply if he does not indicate a choice.[7657]

The reference in s 980(2) of the CA 2006 to the terms of the offer is to be read accordingly.

Section 980(3) of the CA 2006 applies whether or not any time-limit or other conditions applicable to the choice under the terms of the offer can still be complied with.[7658]

If the consideration offered to or (as the case may be) chosen by the shareholder is not cash and the offeror is no longer able to provide it,[7659] or was to have been provided by a third party who is no longer bound or able to provide it,[7660] the consideration is to be taken to consist of an amount of cash, payable by the offeror, which at the date of the notice is equivalent to the consideration offered or (as the case may be) chosen.

At the end of six weeks from the date of the notice the offeror must immediately send a copy of the notice to the company,[7661] and pay or transfer to the company the consideration for the shares to which the notice relates.[7662]

Where the consideration consists of shares or securities to be allotted by the offeror, the reference in para (b) to the transfer of the consideration is to be read as a reference to the allotment of the shares or securities to the company.

If the shares to which the notice relates are registered, the copy of the notice sent to the company under s 980(6)(a) of the CA 2006 must be accompanied by an instrument of transfer executed on behalf of the holder of the shares by a person appointed by the offeror.[7663]

On receipt of that instrument the company must register the offeror as the holder of those shares.

If the shares to which the notice relates are transferable by the delivery of warrants or other instruments, the copy of the notice sent to the company under s 980(6)(a) of the CA 2006 must be accompanied by a statement to that effect.

On receipt of that statement the company must issue the offeror with warrants or other instruments in respect of the shares, and those already in issue in respect of the shares become void.[7664]

The company must hold any money or other consideration received by it under s 980(6)(b) of the CA 2006 on trust for the person who, before the offeror acquired them, was entitled to the shares in respect of which the money or other consideration was received.

[7656] CA 2006, s 981(3)(a).   [7657] CA 2006, s 981(3)(b).   [7658] CA 2006, s 981(4).
[7659] CA 2006, s 981(5)(a).   [7660] CA 2006, s 981(5)(b).   [7661] CA 2006, s 981(6)(a).
[7662] CA 2006, s 981(6)(b).   [7663] CA 2006, s 981(7).   [7664] CA 2006, s 981(8).

Section 982 of the CA 2006 contains further provision about how the company should deal with such money or other consideration.[7665]

It is clarified that where an offer of shares, or a mixture of shares and cash, is made, and it is no longer possible when the offeror exercises his right of squeeze-out to give the consideration in shares, the offeror should pay the cash equivalent irrespective of whether the shareholders had previously been offered a choice (i.e. whether the offer was 'mix and match' or not). Parallel changes are made as regards sell-out (s 985(5) of the CA 2006).

Further provision about consideration helds on trust under section 981(9)

28.50 Section 982 of the CA 2006 applies where an offeror pays or transfers consideration to the company under section 981(6) of the CA 2006.[7666]

The company must pay into a separate bank account that complies with s 982(3) of the CA 2006 any money it receives under para (b) of s 981(6) of the CA 2006,[7667] and any dividend or other sum accruing from any other consideration it receives under that paragraph.[7668]

A bank account complies with this subsection if the balance on the account bears interest at an appropriate rate,[7669] and can be withdrawn by such notice (if any) as is appropriate.[7670]

If the person entitled to the consideration held on trust by virtue of s 981(9) of the CA 2006 cannot be found,[7671] and s 985(5) of the CA 2006 applies,[7672] the consideration (together with any interest, dividend or other benefit that has accrued from it) must be paid into court.

Section 982(5) of the CA 2006 applies where reasonable enquiries have been made at reasonable intervals to find the person,[7673] and 12 years have elapsed since the consideration was received, or the company is wound up.[7674]

In relation to a company registered in Scotland, s 982(7) and (8) of the CA 2006 apply instead of s 984(4) of the CA 2006.[7675]

If the person entitled to the consideration held on trust by virtue of s 981(9) of the CA 2006 cannot be found and s 982(5) of the CA 2006 applies (a) the trust terminates;[7676] (b) the company or (if the company is wound up) the liquidator must sell any consideration other than cash and any benefit other than cash that has accrued from the consideration;[7677] and (c) a sum representing (i) the consideration so far as it is cash,[7678] (ii) the proceeds of any sale under para (b),[7679] and (iii) any interest, dividend or other benefit that

---

[7665] CA 2006, s 981(9).   [7666] CA 2006, s 982(1).   [7667] CA 2006, s 982(2)(a).
[7668] CA 2006, s 982(2)(b).   [7669] CA 2006, s 982(3)(a).   [7670] CA 2006, s 982(3)(b).
[7671] CA 2006, s 982(4)(a).   [7672] CA 2006, s 982(4)(b).   [7673] CA 2006, s 982(5)(a).
[7674] CA 2006, s 982(5)(b).   [7675] CA 2006, s 982(6).   [7676] CA 2006, s 982(7)(a).
[7677] CA 2006, s 982(7)(b).   [7678] CA 2006, s 982(7)(c)(i).   [7679] CA 2006, s 982(7)(c)(ii).

has accrued from the consideration,[7680] must be deposited in the name of the Accountant of Court in a separate bank account complying with s 982(3) of the CA 2006 and the receipt for the deposit must be transmitted to the Accountant of Court.

Section 58 of the Bankruptcy (Scotland) Act 1985 (c 66) (so far as consistent with this Act) applies (with any necessary modifications) to sums deposited under s 982(7) of the CA 2006 as it applies to sums deposited under s 57(1)(a) of that Act.[7681]

The expenses of any such enquiries as are mentioned in s 982(5) of the CA 2006 may be paid out of the money or other property held on trust for the person to whom the enquiry relates.[7682]

'Sell-out'

Right of a minority shareholder to be bought out by offeror

28.51 Section 983 of the CA 2006 deals with right of a minority shareholder to be bought out by an offerror. Section 983(2) and (3) of the CA 2006 applies in a case where a takeover offer relates to all the shares in a company.

For this purpose a takeover offer relates to all the shares in a company if it is an offer to acquire all the shares in the company within the meaning of s 974 of the CA 2006.[7683] The holder of any voting shares to which the offer relates who has not accepted the offer may require the offeror to acquire those shares if, at any time before the end of the period within which the offer can be accepted: (a) the offeror has by virtue of acceptances of the offer acquired or unconditionally contracted to acquire some (but not all) of the shares to which the offer relates;[7684] and (b) those shares, with or without any other shares in the company that he has acquired or contracted to acquire (whether unconditionally or subject to conditions being met) (i) amount to not less than 90 per cent; in value of all the voting shares in the company (or would do so but for s 990(1) of the CA 2006),[7685] and (ii) carry not less than 90 per cent of the voting rights in the company (or would do so but for s 990(1) of the CA 2006).[7686]

The holder of any non-voting shares to which the offer relates who has not accepted the offer may require the offeror to acquire those shares if, at any time before the end of the period within which the offer can be accepted: (a) the offeror has by virtue of acceptances of the offer acquired or unconditionally contracted to acquire some (but not all) of the shares to which the offer relates;[7687] and (b) those shares, with or without any other shares in the company that he has acquired or contracted to acquire (whether unconditionally

[7680] CA 2006, s 982(7)(c)(iii).   [7681] CA 2006, s 982(8).   [7682] CA 2006, s 982(9).
[7683] CA 2006, s 983(1).   [7684] CA 2006, s 983(2)(a).   [7685] CA 2006, s 983(2)(b)(i).
[7686] CA 2006, s 983(2)(b)(ii).   [7687] CA 2006, s 983(3)(a).

or subject to conditions being met), amount to not less than 90 per cent in value of all the shares in the company (or would do so but for s 990(1) of the CA 2006).[7688]

If a takeover offer relates to shares of one or more classes and at any time before the end of the period within which the offer can be accepted (a) the offeror has by virtue of acceptances of the offer acquired or unconditionally contracted to acquire some (but not all) of the shares of any class to which the offer relates;[7689] and (b) those shares, with or without any other shares of that class that he has acquired or contracted to acquire (whether unconditionally or subject to conditions being met) (i) amount to not less than 90 per cent in value of all the shares of that class,[7690] and (ii) in a case where the shares of that class are voting shares, carry not less than 90 per cent of the voting rights carried by the shares of that class.[7691]

The holder of any shares of that class to which the offer relates who has not accepted the offer may require the offeror to acquire those shares.

For the purposes of s 983(2)–(4) of the CA 2006, in calculating 90 per cent of the value of any shares, shares held by the company as treasury shares are to be treated as having been acquired by the offeror.[7692]

Section 983(7) of the CA 2006 applies where (a) a shareholder exercises rights conferred on him by s 983(2), (3) or (4) of the CA 2006;[7693] (b) at the time when he does so, there are shares in the company that the offeror has contracted to acquire subject to conditions being met, and in relation to which the contract has not become unconditional;[7694] and (c) the requirement imposed by s 983(2)(b), (3)(b) or (4)(b) of the CA 2006 (as the case may be) would not be satisfied if those shares were not taken into account.[7695]

The shareholder is treated for the purposes of s 985 of the CA 2006 as not having exercised his rights under this section unless the requirement imposed by para (b) of s 983(2), (3) or (4) of the CA 2006 (as the case may be) would be satisfied if (a) the reference in that paragraph to other shares in the company that the offeror has contracted to acquire unconditionally or subject to conditions being met were a reference to such shares that he has unconditionally contracted to acquire;[7696] and (b) the reference in that subsection to the period within which the offer can be accepted were a reference to the period referred to in s 984(2).[7697]

A reference in s 983(2)(b), (3)(b), (4)(b), (6) or (7) of the CA 2006 to shares that the offeror has acquired or contracted to acquire includes a reference to shares that an associate of his has acquired or contracted to acquire.[7698]

It is clarified that, in addition to shares acquired by the offeror, shares subject to both conditional and unconditional contracts of acquisition are

---

[7688] CA 2006, s 983(3)(b).   [7689] CA 2006, s 983(4)(a).   [7690] CA 2006, s 983(4)(b)(i).
[7691] CA 2006, s 983(4)(b)(ii).   [7692] CA 2006, s 983(5).   [7693] CA 2006, s 983(6)(a).
[7694] CA 2006, s 983(6)(b).   [7695] CA 2006, s 983(6)(c).   [7696] CA 2006, s 983(7)(a).
[7697] CA 2006, s 983(7)(b).   [7698] CA 2006, s 983(8).

included in calculating whether the sell-out threshold has been reached. As a result of this change, there might be circumstances where the 90 per cent threshold required for sell-out to be exercised was reached only because of shares that the offeror had conditionally contracted to acquire. However, if the conditions of such contracts were not fulfilled, the offeror could in fact find that he was being required to buy a minority shareholder's shares even though the offeror had not actually acquired 90 per cent of the shares. So s 983 of the CA 2006 also provides that, if that is the case at the time when the minority shareholder exercises his right of sell-out, the offeror does not have to purchase the shares unless he has acquired or unconditionally contracted to acquire 90 per cent or more of the shares by the time the period referred to in s 984(2) of the CA 2006 (the period within which shareholders can exercise sell-out rights) ends. (A corresponding change is made in s 979(6) and (7) of the CA 2006 to prevent minority shareholders in this situation who have to wait to see if they can exercise sell-out from being squeezed out in the meantime.)

Further provisions about rights conferred by s 983 of the CA 2006

28.52 Section 984 of the CA 2006 deals with the provision about rights conferred by s 983 of the CA 2006. Rights conferred on a shareholder by s 983(2), (3) or (4) of the CA 2006 are exercisable by a written communication addressed to the offeror.[7699]

Rights conferred on a shareholder by s 983(2), (3) or (4) of the CA 2006 not exercisable after the end of the period of three months from the end of the period within which the offer can be accepted,[7700] or if later, the date of the notice that must be given under s 984(3) of the CA 2006 below.[7701]

Within one month of the time specified in s 984(2), (3) or (4) of the CA 2006 (as the case may be) of that section, the offeror must give any shareholder who has not accepted the offer notice in the prescribed manner of the rights that are exercisable by the shareholder under that subsection,[7702] and the period within which the rights are exercisable.[7703]

If the notice is given before the end of the period within which the offer can be accepted, it must state that the offer is still open for acceptance.

Section 984(3) of the CA 2006 does not apply if the offeror has given the shareholder a notice in respect of the shares in question under s 979 of the CA 2006.[7704]

An offeror who fails to comply with s 984(3) of the CA 2006 commits an offence.[7705] If the offeror is a company, every officer of that company who is in

---

[7699] CA 2006, s 984(1).   [7700] CA 2006, s 984(2)(a).   [7701] CA 2006, s 984(2)(b).
[7702] CA 2006, s 984(3)(a).   [7703] CA 2006, s 984(3)(b).   [7704] CA 2006, s 984(4).
[7705] CA 2006, s 984(5).

default or to whose neglect the failure is attributable also commits an offence.

If an offeror other than a company is charged with an offence for failing to comply with s 984(3) of the CA 2006, it is a defence for him to prove that he took all reasonable steps for securing compliance with that subsection.[7706]

A person guilty of an offence under this section is liable on conviction on indictment, to a fine;[7707] and on summary conviction, to a fine not exceeding the statutory maximum and, for continued contravention, a daily default fine not exceeding one-fiftieth of the statutory maximum.[7708]

Effect of a requirement under section 983 of the CA 2006

28.53 Section 985 of the CA 2006 deals with effect of a requirement under s 953 of the CA 2006. Subject to s 986 of the CA 2006, this section applies where a shareholder exercises his rights under s 983 of the CA 2006 in respect of any shares held by him.[7709]

The offeror is entitled and bound to acquire those shares on the terms of the offer or on such other terms as may be agreed.[7710]

Where the terms of an offer are such as to give the shareholder a choice of consideration (a) the shareholder may indicate his choice when requiring the offeror to acquire the shares;[7711] and (b) the notice given to the shareholder under s 984(3) of the CA 2006: (i) must give particulars of the choice and of the rights conferred by this subsection,[7712] and (ii) may state which consideration specified in the offer will apply if he does not indicate a choice.[7713]

The reference in s 985(2) of the CA 2006 to the terms of the offer is to be read accordingly.

Section 985(3) of the CA 2006 applies whether or not any time-limit or other conditions applicable to the choice under the terms of the offer can still be complied with.[7714]

If the consideration offered to or (as the case may be) chosen by the shareholder is not cash and the offeror is no longer able to provide it,[7715] or if it was to have been provided by a third party who is no longer bound or able to provide it,[7716] the consideration is to be taken to consist of an amount of cash, payable by the offeror, that at the date when the shareholder requires the offeror to acquire the shares is equivalent to the consideration offered or (as the case may be) chosen.

[7706] CA 2006, s 984(6).   [7707] CA 2006, s 984(7)(a).   [7708] CA 2006, s 984(7)(b).
[7709] CA 2006, s 985(1).   [7710] CA 2006, s 985(2).   [7711] CA 2006, s 985(3)(a).
[7712] CA 2006, s 985(3)(b)(i).   [7713] CA 2006, s 985(3)(b)(ii).   [7714] CA 2006, s 985(4).
[7715] CA 2006, s 985(5)(a).   [7716] CA 2006, s 985(5)(b).

Supplementary

Applications to the court

28.54 Section 986 of the CA 2006 deals with applications to the court. Where a notice is given under s 979 of the CA 2006 to a shareholder the court may, on an application made by him, order that the offeror is not entitled and bound to acquire the shares to which the notice relates,[7717] or that the terms on which the offeror is entitled and bound to acquire the shares shall be such as the court thinks fit.[7718]

An application under s 986(1) of the CA 2006 must be made within six weeks from the date on which the notice referred to in that subsection was given.[7719]

If an application to the court under s 986(1) of the CA 2006 is pending at the end of that period, s 981(6) of the CA 2006 does not have effect until the application has been disposed of.

Where a shareholder exercises his rights under s 983 of the CA 2006 in respect of any shares held by him, the court may, on an application made by him or the offeror, order that the terms on which the offeror is entitled and bound to acquire the shares shall be such as the court thinks fit.[7720]

On an application under s 986(1) or (3) of the CA 2006, the court may not require consideration of a higher value than that specified in the terms of the offer (the offer value) to be given for the shares to which the application relates unless the holder of the shares shows that the offer value would be unfair;[7721] the court may not require consideration of a lower value than the offer value to be given for the shares.[7722]

No order for costs or expenses may be made against a shareholder making an application under s 986(1) or (3) of the CA 2006 unless the court considers that: (a) the application was unnecessary, improper or vexatious;[7723] (b) there has been unreasonable delay in making the application;[7724] or (c) there has been unreasonable conduct on the shareholder's part in conducting the proceedings on the application.[7725]

A shareholder who has made an application under s 986(1) or (3) of the CA 2006 must give notice of the application to the offeror.[7726]

An offeror who is given notice of an application under s 986(1) or (3) of the CA 2006 must give a copy of the notice to any person (other than the applicant) to whom a notice has been given under s 979 of the CA 2006;[7727] any person who has exercised his rights under s 983 of the CA 2006.[7728]

An offeror who makes an application under s 986(3) of the CA 2006 must

---

[7717] CA 2006, s 986(1)(a).   [7718] CA 2006, s 986(1)(b).   [7719] CA 2006, s 986(2).

[7720] CA 2006, s 986(3).   [7721] CA 2006, s 986(4)(a).   [7722] CA 2006, s 986(4)(b).

[7723] CA 2006, s 986(5)(a).   [7724] CA 2006, s 986(5)(b).   [7725] CA 2006, s 986(5)(c).

[7726] CA 2006, s 986(6).   [7727] CA 2006, s 986(7)(a).   [7728] CA 2006, s 986(7)(b).

give notice of the application to any person to whom a notice has been given under s 979 of the CA 2006;[7729] and to any person who has exercised his rights under s 983 of the CA 2006.[7730]

Where a takeover offer has not been accepted to the extent necessary for entitling the offeror to give notices under s 979(2) or (4) of the CA 2006 the court may, on an application made by him, make an order authorising him to give notices under that subsection if it is satisfied that: (a) the offeror has after reasonable enquiry been unable to trace one or more of the persons holding shares to which the offer relates;[7731] (b) the requirements of that subsection would have been met if the person, or all the persons, mentioned in para (a) above had accepted the offer;[7732] and (c) the consideration offered is fair and reasonable.[7733]

This is subject to s 986(10) of the CA 2006.

The court may not make an order under s 986(9) of the CA 2006 unless it considers that it is just and equitable to do so having regard, in particular, to the number of shareholders who have been traced but who have not accepted the offer.[7734]

Section 986 of the CA 2006 provides that a shareholder receiving a squeeze-out notice may make an application to the court (within six weeks of receiving the notice) seeking to overturn an offeror's intention to purchase his shares compulsorily (or the terms of that purchase). A requirement that the offeror be promptly notified of such an application is now included (this was not previously required by s 430C of the CA 1985). As a consequence of this requirement, it is also required that the offeror is obliged, at the earliest opportunity, to notify shareholders who are being squeezed out. or who are exercising their rights of sell-out, and are not party to a s 986 (CA 2006) application, that proceedings have been initiated.

Joint offers

28.55 Section 987 of the CA 2006 states that in the case of a takeover offer made by two or more persons jointly, this Chapter has effect as follows.[7735]

The conditions for the exercise of the rights conferred by s 979 of the CA 2006 are satisfied (a) in the case of acquisitions by virtue of acceptances of the offer, by the joint offerors acquiring or unconditionally contracting to acquire the necessary shares jointly;[7736] (b) in other cases, by the joint offerors acquiring or unconditionally contracting to acquire the necessary shares either jointly or separately.[7737]

The conditions for the exercise of the rights conferred by s 983 of the CA 2006 are satisfied (a) in the case of acquisitions by virtue of acceptances of

---

[7729] CA 2006, s 986(8)(a).   [7730] CA 2006, s 986(8)(b).   [7731] CA 2006, s 986(9)(a).
[7732] CA 2006, s 986(9)(b).   [7733] CA 2006, s 986(9)(c).   [7734] CA 2006, s 986(10).
[7735] CA 2006, s 987(1).   [7736] CA 2006, s 987(2)(a).   [7737] CA 2006, s 987(2)(b).

the offer, by the joint offerors acquiring or unconditionally contracting to acquire the necessary shares jointly;[7738] (b) in other cases, by the joint offerors acquiring or contracting (whether unconditionally or subject to conditions being met) to acquire the necessary shares either jointly or separately.[7739]

Subject to the following provisions, the rights and obligations of the offeror under s 979 to 985 of the CA 2006 are respectively joint rights and joint and several obligations of the joint offerors.[7740]

A provision of ss 979–986 of the CA 2006 that requires or authorises a notice or other document to be given or sent by or to the joint offerors is complied with if the notice or document is given or sent by or to any of them (but see s 987(6) of the CA 2006).[7741]

The statutory declaration required by s 980(4) of the CA 2006 must be made by all of the joint offerors and, where one or more of them is a company, signed by a director of that company.[7742]

In ss 974–977, 979(9), 981(6), 983(8) and 988, references to the offeror are to be read as references to the joint offerors or any of them.[7743]

In ss 981(7) and (8) of the CA 2006, references to the offeror are to be read as references to the joint offerors or such of them as they may determine.[7744]

In ss 981(5)(a) and 985(5)(a) of the CA 2006, references to the offeror being no longer able to provide the relevant consideration are to be read as references to none of the joint offerors being able to do so.[7745]

In s 986 of the CA 2006, references to the offeror are to be read as references to the joint offerors, except that (a) an application under s 987(3) or (9) of the CA 2006 may be made by any of them,[7746] and (b) the reference in s 987(9)(a) of the CA 2006 to the offeror having been unable to trace one or more of the persons holding shares is to be read as a reference to none of the offerors having been able to do so.[7747]

Interpretation

Associates

28.56 Section 988 of the CA 2006 is concerned with the definition of associates. The term 'associate', in relation to an offeror, means:

(a)   a nominee of the offeror;[7748]
(b)   a holding company, subsidiary or fellow subsidiary of the offeror or a nominee of such a holding company, subsidiary or fellow subsidiary;[7749]

[7738] CA 2006, s 987(3)(a).   [7739] CA 2006, s 987(3)(b).   [7740] CA 2006, s 987(4).
[7741] CA 2006, s 987(5).   [7742] CA 2006, s 987(6).   [7743] CA 2006, s 987(7).
[7744] CA 2006, s 987(8).   [7745] CA 2006, s 987(9).   [7746] CA 2006, s 987(10)(a).
[7747] CA 2006, s 987(10)(b).   [7748] CA 2006, s 988(1)(a).   [7749] CA 2006, s 988(1)(b).

(c)   a body corporate in which the offeror is substantially interested;[7750]
(d)   a person who is, or is a nominee of, a party to a share acquisition agreement with the offeror;[7751] or
(e)   (where the offeror is an individual) his spouse or civil partner and any minor child or step-child of his.[7752]

For the purposes of s 988(1)(b) of the CA 2006 a company is a fellow subsidiary of another body corporate if both are subsidiaries of the same body corporate but neither is a subsidiary of the other.[7753]

For the purposes of s 988(1)(c) of the CA 2006 an offeror has a substantial interest in a body corporate if the body or its directors are accustomed to act in accordance with his directions or instructions,[7754] or he is entitled to exercise or control the exercise of one-third or more of the voting power at general meetings of the body.[7755]

Section 823(2) and (3) of the CA 2006 (which contains provision about when a person is treated as entitled to exercise or control the exercise of voting power) applies for the purposes of this subsection as they apply for the purposes of that section.

For the purposes of s 988(1)(d) of the CA 2006, an agreement is a share acquisition agreement if:

(a)   it is an agreement for the acquisition of, or of an interest in, shares to which the offer relates;[7756]
(b)   it includes provisions imposing obligations or restrictions on any one or more of the parties to it with respect to their use, retention or disposal of such shares, or their interests in such shares, acquired in pursuance of the agreement (whether or not together with any other shares to which the offer relates or any other interests of theirs in such shares);[7757] and
(c)   it is not an excluded agreement (see s 988(5) of the CA 2006).[7758]

An agreement is an 'excluded agreement' if it is not legally binding, unless it involves mutuality in the undertakings, expectations or understandings of the parties to it,[7759] or if it is an agreement to underwrite or sub-underwrite an offer of shares in a company, provided the agreement is confined to that purpose and any matters incidental to it.[7760]

The reference in s 988(4)(b) of the CA 2006 to the use of interests in shares is to the exercise of any rights or of any control or influence arising from those interests (including the right to enter into an agreement for the exercise, or for control of the exercise, of any of those rights by another person).[7761]

[7750] CA 2006, s 988(1)(c).   [7751] CA 2006, s 988(1)(d).   [7752] CA 2006, s 988(1)(e).
[7753] CA 2006, s 988(2).   [7754] CA 2006, s 988(3)(a).   [7755] CA 2006, s 988(3)(b).
[7756] CA 2006, s 988(4)(a).   [7757] CA 2006, s 988(4)(b).   [7758] CA 2006, s 988(4)(c).
[7759] CA 2006, s 988(5)(a).   [7760] CA 2006, s 988(5)(b).   [7761] CA 2006, s 988(5)(c).

The terms 'agreement' includes any agreement or arrangement.[7762] References to provisions of an agreement include undertakings, expectations or understandings operative under an arrangement;[7763] and any provision whether express or implied and whether absolute or not.[7764]

Convertible securities

28.57 Section 989 of the CA 2006 deals with convertible securities. For the purposes of this Chapter securities of a company are treated as shares in the company if they are convertible into or entitle the holder to subscribe for such shares.

References to the holder of shares or a shareholder are to be read accordingly.[7765]

Section 989(1) of the CA 2006 is not to be read as requiring any securities to be treated as shares of the same class as those into which they are convertible or for which the holder is entitled to subscribe,[7766] or as shares of the same class as other securities by reason only that the shares into which they are convertible or for which the holder is entitled to subscribe are of the same class.[7767]

Debentures carrying voting rights

28.58 Section 990 of the CA 2006 deals with debentures carrying voting rights. For the purposes of this Chapter debentures issued by a company to which s 990(2) of the CA 2006 applies are treated as shares in the company if they carry voting rights.[7768]

This subsection applies to a company that has voting shares, or debentures carrying voting rights, which are admitted to trading on a regulated market.[7769]

In this Chapter, in relation to debentures treated as shares by virtue of s 980(1) of the CA 2006 references to the holder of shares or a shareholder are to be read accordingly;[7770] and references to shares being allotted are to be read as references to debentures being issued.[7771]

The following are defined terms under Chapter 3:

- 'the company' means the company whose shares are the subject of a takeover offer; 'date of the offer' means:

    (a) where the offer is published, the date of publication;

[7762] CA 2006, s 988(7)(a).   [7763] CA 2006, s 988(7)(b)(i).   [7764] CA 2006, s 988(7)(b)(ii).
[7765] CA 2006, s 989(1).   [7766] CA 2006, s 989(2)(a).   [7767] CA 2006, s 989(2)(b).
[7768] CA 2006, s 990(1).   [7769] CA 2006, s 990(2).   [7770] CA 2006, s 990(3)(a).
[7771] CA 2006, s 990(3)(b).

(b)   where the offer is not published, or where any notices of the offer are given before the date of publication, the date when notices of the offer (or the first such notices) are given;

and references to the date of the offer are to be read in accordance with s 974(7) (revision of offer terms) where that applies;

- 'non-voting shares' means shares that are not voting shares;
- 'offeror' means (subject to s 987 of the CA 2006) the person making a takeover offer;
- 'voting rights' means rights to vote at general meetings of the company, including rights that arise only in certain circumstances;
- 'voting shares' means shares carrying voting rights.

For the purposes of this Chapter a person contracts unconditionally to acquire shares if his entitlement under the contract to acquire them is not (or is no longer) subject to conditions or if all conditions to which it was subject have been met.

A reference to a contract becoming unconditional is to be read accordingly.

Amendments to Part 7 of the Companies Act 1985

28.59 Chapter 4 is concerned with amendments to Part 7 of the CA 1985.

Matters to be dealt with in the directors' report

28.60 Section 992 of the CA 2006 is concerned with matters to be dealt with in the directors' report.

Part 7 of the CA 1985 (c 6) (accounts and audit) is amended as follows.[7772] In Schedule 7 (matters to be dealt with in the directors' report), after Part 6 insert:[7773]

Disclosure required by certain publicly-traded companies

This Part of this Schedule applies to the directors' report for a financial year if the company had securities carrying voting rights admitted to trading on a regulated market at the end of that year.

The report shall contain detailed information, by reference to the end of that year, on the following matters:

(a)   the structure of the company's capital, including in particular:

(i)   the rights and obligations attaching to the shares or, as the case may be, to each class of shares in the company, and

---

[7772] CA 2006, s 992(1).   [7773] CA 2006, s 992(2).

(ii)   where there are two or more such classes, the percentage of the total share capital represented by each class;

(b)   any restrictions on the transfer of securities in the company, including in particular:

(i)   limitations on the holding of securities, and

(ii)   requirements to obtain the approval of the company, or of other holders of securities in the company, for a transfer of securities;

(c)   in the case of each person with a significant direct or indirect holding of securities in the company, such details as are known to the company of:

(i)   the identity of the person,

(ii)   the size of the holding, and

(iii)   the nature of the holding;

(d)   in the case of each person who holds securities carrying special rights with regard to control of the company:

(i)   the identity of the person, and

(ii)   the nature of the rights;

(e)   where:

(i)   the company has an employees' share scheme, and

(ii)   shares to which the scheme relates have rights with regard to control of the company that are not exercisable directly by the employees,

how those rights are exercisable;

(f)   any restrictions on voting rights, including in particular:

(i)   limitations on voting rights of holders of a given percentage or number of votes,

(ii)   deadlines for exercising voting rights, and

(iii)   arrangements by which, with the company's co-operation, financial rights carried by securities are held by a person other than the holder of the securities;

(g)   any agreements between holders of securities that are known to the company and may result in restrictions on the transfer of securities or on voting rights;

(h)   any rules that the company has about:

(i)   appointment and replacement of directors, or

(ii)   amendment of the company's Articles of Association;

(i)   the powers of the company's directors, including in particular any powers in relation to the issuing or buying back by the company of its shares;

(j)   any significant agreements to which the company is a party that take effect, alter or terminate upon a change of control of the company following a takeover bid, and the effects of any such agreements;

(k) any agreements between the company and its directors or employees providing for compensation for loss of office or employment (whether through resignation, purported redundancy or otherwise) that occurs because of a takeover bid.

For the purposes of sub-para (2)(a) a company's capital includes any securities in the company that are not admitted to trading on a regulated market.

For the purposes of sub-para (2)(c) a person has an indirect holding of securities if:

(a) they are held on his behalf, or

(b) he is able to secure that rights carried by the securities are exercised in accordance with his wishes.

Sub-para (2)(j) does not apply to an agreement if:

(a) disclosure of the agreement would be seriously prejudicial to the company, and

(b) the company is not under any other obligation to disclose it.

In this para

• 'securities' means shares or debentures;
• 'takeover bid' has the same meaning as in the Takeovers Directive;
• 'the Takeovers Directive' means Directive 2004/25/EC of the European Parliament and of the Council;

'voting rights' means rights to vote at general meetings of the company in question, including rights that arise only in certain circumstances.

In section 234ZZA (requirements of directors' reports), at the end of subs (4) (contents of Schedule 7) insert:[7774]

Part 7 specifies information to be disclosed by certain publicly-traded companies.

After that subsection insert:[7775]

(5) A directors' report shall also contain any necessary explanatory material with regard to information that is required to be included in the report by Part 7 of Schedule 7.

In s 251 (summary financial statements), after subs (2ZA) insert:[7776]

(2ZB) A company that sends to an entitled person a summary financial statement instead of a copy of its directors' report shall:

[7774] CA 2006, s 992(3).   [7775] CA 2006, s 992(4).   [7776] CA 2006, s 992(5).

(a)   include in the statement the explanatory material required to be included in the directors' report by section 234ZZA(5), or

(b)   send that material to the entitled person at the same time as it sends the statement.

For the purposes of para (b), subss (2A)–(2E) apply in relation to the material referred to in that paragraph as they apply in relation to a summary financial statement.

The amendments made by this section apply in relation to directors' reports for financial years beginning on or after 20 May 2006.[7777]

This section implements Article 10 of the CA the Takeovers Directive. Article 10.1 and 10.2 require companies admitted to trading on a regulated market to provide in their annual reports detailed information relating to matters such as the control and share structures of the company. It is, therefore, provided by amendment to Part 7 of the CA 2006 that the information required by the Directive must be set out in the directors report.

Additionally, Article 10.3 of the Directive requires boards of companies to present an explanatory report to shareholders on the issues referred to in Article 10.1 and 10.2 at the company's annual general meeting. This section requires this additional explanatory material to be contained in the directors' report submitted to the annual meeting of shareholders.

Section 992(5) of the CA 2006 amends s 251 of the CA 1985 on summary financial statements. It provides for the explanatory material required by Article 10.3 of the Takeovers Directive either to be included in the summary financial statement or to accompany it.

Failure to include either the information concerning control and share structures or explanatory material in the annual report will attract existing criminal sanctions under s 234(5) of the CA 1985 (directors responsible for the failure to comply with provisions related to the directors report to be liable to a fine).

Section 992(6) of the CA 2006 provides that these new provisions apply in relation to directors' reports for financial years beginning on or after 20 May 2006 (the date by which the Directive had to be implemented).

These are general requirements are designed to bring greater transparency to the market, and apply to all relevant companies whether or not they are involved in a takeover. Accordingly, the requirements will apply to all companies registered in the UK that have voting shares traded on a regulated market, whether or. not that includes an official listing on the London Stock Exchange.

[7777] CA 2006, s 992(6).

Under Part 15 of the CA 2006 (s 416), the Secretary of State may in future make regulations as to the contents of directors' reports, and those regulations will be able to incorporate the provisions introduced by s 992(2)–(4) of the CA 2006. Regulations under ss 427 and 428 of the CA 2006 will be able to make provision for the additional explanatory material statement, rather than the full accounts and report.

Chapter 29

Dissolution and Restoration to the Register

Introduction

29.1 Part 31 of the CA 2006 addresses the dissolution and restoration to the register of a company.

It comprises three Chapters. Chapter 1 is concerned with striking off, and the registrar's power to strike off a defunct company as well as voluntary striking off. Chapter 2 addresses what happens to the property of a dissolved company including vesting as *bona vacantia*, and effect of a Crown disclaimer. Chapter 3 contains provisions on restoration to the register, including administrative restoration to the register and restoration to the register by the court.

Dissolution And Restoration To The Register

Striking off

29.2 Chapter 1 is concerned with striking off. It contains 12 sections. It examines the registrar's role in striking off a defunct company as well as voluntary striking off.

Registrar's power to strike off a defunct company

Power to strike off a company not carrying on business or in operation

29.3 Section 1000 of the CA 2006 deals with the registrar's power to strike off a company for not carrying on business or not being in operation. If the registrar has reasonable cause to believe that a company is not carrying on business or is not in operation, the registrar may send to the company by post a letter inquiring whether the company is carrying on business or in operation.[7778]

[7778] CA 2006, s 1000(1).

If the registrar does not within one month of sending the letter receive any answer to it, the registrar must within 14 days after the expiration of that month send to the company by post a registered letter referring to the first letter, and stating that no answer to it has been received,[7779] and that if an answer is not received to the second letter within one month from its date,[7780] a notice will be published in the Gazette with a view to striking the company's name off the register.

If the registrar receives an answer to the effect that the company is not carrying on business or in operation,[7781] or does not within one month after sending the second letter receive any answer,[7782] the registrar may publish in the Gazette, and send to the company by post, a notice that at the expiration of three months from the date of the notice the name of the company mentioned in it will, unless cause is shown to the contrary, be struck off the register and the company will be dissolved.

At the expiration of the time mentioned in the notice the registrar may, unless cause to the contrary is previously shown by the company, strike its name off the register.[7783]

The registrar must publish notice in the Gazette of the company's name having been struck off the register.[7784] On the publication of the notice in the Gazette the company is dissolved.[7785]

However the liability (if any) of every director, managing officer and member of the company continues and may be enforced as if the company had not been dissolved,[7786] and nothing in s 1000 of the CA 2006 affects the power of the court to wind up a company the name of which has been struck off the register.[7787]

Duty to act in case of a company being wound up

29.4 Section 1001 of the CA 2006 applies to situations where there is a duty to act in case of company being wound up. If, in a case where a company is being wound up (a) the registrar has reasonable cause to believe (i) that no liquidator is acting,[7788] or (ii) that the affairs of the company are fully wound up;[7789] and (b) the returns required to be made by the liquidator have not been made for a period of six consecutive months,[7790] the registrar must publish in the Gazette and send to the company or the liquidator (if any) a notice that at the expiration of three months from the date of the notice the name of the company mentioned in it will, unless cause is shown to the contrary, be struck off the register and the company will be dissolved.

[7779] CA 2006, s 1000(2)(a).   [7780] CA 2006, s 1000(2)(b).   [7781] CA 2006, s 1000(3)(a).
[7782] CA 2006, s 1000(3)(b).   [7783] CA 2006, s 1000(4).   [7784] CA 2006, s 1000(5).
[7785] CA 2006, s 1000(6).   [7786] CA 2006, s 1000(7)(a).   [7787] CA 2006, s 1000(7)(b).
[7788] CA 2006, s 1001(1)(a)(i).   [7789] CA 2006, s 1001(1)(a)(ii).
[7790] CA 2006, s 1001(1)(b).

At the expiration of the time mentioned in the notice the registrar may, unless cause to the contrary is previously shown by the company, strike its name off the register.[7791]

The registrar must publish notice in the Gazette of the company's name having been struck off the register.[7792] On the publication of the notice in the Gazette the company is dissolved.[7793]

However the liability (if any) of every director, managing officer and member of the nothing in s 1001 of the CA 2006 affects the power of the court to wind up a company the name of which has been struck off the register.[7794]

Supplementary provisions as to service of a letter or notice

29.5 Section 1002 of the CA 2006 deals with supplementary provisions as to service of letter or notice. A letter or notice to be sent under ss 1000 or 1001 of the CA 2006 to a company may be addressed to the company at its registered office or, if no office has been registered, to the care of some officer of the company.[7795]

If there is no officer of the company whose name and address are known to the registrar, the letter or notice may be sent to each of the persons who subscribed to the memorandum (if their addresses are known to the registrar).[7796]

A notice to be sent to a liquidator under s 1001 of the CA 2006 may be addressed to him at his last known place of business.[7797]

Voluntary striking off

Striking off on application by a company

29.6 Section 1003 of the CA 2006 applies to striking off on application by a company, also known as 'voluntary striking off'. On application by a company, the registrar of companies may strike the company's name off the register.[7798]

The application must be made on the company's behalf by its directors or by a majority of them,[7799] and must contain the prescribed information.[7800]

The registrar may not strike a company off under this section until after the expiration of three months from the publication by the registrar in the Gazette of a notice stating that the registrar may exercise the power under this section in relation to the company,[7801] and inviting any person to show cause why that should not be done.[7802]

[7791] CA 2006, s 1001(2).   [7792] CA 2006, s 1001(3).   [7793] CA 2006, s 1001(4).
[7794] CA 2006, s 1001(5)(b).   [7795] CA 2006, s 1002(1).   [7796] CA 2006, s 1002(2).
[7797] CA 2006, s 1002(3).   [7798] CA 2006, s 1003(1).   [7799] CA 2006, s 1003(2)(a).
[7800] CA 2006, s 1003(2)(b).   [7801] CA 2006, s 1003(3)(a).   [7802] CA 2006, s 1003(3)(b).

The registrar must publish notice in the Gazette of the company's name having been struck off.[7803] On the publication of the notice in the Gazette the company is dissolved.[7804]

However the liability (if any) of every director, managing officer and member of the company continues and may be enforced as if the company had not been dissolved,[7805] and nothing in s 1003 of the CA 2006 affects the power of the court to wind up a company the name of which has been struck off the register.[7806]

Section 652A of the CA 1985 provided that, in certain circumstances, a private company could apply to the registrar to be struck off the register. Section 1003 of the CA 2006 amends s 652A to provide that a public company, too, may so apply.

Circumstances in which an application cannot be made: activities of companies

29.7 Section 1004 of the CA 2006 deals with the circumstances in which an application for striking off may not be made. An application under s 1003 of the CA 2006 (application for voluntary striking off) on behalf of a company must not be made if, at any time in the previous three months, the company has (a) changed its name;[7807] (b) traded or otherwise carried on business;[7808] (c) made a disposal for value of property or rights that, immediately before ceasing to trade or otherwise carry on business, it held for the purpose of disposal for gain in the normal course of trading or otherwise carrying on business;[7809] or (d) engaged in any other activity, except one which is (i) necessary or expedient for the purpose of making an application under that section, or deciding whether to do so,[7810] (ii) necessary or expedient for the purpose of concluding the affairs of the company,[7811] (iii) necessary or expedient for the purpose of complying with any statutory requirement,[7812] or (iv) specified by the Secretary of State by order for the purposes of this sub-paragraph.[7813]

For the purposes of this section, a company is not to be treated as trading or otherwise carrying on business by virtue only of the fact that it makes a payment in respect of a liability incurred in the course of trading or otherwise carrying on business.[7814]

The Secretary of State may by order amend s 1004(1) of the CA 2006 for the purpose of altering the period in relation to which the doing of the things mentioned in paras (a)–(d) of that subsection is relevant.[7815]

[7803] CA 2006, s 1003(4).   [7804] CA 2006, s 1003(5).   [7805] CA 2006, s 1003(6)(a).
[7806] CA 2006, s 1003(6)(b).   [7807] CA 2006, s 1004(1)(a).   [7808] CA 2006, s 1004(1)(b).
[7809] CA 2006, s 1004(1)(c).   [7810] CA 2006, s 1004(1)(d)(i).
[7811] CA 2006, s 1004(1)(d)(ii).   [7812] CA 2006, s 1004(1)(d)(iii).
[7813] CA 2006, s 1004(1)(d)(iv).   [7814] CA 2006, s 1004(2).   [7815] CA 2006, s 1004(3).

An order under this section is subject to negative resolution procedure.[7816]

It is an offence for a person to make an application in contravention of this section.[7817]

In proceedings for such an offence it is a defence for the accused to prove that he did not know, and could not reasonably have known, of the existence of the facts that led to the contravention.[7818]

A person guilty of an offence under s 1004 of the CA 2006 is liable on conviction on indictment, to a fine;[7819] and on summary conviction, to a fine not exceeding the statutory maximum.[7820]

Circumstances in which an application cannot be made: other proceedings not concluded

29.8 Section 1005 of the CA 2006 states that an application under s 1003 of the CA 2006 (application for voluntary striking off) on behalf of a company, must not be made at a time when (a) an application to the court under Part 26 of the CA 2006 has been made on behalf of the company for the sanctioning of a compromise or arrangement and the matter has not been finally concluded;[7821] (b) a voluntary arrangement in relation to the company has been proposed under Part 1 of the Insolvency Act 1986 (c 45) or Part 2 of the Insolvency (Northern Ireland) Order 1989 (SI 1989/2405 (NI 19)) and the matter has not been finally concluded;[7822] (c) the company is in administration under Part 2 of that Act or Part 3 of that Order;[7823] (d) para 44 of Schedule B1 to that Act or para 45 of Schedule B1 to that Order applies (interim moratorium on proceedings where an application to the court for an administration order has been made or notice of intention to appoint an administrator has been filed);[7824] (e) the company is being wound up under Part 4 of that Act or Part 5 of that Order, whether voluntarily or by the court, or a petition under that Part for winding up of the company by the court has been presented and not finally dealt with or withdrawn;[7825] (f) there is a receiver or manager of the company's property;[7826] (g) the company's estate is being administered by a judicial factor.[7827]

For the purposes of s 1005(1)(a) of the CA 2006, the matter is finally concluded if the application has been withdrawn,[7828] or the application has been finally dealt with without a compromise or arrangement being sanctioned by the court,[7829] or a compromise or arrangement has been sanctioned by the court and has, together with anything required to be done under any

---

[7816] CA 2006, s 1004(4).   [7817] CA 2006, s 1004(5).   [7818] CA 2006, s 1004(6).
[7819] CA 2006, s 1004(7)(a).   [7820] CA 2006, s 1004(7)(b).   [7821] CA 2006, s 1005(1)(a).
[7822] CA 2006, s 1005(1)(b).   [7823] CA 2006, s 1005(1)(c).   [7824] CA 2006, s 1005(1)(d).
[7825] CA 2006, s 1005(1)(e).   [7826] CA 2006, s 1005(1)(f).   [7827] CA 2006, s 1005(1)(g).
[7828] CA 2006, s 1005(2)(a).   [7829] CA 2006, s 1005(2)(b).

provision made in relation to the matter by order of the court, been fully carried out.[7830]

For the purposes of s 1005(1)(b) of the CA 2006, the matter is finally concluded if (a) no meetings are to be summoned under section 3 of the Insolvency Act 1986 (c 45) or Article 16 of the Insolvency (Northern Ireland) Order 1989;[7831] (b) meetings summoned under that section or Article fail to approve the arrangement with no, or the same, modifications;[7832] (c) an arrangement approved by meetings summoned under that section, or in consequence of a direction under s 6(4)(b) of that Act or Article 19(4)(b) of that Order, has been fully implemented;[7833] or (d) the court makes an order under section 6(5) of that Act or Article 19(5) of that Order revoking approval given at previous meetings and, if the court gives any directions under s 6(6) of that Act or Article 19(6) of that Order, the company has done whatever it is required to do under those directions.[7834]

It is an offence for a person to make an application in contravention of this section.[7835]

In proceedings for such an offence it is a defence for the accused to prove that he did not know, and could not reasonably have known, of the existence of the facts that led to the contravention.[7836]

A person guilty of an offence under s 1005 of the CA 2006 is liable on conviction on indictment, to a fine;[7837] and on summary conviction, to a fine not exceeding the statutory maximum.[7838]

Copy of application to be given to members, employees, etc

29.9 Section 1006 of the CA 2006 deals with the copy of application to be given to certain person.

A person who makes an application under s 1003 of the CA 2006 (application for voluntary striking off) on behalf of a company must secure that, within seven days from the day on which the application is made, a copy of it is given to every person who at any time on that day is (a) a member of the company;[7839] (b) an employee of the company;[7840] (c) a creditor of the company;[7841] (d) a director of the company;[7842] (e) a manager or trustee of any pension fund established for the benefit of employees of the company;[7843] or (f) a person of a description specified for the purposes of this paragraph by regulations made by the Secretary of State.[7844] The regulations under para (f) are subject to negative resolution procedure.

[7830] CA 2006, s 1005(2)(c).　　[7831] CA 2006, s 1005(3)(a).　　[7832] CA 2006, s 1005(3)(b).

[7833] CA 2006, s 1005(3)(c).　　[7834] CA 2006, s 1005(3)(d).　　[7835] CA 2006, s 1005(4).

[7836] CA 2006, s 1005(5).　　[7837] CA 2006, s 1005(6)(a).　　[7838] CA 2006, s 1005(6)(b).

[7839] CA 2006, s 1006(1)(a).　　[7840] CA 2006, s 1006(1)(b).　　[7841] CA 2006, s 1006(1)(c).

[7842] CA 2006, s 1006(1)(d).　　[7843] CA 2006, s 1006(1)(e).　　[7844] CA 2006, s 1006(1)(f).

Section 1006(1) of the CA 2006 does not require a copy of the application to be given to a director who is a party to the application.[7845]

The duty imposed by s 1006 of the CA 2006 ceases to apply if the application is withdrawn before the end of the period for giving the copy application.[7846]

A person who fails to perform the duty imposed on him by this section commits an offence.

If he does so with the intention of concealing the making of the application from the person concerned, he commits an aggravated offence.[7847]

In proceedings for an offence under s 1006 of the CA 2006 it is a defence for the accused to prove that he took all reasonable steps to perform the duty.[7848]

A person guilty of an offence under this section (other than an aggravated offence) is liable on conviction on indictment, to a fine;[7849] on summary conviction, to a fine not exceeding the statutory maximum.[7850]

A person guilty of an aggravated offence under s 1006 of the CA 2006 is liable on conviction on indictment, to imprisonment for a term not exceeding seven years or a fine (or both);[7851] and on summary conviction (i) in England and Wales, to imprisonment for a term not exceeding 12 months or to a fine not exceeding the statutory maximum (or both);[7852] (ii) in Scotland or Northern Ireland, to imprisonment for a term not exceeding six months, or to a fine not exceeding the statutory maximum (or both).[7853]

Copy of application to be given to new members, employees, etc.

29.10 Section 1007 of the CA 2006 requires a copy of the application for striking off to be give to new members, etc. It applies in relation to any time after the day on which a company makes an application under s 1003 of the CA 2006 (application for voluntary striking off) and before the day on which the application is finally dealt with or withdrawn.[7854]

A person who is a director of the company at the end of a day on which a person (other than himself) becomes (a) a member of the company;[7855] (b) an employee of the company;[7856] (c) a creditor of the company;[7857] (d) a director of the company;[7858] (e) a manager or trustee of any pension fund established for the benefit of employees of the company;[7859] or (f) a person of a description specified for the purposes of this paragraph by regulations made by the Secretary of State,[7860] must secure that a copy of the application is given to that person within seven days from that day.

[7845] CA 2006, s 1006(2).　　[7846] CA 2006, s 1006(3).　　[7847] CA 2006, s 1006(4).
[7848] CA 2006, s 1006(5).　　[7849] CA 2006, s 1006(6)(a).　　[7850] CA 2006, s 1006(6)(b).
[7851] CA 2006, s 1006(7)(a).　　[7852] CA 2006, s 1006(7)(b)(i).
[7853] CA 2006, s 1006(7)(b)(ii).　　[7854] CA 2006, s 1007(1).　　[7855] CA 2006, s 1007(2)(a).
[7856] CA 2006, s 1007(2)(b).　　[7857] CA 2006, s 1007(2)(c).　　[7858] CA 2006, s 1007(2)(d).
[7859] CA 2006, s 1007(2)(e).　　[7860] CA 2006, s 1007(2)(f).

Regulations under para (f) are subject to negative resolution procedure.

The duty imposed by this section ceases to apply if the application is finally dealt with or withdrawn before the end of the period for giving the copy application.[7861]

A person who fails to perform the duty imposed on him by this section commits an offence. If he does so with the intention of concealing the making of the application from the person concerned, he commits an aggravated offence.[7862]

In proceedings for an offence under s 1007 of the CA 2006 it is a defence for the accused to prove that at the time of the failure he was not aware of the fact that the company had made an application under s 1003 of the CA 2006,[7863] or that he took all reasonable steps to perform the duty.[7864]

A person guilty of an offence under s 1007 of the CA 2006 (other than an aggravated offence) is liable on conviction on indictment, to a fine;[7865] on summary conviction, to a fine not exceeding the statutory maximum.[7866]

A person guilty of an aggravated offence under s 1007 of the CA 2006 is liable on conviction on indictment, to imprisonment for a term not exceeding seven years or a fine (or both);[7867] on summary conviction in England and Wales, to imprisonment for a term not exceeding 12 months or to a fine not exceeding the statutory maximum (or both);[7868] in Scotland or Northern Ireland, to imprisonment for a term not exceeding six months, or to a fine not exceeding the statutory maximum (or both).[7869]

Copy of application: provisions as to service of documents

29.11 Section 1008 of the CA 2006 deals with the copy of the application with regard to provisions as to the service of documents. The following provisions apply for the purposes of s 1006 of the CA 2006 (copy of application to be given to members, employees, etc.), and s 1007 of the CA 2006 (copy of application to be given to new members, employees, etc.).[7870]

A document is treated as given to a person if it is delivered to him,[7871] or left at his proper address,[7872] or sent by post to him at that address.[7873]

For the purposes of s 1008(2) of the CA 2006 and s 7 of the Interpretation Act 1978 (c 30) (service of documents by post) as it applies in relation to that subsection, the proper address of a person is (a) in the case of a firm incorporated or formed in the United Kingdom, its registered or principal office;[7874] (b) in the case of a firm incorporated or formed outside the United Kingdom (i) if it has a place of business in the United Kingdom, its principal

---

[7861] CA 2006, s 1007(3).   [7862] CA 2006, s 1007(4).   [7863] CA 2006, s 1007(5)(a).

[7864] CA 2006, s 1007(5)(b).   [7865] CA 2006, s 1007(6)(a).   [7866] CA 2006, s 1007(6)(b).

[7867] CA 2006, s 1007(7)(a).   [7868] CA 2006, s 1007(7)(b)(i).

[7869] CA 2006, s 1007(7)(b)(ii).   [7870] CA 2006, s 1008(1).   [7871] CA 2006, s 1008(2)(a).

[7872] CA 2006, s 1008(2)(b).   [7873] CA 2006, s 1008(3)(a).   [7874] CA 2006, s 1008(3)(b)(i).

office in the United Kingdom,[7875] or (ii) if it does not have a place of business in the United Kingdom, its registered or principal office;[7876] (c) in the case of an individual, his last known address.[7877]

In the case of a creditor of the company a document is treated as given to him if it is left or sent by post to him at the place of business of his with which the company has had dealings by virtue of which he is a creditor of the company,[7878] or if there is more than one such place of business, at each of them.[7879]

Circumstances in which an application to be withdrawn

29.12 Section 1009 of the CA 2006 applies where, at any time on or after the day on which a company makes an application under s 1003 of the CA 2006 (application for a voluntary striking off) and before the day on which the application is finally dealt with or withdrawn (a) the company (i) changes its name,[7880] (ii) trades or otherwise carries on business,[7881] (iii) makes a disposal for value of any property or rights, other than those which it was necessary or expedient for it to hold for the purpose of making, or proceeding with, an application under that section,[7882] or (iv) engages in any activity, except one to which ss 1009(4) of the CA 2006 applies;[7883] (b) an application is made to the court under Part 26 of the CA 2006 on behalf of the company for the sanctioning of a compromise or arrangement;[7884] (c) a voluntary arrangement in relation to the company is proposed under Part 1 of the Insolvency Act 1986 (c 45) or Part 2 of the Insolvency (Northern Ireland) Order 1989 (SI 1989/ 2405 (NI 19));[7885] (d) an application to the court for an administration order in respect of the company is made under para 12 of Schedule B1 to that Act or para 13 of Schedule B1 to that Order;[7886] (e) an administrator is appointed in respect of the company under para 14 or 22 of Schedule B1 to that Act or para 15 or 23 of Schedule B1 to that Order, or a copy of a notice of intention to appoint an administrator of the company under any of those provisions is filed with the court;[7887] (f) there arise any of the circumstances in which, under s 84(1) of that Act or Article 70 of that Order, the company may be voluntarily wound up;[7888] (g) a petition is presented for the winding up of the company by the court under Part 4 of that Act or Part 5 of that Order;[7889] (h) a receiver or manager of the company's property is appointed;[7890] or (i) a judicial factor is appointed to administer the company's estate.[7891]

[7875] CA 2006, s 1008(3)(b)(ii).   [7876] CA 2006, s 1008(3)(c).
[7877] CA 2006, s 1008(4)(a).   [7878] CA 2006, s 1008(4)(b).
[7879] CA 2006, s 1009(1)(a)(i).   [7880] CA 2006, s 1009(1)(a)(i).
[7881] CA 2006, s 1009(1)(a)(ii).   [7882] CA 2006, s 1009(1)(a)(iii).
[7883] CA 2006, s 1009(1)(a)(iv).   [7884] CA 2006, s 1009(1)(b).
[7885] CA 2006, s 1009(1)(c).   [7886] CA 2006, s 1009(1)(d).   [7887] CA 2006, s 1009(1)(e).
[7888] CA 2006, s 1009(1)(f).   [7889] CA 2006, s 1009(1)(g).   [7890] CA 2006, s 1009(1)(h).
[7891] CA 2006, s 1009(1)(i).

A person who, at the end of a day on which any of the events mentioned in subs (1) occurs, is a director of the company must secure that the company's application is withdrawn forthwith.[7892]

For the purposes of s 1009(1)(a) of the CA 2006, a company is not treated as trading or otherwise carrying on business by virtue only of the fact that it makes a payment in respect of a liability incurred in the course of trading or otherwise carrying on business.[7893]

The excepted activities referred to in s 1009(1)(a)(iv) of the CA 2006 are (a) any activity necessary or expedient for the purposes of (i) making, or proceeding with, an application under s 1003 of the CA 2006 (application for voluntary striking off),[7894] (ii) concluding affairs of the company that are outstanding because of what has been necessary or expedient for the purpose of making, or proceeding with, such an application, or (iii) complying with any statutory requirement;[7895] (b) any activity specified by the Secretary of State by order for the purposes of this subsection.[7896] An order under para (b) is subject to negative resolution procedure.

A person who fails to perform the duty imposed on him by s 1009 of the CA 2006 commits an offence.[7897]

In proceedings for an offence under s 1009 of the CA 2006 it is a defence for the accused to prove that at the time of the failure he was not aware of the fact that the company had made an application under s 1003 of the CA 2006,[7898] or that he took all reasonable steps to perform the duty.[7899]

A person guilty of an offence under s 1009 of the CA 2006 is liable on conviction on indictment, to a fine;[7900] and on summary conviction, to a fine not exceeding the statutory maximum.[7901]

Withdrawal of an application

29.13 Section 1010 of the CA 2006 states that an application under s 1003 of the CA 2006 is withdrawn by notice to the registrar.

Meaning of 'creditor'

29.14 Section 1011 of the CA 2006 defines a 'creditor' for the purposes of Chapter 1. The term includes a contingent or prospective creditor.

Property of a Dissolved Company

29.15 Chapter 2 of Part 31 of the CA 2006 is concerned with the property of the dissolved company once the company has been struck off.

[7892] CA 2006, s 1009(2).   [7893] CA 2006, s 1009(3).   [7894] CA 2006, s 1009(4)(a)(i).
[7895] CA 2006, s 1009(4)(a)(ii).   [7896] CA 2006, s 1009(4)(a)(iii).
[7897] CA 2006, s 1009(4)(b).   [7898] CA 2006, s 1009(5).   [7899] CA 2006, s 1009(6)(a).
[7900] CA 2006, s 1009(6)(b).   [7901] CA 2006, s 1009(7)(a).

vesting as *bona vacantia*

... ... of *dissolved company to be* bona vacantia

29.16 Section 1012 of the CA 2006 states that when a company is dissolved, all property and rights whatsoever vested in or held on trust for the company immediately before its dissolution (including leasehold property, but not including property held by the company on trust for another person), are deemed to be *bona vacantia* and accordingly belong to the Crown, or to the Duchy of Lancaster or to the Duke of Cornwall for the time being (as the case may be),[7902] and vest and may be dealt with in the same manner as other *bona vacantia* accruing to the Crown, to the Duchy of Lancaster or to the Duke of Cornwall.[7903]

Section 1012(1) of the CA 2006 applies subject to the possible restoration of the company to the register under Chapter 3 to Part 31 of the CA 2006 (see s 1034 of the CA 2006).[7904]

Crown disclaimer of property vesting as bona vacantia

29.17 Section 1013 of the CA 2006 deals with Crown disclaimers of property vesting as *bona vacantia*. Where property vests in the Crown under s 1012 of the CA 2006, the Crown's title to it under that section may be disclaimed by a notice signed by the Crown representative, that is to say the Treasury Solicitor, or, in relation to property in Scotland, the Queen's and Lord Treasurer's Remembrancer.[7905]

The right to execute a notice of disclaimer under s 1013 of the CA 2006 may be waived by or on behalf of the Crown either expressly or by taking possession.[7906]

A notice of disclaimer must be executed within three years after the date on which the fact that the property may have vested in the Crown under s 1012 of the CA 2006 first comes to the notice of the Crown representative,[7907] or if ownership of the property is not established at that date, the end of the period reasonably necessary for the Crown representative to establish the ownership of the property.[7908]

If an application in writing is made to the Crown representative by a person interested in the property requiring him to decide whether he will or will not disclaim, any notice of disclaimer must be executed within 12 months after the making of the application or such further period as may be allowed by the court.[7909]

[7902] CA 2006, s 1012(1)(a). [7903] CA 2006, s 1012(1)(b). [7904] CA 2006, s 1012(2).
[7905] CA 2006, s 1013(1). [7906] CA 2006, s 1013(2). [7907] CA 2006, s 1013(3)(a).
[7908] CA 2006, s 1013(3)(b). [7909] CA 2006, s 1013(4).

A notice of disclaimer under s 1013 of the CA 2006 is of no effect if it is shown to have been executed after the end of the period specified by s 1013(3) or (4) of the CA 2006.[7910]

A notice of disclaimer under s 1013 of the CA 2006 must be delivered to the registrar and retained and registered by him.[7911]

Copies of it must be published in the Gazette and sent to any persons who have given the Crown representative notice that they claim to be interested in the property.[7912]

This section applies to property vested in the Duchy of Lancaster or the Duke of Cornwall under s 1012 of the CA 2006 as if for references to the Crown and the Crown representative there were respectively substituted references to the Duchy of Lancaster and to the Solicitor to that Duchy, or to the Duke of Cornwall and to the Solicitor to the Duchy of Cornwall, as the case may be.[7913]

Where a company is dissolved while still holding property, that property passes to the Crown. Section 656 of the CA 1985 provided that the Crown's title to the property could be disclaimed by a notice signed by the Crown representative. Under the CA 1985, this disclaimer was generally required to be executed within 12 months of the date on which vesting of the property came to the notice of the Crown representative. Section 1013 of the CA 2006 extends the 12-month period in restating the relevant provisions to three years, and provides that if ownership of the property is not established when the Crown representative first has notice that the property may have vested, that period runs from the end of the period reasonably necessary for the Crown representative to establish ownership. Section 656 of the CA 1985 also provided that a disclaimer may be made within three years of the Crown representative receiving an application from an interested party. Section 1013 of the CA 2006 has changed this to 12 months.

Effect of Crown disclaimer

29.18 Section 1014 of the CA 2006 deals with the effect of a Crown disclaimer. Where notice of a disclaimer is executed under s 1013 of the CA 2006 as respects any property, that property is deemed not to have vested in the Crown under s 1012 of the CA 2006.[7914]

The following sections contain provisions as to the effect of the Crown disclaimer, namely: ss 1015–1019 of the CA 2006 apply in relation to property in England and Wales or Northern Ireland; ss 1020–1022 of the CA 2006 apply in relation to property in Scotland.[7915]

[7910] CA 2006, s 1013(5).   [7911] CA 2006, s 1013(6).   [7912] CA 2006, s 1013(7).
[7913] CA 2006, s 1013(8).   [7914] CA 2006, s 1014(1).   [7915] CA 2006, s 1014(2).

Effect of Crown disclaimer: England and Wales and Northern Ireland

General effect of disclaimers

29.19 Section 1015 of the CA 2006 sets out the general effect of disclaimers. The Crown's disclaimer operates so as to terminate, as from the date of the disclaimer, the rights, interests and liabilities of the company in or in respect of the property disclaimed.[7916]

It does not, except so far as is necessary for the purpose of releasing the company from any liability, affect the rights or liabilities of any other person.[7917]

Disclaimer of leaseholds

29.20 Section 1016 of the CA 2006 sets out the disclaimer of leaseholds. The disclaimer of any property of a leasehold character does not take effect unless a copy of the disclaimer has been served (so far as the Crown representative is aware of their addresses) on every person claiming under the company as under a lessee or mortgagee, and either no application under s 1017 of the CA 2006 (power of court to make vesting order) is made with respect to that property before the end of the period of 14 days beginning with the day on which the last notice under this paragraph was served,[7918] or where such an application has been made, the court directs that the disclaimer shall take effect.[7919]

Where the court gives a direction under s 1016(1)(b) of the CA 2006 it may also, instead of or in addition to any order it makes under s 1017 of the CA 2006, make such order as it thinks fit with respect to fixtures, tenants' improvements and other matters arising out of the lease.[7920]

The term 'Crown representative' means (a) in relation to property vested in the Duchy of Lancaster, the Solicitor to that Duchy;[7921] (b) in relation to property vested in the Duke of Cornwall, the Solicitor to the Duchy of Cornwall;[7922] (c) in relation to property in Scotland, the Queen's and Lord Treasurer's Remembrancer;[7923] (d) in relation to other property, the Treasury Solicitor.[7924]

Power of court to make a vesting order

29.21 Section 1017 of the CA 2006 deals with the power of court to make a vesting order. The court may on application by a person who claims an

---

[7916] CA 2006, s 1015(1). [7917] CA 2006, s 1015(2). [7918] CA 2006, s 1016(1)(a).
[7919] CA 2006, s 1016(1)(b). [7920] CA 2006, s 1016(2). [7921] CA 2006, s 1016(3)(a).
[7922] CA 2006, s 1016(3)(b). [7923] CA 2006, s 1016(3)(c). [7924] CA 2006, s 1016(3)(d).

interest in the disclaimed property,[7925] or is under a liability in respect of the disclaimed property that is not discharged by the disclaimer,[7926] make an order under this section in respect of the property.

An order under s 1017 of the CA 2006 is an order for the vesting of the disclaimed property in, or its delivery to a person entitled to it (or a trustee for such a person),[7927] or a person subject to such a liability as is mentioned in s 1017(1)(b) of the CA 2006 (or a trustee for such a person).[7928]

An order under s 1017(2)(b) of the CA 2006 may only be made where it appears to the court that it would be just to do so for the purpose of compensating the person subject to the liability in respect of the disclaimer.[7929]

An order under this section may be made on such terms as the court thinks fit.[7930]

On a vesting order being made under this section, the property comprised in it vests in the person named in that behalf in the order without conveyance, assignment or transfer.[7931]

Protection of persons holding under a lease

29.22 Section 1018 of the CA 2006 applies to the protection of persons holding under a lease. The court must not make an order under s 1017 of the CA 2006 vesting property of a leasehold nature in a person claiming under the company as underlessee or mortgagee except on terms making that person subject to the same liabilities and obligations as those to which the company was subject under the lease,[7932] or if the court thinks fit, subject to the same liabilities and obligations as if the lease had been assigned to him.[7933]

Where the order relates to only part of the property comprised in the lease, s 1018(1) of the CA 2006 applies as if the lease had comprised only the property comprised in the vesting order.[7934]

A person claiming under the company as underlessee or mortgagee who declines to accept a vesting order on such terms is excluded from all interest in the property.[7935]

If there is no person claiming under the company who is willing to accept an order on such terms, the court has power to vest the company's estate and interest in the property in any person who is liable (whether personally or in a representative character, and whether alone or jointly with the company) to perform the lessee's covenants in the lease.[7936]

[7925] CA 2006, s 1017(1)(a).   [7926] CA 2006, s 1017(1)(b).   [7927] CA 2006, s 1017(2)(a).
[7928] CA 2006, s 1017(2)(b).   [7929] CA 2006, s 1017(3).   [7930] CA 2006, s 1017(4).
[7931] CA 2006, s 1017(5).   [7932] CA 2006, s 1018(1)(a).   [7933] CA 2006, s 1018(1)(b).
[7934] CA 2006, s 1018(2).   [7935] CA 2006, s 1018(3).   [7936] CA 2006, s 1018(4).

The court may vest that estate and interest in such a person freed and discharged from all estates, incumbrances and interests created by the company.[7937]

Land subject to rentcharge

29.23 Section 1019 of the CA 2006 states that where in consequence of the disclaimer land that is subject to a rentcharge vests in any person, neither he nor his successors in title are subject to any personal liability in respect of sums becoming due under the rentcharge, except sums becoming due after he, or some person claiming under or through him, has taken possession or control of the land or has entered into occupation of it.

Effect of a Crown disclaimer: Scotland

General effect of a disclaimer

29.24 Section 1020 of the CA 2006 sets out the general effect of disclaimer. The Crown's disclaimer operates to determine, as from the date of the disclaimer, the rights, interests and liabilities of the company, and the property of the company, in or in respect of the property disclaimed.[7938]

It does not (except so far as is necessary for the purpose of releasing the company and its property from liability) affect the rights or liabilities of any other person.[7939]

Power of court to make a vesting order

29.25 Section 1021 of the CA 2006 deals with the power of the court to make a vesting order. The court may on application by a person who either claims an interest in disclaimed property or is under a liability not discharged by this Act in respect of disclaimed property, and on hearing such persons as it thinks fit,[7940] make an order for the vesting of the property in or its delivery to any persons entitled to it, or to whom it may seem just that the property should be delivered by way of compensation for such liability, or a trustee for him.[7941]

The order may be made on such terms as the court thinks fit.[7942]

On a vesting order being made under this section, the property comprised in it vests accordingly in the person named in that behalf in the order, without conveyance or assignation for that purpose.[7943]

[7937] CA 2006, s 1018(5).   [7938] CA 2006, s 1020(1).   [7939] CA 2006, s 1020(2).
[7940] CA 2006, s 1021(1)(a).   [7941] CA 2006, s 1021(1)(b).   [7942] CA 2006, s 1021(2).
[7943] CA 2006, s 1021(3).

Protection of persons holding under a lease

29.26 Section 1022 of the CA 2006 deals with the protection of persons holding under a lease. Where the property disclaimed is held under a lease, the court must not make a vesting order in favour of a person claiming under the company, whether as sub-lessee,[7944] or as creditor in a duly registered or (as the case may be) recorded heritable security over a lease,[7945] except on the following terms.

The person must by the order be made subject to the same liabilities and obligations as those to which the company was subject under the lease in respect of the property,[7946] or if the court thinks fit, only to the same liabilities and obligations as if the lease had been assigned to him.

In either event (if the case so requires) the liabilities and obligations must be as if the lease had comprised only the property comprised in the vesting order.[7947]

A sub-lessee or creditor declining to accept a vesting order on such terms is excluded from all interest in and security over the property.[7948]

If there is no person claiming under the company who is willing to accept an order on such terms, the court has power to vest the company's estate and interest in the property in any person liable (either personally or in a representative character, and either alone or jointly with the company) to perform the lessee;s obligations under the lease.[7949]

The court may vest that estate and interest in such a person freed and discharged from all interests, rights and obligations created by the company in the lease or in relation to the lease.[7950]

For the purposes of this section a heritable security is duly recorded if it is recorded in the Register of Sasines,[7951] and is duly registered if registered in accordance with the Land Registration (Scotland) Act 1979 (c 33).[7952]

Supplementary provisions

Liability for rentcharge on a company's land after dissolution

29.27 Section 1023 of the CA 2006 applies where on the dissolution of a company, land in England and Wales or Northern Ireland that is subject to a rentcharge vests by operation of law in the Crown or any other person (the proprietor).[7953]

Neither the proprietor nor his successors in title are subject to any personal liability in respect of sums becoming due under the rentcharge, except sums

---

[7944] CA 2006, s 1022(1)(a).   [7945] CA 2006, s 1022(1)(b).   [7946] CA 2006, s 1022(2)(a).
[7947] CA 2006, s 1022(2)(b).   [7948] CA 2006, s 1022(3).   [7949] CA 2006, s 1022(4).
[7950] CA 2006, s 1022(5).   [7951] CA 2006, s 1022(6)(a).   [7952] CA 2006, s 1022(6)(b).
[7953] CA 2006, s 1023(1).

becoming due after the proprietor, or some person claiming under or through him, has taken possession or control of the land or has entered into occupation of it.[7954]

The term 'company' includes any body corporate.[7955]

Restoration to the register

29.28 Under CA 1985, where a company had been struck off the register, mechanisms were available (ss 651 and 653 of the CA 1985) whereby the company could be restored to the register following a court order. The Company Law Review Group[7956] recommended that an alternative, administrative restoration procedure should be available in certain circumstances. Sections 1024–1028 of the CA 2006 make provisions implementing the recommendation.

Administrative restoration to the register

Application for administrative restoration to the register

29.29 Section 1024 of the CA 2006 of the CA 2006 states that an application may be made to the registrar to restore to the register a company that has been struck off the register under s 1000 or s 1001 of the CA 2006 (power of registrar to strike off a defunct company).[7957]

An application under this section may be made whether or not the company has in consequence been dissolved.[7958]

An application under this section may only be made by a former director or former member of the company.[7959]

An application under this section may not be made after the end of the period of six years from the date of the dissolution of the company.[7960]

For this purpose an application is made when it is received by the registrar.

This section provides that an application may be made to restore a company that had been struck off under s 1000 or 1001 of the CA 2006; that it can be made whether or not the company has also been dissolved; that the application must be made by a former director or former member of the company, and that it must be made within six years of the date of dissolution.

Requirements for administrative restoration

29.30 Section 1025 of the CA 2006 sets out the requirement for administrative restorations. On an application under s 1024 of the CA 2006, the

---

[7954] CA 2006, s 1023(2).   [7955] CA 2006, s 1023(3).   [7956] *Final Report*, pp 227–229.
[7957] CA 2006, s 1024(1).   [7958] CA 2006, s 1024(2).   [7959] CA 2006, s 1024(3).
[7960] CA 2006, s 1024(4).

registrar shall restore the company to the register if, and only if, the following conditions are met.[7961]

The first condition is that the company was carrying on business or in operation at the time of its striking off.[7962]

The second condition is that, if any property or right previously vested in or held on trust for the company has vested as *bona vacantia*, the Crown representative has signified to the registrar in writing consent to the company's restoration to the register.[7963]

It is the applicant's responsibility to obtain that consent and to pay any costs (in Scotland, expenses) of the Crown representative in dealing with the property during the period of dissolution,[7964] or in connection with the proceedings on the application,[7965] that may be demanded as a condition of giving consent.

The third condition is that the applicant has delivered to the registrar such documents relating to the company as are necessary to bring up to date the records kept by the registrar,[7966] and paid any penalties under s 453 of the CA 2006 or corresponding earlier provisions (civil penalty for failure to deliver accounts) that were outstanding at the date of dissolution or striking off.[7967]

The term 'Crown representative' means (a) in relation to property vested in the Duchy of Lancaster, the Solicitor to that Duchy;[7968] (b) in relation to property vested in the Duke of Cornwall, the Solicitor to the Duchy of Cornwall;[7969] (c) in relation to property in Scotland, the Queen's and Lord Treasurer's Remembrancer;[7970] (d) in relation to other property, the Treasury Solicitor.[7971]

Section 1025 of the CA 2006 sets out the requirements for restoration, including the conditions that the company was carrying on business or in operation at the time of its striking off; that the Crown representative has given any consent that may be necessary; and that the applicant has delivered any documents necessary to bring the registrar's records up to date and has paid any penalties due at the date of dissolution or striking off.

Application to be accompanied by a statement of compliance

29.31 Section 1026 of the CA 2006 deals with the application to be accompanied by a statement of compliance. An application under s 1024 of the CA 2006 (application for administrative restoration to the register) must be accompanied by a statement of compliance.[7972]

The statement of compliance required is a statement that the person making the application has standing to apply (see s 1024(3) of the CA

[7961] CA 2006, s 1025(1).   [7962] CA 2006, s 1025(2).   [7963] CA 2006, s 1025(3).
[7964] CA 2006, s 1025(4)(a).   [7965] CA 2006, s 1025(4)(b).   [7966] CA 2006, s 1025(5)(a).
[7967] CA 2006, s 1025(5)(b).   [7968] CA 2006, s 1025(6)(a).   [7969] CA 2006, s 1025(6)(b).
[7970] CA 2006, s 1025(6)(c).   [7971] CA 2006, s 1025(6)(d).   [7972] CA 2006, s 1026(1).

2006),[7973] and that the requirements for administrative restoration (see s 1025 of the CA 2006) are met.[7974]

The registrar may accept the statement of compliance as sufficient evidence of those matters.[7975]

Section 1026 of the CA 2006 provides that an application for restoration must be accompanied by a statement that the applicant has the necessary standing to make the application, and that the requirements for administrative restoration have been met. The registrar may accept the statement of compliance as sufficient evidence of the matters stated in it.

Registrar's decision on applications for administrative restoration

29.32 Section 1027 of the CA 2006 states that the registrar must give notice to the applicant of the decision on an application under s 1024 of the CA 2006 (applications for administrative restoration to the register).[7976]

If the decision is that the company should be restored to the register, the restoration takes effect as from the date that notice is sent.[7977]

In the case of such a decision, the registrar must enter on the register a note of the date as from which the company's restoration to the register takes effect,[7978] and cause notice of the restoration to be published in the Gazette.[7979]

The notice under s 1027(3)(b) of the CA 2006 must state the name of the company or, if the company is restored to the register under a different name (see s 1033 of the CA 2006), that name and its former name,[7980] the company's registered number,[7981] and the date as from which the restoration of the company to the register takes effect.[7982]

This section provides that the registrar must give notice of his decision and that (if the decision is that the company is restored) the restoration takes effect from the date that notice is sent. The clause also sets out the consequential actions the registrar must take.

Effect of administrative restoration

29.33 Section 1028 of the CA 2006 deals with the effect of administrative restoration. The general effect of administrative restoration to the register is that the company is deemed to have continued in existence as if it had not been dissolved or struck off the register.[7983]

The company is not liable to a penalty under s 453 of the CA 2006 or any corresponding earlier provision (civil penalty for failure to deliver accounts)

[7973] CA 2006, s 1026(2)(a).   [7974] CA 2006, s 1026(2)(b).   [7975] CA 2006, s 1026(3).
[7976] CA 2006, s 1027(1).   [7977] CA 2006, s 1027(2).   [7978] CA 2006, s 1027(3)(a).
[7979] CA 2006, s 1027(3)(b).   [7980] CA 2006, s 1027(4)(a).   [7981] CA 2006, s 1027(4)(b).
[7982] CA 2006, s 1027(4)(c).   [7983] CA 2006, s 1028(1).

for a financial year in relation to which the period for filing accounts and reports ended after the date of dissolution or striking off,[7984] and before the restoration of the company to the register.[7985]

The court may give such directions and make such provision as seems just for placing the company and all other persons in the same position (as nearly as may be) as if the company had not been dissolved or struck off the register.[7986]

An application to the court for such directions or provision may be made any time within three years after the date of restoration of the company to the register.[7987]

Section 1028 of the CA 2006 provides that the effect of restoration is that the company is deemed to have continued in existence as if it had not been struck off, and that application may be made to the court within three years of restoration for the court to make such directions as may be needed to place the company itself, and other persons, in the same position as they would have been had the company not been struck off.

Restoration to the register by the court

29.34 Sections 1029–1032 of the CA 2006 bring together two separate procedures for a company to be restored to the register by court order (under ss 651 and 653 of the CA 1985). The Company Law Review Group recommended[7988] that the two separate procedures may be replaced by a single new procedure, which should largely be based on the precedent of the procedure under s 653 of the CA 1985.

Application to court for restoration to the register

29.35 Section 1029 of the CA 2006 deals with application to court for restoration to the registrar. An application may be made to the court to restore to the register a company (a) that has been dissolved under Chapter 9 of Part 4 of the Insolvency Act 1986 (c 45) or Chapter 9 of Part 5 of the Insolvency (Northern Ireland) Order 1989 (SI 1989/2405 (NI 19)) (dissolution of company after winding up);[7989] (b) that is deemed to have been dissolved under para 84(6) of Schedule B1 to that Act or para 85(6) of Schedule B1 to that Order (dissolution of company following administration);[7990] or (c) that has been struck off the register (i) under s 1000 or 1001 of the CA 2006 (power of registrar to strike off defunct company),[7991] or (ii) under s 1003 of the CA

[7984] CA 2006, s 1028(2)(a).   [7985] CA 2006, s 1028(2)(b).   [7986] CA 2006, s 1028(3).

[7987] CA 2006, s 1028(4).   [7988] *Final Report* pp 227–229.   [7989] CA 2006, s 1029(1)(a).

[7990] CA 2006, s 1029(1)(b).   [7991] CA 2006, s 1029(1)(c)(i).

2006 (voluntary striking off),[7992] whether or not the company has in consequence been dissolved.

An application under this section may be made by (a) the Secretary of State;[7993] (b) any former director of the company;[7994] (c) any person having an interest in land in which the company had a superior or derivative interest;[7995] (d) any person having an interest in land or other property (i) that was subject to rights vested in the company,[7996] or (ii) that was benefited by obligations owed by the company;[7997] (e) any person who but for the company's dissolution would have been in a contractual relationship with it;[7998] (f) any person with a potential legal claim against the company;[7999] (g) any manager or trustee of a pension fund established for the benefit of employees of the company;[8000] (h) any former member of the company (or the personal representatives of such a person);[8001] (i) any person who was a creditor of the company at the time of its striking off or dissolution;[8002] (j) any former liquidator of the company;[8003] (k) where the company was struck off the register under s 1003 of the CA 2006 (voluntary striking off), any person of a description specified by regulations under s 1006(1)(f) or 1007(2)(f) of the CA 2006 (persons entitled to notice of application for voluntary striking off), or by any other person appearing to the court to have an interest in the matter.[8004]

The section sets out that an application may be made for the restoration of companies that have been dissolved, are deemed to be dissolved, or have been struck off under the various provisions set out in s 1029(1) of the CA 2006. Section 1029(2) of the CA 2006 sets out the persons who may make such an application.

When application to the court may be made

29.36 Section 1030 of the CA 2006 sets out when application to the court may be made. An application to the court for restoration of a company to the register may be made at any time for the purpose of bringing proceedings against the company for damages for personal injury.[8005]

No order shall be made on such an application if it appears to the court that the proceedings would fail by virtue of any enactment as to the time within which proceedings must be brought.[8006]

In making that decision the court must have regard to its power under s 1032(3) of the CA 2006 (power to give consequential directions, etc.) to

---

[7992] CA 2006, s 1029(1)(c)(ii).   [7993] CA 2006, s 1029(2)(a).
[7994] CA 2006, s 1029(2)(b).   [7995] CA 2006, s 1029(2)(c).   [7996] CA 2006, s 1029(2)(d)(i).
[7997] CA 2006, s 1029(2)(d)(ii).   [7998] CA 2006, s 1029(2)(e).
[7999] CA 2006, s 1029(2)(f).   [8000] CA 2006, s 1029(2)(g).   [8001] CA 2006, s 1029(2)(h).
[8002] CA 2006, s 1029(2)(i).   [8003] CA 2006, s 1029(2)(j).   [8004] CA 2006, s 1029(2)(k).
[8005] CA 2006, s 1030(1).   [8006] CA 2006, s 1030(2).

direct that the period between the dissolution (or striking off) of the company and the making of the order is not to count for the purposes of any such enactment.[8007]

In any other case an application to the court for the restoration of a company to the register may not be made after the end of the period of six years from the date of the dissolution of the company, subject as follows.[8008]

In a case where the company has been struck off the register under s 1000 or 1001 of the CA 2006 (power of the registrar to strike off a defunct company),[8009] an application to the registrar has been made under s 1024 of the CA 2006 (application for administrative restoration to the register) within the time allowed for making such an application,[8010] and the registrar has refused the application, an application to the court under this section may be made within 28 days of notice of the registrar's decision being issued by the registrar, even if the period of six years mentioned in s 1030(4) of the CA 2006 above has expired.[8011]

For the purposes of s 1030 of the CA 2006: (a) 'personal injury' includes any disease and any impairment of a person's physical or mental condition;[8012] and (b) references to damages for personal injury include (i) any sum claimed by virtue of s 1(2)(c) of the Law Reform (Miscellaneous Provisions) Act 1934 (c 41) or section 14(2)(c) of the Law Reform (Miscellaneous Provisions) Act (Northern Ireland) 1937 (1937, c 9 (NI)) (funeral expenses)),[8013] and (ii) damages under the Fatal Accidents Act 1976 (c 30), the Damages (Scotland) Act 1976 (c 13) or the Fatal Accidents (Northern Ireland) Order 1977 (SI 1977/1251 (NI 18)).[8014]

Under the CA 1985, applications to the court under s 651 of the CA 1985 had to be made within two years, and under s 653 of the CA 2006 within 20 years. Section 1030 of the CA 2006 provides that the time limit for the new single procedure will generally be six years, although special provision is made (s 1030(5) of the CA 2006) for situations where an application for administrative restoration has been made and refused. Section 1030(1) of the CA 2006 makes clear that there is no time limit where the application is for the purpose of bringing proceedings against the company for damages for personal injury.

Decisions on application for restoration by the court

29.37 Section 1031 of the CA 2006 deals with decisions on application for restoration by the court. On an application under s 1029 of the CA 2006 the

---

[8007] CA 2006, s 1030(3).   [8008] CA 2006, s 1030(4).   [8009] CA 2006, s 1030(5)(a).
[8010] CA 2006, s 1030(5)(b).   [8011] CA 2006, s 1030(5)(c).   [8012] CA 2006, s 1030(6)(a).
[8013] CA 2006, s 1030(6)(b)(ii).   [8014] CA 2006, s 1030(6)(b)(ii).

court may order the restoration of the company to the register if the company was struck off the register under s 1000 or 1001 of the CA 2006 (power of the registrar to strike off defunct companies) and the company was, at the time of the striking off, carrying on business or in operation;[8015] or if the company was struck off the register under s 1003 of the CA 2006 (voluntary striking off) and any of the requirements of ss 1004–1009 of the CA 2006 was not complied with;[8016] or if in any other case the court considers it just to do so.[8017]

If the court orders restoration of the company to the register, the restoration takes effect on a copy of the court's order being delivered to the registrar.[8018]

The registrar must cause to be published in the Gazette notice of the restoration of the company to the register.[8019]

The notice must state the name of the company or, if the company is restored to the register under a different name (see s 1033 of the CA 2006), that name and its former name,[8020] the company's registered number,[8021] and the date on which the restoration took effect.[8022]

This section sets out the circumstances in which the court may order restoration (including any case in which the court considers it just to do so) and provides that restoration takes effect when the court's order is delivered to the registrar. It also requires the registrar to give appropriate public notice of the restoration.

Effect of court orders for restoration to the register

29.38 Section 1032 of the CA 2006 sets out the effect of a court order for restoration to the registrar. The general effect of an order by the court for restoration to the register is that the company is deemed to have continued in existence as if it had not been dissolved or struck off the register.[8023]

The company is not liable to a penalty under s 453 of the CA 2006 or any corresponding earlier provision (civil penalties for failure to deliver accounts) for a financial year in relation to which the period for filing accounts and reports ended after the date of dissolution or striking off,[8024] and before the restoration of the company to the register.[8025]

The court may give such directions and make such provision as seems just for placing the company and all other persons in the same position (as nearly as may be) as if the company had not been dissolved or struck off the register.[8026]

[8015] CA 2006, s 1031(1)(a).   [8016] CA 2006, s 1031(1)(b).   [8017] CA 2006, s 1031(1)(c).
[8018] CA 2006, s 1031(2).   [8019] CA 2006, s 1031(3).   [8020] CA 2006, s 1031(4)(a).
[8021] CA 2006, s 1031(4)(b).   [8022] CA 2006, s 1031(4)(c).   [8023] CA 2006, s 1032(1).
[8024] CA 2006, s 1032(2)(a).   [8025] CA 2006, s 1032(2)(b).   [8026] CA 2006, s 1032(3).

The court may also give directions as to (a) the delivery to the registrar of such documents relating to the company as are necessary to bring up to date the records kept by the registrar;[8027] (b) the payment of the costs (in Scotland, expenses) of the registrar in connection with the proceedings for the restoration of the company to the register;[8028] (c) where any property or right previously vested in or held on trust for the company has vested as *bona vacantia*, the payment of the costs (in Scotland, expenses) of the Crown representative (i) in dealing with the property during the period of dissolution,[8029] or (ii) in connection with the proceedings on the application.[8030]

The term 'Crown representative' means (a) in relation to property vested in the Duchy of Lancaster, the Solicitor to that Duchy;[8031] (b) in relation to property vested in the Duke of Cornwall, the Solicitor to the Duchy of Cornwall;[8032] (c) in relation to property in Scotland, the Queen's and Lord Treasurer's Remembrancer;[8033] (d) in relation to other property, the Treasury Solicitor.[8034]

This section provides that the effect of restoration is that the company is deemed to have continued in existence as if it had not been struck off and that the court may make such directions as are needed to place the company itself, and other persons, in the same position as they would have been had the company not been struck off. The court may also make directions as to the issues set out in s 1032(4) of the CA 2006 to do with the company's file at Companies House and costs.

Supplementary provisions

Company's name on restoration

29.39 Section 1033 of the CA 2006 deals with the company's name on registration. A company is restored to the register with the name it had before it was dissolved or struck off the register, subject to the following provisions.[8035]

If at the date of restoration the company could not be registered under its former name without contravening s 66 of the CA 2006 (name not to be the same as another in the registrar's index of company names), it must be restored to the register (a) under another name specified (i) in the case of administrative restoration, in the application to the registrar,[8036] or (ii) in the case of restoration under a court order, in the court's order;[8037] or (b) as if its registered number was also its name.[8038]

[8027] CA 2006, s 1032(4)(a).   [8028] CA 2006, s 1032(4)(b).   [8029] CA 2006, s 1032(4)(c)(i).
[8030] CA 2006, s 1032(4)(c)(ii).   [8031] CA 2006, s 1032(5)(a).
[8032] CA 2006, s 1032(5)(b).   [8033] CA 2006, s 1032(5)(c).   [8034] CA 2006, s 1032(5)(d).
[8035] CA 2006, s 1033(1).   [8036] CA 2006, s 1033(2)(a)(i).
[8037] CA 2006, s 1033(2)(a)(ii).   [8038] CA 2006, s 1033(2)(b).

References to a company's being registered in a name, and to registration in that context, shall be read as including the company's being restored to the register.

If a company is restored to the register under a name specified in the application to the registrar, the provisions of s 80 of the CA 2006 (change of name: registration and issue of a new certificate of incorporation), and s 81 of the CA 2006 (change of name: effect),apply as if the application to the registrar were notice of a change of name.[8039]

If a company is restored to the register under a name specified in the court's order, the provisions of s 80 of the CA 2006 (change of name: registration and issue of a new certificate of incorporation), and s 81 of the CA 2006 (change of name: effect) apply as if the copy of the court order delivered to the registrar were notice of a change a name.[8040]

If the company is restored to the register as if its registered number was also its name the company must change its name within 14 days after the date of the restoration;[8041] the change may be made by resolution of the directors (without prejudice to any other method of changing the company's name);[8042] the company must give notice to the registrar of the change,[8043] and ss 80 and 81 of the CA 2006 apply as regards the registration and effect of the change.[8044]

If the company fails to comply with s 1033(5)(a) or (c) of the CA 2006 an offence is committed by the company,[8045] and every officer of the company who is in default.[8046] A person guilty of an offence under s 1032(6) of the CA 2006 is liable on summary conviction to a fine not exceeding level 5 on the standard scale and, for continued contravention, a daily default fine not exceeding one-tenth of level 5 on the standard scale.[8047]

This section establishes the fundamental position that a company is restored to the register with the name it had before it was struck off, but also makes new provision for circumstances where restoration of a company would have the effect that two companies with the same or very similar names would appear in the registrar's index. There is a procedure for the restored company to change its name.

Effect of restoration to the register where a property has vested as bona vacantia

29.40 Section 1034 of the CA 2006 deals with the effect of restoration to the registrar where property has vested as *bona vacantia*. The person in whom any property or right is vested by s 1012 of the CA 2006 (property of

---

[8039] CA 2006, s 1033(3).   [8040] CA 2006, s 1033(4).   [8041] CA 2006, s 1033(5)(a).
[8042] CA 2006, s 1033(5)(b).   [8043] CA 2006, s 1033(5)(c).   [8044] CA 2006, s 1033(5)(d).
[8045] CA 2006, s 1033(6)(a).   [8046] CA 2006, s 1033(6)(b).   [8047] CA 2006, s 1033(7).

dissolved company to be *bona vacantia*) may dispose of, or of an interest in, that property or right despite the fact that the company may be restored to the register under Chapter 3 of the CA 2006.[8048]

If the company is restored to the register (a) the restoration does not affect the disposition (but without prejudice to its effect in relation to any other property or right previously vested in or held on trust for the company);[8049] and (b) the Crown or, as the case may be, the Duke of Cornwall shall pay to the company an amount equal to (i) the amount of any consideration received for the property or right or, as the case may be, the interest in it,[8050] or (ii) the value of any such consideration at the time of the disposition,[8051] or, if no consideration was received an amount equal to the value of the property, right or interest disposed of, as at the date of the disposition.

There may be deducted from the amount payable under subs (2)(b) the reasonable costs of the Crown representative in connection with the disposition (to the extent that they have not been paid as a condition of administrative restoration or pursuant to a court order for restoration).[8052]

Where a liability accrues under s 1033(2) of the CA 2006 in respect of any property or right, which before the restoration of the company to the register had accrued as *bona vacantia* to the Duchy of Lancaster, the Attorney General of that Duchy shall represent Her Majesty in any proceedings arising in connection with that liability.[8053]

Where a liability accrues under s 1033(2) of the CA 2006 in respect of any property or right, which before the restoration of the company to the register had accrued *as bona vacantia* to the Duchy of Cornwall, such persons as the Duke of Cornwall (or other possessor for the time being of the Duchy) may appoint shall represent the Duke (or other possessor) in any proceedings arising out of that liability.[8054]

The term 'Crown representative' means (a) in relation to property vested in the Duchy of Lancaster, the Solicitor to that Duchy;[8055] (b) in relation to property vested in the Duke of Cornwall, the Solicitor to the Duchy of Cornwall;[8056] (c) in relation to property in Scotland, the Queen's and Lord Treasurer's Remembrancer;[8057] (d) in relation to other property, the Treasury Solicitor.[8058]

This section replaces s 655 of the CA 1985 with little change of substance. However, it makes a new provision (s 1033(3) of the CA 2006) that, where a company's property has passed to the Crown and been disposed of, Crown, in reimbursing the newly-restored company, may deduct the reasonable costs of sale that were incurred.

[8048] CA 2006, s 1034(1).   [8049] CA 2006, s 1034(2)(a).   [8050] CA 2006, s 1034(2)(b)(i).
[8051] CA 2006, s 1034(2)(b)(ii).   [8052] CA 2006, s 1034(3).   [8053] CA 2006, s 1034(4).
[8054] CA 2006, s 1034(5).   [8055] CA 2006, s 1034(6)(a).   [8056] CA 2006, s 1034(6)(b).
[8057] CA 2006, s 1034(6)(c).   [8058] CA 2006, s 1034(6)(d).

Chapter 30

Offences under the Companies Acts

Introduction

30.1 Part 36 of the CA 2006 addresses the offences under the Companies Acts. It comprises 13 sections.

The Company Law Review Group sought to draw out the basis on which criminal liability for a breach of Companies Acts requirements was allocated under the CA 1985 to companies and to officers of companies. They stated in their *Final Report* that a reformed Companies Act must be underpinned by effective and proportionate sanctions and enforcement.

The key changes in the CA 2006 are refinements to the 'officer in default' framework, to make it clearer which individuals in which circumstances may be liable for a breach; and removal of criminal liability from the company itself in certain circumstances.

The general principle adopted as to whether a company should be liable for a breach of the requirements of Companies Acts is that, where the only victims of the offence are the company or its members, the company should not be liable for the offence. On the other hand, where members or the company are potential victims, but not the only ones, then the company should be potentially liable for a breach, whether or not the offence may also harm the company or its members.

Liability of officer in default

Liability of officer in default

30.2 Section 1,121 of the CA 2006 sets out the liability of officer in default. It applies for the purposes of any provision of the Companies Acts to the effect that, in the event of contravention of an enactment in relation to a company, an offence is committed by every officer of the company who is in default.[8059]

[8059] CA 2006, s 1121(1).

The term 'officer' includes any director, manager or secretary,[8060] and any person who is to be treated as an officer of the company for the purposes of the provision in question.[8061]

An officer is 'in default' for the purposes of the provision, if he authorises or permits, participates in, or fails to take all reasonable steps to prevent, the contravention.[8062]

Section 1121 of the CA 2006 specifies which persons may be liable as an officer of a company, for an offence committed by the company under the CA 2006 or the other Companies Acts. It only applies where another provision expressly states that an offence is commited by every officer of a company who is in default.

An 'officer' of a company is defined as including a director, manager or (company) secretary, and any person who is to be treated as an officer of the company for the purposes of the provisions in question. An officer is liable for an offence when he is 'in default', meaning he authorises or permits, participates in, or fails to take all reasonable steps to prevent the offence being committed.

Liability of company as officer in default

30.3 Section 1122 of the CA 2006 states that where a company is an officer of another company, it does not commit an offence as an officer in default unless one of its officers is in default.[8063]

Where any such offence is committed by a company the officer in question also commits the offence and is liable to be proceeded against and punished accordingly.[8064]

The terms 'officer' and 'in default' have the meanings given by s 1121 of the CA 2006.[8065]

Under this provision, where a company is an officer of another company, liability for a breach of company law can be fixed upon the company as an officer only if one of its officers is in default.

Application to bodies other than companies

30.4 Section 1123 of the CA 2006 states that s 1121 of the CA 2006 (liability of officers in default) applies to a body other than a company as it applies to a company.[8066]

As it applies in relation to a body corporate other than a company (a) the reference to a director of the company shall be read as referring (i) where the body's affairs are managed by its members, to a member of the body,[8067] (ii) in

---

[8060] CA 2006, s 1121(2)(a). [8061] CA 2006, s 1121(2)(b). [8062] A 2006, s 1121(3).
[8063] CA 2006, s 1122(1). [8064] CA 2006, s 1122(2). [8065] CA 2006, s 1122(3).
[8066] CA 2006, s 1123(1). [8067] CA 2006, s 1123(2)(a)(i).

any other case, to any corresponding officer of the body;[8068] and (b) the reference to a manager or secretary of the company shall be read as referring to any manager, secretary or similar officer of the body.[8069]

As it applies in relation to a partnership the reference to a director of the company shall be read as referring to a member of the partnership,[8070] and the reference to a manager or secretary of the company shall be read as referring to any manager, secretary or similar officer of the partnership.[8071]

As it applies in relation to an unincorporated body other than a partnership (a) the reference to a director of the company is to be read as referring (i) where the body's affairs are managed by its members, to a member of the body,[8072] (ii) in any other case, to a member of the governing body;[8073] and (b) the reference to a manager or secretary of the company is to be read as referring to any manager, secretary or similar officer of the body.[8074]

Section 1123 of the CA 2006 provides that s 1121 of the CA 2006 applies to persons in bodies other than companies, where their role is equivalent to that of an officer of a company. It makes specific provisions for bodies corporate, partnerships and unincorporated bodies.

Offences under the Companies Act 1985

Amendments of the Companies Act 1985

30.5 Section 1124 of the CA 2006 deals with amendments under the CA 1985. Schedule 3 of the CA 2006 contains amendments of the Companies Act 1985 (c 6) relating to offences.

This section introduces Schedule 3 of the CA 2006, which contains amendments to the CA relating to offences that remain in Parts 14 and 15 of the CA 1985.

Many of these amendments are necessary due to the repeal by the CA 2006 of Schedule 24 of the CA 1985. Schedule 24 set out the level of punishment for offences under the CA 1985. The provisions in Parts 14 and 15 of the CA 1985 are amended so that the applicable punishments are now included alongside the description of the offence instead of in Schedule 24.

Schedule 3 of the CA 2006 also makes amendments to the offences provisions remaining in Parts 14 and 15 of the CA 1985 to reflect the (non-textual) changes made to the Act by the Criminal Justice Act 2003. Section 282 of the Criminal Justice Act increases from six months to 12 months the maximum term of imprisonment to which a person is liable on summary conviction of an offence triable either way, and s 154(1) of that Act gives power to

[8068] CA 2006, s 1123(2)(a)(ii).   [8069] CA 2006, s 1123(2)(b).
[8070] CA 2006, s 1123(3)(a).   [8071] CA 2006, s 1123(3)(b).   [8072] CA 2006, s 1123(4)(a)(i).
[8073] CA 2006, s 1123(4)(a)(ii).   [8074] CA 2006, s 1123(4)(b).

magistrates to impose a 12-month term of imprisonment. The increased penalties only apply in England and Wales; in Scotland and Northern Ireland the maximum term of imprisonment that may be imposed on summary conviction remains six months. When the Act received Royal Assent, neither s 282 nor s 154(1) of the Criminal Justice Act 2003 had come into force (which the reason for the transitory provision in s 1131).

A number of the amendments make reference to 'the statutory maximum fine'. This was set at £5,000 at the time the Act received Royal Assent.

Schedule 3 of the CA 2006 makes only one substantive change to the offence provisions in Parts 14 and 15. This is to include a daily default fine, of one-fiftieth of the statutory maximum, for continued contravention of s 444(3) of the CA 2006 (failure to provided information about interests in shares). The levels of fine are:

- Level 1: £200;
- Level 2: £500;
- Level 3: £1,000;
- Level 4: £2,500;
- Level 5: £5,000.

The statutory maximum has also been set at £5,000 since the CA 2006 received Royal Assent.

General provisions

Meaning of 'daily default fine'

30.6 Section 1125 of the CA 2006 defines the expression 'daily default fine'. It defines what is meant in the Companies Acts, where it is provided that a person guilty of an offence is liable on summary conviction to a fine not exceeding a specified amount 'and, for continued contravention, a daily default fine' not exceeding a specified amount.[8075]

This means that the person is liable on a second or subsequent summary conviction of the offence to a fine not exceeding the latter amount for each day on which the contravention is continued (instead of being liable to a fine not exceeding the former amount).[8076]

Section 1125 of the CA 2006 replaces s 730(4) of the CA 1985.

Consents required for certain prosecutions

30.7 Section 1126 of the CA 2006 deals with consents required for certain prosecutions. It applies to proceedings for an offence under any of the

---

[8075] CA 2006, s 1125(1).   [8076] CA 2006, s 1125(2).

following provisions: namely, s 458, 460 or 949 of the CA 2006 of this Act (offences of unauthorised disclosure of information); s 953 of the CA 2006 of this Act (failure to comply with rules about takeover bid documents); s 448, 449, 450, 451 or 453A of the CA 1985 (c 6) (offences in connection with company investigations); s 798 of the CA 2006 or s 455 of the CA 1985 (offence of attempting to evade restrictions on shares).[8077]

No such proceedings are to be brought in England and Wales except by or with the consent of (a) in the case of an offence under (i) ss 458, 460 or 949 of the CA 2006,[8078] (ii) s 953 of the CA 2006,[8079] or (iii) ss 448, 449, 450, 451 or 453A of the CA 1985,[8080] the Secretary of State or the Director of Public Prosecutions; (b) in the case of an offence under s 798 of the CA 2006 or s 455 of the CA 1985, the Secretary of State.[8081]

No such proceedings are to be brought in Northern Ireland except by or with the consent of (a) in the case of an offence under (i) ss 458, 460 or 949 of the CA 2006,[8082] (ii) s 953 of the CA 2006,[8083] or (iii) ss 448, 449, 450, 451 or 453A of the CA 1985,[8084] the Secretary of State or the Director of Public Prosecutions for Northern Ireland; (b) in the case of an offence under s 798 of the CA 2006 or s 455 of the CA 1985, the Secretary of State.[8085]

This section provides that certain proceedings can only be brought with the consent of specified persons. It replaces s 732(1) and (2) of the CA 1985.

Summary proceedings: venue

30.8 Section 1127 of the CA 2006 states that summary proceedings for any offence under the Companies Acts may be taken against a body corporate, at any place at which the body has a place of business,[8086] and against any other person, at any place at which he is for the time being.[8087]

This is without prejudice to any jurisdiction exercisable apart from this section.[8088]

Section 1127 of the CA 2006 restates s 731(1) of the CA 1985. It specifies the possible venues for summary proceedings for any breach of Companies Acts requirements. For a body corporate the venue may be any place at which the body corporate has place of business, and for any other person, it may be any place that the person is.

[8077] CA 2006, s 1126(1).
[8078] CA 2006, s 1126(2)(a)(i).
[8079] CA 2006, s 1126(2)(a)(ii).
[8080] CA 2006, s 1126(2)(a)(iii).
[8081] CA 2006, s 1126(2)(b).
[8082] CA 2006, s 1126(3)(a)(i).
[8083] CA 2006, s 1126(3)(a)(ii).
[8084] CA 2006, s 1126(3)(a)(iii).
[8085] CA 2006, s 1126(3)(b).
[8086] CA 2006, s 1127(1)(a).
[8087] CA 2006, s 1127(1)(b).
[8088] CA 2006, s 1127(2).

Summary proceedings: time limit for proceedings

30.9 Section 1128 of the CA 2006 is concerned with summary proceedings with respect to time limits for proceedings. Information relating to an offence under the Companies Acts that is triable by a magistrates' court in England and Wales may be so tried if it is laid at any time within three years after the commission of the offence,[8089] and within 12 months after the date on which evidence sufficient in the opinion of the Director of Public Prosecutions or the Secretary of State (as the case may be) to justify the proceedings comes to his knowledge.[8090]

Summary proceedings in Scotland for an offence under the Companies Acts (a) must not be commenced after the expiration of three years from the commission of the offence;[8091] (b) subject to that, may be commenced at any time (i) within 12 months after the date on which evidence sufficient in the Lord Advocate's opinion to justify the proceedings came to his knowledge,[8092] or (ii) where such evidence was reported to him by the Secretary of State, within 12 months after the date on which it came to the knowledge of the latter.[8093]

Section 136(3) of the Criminal Procedure (Scotland) Act 1995 (c 46) (date when proceedings are deemed to be commenced) applies for the purposes of this subsection as for the purposes of that section.

A magistrates' court in Northern Ireland has jurisdiction to hear and determine a complaint charging the commission of a summary offence under the Companies Acts provided that the complaint is made within three years from the time when the offence was committed,[8094] and within 12 months from the date on which evidence sufficient in the opinion of the Director of Public Prosecutions for Northern Ireland or the Secretary of State (as the case may be) to justify the proceedings comes to his knowledge.[8095]

For the purposes of this section a certificate of the Director of Public Prosecutions, the Lord Advocate, the Director of Public Prosecutions for Northern Ireland or the Secretary of State (as the case may be) as to the date on which such evidence as is referred to above came to his notice is conclusive evidence.[8096]

This section restates s 731(2)–(4) of the CA 1985. It sets out time limits for summary proceedings. The prosecution must be commenced within three years of the offence being committed, and within one year of the prosecuting authorities receiving sufficient evidence to justify the prosecution.

[8089] CA 2006, s 1128(1)(a).   [8090] CA 2006, s 1128(1)(b).   [8091] CA 2006, s 1128(2)(a).
[8092] CA 2006, s 1128(2)(b)(i).   [8093] CA 2006, s 1128(2)(b)(ii).
[8094] CA 2006, s 1128(3)(a).   [8095] CA 2006, s 1128(3)(b).   [8096] CA 2006, s 1128(4).

Legal professional privilege

30.10 Section 1129 of the CA 2006 deals with legal professional privilege. In proceedings against a person for an offence under the Companies Acts, nothing in those Acts is to be taken to require any person to disclose any information that he is entitled to refuse to disclose on grounds of legal professional privilege (in Scotland, confidentiality of communications).

This section states s 732(3) of the CA 1985, and applies its provisions to all offences under the Companies Acts rather than just those instituted by the Director of Public prosecutions or the Secretary of State. It provides that the Companies Acts provisions on offences are not to be read as requiring any person to disclose information that is protected by legal professional privilege.

Proceedings against unincorporated bodies

30.11 Section 1130 of the CA 2006 deals with proceedings against unincorporated bodies. Proceedings for an offence under the Companies Acts alleged to have been committed by an unincorporated body must be brought in the name of the body (and not in that of any of its members).[8097]

For the purposes of such proceedings (a) any rules of court relating to the service of documents have effect as if the body were a body corporate;[8098] and (b) the following provisions apply as they apply in relation to a body corporate (i) in England and Wales, s 33 of the Criminal Justice Act 1925 (c 86) and Schedule 3 to the Magistrates' Courts Act 1980 (c 43),[8099] (ii) in Scotland, ss 70 and 143 of the Criminal Procedure (Scotland) Act 1995 (c 46),[8100] (iii) in Northern Ireland, s 18 of the Criminal Justice Act (Northern Ireland) 1945 (c 15 (NI)) and Article 166 of and Schedule 4 to the Magistrates' Courts (Northern Ireland) Order 1981 (SI 1981/1675 (NI 26)).[8101]

A fine imposed on an unincorporated body on its conviction of an offence under the Companies Acts must be paid out of the funds of the body.[8102]

This section restates s 734(1)–(4) of the CA 1985. It provides for proceedings for offences under the Companies Acts committed by unincorporated bodies to be brought against such bodies as if they corporate bodies.

Imprisonment on summary conviction in England and Wales: transitory provision

30.12 Section 1131 of the CA 2006 applies to any provision of the Companies Acts that provides that a person guilty of an offence is liable on

---

[8097] CA 2006, s 1130(1).   [8098] CA 2006, s 1130(2)(a).   [8099] CA 2006, s 1130(2)(b)(i).
[8100] CA 2006, s 1130(2)(b)(ii).   [8101] CA 2006, s 1130(2)(b)(iii).
[8102] CA 2006, s 1130(3).

summary conviction in England and Wales to imprisonment for a term not exceeding 12 months.[8103]

In relation to an offence committed before the commencement of s 154(1) of the Criminal Justice Act 2003 (c 44), for '12 months' substitute 'six months'.[8104]

Section 1131 of the CA 2006 provides for the period before the commencement of s 154(1) of the Criminal Justice Act 2003, which made new provision about the powers of magistrates' courts in England and Wales to impose sentences of imprisonment on summary conviction. For offences committed before s 154(1) was brought into force, the maximum term of imprisonment in England and Wales for a person guilty of an offence on summary conviction under the Companies Acts was six months instead of 12 months.

Production and inspection of documents

Production and inspection of documents where an offence suspected

30.13 Section 1132 of the CA 2006 states that an application under this section may be made in England and Wales, to a judge of the High Court by the Director of Public Prosecutions, the Secretary of State or a chief officer of police;[8105] in Scotland, to one of the Lords Commissioners of Justiciary by the Lord Advocate;[8106] in Northern Ireland, to the High Court by the Director of Public Prosecutions for Northern Ireland, the Department of Enterprise, Trade and Investment or a chief superintendent of the Police Service of Northern Ireland.[8107]

If on an application under this section there is shown to be reasonable cause to believe that any person has, while an officer of a company, committed an offence in connection with the management of the company's affairs,[8108] and that evidence of the commission of the offence is to be found in any documents in the possession or control of the company,[8109] an order under this section may be made.

The order may authorise any person named in it to inspect the documents in question, or any of them, for the purpose of investigating and obtaining evidence of the offence,[8110] or require the secretary of the company, or such other officer of it as may be named in the order, to produce the documents (or any of them) to a person named in the order at a place so named.[8111]

This section applies also in relation to documents in the possession or control of a person carrying on the business of banking, so far as they relate to the company's affairs, as it applies to documents in the possession or

[8103] CA 2006, s 1131(1).   [8104] CA 2006, s 1131(2)(a).   [8105] CA 2006, s 1132(1)(a).
[8106] CA 2006, s 1132(1)(b).   [8107] CA 2006, s 1132(1)(c).   [8108] CA 2006, s 1132(2)(a).
[8109] CA 2006, s 1132(2)(b).   [8110] CA 2006, s 1132(3)(a).   [8111] CA 2006, s 1132(3)(b).

control of the company, except that no such order as is referred to in subs (3)(b) may be made by virtue of this subsection.[8112]

The decision under this section of a judge of the High Court, any of the Lords Commissioners of Justiciary or the High Court is not appealable.[8113]

In this section 'document' includes information recorded in any form.[8114]

This section restates s 721 of the CA 1985. It makes provisions about orders for the production of documents where there is reasonable causes to believe that an offence has been committed.

Supplementary

Transitional provision

30.14 Section 1133 of the CA 2006 states that the provisions of this Part except s 1132 of the CA 2006 do not apply to offences committed before the commencement of the relevant provision.

This section provides that this Part of the Act (with the exception of s 1132 of the CA 2006) does not apply to offences committed before the commencement of the provision relevant to the offence.

[8112] CA 2006, s 1132(4).　　　[8113] CA 2006, s 1132(5).　　　[8114] CA 2006, s 1132(6).

Transparency Obligations and Related Matters

Introduction

31.1 The EC Transparency Directive[8115] came into effect in the UK on 20 January 2007. The Directive covers a wide spectrum of issues ranging from dissemination of information, notification of major shareholdings, and new requirements on the content and timing of periodic financial information such as annual reports and half-yearly reports.

The CA 2006 gives powers to the Financial Services Authority to make rules for the purposes of implementing the Directive. The FSA has now amended the Listing Rules and updated the Disclosure Rules Sourcebook – now known as the Disclosure and Transparency Rules.

There are new shorter deadlines for annual and half-yearly reports; the introduction of Interim Management Statements in the form of quarterly trading updates; a removal of the requirement to send out half-yearly reports to all shareholders, or to place an advertisement setting out the content in a national newspaper; and the preliminary results statements will be voluntary. The changes will not apply to all quoted companies immediately. They will apply according to the start date of the issuer's accounting year.

Part 43 of the CA 2006 is concerned with transparency obligations and related matters.

Sections 1265, 1266, 1267, 1268, 1270, 1271 and 1272 in Part 43 of the CA 2006 implement Directive 2004/109/EC on the harmonisation of transparency requirements in relation to information about issuers whose securities are admitted to trading on a regulated market and amending Directive 2001/34/EC. Section 1266 of the CA 2006 inserts seven new sections into Part 6 of the Financial Services and Markets Act 2000; ss 89A, 89B, 89C, 89D, 89E, 89F and 89G. The new sections give power to the competent authority (at present the Financial Services Authority (FSA)) to make rules for the purposes of the Transparency Directive (2004/109/EC) (Transparency

---

[8115] Directive 2004/109/EC of the European Parliament and of the Council of 15 December 2004.

Directive) and connected regulatory purposes. Sections 1267 and 1268 of the CA 2006 insert three and four sections, respectively, into Part 6 of FSMA 2000 (89H–89N) setting out the regulatory powers of the FSMA 2000 in connection with the Directive. Section 1270 of the CA 2006 inserts new ss 90A and 90B into FSMA 2000, which set out the issuers' liability in damages for disclosures required under the Transparency Directive, and s 1271 of the CA 2006 inserts a new s 100A into FSMA 2000, setting out provisions in relation to the exercise of the FSA's powers where the UK is a host member state.

The Transparency Directive imposes minimum harmonisation requirements on the information to be provided to the public, about issuers whose securities are traded on a regulated market, and the control of votes attached to shares in those issuers. It permits Member States to impose more stringent requirements on entities that they regulate but Member States, i.e. those states in which the issuers securities are traded on a regulated market, but whose competent authority are not responsible for primary oversight of that issuer, are not permitted to impose any requirements more stringent than those contained in the Transparency Directive.

There are three main categories of obligation that are imposed under the Transparency Directive, and that the FSA's transparency rules will implement in respect of UK markets and issuers: first, requirements for issuers to make public, at regular intervals, information about their financial position and the progress and management of the business of the issuer; second, requirements for holders of votes attached to shares of issuers to notify the issuers when the number of votes they control reaches specified proportions of the total votes available; and third, requirements for issuers to treat the holders of the same securities equally.

The detailed and technical provisions about the required notifications, disclosures and treatment of security-holders will be prescribed in rules made by the FSA under the new rule-making power at s 89A of the Financial Services and Markets Act 2000. The FSA is required by that Act to carry out consultation and a cost – benefit analysis when making any rules under this power.

Having the power to make these rules will promote the harmonisation of practice with other EU jurisdictions, and help enhance investor confidence through increased transparency of the financial markets.

Responsibility for the transposition of the Transparency Directive lies both with HM Treasury and with the FSA. The measures in the CA 2006 that implement the Transparency Directive are the responsibility of HM Treasury.

The transparency obligations directive

31.2 Section 1265 of the CA 2006 states that Part 6 of the Financial Services and Markets Act 2000 (c 8) (which makes provision about official listings, prospectus requirements for transferable securities, etc.), in s 103(1) (interpretation), at the appropriate place insert:

> the transparency obligations directive' means Directive 2004/109/EC of the European Parliament and of the Council relating to the harmonisation of transparency requirements in relation to information about issuers whose securities are admitted to trading on a regulated market.

The objective of s 1265 of the CA 2006 is to insert a definition of the 'transparency obligations directive' at the appropriate place in Part 6 of the Financial Services and Markets Act 2000 (FSMA).

Transparency obligations

Transparency rules

31.3 After s 89 of the Financial Services and Markets Act 2000 the following is inserted:[8116]

Transparency obligations

89A Transparency rules

(1) The competent authority may make rules for the purposes of the transparency obligations directive.

(2) The rules may include provision for dealing with any matters arising out of or related to any provision of the transparency obligations directive.

(3) The competent authority may also make rules:

    (a) for the purpose of ensuring that voteholder information in respect of voting shares traded on a UK market other than a regulated market is made public or notified to the competent authority;

    (b) providing for persons who hold comparable instruments (see section 89F(1)(c)) in respect of voting shares to be treated, in the circumstances specified in the rules, as holding some or all of the voting rights in respect of those shares.

(4) Rules under this section may, in particular, make provision:

    (a) specifying how the proportion of:

        (i) the total voting rights in respect of shares in an issuer, or

        (ii) the total voting rights in respect of a particular class of shares in an issuer, held by a person is to be determined;

    (b) specifying the circumstances in which, for the purposes of any determination of the voting rights held by a person (P) in respect of

[8116] CA 2006, s 1266(1).

voting shares in an issuer, any voting rights held, or treated by virtue of subsection (3)(b) as held, by another person in respect of voting shares in the issuer are to be regarded as held by P;

(c)   specifying the nature of the information which must be included in any notification;

(d)   about the form of any notification;

(e)   requiring any notification to be given within a specified period;

(f)   specifying the manner in which any information is to be made public and the period within which it must be made public;

(g)   specifying circumstances in which any of the requirements imposed by rules under this section does not apply.

(5)   Rules under this section are referred to in this Part as 'transparency rules'.

(6)   Nothing in sections 89B to 89G affects the generality of the power to make rules under this section.

89B Provision of voteholder information

(1)   Transparency rules may make provision for voteholder information in respect of voting shares to be notified, in circumstances specified in the rules:

(a)   to the issuer, or

(b)   to the public,

or to both.

(2)   Transparency rules may make provision for voteholder information notified to the issuer to be notified at the same time to the competent authority.

(3)   In this Part 'voteholder information' in respect of voting shares means information relating to the proportion of voting rights held by a person in respect of the shares.

(4)   Transparency rules may require notification of voteholder information relating to a person:

(a)   initially, not later than such date as may be specified in the rules for the purposes of the first indent of Article 30.2 of the transparency obligations directive, and

(b)   subsequently, in accordance with the following provisions.

(5)   Transparency rules under subsection (4)(b) may require notification of voteholder information relating to a person only where there is a notifiable change in the proportion of:

(a)   the total voting rights in respect of shares in the issuer, or

(b)   the total voting rights in respect of a particular class of share in the issuer,

held by the person.

(6)   For this purpose there is a 'notifiable change' in the proportion of voting rights held by a person when the proportion changes:

(a) from being a proportion less than a designated proportion to a propor-
     tion equal to or greater than that designated proportion,

(b) from being a proportion equal to a designated proportion to a propor-
     tion greater or less than that designated proportion, or

(c) from being a proportion greater than a designated proportion to a
     proportion equal to or less than that designated proportion.

(7) In subsection (6) 'designated' means designated by the rules.

89C Provision of information by issuers of transferable securities

(1) Transparency rules may make provision requiring the issuer of transferable
     securities, in circumstances specified in the rules:
     (a) to make public information to which this section applies, or
     (b) to notify to the competent authority information to which this section
          applies,
     or to do both.

(2) In the case of every issuer, this section applies to:
     (a) information required by Article 4 of the transparency obligations
          directive;
     (b) information relating to the rights attached to the transferable securities,
          including information about the terms and conditions of those secur-
          ities which could indirectly affect those rights; and
     (c) information about new loan issues and about any guarantee or security
          in connection with any such issue.

(3) In the case of an issuer of debt securities, this section also applies to infor-
     mation required by Article 5 of the transparency obligations directive.

(4) In the case of an issuer of shares, this section also applies to:
     (a) information required by Article 5 of the transparency obligations
          directive;
     (b) information required by Article 6 of that directive;
     (c) voteholder information:
          (i)   notified to the issuer, or
          (ii) relating to the proportion of voting rights held by the issuer in
                respect of shares in the issuer;
     (d) information relating to the issuer's capital; and
     (e) information relating to the total number of voting rights in respect of
          shares or shares of a particular class.

89D Notification of voting rights held by issuer

(1) Transparency rules may require notification of voteholder information relat-
     ing to the proportion of voting rights held by an issuer in respect of voting
     shares in the issuer:

(a)   initially, not later than such date as may be specified in the rules for the purposes of the second indent of Article 30.2 of the transparency obligations directive, and

(b)   subsequently, in accordance with the following provisions.

(2)   Transparency rules under subsection (1)(b) may require notification of voteholder information relating to the proportion of voting rights held by an issuer in respect of voting shares in the issuer only where there is a notifiable change in the proportion of:

(a)   the total voting rights in respect of shares in the issuer, or

(b)   the total voting rights in respect of a particular class of share in the issuer, held by the issuer.

(3)   For this purpose there is a 'notifiable change' in the proportion of voting rights held by a person when the proportion changes:

(a)   from being a proportion less than a designated proportion to a proportion equal to or greater than that designated proportion,

(b)   from being a proportion equal to a designated proportion to a proportion greater or less than that designated proportion, or

(c)   from being a proportion greater than a designated proportion to a proportion equal to or less than that designated proportion.

(4)   In subsection (3) 'designated' means designated by the rules.

89E Notification of proposed amendment of issuer's constitution

Transparency rules may make provision requiring an issuer of transferable securities that are admitted to trading on a regulated market to notify a proposed amendment to its constitution:

(a)   to the competent authority, and

(b)   to the market on which the issuer's securities are admitted,

at times and in circumstances specified in the rules.

89F Transparency rules: interpretation, etc.

(1)   For the purposes of sections 89A to 89G:

(a)   the voting rights in respect of any voting shares are the voting rights attached to those shares,

(b)   a person is to be regarded as holding the voting rights in respect of the shares:

(i)   if, by virtue of those shares, he is a shareholder within the meaning of Article 2.1(e) of the transparency obligations directive;

(ii)   if, and to the extent that, he is entitled to acquire, dispose of or exercise those voting rights in one or more of the cases mentioned in Article 10(a)–(h) of the transparency obligations directive;

    (iii) if he holds, directly or indirectly, a financial instrument which results in an entitlement to acquire the shares and is an Article 13 instrument, and

  (c) a person holds a 'comparable instrument' in respect of voting shares if he holds, directly or indirectly, a financial instrument in relation to the shares which has similar economic effects to an Article 13 instrument (whether or not the financial instrument results in an entitlement to acquire the shares).

(2) Transparency rules under section 89A(3)(b) may make different provision for different descriptions of comparable instrument.

(3) For the purposes of sections 89A to 89G two or more persons may, at the same time, each be regarded as holding the same voting rights.

(4) In those sections:

- 'Article 13 instrument' means a financial instrument of a type determined by the European Commission under Article 13.2 of the transparency obligations directive;

- 'UK market' means a market that is situated or operating in the United Kingdom; 'voting shares' means shares of an issuer to which voting rights are attached.

89G Transparency rules: other supplementary provisions

(1) Transparency rules may impose the same obligations on a person who has applied for the admission of transferable securities to trading on a regulated market without the issuer's consent as they impose on an issuer of transferable securities.

(2) Transparency rules that require a person to make information public may include provision authorising the competent authority to make the information public in the event that the person fails to do so.

(3) The competent authority may make public any information notified to the authority in accordance with transparency rules.

(4) Transparency rules may make provision by reference to any provision of any rules made by the Panel on Takeovers and Mergers under Part 28 of the Companies Act 2006.

(5) Sections 89A to 89F and this section are without prejudice to any other power conferred by this Part to make Part 6 rules.

The effectiveness for the purposes of s 155 of the Financial Services and Markets Act 2000 (c 8) (consultation on proposed rules) of things done by the Financial Services Authority before this section comes into force with a view to making transparency rules (as defined in the provisions to be inserted in that Act by subs (1) above) is not affected by the fact that those provisions were not then in force.[8117]

Section 1266 of the CA 2006 inserts seven new sections into Part 6 of FSMA 2000: ss 89A, 89B, 89C, 89D 89E 89F and 89G. Part 6 of FSMA 2000 deals with certain aspects of the regulation of securities that are traded on regulated markets in the UK. These new sections make provision about rules that may be made by the 'competent authority' (which is the Financial Services Authority (the Authority)) for the purposes of the Transparency Directive (2004/109/EC) 'transparency rules'.

Section 89A(1) of FSMA 2000 enables the Authority to make transparency rules to implement the Transparency Directive in the UK. Section 89A(2) FSMA 2000 enables the rules to include provision for any matter arising out of or related to the Directive provisions.

The Transparency Directive itself covers issuers whose securities are traded on regulated markets, and people who hold voting rights attached to shares in such issuers. The scope of the rule-making power allows the rules to address other matters arising from the Directive's implementation, for example, to ensure that secondary legislation adopted by the Commission can be incorporated into the transparency rules, and that optional aspects of the Directive can be implemented, where the Authority considers this appropriate. It is expected that rules made under s 89A(1) of the FSMA 2000 will implement the Transparency Directive by requiring holders of votes attached to shares in issuers to make disclosure about their holdings at certain thresholds (see new s 89B of the FSMA 2000):

- requiring issuers to make public their annual accounts and reports, prepared in accordance with the EU International Accounts Standards Regulation (Regulation (EC) 1606/2002), and, where appropriate, half-yearly and interim management statements about their business (see new s 89C of the FSMA 2000);
- requiring issuers to make notification about voting rights held by themselves in respect of their own voting shares (see new s 89D of the FSMA 2000);
- requiring issuers to notify the Authority and the market of any proposed change to their constitution (see new s 89E of the FSMA 2000).

Section 89A(3)(a) of the FSMA 2000 allows the Authority to make rules about disclosures of voteholdings to UK markets that are not regulated markets (within the meaning of s 103(1) of the FSMA 2000) (such as the AIM). Section 89A(3)(b) of the FSMA 2000 enables the Authority to make rules about disclosure in relation to certain comparable instruments in respect of voting shares. These are instruments that give the holder a level of economic,

[8117] CA 2006, s 1266(2).

as opposed to legal, control over votes attached to shares. An example of the type of instrument that the rules could extend to cover is a contract for difference, known as a 'CFD'.

Section 89A(4) of the FSMA 2000 specifies further matters that the rules may cover. These include: how the proportion of voting rights held by an issuer is to be determined; when voting rights held by one person may be regarded as being held by another; the nature, form, timing and presentation of any notification; and the circumstances in which any of the requirements of s 89A of the FSMA 2000 may not apply.

The new s 89B of the FSMA 2000 sets out provisions for notifications by voteholders under transparency rules. Section 89B(1) of the FSMA 2000 specifies that notification can be required to be made to the issuer or to the public or to both. Under s 89B(2) of the FSMA 2000, rules may provide for such information to be notified at the same time to the Authority.

Section 89B(5) FSMA 2000 sets out the circumstances in which voteholders may be required to notify of a change in the proportion of voting rights (i.e. when a proportion crosses above or below, or reaches, a proportion designated in the rules).

A new s 89C of the FSMA 2000 sets out provisions for issuers of transferable securities to provide information under transparency rules. Section 89C(1) of the FSMA 2000 clarifies that information can be required to be given to the public or the Authority or both.

The rules cover annual financial reports (both financial statements and management reports) and, for certain issuers, half-yearly financial reports and interim management statements, as required by the Transparency Directive. The rules can also require issuers to disclose certain other information relating to voteholder information, information about the different classes of share they have issued and the total number of voting rights attached to each class, their own voteholdings, their capital, and information about new loan issues.

The new s 89D of the FSMA 2000 enables the rules to provide for issuers to make notification of the proportion of voting rights they hold in respect of their own voting shares. Section 89D(1)(a) of the FSMA 2000 permits rules to set the initial notification period in accordance with the requirements of the Transparency Directive at Article 30.2. Sections (1)(b), (2) and (3) of the FSMA 2000 set out the circumstances under which issuers of transferable securities must notify of a change in the proportion of voting rights (i.e. when a proportion crosses above or below, or reaches, a proportion designated in the rules).

The new s 89E of the FSMA 2000 enables the rules to provide that an issuer of transferable securities admitted to trading on a regulated market must notify a proposed amendment to its constitution to the Authority and to the market.

The new s 89F of the FSMA 2000 defines a number of terms used in ss 89A–89G of the FSMA 2000.

The new s 89G of the FSMA 2000 sets out further supplementary provisions relating to transparency rules. Section 89G(1) of the CA 2006 enables the Authority to make rules imposing the same obligations on a person who has applied for the admission of transferable securities to trading on a regulated market without the issuer's consent as they impose on an issuer of transferable securities. Section 89G(2) of the FSMA 2000 enables the Authority to make rules to allow it to make public information that voteholders or issuers are required to make public, where they fail to do so themselves. Section 89G(3) of the FSMA 2000 will enable the Authority to make public information notified to it in accordance with transparency rules.

There is some overlap between notifications required by the Panel on Takeovers and Mergers in the rules made under Part 28 of the CA 2006, and notifications required by the Transparency Directive. Section 89G(4) of the CA 2006 enables transparency rules to cross-refer to rules made by the Panel under Part 28, which will enable greater alignment between the two sets of rules.

A competent authority's power to call for information

31.4 Section 1267 of the CA 2006 states that in Part 6 of the Financial Services and Markets Act 2000 after the sections inserted by s 1266 of the CA 2006 above insert:

Power of competent authority to call for information

89H Competent authority's power to call for information

(1) The competent authority may by notice in writing given to a person to whom this section applies require him:

    (a) to provide specified information or information of a specified description, or

    (b) to produce specified documents or documents of a specified description.

(2) This section applies to:

    (a) an issuer in respect of whom transparency rules have effect;

    (b) a voteholder;

    (c) an auditor of:

        (i) an issuer to whom this section applies, or

        (ii) a voteholder;

    (d) a person who controls a voteholder;

    (e) a person controlled by a voteholder;

    (f) a director or other similar officer of an issuer to whom this section applies;

(g) a director or other similar officer of a voteholder or, where the affairs of a voteholder are managed by its members, a member of the voteholder.

(3) This section applies only to information and documents reasonably required in connection with the exercise by the competent authority of functions conferred on it by or under sections 89A to 89G (transparency rules).

(4) Information or documents required under this section must be provided or produced:

(a) before the end of such reasonable period as may be specified, and

(b) at such place as may be specified.

(5) If a person claims a lien on a document, its production under this section does not affect the lien.

89I Requirements in connection with call for information

(1) The competent authority may require any information provided under section 89H to be provided in such form as it may reasonably require.

(2) The competent authority may require:

(a) any information provided, whether in a document or otherwise, to be verified in such manner as it may reasonably require;

(b) any document produced to be authenticated in such manner as it may reasonably require.

(3) If a document is produced in response to a requirement imposed under section 89H, the competent authority may:

(a) take copies of or extracts from the document; or

(b) require the person producing the document, or any relevant person, to provide an explanation of the document.

(4) In subsection (3)(b) 'relevant person', in relation to a person who is required to produce a document, means a person who:

(a) has been or is a director or controller of that person;

(b) has been or is an auditor of that person;

(c) has been or is an actuary, accountant or lawyer appointed or instructed by that person; or

(d) has been or is an employee of that person.

(5) If a person who is required under section 89H to produce a document fails to do so, the competent authority may require him to state, to the best of his knowledge and belief, where the document is.

89J Power to call for information: supplementary provisions

(1) The competent authority may require an issuer to make public any information provided to the authority under section 89H.

(2) If the issuer fails to comply with a requirement under subsection (1), the competent authority may, after seeking representations from the issuer, make the information public.

(3) In sections 89H and 89I (power of competent authority to call for information):

- 'control' and 'controlled' have the meaning given by subsection (4) below;
- 'specified' means specified in the notice;
- 'voteholder' means a person who:
  (a) holds voting rights in respect of any voting shares for the purposes of sections 89A to 89G (transparency rules), or
  (b) is treated as holding such rights by virtue of rules under section 89A(3)(b).

(4) For the purposes of those sections a person ('A') controls another person ('B') if:

(a) A holds a majority of the voting rights in B,

(b) A is a member of B and has the right to appoint or remove a majority of the members of the board of directors (or, if there is no such board, the equivalent management body) of B,

(c) A is a member of B and controls alone, pursuant to an agreement with other shareholders or members, a majority of the voting rights in B, or

(d) A has the right to exercise, or actually exercises, dominant influence or control over B.

(5) For the purposes of subsection (4)(b):

(a) any rights of a person controlled by A, and

(b) any rights of a person acting on behalf of A or a person controlled by A, are treated as held by A.

Section 1267 of the CA 2006 inserts three new sections into Part 6 of the FSMA 2000: ss 89H–89J. The new s 89H of the FSMA 2000 permits the Authority to call for information from specified persons, set out in s 89H(2) of the FSMA 2000, including issuers of shares and their auditors and directors, and voteholders and their auditors, directors and persons controlling or controlled by voteholders. Section 89H(3) of the FSMA 2000 limits the Authority to requesting information and documents reasonably required in connection with the transparency rules. Section 89H(4) of the FSMA 2000 enables the Authority to determine the timeframe for the production and provision of information, and the location for the information to be provided. Section 89H(5) of the FSMA 2000 makes it clear that the production of the material as required by this section does not affect any lien on a document.

The new s 89I of the FSMA 2000 sets outs the requirements connected with the Authority's power to call for information. The Authority will be empowered to specify the form of the information or documents it calls for under s 89H(1) of the FSMA 2000, and may require its authentication or verification (s 89I(2) of the FSMA 2000). The Authority is permitted, under s 89I(3) of the FSMA 2000, to take copies of and extracts from the documentation provided, and may also require the persons providing the information, or any 'relevant person' within the meaning of s 89I(4) of the FSMA 2000 (which includes directors, auditors, actuaries, accountants, lawyers and employees), to submit an explanation of any documentation produced.

If a person fails to comply with the requirement to produce a document, the Authority is permitted under s 89I(5) of the FSMA 2000 to require a person to state where the document is. The new s 89J of the FSMA 2000 sets out supplementary provisions in relation to the competent authority's power to call for information in ss 89H and 89I of the FSMA 2000.

Powers exercisable in case of an infringement of
transparency obligation

31.5 Section 1268 of the CA 2006 states that in Part 6 of the Financial Services and Markets Act 2000 (c 8), after the sections inserted by s 1267 of the CA 2006 above insert:

Powers exercisable in case of infringement of transparency obligation

89K Public censure of issuer

(1) If the competent authority finds that an issuer of securities admitted to trading on a regulated market is failing or has failed to comply with an applicable transparency obligation, it may publish a statement to that effect.

(2) If the competent authority proposes to publish a statement, it must give the issuer a warning notice setting out the terms of the proposed statement.

(3) If, after considering any representations made in response to the warning notice, the competent authority decides to make the proposed statement, it must give the issuer a decision notice setting out the terms of the statement.

(4) A notice under this section must inform the issuer of his right to refer the matter to the Tribunal (see s 89N of the FSMA 2000) and give an indication of the procedure on such a reference.

(5) In this section 'transparency obligation' means an obligation under:

   (a) a provision of transparency rules, or

   (b) any other provision made in accordance with the transparency obligations directive.

(6) In relation to an issuer whose home State is a member State other than the United Kingdom, any reference to an applicable transparency obligation must be read subject to s 100A(2).

89L Power to suspend or prohibit trading of securities

(1)   This section applies to securities admitted to trading on a regulated market.

(2)   If the competent authority has reasonable grounds for suspecting that an applicable transparency obligation has been infringed by an issuer, it may:

    (a)   suspend trading in the securities for a period not exceeding ten days,

    (b)   prohibit trading in the securities, or

    (c)   make a request to the operator of the market on which the issuer's securities are traded:

        (i)   to suspend trading in the securities for a period not exceeding ten days, or

        (ii)   to prohibit trading in the securities.

(3)   If the competent authority has reasonable grounds for suspecting that a provision required by the transparency obligations directive has been infringed by a voteholder of an issuer, it may:

    (a)   prohibit trading in the securities, or

    (b)   make a request to the operator of the market on which the issuer's securities are traded to prohibit trading in the securities.

(4)   If the competent authority finds that an applicable transparency obligation has been infringed, it may require the market operator to prohibit trading in the securities.

(5)   In this section 'transparency obligation' means an obligation under:

    (a)   a provision contained in transparency rules, or

    (b)   any other provision made in accordance with the transparency obligations directive.

(6)   In relation to an issuer whose home State is a member State other than the United Kingdom, any reference to an applicable transparency obligation must be read subject to section 100A(2).

89M Procedure under section 89L

(1)   A requirement under section 89L takes effect:

    (a)   immediately, if the notice under subsection (2) states that that is the case;

    (b)   in any other case, on such date as may be specified in the notice.

(2)   If the competent authority:

    (a)   proposes to exercise the powers in section 89L in relation to a person, or

    (b)   exercises any of those powers in relation to a person with immediate effect,

    it must give that person written notice.

(3)   The notice must:

(a)   give details of the competent authority's action or proposed action;

(b)   state the competent authority's reasons for taking the action in question and choosing the date on which it took effect or takes effect;

(c)   inform the recipient that he may make representations to the competent authority within such period as may be specified by the notice (whether or not he had referred the matter to the Tribunal);

(d)   inform him of the date on which the action took effect or takes effect;

(e)   inform him of his right to refer the matter to the Tribunal (see section 89N) and give an indication of the procedure on such a reference.

(4)   The competent authority may extend the period within which representations may be made to it.

(5)   If, having considered any representations made to it, the competent authority decides to maintain, vary or revoke its earlier decision, it must give written notice to that effect to the person mentioned in subsection (2).

89N Right to refer matters to the Tribunal

A person:

(a)   to whom a decision notice is given under s 89K of the FSMA 2000 (public censure), or

(b)   to whom a notice is given under s 89M FSMA 2000 (procedure in connection with suspension or prohibition of trading), may refer the matter to the Tribunal.

Section 1268 of the CA 2006 inserts four new sections into Part 6 of the FSMA 2000: ss 89K–89N. The four new sections set out the Authority's powers in case of infringement of transparency obligations. Section 89K of the FSMA 2000 enables the Authority to make a public statement if an issuer is failing or has failed to comply with its obligations. It may only do so after it has issued a warning notice to the issuer (s 89K(2) of the FSMA 2000), and after any representations from the issuer, it has provided the issuer with a decision notice (s 89K(3) of the FSMA 2000). Section 89K(4) of the FSMA 2000 requires the Authority to provide the issuer with notice that it has a right to refer the matter to the Tribunal.

The new s 89L of the FSMA 2000 gives the Authority the power, in certain circumstances, to suspend or prohibit trading of securities admitted to trading on a regulated market, or to request the market operator to suspend or prohibit such trading. The powers are to be used where the Authority suspects (ss 89L(2) and (3) of the FSMA 2000) or finds (s 89L4 of the FSMA 2000) applicable breaches of transparency obligations. The Authority's powers to request a market operator to prohibit trading could be used where an issuer whose home Member State is the UK is listed in an EEA State.

Section 89M of the FSMA 2000 sets out the procedures relating to the suspension and prohibition powers of the Authority set out in s 89L of the FSMA 2000.

The new s 89N of the FSMA 2000 sets out the right for those who receive a decision notice or a notice under s 89M of the FSMA 2000 to refer matters to the Tribunal.

Other matters

Corporate governance rules

31.6 Section 1269 of the CA 2006 states that in Part 6 of the Financial Services and Markets Act 2000 (c 8), after the sections inserted by s 1268 of the CA 2006 above insert:

Corporate governance

89O Corporate governance rules

(1) The competent authority may make rules ('corporate governance rules'):
  (a) for the purpose of implementing, enabling the implementation of or dealing with matters arising out of or related to, any Community obligation relating to the corporate governance of issuers who have requested or approved admission of their securities to trading on a regulated market;
  (b) about corporate governance in relation to such issuers for the purpose of implementing, or dealing with matters arising out of or related to, any Community obligation.

(2) 'Corporate governance', in relation to an issuer, includes
  (a) the nature, constitution or functions of the organs of the issuer;
  (b) the manner in which organs of the issuer conduct themselves;
  (c) the requirements imposed on organs of the issuer;
  (d) the relationship between the different organs of the issuer;
  (e) the relationship between the organs of the issuer and the members of the issuer or holders of the issuer's securities.

(3) The burdens and restrictions imposed by rules under this section on foreign-traded issuers must not be greater than the burdens and restrictions imposed on UK-traded issuers by:
  (a) rules under this section; and
  (b) listing rules.

(4) For this purpose:
  • 'foreign-traded issuer' means an issuer who has requested or approved admission of the issuer's securities to trading on a regulated market situated or operating outside the United Kingdom;

- 'UK-traded issuer' means an issuer who has requested or approved admission of the issuer's securities to trading on a regulated market situated or operating in the United Kingdom.

(5) This section is without prejudice to any other power conferred by this Part to make Part 6 rules.

Section 1269 of the CA 2006 inserts new s 89O of the FSMA 2000, which gives the Authority a power (under Part 6 of of the FSMA 2000) to make rules implementing, enabling the implementation of or dealing with matters arising out of Community obligations on corporate governance of issuers on a regulated market.

This rule-making power will enable the Authority to make corporate governance rules to cover issuers for whom the UK is the home Member State, and whose securities are traded on a regulated market in the UK or elsewhere in the EEA.

Section 89O(2) of the FSMA 2000 sets out the type of corporate governance provision covered by this rule making power. These include:

- the nature, constitution or functions of the organs of issuers;
- the manner in which organs of the issuer conduct themselves;
- the requirements imposed on organs of the issuer;
- the relationship between the different organs of the issuer;
- the relationship between the organs of the issuer and the members of the issuer (or holders of the issuer's securities).

Section 89O(3) FSMA 2000 provides that greater burdens must not be imposed by corporate governance rules on issuers whose securities are traded outside the UK than those imposed by rules or listing rules on issuers with securities on UK markets.

Liability for false or misleading statements in certain publications

31.7 Section 1270 of the CA 2006 states that in Part 6 of the Financial Services and Markets Act 2000 (c 8), after s 90 of the FSMA 2000 insert:

90A Compensation for statements in certain publications

(1) The publications to which this section applies are:
   (a) any reports and statements published in response to a requirement imposed by a provision implementing Article 4, 5 or 6 of the transparency obligations directive; and
   (b) any preliminary statement made in advance of a report or statement to be published in response to a requirement imposed by a provision

implementing Article 4 of that directive, to the extent that it contains information that it is intended:

    (i)   will appear in the report or statement, and

    (ii) will be presented in the report or statement in substantially the same form as that in which it is presented in the preliminary statement.

(2) The securities to which this section applies are:

    (a) securities that are traded on a regulated market situated or operating in the United Kingdom; and

    (b) securities that:

        (i)   are traded on a regulated market situated or operating outside the United Kingdom, and

        (ii) are issued by an issuer for which the United Kingdom is the home Member State within the meaning of Article 2.1(i) of the transparency obligations directive.

(3) The issuer of securities to which this section applies is liable to pay compensation to a person who has:

    (a) acquired such securities issued by it; and

    (b) suffered loss in respect of them as a result of:

        (i)   any untrue or misleading statement in a publication to which this section applies, or

        (ii) the omission from any such publication of any matter required to be included in it.

(4) The issuer is so liable only if a person discharging managerial responsibilities within the issuer in relation to the publication:

    (a) knew the statement to be untrue or misleading or was reckless as to whether it was untrue or misleading; or

    (b) knew the omission to be dishonest concealment of a material fact.

(5) A loss is not regarded as suffered as a result of the statement or omission in the publication unless the person suffering it acquired the relevant securities:

    (a) in reliance on the information in the publication; and

    (b) at a time when, and in circumstances in which, it was reasonable for him to rely on that information.

(6) Except as mentioned in subsection (8):

    (a) the issuer is not subject to any other liability than that provided for by this section in respect of loss suffered as a result of reliance by any person on:

        (i)   an untrue or misleading statement in a publication to which this section applies, or

        (ii) the omission from any such publication of any matter required to be included in it, and

(b) a person other than the issuer is not subject to any liability, other than to the issuer, in respect of any such loss.

(7) Any reference in subsection (6) to a person being subject to a liability includes a reference to another person being entitled as against him to be granted any civil remedy or to rescind or repudiate an agreement.

(8) This section does not affect:

(a) the powers conferred by sections 382 and 384 (powers of the court to make a restitution order and of the Authority to require restitution);

(b) liability for a civil penalty;

(c) liability for a criminal offence.

(9) For the purposes of this section:

(a) the following are persons 'discharging managerial responsibilities' in relation to a publication:

(i) any director of the issuer (or person occupying the position of director, by whatever name called),

(ii) in the case of an issuer whose affairs are managed by its members, any member of the issuer,

(iii) in the case of an issuer that has no persons within sub-paragraph (i) or (ii), any senior executive of the issuer having responsibilities in relation to the publication.

(b) references to the acquisition by a person of securities include his contracting to acquire them or any interest in them.

90B Power to make further provision about liability for published information

(1) The Treasury may by regulations make provision about the liability of issuers of securities traded on a regulated market, and other persons, in respect of information published to holders of securities, to the market or to the public generally.

(2) Regulations under this section may amend any primary or subordinate legislation, including any provision of, or made under, this Act.

Section 1270 of the CA 2006 inserts ss 90A and 90B of the FSMA 2000 and establishes a regime for civil liability to third parties by issuers admitted to trading on a regulated market in respect of disclosure made public in response to provisions implementing obligations imposed by the Transparency Directive.

Although no issuer has been found liable in damages under English law in respect of statements made in narrative reports or financial statements, the law relating to financial markets and to the obligations of issuers to investors on those markets has been developing, in the light of increased regulation of both domestic and European origin. The Transparency Directive has continued that process and increased the level of uncertainty as to whether any actionable duty is owed by an issuer and its directors to investors.

The Transparency Directive sets out the periodic financial disclosures that must be made by issuers admitted to trading on a regulated market. Articles 4 and 5 of the Transparency Directive provide for annual and half-yearly reports, including management statements, to be made public, and requires statements made by persons responsible within the issuer for these disclosures (the directors in the case of a public company) that these give a true and fair view, and that the management report includes a fair review of certain matters. Article 6 requires the disclosure of interim management statements.

The Transparency Directive also sets out the minimum requirements for a liability regime that must be adopted by the UK at Article 7, and recital (17) states 'Member States should remain free to determine the extent of the liability'.

These provisions give considerable flexibility to Member States in the liability regime they choose to adopt in respect of disclosures under the Directive. The Government has established an exhaustive regime in relation to ensuring the delivery and accuracy of these reports including criminal offences, administrative penalties and actions for civil damages. The provisions in this section relate only to the position in respect of the civil liability of issuers on regulated markets to investors in their securities. The liability regime does not cover issuers on exchange-regulated markets. Their position remains unchanged by implementation of the Transparency Directive.

While it is intended that there be no additional liability under the Directive in respect of the disclosures to which it relates, the regime leaves undisturbed any other liability owed by directors to the issuer and to members of the company under UK and other national law, and any liability under other FSA rules. It also leaves undisturbed any liability of the issuer in respect of any loss or damage arising otherwise than as a result of acquiring securities in reliance on the relevant statement or report.

The primary liability of directors and issuers for the accuracy of the required disclosures comprises criminal offences and administrative penalties under the provisions of Part 15 of the CA 2006 and Part 6 of FSMA. The provisions in Part 6 require compliance with FSA rules giving effect to the obligations in the Directive and provide for penalties in respect of failure to comply with the rules. In addition, restitution can potentially be ordered by the court, on application of the Authority or Secretary of State, under s 382 of the FSMA 2000 or by the Authority directly under s 384 of the FSMA 2000.

The Government's intention in developing a civil liability regime has been to provide certainty in an uncertain area and to ensure that the potential scope of liability is reasonable, in relation both to expectations and the likely state of the law after the implementation of the Transparency Directive. In particular, the Government was anxious not to extend unnecessarily the scope of any duties that might be owed to investors or wider classes of third parties, in order to protect the interests of company members, employees and creditors. However, as the state of the law after the implementation of the Transparency Directive was not certain, the Government has taken a power, at new section 90B, that enabled the provision introduced by s 1270 of the CA of the 2006 to be added to or amended if a wider or narrower civil liability regime were deemed appropriate.

Subsection (1)(a) of the new s 90A of the FSMA 2000 provides that the civil liability regime set out in that section applies to those reports and statements required by provisions implementing Articles 4–6 of the Transparency Directive. Depending on transparency rules, we would expect this to include annual and half-yearly financial statements and management reports, the sign-off by directors or other responsible parties, as well as interim management statements.

Section 90A(1)(b) of the FSMA 2000 adds to the scope of the regime the information included in preliminary announcements of results made in advance of the reports and statements required by provision implementing Article 4 of the Transparency Directive, but only to the extent that it is intended that the information will appear in the final report or statement and be presented in substantially the same form as that in which it is presented in the preliminary announcement.

Section 90A(2) of the FSMA 2000 sets the scope of the civil liability regime to cover securities of all issuers for which the UK is the home Member State (whether the regulated market on which they are traded is situated in or outside the UK), as well as to cover those issuers whose securities are traded on a regulated market situated in the UK and for whom the UK is the host Member State. UK holders of securities of other issuers (i.e. those for whom the UK is neither a host nor a home State) will not be able to rely on the rights of action set out.

Section 90A(3) of the FSMA 2000 provides that issuers of such securities are liable to pay compensation to a person who has acquired those securities and has suffered loss in respect of them as a result of any untrue or misleading statement in a publication to which this section applies, or an omission of a required statement from such a statement.

Section 90A(4) of the FSMA 2000, however, limits the liability of the issuer to circumstances where a 'person discharging managerial responsibilities' in relation to the publication within the issuer (see s 90A(9) of the FSMA 2000) knows the statement to be untrue or misleading, or is reckless as to whether the statement is untrue or misleading, or, in the case of omissions, where it is known to be a dishonest concealment of a material fact.

Section 90A(5) of the FSMA 2000 provides that loss will not be regarded as having been suffered for the purposes of s 90A(3) of the FSMA 2000 unless the person suffering it acquired the relevant securities in reliance on the information in the publication and at a time when and in circumstances where it was reasonable to rely on that publication.

Section 90A(6) of the FSMA 2000 limits the liability with regard to untrue or misleading statements, or omissions, in documents to which the section applies. It sets out that issuers are not liable for any liability other than that provided for by the section and that any person who is not the issuer is not liable, other than to the issuer.

Section 90A(8) of the FSMA 2000 clarifies that the section does not affect Part 6 of the FSMA 2000 conferring liability for a civil penalty, liability for a criminal offence or the right to seek restitution.

Section 90A(9) of the FSMA 2000 sets out the persons who are to be considered as discharging managerial responsibilities for the purposes of the section. This is any director of the issuer, or where the issuer's affairs are managed by the members, a member of the issuer. In the case where the issuer does not have directors, or members, any senior executive with responsibilities in relation to the publication is considered as discharging managerial responsibilities.

Subsection (1) of the new section 90B of the FSMA 2000 establishes a power to make further provision about liability for published information. The new section allows the Treasury by regulations to amend any primary or subordinate legislation relating to the liability of issuers and others in respect of information, including the regime set out in the new s 90A of the FSMA 2000. The exercise of the proposed power could, for example, result in that regime or some other appropriate regime applying to other classes of information, such as information that is required to be disclosed by issuers to shareholders or markets under the Market Abuse Directive ('MAD').

Regulations made under the section would be made using affirmative procedure (see the amendment on s 429(2) of the FSMA 2000 made by para 12 of Schedule 15).

Exercise of powers where UK is a host member State

31.8 Section 1271 of the CA 2006 provides that in Part 6 of the Financial Services and Markets Act 2000 (c 8), after s 100 FSMA 2000 insert:

100A Exercise of powers where UK is host Member State

(1) This section applies to the exercise by the competent authority of any power under this Part exercisable in case of infringement of:

   (a) a provision of prospectus rules or any other provision made in accordance with the prospectus directive; or

   (b) a provision of transparency rules or any other provision made in accordance with the transparency obligations directive,

   in relation to an issuer whose home State is a member State other than the United Kingdom.

(2) The competent authority may act in such a case only in respect of the infringement of a provision required by the relevant directive. Any reference

to an applicable provision or applicable transparency obligation shall be read accordingly.

(3) If the authority finds that there has been such an infringement, it must give a notice to that effect to the competent authority of the person's home State requesting it:

    (a) to take all appropriate measures for the purpose of ensuring that the person remedies the situation that has given rise to the notice; and

    (b) to inform the authority of the measures it proposes to take or has taken or the reasons for not taking such measures.

(4) The authority may not act further unless satisfied:

    (a) that the competent authority of the person's home State has failed or refused to take measures for the purpose mentioned in subsection (3)(a); or

    (b) that the measures taken by that authority have proved inadequate for that purpose.

    This does not affect exercise of the powers under section 87K(2), 87L(2) or (3) or 89L(2) or (3) (powers to protect market).

(5) If the authority is so satisfied, it must, after informing the competent authority of the person's home State, take all appropriate measures to protect investors.

(6) In such a case the authority must inform the Commission of the measures at the earliest opportunity.

Section 1271 of the CA 2006 inserts a new section into Part 6 of the FSMA 2000: s 100A. The new s 100A of the FSMA 2000 sets out the Authority's ability to exercise powers in relation to infringements of prospectus rules and transparency rules or related provisions where issuers' home State is not the UK. Section 100A(2) of the FSMA 2000 clarifies that the enforcement powers extend only to cover infringements required by the relevant directive. Section 1000A(3) of the FSMA 2000 sets out the process by which the Authority must engage with the home State competent authority when it finds there has been an infringement. Section 100A(4) of the FSMA 2000 sets out limitations on the Authority's ability to act in those circumstances, but s 100A(5) of the FSMA 2000 provides that, in the appropriate circumstances, it must take all appropriate measures to protect investors.

Section 100A(6) of the FSMA 2000 imposes an obligation on the Authority to inform the Commission where it takes action to protect investors.

Transparency obligations and related matters: minor and consequential amendments

31.9 Schedule 15 to this Act makes minor and consequential amendments in connection with the provision made by this Part.[8118] In that Schedule:[8119]

> Part 1 contains amendments of the Financial Services and Markets Act 2000 (c 8).
>
> Part 2 contains amendments of the Companies (Audit, Investigations and Community Enterprise) Act 2004 (c 27).
>
> Section 1272 of the CA 2006 introduces Schedule 15, which makes minor and consequential amendments to FSMA related to the provision in ss 1265–1271 of the CA 2006. The Schedule also makes amendments to the C(AICE)Act 2004.
>
> Part 1 of Schedule 15 makes minor and consequential amendments to the FSMA 2000.
>
> Paragraph 2 amends s 73 of the FSMA 2000 to extend, for the purposes of the transparency rules (which can apply to non-regulated UK markets), the factors to which the Authority must have regard when making rules under Part 6 FSMA 2000, so that these extend to effects on markets other than regulated markets.
>
> Paragraph 3 amends s 73A of the FSMA 2000 to provide that transparency rules and corporate governance rules are 'Part 6 rules' for the purposes of Part 6 of the FSMA 2000. But para 3 also makes clear that these rules are distinct and separate from other Part 6 rules, such as the listing rules, disclosure rules and prospectus rules. These different kinds of rules impose different, and sometimes overlapping, obligations on different groups of issuers.
>
> Paragraph 6 amends the penalty regime for breaches of Part 6 rules in s 91 of the FSMA 2000, so that it applies also to non-compliance with transparency rules, provisions made under the Transparency Directive, and corporate governance rules.
>
> Paragraph 8 amends s 97 of the FSMA 2000 to enable the Authority to appoint a person to carry out investigations into breaches of the transparency rules or related provisions or the corporate governance rules.
>
> Paragraph 9 amends s 99 of the FSMA 2000, which relates to fees, so as to enable the Authority to levy fees under the transparency rules.
>
> Paragraphs 10 and 11 amend two definitions in Part 6 of the FSMA 2000 ('transferable securities' in s 1024 and 'regulated market' in s 103) to refer to the up-to-date Community legislation (i.e. the Markets in

---

[8118] CA 2006, s 1272(1).   [8119] CA 2006, s 1272(2).

Financial Instruments Directive (2004/39)). These paragraphs also add definitions for the purposes of the provisions on transparency rules.

Paragraph 12 adds regulations made under the new s 90B of the FSMA 2000 to the list of statutory instruments subject to the affirmative procedure in s 429(2) of the FSMA 2000.

Paragraphs 14 and 15 amend ss 14 and 15 of the C(AICE) Act 2004. The amendments mean that periodic accounts and reports of issuers required under corporate governance rules or transparency rules may be examined by the FRRP.

Corporate governance regulations

31.10 Section 1273 of the CA 2006 states that the Secretary of State may make regulations:

(a) for the purpose of implementing, enabling the implementation of or dealing with matters arising out of or related to, any Community obligation relating to the corporate governance of issuers who have requested or approved admission of their securities to trading on a regulated market;[8120]
(b) about corporate governance in relation to such issuers for the purpose of implementing, or dealing with matters arising out of or related to, any Community obligation.[8121]

'Corporate governance', in relation to an issuer, includes:

(a) the nature, constitution or functions of the organs of the issuer;[8122]
(b) the manner in which organs of the issuer conduct themselves;[8123]
(c) the requirements imposed on organs of the issuer;[8124]
(d) the relationship between different organs of the issuer;[8125]
(e) the relationship between the organs of the issuer and the members of the issuer or holders of the issuer's securities.[8126]

The regulations may:

(a) make provision by reference to any specified code on corporate governance that may be issued from time to time by a specified body;[8127]
(b) create new criminal offences (subject to subs (4));[8128]

[8120] CA 2006, s 1273(1)(a).   [8121] CA 2006, s 1273(1)(b).   [8122] CA 2006, s 1273(2)(a).
[8123] CA 2006, s 1273(2)(b).   [8124] CA 2006, s 1273(2)(c).   [8125] CA 2006, s 1273(2)(d).
[8126] CA 2006, s 1273(2)(e).   [8127] CA 2006, s 1273(3)(a).   [8128] CA 2006, s 1273(3)(b).

(c)   make provision excluding liability in damages in respect of things done or omitted for the purposes of, or in connection with, the carrying on, or purported carrying on, of any specified activities.[8129]

'Specified' here means specified in the regulations.

The regulations may not create a criminal offence punishable by a greater penalty than:

(a)   on indictment, a fine;[8130]
(b)   on summary conviction, a fine not exceeding the statutory maximum or (if calculated on a daily basis) £100 a day.[8131]

Regulations under this section are subject to negative resolution procedure.[8132]

In this section 'issuer', 'securities' and 'regulated market' have the same meaning as in Part 6 of the Financial Services and Markets Act 2000 (c 8).[8133]

Section 1273 of the CA 2006 provides the Secretary of State with a regulation-making power similar to the power given to the Authority in new s 89O of the FSMA 2000 inserted by s 1269 of the CA 2006.

The Secretary of State may make regulations for the purposes of implementing, enabling the implementation of or dealing with matters arising out of Community obligations on corporate governance for UK companies, whose securities are traded on a regulated market in the UK or elsewhere in the EEA.

Section 1273(3)(a) of the CA 2006 allows for regulations to be made by reference to any code regulating corporate governance. This could include, for example, the Combined Code on Corporate Governance (issued by the Financial Reporting Council).

Section 1273(4) of the CA 2006 specifies that any criminal offence created by the regulations may not impose a greater penalty than an unlimited fine.

Section 1273(5) of the CA 2006 provides for regulations to be made by way of negative resolution. However, by virtue of s 1292(4) of the CA 2006, it will also be possible to make regulations under this power by affirmative procedure.

Provisions implementing the Transparency Directive

31.11 The table below describes the substantive provisions in the CA 2006 implementing the Transparency Directive.

[8129] CA 2006, s 1273(3)(c).   [8130] CA 2006, s 1273(4)(a).   [8131] CA 2006, s 1273(4)(b).
[8132] CA 2006, s 1273(5).   [8133] CA 2006, s 1273(6).

Part 43 of the CA 2006: Transparency obligations and related matters		
Article	**Objective**	**Implementation under CA 2006**
1.	Sets out scope of the Directive and two derogations from the requirements of the Directive. The Member States may apply the derogations in respect of securities issued by the government, local government or a state's national central bank.	Part 43 of the Act inserts new provisions into the Financial Services and Markets Act 2000 (FSMA) to give the Financial Services Authority power to make Transparency Rules. Most provisions in the Transparency Directive will be implemented by the FSA's Transparency Rules. Other provisions in the Act or in FSMA implement the other requirements. If the derogations are to be implemented, the FSA's Transparency Rules will do this.
2.	Provides various definitions used in the Directive.	These will be applied in Transparency Rules, or apply in relation to the implementation of the Article to which they relate.
3.	Limits the circumstances in which Member States may impose more stringent requirements than those contained in the Directive on issuers of securities and holders of interests in those issuers' shares.	Transparency Rules and new, s 100A(2) of the FSMA introduced by s 1271 of the Act.
4.	Requires issuers of securities that are traded on regulated markets to make public their annual financial report consisting of their audited financial statements and management report.	Transparency Rules: see in particular new ss 89A and 89C of FSMA, inserted by s 1266 of the Act.
5.	Requires issuers of shares or debt securities that are traded on a regulated market to make public a half-yearly financial report.	Transparency Rules: see in particular new ss 89A and 89C of FSMA, inserted by s 1266 of the Act.
6.	Requires issuers whose shares are traded on a regulated market to make public an interim quarterly statement.	Transparency Rules: see in particular new ss 89A and 89C of FSMA, inserted by s 1266 of the Act.
7.	Requires Member States to ensure that responsibility for the information to be drawn up and made public in accordance with Articles 4, 5, 6 and 16 lies at least with the issuer or its administrative,	Provisions relating to liability inserted into FSMA as new ss 90A and 90B by s 1270 of the Act.

	management or supervisory bodies and to ensure that their laws, regulations and administrative provisions on liability apply to the issuers, the bodies referred to in this article or the persons responsible within the issuers.	
8.	Provides various exemptions from the requirements of articles 4, 5 and 6 including to optional exemptions.	Transparency Rules.
9.	Provides that where a shareholder with a significant level of holding acquires or disposes of shares of an issuer whose shares are admitted to trading on a regulated market and to which voting rights are attached, such shareholder notifies the issuer of the proportion of voting rights in the issuer held by the shareholder as a result of the acquisition or disposal where that proportion reaches, exceeds or falls below the thresholds of 5, 10, 15, 20, 25, 30, 50 and 75 per cent.	Transparency Rules: see in particular new ss 89A and 89B of FSMA, inserted by s 1266 of the Act.
10.	The notification requirements in Article 9 shall also apply to a natural person or legal entity to the extent it is entitled to acquire, to dispose of, or to exercise voting rights in any of the cases set out in the Article or a combination of them. (Voting rights acquired through agreement or interest.)	Transparency Rules.
11.	Exempt shares provided to or by the members of the ESCB in certain circumstances from the notification requirements imposed by Articles 9 and 10.	Transparency Rules.
12.	Sets out the information that must be included in the notification under Articles 9 and 10 and includes provision on the timing of the notification and when aggregation of holdings required. Paragraph (6) requires the issuer to make public all information contained within a notification within three days.	Transparency Rules.

13.	Requires the holders of financial instruments, which are to be specified by the Commission, to notify the issuer of their control of votes in accordance with the requirements in Article 9.	Transparency Rules.
14.	Requires an issuer of shares admitted to trading on a regulated market to make public the proportion of its own shares that it holds when those proportions reach, exceed or fall below the thresholds of 5 or 10 per cent.	Transparency Rules: see in particular new ss 89A and 89C of FSMA, inserted by s 1266 of the Act.
15.	Requires the Member State to ensure that an issuer of shares traded on a regulated market, makes public the total number of voting rights and capital at the end of each month during which the number changes.	Transparency Rules.
16.	Requires issuers of securities to make public information about any changes in the rights attached to their securities and any new loan issues and any guarantee or security in respect of such loans.	Transparency Rules: see in particular new ss 89A and 89C of FSMA, inserted by s 1266 of the Act.
17.	Requires issuers of shares admitted to trading on a regulated market to treat their shareholders, who are in the same position, equally. It provides for information to be distributed in particular ways and for shareholders to be able to exercise their rights in specified ways.	Transparency Rules.
18.	Makes similar provision as that contained in Article 17 but in respect of issuers whose debt securities are admitted to trading on a regulated market.	Transparency Rules.
19.	Requires issuers to file information that they are required to make public under the Directive, with the FSA and permits the FSA to publish that information itself. It also requires issuers to inform the FSA and the regulated market to which its securities are admitted of any proposed change to its instrument of incorporation.	Transparency Rules.

20.	Sets out the rules for determining which language the issuer must use to disclose regulated information in various circumstances.	Transparency Rules.
21.	Requires issuers to disclose regulated information in a manner ensuring fast access to such information on a non-discriminatory basis. Also requires each Member State to have an officially appointed mechanism for the central storage of regulated information.	Transparency Rules.
22.	Requires the competent authorities of the Member States (for the UK it is the FSA) to draw up guidelines to create an electronic network at national level to share information between the various competent authorities, operators of regulated markets and national company registers. Such guidelines must aim to further facilitate public access to be disclosed under this Directive, Directive 2003/6/EC (the Market Abuse Directive) and Directive 2003/71/EC (Prospectus Directive).	The FSA will draw up guidelines in accordance with the obligations under this Article.
23.	Enables the FSA to exempt issuers based in third countries from certain disclosure requirements if there are equivalent provisions in the third country. Requires the FSA to ensure that where a third country issuer is regulated in the UK for EU purposes, any information which may be important to the public in the Community is disclosed in accordance with Articles 20 and 21.	Transparency Rules.
24.	Requires each Member State to designate a central competent authority responsible for ensuring that the Directive is applied and to give that competent authority specified powers which are necessary for the performance of its functions. Permits each Member State to designate a competent authority for examining that information is drawn up in accordance with the relevant reporting framework.	The central competent authority in the UK will be the FSA, by virtue of the amendments being inserted into Part 6 of FSMA. The FSA already has various powers under FSMA. Other powers for the FSA to perform its functions are contained in new FSMA ss 89H–89N inserted by ss 1267 and 1268 of the Act. The Act provides power to designate a competent authority for reporting framework purposes

		by amending the Companies (Audit, Investigations and Community Enterprise) Act 2004. See Schedule 15 (Part 2) of the Act.
25.	Imposes a requirement for professional secrecy on those who work for the competent authority and requires cooperation between the competent authorities of the various Member States.	FSMA already contains provisions relating to professional secrecy for those who work for the FSA and the Companies (Audit, Investigations and Community Enterprise) Act 2004 also contains provisions in relation to authorities appointed under that Act.
26.	Provides for host Member States to take action in relation to infringements where an issuer or security holder continues to infringe the requirements of the Directive.	The new s 100A of the FSMA introduced by s 1271 of the Act.
27.	Sets out the committee procedure for the Commission to make implementing measures required by the Directive.	No implementing provision required.
28.	Requires, without prejudice to the right of Member States to impose criminal penalties, Member States to ensure, in conformity with their national law that at least the appropriate administrative measure may be taken or civil and/or administrative penalties imposed in respect of the persons responsible.	Schedule 15 (Part 1) of the Act amends s 91 of FSMA to enable the FSA to impose financial penalties for breach of the Transparency Rules.
29.	Requires a right of appeal to the courts to be in place.	No further implementation is required. FSMA already makes provision for appeals of FSA decisions to the Financial Services and Markets Tribunal and to the Court of Appeal.
30–35	These articles contain transitional and final provisions, including the date by which the Directive must be transposed – 20 January 2007.	No specific implementation is required for most of these provisions. The new ss 89B(4) and 89D(1) introduced by s 1266 of the Act make provision for transitional arrangements.

Control of Political Donations and Expenditure

Introduction

The position before CA 2006

32.1 In October 1998, the Committee of Standards in Public Life presented to the Prime Minister its report on the funding of political parties in the United Kingdom. The report recommended that any company intending to make a donation (whether in cash or in kind and including any sponsorship, or loans or transactions at a favourable rate) to a political party or organisation, should be required to have the prior authority of its shareholders. The Government accepted this recommendation and implemented it through the Political Parties, Elections and Referendums Act 2000 (the PPERA). The new regime of control for political donations and expenditures was set out in Part 10A of the CA 1985, as inserted by s 139 of Schedule 19 to the PPERA.

The position under CA 2006

32.2 Part 14 of the CA 2006 restates the existing provisions in a style consistent with the other sections, but most of the key elements of the framework established by the PPERA will remain. The following aspects should be noted:

- companies will continue to be prohibited from making a donation to a political party or other political organisation or from incurring political expenditure, unless the donation or the expenditure has been authorised, in a typical case by the members of the company;
- a 'political donation' will continue to be defined by reference to ss 50–52 of the PPERA and for this purpose, amendments made to the PPERA by the Electoral Administration Act 2006 (which remove from the definition of 'donations' loans made otherwise than on commercial terms) will be disregarded;
- an approval resolution may authorise the making of donations and

incurring of expenditure for a period of not more than four years commencing with the date of the passing of the resolution up to a value specified in the resolution;

- donations or expenditure by a subsidiary must, in general, be authorised by a resolution of the members of the subsidiary and of the holding company; and the directors of such holding company will continue to be liable for unauthorised donations by the subsidiary company;

- a company need not to seek prior shareholder consent for donations to a political party or organisation unless the aggregate amount of any such donation together with any other relevant donations made by the company and other companies in the group of which it is a member in the previous 12 months exceeds £5,000;

- there are to be no criminal sanctions in relation to the making of unauthorised donations or the incurring of unauthorised political expenditure;

- civil remedies are to be available to a company in the event of breach of the prohibitions, and are to be pursued in the normal manner by the company. There will continue to be available an action under which shareholders may enforce on behalf of the company any of the remedies available to a company.

The main changes from Part 10A of the CA 1985 are that:

- in line with the general approach in the CA 2006, references to the general meeting are removed, to make it clearer that private companies can authorise donations and/or expenditure by written resolution;

- a holding company must authorise a donation or expenditure by a subsidiary company only if it is a 'relevant holding company' (that is, the ultimate holding company or, where such company is not a 'UK registered company' the holding company highest up the chain that is a 'UK registered company)';

- a holding company is to be permitted to seek authorisation of donations and expenditure in respect of both the holding company itself and or more subsidiaries (including wholly-owned subsidiaries) through a single approval resolution (s 367(1) of the CA 2006);

- companies are permitted to table separate approval resolutions in respect of donations to political parties and donations to other political organisations (s 367(3) of the CA 2006);

- companies are required to seek authorisation for donations to independent candidates at any election to public office held in the UK or other EU member state and for expenditure by the company relating to independent election candidates;

- the sections provide greater clarity for companies about the provisions of facilities (for example, meeting rooms) for trade union officials by introducing a specific exemptions for donations to trade unions (s 374 of the CA 2006). The CA 2006 does not introduce a specific exemption in relation to paid leave or local councilors because this does not constitute a political donation under either Part 10A of the CA 1985 or the CA 2006;

- there are important changes to the rules on ratification and liability in cases of unauthorised donations or expenditure;
- the special rules in respect of the parent company of a non-GB subsidiary undertaking (ss 347E and 347G of the CA 1985) are not reproduced;
- the new provisions will apply to Northern Ireland.

Introductory

32.3 Section 362 of the CA 2006 states that Part 14 of the CA 2006 applies for controlling political donations made by companies to political parties, to other political organisations and to independent election candidates;[8134] and political expenditure incurred by companies.[8135]

The objective of s 362 of the CA 2006 is to explain that Part 14 of the CA 2006 relates to political expenditure and to political donations made by companies to political parties, political organisations and independent election candidates.

Political parties, organisations, etc. to which this Part applies

32.4 Section 363 of the CA 2006 is concerned with donations and expenditure in respect of political parties and organisations. It applies to a political party if it is registered under Part 2 of the Political Parties, Elections and Referendums Act 2000 (c 41);[8136] or it carries on, or proposes to carry on, activities for the purposes of or in connection with the participation of the party in any election or elections to public office held in a member State other than the United Kingdom.[8137]

Part 14 of the CA 2006 applies to an organisation (a political organisation) if it carries on, or proposes to carry on, activities that are capable of being reasonably regarded as intended to affect public support for a political party to which, or an independent election candidate to whom, this Part applies;[8138] or to influence voters in relation to any national or regional referendum held under the law of the United Kingdom or another member State.[8139]

Part 14 of the CA 2006 applies to an independent election candidate at any

---

[8134] CA 2006, s 362(a).   [8135] CA 2006, s 362(b).   [8136] CA 2006, s 363(1)(a).
[8137] CA 2006, s 363(1)(b).   [8138] CA 2006, s 363(2)(a).   [8139] CA 2006, s 363(2)(b).

election to public office held in the United Kingdom or another member State.[8140]

Any reference in the following provisions of Part 14 of the CA 2006 to a political party, political organisation or independent election candidate, or to political expenditure, is to a party, organisation, independent candidate or expenditure to which this Part applies.[8141]

The objective of s 363 of the CA 2006 is to establish the general scope of the provisions by explaining how they apply in respect of donations to (a) political parties; (b) political organisations other than political parties; and (c) independent election candidates at any election to public office; and to political expenditure by the company.

Meaning of 'political donation'

32.5 Section 364 of the CA 2006 states that the following provisions will apply for the purposes of Part 14 of the CA 2006 as regards the meaning of 'political donation'.[8142]

In relation to a political party or other political organisation the term 'political donation' means anything that in accordance with ss 50–52 of the Political Parties, Elections and Referendums Act 2000 (i) constitutes a donation for the purposes of Chapter 1 of Part 4 of that Act (control of donations to registered parties);[8143] or (ii) would constitute such a donation, reading references in those sections to a registered party as references to any political party or other political organisation,[8144] and s 53 of that Act applies, in the same way, for the purpose of determining the value of a donation.[8145]

In relation to an independent election candidate, the term 'political donation' means anything that, in accordance with ss 50–52 of that Act, would constitute a donation for the purposes of Chapter 1 of Part 4 of that Act (control of donations to registered parties) reading references in those sections to a registered party as references to the independent election candidate;[8146] and s 53 of that Act applies, in the same way, for the purpose of determining the value of a donation.[8147]

For the purposes of s 364 of the CA 2006, ss 50 and 53 of the Political Parties, Elections and Referendums Act 2000 (c 41) (definition of 'donation' and value of donations) will be treated as if the amendments to those sections made by the Electoral Administration Act 2006 (which remove from the definition of 'donation' loans made otherwise than on commercial terms) had not been made.[8148]

[8140] CA 2006, s 363(3).   [8141] CA 2006, s 363(4).   [8142] CA 2006, s 364(1).
[8143] CA 2006, s 364(2)(a)(i).   [8144] CA 2006, s 364(2)(a)(ii).   [8145] CA 2006, s 364(2)(b).
[8146] CA 2006, s 364(3)(a).   [8147] CA 2006, s 364(3)(b).   [8148] CA 2006, s 364(4).

Section 364 of the CA 2006 defines a 'political donation' for the purposes of Part 14 of the CA 2006 by reference to ss 50–52 of the Political Parties, Elections and Referendums Act 2000. For this purpose, amendments made to the 2000 Act by the Electoral Administration Act 2006 (which remove from the definition of 'donation' loans made otherwise than on commercial terms) are disregarded. Section 364 of the CA 2006 reproduces the effect of s 347A(4) of the CA 1985, except that it includes donations to independent election candidates.

Meaning of 'political expenditure'

32.6 Section 365 of the CA 2006 sets out the meaning of 'political expenditure'. It defines 'political expenditure', in relation to a company, to mean expenditure incurred by the company on (a) the preparation, publication or dissemination of advertising or other promotional or publicity material (i) of whatever nature;[8149] and (ii) however published or otherwise disseminated.[8150] that at the time of publication or dissemination, is capable of being reasonably regarded as intended to affect public support for a political party or other political organisation, or an independent election candidate; or (b) activities on the part of the company that are capable of being reasonably regarded as intended (i) to affect public support for a political party or other political organisation, or an independent election candidate;[8151] or (ii) to influence voters in relation to any national or regional referendum held under the law of a member State.[8152]

A political donation does not count as political expenditure.[8153]

Section 365 of the CA 2006 defines 'political expenditure' for the purposes of Part 14 of the CA 2006. It reproduces the effect of s 347A(5) of the CA 1985, except that it extends the definition to expenditure incurred by the company in relation to independent election candidates.

Authorisation required for donations or expenditure

32.7 Section 366 of the CA 2006 states that a company must not make a political donation to a political party or other political organisation, or to an independent election candidate,[8154] or incur any political expenditure,[8155] unless the donation or expenditure is authorised in accordance with the following provisions.

The donation or expenditure must be authorised (a) in the case of a company that is not a subsidiary of another company, by a resolution of the

---

[8149] CA 2006, s 365(1)(a)(i).   [8150] CA 2006, s 365(1)(a)(ii).   [8151] CA 2006, s 365(1)(b)(i).
[8152] CA 2006, s 365(1)(b)(ii).   [8153] CA 2006, s 365(2).   [8154] CA 2006, s 366(1)(a).
[8155] CA 2006, s 366(1)(b).

members of the company;[8156] (b) in the case of a company that is a subsidiary of another company by (i) a resolution of the members of the company,[8157] and (ii) a resolution of the members of any relevant holding company.[8158]

No resolution is required on the part of a company that is a wholly-owned subsidiary of a UK company.[8159]

For the purposes of s 366(2)(b)(ii) of the CA 2006, the term 'relevant holding company' means a company that, at the time the donation was made or the expenditure was incurred, was a holding company of the company by which the donation was made or the expenditure was incurred,[8160] was a UK registered company,[8161] and was not a subsidiary of another UK registered company.[8162]

The resolution or resolutions required by s 366 of the CA 2006 must comply with s 367 of the CA 2006 (form of authorising resolution);[8163] and must be passed before the donation is made or the expenditure incurred.[8164]

Nothing in s 366 of the CA 2006 enables a company to be authorised to do anything that it could not lawfully do apart from the section.[8165]

Section 366 of the CA 2006 prohibits a company from making a donation or incurring political expenditure, unless the transaction or the expenditure is authorised by a resolution of the members of the company. If the company is a subsidiary of another company, a resolution may instead, or in addition, be required from the members of the holding company. Sections 1159 and 1160 and Schedule 6 of the CA 2006 provide the definition of 'subsidiary'. Section 366 of the CA 2006 reproduces the effect of s 347C(1) and (6) and s 347D of the CA 1985, except that:

- in line with our general approach in CA 2006, the section does not refer to the general meeting, to make it clear that private companies can authorise donations and/or expenditure by written resolution;
- a donation or expenditure by a subsidiary company must be authorised by the members of the company and by members of a 'relevant holding company' (rather than by the members of each holding company within a group). A 'relevant holding company' is the ultimate holding company or, where such a company is not a 'UK registered company', the holding company highest up the chain which is a 'UK registered company';
- a resolution is not required on the part of a company that is wholly-owned subsidiary of a 'UK registered company' (rather than of any holding company, as in s 347D of the CA 1985);

[8156] CA 2006, s 366(2)(a).   [8157] CA 2006, s 366(2)(b)(i).   [8158] CA 2006, s 366(2)(b)(ii).
[8159] CA 2006, s 366(3).   [8160] CA 2006, s 366(4)(a).   [8161] CA 2006, s 366(4)(b).
[8162] CA 2006, s 366(4)(c).   [8163] CA 2006, s 366(5)(a).   [8164] CA 2006, s 366(5)(b).
[8165] CA 2006, s 366(6).

the section does not reproduce the prohibition (in s 347C(5) of the CA 1985) on retrospective ratification of breaches of the rules.

Form of authorising resolution

32.8 Section 367 of the CA 2006 states that a resolution conferring authorisation for the purposes of Part 14 of the CA 2006 may relate to the company passing the resolution,[8166] or one or more subsidiaries of that company,[8167] or the company passing the resolution and one or more subsidiaries of that company.[8168]

A resolution may be expressed to relate to all companies that are subsidiaries of the company passing the resolution at the time the resolution is passed,[8169] or at any time during the period for which the resolution has effect, without identifying them individually.[8170]

The resolution may authorise donations or expenditure under one or more of the following heads: donations to political parties or independent election candidates;[8171] donations to political organisations other than political parties;[8172] political expenditure.[8173]

The resolution must specify a head or heads in the case of a resolution under s 367(2) of the CA 2006, for all of the companies to which it relates taken together;[8174] in the case of any other resolution, for each company to which it relates.[8175]

The resolution must be expressed in general terms conforming with s 367(2) of the CA 2006 and must not purport to authorise particular donations or expenditure.[8176]

For each of the specified heads the resolution must authorise donations or, as the case may be, expenditure up to a specified amount in the period for which the resolution has effect (see s 368 of the CA 2006).[8177]

The resolution must specify such amounts in the case of a resolution under s 367(2) of the CA 2006, for all of the companies to which it relates taken together;[8178] and in the case of any other resolution, for each company to which it relates.[8179]

Section 367 of the CA 2006 provides that an authorising resolution may identify the subsidiaries, the heads of donations or expenditure, and the amounts that it authorises. Section 367 of the CA 2006 reproduces the effect of s 347C(2) and (4) of the CA 1985, but with the following changes. First, under s 367(1) and (2) of the CA 2006, a holding company may seek authorisation of donations and expenditure in respect of both itself and one or

---

[8166] CA 2006, s 367(1)(a).   [8167] CA 2006, s 367(1)(b).   [8168] CA 2006, s 367(1)(c).
[8169] CA 2006, s 367(2)(a).   [8170] CA 2006, s 367(2)(b).   [8171] CA 2006, s 367(3)(a).
[8172] CA 2006, s 367(3)(b).   [8173] CA 2006, s 367(3)(c).   [8174] CA 2006, s 367(4)(a).
[8175] CA 2006, s 367(4)(b).   [8176] CA 2006, s 367(5).   [8177] CA 2006, s 367(6).
[8178] CA 2006, s 367(7)(a).   [8179] CA 2006, s 367(7)(b).

more of its subsidiaries (including wholly-owned subsidiaries) in a single approval resolution. The subsidiaries do not need to be named in the resolution if it applies to all holding company's subsidiaries. Second, under s 367(3) of the CA 2006, a company may pass separate approval resolutions in respect of donations to political parties and donations to other political organisations.

Period for which resolution has effect

32.9 Section 368 of the CA 2006 deals with the period from which the resolution has effect.

A resolution conferring authorisation for the purposes of Part 14 of the CA 2006 has effect for a period of four years beginning with the date on which it is passed, unless the directors determine, or the articles require, that it is to have effect for a shorter period beginning with that date.[8180]

The power of the directors to make a determination under this section is subject to any provision of the articles that operates to prevent them from doing so.[8181]

This section provides that an approval resolution may seek authorisation for the making of donations and incurring of expenditure for a period of not more than four years. It reproduces the effect of s 347C(3)(b) of the CA 1985.

Liability of directors in case of unauthorised donation or expenditure

32.10 Sections 369–373 of the CA 2006 are concerned with remedies in case of unauthorised donations or expenditure.

Section 369 of the CA 2006 applies where a company has made a political donation or incurred political expenditure without the authorisation required by this Part.[8182]

The directors in default are jointly and severally liable to make good to the company the amount of the unauthorised donation or expenditure, with interest;[8183] and to compensate the company for any loss or damage sustained by it as a result of the unauthorised donation or expenditure having been made.[8184]

The directors in default are those who, at the time the unauthorised donation was made or the unauthorised expenditure was incurred, were directors of the company by which the donation was made or the expenditure was incurred,[8185] and where that company was a subsidiary of a relevant holding company, and the directors of the relevant holding company failed to take all

---

[8180] CA 2006, s 368(1).   [8181] CA 2006, s 368(2).   [8182] CA 2006, s 369(1).
[8183] CA 2006, s 369(2)(a).   [8184] CA 2006, s 369(2)(b).   [8185] CA 2006, s 369(3)(a).

reasonable steps to prevent the donation being made or the expenditure being incurred,[8186] the directors of the relevant holding company.

For the purposes of s 369(3)(b) of the CA 2006 a 'relevant holding company' means a company that, at the time the donation was made or the expenditure was incurred was a holding company of the company by which the donation was made or the expenditure was incurred,[8187] was a UK registered company,[8188] and was not a subsidiary of another UK-registered company.[8189]

The 'interest' referred to in s 369(2)(a) of the CA 2006 is interest on the amount of the unauthorised donation or expenditure, so far as not made good to the company in respect of the period beginning with the date when the donation was made or the expenditure was incurred,[8190] and at such rate as the Secretary of State may prescribe by regulations.[8191] Section 379(2) of the CA 2006 (construction of references to date when donation made or expenditure incurred) does not apply for the purposes of this subsection.[8192]

Where only part of a donation or expenditure was unauthorised, this section applies only to so much of it as was unauthorised.[8193]

The objective of s 369 of the CA 2006 is to impose civil liability on directors where unauthorised donations are made or unauthorised political expenditure is incurred. The liabilities are owed to the company and are to be pursued in the normal manner by the company; that is, they will be pursued by the directors in the exercise of the management powers conferred by the Articles of Association, and directors will be subject to the general duties set out in Chapter 2 of Part 10 in the conduct of the company's business. In addition, s 370 of the CA 2006 provides for enforcement by shareholder action.

Section 369 of the CA 2006 largely reproduces the effect of s 347F of the CA 1985, but only a director of the company and of a 'relevant holding company' may be liable in respect of unauthorised expenditure. This reflects the new rules relating to the authorisation of donations or expenditure by subsidiaries in s 366 of the CA 2006. Further, directors of the 'relevant holding company' will not be liable for an unauthorised political donation or unauthorised political expenditure by a subsidiary if they took 'all reasonable steps to prevent the donation being made or the expenditure being incurred'.

The conditions under which directors may be exempted from liability (previously set out in s 347H of the CA 1985) are not reproduced in the new regime.

[8186] CA 2006, s 369(3)(b).   [8187] CA 2006, s 369(4)(a).   [8188] CA 2006, s 369(4)(b).
[8189] CA 2006, s 369(4)(c).   [8190] CA 2006, s 369(5)(a).   [8191] CA 2006, s 369(5)(b).
[8192] CA 2006, s 369(5)(c).   [8193] CA 2006, s 369(6).

Enforcement of directors' liabilities by shareholder action

32.11 Section 370 of the CA 2006 states that any liability of a director under s 369 of the CA 2006 is enforceable in the case of a liability of a director of a company to that company, by proceedings brought under this section in the name of the company by an authorised group of its members;[8194] in the case of a liability of a director of a holding company to a subsidiary, by proceedings brought under this section in the name of the subsidiary by an authorised group of members of the subsidiary;[8195] or an authorised group of members of the holding company.[8196]

This is in addition to the right of the company to which the liability is owed bringing proceedings itself to enforce the liability.[8197]

An 'authorised group' of members of a company means the holders of not less than 5 per cent in nominal value of the company's issued share capital,[8198] or if the company is not limited by shares, not less than 5 per cent of its members,[8199] or not less than 50 of the company's members.[8200]

The right to bring proceedings under s 370 of the CA 2006 is subject to s 371 of the CA 2006.[8201] Nothing in s 370 of the CA 2006 affects any right of a member of a company to bring or continue proceedings under Part II (derivative claims or proceedings).[8202]

Section 370 of the CA 2006 provides a mechanism by which an authorised group of shareholders may enforce on behalf of the company any liability under s 369 of the CA 2006. In the case of a company limited by shares, an action may be brought by a group of shareholders if they are at least 50 in number, or hold at least 5 per cent of the issued share capital. This section reproduces the effect of s 347I of the CA 1985, except that, in a case where liability is owed by directors of a holding company in relation to a donation made by a subsidiary, the action may be brought by shareholders of the subsidiary or of the holding company.

Enforcement of directors' liabilities by shareholder action: supplementary

32.12 Section 371 of the CA 2006 provides that a group of members of a company may not bring proceedings under s 370 of the CA 2006 in the name of the company unless (a) the group has given written notice to the company stating (i) the cause of action and a summary of the facts on which the proceedings are to be based,[8203] (ii) the names and addresses of the members of the company comprising the group,[8204] and (iii) the grounds on which it is

---

[8194] CA 2006, s 370(1)(a).   [8195] CA 2006, s 370(1)(b)(i).   [8196] CA 2006, s 370(1)(b)(ii).
[8197] CA 2006, s 370(2).   [8198] CA 2006, s 370(3)(a).   [8199] CA 2006, s 370(3)(b).
[8200] CA 2006, s 370(3)(c).   [8201] CA 2006, s 370(4).   [8202] CA 2006, s 370(5).
[8203] CA 2006, s 371(1)(a)(i).   [8204] CA 2006, s 371(1)(a)(ii).

alleged that those members constitute an authorised group;[8205] and (b) not less than 28 days have elapsed between the date of the giving of the notice to the company and the bringing of the proceedings.[8206]

Where such a notice is given to a company, any director may apply to the court within the period of 28 days beginning with the date of the giving of the notice for an order directing that the proposed proceedings shall not be brought, on one or more of the following grounds: (a) that the unauthorised amount has been made good to the company;[8207] (b) that proceedings to enforce the liability have been brought, and are being pursued with due diligence, by the company;[8208] and (c) that the members proposing to bring proceedings under this section do not constitute an authorised group.[8209]

Where an application is made on the ground mentioned in s 371(2)(b) of the CA 2006, the court may as an alternative to directing that the proposed proceedings under s 370 of the CA 2006 are not to be brought, direct (a) that such proceedings may be brought on such terms and conditions as the court thinks fit;[8210] and (b) that the proceedings brought by the company (i) shall be discontinued,[8211] or (ii) may be continued on such terms and conditions as the court thinks fit.[8212]

The members by whom proceedings are brought under s 370 of the CA 2006 owe to the company in whose name they are brought, the same duties in relation to the proceedings as would be owed by the company directors if the proceedings were being brought by the company. But proceedings to enforce any such duty may be brought by the company only with the permission of the court.[8213]

Proceedings brought under s 370 of the CA 2006 may not be discontinued or settled by the group except with the permission of the court, which may be given on such terms as the court thinks fit.[8214]

Section 371 of the CA 2006 makes further provision in relation to proceedings brought under s 370 of the CA 2006. It reproduces the effect of s 3471 of the CA 1985. The group of shareholders wanting to take action under s 370 of the CA 2006 must give written notice to the company at least 28 days in advance of bringing the proceedings. Any director of the company has the right to apply to the court within 28 days of when the notice was given to request that the proceedings not be brought.

Section 371 of the CA 2006 also provides that if the liability is already being pursued with due diligence by the company, the court may direct that the proceedings brought by the group of shareholders are either discontinued or brought on such terms and conditions as the court sees fit.

[8205] CA 2006, s 371(1)(a)(iii).   [8206] CA 2006, s 371(1)(b).   [8207] CA 2006, s 371(2)(a).
[8208] CA 2006, s 371(2)(b).   [8209] CA 2006, s 371(2)(c).   [8210] CA 2006, s 371(3)(a).
[8211] CA 2006, s 371(3)(b)(i).   [8212] CA 2006, s 371(3)(b)(ii).   [8213] CA 2006, s 371(4).
[8214] CA 2006, s 371(5).

Costs of shareholder action

32.13 Section 372 of the CA 2006 applies in relation to proceedings brought under s 370 of the CA 2006 in the name of the company (the company) by an authorised group of members of a company (the group).[8215]

The group may apply to the court for an order directing the company to indemnify the group in respect of costs incurred or to be incurred by the group in connection with the proceedings. The court may make such an order on such terms as it thinks fit.[8216]

The group is not entitled to be paid any such costs out of the assets of the company except by virtue of such an order.[8217]

If no such order has been made with respect to the proceedings, then if the company is awarded costs in connection with the proceedings, or it is agreed that costs incurred by the company in connection with the proceedings should be paid by any defendant, the costs shall be paid to the group;[8218] and if any defendant is awarded costs in connection with the proceedings, or it is agreed that any defendant should be paid costs incurred by him in connection with the proceedings, the costs shall be paid by the group.[8219]

In the application of this section to Scotland for 'costs' read 'expenses' and for 'defendant' read 'defender'.[8220]

Section 372 of the CA 2006 provides that the authorised group of members of a company are not to be entitled as of right to have the cost of the shareholders' action met from the funds of the company, but have the right to apply to the court for an indemnity out of the company's assets in respect of costs incurred or to be incurred in a shareholders' action. The court would have full discretion to grant such an indemnity on such terms as it thinks fit. The section reproduces the effect of s 347J of the CA 1985.

Information for purposes of a shareholders' action

32.14 Section 373 of the CA 2006 deals with the aspect of information for the shareholder action. Where proceedings have been brought under s 370 of the CA 2006 by an authorised group, the group is entitled to require the company to provide it with all information relating to the subject matter of the proceedings that is in the company's possession or under its control, or that it can reasonably obtain.[8221]

If the company, having been required by the group to do so, refuses to provide the group with all or any of that information, the court may, on an application made by the group, make an order directing the company,[8222] and any of its officers or employees specified in the application,[8223] to provide the

---

[8215] CA 2006, s 372(1).   [8216] CA 2006, s 372(2).   [8217] CA 2006, s 372(3).
[8218] CA 2006, s 372(4)(a).   [8219] CA 2006, s 372(4)(b).   [8220] CA 2006, s 372(5).
[8221] CA 2006, s 373(1).   [8222] CA 2006, s 373(2)(a).   [8223] CA 2006, s 373(2)(b).

group with the information in question in such form and by such means as the court may direct.

Section 373 of the CA 2006 provides that the authorised group of members of a company is entitled, once the action is commenced, to be provided by the company in whose name it is brought with all information possessed by the company, in its control or obtainable by it relating to the subject matter of the action. It reproduces the effect of s 347K of the CA 1985.

Exemptions

32.15 Sections 374–378 of the CA 2006 are concerned with exemptions. These sections set out five exemptions from the requirement for prior shareholder authorisation.

First, s 374 of the CA 2006 creates a new exemption in relation to donations to trade unions (including trade unions in countries other than the UK). The exemption covers donations such as the provision of company rooms for trade union meetings, the use of company vehicles by trade union officials and paid time off for trade union officials. However, a donation to a trade union's political fund is not covered by the exemption.

Second, s 375 of the CA 2006 restates the exemption in s 347B of the CA 1985 in respect of subscriptions paid to a trade association for membership of the association, except that it is not restricted to trade associations that carry out their activities mainly in the EU.

Third, s 376 of the CA 2006 restates the exemption in s 347B of the CA 1985 in respect of donations to all-party parliamentary groups.

Fourth, s 377 of the CA 2006 restates the exemption in s 347B of the CA 1985 for political expenditure that is exempt by virtue of an order by the Secretary of State. An order made by statutory instrument under this section may confer an exemption on companies or expenditure of any description or category specified in the order. A parallel power in s 347B(8)–(11) of the CA 1985 was used in 2001 to exempt business activities such as the publication of newspapers, which by their very nature, involve the publication or dissemination of materials that seeks to influence the views of members of the public.

Fifth, s 378 of the CA 2006 restates the exemption in s 347B of the CA 1985 under which authorisation for donations is not required unless the donation or aggregate amount of the donations by the company exceeds £5,000 in a 12-month period. Donations by other group companies (including subsidiaries) must be taken into account in calculating whether the £5,000 threshold has been exceeded.

Trade unions

32.16 Section 374 of the CA 2006 deals with exemptions for trade unions. It states that a trade union is not a political organisation for the purposes of Part 14 of the CA 2006.[8224]

A trade union is also not a political organisation for the purposes of s 365 of the CA 2006 (meaning of 'political expenditure').[8225]

The term 'trade union' has the meaning given by s 1 of the Trade Union and Labour Relations (Consolidation) Act 1992 (c 52) or Article 3 of the Industrial Relations (Northern Ireland) Order 1992 (SI 1992/807 (NI 5)).[8226]

The term 'political fund' means the fund from which payments by a trade union in the furtherance of political objects are required to be made by virtue of s 82(1)(a) of that Act or Article 57(2)(a) of that Order.[8227]

Subscription for membership of a trade association

32.17 Section 375 of the CA 2006 deals with subscription for membership of a trade association. A subscription paid to a trade association for membership of the association is not a political donation for the purposes of Part 14 of the CA 2006.[8228]

A 'trade association' means an organisation formed for the purpose of furthering the trade interests of its members, or of persons represented by its members, and 'subscription' does not include a payment to the association to the extent that it is made for the purpose of financing any particular activity of the association.[8229]

All-party parliamentary groups

32.18 Section 376 of the CA 2006 states that an all-party parliamentary group is not a political organisation for the purposes of Part 14 of the CA 2006.[8230]

The term an 'all-party parliamentary group' means an all-party group composed of members of one or both of the Houses of Parliament (or of such members and other persons).[8231]

Political expenditure exempted by order

32.19 Section 377 of the CA 2006 states that authorisation under Part 14 of the CA 2006 is not needed for political expenditure that is exempt by virtue of an order of the Secretary of State under this section.[8232]

[8224] CA 2006, s 374(1). [8225] CA 2006, s 374(2). [8226] CA 2006, s 374(3).
[8227] CA 2006, s 374(3). [8228] CA 2006, s 375(1). [8229] CA 2006, s 375(2).
[8230] CA 2006, s 376(1). [8231] CA 2006, s 376(2). [8232] CA 2006, s 377(1).

An order may confer an exemption in relation to companies of any description or category specified in the order;[8233] or expenditure of any description or category so specified (whether framed by reference to goods, services or other matters in respect of which such expenditure is incurred or otherwise),[8234] or both.

If or to the extent that expenditure is exempt from the requirement of authorisation under Part 14 of the CA 2006 by virtue of an order under this section, it shall be disregarded in determining what donations are authorised by any resolution of the company are passed for the purposes of this Part.[8235]

An order under this section is subject to affirmative resolution procedure.[8236]

Donations not amounting to more than £5,000 in any 12-month period

32.20 Section 378 of the CA 2006 states that authorisation under Part 14 of the CA 2006 is not needed for a donation except to the extent that the total amount of that donation;[8237] and other relevant donations made in the period of 12 months ending with the date on which that donation is made,[8238] exceeds £5,000.

The term 'donation' means a donation to a political party or other political organisation or to an independent election candidate; and 'other relevant donations' means (a) in relation to a donation made by a company that is not a subsidiary, donations made by that company or by any of its subsidiaries;[8239] (b) in relation to a donation made by a company that is a subsidiary, donations made by that company, by any holding company of that company or by any other subsidiary of any such holding company.[8240]

If or to the extent that a donation is exempt by virtue of this section from the requirement of authorisation under Part 14 of the CA 2006, it will be disregarded in determining what donations are authorised by any resolution passed for the purposes of this Part.[8241]

Supplementary provisions

Minor definitions

32.21 Section 379 of the CA 2006 defines a 'director' to include a shadow director; and the term 'organisation' includes any body corporate or unincorporated association and any combination of persons.[8242]

[8233] CA 2006, s 377(2)(a).   [8234] CA 2006, s 377(2)(b).   [8235] CA 2006, s 377(3).
[8236] CA 2006, s 377(4).   [8237] CA 2006, s 378(1)(a).   [8238] CA 2006, s 378(1)(b).
[8239] CA 2006, s 378(2)(a).   [8240] CA 2006, s 378(2)(b).   [8241] CA 2006, s 378(3).
[8242] CA 2006, s 379(1).

Section 379(2) of the CA 2006 states that except as otherwise provided, any reference in Part 14 of the CA 2006 to the time at which a donation is made or expenditure is incurred is, in a case where the donation is made or expenditure incurred in pursuance of a contract, any earlier time at which that contract is entered into by the company.

The Companies (Political Exemption) Order 2007

32.22 A draft of The Companies (Political Exemption) Order 2007 (SI 2081) has been prepared by the Government. This Order exempts certain of types of political expenditure by companies from the requirement for shareholder authorisation under Part 14 of the CA 2006, if it is incurred by new companies.

The expenditure exempted, described in article 3 of the Order, is that incurred in the preparation, publication and dissemination of news material that is capable of being reasonably regarded as intended to affect public support for a political party or other political organisation, or an independent election candidate, or to influence voters in relation to any national or regional referendum held under the law of a member State.

The companies exempted, described in article 4 of the Order, are those whose ordinary course of business includes the preparation, publication or dissemination to the public, or any part of the public, of news material. It is irrelevant by what means or modes the news material is to be prepared, published or disseminated; where the public or part of it to which such material is published or disseminated is located; or how the public or part of it to which such material is published or disseminated is identified or described. (see article 4(2) of the Order).

This Order replaces the Companies (EU Political Expenditure) Exemption Order 2001, which was made under s 347B of the CA 1985. Section 347B of the CA 1985 is repealed by s 1295 of, and Schedule 16 to, the CA 2006 with effect from the date on which this Order comes into force in Great Britain.

Chapter 33

Miscellaneous

Introduction

33.1 This chapter addresses some of the miscellaneous areas of company law set out in various parts the CA 2006. They are (i) fraudulent trading; (ii) company investigations; (iii) companies: supplementary provisions; (iv) companies: minor amendments; (v) miscellaneous provisions; (vi) Northern Ireland.

Fraudulent Trading

33.2 Part 39 of the CA 2006 sets out the offence of fraudulent trading.

Section 993(1) of the CA 2006 states that where any business of a company is carried on with intent to defraud creditors of the company, or creditors of any other person, or for any fraudulent purpose, every person who is knowingly a party to the carrying on of the business in that manner, commits an offence.

This applies whether or not the company has been, or is in the course of being, wound up.[8243]

A person guilty of an offence under s 993 of the CA 2006 is liable on conviction or indictment, to imprisonment for a term not exceeding ten years of a fine (or both);[8244] on summary conviction in England and Wales, to imprisonment for a term not exceeding 12 months or a fine not exceeding the statutory maximum (or both);[8245] in Scotland or Northern Ireland, to imprisonment for a term not exceeding six months or a fine not exceeding the statutory maximum (or both).[8246]

Section 993 of the CA 2006 restates s 458 of the CA 1985, but in doing so, it also increases the maximum sentence for the offence from seven years' imprisonment to ten years.

[8243] CA 2006, s 993(2).   [8244] CA 2006, s 993(3)(a).   [8245] CA 2006, s 993(3)(b)(i).
[8246] CA 2006, s 993(3)(b)(ii).

Company Investigations

33.3 The CA 2006 amends the CA 1985 in respect of company investigations, which is one of the company law areas remaining under the CA 1985.

Powers of Secretary of State to give directions to inspectors

33.4 Section 1035 of the CA 2006 is concerned with the powers of the Secretary of State to give directions to inspectors. It states:

(1) In Part 14 of the CA 1985 (c 6) (investigation of companies and their affairs), after s 446 insert:

Powers of Secretary of State to give directions to inspectors

446A General powers to give directions

(1) In exercising his functions an inspector shall comply with any direction given to him by the Secretary of State under this section.

(2) The Secretary of State may give an inspector appointed under section 431, 432(2) or 442(1) a direction:

    (a) as to the subject matter of his investigation (whether by reference to a specified area of a company's operation, a specified transaction, a period of time or otherwise); or

    (b) which requires the inspector to take or not to take a specified step in his investigation.

(3) The Secretary of State may give an inspector appointed under any provision of this Part a direction requiring him to secure that a specified report under section 437:

    (a) includes the inspector's views on a specified matter;

    (b) does not include any reference to a specified matter;

    (c) is made in a specified form or manner; or

    (d) is made by a specified date.

(4) A direction under this section:

    (a) may be given on an inspector's appointment;

    (b) may vary or revoke a direction previously given; and

    (c) may be given at the request of an inspector.

(5) In this section:

    (a) a reference to an inspector's investigation includes any investigation he undertakes, or could undertake, under section 433(1) (power to investigate affairs of holding company or subsidiary);

    (b) 'specified' means specified in a direction under this section.

446B Direction to terminate investigation

(1) The Secretary of State may direct an inspector to take no further steps in his investigation.

(2) The Secretary of State may give a direction under this section to an inspector appointed under section 432(1) or 442(3) only on the grounds that it appears to him that:

(a)   matters have come to light in the course of the inspector's investigation which suggest that a criminal offence has been committed; and

(b)   those matters have been referred to the appropriate prosecuting authority.

(3) Where the Secretary of State gives a direction under this section, any direction already given to the inspector under section 437(1) to produce an interim report, and any direction given to him under section 446A(3) in relation to such a report, shall cease to have effect.

(4) Where the Secretary of State gives a direction under this section, the inspector shall not make a final report to the Secretary of State unless:

(a)   the direction was made on the grounds mentioned in subsection (2) and the Secretary of State directs the inspector to make a final report to him; or

(b)   the inspector was appointed under section 432(1) (appointment in pursuance of order of the court).

(5) An inspector shall comply with any direction given to him under this section.

(6) In this section, a reference to an inspector's investigation includes any investigation he undertakes, or could undertake, under section 433(1) (power to investigate affairs of holding company or subsidiary).

In s 431 of that Act (inspectors' powers during investigation) in subs (1), for 'report on them in such manner as he may direct', substitute 'report the result of their investigations to him'.

In section 432 of that Act (other company investigations) in subs (1) for 'report on them in such manner as he directs', substitute 'report the result of their investigations to him'.

In section 437 of that Act (inspectors' reports):

(a)   in subs (1) omit the second sentence; and

(b)   subss (1B) and (1C) shall cease to have effect.

In s 442 of that Act (power to investigate company ownership), omit subs (2).

Section 1035(1) of the CA 2006 inserts new ss 446A and 446B into the CA 2006, which provide new powers for the Secretary of State to give directions to inspectors with which they are obliged to comply: ss 446A(1) and 446(B)(5).

Powers to appoint inspectors

33.5 The CA 1985 gave the Secretary of State the power to appoint competent inspectors to carry out inspections, and report the result to him, in a number of circumstances. Under this Act, there were three categories of investigations:

- investigations into the affairs of companies;
- investigations into the membership or control of companies; and
- investigations of dealings in share options by company directors and their families and failure to disclose interests in shares.

Investigations by inspectors into the affairs of companies and certain other bodies corporate could be initiated under ss 431 and 432 of the CA 1985. Such inspections could be launched on the application of a company or a proportion of its members, or on the Secretary of State's own initiative, and must be carried out where the court orders it.

Investigations by inspectors into the membership or control of companies can be initiated under s 442 of the CA 1985. The Secretary of State could launch such an inspection on his own initiative under s 442(1), and was obliged to do so in cases where the requisite number of members of a company applied.

Inspections in the third category, under s 446, related to suspected contraventions of certain provisions of Part 10 of the CA 1985. The CA 2006 repeals the relevant provisions of Part 10 (see s 1177) and s 446 is repealed in consequence.

Two inspectors were generally appointed to carry out an inspection – usually a QC, and a partner in one of the leading accountancy firms.

Inspectors were appointed to investigate and to report the results of their investigations to the Secretary of State. At the end of the inspection, the inspectors generally had a duty to make a final report to the Secretary of State. The inspectors could also make an interim reports during the course of the inspection, and the Secretary of State could direct them to do so.

Unless the appointment was made under s 432 of the CA 1985 on terms that any report is not for publication (s 432 (2A)), interim and final reports were publishable; the Secretary of State had discretion to publish an interim or final report under s 437 (3) of the CA 1985. The availability of a published report is a crucial aspect of the inspection system.

Changes brought in by CA 2006

33.6 The CA 2006 confers new powers on the Secretary of State to bring to an end an investigation when it is no longer in the public interest to continue with it, to revoke the appointment of an inspector and issue directions about the scope of an investigation, its duration and certain other matters.

The main purpose of these sections is to give the Secretary of State power to take appropriate action where an investigation appears to be taking too long. The sections also provide for situations not currently explicitly provided for, such as the resignation or death of inspectors, and the ability to appoint replacement of inspectors.

The details of these changes and the circumstances in which the changes will apply are set out below.

Subsection (1) inserts new ss 446A and 446B into the CA 1985, which provide new powers for the Secretary of State to give directions to inspectors with which they are obliged to comply (new ss 446A(1) and 446B(5)).

Resignation, removal and replacement of inspectors

33.7 Section 1036 of the CA 2006 inserts new provisions in the CA 1985 on resignation, removal and replacement of inspectors. It states:

> After section 446B of the CA 1985 (c 6) (inserted by s 1035 above) insert:
>
> Resignation, removal and replacement of inspectors
>
> 446C Resignation and revocation of appointment
> (1) An inspector may resign by notice in writing to the Secretary of State.
> (2) The Secretary of State may revoke the appointment of an inspector by notice in writing to the inspector.
>
> 446D Appointment of replacement inspectors
> (1) Where:
>   (a) an inspector resigns;
>   (b) an inspector's appointment is revoked; or
>   (c) an inspector dies;
>   the Secretary of State may appoint one or more competent inspectors to continue the investigation.
> (2) An appointment under subsection (1) shall be treated for the purposes of this Part (apart from this section) as an appointment under the provision of this Part under which the former inspector was appointed.
> (3) The Secretary of State must exercise his power under subsection (1) so as to secure that at least one inspector continues the investigation.
> (4) Subsection (3) does not apply if:
>   (a) the Secretary of State could give a replacement inspector a direction under section 446B (termination of investigation); and
>   (b) such a direction would (under subsection (4) of that section) result in a final report not being made.
> (5) In this section, references to an investigation include any investigation the former inspector conducted under section 433(1) (power to investigate affairs of holding company or subsidiary).

Power to obtain information from former inspectors, etc.

33.8 Section 1037 of the CA 2006 inserts new provisions in the CA 1985 on power to obtain information from former inspectors. It states:

(1) After section 446D of the CA 1985 (c 6) (inserted by s 1036 above) insert:

Power to obtain information from former inspectors, etc.

446E Obtaining information from former inspectors, etc.

(1) This section applies to a person who was appointed as an inspector under this Part:

(a) who has resigned; or

(b) whose appointment has been revoked.

(2) This section also applies to an inspector to whom the Secretary of State has given a direction under section 446B (termination of investigation).

(3) The Secretary of State may direct a person to whom this section applies to produce documents obtained or generated by that person during the course of his investigation to:

(a) the Secretary of State; or

(b) an inspector appointed under this Part.

(4) The power under subsection (3) to require production of a document includes power, in the case of a document not in hard copy form, to require the production of a copy of the document:

(a) in hard copy form; or

(b) in a form from which a hard copy can be readily obtained.

(5) The Secretary of State may take copies of or extracts from a document produced in pursuance of this section.

(6) The Secretary of State may direct a person to whom this section applies to inform him of any matters that came to that person's knowledge as a result of his investigation.

(7) A person shall comply with any direction given to him under this section.

(8) In this section:

(a) references to the investigation of a former inspector or inspector include any investigation he conducted under section 433(1) (power to investigate affairs of holding company or subsidiary); and

(b) 'document' includes information recorded in any form.

(2) In section 451A of that Act (disclosure of information by Secretary of State or inspector), in subsection (1)(a) for '446' substitute '446E'.

(3) In section 452(1) of that Act (privileged information) for '446' substitute '446E'.

Power to require production of documents

33.9 Section 1038 of the CA 2006 inserts new provisions in the CA 1985 on power to require production of documentation.

(1) In s 434 of the CA 1985 (c 6) (production of documents and evidence to inspectors), for subs (6) substitute:

(6) In this section 'document' includes information recorded in any form.

(7) The power under this section to require production of a document includes power, in the case of a document not in hard copy form, to require the production of a copy of the document:

(a) in hard copy form; or

(b) in a form from which a hard copy can be readily obtained.

(8) An inspector may take copies of or extracts from a document produced in pursuance of this section.

(2) In s 447 of the CA 1985 (power of the Secretary of State to require documents and information), for subsection (9) substitute:

(9) The power under this section to require production of a document includes power, in the case of a document not in hard copy form, to require the production of a copy of the document.

(a) in hard copy form; or

(b) in a form from which a hard copy can be readily obtained.

Disqualification orders: consequential amendments

33.10 Section 1039 of the CA 2006 deals with disqualification orders and inserts new provision in the Company Directors' Disqualification Act 1986. It states:

In section 8(1A)(b)(i) of the Company Directors' Disqualification Act 1986 (c 46) (disqualification after investigation of company: meaning of 'investigative material'):

(a) after 'section' insert '437, 446E,'; and

(b) after '448' insert, '451A'.

Companies: Supplementary Provisions

33.11 Part 37 of the CA 2006 deals with supplementary provisions governing companies. They are concerned with: company records; service addresses; sending or supplying documents or information; requirements as to independent valuation; notices of the appointment of certain officers; and courts and legal proceedings.

Meaning of 'company records'

33.12 Section 1134 of the CA 2006 sets out the definition of 'company records' referred to in various sections. The term 'company records' means any register, index, accounting records, agreement, memorandum, minutes or other document required by the Companies Acts to be kept by a company;[8247] and any register kept by a company of its debenture holders.[8248]

Forms of company records

33.13 Section 1135 of the CA 2006 states that the company records may be kept in hard copy or electronic form;[8249] and may be arranged in such manner as the directors of the company think fit,[8250] provided the information in question is adequately recorded for future reference.

Where the records are kept in electronic form, they must be capable of being reproduced in hard copy form.[8251]

If a company fails to comply with this section, an offence is committed by every officer of the company who is in default.[8252] A person guilty of an offence under s 1135 of the CA 2006 is liable on summary conviction to a fine not exceeding level 3 on the standard scale and, for continued contravention, a daily default fine not exceeding one-tenth of level 3 on the standard scale.[8253]

Any provision of an instrument made by a company before 12 February 1979 that requires a register of holders of the company's debentures to be kept in hard copy form is to be read as requiring it to be kept in hard copy or electronic form.[8254]

Regulations about where certain company records to be kept available for inspection

Section 1136 of the CA 2006 states that the Secretary of State may make provision by regulations specifying places other than a company's registered office at which company records required to be kept available for inspection under a relevant provision may be so kept in compliance with that provision.[8255]

The 'relevant provisions' are:[8256]

[8247] CA 2006, s 1134(a).   [8248] CA 2006, s 1134(b).   [8249] CA 2006, s 1135(1)(a).
[8250] CA 2006, s 1135(1)(b).   [8251] CA 2006, s 1135(2).   [8252] CA 2006, s 1135(3).
[8253] CA 2006, s 1135(4).   [8254] CA 2006, s 1135(5).
[8255] CA 2006, s 1136(1). See the Companies (Company Records and Fees) Regulations 2007.
[8256] CA 2006, s 1136(2).

s 114 of the CA 2006 (register of members);

s 162 of the CA 2006 (register of directors);

s 228 of the CA 2006 (directors' service contracts);

s 237 of the CA 2006 (directors' indemnities);

s 275 of the CA 2006 (register of secretaries);

s 358 of the CA 2006 (records of resolutions etc);

s 702 of the CA 2006 (contracts relating to purchase of own shares);

s 720 of the CA 2006 (documents relating to redemption or purchase of own shares out of capital by private company);

s 743 of the CA 2006 (register of debenture holders);

s 805 of the CA 2006 (report to members of outcome of investigation by public company into interests in its shares);

s 809 of the CA 2006 (register of interests in shares disclosed to public company);

s 877 of the CA 2006 (instruments creating charges and register of charges: England and Wales);

s 892 of the CA 2006 (instruments creating charges and register of charges: Scotland).

The regulations may specify a place by reference to the company's principal place of business, the part of the United Kingdom in which the company is registered, the place at which the company keeps any other records available for inspection or in any other way.[8257]

The regulations may provide that a company does not comply with a relevant provision by keeping company records available for inspection at a place specified in the regulations unless conditions specified in the regulations are met.[8258]

The regulations need not specify a place in relation to each relevant provision;[8259] they may specify more than one place in relation to a relevant provision.[8260]

A requirement under a relevant provision to keep company records available for inspection is not complied with by keeping them available for inspection at a place specified in the regulations unless all the company's records subject to the requirement are kept there.[8261]

Regulations under this section are subject to negative resolution procedure.[8262]

Regulations about inspection of records and provision of copies

33.14 Section 1137 of the CA 2006 states that the Secretary of State may make provision by regulations, as to the obligations of a company that is

---

[8257] CA 2006, s 1136(3).   [8258] CA 2006, s 1136(4).   [8259] CA 2006, s 1136(5)(a).
[8260] CA 2006, s 1136(5)(b).   [8261] CA 2006, s 1136(6).   [8262] CA 2006, s 1136(7).

required by any provision of the Companies Acts to keep available for inspection any company records;[8263] or to provide copies of any company records.[8264]

A company that fails to comply with the regulations is treated as having refused inspection or, as the case may be, having failed to provide a copy.[8265]

The regulations may make provision as to the time, duration and manner of inspection, including the circumstances in which and extent to which the copying of information is permitted in the course of inspection;[8266] and define what may be required of the company as regards the nature, extent and manner of extracting or presenting any information for the purposes of inspection or the provision of copies.[8267]

Where there is power to charge a fee, the regulations may make provision as to the amount of the fee and the basis of its calculation.[8268]

Nothing in any provision of the CA 2006 or in the regulations is to be read as preventing a company from affording more extensive facilities than are required by the regulations;[8269] or where a fee may be charged, from charging a lesser fee than that prescribed or none at all.[8270]

Regulations under this section are subject to negative resolution procedure.[8271]

Duty to take precautions against falsification

33.15 Section 1138 of the CA 2006 states that where company records are kept otherwise than in bound books, adequate precautions must be taken to guard against falsification;[8272] and to facilitate the discovery of falsification.[8273]

If a company fails to comply with s 1138 of the CA 2006, an offence is committed by every officer of the company who is in default.[8274] A person guilty of an offence under s 1138 of the CA 2006 is liable on summary conviction to a fine not exceeding level 3 on the standard scale and, for continued contravention, a daily default fine not exceeding one-tenth of level 3 on the standard scale.[8275]

This section does not apply to the documents required to be kept under s 228 of the CA 2006 (copy of directors' service contract or memorandum of its terms);[8276] or s 237 of the CA 2006 (qualifying indemnity provision).[8277]

[8263] CA 2006, s 1137(1)(a).   [8264] CA 2006, s 1137(1)(b).   [8265] CA 2006, s 1137(2).
[8266] CA 2006, s 1137(3)(a).   [8267] CA 2006, s 1137(3)(b).   [8268] CA 2006, s 1137(4).
[8269] CA 2006, s 1137(5)(a).   [8270] CA 2006, s 1137(5)(b).   [8271] CA 2006, s 1137(6).
[8272] CA 2006, s 1138(1)(a).   [8273] CA 2006, s 1138(1)(b).   [8274] CA 2006, s 1138(2).
[8275] CA 2006, s 1138(3).   [8276] CA 2006, s 1138(4)(a).   [8277] CA 2006, s 1138(4)(b).

Service addresses

33.16 Sections 1139–1142 of the CA 2006 are concerned with service addresses.

Service of documents on a company

33.17 Section 1139 of the CA 2006 states that a document may be served on a company registered under CA 2006 by leaving it at, or sending it by post to, the company's registered office.

A document may be served on an overseas company whose particulars are registered under s 1046 of the CA 2006 by leaving it at, or sending it by post to, the registered address of any person resident in the United Kingdom who is authorised to accept service of documents on the company's behalf;[8278] or if there is no such person, or if any such person refuses service or service cannot for any other reason be effected, by leaving it at or sending by post to any place of business of the company in the United Kingdom.[8279]

A person's 'registered address' means any address for the time being shown as a current address in relation to that person in the part of the register available for public inspection.[8280]

Where a company registered in Scotland or Northern Ireland carries on business in England and Wales, the process of any court in England and Wales may be served on the company by leaving it at, or sending it by post to, the company's principal place of business in England and Wales, addressed to the manager or other head office in England and Wales of the company.

Where process is served on a company under this subsection, the person issuing out the process must send a copy of it by post to the company's registered office.[8281]

Further provision as to service and other matters is made in the company communications provisions (see s 1143 of the CA 2006).[8282]

Service of documents on directors, secretaries and others

33.18 Section 1140 of the CA 2006 states that a document may be served on a person to whom this section applies by leaving it at, or sending it by post to, the person's registered address.[8283]

Section 1140 of the CA 2006 applies to:

(a) a director or secretary of a company;[8284]
(b) in the case of an overseas company whose particulars are registered

---

[8278] CA 2006, s 1139(2)(a).   [8279] CA 2006, s 1139(2)(b).   [8280] CA 2006, s 1139(3).
[8281] CA 2006, s 1139(4).   [8282] CA 2006, s 1139(5).   [8283] CA 2006, s 1140(1).
[8284] CA 2006, s 1140(2)(a).

under s 1046 of the CA 2006, a person holding any such position as may be specified for the purposes of this section by regulations under that section;[8285]

(c) a person appointed in relation to a company as (i) a judicial factor (in Scotland),[8286] (ii) a receiver and manager appointed under s 18 of the Charities Act 1993 (c. 10),[8287] or (iii) a manager appointed under s 47 of the Companies (Audit, Investigations and Community Enterprise) Act 2004 (c 27).[8288]

Section 1140 of the CA 2006 applies whatever the purpose of the document in question. It is not restricted to service for purposes arising out of or in connection with the appointment or position mentioned in s 1140(2) of the CA 2006, or in connection with the company concerned.[8289]

For the purposes of this section, a person's 'registered address' means any address for the time being shown as a current address in relation to that person, in the part of the register available for public inspection.[8290]

If notice of a change of that address is given to the registrar, a person may validly serve a document at the address previously registered until the end of the period of 14 days beginning with the date on which notice of the change is registered.[8291]

Service may not be effected by virtue of this section at an address (a) if notice has been registered of the termination of the appointment in relation to which the address was registered, and the address is not a registered address of the person concerned in relation to any other appointment;[8292] (b) in the case of a person holding any such position as is mentioned in s 1140(2)(b) of the CA 2006, if the overseas company has ceased to have any connection with the United Kingdom, by virtue of which it is required to register particulars under s 1046 of the CA 2006.[8293]

Further provision as to service and other matters is made in the company communications provisions (see s 1143 of the CA 2006).[8294]

Nothing in this section is to be read as affecting any enactment or rule of law under which permission is required for service out of the jurisdiction.[8295]

Service addresses

33.19 Section 1141 of the CA 2006 states that in the Companies Acts, a 'service address', in relation to a person, means an address at which documents may be effectively served on that person.[8296]

[8285] CA 2006, s 1140(2)(b). [8286] CA 2006, s 1140(2)(c)(i).
[8287] CA 2006, s 1140(2)(c)(ii). [8288] CA 2006, s 1140(2)(c)(iii).
[8289] CA 2006, s 1140(3). [8290] CA 2006, s 1140(4). [8291] CA 2006, s 1140(5).
[8292] CA 2006, s 1140(6)(a). [8293] CA 2006, s 1140(6)(b). [8294] CA 2006, s 1140(7).
[8295] CA 2006, s 1140(8). [8296] CA 2006, s 1141(1).

The Secretary of State may by regulations specify conditions with which a service address must comply.[8297]

Regulations under this section are subject to negative resolution procedure.[8298]

Requirement to give a service address

33.20 Section 1,142 of the CA 2006 states that any obligation under the Companies Acts to give a person's address is, unless otherwise expressly provided, to give a service address for that person.

Sending or supplying documents or information

33.21 Sections 1,143–1,148 of the CA 2006 deal with sending or supplying documents or information.

The company communications provisions

33.22 Section 1143 of the CA 2006 states that the provisions of ss 1144–1148 and Schedules 4 and 5 of the CA 2006 (the company communications provisions) apply for the purposes of any provision of the Companies Acts, which authorises or requires documents or information to be sent or supplied by or to a company.[8299]

The company communications provisions have effect subject to any requirements imposed, or contrary provision made, by or under any enactment.[8300]

In particular, in their application in relation to documents or information to be sent or supplied to the registrar, they have effect subject to the provisions of Part 35 of the CA 2006.[8301]

For the purposes of s 1143(2) of the CA 2006, provision is not to be regarded as contrary to the company communications provisions, by reason only of the fact that it expressly authorises a document or information to be sent or supplied in hard copy form, in electronic form or by means of a website.[8302]

Sending or supplying documents or information

33.23 Section 1144 of the CA 2006 states that documents or information to be sent or supplied to a company, must be sent or supplied in accordance with the provisions of Schedule 4 of the CA 2006.[8303]

[8297] CA 2006, s 1141(2). See regulation 14 of the Companies (Annual Return and Service Addresses) Regulations 2007.
[8298] CA 2006, s 1141(3).   [8299] CA 2006, s 1143(1).   [8300] CA 2006, s 1143(2).
[8301] CA 2006, s 1143(3).   [8302] CA 2006, s 1143(4).   [8303] CA 2006, s 1144(1).

Documents or information to be sent or supplied by a company, must be sent or supplied in accordance with the provisions of Schedule 5 of the CA 2006.[8304]

The provisions referred to in s 1144(2) of the CA 2006 apply (and those referred to in s 1144(1) of the CA 2006 do not apply), in relation to documents or information that are to be sent or supplied by one company to another.[8305]

Right to hard copy version

33.24 Section 1145 of the CA 2006 states that where a member of a company or a holder of a company's debentures has received a document or information from the company otherwise than in hard copy form, he is entitled to require the company to send him a version of the document or information in hard copy form.[8306]

The company must send the document or information in hard copy form within 21 days of receipt of the request from the member or debenture holder.[8307]

The company may not make a charge for providing the document or information in that form.[8308]

If a company fails to comply with s 1144 of the CA 2006, an offence is committed by the company and every officer of it who is in default.[8309] A person guilty of an offence under s 1144 of the CA 2006 is liable on summary conviction to a fine not exceeding level 3 on the standard scale and, for continued contravention, a daily default fine not exceeding one-tenth of level 3 on the standard scale.[8310]

Requirement of authentication

33.25 Section 1146 of the CA 2006 applies in relation to the authentication of a document or information sent or supplied by a person to a company.[8311]

A document or information sent or supplied in hard copy form, is sufficiently authenticated if it is signed by the person sending or supplying it.[8312]

A document or information sent or supplied in electronic form is sufficiently authenticated, if the identity of the sender is confirmed in a manner specified by the company;[8313] or where no such manner has been specified by the company, if the communication contains or is accompanied by a statement of the identity of the sender and the company has no reason to doubt the truth of that statement.[8314]

[8304] CA 2006, s 1144(2).   [8305] CA 2006, s 1144(3).   [8306] CA 2006, s 1144(1).
[8307] CA 2006, s 1144(2).   [8308] CA 2006, s 1144(3).   [8309] CA 2006, s 1144(4).
[8310] CA 2006, s 1144(5).   [8311] CA 2006, s 1146(1).   [8312] CA 2006, s 1146(2).
[8313] CA 2006, s 1146(3)(a).   [8314] CA 2006, s 1146(3)(b).

Where a document or information is sent or supplied by one person on behalf of another, nothing in s 1144 of the CA 2006 affects any provision of the company's articles, under which the company may require reasonable evidence of the authority of the former, to act on behalf of the latter.[8315]

Deemed delivery of documents and information

33.26 Section 1147 of the CA 2006 applies in relation to documents and information sent or supplied by a company.[8316]

Where the document or information is sent by post (whether in hard copy or electronic form) to an address in the United Kingdom;[8317] and the company is able to show that it was properly addressed, prepaid and posted,[8318] it is deemed to have been received by the intended recipient 48 hours after it was posted.

Where the document or information is sent or supplied by electronic means;[8319] and the company is able to show that it was properly addressed,[8320] it is deemed to have been received by the intended recipient 48 hours after it was sent.

Where the document or information is sent or supplied by means of a website, it is deemed to have been received by the intended recipient when the material was first made available on the website;[8321] or if later, when the recipient received (or is deemed to have received) notice of the fact that the material was available on the website.[8322]

In calculating a period of hours for the purposes of this section, no account will be taken of any part of a day that is not a working day.[8323]

Section 1147 of the CA 2006 applies subject to:

(a) in its application to documents or information sent or supplied by a company to its members, any contrary provision of the company's articles;[8324]

(b) in its application to documents or information sent or supplied by a company to its debentures holders, any contrary provision in the instrument constituting the debentures;[8325]

(c) in its application to documents or information sent or supplied by a company to a person otherwise than in his capacity as a member or debenture holder, any contrary provision in an agreement between the company and that person.[8326]

[8315] CA 2006, s 1146(4).   [8316] CA 2006, s 1147(1).   [8317] CA 2006, s 1147(2)(a).

[8318] CA 2006, s 1147(2)(b).   [8319] CA 2006, s 1147((3)(a).   [8320] CA 2006, s 1147(3)(b).

[8321] CA 2006, s 1147(4)(a).   [8322] CA 2006, s 1147(4)(b).   [8323] CA 2006, s 1147(5).

[8324] CA 2006, s 1148(6)(a).   [8325] CA 2006, s 1148(6)(b).   [8326] CA 2006, s 1148(6)(c).

Interpretation of company communications provisions

33.27 Section 1148 of the CA 2006 deals with the interpretation of company communication provisions. In the company communications provisions the term 'address' includes a number or address used for the purposes of sending or receiving documents or information by electronic means; 'company' includes any body corporate; and 'document' includes summons, notice, order or other legal process and registers.[8327]

References in the company communications provisions to provisions of the Companies Acts authorising or requiring a document or information to be sent or supplied include all such provisions, whatever expression is used, and references to documents or information being sent or supplied shall be construed accordingly.[8328]

References in the company communications provisions to documents or information being sent or supplied by or to a company, include references to documents or information being sent or supplied by, or to the directors of a company acting on behalf of the company.[8329]

Requirements as to independent valuation

33.28 Sections 1149–1153 of the CA 2006 deal with the requirements as to independent valuation for the purposes of certain provisions of the CA 2006.

Application of valuation requirements

33.29 Section 1149 of the CA 2006 states that the provisions of ss 1150–1153 of the CA 2006 apply to the valuation and report required by s 93 of the CA 2006 (re-registration as public company: recent allotment of shares for non-cash consideration); s 593 of the CA 2006 (allotment of shares of public company in consideration of non-cash asset); s 599 of the CA 2006 (transfer of non-cash asset to public company).

Valuation by qualified independent person

33.30 Section 1150 of the CA 2006 states that the valuation and report must be made by a person (the valuer) who is eligible for appointment as a statutory auditor (see s 1212 of the CA 2006);[8330] and meets the independence requirement in s 1151 of the CA 2006.[8331]

However, where it appears to the valuer to be reasonable for the valuation of the consideration, or part of it, to be made by (or for him to accept a valuation made by) another person who:

[8327] CA 2006, s 1148(1).   [8328] CA 2006, s 1148(2).   [8329] CA 2006, s 1148(3).
[8330] CA 2006, s 1150(1)(a).   [8331] CA 2006, s 1150(1)(b).

(a) appears to him to have the requisite knowledge and experience to value the consideration or that part of it;[8332] and

(b) is not an officer or employee of (i) the company,[8333] or (ii) any other body corporate that is that company's subsidiary or holding company or a subsidiary of that company's holding company,[8334] or a partner of or employed by any such officer or employee,

he may arrange for or accept such a valuation, together with a report that will enable him to make his own report under this section.

The references in 1150(2)(b) of the CA 2006 to an officer or employee do not include an auditor.[8335]

Where the consideration or part of it is valued by a person other than the valuer himself, the latter's report must state that fact and shall also state the former's name and what knowledge and experience he has to carry out the valuation;[8336] and describe so much of the consideration as was valued by the other person, and the method used to value it, and specify the date of that valuation.[8337]

The independence requirement

33.31 Section 1151 of the CA 2006 states that a person meets the independence requirement for the purposes of s 1150 of the CA 2006 only if:

(a) he is not (i) an officer or employee of the company,[8338] or (ii) a partner or employee of such a person, or a partnership of which such a person is a partner;[8339]

(b) he is not (i) an officer or employee of an associated undertaking of the company,[8340] or (ii) a partner or employee of such a person, or a partnership of which such a person is a partner;[8341] and

(c) there does not exist between (i) the person or an associate of his,[8342] and (ii) the company or an associated undertaking of the company,[8343] a connection of any such description as may be specified by regulations made by the Secretary of State.

An auditor of the company is not regarded as an officer or employee of the company for this purpose.[8344]

The term 'associated undertaking' means a parent undertaking or

[8332] CA 2006, s 1150(2)(a).
[8333] CA 2006, s 1150(2)(b)(i).
[8334] CA 2006, s 1150(2)(b)(ii).
[8335] CA 2006, s 1150(3).
[8336] CA 2006, s 1150(4)(a).
[8337] CA 2006, s 1150(4)(b).
[8338] CA 2006, s 1151(a)(i).
[8339] CA 2006, s 1151(1)(a)(ii).
[8340] CA 2006, s 1151(1)(b)(i).
[8341] CA 2006, s 1151(1)(b)(ii).
[8342] CA 2006, s 1151(1)(c)(i).
[8343] CA 2006, s 1151(1)(c)(ii).
[8344] CA 2006, s 1151(2).

subsidiary undertaking of the company;[8345] or a subsidiary undertaking of a parent undertaking of the company;[8346] and 'associate' has the meaning given by s 1152 of the CA 2006.

Regulations under this section are subject to negative resolution procedure.[8347]

Meaning of 'associate'

33.32 Section 1152 of the CA 2006 defines 'associate' for the purposes of s 1151 of the CA 2006 (valuation: independence requirement).[8348]

In relation to an individual, 'associate' means:

(a)   that individual's spouse or civil partner or minor child or step-child;[8349]
(b)   any body corporate of which that individual is a director;[8350] and
(c)   any employee or partner of that individual.[8351]

In relation to a body corporate, 'associate' means:

(a)   any body corporate of which that body is a director;[8352]
(b)   any body corporate in the same group as that body;[8353] and
(c)   any employee or partner of that body or of any body corporate in the same group.[8354]

In relation to a partnership that is a legal person under the law by which it is governed, 'associate' means:

(a)   any body corporate of which that partnership is a director;[8355]
(b)   any employee of or partner in that partnership;[8356] and
(c)   any person who is an associate of a partner in that partnership.[8357]

In relation to a partnership that is not a legal person under the law by which it is governed, 'associate' means any person who is an associate of any of the partners.[8358]

In this section, in relation to a limited liability partnership, for 'director', read 'member'.[8359]

[8345] CA 2006, s 1151(3)(a).   [8346] CA 2006, s 1151(3)(b).   [8347] CA 2006, s 1151(4).
[8348] CA 2006, s 1152(1).   [8349] CA 2006, s 1152(2)(a).   [8350] CA 2006, s 1152(2)(b).
[8351] CA 2006, s 1152(2)(c).   [8352] CA 2006, s 1152(3)(a).   [8353] CA 2006, s 1152(3)(b).
[8354] CA 2006, s 1152(3)(c).   [8355] CA 2006, s 1152(4)(a).   [8356] CA 2006, s 1152(4)(b).
[8357] CA 2006, s 1152(4)(c).   [8358] CA 2006, s 1152(5).   [8359] CA 2006, s 1152(6).

Valuer entitled to full disclosure

33.33 Section 1153 of the CA 2006 states that a person carrying out a valuation or making a report with respect to any consideration proposed to be accepted or given by a company, is entitled to require from the officers of the company such information and explanation as he thinks necessary to enable him to carry out the valuation or make the report;[8360] and provide any note required by s 596(3) or 600(3) of the CA 2006 (note required where a valuation is carried out by another person).[8361]

A person who knowingly or recklessly makes a statement to which this subsection applies that is misleading, false or deceptive in a material particular commits an offence.[8362]

Section 1153 (2) of the CA 2006 applies to a statement made (whether orally or in writing) to a person carrying out a valuation or making a report;[8363] and conveying or purporting to convey any information or explanation which that person requires, or is entitled to require, under subs (1).[8364]

A person guilty of an offence under s 1153 (2) of the CA 2006 is liable on conviction on indictment, to imprisonment for a term not exceeding two years or a fine (or both);[8365] on summary conviction in England and Wales, to imprisonment for a term not exceeding 12 months or to a fine not exceeding the statutory maximum (or both);[8366] in Scotland or Northern Ireland, to imprisonment for a term not exceeding six months, or to a fine not exceeding the statutory maximum (or both).[8367]

Notice of appointment of certain officers

Duty to notify registrar of certain appointments, etc.

33.34 Section 1154 of the CA 2006 states that notice must be given to the registrar of the appointment in relation to a company of a judicial factor (in Scotland);[8368] a receiver and manager appointed under s 18 of the Charities Act 1993 (c 10);[8369] or a manager appointed under s 47 of the Companies (Audit, Investigations and Community Enterprise) Act 2004 (c 27).[8370]

The notice must be given:

(a)   in the case of appointment of a judicial factor, by the judicial factor;[8371]
(b)   in the case of appointment of a receiver and manager under s 18 of the Charities Act 1993 (c 10), by the Charity Commission;[8372]

[8360] CA 2006, s 1153(1)(a).   [8361] CA 2006, s 1153(1)(b).   [8362] CA 2006, s 1153(2).
[8363] CA 2006, s 1153(3)(a).   [8364] CA 2006, s 1153(3)(b).   [8365] CA 2006, s 1153(4)(a).
[8366] CA 2006, s 1153(4)(b)(i).   [8367] CA 2006, s 1153(4)(b)(ii).
[8368] CA 2006, s 1154(1)(a).   [8369] CA 2006, s 1154(1)(b).   [8370] CA 2006, s 1154(1)(c).
[8371] CA 2006, s 1154(2)(a).   [8372] CA 2006, s 1154(2)(b).

(c) in the case of appointment of a manager under s 47 of the Companies (Audit, Investigations and Community Enterprise) Act 2004, by the Regulator of Community Interest Companies.[8373]

The notice must specify an address at which service of documents (including legal process) may be effected on the person appointed.[8374]

Notice of a change in the address for service may be given to the registrar by the person appointed.

Where notice has been given under this section of the appointment of a person, noti . must also be given to the registrar of the termination of the appointment.[8375]

This notice must be given by the person specified in subs (2).

Offence of failure to give notice

33.35 Section 1156 of the CA 2006 states that if a judicial factor fails to give notice of his appointment in accordance with s 1154 of the CA 2006 within a period of 14 days of the appointment, he commits an offence.[8376] A person guilty of an offence under this section is liable on summary conviction to a fine not exceeding level 5 on the standard scale and, for continued contravention, a daily default fine not exceeding one-tenth of level 5 on the standard scale.[8377]

Courts and legal proceedings

Meaning of 'the court'

33.36 Section 1,156 of the CA 2006 states that except as otherwise provided, in the Companies Acts 'the court' means:

(a) in England and Wales, the High Court or (subject to s 1156(3) of the CA 2006) a county court;[8378]
(b) in Scotland, the Court of Session or the sheriff court;[8379]
(c) in Northern Ireland, the High Court.[8380]

The provisions of the Companies Acts conferring jurisdiction on 'the court' as defined above have effect subject to any enactment or rule of law relating to the allocation of jurisdiction or distribution of business between courts in any part of the United Kingdom.[8381]

[8373] CA 2006, s 1154(2)(c). [8374] CA 2006, s 1154(3). [8375] CA 2006, s 1154(4).
[8376] CA 2006, s 1155(1). [8377] CA 2006, s 1155(2). [8378] CA 2006, s 1156(1)(a).
[8379] CA 2006, s 1156(1)(b). [8380] CA 2006, s 1156(1)(c), [8381] CA 2006, s 1156(2).

The Lord Chancellor may, with the concurrence of the Lord Chief Justice, by order exclude a county court from having jurisdiction under the Companies Acts;[8382] and for the purposes of that jurisdiction attach that court's district, or any part of it, to another county court.[8383]

The Lord Chief Justice may nominate a judicial office holder (as defined in s 109(4) of the Constitutional Reform Act 2005 (c 4)) to exercise his functions under s 1156(3) of the CA 2006.[8384]

Power of court to grant relief in certain cases

33.37 Section 1157 of the CA 2006 states that if in proceedings for negligence, default, breach of duty or breach of trust against an officer of a company;[8385] or a person employed by a company as auditor (whether he is or is not an officer of the company),[8386] it appears to the court hearing the case that the officer or person is or may be liable, but that he acted honestly and reasonably, and that having regard to all the circumstances of the case (including those connected with his appointment) he ought fairly to be excused, the court may relieve him, either wholly or in part, from his liability on such terms as it thinks fit.

If any such officer or person has reason to apprehend that a claim will or might be made against him in respect of negligence, default, breach of duty or breach of trust he may apply to the court for relief;[8387] and the court has the same power to relieve him as it would have had if it had been a court before which proceedings against him for negligence, default, breach of duty or breach of trust had been brought.[8388]

Where a case to which s 1157(1) of the CA 2006 applies is being tried by a judge with a jury, the judge, after hearing the evidence, may, if he is satisfied that the defendant (in Scotland, the defender) ought in pursuance of that subsection to be relieved either in whole or in part from the liability sought to be enforced against him, withdraw the case from the jury and forthwith direct judgment to be entered for the defendant (in Scotland, grant decree of absolvitor) on such terms as to costs (in Scotland, expenses) or otherwise as the judge may think proper.[8389]

Companies: Interpretation

33.38 Sections 1158–1174 of the CA 2006 deal with interpretation provisions.

[8382] CA 2006, s 1156(3)(a).   [8383] CA 2006, s 1156(3)(b).   [8384] CA 2006, s 1156(4).
[8385] CA 2006, s 1157(1)(a).   [8386] CA 2006, s 1157(1)(b).   [8387] CA 2006, s 1157(2)(a).
[8388] CA 2006, s 1157(2)(b).   [8389] CA 2006, s 1157(3).

Meaning of 'UK-registered company'.

33.39 Section 1158 of the CA 2006 states that in the Companies Acts 'UK-registered company' means a company registered under the CA 2006.

The expression does not include an overseas company that has registered particulars under s 1046 of the CA 2006.

Meaning of 'subsidiary' and related expressions

Meaning of 'subsidiary', etc.

33.40 Section 1159 of the CA 2006 states that a company is a 'subsidiary' of another company, its 'holding company', if that other company:

(a) holds a majority of the voting rights in it;[8390] or
(b) is a member of it and has the right to appoint or remove a majority of its board of directors;[8391] or
(c) is a member of it and controls alone, pursuant to an agreement with other members, a majority of the voting rights in it;[8392]

or if it is a subsidiary of a company that is itself a subsidiary of that other company.

A company is a 'wholly-owned subsidiary' of another company if it has no members except that other and that other's wholly-owned subsidiaries or persons acting on behalf of that other or its wholly-owned subsidiaries.[8393]

Schedule 6 of the CA 2006 contains provisions explaining expressions used in this section and otherwise supplementing this section.[8394]

In this section and that Schedule, the term 'company' includes any body corporate.[8395]

Meaning of 'subsidiary', etc: power to amend

33.41 Section 1160 of the CA 2006 states that the Secretary of State may by regulations amend the provisions of s 1159 of the CA 2006 (meaning of 'subsidiary', etc.) and Schedule 6 of the CA 2006 (meaning of 'subsidiary', etc.: supplementary provisions) so as to alter the meaning of the expressions 'subsidiary', 'holding company' or 'wholly-owned subsidiary'.[8396]

Regulations under this section are subject to negative resolution procedure.[8397]

[8390] CA 2006, s 1159(1)(a).   [8391] CA 2006, s 1159(1)(b).   [8392] CA 2006, s 1159(1)(c).
[8393] CA 2006, s 1159(2).   [8394] CA 2006, s 1159(3).   [8395] CA 2006, s 1159(4).
[8396] CA 2006, s 1160(1).   [8397] CA 2006, s 1160(2).

Any amendment made by regulations under this section does not apply for the purposes of enactments outside the Companies Acts unless the regulations so provide.[8398]

So much of s 23(3) of the Interpretation Act 1978 (c 30) as applies s 17(2)(a) of that Act (effect of repeal and re-enactment) to deeds, instruments and documents other than enactments does not apply in relation to any repeal and re-enactment effected by regulations under this section.[8399]

Meaning of 'undertaking' and related expressions

33.42 Section 1161 of the CA 2006 states that in the Companies Acts, 'undertaking' means a body corporate or partnership;[8400] or an unincorporated association carrying on a trade or business, with or without a view to profit.[8401]

In the Companies Acts, references to shares:

(a)　in relation to an undertaking with capital but no share capital, are to rights to share in the capital of the undertaking;[8402] and

(b)　in relation to an undertaking without capital, are to interests conferring any right to share in the profits or liability to contribute to the losses of the undertaking;[8403] or giving rise to an obligation to contribute to the debts or expenses of the undertaking in the event of a winding up.[8404]

Other expressions appropriate to companies shall be construed, in relation to an undertaking that is not a company, as references to the corresponding persons, officers, documents or organs, as the case may be, appropriate to undertakings of that description.[8405]

This is subject to provision in any specific context providing for the translation of such expressions.

References in the Companies Acts to 'fellow subsidiary undertakings' are to undertakings that are subsidiary undertakings of the same parent undertaking but are not parent undertakings or subsidiary undertakings of each other.[8406]

In the Companies Acts, 'group undertaking, in relation to an undertaking, means an undertaking that is a parent undertaking or subsidiary undertaking of that undertaking;[8407] or a subsidiary undertaking of any parent undertaking of that undertaking.[8408]

[8398] CA 2006, s 1160(3).　　[8399] CA 2006, s 1160(4).　　[8400] CA 2006, s 1161(1)(a).
[8401] CA 2006, s 1161(1)(b).　　[8402] CA 2006, s 1161(2)(a).
[8403] CA 2006, s 1161(2)(b)(i).　　[8404] CA 2006, s 1161(2)(b)(ii).
[8405] CA 2006, s 1161(3).　　[8406] CA 2006, s 1161(4).　　[8407] CA 2006, s 1161(5)(a).
[8408] CA 2006, s 1161(5)(b).

Parent and subsidiary undertakings

33.43 Section 1162 of the CA 2006 states that this section (together with Schedule 7 of the CA 2006) defines 'parent undertaking' and 'subsidiary undertaking' for the purposes of the Companies Acts.[8409]

An undertaking is a parent undertaking in relation to another undertaking, a subsidiary undertaking, if:

(a) it holds a majority of the voting rights in the undertaking;[8410] or
(b) it is a member of the undertaking and has the right to appoint or remove a majority of its board of directors;[8411] or
(c) it has the right to exercise a dominant influence over the undertaking by virtue of provisions contained in the undertaking's articles;[8412] or by virtue of a control contract;[8413] or
(d) it is a member of the undertaking and controls alone, pursuant to an agreement with other shareholders or members, a majority of the voting rights in the undertaking.[8414]

For the purposes of subs (2), an undertaking is to be treated as a member of another undertaking:

(a) if any of its subsidiary undertakings is a member of that undertaking;[8415] or
(b) if any shares in that other undertaking are held by a person acting on behalf of the undertaking or any of its subsidiary undertakings.[8416]

An undertaking is also a parent undertaking in relation to another undertaking, a subsidiary undertaking, if it has the power to exercise, or actually exercises, dominant influence or control over it,[8417] or it and the subsidiary undertaking are managed on a unified basis.[8418]

A parent undertaking is to be treated as the parent undertaking of undertakings in relation to which any of its subsidiary undertakings are, or are to be treated as, parent undertakings; and references to its subsidiary undertakings shall be construed accordingly.[8419]

Schedule 7 of the CA 2006 contains provisions explaining expressions used in this section and otherwise supplementing this section.[8420]

In this section and Schedule 7 references to shares, in relation to an undertaking, are to allotted shares.[8421]

[8409] CA 2006, s 1162(1).   [8410] CA 2006, s 1162(2)(a).   [8411] CA 2006, s 1162(2)(b).
[8412] CA 2006, s 1162(2)(c)(i).   [8413] CA 2006, s 1162(2)(c)(ii).
[8414] CA 2006, s 1162(2)(d).   [8415] CA 2006, s 1162(3)(a).   [8416] CA 2006, s 1162(3)(b).
[8417] CA 2006, s 1162(4)(a).   [8418] CA 2006, s 1162(4)(b).   [8419] CA 2006, s 1162(5).
[8420] CA 2006, s 1162(6).   [8421] CA 2006, s 1162(7).

Other definitions

'Non-cash asset'

33.44 Section 1163 of the CA 2006 states that in the Companies Acts 'non-cash asset' means any property or interest in property, other than cash.

For this purpose 'cash' includes foreign currency.[8422]

A reference to the transfer or acquisition of a non-cash asset includes the creation or extinction of an estate or interest in, or a right over, any property;[8423] and the discharge of a liability of any person, other than a liability for a liquidated sum.[8424]

Meaning of 'banking company' and 'banking group'

33.45 Section 1164 of the CA 2006 defines 'banking company' and 'banking group' for the purposes of the Companies Acts.[8425]

The term 'Banking company' means a person who has permission under Part 4 of the Financial Services and Markets Act 2000 (c 8) to accept deposits, other than a person who is not a company;[8426] and a person who has such permission only for the purpose of carrying on another regulated activity in accordance with permission under that Part.[8427]

The definition in s 1164 (2) of the CA 2006 must be read with s 22 of that Act, any relevant order under that section and Schedule 2 to that Act.[8428]

References to a banking group are to a group where the parent company is a banking company or where the parent company's principal subsidiary undertakings are wholly or mainly credit institutions;[8429] and the parent company does not itself carry on any material business apart from the acquisition, management and disposal of interests in subsidiary undertakings.[8430]

'Group' here means a parent undertaking and its subsidiary undertakings.

For the purposes of s 1164 (4) of the CA 2006:

(a) a parent company's principal subsidiary undertakings are the subsidiary undertakings of the company whose results or financial position would principally affect the figures shown in the group accounts,[8431] and

(b) the management of interests in subsidiary undertakings includes the provision of services to such undertakings.[8432]

[8422] CA 2006, s 1163(1). [8423] CA 2006, s 1163(2)(a). [8424] CA 2006, s 1163(2)(b).
[8425] CA 2006, s 1164(1). [8426] CA 2006, s 1164(2)(a). [8427] CA 2006, s 1164(2)(b).
[8428] CA 2006, s 1164(3). [8429] CA 2006, s 1164(4)(a). [8430] CA 2006, s 1164(4)(b).
[8431] CA 2006, s 1164(5)(a). [8432] CA 2006, s 1164(5)(b).

Meaning of 'insurance company' and related expressions

33.46 Section 1165 of the CA 2006 defines 'insurance company', 'authorised insurance company', 'insurance group' and 'insurance market activity' for the purposes of the Companies Acts.[8433]

An 'authorised insurance company' means a person (whether incorporated or not) who has permission under Part 4 of the Financial Services and Markets Act 2000 (c 8) to effect or carry out contracts of insurance.[8434]

An 'insurance company' means:

(a) an authorised insurance company;[8435] or
(b) any other person (whether incorporated or not) who: (i) carries on insurance market activity,[8436] or (ii) may effect or carry out contracts of insurance under which the benefits provided by that person are exclusively or primarily benefits in kind in the event of accident to or breakdown of a vehicle.[8437]

Neither expression includes a friendly society within the meaning of the Friendly Societies Act 1992 (c 40).[8438]

References to an insurance group, are to a group where the parent company is an insurance company, or where the parent company's principal subsidiary undertakings are wholly or mainly insurance companies;[8439] and the parent company does not itself carry on any material business apart from the acquisition, management and disposal of interests in subsidiary undertakings.[8440]

'Group' here means a parent undertaking and its subsidiary undertakings. For the purposes of s 1165 (5) of the CA 2006:

(a) a parent company's principal subsidiary undertakings are the subsidiary undertakings of the company, whose results or financial position would principally affect the figures shown in the group accounts;[8441] and
(b) the management of interests in subsidiary undertakings includes the provision of services to such undertakings.[8442]

'Insurance market activity' has the meaning given in s 316(3) of the Financial Services and Markets Act 2000.[8443]

References in this section to contracts of insurance and to the effecting or carrying out of such contracts must be read with s 22 of that Act, any relevant order under that section and Schedule 2 to that Act.[8444]

[8433] CA 2006, s 1165(1).　　[8434] CA 2006, s 1165(2).　　[8435] CA 2006, s 1165(3)(a).
[8436] CA 2006, s 1165(3)(b)(i).　　[8437] CA 2006, s 1165(3)(b)(ii).
[8438] CA 2006, s 1165(4).　　[8439] CA 2006, s 1165(5)(a).　　[8440] CA 2006, s 1165(5)(b).
[8441] CA 2006, s 1165(6)(a).　　[8442] CA 2006, s 1165(6)(b).　　[8443] CA 2006, s 1165(7).
[8444] CA 2006, s 1165(8).

'Employees' share scheme'

33.47 Section 1166 of the CA 2006 states that for the purposes of the Companies Acts, an employees' share scheme is a scheme for encouraging or facilitating the holding of shares in or debentures of a company by or for the benefit of:

(a) the bona fide employees or former employees of:

    (i)   the company,

    (ii)   any subsidiary of the company, or

    (iii) the company's holding company or any subsidiary of the company's holding company, or

(b) the spouses, civil partners, surviving spouses, surviving civil partners, or minor children or step-children of such employees or former employees.

Meaning of 'prescribed'

33.48 Section 1167 of the CA 2006 states that in the Companies Acts, 'prescribed' means prescribed (by order or by regulations) by the Secretary of State.

Hard copy and electronic form and related expressions

33.49 Section 1168 of the CA 2006 states that the following provisions apply for the purposes of the Companies Acts.[8445]

A document or information is sent or supplied in hard copy form, if it is sent or supplied in a paper copy or similar form capable of being read.

References to hard copy have a corresponding meaning.[8446]

A document or information is sent or supplied in electronic form if it is sent or supplied by electronic means (for example, by e-mail or fax);[8447] or by any other means while in an electronic form (for example, sending a disk by post).[8448]

References to electronic copy have a corresponding meaning.

A document or information is sent or supplied by electronic means, if it is sent initially and received at its destination by means of electronic equipment for the processing (which expression includes digital compression) or storage of data;[8449] and entirely transmitted, conveyed and received by wire, by radio, by optical means or by other electromagnetic means.[8450]

References to electronic means have a corresponding meaning.

A document or information authorised or required to be sent or supplied

---

[8445] CA 2006, s 1168(1).   [8446] CA 2006, s 1168(2).   [8447] CA 2006, s 1168(3)(a).
[8448] CA 2006, s 1168(3)(b).   [8449] CA 2006, s 1168(4)(a).   [8450] CA 2006, s 1168(4)(b).

in electronic form, must be sent or supplied in a form, and by a means, that the sender or supplier reasonably considers will enable the recipient to read it;[8451] and to retain a copy of it.[8452]

For the purposes of this section, a document or information can be read only if it can be read with the naked eye;[8453] or to the extent that it consists of images (for example photographs, pictures, maps, plans or drawings), it can be seen with the naked eye.[8454]

The provisions of this section apply whether the provision of the Companies Acts in question uses the words 'sent' or 'supplied' or uses other words (such as 'deliver', 'provide', 'produce' or, in the case of a notice, 'give') to refer to the sending or supplying of a document or information.[8455]

Dormant companies

33.50 Section 1169 of the CA 2006 states that for the purposes of the Companies Acts, a company is 'dormant' during any period in which it has no significant accounting transaction.[8456]

A 'significant accounting transaction' means a transaction that is required by s 386 of the CA 2006 to be entered in the company's accounting records.[8457]

In determining whether or when a company is dormant, the following is to be disregarded: (a) any transaction arising from the taking of shares in the company by a subscriber to the memorandum, as a result of an undertaking of his in connection with the formation of the company;[8458] (b) any transaction consisting of the payment of (i) a fee to the registrar on a change of the company's name,[8459] (ii) a fee to the registrar on the re-registration of the company,[8460] (iii) a penalty under s 453 (penalty for failure to file accounts),[8461] or (iv) a fee to the registrar for the registration of an annual return.[8462]

Any reference in the Companies Acts to a body corporate other than a company being dormant has a corresponding meaning.[8463]

Meaning of 'EEA State' and related expressions

33.51 Section 1170 of the CA 2006 states that in the Companies Acts:

'EEA State' means a state which is a Contracting Party to the Agreement on the European Economic Area signed at Oporto on 2 May 1992 (as it has effect from time to time);

[8451] CA 2006, s 1168(5)(a).   [8452] CA 2006, s 1168(5)(b).   [8453] CA 2006, s 1168(6)(a).
[8454] CA 2006, s 1168(6)(b).   [8455] CA 2006, s 1168(7).   [8456] CA 2006, s 1169(1).
[8457] CA 2006, s 1169(2).   [8458] CA 2006, s 1169(3)(a).   [8459] CA 2006, s 1169(3)(b)(i).
[8460] CA 2006, s 1169(3)(b)(ii).   [8461] CA 2006, s 1169(3)(b)(iii).
[8462] CA 2006, s 1169(3)(b)(iv).   [8463] CA 2006, s 1169(4).

'EEA company' and 'EEA undertaking' mean a company or undertaking governed by the law of an EEA State.

The former Companies Acts

33.52 Section 1171 of the CA 2006 states that in the Companies Acts:

'the former Companies Acts' means:

(a)   the Joint Stock Companies Acts, the Companies Act 1862 (c 89), the Companies (Consolidation) Act 1908 (c 69), the Companies Act 1929 (c 23), the Companies Act (Northern Ireland) 1932 (c 7 (NI)), the Companies Acts 1948 to 1983, the Companies Act (Northern Ireland) 1960 (c 22 (NI)), the Companies (Northern Ireland) Order 1986 (SI 1986/1032 (NI 6)) and the Companies Consolidation (Consequential Provisions) (Northern Ireland) Order 1986 (SI 1986/1035 (NI 9)), and

(b)   the provisions of the Companies Act 1985 (c 6) and the Companies Consolidation (Consequential Provisions) Act 1985 (c 9) that are no longer in force;

'the Joint Stock Companies Acts' means the Joint Stock Companies Act 1856 (c 47), the Joint Stock Companies Acts 1856, 1857 (20 & 21 Vict c 14), the Joint Stock Banking Companies Act 1857 (c 49), and the Act to enable Joint Stock Banking Companies to be formed on the principle of limited liability (1858, c 91), but does not include the Joint Stock Companies Act 1844 (c 110).

General

References to requirements of this Act

33.53 Section 1172 of the CA 2006 states that references in the company law provisions of this Act to the requirements of this Act, include the requirements of regulations and orders made under it.

Minor definitions: general

33.54 Section 1173 of the CA 2006 deals states that in the Companies Acts:

- 'body corporate' and 'corporation' include a body incorporated outside the United Kingdom, but do not include:

(a)   a corporation sole; or

(b)   a partnership that, whether or not a legal person, is not regarded as a body corporate under the law by which it is governed;

- 'credit institution' means a credit institution as defined in Article 4.1(a) of Directive 2006/48/EC of the European Parliament and of the Council relating to the taking up and pursuit of the business of credit institutions;
- 'financial institution' means a financial institution within the meaning of Article 1.1 of the Council Directive on the obligations of branches established in a Member State of credit and financial institutions having their head offices outside that Member State regarding the publication of annual accounting documents (the Bank Branches Directive, 89/117/EEC);
- 'firm' means any entity, whether or not a legal person, that is not an individual and includes a body corporate, a corporation sole and a partnership or other unincorporated association;
- 'the Gazette; means:

  (a) as respects companies registered in England and Wales, the London Gazette;
  (b) as respects companies registered in Scotland, the Edinburgh Gazette; and
  (c) as respects companies registered in Northern Ireland, the Belfast Gazette;

- 'hire-purchase agreement' has the same meaning as in the Consumer Credit Act 1974 (c 39);
- 'officer', in relation to a body corporate, includes a director, manager or secretary;
- 'parent company' means a company that is a parent undertaking (see s 1162 and Schedule 7);
- 'regulated activity' has the meaning given in s 22 of the Financial Services and Markets Act 2000 (c 8);
- 'regulated market' has the same meaning as in Directive 2004/39/EC of the European Parliament and of the Council on markets in financial instruments (see Article 4.1(14));
- 'working day', in relation to a company, means a day that is not a Saturday or Sunday, Christmas Day, Good Friday or any day that is a bank holiday under the Banking and Financial Dealings Act 1971 (c 80) in the part of the United Kingdom where the company is registered.

In relation to an EEA State that has not implemented Directive 2004/39/EC of the European Parliament and of the Council on markets in financial instruments, the following definition of 'regulated market' has effect in place of that in subs (1): 'regulated market' has the same meaning as it has in Council Directive 93/22/EEC on investment services in the securities field.[8464]

[8464] CA 2006, s 1173(2).

Index of defined expressions

33.55 Section 1174 of the CA 2006 states that Schedule 8 of the CA 2006 contains an index of provisions defining or otherwise explaining expressions used in the Companies Acts.

Companies: Minor Amendments

Removal of special provisions about accounts and audit of charitable companies

33.56 Section 1175 of the CA 2006 states that Part 7 of the CA 1985 (c 6) and Part 8 of the Companies (Northern Ireland) Order 1986 (accounts and audit) are amended in accordance with Schedule 9 to this Act so as to remove the special provisions about companies that are charities.[8465]
   In that Schedule:

   Part 1 contains repeals and consequential amendments of provisions of the CA 1985;
   Part 2 contains repeals and consequential amendments of provisions of the Companies (Northern Ireland) Order 1986.[8466]

Power of Secretary of State to bring civil proceedings on a company's behalf

33.57 Section 1176 of the CA 2006 states that s 438 of the CA 1985 (power of Secretary of State to bring civil proceedings on a company's behalf) will cease to have effect.[8467]
   In s 439 of that Act (expenses of investigating company's affairs):[8468]

(a)   in subs (2) omit ', or is ordered to pay the whole or any part of the costs of proceedings brought under section 438';
(b)   omit subss (3) and (7) (which relate to s 438);
(c)   in subs (8):

   (i)   for 'subsections (2) and (3)' substitute 'subsection (2)'; and
   (ii) omit '; and any such liability imposed by subsection (2) is (subject as mentioned above) a liability also to indemnify all persons against liability under subsection (3)'.

[8465] CA 2006, s 1175(1).   [8466] CA 2006, s 1175(2).   [8467] CA 2006, s 1176(1).
[8468] CA 2006, s 1176(2).

In s 453(1A) of the CA 1985 (investigation of overseas companies: provisions not applicable), omit para (b) (which relates to s 438).[8469]

Nothing in this section affects proceedings brought under s 438 of the CA 1985 before the commencement of this section.[8470]

Repeal of certain provisions about company directors

33.58 Section 1177 of the CA 2006 states that the following provisions of Part 10 of the CA the CA 1985 will cease to have effect:

s 311 (prohibition on tax-free payments to directors);
ss 323 and 327 (prohibition on directors dealing in share options);
ss 324–326 and 328–329, and Parts 2–4 of Schedule 13 (register of directors' interests);
ss 343 and 344 (special procedure for disclosure by banks).

Repeal of requirement that certain companies publish periodical statements

33.59 Section 1178 of the CA 2006 states that the following provisions will cease to have effect: s 720 of the CA 1985 (c 6) (certain companies to publish periodical statements), and Schedule 23 of the CA 1985 (form of statement under s 720).

Repeal of requirement that Secretary of State prepares annual report

33.60 Section 1179 of the CA 2006 states that s 729 of the CA 1985 (annual report to Parliament by Secretary of State on matters within the Companies Acts) shall cease to have effect.

Repeal of certain provisions about company charges

33.61 Section 1180 of the CA 2006 states that Part 4 of the CA 1989 (c 40) (registration of company charges), which had not been brought into force, is repealed.

Access to constitutional documents of RTE and RTM companies

33.62 Section 1181 of the CA 2006 the Secretary of State may by order amend Chapter 1 of Part 1 of the Leasehold Reform, Housing and Urban Development Act 1993 (c 28) for the purpose of facilitating access to the

---

[8469] CA 2006, s 1176(3).　　[8470] CA 2006, s 1176(4).

provisions of the articles or any other constitutional document of RTE companies;[8471] amend Chapter 1 of Part 2 of the Commonhold and Leasehold Reform Act 2002 (c 15) (leasehold reform) for the purpose of facilitating access to the provisions of the articles or any other constitutional document of RTM companies.[8472]

References in s 1181(1) of the CA 2006 to provisions of a company's articles or any other constitutional document include any provisions included in those documents by virtue of any enactment.[8473]

An order under this section is subject to negative resolution procedure.[8474]

In this section:[8475]

> 'RTE companies' has the same meaning as in Chapter 1 of Part 1 of the Leasehold Reform, Housing and Urban Development Act 1993;
> 'RTM companies' has the same meaning as in Chapter 1 of Part 2 of the Commonhold and Leasehold Reform Act 2002.

Miscellaneous Provisions

33.63 Sections 1274–1283 of the CA 2006 deals with miscellaneous provisions.

Regulation of actuaries, etc.
Grants to bodies concerned with actuarial standards, etc.

33.64 Section 1274 of the CA 2006 states that s 16 of the Companies (Audit, Investigations and Community Enterprise) Act 2004 (c 27) (grants to bodies concerned with accounting standards etc) is amended as follows.[8476]

In subs (2) (matters carried on by bodies eligible for grants) for para (l) substitute:[8477]

> (l) issuing standards to be applied in actuarial work;
> (m) issuing standards in respect of matters to be contained in reports or other communications required to be produced or made by actuaries or in accordance with standards within para (l);
> (n) investigating departures from standards within para (l) or (m);
> (o) taking steps to secure compliance with standards within para (l) or (m);
> (p) carrying out investigations into public interest cases arising in connection with the performance of actuarial functions by members of professional actuarial bodies;

[8471] CA 2006, s 1181(1)(a).   [8472] CA 2006, s 1181(1)(b).   [8473] CA 2006, s 1181(2).
[8474] CA 2006, s 1181(3).   [8475] CA 2006, s 1181(4).   [8476] CA 2006, s 1274(1).
[8477] CA 2006, s 1274(2).

(q)   holding disciplinary hearings relating to members of professional actuarial bodies following the conclusion of investigations within para (p);

(r)   deciding whether (and, if so, what) disciplinary action should be taken against members of professional actuarial bodies to whom hearings within para (q) related;

(s)   supervising the exercise by professional actuarial bodies of regulatory functions in relation to their members;

(t)   overseeing or directing any of the matters mentioned above.

In subs (5) (definitions) at the appropriate places insert:[8478]

'professional actuarial body' means:

(a) the Institute of Actuaries; or

(b) the Faculty of Actuaries in Scotland,

and the 'members' of a professional actuarial body include persons who, although not members of the body, are subject to its rules in performing actuarial functions;

'regulatory functions', in relation to professional actuarial bodies, means any of the following:

(a) investigatory or disciplinary functions exercised by such bodies in relation to the performance by their members of actuarial functions,

(b) the setting by such bodies of standards in relation to the performance by their members of actuarial functions, and

(c) the determining by such bodies of requirements in relation to the education and training of their members.

Levy to pay expenses of bodies concerned with actuarial standards, etc.

33.65 Section 1275 of the CA 2006 states that s 17 of the Companies (Audit, Investigations and Community Enterprise) Act 2004 (c 27) (levy to pay expenses of bodies concerned with actuarial standards, etc.) is amended in accordance with subss (2)–(5).[8479]

In subs (3)(a) after 'to which' insert '. . ., or persons within subsection (3A) to whom, . . .'.[8480]

After subs (3) insert:[8481]

(3A) The following persons are within this subsection:

(a)   the administrators of a public service pension scheme (within the meaning of section 1 of the Pension Schemes Act 1993);

[8478] CA 2006, s 1274(3).   [8479] CA 2006, s 1275(1).   [8480] CA 2006, s 1275(2).
[8481] CA 2006, s 1275(3).

(b)   the trustees or managers of an occupational or personal pension scheme (within the meaning of that section).

After subs (4)(b) insert:[8482]

(c)   make different provision for different cases.

After subs (12) insert:[8483]

(13)If a draft of any regulations to which subsection (10) applies would, apart from this subsection, be treated for the purposes of the standing orders of either House of Parliament as a hybrid instrument, it is to proceed in that House as if it were not such an instrument.

The above amendments have effect in relation to any exercise of the power to make regulations under s 17 of the Companies (Audit, Investigations and Community Enterprise) Act 2004 after this section comes into force, regardless of when the expenses to be met by the levy in respect of which the regulations are made were incurred.[8484]

In Schedule 3 to the Pensions Act 2004 (c 35) (disclosure of information held by the Pensions Regulator), in the entry relating to the Secretary of State, in the second column, for 'or' at the end of para (g) substitute:[8485]

(ga)   Section 17 of the Companies (Audit, Investigations and Community Enterprise) Act 2004 (levy to pay expenses of bodies concerned with accounting standards, actuarial standards etc), or . . .

Application of provisions to Scotland and Northern Ireland

33.66 Section 1276 of the CA 2006 states that s 16 of the Companies (Audit, Investigations and Community Enterprise) Act 2004 (grants to bodies concerned with accounting standards, etc.) is amended as follows.[8486]

For subs (6) (application of section to Scotland) substitute:[8487]

(6)   In their application to Scotland, subsection (2)(a) to (t) are to be read as referring only to matters provision relating to which would be outside the legislative competence of the Scottish Parliament.

In subs (2) in para (c), after '1985 (c 6)' insert 'or the 1986 Order'.[8488]

[8482] CA 2006, s 1275(4).   [8483] CA 2006, s 1275(5).   [8484] CA 2006, s 1275(6).
[8485] CA 2006, s 1275(7).   [8486] CA 2006, s 1276(1).   [8487] CA 2006, s 1276(2).
[8488] CA 2006, s 1276(3).

In subs (5):[8489]

(a) in the definition of 'company' after '1985 (c 6)' insert 'or the 1986 Order';

(b) in the definition of 'subsidiary' after '1985' insert 'or Article 4 of the 1986 Order'; and

(c) after that definition insert: ' "the 1986 Order" means the Companies (Northern Ireland) Order 1986 (SI 1986/1032 (NI 6))'.

In s 66 of that Act (extent), in subs (2) (provisions extending to Northern Ireland, as well as England and Wales and Scotland) for '17' substitute '16 to 18'.[8490]

Information as to exercise of voting rights by institutional investors

Power to require information about exercise of voting rights

33.67 Section 1277 of the CA 2006 states that the Treasury or the Secretary of State may make provision by regulations requiring institutions to which this section applies, to provide information about the exercise of voting rights attached to shares to which this section applies.[8491]

This power is exercisable in accordance with:[8492]

s 1278 of the CA 2006 (institutions to which information provisions apply);

s 1279 of the CA 2006 (shares to which information provisions apply); and

s 1280 of the CA 2006 (obligations with respect to provision of information).

In this section and the sections mentioned above:[8493]

(a) references to a person acting on behalf of an institution include:

(i) any person to whom authority has been delegated by the institution to take decisions as to any matter relevant to the subject matter of the regulations, and

(ii) such other persons as may be specified; and

(b) 'specified' means specified in the regulations.

[8489] CA 2006, s 1276(4).   [8490] CA 2006, s 1276(5).   [8491] CA 2006, s 1277(1).
[8492] CA 2006, s 1277(2).   [8493] CA 2006, s 1277(3).

The obligation imposed by regulations under this section is enforceable by civil proceedings brought by any person to whom the information should have been provided, or a specified regulatory authority.[8494]

Regulations under this section may make different provision for different descriptions of institution, different descriptions of shares and for other different circumstances.[8495]

Regulations under this section are subject to affirmative resolution procedure.[8496]

Institutions to which information provisions apply

33.68 Section 1278 of the CA 2006 states that the institutions to which s 1277 of the CA 2006 applies are:[8497]

(a) unit trust schemes within the meaning of the Financial Services and Markets Act 2000 (c 8) in respect of which an order is in force under s 243 of that Act;

(b) open-ended investment companies incorporated by virtue of regulations under s 262 of that Act;

(c) companies approved for the purposes of s 842 of the Income and Corporation Taxes Act 1988 (c 1) (investment trusts);

(d) pension schemes as defined in s 1(5) of the Pension Schemes Act 1993 (c 48) or the Pension Schemes (Northern Ireland) Act 1993 (c 49);

(e) undertakings authorised under the Financial Services and Markets Act 2000 to carry on long-term insurance business (that is, the activity of effecting or carrying out contracts of long-term insurance within the meaning of the Financial Services and Markets (Regulated Activities) Order 2001 (SI 2001/544);

(f) collective investment schemes that are recognised by virtue of s 270 of the CA that Act (schemes authorised in designated countries or territories).

Regulations under that section may:[8498] provide that the section applies to other descriptions of institution; provide that the section does not apply to a specified description of institution.

The regulations must specify by whom, in the case of any description of institution, the duty imposed by the regulations is to be fulfilled.[8499]

[8494] CA 2006, s 1277(4).   [8495] CA 2006, s 1277(5).   [8496] CA 2006, s 1277(6).
[8497] CA 2006, s 1278(1).   [8498] CA 2006, s 1278(2).   [8499] CA 2006, s 1278(3).

Shares to which information provisions apply

33.69 Section 1279 of the CA 2006 states that the shares to which s 1277 of the CA 2006 applies are shares of a description traded on a specified market;[8500] and in which the institution has, or is taken to have, an interest.[8501]

Regulations under that section may provide that the section does not apply to shares of a specified description.

For this purpose an institution has an interest in shares if the shares, or a depositary certificate in respect of them, are held by it, or on its behalf.[8502]

A 'depositary certificate' means an instrument conferring rights (other than options) in respect of shares held by another person, and the transfer of which may be effected without the consent of that person.

Where an institution has an interest in a specified description of collective investment scheme (within the meaning of the Financial Services and Markets Act 2000 (c 8));[8503] or in any other specified description of scheme or collective investment vehicle,[8504] it is taken to have an interest in any shares in which that scheme or vehicle has or is taken to have an interest.

For this purpose, a scheme or vehicle is taken to have an interest in shares if it would be regarded as having such an interest in accordance with subs (2) if it were an institution to which s 1277 of the CA 2006 applied.[8505]

Obligations with respect to provision of information

33.70 Section 1280 of the CA 2006 states that regulations under s 1277 of the CA 2006 may require the provision of specified information about:

(a) the exercise or non-exercise of voting rights by the institution or any person acting on its behalf;[8506]
(b) any instructions given by the institution or any person acting on its behalf as to the exercise or non-exercise of voting rights;[8507] and
(c) any delegation by the institution or any person acting on its behalf of any functions in relation to the exercise or non-exercise of voting rights or the giving of such instructions.[8508]

The regulations may require information to be provided in respect of specified occasions or specified periods.[8509]

Where instructions are given to act on the recommendations or advice of another person, the regulations may require the provision of information about what recommendations or advice were given.[8510]

[8500] CA 2006, s 1279(1)(a).   [8501] CA 2006, s 1279(1)(b).   [8502] CA 2006, s 1279(2).
[8503] CA 2006, s 1279(3)(a).   [8504] CA 2006, s 1279(3)(b).   [8505] CA 2006, s 1279(4).
[8506] CA 2006, s 1280(1)(a).   [8507] CA 2006, s 1280(1)(b).   [8508] CA 2006, s 1280(1)(c).
[8509] CA 2006, s 1280(2).   [8510] CA 2006, s 1280(3).

The regulations may require information to be provided in such manner as may be specified,[8511] and to such persons as may be specified, or to the public, or both.[8512]

The regulations may provide:

(a)   that an institution may discharge its obligations under the regulations by referring to information disclosed by a person acting on its behalf,[8513] and

(b)   that in such a case it is sufficient, where that other person acts on behalf of more than one institution, that the reference is to information given in aggregated form, that is:

   (i)   relating to the exercise or non-exercise by that person of voting rights on behalf of more than one institution,[8514] or

   (ii)   relating to the instructions given by that person in respect of the exercise or non-exercise of voting rights on behalf of more than one institution,[8515] or

   (iii)   relating to the delegation by that person of functions in relation to the exercise or non-exercise of voting rights, or the giving of instructions in respect of the exercise or non-exercise of voting rights, on behalf of more than one institution.[8516]

References in this section to instructions are to instructions of any description, whether general or specific, whether binding or not and whether or not acted upon.[8517]

Disclosure of information under the Enterprise Act 2002

Disclosure of information under the Enterprise Act 2002

33.71 Section 1281 of the CA 2006 states that in Part 9 of the Enterprise Act 2002 (c 40) (information), after s 241 insert:

   241A Civil proceedings

   (1)   A public authority which holds prescribed information to which section 237 applies may disclose that information to any person:

      (a)   for the purposes of, or in connection with, prescribed civil proceedings (including prospective proceedings) in the United Kingdom or elsewhere, or

---

[8511] CA 2006, s 1280(4)(a).   [8512] CA 2006, s 1280(4)(b).   [8513] CA 2006 s 1280(5)(a).
[8514] CA 2006, s 1280(5)(b)(i).   [8515] CA 2006, s 1280(5)(b)(ii).
[8516] CA 2006, s 1280(5)(b)(iii).
[8517] CA 2006, s 1280(6).

(b) for the purposes of obtaining legal advice in relation to such proceedings, or

(c) otherwise for the purposes of establishing, enforcing or defending legal rights that are or may be the subject of such proceedings.

(2) Subsection (1) does not apply to:

(a) information which comes to a public authority in connection with an investigation under Part 4, 5 or 6 of the 1973 Act or under section 11 of the Competition Act 1980;

(b) competition information within the meaning of section 351 of the Financial Services and Markets Act 2000;

(c) information which comes to a public authority in connection with an investigation under Part 3 or 4 or section 174 of this Act;

(d) information which comes to a public authority in connection with an investigation under the Competition Act 1998 (c 41).

(3) In subsection (1) 'prescribed' means prescribed by order of the Secretary of State.

(4) An order under this section:

(a) may prescribe information, or civil proceedings, for the purposes of this section by reference to such factors as appear to the Secretary of State to be appropriate;

(b) may prescribe for the purposes of this section all information, or civil proceedings, or all information or civil proceedings not falling within one or more specified exceptions;

(c) must be made by statutory instrument subject to annulment in pursuance of a resolution of either House of Parliament.

(5) Information disclosed under this section must not be used by the person to whom it is disclosed for any purpose other than those specified in subsection (1).

Expenses of winding up

Payment of expenses of winding up

33.72 Section 1282 of the CA 2006 inserts the following provision:

(1) In Chapter 8 of Part 4 of the Insolvency Act 1986 (c 45) (winding up of companies: provisions of general application), before s 176A (under the heading 'Property subject to floating charge') insert:[8518]

[8518] CA 2006, s 1282(1).

176ZA Payment of expenses of winding up (England and Wales)

(1)   The expenses of winding up in England and Wales, so far as the assets of the company available for payment of general creditors are insufficient to meet them, have priority over any claims to property comprised in or subject to any floating charge created by the company and shall be paid out of any such property accordingly.

(2)   In subsection (1):

(a)   the reference to assets of the company available for payment of general creditors does not include any amount made available under section 176A(2)(a);

(b)   the reference to claims to property comprised in or subject to a floating charge is to the claims of:

(i)   the holders of debentures secured by, or holders of, the floating charge, and

(ii)   any preferential creditors entitled to be paid out of that property in priority to them.

(3)   Provision may be made by rules restricting the application of subsection (1), in such circumstances as may be prescribed, to expenses authorised or approved:

(a)   by the holders of debentures secured by, or holders of, the floating charge and by any preferential creditors entitled to be paid in priority to them, or

(b)   by the court.

(4)   References in this section to the expenses of the winding up are to all expenses properly incurred in the winding up, including the remuneration of the liquidator.

(2) In Chapter 8 of Part 5 of the Insolvency (Northern Ireland) Order 1989 (SI 1989/2405 (NI 19)) (winding up of companies: provisions of general application), before Article 150A (under the heading 'Property subject to floating charge') insert:[8519]

150ZA Payment of expenses of winding up

(1)   The expenses of winding up, so far as the assets of the company available for payment of general creditors are insufficient to meet them, have priority over any claims to property comprised in or subject to any floating charge created by the company and shall be paid out of any such property accordingly.

(2)   In para (1):

(a)   the reference to assets of the company available for payment of general

---

[8519] CA 2006, s 1282(2).

creditors does not include any amount made available under Article 150A(2)(a);

(b) the reference to claims to property comprised in or subject to a floating charge is to the claims of:

    (i) the holders of debentures secured by, or holders of, the floating charge, and

    (ii) any preferential creditors entitled to be paid out of that property in priority to them.

(3) Provision may be made by rules restricting the application of para (1), in such circumstances as may be prescribed, to expenses authorised or approved:

    (a) by the holders of debentures secured by, or holders of, the floating charge and by any preferential creditors entitled to be paid in priority to them, or

    (b) by the Court.

(4) References in this Article to the expenses of the winding up are to all expenses properly incurred in the winding up, including the remuneration of the liquidator.

Commonhold associations

Amendment of memorandum or articles of commonhold association

33.73 Section 1283 of the CA 2006 states that in para 3(1) of Schedule 3 to the Commonhold and Leasehold Reform Act 2002 (c 15) (alteration of memorandum or articles by commonhold association to be of no effect until altered version registered with Land Registry) for 'An alteration of the memorandum or Articles of Association' substitute 'Where a commonhold association alters its memorandum or articles at a time when the land specified in its memorandum is commonhold land, the alteration'.

Northern Ireland

33.74 This is governed by Part 45 of the CA 2006.

Extension of Companies Acts to Northern Ireland

33.75 Section 1284 of the CA 2006 states that the Companies Acts as defined by this Act (see s 2) extend to Northern Ireland.[8520]

The Companies (Northern Ireland) Order 1986 (SI 1986/1032 (NI 6)), the Companies Consolidation (Consequential Provisions) (Northern Ireland)

[8520] CA 2006, s 1284(1).

Order 1986 (SI 1986/1035 (NI 9)) and Part 3 of the Companies (Audit, Investigations and Community Enterprise) Order 2005 (SI 2005/1967 (NI 17)) shall cease to have effect accordingly.[8521]

Extension of GB enactments relating to SEs

33.76 Section 1285 of the CA 2006 states that the enactments in force in Great Britain relating to SEs extend to Northern Ireland.[8522]

The following enactments will cease to have effect accordingly:[8523]

(a)   the European Public Limited Liability Company Regulations (Northern Ireland) 2004 (SR 2004/417); and
(b)   the European Public Limited Liability Company (Fees) Regulations (Northern Ireland) 2004 (SR 2004/418).

In this section 'SE' means a European Public Limited Liability Company (or Societas Europaea) within the meaning of Council Regulation 2157/2001/EC of 8 October 2001 on the Statute for a European Company.[8524]

Extension of GB enactments relating to certain other forms of business organisation

33.77 Section 1286 of the CA 2006 states that the enactments in force in Great Britain relating to:

(a)   limited liability partnerships;
(b)   limited partnerships;
(c)   open-ended investment companies; and
(d)   European Economic Interest Groupings,

extend to Northern Ireland.[8525]

The following enactments shall cease to have effect accordingly:[8526]

(a)   the Limited Liability Partnerships Act (Northern Ireland) 2002 (c 12 (NI));
(b)   the Limited Partnerships Act 1907 (c 24) as it formerly had effect in Northern Ireland;
(c)   the Open-Ended Investment Companies Act (Northern Ireland) 2002 (c 13 (NI));
(d)   the European Economic Interest Groupings Regulations (Northern Ireland) 1989 (SR 1989/216).

[8521] CA 2006, s 1284(2).   [8522] CA 2006, s 1285(1).   [8523] CA 2006, s 1285(2).
[8524] CA 2006, s 1285(3).   [8525] CA 2006, s 1286(1).   [8526] CA 2006, s 1286(2).

Extension of enactments relating to business names

33.78 Sections 1287 of the CA 2006 states that the provisions of Part 41 of this Act (business names) extend to Northern Ireland.[8527]

The Business Names (Northern Ireland) Order 1986 (SI 1986/1033 (NI 7)) shall cease to have effect accordingly.[8528]

[8527] CA 2006, s 1287(1).   [8528] CA 2006, s 1287(2).

Index

EC Directives 29, 97, 108, 130
First Company Law Directive 21n, 109, 178, 231, 244, 248–9, 366, 517, 525, 531, 533, 534, 535, 540, 542, 543, 544, 549, 554, 555
Second Company Law Directive 21n, 75, 79, 186, 619, 627–8, 642, 668–9, 672, 676, 773
Third Council Directive 1068
Fourth Company Law Directive 21n, 878, 935, 941
Sixth Council Directive 1068
Seventh Company Law Directive 21, 864, 866, 878, 935
Eighth Company Law Directive 21, 935, 991
Eleventh Company Law Directive 85, 86, 87, 201, 202, 203
Twelfth Company Law Directive 331, 482
Accounts Modernisation Directive 851, 854
Audit Directive 935, 959
Bank Branches Directive 206, 866, 1263
Credit Institutions Directive 993, 1263
Market Abuse Directive 1208
on Takeover bids 130, 893, 1092, 1093, 1095, 1096, 1097, 1100, 1101, 1102, 1103, 1107, 1115–16, 1117, 1118, 1120, 1121, 1122, 1124–5, 1126, 1127, 1135, 149, 1150
Transparency 130, 157, 717, 1187–94, 1195, 1196, 1199–1200, 1203–4, 1205, 1206–7, 1212–17
election candidates 1219, 1220–21, 1222, 1224
electronic communications 2, 52, 53, 72, 75, 76, 81, 82, 114, 125n, 139n, 151, 167–8, 525–6, 559–60, 575–6, 596, 1037–8
to include company particulars 161, 167
electronic incorporation 132, 162
enlightened shareholder value 42–4, 45n, 88, 115, 390n, 395, 399–402, 431, 432
e-mail 114, 159, 167, 541, 571, 1260
to include company particulars 161
employees 3, 37n, 40, 41, 43n, 44, 64, 69, 88, 89n, 90, 101, 102, 105, 106, 111, 113, 150, 389, 390, 399, 401

application for striking off to be given to 1157, 1158, 1159
corporate social responsibilities 237
directors' regard to interest of 404–8
gratuitous distributions to 372
information in accounts 874–5, 881
liability of senior 122
number of 848, 849, 926, 927
provision for on cessation 491–3
share scheme 264, 338–40, 376, 495, 622–3, 634, 646, 769–70, 771, 777, 805, 806, 1148, 1260
South Africa 414n
Enron 13, 105, 107, 109, 110n
environment, company impact on 3, 40, 45, 71, 89, 90, 101, 113, 390, 395, 401, 402, 404n, 409–12, 427, 431, 881, 882
equity securities 152, 617, 630–40
existing shareholders rights of pre-emption 631–40
meaning of 630–1
European Convention on Human Rights 39n
European Court of Justice 85
European Economic Area (EEA) 201, 203, 204, 340, 341, 366, 517, 632, 633, 639, 803, 804, 807, 850, 851, 858, 860, 862, 863, 864, 865, 866, 868, 1100, 1103, 1115, 1122, 1125, 1129, 1132, 1201, 1203, 1212, 1261–2, 1263
meaning 1261–2
European Economic Community 21
European Economic Interest Groupings 136, 550, 1276
euros 264, 618, 672, 675, 930
extraordinary general meeting (EGM) 72, 73, 79, 80, 1123
notice period 80, 120
requisitioned by shareholders 80

fairness 69, 369, 416, 986
family members
definition 495, 496
interest in shares 738, 739
shareholders of same company 375, 383n, 415
fees
payable to registrar 521–2
statutory auditors 1029
takeovers 1110, 1112